State	Registration deadline before election	Early voting permitted?	Identification required to vote?*	More information
Nebraska	Third Friday prior to election by mail or online; second Friday prior to election in person	Yes	No	sos.nebraska.gov
Nevada	28 days by mail; 5 days online; Election-Day registration permitted	Yes (all voting by mail)	No	nvsos.gov
New Hampshire	6–13 days (varies by county); Election-Day registration permitted	No	ID requested; photo not required	sos.nh.gov
New Jersey	21 days	Yes	No	njelections.org
New Mexico	28 days by mail or online; in-person Election-Day registration permitted	Yes	No	sos.state.nm.us
New York	10 days	Yes	No	elections.ny.gov
North Carolina	25 days	Yes	Photo ID required	ncsbe.gov
North Dakota	No voter registration required	Yes	ID required; photo not required	vote.nd.gov
Ohio	30 days	Yes	Photo ID required	sos.state.oh.us
Oklahoma	25 days	Yes	ID requested; photo not required	ok.gov/elections
Oregon	21 days	Yes	No	sos.oregon.gov
Pennsylvania	15 days	Yes	ID required only for first-time PA voters	votespa.com
Rhode Island	30 days; Election-Day registration permitted for presidential races only	Yes	Photo ID requested	elections.ri.gov
South Carolina	30 days	Yes	ID requested; photo not required	scvotes.org
South Dakota	15 days in person or by mail; no online registration	Yes	Photo ID requested	sdsos.gov
Tennessee	30 days	Yes	Photo ID required	tn.gov/sos/election
Texas	30 days; no online registration	Yes	Photo ID requested	votetexas.gov
Utah	11 days by mail or online; no in-person deadline	Yes (all voting by mail)	ID requested; photo not required	elections.utah.gov
Vermont	No registration deadline; Election-Day registration permitted	Yes (all voting by mail)	No	sos.vermont.gov/elections/voters
Virginia	22 days by mail or online; in-person Election-Day registration permitted	Yes	ID requested; photo not required	elections.virginia.gov
Washington	8 days by mail or online; Election-Day registration permitted	Yes (all voting by mail)	ID requested; photo not required	sos.wa.gov/elections/
West Virginia	21 days	Yes	ID requested; photo not required	sos.wv.gov
Wisconsin	20 days by mail or online; Election-Day registration permitted	Yes	Photo ID required	myvote.wi.gov
Wyoming	14 days by mail; Election-Day registration permitted ; no online registration	Yes	ID required; photo not required	sos.wyo.gov

Sources: Project Vote Smart, https://justfacts.votesmart.org/elections/voter-registration (accessed 10/9/24); National Conference of State Legislatures, www.ncsl.org (accessed 10/9/24).

*In states where an ID is "requested," voters who do not bring ID to the polls may be required to sign an affidavit of identity, vote on a provisional ballot, have a poll worker vouch for their identity, or take additional steps after Election Day to make sure their vote is counted.

Note: Voter registration requirements and deadlines may be altered at any time in accordance with changes in state law. Please go to vote.org or your secretary of state's website to learn more about how to vote in your state.

USE CROSSWALK
NO PARKING ANY TIME
ROBERT EVANS HUGHES
CUYAHOGA COUNTY
BOARD OF
2925

Eighth Edition, Election Update

American Politics Today

William T. Bianco
Indiana University, Bloomington

David T. Canon
University of Wisconsin, Madison

W. W. NORTON & COMPANY
Independent Publishers Since 1923

W. W. Norton & Company has been independent since its founding in 1923, when William Warder Norton and Mary D. Herter Norton first published lectures delivered at the People's Institute, the adult education division of New York City's Cooper Union. The firm soon expanded its program beyond the Institute, publishing books by celebrated academics from America and abroad. By midcentury, the two major pillars of Norton's publishing program—trade books and college texts—were firmly established. In the 1950s, the Norton family transferred control of the company to its employees, and today—with a staff of five hundred and hundreds of trade, college, and professional titles published each year—W. W. Norton & Company stands as the largest and oldest publishing house owned wholly by its employees.

Copyright © 2025, 2023, 2021, 2019, 2017, 2015, 2013, 2011, 2009 by W. W. Norton & Company, Inc.
All rights reserved
Printed in Canada

Editor: Laura Wilk
Project Editor: Sarah McGinnis
Editorial Assistant: Anna Chung
Managing Editors, College: Kim Yi and Carla Talmadge
Senior Production Manager: Richard Bretan
Media Editor: Spencer Richardson-Jones
Associate Media Editor: Lexi Malakhoff
Media Editorial Assistant: Ethan Patrick
Ebook Producer: Emily Schwoyer
Senior Media Producer: Katie Pellegrino
Media Producer: Lindsey Heale
Junior Media Producer: Daria Turner
Marketing Manager, Political Science: Marlee Lisker
Design Director: Jillian Burr
Text Designer: Open, NY
Photo Editor: Amla Sanghvi
Photo Researchers: Julie Tesser and Jane Sanders Miller
Manager, Photo Department: Melinda Patelli
Director of College Permissions: Megan Schindel
College Permissions Manager: Elizabeth Trammell
Composition: KnowledgeWorks Global Ltd.
Manufacturing: Transcontinental Inc.

Permission to use copyrighted material is included on p. A67.

ISBN 978-1-324-07198-3

W. W. Norton & Company, Inc., 500 Fifth Avenue, New York, N.Y. 10110
www.wwnorton.com
W. W. Norton & Company Ltd., 15 Carlisle Street, London W1D 3BS

1 2 3 4 5 6 7 8 9 0

For our families,
Regina, Anna, and Catherine,
Sarah, Neal, Katherine, and Sophia,
who encouraged, empathized, and
helped, with patience,
grace, and love.

About the Authors

William T. Bianco

is professor of political science at Indiana University, Bloomington, where he is also director of the Indiana Political Analysis Workshop (IPAW). His research focuses on congressional institutions, representation, and science policy. He received his undergraduate degree from SUNY Stony Brook and his MA and PhD from the University of Rochester. He is the author of *Trust: Representatives and Constituents; American Politics: Strategy and Choice*; and numerous articles on American politics. His research and graduate students have received funding from the National Science Foundation and the National Council for Eurasian and East European Research. He has also served as a consultant to congressional candidates and party campaign committees, as well as to the U.S. Department of Energy, the U.S. Department of Health and Human Services, and other state and local government agencies. He was also a Fulbright Senior Scholar in Moscow, Russia, during 2011–2012.

David T. Canon

is a professor emeritus in the political science department at the University of Wisconsin, Madison. He served as chair of the department from 2014–2017 and in Fall 2020. He received his PhD from the University of Minnesota and his BA from Indiana University, Bloomington. His teaching and research interests were in American political institutions, especially Congress, and racial representation. He is the author of *Race, Redistricting, and Representation* (winner of the Richard F. Fenno, Jr. Prize for the best book on legislative politics); *The Dysfunctional Congress?* (with Kenneth Mayer); and *Actors, Athletes, and Astronauts: Political Amateurs in the U.S. Congress*. He served as the editor of the *Election Law Journal* and as the Congress editor of *Legislative Studies Quarterly*. He was an AP® consultant and taught in the University of Wisconsin Summer AP® Institute for U.S. Government & Politics from 1997–2022. Professor Canon is the recipient of a University of Wisconsin Chancellor's Distinguished Teaching Award.

Contents in Brief

Contents

Part II: Politics

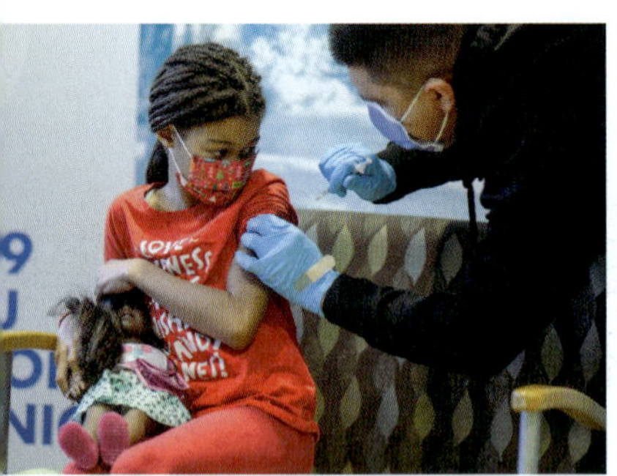

7. The Media 252

8. Political Parties 284

9. Elections 322

10. Interest Groups 368

Part III: Institutions

14. The Courts 528

Part IV: Policy

15. Economic Policy 574

OBAMACARE

17. Foreign Policy 662

Appendix

Preface

Welcome to the Eighth Edition Election Update to *American Politics Today*. In this edition, we continue our commitment to being "ruthlessly contemporary" by focusing on extensive revisions on three topics: the dynamic 2024 elections (Chapter 9), key congressional developments (Chapter 11), and consequential Supreme Court decisions (Chapter 14). While we have made updates throughout the book, we have focused on our efforts in these areas in both the book and student and instructor resources.

This book is based on three simple premises: politics is conflictual, political process matters, and politics is everywhere. It reflects our belief that politics is explainable, that political outcomes can be understood in terms of decisions made by individuals—and that the average college undergraduate can make sense of the political world in these terms. It focuses on contemporary American politics, the events and outcomes that our students have lived through and know something about. The result, we believe, is a book that provides an accessible but rigorous account of the American political system.

American Politics Today is also the product of our dissatisfaction. Thirty years ago, we were assistant professors together at the same university, assigned to teach the introductory class in alternate semesters. Though our graduate training was quite different, we found that we shared a deep disappointment with available texts. Their wholesale focus on grand normative concepts such as civic responsibility or their use of advanced analytic themes left students with little idea of how American politics really works, how events in Washington, D.C., affect their everyday lives, and how to piece together all the facts about American politics into a coherent explanation of why things happen as they do. These texts did not engender excitement, fascination, or even passing interest. What they did was put students to sleep.

As with previous editions, the overarching goal of the Election Update Edition is to describe what happens in American politics but also to explain behavior and outcomes. In part we wish to counter the widespread belief among students that politics is too complicated, too chaotic, or too secretive to make sense of. More than that, we want to empower our students, to demonstrate that everyday American politics is relevant to their lives. This emphasis is also a response to the typical complaint about American government textbooks—that they are full of facts but devoid of useful information and that after students finish reading, they are no better able to answer "why" questions than they were before they cracked open the book.

In this updated edition, we maintain our focus on conflict and compromise in American politics—identifying what Americans agree and disagree about and assessing how conflict shapes American politics, from campaign platforms to policy outcomes. Though this emphasis seems especially timely given recent elections and the social movements and dynamic global events that preceded them, our aim is to go beyond these events to identify a fundamental constant in American politics: the reality that much of politics is driven by disagreements over the scope and form of government policy and that compromise is an essential component of virtually all significant changes in government policy. Indeed, it is impossible to imagine politics without conflict. Conflict was embedded in the American political system by the Founders, who set up a system of checks and balances to make sure that no single group could dominate. The Constitution's division of power guarantees that enacting and implementing laws will involve conflict and compromise. Furthermore, the Constitution itself was constructed as one long series of compromises. Accordingly, despite the general dislike people have for conflict, our students must recognize that conflict and compromise lie at the heart of politics.

Throughout the text, we emphasize common sense, showing students that politics inside the Beltway is often strikingly similar to the students' own everyday interactions. For example, what sustains policy compromises made by members of Congress? The fact that the members typically have long careers, that they interact frequently with each other, and that they only deal with colleagues who have kept their word in the past. These strategies are not unique to the political world. Rather, they embody rules of thumb that most people follow (or are at least aware of) in their everyday interactions. In short, we try to help students understand American politics by emphasizing how it is not all that different from the world they know.

This focus on common sense is coupled with many references to the political science literature. We believe that contemporary research has something to say about prediction and explanation of events that students care about—and that these insights can be taught without turning students into game theorists or statisticians. Our text presents the essential insights of contemporary research, motivated by real-world political phenomena and explained using text or simple diagrams. This approach gives students a set of tools for understanding politics, provides an introduction to the political science literature, and matches up well with students' commonsense intuitions about everyday life. Moreover, by showing that academic scholarship is not a blind alley or irrelevant, this approach helps bridge the gap between an instructor's teaching and his or her research.

In this edition, we also had the opportunity to continue to enhance our resources to support teaching and learning so that they better reflect where students are today. That means reshaping the book to include cutting-edge scholarship and also tools that support student success to ensure all students understand why they should care about American government. In conjunction with these changes to the text, we wanted to integrate meaningful pedagogical support through the following resources:

The **Norton Illumine Ebook** supports engagement, assessment, and self-reflection as students learn. Each learning objective now features new **Check Your Understanding** questions that provide an opportunity for students to ensure they have grasped the main concepts. Students see how they have performed, and this completion grade reports to your learning management system, allowing you to confirm student reading.

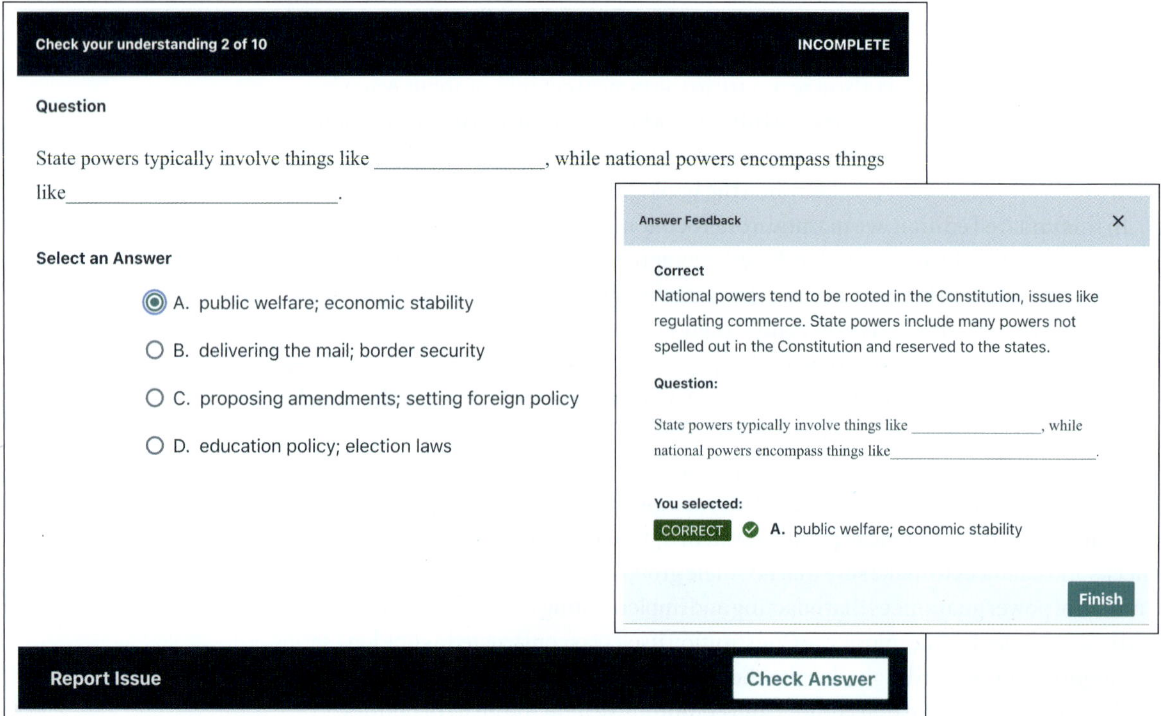

Dynamic Data Figures give students more opportunities to build their quantitative literacy skills by exploring trends over time in select figures, maps, and graphs in each chapter.

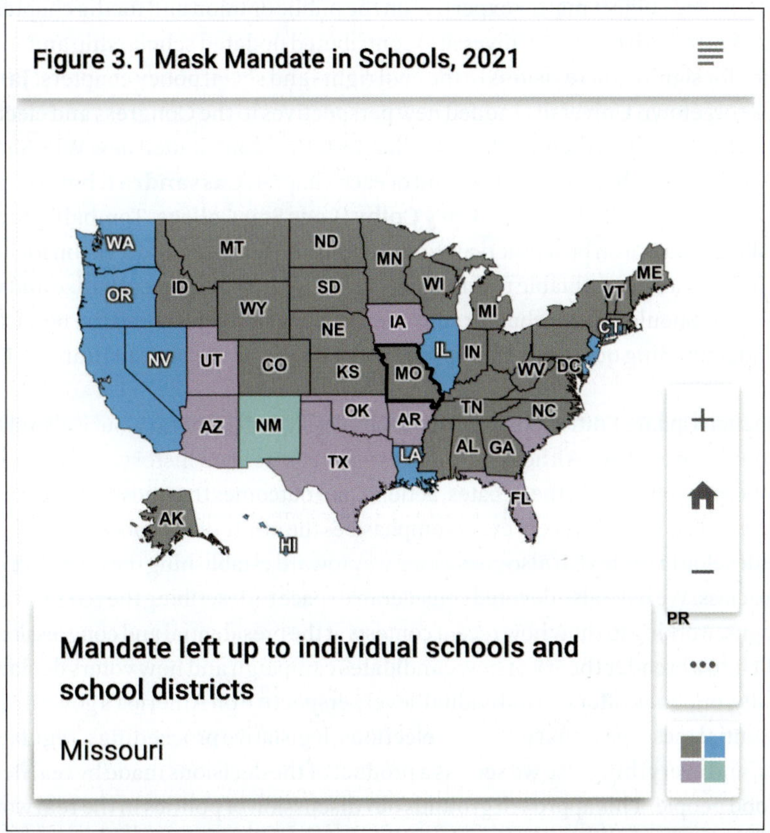

Why Should I Care? end-of-chapter summaries connect the dots across the learning objectives and encourage students to reflect on how the topic of the chapter shapes the world in which we live.

CHECK YOUR UNDERSTANDING

"Why Should I Care?"

The Constitution clearly creates a federal system that consists of states and a national governing body, giving to each distinct functions and authorities. However, the Constitution does not paint a comprehensive picture of all the different potential interactions and ways in which the divisions between the national government and the states might arrive in conflict, especially in a digital age characterized by increasingly complex and interconnected economies, digital commerce and connections, and ever more diverse understandings about humanity. The framers of the Constitution, through compromises at the Constitutional Convention, understandings of their own limitations of knowledge and imagination, and intentional areas of vagueness built into the Constitution and its subsequent amendments, did not seek to prescribe solutions to future disputes over authority; rather, they defined the framework that would be used to find solutions.

How do we see that in action today? States have long served as what Justice Louis Brandeis labeled "laboratories of democracy," designing and implementing laws, policies, and institutions to answer the needs and demands of the public they serve. Often the policy experiments in the states have yielded significant positive outcomes later adopted by other states and the national government, such as Wyoming granting voting rights to women by 1869, fifty-one years before the ratification of the Nineteenth Amendment, and the expanded access to health insurance passed in Massachusetts under Governor Mitt Romney that later became the framework for the Affordable Care Act during the Obama administration. But experimentation with policies in states have not always had positive outcomes. Issues like legal racial segregation, child labor, and lax environmental policies have often triggered expanded federal involvement as states either created or neglected harmful situations. Today, states often turn to the federal government for help in addressing economic and natural disasters—like the COVID-19 pandemic, wildfires in the West, and flooding after storms in coastal states like Texas, Louisiana, and South Carolina—that overwhelm state infrastructures, a benefit of federalism that even the most anti–big government states embrace in times of trouble.

In her Senate confirmation hearing as the first Black woman to be nominated to the U.S. Supreme Court, Justice Ketanji Brown Jackson was asked by Texas senator John Cornyn if she agreed with the 2015 decision of the Supreme Court in *Obergefell v. Hodges* that granted constitutional protections nationally to same-sex couples or if marriage was legally best left to the states to decide. Senator Cornyn's question demonstrates the ongoing debates over what the appropriate limits and divisions of power between the states and the national government are.

We couldn't have made these changes all on our own, so we put together an advisory board of instructors at diverse institutions to support the development of these elements. Their contributions, support, and expertise helped us strengthen the core content and pedagogical elements. **Amber Boydstun** (University of California, Davis) provided subject matter expertise on the public opinion and media chapters. **Candis Watts Smith** (Duke University) contributed updated scholarship and guidance for significant revisions to the civil rights and social policy chapters. **Jamil Scott** (Georgetown University) added new perspectives to the Congress and elections chapters. In addition to their work on the chapters, they contributed new Why Should I Care? summaries that appear at the end of each chapter. **Cassandra Khatri** (Lone Star College, University Park) and **Cory Colby** (Lone Star College, Tomball) provided invaluable guidance on best practices for teaching and learning and a vision for how to make the book a more valuable tool for students. They helped conceptualize and write the new Why Should I Care? chapter summaries. Cory Colby authored the new Check Your Understanding questions that appear in the book and the Norton Illumine Ebook.

This Election Update Edition continues to be ruthlessly contemporary, but it also places recent events in context. Although we do not ignore American history, our stress is on contemporary politics—on the debates, actions, and outcomes that most college students are aware of. Focusing on recent events emphasizes the utility of the concepts and insights that we develop in the text. It also goes a long way toward establishing the relevance of the intro class. We have also devoted considerable space to describing the 2022 and 2024 campaigns, working to show how recent contests at the presidential and congressional levels fit into a broader theory of how candidates campaign and how voters decide.

Finally, our book offers an individual-level perspective on America's government. The essential message is that politics—elections, legislative proceedings, regulatory choices, and everything else we see—is a product of the decisions made by real flesh-and-blood people. This approach grounds our discussion of politics in the real world. Many texts focus on abstractions such as "the eternal debate," "the great questions," or "the pulse of democracy." We believe that these constructs don't explain where the debate, the questions, or even democracy come from. Nor do they help students understand what's going on in Washington, D.C., and elsewhere, as it's not obvious that the participants themselves care much about these sorts of abstractions—quite the opposite, in fact.

We replace these constructs with a focus on real people and actual choices. The primary goal is to make sense of American politics by understanding why politicians, bureaucrats, judges, and citizens act as they do. That is, we are grounding our description of American politics at the most fundamental level—an individual facing a decision. How, for example, does a voter choose among candidates? Stated that way, it is reasonably easy to talk about where the choice came from, how the individual might evaluate different options, and why one choice might look better than the others. Voters' decisions may be understood by examining the different feasible strategies they employ (issue voting, retrospective evaluations, stereotyping, and so on) and by asking why some voters use one strategy while others use a different one.

By focusing on individuals and choices, we can place students in the shoes of the decision makers, and in so doing, give them insight into why people act as they do. We can discuss, for example, why a House member might favor enacting wasteful pork-barrel spending, even though a proposal full of such projects will make his constituents economically worse off—and why constituents might reward such behavior, even if they suspect the truth. By taking this approach, we are not trying to let legislators off the hook. Rather, we believe that any real understanding of the political process must begin with a sense of the decisions the participants make and why they make them.

Focusing on individuals also segues naturally into a discussion of consequences, allowing us to move from examining decisions to describing and evaluating outcomes. In this way, we can show students how large-scale outcomes in politics, such as inefficient programs, don't happen by accident or because of malfeasance. Rather, they are the predictable results of choices made by individuals (here, politicians and voters).

The policy chapters in the Full and Essentials Editions also represent a distinctive feature of this book. The discussion of policy at the end of an intro class often fits awkwardly with the material covered earlier. It is supposed to be a culmination of the semester-long discussion of institutions, politicians, and political behavior, but instead it often becomes an afterthought that gets discarded when time runs out in the last few weeks of class. Our policy chapters explicitly draw on previous chapters' discussions of the actors that shape policy: the president, Congress, the courts, interest groups, and parties. By doing so, these chapters show how all the pieces of the puzzle fit together.

Finally, this book reflects our experience as practicing scholars and teachers, as well as interactions with more than 20,000 students in introductory classes at several universities. Rather than thinking of the intro class as a service obligation, we believe it offers a unique opportunity for faculty to develop a broader sense of American politics and American political science, while at the same time giving students the tools they need to behave as knowledgeable citizens or enthusiastic political science majors. We hope that it works for you as well as it does for us.

Features of the Text and Media Package

The book's "three key ideas"

are fully integrated throughout the text.

- **Politics Is Conflictual** and conflict and compromise are a normal, healthy part of politics. The questions debated in elections and the policy options considered by people in government are generally marked by disagreement at all levels. Making policy typically involves important issues on which people disagree, sometimes strongly; so compromise, bargaining, and tough choices about trade-offs are often necessary.
- **Political Process Matters** because it is the mechanism we have established to resolve conflicts and achieve compromise. Governmental actions result from conscious choices made by voters, elected officials, and bureaucrats. The media often cover political issues in the same way they do sporting events, and though this makes for entertaining news, it also leads citizens to overlook the institutions, rules, and procedures that have a decisive influence on American life. Politics really is not just a game.
- **Politics Is Everywhere** in that the results of the political process affect all aspects of Americans' everyday lives. Politics governs what people can and cannot do, their quality of life, and how they think about events, other people, and situations.

Updated chapter openers and conclusions

present two sides of a controversy that has dominated media headlines—and about which people have passionate, emotion-driven opinions from both points of view—framed by quotes from politicians, pundits, and everyday people who hold these views. These include the future of democracy (The Constitution and the Founding), Biden's decision to step out of the race (Political Parties), and Kamala Harris's historic run for the White House (The Presidency). The Unpacking the Conflict sections at the end of each chapter show how the nuts and bolts of the chapter topic can be applied to help students understand both sides of these debates.

New coverage of the 2024 elections and the Biden administration

provides numerous graphics analyzing the 2022 and 2024 elections and the Biden presidency, including coverage of current issues, such as the economy, recent Supreme Court decisions, and the U.S. response to the conflicts in the Middle East and between Russia and Ukraine.

Organization around chapter goals

stresses learning objectives and mastery of core material.

- **Chapter Goals** appear at the beginning of the chapter and then recur at the start of the relevant sections throughout the chapter to create a more active reading experience that emphasizes important learning objectives.

Special features support student success

by reinforcing the three key ideas while introducing other important ways to think about American politics.

- **Check Your Understanding** questions with rich answer feedback following each main section of the Norton Illumine Ebook support students and give them opportunities to practice. Written by Cory Colby, these new questions incorporate popular culture references, hypothetical scenarios, and other applied question stems to ensure the students can see how the concepts play out in their daily lives, and ensure they get the remediation they need before moving on. Students' progress is tracked as they work toward completion through easy-to-use assignment tools and learning management system (LMS) integration.
- **Why Should I Care?** chapter conclusions break down the core concepts and provide examples of how these concepts impact students' own lives. Building on the popular Why Should I Care? section summaries, these offer opportunities for students to make sense of what they are learning in a way that matters to them.
- **The Media Checklist for Assessing Reporting on Politics infographic** provides a five-step framework for best practices for assessing media sources ranging from tweets to news articles.
- **How It Works: In Theory/How It Works: In Practice graphics,** many new to this edition, highlight key political processes and structures and build graphical literacy. The new feature in the Elections chapter explores the Electoral College and the strategy deployed in 2024.
- **What Do the Facts Say? features** develop quantitative reasoning skills by teaching students to read and interpret data on important political issues and current events. Five special features focus on honing students' media literacy skills by breaking down various media sources, including tweets, articles, and quotations, using the framework introduced in the Media Checklist for Assessing Reporting on Politics.
- **Did You Know? features and pull quotes** give students tidbits of information that may induce questions and even inspire students to get involved.
- **Take a Stand features** address contemporary issues in a pro/con format and invite students to consider how they would argue their own position on the topic. Each feature concludes with critical-thinking questions. New and updated features include discussion on fighting climate change with market forces or regulation.
- **Nuts & Bolts features** provide students with concise explanations of key concepts, like the difference between civil liberties and civil rights, different kinds of gerrymanders, and brief summaries of campaign finance rules. These features provide an easy way for quick study and review.

Tools for a dynamic classroom

- The **Norton Illumine Ebook** makes high-quality content shine brighter through engaging and motivational features that illuminate core concepts for all students in a supportive, accessible, and low-stakes environment. Check Your Understanding questions with rich feedback motivate students and build confidence in their learning, and embedded Dynamic Data Figures offer opportunities to build quantitative literacy through in-depth analysis. The active reading experience also includes the ability to highlight, take notes, search, read offline, and more. Instructors can promote student accountability by adding their own content and notes and through easy-to-use assignment tools in their LMS.

- **InQuizitive, Norton's adaptive learning tool,** accompanies the Eighth Edition Election Update of *American Politics Today* and reinforces reading comprehension with a focus on the foundations of government and major political science concepts. Guiding feedback helps students understand why their answers were right or wrong and steers them back to the text. To try it out, go to https://digital.wwnorton.com/amerpoltoday8update.
- **The Evaluating Sources InQuizitive module,** like the current How to Read Charts and Graphs tutorial, walks students step by step through identifying and understanding what a source is, how it is used in an argument, and whether it is a valid source or not (such as fake news). Paired with the Media Checklist, this module will help students be better prepared than ever to understand and evaluate the news.
- **Features for your Learning Management System (LMS)** allow you to easily bring Norton's high-quality digital content into your existing LMS. The content is fully editable and adaptable to your course needs. The Norton Coursepack for *American Politics Today,* Eighth Edition Election Update, contains the following activities and quizzes:
    - **How to Read Charts and Graphs tutorial** that provides students with extra practice and guidance interpreting common representations of data that they will encounter in this textbook and in the world,
    - **Simulations** tied to each chapter that allow students to inhabit the role of various political actors to help them better understand political decision making,
    - **How It Works: In Theory/How It Works: In Practice animated graphics,** with assessment, that guide students through understanding political processes and institutions,
    - **What Do the Facts Say? activities** that give students more practice with quantitative skills and more familiarity with how political scientists know what they know, and
    - **Take a Stand exercises** that present students with multiple sides of contemporary debates and ask them to consider and refine their own views based on what they've learned.
- **The test bank** contains more than 1,800 questions tagged to chapter learning objectives and keyed to Bloom's taxonomy.
- **An Interactive Instructor's Guide (IIG)** includes chapter outlines, class activities, and discussion questions, and suggestions for additional resources to engage students.
- **Instructor PowerPoints** contain fully customizable lecture slides with clicker questions and How It Works: In Theory and How It Works: In Practice animated PowerPoint slides for optimal classroom presentation.

Acknowledgments

This Election Update Edition of *American Politics Today* is again dedicated to our families. Our wives, Regina and Sarah, have continued to accommodate our deadlines and schedules and have again served as our most accurate critics and sources of insight and inspiration. Our children have again been forced to contend with politics and textbook writing as a perennial topic of conversation in their visits home, and have responded with critiques and ideas of their own, which appear throughout the text. In light of important recent and ongoing discussions, we wanted to note that consistent with our strong commitment to diversity and our belief that all should be treated with respect, we are capitalizing the names of all racial, religious, and ethnic groups.

Our colleagues at Indiana University and the University of Wisconsin (and before that, Duke University for both of us) provided many opportunities to talk about American politics and teaching this course.

Bill thanks his colleagues at Indiana University and elsewhere, including Christine Barbour, John Brehm, Laura Bucci, Ted Carmines, Chris DeSante, Mike Ensley, Bernard Fraga, Matthew Hayes, Yanna Krupnikov, Lin Ostrom, Regina Smyth, Steven Webster, Will Winecoff, and Jerry Wright, for sharp insights and encouragement at crucial moments. He is also grateful to many teaching assistants who have helped him organize and teach the intro class at three universities. Finally, he thanks the students at the Higher School of Economics in Moscow, Russia, where he taught the introductory class as a Fulbright Scholar in 2012.

David gives special thanks to Ken Mayer, whose daily "reality checks" and consistently thoughtful professional and personal advice are greatly appreciated. Barry Burden, Kathy Cramer, Ben Marquez, Ryan Owens, Ellie Powell, Howard Schweber, Alex Tahk, Dave Weimer, Susan Yackee, and all the great people at Wisconsin have provided a wonderful community within which to teach and research American politics. John Coleman, who has moved on to become a dean at the University of Minnesota, also deserves special thanks as a former member of the intro American team and good friend and colleague. David would also like to thank the students at the University of Debrecen in Hungary, where he taught American politics as a Fulbright Scholar in 2003–2004, and the Eberhard Karls University of Tübingen, Germany, where he taught as a Fulbright Scholar in 2011–2012. The Hungarian students' unique perspective on democracy, civil liberties, and the role of government required David to think about American politics in a different way. The German students' views on the role of political parties, campaigns, and the social welfare state also provided a strong contrast to the views of his American students.

Both of us are grateful to the political science faculty at Duke University, who, in addition to giving us our first academic jobs, worked to construct a hospitable and invigorating place to research and to teach. In particular, Rom Coles, Ruth Grant, John Aldrich, Tom Spragens, Taylor Cole, and David Barber were model teachers, colleagues, and scholars. We both learned to teach by watching them, and we are better instructors and scholars for it.

We are indebted to the outstanding people at W. W. Norton who have been our full partners through all eight editions. Our editor Laura Wilk is a graceful, insightful taskmaster, and her new perspective has improved the text immensely. Steve Dunn was responsible for getting the process started and providing good counsel from beginning to end. Roby Harrington has been a source of constant encouragement and feedback. Sarah McGinnis has been a superb project editor, bringing to the project her talent for clarity of words and visuals. Amla Sanghvi put together an excellent photo program. Elizabeth Trammell cleared permissions for the figures and tables. Rich Bretan handled production with efficiency and good humor. Jillian Burr and Open design studio created a beautiful design for the book's interior and cover. Spencer Richardson-Jones, Lexi Malakhoff, and Ethan Patrick's clear vision for the ever-more-complex and rich digital media package has been a major help. And Marlee Lisker is our fearless marketer. We also would like to thank Peter Lesser, Aaron Javsicas, and Ann Shin for their outstanding work on earlier editions. The entire crew at Norton has been incredibly professional and supportive in ways we never expected when we started writing this book. Signing with them 20 years ago was an eyes-shut home run.

We are also indebted to the many reviewers who have commented on the text.

First Edition Reviewers

Dave Adler, *Idaho State University*
Rick Almeida, *Francis Marion University*
Jim Bailey, *Arkansas State University–Mountain Home*
Todd Belt, *University of Hawaiʻi at Hilo*
Scott Buchanan, *Columbus State University*
Randy Burnside, *Southern Illinois University, Carbondale*
Carolyn Cocca, *SUNY College at Old Westbury*
Tom Dolan, *Columbus State University*
Dave Dulio, *Oakland University*
Matt Eshbaugh-Soha, *University of North Texas*
Kevin Esterling, *University of California, Riverside*
Peter Francia, *East Carolina University*
Scott Frisch, *California State University, Channel Islands*
Sarah Fulton, *Texas A&M University*
Keith Gaddie, *University of Oklahoma*
Joe Giammo, *University of Arkansas at Little Rock*
Kate Greene, *University of Southern Mississippi*
Steven Greene, *North Carolina State University*
Phil Habel, *Southern Illinois University, Carbondale*
Charles Hartwig, *Arkansas State University, Jonesboro*
Ted Jelen, *University of Nevada, Las Vegas*
Jennifer Jensen, *Binghamton University, SUNY*
Terri Johnson, *University of Wisconsin–Green Bay*
Luke Keele, *Ohio State University*
Linda Keith, *The University of Texas at Dallas*
Chris Kelley, *Miami University*
Jason Kirksey, *Oklahoma State University*
Jeffrey Kraus, *Wagner College*
Chris Kukk, *Western Connecticut State University*
Mel Kulbicki, *York College*
Joel Lieske, *Cleveland State University*
Steve Light, *University of North Dakota*
Baodong (Paul) Liu, *University of Utah*
Ken Long, *University of Saint Joseph, Connecticut*
Michael Lynch, *University of Kansas*
Cherie Maestas, *Florida State University*
Tom Marshall, *The University of Texas at Arlington*
Scott McClurg, *Southern Illinois University, Carbondale*
Jonathan Morris, *East Carolina University*
Jason Mycoff, *University of Delaware*
Sean Nicholson-Crotty, *University of Missouri, Columbia*
Timothy Nokken, *Texas Tech University*
Sandra O'Brien, *Florida Gulf Coast University*
John Orman, *Fairfield University*
L. Marvin Overby, *University of Missouri, Columbia*
Catherine Paden, *Simmons College*
Dan Ponder, *Drury University*
Paul Posner, *George Mason University*
David Redlawsk, *University of Iowa*
Russell Renka, *Southeast Missouri State University*
Travis Ridout, *Washington State University*
Andy Rudalevige, *Dickinson College*
Denise Scheberle, *University of Wisconsin–Green Bay*
Tom Schmeling, *Rhode Island College*
Pat Sellers, *Davidson College*
Dan Smith, *Northwest Missouri State University*
Dale Story, *The University of Texas at Arlington*
John Vile, *Middle Tennessee State University*
Mike Wagner, *University of Nebraska*
Dave Wigg, *St. Louis Community College*
Maggie Zetts, *Purdue University*

Second Edition Reviewers

Danny Adkison, *Oklahoma State University*
Hunter Bacot, *Elon College*
Tim Barnett, *Jacksonville State University*
Robert Bruhl, *University of Illinois at Chicago*
Daniel Butler, *Yale University*
Jennifer Byrne, *James Madison University*
Jason Casellas, *The University of Texas at Austin*
Jeffrey Christiansen, *Seminole State College*
Richard Conley, *University of Florida*
Michael Crespin, *University of Georgia*
Brian DiSarro, *California State University, Sacramento*
Ryan Emenaker, *College of the Redwoods*
John Evans, *California State University, Northridge*
John Fliter, *Kansas State University*
Jimmy Gleason, *Purdue University*
Dana Glencross, *Oklahoma City Community College*
Jeannie Grussendorf, *Georgia State University*
Phil Habel, *Southern Illinois University, Carbondale*
Lori Han, *Chapman University*
Katy Harriger, *Wake Forest University*
Richard Himelfarb, *Hofstra University*
Doug Imig, *University of Memphis*
Daniel Klinghard, *College of the Holy Cross*
Eddie Meaders, *University of North Texas*
Kristy Michaud, *California State University, Northridge*
Kris Miler, *University of Illinois at Urbana-Champaign*
Melinda Mueller, *Eastern Illinois University*
Michael Mundt, *Oakton Community College*
Emily Neff-Sharum, *The University of North Carolina at Pembroke*
David Nice, *Washington State University*
Tim Nokken, *Texas Tech University*
Stephen Nuño, *Northern Arizona University*
Richard Powell, *University of Maine, Orono*
Travis Ridout, *Washington State University*
Sara Rinfret, *University of Wisconsin–Green Bay*
Martin Saiz, *California State University, Northridge*
Gabriel Ramon Sanchez, *University of New Mexico*
Charles Shipan, *University of Michigan*
Dan Smith, *Northwest Missouri State University*
Rachel Sondheimer, *United States Military Academy*
Chris Soper, *Pepperdine University*
Walt Stone, *University of California, Davis*
Greg Streich, *University of Central Missouri*
Charles Walcott, *Virginia Tech*
Rick Waterman, *University of Kentucky*
Edward Weber, *Washington State University*
Jack Wright, *Ohio State University*

Third Edition Reviewers

Steve Anthony, *Georgia State University*
Marcos Arandia, *North Lake College*
Richard Barberio, *SUNY Oneonta*
Jody Baumgartner, *East Carolina University*
Brian Berry, *The University of Texas at Dallas*
David Birch, *Lone Star College–Tomball*
Eileen Burgin, *University of Vermont*
Randolph Burnside, *Southern Illinois University, Carbondale*
Kim Casey, *Northwest Missouri State University*
Christopher Chapp, *University of Wisconsin–Whitewater*
Daniel Coffey, *University of Akron*
William Corbett, *The University of Texas at El Paso*
Jonathan Day, *Western Illinois University*
Rebecca Deen, *The University of Texas at Arlington*
Brian DiSarro, *California State University, Sacramento*
Nelson Dometrius, *Texas Tech University*
Stan Dupree, *College of the Desert*
David Edwards, *The University of Texas at Austin*
Ryan Emenaker, *College of the Redwoods*
John Evans, *University of Wisconsin–Eau Claire*
Brandon Franke, *Blinn College, Bryan*
Rodd Freitag, *University of Wisconsin–Eau Claire*
Donna Godwin, *Trinity Valley Community College*
Craig Goodman, *Texas Tech University*
Amy Gossett, *Lincoln University*
Tobin Grant, *Southern Illinois University*
Stephanie Hallock, *Harford Community College*
Alexander Hogan, *Lone Star College–CyFair*
Marvin King, *University of Mississippi*
Timothy LaPira, *James Madison University*
Mary Linder, *Grayson University*
Christine Lipsmeyer, *Texas A&M University*
Michael Lyons, *Utah State University*
Jill Marshall, *The University of Texas at Arlington*

Thomas Masterson, *Butte College*
Daniel Matisoff, *Georgia Institute of Technology*
Jason McDaniel, *San Francisco State University*
Mark McKenzie, *Texas Tech University*
Leonard McNeil, *Contra Costa College*
Melissa Merry, *University of Louisville*
Ann Mezzell, *Lincoln University*
Eric Miller, *Blinn College, Bryan*
Jonathan Morris, *East Carolina University*
Leah Murray, *Weber State University*
Farzeen Nasri, *Ventura College*
Brian Newman, *Pepperdine University*
David Nice, *Washington State University*
Stephen Nichols, *California State University San Marcos*
Tim Nokken, *Texas Tech University*
Barbara Norrander, *University of Arizona*
Andrew Reeves, *Boston University*
Michelle Rodriguez, *San Diego Mesa College*
Dan Smith, *Northwest Missouri State University*
Christopher Soper, *Pepperdine University*
Jim Startin, *The University of Texas at San Antonio*
Jeffrey Stonecash, *Syracuse University*
Linda Trautman, *Ohio University*
Kevin Unter, *University of Louisiana Monroe*
Michelle Wade, *Northwest Missouri State University*
Michael Wagner, *University of Nebraska-Lincoln*
Adam Warber, *Clemson University*
Wayne Wolf, *South Suburban College*

Fourth Edition Reviewers

Rickert Althaus, *Southeast Missouri State University*
Eric K. Austin, *Montana State University*
Evelyn Ballard, *Houston Community College Southeast*
Jim Battista, *University at Buffalo, SUNY*
Kenneth C. Blanchard Jr., *Northern State University*
Heidi Brockmann, *United States Military Academy*
Adriana Buliga-Stoian, *Mount Mercy University*
Abbe Allen DeBolt, *Sandhills Community College*
John C. Evans, *University of Wisconsin-Eau Claire*
Babette Faehmel, *Schenectady County Community College*
Daniel Fuerstman, *State College of Florida*
Stephanie Hallock, *Harford Community College*
John Hitt, *North Lake College*
Debra Jenke, *Angelina College*
Ronald A. Kuykendall, *Trident Technical College*
Paul Lewis, *Arizona State University*
Mary Linder, *Grayson College*
Michael Lyons, *Utah State University*
Wendy Martinek, *Binghamton University, SUNY*
Melissa Merry, *University of Louisville*
Javan "J. D." Mesnard, *Mesa Community College*
Monique Mironesco, *University of Hawai'i-West O'ahu*
Tim Nokken, *Texas Tech University*
David Parker, *Montana State University*
Sylvia Peregrino, *El Paso Community College*
Blayne Primozich, *El Paso Community College*
Bryan Rasmussen, *Collin College*
Suzanne M. Robbins, *George Mason University*
Susan Roomberg, *The University of Texas at San Antonio*
Michael Shamgochian, *Worcester State University*
Geoffrey Shine, *Wharton County Junior College*
Rachel Milstein Sondheimer, *United States Military Academy*
Gregory Streich, *University of Central Missouri*
Jeremy Teigen, *Ramapo College*
Dave Wells, *Arizona State University*

Fifth Edition Reviewers

Leslie Baker, *Mississippi State University*
Evelyn Ballard, *Houston Community College*
Jim Battista, *University at Buffalo, SUNY*
Nathaniel A. Birkhead, *Kansas State University*
William Blake, *Indiana University, Purdue University Indianapolis*
Kenneth C. Blanchard Jr., *Northern State University*
Michael P. Bobic, *Glenville State College*
Ben Christ, *Harrisburg Area Community College*
Rosalyn Crain, *Houston Community College, Northwest College*
Brian Cravens, *Blinn College-Schulenburg*
Stephanie R. Davis, *University of South Carolina*
Christi Dayley, *Weatherford College*
Justin B. Dyer, *University of Missouri*
Jonathan P. Euchner, *Missouri Western State University*
John W. Eyster, *University of Wisconsin-Whitewater*
Eddie Feng, *Weatherford College*
John P. Flanagan, *Weatherford College*
Peter L. Francia, *East Carolina University*
Daniel Fuerstman, *State College of Florida*
Willie Hamilton, *Mt. Jacinto College*
David Huseman, *Butler County Community College*
Debra Jenke, *Angelina College*

Catherine Johnson, *Weatherford College*
Joshua Kaplan, *University of Notre Dame*
Tim LaPira, *James Madison University*
Alan Lehmann, *Blinn College*
Morris Levy, *University of Southern California*
Michael S. Lynch, *University of Georgia*
Rob Mellen Jr., *Mississippi State University*
Timothy Nokken, *Texas Tech University*
Anthony O'Kegan, *Los Angeles Valley College*
Hyung Lae Park, *El Paso Community College*
Donna Rhea, *Houston Community College*
Joseph Romance, *Fort Hays State University*
Sam Scinta, *Viterbo University*
Michael Shamgochian, *Worcester State University*
Abram J. Trosky, *United States Coast Guard Academy*
Lenore VanderZee, *SUNY Canton*
Ronald W. Vardy, *Wharton County Community College; University of Houston*
Gordan Vurusic, *Grand Rapids Community College*
Jeremy Walling, *Southeast Missouri State University*

Sixth Edition Reviewers

Brent Andersen, *University of Maine at Presque Isle*
Nick Anspach, *York College of Pennsylvania*
Nick Beatty, *Missouri State University*
Todd Belt, *University of Hawai'i*
Mark Brewer, *University of Maine*
Mark Checchia, *Old Dominion University*
Tom Copeland, *Biola University*
Todd Curry, *The University of Texas at El Paso*
Erin Engels, *Indiana University School of Liberal Arts at IUPUI*
Greg Granger, *Northwestern State University of Louisiana*
Jeanette Harvie, *California State University, Los Angeles*
Susan Haynes, *Lipscomb University*
Carol Jasieniecki, *Santiago Canyon College*
Alana Jeydel, *American River College*
Travis Johnston, *University of Massachusetts Boston*
Jesse Kapenga, *The University of Texas at El Paso*
Cassandra Khatri, *Lone Star College—University Park*
David Kimball, *University of Missouri—St. Louis*
Keith Knutson, *Viterbo University*
Julie Lane, *University of North Carolina Wilmington*
Tim LaPira, *James Madison University*
Beth Leech, *Rutgers University*
Eric Loepp, *University of Wisconsin—Whitewater*
Darrell Lovell, *Lone Star College—University Park*
Drew McMurray, *Wabash Valley College*
Melissa Merry, *University of Louisville*
Akira Ruddle Miyamoto, *University of Hawai'i*
James Newman, *Southeastern Missouri State University*
Timothy Nokken, *Texas Tech University*
Stephen Northam, *University of North Georgia*
Hyung Park, *El Paso Community College*
Yuhua Qiao, *Missouri State University*
Jason Sides, *Southeastern Missouri State University*
Anand Edward Sokhey, *University of Colorado Boulder*
Herschel Thomas, *The University of Texas at Arlington*
Paul Weizer, *Fitchburg State University*
Maryann Zihala, *Ozarks Technical Community College*

Seventh Edition Reviewers

Audrey Ambrosino, *Middlesex Community College*
Brent Andersen, *University of Maine, Presque Isle*
Sean Anderson, *California State University Stanislaus*
John Aughenbaugh, *Virginia Commonwealth University*
Manuel Avalos, *University of Southern Maine*
Bruce Brady, *Norfolk Public Schools*
Cynthia Breneman, *Erie Community College, City Campus*
Kizmet Chandler, *Nitro High School*
Anne Comiskey, *St. Mary's Dominican High School*
Mark Drake, *West Bend West High School*
Denise Dupas, *Del Norte High School*
Erin Engels, *Indiana University-Purdue University Indianapolis*
John C. Evans, *Century College*
Frank Franz, *James Madison High School*
Annika Hagley, *Roger Williams University*
Rick Henderson, *Texas State University*
Josh Herring, *Jones County High School*
Mark Jendrysik, *University of North Dakota*
Jerrod Kelly, *North Carolina Wesleyan College*
Daniel Kirsch, *California State University, Sacramento*
Ronald Kuykendall, *Trident Technical College*
Denise Lutz, *East Meadow High School*
Thomas Marshall, *University of Texas at Arlington*
Laura Matthews, *Rochester High School*
Markie McBrayer, *University of Idaho*
Dylan McLean, *University of West Georgia*
Peter Meinberg, *Hartford Union High School*
Wendel Morden, *Shadow Hills High School*
Anthony Nownes, *University of Tennessee*
Anthony Peek, *Baton Rouge Magnet High School*
Joseph Pelletier, *Bangor High School*

Curt Portzel, *Pepperdine University*
Christina Rice, *Thomas M. Wootton High School*
Heather M. Rice, *Slippery Rock University of Pennsylvania*
Suzanne Robbins, *University of Florida*
Michael Romano, *Shenandoah University*
Marc Schwarz, *Pflugerville Independent School District*
Jeffrey Sher, *McKinney North High School*
Rebecca Small, *Fairfax County Public Schools*
Christine Soderquist, *Kenowa Hills High School*
Bob Turner, *Skidmore College*
Greg Wall, *Amador High School*
Paul Weizer, *Fitchburg State University*
Dave Wells, *Arizona State University*
Adam Wemmer, *Pacifica High School*

Eighth Edition Reviewers

Brent Anderson, *University of Maine at Presque Isle*
Andrew Aoki, *Augsburg University*
Manuel Avalos, *University of Southern Maine-Gorham Campus*
Leslie Baker, *Mississippi State University*
Kylee Britzman, *Lewis-Clark State College*
Jane Bryant, *John A. Logan College*
Michael Chan, *California State University–Long Beach*
Frank Colucci, *Purdue University Northwest*
Evan Crawford, *University of San Diego*
Bryan Dubin, *Oakland Community College*
Brian Fife, *Lehigh University*
William Garst, *Fresno State University*
John Givens, *Kennesaw State University*
Stephanie Hallock, *Harford Community College*
Lisa Kissopoulos, *University of Cincinnati*
Jill Lane, *North Seattle College*
Daewoo Lee, *Columbus State University*
Julie Lester, *Middle Georgia State University*
Michael Lynch, *University of Georgia*
Domenic Maffei, *Caldwell University*
Thomas Marshall, *University of Texas at Arlington*
Stephen Meinhold, *University of North Carolina–Wilmington*
Honey Minkowitz, *North Carolina Wesleyan University*
Hayley Munir, *Albright College*
Nicholas Pyeatt, *Pennsylvania State University–Altoona*
Heather M. Rice, *Slippery Rock University of Pennsylvania*
Jennifer Ross, *Lone Star College*
Cynthia Simon, *William Patterson University*
Chris Soper, *Pepperdine University*
Nicola Walters, *Humboldt University*
Paul Weizer, *Fitchburg State University*

Eighth Edition Election Update Reviewers

Robert H. Bruhl, *University of Illinois at Chicago*
Nathan Carrington, *University of Louisiana at Lafayette*
David Fleming, *Furman University*
Heidi Getchell-Bastien, *MassBay Community College*
Joon Kil, *Irvine Valley College*
Lisa Kissopoulos, *University of Cincinnati, Clermont College*
Jeffrey Kraus, *Wagner College*
Benjamin Gonzalez O'Brien, *San Diego State University*
Tessa Provins, *University of Pittsburgh*
Jesse Richman, *Old Dominion University*
Henry Srebrnik, *University of Prince Edward Island*
Pinar Tremblay, *Cal Poly, Pomona-CPP*
Brian Turnbull, *University of South Florida*
Adam L. Warber, *Clemson University*

We would like to thank Cory Colby for his thoughtful and considered suggestions for improving the text, as well as his work on the Check Your Understanding questions. His innovative teaching strategies make this a valuable resource for instructors. Danny Fuerstman provided invaluable feedback on the text, as well as led the development of InQuizitive. We're grateful for his commitment to the project and thoughtful feedback. We would also like to thank Eric Loepp for his thought leadership on online teaching, and his efforts authoring and enhancing the PowerPoints that accompany the text. It is a humbling experience to have so many smart people involved in the process of writing and revising this book. Their reviews are often critical but always insightful, and you the reader are the beneficiaries of their efforts. In many cases, the improvements in this edition are the direct result of their suggestions. They have our profound thanks.

William T. Bianco
David T. Canon
November 2024

American Politics Today

Eighth Edition, Election Update

1

Understanding American Politics

How does politics work and why does politics matter?

» **"Republican, Democrat, anybody else, we are all in this together. I believe for the most part you can trust respected medical authorities. I believe I'm one of them, so I think you can trust me . . . [and other experts] who have a track record of telling the truth."[1]**

Dr. Anthony Fauci, Director, National Institute of Allergy and Infectious Diseases, July 2020

« **"Make no mistake—the threat of bringing masks back is not a decision based on science, but a decision conjured up by liberal government officials who want to continue to live in a perpetual pandemic state."[2]**

Kevin McCarthy, House Republican leader, July 2021

Politics is conflictual. We saw this firsthand during the COVID-19 pandemic as federal and state governments enacted restrictions—including mask and vaccine mandates—that some say threatened their civil liberties. Informed opinions are essential to a democracy.

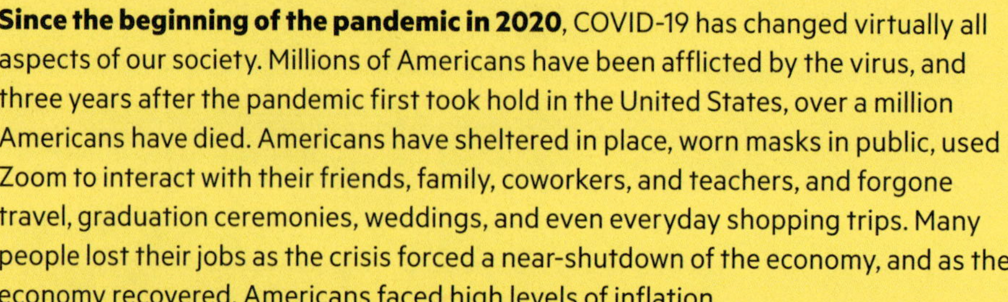

Since the beginning of the pandemic in 2020, COVID-19 has changed virtually all aspects of our society. Millions of Americans have been afflicted by the virus, and three years after the pandemic first took hold in the United States, over a million Americans have died. Americans have sheltered in place, worn masks in public, used Zoom to interact with their friends, family, coworkers, and teachers, and forgone travel, graduation ceremonies, weddings, and even everyday shopping trips. Many people lost their jobs as the crisis forced a near-shutdown of the economy, and as the economy recovered, Americans faced high levels of inflation.

The pandemic also highlighted the federal government's role as a nonpartisan provider of information, expertise, and services to American citizens, as the quote

CHAPTER GOALS

Describe the basic functions of government (pp. 4–9)

Define *politics* and identify three key ideas that help explain politics (pp. 9–15)

Identify major sources of conflict in American politics (pp. 16–21)

Explain how the American values of democracy, liberty, and equality work to resolve political conflict (pp. 21–24)

Understand how to interpret, evaluate, and use political information (pp. 24–28) from Dr. Fauci illustrates. Throughout the pandemic, federal emergency management personnel and National Guard troops staffed hospitals and distributed food and supplies. Operation Warp Speed, initiated by the Trump administration, funded efforts to develop and produce vaccines against COVID-19. The postal service delivered online purchases. In all, federal agencies provided over $6 trillion in assistance to individuals and businesses.

While some of the government's response to COVID-19 received broad support, many issues were intensely controversial. In the early days of the pandemic, some Republicans argued that Democrats were using the pandemic to expand the size and reach of government. As the pandemic evolved, Republicans and Democrats disagreed over when to reopen businesses and schools, the need for federal assistance packages, and the value of mask and vaccine mandates. These events illustrate one of the central arguments of this text: that American politics is almost always conflictual, and that arguments over public policy generally reflect real disagreements about what government should or should not do.

In addition, the pandemic illustrates a deeper issue in contemporary American politics: while there are many information sources, it is often hard to determine which are reliable—which stories are "fake news" and which are not. Americans' propensity to share information through social media means that outlandishly false stories can get widespread attention. Over the last three years, we have been bombarded with stories that said the pandemic was a military operation by a foreign government, that the virus could be treated with medicines intended for livestock, and that vaccines came with microchips that would allow Bill Gates to control our thoughts. None of these stories are true—but in a world where the public is overwhelmed with political information, it is easy to see why some truly fake news gets taken seriously—and why political actors from all sides might want to misinform the public.

If Americans can't even agree on which news is "fake," how can we know what to trust? In a complex world, how do Americans understand, evaluate, and act on the political information that they encounter when our political leaders disagree? In part, we will explore these questions throughout the book because the answers can tell us a lot about important political outcomes, including how people vote, what kinds of candidates win elections, and why some policies get enacted in Congress while others are defeated. At the same time, we hope to give you some ideas about how to find the information you need to make up your own mind about political debates.

DESCRIBE THE BASIC FUNCTIONS OF GOVERNMENT

Making sense of American government and politics

The premise of this book is simple: *American politics makes sense.* What happens in elections, in Washington, D.C., and everywhere else has a logical and often simple explanation. By the end of this book, we hope you get really good at analyzing the politics you see everywhere—in the news and in your own life.

This claim may seem unrealistic or even naive. On the surface, American politics often makes no sense. Polls show strong support for extreme, unconstitutional, or downright silly proposals. Candidates put more time into insulting their opponents than into making credible campaign promises. Members of Congress seem more interested in beating their political opponents than in getting something done, and the Democratic and Republican caucuses agree on virtually nothing.

Regardless of how you think about these events, it is important to remember two things. First, we are not claiming that all the people in politics are good, that citizens are well informed, that the right candidates always win elections, that legislative debate leads to thoughtful compromise, or that government decisions serve the public interest. In concrete terms, Dr. Fauci is not an infallible saint—nor is your least-liked politician an irredeemable sinner. What we are saying is that the political process is largely predictable and that we can reason from some basic principles about politics to develop a better understanding of why things happen in Washington.

Second, for all the turmoil surrounding the 2020 presidential election (including court cases, public debate, and violent actions), the basic rules of democracy still hold in America: votes were counted as they were supposed to be, and power was transferred to the winner. The polarization, distrust, and anger that seem to be core features of contemporary American politics are actually nothing new. Many people, we believe, are hostile toward American politics because they don't understand the political process, feel helpless to influence election outcomes or policy making, and believe that it is impossible to work within the system to change things (even deeply flawed practices such as racially biased policing). Here again, while these beliefs might be somewhat stronger than they were a generation ago, Americans have always been skeptical of politicians and political parties since the Founding.

To be clear, it is *not* our goal to turn you into a political junkie, a policy wonk, or a Democrat, Republican, or anything else. You don't need to like politics to make sense of it, but we hope that after finishing this book you will have a basic understanding of how the political process works and why it matters.

One of our goals is to help you take an active role in the political process, if you want to. A democracy allows citizens to defer complicated policy decisions to their elected leaders, but a democracy works better when citizens organize to make demands of government, monitor what politicians do, and hold them accountable at

Conflicts within the government—say, over immigration policy or a woman's right to an abortion—often reflect real divisions among American citizens about what government should do about certain issues. Groups on all sides of controversial issues pressure the government to enact their preferred policies.

the voting booth. This book will help you be an effective participant by providing the analytical skills you need to make sense of politics, even when it initially appears to make no sense at all.

We are not going to spend time talking about how American politics should be. Rather, our focus will be on explaining American politics as it is. Here are some other questions we will examine:

- Why don't people vote? Why *do* people vote? How do they decide whom to vote for?
- Why do so many people mistrust politicians and the political system?
- Why can't Congress get things done?
- Why is the Supreme Court so political?
- Can presidents do whatever they want? Why can't they do more?
- How much power do bureaucrats have?
- Are the media biased?

We will answer these questions and many others by applying three key ideas about the nature of politics: politics is conflictual, political process matters, and politics is everywhere. But first, we begin with an even more basic question: Why do we have a government?

Why do we have a government?

government
The system for implementing decisions made through the political process.

As we prepare to address this question, let's agree on a definition: **government** is the system for implementing decisions made through the political process. All countries have some form of government, which in general serves two broad purposes: to provide order and to promote the general welfare.

To Provide Order At a basic level, the answer to the question "Why do we have a government?" seems obvious: without government, there would be chaos. As the seventeenth-century British philosopher Thomas Hobbes said, life in the "state of nature" (that is, without government) would be "solitary, poor, nasty, brutish, and short."[3] Without government, there would be no laws—people could do whatever they wanted. Even if people tried to develop informal rules, there would be no way to guarantee enforcement of those rules. Accordingly, some of the most important roles of government are policing and providing national security.

The Founders of the United States noted this crucial role in the Constitution's preamble: two of the central goals of government are to "provide for the common defense" and to "insure domestic Tranquility." The former refers to military protection against foreign invasion and the defense of our nation's common security interests. The latter refers to policing and law enforcement within the nation, which today includes the National Guard, the Federal Bureau of Investigation (FBI), the Department of Homeland Security, state and local police, and the courts. So at a minimal level, government is necessary to provide security.

However, there's more to government than that. The Founders cited the desire to "establish Justice . . . and secure the Blessings of Liberty to ourselves and our Posterity." But do we need government to do these things? It may be obvious that the police power of the nation is required to prevent anarchy, but can't people have justice and liberty without government? In a perfect world, maybe, but the Founders had a more realistic view of human nature. As James Madison, one of the founding fathers (and the fourth president of the United States), said, "But what is government itself, but the greatest of all reflections on human nature? If men were angels, no government would be necessary. If angels were to govern men, neither external nor internal controls on government would be necessary."[4] Furthermore, Madison continued, people have a variety of interests that have "divided mankind into parties, inflamed them with mutual animosity, and rendered them much more disposed to vex and oppress each other than to co-operate for their common good."[5] That is, without government, we would quickly be headed toward Hobbes's nasty and brutish state of nature because of differences in opinion about what society should look like. Having a government means that people cannot act unilaterally against each other, but it also creates a new problem: people will try to use the government and its powers to impose their views on the rest of society.

Madison's view of human nature might sound pessimistic, but it was also realistic. He assumed that people were self-interested: we want what is best for ourselves and for our families, and to satisfy those interests we tend to form groups with like-minded people. Madison saw these groups, which he called **factions**, as being opposed to the public good, and his greatest fear was of tyranny by a faction imposing its will on the rest of the nation. For example, if one group took power and established an official state religion, that faction would be tyrannizing people who practiced a different religion. This type of oppression is precisely why many of the early American colonists fled Europe in the first place.

factions
Groups of like-minded people who try to influence the government. American government is set up to avoid domination by any one of these groups.

As we will discuss in Chapters 2 and 3, America's government seeks to control the effects of factions by dividing government power in three main ways. First, the **separation of powers** divides the government into three branches—judicial, executive, and legislative—and assigns distinct duties to each branch. Second, the system of **checks and balances** gives each branch some power over the other two. (For example, the president can veto legislation passed by Congress; Congress can impeach the president; and the Supreme Court has the power to interpret laws written by Congress to determine whether they are constitutional.) Third, **federalism** divides power yet again by allotting different responsibilities to local, state, and national government. With power divided in this fashion, Madison reasoned, no single faction could dominate the government.

separation of powers
The division of government power across the judicial, executive, and legislative branches.

checks and balances
A system in which each branch of government has some power over the others.

federalism
The division of power across the local, state, and national levels of government.

To Promote the General Welfare The preamble to the Constitution also states that the federal government exists to "promote the general Welfare." This means tackling the hard problems that Americans cannot solve on their own, such as taking care of the poor, the sick, and the aged, and dealing with global issues like climate change, pandemics, terrorist threats, and wars in other countries. However, government intervention is not inevitable—people can decide that these problems aren't worth solving. But if people *do* want to address these large problems, government action is necessary because **public goods** such as environmental protection or national defense are not efficiently provided by the free market, either because of **collective action problems** or for other reasons.

public goods
Services or actions (such as protecting the environment) that, once provided to one person, become available to everyone. Government is typically needed to provide public goods because they will be underprovided by the free market.

collective action problems
Situations in which the members of a group would benefit by working together to produce some outcome, but each individual is better off refusing to cooperate and reaping benefits from those who do the work.

It is easy for two people or even a small group to tackle a common problem without the help of government, but 1,000 people (to say nothing of the more than 334 million in the United States today) would have a very difficult time. They would suffer from the **free rider problem**—that is, because it is in everyone's own interest to let someone else do the work, the danger is that no one will contribute, even though everyone wants the outcome that collective contributions would create. A government representing more than 334 million people can provide public goods that all those people acting on their own would be unable to provide, so people elect leaders and pay taxes to provide those public goods.

free rider problem
The incentive to benefit from others' work without making a contribution, which leads individuals in a collective action situation to refuse to work together.

Collective action problems are common in modern society. Education is a great example. You benefit personally from your primary, secondary, and college education in terms of the knowledge and experience you gain, and from the higher salary and better job you will earn because of your college degree. However, society also benefits from your education. Your employer will benefit from your knowledge and skills, as will people you interact with. If education were provided solely by the free market, those who could afford schooling would be educated, but the rest would not, leaving a large segment of society with little or no education and therefore unemployable. So public education, like many important services, benefits all levels of society and must be provided by the government for the general welfare.

Now that we understand *why* we have a government, the next question is, *What* does the government do to "insure domestic Tranquility" and "promote the general Welfare"? Many visible components of the government promote these goals, from the police and armed services to the Internal Revenue Service, Federal Reserve, Postal Service, Social Security Administration, National Aeronautics and Space Administration, Department of Education, and Food and Drug Administration. In fact, it is hard to find an aspect of everyday life that does not involve the government in some way, as a provider of public goods, as a protector of civil liberties, as an enforcer of laws and property rights, or as a regulator of individual or corporate behavior. What makes politics both interesting and important is that in most of these cases, Americans disagree on what kinds of public goods the government should provide, or whether government should be involved at all.

Forms of government

While all governments must provide order and promote the general welfare, different types of governments accomplish this in various ways. Greek political philosopher Aristotle, writing in the fourth century BC, developed a classification scheme for governments that is still surprisingly useful. Aristotle distinguished three pure types of government based on the number of rulers versus the number of people ruled: monarchy (rule by one), aristocracy (rule by the few), and polity (rule by the many, such as the general population—this is the most general description of a democracy).

Two important government functions described in the Constitution are to "provide for the common defense" and "insure domestic Tranquility." The military and local police are two of the most commonly used forces the government maintains to fulfill those roles.

There are many ways to implement democracy. In its purest form, a democracy is a system in which citizens make policy choices directly, such as through referenda. However, all current democracies, including America's national government, are organized as republics, a form of democracy in which elected representatives make policy decisions on behalf of citizens. Republics throughout the world are organized very differently. For example, they allocate power differently among the executive, legislative, and judicial branches. Presidential systems such as the one we have in the United States tend to follow a separation of powers among the three branches, while parliamentary systems such as the one in the United Kingdom elect the chief executive from the legislature, resulting in much closer coordination between those two branches.

An additional distinction is the relationship among different levels of government. In a federal system (such as the United States), power is shared among the local, state, and national levels of government. In a unitary system (such as France or Japan), all power is held at the national level, and local governments must comply with orders from the central government. A confederation (like Switzerland) is a less common form of government in which states retain their sovereignty and autonomy but form a loose association at the national level.

DID YOU KNOW?

63%

of the world's population lives in countries considered to be free or partly free. Most countries considered not free are in Asia or Africa.

Source: Freedom House.

What is politics?

DEFINE *POLITICS* AND IDENTIFY THREE KEY IDEAS THAT HELP EXPLAIN POLITICS

We define **politics** as the process that determines what government does—whether and how it provides different public and private goods. You may consider politics the same thing as government, but we see government as the institutions that carry out the decisions made through the political process. Many aspects of our discussion of politics will probably sound familiar because your life involves politics on a regular basis. This may sound a little abstract, but it should become clear in light of the three key ideas of this book (see the How It Works graphic on p. 11).

politics
The process that determines what government does.

First, *politics is conflictual*. The questions debated in election campaigns and in Washington and the options considered by policy makers generally involve disagreement at all levels. The federal government does not spend much time resolving questions that everyone agrees on the answers to. Rather, making government policy involves issues on which people disagree, sometimes strongly, which makes compromise difficult—and this is a normal, healthy part of politics. Although compromise may be difficult to achieve, it is often necessary to produce outcomes that can be enacted and implemented.

Second, *political process matters*. Governmental actions don't happen by accident—they result from conscious choices made by elected officials and bureaucrats. Politics puts certain individuals into positions of power and makes the rules that structure their choices. The media often cover political campaigns the way they would report on a boxing match or the Super Bowl, focusing on the competition, rivalries, and entertaining stories, which can lead people to overlook the institutions, rules, and procedures that have a decisive influence on politics. Indeed, the political process is in part a mechanism for resolving conflict.

The most obvious example of the political process at work is elections, which democracies use to resolve a fundamental conflict: deciding who should lead the country and make policy choices. Another are the rules of the Senate discussed in Chapter 11, where 60 votes (more than a 51-vote majority) are required to enact most policy proposals.

Third, *politics is everywhere*. Decisions about what government should do or who should be in charge are integral to society, and they influence the everyday lives of all Americans. Politics helps determine what people can and cannot do, their quality of life, and how they think about events, people, and situations. Moreover, people's political thought and behavior are driven by the same types of calculations and decision-making rules that shape beliefs and actions in other parts of life. For example, deciding which presidential candidate to vote for is not so different from deciding which college to attend. For candidates, you might consider issue positions, character, and leadership ability, while for college you would weigh how schools fit your academic goals, how much tuition you can afford, and where different schools are located. In both cases you are consciously making a decision that will satisfy the criteria most important to you, given known budgetary and academic constraints.

Politics is conflictual

Political scientists have long recognized the central role of conflict in politics. In fact, one prominent theory in the mid-twentieth century saw conflict between interest groups as explaining most outcomes in American politics. The political scientist E. E. Schattschneider argued that the scope of political conflict—that is, how many people are involved in the fight—determines who wins in politics.[6] Others have argued that some conflict is helpful for group decision-making: if nobody challenges a widely shared but flawed view, people may convince themselves that the obvious flaws are not a problem.[7] Bureaucratic politics, congressional politics, elections, and even Supreme Court decision-making have all been studied through the lens of political conflict.[8]

Despite the consensus that conflict in politics is inevitable, most people do not like conflict, either in their personal lives or in politics. You probably have heard people say that the three topics one should not discuss in polite company are money, religion, and politics. Indeed, political scientists have found strong evidence that people avoid discussing politics in order to maintain social harmony.[9]

Conflict is inherent in American politics. Here, supporters and opponents of abortion rights argue in front of the Supreme Court building in Washington on the day the Court heard arguments in *Dobbs v. Jackson Women's Health Organization*, the 2022 case over the timeframe for allowing a woman to terminate a pregnancy. The Supreme Court ultimately ruled in favor of the plaintiff, overturning the landmark 1973 case *Roe v. Wade*.

How it works: **in theory**

Three Key Ideas for Understanding Politics

Politics Is Conflictual

Conflict and compromise are natural parts of politics. Political conflict over issues like the national debt, abortion, and health care **reflects disagreements among the American people** and often requires compromises within government.

Political Process Matters

How political conflicts are resolved is important. Elections determine who represents citizens in government. **Rules and procedures determine who has power** in Congress and other branches of government.

Politics Is Everywhere

What happens in government affects our lives in countless ways. Policies related to jobs and the economy, food safety and nutrition, student loans, and many other areas shape **our everyday lives**. We see political information in the news and encounter political situations in many areas of our lives.

Critical Thinking

1. **One implication of the idea that politics is conflictual is that politicians** may not want to negotiate compromises on important policy questions. Why do you think politicians sometimes refuse to compromise rather than work together to get things done?
2. **Think back to the discussion** of fake news at the beginning of this chapter. In what ways do disagreements over what constitutes "fake" news illustrate the three key ideas described here?

Many people apply their disdain for conflict to politicians as well. "Why is there so much partisan bickering?" our students frequently ask. "Why can't they just get along?" This dislike of conflict, and of politics more generally, produces a desire for what political scientists John R. Hibbing and Elizabeth Theiss-Morse call "stealth democracy"—that is, nondemocratic practices such as running government like a business or taking action without political debate. In essence, this idea reflects the hope that everything would be better if we could just take the politics out of politics. Hibbing and Theiss-Morse argue that to combat this belief, we need to do a better job of educating people about conflict and policy differences and that the failure to do so "is encouraging students to conclude that real democracy is unnecessary and stealth democracy will do just fine."[10] Conflict cannot be avoided in politics; ignoring fundamental disagreements will not make conflict go away.

The argument over abortion is a good example. Abortion rights have been a perennial topic of debate since a 1973 Supreme Court decision held that state laws banning abortion were unconstitutional (although this ruling was ultimately overturned in 2022). Surveys about abortion rights show that public opinion spans a wide range of policy options, with little agreement about which policy is best. (In Chapter 6, we will examine the political implications of this kind of broad disagreement.) Such conflicts reflect intense differences of opinion that are rooted in self-interest, ideology, and personal beliefs. Moreover, in such situations, no matter what Congress does, many people will be unhappy with the result. You might expect that politicians will ultimately find a compromise that satisfies everyone, but this is not always true. In many cases (abortion rights are a good example), no single policy choice satisfies even a slight majority of elected officials or citizens.

One consequence of political conflict is that one party's policy victories last only until the other party wins control of government. In his first week in office, for example, President Biden signed executive orders to investigate and reevaluate key components of President Trump's signature "America First" immigration policy, including restrictions on immigration and separating migrant families at the borders.

The idea that conflict is nearly always a part of politics should be no surprise. Situations in which everyone (or almost everyone) agrees about what government should be doing are easy to resolve: either a popular new policy is enacted or an unpopular issue is avoided, and the debate moves off the political agenda. Although issues where there is consensus resolve quickly and disappear, conflictual issues remain on the agenda as the winners try to extend their gains and the losers work to roll back policies. Thus, one reason that abortion rights is a perennial issue in campaigns and congressional debates is that there is no national consensus on when to allow abortions, no indication that the issue is becoming less important to citizens or elected officials, and no sign of a compromise policy that would attract widespread support.

An important consequence of the inevitable conflicts in American politics is that compromise and bargaining are essential to getting things done. Politicians who bargain with opponents are not necessarily abandoning their principles; striking a deal may be the only way to make some of the policy changes they want. Moreover, agreement sometimes exists even in the midst of controversy. For example, surveys that measure attitudes about abortion find widespread support for measures such as prohibiting government funding for abortions, requiring parental notification when a minor has an abortion, or requiring doctors who perform the procedure to present their patients with information on alternatives such as adoption, while only 15–25 percent (depending on the survey) think that abortion should always be illegal.[11]

Disagreement is something normal.

—Dalai Lama

Another consequence of conflict is that it is almost impossible to get exactly what you want from the political process. Even when a significant percentage of the population is united behind common goals—such as supporters of Donald Trump after the 2016 election, who demanded the repeal of Obamacare—these individuals almost always find that translating these demands into policy change requires them to accept something short of their ideal. Even with Democratic gains in the 2020 election, supporters of initiatives such as free college tuition or Medicare for All have found that they must accept more modest changes or risk winning nothing at all. The need for compromise does not mean that change is impossible, but rather means that what is achievable often falls short of individuals' demands.

Political process matters

The political process is often described like a sporting event. Election coverage often emphasizes the "horse race" (who's ahead in the latest poll), and accounts of negotiations between the president and Congress often make the process sound like a poker game. This emphasis overlooks an important point: politics is the process that determines what government does, none of which is inevitable. Public policy—everything from defending the nation to spending on Medicare—is up for grabs. Changes in federal policy can have profound consequences for large swaths of the population. Politics is not just a game.

Elections are an excellent example. Elections allow voters to give fellow citizens the power to enact laws, write budgets, and appoint senior bureaucrats and federal judges. It matters who gets elected. In the first two years after the 2020 election produced unified Democratic control of the presidency and Congress, many Trump-era environmental and employment regulations were repealed, the United States rejoined the Paris Agreement on climate change, and there were major increases in spending for government social programs. After the 2022 midterms, when Republicans gained control of the House, Democrats were unable to enact additional policy gains. Clearly, political process matters: if the 2020 or 2022 elections had gone the other way, outcomes in all these important areas would have been significantly different.

Yet politics is more than elections. As you will see, many unelected members of the federal bureaucracy have influence over what government does by virtue of their roles in developing and implementing government policies. The same is true for federal judges, who review government actions to see if they are consistent with the Constitution and other federal laws. These individuals' decisions are part of the political process, even though they are not elected to their positions.

Ordinary citizens are also part of politics. They can vote; donate time or money to interest groups, party organizations, or individual candidates; or demand action from these groups or individuals by writing letters, sending emails, or participating in public protest. Such actions can influence government policy, either by determining who holds the power to directly change policy or by signaling to policy makers which options have public support.

The political process mattered in the 2020 election, from determining who the candidates were to affecting which states received the most attention from campaigns. Both Joe Biden and Donald Trump spent a lot of time campaigning in Florida in a bid to win the state's Electoral College votes.

I'll let you write the substance, you let me write the procedure, and I'll screw you every time.

—John Dingell, former U.S. representative

Another important element of politics is the web of rules and procedures that determines who has the power to make choices about government policy. These rules range from the requirement that the president must be born a U.S. citizen, to the rules that structure debates and voting in the House and the Senate, to the procedures for approving new federal regulations. Seemingly innocuous rules can have an enormous impact on what can or does happen, which means that choices about these rules are actually choices about outcomes. The ability to determine political rules empowers the people who make those choices.

Politics is everywhere

Even though most Americans have little interest in politics, most of us encounter it every day. When you read the newspaper, watch television, go online, or listen to the radio, you'll almost surely encounter a political story. When you are walking down the street, you may see billboards, bumper stickers, or T-shirts advertising a candidate, a political party, an interest group, or an issue position. Someone may ask you to sign a petition. You may walk past an unhoused person and wonder whether a winning candidate followed through on their promise to help. You may glance at a headline about a Black Lives Matter protest and wonder why the protection of civil rights is such an enduring problem in America.

Many people have an interest in putting politics in front of us on a daily basis. Interest groups, political parties, and candidates work to raise public awareness of the political process and to shape what people know and want. Moreover, the news media offer extensive coverage of elections, governing, and how government policies affect ordinary Americans. Through efforts like these, politics really is everywhere.

Politics is also a fundamental part of how Americans think about themselves. Virtually all of us can name our party identification (Democrat, Republican, or Independent)[12] and can place our views on a continuum between liberal and conservative.[13]

Politics is everywhere in another important way, too: actions by the federal government touch virtually every aspect of your life. Figure 1.1 shows a time line for a typical college student on a typical day. As you can see, from the moment this student wakes up until the end of the day, their actions are influenced by federal

FIGURE 1.1

Government in a Student's Daily Life

On a typical day, the government plays a critical role in a student's daily life through federal programs, regulation, and spending. In addition to what is listed here, in what other aspects of your life does government play a part?

7:30	Wake up in an apartment building funded by a federal program.
8:00	Eat cereal regulated by the Food and Drug Administration.
8:15	Get dressed in clothing subject to import tariffs and regulations.
8:30	Check weather app that that uses data from the National Weather Service.
9:00	Check email using Internet developed with federal funding.
10:00	Drive to school in car whose design is shaped by federal regulations.
10:30	Drive past post office, military recruitment office, and environmental cleanup site.
11:00	Attend lecture by professor whose research receives federal funding.
4:00	Ride home from school on federally subsidized mass transit.
7:30	Pay bursar bill using federally funded student loan.
8:00	Text friend on cellular network regulated by the Federal Communications Commission.
10:00	Stream TV program on station that has federal license.

programs, spending, and regulations. Moreover, this chart omits actions by state and local governments, which are very active in areas such as education policy and law enforcement. As you will see in later chapters, it's not surprising that the federal government touches your everyday life in many ways. The federal government is extraordinarily large regardless of whether you measure it in terms of spending (more than $4.4 trillion a year), number of employees (over 2 million, not including contract workers and Postal Service employees), or regulations (over 180,000 pages in the *Code of Federal Regulations*).[14]

Moreover, the idea that politics is everywhere has a deeper meaning: people's political behavior is similar to their behavior in the rest of their lives. For example, collective action problems occur when you live with roommates and need to keep common areas neat and clean. Everyone has an interest in a clean area, but each person is inclined to let someone else do the work. The same principles help us understand campus protests over tuition hikes, alcohol bans, or changes in graduation requirements in terms of which kinds of issues and circumstances foster cooperation. In each case, individual free riders acting in their own self-interest may undermine the outcome that most people prefer.

Similarly, convincing like-minded individuals to contribute to a political group's lobbying efforts is no easy task. Each would-be contributor of time or money also has the opportunity to be a free rider who refuses to participate yet reaps the benefits of others' participation. Because of these difficulties, some groups of people with common goals remain unorganized. College students are a good example: many want more student aid and lower interest rates on government-subsidized student loans, but they fail to organize politically toward those ends.

This similarity between behavior in political situations and in the rest of life is no surprise; everything that happens in politics is the result of individuals' choices. And the connections between politics and everyday life mean you already know more about politics than you realize.

The idea that "politics is everywhere" means that government actions touch virtually all aspects of our lives, from regulating the business of social media companies to ensure they don't grow too powerful to mandating equal funding for men's and women's sports in high schools and colleges. Moreover, everyday life often helps us make sense of politics and politicians; for example, U.S. senator Ted Cruz joked, "The Democrats are the party of Lisa Simpson and Republicans are happily the party of Homer, Bart, Maggie and Marge," riffing on the perceived elitism of Lisa in comparison to the rest of her down-to-earth and highly relatable (and amusing) family members.

Just because you do not take an interest in politics does not mean that politics will not take an interest in you.

—**Pericles,** ancient Greek lawmaker

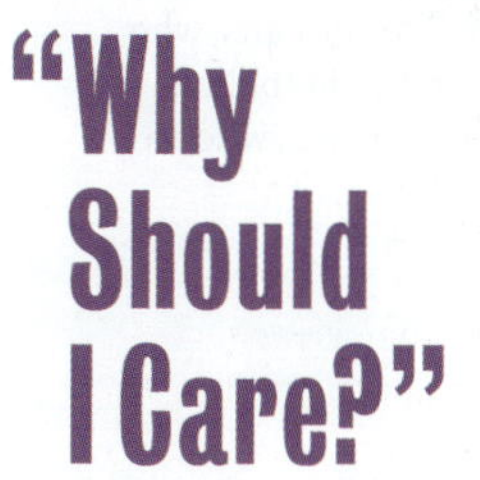

When you are trying to make sense of a political situation, think first of the three key ideas that we have just discussed. Focusing on conflict helps you understand what is at stake. Focusing on rules helps explain the strategies that participants use to achieve their goals. And the idea that politics is everywhere is there to remind you that conflicts over government policy are not things that happen only to other people—for better or worse, the outcome of political conflicts can touch virtually all aspects of our lives.

Sources of conflict in American politics

Where does political conflict come from? The reality is that conflict must be addressed in order to find compromise and enact policy. Sometimes, however, disagreements resist resolution because of inherent differences among people and their opinions about government and politics.

Economic interests

People's economic interests today vary widely, and they constitute a source of conflict in politics. In contrast, relative economic equality was a defining characteristic of our nation's early history—at least among White men—since small landowners, businessmen, craftsmen, and their families constituted a large majority of the nation's population. Compared with our European counterparts, the United States has, historically, been relatively free from class-based politics. Over time, our nation has become more stratified by class, to the point that the United States now has one of the highest levels of income inequality among developed nations. Nonetheless, a broad commitment to the **free market** (an economic system based on competition among businesses without government interference) and to *economic individualism* (the autonomy of individuals to manage their own financial decisions without government interference) remains central to our national identity.

free market
An economic system based on competition among businesses without government interference.

Despite this basic consensus on economic principles and a history relatively free of class-based politics, there are important differences among American citizens, interest groups, and political parties in terms of their economic interests and favored economic policies. Democratic politicians and activists tend to favor more **redistributive tax policies** (that is, tax policies that attempt to create greater social equality, such as taxing the rich at higher rates than the middle class or the poor, as in the wealth tax proposed by a 2020 Democratic presidential candidate, Senator Elizabeth Warren) and social spending on programs for the poor. Democrats are also more inclined to regulate industry to protect the environment and ensure worker and product safety, but they tend to favor fewer restrictions on the personal behavior of individuals. Republicans favor lower taxes and less spending on social policies. They are also more supportive than Democrats of the free market and less inclined to interfere with business interests, although many Republicans favor regulation of individual behaviors, such as abortion, same-sex marriage, and marijuana consumption.

redistributive tax policies
Policies, generally favored by Democratic politicians, that use taxation to attempt to create social equality (for example, higher taxation of the rich to provide programs for the poor).

Cultural values

Another source of conflict in American politics is differing cultural values. For example, political analysts often focus attention on the **culture wars** in the United States between "red-state" Americans, who tend to have strong religious beliefs, and "blue-state" Americans, who tend to be more secular. (The color coding of the states comes from the election-night maps on television that show the states carried by Republican candidates in red and those won by Democrats in blue—but see the What Do the Facts Say? feature for a more nuanced take on this.)

culture wars
Political conflict in the United States between "red-state" Americans, who tend to have strong religious beliefs, and "blue-state" Americans, who tend to be more secular.

Although the precise makeup and impact of "values voters" is still debated, there is no doubt that many Americans disagree on cultural and moral issues. These include the broad category of "family values" (such as whether and how to regulate

Purple America: The 2020 Presidential Election

The media create maps of the country on election night with red states indicating where Republicans win and blue states where Democrats win, like the top map here. But what do we see if we look beyond the state level to the county level? And what if we look not just at who won and who lost, but which party was stronger relative to the other? This is what the bottom map, created by Robert Vanderbei at Princeton University, shows. The simple view of two Americas—Republican versus Democrat, red versus blue—starts to look a lot more purple.

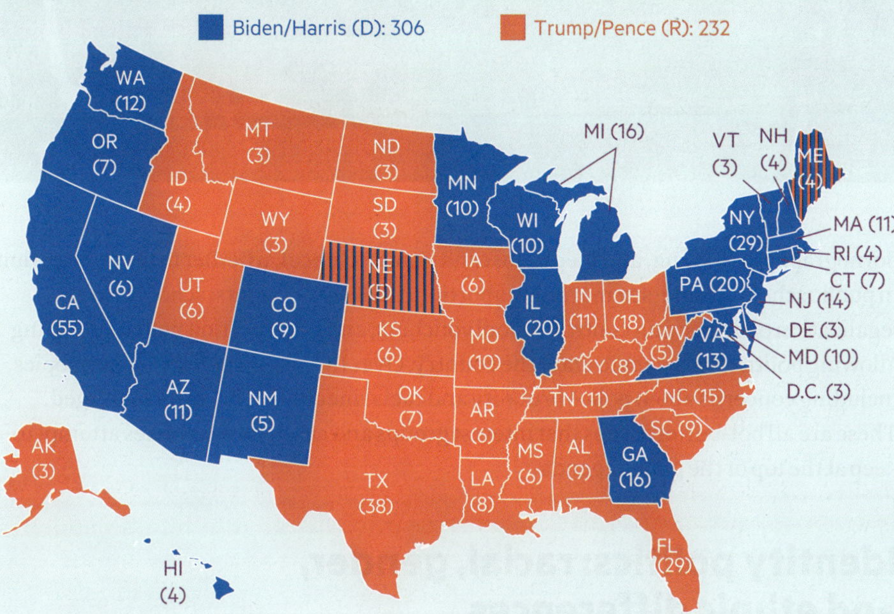

Note: Two states split their electoral votes: in Maine, Trump received 1 vote and Biden 3; in Nebraska, Trump received 4 votes and Biden 1.

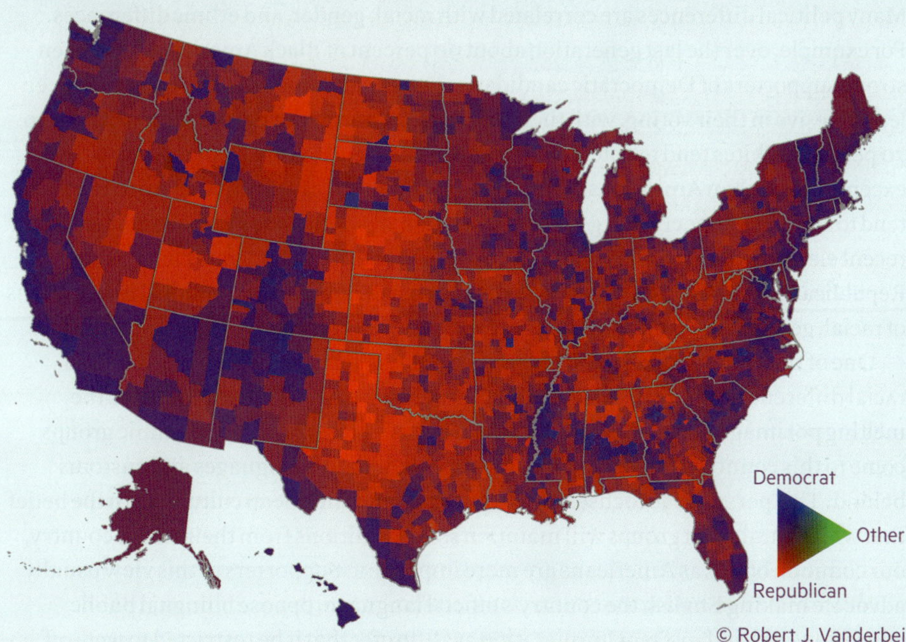

Source: Provided by Robert J. Vanderbei, Princeton University, "2020 Presidential Election, Purple America," https://vanderbei.princeton.edu/JAVA/election2020/ (accessed 11/1/21).

WHAT DO THE FACTS SAY?

Think about it

- **Which sections of the country** were the strongest for Biden, and which were strongest for Trump?
- **In the bottom map,** which areas are the most mixed (purple)?
- **Over the next 20 years,** the nation will become more racially and ethnically diverse. How do you think these maps will change in light of this growing diversity?

Differing cultural values are a significant source of conflict among groups of voters in the United States. Pictured here are students in Odessa, Texas, protesting a school district policy that changed the names of the "invocation" and "benediction" to "opening" and "closing" at their graduation ceremony.

Civil and voting rights contributed to the realignment of the South in the second half of the twentieth century, as more Whites began supporting the Republican Party, and the Democratic Party came to be seen as the champion of minority rights. Here, Black and White Americans in Alabama wait in line together to vote at a city hall after the enactment of the 1965 Voting Rights Act.

pornography, gambling, and media obscenity and violence); whether to teach evolution in public schools; same-sex marriage; abortion; LGBTQIA+ rights; school prayer; legalization of drugs; gun control; school vouchers; and immigration policy, including allowing political refugees to enter the country. Over the last several years, new topics, including concerns about police brutality and racial inequality, have also emerged. These are all hot-button issues that interest groups and activists on all sides attempt to keep at the top of the policy agenda.

Identity politics: racial, gender, and ethnic differences

Many political differences are correlated with racial, gender, and ethnic differences. For example, over the last generation about 90 percent of Black Americans have been strong supporters of Democratic candidates. Other racial and ethnic groups have been less cohesive in their voting, with their support for a particular party ranging from 55 to 70 percent. Whites tend to vote Republican; Latinos tend to vote Democratic, with the exception of Cuban Americans, who tend to vote Republican; and Asian Americans tend to support Democrats. A gender gap in national politics has also been evident in recent elections, with women being more likely to vote for Democrats and men for Republicans. Because these tendencies are not fixed, however, the political implications of racial, gender, and ethnic differences can change over time.

One of the enduring debates in American politics concerns whether ethnic and racial differences *should* be tied to political interests. One perspective reflects the melting pot image of America, which holds that as different racial and ethnic groups come to this country, they should mostly leave their native languages and customs behind. This perspective focuses on assimilation into American culture, with the belief that while immigrant groups will maintain some traditions from their native country, our common bonds as Americans are more important. Supporters of this view usually advocate making English the country's official language, oppose bilingual public education, and, if they favor immigration at all, prefer that it be restricted to well-off people from English-speaking countries.

However, there are varied alternatives to the melting pot view. These range from racial separatists such as the Nation of Islam, whose members see White-dominated society as oppressive and discriminatory, to multiculturalists, who argue that there is strength in diversity and embrace a "tossed salad" version of assimilation (that is, each ingredient remains distinct but contributes to the overall quality of the salad).[15] In general, people holding this viewpoint favor less restrictive immigration laws and oppose policies that encourage immigrants to assimilate. Given that immigrant groups also differ from the population in terms of education levels, occupation, family size, and other factors, it should not be surprising that members of these groups have their own ideas about what government should and should not do.

This debate over culture is one reason why recent discussions about immigration law have been so conflictual—the two sides start from very different premises about the value of diversity. But regardless of how this debate is resolved, our multiracial makeup is clear, as Figure 1.2 shows. In fact, trends in population growth suggest that by 2060 or so, Whites will no longer constitute a majority of the U.S. population. The extent to which this diversity continues to be a source of political conflict depends on the broader role of race in our society. As long as there are racial differences in employment, education, health, housing, and crime, and as long as racial discrimination is present in our society, race will continue to be a source of political conflict, as the ongoing Black Lives Matter protests and debates over critical race theory illustrate.

Many of the same observations apply to gender and politics. The women's movement is usually viewed as beginning in 1848 at the first Women's Rights Convention in Seneca Falls, New York. The fight for women's suffrage and legal rights dominated the movement through the late nineteenth and early twentieth centuries, with women gaining the right to vote in 1920 after passage of the Nineteenth Amendment to the Constitution—although in practice, voting rights for women of color were restricted in many areas until the 1960s. Beginning in the 1960s and 1970s, feminism and the women's liberation movement highlighted a broad range of issues: workplace issues such as maternity leave, equal pay, and sexual harassment; reproductive rights and abortion; domestic violence; and sexual violence.

The Racial Composition of the United States

FIGURE 1.2

Only about 60 percent of Americans describe themselves as White. Moreover, the proportion of Hispanics and Latinos in the population is about 19 percent and rising, although this category contains many distinct subgroups. What changes would you expect in American politics and federal policy if the actual population in 2060 matches the projections?

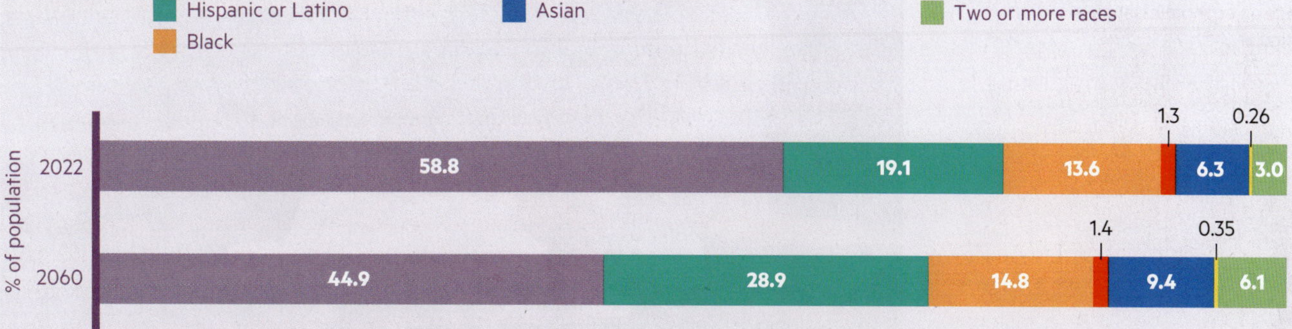

Source: Census data aggregated by author. Raw data available at www.census.gov/programs-surveys/popproj/data/tables.html (accessed 2/26/24).

While progress has occurred on many fronts, including electing women to political office, gender remains an important source of political disagreement and identity politics. While the Congress elected in 2022 has more than 120 female House members and more than 20 female senators, these percentages are far lower than in the general population, and many other nations have a higher percentage of women in elected office. Gender politics became even more central in recent years, particularly in light of the #MeToo movement that has drawn attention to sexual assault and revisions to state abortion laws after the repeal of *Roe v. Wade* (see Chapter 5 for additional details on contemporary civil rights politics).

ideology
A cohesive set of ideas and beliefs used to organize and evaluate the political world.

conservative
The side of the ideological spectrum defined by support for lower taxes, a free market, and a more limited government; generally associated with Republicans.

liberal
The side of the ideological spectrum defined by support for stronger government programs and more market regulation; generally associated with Democrats.

libertarians
Those who prefer very limited government and therefore tend to be conservative on issues such as social welfare policy, environmental policy, and government funding for education but liberal on issues involving personal liberty such as free speech, abortion, and the legalization of drugs.

Ideology

Another source of differences in interests is **ideology**: a cohesive set of ideas and beliefs that allows an individual to organize and evaluate the political world. Ideology may seem most obviously related to political interests through political parties, since Republicans tend to be **conservative** and Democrats tend to be **liberal**. While this is true in a relative sense (most Republicans are more conservative than most Democrats), few Americans consider their own views ideologically extreme.[16]

Ideology shapes beliefs about more specific policies. Conservatives promote traditional social practices and favor lower taxes, a free market, and a more limited government, whereas liberals support social tolerance, stronger government programs, and more market regulation. However, the picture gets cloudy if we look more closely. **Libertarians**, for example, prefer very limited government—they believe government should provide for the national defense and should have only a few other narrowly defined responsibilities. Because they are at the extreme end of the ideological continuum on this issue, libertarians are generally conservative in areas such as social welfare policy, environmental policy, and government funding for education and generally liberal on issues involving personal liberty such as free speech, abortion, and the legalization of drugs. For libertarians, the consistent ideological theme is limiting the role of government in our lives.

Though he is formally affiliated with the Republican Party, Senator Rand Paul of Kentucky is often associated with libertarianism and is well known for taking a libertarian conservative stance on economic issues, in particular.

Personal ideologies are not always consistent. Someone can be both a fiscal conservative (favoring balanced budgets) and a social liberal (favoring the pro-choice position on abortion and marital rights for gay men and lesbians), or a liberal on foreign policy issues (supporting humanitarian aid and opposing military intervention overseas) and a conservative on moral issues (being pro-life on abortion and opposing stem-cell research). Ideology is a significant source of conflict in politics, and it does not always operate in a straightforward manner. In Chapter 6, we explore whether America is becoming more ideological and polarized, deepening our conflicts and making compromise more difficult.

Even so, there are clear areas of agreement in American politics, even on issues that once divided us. For example, while there is still considerable disagreement over same-sex marriage, public opinion has clearly shifted toward accepting these unions. Along the same lines, two generations ago Americans were divided on the legality of mixed-race marriage, while today very few people would object. Thus, even though conflict is a constant in American politics, it is wrong to say that we are divided into two groups, red and blue, that oppose each other on all issues of significance.

DID YOU KNOW?

25%

of millennials give consistently liberal responses across a range of policy questions, while 2 percent give consistently conservative responses.

Source: Pew Research Center.

The first step in understanding any political conflict is to determine who wants what. Who is involved? What do they, or their side, want? In modern American politics, citizens' demands are often connected to their economic interests, values, race, gender, ethnicity, and ideology. As a result, the group affiliations of individuals often tell us a lot about what they want from candidates and the government, and why they want it.

"Why Should I Care?"

Resolving conflict: democracy and American political values

EXPLAIN HOW THE AMERICAN VALUES OF DEMOCRACY, LIBERTY, AND EQUALITY WORK TO RESOLVE POLITICAL CONFLICT

When we say that rules shape how conflicts are worked out in American politics, most of the time we are referring to formal (written-down) constraints that describe how the actions taken by each participant shape the ultimate outcome. For example, most American House and Senate elections are decided using plurality rule (whichever candidate gets the most votes wins), while a few states require winners to receive an absolute majority (50 percent + 1) of votes cast. However, some of the most important rules are not written down—these **norms** constitute America's political culture, or a collective idea of how a government and society should operate, including democracy, equality, and liberty, and more specific ideas about everyday political interactions.[17] For example, sometimes during a close vote in the Senate, if one senator cannot be present because of a personal matter, a senator from the other side will refrain from voting, so that the first senator's absence does not change the outcome. (This actually happened during the vote to appoint Brett Kavanaugh to the Supreme Court. Senator Lisa Murkowski, who opposed Kavanaugh, voted "present" rather than "no" to offset the absence of Kavanaugh-supporting senator Steven Daines, who was attending his daughter's wedding.)

norms
Unwritten rules and informal agreements among citizens and elected officials about how government and society should operate.

Democracy

democracy
Government by the people. In most contexts, this means representative democracy in which the people elect leaders to enact policies. Democracies must have fair elections with at least two options.

The idea of democracy means that policy disagreements are ultimately resolved through decisions made by citizens, such as their votes in elections. In the simplest terms, "**democracy**" means government by the people. As put into practice, this typically means representative democracy rather than direct democracy—that is, the people elect representatives who decide policies and pass laws rather than determining those things directly. There are some examples of direct democracy in the United States, such as the New England town meeting and the referendum process, through which people in a state directly determine policy.[18] But for the most part, Americans elect politicians to represent us, from school board and city council members at the local level, to state legislators and governors at the state level, to U.S. House members, senators, and the president at the national level.

Democracy is not the only way to resolve conflict, nor do all societies have as strong a belief in democracy as in America. One mechanism used by authoritarian governments is to suppress conflict though violence and limitations on freedom. Some governments, such as those of China and Russia, control political outcomes while allowing somewhat free markets. The Iranian government is a theocracy, in which religious leaders have a veto over the government's policy choices. And some countries, such as the oil sheikdoms in the Middle East, like the United Arab Emirates, have a monarchy, in which rulers are determined by heredity. While nondemocratic systems vary widely in terms of their structure and their popularity, the common thread is that some individual or group is in charge of the country and the policy-making process and cannot be removed except by revolution.

In contrast, democracies select rulers and resolve conflict through voting and elections. When the second president of the United States, John Adams, turned over power to his bitter rival, Thomas Jefferson, after losing a hotly contested election in 1800, his departure demonstrated that democratic government by the people had real meaning—electoral winners get to exercise power, while losers go home to strategize about how to increase their popularity and win the next election. Democracy depends on the consent of the governed: if the views of the people change, then the government must eventually be responsive to those views or the people will choose new leaders. It also means that citizens must accept election results as authoritative—you have to obey the laws passed by a new Congress, even if you voted for the other party's candidates.

Liberty

liberty
Political freedom, such as the freedom of speech, press, assembly, and religion. These and other legal and due process rights protecting individuals from government control are outlined in the Bill of Rights of the U.S. Constitution.

To the Founders, **liberty** was a central principle for their new government: they believed that people must have the freedom to express their political views, with the understanding that conflict may arise between different views expressed by different people. The Bill of Rights of the Constitution (discussed in Chapter 4) outlines the nature of those liberties: the freedom of speech, press, assembly, and religion, as well as many legal and due process rights protecting individuals from government control.

Liberty also means that within broad limits, people are free to determine what they want from government and to organize themselves to demand their preferred policies from elected officials. Thus, in the case of immigration policy, it is acceptable to hold the view that America should have open borders, and it is also acceptable to demand (and lobby Congress to enact) a complete ban on immigration—or to hold any view in between these extremes.

A system in which individuals are free to form their own views about what government should do virtually guarantees conflict over government policy. James Madison recognized this essential trade-off between liberty and conflict. He argued that suppressing conflict by limiting freedom was "worse than the disease" (worse than conflict). To put it another way, any political system that prioritizes liberty will have conflict.

Another consequence of valuing liberty (and the inevitable conflict over policy that results) is the need for compromise in the policy-making process. In most policy areas, Americans and their elected officials hold a wide range of views, with no consensus on what government should do. Getting something done requires fashioning an agreement that gives no one what they really want but is nevertheless better than nothing. Standing on principle and refusing to compromise may sound like a noble strategy, but it often results in getting none of what you want, as other individuals or groups work to change policy without your involvement.

Equality

Another principle of democracy is **equality**. Even though the Declaration of Independence boldly declared that "all men are created equal," this did not mean that all people were entitled to the same income or even the same social status (and the Founders obviously ignored slavery as well). Instead, the most widely embraced notion of equality in the United States today is the equality of opportunity—that is, everyone should have the same chance to realize their potential. Political equality also means that people are treated the same in the political system. Everyone has one vote in an election, and everyone is equal in the eyes of the law—that is, we are all subject to the same rules that limit how we can lobby, contribute, work for a candidate, or express our opinions.

equality
In the context of American politics, "equality" means equality before the law, political equality (one person, one vote), and equality of opportunity (the equal chance for everyone to realize their potential) but not material equality (equal income or wealth).

In practice, political equality has not always existed in America, and it does not completely exist today. In our early history, only White men could vote, and in many states those men needed to be property owners in order to vote. Slowly, political equality expanded as property requirements were dropped; Black men (in 1870), women (in 1920)—though restrictions for people of color persisted into the 1960s—and 18- to 20-year-olds (in 1971) got the right to vote. (For more on the expansion of the right to vote, see Chapter 5.) Today, wealthy people clearly can have their voices heard more easily than poor people can (through campaign contributions or independent expenditures on political ads). Similarly, requiring photo IDs for voting or placing restrictions on early voting and voting by mail constrains some groups (including historically marginalized communities) more than others.

In democracies like the United States, voting is one of the most visible ways citizens use the political process to express their opinions and resolve conflict.

Like democracy, political equality also contributes to resolving conflict. First, if people know that they will be treated equally by the political system, they are more likely to respect the system. Indeed, one of the triggers for revolutions around the world is reaction against rigged elections or policies that benefit only the supporters of winning candidates. Political equality also gives us cues about how to get involved in politics. Most fundamentally, it suggests that the way to change policy is to elect candidates who share your views, rather than appealing to a friend or relative who works in the government or offering a bribe to a bureaucrat.

While America's political culture has many other aspects, the concepts of democracy, liberty, and equality are central to understanding how American politics works. Agreement on these principles helps lessen conflicts and limit their scope. For example, when Republican senators lost the battle to prevent Biden's Supreme Court nominee Ketanji Brown Jackson from being appointed, they didn't have to worry that Biden would remove them from office or throw them in jail for opposing Jackson.

Moreover, Republicans had a clear path to preventing Biden from appointing more justices like Jackson: regain control of the Senate or win the presidency. Americans and their elected officials have been willing to grant one another political equality and to take political defeats in stride because there is agreement on the basic boundaries of political debate. Again, this consensus does not imply there is no conflict—quite the contrary. However, conflict is easier to resolve if it is over a narrower range of options.

Not surprisingly, many aspects of America's political culture will come up throughout this book. You also might want to look out for them when you are watching the news or reading about national politics. When Democrats in Congress talk about the need to provide health insurance for all Americans, they are emphasizing equality—and when Republicans argue that minimizing government involvement and allowing people more choice (even if it means some people cannot afford insurance) will lead to a better system, they are emphasizing liberty. Moreover, as this example suggests, part of the conflict in American politics is over which aspect of political culture should carry the day. The fact that issues such as health care have been central in recent elections is a reminder of the importance of elections in a democracy and our belief that elections are one venue where conflicts are debated and resolved.

"Why Should I Care?"

To truly understand American politics, you must understand America's core values: democracy, liberty, and equality. These values set broad limits on how political conflicts will be resolved. Democracy implies that the people are the ultimate authority over political outcomes. Liberty implies that people are able to express whatever demands they want and to choose among a wide range of strategies in trying to shape the outcomes of political decisions. And equality means that everyone has an equal share of decision-making power. Despite conflicts over their interpretations, most Americans believe in these core values, and reminding ourselves of this can help us work toward resolving political conflicts.

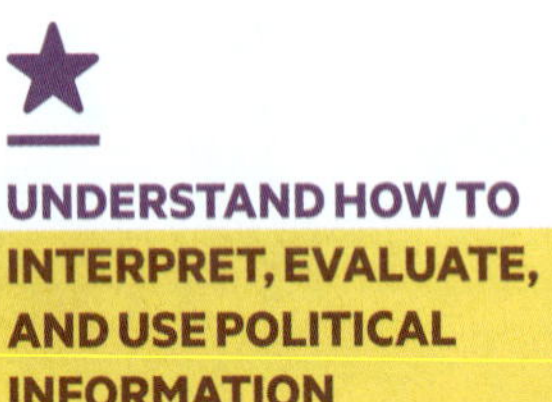

How to be a critical consumer of politics

One of the biggest problems in understanding American politics today is deciding whom you should believe. If you want to justify a particular policy solution or point of view on any political issue, you can find a source that will help you do just that. Would free college tuition for all create a well-informed American citizenry? There are people who think so—and who have spent a great deal of time making this argument on free and paid media. Alternatively, would making college free do nothing except increase enrollments? There are plenty of easily accessible arguments for this position as well.

The further a society drifts from the truth, the more it will hate those who speak it.

—George Orwell, novelist

In one sense, the mountain of available information is an amazing asset. If you want to learn about politics, there are many more sources available now compared with generations ago, from mainstream media to a large number of political observers who put together websites, podcasts, Twitter feeds, or other social media sites. The problem is, if two sources disagree, whom should you believe? If a source makes an extraordinary claim ("Space aliens control Congress!"), when should you take it seriously—at least seriously enough to research the claim? What rules should you follow to become well informed without being misled?

The Media Checklist for Assessing Reporting on Politics on page 26 provides some general guidelines for learning about politics. We will be referring to these rules throughout the text, to help you understand how to put them into practice.

Consider the Author While it is true that the rise of the Internet and social media allows virtually anyone to report on politics, authors are not created alike. Some reporters have covered American politics for several decades and have a track record for cultivating sources, uncovering information, or analyzing and interpreting events. Other reporters essentially come out of nowhere, offering insights on a brand-new blog or website. Other things being equal, whom should you believe—someone who has produced reliable reporting in the past or someone whose abilities can't be evaluated? Think about it this way: Whom do you want to fix your car—someone who's been fixing cars for 30 years and has thousands of satisfied customers (including your best friend, once a mechanic herself) or the newbie who just opened a shop last week? The answer is easy: unless the newbie has some identifiable edge, go with the track record.

Look for Verifiable Evidence Another important criterion for evaluating political reports is to see if they provide evidence to back up their claims. Anyone can say that free tuition will create a well-informed citizenry. However, this argument is more credible if it comes with supporting data, such as a study showing that college graduates are better informed than people who never attended. As engineer David Akin once put it, "Analysis without numbers is only an opinion." It's also important for the article to include enough information about the source so that it can be found without too much searching. That way, readers can examine the source themselves to verify that evidence was reported fairly. Of course, many reports on American politics rely on anonymous sources—in these cases, the author's reputation looms especially large in the decision of whether to take the story seriously.

Think about the Size of the Claim Evidence should also match the claims being made by a reporter. If someone claims that space aliens control Congress, we need more than their word to believe the report. In fact, in an era when everyone has access to Photoshop, pictures would not be enough. We'd probably want a news conference with a space alien and congressional leaders in which the full plot is revealed in detail. As the astronomer Carl Sagan often said, "Extraordinary claims require extraordinary evidence." The problem, of course, is that in many cases available evidence is fragmentary, contradictory, or even nonexistent. For example, one persistent rumor over the last few years was that the Russian government has some sort of embarrassing information about former President Trump and that it was controlling his actions by threatening to release it. However, there is no hard evidence to back up these claims, and there are many other possible explanations for Trump's allegedly pro-Russia actions. Which is to say, some of the time, it makes sense to disregard a potentially explosive story because those reporting it cannot prove what they claim to be true.

Read Multiple Reports A story about a political event or outcome is more credible if it is consistent with other reports. For example, in the aftermath of the 2020 election, reports circulated on social media that on the night of Election Day, boxes containing thousands of forged ballots had been delivered by an unmarked truck to a vote-counting site in Detroit, Michigan, a state that Democrat Joe Biden narrowly won over Republican Donald Trump. These are troubling reports to be sure. However, investigations by several teams of reporters from different newspapers found no discrepancies in the vote counts. Several judges (including some Republicans) ruled that the ballot-stuffing claims were totally bogus. And a press photographer reported that he may well have inadvertently caused the rumors in the first place, as he had used a rental truck to deliver several large boxes of video

Media Checklist for Assessing Reporting on Politics

1 Says Who?

Evaluate the author's reputation
The Internet and social media allow virtually anyone to report on politics, but authors are not created alike. Trust reporters who have experience covering American politics.

2 Fact or "Fake News"?

Verify the information
Good reporting is the result of good sources, and you should always be able to identify and find the source without too much searching. Take a look at the source yourself—whether it is data, polling results, or even a journal article—to verify that evidence was reported fairly.

3 What's the Impact?

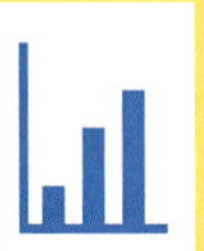

Assess the extent of the claim
As the astronomer Carl Sagan once put it, "Extraordinary claims require extraordinary evidence." Evidence should also match the claims being made by reporters. We need more than their word to believe what they are saying.

4 Who Agrees?

Corroborate the report
A story about a political event or outcome is more credible if it is consistent with other reports. Make sure you verify that other credible sources of news and reporters are saying the same thing.

5 Tell Me More!

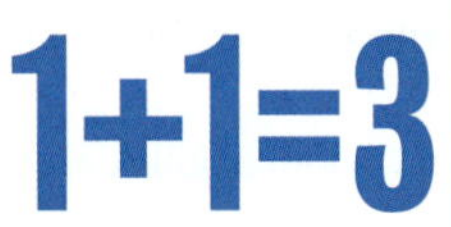

Assess if the explanation is too simple
Be skeptical about simple explanations for political outcomes. Complex outcomes are rarely explained by a single factor.

camera equipment to document the vote count. We'll talk more about election administration in Chapter 9. For now, these examples illustrate the dangers of relying on a single information source.

Some sources are also better than others. Most of the time, major news organizations like the *New York Times* or the *Washington Post* get the story right—they have large staffs of smart, experienced reporters, and working to publish accurate reports reinforces their reputation (and helps sell subscriptions and advertising). In contrast, anonymous Twitter or Facebook sources have nothing to lose from inaccurate stories. This is not to say that the *Times* and the *Post* are always right and anonymous sources always wrong. Rather, it's generally a good idea to focus on the sources who have strong incentives to be truthful about their reporting.

"All the News That's Fit to Print"

The New York Times

VOL. CLXX ... No. 58,871 — NEW YORK, SUNDAY, NOVEMBER 8, 2020 — $6.00

Late Edition
Today, mostly sunny, warm for early November, high 72. Tonight, clear, mild, low 54. Tomorrow, sunshine, patchy clouds, remaining warm, high 71. Weather map, Page 21.

BIDEN BEATS TRUMP

RACE IS FINALLY CALLED AFTER RECORD TURNOUT; CHAOTIC TERM ENDS WITH RARE INCUMBENT LOSS

Harris Will Become the Country's First Female Vice President

By JONATHAN MARTIN and ALEXANDER BURNS

Joseph Robinette Biden Jr. was elected the 46th president of the United States on Saturday, promising to restore political normalcy and a spirit of national unity to confront raging health and economic crises, and making Donald J. Trump a one-term president after four years of tumult in the White House.

Mr. Biden's victory amounted to a repudiation of Mr. Trump by millions of voters exhausted with his divisive conduct and chaotic administration, and was delivered by an unlikely alliance of women, people of color, old and young voters and a sliver of disaffected Republicans. Mr. Trump is only the third elected president since World War II to lose re-election, and the first in more than a quarter-century.

The result also provided a history-making moment for Mr. Biden's running mate, Senator Kamala Harris of California, who will become the first woman to serve as vice president.

With his triumph, Mr. Biden, who turns 78 later this

Beware of Simple Explanations In general, you should be skeptical about simple explanations for political outcomes. For example, one explanation for the failure of the presidential campaign of Republican Nikki Haley during the 2024 Republican nomination process was that Americans were not ready to elect a female president. However, this account ignores the fact that throughout America women are routinely elected as mayors, governors, and members of Congress—and, after Kamala Harris's win in the 2020 election, as vice president. This is not to say that attitudes about gender did not play a role in Haley's defeat but rather to note that this outcome was the result of many factors working together. Complex outcomes are rarely explained by a single factor.

When assessing reporting on politics, it is important to consider the source of the information. Though they are not immune from error, print sources, like the *New York Times*, have strong incentives to be truthful about their reporting.

Finally, you might ask, If I'm supposed to be skeptical, why should I believe anything in this book? The answer is that throughout this book we've strived to follow all the rules presented here. Our aim is to describe how American politics works, rather than to make an argument about how it *should* work. We are social scientists, not partisans or cheerleaders. Rather than shaping your preferences, our goal is to give you the tools to understand, evaluate, and interpret political information and to help you be an informed, effective participant in the political process. As we always tell our students, "My goal is not to tell you *what* to think, but to help you learn *how* to think about politics." We emphasize facts and data (often from multiple sources, with citations and references) because the first step in understanding why things happen is to learn the details of actual events. And while we believe that American politics makes sense and that you can learn to make sense of it, we avoid simple explanations, as these generally do not provide much insight into political behavior or policy outcomes.

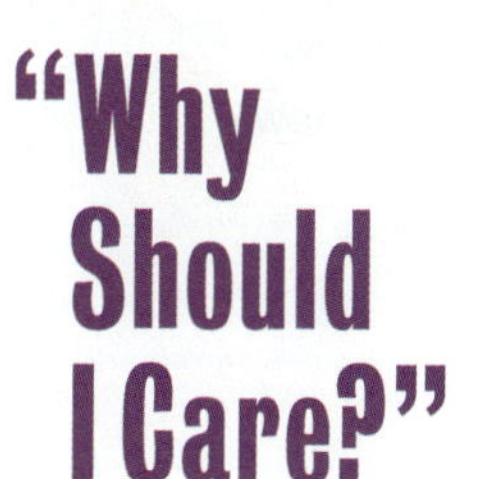

Which reports about American politics should we take seriously? Those whose authors have reputations for insight and reliability, those that present appropriate evidence given their claims, those that are consistent with what other reporters are saying, and those that reflect the complexity of America's society and its government.

Unpacking the Conflict

As we consider the three key ideas about politics that we've discussed in this chapter—politics is conflictual, political process matters, and politics is everywhere—let's return to the problem of defining "fake news" discussed at the beginning of the chapter. If Americans can't even agree on which news is "fake," how can we know what to trust? Where can we learn how to keep ourselves safe from COVID-19 or assess whether government has behaved well or poorly?

Understanding that politics is conflictual reveals important details about the fight over information and the media, including coverage of the pandemic. Because media coverage shapes public support, politicians and political actors want stories that said good things about their performance and policy aims. But the job of a reporter is not to support politicians—it's to provide a combination of facts and analysis that captures the situation. Virtually all politicians have felt at times that they were being treated unfairly by the media. But those feelings reflect the different goals held by presidents and the people who report on their performance. It's all about conflict, not fake news.

Understanding that process matters also provides insight into fake news. One reason why presidents complain about press coverage is that there is very little they can do to stop the media from publishing critical stories. This is because of the First Amendment to our Constitution, which guarantees a free press. Presidents can fume in private and publish critical tweets, but they have only marginal influence over what is written about them. Former president Trump, for example, may have wished that the impact of the pandemic was not front-page news during the 2020 presidential campaign. However, there was no way for him to influence press coverage.

Finally, the media's coverage of presidents and other politicians illustrates the fact that politics is everywhere. Government's role in dealing with COVID-19 got attention because these decisions affect our lives directly and indirectly. You might prefer that all the stories about COVID-19 were replaced by additional coverage of your hobbies, favorite sports team, or other interests. But even if you ignore politics, politics does not ignore you. Decisions made in Washington have a profound impact on your life, whether you want them to or not.

As you read this book, we hope you will learn important "nuts and bolts" of the American political process as well as some political history that will help you gauge the likely accuracy of what you learn from news reports and help you determine if there might be more to the story than the narratives that are being presented. In general, your reading in this book will focus on contemporary questions, debates, and examples—the kinds of stories that constitute a lot of political news coverage—to illustrate broader points about our nation's political system.

Although you will no doubt disagree with—or even be angry about—some aspects of American politics and some media coverage, our goal is to provide you with the tools to understand *why* government operates as it does. Again, we are not arguing that the federal government is perfect, that one party's agenda (or leadership) is better than the other's, or that imperfect responses to policy problems are inevitable. Rather, we believe that any attempt to explain these outcomes or to devise ways to prevent similar problems requires an understanding of why they happened in the first place. After reading this book, you will have a better sense of how American politics really works and why it matters.

"What's Your Take?"

Is the media the "watchdog" that protects democracy, or is it an out-of-control, self-serving, biased group of partisans?

And if Americans can't even agree on which news is "fake," how can we know what to trust?

CHECK YOUR UNDERSTANDING

"Why Should I Care?"

In this introductory chapter, you are encouraged to take what you already know and use it to fashion the lens through which you will view the rest of the content covered in the course. If you find yourself being frustrated by pundits on the news, consider that their ideas are based in their fundamental understanding of the world as it exists. Politics is a puzzle where each actor, institution, procedure, and decision fits together to form a complete picture. While the goal of this class is for you to leave being able to identify each of the different pieces and understand which way they need to be oriented so that they fit together, the goal of this chapter is to help you begin to understand how to make sense of the picture they create.

Democracy in the United States is the means through which we activate our government to help solve our collective action problems, including working to support the most equitable distribution of public goods, or resources, possible. One of the ways to think about the differences in the political parties in our government, which will be addressed in more detail later, is that each party's ideology centers on identifying what actually is a "public good" and how to manage the free rider problem relative to those goods. Politics is the act of attempting to persuade voters to join one party or the other in their perception of the world around them and most importantly to give them votes so that they can turn their belief into law. In short, democracy is the path which our ideas and beliefs take to become the policies that govern American society.

Throughout this course, you will be introduced to the fundamental nuts and bolts—or processes and procedures—of our governmental institutions. Understanding the skeleton of the branches of our government that are found in the Constitution will help you understand the actions—or policies—that the government implements. Additionally, understanding these rules of the game will help you to understand how people like you can influence government actions through your vote and protest.

Successful governments work in concert with the people they govern, and you are encouraged to consider the role that you play in holding government to the standards that you believe. This is a good question to ask yourself as you read each chapter: What role do I play here?

1. The significant expansion of the federal government during the twentieth century can primarily be attributed to the efforts of the government to achieve which of the goals stated by the authors of the Preamble to the Constitution?

a "provide for the common defense"

b "promote the general Welfare"

c "insure domestic Tranquility"

d "secure the Blessings of Liberty to ourselves and our Posterity"

2. The beliefs about human nature Madison and the framers developed from the work of Hobbes and Locke guided them in developing mechanisms in the American structure of government that accomplished which function?

a Popular control of government

b Balancing interests against one another

c Proportional representation of states in the legislature

d Vesting the executive power in a single executive

3. The lack of familiarity with the institutions of government leads many Americans to distrust the system and misunderstand what they can expect from government, but studying American government and politics shows that these American institutions

a follow a natural progression that allows engaged individuals to organize, influence government, and hold officials accountable.

b has followed roughly the same trajectory of declining trust and growing ineffectiveness of other Western nations.

c illustrate the defects of free market individualism and democratic structures.

d are unique among the developed world and stand out as a model for other nations.

4. People who disengage from the political process because they believe it is too full of conflict misunderstand what concept about the American political process?

a The conflict within the system will not resolve unless more Americans are engaged in the political process.

b Changes through amendments to the Constitution have made conflict a greater part of American society.

c Living in a free society means that conflict in deciding public policy is inevitable.

d A lack of clear political ideologies has increased conflict in American political institutions.

5. The defeat of President Trump in 2020, along with other one-term U.S. presidents who sought reelection, illustrates which valuable concept about the American political process?

a Political parties can powerfully manipulate electoral institutions to change the outcome of an election.

b Interest groups and other factions within American society wield significant political power when selecting political leaders.

c Checks and balances allow the other branches of government to play an important role in presidential elections.

d Americans who are unhappy with policy makers and policy decisions can effect changes in policy by engaging in the political system.

6. In the wake of the 2020 presidential election, many states passed laws that restricted voter registration and voting processes. This effort to change election laws best illustrates which idea about American politics?

a Policy makers understand that the rules of the political process can significantly impact outcomes.

b Compromise in developing public policy is important to achieving the creation of policies that enjoy strong public support.

c Access to elections in American society continues a historic trend of expanding access for greater numbers of people from diverse communities and backgrounds.

d Media that cover campaigns like sports competitions cause Americans to make policy decisions without important knowledge about political institutions.

7. Suppose a likely voter responds to a public opinion poll by saying her vote in the upcoming election centers on the issues of raising taxes on the "super-rich" and raising the minimum wage to a "living wage." Based on this, the respondent is most likely to identify with which political ideology?

a Libertarian

b Conservative

c Liberal

d Democratic

8. Election maps often used by media and political parties that show solid-colored red and blue states reflect which problem in the political process in the United States?

a American politics is deeply polarized in ways that are leading to greater divisions and more common violent political interactions.

b Characterizations of solidly "red" and "blue" states creates a misleading perception about the realities of the people who vote in the United States.

c "Blue" and "red" states are almost equally divided, just like the voters of the American electorate.

d Presidential elections drive up voter turnout in rural states compared with the voter turnout in midterm elections.

9. In a plural society like the United States, where there are many different cultural, ethnic, racial, religious, and other demographic groups, the ideas of liberty, equality, and democracy serve what function?

a Areas that create divisions among the groups because of ideological disagreements over interpretations of the ideas

b Critical concepts embedded and clearly described within the body of the American Constitution and other founding documents

c Broadly shared areas of general agreement that allow for common understandings and foundations for political compromise

d Sources of growing unrest as Americans become disenchanted with ideals they see as unfulfilled

10. The fact that the United States has a much larger wealth disparity and distinctly separate economic interests than when the framers wrote the Constitution is likely to contribute to which of the following scenarios in American politics?

- a Increased calls for tax cuts to stimulate the economy to put upward pressure on wages
- b Greater trust in government and political institutions as the wealthy reinvest resources into the markets to stimulate growth
- c Stronger engagement of American voters in campaigns and elections to revitalize the system
- d Growing distrust of the government and political leaders to act in the best interest of Americans

11. Suppose the *New York Times* newspaper revealed evidence that a popular political candidate was trading favors for campaign donations. When confronted with such stories, which of these is the primary question students of political science should ask when considering whether they should believe the claim?

- a "What is the reputation of the person or organization providing the information?"
- b "Is the *New York Times* a liberal- or conservative-leaning news organization?"
- c "How large were these campaign contributions?"
- d "What are the candidate's press secretary's comments on the issue?"

12. Which of the following items is most likely to be a story that the public can trust to be accurate?

- a A segment on National Public Radio's *Marketplace* reporting the most recent employment figures that features commentary from the White House chief economic adviser
- b An episode of the *Alex Jones Show* that features political candidates highlighting the failures of the Biden administration
- c A shared post on Facebook that features a link to a statement from the former White House senior counselor to President Trump about her perspective on Trump's prospects for success in a future election
- d A podcast with a large following that has large numbers of testimonies about the effectiveness of home remedies to treat seasonal illnesses

Use INQUIZITIVE to help you study and master this material.

2

The Constitution and the Founding

What are the rules of the political game?

» **"Joe Biden will forever be remembered as not only the most corrupt and incompetent president in the history of our country—but perhaps even more importantly, the president who together with a band of his closest Thugs, Misfits, and Marxists tried to destroy American democracy!"[1]**
President Donald Trump

« **"Donald Trump's campaign is about him. Not America, not you. Donald Trump's campaign is obsessed with the past. Not the future. He's willing to sacrifice our democracy to put himself in power. . . . Once again, he's saying he won't honor the results of the election if he loses."[2]**
President Joe Biden

With this framing by the two major-party candidates in 2024, the presidential election was widely viewed as a referendum on the future of democracy. Early in the campaign, a poll revealed that 62 percent of Americans (including a majority of Democrats and Republicans) believed that democracy would be at risk, depending on who won.[3] Supporters of Joe Biden were worried about a peaceful transition of power, given the attempt to stop Congress from counting the electoral votes on January 6, 2021, and Donald Trump's regular comments about stolen elections. Trump's supporters continued to worry about voter fraud.

The Constitution clearly provides the basis for resolving conflict through elections and representative government rather than by taking up arms. Losers of one round of elections know that they can compete in the next election and that their voices can be heard in another part of the government.

The contrasting fears about the future of democracy are rooted in polarized views about how our Constitution shapes our political system. Many on the right see the expansion of federal power—which began with Teddy Roosevelt, exploded during the New Deal of the 1930s and Great Society of the 1960s, and continued with President Obama's health care reform and Biden's climate change policies—as constitutional overreach. Those on the left say the Constitution was intended to create a strong national government while limiting state power, and therefore an active policy agenda

CHAPTER GOALS

Describe the historical circumstances that led to the Constitutional Convention of 1787 (pp. 34–42)

Analyze the major issues debated by the framers of the Constitution (pp. 42–52)

Contrast the arguments of the Federalists with those of the Antifederalists (pp. 52–55)

Outline the major provisions of the Constitution (pp. 55–63)

Explore how the meaning of the Constitution has evolved (pp. 63–71) is well within the government's constitutional powers. Those opposing views of the constitutional basis for national policy have evolved into polarizing arguments that our democracy is dead if the "other side" wins.

Some historical context may help. Differences of opinion about the Constitution have been part of American politics since the debates over its ratification. Unfortunately, the Constitution itself provides few definitive answers because its language was intentionally written to be general so it would stand the test of time. Consequently, in every major political debate in our history, both sides have claimed to ground their views in the Constitution. Proslavery and antislavery factions during the pre–Civil War period, New Deal supporters and opponents during the Great Depression, and civil rights activists and segregationists all claimed to have the Constitution on their side, whether the dispute was over a broad or narrow interpretation of the commerce clause, the Fourteenth Amendment, or the Tenth Amendment. Today's vigorous debate about the proper scope of the national government's powers on abortion, climate change, immigration, and executive power is only the most recent chapter in this perpetual conflict.

Despite that uncertainty, the Constitution clearly provides the basis for resolving conflict through elections and representative government rather than by taking up arms. Losers of one round of elections know that they can compete in the next election and that their voices can be heard in another part of the government. The historic stability in our political system may be attributed to the hallmark characteristic of U.S. constitutional government: the separation of power across the levels of government (national, state, and local) and within government (legislative, executive, and judicial), and the checks and balances of power across the institutions of government.

This stability does not mean that the Constitution resolves our political conflicts. The Founders recognized that self-interest and conflict are inherent parts of human nature and cannot be eliminated, so they attempted to control conflict by dispersing power across different parts of government. This means that parts of the political system are always competing with one another in pursuit of various interests: for example, some Republicans want states to determine abortion policy while others prefer a national law banning all abortions. Most Democrats see abortion as a constitutionally protected right. This creates a conflictual process that is often criticized as being mired in "gridlock" and "partisan bickering." But that is the system our Founders created. Think about it this way: dictatorships do not have political conflict because dissenters are sent to jail or killed. We experience political conflict in this country because there is free and open competition between different interests and ideas. Why is conflict inherent in our political system? And what does the Constitution say about how we deal with that conflict?

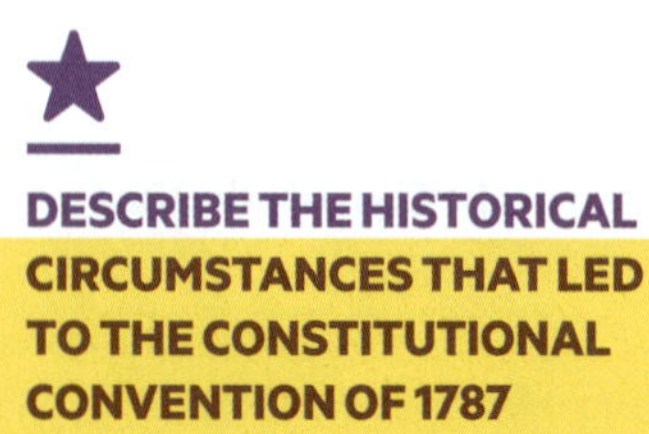
DESCRIBE THE HISTORICAL CIRCUMSTANCES THAT LED TO THE CONSTITUTIONAL CONVENTION OF 1787

The historical context of the Constitution

The Constitution was created through conflict and compromise, and understanding its historical context can help clarify *why* the framers made the specific choices they did and how those choices influence our understanding of the Constitution today. The first event that led many American colonists to question the fairness of British rule and shape their ideas about self-governance was the Stamp Act of 1765, which imposed a tax on many publications and legal documents in the colonies. The British Parliament enacted the tax to help pay for the French and Indian War (1754–1763), which those lawmakers thought was only reasonable because the American colonies had benefited from the protection of British troops during the war. However, many colonists saw this as unfair "taxation without representation," because they had no representation in British Parliament and thus had no say in the passage of the act. A series of escalating events moved the colonies closer to their inevitable break with Great Britain. These included the British-imposed Tea Act (1773) and the resulting Boston Tea Party later that year, in which colonists dumped tea from the British East India Company into the harbor rather than pay the new tax on tea. The British Parliament responded to the Tea Party with the Coercive Acts (or Intolerable Acts) of 1774 in a series of moves aimed at making sure the colonists paid for the tea they had destroyed, and designed to break the pattern of the colonists' resistance to British rule. Attempts at a political solution failed, so the Continental Congress declared independence from Britain on July 4, 1776.[4]

Articles of Confederation
Sent to the states for ratification in 1777, these were the first attempt at a new American government. It was later decided that the Articles restricted national government too much, and they were replaced by the Constitution.

limited government
A political system in which the powers of the government are restricted to prevent tyranny by protecting property and individual rights.

The Articles of Confederation: the first attempt at government

The radical nature of the break with Great Britain cannot be overstated. Throughout the Revolutionary (1775–1783) and early post-Revolutionary era (1783–1787), the future of the American colonies was very much in doubt, mostly because of deep divisions among the colonists. While many Americans were eager to sever ties with the oppressive British government and establish a new nation that rejected the trappings of royalty, there was still a large contingent of Tories (supporters of the British monarchy) and probably an even larger group of Americans who wished the conflict would just go away. Although public opinion on the matter is impossible to know, John Adams, the second president of the United States, estimated that the Second Continental Congress was about equally divided between Tories, "true blue" revolutionaries, and "those too cautious or timid to take a position one way or the other."[5] Contemporary historians estimate that about 20 percent of colonists were Tories, 40 percent revolutionaries, and 40 percent neutral. Also, unlike the Civil War, which pitted regions of the country against each other, the Revolutionary War witnessed neighbor fighting neighbor, in often brutal combat.[6] This context of uncertainty and conflict made the Founders' task of creating a lasting republic extremely difficult.

The first attempt to structure an American government, the **Articles of Confederation**, swung too far in the direction of decentralized and **limited government**. The Articles were written in the summer of 1776 during the Second Continental Congress, which had also authorized and approved the Declaration of Independence. They were submitted to all 13 states in 1777 for approval, but they did not take effect until the last state ratified them in 1781. However, in the absence of

Under the Articles of Confederation, the weak national government was unable to raise enough money from the states to support American troops in the Revolutionary War. General George Washington's men lacked food, clothing, and sufficient arms and munitions until they were assisted by the French. As many as 2,000 troops are thought to have perished from starvation, cold, and disease at Valley Forge, Pennsylvania, where they spent six months during the winter of 1777–1778.

FIGURE 2.1

Constitutional Time Line

The sequence of important events leading to independence and the writing and ratification of the Constitution.

1774 — **September** First Continental Congress

1775 — **May** Second Continental Congress

1776 — **January** First publication of Thomas Paine's *Common Sense*; **July** Congress adopts the Declaration of Independence

1777 — **November 15** Articles of Confederation adopted by Congress, sent to the states for ratification

1778 — **February 6** Treaty of Alliance with France

1779

1780

1781 — **March 1** Articles of Confederation are ratified by the requisite number of states; **October 19** Cornwallis surrenders the British army at Yorktown

1775–1783 Revolutionary War

Source: Compiled by the authors.

any alternative, the Articles of Confederation served as the basis for organizing the government during the Revolutionary War (see Figure 2.1).

monarchy
A form of government in which power is held by a single person, or monarch, who typically comes to power through inheritance rather than election.

In their zeal to reject **monarchy**, the authors of the Articles did not even include provisions for a president or any other executive leader. Instead, they assigned all national power to a Congress in which each state had a single vote. Members of Congress were elected by state legislatures rather than directly by the people. There was no judicial branch; all legal matters were left to the states, with the exception of disputes among the states, which would be resolved by special panels of judges appointed on an as-needed basis by Congress. To limit the power of government, the authors of the Articles gave each state veto power over any changes to the Articles and required approval from 9 of the 13 states on any legislation. Even more important, the states maintained autonomy and did not sacrifice any significant power to the national government; thus, government power was decentralized in the states, rather than centralized in the national government. For example, both the national government and the states could make treaties and coin money.

Congress also lacked any real authority over the states. For example, Congress could suggest the amount of money each state owed to support the Revolutionary army but could not enforce payment. This meant that General George Washington's troops were in dire straits, lacking basic food and clothing—to say nothing about the arms and munitions they needed to defeat the British. At first, Congress tried to compel the states to support their own troops, but this appeal failed. Desperate for funds, Congress tried in 1781 to give itself the power to raise taxes, but the measure was vetoed by Rhode Island, which represented less than 2 percent of the nation's population! If France had not come to the aid of the American army with much-needed funds and troops, the weakness of the national government could have led to defeat.[7]

After the Revolutionary War ended with the Treaty of Paris in September 1783, the inability to raise revenue through taxes continued to plague Congress. The new government owed millions of dollars in war debts to foreign governments and domestic

October 27
Federalist Papers begin appearing in New York newspapers

September 14
Annapolis delegates decide that Articles need to be fixed

September 17
Constitution signed

June 21
Constitution ratified when New Hampshire is the ninth state to ratify

May 25
Constitutional Convention begins in Philadelphia

September 3
Treaty of Paris signed, ending the Revolutionary War

August 1786–January 1787
Shays's Rebellion

March 4
Constitution takes effect

1782 1783 1784 1785 1786 1787 1788 1789

1781–1789 Articles of Confederation period

creditors. Because it had no way to make the states pay their share, Congress proposed an amendment to the Articles that would allow the national government to collect import duties to put toward paying off the debt. However, New York, the busiest seaport in the nation, did not want to share its revenue and vetoed the amendment. Foreign trade also suffered because of the weak national government. If a foreign government negotiated a trade arrangement with Congress, it could be vetoed or amended by a state government, so a foreign country wanting to conduct business with the United States might have to negotiate separate agreements with Congress and each state legislature. Even trade among the states was complicated and inefficient: each state could make its own currency, exchange rates varied, and many states charged tolls and fees to export goods across state lines. (Just imagine how difficult interstate commerce would be today if you had to exchange currency at every state line and if the value of your currency varied depending on which state you were in.)

A small group of leaders decided that something had to be done. A group from Virginia urged state legislatures to send delegates to a convention on interstate commerce in Annapolis, Maryland, in September 1786. Only five states sent delegates. However, Alexander Hamilton and James Madison salvaged success from the convention by getting those delegates to agree to convene again in Philadelphia the following May. Delegates to the Annapolis Convention also agreed that the next convention would examine the defects of the current government and "devise such further provisions as shall appear to them necessary to render the Constitution of the Federal Government adequate to the exigencies of the Union."[8]

The issues that motivated the Annapolis Convention gained new urgency as events unfolded over the next several months. Economic chaos and depression in the years after the war had caused many farmers to lose their land because they could not pay their debts or state taxes. Frustration mounted throughout the latter half of 1786, and early in 1787 a former captain in the Revolutionary army, Daniel Shays, led a force of 1,500 men in an attempt to take over the Massachusetts state government arsenal in

Springfield. Their goal was to force the state courts to stop prosecuting debtors and taking their land, but the rebels were repelled by a state militia. Similar protests on a smaller scale took place in Pennsylvania and Virginia. Some state legislatures gave in to the debtors' demands, causing national leaders to fear that **Shays's Rebellion** had exposed fundamental discontent with the new government. The very future of the fledgling nation was at risk.

Shays's Rebellion
An uprising of about 1,500 men in Massachusetts in 1786 and 1787 to protest oppressive laws and gain payment of war debts. The unrest prompted calls for a new constitution.

The rebellion exposed the central flaws of the government under the Articles of Confederation. If its leaders could not build a political system that addressed the problems of state sovereignty, redundant or conflicting responsibilities (such as coining money, foreign policy and trade, and taxing power), and the resulting political and economic chaos, then the United States would not be able to unite. Something clearly needed to be done.

Political theories of the framers

Although the leaders who gathered in Philadelphia in the summer of 1787 to write the Constitution were chastened by the failure of the Articles of Confederation, these men still shared many of the principles that had motivated the Revolution. There continued to be broad consensus on three key principles: (1) popular control of government through a republican democracy, (2) a rejection of monarchy, and (3) limitations on government power that would protect individual rights and personal property (that is, protect against tyranny).

Republicanism First among these principles was rejection of monarchy in favor of a form of government based on self-rule. **Republicanism** as understood by the framers is a government in which elected leaders represent the views of the people. Thomas Paine, an influential political writer of the Revolutionary era, wrote a pamphlet titled *Common Sense* in 1776 that was a widely read indictment of monarchy and an endorsement of the principles that fueled the Revolution and underpinned the framers' thinking.[9] Paine wrote that monarchy was the "most bare-faced falsity ever imposed

republicanism
As understood by James Madison and the framers, the belief that a form of government in which the interests of the people are represented through elected leaders is the best form of government. Our form of government is known as a republican democracy.

The Founders wanted to create a constitution that was general enough to stand the test of time. Their approach succeeded, and the U.S. Constitution is the oldest written constitution still in use today. However, by leaving some passages open to interpretation, they also set the stage for conflict over the meaning of the Constitution. This painting depicts the signing of the document at the Constitutional Convention of 1787.

on mankind" and that the common interests of the community should be served by elected representatives.

The Founders' views of republicanism, together with liberal principles of liberty and individual rights, shaped their vision of the proper form of government. The best expression of these principles is found in Thomas Jefferson's inspirational words in the Declaration of Independence:

We hold these truths to be self-evident, that all men are created equal, that they are endowed by their Creator with certain unalienable Rights, that among these are Life, Liberty, and the pursuit of Happiness. That to secure these rights, Governments are instituted among Men, deriving their just powers from the consent of the governed. That whenever any Form of Government becomes destructive of these ends, it is the Right of the People to alter or to abolish it, and to institute new Government.

Three crucial ideas are packed into this passage: equality, self-rule, and natural rights. Equality was not given much attention in the Constitution (later in this chapter we discuss how the problem of slavery was handled), but the notion that a government gains its legitimacy from the "consent of the governed" (the idea of **popular sovereignty**) and that its central purpose is to uphold the "unalienable" or **natural rights** of the people was central to the framers. The "right of the people to alter or abolish" a government that did not protect these rights served both to justify the revolt against the British and to remind the framers of their continuing obligation to make sure that those rights were maintained. The leaders who met in Philadelphia thought the Articles of Confederation had become "destructive to those ends" and therefore needed to be altered.

popular sovereignty
The idea that government gains its legitimacy through regular elections in which the people living under that government participate to elect their leaders.

natural rights
Also known as "unalienable rights," these rights are defined in the Declaration of Independence as "Life, Liberty, and the pursuit of Happiness." The Founders believed that upholding these rights should be the government's central purpose.

Seventeenth-century political philosopher John Locke greatly influenced the Founders. Many ideas discussed in Locke's writing appear in the Declaration of Independence and the Constitution.

Paine, Jefferson, Madison, and other political thinkers of the American Founding broke new ground in laying out the principles of republican democracy, but they also built on the ideas of political philosophers of their era. As mentioned in Chapter 1, Thomas Hobbes argued that government was necessary to prevent people from living in an anarchic "state of nature" in which life would be "nasty, brutish, and short."[10] However, Hobbes's central conclusion was undemocratic: he believed that a single king must rule because any other form of government would produce warring factions. Another influential seventeenth-century philosopher, John Locke, took the notion of the consent of the governed in determining a government's legitimacy in a more democratic direction. He discussed many of the ideas that later appeared in the Declaration of Independence and the Constitution, including natural rights, property rights, the need for a vigorous executive branch that would be checked by a legislative branch, and self-rule through elections.[11] Baron de Montesquieu, an eighteenth-century political thinker, also influenced the framers. Although he did not use the term "separation of powers," Montesquieu argued in *The Spirit of the Laws* (1748) that no two, let alone three, functions of government (judicial, legislative, and executive) should be controlled by one branch. He also argued that in order to preserve liberty, one branch of government should be able to check the excesses of the other branches.

Human Nature and Its Implications for Democracy The most comprehensive statement of the framers' political philosophy and democratic theory was a series of essays written by James Madison, Alexander Hamilton, and John Jay titled the *Federalist Papers*. These essays explained and justified the framework of government created by the Constitution; they also revealed the framers' view of human nature and its implications for democracy. The framers' view of human nature as basically being driven by self-interest led to Madison's assessment that "[i]n framing a government which is to be administered by men over men, the great difficulty lies in this: you must first enable the government to control the governed; and in the next place oblige it to control itself." This analysis, which comes from *Federalist 51*, is often considered the clearest articulation of the need for republican government and a system of separated powers.

In *Federalist 10*, Madison described the central problem for government as the need to control factions. He argued that governments cannot control the causes of factions because differences of opinion—based on the fallibility of reason; differences in wealth, property, and native abilities; and attachments to different leaders—are part of human nature. The only way to eliminate factions would be to either curtail liberty or try to make everyone the same. The first remedy Madison called "worse than the disease" of factions themselves, and the second he found "as impracticable as the first would be unwise." Because people are driven by self-interest, which sometimes conflicts with the common good, government must, however, try to control the effects of factions. This was the task facing the framers at the Constitutional Convention.

Economic interests

Political ideas were central to the framers' thinking at the Constitutional Convention, but economic context and interests were equally important. First, while there were certainly class differences among Americans in the late eighteenth century, they were insignificant compared with the inequalities found in Europe. America did not have the history of feudalism that had created tremendous inequality in Europe between landowners and propertyless serfs who worked the land. In contrast, most Americans owned small farms or worked as middle-class artisans and craftsmen. Thus, while political equality did not figure prominently in the Constitution, citizens' relative economic equality did influence the context of debates at the Constitutional Convention.

Second, despite Americans' general economic equality, there were significant regional economic differences. The South was largely agricultural, with cotton and

The economic context of the American Founding had an important impact on the framing of the Constitution. Most Americans worked on small farms or as artisans or business owners, which meant that economic power was broadly distributed. This woodcut shows New York City around the time the Constitution was written, viewed from upper Manhattan.

tobacco plantations that depended on the labor of enslaved people. The region favored free trade because of its export-based economy (bolstered by westward expansion) and the trading of enslaved people. The middle Atlantic and northern states, however, had smaller farms and a broad economic base of manufacturing, fishing, and trade. These states favored government-managed trade and commercial development.

Despite these different interests, people in many sectors of the economy favored a stronger national government and reform of the Articles of Confederation (see Nuts & Bolts 2.1). Creditors wanted a government that could pay off its debts to them, southern farmers wanted free trade that could be efficiently promoted only by a central government, and manufacturers and traders wanted a single national currency and uniform interstate commerce regulations. However, there was a deep division between those who supported empowering the national government and those who still favored strong state governments and a weak national government. These two groups became known as the **Federalists** and the **Antifederalists**. Now the stage was set for a productive but contentious convention.

Federalists
Those at the Constitutional Convention who favored a strong national government and a system of separated powers.

Antifederalists
Those at the Constitutional Convention who favored strong state governments and feared that a strong national government would be a threat to individual rights.

NUTS & BOLTS 2.1

Comparing the Articles of Confederation and the Constitution

Issue	Articles of Confederation	Constitution
Legislature	Unicameral Congress	Bicameral Congress divided into the House of Representatives and the Senate
Members of Congress	Between two and seven per state (the number was determined by each state)	Two senators per state; representatives apportioned according to population of each state
Voting in Congress	One vote per state	One vote per representative or senator
Selection of members	Appointed by state legislatures	Representatives elected by popular vote; senators appointed by state legislatures
Chief executive	None (there was an Executive Council within Congress, but it had limited executive power)	President
National judiciary	No general federal courts	Supreme Court; Congress authorized to establish national judiciary
Amendments to the document	When approved by all states	When approved by two-thirds of each house of Congress and three-fourths of the states
Power to coin money	Federal government and the states	Federal government only
Taxes	Apportioned by Congress, collected by the states	Apportioned and collected by Congress
Ratification	Unanimous consent required	Consent of nine states required

Source: Compiled by the authors.

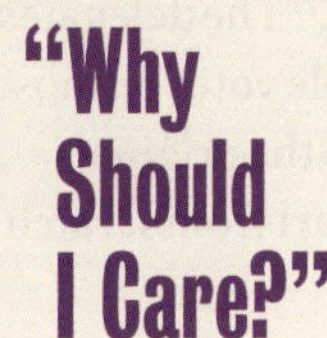

The Constitution, which to this day outlines the rules for American government, provides for a strong federal government. This resolved many of the challenges that handicapped the early republic under the Articles of Confederation.

"Why Should I Care?"

The historical context and political ideas that shaped the thinking of the framers still resonate today. While we are centuries removed from the oppressive rule of the British monarchy, most Americans still support the ideas of representative democracy and limited government that replaced it. The division between the Federalists and Antifederalists on how to best create a representative government that protected our freedom is evident today in ongoing debates about the proper role of the government in our everyday lives.

ANALYZE THE MAJOR ISSUES DEBATED BY THE FRAMERS OF THE CONSTITUTION

The politics of compromise at the Constitutional Convention

The central players at the Constitutional Convention were James Madison, Gouverneur Morris, Edmund Randolph, James Wilson, Benjamin Franklin, and George Washington, who was the unanimous choice to preside over the convention (despite his initial decision not to attend). Several of the important leaders of the Revolution were not present. Patrick "Give me Liberty, or give me Death!" Henry was selected to attend but declined to do so, as he opposed any changes in the Articles, saying he "smelled a rat." Indeed, those who were opposed to a stronger national government largely avoided the convention. Other prominent leaders who did not attend included Thomas Jefferson and J ohn Adams, who were working overseas as U.S. diplomats, and Thomas Paine, who was back in England. Moreover, John Hancock and Samuel Adams were not selected to attend. The delegates met in secret to encourage open, uncensored debate.

Although there was broad consensus among the delegates that the Articles of Confederation needed to be changed, there were many tensions over the issues that required political compromise (see Nuts & Bolts 2.2). Among them were the following:

- majority rule versus minority rights
- large states versus small states
- legislative power versus executive power (and how to elect the executive)
- national power versus state and local power
- states that allowed slavery versus states that did not

These complex and competing interests meant that the delegates had to focus on pragmatic, achievable solutions rather than on proposals that represented particular groups' ideals but that could not gain majority support. Robert A. Dahl, a leading democratic theorist of the twentieth century, argues that it was impossible for the Constitution to "reflect a coherent, unified theory of government" because so much compromising and vote trading were required to find common ground.[12] The delegates tackled the problems one at a time, holding lengthy debates and multiple votes on most issues. The most important initial decision they made was to give up on the original plan to revise the Articles of Confederation; instead, they decided to start from scratch with a new blueprint for government.

DID YOU KNOW?

The average age of the delegates to the Constitutional Convention was

42

Four of the delegates were in their 20s, and 14 were in their 30s.

Source: teachingamericanhistory.org

NUTS & BOLTS 2.2

Major Compromises at the Constitutional Convention

Conflict	Position of the large states	Position of the small states	Compromise
Apportionment in Congress	By population	State equality	Great Compromise created the Senate and House
Method of election to Congress	By the people	By the states	House elected by the people; Senate elected by the state legislatures*
Electing the executive (president)	By Congress	By the states	By the Electoral College
Who decides federal–state conflicts?	Some federal authority	State courts	State courts to decide†
	Position of the states that allowed slavery	**Position of the states that did not allow slavery**	**Compromise**
Control over commerce	By the states	By Congress	By Congress, but with 20-year exemption for the importation of enslaved people
Counting enslaved people toward apportionment	Counted 1:1 like citizens	Not counted	Three-Fifths Compromise
	Position of the Federalists	**Position of the Antifederalists**	**Compromise**
Protection for individual rights‡	Secured by state constitutions; national Bill of Rights not needed	National Bill of Rights needed	Bill of Rights passed by the 1st Congress; ratified by all states as of December 1791

*This was changed by the Seventeenth Amendment in 1913, which allowed for the direct election by the people of two senators from each state.
†This was changed by the Judiciary Act of 1789, which provided for appeals from state to federal courts.
‡This issue was raised but not resolved until after the convention.
Source: Compiled by the authors.

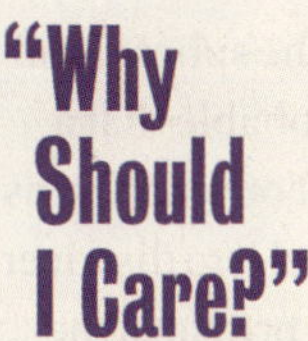

As we noted in Chapter 1, politics is conflictual. People will always have different goals and objectives. Adhering to one's principles is admirable, but unless one is willing to compromise, no one will get anything they want in politics—or in life. The success of the Constitution is a result of compromises outlined above.

Majority rule versus minority rights

A central problem for any representative democracy is protecting minority rights within a system ruled by the majority. The framers thought of this issue not in terms of racial and ethnic minorities (as we might today), but in terms of regional and economic minorities. How could the framers be sure that small landowners and poorer people would not impose onerous taxes on the wealthier minority? How could they guarantee that dominant agricultural interests would not impose punitive tariffs on manufacturing while allowing free export of farmed commodities? The answers to these questions can be found in Madison's writings on the problem of factions in *Federalist 10*.

Madison defined a "faction" as a group motivated by selfish interests against the common good. If these interests prevailed, it could produce the very kind of tyranny that the Americans had fought to escape during the Revolutionary War. Madison was especially concerned about tyranny by majority factions because in a democracy, minority tyranny would be controlled by the republican principle: the majority could simply vote out the minority faction. If, however, the majority always rules, majority tyranny could be a real problem. Given the understanding of selfish human nature that Madison so clearly outlined, a populist, majoritarian democracy would not necessarily promote the common good. John Jay expressed his concern about popular majorities in strong terms: "The wise and the good never form the majority of any large society, and it seldom happens that their measures are uniformly adopted; or that they can always prevent being overborne themselves by the strong and almost never-ceasing union of the wicked and the weak."[13] However, if too many protections were provided to minority and regional interests, the collective interest would not be served because constructive changes could be vetoed too easily, as under the Articles of Confederation.

Madison's solution to this problem provided the justification for our form of government. He argued that to control majority tyranny, factions must be set against one another to counter each other's ambitions and prevent the tyranny of any single majority faction. This was to be accomplished through the "double protection" of the separation of powers within the national government in the form of checks and balances, and by further dividing power across the levels of state and local governments through the system of federalism (which we will discuss in detail in the next chapter). Popular majorities were also controlled, as we discuss below, by the indirect election of the president through the Electoral College and senators by state legislatures.

James Madison argued that it is beneficial to put the interests of one group in competition with the interests of other groups, so that no one group can dominate government. He hoped to achieve this through the separation of powers across different branches of the national government and across the national, state, and local levels.

Madison also argued that additional protection against majority tyranny would come from the "size principle." That is, the new nation would be a large and diverse republic in which majority interests would be less likely to organize and therefore less able to dominate. According to Madison in *Federalist 10*, "Extend the sphere, and you take in a greater variety of parties and interests; you make it less probable that a majority of the whole will have a common motive to invade the rights of other citizens; or if such a common motive exists, it will be more difficult for all who feel it to discover their own strength, and to act in unison with each other."[14] This insight provides the basis for modern **pluralism**, a political theory that makes the same argument about the crosscutting interests of groups today.

pluralism
The idea that having a variety of parties and interests within a government will strengthen the system, ensuring that no group possesses total control.

The precise contours of Madison's solution still had to be hammered out at the convention, but the general principle pleased both the Antifederalists and the Federalists. State governments would maintain some autonomy, but the national government would become stronger than it had been under the Articles. The issue was striking the appropriate balance: none of the framers favored a pure populist majoritarian democracy, and few wanted to protect minority rights to the extent that the Articles had.

Small states versus large states

The question of the appropriate balance came to an immediate head in a debate between small-population and large-population states over representation in the national legislature. Under the Articles, every state had a single vote, but this did not seem fair to large states. They pushed for representation based on population. This proposal, along with others that would strengthen the national government, was the

Virginia Plan. The small states countered with the **New Jersey Plan**, which proposed maintaining equal representation for every state. Rhode Island, the smallest state, was so concerned about small-state power that it boycotted the convention. Tensions were running high; this issue appeared to have all the elements of a deal breaker, and there seemed to be no way to resolve the impasse.

Just as it appeared that the convention might grind to a halt before it really got started, Connecticut proposed what became known as the **Great Compromise**, or Connecticut Compromise. The plan suggested establishing a Congress with two houses: the Senate would have two senators from each state, and in the House of Representatives each state's number of representatives would be based on its population. At first glance, the Connecticut Compromise seems to make perfect sense: as the seventh of 13 states in terms of population, Connecticut was positioned to offer a compromise that would appeal to both large and small states. But the situation was actually much more complicated. First, Rhode Island did not attend the convention, so there was no true median state (with only 12 states at the convention, no one stood alone at the center). Second, given that each state had one vote at the convention, the smallest states could have easily outvoted the biggest ones and insisted on equal representation for each state.

Why didn't the smaller states impose their view? Two of the smaller states, Georgia and South Carolina, focused on their future growth, so they supported representation based on population, the Virginia Plan. But when other smaller states balked at their loss of power, the Connecticut Compromise was able to win the support of North Carolina (and Massachusetts's delegates were divided), so the compromise passed 5–4–1.

Despite this more complex picture, an analysis of all 569 votes at the Constitutional Convention clearly shows that Connecticut occupied a pivotal place at the convention. As the graphs in Figure 2.2 illustrate, Connecticut was in the middle in terms of

Virginia Plan
A plan proposed by the larger states during the Constitutional Convention that based representation in the national legislature on population. The plan also included a variety of other proposals to strengthen the national government.

New Jersey Plan
A plan that was suggested in response to the Virginia Plan; smaller states at the Constitutional Convention proposed that each state should receive equal representation in the national legislature, regardless of size.

Great Compromise
A compromise between the large and small states, proposed by Connecticut, in which Congress would have two houses: a Senate with two legislators per state and a House of Representatives in which each state's representation would be based on population (also known as the Connecticut Compromise).

FIGURE 2.2

Connecticut's Pivotal Place at the Constitutional Convention

Though there were many disagreements over the details of America's new constitution, one of the most intense focused on how states would be represented in Congress, either allocating representatives equally or based on population. After other plans were considered and rejected, the Connecticut Compromise won out. Why do you think Connecticut was well positioned to find a compromise? How do these graphs help us understand why the Virginia and New Jersey Plans were in conflict and ultimately rejected?

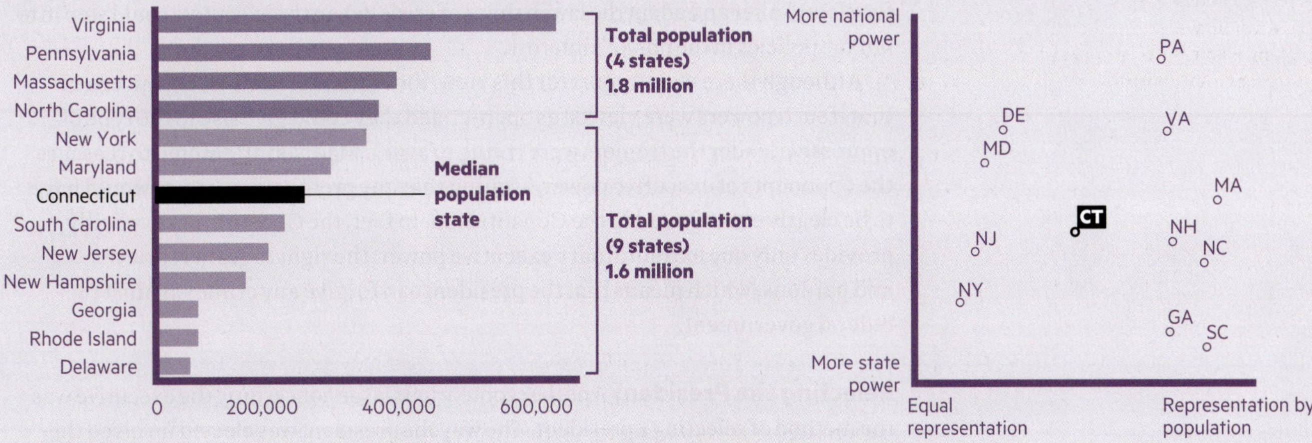

Source: Keith L. Dougherty and Jac C. Heckelman, "A Pivotal Voter from a Pivotal State: Roger Sherman at the Constitutional Convention," *American Political Science Review* 100:2 (May 2006): 298.

desire for representation based on population and in terms of desire for more state power. Connecticut is right in the center of these graphs—no wonder it could broker a compromise!

Legislative power versus executive power

An equally difficult challenge was how to divide power at the national level. Here the central issues revolved around the executive: the president. How much power should the president have relative to the legislative branch? (The courts also figured here, but they were less central to the discussions.) And how would the president be elected?

Limiting Presidential Power The delegates knew what they did not want: the king of England and his colonial governors were viewed as tramplers of liberty. But many delegates rejected outright the idea of a single executive because they believed it was impossible to have an executive who would not be oppressive. Edmund Randolph proposed a three-person executive for this reason, arguing that a single executive would be the "fetus of monarchy." The Virginia Plan envisioned a single executive who would share some legislative power with federal judges in a Council of Revision with the power to veto legislation passed by Congress (however, the veto could be overridden by a simple majority vote in Congress). The delegates finally agreed on the single executive because he would have the most "energy, dispatch, and responsibility for the office" (as explained in *Federalist 70*), but they constrained the president's power through the system of checks and balances. One significant power they granted to the executive was the veto. It could be overridden by Congress, but only with the support of two-thirds of both chambers. This requirement gave the president a significant role in the legislative process.

Hamilton and the other New Yorkers favored a strong executive. This was probably because the governorship of New York closely resembled the type of executive that the Constitution envisioned. The governor of New York was elected by the people rather than by the legislature, served for three years, and was eligible for reelection. The office also had a legislative veto power and considerable control over appointments to politically controlled jobs. The arguments the New Yorkers made on behalf of the strong executive relied heavily on the philosophy of John Locke. Locke saw the general superiority of a government of laws created by legislatures, but he also saw the need for an executive with more flexible leadership powers, or what he called "prerogative powers." Legislatures are unable, Locke wrote, "to foresee, and so by laws to provide for all accidents and necessities."[15] They also are, by virtue of their size and unwieldiness, too slow to alter and adapt the law in times of crisis, when the executive could step in to pursue policies in the public's interest.

Although there was support for this view, the Antifederalists were concerned that if such powers were viewed as open-ended they could give rise to the type of oppressive leader the framers were trying to avoid. Madison attempted to reassure the opponents of executive power, arguing that any prerogative powers would have to be clearly enumerated in the Constitution. In fact, the Constitution explicitly provides only one extraordinary executive power: the right to grant reprieves and pardons, which means that the president can forgive any crimes against the federal government.

Selecting the President Another contentious issue concerning the executive was the method of selecting a president. The way the president was elected involved the issues of majority rule and minority rights, state versus national power, and the nature of executive power itself. Would the president be elected by the nation as a whole, by the states, or by coalitions within Congress? If the state-level governments played a central role, would this mean that the president could not speak for national interests? If Congress elected the president, could the executive still provide a check on the legislative branch?

Most Americans do not realize that (1) our presidential system is unique and (2) we came close to having a parliamentary system, which is the form of government that exists in most other established democracies. In a **parliamentary system**, the executive branch depends on the support of the legislative branch. The Virginia Plan proposed that Congress elect the president, just as Parliament elects the British prime minister. However, facing lingering concerns that a congressionally elected president would be too beholden to that body, a committee of framers subsequently made the following recommendations: (1) that the president be selected by an Electoral College, representation in which would be based on the number of representatives and senators each state has in Congress, and (2) that members of each state's legislature would determine the method for choosing their state's electors.[16] The delegates ultimately approved this recommendation.

parliamentary system
A system of government in which legislative and executive power are closely joined. The legislature (parliament) selects the chief executive (prime minister), who forms the cabinet from members of the parliament.

Why did the delegates favor this complicated, indirect way of electing the president? As with good compromises, all sides could claim victory to some extent. Advocates of state power were happy because state legislatures played a central role in presidential elections; those who worried about the direct influence of the people liked the indirect manner of election; and proponents of strong executive power were satisfied that the president would not simply be an agent of Congress.

However, the solution had its flaws and did not work out the way the framers intended. First, if the Electoral College was supposed to provide an independent check on the voters, it never played this role because of the quick emergence of political parties (which the framers did not anticipate). Electors became agents of the parties, as they remain today, rather than independent actors who would use their judgment to pick the most qualified candidate for president.

Second, the basic math of how the number of electors was determined (the size of the congressional delegation) magnified the impact of two other compromises at the convention, the Connecticut Compromise and the Three-Fifths Compromise. Because each state had a minimum of three electors (one House member, plus two senators), smaller states had proportionately more representation in the Electoral College than large states. For example, today, the smallest states such as Wyoming and Vermont have 200,000 people per electoral vote, while the largest states, such as California and Texas, have about 740,000 people per electoral vote. Given that the Republican Party wins more of the smaller, rural states, this small-state bias of the Electoral College can actually determine the outcome of an election. In 2000, Democrat Al Gore would have beaten Republican George W. Bush if the two-elector bonus for each state was removed. Similarly, the Three-Fifths Compromise gave additional voting power to states that allowed slavery in the pre–Civil War period, given the increase in the size of their House delegations (and therefore, electoral votes; see the What Do the Facts Say? feature on p. 50).

Third, the emergence of parties created a serious technical error in the Constitution: the provision that gave each elector two votes and elected the candidate with the most votes as president and the second-place finisher as vice president. With electors acting as agents of parties, they ended up casting one vote each for the presidential and vice-presidential candidate of their own party. This created a tie in the 1800 presidential election when Thomas Jefferson and Aaron Burr each received 73 electoral votes. The problem was fixed by the Twelfth Amendment, which required that electors cast separate ballots for president and vice president.

Jefferson: You hear this guy? Man openly campaigns against me, talking 'bout "I look forward to our partnership!"
Madison: It is crazy that the guy who comes in second gets to be vice president.
Jefferson: OOOH! Y'know what, we can change that! Y'know why?
Madison: Why?
Jefferson: 'Cause I'm the president!

—***Hamilton,*** the musical

National power versus state and local power

Tensions over the balance of power cut across virtually every debate at the convention. The issues included presidential versus legislative power, whether the national government could supersede state laws, apportionment in the legislature, slavery, regulation of commerce and taxation, and the amendment process. The overall compromise that addressed these tensions was the second of Madison's "double protections," the system of federalism, which divided power between autonomous levels of government that controlled different areas of policy.

Federalism is such an important topic that we devote the entire next chapter to it, but two brief points about it are important here. First, the Tenth Amendment, which was added as part of the Bill of Rights shortly after ratification, was a concession to the Antifederalists, who were concerned that the national government would gain too much power in the new political system. The Tenth Amendment says: "The powers not delegated to the United States by the Constitution, nor prohibited by it to the States, are reserved to the States respectively, or to the people." This definition of **reserved powers** was viewed as setting outer limits on the reach of national power.

reserved powers
As defined in the Tenth Amendment, powers that are not given to the national government by the Constitution, or not prohibited to the states, are reserved to the states or the people.

Between 1918 and 1937 and then again starting in the 1990s, the Supreme Court has frequently invoked the Tenth Amendment to nullify various laws passed by Congress as unconstitutional intrusions on the reserved powers of the states (see the discussion in Chapter 3 of the Supreme Court's recent preference for state-centered federalism). The Tenth Amendment continues to play an important role in current debates about the proper level of national power. For example, conservative Republicans argue that the states and the private sector, not the national government, should have the primary responsibility for health care policy, while Democrats in state and local government served as a check on President Trump's policy agenda concerning immigration and climate change (among other issues), while state Republicans have checked President Biden's policies on COVID-19 vaccines and election laws.

national supremacy clause
The part of Article VI, Section 2, of the Constitution stating that the Constitution and the laws and treaties of the United States are the "supreme Law of the Land," meaning national laws take precedence over state laws if the two conflict.

Second, the **national supremacy clause** of the Constitution (Article VI) says that any national law is the supreme law of the land and takes precedence over any state law that conflicts with it. This is especially important in areas where the national and state governments have overlapping responsibilities for policy.

States that allowed slavery versus states that did not

Slavery was another nearly insurmountable issue for the delegates. Southern states would not agree to any provisions limiting slavery; indeed, about 25 of the 55 delegates to the Constitutional Convention owned enslaved people.[17] Although the states that did not allow slavery were opposed to the practice, they were not willing to scuttle the entire Constitution by taking a principled stand. Even after these basic positions had been recognized, many unresolved issues remained. Could the importation of enslaved people be restricted in the future? How would northern states deal with enslaved people who had escaped to freedom? Most important in terms of the politics of the issue, how would the enslaved population be counted for the purpose of congressional representation in states that allowed slavery? The deals that the convention delegates cut on the issue of slavery illustrate the two most common forms of compromise: splitting the difference and logrolling (trading votes). Splitting the difference is familiar to anyone who has haggled over the price of a car or bargained for something at a flea market; you end up meeting halfway, or splitting the difference. Logrolling occurs when politicians trade votes for one another's pet projects, for example, support for dairy subsidies in one district in exchange for opening up more federal lands for mining in another.

The delegates went through similar negotiations over how enslaved people would be counted for purposes of states' congressional representation. The states had been through this debate once before, when they addressed the issue of taxation under the Articles of Confederation. At that point, the states that allowed slavery had argued that enslaved people should not be counted because they did not receive the same benefits as citizens and were not the same burden to the government. States that did not allow slavery had countered that enslaved people should be counted the same way as citizens when determining a state's fair share of the tax burden. The sides had reached a compromise by agreeing that each enslaved person would count as three-fifths of a person for purposes of taxation. The arguments over the issue of representation became even more contentious at the Constitutional Convention, where the positions were reversed, with states that allowed slavery arguing that enslaved people should be counted like everyone else for the purposes of determining the number of House representatives for each state. Once again, both sides managed to agree on the **Three-Fifths Compromise** (see the What Do the Facts Say? feature on p. 50).

Three-Fifths Compromise The states' decision during the Constitutional Convention to count each enslaved person as three-fifths of a person in a state's population for the purposes of determining the number of House members and the distribution of taxes.

The other two issues, the importation of enslaved people and dealing with enslaved people who had escaped to freedom, were handled by logrolling combined with an element of splitting the difference. Logrolling is more likely to occur than splitting the difference when the issue cannot be neatly divided. For example, northern states either would be obligated to return freedom seekers to their southern owners or would not; there was no way to split the difference. On issues like this with no clear middle

WANTED,
ONE HUNDRED
NEGROES,
From 12 to 30 years old, for which a good price will be given.
THEY are to be ſent out of the ſtate, therefore we ſhall not be particular reſpecting the character of any of them—Hearty and well made is all that is neceſſary.
Moſes Auſtin & Co.
Richmond, Dec. 15, 1787.

This advertisement from a slave-trading company appeared in a Richmond, Virginia, newspaper shortly after the Constitution was signed. Slavery is often referred to as the "original sin" of our nation and proved to be very problematic at the Constitutional Convention: Would there be limits on the importation of enslaved people? How would enslaved people who had escaped to freedom be dealt with by states that did not allow slavery? And how would enslaved people be counted for the purposes of congressional representation?

WHAT DO THE FACTS SAY?

Think about it

- **How many additional seats in the House did southern states get** as a result of the Three-Fifths Compromise, relative to the number of seats they would have had if enslaved people had not been counted at all?
- **How many additional seats in the House would southern states have gotten** if enslaved people had been counted as full members of the population?
- **How did the Three-Fifths Compromise** have an impact on the Electoral College? (Remember: each state's number of electors is equal in number to its combined total of representatives in the House and senators.)

The Three-Fifths Compromise

The Three-Fifths Compromise is often described as the "original sin" of the Constitution, but less recognized is the impact that it had on the Electoral College. The figure shows the number of each state's House members in the 1790s based on the Three-Fifths Compromise, and then how many representatives they would have had if only the free population had been counted or if the total population, including enslaved people, had been counted.

Number of House members

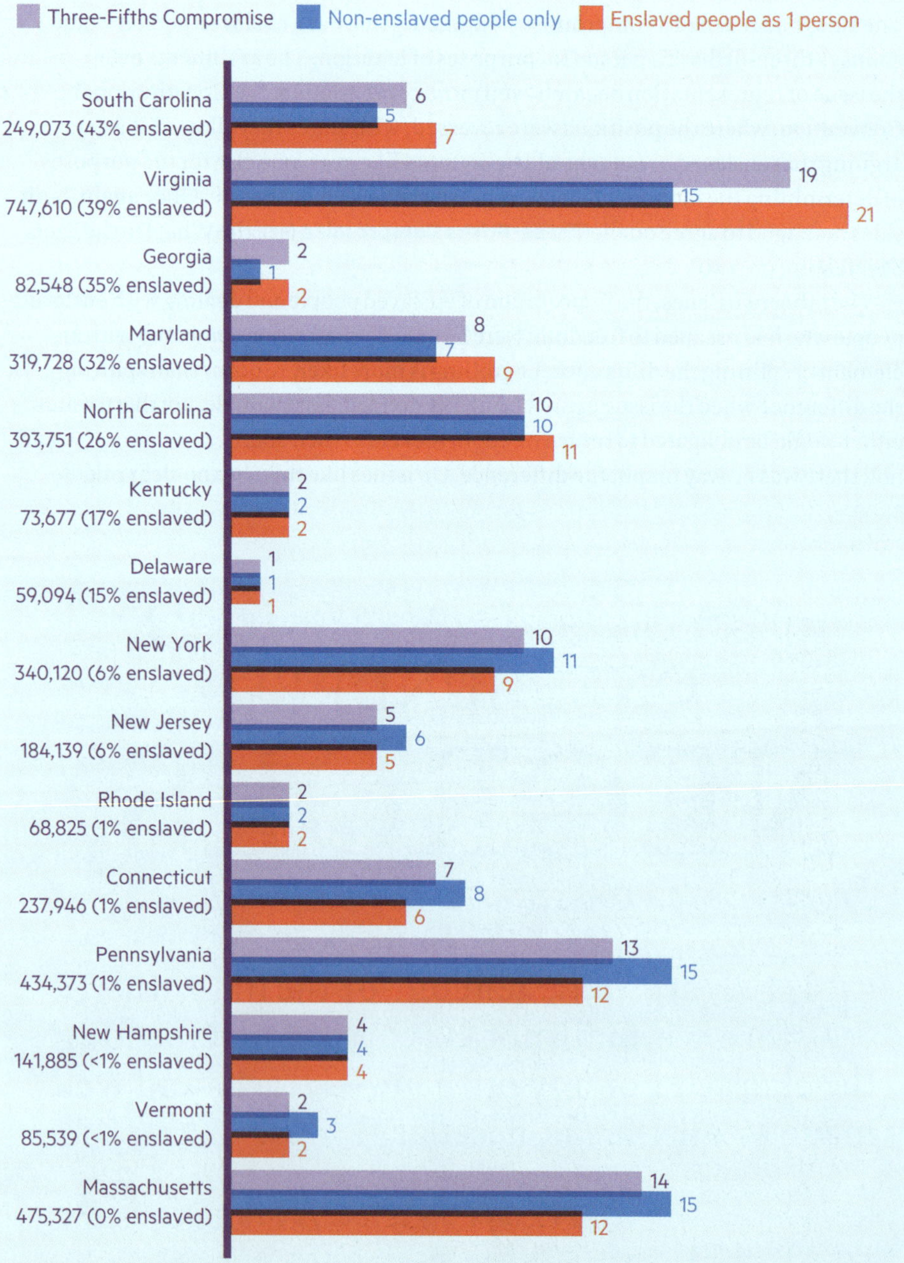

State	Three-Fifths Compromise	Non-enslaved people only	Enslaved people as 1 person
South Carolina 249,073 (43% enslaved)	6	5	7
Virginia 747,610 (39% enslaved)	19	15	21
Georgia 82,548 (35% enslaved)	2	1	2
Maryland 319,728 (32% enslaved)	8	7	9
North Carolina 393,751 (26% enslaved)	10	10	11
Kentucky 73,677 (17% enslaved)	2	2	2
Delaware 59,094 (15% enslaved)	1	1	1
New York 340,120 (6% enslaved)	10	11	9
New Jersey 184,139 (6% enslaved)	5	6	5
Rhode Island 68,825 (1% enslaved)	2	2	2
Connecticut 237,946 (1% enslaved)	7	8	6
Pennsylvania 434,373 (1% enslaved)	13	15	12
New Hampshire 141,885 (<1% enslaved)	4	4	4
Vermont 85,539 (<1% enslaved)	2	3	2
Massachusetts 475,327 (0% enslaved)	14	15	12

Note: These numbers reflect total populations according to the 1790 census.

Source: U.S. Census Bureau, "Return of the Whole Number of Persons within the Several Districts of the United States," www2.census.gov/library/publications/decennial/1790/number_of_persons/1790a-02.pdf (accessed 5/3/22); calculations are by the authors.

ground, opposing sides will look for other issues on which they can trade votes. In this case, the states that did not allow slavery saw an opportunity to push for more national government control over commerce and trade than was provided under the Articles, a change that the states that allowed slavery opposed. A logroll—or vote trade—developed as a way to compromise the competing regional interests of slavery and regulation of commerce. Northern states agreed to return freedom seekers (the Fugitive Slave Clause), and southern states agreed to allow Congress to pass laws regulating commerce and taxing imports with a simple majority vote (rather than the supermajority required under the Articles).

The importation of enslaved people was included as part of this logroll, along with some split-the-difference negotiating. Northern states wanted to allow future Congresses to ban the importation of enslaved people; southern states wanted to allow the importation of enslaved people to continue indefinitely, arguing that slavery was essential to produce their labor-intensive crops. After much negotiation among the states, the final language of the Article resulting from this part of the logroll prevented a constitutional amendment from banning the trading of enslaved people until 1808.[18]

From a modern perspective, it is difficult to understand how the framers could have taken such a purely political approach to the moral issue of slavery. Many of the delegates believed slavery was immoral, yet they were willing to negotiate for the southern states' support of the Constitution. Some southern delegates were apologetic about slavery, even as they argued for protecting their interests. Many constitutional scholars view the convention's treatment of slavery as its central failure. In fairness to the delegates, the issue of slavery could not be settled, since the goal was to create a document that all states would support. However, the delegates' inability to resolve this issue meant that it would simmer below the surface for the next 70 years, finally boiling over into the bloodiest of all American wars: the Civil War.

The convention ended on a relatively harmonious note with Benjamin Franklin moving for adoption. Franklin's motion was worded ambiguously to allow those who still had reservations to sign the Constitution anyway. Franklin's motion was in the

DID YOU KNOW?

At only about

8,700

words, the U.S. Constitution is much shorter than the average state constitution (39,604 words).

Source: PARCA, Tableau Public

Union and Confederate troops clashed in close combat in Gettysburg, Pennsylvania, in July 1863. It was the turning point of the war, and the bloodiest single conflict, claiming an estimated 51,000 lives. The inability of the framers to resolve the issue of slavery allowed tensions over the issue to grow throughout the early nineteenth century, culminating in the Civil War.

"following convenient form": "Done in Convention by the unanimous consent of the States present the 17th of September. . . . In Witness whereof we have hereunto subscribed our names." His clever wording meant that the signers were only bearing witness to the approval by the states and therefore could still, in good faith, oppose substantial parts of the document. Franklin's motion passed with 10 ayes, no nays, and one delegation divided. All but three of the remaining delegates signed.

"Why Should I Care?"

Politicians today have a very difficult time compromising on issues like gun control, abortion rights, and even the proper levels of taxation and spending. At the Constitutional Convention, the framers had to struggle with fundamental issues such as executive power and state versus national power as well as incredibly divisive issues like slavery. The framers were facing uncertainty about the very survival of their new nation and the nearly impossible task of creating a new framework that would allow our nation to not only survive but also flourish. Yet the framers were able to arrive at workable compromises on all of these issues. Without compromise, our nation would not exist. When you hear a politician today say, "I am going to stick to my principles; I am not going to compromise," reflect on the fact that governing is not possible without compromise. "Compromise" is not a dirty word; it is an essential feature of politics. We may get a chance to see if today's politicians are as able to compromise as the Founders: 15 states have passed legislation calling for a new constitutional convention, with legislation introduced in 17 more states.[19]

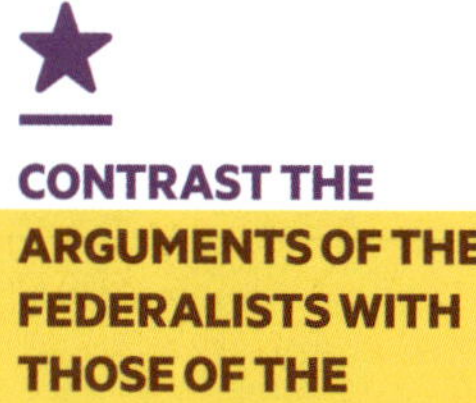
CONTRAST THE ARGUMENTS OF THE FEDERALISTS WITH THOSE OF THE ANTIFEDERALISTS

Ratification

Article VII of the Constitution, which described the process for ratifying the document, was also designed to maximize its chance of success. Only nine states were needed to ratify, unlike under the unanimity rule that had applied to changing the Articles of Confederation. Equally important, ratification votes would be taken in state conventions set up specifically for that purpose, bypassing the state legislatures, which would be more likely to resist some of the Constitution's state–federal power-sharing arrangements.

The near-unanimous approval at the Constitutional Convention's end masked the very strong opposition that remained. Many delegates simply left the convention when it became clear that things were not going their way (overall, 74 delegates were elected to go, 55 attended, and 39 signed the Constitution). Rhode Island sent no delegates and refused to appoint a ratification convention. More ominously, New York seemed dead set against the Constitution, and Pennsylvania, Virginia, and Massachusetts were split. The ratifying conventions in each state subjected the Constitution to intense scrutiny, as attendees examined every sentence for possible objections. A national debate raged over the next nine months.

The Antifederalists' concerns

The Antifederalists were most worried about the role of the president, the transfer of power from the states to the national government, and the lack of specific guarantees of civil liberties. In short, they feared that a strong, centralized national government would become tyrannical and they favored a small, decentralized republic. This

This engraving by Amos Doolittle titled *The Looking Glass for 1787* satirizes some of the issues raised in the debate over the ratification of the Constitution. The wagon in the center is carrying Connecticut and sinking into the mud under the weight of debts and paper money as "Federalists" and "Antifederalists" try to pull it out.

concern was summarized in Brutus 1, an Antifederalist paper believed to have been written by Robert Yates, a New York judge and delegate to the Constitutional Convention: the Constitution would create a federal government that would "possess absolute and uncontrollable power."[20] The doubts about the single central executive were expressed by Patrick Henry, a leading Antifederalist. Speaking to the Virginia ratifying convention, Henry was mocking in his indictment: "Your president may easily become a king. . . . There will be no checks, no real balances in this government."[21] Even Thomas Jefferson complained that the president would control the armed forces and could be reelected indefinitely.[22] State power and the ability to regulate commerce were also central concerns. States such as New York would lose substantial revenue if they could no longer charge tariffs on goods that came into their ports. Other states were concerned that they would pay a disproportionate share of national taxes.

The Antifederalists' foremost objection was to the lack of protections for civil liberties in the new political system. During the last week of the convention, Elbridge Gerry and George Mason offered a resolution "to prepare a Bill of Rights." However, the resolution was unanimously defeated by the state delegations. Some believed that the national government posed no threat to liberties, such as freedom of the press, because it did not have the power to restrict them in the first place. Others thought that because it would be impossible to enumerate all rights, it was better to list none at all. Federalists such as Roger Sherman argued that state constitutions, most of which protected freedom of speech, freedom of the press, right to a trial by jury, and other civil liberties, would be sufficient to protect liberty. However, many Antifederalists still wanted assurances that the *national* government would not trample their rights.

> **A lady asked Dr. [Benjamin] Franklin, "Well, Doctor, what have we got—a republic or a monarchy?"**
>
> **"A republic," replied the Doctor, "if you can keep it."**
>
> **—James McHenry,** *The Records of the Federal Convention of 1787*

The Federalists' strategies

The Antifederalists had many strong arguments, and there was no denying that the Constitution was really a "leap in the dark"—many of the ideas of the document had never been tested, so the experiment in government had high risks and no

Alexander Hamilton authored a majority of the *Federalist Papers* and was a strong advocate for ratification of the Constitution.

guarantee of success. To try to reassure opponents of the Constitution, the Federalists counterattacked on several fronts. First, supporters of the Constitution gained the upper hand in the debate by claiming the term "federalist." It is a common tactic in debates to co-opt a strong point of the opposing side as a positive for your side. The opponents of the Constitution probably had a stronger claim than its supporters to being federalists—that is, those who favor and emphasize the autonomous power of the state governments. Today, for example, the Federalist Society is a conservative group organized around the principles of states' rights and limited government. By calling themselves Federalists, the supporters of the Constitution asserted that they were the true protectors of states' interests, which irritated the Antifederalists to no end. The Antifederalists also had the rhetorical disadvantage of having "anti" attached to their name, thereby being defined in terms of their opponents' position rather than their own. But the problem was more than just rhetorical: the Federalists pointed out that the Antifederalists did not have their own plan to solve the problems created by the Articles and therefore were cast as defenders of the status quo, which the Federalists viewed as unsustainable.

Second, as we mentioned earlier, the Federalists published the *Federalist Papers*. Although originally published in New York newspapers, they were widely read throughout the nation. The *Federalist Papers* were essentially one-sided arguments aimed at changing public opinion. The authors downplayed potentially unpopular aspects of the new system, such as the power of the president, while emphasizing points they knew would appeal to the opposition. Despite the authors' biased arguments, the *Federalist Papers* are considered the best comprehensive discussion of the political theory underlying the Constitution, such as the framers' views of self-interested human nature and the dangers of factions, and their interpretations of many of the document's key provisions, such as the meaning of impeachment, as we will discuss below.

Bill of Rights
The first 10 amendments to the Constitution; they protect individual rights and liberties.

Third, the Federalists agreed that the new Congress's first order of business would be to add a **Bill of Rights** to the Constitution to protect individual rights and liberties. This promise was essential for securing the support of New York, Massachusetts, and Virginia. The ninth state, New Hampshire, ratified the Constitution on June 21,

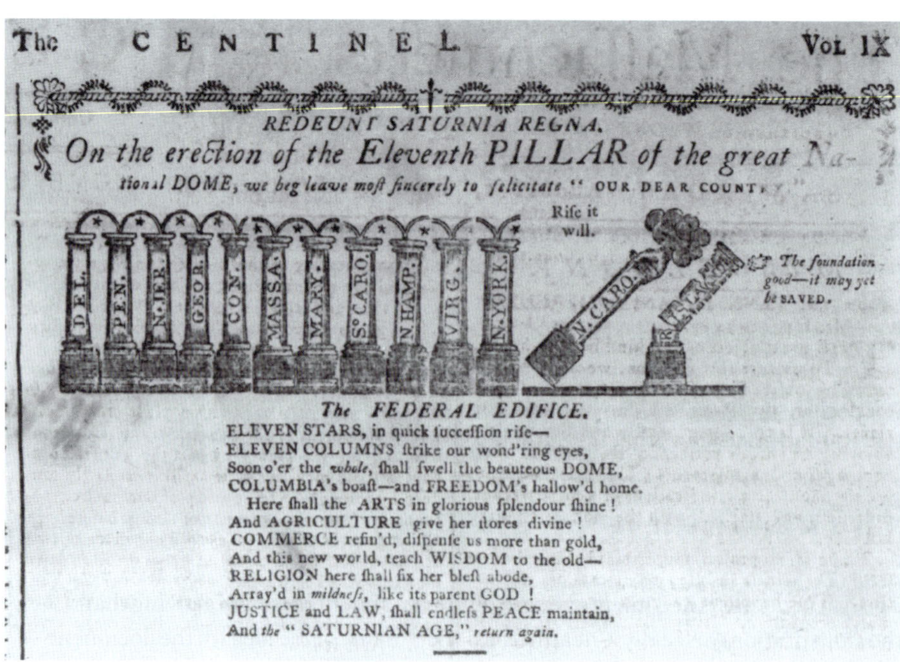

The CENTINEL. Vol. IX

REDEUNT SATURNIA REGNA.

On the erection of the Eleventh PILLAR of the great National DOME, we beg leave most sincerely to felicitate " OUR DEAR COUNTRY "

The FEDERAL EDIFICE.

ELEVEN STARS, in quick ſucceſſion riſe—
ELEVEN COLUMNS ſtrike our wond'ring eyes,
Soon o'er the *whole*, ſhall ſwell the beauteous DOME,
COLUMBIA's boaſt—and FREEDOM's hallow'd home.
Here ſhall the ARTS in glorious ſplendour ſhine!
And AGRICULTURE give her ſtores divine!
COMMERCE refin'd, diſpenſe us more than gold,
And this new world, teach WISDOM to the old—
RELIGION here ſhall fix her bleſt abode,
Array'd in *mildneſs*, like its parent GOD!
JUSTICE and LAW, ſhall endleſs PEACE maintain,
And *the* " SATURNIAN AGE," *return again.*

This political cartoon from 1788 depicts the erection of the "eleventh pillar of the great national dome" when New York became the eleventh state to ratify the Constitution, leaving only North Carolina and Rhode Island (shown as still wobbling in this cartoon) to ratify the document.

1788, but New York and Virginia were still dragging their heels, and their support was viewed as necessary for the legitimacy of the United States, even if it technically was not needed. By the end of the summer, both Virginia and New York finally voted for ratification. Rhode Island and North Carolina refused to ratify until Congress made good on its promise of a Bill of Rights (our civil liberties, which are guaranteed in the Bill of Rights, will be examined in Chapter 4). The 1st Congress submitted 12 amendments to the states, and 10 were ratified by all the states as of December 15, 1791.

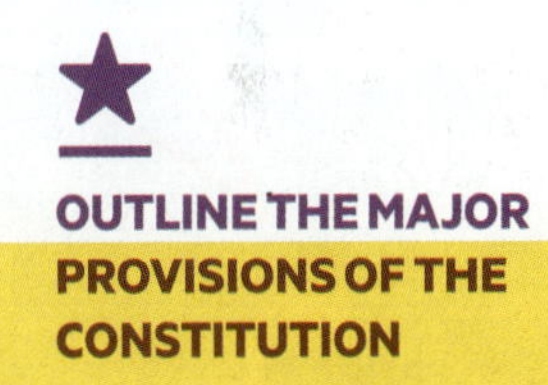

The ratifying conventions in each state subjected the Constitution to intense scrutiny, as attendees examined every sentence for possible objections. A national debate raged over the next nine months, framed by the arguments of the Federalists and the Antifederalists. As we explained in Chapter 1, all politics is conflictual, but ultimately compromise is necessary in order to move forward. The resulting compromise between these two groups was the addition of the Bill of Rights, securing the civil liberties we hold as central American values to this day.

The Constitution: a framework for government

OUTLINE THE MAJOR PROVISIONS OF THE CONSTITUTION

The Constitution certainly has its flaws, primarily its undemocratic qualities: the indirect election of senators and the president, the compromises that suppressed the issue of slavery (indeed, the words "slave" and "slavery" do not appear in the Constitution), the overrepresentation of small states in the Senate, and the absence of any general statement about citizens' right to vote. Some of the flaws have been addressed by amending the Constitution (slavery and the indirect election of senators), but the others persist and have even gotten more extreme, such as the small-state bias of the Senate. In the 1790 Census, the difference between the largest and smallest state was about 10:1 (Virginia at 747,610 and Kentucky at 73,677). In the 2020 Census, it was 68:1 (California 39.6 million and Wyoming, 581,075). The smallest 25 states, representing 54 million people, have the same number of senators as the biggest 25 states that have 331 million people. The partisan implications of the small-state bias are mitigated by the fact that there are large and small Democratic and Republican states. However, the 50 Democratic senators in 2022 represent about 41 million more Americans than the 50 Republican senators. Despite the flaws of the original document, given the delegates' political context and the various factions that had to be satisfied, the Constitution's accomplishments are substantial.

The document's longevity is testimony to the framers' foresight in crafting a flexible framework for government. Perhaps its most important feature is the system of separation of powers and checks and balances that prevents majority tyranny while maintaining sufficient flexibility for decisive leadership during times of crisis (such as the Civil War, the Great Depression, and World War II). The system of checks and balances means that each branch of national government has certain exclusive powers, some shared powers, and the ability to check the other two branches (see the How It Works graphic on pp. 56–57).

The Constitution is the guide which I never will abandon.

—President George Washington

How it works: in theory

Checks and Balances

The Constitution stipulates that if one branch tries to assert too much power, the other branches have certain key powers that allow them to fight back and restore the balance.

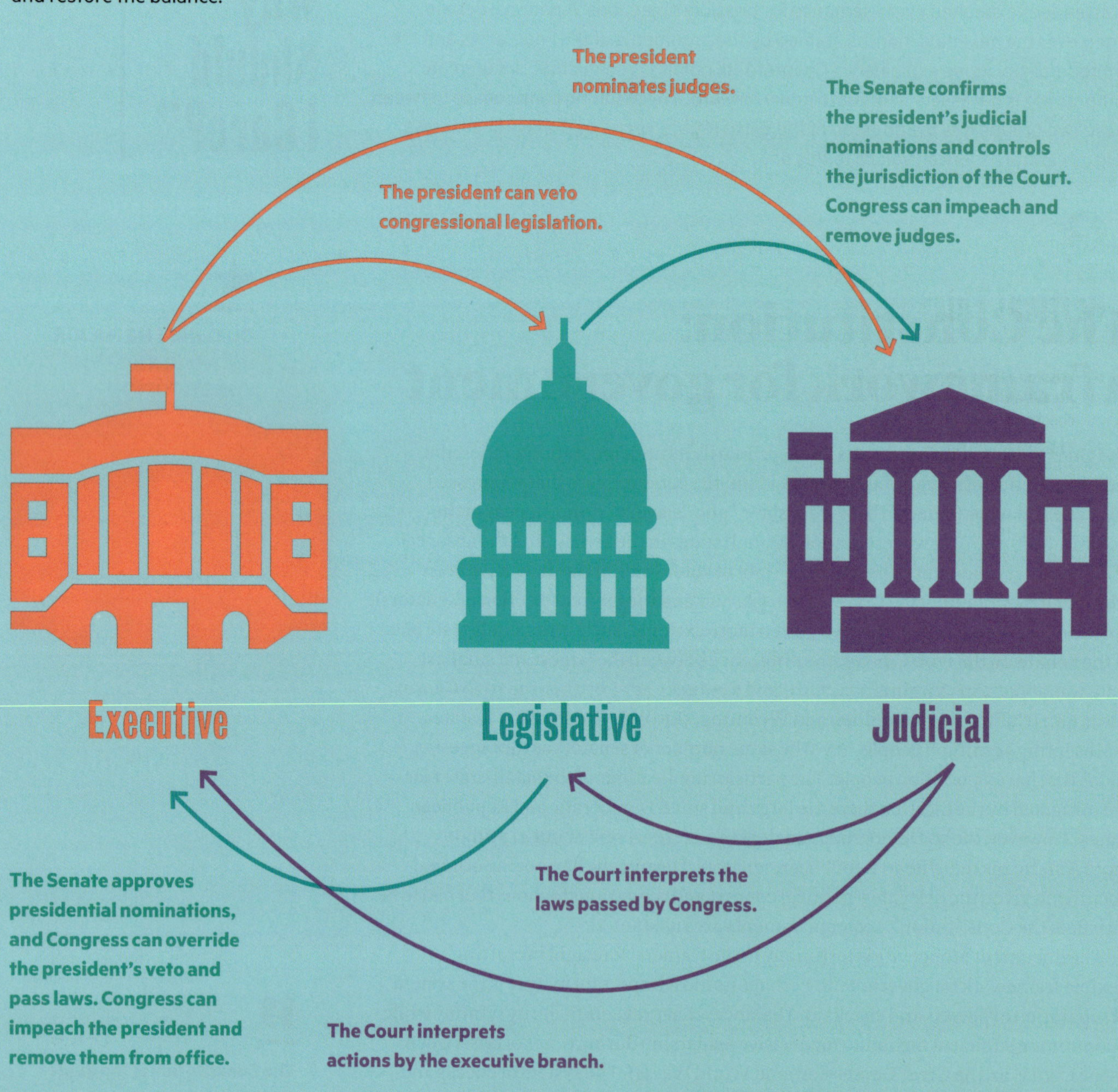

How it works: **in practice**

Checks and Balances: The DREAM Act

For more than 20 years, majorities of Americans have supported versions of the Development, Relief, and Education for Alien Minors (DREAM) Act, which would provide a path to citizenship for "Dreamers," children who were brought to this country without documentation by their parents. About two-thirds of Americans support the idea, yet Congress has not yet acted on the legislation.

Critical Thinking

1. **What are the advantages and disadvantages** of our systems of checks and balances?
2. **The Dreamers have been supported by Republican and Democratic presidents**, majorities in the House and Senate, and two-thirds of the American people. Yet our political system has been unable to pass a law protecting their legal status. What is the key part of our system that creates this gridlock? Do you think that feature of our system should be changed?

A slow start.

August 1, 2001: Senators Dick Durbin (D-IL) and Orrin Hatch (R-UT) **introduce the first version of the DREAM Act**. It dies in committee.

POTUS is on board!

January 23, 2007: President George W. Bush **calls for comprehensive immigration reform** in his State of the Union address, including action on the Dreamers.

Nope!

October 24, 2007: **A Senate filibuster kills the DREAM Act** by a vote of 52–44 (60 votes were needed to pass).

New POTUS, but still nope!

Jan. 2009–Dec. 2010: President Barack Obama supports the Dreamers. Several versions of the act pass the House, but **once again die in the Senate**.

POTUS is tired of "nope."

June 15, 2012: President Obama issues an executive order on the Deferred Action for Childhood Arrivals (DACA) program **giving Dreamers temporary protection** but no path to citizenship.

Parents too!

November 20, 2014: President Obama's executive order, the Deferred Action for Parents of Americans and Lawful Permanent Residents (DAPA) program, **defers deportation for about four million undocumented immigrants** with citizen children and allows them to work legally. It also expands DACA.

See you in court.

Dec. 2014–June 2016: Texas and 16 other states file a lawsuit against DAPA and DACA. Lower courts block DAPA and the expanded DACA. **The Supreme Court deadlocks 4–4 in *United States v. Texas***, so the lower court ruling holds.

New POTUS.

June 2017: President Donald Trump says **if Congress can't pass an act within six months**, DACA will be rescinded.

A trade?

President Trump **proposes a path to citizenship for up to 1.8 million Dreamers**, in exchange for $25 billion for a border wall and cuts to legal immigration. Several versions of this proposal are killed by filibusters in the Senate.

SCOTUS to the rescue.

June 18, 2020: The Supreme Court says the president had the power to cancel DACA, but the process violated the Administrative Procedure Act, **so DACA remains in effect**.

Here we go again . . .

On his first day in office, President Joe Biden's executive order reinstates DACA, but that order is challenged in court. **A federal judge bars new applications to the program** but allows current Dreamers to stay in the program as the case is appealed. Congress remains deadlocked.

Exclusive powers

The framers viewed Congress as the "first branch" of government and granted it significant exclusive powers. With the House of Representatives elected by popular vote and the Senate indirectly elected by state legislatures, Congress was designed to be both the voice of the people and an institution more removed from the people, with an important role in domestic and foreign policy. Congress was given the specific **enumerated powers** to raise revenue for the federal government through taxes and borrowing, regulate interstate and foreign commerce, coin money, establish post offices and roads, grant patents and copyrights, create the system of federal courts, declare war, "raise and support armies," make rules for the military, and create and maintain a navy. Most important is the so-called **power of the purse**—control over taxation and spending—given to Congress in Article I, Section 8, of the Constitution: "No money shall be drawn from the Treasury, but in consequence of appropriations made by law." Or, as Madison put it, "the legislative department alone has access to the pockets of the people."

enumerated powers
Powers explicitly granted to Congress, the president, or the Supreme Court in the first three articles of the Constitution. Examples include Congress's power to "raise and support Armies" and the president's power as commander in chief.

power of the purse
The constitutional power of Congress to raise and spend money. Congress can use this as a negative or checking power over the other branches by freezing or cutting their funding.

necessary and proper clause
The part of Article I, Section 8, of the Constitution that grants Congress the power to pass all laws related to its expressed powers; also known as the elastic clause.

Congress's exclusive powers take on additional significance through the **necessary and proper clause**, also known as the elastic clause. It gives Congress the flexibility to "make all Laws which shall be necessary and proper for carrying into Execution the foregoing Powers, and all other Powers vested by this Constitution in the Government of the United States, or in any Department or Officer thereof." This broad grant of power meant that Congress could pass laws related to any of its exclusive powers. For example, although the Constitution did not explicitly mention Congress's right to compel people to serve in the military, its power to enact a draft was clearly given by the necessary and proper clause, in conjunction with its power to "raise and support Armies."

In contrast to Congress's numerous and specific exclusive powers, the Constitution grants very limited exclusive powers to the president. The president is the commander in chief of the armed forces, has power to receive ambassadors and foreign ministers, and may issue pardons. While these powers are fewer in number than those of Congress, they are consequential. For example, President Trump pulled out of the

Congress alone has "the power of the purse" to fund government programs. For example, in 2021 it passed the bipartisan Infrastructure and Jobs Act which provided money for projects as diverse as tribal highways, reducing carbon emissions, and studying self-driving vehicles. President Biden campaigned in support of the legislation, including test driving an electric Hummer at a Detroit General Motors factory.

Paris Agreement on climate change, the Trans-Pacific Partnership, the Iran nuclear agreement, and the Intermediate-Range Nuclear Forces (INF) Treaty, and imposed an extensive travel ban for national security reasons. He pulled U.S. troops out of northern Syria, engaged in a lengthy trade war with China, moved the U.S. embassy in Israel to Jerusalem, and threatened war with North Korea. President Biden reversed some of these policies. For example, on his first day in office he issued an executive order ending Trump's travel ban and recommitted the United States to the global effort to reduce carbon emissions.[23] In 2022, Biden also pardoned anyone convicted of a federal crime for simple possession of marijuana.[24]

The president's most important powers are contained in the executive powers clause that says, "The executive power shall be vested in a President of the United States of America," and in the directive to ensure "that the laws are faithfully executed." As we see later in the chapter, these Article II clauses impart most of the president's power.

The courts did not receive nearly as much attention in the Constitution as either Congress or the president. Alexander Hamilton argued in *Federalist 78* that the Supreme Court would be the "least dangerous branch," because it had "neither the power of the purse nor the sword." The most important positive powers that the framers gave the Supreme Court were lifetime tenure for justices "during good behaviour" and relative independence from the other two branches. The critical negative power of judicial review, the ability to strike down the laws and actions of other branches, will be discussed later in this chapter.

Shared powers

Along with dividing the exclusive powers between branches, the Constitution's system of checks and balances designates some shared powers. These are areas where no branch has exclusive control. For example, the president has the power to negotiate treaties and make appointments to the federal courts and other government offices, but these executive actions are to be undertaken with the "advice and consent" of the

The president and the Senate share the appointment power to many federal offices: the president makes the nominations, and the Senate provides its "advice and consent." The nomination of Saule Omarova, a professor of law at Cornell University, to be the Treasury's lead bank regulator was extremely contentious and prompted several days of Senate hearings. The Senate panel raised issues concerning her education in Russia and views on bank oversight they thought would conflict with the job. Ultimately, Omarova withdrew her candidacy.

Senate, which means they were intended to be shared powers. In the twentieth century, these particular powers became executive centered, with the Senate providing almost no advice to the president and routinely giving its consent (often disapprovingly called rubber-stamping). However, the Senate can assert its shared power, as shown by the Senate's blocking of several of President George W. Bush's and President Barack Obama's lower-court nominees and Obama's nomination of Merrick Garland to the Supreme Court in 2016.

The war powers, which include decisions about when and how to use military force, were also intended to be shared. After serious disagreements, the ultimate compromise that the framers reached shows checks and balances at work, with the president serving as the commander in chief of the armed forces and Congress having the power to declare war and to appropriate the funds to conduct a war. One other goal of the Founders in making the war powers a shared power was to ensure civilian control of the military. By providing a role for both Congress and the president, the Constitution made it more likely that this important democratic principle would be maintained. George Washington set a critical precedent for this before the Constitution was written when he resigned his commission as commander in chief of the Continental Army. Congress had given Washington complete authority over conduct of the Revolutionary War, and many in Congress wanted him to continue to rule, almost as a king. Washington knew that it was essential for the new nation to have democratically elected leaders control the military. By resigning his commission, he made it clear that any future leadership role he would play (and it was widely assumed by the Founders that he would be the first president) would be as a civilian rather than a general.

Since very early in our nation's history, the president has taken a lead role in the war powers, often making the decision to use military force. Presidents have authorized the use of American troops on hundreds of occasions, but Congress has declared war only five times. Of these, Congress debated the merits of entering only one war, the War of 1812. The other "declarations" recognized a state of war that already existed. (For example, after Japan bombed Pearl Harbor, Hawaii, in 1941, Congress's subsequent declaration of war formally recognized what everyone already knew.) As the 2003 invasion of Iraq demonstrated, if a president is intent on going to war, Congress must go along or get out of the way. President Trump's authorization of strikes against ISIS in Syria and subsequent removal of troops from the Turkish border and President Biden's removal of troops from Afghanistan demonstrate that the president has substantial power in situations that are short of full-scale war.

Because the president's war powers have grown significantly, some fear that the president could lead us into a full-scale war on their own. But the president's war powers are not unlimited. Since the Vietnam War, Congress has tried to redress the imbalance in the war powers in a variety of ways. In 1970, Congress passed a resolution that prevented any funds from supporting ground troops in Laos or Cambodia (nations that bordered Vietnam). Congress passed the War Powers Resolution in 1973 to further limit the president's war powers (this will be discussed in more detail in Chapter 17). In 2013, Congress was strongly opposed to a military strike against Syria in response to its use of chemical weapons against its own people. A showdown with President Obama, who favored a strike, was averted when Syria agreed to allow weapons inspectors to destroy its chemical weapons stockpile. These examples show that although the president continues to dominate the war powers, Congress can assert its power when it has the will—just as it can by advising the president in treaty negotiations or by withholding approval of the president's nominees for appointed positions. Congress can also express its displeasure when the president acts unilaterally against its will, as it did when the House voted 354–60 to condemn Trump's withdrawal of American forces from northern Syria.[25]

This painting, which hangs in the Capitol rotunda, shows General George Washington resigning his commission as commander in chief of the Continental Army. This set the precedent that democratically elected officials would control the U.S. military.

Negative or checking powers

The last part of the system of checks and balances is the negative power that the branches have over one another. These powers are especially important to ensure that no single branch dominates the national government.

Congressional Checks Congress has two important negative checks on the other branches: impeachment and the power of the purse. The **impeachment** power allows Congress to remove the president, vice president, or other "officers of the United States" (including federal judges) for abuses of power—specifically, "Treason, Bribery, or other High Crimes or Misdemeanors." The framers placed this central check with Congress as part of the overall system of checks and balances.

impeachment
A negative or checking power over the other branches that allows Congress to remove the president, the vice president, or other "officers of the United States" (including federal judges) for abuses of power.

Through the power of the purse, Congress can punish executive agencies by freezing or cutting their funding or holding hearings on, investigations into, or audits of their operations to make sure money is being spent properly. Congress can also freeze judges' salaries to show displeasure with court decisions, and it has the power to limit the issues that federal courts can consider. Congress can also limit the discretion of judges in other ways, such as by setting federal sentencing guidelines that recommend a range of years in prison that should be served for various crimes. Even today, the system of checks and balances is not fixed in stone but evolves according to the changing political climate.

In addition to these two formal constitutional checks, Congress may limit presidential power through its legislative powers of lawmaking and oversight. When Congress is controlled by a different party than the president, such checking is common; for example, in the last six years of Obama's presidency, Republicans in Congress tried to stop much of his agenda. But even under unified government, as in the first two years of Trump's presidency, Congress can check presidential power. Republicans passed stronger sanctions against Russia, investigated Russian interference in our elections, failed to provide full funding for the wall at the U.S.-Mexico border, and failed to "repeal and replace" the Affordable Care Act (Obamacare), all in the face of Trump's opposition.

Presidential Checks The framers placed important checks on congressional power as well, and the president's most important check on Congress is the veto. Again, there was very little agreement on this topic. The Antifederalists argued that it was "a political error of the greatest magnitude, to allow the executive power a negative, or in fact any kind of control over the proceedings of the legislature." But the Federalists worried that Congress would slowly strip away presidential powers and leave the president too weak. In the end, the Federalist view that the president needed some protections against the "depredations" of the legislature won the day. However, the veto has developed into a major policy-making tool for the president, which is probably broader than the check against "depredations" envisioned by the framers.

The president does not have any formal check on the courts other than the power to appoint judges. However, presidents have, at various times, found unconventional ways to try to influence the courts. For example, Franklin Delano Roosevelt tried to "pack the Court" by expanding the size of the Supreme Court with justices who would be sympathetic to his New Deal policies (President Biden resisted pressure from liberal Democrats to do the same). More recently, George W. Bush attempted to expand the reach of executive power in the War on Terror by taking over some functions within the executive branch that the courts had previously performed, such as defining which suspected terrorists would have legal rights. However, the Supreme Court struck down some of these policies as unconstitutional violations of defendants' due process rights.[26] President Obama changed many of Bush's policies, such as harsh interrogation methods and excessive secrecy. But other Bush-era policies were either more difficult to change than Obama anticipated, such as the detainment of enemy combatants in the prison at Guantánamo Bay, or deemed necessary to fight terrorism, such as indefinite detention without trial for suspected terrorists who were arrested outside combat areas.[27] President Trump continued these policies and created other new ones, such as the travel ban aimed at specific countries that are viewed as terrorist threats (see the How It Works graphic in this chapter), and many of those policies persist in the Biden administration. Critics claim that the expansion of executive power in order to fight terrorism has threatened the institutional balance of power by giving the president too much control over functions previously carried out by the courts.[28]

The Constitution attempts to strike a balance between protecting our civil liberties from government intrusion and providing for a government strong enough to protect our national security. In this photo, a security officer is using facial recognition technology to identify a woman before she boards a plane at Dulles International Airport. Although this technology poses several benefits for law enforcement, critics argue that it could be misused in ways that infringe upon the basic civil rights of U.S. citizens. For example, in China facial recognition technology is used to identify and arrest citizens for jaywalking.

Judicial Review The Constitution did not provide the Supreme Court with any negative checks on the other two branches. Instead, the Court itself (in the landmark decision of *Marbury v. Madison* in 1803) established the practice of **judicial review**, the ability of the Supreme Court to strike down a law or an executive branch action as unconstitutional. For example, in 2022, the Supreme Court restricted the ability of the Environmental Protection Agency (EPA) to regulate carbon emissions in the case *West Virginia v. EPA*. According to Madison's notes, nine of the eleven framers who spoke on the topic clearly favored explicitly granting the Supreme Court the power of judicial review, but the issue was not resolved at the convention. In several states assertive courts had struck down state laws, and delegates from those states resisted giving an unelected national court similar power over the entire country.

judicial review
The Supreme Court's power to strike down a law or an executive branch action that it finds unconstitutional.

Although judicial review is not explicitly mentioned in the Constitution, supporters of the practice justify it by pointing to the supremacy clause, which states that the "Constitution, and the Laws of the United States which shall be made in Pursuance thereof . . . shall be the supreme Law of the Land." As Chief Justice John Marshall argued in *Marbury v. Madison*, to enforce the Constitution as the supreme law of the land, the Court must determine which laws are "in pursuance thereof." Critics of judicial review argue that the Constitution is supreme because it gains its legitimacy from the people and that therefore elected officials—Congress and the president—should be the primary interpreters of the Constitution rather than the courts. This dispute may never be fully resolved, but Marshall's bold assertion of judicial review made the Supreme Court an equal partner in the system of separate powers and checks and balances rather than "the least dangerous branch" that the framers described.

"Why Should I Care?"

If you remember anything from your elementary civics class, it is probably some foggy notion of the system of checks and balances and separation of powers. But why is this system so important? This institutional framework provides the basis for our government and explains the nature of political conflict and outcomes. When the government shuts down because of a dispute over spending or the Senate blocks the president's court nominees, this is because the president and Congress have different roles but can check each other's powers. Understanding checks and balances and separation of powers helps us be realistic about what government can do and shows us that all parts of the government are critical, but none are dominant, in making policy and enforcing laws.

Is the Constitution a "living" document?

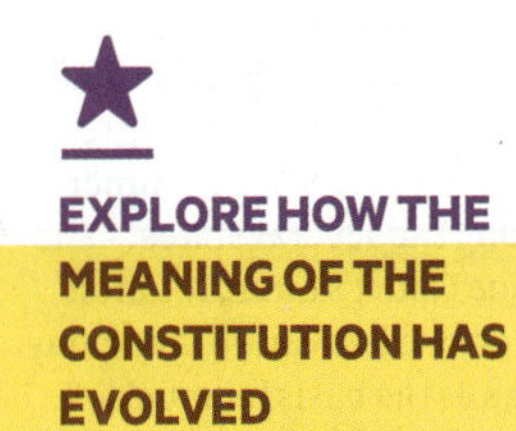

Polls suggest that many Americans are unfamiliar with the Constitution's basic provisions. Indeed, a national poll found that only 26 percent could name all three branches of the U.S. government, while 31 percent could not identify even one; 12 percent believed there was a constitutional right to own a pet, and 34 percent thought there was a right to own a home.[29] Even more disconcerting, another poll showed that 52 percent could name at least two members of Bart Simpson's family, while only 28 percent could list more than one of their five First Amendment rights.[30] In the face of such public ignorance, can the Constitution provide the blueprint for modern democratic governance? If so, how has it remained relevant after more than 230 years? The answer to the first question, in our opinion, is clearly yes. Although the United States falls short on many measures of an ideal democracy, the Constitution remains relevant in part because it embodies many of the central values of American citizens: liberty and freedom, majority rule and minority rights, equal protection for all citizens under the laws, and a division of power across and within levels of government. The Constitution presents a list of substantive values, largely within the Bill of Rights, aimed at legally protecting certain individual rights that we still consider basic and necessary. The Constitution also sets out the institutional framework within which the government operates.

But these observations raise the question of *why* the Constitution remains relevant today. Why does this framework of government still work? How can the framers' values still be meaningful to us? There are at least three components of the Constitution that allow it to continue as a "living" document: the ambiguity in central passages that permits flexible interpretation, the amending process, and the document's own designation of multiple interpreters of the Constitution. These factors have allowed the Constitution to evolve with the changing values and norms of the nation (see the Take a Stand feature on p. 65).

The people made the Constitution, and the people can unmake it. It is the creature of their will, and lives only by their will.

—John Marshall, chief justice, 1801–1835

Ambiguity

The Constitution's inherent ambiguity is a characteristic that has kept the document relevant to this day. Key passages were written in very general language, which has allowed the Constitution to evolve along with changing norms, values, and political contexts. This ambiguity was a political necessity: not only were the framers aware that the document would need to survive for generations, but in many instances the language that they chose was simply the only wording that all the framers could agree on.

Three of the most important parts of the Constitution are also among its most ambiguous: the necessary and proper (or elastic) clause, the **executive powers clause**, and the **commerce clause**. As discussed earlier, the necessary and proper clause gives Congress the power to enact laws that are related to its enumerated powers, or those that are explicitly granted. But what does "necessary and proper" mean? For the most part, Congress gets to answer that question.

executive powers clause
The part of Article II, Section 1, of the Constitution that states: "The executive Power shall be vested in a President of the United States of America." This broad statement has been used to justify many assertions of presidential power.

commerce clause
The part of Article I, Section 8, of the Constitution that gives Congress "the power to regulate Commerce . . . among the several States." The Supreme Court's interpretation of this clause has varied, but today it serves as the basis for much of Congress's legislation.

The executive powers clause is even more vague: Article II begins with the words "The executive Power shall be vested in a President of the United States of America." This sentence has served to justify a broad range of presidential actions because it does not define any boundaries for the "executive powers" it grants. The vague wording was necessary because the Constitutional Convention delegates could not agree on a definition of executive power. The wording also had the desirable consequence of making the clause flexible enough to serve the country both in times that require strong presidential action (such as the Civil War, the Great Depression, or World War II) and in times when the president was not as central (such as the "golden age of Congress" in the late nineteenth century).

Perhaps the best illustration of the importance of ambiguity in the Constitution is the commerce clause, which gives Congress "the power to regulate commerce . . . among the several States." What is "commerce" and what exactly does "among the states" mean? Different interpretations have reflected prevailing norms of the time. In the nineteenth century, when the national government was relatively weak and more

TAKE A STAND

A Living Constitution?

Should the Constitution be viewed as a flexible framework or a document that has fixed meaning? The public is fairly split on this issue, with 55 percent saying that constitutional interpretation should be based on "what it means in current time" (the living Constitution approach) and 41 percent saying that it should be based on "what it originally meant" (originalism). However, there is a deep partisan divide on this issue, with 78 percent of Democrats taking the living Constitution approach and 77 percent of Republicans supporting originalism.[a]

There is a vigorous debate among justices of the Supreme Court as to whether the Constitution is a living document or should be interpreted more strictly according to the original intent of the framers.

The meaning of the Constitution doesn't change. Justice Clarence Thomas is perhaps the strongest advocate of the originalist view. He wrote: "Let me put it this way; there are really only two ways to interpret the Constitution—try to discern as best we can what the framers intended or make it up."[b] Former chief justice William Rehnquist, although generally adhering to the originalist view, took a more nuanced approach. He favorably cited a 1920 Supreme Court opinion by Oliver Wendell Holmes: "When we are dealing with words that also are a constituent act, like the Constitution of the United States, we must realize that they have called into life a being the development of which could not have been foreseen completely by the most gifted of its begetters."[c] John Marshall in *McCulloch v. Maryland* also endorsed this view, saying the Constitution was "intended to endure for ages to come, and consequently to be adapted to the various crises of human affairs." Rehnquist said that "scarcely anyone would disagree" with the idea that the Constitution was written broadly enough to allow principles such as the prohibition against illegal searches and seizures to apply to technologies, such as the telephone or the Internet, that could not have been envisioned by the framers.[d]

However, according to this view, the *meaning* of the Constitution cannot change with the times. Rehnquist wrote that "mere change in public opinion since the adoption of the Constitution, unaccompanied by a constitutional amendment, should not change the meaning of the Constitution. A merely temporary majoritarian groundswell should not abrogate some individual liberty truly protected by the Constitution."[e] Therefore, recent rulings restricting the death penalty (which is clearly endorsed by the Constitution), expanding gay rights, or allowing children to testify remotely against their sexual abusers rather than having to confront them directly in court (as guaranteed by the Sixth Amendment) would all be inconsistent with the originalist view. This view would also hold that anything other than relying on the meaning of the words of the Constitution allows justices to "legislate from the bench," which is undemocratic given that the judges are not elected.

The meaning of the Constitution changes with the times. Proponents of a living Constitution argue for a more flexible view. Justice Thurgood Marshall advocated a living Constitution, noting that the framers "could not have imagined, nor would they have accepted, that the document they were drafting would one day be construed by a Supreme Court to which had been appointed a woman and the descendent of an African slave."[f] If the meaning of the Constitution is fixed, then the Court would have to uphold a state law allowing the death penalty for horse stealing, which was common during the Founding era. Executing horse thieves, or, more realistically, executing children and the mentally impaired (which was allowed in some states until the early 2000s), is unacceptable in a modern society, even if it would be allowed by a strict reading of the Constitution.

The answer to the question about how justices should interpret the Constitution ultimately depends on one's broader views of the proper role of the Court within a representative democracy. Should justices be constrained by the original meaning of the Constitution, or should that meaning evolve over time?

take a stand

1. If you were on the Supreme Court, would you adopt an originalist or a living Constitution approach? Justify your position.
2. Based on the originalist view, should a state be allowed to execute whomever it wants to, including minors (or horse thieves)? Based on the living Constitution approach, should limits be placed on justices to prevent them from "legislating from the bench"?

power was held at the state level, the Supreme Court interpreted the clause to mean that Congress could not regulate commerce that was entirely within the boundaries of a single state (*intra*state, as opposed to *inter*state, commerce). Because manufacturing typically occurred within the boundaries of a given state, this ruling led to a distinction between manufacturing and commerce, which had significant implications. For example, Congress could not regulate working hours, worker safety, or child labor given that these were defined as part of manufacturing rather than commerce. In the New Deal era of the mid-1930s, the Court adopted a more expansive interpretation of the commerce clause that largely obliterated the distinction between intrastate and interstate commerce. This view was strengthened in the 1960s when the Supreme Court upheld a civil rights law that, among other things, prevented owners of hotels and restaurants from discriminating against Black Americans. For nearly 60 years this interpretation held. More recently the Supreme Court has tightened the scope of Congress's powers to regulate commerce,[31] but the clause still serves as the basis for most important national legislation. The commerce clause has been unchanged since 1789, but its ambiguous wording has been used to justify or restrict a varying array of legislation.

Impeachment is another good example of the Constitution's ambiguity. President Trump was impeached twice, first for his abuse of power in withholding military aid from Ukraine until they investigated Joe and Hunter Biden and second for his role in the January 6 insurrection. The Senate failed to convict him because senators had different interpretations of the meaning of Article II, Section 4. It says, "The President, Vice President and all civil Officers of the United States, shall be removed from Office on Impeachment for, and Conviction of, Treason, Bribery, or other High Crimes and Misdemeanors." Treason and bribery are pretty clear, but what is a "high crime and misdemeanor"? When the words of the Constitution are unclear, scholars first look to two sources to figure out the framers' intent: James Madison's notes to the Constitutional Convention and the *Federalist Papers*. Madison's notes reveal that initially the framers planned to limit impeachment to treason and bribery, but George Mason objected that the narrowness of those terms would excuse some impeachable behavior and "will not reach many great and dangerous offenses." So the framers added "high crimes and misdemeanors." At the time, misdemeanor meant "misconduct or misbehavior," so the term would have applied to a general abuse of power.

Alexander Hamilton argued that impeachment is for "offenses which proceed from the misconduct of public men, or, in other words, from the abuse or violation of public trust. They are of a nature which may with peculiar propriety be denominated POLITICAL, as they relate chiefly to injuries done immediately to the society itself."[32] Senators who decided to acquit Trump believed that only criminal offenses warranted removal. Because impeachment is inherently a political process, not a legal process, impeachment means whatever a given House and Senate say that it means.

One consequence of this ambiguity is that both sides of every major political debate in our history have claimed to ground their views in the Constitution. Proslavery and antislavery factions during the pre–Civil War period, New Deal supporters and opponents during the Great Depression, and civil rights activists and segregationists all claimed to have the Constitution on their side, whether the dispute was over a broad or narrow interpretation of the commerce clause, impeachment, the Fourteenth Amendment, or the Tenth Amendment. Today's vigorous debate about the proper scope of the national government's powers on issues such as health care, immigration, abortion, and economic policy is only the most recent chapter in this perpetual conflict.

Changing the Constitution

The most obvious way that the Constitution keeps up with the times is by allowing for changes to its language (see Nuts & Bolts 2.3). The framers broadly supported the idea behind Article V, which lays out the formal process for amending the Constitution: the people must control their own political system, which includes the ability to change it through a regular, nonviolent process. George Washington called constitutional amendments "explicit and authentic acts," and Thomas Jefferson was adamant that each generation needed to have the power to change the Constitution. Toward the end of his life, he wrote in a letter to James Madison:

Some men look at constitutions with sanctimonious reverence, and deem them like the ark of the covenant, too sacred to be touched. They ascribe to the men of the preceding age a wisdom more than human, and suppose what they did to be beyond amendment. I knew that age well; I belonged to it and labored with it. . . . It was very like the present. . . . Let us not weakly believe that one generation is not as capable as another of taking care of itself.[33]

Proposal and Ratification Although there was strong consensus on including in the Constitution a set of provisions for amending it, there was no agreement on how this should be done. The Virginia Plan envisioned a relatively easy process of changing the Constitution "whensoever it shall seem necessary" by means of ratification by the people, whereas the New Jersey Plan proposed a central role for state governments.

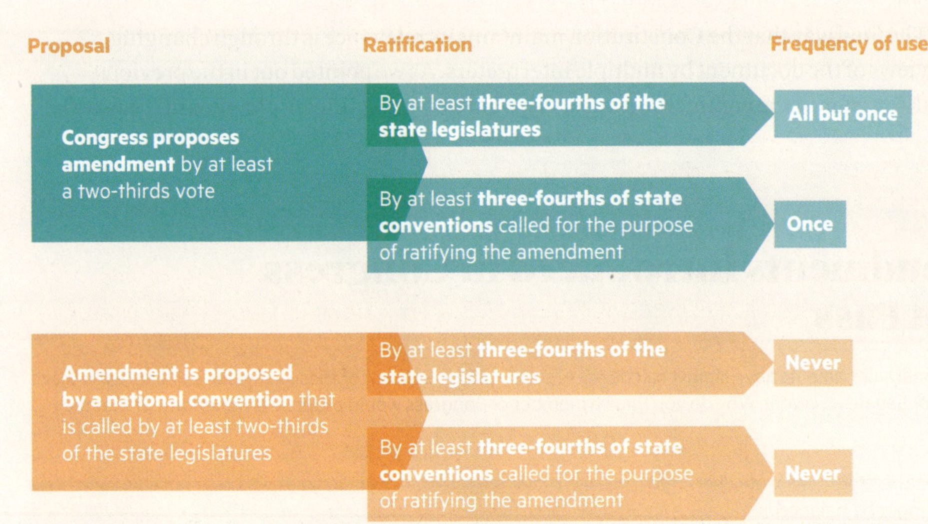

NUTS & BOLTS 2.3

Amending the Constitution

This flowchart shows how amendments to the Constitution can be proposed and ratified and the frequency with which each method has been used. Interestingly, the president is not a part of the formal process of amending the Constitution.

Source: Compiled by the authors.

"Why Should I Care?"

The amendment process reflects the idea that the people must control their own political system, which includes the ability to change it through a regular, nonviolent process. Would the country have survived the Civil War if not for the ability to amend the Constitution? Would the Senate be as representative as it is now? How does this process serve as a safeguard for the future?

Madison suggested the plan that was eventually adopted, which once again accommodated both those who wanted a stronger national government and those who favored the states.

Article V describes the two steps necessary to change the Constitution: proposal and ratification. Congress may *propose* an amendment that has the approval of two-thirds of the members in both houses, or an amendment may be proposed by a national convention that has been called by two-thirds of the states' legislatures. In either case, the amendment must be *ratified* by three-fourths of the states' legislatures or state conventions (see Nuts & Bolts 2.3). A national convention has never been used to propose an amendment, and every amendment except for the Twenty-First, which repealed Prohibition, has been ratified by state legislatures rather than state conventions.

A Range of Amendments Amendments have ranged from fairly narrow, technical corrections of errors in the original document (Eleventh and Twelfth Amendments) to important topics such as abolishing slavery (Thirteenth Amendment), mandating equal protection of the laws for all citizens (Fourteenth Amendment), providing for the popular election of senators (Seventeenth Amendment), giving Black men and then women the right to vote (Fifteenth and Nineteenth Amendments), and allowing a national income tax (Sixteenth Amendment). Potential constitutional amendments have addressed many other issues, with more than 10,000 proposed; of those, 33 were sent to the states and 27 have made it through the amending process (the first 10 came at once in the Bill of Rights). Table 2.1 shows several amendments that were introduced but not ratified.

Multiple interpreters

The final way that the Constitution maintains its relevance is through changing views of the document by multiple interpreters. As we pointed out in the previous discussion of the commerce clause, there have been significant changes in the way the

TABLE 2.1

Recent Amendments Introduced in Congress That Did Not Pass

Many proposed constitutional amendments have almost no chance of passing. Indeed, most of those listed here did not even make it to the floor of the House or Senate for a vote. Why do you think a member of Congress would propose an amendment that they knew would fail?

Congress	Proposed amendments
118th Congress (2023–2024)	Require that the federal budget be balanced. Protect the rights of parents concerning the upbringing, education, and care of their children. Protect the voting rights of the citizens of the United States. Amend the First Amendment to allow limitations on federal campaign contributions and expenditures.
117th Congress (2021–2022)	Reduce the voting age to 16. Repeal the Sixteenth Amendment (income tax). Establish health care as a right for the people of the United States.
116th Congress (2019–2020)	Limit the pardon power of the president (so he cannot pardon himself). Provide equal rights for men and women. Limit the number of terms a representative or senator may serve.

Source: Compiled by the authors from www.congress.gov (accessed 10/4/24).

Amending the Constitution is difficult and can be controversial. Some amendments that are widely accepted today, like the Nineteenth Amendment giving women the right to vote, were intensely debated prior to their ratification.

Constitution structures the policy-making process, even though the pertinent text of the Constitution has not changed.[34] This point is best understood by examining the concept of **implied powers**—that is, powers that are not explicitly stated in the Constitution but can be inferred from an enumerated power. The Supreme Court often defines the boundaries of implied powers, but Congress, the president, and the public can also play key roles.

implied powers
Powers supported by the Constitution that are not expressly stated in it.

Three of the earliest examples of implied powers show the president, the Supreme Court, and Congress each interpreting the Constitution and contributing to its evolving meaning. The first involved the question of how active the president should be in stating national foreign policy principles. In issuing his famous proclamation of neutrality in 1793, George Washington unilaterally set forth a national foreign policy, even though the president's power to do so is not explicitly stated in the Constitution. Alexander Hamilton defended the presidential power to make such a proclamation as implied in both the executive powers clause and the president's explicitly granted powers in the area of foreign policy (receiving ambassadors, negotiating treaties, and serving as commander in chief). Thomas Jefferson, in contrast, thought it was a terrible idea for presidents to have that kind of power. He preferred that such general policy statements be left to Congress.

The Supreme Court first made its mark on the notion of implied powers in a landmark case involving the creation of a national bank. In *McCulloch v. Maryland* (1819), the Court ruled that the federal government had the power to create a national bank and denied the state of Maryland the right to tax a branch of that bank. The Court said it was not necessary for the Constitution to expressly grant Congress the power to create the bank; rather, it was implied in Congress's power over financial matters and from the necessary and proper clause of the Constitution.

Congress got into the act with an early debate over the president's implied power to remove appointed officials. The Constitution clearly gives the president the power to make appointments to cabinet positions and other top executive branch offices, but it is silent on how these people can be removed. This was one of the most difficult issues that faced the 1st Congress, and members spent more than a month debating the topic. The record of the debate is the most thorough examination of implied powers ever conducted in Congress. However, Congress ended up not taking any action on the issue, which left the president's removal power implicit in the Constitution.

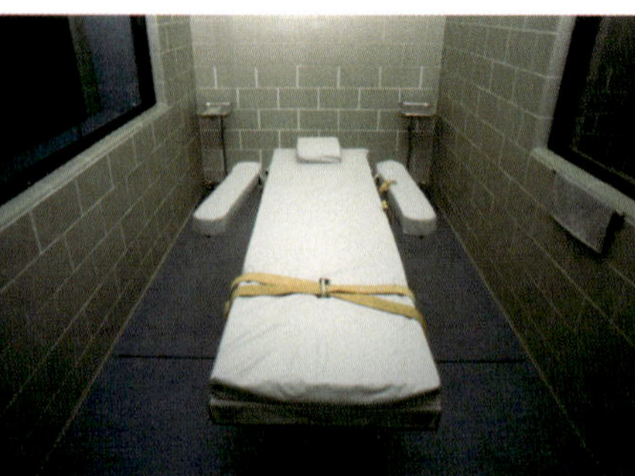

The Eighth Amendment's ban on "cruel and unusual punishments" is generally viewed as excluding capital punishment, but the execution of juveniles and the mentally impaired has been found unconstitutional. This picture shows the lethal injection chamber at the Arizona State Prison in Florence.

Issues concerning implied powers continue to surface. The president's appointment powers have recently evolved as the Senate has played a much more aggressive role in providing its "advice and consent" on presidential nominations to the federal courts. As we explore in Chapter 14, in the past 25 years the Senate has blocked court appointments at a significantly higher rate than it did in the first half of the twentieth century. The relevant language in the Constitution is the same, yet the Senate's understanding of its role in this important process has changed. The president's power to remove appointees also recently came into play in May 2017 when President Trump fired FBI director James Comey, who was investigating the Trump campaign's connections to Russia. This situation raised the constitutional question of when (or whether) the president's removal of one of their appointees constitutes an obstruction of justice. Presidential use of executive powers to go around Congress when it declines to act on issues the president deems important also demonstrates the ambiguous nature of constitutional powers. For example, Trump's use of executive orders to impose a travel ban on specific countries to limit the threat of terrorism and Biden's executive order on COVID-19 vaccines were viewed as either appropriate and necessary executive action or "constitutional overreach," depending on whom you ask.

Public opinion and social norms also influence the prevailing interpretation of the Constitution, as is evident in the evolving meanings of capital punishment (the death penalty) and freedom of speech. When the Constitution was written, capital punishment was broadly accepted, even for horse thieves. The framers were concerned only that people not be "deprived of life, liberty, or property without the due process of law." Therefore, the prohibition in the Eighth Amendment against "cruel and unusual punishments" certainly did not mean to the framers that the death penalty was unconstitutional. However, in 1972 the Supreme Court struck down capital punishment as unconstitutional because it was being applied arbitrarily.[35] Subsequently, after procedural changes were made, the Court once again upheld the practice. However, the Court has since decided that capital punishment for minors and mentally impaired people constitutes cruel and unusual punishment—decisions that reflect modern sensibilities but not the thinking of the framers.[36] Similarly, the text of the First Amendment protections for freedom of speech has never changed, but the Supreme Court has been willing to uphold significant limitations on free speech, especially in wartime. When external threats are less severe, the Court has been more tolerant of controversial speech.

The line between a new interpretation of the Constitution and constitutional change is difficult to define. Clearly, not every new direction taken by the Supreme Court or new interpretation of the constitutional roles of the president or Congress is comparable to a constitutional amendment. In one respect, a constitutional amendment is much more permanent than a new interpretation by the Court. For example, the Court could not unilaterally decide that 18- to 20-year-olds, women, and Black Americans no longer have the right to vote. Constitutional amendments expanded the right to vote to include these groups, and only further amendments could either expand or restrict the right to vote. However, gradual changes in constitutional interpretation are probably just as important as the amending process in explaining the Constitution's ability to keep pace with the times. For example, although the Civil War amendments produced lasting and significant changes in the Constitution, during the New Deal shifts in constitutional interpretation helped establish a huge growth in national power without changing a single word of the document.

One of the most remarkable things about the Constitution is its longevity. While there are intense debates about whether a "living Constitution" is a good thing, there is no doubt that its ability to change with the times, whether because of its amending process, multiple interpreters, or ambiguity, has helped make it the oldest constitution in the world. People may joke that the Constitution isn't relevant anymore, but it shapes the boundaries for all of today's policy debates and institutional struggles.

"Why Should I Care?"

Unpacking the Conflict

As we discussed at the beginning of this chapter, the 2024 elections raised many questions about the strength and resilience of our Constitution. Considering all that we know about how the Constitution works, was American democracy in danger? Is our system of checks and balances working?

While there are many aspects of politics today that were not anticipated by our founders, most significantly partisan politics and a bifurcated media and social media that deeply divide our country, a look at the facts indicates that the Constitution is working just as the Founders intended. The Trump presidency and the first two years of Biden's term illustrate many of the themes of this chapter, such as the conflictual nature of politics established by the Constitution (there has been plenty of conflict!) and the fact that multiple interpreters and ambiguous language provide the flexibility for our political system to respond to challenging times. Most significantly, elections served their function of imposing accountability, and there was a peaceful transition of power.

To protect against majority tyranny, the separation of powers and the system of checks and balances in our political system divide power by giving each branch of government the power to check the others (and the additional check of divided power across levels of government). Therefore, when the presidency starts to drift out of the mainstream of American politics, Congress, the courts, and state governments can reel it back in. We've seen throughout the chapter how our constitutional system has allowed the courts and Congress to effectively check the more extreme aspects of Trump's agenda that have alarmed pundits on the left, from Trump's proposed immigration and environmental policies, to the failure to "repeal and replace" Obamacare, to the early versions of his travel bans, to his relationship with Russia, and most significantly, to the attempt to overturn the results of the 2020 election. Similarly, when Democrats reached too far with their infrastructure and "Build Back Better" bills, Joe Manchin (D-WV) said "no" and they had to scale back their plans (a smaller version of Build Back Better that focused on climate change was enacted in August 2022). While these checks frustrate partisan Democrats and Republicans alike, this self-corrective feature of our constitutional system means that no branch of government will attain disproportionate power for very long, and it has kept the political system stable.

Even more fundamentally, also as noted in the introduction, the Constitution promotes long-term stability by providing the basis for resolving conflict through elections and representative government rather than by taking up arms. Midterm elections provide an example of how losers of one round of elections may compete in the next election to regain some of the political ground they lost. Indeed, after heavy losses in 2016, Democrats were especially energized for the competitive 2018 midterms and taking back the presidency two years later. Similarly, in the 2022 midterm elections, Republican voters had a chance to express their displeasure with the Biden administration. While Republicans' gains fell short of the "red wave," they were hoping for, they were able to regain control of the House and campaigned hard to regain the presidency in 2024. Congress, the president, and the Supreme Court all must interpret the Constitution in the normal course of fulfilling their institutional roles, which also helps preserve an institutional balance of power. Having multiple interpreters of the Constitution is built into our system. The Trump presidency also compelled the general public to become more interested in the Constitution.[37] Maybe with enough attention, those public-opinion polls showing that Americans are more familiar with *The Simpsons* than with the three branches of government can be reversed. If Americans are more informed about the Constitution, they can become even more significant interpreters of the Constitution.

Finally, the general and ambiguous language of the Constitution means that both supporters and opponents of the president can find evidence for their views. Supporters of President Trump believe that his two impeachments were partisan "witch hunts," while his critics believe they were justified attempts to impose accountability. Ultimately, the Senate decided not to convict him, but the voters decided they wanted a change. Therefore, the broader health of our American democracy will continue to be determined by the outcome of the political process and democratic elections as established by the Constitution. While there is no guarantee that our nation will be around for another 230 years, these past eight years have demonstrated the Constitution's resilience and strength once again.

A leading constitutional scholar, Walter Murphy, addressed the relevance of the Constitution this way: "The ideals it enshrines, the processes it prescribes, and the actions it legitimizes must either help to change its citizenry or at a minimum reflect their current values. If a constitution does not articulate, at least in general terms, the ideals that form or will re-form its people and express the political character they have . . . , it will soon be replaced or atrophy."[38] The Constitution's ability to change with the times and reflect its citizens' values has enabled it to remain relevant and important today. Its flexibility and general language mean that there will never be definitive answers to the conflict over its meaning, but they ensure that these debates will be enduring and meaningful.

"What's Your Take?"

Did the Capitol insurrection of January 6, 2021, threaten democracy?

Or did our system of government as laid out in the Constitution work to keep conflicts over Trump's policies in check?

CHECK YOUR UNDERSTANDING

"Why Should I Care?"

"A republic, if you can keep it," is reported to have been the response of Benjamin Franklin, one of only six individuals present at both the signing of the Declaration of Independence and the signing of the Constitution, as he met the inquiry of a woman outside the Constitutional Convention who wanted to know what kind of government the delegates had proposed in the new Constitution. What many overlook in this story is that the woman's question was one held by most Americans as the men gathered in Philadelphia, who had come with their own interests and biases, made a second attempt at creating a national government that could withstand the conflicting pressures of autonomous state governments; different economic interests, including the issue of enslavement; culturally diverse populations; and the vastness of an increasingly large territory that had led to the collapse of the Articles of Confederation.

The ability to keep the republic, as Franklin noted, would be not only in the willingness of the states to ratify the new Constitution but in the craftsmanship of the document itself. The Constitution clearly established the ordered federal relationship between the states and the national government, checks and balances among the branches of government, and reciprocity among the states. Intentional ambiguities allowed for public opinions, social norms, and political realities of the times to influence the prevailing interpretations of the Constitution, allowing it to retain its relevance more than two centuries after ratification.

Over time, the ability of the Constitution to be formally amended to fix structural issues and codify new protections for Americans has allowed the American government to address pressures of social, economic, and both domestic and international political crises while remaining true to the fundamentals reached through hard-fought compromise at the Constitutional Convention.

How to determine the meaning of the Constitution as it should be applied today remains hotly contested in American politics, with a spectrum of opinions represented throughout the public. What remains true is that the principles of American government embedded in the Constitution by the framers, and implanted by reformers, remain the undergirding elements of American life today. Important discussions about the appropriate applications of the Constitution, the balance between states and the national government, the limitations of power, and the need for intervention into parts of American life are ongoing and exist within all aspects of society, from classrooms and family dining tables to Congress and the Supreme Court. The effects of these debates and discussions play out in our system of government through elections, interest groups, political parties, and even individual activism seeking to turn ideas about the Constitution into public policy, which you will learn about in subsequent chapters.

1. The underlying cause of the failure of the Articles of Confederation is that

a there were no mechanisms for overcoming the conflicting individual interests of member states.

b the national government had repeatedly ignored requests from the states to deal with economic issues.

c checks on the legislative branch were insufficient to limit the power of the Congress.

d Federalists and Antifederalists were unable to resolve their political disputes.

2. Most of the delegates to the Constitutional Convention would likely have agreed with which statement?

a "If you leave people alone, they will generally find a way to work things out to the benefit of the overall group."

b "The least government of all is the best government of all."

c "The struggle of leaders is to determine how to control the selfishness of people without asserting too much power."

d "Even acts of government that may be unethical are justified to keep order in society and the economy."

3. The Constitution created political structures that intentionally

a gave states greater power than the national government.

b placed most government institutions beyond the reach of the voters.

c defined the liberties from which government would be restrained.

d favored majoritarian control of government.

4. Contrary to what many believe, the Constitution was the result of

a a well-structured plan for government proposed by the delegates from Virginia.

b intense political maneuvering of delegates from states with large populations.

c singular compromises between competing interests on numerous individual issues.

d ideologically principled individuals who were able to set aside their individual and regional interests for the good of the nation.

5. Select the quote that is most in line with the position of the Antifederalist perspectives about the changes the proposed Constitution would make to the national government.

a "But remember, when the people once part with power, they can seldom or never resume it again but by force. Many instances can be produced in which the people have voluntarily increased the powers of their rulers; but few, if any, in which rulers have willingly abridged their authority."

b "Among the numerous advantages promised by a well-constructed union, none deserves to be more accurately developed than its tendency to break and control the violence of faction."

c "The authorities essential to the common defense are these: to raise armies; to build and equip fleets; to prescribe rules for the government of both; to direct their operations; to provide for their support."

d "A feeble executive implies a feeble execution of the government. A feeble execution is but another phrase for a bad execution; and a government ill executed, whatever it may be in theory, must be, in practice, a bad government."

6. Why were the Federalists concerned about listing the rights and liberties of Americans in the body of the Constitution itself?

a They did not want to hamper the government from making laws they believed to be necessary to limit certain rights.

b They believed that by creating an enumeration of rights and liberties it could be seen in the future that these were the only ones the people were given.

c They believed the people were the best protectors of their own rights and liberties without the government becoming involved in listing them out.

d They felt that human nature prevented the government from needing to create specific protections within the structures of government.

7. Presidents nominate Supreme Court justices, subject to approval by the Senate, to lifetime positions on the Court. Which constitutional principle best illustrates this relationship?

a Federalism

b Popular sovereignty

c Republicanism

d Checks and balances

8. The significant powers of Congress are mostly defined in ____________ of the Constitution.

- **a** Article II, Section 1
- **b** Article V
- **c** Article I, Section 8
- **d** Article III, Section 2

9. The Constitution continues to remain relevant as a governing document even in an age of digital technologies, globally interconnected economies, and an ever-diversifying population because

- **a** the continuous amendment of the Constitution has expanded its authority to include these modern realities.
- **b** states have deferred much of their authority to the national government in being able to regulate these issues.
- **c** there are shared beliefs among Americans about the meaning of the Constitution and public policy priorities.
- **d** flexibility was intentionally built into the wording of the Constitution so that it could adapt to the changing realities of the nation.

10. The inclusion of the Ninth and Tenth Amendments in the Bill of Rights gives us what understanding about the thinking of the framers?

- **a** The American people and the state governments needed to be clearly seen as under the supremacy of the national government.
- **b** The authority of the government was understood to be limited, with undefined rights of people and states existing outside of the federal government's control.
- **c** The states were given authority to both restrict the rights of the people and challenge the national authority in areas where the states disagreed.
- **d** It was necessary to specify the rights and liberties of the people and powers of the states within the political structures of the United States.

11. The vestment clause of Article II, the necessary and proper clause of Article I, and the power of judicial review that rests with the Supreme Court have had what impact on the structure of power within the American system of government?

- **a** Increase in national power over the states
- **b** Expanded influence of states
- **c** Greater emphasis on the rulemaking authority of bureaucratic agencies
- **d** Growing influence of interest groups and corporations

Use INQUIZITIVE *to help you study and master this material.*

3

Federalism

States or the federal government: who's got the power?

"Schools that have had masks in place were three and a half times less likely to have school outbreaks requiring school closure. So, right now, we are going to continue to recommend masks in all schools for all people in those schools."[1]

Dr. Rochelle Walensky, director, Centers for Disease Control

"[Biden] is obsessed with having the government force kindergarteners to wear masks all day in school. In Florida, we believe that that's the parents' decision. Joe Biden thinks the federal government should come and overrule the parents and force these young kids to wear these masks."[2]

Florida governor Ron DeSantis

One of the most notable aspects of the COVID-19 pandemic has been the variation in local responses. Throughout the crisis, communities across the country made very different decisions on business closures, public gatherings, vaccination priorities, and mask wearing. One of the most contentious issues was whether or not elementary and high school students should be required to wear masks in school. Figure 3.1 shows cross-state variation in mask mandates for these students as of September 2021: 10 states mandated masks in their public schools, eight banned mandates, and the remaining states left it up to local districts to decide.

The Biden administration made no secret of its support for mask mandates. Even so, while the federal government required masks in public transportation and in federal buildings, it did not order states and local communities to implement similar policies. States opposed to mask mandates went to great lengths to enforce their policies: for example, Florida governor (and 2024 Republican presidential candidate) Ron DeSantis withheld state education aid from districts that implemented a mandate in violation of state law.

How strictly should the government regulate protocols to combat the COVID-19 pandemic, such as requiring children to wear masks in schools? Not only do many individual Americans disagree on this issue, but so do many elected officials, including Florida governor Ron DeSantis, who has argued that the decision should be left up to the individual.

CHAPTER GOALS

Define *federalism* and explain its significance (pp. 79–82)

Explain what the Constitution says about federalism (pp. 82–85)

Trace the major shifts in state and federal government power over time (pp. 86–94)

Describe the major trends and debates in federalism today (pp. 94–103)

Analyze the arguments for and against a strong federal government (pp. 103–108)

FIGURE 3.1

Mask Mandates in Schools, 2021

States across the country varied widely in their implementation of mask mandates in schools during the COVID-19 pandemic. Are there any political differences between the states that chose to implement (or ban) mask mandates?

Source: Katharina Buchholz, "Where Schools Have to Follow Mask Mandates," Statista, www.statista.com/chart/25525/school-mask-mandates-by-us-state/ (accessed 12/21/21).

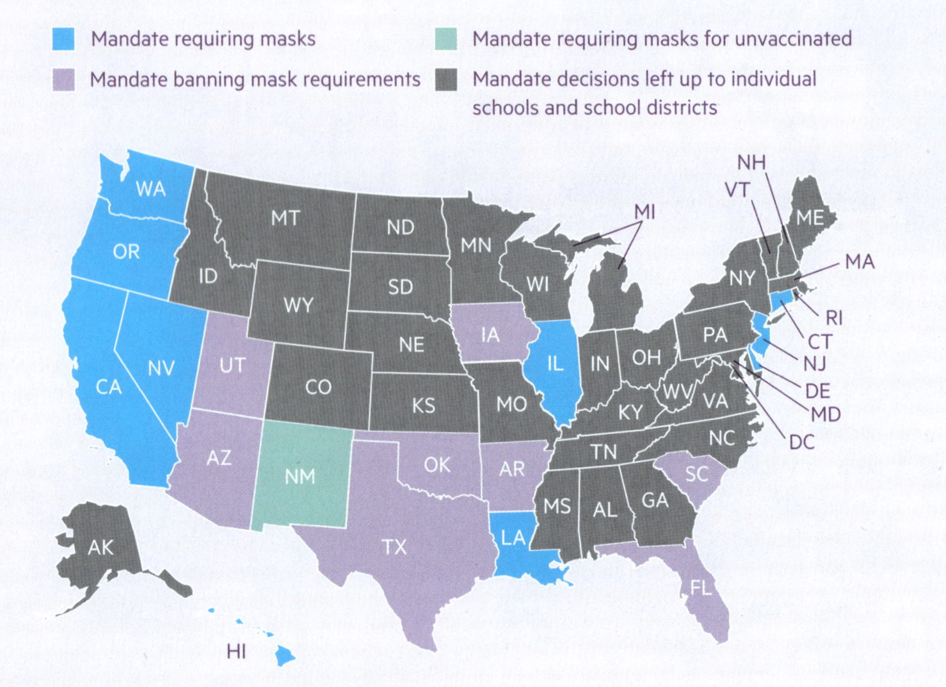

This conflict over mask mandates reflects a fundamental feature of America's government: federalism. In areas such as education, law enforcement, and environmental policy, the federal government has limited power to effect policy at the state and local level. Because of federalism, your experiences with government, including the services you receive, the laws you are supposed to obey, and the regulations that constrain your actions, differ depending on where you live.

One of the reasons we have a federal system is the desire to limit the power of the national government (see Chapter 2). Federalism also enables state and local governments to take account of citizens' demands or local conditions—information that might not be available to decision makers in Washington. By giving power to state and local governments, federalism can increase citizen satisfaction and governmental efficiency.

However, as the fight over mask mandates suggests, federalism is more than a way to increase responsiveness and efficiency. In many policy areas, federalism sets up conflicts between different levels of government over who gets to make policy choices. At the national level, policy makers such as CDC director Rochelle Walensky argued that mandates would prevent the spread of the virus and lower the chances of a new variant emerging. In states opposed to mandates, officials argued that masks were largely ineffective and that citizens deserved to make their own choices about personal safety. These two views of the world are incompatible. The question is, whose preferences will become law?

The conflict over mask mandates is a great example of the tensions created by a federal system, and the reality that the benefits and responsibilities of citizenship (including COVID-19 restrictions but also everything from educational opportunities to tax rates) vary a lot depending on where you live. When local and federal officials disagree about mask mandates and other policy questions, who wins? What are the responsibilities of the states, and what is the domain of the national government?

What happens when levels of government disagree? How have the answers to these questions changed over the course of American history—and how does federalism work today?

What is federalism and why does it matter?

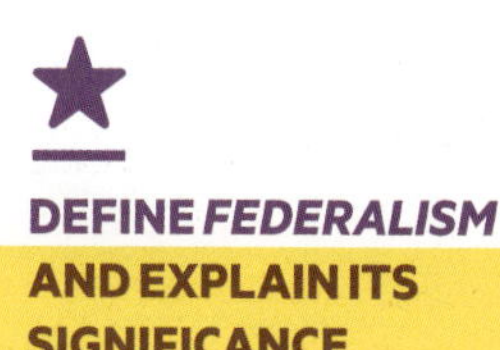

DEFINE *FEDERALISM* AND EXPLAIN ITS SIGNIFICANCE

Federalism is a form of government that divides sovereign power across at least two political units. Dividing **sovereign power** simply means that each unit of government (in the United States, national, state, and local governments) has some degree of authority and autonomy. This division of power across levels of government is central to the system of separated powers in the United States (see Chapter 2). Dividing power across levels of government seems like a simple concept, but as we will see later in this chapter, the political battles over *how* that power is divided have been intense. (One important note on terminology: while the national government in Washington, D.C., is referred to as the federal government, it is only one part of the federal system that combines national, state, and local governments.)

federalism
The division of power across the local, state, and national levels of government.

sovereign power
The supreme power of an independent state to regulate its internal affairs without foreign interference.

In practical terms, federalism is about intergovernmental relations: How do the different levels of government interact, and how is power divided? But even that may seem a little abstract. Why does federalism matter? On a broad range of issues, the level of government that dictates policy can make a real difference, simply because preferences vary across these levels. Sometimes these disagreements reflect different beliefs about what citizens want from government. But more commonly, conflicts result from differences of opinion about what government should be doing. In the case of COVID-19 policy, for example, the national government, represented by President Biden and the Centers for Disease Control, favors mask mandates, vaccine mandates, and other measures that compel individuals to do things they might not want to do. While some state and local politicians (as well as their supporters) hold similar feelings, others, such as Florida's Governor DeSantis and many other citizens, disagree. This divergence between the policies desired by

The relationship between the national government and states and territories involves cooperation as well as competition. During the COVID-19 pandemic, FEMA partnered with local officials to provide emergency support, including setting up and running vaccination sites throughout the country to accommodate the unprecedented number of civilians needing to receive two doses of the most readily available vaccines.

politicians at different levels of government means that decisions about federalism (which level of government does what) affect how laws are ultimately interpreted and enforced.

The fact that many policies are administered by multiple levels of government provides multiple access points for citizens and groups who want to influence the details of these policies. Finally, conflicts over federalism create a key role for the federal courts, as their power to interpret the Constitution makes them the ultimate arbiter of conflicts between federal and state governments. As we will see, at various points in American history (including recent years), changes in the composition of the Supreme Court have had important consequences for the balance of power between different levels of government.

Levels of government and their degrees of autonomy

A distinguishing feature of federalism is that each level of government has some degree of autonomy from the other levels—that is, each level can carry out some policies without interference from the others. In the United States, this means that the national and state governments have distinct powers and responsibilities (see Nuts & Bolts 3.1). The national government, for example, has **exclusive powers** for national defense and foreign policy. That is, we have a U.S. Army, but states do not have their own armed forces (the National Guard is actually a branch of the army). State and local governments have primary responsibility for conducting elections and promoting public safety, or **police powers**. So, for example, Minneapolis police officers accused of murder in the death of George Floyd in 2020 were prosecuted in state courts, not federal. In other areas, such as transportation, the different levels of government have **concurrent powers**—they share responsibilities. Road projects, for example, are generally executed by state agencies but receive federal funds. The national government has also taken on additional responsibilities through implied powers that are inferred from the powers explicitly granted in the Constitution (see Chapter 2 and later in this chapter).

exclusive powers
Policy-making responsibilities that are exercised only by the national government.

police powers
Responsibilities that include the power to enforce laws and provide for public safety.

concurrent powers
Responsibilities for particular policy areas, such as transportation, that are shared by federal, state, and local governments.

Local governments—cities, towns, school districts, and counties—are not autonomous units of government; they are creatures of state governments. State governments create local governments and control the types of activities they can engage in by specifying in the state charter what local governments can do and cannot do.

A comparative perspective

It is useful to compare U.S. federalism with forms of government in other countries. Just because a nation is composed of states does not mean that it is a federal system. The key factor in determining whether a system is federal or not is the autonomy of the political subunits. The United Kingdom, for example, is made up of England, Scotland, Wales, and Northern Ireland. In 1998, the British Parliament created a new Scottish government and gave it authority in a broad range of areas. However, Parliament retained the right to unilaterally dissolve the Scottish government; therefore, the subunit (Scotland) is not fully autonomous. This type of government, in which power is centralized at the national level, is a **unitary government**. Unitary governments

unitary government
A system in which the national, centralized government holds ultimate authority. It is the most common form of government in the world.

National and State Responsibilities

National government powers	State government powers	Concurrent powers
Print money	Issue licenses	Collect taxes
Regulate interstate commerce and international trade	Regulate intrastate (within the state) businesses	Build roads
Make treaties and conduct foreign policy	Conduct elections	Borrow money
Declare war	Establish local governments	Establish courts
Provide an army and navy	Ratify amendments to the Constitution	Make and enforce laws
Establish post offices	Promote public health and safety	Charter banks and corporations
Make laws necessary and proper to carry out these powers	May exert powers the Constitution does not delegate to the national government or does not prohibit the states from using	Spend money for the general welfare; take private property for public purposes, with just compensation
Powers denied to the national government	**Powers denied to state governments**	
May not violate the Bill of Rights	May not enter into treaties with other countries	
May not impose export taxes among states	May not print money	
May not use money from the Treasury without an appropriation from Congress	May not tax imports or exports	
May not change state boundaries	May not interfere with contracts	
	May not suspend a person's rights without due process	

Source: Compiled by the authors.

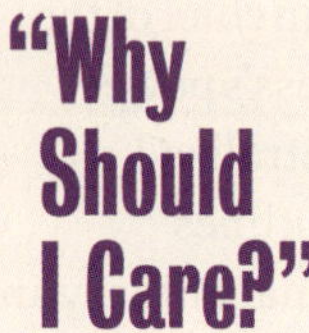

These provisions of the Constitution define the scope of policy conflict between the state and federal governments—which powers are given exclusively to one level, which are shared, and, most important, which are left unallocated. Modern fights over federalism start with these provisions and how they should be interpreted.

are the most common in the modern world (about 80 percent); other examples include Israel, Italy, France, Japan, and Sweden. Although U.S.-style federalism is not as common, Australia, Canada, and Germany, among others, share this form of government. At the opposite end of the spectrum is a **confederal government**, in which the states have most of the power. This was the first type of government in the United States under the Articles of Confederation, but there are very few modern examples.

confederal government
A form of government in which states hold power over a limited national government.

"Why Should I Care?"

Federalism explains why laws and regulations may differ from state to state; it allows for differences of opinion across regions. For example, how do your state's opinions on mask mandates differ from Florida's? How does federalism allow your state to respond differently to address public health crises? This is federalism in action.

EXPLAIN WHAT THE CONSTITUTION SAYS ABOUT FEDERALISM

Balancing national and state power in the Constitution

Although the Founders wanted a national government that was stronger than it had been under the Articles of Confederation, they also wanted to preserve states' autonomy. These goals are reflected in different parts of the Constitution, which provides ample support for advocates of both strong state governments and a strong national government. The nation-centered position has its roots in the document's preamble, which begins, "We the People of the United States." The Articles of Confederation, by contrast, began, "We the undersigned delegates of the States." The Constitution's phrasing emphasizes the nation over the separate states—although as we will see, it also allocates significant powers to the states.

A strong national government

DID YOU KNOW?

Under the Articles of Confederation, all

13

states had their own militia and navy.

Most of the Founders wanted a strong national government to provide national security and a healthy and efficient economy, so they included various powers in the Constitution for the federal government. In terms of national security, Congress was granted the power to raise and support armies, declare war, and "suppress Insurrections and repel Invasion," while the president, as commander in chief of the armed forces, would oversee the conduct of war (see Chapter 2). Congress's power to regulate interstate commerce promoted economic efficiency and centralized an important economic power at the national level. The Constitution outlines restrictions on state power that contribute to the centralization of national military and economic power: states were *prohibited* from entering into "any Treaty, Alliance, or Confederation" or keeping troops or "Ships of War" during peacetime. They also could not coin money or impose duties on imports or exports (see Article I, Section 10).

The necessary and proper clause (Article I, Section 8) was another broad grant of power to the national government: it gave Congress the power "[t]o make all Laws which shall be necessary and proper for carrying into Execution the foregoing Powers." Similarly, the national supremacy clause (Article VI) says that the Constitution and all laws and treaties that are made under the Constitution shall be the "supreme Law of the Land" and that "the Judges in every State shall be bound thereby, any Thing in the Constitution or Laws of any State to the Contrary notwithstanding." This is perhaps the clearest statement of the nation-centered focus of the Constitution. If any state law or constitution conflicts with national law or the Constitution, the national perspective wins. Thus, in the case of same-sex marriages, once the Supreme Court ruled in 2015

Jim Obergefell, the plaintiff in the *Obergefell v. Hodges* Supreme Court case that legalized same-sex marriage nationwide, is backed by supporters of the ruling on the steps of the Texas capitol during a rally on June 29, 2015, in Austin. This ruling shows the power of the supremacy clause, as it struck down laws in 14 states.

that all laws prohibiting same-sex marriage were unconstitutional, elected officials at all levels knew that if they enacted new prohibitions, the laws would be immediately invalidated by the courts.

You might be thinking, "Wait a minute, if the Constitution and the federal government always win, how could Florida ban mask mandates even though the Biden administration favored them?" The answer is not simple. (See the What Do the Facts Say? feature on p. 84.) For one thing, there is no constitutional provision that directly gives the federal government control over public health. Existing laws give the president authority over the military, federal contractors, and people using public transportation—using this authority, the federal government has ordered military personnel and employees of federal contractors to get vaccinated against COVID-19 and mandated masks for people using public transit, like airplanes. However, courts would likely find that a blanket mandate is in violation of the First and Tenth Amendments to the Constitution—although there is disagreement on this point, and we won't know for sure until a case is decided.[3]

The controversy illustrates that even after 230 years, there still is disagreement over how the Constitution divides power between the federal government and the states. As we will see, when conflicts between the federal and local governments arise, the federal government can try to persuade local governments by offering grants or other forms of aid to induce cooperation, but it often cannot simply order local governments to comply with its wishes.

State powers and limits on national power

Despite the Founders' nation-centered bias, many parts of the Constitution also address state powers and set limits on national power. Article II gives the states the power to choose electors for the Electoral College, and Article V grants the states a central role in the process of amending the Constitution. Three-fourths of the states must ratify any constitutional amendment (either through conventions or through their state legislatures, as specified by Congress), but the states can also bypass Congress in proposing amendments if two-thirds of the states call for a Constitutional Convention (this route to amending the Constitution has never been used).

WHAT DO THE FACTS SAY?

Did Florida "Fare Much Better" Than Other States Despite No Mask Mandates during COVID-19?

One of the most important rules when reading a news story about a controversial issue is to look for sources and documentation. We all want media coverage that gives "just the facts"—but a good article also tells readers where the facts came from, so that they can be checked and verified. This is particularly true when a story relies on quotes from participants in a political conflict, as their comments may be designed to persuade rather than inform.

Let's look at an example from Breitbart News' (a conservative media source) coverage of COVID-19 case rates in Florida during fall 2021. Over the summer, Florida had seen a sharp increase cases and deaths—nearly 1.2 million cases and over 32,000 deaths. In fact, during this time, Florida accounted for 17 percent of U.S. deaths from COVID-19, despite the fact that it has only 6.5 percent of the total population.[b]

A Breitbart article published on October 19, 2021, noted that the surge had abated and that Florida now had one of the lowest rate of new infections in the country.

The central argument of the Breitbart story: mask mandates don't work. "Florida's Gov. Ron DeSantis (R) never implemented a statewide mask mandate during the pandemic and received tremendous pushback from blue state governors, such as former New York Gov. Andrew Cuomo (D), whose states ended up faring far worse in terms of fatalities and economic impacts," the article reports.

It is true that the time of the Breitbart article, Florida had one of the lowest COVID-19 case rates in the country—you can confirm this fact by looking at the official statistics maintained by the Centers for Disease Control. But one of the central features of the pandemic is that caseloads have varied widely over time and across regions. This variation probably reflects differences in populations, access to health care, the spread of natural immunity, vaccination rates, the spread of new COVID-19 variants, and other factors—but scientists are still working to make sense of the data. It does not make sense to draw conclusions about mask mandates by comparing caseloads in New York and Florida without considering these other factors.

In fact, Florida's low caseloads highlighted by Breitbart are an illustration of this problem. One reason why Florida's case rate was low in mid-October 2021 was that it had been extraordinarily high in the months prior to that, so that a sizable fraction of the people who were vulnerable had already caught the disease. As a reporter for the *Washington Post* put it, "this is a bit like boasting that your forest hasn't caught fire since your recent forest fire."[c] Another reason was Florida's success in distributing vaccines to vulnerable groups in the state, particularly senior citizens.

The point is not that you should think every story on Breitbart is fake. Rather, when trying to make sense of American politics, you should consider both the facts reported in a story and the interpretations of these facts. As you see in this case, it is easy to misinterpret a set of facts (either inadvertently or deliberately) and arrive at a very incorrect view of what is actually going on. You should be particularly suspicious when a story simply asserts what facts mean without citing sources or documentation.

"Florida, which came under a constant stream of criticism from corporate media outlets and blue state leaders throughout the Chinese coronavirus pandemic, is faring better than nearly every other state in the country in terms of case averages per capita, as the state's two-week average of cases dropped by 33 percent."[a]

—**Breitbart News,** 2021

Think about it

- **What are some credible sources** of news you go to for "just the facts"? What do you do when you can't validate the information in a second source?
- **What are the dangers** of spreading misleading or incorrect information? How might these errors lead people to make uninformed decisions?

There are also limitations on Congress's authority over the states. For example, although Congress was given the power to regulate interstate commerce, it cannot regulate commerce that occurs entirely within a state. Moreover, Congress cannot favor one state over another in regulating commerce, and it cannot impose a tax on any good that is shipped from one state to another.

While Article I of the Constitution enumerates many specific powers for Congress, the list of state powers is much shorter. One could interpret this as more evidence for the nation-centered perspective, but at the time of the Founding the expectation was that most power would be exercised at the state level. Therefore, the federal powers that were exceptions to this rule had to be clearly specified, and state governments received authority over all other matters. The Tenth Amendment supports this view: "The powers not delegated to the United States by the Constitution, nor prohibited by it to the states, are reserved to the states respectively, or to the people."

Clauses that favor both perspectives

Article IV of the Constitution includes provisions that favor both the state-centered and the nation-centered perspectives. For example, its **full faith and credit clause** specifies that states must respect one another's laws, granting citizens the "Full Faith and Credit" of their home state's laws if they go to another state. At the same time, however, the article's **privileges and immunities clause** says that citizens of each state are "entitled to all Privileges and Immunities" of citizens in the other states, which means that states must treat visitors from other states the same as their own residents.

full faith and credit clause
The part of Article IV of the Constitution requiring that each state's laws be honored by the other states. For example, a legal marriage in one state must be recognized across state lines.

privileges and immunities clause
The part of Article IV of the Constitution requiring that states must treat nonstate residents within their borders as they would treat their own residents. This was meant to promote commerce and travel between states.

There are many examples of the full faith and credit clause and privileges and immunities clause at work today. If you have a Michigan driver's license and are traveling to Texas, you do not need to stop at every state line to get a new license; each state will honor your Michigan license. Similarly, a legal marriage in one state (even a same-sex marriage) must be honored by another state. But not all state licenses are subject to full faith and credit: if you have an open or concealed-carry gun permit in one state, that does not automatically give you the right to carry a firearm in another state. Similarly, states do not have to permit nonresidents to vote in state elections, and public colleges and universities may charge out-of-state residents higher tuition than in-state residents. Therefore, the privileges and immunities clause cuts both ways on the question of the balance of power: it allows the states to determine and uphold their own laws autonomously, but it also emphasizes that national citizenship is more important than state citizenship.

"Why Should I Care?"

Why is it important to understand the Constitution's role in federalism? The Constitution sets the boundaries for the battles over state and federal power. For example, no state can decide to print its own currency, and the U.S. government cannot take over the public schools. But within those broad boundaries, the balance between national and state power at any given point in history is a political decision, the product of choices made by elected leaders and the courts. The struggle over mask mandates is a perfect example: the Biden administration wanted to impose these mandates, and the governors of states such as Florida and Texas wanted to ban them.

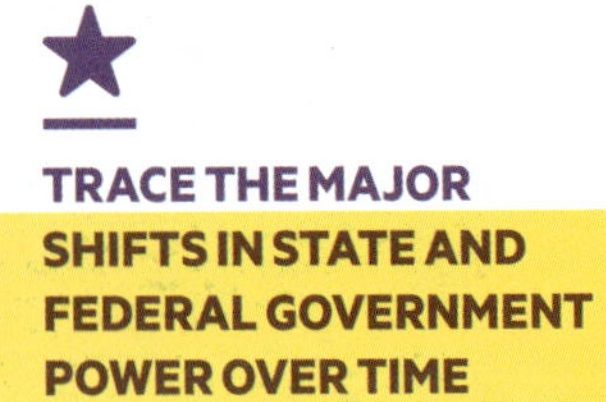

TRACE THE MAJOR SHIFTS IN STATE AND FEDERAL GOVERNMENT POWER OVER TIME

The evolving concept of federalism

The nature of federalism has changed as the size and functions of the national and state governments have evolved. In the first century of our nation's history, the national government played a relatively limited role and the boundaries between the levels of government were distinct. As the national government took on more power in the twentieth century, intergovernmental relations became more cooperative and the boundaries less distinct. Even within this more cooperative framework, federalism remains a source of conflict within our political system, both because the levels of government share lawmaking authority and because they may disagree over the details of government policy.

The early years

As the United States gained its footing, clashes between the advocates of state-centered and nation-centered federalism turned into a partisan struggle. The Federalists—the party of George Washington, John Adams, and Alexander Hamilton—controlled the new government for its first 12 years and favored strong national power. One of their strongest allies was Chief Justice John Marshall, who wrote several landmark Supreme Court decisions that enhanced the power of the national government. The Federalists' opponents, the Democratic-Republicans, led by Thomas Jefferson and James Madison, favored state power, or, as it came to be known, **dual federalism**. Dual federalism, as we will discuss, was the guiding principle of Marshall's successor as chief justice, Roger Taney. Table 3.1 highlights several important decisions resolved during Marshall's and Taney's tenures on the Court.

dual federalism
The form of federalism favored by Chief Justice Roger Taney, in which national and state governments are seen as distinct entities providing separate services. This model limits the power of the national government.

TABLE 3.1 Early Landmark Supreme Court Decisions on Federalism

Case	Holding and significance for states' rights	Direction of the decision
Chisholm v. Georgia (1793)	Held that citizens of one state could sue another state; led to the Eleventh Amendment, which prohibited such lawsuits.	Less state power
McCulloch v. Maryland (1819)	Upheld the national government's right to create a bank and reaffirmed the idea of "national supremacy."	Less state power
Gibbons v. Ogden (1824)	Held that Congress, rather than the states, has broad power to regulate interstate commerce.	Less state power
Barron v. Baltimore (1833)	Endorsed a notion of "dual federalism" in which the rights of a U.S. citizen under the Bill of Rights did not apply to that same person under state law.	More state power
Dred Scott v. Sandford (1857)	Sided with southern states' view that enslaved people were property and ruled that the Missouri Compromise violated the Fifth Amendment, because making slavery illegal in some states deprived owners of enslaved people of property. Contributed to the start of the Civil War.	More state power

Source: Compiled by the authors.

Establishing National Supremacy The first confrontation came when the Federalists established a national bank in 1791, followed by a second national bank in 1816. At that time, the state of Maryland, which was controlled by the Democratic-Republicans, tried to tax the National Bank's Baltimore branch out of existence. However, the bank refused to pay the tax, creating a conflict that sent the case to the Supreme Court. In the landmark decision *McCulloch v. Maryland* (1819), Marshall's Court held that even though the word "bank" does not appear in the Constitution, Congress's power to create one is implied through its relevant enumerated powers—such as the power to coin money, levy taxes, and borrow money. The Court also ruled that Maryland did not have the right to tax the bank because of the Constitution's national supremacy clause.

A few years later, Marshall's Court held in *Gibbons v. Ogden* (1824) that Congress has broad power to regulate interstate commerce. The ruling struck down a New York law that had granted a monopoly to a private company that was operating steamboats on the Hudson River between New York and New Jersey. By granting this monopoly, New York was interfering with interstate commerce, a power reserved to Congress by the Constitution. Even in the modern era, this ruling underlies many of the federal government's regulations on businesses, which are based on the expectation that virtually any commercial activity will involve buying and selling across state lines.

The emergence of states' rights and dual federalism

Under Marshall's successor, Chief Justice Roger Taney, Court decisions involving federalism shifted to reflect a new concept: dual federalism. According to the system of dual federalism, the national and state governments are considered distinct, with little overlap in their activities or the services they provide. In this view, the national government's activities are confined to powers strictly enumerated in the Constitution.

Dual federalism was expressed most consequentially in the *Dred Scott v. Sandford* decision of 1857. Dred Scott was an enslaved man who had lived for many

In the early 1800s, the Supreme Court confirmed the national government's right to regulate commerce between the states. The state of New York granted a monopoly to a ferry company serving ports in New York and New Jersey, but this was found to interfere with interstate commerce and was therefore subject to federal intervention.

years with his owner in the free state of Illinois and the free Wisconsin Territory but was living in Missouri, a state that allowed slavery, when his owner died. Scott petitioned for his freedom under the Missouri Compromise, which had made slavery illegal in any free state. The Court did not grant Scott his freedom. Its majority decision held that enslaved people were not citizens but private property; therefore, the Missouri Compromise's ban on slavery in certain territories violated the Fifth Amendment because it deprived citizens (owners of enslaved people) of their property without the due process of law. Put another way, the *Dred Scott* decision said that state law, not federal, determined the legal status of enslaved people.

Contrasting Marshall's decisions in favor of national power with Taney's decisions in favor of state power highlights the profound policy consequences of judicial decisions. The Taney Court's decision that the Missouri Compromise was unconstitutional is consistent with a dual federalism interpretation of the Constitution—but it also sustained the legality of slavery in southern states and halted attempts by representatives from the North to limit the spread of slavery into the western territories. There is no doubt that Taney favored this outcome on policy grounds. In this way, debates about dual federalism during this time were really about the legality of slavery, its expansion into new states, and the rights of formerly enslaved people in free states.

states' rights
The idea that states are entitled to a certain amount of self-government, free of federal government intervention. This became a central issue in the period leading up to the Civil War.

Arguments about dual federalism are sometimes framed using the concept of **states' rights**: the idea that states retain some powers under the Constitution (specifically those reserved by the Tenth Amendment) and can ignore federal policies that encroach on these powers. The key question is, where does federal authority end and state authority begin? Some people argue that southern states fought the Civil War to preserve the concept of states' rights, but this argument is incorrect. Southern secessionists were not interested in states' rights per se; what they wanted was to continue slavery without federal intervention. States' rights was a convenient rationale for their proslavery position.

Modern political debates also use states' rights as a cover for substantive policy disagreements. Some opposition to expanding protections for LGBTQIA+ individuals is justified using a states' rights argument, that the federal government does not have the power to dictate "one size fits all" policy choices for communities throughout the nation. For example, some states require proof of sexual reassignment surgery before changing the name and gender on an individual's birth certificate, while others have much looser requirements. If the federal government tried to impose uniform standards, some opponents would likely cite states' rights as their justification. Of course, their opposition is not driven by a belief about the limits of federal power—rather, it is their opposition to changing the birth certificate regulations.

After the Civil War, constitutional amendments banned slavery (Thirteenth Amendment), prohibited states from denying citizens due process or the equal protection of the laws (Fourteenth Amendment), and gave newly freed men the right to vote (Fifteenth Amendment). Congress also passed the 1875 Civil Rights Act (although it was later overturned by the Supreme Court). The Fourteenth Amendment was the most important in terms of federalism because it was the constitutional basis for many of the civil rights laws passed by the federal government during Reconstruction. The Civil War fundamentally changed the way Americans thought about the relationship between the national government and the states: before the war people said "the United States *are* . . . ," but after the war they said "the United States *is* . . ."

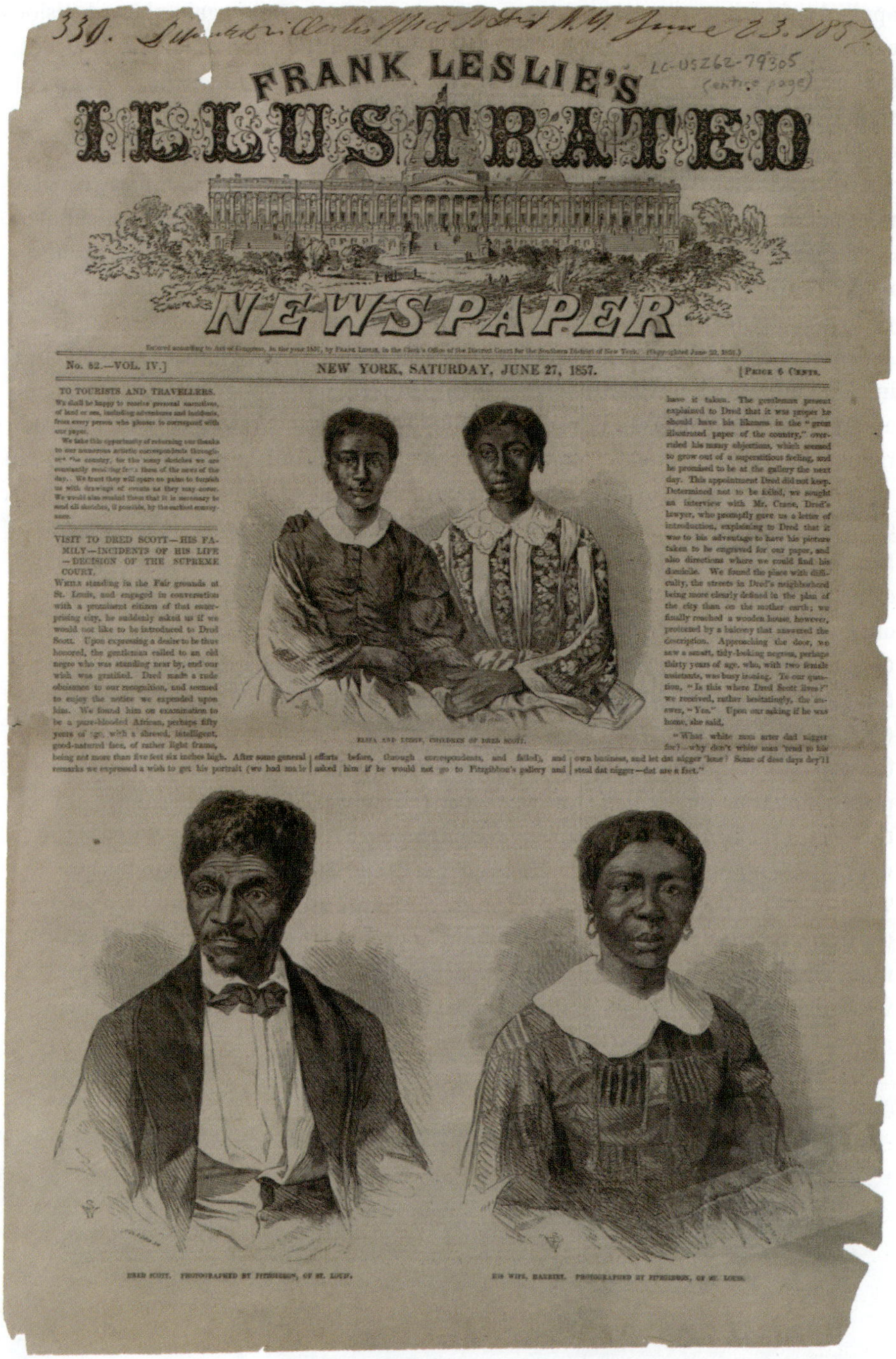

FRANK LESLIE'S ILLUSTRATED NEWSPAPER

Entered according to Act of Congress, in the year 1857, by Frank Leslie, in the Clerk's Office of the District Court for the Southern District of New York. (Copyrighted June 20, 1857.)

No. 82.—VOL. IV.] NEW YORK, SATURDAY, JUNE 27, 1857. [PRICE 6 CENTS.

TO TOURISTS AND TRAVELLERS.

We shall be happy to receive personal narratives, of land or sea, including adventures and incidents, from every person who pleases to correspond with our paper.

We take this opportunity of returning our thanks to our numerous artistic correspondents throughout the country, for the many sketches we are constantly receiving from them of the news of the day. We trust they will spare no pains to furnish us with drawings of events as they may occur. We would also remind them that it is necessary to send all sketches, if possible, by the earliest conveyance.

VISIT TO DRED SCOTT—HIS FAMILY—INCIDENTS OF HIS LIFE—DECISION OF THE SUPREME COURT.

While standing in the Fair grounds at St. Louis, and engaged in conversation with a prominent citizen of that enterprising city, he suddenly asked us if we would not like to be introduced to Dred Scott. Upon expressing a desire to be thus honored, the gentleman called to an old negro who was standing near by, and our wish was gratified. Dred made a rude obeisance to our recognition, and seemed to enjoy the notice we expended upon him. We found him on examination to be a pure-blooded African, perhaps fifty years of age, with a shrewd, intelligent, good-natured face, of rather light frame, being not more than five feet six inches high. After some general remarks we expressed a wish to get his portrait (we had made efforts before, through correspondents, and failed), and asked him if he would not go to Fitzgibbon's gallery and have it taken. The gentleman present explained to Dred that it was proper he should have his likeness in the "great illustrated paper of the country," overruled his many objections, which seemed to grow out of a superstitious feeling, and he promised to be at the gallery the next day. This appointment Dred did not keep. Determined not to be foiled, we sought an interview with Mr. Crane, Dred's lawyer, who promptly gave us a letter of introduction, explaining to Dred that it was to his advantage to have his picture taken to be engraved for our paper, and also directions where we could find his domicile. We found the place with difficulty, the streets in Dred's neighborhood being more clearly defined in the plan of the city than on the mother earth; we finally reached a wooden house, however, protected by a balcony that answered the description. Approaching the door, we saw a smart, tidy-looking negress, perhaps thirty years of age, who, with two female assistants, was busy ironing. To our question, "Is this where Dred Scott lives?" we received, rather hesitatingly, the answer, "Yes." Upon our asking if he was home, she said,

"What white man arter dat nigger for?—why don't white man 'tend to his own business, and let dat nigger 'lone? Some of dese days dey'll steal dat nigger—dat are a fact."

ELIZA AND LIZZIE, CHILDREN OF DRED SCOTT.

DRED SCOTT. PHOTOGRAPHED BY FITZGIBBON, OF ST. LOUIS.

HIS WIFE, HARRIET. PHOTOGRAPHED BY FITZGIBBON, OF ST. LOUIS.

LC-USZ62-79305 (entire page)

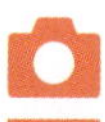

The *Dred Scott* decision, covered here in *Frank Leslie's Illustrated Newspaper,* was the subject of much public interest when it was handed down in 1857. The decision inflamed tensions between states that allowed slavery and states that did not, and it vindicated those who saw state law as superior to federal law.

The Supreme Court and Limited National Government The assertion of power by Congress during Reconstruction was short-lived, as the Supreme Court soon stepped in again to limit the power of the national government. In 1873, the Court reinforced the notion of dual federalism, ruling that the Fourteenth Amendment did not change the balance of power between the national and state governments. Specifically, the Court ruled that the Fourteenth Amendment right to due process and equal treatment under the law applied to individuals' rights only as citizens of the United States, not to their state citizenship.[4] By extension, freedom of speech, freedom of the press, and the other liberties protected in the Bill of Rights applied only to laws passed by Congress, not to state laws. Here again, these decisions can be read as an articulation of a theoretical interpretation of the Constitution, but they are also part of a broader, more concrete debate over how much the government should regulate interactions between individuals, or between individuals and corporations.

In 1883, the Court overturned the 1875 Civil Rights Act, which had guaranteed equal treatment in public accommodations. The Court argued that the Fourteenth Amendment did not give Congress the power to regulate private conduct, such as whether a White restaurant owner had to serve a Black customer; it affected only the conduct of state governments, not individuals in these states.[5] This narrow view of the Fourteenth Amendment left the national government powerless to prevent southern states from implementing state and local laws that led to complete segregation of Black Americans and White Americans in the South (called Jim Crow laws) and the denial of many basic rights to Black Americans after northern troops left the South at the end of Reconstruction.

The Supreme Court also limited the reach of the national government by curtailing Congress's authority to regulate the economy through its commerce clause powers. In a series of cases in the late nineteenth and early twentieth centuries, the Supreme Court endorsed a view of laissez-faire—French for "leave alone"—capitalism aimed at protecting business from regulation by the national government. To this end, the Court defined clear boundaries between *inter*state and *intra*state commerce, ruling that Congress could not regulate any economic activity that occurred *within* a state (intrastate). The Supreme Court let some national legislation that was connected to interstate commerce stand, such as the Sherman Antitrust Act (1890), which placed limits on monopolies. However, when the national government tried to use this act to break up a cartel of four sugar companies that controlled 98 percent of the nation's sugar production, the Court ruled that Congress did not have this power. The Court's decision argued that the commerce clause allowed Congress to regulate the transportation of goods, not their manufacture, and the sugar in question was made within a single state. Even if the sugar was sold throughout the country, this was "incidental" to its manufacture.[6] On the same grounds, the Court struck down attempts by Congress to regulate child labor.[7]

After the Supreme Court struck down the 1875 Civil Rights Act, southern states were free to impose Jim Crow laws. These state and local laws led to complete racial segregation, even for public waiting rooms.

Cooperative federalism

From the early years of the twentieth century through the 1930s, a new era of American federalism emerged in which the national government became much more involved in activities that were formerly reserved for the states, such as transportation, civil rights, agriculture, social welfare, and management-labor relations. At first, the Supreme Court resisted this broader reach of national power, clinging to its nineteenth-century conception of dual federalism.[8] But as commerce became more national, the distinctions between interstate and intrastate commerce, and between manufacture and transportation, became increasingly difficult to sustain. Starting in 1937 with the landmark ruling *National Labor Relations Board v. Jones and Laughlin Steel Corporation*, the Supreme Court largely discarded these distinctions and gave Congress far more latitude to shape economic and social policy for the nation.[9]

Shifting National–State Relations The type of federalism that emerged in this era is called **cooperative federalism**, or "marble cake" federalism, as opposed to the "layer cake" model of dual federalism.[10] As the image of a marble cake suggests, the boundaries of state and national responsibilities are less well defined than they are under dual federalism. With the increasing industrialization and urbanization of the late 1930s and 1940s, along with the Great Depression, more complex problems arose that could not be solved at one level of government. Cooperative federalism adopted a more practical focus on intergovernmental relations and the efficient delivery of services. State and local governments maintained a level of influence as the implementers of national programs, but the national government played an enhanced role as the initiator, director, and funder of key policies.

cooperative federalism
A form of federalism in which national and state governments work together to provide services efficiently. This form emerged in the late 1930s, representing a profound shift toward less concrete boundaries of responsibility in national–state relations.

"Cooperative federalism" accurately describes this important shift in national-state relations in the first half of the twentieth century, but it only partially captures the complexity of modern federalism. The marble cake metaphor falls short in one important way: the lines of authority and patterns of cooperation are not as messy as implied by the gooey flow of chocolate through white cake. Instead, the 1960s metaphor of **picket fence federalism** is a better description of cooperative federalism in action. As the How It Works graphic on pages 92–93 shows, each picket of the fence represents a different policy area, and the horizontal boards that hold the pickets together represent the different levels of government. This is a much more orderly image than the marble cake provides, and it illustrates important implications about how policy is made across levels of government.

picket fence federalism
A more refined and realistic form of cooperative federalism in which policy makers within a particular policy area work together across the levels of government.

The most important point to be drawn from this analogy is that activity in the cooperative federal system occurs *within* pickets of the fence—that is, within policy areas. Policy makers within a given policy area will have more in common with others in that area (even if they are at different levels of government) than they do with people who work in different areas (even if they are at the same level of government). For example, someone working in a state's Department of Natural Resources will have more contact with people working in local park programs and the national Department of the Interior than with people who also work at the state level but who focus on, say, public health.

Cooperative federalism, then, is likely to emerge within policy areas rather than across them. This may create problems for the chief executives who are trying to run the show (mayors, governors, the president), as rivalries develop among

How it works: in theory

Versions of Federalism

Version 1:

Layer Cake Federalism

1789–1937

No interactions between the levels of government.

National

State

Local

Version 2:

Marble Cake Federalism

1937–today

Interactions between the levels of government are common.

Version 3:

Picket Fence Federalism

1960s–today

Horizontal boards represent different levels of government, and the pickets are policy areas within which coordination happens across those levels.

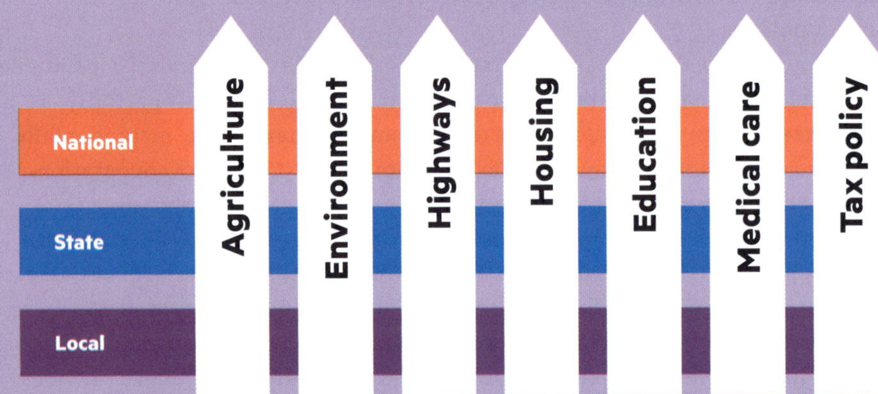

Version 4:

Coercive Federalism

1970s–today

National government uses regulations, mandates, and conditions to pressure states to fall into line with national policy goals.

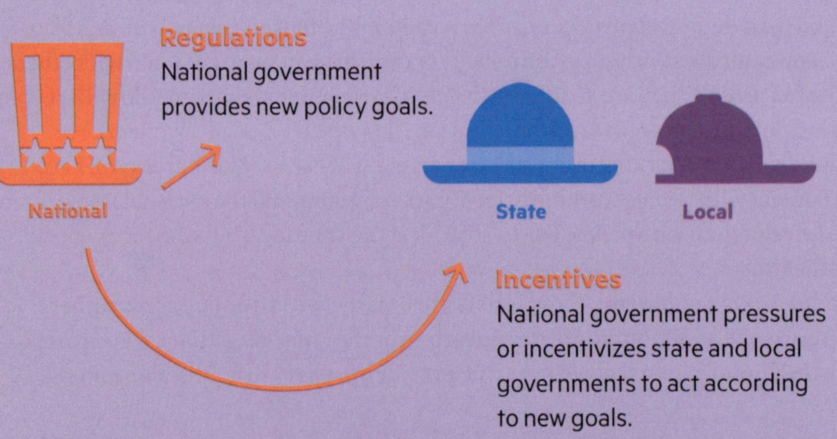

How it works: in practice

Federalism and Environmental Policy

This is who carries out environmental policy in . . .

The national government:
Environmental Protection Agency (EPA),
Department of the Interior,
Department of Energy

The state government:
State department of natural resources, state park service, state environmental protection agencies

The local government:
City park system, city and county oversight boards for land use policy and zoning

Environmental policy shows contemporary federalism in action. As you can see on the right, all levels of government combine to effect environmental policy (exemplifying picket fence federalism). Also, the national government provides both rules and incentives for state and local governments to change their environmental policies (exemplifying coercive federalism).

Congress passed new acts.

Over the last several decades, Congress has passed the **Coastal Zone Management Act**, the **Clean Water Act**, the **Endangered Species Act**, and the **Clean Air Act**.

What does that mean?

This legislation has provided states and localities with **federal regulations and mandates**.

Stricter rules . . .

During the Obama administration, **the EPA set tougher limits on ozone and water pollution** and proposed stricter limits on carbon emissions.

But also incentives.

Other federal programs **provided grants and tax incentives** to encourage use of renewable energy technologies.

Change happens.

Beginning in 2017, the Trump administration **repealed many of the new EPA regulations** but left the tax credits and grant programs largely intact.

The states fight back.

Fifteen states **sued the federal government**, claiming that the regulatory rollbacks violated the Clean Air Act.

Elections matter.

The state lawsuits became irrelevant after Joe Biden's election in 2020. His EPA appointees **decided against pursuing the Clean Power Plan,** preferring to begin an effort to set more ambitious targets for reductions in power plant emissions.

But so do courts.

In June 2022, the Supreme Court ruled that **the EPA could not use the Clean Air Act to justify regulation of carbon emissions** by power plants, putting new regulations on hold until Congress acts or another rationale is identified.

Critical Thinking

1. **Which do you think is a more effective tool** to change environmental policy—the "stick" of regulation or the "carrot" of incentives? Why?
2. **Should the government provide tax credits and other incentives** for things like renewable energy, or leave such things up to the free market?

Franklin Delano Roosevelt's New Deal shifted more power than ever to the national government. Through major new programs to address the Great Depression, such as the Works Progress Administration construction projects pictured here, the federal government expanded its reach into areas that had been primarily the responsibility of state and local governments.

policy agencies competing for funds. Also, contact within policy areas is not always cooperative. (Think of detective shows in which the FBI arrives to investigate a local crime and pulls rank on the town sheriff, provoking resentment from local law-enforcement officials.) This is the inefficient side of picket fence federalism in action.

"Why Should I Care?"

Why is it important to understand the history of federalism? You might think that the Civil War ended the debates over nation-centered versus state-centered federalism (in favor of the national government), but disputes today over immigration, health care, welfare, and education policy all revolve around the balance of power between the levels of government. State legislatures that talk about ignoring federal criticisms of their policy choices are invoking the same arguments used by advocates of states' rights in the 1830s and 1840s concerning tariffs and slavery.

DESCRIBE THE MAJOR TRENDS AND DEBATES IN FEDERALISM TODAY

Federalism today

Federalism today is a complex mix of all the types of federalism that our nation's political system has experienced in the past. Our current system is predominantly characterized by cooperative federalism, but it has retained strong elements of national supremacy, dual federalism, and states' rights (see Nuts & Bolts 3.2). Debates over the appropriate role of the federal and state governments continue to occur in areas such as government surveillance of individuals (especially after September 11) and funding of social-welfare programs like public school education and health care. (For more details on these programs, see Chapter 16.) And the courts continue to play a key role in deciding the constitutionality of new laws and regulations.

NUTS & BOLTS 3.2

The Evolution of Federalism

Type of federalism	Period	Characteristics
Dual federalism (layer cake)	1789–1937	The national and state governments were viewed as very distinct with little overlap in their activities or the services they provided. Within this period, federalism could have been state centered or nation centered, but relations between levels of government were limited.
Cooperative federalism (marble cake)	1937–present	This indicates greater cooperation and collaboration between the levels of government.
Fiscal federalism	1937–present	This system of transfer payments or grants from the national government to lower-level governments involves varying degrees of national control over how the money is spent: categorical grants give the national government a great deal of control, whereas block grants involve less national control.
Picket fence federalism	1960–present	This version of cooperative federalism emphasizes that policy makers within a given policy area have more in common with others in their area at different levels of government than with people at the same level of government who work on different issues.
Coercive federalism	1970s–present	This involves federal preemptions of state and local authority and unfunded mandates on state and local governments to force the states to change their policies to match national goals or policies established by Congress.

Source: Compiled by the authors.

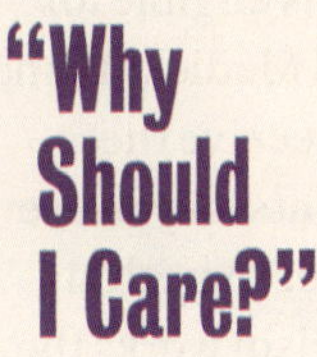

Over the 240 years of American history, shifts in citizen demands and the expansion of the federal government have changed the nature of policy conflicts between state and federal governments. Even so, the fact that many policy responsibilities are shared or left undetermined, coupled with the fact that politics is conflictual, means that the federal government and the states will always be arguing over who gets to do what.

Cooperative federalism lives on: fiscal federalism

Cooperative federalism refers to situations in which federal and state governments share responsibility for delivering a policy. In the case of the Medicaid program that provides health coverage for low-income adults (and the equivalent Medicare program for senior citizens), programs in each state are administered by state agencies operating under federal guidelines, sometimes with waivers. In the modern era, the federal government has also become involved in funding and setting requirements for K–12 education as well as paying for welfare benefits and food stamps for poor people, policies that were long considered local responsibilities. And to schools, to health care providers, and even to individuals for rental assistance and extended unemployment benefits.

Most examples of cooperative federalism involve some element of **fiscal federalism**, a system whereby the federal government provides some of the funds needed to sustain the state programs that deliver services to citizens. For example, the federal government pays a large share of state Medicaid costs and a portion of the funding for local school districts. At one level, fiscal federalism is a way for the federal government to help states deal with responsibilities that outstrip their

fiscal federalism
A form of federalism in which federal funds are allocated to the lower levels of government through transfer payments or grants.

One of the Biden administration's campaign promises was to create and expand partnerships with states to offer free prekindergarten. Here, Secretary of Education Miguel Cardona and First Lady Dr. Jill Biden, who is a teacher, engage with children who would benefit from the expanded investment in education. These proposals were not enacted by Congress.

financial resources. However, fiscal federalism also gives the federal government a way to influence the kinds of policies implemented at the state level. In theory, states have large amounts of discretion in terms of determining who is eligible for Medicaid or the fees paid to doctors. However, the promise of federal Medicaid funds comes with program requirements that state agencies must meet to receive these funds. This type of relationship may sound familiar. When your parents let you use the car or lent you $50, was it "no strings attached"? Or did they expect something in return—such as help with yard work or other chores? Fiscal federalism works the same way, as the federal government tries to use its resources to gain control over state policies.

An extreme version of fiscal federalism is **coercive federalism**, which is the use of federal mandates or conditions to force or entice the states to change their policies to match national goals or policies established by Congress. A related concept, **federal preemption**, occurs when the federal government passes a law that overrides state law or makes it impossible for a state to enact its own statute. The Clean Air and Clean Water Acts, the Americans with Disabilities Act (ADA) (which promotes making public buildings and commercial facilities more accessible to those with disabilities), and the Motor Voter Act (which requires states to provide voter registration services at motor vehicle departments) are all laws that forced states to change their policies. In recent years, Democrats at the national level also tried to enact laws that would set uniform standards for voter registration, early voting, and voting by mail.

The laws most objectionable to the states are **unfunded mandates**, which require states to do certain things but carry no federal money to pay for them. Republican criticism of unfunded mandates in the 1990s led to passage of the Unfunded Mandate Reform Act of 1995. This act made it more difficult for Congress to impose these mandates on the states; it required a separate vote on mandates that imposed costs of more than $50 million, and it required a Congressional Budget Office estimate of exactly how much such mandates would cost the states. Although this law could not prevent unfunded mandates, Republicans hoped that bringing more attention to the practice would create political pressure against such policies.

coercive federalism
A form of federalism in which the federal government pressures the states to change their policies by using regulations, mandates, or conditions (often involving threats to withdraw federal funding).

federal preemption
Imposition of national priorities on the states through national legislation that is based on the Constitution's supremacy clause.

unfunded mandates
Federal laws that require the states to do certain things but do not provide state governments with funding to implement these policies.

Types of Federal Aid to States The method used to transfer resources from the federal government to states and localities often determines the effectiveness of fiscal federalism. Today, most federal aid comes in two forms. **Categorical grants** are for specific purposes—they have strings attached. Funds that help states run their Medicaid programs, for example, are delivered as categorical grants. **Block grants** are financial aid to states for use within a specific policy area, but within that area the states have discretion on how to spend the money. An example of a block grant is TANF (Temporary Assistance for Needy Families), which is federal money given to states to help fund their welfare programs. However, in contrast to Medicaid, federal welfare funds are given without restrictions about how the states determine benefits or the eligibility of welfare recipients. As a result, both factors vary across states. Since the 1970s, grants to the states as a proportion of the size of the national economy (gross domestic product, or GDP) have been relatively constant, whereas the rate of state and local spending has continued to inch up.

categorical grants
Federal aid to state or local governments that is provided for a specific purpose, such as a mass-transit program within the transportation budget or a school lunch program within the education budget.

block grants
Federal aid provided to a state government to be spent within a certain policy area but that the state can decide how to spend within that area.

Advocates of cooperative federalism often promote block grants as the best way for the levels of government to work together to solve problems: the national government identifies problem areas and then provides money to the states to help solve them. The problem is that state governments may disagree with the president or Congress on how these programs should be implemented, which creates a temptation for the federal government to move to categorical grants to shape state policy. For example, in the case of extended unemployment benefits enacted because of the COVID-19 pandemic, some Republican states curtailed these programs early and returned funds to the federal government.

A separate argument for block grants is made by people who believe that state governments are better informed about local conditions—as well as people who prefer the results of state-led policies to a situation wherein states must obey federal directives. For example, Republican attempts to repeal the Affordable Care Act (the ACA, or "Obamacare") have proposed transforming the program into a block grant to state governments, arguing along the lines of the quote from Nobel Laureate Elinor Ostrom—that local decision makers are often better informed about citizen needs. While Ostrom's work shows that decentralization can lead to more efficient, effective policies, it appears that these efforts by Republicans are more about saving money and reducing services, as the block grants they propose would not cover predicted increases in health care costs.

Expanding national power

Despite the overall shift toward cooperative federalism, strong overtones of national government supremacy remain. Three important characteristics of American politics in the past 60 years have reinforced the role of the national government: (1) reliance on the national government in times of crisis and war; (2) the "rights revolution" of the 1950s and 1960s, as well as the Great Society programs of the 1960s; and (3) the rise of coercive federalism.

Crisis and War Reliance on the national government in times of crisis and war has always been a characteristic of American politics. Even in the 1800s, during the period of dual federalism and strong state power, the national government's strong actions were needed during the Civil War to hold the nation together. Policy responses to the major crises of the twentieth century (the Great Depression's New Deal policies, the massive mobilization for World War II), as well as the response to the banking meltdown of 2008–2009, also dramatically shifted the balance of power toward

"Bureaucrats sometimes do not have the correct information, while citizens and users of resources do."

—Elinor Ostrom, Nobel laureate

Washington. More recently, as the COVID-19 pandemic spread across the country, the federal government sent over $6 trillion in assistance to individuals, businesses, and state and local governments, shifting the balance of power.

The "Rights Revolution" and Great Society Programs The "rights revolution" initiated by the Supreme Court, as well as Lyndon Johnson's Great Society programs, contributed to increased national control over state policies. Landmark Court decisions thrust the national government into policy areas that had typically been reserved to the states. In the school desegregation and busing cases of the 1950s and 1960s, for example, the Court upheld the national goal of promoting racial equality and fighting discrimination over the earlier norm of local control of school districts.[11] The "one person, one vote" decisions, which required that the populations of legislative districts be equalized when district lines were redrawn, put the federal courts at the center of another policy area that had always been left to the states.[12] The rights revolution also applied to police powers, another area of traditional state control, including protection against self-incrimination and preventing illegally obtained evidence from being used in a criminal trial.[13]

These Court actions were paralleled by a burst of legislation that tackled civil rights, education, the environment, medical care for the poor, and housing. These so-called Great Society policies made the national government much more active in policy areas previously controlled by state and local governments. For example, after passage of the 1965 Voting Rights Act, federal marshals were sent to the South to make sure that Black Americans were allowed to vote.

In the 1960s, the national government also expanded its reach through a large increase in categorical grants, although most of these funds came with strings attached. For example, the 1964 Civil Rights Act required nondiscrimination as a condition for receiving any kind of federal grants. The Elementary and Secondary Education Act of 1965 gave the federal government heightened control over public education by attaching conditions to federal grant money.

More Unfunded Mandates Despite the legislation enacted by Congress designed to curb unfunded mandates, the practice has continued. President Barack Obama's administration required state governments to adopt policies preventing discrimination against the disabled and mandated reforms to local school lunch menus. The Trump administration's crackdown on undocumented immigrants had an unfunded mandate: if local police arrested someone suspected of being undocumented, they were expected to keep these suspects in custody until federal authorities arrived, even though the federal government did not pay them for the cost of the detention. More recently, the Biden administration's Environmental Protection Agency mandated that local water utilities review their preparedness against cybersecurity attacks, but did not provide any funds for the review.

The fact that members of Congress enact unfunded mandates makes sense given the themes of this textbook. First, politics is about conflict, and when there is disagreement between the federal and state government over what policies should look like, we should expect each side to do whatever it can to advance its own priorities. Second, the rules matter. The fact that the Constitution prioritizes federal law over state law, coupled with increased federal aid to state and local governments, gives the federal government considerable leverage to get its way when conflicts arise. In the case of suspected undocumented immigrants, the Trump administration threatened to withhold various forms of federal aid to communities that refused to hold suspects for transfer, although it never actually did so, and it is questionable whether aid cutoffs would survive a court challenge.

The states fight back

Most Americans support some of the policies that have been imposed on the states: racial equality, clean air and water, a fair legal process, safer highways, and equal access to the voting booth. At the same time, there has always been considerable opposition in some states to federal mandates, whether unfunded or otherwise. For example, about 20 states have refused to accept federal funds to expand Medicaid as outlined in the Affordable Care Act. While the law initially did not give states the flexibility to opt out of the expansion, the Supreme Court found that mandating that states expand their Medicaid programs to receive these funds was unconstitutional.

States appear to be reversing their traditional role of resisting change and protecting the status quo. In recent years, some states such as California and Colorado have refused to accept national pollution standards that are too lenient or the lack of national action on issues such as global warming. Many policies to address climate change—including the development of renewable energy sources, carbon emissions limits, and carbon cap-and-trade programs—have been advocated or enacted at the state level.[14] To take another example, Kansas and Montana passed laws holding that federal gun laws do not apply to guns manufactured in their states (and making it a felony to try to enforce those laws).[15] Many such state laws will not stand up in federal court; the Montana gun law was struck down. But the laws are clearly a reflection of state frustration with assertions of federal power and with the policy goals that underlie these assertions. Simply put, local elected officials and their constituents often disagree with federal directives. From this perspective, federalism provides a way for state and local officials to shape public policy in ways that favor their own policy goals.

Federalism provides a way for states to shape public policy to support their citizens' policy goals. But it doesn't always work out. For example, in 2021, Montana passed a law prohibiting "the enforcement of any federal ban or regulation of firearms, magazines, ammunition, ammunition components, or firearm accessories," reinforcing the state's strong commitment to the Second Amendment right to bear arms. The law was subsequently struck down in federal court.

States have one important advantage over the national government when it comes to experimenting with new policies: their numbers. There are 50 states potentially trying a mix of different policies—another reason that advocates of state-centered federalism see the states as the proper repository of government power. In this view, such a mix of policies produces **competitive federalism**—competition among states to provide the best policies to attract businesses, create jobs, and maintain a healthy social fabric.[16] For example, one of the arguments in favor of repealing Obamacare and giving the program's funds to states as a block grant was that state governments might develop better, more efficient ways to deliver health care without having to meet federal requirements.

competitive federalism
A form of federalism in which states compete to attract businesses and jobs through the policies they adopt.

Fighting for states' rights: the role of the modern Supreme Court

Just as the Supreme Court played a central role in defining dual federalism in the nineteenth and early twentieth centuries and in opening the door to a more nation-centered cooperative federalism in the late 1930s, today's Court is once again reshaping federalism. But this time the move is decidedly in the direction of state power (see Table 3.2 on p. 100).

The Tenth Amendment On paper, it seems that the Tenth Amendment would be at the center of any resurgence of state power because it ensures that all powers not delegated to the national government are reserved to the states or to the people. Until recent years, this amendment had been overshadowed by federal supremacy—state

"Crucial to understanding federalism in modern day America is the concept of mobility, or 'the ability to vote with your feet.' If you don't support the death penalty and citizens packing a pistol—don't come to Texas. If you don't like medicinal marijuana and gay marriage, don't move to California."

—Rick Perry, former Texas governor

TABLE 3.2

Recent Important Supreme Court Decisions on Federalism

Case	Holding and significance for states' rights	Direction of the decision
United States v. Lopez (1995)	Carrying a gun in a school did not fall within "interstate commerce"; thus, Congress could not prohibit the possession of guns on school property.	More state power
City of Boerne v. Flores (1997)	The Court struck down the Religious Freedom Restoration Act as an overly broad attempt to curtail the state-sponsored harassment of religion, saying that national legislation aimed at remedying states' discrimination must be "congruent and proportional" to the harm.	More state power
United States v. Morrison (2000)	The Court struck down part of the Violence Against Women Act, saying that Congress did not have the power under the commerce clause to provide a national remedy for gender-based crimes.	More state power
Alabama v. Garrett (2001)	The Court struck down the portion of the ADA that applied to the states, saying that state governments are not required to make special accommodations for the disabled.	More state power
Nevada Department of Human Resources v. Hibbs (2003)	The Court upheld Congress's power to apply the 1993 Family Leave Act to state employees as "appropriate legislation" under Section 5 of the Fourteenth Amendment.	Less state power
United States v. Bond (2011)	The Court upheld an individual's right to challenge the constitutionality of a federal law under the Tenth Amendment.	More state power
National Federation of Independent Business v. Sebelius (2012)	The Court upheld most provisions of the ACA but struck down the expansion of Medicaid as an unconstitutional use of coercive federalism (states could voluntarily take the additional funding to cover the expansion, but they would not lose existing funds if they opted out).	Mixed
United States v. Windsor (2013)	The Court held that Section 3 of the Defense of Marriage Act (DOMA) was unconstitutional because it denied federal benefits to same-sex couples who were legally married under state law.	More state power
Shelby County v. Holder (2013)	The Court struck down Section 4 of the Voting Rights Act on the grounds that it violated the "equal sovereignty" of the states.	More state power
Carson v. Makin (2022)	The Court struck down a Maine law that prevented school vouchers from being used to pay for attending religion-based private schools.	More state power
New York State Rifle & Pistol Association Inc. v. Bruen (2022)	The Court struck down a New York State law that allowed concealed carry of firearms only if a citizen could show they had "proper cause" for doing so.	Less state power
Dobbs v. Jackson Women's Health Organization (2022)	The Court reversed the *Roe v. Wade* abortion rights decision, holding that individual states have the power to regulate abortions.	More state power

Source: Compiled by the authors.

laws contradicting the Constitution or federal laws and regulations were generally found to be unconstitutional. For example, state laws enforcing racial segregation were deemed unconstitutional because they conflicted with the equal protection clause of the Fourteenth Amendment. Similarly, a state law concerning public education, traditionally a state power, is void if it conflicts with the Constitution or with a national law that is based on an enumerated power. For example, a state could not compel an 18-year-old to attend school if the student had been drafted to serve in the army. Under the Tenth Amendment, the constitutionally enumerated national power to "raise and support armies" would override the reserved state power to support public education.

However, with the appointment of three conservative justices between 1986 and 1991 who favored a stronger role for the states, the Court started to limit the national government's reach. One common thread in these decisions was to require that Congress provide an unambiguous statement of its intent for a particular law to overrule state authority. For example, the Court ruled that the Missouri constitution, which requires state judges to retire by age 70, did not violate the Age Discrimination in Employment Act because Congress did not make its intentions "unmistakably clear in the language of the statute."[17]

The Fourteenth Amendment The Supreme Court has also empowered states by limiting the applicability of the Constitution's Fourteenth Amendment to state laws. The Fourteenth Amendment was intended to give the national government broad control over the potentially discriminatory laws of southern states after the Civil War. Section 1 guarantees that no state shall make or enforce any law depriving any person of "life, liberty, or property, without due process of law" or denying any person the "equal protection of the laws," and Section 5 empowers Congress "to enforce" those guarantees by "appropriate legislation." Throughout most of the twentieth century, the Court interpreted Section 5 to give Congress broad discretion to pass legislation to remedy bad state laws. For example, discriminatory application of literacy tests prevented millions of Black Americans from voting in the South before the Voting Rights Act was passed in 1965.

"The immense size and power of the Government of the United States ought not obscure its fundamental character. It remains a Government of enumerated powers."

—Sandra Day O'Connor, former Supreme Court justice

As part of the federalism revolution of the 1990s, the Court started to chip away at Congress's Fourteenth Amendment powers. In one important case in 1997, the Supreme Court struck down the Religious Freedom Restoration Act as an overly broad attempt to curtail state-sponsored harassment based on religion. This case established a new standard to justify **remedial legislation**—that is, national legislation that fixes discriminatory state law—under Section 5 of the Fourteenth Amendment, saying, "There must be a congruence and proportionality between the injury to be prevented or remedied and the means adopted to that end."[18] In one application of the new standard for remedial legislation, the Court ruled that the Age Discrimination in Employment Act of 1967 could not be applied to state employees because it was not "appropriate legislation."[19] Two applications of this logic also applied to the Eleventh Amendment, which originally was interpreted to mean that residents of one state could not sue other (non-home-state) state governments. More recently, the Supreme Court has expanded the reach of the Eleventh Amendment through the concept of **states' sovereign immunity**. States are now immune from a much broader range of lawsuits in state and federal court.

remedial legislation
National laws that address discriminatory state laws. Authority for such legislation comes from Section 5 of the Fourteenth Amendment.

states' sovereign immunity
Based on the Eleventh Amendment, immunity that prevents state governments from being sued by private parties in federal court unless the state consents to the suit.

The Commerce Clause Another category of cases that have been decided in favor of more state power concerns the commerce clause of the Constitution. The first Court case to limit Congress's commerce powers since the New Deal of the 1930s came in 1995. The case involved the Gun-Free School Zones Act of 1990, which Congress passed in response to the increase in school shootings around the nation. The law made it a federal offense to have a gun within 1,000 feet of a school. Congress assumed that it had the power to pass this legislation, given the Court's expansive interpretation of the commerce clause over the previous 55 years, even though it concerned a traditional area of state power. Although it was a stretch to claim that carrying a gun in or around a school was related to interstate commerce, Congress might have been able to demonstrate the point by showing that (1) most guns are made in one state and sold in another (thus commercially crossing state lines); (2) crime affects the economy and commerce; and (3) the quality of education, which is also crucial to the economy, is harmed if students and teachers are worrying about guns in their schools. However, members of Congress did not present this evidence.

Alfonso Lopez, a senior at Edison High School in San Antonio, Texas, was arrested for carrying a concealed .38-caliber handgun with five bullets in it, in violation of the Gun-Free School Zone Act. Attorneys for Lopez moved to dismiss the charges, arguing that the law was unconstitutional because carrying a gun in a school could not be regulated as "interstate commerce." The Court agreed in *United States v. Lopez*,[20] and the ruling was widely viewed as a warning shot over Congress's bow. If Congress wanted to encroach on the states' turf in the future, it would have to demonstrate that the law in question was a legitimate exercise of the commerce clause powers.

The next time Congress passed legislation that affected law enforcement at the state level, it was careful to document the impact on interstate commerce. The Violence Against Women Act was passed in 1994 with strong bipartisan support after testimony and evidence were entered into the record showing the links between violence against women and commerce. Despite the evidence Congress presented, the Supreme Court ruled that Congress did not have the power under the commerce clause to make a national law that gave victims of gender-motivated violence the right to sue their attackers in federal court (the Court struck down only that part of the law, however; the program funding remained unaffected and was reauthorized in 2013 and again in 2019).[21]

The impact of these cases goes well beyond setting limits on the federal government's ability to regulate commerce. Not only has the Supreme Court set new limits on Congress's ability to address national problems, but it has also clearly stated that the Court alone will determine which rights warrant protection by Congress. However, it is important to recognize that the Court does not consistently rule against Congress; it often rules against the states. For example, the Court has struck down state laws limiting gay rights as a violation of the equal protection clause of the Fourteenth Amendment.[22] And although the Court rejected the commerce clause as the constitutional justification for national health care reform, it did uphold the ACA based on Congress's taxing power.[23]

It's also important to keep in mind that the national government still has the upper hand in the balance of power and has many tools at its disposal to blunt the impact of any Court decision. Congress can pass new laws to clarify its legislative intent and overturn any of the Court cases that involved statutory interpretation. Congress can also use its financial power to impose its will on the states, although this power is not unlimited. For example, in a 2012 case dealing with Obamacare's requirement that states expand Medicaid coverage in order to receive federal subsidies for the program, the Court ruled that the threat embodied in this requirement was a "gun to the head,"[24] meaning states did not have a real choice: without the subsidies, no state could afford to provide Medicaid coverage on its own, even without the expansion in coverage. This was the first time the Court limited Congress's coercive budgetary power over the states, and the boundaries of the new limits will have to be decided in future cases.

The *Lopez* decision struck down the 1990 Gun-Free School Zones Act, ruling that Congress did not have the power to forbid people to carry guns near schools. After the shooting of 34 people at Marjory Stoneman Douglas High School in Parkland, Florida, on February 14, 2018, students led renewed calls nationwide for strengthening gun control laws.

The impact of this decision changed slowly over time: as of 2024, all but 10 states have accepted Medicaid expansion, reflecting the large federal subsidies that come with this decision.

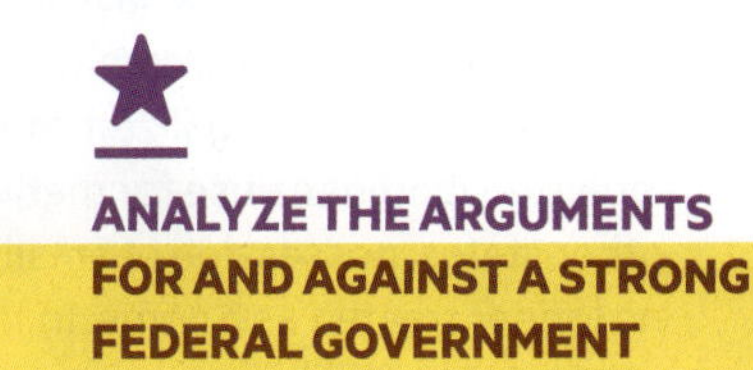

Why is it important to understand federalism today? More than at any time in U.S. history, the question of which branch of government has power over a particular policy is up for interpretation. This change gives elected officials new opportunities to influence policy—rather than changing the policy itself, they can influence decisions about which level of government implements the policy.

Assessing federalism

★

ANALYZE THE ARGUMENTS FOR AND AGAINST A STRONG FEDERAL GOVERNMENT

There is much to recommend federalism as a cornerstone of our political system. However, there are disadvantages as well, such as inefficiency in the policy process and inequality in policy outcomes. This section will assess the advantages, disadvantages, and ideological complexities of federalism.

Policy preferences

Issues concerning federalism often seem to break down along traditional liberal and conservative lines. Liberals generally favor strong national power to fight discrimination against women, historically marginalized groups, disabled people, the LGBTQIA+ community, and the elderly, and they push for progressive national policies on issues such as protecting the environment, providing national health care, and supporting the poor. Conservatives, in contrast, tend to favor limiting intrusion from the national government and allowing the states to decide their own mix of social welfare and regulatory policies, including how aggressively they will protect various groups from discrimination. In this way, individuals' feelings about federalism are connected to their policy preferences and their judgments about what kinds of policies should emerge from different levels of government.

However, assessing the implications of having policies carried out by one level of government or another is not always so simple. In recent years the tables have turned, so that liberals are arguing for states' rights while conservatives are advocating the virtues of uniform national laws. On a broad range of new issues, such as LGBTQIA+ rights, aid in dying, and the recreational use of marijuana (see the Take a Stand feature on p. 104), some state governments have enacted socially liberal legislation in recent years. As a result, liberals who might have favored a strong national government as a way of implementing their policy goals have found themselves arguing for states' rights, and conservatives have ended up arguing for the virtues of centralizing power.

"[A] state may, if its citizens choose, serve as a laboratory; and try novel social and economic experiments without risk to the rest of the country."

—Louis Brandeis,
former Supreme Court justice

Advantages of a strong role for the states

In addition to pointing out the policy implications of federalism, any assessment of federalism today must consider the advantages and disadvantages for our political system. The advantages of a strong role for the states can be summarized in four main

TAKE A STAND

Recreational Marijuana and Federalism

Should the federal government be able to tell a state that it cannot allow the recreational use of marijuana? While the use and possession of marijuana are illegal under federal law, more than 23 states have legalized nonmedical use. In most of these states, commercial activity (growing and sale) has also been legalized. More than 35 states have legalized marijuana use for medical purposes. And in most other states, possession of small amounts of marijuana is no longer treated as a crime. In the coming years, several other states are likely to move toward partial or complete legalization.

The federal government should be "hands off." Until recently, the federal government responded to these changes in state law by adopting a "hands off" policy. The so-called Cole Memo (named after Obama administration deputy associate attorney general James Cole) stated that the federal government would not prosecute marijuana cases unless there had been a violation of both state and federal law. This policy reflected an attitude within the Obama Justice Department that prosecution of marijuana cases was not a high priority. Moreover, some Justice Department staff members (and perhaps President Obama) probably favored federal legalization. However, this step would have required congressional approval, which would have been unlikely during Obama's administration given the Republican majority in the House. Thus, deferring to state law helped move parts of the country toward decriminalization without requiring additional legislative action and allowed public support for legalization to build. Opponents of marijuana legalization in Congress may eventually be forced to reconsider their position based on the tides of public opinion.

The federal government should be "hands on." The situation changed after the election of Donald Trump. Throughout 2017, the Trump Justice Department argued that the federal government needed to be more aggressive in its enforcement of marijuana laws as a means of reducing drug abuse, fighting criminal organizations, and decreasing violent crime. In January 2018, then–attorney general Sessions formally rescinded the Cole Memo, although his new guidelines did not order U.S. attorneys to give marijuana prosecutions a higher priority, distinguish between medical or recreational use, or provide additional resources for anti-marijuana efforts. Sessions did not order states to change their laws or compel local law-enforcement agencies to enforce federal law.

Federal drug enforcement agents raid a medical marijuana club.

Somewhat surprisingly, the Biden administration has not reversed the Trump-era policies, so federal policy remains formally opposed to legalization but largely leaves the decision up to the states. However, there are efforts within federal agencies to change how cannabis is classified under federal regulations so that it can be legally dispensed by prescription. At the same time, federal laws that criminalize marijuana cultivation, possession, and sale remain on the books, although they are not enforced.

take a stand

1. As a matter of policy, should marijuana be legalized in all cases or just some cases—ranging from complete legalization to legalization only for medical use when prescribed by a doctor? If some possession is legal, what should policies be for growth and sale?

2. Do you tend to support a state-centered or a nation-centered perspective on federalism? Now revisit your answers to question 1. Are your positions more consistent with your views on federalism or with your policy concerns?

points: (1) states can be laboratories of democracy, (2) state and local governments are closer to the people, (3) states provide more access to the political system, and (4) states provide an important check on national power.

The first point refers to the role that states can play as the source of policy diversity and innovation. If many states are trying to solve problems creatively, their efforts can complement those of the national government. Successful policies first adopted at the state level often percolate up to the national level. Consider health care. Many provisions of Obamacare were taken from the highly successful state-level program in Massachusetts. Similarly, climate change initiatives emerging in California and other states may provide templates for federal action in the future.

Second, government that is closer to the people can encourage participation in the political process and may be more responsive to local needs. Local politicians know better what their constituents want than further-removed national politicians do. On the one hand, if voters want higher taxes to pay for more public benefits, such as public parks and better schools, they can enact these changes at the state and local levels. On the other hand, if they prefer lower taxes and fewer services, local politicians can be responsive to those desires. In addition, local government provides a broad range of opportunities for direct involvement in politics, from working on local political campaigns to attending school board or city council meetings, which may increase the input that citizens have in the establishment of new policies.

Third, our federalist system provides more access points for interested parties (stakeholders) to influence government policy. For example, the court system allows citizens to pursue complaints under state or federal law. If a group, such as anti-abortion activists, loses at the federal level, it can try to enact similar legislation at the state level. Likewise, cooperative federalism can draw on the strengths of different levels of government to solve problems. A local government may recognize a need and respond to it more quickly than the national government can, but if additional resources are needed to address the problem, the municipality may be able to turn to the state or national government for help—as in the case of the COVID-19 pandemic, where the federal government provided massive amounts of aid to individuals, states, and businesses.

Finally, federalism can provide a check on national tyranny. Competitive federalism ensures that Americans have a broad range of social policies, levels of taxation and

DID YOU KNOW?

Owing to a state program that is similar to Obamacare, only

2.8%

of people in Massachusetts don't have health insurance. In Texas, 17.7 percent of people do not have health insurance—the highest percentage in the nation.

Source: Census.gov.

Government that is closer to the people can encourage participation in the political process and may be more responsive to local needs. These demonstrators outside a school board meeting in Leesburg, Virginia, for example, expressed concerns about curriculum changes they felt would expose their children to ideas with which they didn't agree. Protests like these led many states to ban teaching critical race theory, a framework for analyzing race and racism in society, in their schools.

FIGURE 3.2

State Spending per Person, 2021

Spending per person varies dramatically by state. What are some of the advantages and disadvantages of living in a low-spending state or in a high-spending state? What type of state would you rather live in? Why?

Source: State and Local Government Finance Data Query System, http://slfdqs.taxpolicycenter.org (accessed 3/1/24).

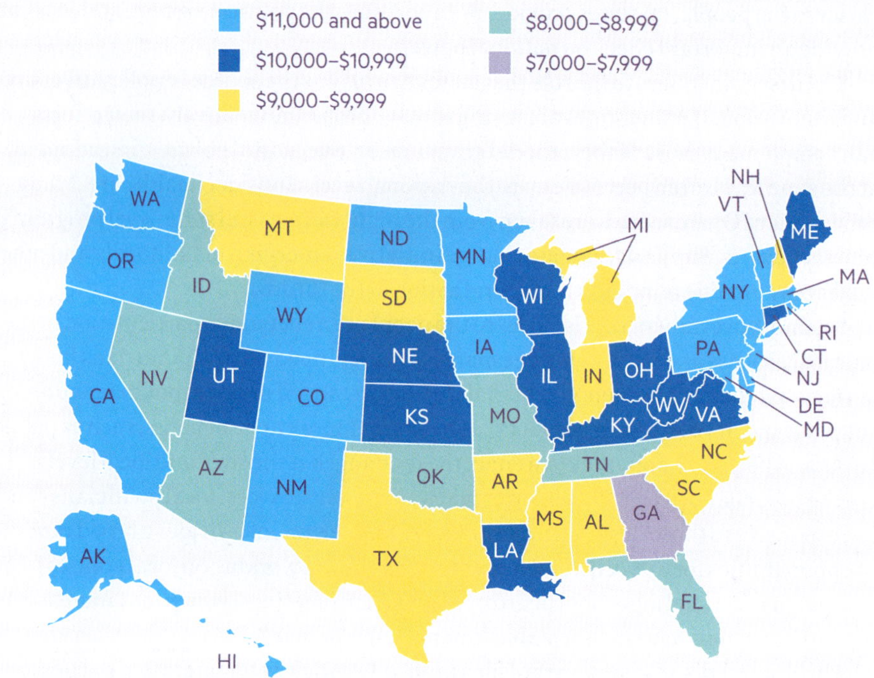

regulation, and public services to choose from (see Figure 3.2). When people "vote with their feet" by deciding whether to move and where to live, they encourage healthy competition among states that would be impossible under a unitary government.

Disadvantages of too much state power

A balanced assessment of federalism must acknowledge that there are problems with a system that gives too much power to the states. The disadvantages include unequal distribution of resources across the states, unequal protection for civil rights, competition that produces a "race to the bottom," and the problem of coordinating local responses to truly national problems.

The resource problem becomes more acute when dealing with national-level problems that affect different areas differently. For example, many communities across the United States are faced with deteriorating public infrastructure, including highways, bridges, and mass transit. Paying for these repairs can outstrip the resources of state and local governments, particularly for a small number of localities that have a disproportionate number of bridges and roads needing repairs. These pressures are one reason why the Biden administration was able to build majority support in Congress for its $550 billion infrastructure spending plan.

Another problem, unequal civil rights protection, is evident in various federalism cases that have passed before the Supreme Court. These clearly show that states are not uniformly willing to protect the civil liberties and civil rights of their citizens. This was critically important during the 1950s and 1960s when the national government forced southern states to end segregation and passed laws outlawing discrimination in housing, employment, transportation, and voting. The Supreme Court recently stepped in to provide equal rights to marry, but states still vary a great deal in terms of antidiscrimination laws based on sexual orientation. Without national laws, there will be large differences in the levels of protection against discrimination based on age,

Historically marginalized groups are more vulnerable to negative repercussions of the power of state and local laws that might not protect their rights, and they cannot appeal to the federal government to provide assistance. This was seen in action in 2020 when the families of victims of police shootings, including Breonna Taylor and George Floyd, had to appeal to the same officials who managed the police for systemic changes.

disability, and sexual orientation. This problem is especially acute for racial, ethnic, and other historically marginalized groups. In a federal system where the national government defers to state and local officials, local policies that discriminate against historically marginalized racial, ethnic, or religious groups can persist because these groups are not large enough in number to demand redress from their elected representatives.

For example, research by computer scientist Emma Pierson and the Stanford Open Policing Project has documented long-standing patterns of police excessive use of force against historically marginalized groups. These patterns are exemplified by the 2020 deaths of George Floyd while being taken into custody by Minneapolis police and Breonna Taylor when Louisville police mistakenly executed a no-knock warrant on her apartment. As we noted earlier, law enforcement is almost exclusively managed by local governments. Thus, under a federal system, citizens cannot ask the national government to intervene; they have to appeal to the very same elected officials who manage (and in some cases created) the system that allowed policy brutality to happen in the first place. Sometimes these complaints trigger action (in the Floyd case, a Minnesota state court convicted a police officer of murder and the city of Minneapolis settled a civil case with Floyd's family), but sometimes they are not (in the Taylor case, the city of Louisville settled with Taylor's family and promised to reform police practices, but a grand jury did not charge the officers with murder).

In addition, competitive federalism can create a "race to the bottom" as states attempt to lure businesses by keeping taxes and social spending low. This can place an unfair burden on states that take a more generous position toward the poor or provide services (low college tuition, for example) that others do not. Thus, overall, there is no clear "winner" in determining the appropriate balance of national and state power. The advantages and disadvantages of our federal system ensure that federalism will always remain a central source of conflict in the policy-making process as the various levels of government fight it out.

Finally, state and local governments might be unable to coordinate their response to truly national problems such as managing a pandemic. If states take different stances on mask mandates, vaccination initiatives, and shutdowns, it does little good to stem the national spread of the virus. Action at the national level is the only way to ensure universal compliance.

"Why Should I Care?"

Today's federal structure offers a complex mix of all previous components of federalism: some elements of national supremacy combine with states' rights for a varied federal landscape. Although the federal and state governments still exercise cooperative federalism to achieve joint policy goals, the federal government has also utilized coercive federalism to impose federal priorities on the states without offering compensation.

Unpacking the Conflict

Considering all that we've discussed in this chapter, let's apply what we know about how federalism works to the example of mask mandates from the beginning of the chapter. When local and federal officials disagree about whether mandates are good or bad, who wins? How can we explain this conflict, or conflicts between federal and state authorities over other policies?

In some policy areas, the lines of authority between federal and state governments are relatively clear, but federalism can be justified as a way to deliver policies more effectively or efficiently. For example, many environmental initiatives over the last generation were designed with the idea that some states and communities would implement policies that deviated from federal standards—and that allowing such flexibility would ensure consideration of local needs or conditions. However, nothing in the Constitution mandates that the federal government allow local discretion—it all depends on what the president and Congress agree with and on what local governments want to do.

> **"Americans chose to be both one great nation and many relatively quite small, local communities."**
>
> —**Martha Derthick,** political scientist

That said, in many policy areas, the boundaries between federal authority and state authority are not always clear, particularly given the rise of cooperative federalism and the use of unfunded mandates. In other areas, such as laws governing the legality of marijuana, federal authority and state authority are genuinely overlapping. Depending on how broad they are, mask mandates fall into one of these two categories. In these situations, the question of whether the federal government can tell states what to do (or whether states have the right to ignore federal directives) has no clear answer. In these situations, politicians' (or citizens') judgments about federalism probably reflect their ideas about which level of government is more likely to give them an outcome they want.

The fight over mask mandates also highlights the view expressed in the quote from Martha Derthick,[25] that Americans are citizens of several levels of government simultaneously. If you asked most people in our nation about their primary geopolitical community, most people would likely say, "I am an American." Yet we have strong attachments to our local communities and state identities. We are members of multiple communities and subject to several different sets of overlapping laws, a fact that has had an indelible impact on our political system and the policy choices that affect our everyday life.

"What's Your Take?"

Should the federal government compel states to adhere to guidelines related to public health, as with mask and vaccine mandates during the COVID-19 pandemic?

Or should state and local officials be able to establish their own guidelines without federal interference?

CHECK YOUR UNDERSTANDING

"Why Should I Care?"

The Constitution clearly creates a federal system that consists of states and a national governing body, giving to each distinct functions and authorities. However, the Constitution does not paint a comprehensive picture of all the different potential interactions and ways in which the divisions between the national government and the states might arrive in conflict, especially in a digital age characterized by increasingly complex and interconnected economies, digital commerce and connections, and ever more diverse understandings about humanity. The framers of the Constitution, through compromises at the Constitutional Convention, understandings of their own limitations of knowledge and imagination, and intentional areas of vagueness built into the Constitution and its subsequent amendments, did not seek to prescribe solutions to future disputes over authority; rather, they defined the framework that would be used to find solutions.

How do we see that in action today? States have long served as what Justice Louis Brandeis labeled "laboratories of democracy," designing and implementing laws, policies, and institutions to answer the needs and demands of the public they serve. Often the policy experiments in the states have yielded significant positive outcomes later adopted by other states and the national government, such as Wyoming granting voting rights to women by 1869, fifty-one years before the ratification of the Nineteenth Amendment, and the expanded access to health insurance passed in Massachusetts under Republican Governor Mitt Romney that later became the framework for the Affordable Care Act during the Obama administration. But experimentation with policies in states have not always had positive outcomes. Issues like legal racial segregation, child labor, and lax environmental policies have often triggered expanded federal involvement as states either created or neglected harmful situations. Today, states often turn to the federal government for help in addressing economic and natural disasters—like the COVID-19 pandemic, wildfires in the West, and flooding after storms in coastal states like Texas, Louisiana, and South Carolina—that overwhelm state infrastructures, a benefit of federalism that even the most anti–big government states embrace in times of trouble.

In her Senate confirmation hearing as the first Black woman to be nominated to the U.S. Supreme Court, Justice Ketanji Brown Jackson was asked by Texas senator John Cornyn if she agreed with the 2015 decision of the Supreme Court in *Obergefell v. Hodges* that granted constitutional protections nationally to same-sex couples or if marriage was legally best left to the states to decide. Senator Cornyn's question demonstrates the ongoing debates over what the appropriate limits and divisions of power between the states and the national government are.

1. Most conflicts that arise in the United States among the levels of government—local, state, and national—center on

- **a** growing disputes about the role of the police and expanded healthcare.
- **b** disputes about what is the appropriate role of government.
- **c** whether or not local governments are exercising their exclusive powers properly.
- **d** rights and liberties guaranteed by the Constitution.

2. State powers typically involve things like __________, while national powers encompass things like __________.

- **a** public welfare : economic stability
- **b** delivering the mail : border security
- **c** proposing amendments : setting foreign policy
- **d** education policy : election laws

3. In ratifying the Constitution, states understood that they would be losing some powers they had under the Articles of Confederation. Most of the powers that states surrendered to the new central government allowed for which of the following?

- **a** Greater economic stability and national security
- **b** Increased protections for laborers and manufacturing regulations
- **c** Improved transportation and consistency in education
- **d** Fewer disputes about the responsibilities of each level of government

4. Not only did the framers of the Constitution outline the supremacy of the national government and national policies, but they also addressed conflicts between states by doing which of the following?

- **a** Assigning Congress the ability to make laws that were necessary to fulfilling their constitutional powers and regulating state actions
- **b** Designating the Supreme Court as the ultimate arbiter of disputes about the meaning of the Constitution
- **c** Instituting a role for states in ratifying proposed amendments to the national constitution
- **d** Creating obligations requiring states to honor the acts and public policies of other states

5. Generally, the balance of power between the state and the national government can be characterized as

- **a** devolution of national powers to the state and local levels.
- **b** increasing state authority.
- **c** giving greater authority to the national government.
- **d** mixed between the growth of state and national powers.

6. How did the ratification of the Thirteenth, Fourteenth, and Fifteenth Amendments set the stage for a modern shift in the power balance between the state and national governments?

- **a** The Supreme Court interpreted them as having limited application to state decisions about civil rights and civil liberties.
- **b** The specific prohibition of states making policies that violate due process or equal protection allowed for the future expansion of national regulations over states.
- **c** The Reconstruction Amendments, as they were called, established a greater assertion of states' rights in creating public policies.
- **d** The abolition of slavery and enfranchisement of Black men guaranteed an ongoing federally protected role for formerly enslaved people in the decades following the Civil War.

7. What does the phrase "picket fence federalism" describe about the nature of federalism today?

- **a** People in government who work in a particular policy area are often connected to people who work in all levels of government who also work in that policy area.
- **b** It is often difficult to determine the basis of authority and areas of responsibility within the collaborating levels of government.
- **c** Most Americans want the levels of government to have clearly defined separations in their areas of responsibility and operations.
- **d** Political parties and their followers have conflicting beliefs about what policy values should be implemented by the government.

8. One of the most significant changes about the relationship between the national and state governments after the Great Depression is the

- **a** movement of the Supreme Court toward protecting state powers under the Tenth Amendment.
- **b** growth of state government regulations when compared with the relatively slow growth of federal regulation.
- **c** increase in financial entanglements and dependence between the state and national governments.
- **d** unchecked growth in the number of unfunded mandates and national government interventions into state affairs.

9. Which statement best describes the disagreement between conservative and liberal ideologies when it comes to federalism?

- **a** Liberals and conservatives disagree on which level (state or national) of government best protects the rights and liberties of Americans.
- **b** Liberals have less faith in the ability of the national government to create policy that reflects the inputs and priorities of the people than do conservatives.
- **c** The national government in acting as a laboratory of democracy is unpredictable.
- **d** Liberals believe that states should implement immigration and public health policy, while conservatives believe that the federal government should be responsible.

10. Perhaps the greatest benefit of a strong national government is

- **a** clearly articulated policy preferences and consistent accountability.
- **b** greater representation of the policy preferences of historically marginalized groups.
- **c** increased ability to coordinate resources and responses to truly national problems.
- **d** ability of states to compete in implementing federal policies to find the best fit for their populations.

Use INQUIZITIVE to help you study and master this material.

4

Civil Liberties

It's a free country . . . right?

"Respect for religious expressions is indispensable to life in a free and diverse Republic. Here, a government entity sought to punish an individual for engaging in a personal religious observance, based on a mistaken view that it has a duty to suppress religious observances even as it allows comparable secular speech. The Constitution neither mandates nor tolerates that kind of discrimination."[1]

—Justice Neil Gorsuch, majority opinion, *Kennedy v. Bremerton School District*

"This case is about whether a public school must permit a school official to kneel, bow his head, and say a prayer at the center of a school event. The Constitution does not authorize, let alone require, public schools to embrace this conduct. . . . This decision does a disservice to schools and the young citizens they serve, as well as to our Nation's longstanding commitment to the separation of church and state."[2]

—Justice Sonia Sotomayor, dissenting opinion, *Kennedy v. Bremerton School District*

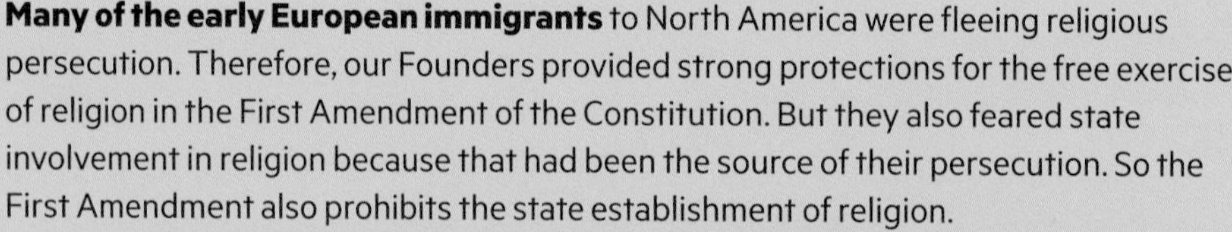

Many of the early European immigrants to North America were fleeing religious persecution. Therefore, our Founders provided strong protections for the free exercise of religion in the First Amendment of the Constitution. But they also feared state involvement in religion because that had been the source of their persecution. So the First Amendment also prohibits the state establishment of religion.

Does allowing prayer on public school grounds infringe on the rights of students of a different faith? Does prohibiting it infringe on free speech rights? Joe Kennedy, a public school football coach, was dismissed from his job at a public high school for leading the team in prayer before games after being asked by administrators to stop. He argued it was a violation of his free speech rights, while the school argued it was ensuring the separation of the church and state.

These two parts of the First Amendment are often in tension, as was true with a recent Supreme Court case involving Joseph Kennedy, a football coach at Bremerton High School in Washington State. Kennedy knelt at the 50-yard line after each football game in prayer, often joined by some of his players. The school asked him to stop, fearing it would be sued for promoting religion in a public school. He refused and the school offered alternatives for more private prayer, but he persisted, so he was suspended and the school decided to not hire him back after the suspension. In response, Kennedy sued the school, saying its actions had violated the free exercise and free speech clauses of the First Amendment, which says that Congress will not establish any state religion, but it will also not restrict the practice of any religion.

CHAPTER GOALS

Define what we mean by *civil liberties* (pp. 114–16)

Explain why the Bill of Rights was added to the Constitution and how it came to apply to the states (pp. 116–20)

Describe the First Amendment liberties related to freedom of religion (pp. 121–27)

Describe the major First Amendment liberties related to freedom of speech (pp. 128–40)

Explore why the Second Amendment's meaning on gun rights is often debated (pp. 141–43)

Describe the protections provided for people accused of a crime (pp. 143–54)

Explain why the rights associated with privacy are often controversial (pp. 154–57)

The lower courts ruled in favor of the school, saying the school was correct to be worried about violating the establishment clause. But in July 2022, the Supreme Court reversed this decision, ruling on the coach's side, saying, "The Constitution neither mandates nor permits the government to suppress such religious expression. The district acted on a mistaken view that it has a duty to suppress religious observances even as it allows comparable secular speech."[3]

Not only did the justices differ on what the Constitution permits and requires concerning religion, they couldn't even agree on the facts of the case, as seen in the two quotations above. The majority opinion states that the coach was "in a sincerely motivated religious exercise that does not involve students" and "lost his job" for "pray[ing] quietly while his students were otherwise occupied." The three dissenters pointed out that after being told by the school that he must stop praying after games with his players, Kennedy made multiple media appearances to publicize his plans to do exactly that (and he carried through those plans). The dissenters also pointed out that players might feel coerced to join, even if they were not required to pray, writing, "This Court has recognized that students face immense social pressure. Students look up to their teachers and coaches as role models and seek their approval. Students also depend on this approval for tangible benefits. Players recognize that gaining the coach's approval may pay dividends small and large, from extra playing time to a stronger letter of recommendation to additional support in college athletic recruiting."[4]

Over the last twenty years the Court has moved to a more accommodating position when it comes to how much religious freedom it must allow before it starts encroaching on someone else's freedom to practice a different religion or not to observe religion at all. If the coach's prayer had been truly private (say, in his car after the game), nobody would object. Only when it was so clearly in the public eye did it become controversial.

Defining the boundaries of our liberties and freedoms, like the free exercise of religion, is messy and complicated. When can the state limit the practice of a person's religion? When we say America is a free country, what does this really mean? Are there limits to those freedoms? If so, how should political actors draw the lines between protected behavior and actions that may be regulated?

Defining civil liberties

The terms "civil rights" and "civil liberties" are often used interchangeably, but there are important differences (see Nuts & Bolts 4.1). To oversimplify a bit, **civil liberties** are about freedom and civil rights are about equality. Given that civil liberties are rooted in the Bill of Rights, it might have been less confusing if it had been called the "Bill of Liberties." (This distinction is discussed further in Chapter 5.)

civil liberties
Constitutionally established guarantees and freedoms that protect citizens, opinions, and property against arbitrary government interference.

Civil liberties are deeply rooted in our key idea that politics is conflictual and involves trade-offs. When the Supreme Court rules on civil liberties cases, it must balance an individual's freedom with government interests and the public good. In some cases, the Court must not only balance these interests but also "draw a line" between permissible and illegal conduct concerning a specific liberty.

Balancing interests

Civil liberties must be balanced against competing interests, because when it comes to our freedoms there are no absolutes. The trade-off between civil liberties and national security in the war on terrorism illustrates this point. Many Americans were concerned

Distinguishing Civil Liberties from Civil Rights

NUTS & BOLTS 4.1

Civil liberties	Civil rights
Basic freedoms and liberties	Protection from discrimination
Rooted in the Bill of Rights and the "due process" protection of the Fourteenth Amendment	Rooted in laws and the "equal protection" clause of the Fourteenth Amendment
Primarily restrict what the government can do to you ("*Congress* shall make no law . . . abridging the freedom of speech")	Protect you from discrimination both by the government and by individuals and enforced through government action

Source: Compiled by the authors.

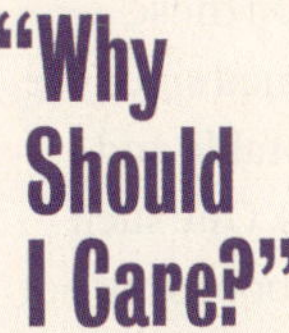

"Why Should I Care?"

One easy way to remember the difference between the two is that civil liberties are about freedom and civil rights concern equality. Also, civil liberties *limit* the actions government can take against you, while civil rights *expand* the actions that you can take as a citizen while also protecting you from discrimination from the government and other citizens.

that civil liberties were being eroded upon discovering that the government was arresting suspected terrorists in the United States and taking them to foreign countries that are less protective of civil liberties—Egypt, Syria, Jordan, and Morocco—to be interrogated through torture.[5] Despite these concerns, even the strongest critic of state-sponsored torture would have to admit that, in some instances, it might be justified. For example, if a nuclear device were set to detonate in Manhattan in three hours, few would insist on protecting the civil liberties of someone who knew where the bomb was hidden. Once we recognize that our freedoms are not absolute, it becomes a question of how they are balanced against other interests, such as national security.

Other interests that compete with civil liberties include public safety and public health. For example, members of some Christian fundamentalist churches regularly handle dangerous snakes in their services, though many states and cities have laws prohibiting the practice. The courts have upheld those laws, saying that "public safety is superior to religious practice."[6] But despite the laws, snake handling in churches continues to be a problem. In 2013, Tennessee Wildlife Resource Agency officials cited Reverend Andrew Hamblin, co-star of the National Geographic Channel reality show *Snake Salvation*, for keeping 53 poisonous snakes and using them in services (an estimated 125 churches still handle snakes). Hamblin was eventually acquitted by a grand jury. A couple of months later, his co-star Reverend Jamie Coots died after being bitten by a rattlesnake in his church and refusing treatment.[7] Similarly, in some states the Amish are forced to place reflective "slow-moving vehicle" (SMV) triangles on their horse-drawn carriages, even if it violates their religious beliefs, because of the paramount concern for public safety.[8] Yet the Amish are not forced to send their children to public schools despite a state law requiring all children to attend school through age 16. In *Wisconsin v. Yoder* (1972), the Court said this law presented "a very real threat of undermining the Amish community and religious practice as it exists today."[9]

These decisions show that balancing interests is never a simple process and involves deciding whether a specific civil liberty or some competing public interest is more compelling in a specific case.

How can conflicts be resolved between civil liberties and other legitimate interests, such as public safety and public health? Sometimes freedom is forced to give way. Courts have upheld bans on the religious practice of snake handling (though several churches have been undeterred by these bans) and upheld laws requiring the Amish to display reflective triangles when driving slow-moving buggies on public roads, despite religious objections to doing so.

Drawing lines

Along with balancing competing interests, court rulings draw the lines defining the limits of permissible conduct by the government or an individual in the context of a specific civil liberty. For example, despite the First Amendment protection of freedom of speech, it is obvious that some speech cannot be permitted. The classic example is falsely yelling "Fire!" in a crowded theater. Therefore, the courts must interpret the law to draw the line between protected speech and impermissible speech.

The same applies to other civil liberties, such as the establishment of religion, freedom of the press, freedom from illegal searches, or other due process rights. For example, the First Amendment prohibits the government from establishing an official religion, which the Court has carefully interpreted over the years to avoid "excessive entanglement" between any religion and the government. On these grounds, government-sponsored prayer in public schools has been banned since the early 1960s. But sometimes it is difficult to draw the line between acceptable and impermissible government involvement concerning religion in schools. One such ruling allowed taxpayer subsidies to fund parochial schools for buying books but not maps. (This odd hairsplitting led the late senator Daniel Patrick Moynihan to quip, "What about atlases?"[10]) Another difficult issue is the Fourth Amendment prohibition against "unreasonable searches and seizures" and the role of drug-sniffing dogs. Here the line drawing involves deciding whether a sniff is a search and, if so, under what circumstances it is reasonable. The Supreme Court has ruled that drug-sniffing dogs searching luggage at an airport or a car that has been stopped for a traffic violation unrelated to drugs is acceptable, but a warrant is required to have a dog sniff for drugs on the porch of a home.[11] Search and seizure cases also involve balancing interests: in this case, the individual freedoms of the target of police action and the broader interests in public order and security.

EXPLAIN WHY THE BILL OF RIGHTS WAS ADDED TO THE CONSTITUTION AND HOW IT CAME TO APPLY TO THE STATES

The origins of civil liberties

Courts define the boundaries of civil liberties, but the other branches of government and the public often get involved as well. The earliest debates during the American Founding illustrate the broad public involvement concerning the basic questions of how our civil liberties would be defined: Should government be limited by an explicit statement of individual liberties? Would these limitations apply to the state governments or just the national government? How should these freedoms evolve as our society changes?

Origins of the Bill of Rights

The original Constitution provided only limited protection of civil liberties: it guaranteed habeas corpus rights (a protection against illegal incarceration) and prohibited bills of attainder (legislation punishing someone for a crime without the benefit of a trial) and ex post facto laws (laws that retroactively change the legal consequences of some behavior). Delegates to the Constitutional Convention made a few attempts to include a broader statement of civil liberties, including one by George Mason and Elbridge Gerry five days before the convention adjourned. But their motion to appoint a committee to draft a bill of rights was rejected. Charles Pinckney and Gerry also tried to add a provision to protect the freedom of the press, but that too was rejected.[12]

Mason and Gerry opposed ratification of the Constitution, partly because it did not include a bill of rights, and many Antifederalists echoed this view, including in the influential Brutus essays, which were written to encourage New Yorkers to reject the Constitution (see especially Brutus 1). In a letter to James Madison, Thomas Jefferson predicted that four states would withhold ratification until a bill of rights was added.[13] Some states ratified the Constitution but urged Congress to draft specific protections for individuals' and states' rights from federal action (they believed protection of civil liberties from state actions should reside in state constitutions). In other states, the Antifederalists who lost the ratification battle continued making their case to the public and Congress. One of the most famous arguments came from the Antifederalists of Pennsylvania, who claimed that a bill of rights was needed to "fundamentally establish those unalienable and personal rights of men, without the full, free, and secure enjoyment of which there can be no liberty, and over which it is not necessary for a good government to have the control."[14] Their statement went on to outline many of those civil liberties that ultimately became the basis for the Bill of Rights.

Madison and other supporters of the Constitution agreed that the 1st Congress would take up the issue, despite their reservations that a Bill of Rights could lead the people into falsely believing that it was an exhaustive list of all their rights. State conventions submitted 124 amendments for consideration. That list was whittled down to 17 by the House and then to 12 by the Senate. This even dozen was approved by the House and sent to the states, which in 1791 ratified the 10 amendments that became the Bill of Rights (see Nuts & Bolts 4.2 on p. 118).[15]

Despite the profound significance of the Bill of Rights, one point limited its reach: it applied only to the laws and actions of the national government and not to those of the states. For example, the First Amendment says that "*Congress* shall make no law" infringing on freedom of religion, speech, and the press, among others. Madison submitted another amendment, which he characterized as "the most valuable of the whole list," requiring states to protect some civil liberties: "The equal rights of conscience, the freedom of speech or of the press, and the right of trial by jury in criminal cases shall not be infringed by any State."[16] But Antifederalists feared another power grab by the Federalists in limiting states' rights, so the proposed amendment was voted down in Congress. This decision proved consequential, because the national government was quite weak for the first half of our nation's history. Because states exercised as much power over people's lives as the national government did, if not more, it would have been more important for the Bill of Rights to limit the reach of the state governments than to limit that of the federal government. Thus, the Bill of Rights played a surprisingly small role for more than a century. The Supreme Court used it only once before 1866 to invalidate a federal action—in the infamous *Dred Scott* case that contributed to the Civil War (see Chapter 3).

Selective incorporation and the Fourteenth Amendment

The significance of the Bill of Rights increased somewhat with the ratification of the Fourteenth Amendment in 1868. It was one of the three **Civil War amendments** that attempted to guarantee equal rights to the newly freed, formerly enslaved people.

Civil War amendments
The Thirteenth, Fourteenth, and Fifteenth Amendments to the Constitution, which abolished slavery and granted civil liberties and voting rights to newly freed people after the Civil War.

NUTS & BOLTS 4.2

The Bill of Rights: A Statement of Our Civil Liberties

First Amendment	Freedom of religion, speech, press, and assembly; the separation of church and state; and the right to petition the government.
Second Amendment	Right to bear arms.
Third Amendment	Protection against the forced quartering of troops in one's home.
Fourth Amendment	Protection from unreasonable searches and seizures; "probable cause" is required for search warrants, which must specifically describe the "place to be searched, and the persons or things to be seized."
Fifth Amendment	Protection from forced self-incrimination or double jeopardy (being tried twice for the same crime); no person can be deprived of life, liberty, or property without due process of law; private property cannot be taken for public use without just compensation; and no person can be tried for a serious crime without the indictment of a grand jury.
Sixth Amendment	Right of the accused to a speedy and public trial by an impartial jury, to an attorney, to confront witnesses, to a compulsory process for obtaining witnesses in their favor, and to counsel in all felony cases.
Seventh Amendment	Right to a trial by jury in civil cases involving common law.
Eighth Amendment	Protection from excessive bail, excessive fines, and cruel and unusual punishment.
Ninth Amendment	The enumeration of specific rights in the Constitution shall not be construed to deny other rights retained by the people. This has been interpreted to include a general right to privacy and other fundamental rights.
Tenth Amendment	Powers not delegated by the Constitution to the national government, nor prohibited by it to the states, are reserved to the states or to the people.

Source: Compiled by the authors.

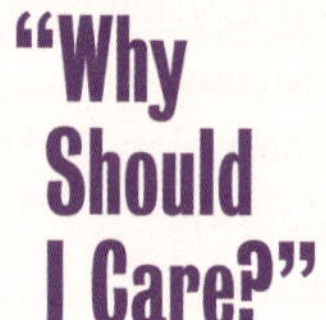

Many of the rights and liberties Americans think of as core American values weren't originally outlined in the Constitution. These first 10 amendments, outlined in the Bill of Rights, affect your daily life: you can practice the religion you choose, you can express your opinions on government actions, and you can choose to carry a gun. Additionally, if you are accused of a crime, the Bill of Rights guarantees your right to a trial by jury and various due process rights.

(The other two Civil War amendments were the Thirteenth, which abolished slavery, and the Fifteenth, which gave formerly enslaved men the right to vote.) Northern politicians were concerned that southerners would deny basic rights to the formerly enslaved people, so the sweeping language of the Fourteenth Amendment was adopted. Section 1 of the Fourteenth Amendment says:

> *All persons born or naturalized in the United States, and subject to the jurisdiction thereof, are citizens of the United States and of the State wherein they reside. No State shall make or enforce any law which shall abridge the privileges or immunities of citizens of the United States; nor shall any State deprive any person of life, liberty, or property, without due process of law; nor deny to any person within its jurisdiction the equal protection of the laws.*

This language was intended to make sure that states would not deny newly freed people the full protection of the law.[17] The **due process clause**, which forbids any state from denying "life, liberty, or property, without due process of law," led to an especially important expansion of civil liberties because the similar clause in the Fifth Amendment had previously been interpreted by the Court to apply only to the federal government.

due process clause
Part of the Fourteenth Amendment that forbids states from denying "life, liberty, or property" to any person without due process of law. (A nearly identical clause in the Fifth Amendment applies only to the national government.)

Evolving Interpretations by the Supreme Court Despite the amendment's clear statement that "no State shall make or enforce any law," in the Supreme Court's first opportunity to interpret the Fourteenth Amendment in 1873 it continued to rule in favor of protecting states from national government actions only, embracing the "dual citizenship" idea set forth in *Barron v. Baltimore* (the 1833 case ruling that the Fifth Amendment's protection of property from being taken by the government without compensation applied only to the federal government, not to state governments; see Chapter 3).[18] Over the next 50 years, a minority of justices tried mightily to strengthen the power of the Fourteenth Amendment and use it to protect civil liberties against state government action. In two early cases involving property rights and self-incrimination, the Supreme Court started to use the Fourteenth Amendment to prohibit state governments from violating individual rights—but stopped short of invoking amendments in the Bill of Rights itself to support their decisions.[19]

This progression culminated in the 1925 case *Gitlow v. New York*. Here the Court said for the first time that the Fourteenth Amendment incorporated one of the amendments in the Bill of Rights (provisions protecting freedom of speech and freedom of the press) and applied it to the states. The case involved Benjamin Gitlow, a radical socialist convicted under New York's Criminal Anarchy Act of 1902 for advocating the overthrow of the government. The Court upheld his conviction, arguing that his writings were the "language of direct incitement," but it also warned state governments that there were limits on such suppression of speech. This decision marked the first time that the Court ruled that a state law could be challenged because it violated an amendment in the Bill of Rights.[20]

Applying Civil Liberties to the States Slowly over the next 50 years, most civil liberties covered in the Bill of Rights were applied to the states on a right-by-right, case-by-case basis through the Fourteenth Amendment. However, this process of **selective incorporation** was not smooth and incremental. Rather, it progressed in surges with flurries of activity in the 1930s and the 1960s (see Table 4.1 on p. 120). As a result, the Bill of Rights has evolved from a narrow range of protections for people from national government actions during the early nineteenth century to a robust set of protections for freedom and liberty that limit national, state, and local government actions today.

selective incorporation
The process through which most of the civil liberties granted in the Bill of Rights were applied to the states on a case-by-case basis through the Fourteenth Amendment.

"Why Should I Care?"

Today the Bill of Rights is one of the most revered and important parts of the Constitution. But it didn't start out that way. Initially, the Bill of Rights applied to only the national government, not the states. But through the Fourteenth Amendment and the process of selective incorporation, the Supreme Court has gradually applied most of the Bill of Rights to the states. While all levels of government must respect our civil liberties today, there are many unresolved areas in terms of balancing interests and drawing lines. The next time you feel strongly about an issue concerning civil liberties, take some time to consider the other side—these questions are often not as black-and-white as they seem. Should speakers who hold extreme, even racist, views be allowed to speak on campus? How do we balance our freedom of speech or freedom from illegal searches with the need for national security?

TABLE 4.1

Selective Incorporation

The process of applying most of the Bill of Rights to the states progressed in two stages. The first, coming in the 1920s and 1930s, applied the First Amendment to the states; the second came a few decades later and involved criminal defendants' rights.

Amendment	Issue	Case
First Amendment	Freedom of speech	*Gitlow v. New York* (1925)
	Freedom of the press	*Near v. Minnesota* (1931)
	Freedom of assembly	*De Jonge v. Oregon* (1937)
	Right to petition the government	*Hague v. CIO* (1939)
	Free exercise of religion	*Hamilton v. Regents of the University of California* (1934); *Cantwell v. Connecticut* (1940)
	Separation of church and state	*Everson v. Board of Education of Ewing Township* (1947)
Second Amendment	Right to bear arms	*McDonald v. Chicago* (2010)
Fourth Amendment	Protection from unreasonable search and seizure	*Wolf v. Colorado* (1949); *Mapp v. Ohio* (1961)*
Fifth Amendment	Protection from forced self-incrimination	*Malloy v. Hogan* (1964)
	Protection from double jeopardy	*Benton v. Maryland* (1969)
Sixth Amendment	Right to a public trial	*In re Oliver* 333 U.S. 257 (1948)
	Right to a fair trial and an attorney in death-penalty cases	*Powell v. Alabama* (1932)
	Right to an attorney in all felony cases	*Gideon v. Wainwright* (1963)
	Right to an attorney in cases involving jail time	*Argersinger v. Hamlin* (1972)
	Right to a jury trial in a criminal case	*Duncan v. Louisiana* (1968)
	Right to cross-examine a witness	*Pointer v. Texas* (1965)
	Right to compel the testimony of witnesses who are vital for the defendant's case	*Washington v. Texas* (1967)
	Right to a unanimous jury verdict	*Ramos v. Louisiana* (2020)
Eighth Amendment	Protection from cruel and unusual punishment	*Robinson v. California* (1962)†
	Protection from excessive bail	*Schilb v. Kuebel* (1971)‡
	Protection from excessive fines	*Timbs v. Indiana* (2019)
Ninth Amendment	Right to privacy and other nonenumerated, fundamental rights	*Griswold v. Connecticut* (1965)§
Not incorporated		
Third Amendment	Prohibition against the quartering of troops in private homes	
Fifth Amendment	Right to indictment by a grand jury	
Seventh Amendment	Right to a jury trial in a civil case	

* *Wolf v. Colorado* applied the Fourth Amendment to the states (which meant that states could not engage in unreasonable searches and seizures); *Mapp v. Ohio* applied the exclusionary rule to the states (which excludes the use in a trial of illegally obtained evidence).

† Some sources list *Louisiana ex rel. Francis v. Resweber* (1947) as the first case that incorporated the Eighth Amendment. While the decision mentioned the Fifth and Eighth Amendments in the context of the due process clause of the Fourteenth Amendment, this argument was not included in the majority opinion that upheld as constitutional the bizarre double electrocution of prisoner Willie Francis (the electric chair malfunctioned on the first attempt but was successful on the second attempt; see Henry J. Abraham and Barbara A. Perry, *Freedom and the Court: Civil Rights and Civil Liberties in the United States*, 8th ed. [Lawrence: University Press of Kansas, 2003], pp. 71–72).

‡ Justice Blackmun "assumed" in this case that "the Eighth Amendment's proscription of excessive bail [applies] to the states through the Fourteenth Amendment," but later decisions did not seem to share this view. However, Justices Stevens and O'Connor agreed with Blackmun's view in *Browning-Ferris v. Kelco Disposal* (1989). Some sources argue that the excessive bail clause of the Eighth Amendment is unincorporated.

§ Justice Goldberg argued for explicit incorporation of the Ninth Amendment in a concurring opinion joined by Justices Warren and Brennan. The opinion of the Court referred more generally to a privacy right rooted in five amendments, including the Ninth, but did not explicitly argue for incorporation.

Source: Compiled by the authors.

Freedom of religion

DESCRIBE THE FIRST AMENDMENT LIBERTIES RELATED TO FREEDOM OF RELIGION

The First Amendment's ringing words are the most famous statement of personal freedoms in the Constitution: "Congress shall make no law respecting an establishment of religion, or prohibiting the free exercise thereof; or abridging the freedom of speech, or of the press; or the right of the people peaceably to assemble, and to petition the Government for a redress of grievances." (The How It Works graphic on pp. 122–23 illustrates how much is packed into this one amendment.)

The First Amendment has two parts that deal with religion: the **establishment clause**, which has been interpreted to mean that Congress cannot sponsor or endorse any particular religion, and the **free exercise clause**, which has been interpreted to mean that Congress cannot interfere with the practice of religion unless there are important secular reasons for doing so. To simplify only slightly, the former says that Congress should not *help* religion and the latter that it should not *hurt* religion. The establishment clause is primarily concerned with drawing lines. For example, does a prayer at a public high school football game or a Nativity scene on government property constitute state sponsorship of religion? The free exercise clause has more to do with balancing interests. Recall the earlier examples of balancing public safety concerns against snake handling in religious services and the use of Amish buggies on highways.

establishment clause
Part of the First Amendment that states, "Congress shall make no law respecting an establishment of religion," which has been interpreted to mean that Congress cannot sponsor or favor any religion.

free exercise clause
Part of the First Amendment that states that Congress cannot prohibit or interfere with the practice of religion unless there are important secular reasons for doing so.

The combination of the establishment and free exercise clauses results in a general policy of noninterference and government neutrality toward religion. As Thomas Jefferson put it in 1802, the First Amendment provides a "wall of eternal separation between church and state." This language continues to be cited in Court cases in which religion and politics intersect.[21] Since both areas carry great moral weight and emotional charge, it's no wonder that vehement debates continue over the appropriateness of the saying "In God We Trust" on our currency, the White House Christmas tree, and whether evolution and "intelligent design" should be taught in public schools. The boundaries of religious expression remain difficult to draw.

The establishment clause and separation of church and state

Determining the boundaries between church and state—the central issue of the establishment clause—is very difficult. As a leading text on civil liberties puts it, the words of the establishment clause—"Congress shall make no law respecting an establishment of religion"—are commanding and clear, but their meaning is entirely unclear. What does the clause allow or forbid?[22] We know that the Founders did not want an official state religion and did not want the government to favor one religion over another, but beyond that it's hard to say. Jefferson's "wall of eternal separation" comment has been used in Court decisions that prohibit state aid for religious activities, but lately the Court has been moving toward a more "accommodationist" perspective that sometimes allows religious activity in public institutions including taxpayer support for religious schools in some cases.

The number, the industry, and the morality of the Priesthood, & the devotion of the people have been manifestly increased by the total separation of the Church from the State.

—President James Madison

Public Prayer The prohibition of prayer in public schools has become the most controversial establishment clause issue. It exploded onto the political scene in 1962 when the Court ruled in *Engel v. Vitale* that the following prayer, written by the New York State Board of Regents and read every day in the state's public schools, violated the establishment clause and the separation of church and state: "Almighty God, we acknowledge our dependence upon Thee, and we beg Thy blessing upon us, our parents, our teachers, and our country."[23] Banning the prayer caused a huge public outcry protesting the perceived attack on religion.

How it works: in theory

The First Amendment

The First Amendment states:
"Congress shall make no law respecting an establishment of religion, or prohibiting the free exercise thereof; or abridging the freedom of speech, or of the press; or the right of the people peaceably to assemble, and to petition the government for a redress of grievances."

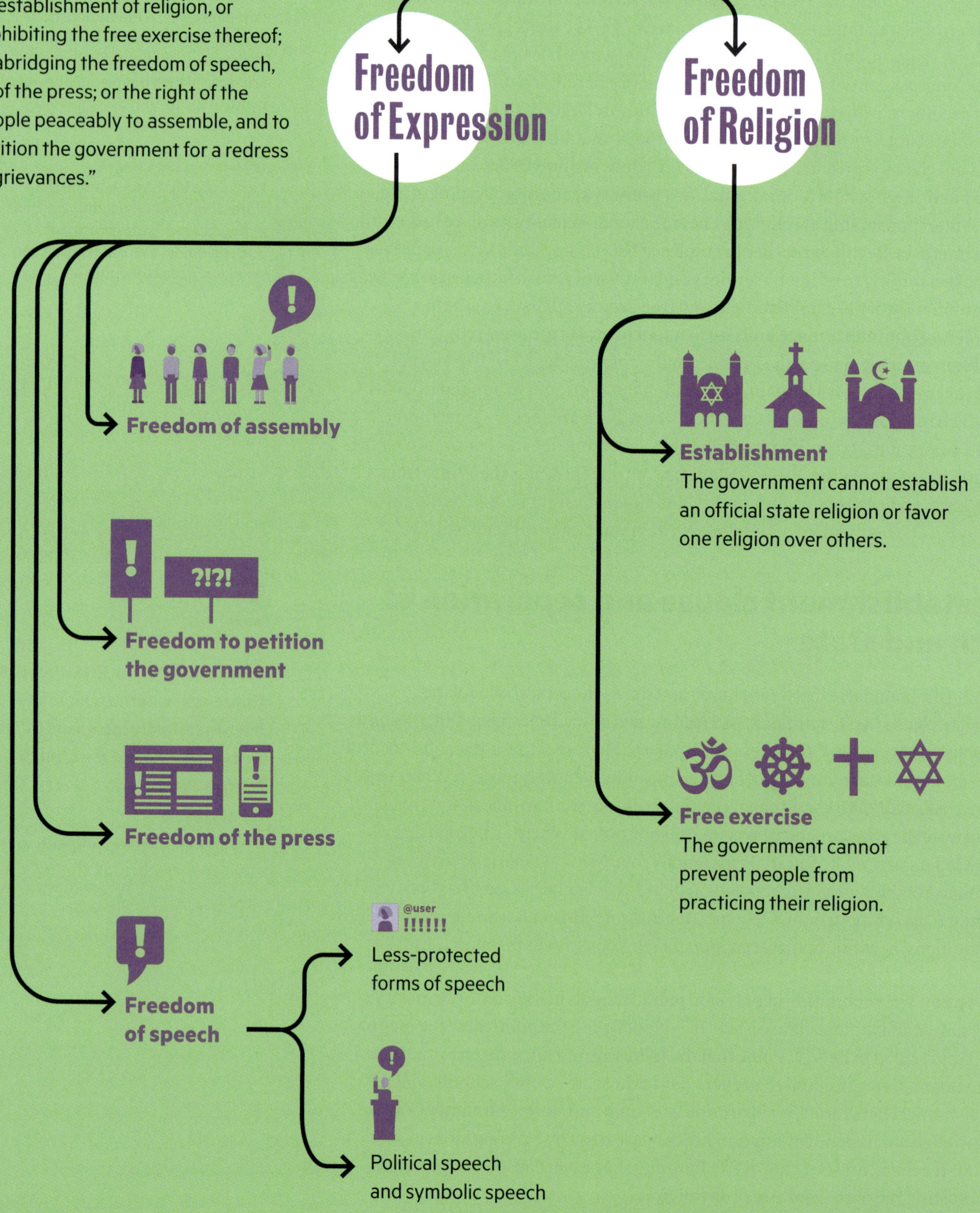

Freedom of Expression

Freedom of assembly

Freedom to petition the government

?!?!

Freedom of the press

Freedom of speech

- @user !!!!!! Less-protected forms of speech
- Political speech and symbolic speech

Freedom of Religion

Establishment
The government cannot establish an official state religion or favor one religion over others.

Free exercise
The government cannot prevent people from practicing their religion.

How it works: **in practice**

Balancing Interests and Drawing Lines: Government and Religion

While the different branches of the First Amendment on the opposite page are an accurate representation of the various aspects of our religious and expressive freedoms, in practice, the implementation of these civil liberties is more complicated.

Free Exercise

When they refused . . .

When Masterpiece Cakeshop **refused to make a wedding cake** for a same-sex couple . . .

They said . . .

The baker didn't have to bake the cake . . . for now (postponing a decision on the broader question).

Here's why.

In cases like these, **courts must balance religious freedom against other state interests**, such as freedom from discrimination.

Establishment Clause

Banned.

Since 1962 the Supreme Court has **banned school prayer as a violation of the establishment clause**.

What about . . . ?

But does the separation of church and state also apply to **a public school football coach who prays after a game with some players**? In 2022, the Court decided by a 6–3 vote that it did not.

It's tough.

The establishment clause often asks courts to **draw lines between what type of religious conduct is allowed** and what would be considered coercive behavior by a state actor (by compelling, for example, someone to pray).

In some cases, the free exercise and establishment clauses are in tension with one another. For example, while the establishment clause prohibits school-sponsored prayer, the free exercise clause guarantees that any student can pray at any time in school on their own, **as long as they are not bothering others**.

Critical Thinking

1. **Balancing interests can be tricky**. Consider these two scenarios in which competing interests are in play: Company policy restricts employees from wearing political T-shirts or buttons at work. A pharmacist denies birth control pills to a customer for religious reasons. Which (if either) do you think should be allowed? Why did you select the one(s) you did?
2. **Drawing lines for a given civil liberty** can also be difficult. What if a high school football coach knelt in a private prayer on the field after a game? Should that be allowed? Or, consider a different scenario: Should Congress be able to start its sessions with a prayer? Reference the First Amendment and its interpretations in your answer.

Over the next 60 years, Congress repeatedly tried, unsuccessfully, to amend the Constitution to allow school prayer. Meanwhile, the Court continued to take a hard line on school-sponsored prayer. In 1985, the Court struck down the practice of observing a mandatory one-minute moment of silence for "meditation or voluntary prayer" in the Alabama public schools, showing that it isn't the *words* of the prayer that are the problem, but the idea of prayer itself.[24] More recently, the Court said that benedictions or prayers at public school graduations and a school policy that allowed an elected student representative to lead a prayer at a high school football game also violated the establishment clause. The former established a strong "coercion test" that prohibited prayers that may appear to be voluntary (students are not required to attend their high school graduation) but in effect are compulsory; private, voluntary student prayer that is not disruptive is allowed.[25] Yet the Court has upheld the practice of opening every session of Congress with a prayer, has let stand without comment a lower-court ruling that allowed a prayer that was planned and led by students (rather than recited as school policy) at a high school graduation, and, most recently, in 2014 upheld prayers by voluntary chaplains for town board meetings in Greece, New York.[26] The latter case was especially significant because the legislative prayers were offered at town meetings that included residents, unlike the previously approved prayers that were intended for the elected leaders only. As discussed in the chapter opener, the Supreme Court mostly ruled to allow Joe Kennedy, a football coach, to pray after games.

Lemon test
The Supreme Court uses this test, established in *Lemon v. Kurtzman*, to determine whether a practice violates the First Amendment's establishment clause.

Aid to Religious Organizations and Religious Symbols The Court has had an even more difficult time coming up with principles to regulate government aid to religious organizations, either directly, through tax dollars, or indirectly, through the use of public space for religious symbols. One early attempt was known as the **Lemon test**, after one of the parties in a 1971 case involving government support for religious schools (*Lemon v. Kurtzman*). This case said that a practice violated the establishment clause if it (1) did not have a "secular legislative purpose," (2) either advanced or inhibited religion, or (3) fostered "an excessive government entanglement with religion."[27] The third part of the test was later found open to interpretation by lower courts and therefore led to conflicting rulings.

The Court started to move away from the Lemon test in a 1984 case involving a crèche owned by the city of Pawtucket, Rhode Island, and displayed in a park owned by a nonprofit corporation. The Court allowed the Nativity display, saying: "The Constitution does not require complete separation of church and state; it affirmatively mandates accommodation, not merely tolerance, of all religions, and forbids hostility toward any."[28] This "endorsement test" simply says that government action is unconstitutional if a "reasonable observer" would think that the action either endorses or disapproves of religion. Later rulings upheld similar religious displays, especially if they conformed to what observers have labeled the "three plastic animals rule"—if the baby Jesus is surrounded by Rudolph the red-nosed reindeer and other secular symbols, the overall display is considered sufficiently nonreligious to pass constitutional muster.[29]

More recently, in a 2019 case the Court upheld the American Legion's right to display a 40-foot cross at a World War I memorial on state property in Bladensburg, Maryland, saying that *Lemon* should not apply in cases that "involve the use, for ceremonial, celebratory, or commemorative purposes, of words or symbols with religious associations." Instead, the Court ruled, "The cross is undoubtedly a Christian symbol, but that fact should not blind us to everything else that the Bladensburg Cross has come to represent. . . . [D]estroying or defacing the Cross that has stood undisturbed for nearly a century would not be neutral and would not further the ideals of respect and tolerance embodied in the First Amendment."[30] Three justices wanted to completely overturn *Lemon* and that finally happened in the case discussed in the chapter opener. Instead of Lemon's "endorsement test," the Court said the Establishment Clause must be interpreted by "reference to historical practices and understandings" consistent with the intentions of the Founders.[31]

In cases involving funding for religious schools, the Court has applied the accommodationist perspective by looking more favorably on providing tax dollars to students' families to subsidize tuition costs at religious schools than on funding parochial schools directly. For example, the Court upheld an Ohio school voucher program that distributed scholarships to needy students so they could attend the Cleveland school of their choice, including private religious schools. The Court said the program did not violate the establishment clause because it allowed students and their families "to exercise genuine choice among options public and private, secular and religious."[32] Critics of the decision pointed out that 96 percent of the students participating in the scholarship program were enrolled in religiously affiliated schools, which amounted to state sponsorship of religious education, something that the Court had not previously allowed. In 2011, the Court expanded taxpayer support for religious education when it upheld an Arizona law that provides state tax credits for contributions to organizations that provide tuition for religious schools.[33] The Court has also ruled that it is acceptable to use federal funds to buy computers and other educational equipment to be used in public and private schools for "secular, neutral, and nonideological programs"[34] and tax dollars for a sign language interpreter for a deaf student who attended a parochial school.[35]

In a landmark 2020 decision, *Espinoza v. Montana Department of Revenue*, the Supreme Court ruled 5–4 that under the free exercise clause, a state could not prevent the use of state-based, publicly funded scholarship funds meant for private school tuition from being applied toward religious school tuition. The case was brought by Montana parents who qualified for these income-based scholarships, and whose children attended a Christian school. The state supreme court ruled that the scholarship funds could not be applied toward the religious school tuition because of a Montana state rule barring the use of "any direct or indirect appropriations or payment" to any religious organizations or schools affiliated with religious organizations. But the U.S. Supreme Court said that the program violated the free exercise clause, as it "bars religious schools from public benefits solely because of the religious character of the schools" and "also bars parents who wish to send their children to a religious school from those same benefits, again solely because of the religious character of the school."[36] The Court reached the same conclusion in a case from Maine, but with a stronger endorsement of free exercise over establishment: in this case, the state attempted to prevent taxpayers' dollars from supporting religious education (in a program that supported students in rural areas of the state not served by public schools), rather than just schools with a religious affiliation (as in the Montana case). However, the Court said that if the state provides funds for rural students to attend private schools, religious schools could not be excluded, even if daily religious services were part of the curriculum.[37]

The free exercise clause

While the freedom of belief is absolute, freedom of religious conduct cannot be unrestricted. That is, you can believe whatever you want without government interference, but if you *act* on those beliefs, the government may regulate your behavior. And while the government has restricted religious conduct in dozens of cases, the freedom of religion has been among the most consistently protected civil liberties.

Hundreds of cases have come before the Court in the area of the free exercise of religion.[38] Here are some examples of the questions they addressed: May Amish

Wisconsin v. Yoder
A 1972 case in which the Supreme Court held that compelling Amish students to attend school past the eighth grade violates the free exercise clause. The ruling opened the door to homeschooling, which is a common practice today.

parents be forced to send their children to schools beyond the eighth grade? (No, as established in **Wisconsin v. Yoder** in 1972.) May religion serve as the basis for attaining "conscientious objector" status and avoiding the draft? (Generally yes, but with many qualifications.) Is animal sacrifice as part of a religious ceremony protected by the First Amendment? (Generally yes.) May Mormons have multiple wives? (No.) May people be forced to work on Friday night and Saturday if those are their days of worship? (No.) Does the First Amendment protect distribution of religious leaflets on public streets? And religious meetings in public parks? (Yes, for both, but the latter is subject to "time, manner, and place" restrictions.) May religious dress be regulated? (Generally not, but in some contexts, such as the military, yes.) Are all prison inmates entitled to hold religious services (apparently yes, but this is still an open question) and grow short beards? (Yes.) Are religious organizations subject to child labor laws? (Yes.) Are death row inmates allowed to have their pastor touch them and pray aloud in the execution chamber? (Yes.) Whew! Keep in mind that this list is by no means exhaustive.

One particular case, brought by plaintiffs who had been fired for using peyote as part of a religious ceremony and then denied unemployment benefits because they had broken the law, had broad implications that defined the general basis for government restrictions of religious expression. The Court ultimately ruled that the state of Oregon had not violated the free exercise clause in denying the plaintiffs unemployment benefits. More significantly, with this ruling the Court announced a new interpretation of the free exercise clause: the government does not need a "compelling interest" in regulating a particular behavior to justify a law that limits a religious practice; it only needs a demonstration that the law in question was a "neutral law of general applicability."[39] In other words, after this decision it would be easier for the government to limit the exercise of religion because the Court would no longer require a "compelling" reason for the restrictions.

Congress responded by passing the Religious Freedom Restoration Act (RFRA) in 1993, reinstating the need to demonstrate a "compelling state interest" before limiting religious freedoms; the act also specified exceptions to the Controlled Substances Act to allow the use of peyote in religious ceremonies. After several cases and congressional actions, the Court made it clear that it would have the final word in deciding when a compelling interest is required in order to limit religious practice.[40] The Court relied on this standard in the controversial 2014 case involving the family-owned Hobby Lobby stores, ruling that a "closely held" private corporation could not be forced to provide contraception to women under the Affordable Care Act if there was a "less restrictive" means available to have the insurance provide it.[41] This was the first time that a corporation was given First Amendment protections based on the religious beliefs of the owners of the corporation. In 2020, the Court extended the opt-out options to private employers on religious or moral grounds. The Court also expanded religious freedom when it approved, for the first time in 2017, direct government payments to a church in support of a secular purpose (in this case, funds for a playground in a church-run day-care center). The Court ruled that churches should have equal access to state grants made available to fund neutral, secular programs.[42]

The Court had an opportunity to overrule the 1990 *Employment Division v. Smith* decision that "neutral laws of general applicability" did not violate the free exercise clause, even if it did limit a religious practice, in a case involving Philadelphia's law that adoption agencies cannot discriminate against gay parents. The Court ruled in favor of Catholic Social Services, which was challenging the law, but did so on narrow grounds that did not overturn *Smith*.[43] But then, in what one expert called the "most important free exercise case since 1990,"[44] the Court blocked California's COVID-related ban

Cake shop owner Jack Phillips did not want to bake a wedding cake for Charlie Craig and David Mullins because it would have violated his religious beliefs. In a narrow ruling that did not settle the broader free exercise question, the Court sided with the baker because he had not been treated fairly by the commission that heard his case.

on in-home religious gatherings, ruling "government regulations are not neutral and generally applicable, and therefore trigger strict scrutiny under the Free Exercise Clause, whenever they treat any comparable secular activity more favorably than religious exercise." That is, because California allowed people to ride a bus, get a haircut, or go shopping during the pandemic, it would have to allow people to gather in homes for Bible study.[45] However, the Court did uphold the Biden administration's mandate to require vaccinations for health care workers, even if the workers claimed it violated their religious beliefs.[46]

In a highly anticipated case, the Court was faced with a difficult question concerning the civil rights of a same-sex couple and the religious beliefs of a cake shop owner. The baker had refused to bake a cake for the couple, saying that doing so would violate his religious beliefs. The Court avoided ruling on this central question because the Colorado Civil Rights Commission, which initially heard the case, did not treat religion in a neutral manner and did not give the baker a fair hearing. While concluding that the baker did not have to bake the cake because of the commission's biased behavior, the Court affirmed that the free exercise clause will not provide a basis for such refusals of service when there is not the expression of hostility to religion and that LGBTQIA+ people have the right to "equal access to goods and services under a neutral and generally applicable public accommodations law."[47]

"Why Should I Care?"

Being familiar with these freedoms and the controversies around them is important because they concern the most deeply personal freedoms debated today. Would you, or do you, send your children to religious schools? Should the government pay for it? If you attend a public college or university, should it be allowed to organize a prayer before a football or basketball game? Should business owners be able to deny equal access to a service (baking a wedding cake) or a public program (health insurance) because of their religious beliefs?

DESCRIBE THE MAJOR FIRST AMENDMENT LIBERTIES RELATED TO FREEDOM OF SPEECH

Freedom of speech, assembly, and the press

As we noted earlier, defining the scope of our civil liberties depends on balancing interests and drawing lines. This is especially true of the First Amendment's freedom of speech, which can be envisioned on a continuum from most to least protected types of speech based on the Supreme Court cases that have tested their limits.

Generally protected expression

Any time you attend a religious service or a political rally, post a tweet, write a blog post or letter to the editor, or express a political idea, you are protected by the First Amendment. However, the nature of this protection is continually evolving due to political forces and shifting constitutional interpretations. For much of our nation's history, freedom of speech and freedom of the press were not strongly protected. Only recently have the courts developed a complex continuum ranging from strongly protected political speech to less protected speech.

Standards for Protection The basis for the continuum of protected speech is rooted in the content of the speech. The Supreme Court has interpreted the law to mean that content-based regulation of speech is not permissible (unless it falls into one of the categories of exceptions we outline later). For example, the Court struck down a local ordinance that banned picketing outside schools except for labor picketing.[48] This ordinance was deemed to be content-based regulation because it favored one form of speech (from labor unions) over others. Such regulation is subject to the **strict scrutiny** standard of judicial review, which means the regulation must be narrowly tailored so that it is the least restrictive on an individual's fundamental right to free speech and the government must demonstrate a compelling state interest to curtail the speech. In most cases, such strict scrutiny by the courts means that the speech will be protected and the regulation will be struck down. If a regulation is content neutral and does not favor any given viewpoint over another, then it is subject to the less demanding **intermediate scrutiny** standard. This means that the government must demonstrate only a substantial interest in curtailing the speech, the interest must be unrelated to the content of the speech, and there must be alternative opportunities for communication.[49]

strict scrutiny
The highest level of scrutiny the courts can use when determining whether a law is constitutional. To meet this standard, the law or policy must be shown to serve a "compelling state interest" or goal, it must be narrowly tailored to achieve that goal, and it must be the least restrictive means of achieving that goal.

intermediate scrutiny
The middle level of scrutiny the courts can use when determining whether a law is constitutional. To meet this standard, the law or policy must be "content neutral," must further an important government interest in a way that is "substantially related" to that interest, and must use means that are a close fit to the government's goal and not substantially broader than is necessary to accomplish that goal.

Political Speech Freedom of speech got off to a rocky start when Congress passed the Alien and Sedition Acts in 1798. The controversial Sedition Act made it a crime to "write, print, utter or publish . . . any false, scandalous and malicious writing or writings against the government of the United States." Supporters of the acts claimed they were necessary to strengthen the national government in response to the French Revolution, but in reality they were an attempt by the governing Federalist Party to neutralize the opposition—the Democratic-Republican Party. As many as 25 people, mostly newspaper editors, were tried under the law and 10 were jailed, including Benjamin Franklin's grandson. The outcry against the laws helped Thomas Jefferson win the presidential election in 1800. Jefferson pardoned the convicted editors, Congress repealed one of the acts in 1802, and the other acts were allowed to expire before the Supreme Court had a chance to rule that they were unconstitutional.

World War I prompted the harshest crackdowns on free speech since the Sedition Act of 1798. The most important case from this period involved the general secretary of the Socialist Party, Charles Schenck, who opposed U.S. involvement in the war. He had printed a leaflet urging young men to resist the draft. Schenck was arrested under the Espionage Act of 1917, which prohibited "interfering with military or naval operations," including the draft. He appealed all the way to the Supreme Court, arguing that the First Amendment permitted him to protest the war and to urge others to resist the draft. But the Court sustained his conviction, noting that free speech is not an absolute right:

The most stringent protection of free speech would not protect a man in falsely shouting fire in a theatre and causing a panic. . . . The question in every case is whether the words used are used in such circumstances and are of such a nature as to create a clear and present danger that they will bring about the substantive evils that Congress has a right to prevent.[50]

This **clear and present danger test** meant that the government could suppress speech it deemed dangerous (in this instance, preventing the government from fighting the war). However, critics of the decision argue that Schenck's actions were not dangerous for the country and should have been allowed.[51]

clear and present danger test
Established in *Schenck v. United States*, this test allowed the government to restrict certain types of speech deemed dangerous.

Justice Oliver Wendell Holmes, author of the *Schenck v. United States* (1919) decision and the clear and present danger test, had a change of heart and dissented in a case later that year that upheld the conviction of six anarchists who supported the cause of the Bolsheviks in Russia. In one of the most famous statements of the importance of the freedom of speech, he touted the "free trade in ideas," saying, "The best test of truth is the power of the thought to get itself accepted in the competition of the market. . . . [W]e should be eternally vigilant against attempts to check the expression of opinion that we loathe and believe to be fraught with death."[52] This notion of the marketplace of ideas in which good ideas triumph over bad is still central to modern defenses of the First Amendment.

Restriction of free thought and free speech is the most dangerous of all subversions. It is the one un-American act that could most easily defeat us.

—William O. Douglas, former Supreme Court justice

Over the next several decades, the Court struggled to draw the line between dangerous speech and words that were simply unpopular. During the Red Scare of the late 1940s and early 1950s, the hunt for communists in government was led by Senator Joe McCarthy, and the Court had many opportunities to defend unpopular speech, but for the most part it declined to do so. For example, in 1951 the Court upheld the conviction of 11 members of the Communist Party under the Smith Act, which banned the advocacy of force or violence against the United States.[53]

Then, in 1969, the Court established a strong protection for free speech, superseding the clear and present danger test, that still holds today. This case involved a leader of the Ku Klux Klan who made a threatening speech at a cross-burning rally that was subsequently shown on television. Twelve hooded figures were shown, many with weapons. The speech said that "revengence [*sic*]" might be taken if "our president, our Congress, our Supreme Court continues to suppress the white, Caucasian race." It continued, "We are marching on Congress July the Fourth, four hundred thousand strong." The Klan leader was convicted under the Ohio law banning "sabotage, violence, or unlawful methods of terrorism as a means of accomplishing industrial or political reform," but the Court unanimously reversed his conviction, arguing that threatening speech could not be suppressed just because it sounded dangerous. Specifically, the **direct incitement test** holds that speech is protected "except where such advocacy is directed to inciting or producing imminent lawless action and is likely to incite or produce such action."[54] Under this standard, most, if not all, of the sedition convictions and limitations on speech during World War I and the Red Scare would have been overturned.

direct incitement test
Established in *Brandenburg v. Ohio*, this test protects threatening speech under the First Amendment unless that speech aims to and is likely to cause imminent "lawless action."

Should free speech be protected even when the ideas are offensive? The Supreme Court ruled that the Westboro Baptist Church had a right to protest at military funerals, even though many Americans found the arguments and approach of the church members deeply offensive.

Perhaps the strongest example of protecting unpopular speech comes from the case of the Westboro Baptist Church (WBC). Between 2005 and 2011 members of the WBC protested at hundreds of funerals of members of the armed services who were killed in Iraq and Afghanistan. However, these are not typical antiwar protests. Instead, the protesters claim that the troops' deaths were God's punishment for "the homosexual lifestyle of soul-damning, nation-destroying filth." The church and its members have drawn strong reactions and counterprotests for their confrontational approach at the military funerals, including their use of signs that say "God Hates Fags," "Thank God for Dead Soldiers," "God Killed Your Sons," and "God Hates America." Critics, including many veterans groups and attorneys general from 48 states, argue that the protests should not be considered protected speech under the First Amendment. The Veterans of Foreign Wars issued a statement saying, "In a time of profound grief and emotional vulnerability, these personal attacks are an affront of the most egregious kind." However, in 2011 the Supreme Court ruled 8–1 that the WBC's protests were protected speech.[55]

symbolic speech
Nonverbal expression, such as the use of signs or symbols. It benefits from many of the same constitutional protections as verbal speech because of its expressive value.

Tinker v. Des Moines School District
In 1969, the Supreme Court ruled that students may wear armbands to protest the Vietnam War. The Court noted that the students "were not disruptive and did not impinge upon the rights of others" and therefore their conduct was protected by the First and Fourteenth Amendments.

Symbolic Speech The use of signs, symbols, or other unspoken acts or methods to communicate in a political manner—**symbolic speech**—enjoys many of the same protections as regular speech. For example, during the Vietnam War the Court protected the right of a war protester to wear an American flag patch sewn on the seat of his pants,[56] high school students' right to wear an armband to protest the war (***Tinker v. Des Moines School District***, 1969),[57] and an individual's right to tape a peace symbol on the flag and fly it upside down outside an apartment window.[58] Lower courts had convicted these protesters under state laws that protected the American flag or under a school policy that prohibited wearing armbands to protest the Vietnam War. In the flag desecration case involving the peace symbol, the Court stated that protected "speech" need not be verbal: "[T]here can be little doubt that appellant communicated through the use of symbols."[59]

A 1989 case provided the strongest protection for symbolic speech yet. The case involved a man who burned a flag outside the 1984 Republican National Convention in Texas, chanting along with other protesters, "America the red, white, and blue, we spit on you. You stand for plunder, you will go under." The Court refrained from critiquing the jingle, but its 5–4 decision overturned the man's conviction under

The American flag is a popular target for protesters: it has been spat upon, shredded, turned into underwear, and burned. Here, protesters burn a U.S. flag as they march through New York City, protesting institutional racism during a Black Lives Matter march in the summer of 2020.

Texas's flag desecration law on the grounds that symbolic political speech is protected by the First Amendment.[60] In response to this unpopular decision, Congress passed the Flag Protection Act of 1989, which the Court also struck down as an unconstitutional infringement on political expression.[61] Congress then attempted to pass a constitutional amendment to overturn the Court decision; the House passed the amendment six times between 1995 and 2005 with the necessary two-thirds vote, but each time the measure failed by a narrow margin in the Senate (by just one vote in 2006). President Trump reignited this debate shortly after he was elected, tweeting, "Nobody should be allowed to burn the American flag—if they do, there must be consequences—perhaps loss of citizenship or year in jail!" However, Republican leaders in Congress have not been interested in revisiting this fight.[62]

Although the Court has protected flag burning and other forms of symbolic speech, there are limits, especially when the symbolic speech conflicts with another substantial governmental interest. Here the critical test is whether the action can be regulated for important reasons unrelated to ideas. If so, then the "intermediate scrutiny" standard will apply. For example, Vietnam War protesters who burned their draft cards were not protected by the First Amendment because their actions interfered with Congress's constitutional authority to "raise and support" armies, and the purpose of the draft was not to suppress speech.[63] The Court also ruled in 2015 that states may ban the use of the Confederate battle flag on state vanity plates. The Sons of Confederate Veterans argued that the battle flag honored their southern heritage, but the state of Texas said it was offensive.[64] The debate over the flag intensified after a "Unite the Right" rally in Charlottesville, Virginia, in which a White supremacist killed a woman and injured 19 others, and demonstrators prominently displayed the Confederate battle flag. According to the Southern Poverty Law Center, at least 312 statues and memorials to Confederate leaders were removed since 2015.[65]

DID YOU KNOW?

73%

of college-educated Black Americans and 45 percent of college-educated White Americans view the Confederate battle flag primarily as a symbol of racism.

Source: YouGov

Money as Speech Spending money in political campaigns may also be protected by the First Amendment, since it provides the means for more conventional types of political speech. Here the central question is whether the government can control campaign contributions and spending for a broader public purpose such as lessening the potential for corruption, or whether such laws violate the First Amendment rights of candidates or their supporters. You probably have heard the old saying "Money talks," which implies that money is speech. Given the importance of advertising in modern campaigns, limitations on raising and spending money could limit the ability of candidates and groups to reach voters with their message. The Court has walked a tightrope on this one, balancing the public interest in honest and ethical elections and the First Amendment rights of candidates and their advocates. The Court has upheld individual candidates' right to spend their own money in federal elections, but presidential candidates give up that right if they accept federal campaign funds (taxpayers' money) in a presidential election. Also, candidates in federal elections are subject to limits on the types and size of contributions they can receive, and they must report all contributions and spending to the Federal Election Commission.[66]

The Bipartisan Campaign Reform Act, which went into effect for the 2004 elections, included a "Millionaires' Amendment" that lifted restrictions on campaign contributions for candidates whose opponents spent more than $350,000 of their own money in the election. This attempt to level the campaign finance playing field was struck down by the Supreme Court in 2008 as a violation of wealthy candidates' First Amendment rights.[67] In 2010 the Court also extended First Amendment rights to corporations and labor unions that want to spend money on campaign ads, and in 2014 it struck down the aggregate (collective) limits placed on individual contributions to candidates and parties (these cases are discussed in more detail in Chapter 9).[68] However, the Court upheld a ban on unlimited "soft money" contributions because they were seen by the Court as the type of contribution with the most potential for corruption.[69]

Student fees as a form of symbolic speech came up in a case in 2000 involving student activity fees at the University of Wisconsin. A group of students argued that they should not have to pay fees to fund groups whose activities they opposed, including a student environmental group, a gay and bisexual student center, a community legal office, an AIDS support network, a campus women's center, and the Wisconsin Student Public Interest Research Group. The Court ruled that mandatory student fees could continue to support the full range of groups as long as the process for allocating money was "viewpoint neutral." The Court also said that student referendums that could add or cut money for specific groups violated viewpoint neutrality. The potential for the majority to censor unpopular views was unacceptable to the Court, since "the whole theory of viewpoint neutrality is that minority views are treated with the same respect as are majority views."[70]

hate speech
Expression that is offensive or abusive, particularly in terms of race, gender, or sexual orientation. It is currently protected under the First Amendment.

Hate Speech Whether or not freedom of speech should apply to **hate speech** has been a controversial issue both on college campuses and in society generally. Do people have a right to say things that are offensive or abusive, especially in terms of race, gender, and sexual orientation? By the mid-1990s, more than 350 public colleges and universities said no by regulating some forms of hate speech.[71]

Many of these speech codes were struck down in federal court, but in the last few years the issue has resurfaced on many college campuses. A variety of "campus climate" issues consumed dozens of schools. Controversial speakers such as Richard Spencer and Milo Yiannopoulos were prevented from speaking on several college campuses. Some see this as "political correctness" run amok, and others call for the creation of "safe spaces" on campuses and limits on hate speech. The president of the University of Missouri resigned in 2015 after students, including the football team, said that he was racially insensitive and not open to their demands for a more inclusive environment on campus. In 2017, Indiana University students petitioned to remove part of a mural that depicts the history of the state using imagery of a burning cross and white-hooded Klansmen. University leaders compromised by leaving the artwork but saying that classes would no longer be held in the lecture hall with the mural.[72]

Drawing the line between protected hate speech and threatening speech that may be limited became especially fraught in the 2023–2024 academic year when protests erupted on college campuses concerning the conflict in Gaza. Most protests supported the Palestinian cause, but divisions quickly emerged concerning antisemitic statements. The presidents of Penn and Harvard were forced to resign after failing to say that calls for the genocide of Jews violated their universities' codes of conduct.[73] Other college presidents were censured by their faculty for cracking down on the pro-Palestinian protests and some for being too sympathetic to the cause.[74]

Another significant issue combines the topics of symbolic speech and hate speech. Can a person who burned a cross on a Black family's lawn be convicted under a city ordinance that prohibits conduct in St. Paul, Minnesota, that "arouses anger, alarm, or resentment in others on the basis of race, color, creed, religion, or gender"? Or is the ordinance an unconstitutional limit on First Amendment rights? The Court said the cross burner could be punished for arson, terrorism, trespassing, or other violations of the law, but he could not be convicted under this ordinance because it was overly broad and vague. The Court said: "Let there be no mistake about our belief that burning a cross in someone's front yard is reprehensible. But St. Paul has sufficient means at its disposal to prevent such behavior without adding the First Amendment to the fire."[75] The city ordinance was unconstitutional because it took selective aim at a disfavored message; it constituted "viewpoint discrimination." However, the Court has since upheld more carefully worded bans of cross burning. Eleven years after the St. Paul case, the Court ruled that Virginia could prohibit cross burning if there was intent to intimidate. The Court also noted that the law was content neutral because it did not engage in viewpoint discrimination: any burning of a cross in a threatening context was illegal.[76]

Speech on the Internet Internet hate speech has become increasingly controversial in recent years. Cyberbullying through social media like Instagram, Twitter, Facebook, and Reddit precipitated several suicides. In 2013, Facebook cracked down on offensive content that glorified violence against women, such as pages with headlines like "Violently Raping Your Friend Just for Laughs."[77] Facebook's "community standards" have a more restrictive definition of hate speech than is allowed by the direct incitement test. While Facebook makes a distinction between humor and serious speech, it "do[es] not permit individuals or groups to attack others based on their race, ethnicity, national origin, religion, sex, gender, sexual orientation, disability or medical condition."[78] This led law professor Jeff Rosen to conclude that "today, lawyers at Google, YouTube, Facebook, and Twitter have more power over who can speak and who can be heard than any president, judge, or monarch."[79] This may sound like hyperbole, but he is right: corporations are not restricted by the First Amendment (which, after all, says "*Congress* shall make no law . . ."). So if Facebook and other social media want to restrict hate speech, they can. Although free speech advocates are concerned about restrictions on Internet hate speech, civil rights groups such as the Anti-Defamation League, the Leadership Conference on Civil and Human Rights, and the National Organization for Women all support the move. Another controversial area of speech on the Internet is political ads. Late in 2019, Twitter announced that it was banning all political ads for the 2020 elections, while Google restricted "micro-targeting" based on ideology, party, or voting history. Facebook, on the other hand, still allows political ads, but with warnings if they are deemed untrue.[80] After the January 6, 2021, attack on the Capitol, Donald Trump was permanently banned from Twitter for false claims he continued to make about the election being stolen. Rep. Marjorie Taylor Greene

There has been debate around free speech online, as well as in public. During the pandemic, social media sites, including Facebook and Twitter, struggled to control the flow of misinformation. As a result, Twitter decided to block users who shared fake news harmful to public safety. Representative Marjorie Taylor Greene (R-GA) was temporarily blocked for repeatedly posting without evidence that vaccines were harmful, including, "Thousands of people are reporting very serious life changing vaccine side effects from taking the vaccine."

Brandi Levy was reprimanded by her high school's cheerleading team for posting a message on social media containing language that was deemed inappropriate, even though the message was not posted while she was at school. The case ultimately made it to the Supreme Court, which ruled that in punishing her, the school had violated Levy's First Amendment rights.

(R-GA) also was permanently banned for various false claims, while Sen. Rand Paul (R-KY), Sen. Ron Johnson (R-WI), and other politicians have received temporary suspensions from Twitter, Facebook, and YouTube.[81]

While social media companies have great latitude in what they permit online, the government has limited power to regulate access to social media. In 2017, the Court struck down a North Carolina law that prohibited sex offenders from accessing or using social media sites, saying that these sites are the "principal sources for knowing current events, checking ads for employment, speaking and listening in the modern public square, and otherwise exploring the vast realms of human thought and knowledge." Therefore, limiting access to social media would prevent the "legitimate exercise of First Amendment rights."[82] Another recent case involved Brandi Levy, who was cut from the varsity cheerleading team and then posted an F-bomb-filled message to Snapchat. She was later reprimanded and suspended from the junior varsity team for the comments even though she wasn't in school at the time. The Court said the school could not regulate her off-campus speech because it had not disrupted school activities.[83]

Freedom of Assembly The right to assemble peaceably has been consistently protected by the Supreme Court.[84] However, when peaceful protests concerning criminal justice reform after the murder of George Floyd (this will be discussed in more detail in the next chapter) turned violent, many states responded by placing limits on assembly. The International Center for Not-for-Profit Law has tracked 235 bills in 45 states since 2017 that would restrict the right to peaceful assembly, with 36 having been enacted into law.[85] One of the most restrictive, an "anti-riot law" in Florida, was barred from being enforced by a federal judge who said the law "could effectively criminalize the protected speech of hundreds, if not thousands of law-abiding Floridians," arguing that the law's definition of a riot is "vague to the point of unconstitutionality."[86] Critically, thousands of peaceful protesters could be defined as "rioters" if some other protesters at the same event become violent. The Supreme Court will eventually have to sort out what type of limitations states can place on the First Amendment right to assemble.

While broad protection is provided for peaceable assemblies, governments may regulate the time, manner, and place of expression as long as these regulations do

After the killing of George Floyd, an unarmed Black man by the police in Minnesota, peaceful protests turned violent when protesters came into conflict with local police. In Cleveland, Ohio, police disbursed a crowd of thousands with tear gas near downtown. Anti-riot legislation would criminalize the act of peaceful assembly like this.

not favor certain groups or messages over others. For example, the Court ruled that anti-abortion protesters were not allowed to picket a doctor's home in Brookfield, Wisconsin, on the grounds that the ordinance banning all residential picketing was content neutral; there was a government interest in preserving the "sanctity of the home, the one retreat to which men and women can repair to escape from the tribulations of their daily pursuits."[87] "Time, manner, and place" restrictions also may be invoked for practical reasons. For instance, if the Ku Klux Klan planned to hold a march around a football stadium on the day of a game, the city council could deny it a permit and could suggest that it choose another day that would not interfere with game day activities. In a case involving a speech by white supremacist Richard Spencer at the University of Florida, the school initially turned down Spencer's request to speak on campus just a month after the tragic events in Charlottesville, saying that it would not have time to provide adequate security for the event. However, it approved the talk for a date a month later.[88]

The legal standard for "time, manner, and place" regulations is that they must be "reasonable." This standard came into play in a 2014 case in which the Court ruled that a Massachusetts state law creating a 35-foot buffer zone around entrances to abortion clinics violated the First Amendment. While the buffer zone was content neutral, it was unreasonable because it was more restrictive than necessary to allow access to the clinics.[89] While the "reasonableness" standard is vague, it allows the courts to balance the right to assemble against other practical considerations.

Freedom of the Press The task of balancing interests is central to many First Amendment cases involving freedom of the press. Which is more important, the First Amendment freedom of the press to disclose details about current events or the Sixth Amendment right to a fair trial, which may require keeping important information out of the public eye? When do national security concerns prevail over journalists' right to keep citizens informed? The general issue here is **prior restraint**, the government's right to prevent the media from publishing something.

prior restraint
A limit on freedom of the press that allows the government to prohibit the media from publishing certain materials.

Prior restraint has never been clearly defined by the Court, but several landmark cases have set a very high bar for applying it. In 1971, the Pentagon Papers case (***New York Times Co. v. United States***) involved disclosure of parts of the top-secret

New York Times Co. v. United States
The Supreme Court ruled in 1971 that the government could not prevent the publication of the Pentagon Papers, which revealed lies about the progress of the war in Vietnam.

report on internal planning for the Vietnam War. This incredibly divided case had nine separate written opinions! In a 6–3 decision the Court said that the government could not prevent the publication of the Pentagon Papers, but at least five justices supported the view that, under some circumstances, the government could use prior restraint—although they could not agree on the standard.[90] For some of the justices, a crucial consideration was the Pentagon Papers' revelation that the U.S. government had lied about its involvement in and the progress of the Vietnam War. Justice Hugo Black noted the importance of this point, saying, "Only a free and unrestrained press can effectively expose deception in government."[91]

The freedom of the press is one of the greatest bulwarks of liberty, and can never be restrained but by despotic governments.

—George Mason, politician and father of the Bill of Rights

The debate over restraining the media heated up in 2010, when WikiLeaks released a classified video of an air strike in Baghdad showing U.S. pilots mistakenly firing on two Reuters reporters and more than 91,000 classified battlefield incident reports from Iraq and Afghanistan and U.S. State Department cables. All of these documents had been leaked by U.S. Army Private First Class Chelsea Manning. This sensational leaking ratcheted up the stakes, and some members of Congress called the leaks treason and urged for prosecution (Manning was tried and convicted in a military court for violations of the Espionage Act and for copying and releasing classified information; she served seven years in prison before President Obama pardoned her, commuting the rest of Manning's 35-year sentence).

President Trump frequently expressed frustration about leaks to the media and aggressively used the Espionage Act to try to stop leaks. Prosecuting government employees for leaking information had been relatively rare until recently; President Obama did it a few times and President Trump pursued eight prosecutions under the law (ironically, Trump was indicted in 2023 under the Act with 31 counts of unauthorized possession of national defense information). It is illegal to leak classified information and the law doesn't allow a balancing test to assess whether the leak was in the public's interest (as in the Pentagon Papers case). First Amendment advocates worry that this "gives the government enormous leverage over journalists and, in the United States, provides them with a detour around First Amendment concerns."[92]

The forms of expression discussed in this section—speech, assembly, and press—all have strong protections based on the First Amendment. The strongest protections

Through her work as an intelligence analyst for the U.S. military, Chelsea Manning downloaded thousands of classified videos, diplomatic cables, reports, and other information that she then gave to the website WikiLeaks in 2010. Though she was released from prison in 2017, Manning has since spent additional time in jail for refusing to testify in additional WikiLeaks-related investigations.

are for content-based expression—that is, if a regulation is trying to limit *what* can be said, the Court applies the strict scrutiny standard and usually strikes down the regulation. However, there are exceptions, such as speech that directly incites an imminent danger. If the regulation is content neutral and does not favor one viewpoint over another, then it is easier to uphold. But even then, the government must have a substantial reason for limiting expression.

Less protected speech and publications

Some forms of speech do not warrant the same level of protection as political speech because they do not contribute to public debate or express ideas that have important social value. Four categories of speech may be more easily regulated by the government than political speech: fighting words, slander and libel, commercial speech, and obscenity. The first two categories may be prevented by the state if certain conditions are met, and the second two receive some protection, but not as much as political speech.

Fighting Words Governments may regulate **fighting words**, "which by their very utterance inflict injury or tend to incite an immediate breach of the peace."[93] Such laws must be narrowly written; it is not acceptable to ban all foul language, and the prohibited speech must target a single person rather than a group. Moreover, the question of whether certain words provoke a backlash depends on the reaction of the targeted person. Inflammatory words directed at Pope Francis would not be fighting words because he would turn the other cheek, whereas the same words yelled at musician Kanye West or actor Alec Baldwin *would* be fighting words because he would probably deck you. The Court clarified the test based on "what persons of common intelligence would understand to be words likely to cause an average addressee to fight."[94] While this provides a somewhat objective test, the fighting words doctrine has still been difficult to apply.

fighting words
Forms of expression that "by their very utterance" can incite violence. These can be regulated by the government but are often difficult to define.

Slander and Libel A more extensive line of cases prohibiting speech concerns **slander**, spoken false statements that damage someone's reputation (defamation), and **libel**, written statements that do the same thing. As in many areas of First Amendment law, it is difficult to draw the line between permissible speech and slander or libel. The current legal standard distinguishes between speech about a public figure, such as a politician or celebrity, and about a regular person. In short, it is much more difficult for public figures to prove libel. A public figure has to demonstrate that the defamatory statement was made with "actual malice" and "with knowledge that it was false or with reckless disregard of whether it was false or not."[95]

slander
Spoken false statements that damage a person's reputation. They can be regulated by the government but are often difficult to distinguish from permissible speech.

libel
Written false statements that damage a person's reputation. They can be regulated by the government but are often difficult to distinguish from permissible speech.

One of the most famous libel cases was brought against *Hustler* magazine by the Reverend Jerry Falwell, a famous televangelist and political activist. Falwell sued *Hustler* for libel and emotional distress after the magazine published a parody of a liquor advertisement depicting him in a "drunken incestuous rendezvous with his mother in an outhouse" (this quote is from the Supreme Court case).[96] The lower court said that the parody wasn't believable, so *Hustler* couldn't be sued for libel, but they awarded Falwell damages for emotional distress. The Court overturned the damages, saying that public figures and public officials must put up with such things, comparing the parody to outrageous political cartoons, which have always been protected by the First Amendment.

While it is extremely difficult to win a slander or libel case, Hulk Hogan's 2016 case against the website Gawker shows that it is not impossible. Hogan sued Gawker—and

Former first lady Melania Trump sued the British tabloid the *Daily Mail* for defamation for an article it published insinuating she had worked as an escort while modeling. She was awarded an estimated $2.9 million in damages and also received a public apology from the paper for publishing inaccurate information.

won a $140 million verdict—for posting a sex tape of him with his friend's wife, Heather Clem, that had been recorded without his knowledge. He ultimately settled with Gawker for $31 million, and the website declared bankruptcy because of the case. The case has broader political implications because it shows that public figures may be able to win damages even when the defamatory content is *true*.[97] Melania Trump also reached a settlement with the *Daily Mail*, a British tabloid, for articles that the outlet published in 2016 falsely claiming that she had once worked for an escort service (the paper printed a retraction, apologized, and paid damages).[98] President Trump vowed to "open up our libel laws" to deter what he claimed were false "fake news" stories. Libel law, however, is controlled by the states, subject to limits from the U.S. Supreme Court, so it is not something that the president can change.[99] Trump also faced a lawsuit from author and columnist Jean Carroll, who alleges that he raped her in the 1990s and then defamed her when he was president, saying "she isn't my type." Two juries found that Trump was liable for sexual abuse and defamation and must pay Carroll $5 million and $83.3 million; the cases are being appealed.[100]

commercial speech
Public expression with the aim of making a profit. It has received greater protection under the First Amendment in recent years but remains less protected than political speech.

Commercial Speech **Commercial speech**, which mostly refers to advertising, has evolved from having almost no protection under the First Amendment to enjoying quite strong protection. One early case involved a business owner who distributed leaflets to advertise rides on his submarine, which was docked in New York City. Under city ordinances, leafleting was permitted only if it was devoted to "information or a public protest," but not for a commercial purpose. The plaintiff changed the leaflet to have his advertisement on one side and a statement protesting a city policy on the other side (clever guy!). He was arrested anyway, and the Supreme Court upheld his conviction, saying that the city council had the right to regulate the distribution of leaflets.[101]

The Court became much more sympathetic to commercial speech in the 1970s when it struck down a law against advertising prescription drug prices and a law prohibiting placing newspaper racks on city streets to distribute commercial publications such as real estate guides.[102] The key decision in 1980 established a test that is still central today: the government may regulate commercial speech if it concerns an illegal activity, if the advertisement is misleading, or if regulating speech directly advances a substantial government interest and the regulation is not excessive. In practice, this test means that commercial speech can be regulated, but the government must have a very good reason to do it.[103]

Commercial speech is protected even when it could be considered offensive. In 2017, the Court sided with the Slants, an Asian-American rock band, in overturning a provision of U.S. patent and trademark law that prohibited the registration of trademarks that "disparage" or "bring . . . into contempt or disrepute" any "persons, living or dead." The Slants, whose application to trademark their band name had been denied, argued that their goal was to reclaim the racial slur against Asian Americans, in the same way that the LGBTQIA+ community over time redefined the use of "queer." The Court agreed, saying, "A law that can be directed against speech found offensive to some portion of the public can be turned against minority and dissenting views to the detriment of all."[104]

An even stronger protection for potentially offensive commercial speech came with the 2019 ruling that struck down bans on trademarking words and symbols that are "immoral" or "scandalous." A clothing designer wanted to trademark the phrase FUCT, which the majority opinion wryly noted was "the equivalent of [the] past participle form of a well-known word of profanity." The Court said that the law banning the trademark was overly broad and violates the First Amendment guarantee of free speech because "it disfavors certain ideas." The dissenters worried that it would lead to more "obscene, vulgar, and profane modes of expression."[105]

Miller test
Established in *Miller v. California*, this three-part test is used by the Supreme Court to determine whether speech meets the criteria for obscenity. If so, it can be restricted by the government.

Obscenity One area in which the press has never experienced complete freedom involves the publication of pornography and material considered obscene. The difficulty arises in deciding where to draw the line. Nearly everyone would agree that child pornography should not be published[106] and that pornography should not be available to minors. However, beyond these points there is not much consensus. For example, some people are offended by nude paintings in art museums, while others enjoy watching hard-core X-rated movies.

Defining obscenity has proven difficult for the courts. In an often-quoted moment of frustration, Justice Potter Stewart wrote that he could not define obscenity, but "I know it when I see it."[107] In its first attempt, the Court ruled that a particular publication could be banned if an "average person, applying contemporary community standards," would find that the material appeals to prurient interests and is "utterly without redeeming social importance."[108] This standard proved unworkable because lower courts differed in their interpretation. The Court took another stab at it in 1973 in a case that gave rise to the **Miller test**, which is still applied today.[109] The test has three standards that must all be met in order for material to be banned as obscene: (1) it appeals to prurient interests, (2) it is "patently offensive," and (3) the work as a whole lacks serious literary, artistic, political, or scientific value. The Court also clarified that *local* community standards were to apply rather than a single national standard, reasoning that what passes for obscenity in Sioux City, Iowa, probably would be considered pretty tame in Las Vegas.

Commercial speech may be protected even if some consider its content offensive. The rock band the Slants won the right to trademark their band name even though it refers to a racial slur against the Asian-American community.

In 2009, the Supreme Court addressed an area of the law that it had not touched for more than 30 years: regulating vulgar language that does not rise to the level of obscenity on broadcast television and radio (but not on cable or other paid-subscription services, which are not regulated as to language). In 1978, the Court ruled that the Federal Communications Commission (FCC) had the power to regulate indecent language, but the FCC had always interpreted that power to cover only repeated use of vulgar words.[110] However, after the use of vulgar words by Bono during the 2003 Golden Globe Awards and by Cher and Nicole Richie during the 2002 and 2003 Billboard Music Awards, the FCC announced that it would no longer tolerate even "isolated uses of sexual and excretory words."

Fox Television challenged this new rule, but in 2009 the Supreme Court upheld the FCC's ban on "fleeting expletives" as "entirely rational" under existing law. (Its opinion also took a swipe at the "foul-mouthed glitteratae from Hollywood.")[111] The Court also ruled the following week that the FCC had not acted capriciously in fining CBS $550,000 for Janet Jackson's infamous "wardrobe malfunction" at the 2004 Super Bowl.[112] However, after sending the cases back to the lower courts and another round of appeals, the Supreme Court ruled that the regulations were unconstitutionally vague and the networks could not be fined. The Court also let stand a lower-court ruling that voided the fine against CBS on similar grounds.[113] But the Court did not address the broader constitutional questions, so the regulation still stands; stronger First Amendment protections for broadcast radio and television will have to come from future cases.

Two more recent cases made clear that violence in published material cannot be regulated in the same way as sexual content. In 2010, the Court struck down a federal law that criminalized depictions "in which a living animal is intentionally maimed, mutilated, tortured, wounded, or killed." The law focused on "crush videos," which show the torture and killing of helpless animals but also included dog fighting and other forms of animal cruelty. In striking down the law, the Court said the First Amendment protected such depictions, even if the underlying behavior itself could be illegal.[114] In 2011, the Court struck down a California law that banned the sale of violent video games to children, saying: "Like the protected books, plays and movies that preceded them, video games communicate ideas—and even social messages—through many familiar literary devices (such as characters, dialogue, plot and music) and through features distinctive to the medium (such as the player's interaction with the virtual world). That suffices to confer First Amendment protection."[115]

"Why Should I Care?"

Even if you are not a journalist, do not engage in political protest, or do not contribute to political campaigns, the freedom of speech, the press, and assembly still shapes the world around you. The "marketplace of ideas" ensures that policies are debated and a range of voices can be heard. Our political leaders are held accountable by the free exchange of ideas and a strong independent media that can criticize their actions. Also, other areas of your everyday life that you may not consider to be "speech," such as video games, are protected by the First Amendment. Having an understanding of the law is especially important when the freedom of the press and free speech are regularly challenged in the political world.

The right to bear arms

EXPLORE WHY THE SECOND AMENDMENT'S MEANING ON GUN RIGHTS IS OFTEN DEBATED

Until recently, the right to bear arms was the only civil liberty that the Supreme Court had played a relatively minor role in defining. Between 1791 and 2007, the Court issued only four rulings directly pertaining to the Second Amendment. The federal courts had always interpreted the Second Amendment's awkward phrasing—"A well regulated Militia, being necessary to the security of a free State, the right of the people to keep and bear Arms, shall not be infringed"—as a right to bear arms within the context of serving in a militia, rather than as an individual right to own a gun.

Although legal conflict over gun ownership has intensified only recently, battles over guns have always been intense in the broader political realm. Interest groups such as the National Rifle Association have long asserted that the Second Amendment guarantees an individual right to bear arms.[116] Critics of this view emphasize the first clause of the amendment and point to the frequent mention of state militias in congressional debates at the time the Bill of Rights was adopted.[117] They argue that the Second Amendment was adopted to reassure Antifederalist advocates of states' rights that state militias, not a national standing army, would provide national security. In this view, the national armed forces and the National Guard have made the Second Amendment obsolete.

Before the Court's recent entry into this debate, Congress and state and local lawmakers had largely defined gun ownership and gun carrying rights, creating significant variation among the states. Wyoming and Montana have virtually no restrictions on gun ownership, for example, whereas California and Connecticut have many. At the national level, Congress tends to respond to crime waves or high-profile assassinations by passing new gun control laws. The broadest one, the Gun Control Act of 1968, was passed in the wake of the assassinations of Robert F. Kennedy and Martin Luther King Jr. The law sets standards for gun dealers, bans the sale of weapons through the mail, and restricts the sale of new machine guns, among other provisions.

Following the assassination attempt on President Reagan in 1981, the push for stronger gun control laws intensified. Spearheading this effort was Sarah Brady, whose husband, James Brady (Reagan's press secretary), was shot and disabled in the assassination attempt. It took nearly 13 years for the campaign to bear fruit, but in 1993 Congress passed and President Clinton signed the Brady Bill, which mandates a background check and a five-day waiting period for any handgun purchase.

But not all gun tragedies lead to more gun control. In 2021, there were 693 mass shootings, defined as incidents in which at least four people were killed or injured, not counting the shooter.[118] By the FBI's definition of an "active shooter" there were 373 incidents from 2000 to 2020, including those in Orlando, Florida; San Bernardino, California; Charleston, South Carolina; and Parkland, Florida.[119] In the deadliest mass shooting by a single gunman, 60 people were killed and 867 injured (411 from gunfire) in October 2017 at a country music festival in Las Vegas. While 45 states have passed 465 new gun safety laws since 2012, including "smart gun" laws, laws concerning mental health and gun ownership, laws regulating ghost guns, laws restricting ownership of assault weapons, and stronger background checks, 39 states now make it relatively easy to get a permit to carry a concealed weapon. Many states have also expanded the places in which guns may be carried, including college campuses, and have passed "stand your ground" laws, which allow gun owners to shoot first if they feel threatened. Twenty-one states allow individuals to buy and carry guns into public spaces without any background check or safety training, compared with just four states in 2014.[120]

While the Constitution guarantees the individual right to bear arms, the shootings at Marjory Stoneman Douglas High School in Parkland, Florida, shocked the nation. Advocates point to self protection as a reason for owning a gun, but others concerned about more mass shootings, like the March for Our Lives movement organized after the Parkland shooting, advocate for restrictive measures.

In 2008, a landmark Supreme Court ruling recognized for the first time an individual right to bear arms for self-defense and hunting.[121] The decision struck down the District of Columbia's ban on handguns, while noting that state and local governments could enforce ownership restrictions, such as preventing felons or the mentally impaired from buying guns. The Court did not apply the Second Amendment to the states in this decision, but it did so two years later in striking down a gun control ordinance in Chicago in ***McDonald v. Chicago*** (2010) and reaffirming the ownership restrictions noted in the Washington, D.C., case.[122] The dissenters in both strongly divided 5–4 decisions lamented the Court's activism in reopening a legal question considered settled for 70 years (in 32 instances since a 1939 Court ruling, appeals courts had affirmed the focus on a collective right—in the context of a militia—rather than an individual right to bear arms, and recognized an individual right only twice between 1939 and 2007).[123]

In 2022, the Court ruled that a state (New York in this case) may not require people to justify why they should be allowed to carry a gun. The Court also opened the door to more challenges to restrictions on gun ownership by replacing the "balancing test" (in which the interests of the state in regulating guns is balanced against the gun owner's Second Amendment right to bear arms), with a tradition test "as informed by history," to make sure a regulation is consistent with America's traditional firearm practices.[124]

There is strong public support for gun ownership in the United States, where there are about 393 million privately owned guns. This accounts for 46 percent of the world's total and is more than twice as high a rate of gun ownership as in the second most heavily armed nation: there are 120.5 guns per 100 people in the United States compared with 52.8 in Yemen. The contrast to our closest allies is even more extreme: there are 34.7 guns per 100 people in Canada, 19.6 in Germany, 4.9 in the United Kingdom, and 0.3 in Japan.[125] The fact that so many Americans support gun ownership, combined with the Supreme Court's endorsement of an individual right to bear arms, means that stronger gun control at the national level is highly unlikely.

However, Congress and the president have taken some limited steps in recent years. After a mass shooting at a Parkland, Florida, high school that killed 17 students in 2018, high school students organized the March for Our Lives, which had 1.2 to 2 million participants in more than 800 cities around the world. In Florida, gun control laws were strengthened by raising the age to buy a gun to 18, banning bump stocks that allow bullets to be fired more rapidly, and introducing a three-day waiting period before buying a long rifle. Congress passed legislation strengthening the

McDonald v. Chicago
The Supreme Court ruled in 2010 that the Second Amendment's right to keep and bear arms for self-defense in one's home is applicable to the states through the Fourteenth Amendment.

DID YOU KNOW?

44,858

people were killed by guns in the United States in 2021. About 54 percent of these deaths were from suicides.

Source: www.gunviolencearchive.org

National Instant Criminal Background Check System and providing $1 billion to fund initiatives intended to enhance school safety, such as the addition of metal detectors. President Trump also signed an executive order banning bump stocks. However, the Supreme Court struck down that order in 2024, saying bump stocks did not make a gun fully automatic (like a machine gun).[126] In his first year in office President Biden issued executive orders and supported policies to limit ghost guns and promote the safe storage of guns and neighborhood-based programs to combat gun violence.[127] Following the school shooting in Uvalde, Texas, Congress passed the most significant gun control legislation in decades, requiring stronger background checks for eighteen- to twenty-one-year-olds, restricting gun ownership for domestic violence offenders who are not married to their partner, providing incentives for states to pass "red flag" laws, and providing funds for school safety and youth mental health programs.[128]

In addition to this limited legislative and executive action, extensive litigation will be necessary to define the acceptable boundaries of gun control and to identify which state and local restrictions will be allowed to stand especially after the recent New York case that established a new "traditions" test for gun regulations. Up to this point, the verdicts have been mixed, with some lower courts upholding limitations on gun ownership (such as laws prohibiting felons from owning guns) and other lower courts striking them down. However, an overwhelming majority of challenges to gun control laws have failed and almost all challenges to gun laws in criminal cases have been unsuccessful. Since the *Heller* decision, the Supreme Court has declined to hear 150 gun cases, which allowed lower court decisions to stand (and upholding regulations in most cases).[129]

Law, order, and the rights of criminal defendants

DESCRIBE THE PROTECTIONS PROVIDED FOR PEOPLE ACCUSED OF A CRIME

Every advanced democracy protects the rights of people who have been accused of a crime. In the United States, the **due process rights** of the Fourth, Fifth, Sixth, and Eighth Amendments include the right to a fair trial, the right to consult a lawyer, freedom from self-incrimination, the right to know what crime you are accused of, the right to confront the accuser in court, and freedom from unreasonable police searches. This means that the Bill of Rights offers protections at every stage of the process, from gathering evidence, charging crimes, conducting a trial, and imposing the punishment.

due process rights
The idea that laws and legal proceedings must be fair. The Constitution guarantees that the government cannot take away a person's "life, liberty, or property, without due process of law." Other specific due process rights are found in the Fourth, Fifth, Sixth, and Eighth Amendments, such as protection from self-incrimination and freedom from illegal searches.

It is difficult to apply the abstract principles of due process to concrete situations in a way that protects civil liberties without jeopardizing order. The Fifth and Fourteenth Amendments specify that life, liberty, and property may not be denied "without due process of law." In general, this language refers to *procedural* restrictions on what government can do and is based on the idea of fairness and justice. The difficulty comes in defining what is fair or just.

The difference between abstract principles of due process and their specific application also raises difficult *political* questions. Most people endorse the principle of "due process of law" and general ideas such as requiring that police legally obtain any evidence used in court. However, when the Supreme Court applies these principles to protect the rights of criminal defendants, there is a public outcry that too many suspects are going free on "legal technicalities," such as having to inform a suspect of their right to talk to an attorney before being questioned by the police. Elected politicians are very vulnerable to such public pressure and have a strong incentive to be "tough on crime," while the courts are left to decide whether a specific case involves a legal technicality or a fundamental civil liberty.

The question of whether government officials can compel companies like Apple to assist them in unlocking phones so they can conduct a search remains contentious. This issue became especially prominent after the 2015 shooting in San Bernardino, California, when the FBI ordered Apple to unlock the suspect's phone. The FBI dropped the lawsuit once it unlocked the phone without Apple's help. But in 2018, Apple announced it had changed the iPhone so it couldn't be unlocked.

The Fourth Amendment: unreasonable searches and seizures

The Fourth Amendment says: "The right of the people to be secure in their persons, houses, papers, and effects, against unreasonable searches and seizures, shall not be violated." Defining "unreasonable" puts us back in the familiar position of drawing lines and balancing interests.

Over the years, the Supreme Court has provided strong protections against searches within a person's physical space, typically defined as their home. With the introduction of new technology—first telephones and wiretapping, then more sophisticated listening and searching devices—the Court has had to confront a broad array of complicated questions. It has attempted to achieve a balance between privacy and security by requiring the courts to approve search warrants, yet continuing to carve out limited exceptions to this general rule.

Searches and Warrants Under most circumstances, a law-enforcement official seeking a search warrant must provide the court with "personal knowledge" of a "probable cause" of specific criminal activity and must outline the evidence that is the target of the search. Broad, general "fishing expeditions" for evidence are not allowed.

School officials must also balance the constitutional rights of students against the need to maintain discipline. But school searches may be permitted with a weaker "reasonable suspicion"; this is because the courts have viewed the schools as "in loco parentis" (that is, as playing the role of surrogate parents for the students). In 1985, the Court ruled in favor of a school official who discovered two girls smoking in a school bathroom and, in searching the purse of one of the girls for cigarettes, found marijuana, a pipe, rolling papers, plastic bags, and enough cash to suggest that the girl was selling marijuana. Yet, in other cases, the Court ruled that there are limits to searches by school officials and that students have the right to privacy. For example, in 2003 school administrators in Safford, Arizona, responding to a tip that a student was in possession of prescription-strength ibuprofen pills, subjected 13-year-old Savana Redding to a strip search. After searching her backpack and outer clothing and finding nothing, the police told Savana "to pull her bra out and to the side and shake it, and to pull out the elastic on her underpants, thus exposing her breasts and pelvic area to some degree." The Court ruled that this search violated her Fourth Amendment rights because "the content of the suspicion failed to match the degree of intrusion."[130]

Police searches inherently involve a clash between public safety and an individual's private freedom from government intrusions. These issues came to the fore with the passage of the Patriot Act of 2001 after the terrorist attacks of September 11. (The official name of this law is the USA PATRIOT Act, which is an acronym for the "Uniting and Strengthening America by Providing Appropriate Tools Required to Intercept and Obstruct Terrorism Act.") Several of the most controversial parts of the act strengthen police surveillance powers; make it easier to conduct "sneak and peek" searches (the police enter a home with a warrant, look for evidence, and do not inform the suspect that their home was searched until months later); broaden Internet surveillance; increase the government's access to individuals' library, banking, and medical records; and permit roving wiretaps for suspected terrorists.

Most police searches conducted without warrants occur because suspects consent to being searched. Officers are not required to tell suspects that they may say no or request a warrant. Here are examples of other instances in which the Court will allow a warrantless search:

- Conducting a search at the time of a legal arrest that "is confined to the immediate vicinity of the arrest."
- Collecting evidence that was not included in the search warrant but is out in the open and in plain view.
- Using a police roadblock to search for information about a crime, to check for illegal immigrants or contraband at borders, or to conduct sobriety checks (but not for random drug searches or license checks), as long as the roadblock stops all drivers.
- Searching containers in cars if the officer has probable cause to suspect criminal activity.
- Searching passengers and the passenger area of a car if the driver has been stopped for a traffic offense (because people in automobiles do not have the same Fourth Amendment protections as people do in their homes).
- Searching an area where the officer thinks there is either a crime in progress or an "armed and dangerous" suspect.
- Searching school lockers, with probable cause.
- Searching for weapons and/or to prevent the destruction of evidence.[131]

Strip searches after an arrest and before the suspect is put in jail were upheld in 2012 by the Supreme Court even when there was no suspicion of illegal substances. The dissenting justices argued that "the humiliation of a visual strip-search" after being "arrested for driving with a noisy muffler, failing to use a turn signal and riding a bicycle without an audible bell" should not be allowed under the Fourth Amendment.[132]

In 2013, the Court ruled that a DNA swab of an arrested suspect is simply for identification and therefore is no more intrusive than a photograph or fingerprint. The late Justice Scalia, a strong defender of privacy rights, wrote in his dissent: "I doubt that the proud men who wrote the charter of our liberties would have been so eager to open their mouths for royal inspection."[133] Scalia argued that DNA evidence could be used to identify the arrestee as a suspect in an unrelated crime and therefore a swab should be taken only if there is probable cause that another crime has also been committed. Another controversial case that deeply divided the Court was the ruling that a warrant was not necessary to draw blood from an unconscious driver (who obviously could not provide consent) under the "exigent-circumstances doctrine" that allows warrantless searches to protect the destruction of evidence.[134]

The Court has generally made it easier for law-enforcement officials to conduct searches without warrants, but two important decisions in the other direction were a 2014 case that required a warrant to search cell phones of people who had been arrested[135] and a 2012 case that required a warrant to place a GPS tracking device on a vehicle. In the latter case, the FBI suspected Antoine Jones of selling cocaine, so agents placed a tracking device on his vehicle without a warrant, monitored his movements for four weeks, and then used the evidence to convict him. Jones was sentenced to life in prison. While the Court required a warrant in this specific case, the basis for the majority's decision was fairly narrow: the placement of the device was a "physical trespass," and the lengthy monitoring of his movement constituted an illegal search.[136] The Court provided additional protection for privacy in 2018 when it ruled that a search warrant is required to access cell phone location records. While the ruling made exceptions for emergencies such as "bomb threats, active shootings, and child abductions," the four dissenting justices feared that law-enforcement officials were losing an important tool in fighting crime.[137] However, in 2021, the Court allowed an appeals court ruling to stand that allowed the search, without probable cause, of documents, emails, photographs, and other files stored on the electronic devices of U.S. citizens when they enter the country.[138]

The Exclusionary Rule Another important concern related to the Fourth Amendment is what to do if the police obtain evidence illegally. Here the need to balance security and privacy becomes concrete. Either the evidence is excluded from a criminal trial to protect privacy rights or it is allowed to support the conviction of the suspect. In 1961, the Fourth Amendment was incorporated (applied to the states through the Fourteenth Amendment) in a case, *Mapp v. Ohio*. This case established for all courts the **exclusionary rule**, which says that illegally or unconstitutionally obtained evidence cannot be used in a criminal trial. Previously, the rule had applied only at the national level.[139]

exclusionary rule
The principle that illegally or unconstitutionally acquired evidence cannot be used in a criminal trial.

In the landmark case, police broke into Dollree Mapp's residence without a warrant, looking for a suspect thought to be hiding in the house. The officers did not find the suspect, but they did find illegal pornographic material, and Mapp was convicted of possessing it. Mapp's lawyer tried to defend her on First Amendment grounds, claiming she had the right to own the pornography, but instead the Court used the opportunity to apply the Fourth Amendment to the states. The Court threw out Mapp's conviction because the police did not have a search warrant, arguing that applying the Fourth Amendment only to the national government and not to the states didn't make any sense: Why should a state's attorney be able to use illegally obtained evidence while a federal prosecutor could not? The justices ruled that for the exclusionary rule to deter illegal searches and seizures, it must apply to law enforcement at both state and national levels.

Subsequently, the Supreme Court began weakening the exclusionary rule. For example, the Court established a "good faith exception" to the exclusionary rule, allowing evidence to be used as long as the officer believed that they had conducted a legal search. In this specific case, the officer had a warrant with the wrong address.[140] Yet another case established an "independent source" exception allowing the use of evidence that was initially obtained in an illegal search but subsequently acquired with a valid warrant. A major new exception was established in 2016 when the Court ruled that drugs found during a search in which an officer stopped a person with no probable cause are admissible as evidence if there was an outstanding arrest warrant for the suspect (in this case for a traffic offense) at the time of the search. Justice Sotomayor pointed out in her dissent that there are 7.8 million outstanding warrants, mostly for traffic and parking violations, which means that this new exception has far-reaching consequences: "The mere existence of a warrant not only gives an officer legal cause to arrest and search a person, it also forgives an officer who, with no knowledge of the warrant at all, unlawfully stops that person on a whim or hunch."[141] The bottom line is that the exclusionary rule remains in effect, but in the last several decades the courts have eased the conditions in which prosecutors can use evidence obtained under questionable circumstances.

Can the police search your home without a warrant? After Dollree Mapp was arrested for possession of pornographic material, the case made its way to the Supreme Court and the search was ruled unconstitutional. This case established the exclusionary rule for evidence that is obtained without a warrant.

Drug Testing Another area of Fourth Amendment law concerns drug testing. The clause granting people the right "to be secure in their persons" certainly seems to cover drug testing. However, the courts have long recognized the right of private companies to test their employees for illegal drugs. Moreover, in professional sports testing for performance-enhancing drugs is increasingly common. Lance Armstrong was stripped of his seven Tour de France titles after admitting in 2013 to doping, and Major League Baseball has struggled to rein in steroid and human growth hormone use by many of its players, including stars such as Alex Rodriguez, Steven Wright, and Francis Martes, who was suspended for the entire 2020 season for his use of performance-enhancing drugs.

What about drug testing by the state? The Court has upheld random drug testing for high school athletes and mandatory drug testing for any junior high or high school students involved in extracurricular activities.[142] In the case of athletes, proponents of the policy asserted that safety concerns should preclude a 260-pound lineman or a pitcher with a 90-mile-per-hour fastball from using drugs. However, the same arguments could not be made for members of the choir, band, debate club, social dance club, or chess club, so this decision to include all extracurricular activities was a particularly strong endorsement of schools' antidrug policies.

The Court has also upheld drug testing of public employees, with one exception. It struck down a Georgia law that would have required all candidates for state office to pass a drug test within 30 days of announcing a run for office, because candidates are not public employees.[143] Rather than appealing to the courts, former senator Ernest Hollings of South Carolina had a different approach to avoid drug testing. When his opponent challenged him to take a drug test, the senator shot back, "I'll take a drug test if you take an IQ test."[144]

The Post–September 11 Politics of Domestic Surveillance The debate over the trade-off between civil liberties and security intensified in 2005 when a White House–approved domestic surveillance program was revealed. At the center of this controversy is the National Security Agency (NSA), which was created during the Korean War in 1952 by President Harry Truman. The agency was initially kept so secret that for many years the government even denied its existence. Insiders joked that the "NSA" stood for "No Such Agency." Today the NSA is responsible for surveillance to protect national security, whereas the FBI is in charge of spying related to criminal activity and the Central Intelligence Agency (CIA) oversees foreign intelligence gathering. Since the terrorist attacks of September 11, 2001, the NSA has been monitoring the phone calls and Internet usage of many U.S. citizens who have had contact with suspected terrorists overseas. These calls were intercepted without the approval of the Foreign Intelligence Surveillance Court (FISC), which was created by Congress in 1978 under the Foreign Intelligence Surveillance Act (FISA) specifically for approving requests for the interception of calls. The NSA was also found to be creating a database of every phone call made within the borders of the United States.

Phone companies AT&T, Verizon, and BellSouth reportedly turned over records of millions of customers' phone calls to the government.[145] In 2013, classified information revealed by Edward Snowden showed that the NSA had monitored the phone calls of German chancellor Angela Merkel and other leaders of allied countries, in addition to collecting email traffic in the United States that contained the email address or phone number of a foreign target. In April 2017, the NSA announced that it would no longer collect information on communications that simply mentioned someone rather than being sent to or from that person (so-called about searches). It also would discontinue "backdoor" searches in which conversations and Internet data from Americans get swooped up in the course of monitoring foreign targets. However, early in 2018, when Congress reauthorized the foreign surveillance for an additional six years, and again in 2024 for two years, it opened the door to allowing "about" collection and "backdoor" searches to start up again.[146]

Critics warn that phone surveillance may be the tip of the iceberg, because the government may be monitoring travel, credit card, and banking records more widely than we think. Government agencies have previously skirted the restrictions in the Privacy Act of 1974 and the Fourth Amendment by purchasing this information from businesses, since the Privacy Act requires disclosure of how the government is using personal information only when the government itself collects the data. The Justice Department spent $19 million in 2005 to purchase commercially gathered data about American citizens, according to a report by the Government Accountability Office. These data are then used to search for suspicious patterns of behavior in a process known as data mining.[147] In 2016, a massive data collection program by AT&T called Project Atmosphere was used by law-enforcement agencies investigating everything from murder to medical fraud.[148]

The debate over domestic surveillance has generated intense disagreement. At one extreme, critics conjure up images of George Orwell's classic novel *1984*, in which Big Brother, a reclusive totalitarian ruler, watches the characters' every move. Critics see the surveillance as a threat to civil liberties and to our system of checks and balances and separation of powers. They believe that when the executive branch refuses to obtain warrants through the FISA court to conduct surveillance, it is taking on too much power without consulting the other branches of government. But supporters of the program argue that getting a court order may take too long, jeopardizing the surveillance necessary to protect the country. Congress tried to strike a balance between these two positions when it enacted the FISA Amendments Act of 2008. This law continued the ban on monitoring the purely domestic communications of Americans without a court order, gave the government authority to intercept international communications, and provided legal immunity to the telecommunications companies that had cooperated in the original wiretapping program. However, the *New York Times* revealed that the NSA had still been engaged in "overcollection" of domestic communication between Americans under the new law, including an attempt to wiretap a member of Congress without a court order. Although the NSA vowed to stop purely domestic surveillance without a court order, technical problems make it difficult to distinguish between communications made within the United States and overseas, and recently declassified information reveals that these searches continued into 2021 and the certification for blanket searches under Section 702 of the law remains controversial.[149]

The director of National Intelligence under Barack Obama, James Clapper, testified at a congressional hearing on possible changes to the FISA as protesters in the background called for an end to government surveillance.

TAKE A STAND

The Fourth Amendment and Digital Privacy

New and future technologies complicate the question of what is a "reasonable" search or even an expectation of any privacy in the digital age. Justice Alito raised this question in oral arguments in a Supreme Court case involving a GPS tracking device. He said, "Technology is changing people's expectations of privacy. . . . Maybe 10 years from now 90 percent of the population will be using social networking sites and they will have on average 500 friends and they will have allowed their friends to monitor their location 24 hours a day, 365 days a year, through the use of their cell phones. Then—what would the expectation of privacy be then?"[a]

More than 10 years have passed since Justice Alito asked this question, and he was right—most of us always carry a personal tracking device (our phones), and everything you do on the Internet is recorded somewhere. New surveillance methods pose even more serious threats to privacy: RFIDs (radio frequency identifications) are the size of a grain of rice and transmit information wirelessly through radio waves; facial recognition software can identify people in a crowd and iris scanners provide quick proof of identity that is more reliable than fingerprints; "smart dust devices"—tiny wireless micromechanical sensors that can detect light and movement—and drones have vast potential for tracking people in any situation.

Data on personal devices such as laptops and smartphones may be subject to search by authorities.

Do we simply have to give up an expectation of privacy in this context? The government must show probable cause to get a warrant to gain access to the content of personal communications. But metadata of Internet searches and cell phone location may be purchased from Internet providers and communication corporations. Should the government be able to buy data to assist in law enforcement?

Buying data violates the Fourth Amendment The Department of Homeland Security has been using commercially available cell phone location records for immigration and border enforcement, and it is likely that it is also used for more general law enforcement.[b] The Supreme Court has yet to decide whether the purchase of such data constitutes a "search" under the Fourth Amendment. The Stored Communications Act of 1986 prohibits communication companies from "knowingly" sharing user data with the government without a warrant. However, the law doesn't apply to data brokers who do not directly deal with consumers. Sen. Ron Wyden (D-OR) and Sen. Rand Paul (R-KY) introduced the "Fourth Amendment Is Not for Sale Act" to close this loophole, arguing, "Doing business online doesn't amount to giving the government permission to track your every movement or rifle through the most personal details of your life. There's no reason information scavenged by data brokers should be treated differently than the same data held by your phone company or email provider."[c]

We shouldn't expect privacy in a digital age There are two types of arguments against this proposed law. First, as Sun Microsystems chief executive Scott McNealy famously said, "You have zero privacy anyway. Get over it."[d] While this flip comment may seem extreme, it is essentially the question raised by Justice Alito about our willingness to share private data with Internet and communications companies. The second argument is that the government needs to do whatever it can to protect us from terrorists and law enforcement should be able to use whatever tools they can. Furthermore, innocent people who have not broken the law have nothing to hide.

take a stand

1. If you had to decide where to draw the line on digital privacy rights, what would you do? Do you think the government should be able to buy location data and other information from Internet data brokers?

2. When should law-enforcement officials have to get a warrant to monitor our behavior?

The Fifth Amendment

Miranda Rights and Self-Incrimination The familiar phrase "I plead the Fifth" has been part of our criminal justice system since the Bill of Rights was ratified, ensuring that a suspect cannot be compelled to provide court testimony that would cause them to be prosecuted for a crime. However, what about outside a court of law? If a police officer coerces a confession out of a suspect, does that amount to self-incrimination?

Coercive police interrogations were allowed until a landmark case in 1966. Ernesto Miranda had been convicted in an Arizona court of kidnapping and rape, on the basis of a confession extracted after two hours of questioning in which he was not read his rights. The Court overturned the conviction, saying that a police interrogation "is inherently intimidating" and in these circumstances "no statement obtained from the defendant can truly be the product of his free choice."[150] To ensure that a confession is truly a free choice, the Court came up with the well-known **Miranda rights**. If police do not read a suspect these rights, nothing the suspect says can be used in court.

Miranda rights
The list of civil liberties described in the Fifth Amendment that must be read to a suspect before anything the suspect says can be used in a trial.

The Court has carved out exceptions to the Miranda rights requirement as more conservative justices gave greater weight to law and order than civil liberties concerns. In one case, police failed to read a suspect his Miranda rights until after they had frisked him, found an empty holster, and asked him where his gun was. The suspect led police to a gun. The lower court dismissed the charges because the gun had been used as incriminating evidence in the trial, but the Supreme Court reinstated the conviction because "concern for public safety must be paramount to adherence to the literal language of the *Miranda* rule."[151]

Although the Court has been willing to carve out limited exceptions to the Miranda rule, in 2000 the Court rejected Congress's attempt to overturn *Miranda* by designating all voluntary confessions as legally admissible evidence. The Court ruled that it, and not Congress, has the power to determine constitutional protections for criminal defendants. The justices also affirmed their intent to protect the Miranda rule,

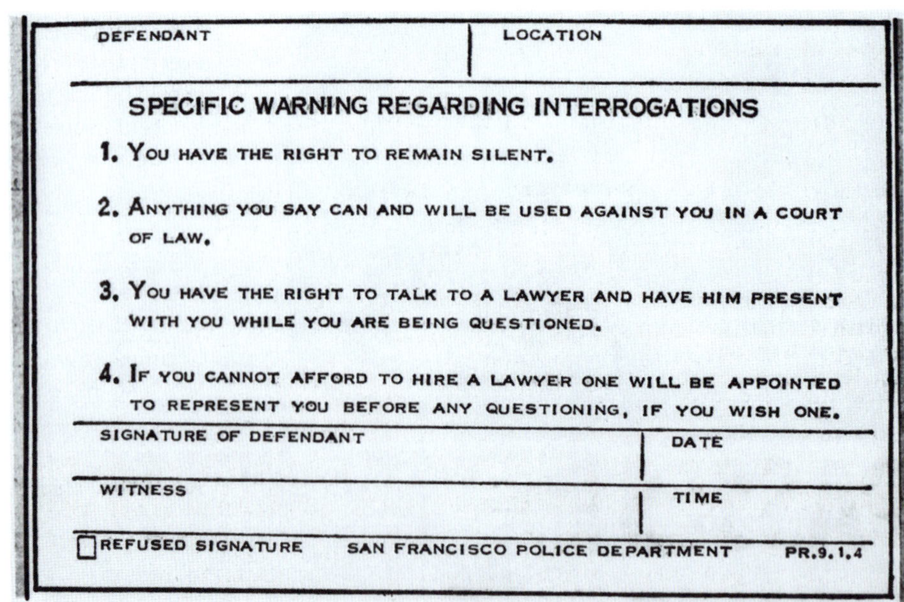
DEFENDANT | LOCATION

SPECIFIC WARNING REGARDING INTERROGATIONS

1. You have the right to remain silent.
2. Anything you say can and will be used against you in a court of law.
3. You have the right to talk to a lawyer and have him present with you while you are being questioned.
4. If you cannot afford to hire a lawyer one will be appointed to represent you before any questioning, if you wish one.

SIGNATURE OF DEFENDANT | DATE

WITNESS | TIME

☐ REFUSED SIGNATURE — SAN FRANCISCO POLICE DEPARTMENT — PR.9.1.4

This is a typical example of the Miranda warning card that police officers carry with them and read to every suspect after an arrest.

saying: "*Miranda* has become embedded in routine police practice to the point where the warnings have become part of our national culture."[152]

Double Jeopardy Another Fifth Amendment right for defendants is protection against being tried more than once for a particular crime. This is known as **double jeopardy** because the suspect is "twice put in jeopardy of life or limb" for a single offense. This prohibition was extended to the states in 1969.[153] But prosecutors can exploit two loopholes in this civil liberty: (1) a suspect may be tried in federal court and state court for the same crime,[154] and (2) if a suspect is found innocent of one set of *criminal* charges brought by the state, they may still be found guilty of the same or closely related offenses based on *civil* charges brought by a private individual.

double jeopardy
Being tried twice for the same crime. This is prevented by the Fifth Amendment.

Usually these loopholes are exploited only in high-profile cases in which there is public or political pressure to get a conviction. For example, in 1992 four Los Angeles police officers were acquitted of beating Rodney King, a driver they had chased for speeding. Before the trial, a bystander's video of the beating had been widely broadcast; subsequently, when people heard the news of the police officers' acquittal, massive riots broke out that lasted three days. Responding to political pressure, President George H. W. Bush urged federal prosecutors to retry the officers not for the *criminal* use of excessive force but for violating Rodney King's *civil* rights. (Two were ultimately found guilty, and two were acquitted.)

Property Rights and Eminent Domain The final part of the Fifth Amendment is at the heart of a hot legal debate over property rights. The clause says, "nor shall private property be taken for public use, without just compensation." For most of American history, this civil liberty has been noncontroversial. When the government needs private property for a public use such as building a highway or a park, it may force a property owner to sell at a fair market value in a practice known as eminent domain.

A new, controversial interpretation of the Fifth Amendment's "takings" clause, however, has attempted to expand the principle of just compensation to cover not only "physical takings" but also "regulatory takings." For example, if the Endangered Species Act protects an animal whose habitat is on your land, you would not be able to develop that property. Thus, its market value would probably be lower than if the endangered species did not live on your land. Therefore, the argument goes, because of this law the government has "taken" some of the value of your land by legally protecting the species, so it should compensate you for your loss.

This issue became even more controversial after a case involving a development project in New London, Connecticut. A working-class neighborhood was sold to a private developer to build a waterfront hotel, office space, and higher-end housing, but a homeowner sued the city to stop the development. The Court supported the local government, saying that "promoting economic development is a traditional and long accepted function of government," so a "plausible public use" is satisfied. Justice O'Connor wrote a strong dissent, saying that the "specter of condemnation hangs over all property. Nothing is to prevent the State from replacing any Motel 6 with a Ritz-Carlton, any home with a shopping mall, or any farm with a factory."[155] In reaction to this decision, legislation or constitutional amendments have been passed in 42 states restricting the use of eminent domain for economic development.[156] This is an evolving area of the law, with several recent cases restoring property rights and an important 2017 case providing another setback for property owners.[157] However, in 2021, the Court rewrote 40 years of precedent by giving property owners protection from temporary regulatory taking rather than just permanent physical taking of property. The case involved a California law that gave labor unions access to private farms to try to organize the farm workers, which the Court ruled violated the property owner's rights

A California law that allowed union representatives to go onto private property to facilitate the organization of labor was challenged in court as farm owners looked to protect their property from regulatory measures. The Supreme Court held that the law constituted a *per se* violation of the Fifth Amendment and could not be enforced without "just compensation" to the property owners.

under the Fifth Amendment. While the ultimate reach of this ruling won't be known for a few years, it will produce more challenges to government regulations designed to protect workers and the public."[158]

The Sixth Amendment: the right to legal counsel and a jury trial

Gideon v. Wainwright
The 1963 Supreme Court case that guaranteed the right to an attorney for the poor or indigent for felony offenses.

The right to an attorney is one of the civil liberties key to criminal law, because the legal system is too complicated for a layperson to navigate. However, at one time, poor people accused of a state felony were forced to defend themselves in court if they could not afford a lawyer (except in cases involving the death penalty, for which the state would provide a lawyer).[159] This changed in 1963 with the celebrated case of **Gideon v. Wainwright**. Clarence Gideon was accused of breaking into a pool hall and stealing beer, wine, and money. He could not afford an attorney, so he tried to defend himself. He did a pretty good job—calling witnesses, cross-examining the prosecutor's witnesses, and providing a good summary argument. However, he was convicted and sentenced to five years in jail, based largely on the testimony of the person who turned out to be the guilty party. The Court unanimously overturned Gideon's conviction, saying: "In our adversary system of criminal justice, any person hauled into court who is too poor to hire a lawyer cannot be assured a fair trial unless counsel is provided for him."[160]

Unlike the exclusionary rule and the protection against self-incrimination, the right to an attorney has been strengthened over time, through both legislation and subsequent Court rulings. One year after *Gideon*, Congress passed the Criminal Justice Act, which provided better legal representation for criminal defendants in federal court; within two years, 23 states had taken similar action. The Court has defined a general right to *effective* counsel (although the bar is set considerably low in terms of defining "effective") and more recently mandated that defense attorneys must conduct any reasonable investigation into possible lines of defense when presenting evidence that could help the defendant.[161] The Court extended this right to effective counsel in cases determined by plea bargains, which is significant because 97 percent of convictions in federal courts and 94 percent in state courts were the result of guilty pleas.[162]

The Sixth Amendment also protects an individual's right to a speedy and public trial by an impartial jury in criminal cases. The Court affirmed the right to a speedy trial in 1967,[163] and today under the Federal Speedy Trial Act a trial must begin within 70 days of the defendant's arrest or first appearance in court. This law was strengthened by a 2006 Court decision stating that a defendant may not waive the right to a speedy trial.[164]

The most important legal disputes over the "impartial jury" issue concern the process of jury selection and peremptory challenges, in which lawyers from each side may eliminate certain people from the jury pool without providing any reason. The Court has ruled that race and gender may not be the basis for a peremptory challenge.[165] The Court has also made clear that racial bias during jury deliberation is not allowed. Although jury deliberations are normally secret, in a 2017 case in which Miguel Peña-Rodriguez was convicted of misdemeanor sexual assault, two jurors told the judge that one of the jurors had demonstrated a bias against Mexican Americans, saying things like "Nine times out of ten Mexican men [are] guilty of being aggressive toward women and young girls." In the majority opinion Justice Kennedy argued that "racial bias in the justice system must be addressed—including, in some instances, after the verdict has been entered" in order to "prevent a systemic loss of confidence in jury verdicts, a confidence that is a central premise of the Sixth Amendment trial right."[166]

The Eighth Amendment: cruel and unusual punishment

The Founders would be surprised by the intense debates over whether the Eighth Amendment prohibition against "cruel and unusual punishments" applies to the death penalty. Clearly, the death penalty was accepted in their time (even stealing a horse was a capital offense!), and the language of the Constitution reflects that. Both the Fifth and Fourteenth Amendments say that a person may not be deprived of "life, liberty, or property, without due process of law," which implies that someone *could* be deprived of life as long as the state followed due process. The death penalty continues to be supported by many people in the United States, with 27 states allowing capital punishment. However, there is a clear overall trend away from the death penalty. Nine U.S. states have abolished the death penalty since 2007 (and three more states have moratoriums on the death penalty imposed by their governors), and dozens of other countries have done so in recent years. There were 11 executions in the United States in 2021, which is the lowest number since 1988 and well below the peak of 98 in 1999.[167] A botched execution in Oklahoma in 2014, in which Clayton Lockett writhed and gasped for nearly 30 minutes when one of the lines filled with the lethal drugs failed, led to renewed calls for abolishing the death penalty.[168]

DID YOU KNOW?

367

people have been exonerated post-conviction in the United States based on DNA evidence since 1989. On average, they spent 14 years in prison prior to their exoneration, and 21 of them had served time on death row.

Source: The Innocence Project

Supreme Court Rulings on the Death Penalty The Supreme Court remained silent on the issue of the death penalty for nearly two centuries. But in 1972 the Court ruled that the death penalty was unconstitutional because the process of applying it was too inconsistent. Congress and 35 states rushed to make their laws compliant with the Court decision. The typical fix was to say more explicitly which crimes were punishable by death and to make capital sentencing a two-step process: first, the determination of guilt or innocence, and second, a sentencing phase if the suspect is found guilty. Four years later, the Court approved these changes and allowed states to bring back the death penalty.[169]

While never again challenging the constitutionality of the death penalty, the Supreme Court has been chipping away at its edges for two decades. The Court has struck down state laws that mandated the death penalty in murder cases and a law requiring a death sentence for rape. It has also prohibited the execution of insane prisoners and abolished the death penalty for the mentally impaired—although the Court left it to the states to define who is "mentally retarded," it has since struck down standards in Florida and Texas that it found to be inappropriate indicators of intellectual capacity.[170] The Court has also prohibited the death penalty for juveniles under the age of 18 and for child rapists.[171] However, in 2021, the Court ruled that judges need not find a juvenile murderer "beyond rehabilitation" before sentencing him to life in prison.[172]

EXPLAIN WHY THE RIGHTS ASSOCIATED WITH PRIVACY ARE OFTEN CONTROVERSIAL

Privacy rights

You may be surprised to learn that the word "privacy" does not appear in the Constitution. **Privacy rights** were first developed in a 1965 case that questioned the constitutionality of an 1879 Connecticut law against using birth control. Estelle Griswold, the director of Planned Parenthood in Connecticut, was arrested nine days after opening a clinic that dispensed contraceptives. She was fined $100 and appealed her conviction. Although she lost in state court, she appealed all the way to the Supreme Court, which overturned her conviction.[173]

privacy rights
Liberties protected by several amendments in the Bill of Rights that shield certain personal aspects of citizens' lives from governmental interference, such as the Fourth Amendment's protection against unreasonable searches and seizures.

In a very fractured decision (there were six different opinions), the Court agreed that the law was outdated, but the justices agreed on little else. Even the justices who based their opinions on an implied constitutional right to privacy cited various constitutional roots. Justice William O. Douglas found privacy implicit in the First Amendment right of association, the Third Amendment's protection against the quartering of troops, the Fourth Amendment's prohibition against unreasonable searches and seizures, the Fifth Amendment's protection against self-incrimination, and the Ninth Amendment's catchall statement "The enumeration in the Constitution, of certain rights, shall not be construed to deny or disparage others retained by the people." These all seem like reasonable grounds for implicit privacy rights except the First Amendment right of association—since the Founders clearly meant political association, not an association with your spouse in bed.

The *Griswold v. Connecticut* case was significant for establishing the constitutional basis for a right to privacy, but the dissenters in the case were concerned about where this right would lead. Justice Black warned that privacy "is a broad, abstract and ambiguous concept" that can be shrunk or expanded in subsequent decisions. He said that Douglas's argument "require[d] judges to determine what is or is not constitutional on the basis of their own appraisal of what laws are unwise or unnecessary. The power to make such decisions is of course that of a legislative body. Surely it has to be admitted that no provision of the Constitution specifically gives such blanket power to courts to exercise such a supervisory veto over the wisdom and value of legislative policies and to hold unconstitutional those laws which they believe to be unwise or dangerous."[174]

Abortion rights

Justice Black's prediction came true eight years later in ***Roe v. Wade***, the landmark ruling that struck down laws in 46 states that limited abortion. Twelve of those states allowed abortions for pregnancies due to rape or incest, to protect the life of the mother,

Roe v. Wade
This 1973 Supreme Court case extended the right of privacy to a woman's decision to have an abortion while recognizing legitimate state interests in potential life and maternal health. The Court noted that the "relative weight of each of these interests varies over the course of pregnancy, and the law must account for this variability."

and in cases of severe fetal abnormalities. The much-criticized trimester analysis in the *Roe* ruling said that in the first trimester, states could not limit abortions; in the second trimester, states could regulate abortions in the interests of the health of the mother; and in the third trimester, states could forbid all abortions except those necessary to protect the health or life of the mother. The justices cited a constitutional basis for abortion rights in the general right to privacy outlined in *Griswold*; the concept of "personal liberty" in the Fourteenth Amendment's due process clause; and the "rights reserved to the people" in the Ninth Amendment.[175]

For nearly 50 years, Court decisions upheld *Roe* but endorsed state restrictions on abortion, such as requiring parental consent, a waiting period, or counseling sessions aimed at convincing the woman not to have an abortion (see the What Do the Facts Say? feature on p. 156 for more on restrictions currently in effect). During that period, *Roe*'s trimester analysis was replaced by a focus on the viability of the fetus. When the fetus would be viable (generally at 22 or 23 weeks), states could ban abortions "except where it is necessary, in appropriate medical judgment, for the preservation of the life or health of the mother."[176]

The pace of state restrictions on abortions accelerated from 2011 to 2013, with more than 200 limitations on abortion services. Laws passed in 2013 by Arkansas and North Dakota limiting abortions as soon as a fetal heartbeat can be detected (as early as six weeks) were struck down by federal courts. In 2013, 22 states enacted 70 new restrictions, including a requirement that abortion doctors have admitting privileges at local hospitals—which would close up to one-third of abortion clinics in affected states.[177] In 2016, the Supreme Court struck down the latter as an "undue burden" on the right to an abortion.[178] In June 2020, the Supreme Court also struck down a Louisiana law that would have limited the number of abortion providers in the state to just one.

When Justice Ruth Bader Ginsburg died shortly before the 2020 elections and was replaced by Amy Coney Barrett, abortion opponents believed they might have the fifth vote needed to overturn *Roe v. Wade*. That prediction came true in 2022 when *Dobbs v. Jackson Women's Health Organization* overturned *Roe*, upholding a Mississippi state law banning nearly all abortions after 15 weeks by a 6–3 vote. Chief Justice Roberts wrote a separate concurring opinion upholding the state law but not overturning *Roe* (five justices joined the opinion overturning *Roe*). The majority opinion emphasized that their decision applied only to abortion and not to same-sex marriage, contraception, and same-sex intimacy. With abortion no longer a constitutionally protected right, the politics of abortion will now shift to the states. While it will take years to sort out, abortion is currently illegal in 14 states and banned after between six and eighteen weeks of pregnancy in seven other states.[179]

Tyron Garner and John Geddes Lawrence after the Supreme Court decision in *Lawrence v. Texas* in 2003 established broad privacy rights for sexual behavior.

LGBTQ rights

Gay rights have typically been thought of more as a civil right (that is, freedom from discrimination) than a civil liberty, so these issues will be discussed in the next chapter. However, several important cases involving sexual relations are rooted in privacy rights. In 1986, the Court had ruled in *Bowers v. Hardwick* that there was no privacy protection or fundamental right for consenting adults to engage in "homosexual sodomy."[180] But in 2003, in *Lawrence v. Texas*, the Court established very broad privacy rights for sexual behavior. The case involved two Houston men, John Geddes Lawrence and Tyron Garner, who were prosecuted for same-sex sodomy after police entered Lawrence's apartment—upon receiving a false tip about an armed man—and found the two having sex. Under Texas law, sodomy was illegal for gays but not for heterosexuals.

WHAT DO THE FACTS SAY?

Abortion Rights Today

The Court's 1973 decision in *Roe v. Wade* made abortion legal throughout the United States, but when the Supreme Court reversed this decision in *Dobbs v. Jackson Women's Health Organization* in 2022 and handed back to the states the power to decide if or when a woman could have an abortion, it created a patchwork of policies across the country demonstrating federalism in action. How do abortion rights look today? What do the numbers say?

Abortion access by state

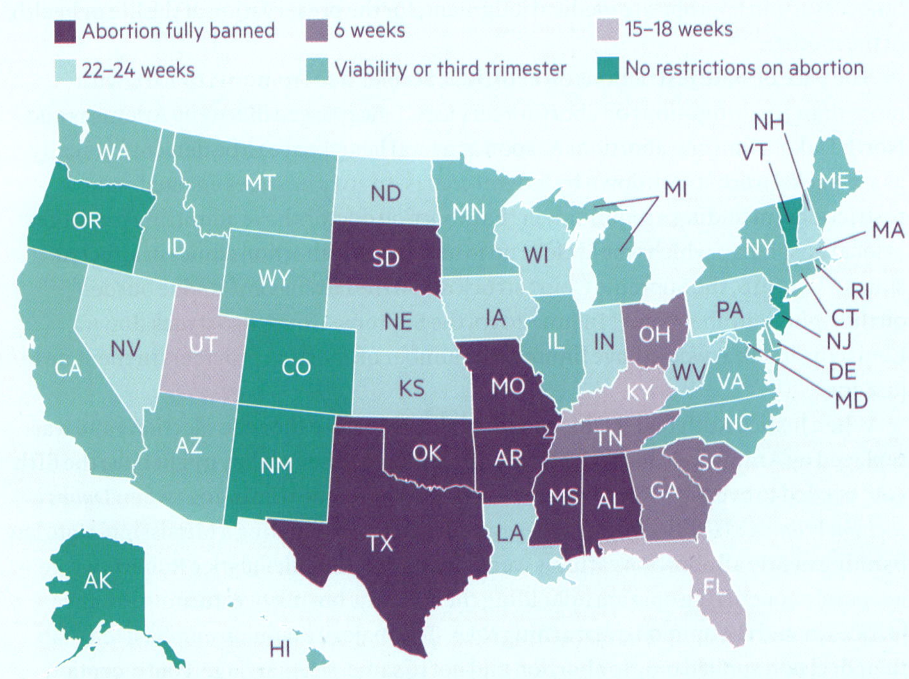

Source: Kaia Hubbar, "Where State Abortion Laws Stand without Roe," *U.S. News and World Report*, July 22, 2022, www.usnews.com/news/best-states/articles/a-guide-to-abortion-laws-by-state (accessed 7/28/22).

Think about it

- **Which states have the most** restrictive policies concerning access to abortions?
- **What do you think the implications** will be for states that neighbor those with more restrictive policies? Would you expect the number of procedures to go up in those states? What effect do you think *Dobbs v. Jackson Women's Health Organization* will have on the number of abortions nationwide?

In a landmark 6–3 ruling, the Supreme Court said that the liberty guaranteed by the Fourteenth Amendment's due process clause allows homosexuals to have sexual relations: "Freedom presumes an autonomy of self that includes freedom of thought, belief, expression, and certain intimate conduct."[181] The decision explicitly overturned *Bowers v. Hardwick* and five members of the majority signed onto the broad "due process" reasoning of the decision, while Justice O'Connor wrote a concurring opinion in which she agreed that the Texas law was unconstitutional but on narrower grounds. With the broader due process logic, a total of 13 state laws that banned sodomy were struck down.

"Why Should I Care?"

Privacy might not seem important. You may think you'll never be accused of a crime or have your privacy invaded or questioned by the government. Indeed, many people think, "I have nothing to hide, so it is fine if the NSA monitors email and Internet traffic to keep tabs on suspected terrorists." What if your email revealed that you had a serious medical or mental health condition? What if the NSA paid special attention to you because of tweets you posted criticizing a government policy? Knowing your rights and how those rights apply to everyone—both criminals and innocent people—will help you make informed decisions about which policies to support.

Unpacking the Conflict

The issue of prayer by a public school football coach raises difficult questions of balancing interests and drawing lines. When can the state limit the practice of a person's religion? When we say America is a free country, what does this really mean? Are there limits to those freedoms? If so, how should political actors draw the lines between protected behavior and actions that may be regulated? The coach's freedom to express his religious views must be balanced against the state's interest in protecting students from feeling compelled to participate in a prayer and its obligation to not participate in establishing a religion. The First Amendment is applicable in these instances because the coach was employed by a public school, but two parts of the First Amendment, the "free exercise" and "establishment" clauses, must be balanced against each other. Public schools must not actively promote religion, but they also cannot prevent an employee from private prayer, even when it is conducted in a very public manner. Balancing interests and drawing lines often involve a very difficult set of questions for the Court.

You exercise your civil liberties every day, whether speaking in public, going to church, being searched at an airport, participating in a political demonstration, writing or reading an article in your school newspaper, or being free from illegal police searches in your home. Because civil liberties are defined as those things the government *cannot* do to you, defining civil liberties is a political process. Often this process is confined to the courts, but for many issues—including free speech, freedom of the press, pornography, criminal rights, abortion, and gun control—it takes place in the broader political world, where defining civil liberties involves balancing competing ideals and interests and drawing lines by interpreting and applying the law. For example, debates over how to balance national security and civil liberties—whether newspapers should publish stories about classified government programs that may threaten civil liberties, or whether government surveillance powers should be strengthened to fight terrorism—will rage for years.

Other cases, such as the protests at military funerals or the protection of the due process rights of suspected criminals and terrorists, illustrate how difficult and politically unpopular it can be to protect our freedoms and liberty. Nearly everyone would agree that the behavior of the members of Westboro Baptist Church is completely outrageous. But protecting the freedom of speech is easy if you agree with what is being spoken. It becomes much more difficult if the freedom protects the rights of homophobic activists to protest at military funerals, defends a person accused of a heinous crime, or gives White supremacists a platform to speak at universities. It is also easy to think about religious freedom when it comes to practicing your own religion, but it becomes more difficult if you think about how your religious expression may influence those who practice another religion, or no religion at all.

"What's Your Take?"

Should coaches and other public school employees be able to pray with their students at school events, like a football game?

Or does this cross the "wall of separation" between church and state and allow too much religious activity in public schools?

CHECK YOUR UNDERSTANDING

"Why Should I Care?"

Much of our lives is spent searching for the definition of who we are. We find friend groups, religion (or not), college majors, jobs, volunteer opportunities, and even partners who speak to our individual needs. We choose our clothes, where we live, how we get from place to place, and where we spend our free time as a means to build up and support our deeply rooted conceptions of who we are.

At the same time, there is no more fraught space in American society than the search for our individual identity. In diverse communities, the exercise of one's personal identity can sometimes conflict with the exercise of another person's personal identity. Our civil liberties are, at their core, the most important part of our social contract with our government: our political leaders promise, with the consent of the governed, to protect our individual liberties and freedoms.

Personal political ideology and experiences provide the lens through which we think about the liberties guaranteed in the Bill of Rights and the other amendments to the Constitution. The way those liberties are put into practice through policy tells us who we are as a country at any given time.

1. An effective way of determining if a case involves civil liberties or civil rights is

- **a** learning whether or not there are discriminatory actions or regulations involved.
- **b** questioning if the government is being restrained or being asked to take action.
- **c** understanding which level of government is primarily involved in the case.
- **d** knowing if the case involves the issue of states' rights.

2. The primary difference between liberty and freedom is that liberty

- **a** is enjoyed by individuals within boundaries that protect the rights of others.
- **b** allows individuals and groups to act without the potential for government intervention.
- **c** requires active involvement of the government to create protections.
- **d** may require the courts to violate the civil rights of other individuals or groups.

3. Judging from what was included by the first Congress in the Bill of Rights, we understand that civil liberties primarily involve which of the following concerns?

- **a** Potential abuses of individuals and factions of the population by state and local governments
- **b** Restricting the power of states in relationship to the new national government
- **c** Codifying a system of checks and balances within the institutions of the national government
- **d** Creating restraints on the potential overreach of the national government

4. How would an individual from the nineteenth century differ in their understanding from an individual in the twenty-first century about the application of the Bill of Rights?

- **a** Individuals in the nineteenth century developed the Doctrine of Selective Incorporation to expand the ability of the national government to restrain acts of lower governments.
- **b** Traditional understandings about the Bill of Rights in the nineteenth century committed the national government to protecting the rights of groups who lacked political or social influence.
- **c** The common understanding in the nineteenth century was that the Bill of Rights did not place restraints on the actions of state or local governments.
- **d** Individual understandings about the Bill of Rights in the nineteenth century represented wide disagreements on how much it empowered the government to act.

5. The primary issue involved in the case of *Engel v. Vitale* was

- **a** the removal of religious activities within public schools.
- **b** the coercive nature of public employees leading religious observations.
- **c** the enforcement of a clearly defined "wall of separation" between church and state.
- **d** the financial support of government institutions for organized religious groups within schools.

6. What statement most accurately describes how the Supreme Court has ruled on issues of religious freedom in the last twenty years?

- **a** The Court has offered greater accommodations of religious beliefs in exempting groups from public policy.
- **b** The Court has increased focus on creating more clear distinctions between government and religious entities.
- **c** The Court expanded the role of government in regulating the economic and political activities of religious organizations.
- **d** The Court permitted expanded regulation of the religious content within free speech activities.

7. The First Amendment protection of free speech is best understood in which of the following ways?

- **a** An absolute protection of the right to speak freely
- **b** The ability to offer ideas, even controversial ones, without fear of government or corporate limitations
- **c** A spectrum with varying degrees of protection dependent on the content and value of the speech
- **d** Wide-ranging areas with significant regulations around unpopular words and ideas

8. The Supreme Court has ruled that symbolic speech such as campaign donations, wearing black arm bands, and burning flags are protected speech, while burning draft cards in protest is not protected speech. What is the distinction between when symbolic speech is protected by the Court and when it is not?

- **a** Which institutions or organizations are being targeted by the protests
- **b** Whether or not the protests disrupt a legitimate function of the government
- **c** What the circumstances are surrounding the time and place of the protests
- **d** What organizations are behind the mobilization of the protests

9. Which description best captures the history of the Supreme Court in its interpretation of the Second Amendment's guarantee of a right to bear arms?

- **a** The Court has historically recognized two distinct protections: a right of states to keep a well-regulated militia and an individual right to own firearms.
- **b** The Court has alternated between interpreting the Second Amendment as an individual right to bear arms or a right to bear arms within the well-regulated militia.
- **c** The Court interpreted the right to bear arms as linked to maintaining a well-regulated militia for the overwhelming majority of the nation's history.
- **d** The Court has reinterpreted a right to bear arms more narrowly after the vast number of mass shootings in modern history.

10. Since the early 2000s, the Supreme Court has

- **a** struck down significant numbers of federal firearms restrictions.
- **b** consistently struck down state and local regulations on owning firearms.
- **c** skewed more toward a less expansive view of the right to bear arms.
- **d** largely deferred to state governments in determining policies around gun ownership.

11. "I plead the Fifth," "You have the right to remain silent," and "You have the right to an attorney" are all phrases that assert protections from which protections within the Constitution and Bill of Rights?

- **a** Due process
- **b** Equal protection
- **c** Bills of attainder
- **d** Eminent domain

12. People found "not guilty" of a crime in federal court may still face which future situation related to the same charges?

- **a** A new criminal trial if evidence against them surfaces
- **b** A state trial for the same or similar crime
- **c** A trial in a different federal court with a different judge and jury
- **d** A plea bargain offer in exchange for a conviction on a lesser charge

13. While the public overwhelmingly believes in a constitutional right to privacy, it remains controversial because

- **a** the language defining privacy in the Constitution is unclear.
- **b** privacy is inferred from the other protections in the Bill of Rights without being included in the text.
- **c** privacy rights have been expanded beyond the original text in the Bill of Rights to include more questionable areas of application.
- **d** there is little evidence that the framers prioritized a right to privacy from the government during the debates at the Constitutional Convention.

14. The concept that sexual behavior between consenting adults, as noted in *Lawrence v. Texas*, cannot be regulated by the government is connected to the liberties associated with the

- **a** First, Third, and Fifth Amendments.
- **b** Fourth, Fifth, and Ninth Amendments.
- **c** First, Sixth, and Eighth Amendments.
- **d** Ninth and Tenth Amendments.

15. The primary difficulty in determining which liberties fall within a "right to privacy" is which of the following?

- **a** The framers of the Constitution didn't make clear what areas were extended an expectation of privacy.
- **b** Privacy issues often include issues and activities that are socially divisive.
- **c** Congress has been hesitant to extend privacy laws to various groups and activities.
- **d** Policies and regulations from states, Congress, and bureaucratic agencies contradict each other.

Use INQUIZITIVE to help you study and master this material.

5

Civil Rights

You can't discriminate against me . . . right?

» **"[George Floyd's death is a] tragic reminder that this was not an isolated incident, but a part of an ingrained systemic cycle of injustice that still exists in this country. I don't think we can move forward unless we take aggressive action to rip out the insidious race-based inequalities that corrupt every part of our society."[1]**
President Joe Biden, May 27, 2020

« **"We should all agree: The answer is not to defund the police. The answer is to fund the police. Fund them with resources and training they need to protect our communities."[2]**
President Joe Biden, March 1, 2022

In 2020 when the killing of an unarmed Black man, George Floyd, by the police set off mass protests across the country against police brutality and racial injustice, the majority of Americans supported the social justice movement. But as the protests continued and the issues discussed expanded to include the movement to reallocate funds—or defund—from the police to social services for historically marginalized communities, some people balked. How far are Americans willing to go to support fairness and equality in this country? We explore the history and future of civil rights in this chapter.

Our civil rights protect us from discrimination by the government and our fellow Americans. This issue came to the fore in 2020 when the killing of an unarmed Black man, George Floyd, by the police set off mass protests across the country against police brutality and racial injustice. Almost everyone would agree that selective enforcement of laws depending on the color of one's skin constitutes discrimination—and is unacceptable. However, opinions on discrimination become less clear-cut in the realm of law enforcement, particularly when it comes to policies aimed at changing policing practices. Early support for the protests dissipated when general ideas about reforming policing evolved into more specific proposals to "defund the police."[3]

This same pattern of support for general ideas, such as "equality for all" and "equal protection of the laws," fades when it comes to specific applications to policies concerning race, ethnicity, gender, and sexual orientation. Indeed, topics such as voting rights, environmental racism, sexual harassment, critical race theory, institutional racism, equal rights for transgender people, "cancel culture," and how race is taught in the public schools have become very divisive in recent years and figured prominently in recent elections.

You probably have experience with questions of discrimination in your own life, beyond the realm of law enforcement. In fact, civil rights are one of the best examples of the idea that politics is everywhere: policies concerning discrimination in the workplace

CHAPTER GOALS

Describe the historical struggles groups have faced in winning civil rights (pp. 164–175)

Analyze inequality among racial, ethnic, and social groups today (pp. 175–181)

Explain the approaches used to bring about change in civil rights policies (pp. 181–203)

Examine affirmative action and other ongoing civil rights issues (pp. 204–210) and in housing and against women, historically marginalized groups, the LGBTQIA+ community, and disabled people affect millions of Americans every day. Consider the following scenarios:

- Scenario 1: You are driving home one night with a few of your friends after a party. It is late at night, but you have not had anything to drink and you are following all traffic laws. Your heart sinks as you see the flashing lights of a squad car signaling you to pull over. As the police officer approaches your car, you wonder if you have been pulled over because you and your friends are Black Americans driving in an all-White neighborhood. Have your civil rights been violated? Change the scene to a car full of White teenagers with all the other facts the same. Can an officer pull them over just because the officer thinks that teenagers are more likely than older people to be engaging in criminal activity?
- Scenario 2: You are a 21-year-old Asian-American woman applying for your first job out of college. After being turned down for a job at an engineering firm, you suspect that you didn't get the job because you are a woman and because management thought that you would not fit in with the "good ol' boy" atmosphere of the firm. Have your civil rights been violated?
- Scenario 3: You and your same-sex partner are told that "your kind" are not welcome in the apartment complex that you want to live in. Should you call a lawyer?
- Scenario 4: You are a White male graduating from high school. You have just received a letter of rejection from the college that was first on your list. You are very disappointed, but then you get angry when a friend tells you that one of your classmates got into the same school even though he had virtually the same grades as you and his SAT scores were a bit lower. Your friend says that it is probably because of the school's affirmative action policy—the classmate who was accepted is Latino. Are you a victim of discrimination? Have your civil rights been violated?

All of these scenarios would seem to be civil rights violations. However, some are, some are not, and some depend on additional considerations (we will return to these examples in the chapter's conclusion). Is it ever acceptable to treat people differently based on the color of their skin, their ethnic background, their gender, or their sexual orientation? More broadly, when is discrimination legal, and when isn't it? How are civil rights in the United States defined today?

DESCRIBE THE HISTORICAL STRUGGLES GROUPS HAVE FACED IN WINNING CIVIL RIGHTS

The context of civil rights

In general, **civil rights** are rights that guarantee individuals freedom from discrimination. In the United States, individuals' civil rights are monitored by the U.S. Commission on Civil Rights, a bipartisan, independent federal commission that was established by the 1957 Civil Rights Act.[4] The commission's mission is to "appraise federal laws and policies," investigate complaints, and collect information regarding citizens who are "being deprived of their right to vote" or who are being discriminated against or denied the "equal protection of the laws under the Constitution because of race, color, religion, sex, age, disability, or national origin." It investigates government actions, such as allegations of racial discrimination in elections, and discriminatory actions of individuals in the workplace, commerce, housing, and education.

civil rights
Rights that guarantee individuals freedom from discrimination. These rights are generally grounded in the equal protection clause of the Fourteenth Amendment and more specifically laid out in laws passed by Congress, such as the 1964 Civil Rights Act.

This definition seems straightforward enough, but confusion may arise when comparing the terms "civil rights" and "civil liberties." They are often used interchangeably, but there are important differences. "Civil liberties" refers to the freedoms guaranteed in the Bill of Rights, such as the freedom of speech, religious expression, and the press, as well as the due process protection of the Fourteenth Amendment. In contrast, civil rights protect all persons from discrimination and are rooted in laws and the equal protection clause of the Fourteenth Amendment. Moreover, civil liberties primarily limit what the government can do to you ("*Congress* shall make no law... abridging the freedom of speech," for example), whereas civil rights protect you from discrimination both by the government and by individuals. As noted in the previous chapter, to oversimplify, civil liberties are about freedom and civil rights are about equality.

Neither civil liberties nor civil rights figured prominently at the Constitutional Convention. Equality is not even mentioned in the Constitution or the Bill of Rights. However, equality was very much on the Founders' minds, as is evident in this ringing passage from the Declaration of Independence: "We hold these truths to be self-evident, that all men are created equal, that they are endowed by their Creator with certain unalienable Rights, that among these are Life, Liberty, and the pursuit of Happiness." Despite the broad language, this was a limited conception of equality. The reference to "men" was intentional: women had no political or economic rights in the late eighteenth century. Similarly, equality did not apply to enslaved people or to Native Americans. Even propertyless White men did not have full political rights until several decades after the Constitution was ratified. Equality and civil rights in the United States have been a continually evolving work in progress.

Black Americans

From the early nineteenth century and the movement for the abolition of slavery until the mid-twentieth century and the civil rights movement, the central focus of civil rights was on the experiences of Black Americans. Other groups received attention more gradually. Starting in the mid-nineteenth century women began their fight for equal rights, and over the next century the civil rights movement expanded to include other groups such as Native Americans, Latinos, and Asian Americans. Most recently, attention has turned to the elderly, disabled people, and the LGBTQIA+ community (lesbian, gay, bisexual, transgender, queer/questioning [one's sexual or gender identity], intersex, and asexual/aromantic/agender people). This part of the chapter will discuss the experiences of each of these groups separately, but each has the common experience of being discriminated against. Also, the discussion of each separate group ignores the **intersectionality** of being part of more than one group (for example, a Latina lesbian). The criticism President Biden faced for saying that he was only going to consider nominating a Black woman to the Supreme Court, *because there had never been a Black woman on the Court*, is an example of the layers of discrimination embedded in our political system.

intersectionality
The complex, cumulative way in which the effects of multiple forms of discrimination (such as racism, sexism, and classism) combine, overlap, or intersect especially in the experiences of marginalized individuals or groups.

Consider that you are a victim of intimate partner violence. Who would you call for help? If you were an undocumented immigrant or a Black transgender woman, would you make the same decision? Intersectionality helps us look at how various combinations of identities can produce very different outcomes and expectations for treatment despite nondiscrimination policies.

Slavery and Its Impact The most divisive civil rights issue with the greatest long-term impact has been slavery and its legacy. Slavery was part of the American economy from nearly the beginning of the nation's history. Dutch traders brought 20 enslaved people to Jamestown, Virginia, in 1619, a year before the Puritans landed at Plymouth Rock. It is impossible to overstate the importance of enslaved people to the southern economy. The 1860 census shows that there were 2.3 million enslaved people in the Deep South (including Georgia, Alabama, South Carolina, Mississippi, and Louisiana), constituting 47 percent of its population, and there were nearly 4 million enslaved people in

Slavery was part of the American economy from 1619 until it was abolished by the Thirteenth Amendment in 1865. The system of slavery in the South created a highly unequal society in which Black Americans were denied virtually all rights. Abolitionists worked to undermine and abolish slavery. Harriet Tubman (right) was instrumental in the success of the Underground Railroad, which brought countless enslaved people to freedom.

the South overall. The economic benefits for owners of enslaved people were clear. By 1860, the per capita income for White Americans in the South was $3,978; in the North, it was $2,040. The South had only 30 percent of the nation's free population, but it had 60 percent of the wealthiest men.[5] However, slavery was not entirely a southern institution. Many businesses in the North benefited from slavery and the trading of enslaved people[6] and every northern state, with the exception of Vermont, had at least a few enslaved people before the Civil War. Some states, such as New York with 21,193 enslaved people in 1790, had quite a few. While slavery was abolished in northern states by 1804, it continued in the North until 1850, at which point New Jersey and Delaware were the only two northern states that still had enslaved people.[7]

Abolitionists worked to rid the nation of slavery as its importance to the South grew, setting the nation on a collision course that would not be resolved until the Civil War. Despite the work of some early abolitionists, the Founders largely ducked the issue (see Chapter 2), and subsequent legislatures and courts did not come any closer to resolving the impasse between the North and South over slavery. The Missouri Compromise of 1820, which limited the expansion of slavery and kept the overall balance between slave states and free states, eased tensions for a while, but the issue persisted. By the 1830s, the abolitionist movement gained considerable strength. Owners of enslaved people became increasingly frustrated with the success of the Underground Railroad, which helped some enslaved people escape to freedom in the North. In 1850, the debate over admitting California as a free state or a slave state (or making it half-free and half-slave) threatened to split the nation once again. As part of the Compromise of 1850, southern states agreed to admit California as a free state, but only if Congress passed the Fugitive Slave Act, which required northern states to treat people who had escaped from slavery as property and return them to their owners. The Compromise also established Utah and New Mexico as territories that could decide for themselves if they would permit slavery. This idea of "popular sovereignty" concerning slavery in new states was fully embraced in the Kansas-Nebraska Act of 1854, thus overturning that central part of the Missouri Compromise.[8]

All possibility of further compromise on the issue ended with the misguided *Dred Scott v. Sandford* decision in 1857. The Supreme Court ruled that at the time of the drafting of the Constitution enslaved people were "considered as a subordinate and inferior class of beings who had been subjugated by the dominant race." Therefore, enslaved people were property rather than citizens and, as such, had no legal rights. The Court also used its power of judicial review for only the second time, ruling that it was unconstitutional for Congress to limit the property rights of owners of enslaved people in the territories. In 1860, believing that slavery was in jeopardy after Abraham Lincoln won the presidency, the southern states seceded from the Union and formed the Confederacy.

When the Civil War ended, national unity was restored and slavery ended, but the price was very high. About 528,000 Americans died in the war, with an astonishingly high casualty rate (25 percent).[9] After the war, Republicans moved quickly to ensure that the changes accomplished by the war could not easily be undone: they promptly adopted the Civil War amendments to the Constitution. The Thirteenth Amendment banned slavery, the Fourteenth guaranteed that states could not deny newly freed people the equal protection of the laws and provided citizenship to anyone born in the United States, and the Fifteenth gave Black men the right to vote. These amendments were ratified within five years of the war, although southern states resisted giving freed people and their descendants "equal protection of the laws" over the next 100 years.

Voting Rights and Obstacles During Reconstruction (1866–1877), Black Americans in the South gained political power through institutions such as the Freedmen's Bureau and the Union League. With the protection of the occupying northern army, Black Americans were able to vote and even hold public office. When federal troops withdrew and the Republican Party abandoned the South, however, Black Americans were almost completely **disenfranchised** (denied the right to vote) through the imposition of residency requirements, poll taxes, literacy tests, physical intimidation, and other forms of disqualification. Southern states also took advantage of a loophole in Section 2 of the Fourteenth Amendment that allowed states to not be penalized for disenfranchising people who had committed crimes. Southern states targeted Black Americans for loitering and petty crimes that were selectively enforced to prevent them from voting.[10] Later the practice known as the "white primary" allowed only White Americans to vote in Democratic primary elections, and given that the Republican Party did not exist in most southern states, Black Americans were effectively disenfranchised. Although most of these provisions were claimed to be race neutral, their impact fell disproportionately on Black voters. For example, the **grandfather clause**, which permitted those who had voted before the war and their descendants to vote even if they did not meet current voting requirements, enabled illiterate White Americans (but not illiterate Black Americans) to avoid the literacy test.[11] Many states also had "understanding" or "good character" exceptions to the literacy tests, which gave election officials substantial discretion over who would be allowed to vote.

The collective impact of these obstacles virtually eliminated Black voting. For example, only 6 percent of Black Americans were registered to vote in Mississippi in 1890 and only 2 percent were registered in Alabama in 1906. After the last post-Reconstruction Black congressman left the House in 1901, 72 years passed before another Black American represented a southern district in Congress. In one Mississippi county in 1947, only 6 out of 13,000 eligible Black Americans were actually registered to vote. Despite the constitutional guarantees of the Fourteenth and Fifteenth Amendments, Black Americans had little access to the political system in the South, and they had little success in winning office at any level in the rest of the nation.[12]

Jim Crow The social and economic position of Black Americans in the South followed a path similar to their political fortunes. Soon after the Civil War ended, sympathetic Republicans passed the Civil Rights Acts of 1866 and 1875, which aimed to outlaw segregation and provide equal opportunity for Black Americans. However, there were no enforcement provisions, and when Reconstruction ended in 1877 the southern states enacted "black codes," or **Jim Crow laws**, that led to complete segregation of the races. Then, in 1883, the Supreme Court ruled that the 1875 Civil Rights Act was unconstitutional because Congress did not have the power to forbid racial discrimination

disenfranchised
To have been denied the ability to exercise a right, such as the right to vote.

grandfather clause
A type of law enacted in several southern states to allow those who were permitted to vote before the Civil War, and their descendants, to bypass literacy tests and other obstacles to voting, thereby exempting White Americans from these tests while continuing to disenfranchise Black Americans and other people of color.

Jim Crow laws
State and local laws that mandated racial segregation in all public facilities in the South, many border states, and some northern communities between 1876 and 1964.

A house divided against itself cannot stand. I believe this government cannot endure permanently half-slave and half-free.

—President Abraham Lincoln

Senator Hiram Revels, the first Black American to serve in the U.S. Congress, represented Mississippi in 1870 and 1871.

in private businesses. Southern states interpreted this decision as a signal that the national government was unconcerned about protecting the rights of Black Americans.

Jim Crow laws forbade interracial marriage and mandated the complete separation of the races for neighborhoods, hotels, apartments, hospitals, schools, restrooms, drinking fountains, restaurants, elevators, and even cemetery plots. In cases where it would have been inconvenient to completely separate the races, as in public transportation, Black Americans had to sit in the back of the bus or in separate cars on the train and give up their seats to White Americans if asked. The Supreme Court validated these practices in *Plessy v. Ferguson* (1896) by establishing the **"separate but equal" doctrine**, officially permitting segregation as long as Black Americans had facilities equal to those of White Americans.

"separate but equal" doctrine
The idea that racial segregation was acceptable as long as the separate facilities were of equal quality; supported by *Plessy v. Ferguson* and struck down by *Brown v. Board of Education*.

In the first several decades after Reconstruction, the rest of the nation mostly ignored the status of Black Americans, because 90 percent of all Black Americans lived in the South. The subjugation of Black Americans in the South went well beyond the separations of the races. A racist criminal justice system ignored widespread lynchings, church burnings, and general intimidation. The Equal Justice Initiative has documented 4,084 "racial terror lynchings" in 12 southern states between the end of Reconstruction in 1877 and 1950.[13] But Black Americans' northward migration to urban areas throughout the first half of the twentieth century transformed the nation's demographic profile and its racial politics. America's "race problem" was no longer just a southern problem. Although conditions for Black Americans were generally better outside the South, they still faced discrimination and lived largely segregated lives throughout the nation. In World Wars I and II, Black soldiers fought and died for their country in segregated units. Professional sports teams were segregated, and Black musicians and artists could not perform in many of the nation's leading theaters. Moreover, Black Americans largely were hired for the lowest-paying menial jobs.

Progress began in the 1940s. The Supreme Court struck down the white primary in 1944, Jackie Robinson broke the color line in Major League Baseball in 1947, and President Harry Truman issued an executive order integrating the U.S. armed services in 1948. Then came the landmark decision ***Brown v. Board of Education*** (1954), which rejected the "separate but equal" doctrine and declared that race-based school segregation violates the Fourteenth Amendment's equal protection clause, followed by *Brown II* (1955), which ordered that public schools be desegregated "with all deliberate speed." These events set the stage for the growing success of the civil rights movement, discussed later in this chapter.

Brown v. Board of Education
(1954) declared that race-based school segregation violates the Fourteenth Amendment's equal protection clause.

Native Americans

The legacy of slavery and racial segregation in the South has been the dominant focus of U.S. civil rights policies, but many other groups have also fought for equal rights. Native Americans were the first group to come in contact with the European immigrants. Although initial relations between the Native Americans and the European settlers were good in many places, the settlers' appetite for more land and their insensitivity to Native-American culture soon led to a state of continual conflict. By the mid-1800s this continual expansion westward was labeled "manifest destiny" and was used to justify systematically removing Native Americans from their land and placing them on reservations. The most infamous example was the removal of 60,000 members of the "Five Civilized Tribes" from the southeastern United States following the enactment of the Indian Removal Act in 1830. Thousands of Native Americans died on the Trail of Tears on their way to reservations in Oklahoma.[14] Also, while the practice differed from the chattel slavery of the South, tens of thousands of Native Americans served in bondage

The Carlisle Indian Industrial School in Carlisle, Pennsylvania, was open from 1879 to 1918. The school's Native-American students were forced to cut their hair and change their names.

in the pre–Civil War West. The practice started with Spanish California's mission system of the late 1700s and continued through the gold rush of the mid-1800s.[15]

Native Americans had no political rights; indeed, the U.S. government was in open conflict with many tribes. The American Indian Wars involved about 1,500 different campaigns authorized by the U.S. government between 1622 and 1924.[16] By the end of the nineteenth century, the Native-American population had shrunk to 250,000 from at least eight times that many before the Europeans arrived (estimates range from a low of 2.1 million to a high of 18 million).[17] While thousands were killed by the military campaigns, most deaths were caused by European diseases for which the Native Americans did not have immunity, with smallpox being the most deadly.[18]

Native Americans did not gain the universal right to vote until 1924, just after women and well after Black men. Although the U.S. government signed treaties with Native-American tribes that recognized them as sovereign nations (not as foreign nations but as "domestic dependent nations"),[19] in practice the government ignored most of the agreements.[20] One of the most devastating abrogations of treaties was the 1887 Dawes Act that compensated individual Native-American families for land they already collectively controlled on reservations. In the nearly 50 years the law was in effect (1887–1934), the Dawes Act took 90 million acres from Native Americans, reducing their land holdings from 138 million to 48 million acres.[21]

Only in recent decades has the government started to uphold its obligations, although compliance remains spotty. For example, in a 2020 decision that was described as a "stunning reaffirmance of the nation's obligations to Native Americans," the Supreme Court ruled that nearly half of Oklahoma that was promised to the Five Civilized Tribes in the 1830s as part of the treaty that started the Trail of Tears remains a reservation for purposes of the statute in question. The law concerned the federal government's jurisdiction, not the state's, over some major crimes committed by a Native American on the reservation.[22] Oklahoma did not exist at the time of the treaty, so the state argued that the treaty should not apply. However, the treaty "solemnly guarantied [*sic*]" the land to the tribe, "forever set apart as a home for said Creek Nation," "no portion [of which] shall ever be embraced or included within . . . any Territory or State." In Justice Gorsuch's majority opinion, he said agreeing with the arguments presented by Oklahoma would be endorsing the "rule of the strong, not the rule of law."[23]

Native Americans have struggled to maintain their cultural history and autonomy in the face of widespread poverty and unemployment and a sustained and concerted effort by the government to force assimilation. The most notorious of these practices was the removal of children from their families to attend Native-American boarding schools that forced assimilation. Founded shortly after the Civil War, these schools continued to operate into the late twentieth century, with a peak attendance of 60,000 Native-American children in 1973. Although Christian missionaries originally ran the schools, the Bureau of Indian Affairs took over the operation of many in the twentieth century. This dark chapter in American history has been referred to by its critics as "cultural genocide."[24]

Founded in 1968, the American Indian Movement (AIM) organized to fight for equal rights and address problems of poverty, discrimination, and police brutality. The occupation of Alcatraz for 19 months in 1969–1971 called attention to the goals

The American Indian Movement was founded in the 1960s to fight systemic discrimination and raise awareness of issues facing Native Americans, including poverty, education, and land rights. The movement included several actions to bring attention to their cause, including the occupation of Alcatraz Island, the location of a decommissioned prison. The group of 89 Native Americans tried to reclaim the land under the 1868 Treaty of Fort Laramie, which states that surplus U.S. land could be ceded to Native Americans.

of the movement and served as a model for activism on these issues for the next fifty years. The history is too voluminous to recount in detail here, but significant actions include occupying Mount Rushmore (1970), the "trail of broken treaties" (1972), the occupation of Wounded Knee (1973), the Longest Walk (1978), Orme Dam (1981), the National Coalition of Racism in Sports and Media (1992, but this is an ongoing campaign, with the most recent success of changing the name of the NFL's Washington Redskins to the Commanders), and protests against the Keystone XL Pipeline (2011), uranium mining near the Grand Canyon (2013), and the Standing Rock Pipeline (2012–2022).[25]

Latinos and Latinas

Latinos have also struggled for political and economic equality. The early history of Latinos in the United States is rooted in the Mexican-American War (1846–1848) and the conquest by the United States of the territory that today makes up most of the southwestern states. The Treaty of Guadalupe Hidalgo ended the war with Mexico ceding to the United States 525,000 square miles (more than half its territory), including parts of present-day Arizona, California, New Mexico, Texas, Colorado, Nevada, and Utah. Mexico also gave up all claims to Texas and recognized the Rio Grande as the boundary. Since that time, Mexicans have resided in large numbers in the Southwest. Although Latinos had long experienced prejudice and discrimination, one of their first major political successes was Cesar Chavez's effort to organize farmworkers in the 1960s and 1970s and end the Bracero program that authorized agricultural workers from Mexico between 1951 and 1964. He established the United Farm Workers Union and forced growers to bargain with 50,000 mostly Mexican-American (but also Filipino) fieldworkers in California and Florida.

Although many Mexican Americans have roots that go back hundreds of years, a majority of Latinos have been in the United States for less than two generations. Consequently, they have become a political force only recently, although they are now the nation's largest historically marginalized group. Latinos' relative lack of political clout when compared with that of Black Americans can be explained by two factors. First, Latinos vote at a much lower rate than Black Americans, in part because

While most Latino voters are loyal to the Democratic Party, they represent an extremely diverse group composed of people from many Latin American nations, and so they rally around diverse issues. Several issues that unite this diverse group include immigration and DACA.

many have language barriers. In addition, about one-third of Latinos cannot vote in national elections because they are not U.S. citizens. Second, unlike Black Americans, Latinos are a relatively diverse group politically, composed of people from many Latin American nations. Most Latino voters are loyal to the Democratic Party, but a majority of Cuban Americans are Republicans. Although this diversity means that Latino voters do not speak with one voice, it brings opportunity for increased political clout in the future. The diversity of partisan attachments among Latinos and their relatively low levels of political involvement mean that both parties are eager to attract them as new voters. In 2016, Donald Trump surprised many experts by winning a higher percentage of the Latino vote (29 percent) than Mitt Romney did in 2012 (27 percent). Trump defied expectations again in 2020, as this percentage increased to 32 percent despite his immigration policies.

Asian Americans and Pacific Islanders

Asian Americans experienced discrimination beginning with their arrival in the United States in the nineteenth century. The first wave of Chinese immigrants came with the 1848 California gold rush. Initially, foreign miners, including Chinese immigrants, were able to stake out their claims along with Americans. But by 1850, when the easy-to-find gold was gone, Americans tried to drive out Chinese immigrants through violence and the Foreign Miners Tax. Subsequently, Chinese immigrants played a crucial role in building the intercontinental railroad between 1865 and 1869. Yet, because they were given the most dangerous jobs, many lost their lives. After the railroad was completed, Chinese workers returned to the West Coast, where they experienced increasing discrimination and violence. Following several race riots, Congress passed the Chinese Exclusion Act of 1882, which prevented Chinese immigrants already in the United States from becoming U.S. citizens—although the Supreme Court later granted their American-born children automatic citizenship under the Fourteenth Amendment.[26] The Chinese Exclusion Act also barred virtually all immigration from China—the first time in U.S. history that a specific ethnic group was singled out in this way. During World War II, more than 110,000 Japanese were placed in internment camps for fear that they were enemy supporters. Although the internment was upheld by the Supreme Court at the time, a 1980 congressional commission determined that it was a "grave injustice" motivated by "racial prejudice, war hysteria and the failure of political leadership."

During World War II, tens of thousands of Japanese Americans were forced to relocate to internment camps. Nearly two-thirds were American citizens, and most lost their homes and jobs.

Eight years later, President Ronald Reagan signed into law the Civil Liberties Act, which paid more than $1.6 billion in reparations to the survivors of the camps and their heirs.[27] In 2018, the Court explicitly overturned the 1944 decision that approved the internment, saying, "The forcible relocation of U.S. citizens to concentration camps, solely and explicitly on the basis of race, is objectively unlawful and outside the scope of presidential authority."[28] In recent decades, a much broader range of Asians have emigrated to the United States, including Koreans, Filipinos, Hmong, Vietnamese, and Indians. This variation in national heritage, culture, and language means that Asian Americans are quite diverse in their political views, partisan affiliation, and voting patterns. The recent

During the COVID-19 pandemic, more than 9,000 incidents of Anti-Asian hate crimes were reported. This rally in New York City's Chinatown was held to raise awareness and fight claims, including those made by President Trump in 2020, that blamed China for the spread of the pandemic.

experience of these immigrants in terms of discrimination has also varied, but since the COVID-19 pandemic, anti-Asian hate crimes have increased by 339 percent.[29] Some claim that climate for these hate crimes was partly created by President Trump, who blamed China for the virus, calling it the "Kung Flu."[30]

Women and civil rights

On the eve of the United States' declaration of independence in 1776, John Adams's wife, Abigail, advised him not to "put such unlimited power in the hands of the husbands. Remember, all men would be tyrants if they could. . . . If particular care and attention is not paid to the ladies, we . . . will not hold ourselves bound by any laws in which we have no voice or representation."[31] John Adams did not listen to his wife. The Constitution did not give women the right to vote, and they were not guaranteed that civil right until the Nineteenth Amendment was ratified in 1920—although 16 states had allowed women to vote before then. Until the early twentieth century, women in most parts of the country could not hold office, serve on juries, bring lawsuits in their own name, own property, or serve as legal guardians for their children. A woman's identity was so closely tied to her husband's that if she married a noncitizen she automatically gave up her citizenship.

protectionism
The idea under which some people have tried to rationalize discriminatory policies by claiming that some groups, like women or Black Americans, should be denied certain rights for their own safety or well-being.

The rationale for these policies was called **protectionism**. The argument was that women were too frail to compete in the business world and needed to be protected by men. This reasoning served in many court cases to deny women equal rights. For example, in 1869 Myra Bradwell requested admission to the Illinois bar to practice law. She was the first woman to graduate from law school in Illinois and the editor of *Chicago Legal News,* and she held all the qualifications to be a lawyer in the state except for one—she was a woman. Her request was denied, and she sued all the way to the Supreme Court. In 1873, the Court ruled that the prohibition against women lawyers did not violate the Fourteenth Amendment's privileges and immunities clause because there was no constitutional right to be an attorney. If the Court had stopped there, the decision would have been unremarkable for its time. But Justice Joseph Bradley went on to provide a classic example of protectionism:

> *The civil law as well as nature itself has always recognized a wide difference in the respective spheres and destinies to man and woman. Man is, or should be, woman's protector and defender. The natural and proper timidity and delicacy which belongs to the female sex evidently unfits it for many of the occupations of civil life. The constitution of the family organization which is founded in the divine ordinance, as well as the nature of things, indicates the domestic sphere as that which properly belongs to the domains and functions of womanhood.*[32]

While protectionist sentiment on the Court had waned by the mid-twentieth century, as recently as 1961 the Court upheld a Florida law that automatically exempted women but not men from compulsory jury duty. The case involved a woman who killed her husband with a baseball bat after he admitted that he was having an affair and wanted to end the marriage. The woman argued that her conviction by an all-male jury violated her Fourteenth Amendment guarantee of "equal protection of the laws" and that a jury panel containing some women would have been more sympathetic to her "temporary insanity" defense. The Court rejected this argument, ruling that the Florida law excluding women from jury duty was reasonable because "despite the enlightened emancipation of women from the restrictions and protections of bygone years, and their entry into many parts of community life formerly considered to be reserved to men, woman still is regarded as the center of home and family life."[33] Apparently, it was unthinkable to the all-male Court that a man might have to stay home from work and take care of the kids while his wife served on a jury (a related point is that businesses at that time would have been unwilling to give men time off from work so their wives could serve on juries). Later in this chapter, we will describe how the Supreme Court has moved away from this discriminatory position and rejected protectionist thinking.

The LGBTQIA+ community

The most recent group to engage in the struggle for civil rights is the LGBTQIA+ community. For most of American history, gays and lesbians lived secret lives and were subject to abuse and discrimination if they openly acknowledged their sexual orientation. The critical moment that spurred the gay rights movement occurred on June 28, 1969, during a routine police raid on the Stonewall Inn in New York City.[34] (Police often raided gay bars to harass patrons and selectively enforce liquor laws.) This time, rather than submitting to the arrests, the customers fought back, throwing stones and beer bottles, breaking windows, and starting small fires. A crowd of several hundred people gathered, and the fighting raged for three nights. The Stonewall rebellion galvanized the gay community by demonstrating the power of collective action.

Since Stonewall, the gay rights movement has made steady progress through a combination of political mobilization and protest, legislative action, and legal action. Public support for gay rights has increased dramatically in recent years. Between two-thirds and three-fourths of Americans (depending on the poll) agree with the national policy established in 2011 that gays may openly serve in the military, whereas a majority of Americans opposed this policy when it was first

In 2016, President Obama designated the historic site of the Stonewall uprising in New York City as a national monument to honor the LGBTQIA+ equality movement.

proposed by President Clinton in 1993. Between 60 and 64 percent of Americans support same-sex marriage according to recent polls, whereas only 35–40 percent held that view in 2009. Seventy-five percent believe that same-sex couples should be able to adopt children (compared with only 14 percent in 1977), 89 percent think that businesses should not be able to discriminate against gays and lesbians, and 63 percent believe that same-sex couples should be entitled to the same benefits as heterosexual couples (whereas only 32 percent think they should not).[35] In May 2012, President Obama endorsed same-sex marriage for the first time (and was the first president to take that position), completing his gradual shift on the issue. In 2015, the Supreme Court ruled that same-sex marriage is legal in all 50 states (we will discuss this and other issues concerning gay and lesbian rights later in the chapter).[36] In the 2016 presidential campaign Donald Trump said, "I will do everything in my power to protect our LGBTQ citizens from the violence and oppression of a hateful foreign ideology. Believe me." But his record on LGBTQIA+ issues was criticized by civil rights supporters.[37] In 2019, the Trump administration banned transgender people from joining the military and prohibited anyone currently in the military from transitioning genders. In 2020, Health and Human Services finalized a rule that would remove nondiscrimination protections for LGBTQIA+ people when it comes to health care and health insurance. However, following the Court's June 2020 landmark civil rights decision protecting gay and transgender people from discrimination in the workplace, two lower courts blocked part of the rule.[38] Then in President Biden's first week in office, he reversed Trump's executive order on transgender persons serving in the military and issued another executive order, "Preventing and Combating Discrimination on the Basis of Gender Identity or Sexual Orientation." In May 2021, he restored anti-bias protections in health care for transgender people.[39]

Why does this history matter for politics today? First, the effects of slavery and Jim Crow laws are still quite evident: legal racial segregation ended nearly 60 years ago, but its legacy—especially evident in the difference that exists in the relative quality of education available to most White Americans and Black Americans—remains. Second, knowing about this history helps us understand where the inequalities (that we discuss in the next section) in our society come from. Finally, active discrimination based on race, gender, and sexual orientation is still evident in our society. Given the importance of race in the everyday lives of millions of Americans and in gaining an understanding of American politics, a grasp of the history that got us to where we are today is an important starting point.

"Why Should I Care?"

The racial divide today

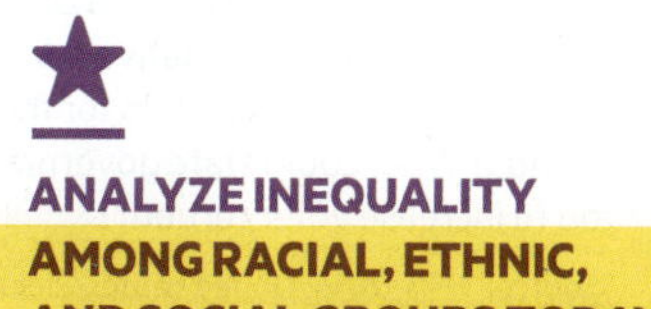

The racial divide today begins with the unequal treatment of racial historically marginalized groups, women, gays, and lesbians and is rooted in the gulf that remains between historically marginalized groups and White Americans, in terms of their objective condition as well as their political views. Although substantial progress has been made in bridging that gulf, political, social, and economic inequalities remain.

Discriminatory treatment

Discrimination is much more common today than many people realize. The Equal Employment Opportunity Commission (EEOC) filed an average of 78,663 charges of employment discrimination each year in the past ten years,[40] while the National Fair Housing Alliance reports an average of 30,000 cases of housing discrimination a year.[41] The Justice Department has won dozens of lawsuits against banks and mortgage lenders who engage in discriminatory practices, winning settlements totaling several hundred million dollars in the past five years.[42]

The experience of a former graduate student in our department who is White and whose wife is Black puts a human face on these statistics. The couple wanted to rent a bigger apartment, so they searched the want ads and made appointments to see some apartments. One landlord told them to meet him in front of the apartment at a specific time. They waited where they were told, but the landlord didn't show up. Later they remembered seeing a car that slowed down and almost stopped but then sped away. They wondered if this was a case of a "drive-by landlord"—one who checks out potential tenants' race from a distance; if they are not White, the landlord skips the appointment and tells them it is rented if they ask. This is exactly what happened. This couple called the landlord, asked what had happened, and were told that the apartment was already rented. To check their suspicions, they had some friends ask about the apartment, and the friends were told it was available. Their friends (both White) made an appointment to meet the landlord, and this time the same car pulled up and stopped. The landlord showed them the apartment and was very friendly. The next day, the graduate student filed a racial discrimination lawsuit.

These types of stories, ranging from irritating and demeaning to serious violations of the law, are familiar to nearly every member of a historically marginalized racial group, woman, and LGBTQIA+ person in the United States. Consider the well-dressed businessman who cannot get a cab in a major city because he is Black, the woman who is sexually harassed by her boss but hesitates to say anything for fear of losing her job, the teenage Latino who is shadowed in the clothing store by a clerk, the Arab American

Bank of America paid

$335 million

in 2011 to settle the largest mortgage discrimination case of its kind.

Source: *New York Times*.

FIGURE 5.1

Turnout in Presidential Elections by Race

Turnout among Black Americans has risen steadily over the last 20 years (with a dip in 2016 that was nearly erased in 2020), while turnout of other groups has remained relatively flat. What do you think accounts for these trends? What could state governments do to increase voter turnout?

Source: 1996–2016: United States Elections Project, "Voter Turnout Demographics," www.electproject.org/home/voter-turnout/demographics; 2020: Kevin Morris, "Large Racial Turnout Gap Persisted in 2020 Elections," Brennan Center for Social Justice, August 6, 2021, www.brennancenter.org/our-work/analysis-opinion/large-racial-turnout-gap-persisted-2020-election (2/3/22).

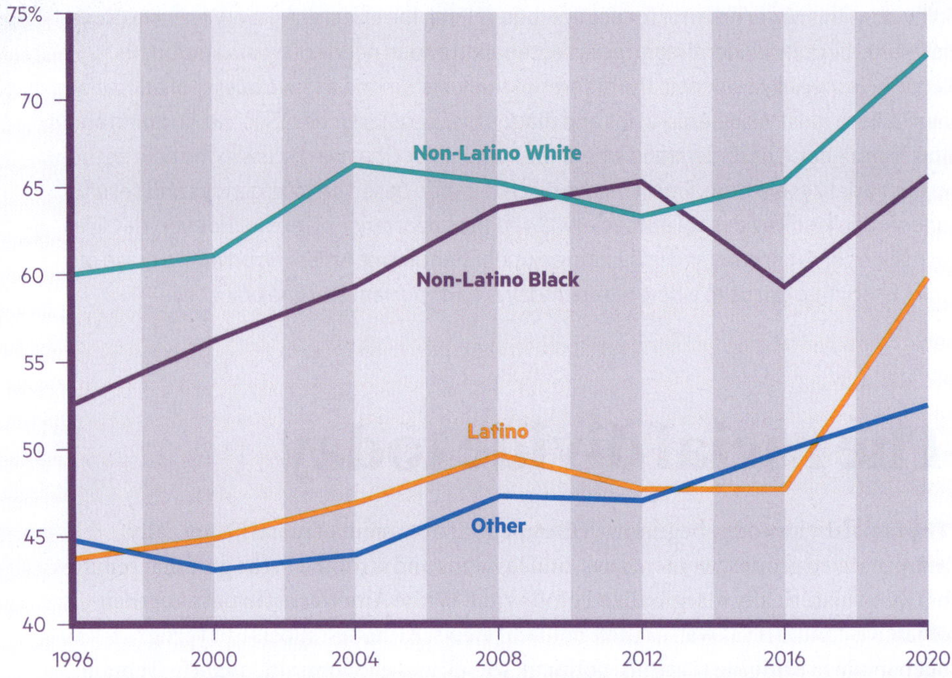

who endures taunts about her head covering, or the lesbian couple who cannot find an apartment. Such personal experiences, as well as extensive government data and academic research, indicate continuing discrimination in our society, despite significant progress in the past generation.

Differences in voting access

The United States has a long history of discriminating against racial and ethnic groups in the election process. Although Black Americans voted at a rate that was quite similar to that of White Americans in presidential elections from 2008 to 2020, their turnout in midterm elections has been somewhat lower than that of White Americans, and other racial and ethnic groups have generally lower turnouts (see Figure 5.1). Much of the difference in voter turnout can be accounted for by education and income, but there still are practices and institutions that specifically depress voter turnout. And many of these deterrents are intentional. The National Association for the Advancement of Colored People (NAACP), the U.S. Commission on Civil Rights, and the Brennan Center for Justice have all documented such practices in elections going back to 2000, including moving and reducing the number of polling places in areas with large populations of historically marginalized groups, changing from district-based to at-large elections (citywide or countywide elections in which there is often a mix of historically marginalized and White voters), using voter challenges to target historically marginalized voters, redistricting to dilute the voting power of historically marginalized groups, withholding information about registration and voting procedures from Black Americans, and "causing or taking advantage of Election Day irregularities."[43]

There are other state practices that are not specifically aimed at voters from historically marginalized groups but that have a disproportionate impact on them. Examples have included removing voters' names from the voting rolls if there wasn't an identical match between the name the voter used when registering to vote and the name as it appeared in another state database (often the database of driver's license information); purging the names of people who had committed felonies from the voting registration lists, which often produced false matches to people with the same names who had not committed a crime; and engaging in voter intimidation and deceptive practices. Moreover, several states use technical barriers to voter registration and voting, limit access to voter registration services at social services offices (even though such access is required by federal law), and use poorly designed ballots.[44]

In recent years many states have restricted access to voting by requiring a photo ID to vote (which has a disproportionate impact on historically marginalized groups because they are less likely to have a photo ID), requiring proof of citizenship to vote, cutting back on early voting days and times, and making it more difficult for people to register to vote.[45] In addition, as we will discuss later, in 2013 the Supreme Court struck down an important part of the 1965 Voting Rights Act (VRA), making it easier for the nine states that had been covered by this provision of the law to implement discriminatory practices. However, legal challenges in many states pushed back against these changes in voting laws. Those supporting voting rights won at least partial victories in eight states against voter ID laws and restrictions on early voting that had a racial impact. Other states also restored the right to vote for those with past criminal convictions.[46] Also, partly in response to the COVID-19 pandemic, which required restrictions on social gatherings and interactions, many states passed laws to make voting easier, such as automatically registering voters and imposing fewer restrictions on early voting and voting by mail. But then 2021 had the largest increase in laws restricting voting access in the last ten years: 19 states passed 34 restrictive voting laws, which accounts for a third of the total number in the past decade. Many of these laws reversed the 2020 changes, for example making it harder to vote by mail, and others made the oversight of the vote-counting process more partisan.[47] Congress attempted to reverse many of these changes while also creating a national holiday for voting and restoring Section 5 of the Voting Right Acts, but the bill was killed early in 2022 by a filibuster in the Senate.[48]

Despite the removal of most formal barriers to voting, since 2014 Latinos have been less likely to vote and participate in politics than White, Black, and Asian Americans. Latino advocacy groups like Mi Familia Vota work to engage and register voters in their local communities.

Health outcomes and environmental racism

On every measure of health—life expectancy, infectious diseases, infant mortality, cancer rates, heart disease, and strokes—the gaps between White Americans and Black Americans are large and, in some cases, increasing. For example, life expectancy for Black Americans is nearly six years shorter than for White Americans (71.8 years for Black Americans compared with 77.6 years for White Americans), the infant mortality rate is more than double for Black Americans (10.8 deaths per 1,000 live births compared with 4.6 deaths per 1,000 live births for White Americans and 4.9 for Latinos), and maternal mortality is two and a half times higher for Black Americans (44 deaths per 100,000 births for Black women compared with 17.9 for White women and 12.6 for Latinas). Similar gaps also exist for incidences of cancer, Type 2 diabetes, strokes, and heart attacks in Black Americans and White Americans.[49] COVID-19 death rates are 2.2 times as high for Native Americans, 1.9 times for Latinos, and 1.7 times for Black Americans when compared with White Americans (while vaccination rates are slightly higher for Native Americans and Latinos compared with White Americans, and a bit lower for Black Americans).[50] While social scientists continue to debate the causes of the racial disparities in health outcomes, an increasing body of evidence indicates that much of the gap is caused by "institutional racism" (also called systemic or structural racism): government policies, social practices, and business-related decisions that perpetuate discrimination. In health care, discrimination happens at three levels: the individual level (between the health care provider and patient), the organizational level (the clinic, hospital, or medical school), and the extra-organizational level (institutions that have regulatory power or government authority, e.g., the Department of Health and Human Services). Examples include implicit bias that leads to different diagnoses and treatment based on race, statistical algorithms of risk assessment that produce racially disparate outcomes, and long-established training practices that discriminate based on race.[51]

Another category of institutional racism is "environmental racism," which refers to practices that make historically marginalized groups much more likely to live in areas affected by pollution, toxic waste, and hazardous chemical sites.[52] One of the most extreme examples of this, uncovered in late 2015 and early 2016, involved the public water supply in Flint, Michigan. In 2014, to save money, the city switched its water supply from Lake Huron to the Flint River. Residents of the poor, majority-Black city soon reported discolored, foul-looking water, but their complaints were ignored by city and state officials. Researchers demonstrated that levels of lead in the water far exceeded safe levels, and 6,000 to 12,000 residents experiencing serious health issues were found to have elevated levels of lead in their blood. President Obama declared the city a disaster area and aid was provided in early 2016, but permanent damage had already been done.[53] More than a dozen officials were charged with felonies for their role in the crisis; none were convicted of the most serious charges, but several pleaded "no contest" to lesser charges. Late in 2021, a federal judge approved a $626.25 million settlement in a class-action lawsuit against the state of Michigan, with about 80 percent of the money going to those who were under 18 at the time of the crisis.[54]

Polluting industries are often placed close to communities with large historically marginalized populations because land is cheaper and historically those areas had less political power to oppose location decisions than wealthy White communities. A report titled *America's Dirty Divide* concludes, "The health effects of these inequalities are staggering. Black Americans are 75 percent more likely to live in close proximity to oil and gas facilities, which emit toxic air pollutants; as a result, these communities often suffer from higher rates of cancer and asthma. Researchers have found that Black children are twice as likely to develop asthma as their peers."[55] Another study found that historically redlined communities (a racist practice used from 1935 through 1968 in the real estate industry to limit investment in neighborhoods with historically marginalized groups) have less access to greenspace today.[56] But communities are starting to fight back as the health effects of environmental racism are documented and publicized.[57]

Criminal justice and hate crimes

The greatest disparity between historically marginalized racial and ethnic groups and White Americans may be in the criminal justice system. Racial profiling subjects many innocent Black Americans to intrusive searches.[58] Tim Scott, a Republican Black senator from South Carolina, said in a speech on the Senate floor that he was pulled over by police officers seven times in one year "for nothing more than driving a new car in the wrong neighborhood." He continued, "I do not know many African-American men who do not have a very similar story to tell—no matter their profession, no matter their income, no matter their disposition in life."[59] Early in 2014, Mayor Bill de Blasio changed New York's policing practices to comply with a federal court ruling concerning the city's aggressive "stop-and-frisk" policy.[60] Racial bias is also evident in the criminal system after the initial arrest. Studies have shown that Black Americans are more likely than White Americans to be convicted for the same crimes and are also more likely to serve longer sentences.[61]

> **There are very few African-American men in this country who haven't had the experience of being followed when they were shopping in a department store. That includes me.**
>
> **—President Barack Obama**

Recently, tensions have been high between historically marginalized communities and the police in the wake of dozens of cases of police shooting unarmed Black men. From 2015 to 2021, police killed 6,972 people in the United States; of those, 1,562 were Black and 1,087 were Latino (see the What Do the Facts Say? feature).[62] Most of these involved tragic

Racial Inequality in Law Enforcement

In 2020, national protests set off by the killing of an unarmed Black man, George Floyd, in Minneapolis, Minnesota, raised the issue of racial inequality in law enforcement and underscored similar killings in Ferguson, Missouri, Baltimore, Maryland, and Staten Island, New York. These graphs show both the total number and the relative number (expressed as a percentage), by race, of people killed by police. Do racial inequalities exist in law enforcement? What do the facts say?

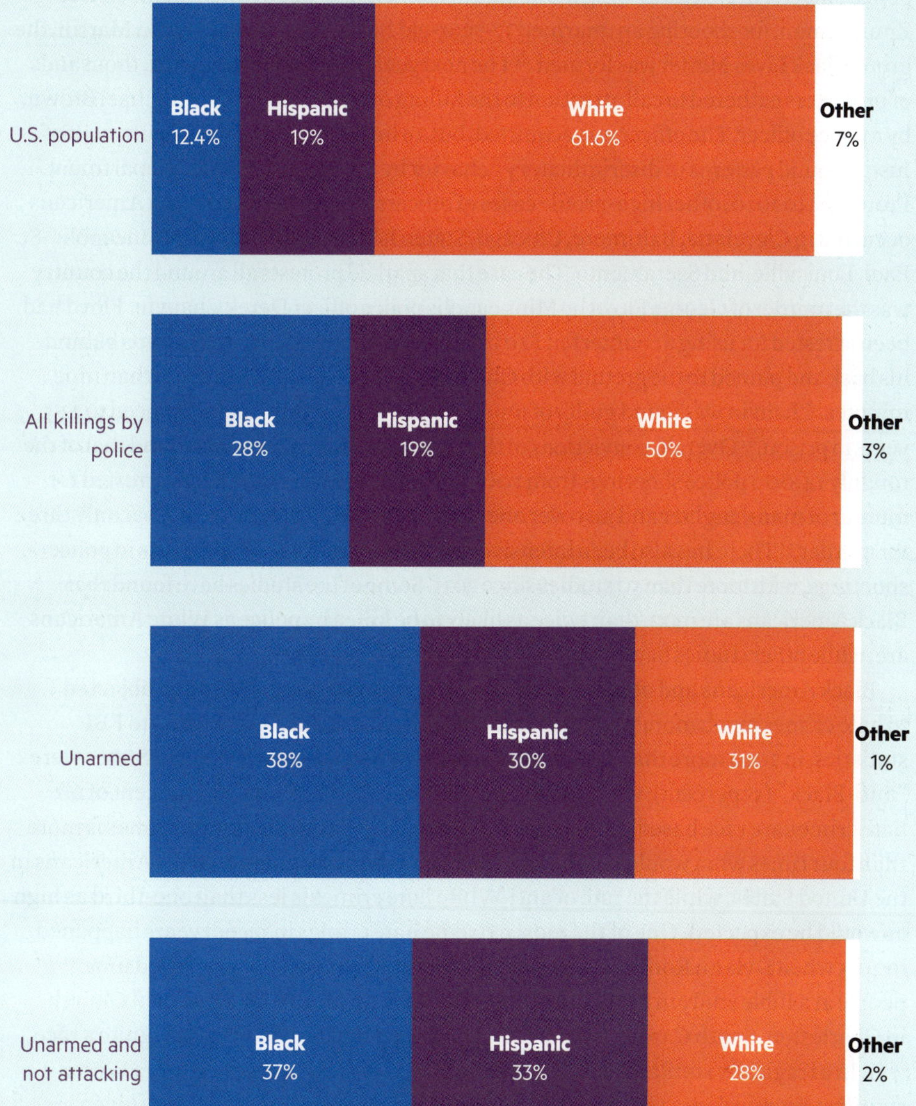

Source: "2021 Police Violence Report," Mapping Police Violence, https://policeviolencereport.org (accessed 7/25/22).

WHAT DO THE FACTS SAY?

Think about it

- **For all victims (total and unarmed),** what racial category had the highest percentage of deaths? What racial category had the highest percentage of victims unarmed and not attacking? What do you think accounts for this difference?
- **Is there a greater racial disparity** in the second chart (which shows all people killed by police) or the third chart (which shows unarmed people)?
- **What, if anything, surprises you** about these numbers? Why?

There have been dozens of high-profile cases in recent years of police shooting unarmed Black men. The killing of George Floyd (memorialized in a mural, left) by White police officer Derek Chauvin in Minneapolis, Minnesota, because Floyd had been suspected of using a counterfeit $20 to make a purchase, set off global protests against policy brutality against Black Americans and started a national dialogue about issues of structural racism and social justice.

circumstances in which police were acting appropriately given existing protocols. But several highly publicized cases reveal negligent and, in some cases, criminal behavior by police officers. In 2013, following the acquittal of a neighborhood watch member, George Zimmerman, for shooting an unarmed 17-year-old Black American, Trayvon Martin, the group Black Lives Matter was formed.[63] The next year in Ferguson, Missouri, thousands of protesters gathered to call attention to the killing of an unarmed man, Michael Brown, by a police officer. The officer was acquitted, but an investigation by the Department of Justice found patterns of discriminatory behavior by the Ferguson Police Department. From 2015 to 2020, other high-profile cases of officers killing unarmed Black Americans occurred in Cleveland, Baltimore, Chicago, Staten Island, Baton Rouge, Minneapolis–St. Paul, Louisville, and Sacramento. The case that sparked protests all around the country was the murder of George Floyd by Minneapolis police officer Derek Chauvin. Floyd had been arrested for using a counterfeit $20 bill. He was handcuffed with his arms behind his back and pinned to the ground with Chauvin's knee on his neck for more than nine minutes. Chauvin was found guilty of murder and manslaughter and sentenced to 22.5 years in prison.[64] Overall, convictions in these cases are rare. One study found that of the roughly 14,000 police shootings from 2005 to 2019, there were 98 officers arrested for murder or manslaughter and just over one-third were convicted of a crime, but only three for murder.[65] There has also been intensive research on the topic of racial bias in police shootings, with more than 50 studies since 2015. Some of the studies have found that Black Americans are more than twice as likely to be killed by police as White Americans are, while other studies have found no significant differences.[66]

Black Americans and other historically marginalized groups are also subjected to hate crimes much more frequently than White Americans.[67] According to FBI statistics, in 2020 more than half of race-related hate crimes in the United States were "anti-Black" (55 percent), while only 17 percent were "anti-White" (63 percent of all hate crimes are race based). This means that the rate of anti-Black hate crimes is more than four times what would be expected based on the percentage of Black Americans in the United States, while the rate of anti-White hate crimes is less than one-third as high as would be expected. One of the most extreme hate crimes in recent years happened in 2015 when Dylann Roof, a 21-year-old White supremacist, shot and killed nine people at a Bible study in the historic Emanuel African Methodist Episcopal Church in Charleston, South Carolina. Roof later confessed that he was trying to ignite a race war. In a tragically similar massacre in a Buffalo, New York, grocery store, a White supremacist murdered ten Black people. He was charged with hate crimes, given his motive "to prevent Black people from replacing white people and eliminating the white race, and to inspire others to commit similar attacks."[68]

This backdrop of racial inequality, discrimination, and violence drives civil rights activists to push their agenda in the three branches of government: legislative, executive, and judicial. In some instances, activists work in several arenas simultaneously; in others, they seek redress in one arena after exhausting alternatives in the others. The civil rights movement, which was crucial in early policy successes, also continues to mobilize from the grass roots.

Key players in the conflict over civil rights

EXPLAIN THE APPROACHES USED TO BRING ABOUT CHANGE IN CIVIL RIGHTS POLICIES

Our civil rights policies are produced by several key players. First, the public becomes involved through social movements to put pressure on the political system to change. But Congress, the president, and the courts all also exert their own influence on policies that define civil rights.

Social movements

From the early women's rights movement and abolitionists of the nineteenth century to the gay rights and civil rights movements of the mid-twentieth century, activists have pressured the political system to change civil rights policies. Through collective action, these social movements have made sure that protecting equal rights remained on the policy agenda.

Women started to push for the right to vote at a convention in 1848 in Seneca Falls, New York. Subsequently, a constitutional amendment to give women the right to vote was regularly introduced in Congress between 1878 and 1913 but never was passed, despite the efforts of women such as Sojourner Truth, Ida B. Wells, Susan B. Anthony, and Elizabeth Cady Stanton. After a parallel movement at the state level had some success, the Nineteenth Amendment, giving women the right to vote, was finally passed in 1919 and ratified in 1920 (see Figure 5.2).

The civil rights movement of the 1950s and 1960s, aimed at ending segregation and guaranteeing equal political and social rights for Black Americans, is the most famous example of a successful social movement (see Figure 5.3). Although the *Brown v. Board of Education* decision, which struck down segregation in public schools, gave the movement a boost, most southern Black Americans saw little change in their daily lives. As White school boards and local governments resisted integration, Black leaders became convinced that the courts would not effect change because of resistance to their decisions. The only way to change the laws was to get the public, both Black and White, to demand change.

The spark came on December 1, 1955, in Montgomery, Alabama, when a woman named Rosa Parks refused to give up her seat on a bus to a White person, as she was required to do by law. Chroniclers often describe Parks as a seamstress who was tired after a long day's work and simply did not want to give up her seat, in order to cast her not as a pioneering activist in a social movement but as an "everyday hero." This is true, but there is more to the story. Local civil rights leaders had been waiting for years for an opportunity to boycott the local bus company because of its segregation policy. They needed a perfect test case—someone who would help draw attention to the cause.

Rosa Parks was just that person. She was a well-educated, law-abiding citizen who had been active in local civil rights organizations. In her book *My Story*, Parks says: "I was . . . no more tired than I usually was at the end of a working day. . . . No, the only tired I was, was tired of giving in."[69] When she was arrested for refusing to give up her seat, local civil rights leaders organized a boycott of the bus company that lasted more than a year. White Americans in Montgomery tried to stop the boycott. The police arrested and fined Black Americans who had arranged a car pooling system to get to work: people waiting for a car to pick them up were arrested for loitering, and car pool drivers

FIGURE 5.2

Women's Rights Time Line

1848	1869	1872	1920	1963	1964	1965
First women's rights convention held in Seneca Falls, New York.	Territory of Wyoming gives women the right to vote.	Congress requires equal pay for equal work for federal employees (but not for private-sector workers).	The Nineteenth Amendment gives women the right to vote (however, this largely only benefits White women, as women of color still face significant barriers to voting, including voter suppression and intimidation at the polls).	Equal Pay Act requires equal pay for equal work.	Title VII of the Civil Rights Act bars employment discrimination based on race, sex, and other grounds.	*Griswold v. Connecticut* legalizes the use of contraceptives by married couples.

Source: Compiled by the authors.

were arrested for lacking appropriate insurance or having too many people in their car. Martin Luther King Jr. was elected leader of the bus boycott, and he was subjected to harassment and violence—his house was firebombed, and he was arrested several times. Finally, a federal district court ruled that Montgomery's segregation policy was unconstitutional, and the Supreme Court upheld the ruling.

Nonviolent Protest On February 1, 1960, four Black students in Greensboro, North Carolina, went to a segregated lunch counter at a local Woolworth's and asked to be served. They sat there for an hour without being served and had to leave when the store closed. When 20 students returned the next day, national wire services picked up the story. Within two weeks, the sit-ins had spread to 11 cities. In some cases, the students were met with violence; in others, they were simply arrested. However, the students continued to respond with passive resistance, and new waves of protesters replaced those who had been arrested. The Student Nonviolent Coordinating Committee (SNCC) was created to coordinate the protests. The Greensboro Woolworth's was integrated on July 26, 1961, but the protests continued in other cities. By August 1961,

Left, a 15-year-old civil rights demonstrator, defying an anti-parade ordinance, is attacked by a police dog in Birmingham, Alabama, on May 3, 1963. Reactions against this police brutality helped spur Congress and the president to enact civil rights legislation. Three months later, civil rights leader Martin Luther King Jr. *(right)* waves to supporters from the steps of the Lincoln Memorial in Washington, D.C. The March on Washington drew an estimated 250,000 people, who heard King deliver his famous "I Have a Dream" speech.

1967	1972	1973	1982	2009	2017	2022
Federal affirmative action policies are extended to women by an executive order.	Title IX of the Education Amendments of 1972 requires equal access to programs for men and women in higher education.	*Roe v. Wade* establishes a constitutional right to abortion.	Thirty-five states ratify the Equal Rights Amendment, passed by Congress in 1971–1972, falling three states short of the number needed to add the amendment to the Constitution. (As of 2020, three additional states ratified the amendment; however, because their approval occurred after the deadline, they don't legally count toward the three-fourths of the states required.)	Lilly Ledbetter Fair Pay Act makes it easier to sue for gender-based pay discrimination.	The social media campaign #MeToo calls attention to sexual violence against women.	*Roe v. Wade* overturned in *Dobbs v. Jackson Women's Health Organization:* abortion rights are now determined by the states.

the sit-ins had 70,000 participants and there had been 3,000 arrests.[70] The sit-ins marked an important shift in the tactics of the civil rights movement: away from the court-based approach, exemplified by the fight against the "separate but equal" doctrine (as we will discuss next), and toward the nonviolent civil disobedience approach that had been successful in Montgomery.

Also during this period, the Freedom Riders were working to get President Kennedy to enforce two Supreme Court decisions that banned segregation in interstate travel, including at bus terminals, in waiting rooms, in restaurants, and in other public facilities related to interstate travel.[71] On May 4, 1961, a group of White and Black Americans boarded two buses in Washington, D.C., headed for New Orleans. The White and Black Americans sat together and went into segregated areas of bus stations together. The trip was uneventful until Rock Hill, South Carolina, where several Freedom Riders were beaten. Then, in Anniston, Alabama, one bus had its tires slashed and was firebombed. The Freedom Riders were beaten as they fled the burning bus. A second group encountered an angry mob at the bus station in Birmingham and was severely beaten with baseball bats and iron pipes. When it became clear that police protection would not be forthcoming, the Freedom Riders abandoned the trip and regrouped in Nashville. After much internal debate, they decided to continue the rides.

Following more violence in Montgomery, President Kennedy intervened and his brother Robert Kennedy, the attorney general, worked out a deal: the Freedom Riders would receive police protection, federal troops would not intervene, and they would face the local courts upon their arrest for "disturbing the peace." The Freedom Rides continued throughout the summer. Their actions successfully drew national attention to the continuing resistance in the South to desegregation rulings, forced the Kennedy administration to take a stand on this issue, and led to a stronger Interstate Commerce Commission ruling banning segregation in interstate travel.[72]

The next significant events occurred in Birmingham, Alabama, in 1963. Birmingham had more racial violence than any southern city, with 18 unsolved bombings of Black churches and homes in a six-year period. The city had closed its parks and golf courses rather than integrate them, and there was no progress on integrating the local schools. A leading supporter of integration had been castrated to intimidate other Black

FIGURE 5.3

Black American Civil Rights Time Line

Government action

1954

May 17
U.S. Supreme Court rules segregated schools are unconstitutional in the *Brown v. Board of Education* decision.

1957

September 9
The Federal Civil Rights Act prohibits discrimination.

September 23
President Eisenhower sends troops to escort Black students into a White high school in Little Rock, Arkansas.

Social movement

1955

December 1
Rosa Parks is arrested for refusing to give up her seat to a White person on a bus in Montgomery, Alabama.

1960

February 1
Black college students, refused service at a lunch counter in Greensboro, North Carolina, launch a sit-in.

1961

May 4
Freedom Riders test a Supreme Court decision that integrated interstate bus travel, sparking violence.

Source: Adapted from "Civil Rights Movement Timeline," History.com, www.history.com/topics/civil-rights-movement-timeline (accessed 2/23/22).

Americans who might advocate integration. The city's police chief, "Bull" Connor, was a strong segregationist who had allowed the attacks on the Freedom Riders. During a peaceful protest in April 1963, Martin Luther King Jr. and many others were arrested. While in solitary confinement, King wrote his now-famous "Letter from Birmingham Jail," an eloquent statement of the principles of nonviolent civil disobedience.

The letter was a response to White religious leaders who had told King in a newspaper ad that his actions were "unwise and untimely" and that "when rights are consistently denied, a cause should be pressed in the courts and in negotiations among local leaders, and not in the streets." King responded with a justification for civil disobedience, writing that everyone had an obligation to follow just laws but an equal obligation to break unjust laws.

King also laid out the four steps of nonviolent campaigns: (1) collection of the facts to determine whether injustices are alive; (2) negotiation with White leaders to change the injustices; (3) self-purification, which involved training to make sure that the civil rights protesters would be able to endure the abuse that they would receive; and (4) direct action (for example, sit-ins and marches) to create the environment in which change could occur, but always in a nonviolent manner. By following these steps, civil rights protesters ensured that their social movement would draw attention to their cause while turning public opinion against their opponents' violent tactics.

Following King's release from jail, the situation escalated. The protest leaders decided to use children in the next round of demonstrations. After more than

As part of the Montgomery Bus Boycott, many Black Americans organized car pools or walked to work.

July 2
President Johnson signs the Civil Rights Act.

August 6
The Federal Voting Rights Act prohibits denying anyone the vote on the basis of color or race.

April 11
Fair Housing Act protects against discrimination in housing.

1964 **1965** **1968**

April 16
Martin Luther King Jr. writes his "Letter from Birmingham Jail," defending nonviolent civil disobedience against unjust laws.

August 28
Martin Luther King Jr. delivers his "I Have a Dream" speech at the March on Washington.

September 15
Four girls are killed when a Baptist church in Birmingham, Alabama, is bombed.

June 21
Three civil rights workers are murdered outside Philadelphia, Mississippi.

February 21
Malcolm X is shot and killed in New York.

March 7
Six hundred voting rights marchers are attacked by police with clubs and whips on the Edmund Pettus Bridge outside Selma, Alabama. On March 21, about 3,200 marchers head out again on a four-day march to Montgomery in support of voting rights.

April 4
Martin Luther King Jr. is slain in Memphis, Tennessee.

1963 **1964** **1965** **1968**

1,000 children were arrested and the jails were overflowing, the police turned fire hoses and police dogs on children who were trying to continue their march. Media coverage of the incident turned the tide of public opinion in favor of the marchers as the country expressed outrage over the violence in Birmingham. Similar protests occurred throughout the South, with more than 1,000 actions in over 100 different southern cities and more than 20,000 people arrested throughout the summer. The demonstration culminated in August 1963, when 250,000 people participated in the March on Washington. King delivered his famous "I Have a Dream" speech and civil rights leaders pressured congressional leaders to pass civil rights legislation.

Protest Today After King's and others' nonviolent protests produced significant successes, mass protest became the preferred tool of many social movements for civil rights and other causes. Vietnam War protesters marched on Washington by the hundreds of thousands in the late 1960s and early 1970s. The women's rights, gay rights, and environmental movements have staged many mass demonstrations in Washington and other major cities. The largest single day of protest in the United States was the Women's March on January 21, 2017, which drew an estimated 4.2 million people in 654 American cities and another 300,000 in 261 cities around the world to protest the election of Donald Trump and call attention to issues concerning women's rights, health care, and immigration reform.[73]

Native Americans' struggles to maintain the security of their cultural lands were at the forefront of controversy over the construction of the Dakota Access Pipeline. In 2016 and 2017, the Standing Rock Sioux tribe led protests against the oil pipeline and its proposed route, which threatened their ancestral lands and clean water supply.

Social movements may also use direct action, rather than mass protests, to advance their causes, as was the case with the protests against the Dakota Access Pipeline in 2016–2017. When an oil pipeline was approved stretching from North Dakota to southern Illinois, the Sioux tribe from the nearby Standing Rock Indian Reservation objected on the grounds that the pipeline's route under the Missouri River posed a threat to their sources of clean water and to their ancient burial grounds. Thousands of protesters occupied the construction site for months in an effort to stop the pipeline, but ultimately law-enforcement officers cleared the protesters with water cannons, tear gas, and rubber bullets. In December 2016, President Obama issued an executive order requiring an environmental impact statement for the part of the pipeline that was to go under the river. However, President Trump overturned that order, and the pipeline was completed in May 2017.[74] A district court judge ordered an environmental impact statement in 2020 and that study is due soon but is unlikely to stop the flow of oil.

The tools of social movements have evolved in recent years to combine the power of social media with mass protest. #BlackLivesMatter started in 2013 on social media but has since expanded to organize mass protests against police killings in many cities across the country. Black Lives Matter is a large, decentralized movement that is not organized under a traditional hierarchy or national leadership. Black Lives Matter activists have thus used a broad range of tactics to raise awareness and put pressure on police departments to change their policies, including marches, "die-ins" (protests in which participants block traffic by lying in the street), and social media campaigns. Many police departments have responded to the organization's concerns about excessive police violence and a lack of accountability by adopting new policies, such as requiring police officers to wear body cameras and complete bias-reduction training programs.[75] The cause received a boost in 2017 when many NFL players kneeled during the playing of the national anthem before games to call attention to racially biased policing and police violence. President Trump pressured NFL owners to force the players to stand, saying that their actions disrespected the flag and the military personnel who serve the country. However, some players continued their protest throughout the season and through the 2021 season.[76] Protesters intensified their call for changes to police practices during the summer of 2020 after police killed George Floyd in Minneapolis and Breonna Taylor in Louisville and shot Jacob Blake in Kenosha. The Black Lives Matter protests that swept the country in 2020 have been called the "largest movement in U.S. history."[77]

The legacy of the civil rights movement has been not only to help change unjust laws but also to provide a new tool for political action across a broad range of policy areas. By putting pressure on political leaders through direct, nonviolent protest, millions of Americans have had their voices heard.

The courts

The Supreme Court has played an important role in defining civil rights, including those pushed for by the social movements just discussed. In the mid-twentieth century, the justices moved away from the "separate but equal" doctrine, required the desegregation of public schools, and upheld landmark civil rights legislation passed by Congress. More recently, they have expanded civil rights for women and the LGBTQIA+ community, but they also have endorsed a color-blind position that some see as a movement away from protecting civil rights.

Challenging "Separate but Equal" in Education In the 1930s, the NAACP, which was established to fight for equal rights for Black people, started a concerted effort to nibble away at the "separate but equal" doctrine. Rather than tackling segregation head-on, the NAACP first challenged an aspect of segregation that would be familiar to the Supreme Court justices: the ways in which states kept Black Americans out of all-White law schools. Another strategy was to challenge admissions practices in law schools outside the Deep South to demonstrate that segregation was not just a "southern problem" and to raise the chances for compliance with favorable Court decisions. A young NAACP attorney named Thurgood Marshall (who later became the first Black Supreme Court justice) argued that the University of Maryland's practice of sending Black students to out-of-state law schools rather than admitting them to the university's all-White law school violated the Black students' civil rights. (The state gave Black students a $200 scholarship, which did not cover the costs of tuition and travel and was not available to all Black students who wanted to attend law school.) In 1936, the circuit court and subsequently the Maryland appeals court rejected this arrangement and ordered that Black students be admitted to the University of Maryland law school.[78]

Over the next 15 years, a series of successful lawsuits slowly chipped away at the idea of "separate but equal." After these victories, there was a debate within the NAACP over whether to continue the case-by-case approach against the "separate but equal" doctrine or to directly challenge the principle itself. The latter approach was risky because it was unclear if the Court was ready to take this bold step, and defeat in the Court would set back the movement. However, the signals increasingly indicated that the Supreme

After King's and others' nonviolent protests produced significant successes, mass protests became the preferred tool of many social movements, such as the Women's March on Washington *(left)* and Black Lives Matter *(right)*.

Court was ready to strike down the "separate but equal" doctrine. In addition to the law school cases, in 1948 the Court ruled that "restrictive covenants"—clauses in real estate contracts that prevented a property owner from selling to a Black American—could not be enforced by state or local courts because the Fourteenth Amendment prohibited the states from denying Black Americans the "equal protection of the laws."[79]

This application of the Fourteenth Amendment was expanded in the landmark ruling *Brown v. Board of Education*. The case arrived on the Court's docket in 1951, was postponed for argument until after the 1952 election, and then was re-argued in December 1953. The ruling was postponed for so long because the Court was keenly aware of the firestorm that would ensue. In its unanimous decision, the Court ruled: "In the field of public education, the doctrine of separate but equal has no place. Separate educational facilities are inherently unequal, depriving the plaintiffs of the equal protection of the laws. Segregated facilities may generate in Black children a feeling of inferiority that may affect their hearts and minds in a way unlikely ever to be undone."[80] The case was significant not only because it required all public schools in the United States to desegregate but also because it used the equal protection clause of the Fourteenth Amendment in a way that had potentially far-reaching consequences.

Nonetheless, the decision was limited because it focused on segregation in schools rather than segregation more generally and it focused on the psychological damage done to Black schoolchildren through segregation rather than on the broader claim that racial classification itself was not allowed by the Constitution. Chief Justice Earl Warren wanted a unanimous vote and knew that two justices would not support a broader ruling that would overturn *Plessy v. Ferguson* and rule segregation unconstitutional in all contexts. Even if segregation in other public places still was legal, the *Brown* ruling provided an important boost to the civil rights movement.

DID YOU KNOW?

82%

of Black students and 81 percent of Latino students attend schools where the majority of the student population is from historically marginalized groups.

Source: National Center for Education Statistics.

The Push to Desegregate Schools In 1955, *Brown v. Board of Education II* addressed the implementation of desegregation and required the states to "desegregate with all deliberate speed."[81] The odd choice of words, "all deliberate speed," was read as a signal by southerners that they could take their time with desegregation. The phrase does seem to be contradictory: being deliberate does not usually involve being speedy. Southern states engaged in "massive resistance" to the desegregation order, as articulated by Harry F. Byrd, the segregationist senator from Virginia. In some cases, they even closed public schools rather than integrate them—and then reopened the schools as "private" segregated schools for which the White students received government vouchers. However, Maryland, Kentucky, Tennessee, Missouri, and the District of Columbia desegregated their schools within two years.

Eight years after *Brown I*, little had changed in the Deep South: fewer than 1 percent of Black children attended school with White children.[82] Through the 1960s, the courts had to battle against continued resistance to integration. In 1971, the Court shifted its focus from **de jure** segregation (segregation mandated by law) to **de facto** segregation (segregation that existed because of segregated housing patterns) and approved school busing as a tool to integrate schools.[83] This approach was extremely controversial. The Court almost immediately limited the application of busing by ruling in a Detroit case that busing could not go beyond the boundaries of a city's school district—that is, students did not have to be bused from suburbs to cities—unless it could be shown that the school district's lines were drawn in an intentionally discriminatory way.[84] This rule encouraged "White flight" from the cities to the suburbs in response to court-ordered busing.

de jure
Relating to actions or circumstances that occur "by law," such as the legally enforced segregation of schools in the American South before the 1960s.

de facto
Relating to actions or circumstances that occur outside the law or "by fact," such as the segregation of schools that resulted from housing patterns and other factors rather than from laws.

In 2007, in perhaps the most important decision on race in education since *Brown*, the Court invalidated voluntary desegregation plans implemented by public school districts in Seattle and Louisville. Both districts set goals for racial diversity and denied school assignment requests if they tipped the racial balance above or below certain

Busing students from one school district to another has been controversial since the 1960s. In Boston in the 1970s, many Black students who were bused into White districts needed police protection against protests.

thresholds. In a ringing endorsement of the color-blind approach, the majority opinion said: "The way to stop discrimination on the basis of race is to stop discriminating on the basis of race." In this case, the discrimination was against White students who wanted to be in schools with few students from historically marginalized groups, rather than Black students who wanted to be in integrated schools.[85]

Expanding Civil Rights for Black Americans Other significant rulings in the 1960s struck down state laws that forbade interracial marriages (16 states had such laws), upheld all significant parts of the Civil Rights Act, and upheld and expanded the scope of the Voting Rights Act (VRA; these important laws will be discussed in the next section). In central cases, the justices ruled that Congress had the power to eliminate segregation in public places, such as restaurants and hotels, under the commerce clause of the Constitution.

The first case involved a hotel in Atlanta that was close to an interstate highway, advertised extensively on the highway, and had a clientele that was about 75 percent from out of state. The Court ruled that this establishment was clearly engaging in interstate commerce, so Congress had the right to regulate it.[86] In the second case, "almost all, if not all," of the patrons of Ollie's Barbecue in Birmingham, Alabama, were local. However, the Court pointed out that meat purchased for the restaurant came from out of state and this constituted 46 percent of the total amount spent on supplies. Therefore, the practice of segregation would place significant burdens on "the interstate flow of food and upon the movement of products generally."[87]

The next important area of cases was in employment law. In 1971, the Court ruled that employment tests, such as written exams or general aptitude tests, that are not related to job performance and that discriminate against Black Americans violate the 1964 Civil Rights Act.[88] This **disparate impact standard** of discrimination means that if the employment practice has a bad *effect* on a racial group, it doesn't matter whether or not the discrimination is *intended*. The Supreme Court and Congress have gone back and forth in defining this concept, but it is still important in workplace discrimination suits. (See Nuts & Bolts 5.1 on p. 190 for the legal definition of race-based workplace discrimination.)

disparate impact standard
The idea that discrimination exists if a practice has a negative effect on a specific group, whether or not this effect was intentional.

The Color-Blind Court and Judicial Activism Recently, the Supreme Court has been gradually imposing a "color-blind jurisprudence" over a range of issues—that is, the Court has reasoned that race should not be considered in determining the outcome

NUTS & BOLTS 5.1

Race-Related Discrimination as Defined by the Equal Employment Opportunity Commission

Race/Color Discrimination

Race discrimination involves treating someone (an applicant or employee) unfavorably because he/she is of a certain race or because of personal characteristics associated with race (such as hair texture, skin color, or certain facial features). Color discrimination involves treating someone unfavorably because of skin color complexion. . . . Discrimination can occur when the victim and the person who inflicted the discrimination are the same race or color.

Race/Color Discrimination and Work Situations

The law forbids discrimination when it comes to any aspect of employment, including hiring, firing, pay, job assignments, promotions, layoff, training, fringe benefits, and any other term or condition of employment.

Race/Color Discrimination and Harassment

It is unlawful to harass a person because of that person's race or color. Harassment can include, for example, racial slurs, offensive or derogatory remarks about a person's race or color, or the display of racially offensive symbols. Although the law doesn't prohibit simple teasing, offhand comments, or isolated incidents that are not very serious, harassment is illegal when it is so frequent or severe that it creates a hostile or offensive work environment or when it results in an adverse employment decision (such as the victim being fired or demoted). The harasser can be the victim's supervisor, a supervisor in another area, a coworker, or someone who is not an employee of the employer, such as a client or customer.

Race/Color Discrimination and Employment Policies/Practices

An employment policy or practice that applies to everyone, regardless of race or color, can be illegal if it has a negative impact on the employment of people of a particular race or color and is not job-related and necessary to the operation of the business.

Source: U.S. Equal Employment Opportunity Commission, "Race/Color Discrimination," www.eeoc.gov (accessed 2/23/22).

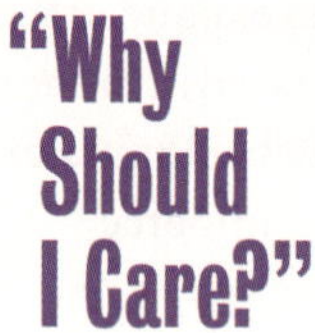

"Why Should I Care?"

As a job applicant, it is essential to know your rights. These guidelines forbid discrimination when it comes to any aspect of employment, including hiring, firing, pay, job assignments, promotions, layoff, training, fringe benefits, and any other term or condition of employment. They also prohibit retaliation against people who complain of discrimination. Everyone is protected from race and color discrimination: White Americans, Black Americans, Asian Americans, Latinos, persons of more than one race, and all other persons, whatever their race, color, or ethnicity.

of certain kinds of cases. One significant area was the 1992 racial redistricting in which 15 new U.S. House districts were drawn to help elect Black Americans and 10 new districts were drawn to help elect Latino members. The resulting dramatic change in the number of representatives from historically marginalized groups in Congress (an increase greater than 50 percent) was rooted in the 1982 amendments to the VRA. Instead of mandating a fair *process*, this law and subsequent interpretation by the Supreme Court mandated that historically marginalized groups have an "equal opportunity" to "elect representatives of their choice" when their numbers and configuration permit. As a result, the legislative redistricting process now had to avoid discriminatory *results* rather than being concerned only with discriminatory *intent*.

However, in a series of decisions starting with the 1993 landmark case *Shaw v. Reno*, the Supreme Court's adherence to a color-blind jurisprudence has thrown the constitutionality of Black-majority districts into doubt. The Court has ruled that Black-majority districts are legal as long as they are "done right."[89] But it has consistently held that if race is the predominant factor in drawing district lines, the districts are unconstitutional because they violate the equal protection clause of the Fourteenth Amendment for the White plaintiffs in these cases. Based on this reasoning, Black-majority districts in North Carolina, Georgia, Louisiana, Virginia, Texas, and Florida have been found to be unconstitutional. In 2001, the Court upheld the re-drawn 12th District in North Carolina, which no longer was a Black-majority district, arguing that when race and partisanship are so intertwined—as they are when 90 percent of Black Americans vote for a Democratic candidate—plaintiffs cannot assume that Black Americans were placed together for racial reasons.[90]

However, racial redistricting remains an unsettled area of the law. According to election law expert Richard Hasen, the Supreme Court's decision in 2019 to no longer decide cases concerning partisan gerrymandering will "force courts to make logically impossible determinations about whether racial reasons or partisan motives predominate when a party gerrymanders for political advantage." That is, a state could re-draw districts on racial grounds (which would not be OK) but claim it was for partisan reasons (which now *is* OK, at least in federal court), and there would be no way for the courts to sort this out.[91] That was exactly what happened in a 2024 case from South Carolina in which the lower court ruled that a district was drawn predominantly on the basis of race, but the Supreme Court disagreed, saying that the legislature's claim of partisan motivation should be accepted unless there was strong evidence to the contrary.[92]

The Court also struck down an important part of the 1965 VRA in a 2013 ruling. This case concerned the "coverage formula" that determines which states have to get approval from the Justice Department before implementing changes in an election law or practice (such as redistricting or closing a polling place). This "preclearance" provision of the law was viewed as one of the best ways to stop discriminatory voting practices because it could prevent them before they were implemented, rather than forcing voters to wait until they went into effect to challenge them. The Court ruled that the coverage formula was an unconstitutional burden on the covered states and was a violation of the Tenth Amendment.[93] The House passed the John Lewis Voting Rights Advancement Act, which would have reinstated this important part of the VRA, but the bill was killed by a filibuster in the Senate in 2022.[94]

In 2021, the Court also weakened Section 2 of the VRA by allowing states to implement voting changes, such as ballot collection practices and throwing out votes that were cast in the wrong precinct, that may have a disproportionate effect on voters from historically marginalized groups. Citing deference to the states' ability to regulate the "time, manner, and place" of elections, the Court said that as long as it was a standard practice existing in 1982 (when Section 2 was last amended), it did not place an undue burden on voters from historically marginalized groups. In her dissent, Justice Kagan lamented the activism of the Court, saying Congress should decide whether Section 2 of the VRA is weakened, not the Court.[95]

The racial redistricting and voting rights cases illustrate that the Supreme Court is increasingly activist in issues involving civil rights: it is generally unwilling to defer to the other branches of government and will assert its view of discrimination and equal protection regardless of what the other branches think (see Chapter 14 for a broader discussion of judicial activism). In some periods, like the 1950s and 1960s, judicial activism has served to further civil rights. More recently, it has served to limit them.

Women's Rights The Supreme Court has also been central in shaping women's civil rights. Until relatively recently, the Court did not apply the Constitution to protect women's rights, despite the Fourteenth Amendment's language that states may not deny any *person* the equal protection of the laws. Apparently, women were not regarded as people when it came to political and economic rights in the nineteenth and early twentieth centuries. These protectionist notions were finally rejected in three cases between 1971 and 1976, when the Court made it much more difficult for states to treat men and women differently.

The first case involved an Idaho state law that gave a man priority over a woman when they were otherwise equally entitled to execute a person's estate. This law was justified on the "reasonable" grounds that it reduced the state courts' workload by having an automatic rule that would limit challenges. But the Court ruled that the law was arbitrary, did not meet the "reasonableness" test, and therefore violated the woman's equal protection rights under the Fourteenth Amendment.[96] The second case involved a female air force officer who wanted to count her husband as a dependent for purposes of health and housing benefits. Under the law at the time, a military man could automatically count his wife as a dependent, but a woman could claim her husband only if she brought in more than half the family income. The Court struck down this practice, saying protectionist laws, "in practical effect, put women not on a pedestal, but in a cage."[97]

rational basis test
The use of evidence to suggest that differences in the behavior of two groups can rationalize unequal treatment of these groups.

These two cases relied on the **rational basis test** for discrimination between men and women (which evolved from the reasonableness test). Along with the strict scrutiny test (see Chapter 4), it allows the Fourteenth Amendment to be applied differently to particular categories of people. Under the rational basis test, states can discriminate against a group of people as long as there is a "rational basis" for the state law in question. Today, for example, states can pass drinking laws that allow only those who are 21 and older to drink on the grounds that traffic fatalities will be lower with that drinking age rather than under a law that allows 18-year-olds to drink.

The strict scrutiny test gives historically marginalized groups the strongest protection as the "suspect classification" under the Fourteenth Amendment, but it has not been applied to women. This test stipulates that there must be a "compelling state interest" to discriminate among people if race is involved. The idea of a suspect classification was first used in a case involving the internment of Japanese Americans during World War II. In a controversial ruling, the Court said that the internment camps were justified on national security grounds, making it one of the few instances in which racial classification has survived strict scrutiny.[98] However, the Supreme Court overturned this ruling in a 2018 case involving President Trump's travel ban.[99]

In 1976, the Court established a third test, the intermediate scrutiny test (see Chapter 4), in a case involving the drinking age. In the early 1970s, some states had a lower drinking age for women than for men on the "rational basis" that 18- to 20-year-old women are more mature than men of that age. (States argued that women were less likely to be drunk drivers and less likely to abuse alcohol than men were.) The new intermediate scrutiny standard meant that the government's policy must be "substantially related" to an "important government objective" to justify the unequal treatment of men and women, so the law was struck down.[100]

The intermediate scrutiny test gives women stronger protections than the rational basis test, but it is not as strong as strict scrutiny (see the How It Works graphic on pp. 194–95). To use the legal jargon, the gender distinction would have to serve an "important government objective," but not a "compelling state interest," in order to withstand intermediate scrutiny.

In many instances, as with the Idaho case, the rights of women were strengthened by this new standard of equal protection. However, in other instances women may actually be more restricted by being treated the same as men. For example, in the drinking age case, instead of dropping the drinking age for men to 18, states raised the age for women to 21. Similarly, the Court struck down an Alabama divorce law in which husbands but not wives could be ordered to pay alimony.[101] Arguably, women would have been better off in these two specific instances under the old discriminatory laws (because they could drink at 18 instead of 21 and did not have to pay alimony in some states). However, the more aggressive application of the Fourteenth Amendment for women was an important step in providing them with the equal protection of the laws, as clearly shown in a Court decision that struck down the male-only admission policy at the Virginia Military Institute (VMI). The majority opinion stated that VMI violated the Fourteenth Amendment's equal protection clause because it failed to show an "exceedingly persuasive justification" for its sex-biased admissions policy.[102]

An important gender-equality case in 2017 concerned the law for determining the citizenship of children born overseas to an unmarried couple when one parent is a citizen and the other is not. Federal law requires a single father to have resided in the United States for five years prior to his child's birth in order for that child to have U.S. citizenship, while a child born overseas to a single American mother would be granted U.S. citizenship if the mother had lived continuously in the United States for just one year prior to the child's birth. The Court ruled that this gender-based distinction was unconstitutional. As with earlier cases involving the drinking age and alimony, the remedy in this case was to make things worse for women in the short term—that is, rather than reducing the residency requirement for men from five years to one, the Court increased it for women to match the longer period for men. However, supporters of women's rights applauded the decision for what it means for gender equality in the long term. One expert on women's rights noted that the gender difference in this law was rooted in outdated notions of parental responsibilities and argued, "Romantic ideals about the uniqueness of motherhood perpetuate the notion that women, rather than men, should assume responsibility for children. They also contribute to negative stereotypes that diminish women as workers, wage earners, and participants in public life."[103]

Two other areas where the Supreme Court has helped advance women's rights are affirmative action and protection against sexual harassment. In 1987, the Court approved affirmative action in a case involving a woman who was promoted over a man despite the fact that he had scored slightly higher than she did on a test. The Court ruled that the promotion was acceptable to make up for past discrimination.[104] And in 1993 the Court made it easier to sue employers for sexual harassment, saying that a woman did not have to reach the point of a nervous breakdown before claiming that she was being harassed; it was enough to demonstrate a pattern of "repeated and unwanted" behavior that created a "hostile workplace environment."[105] Later rulings stated that if a single act is flagrant, the conduct does not have to be repeated to create a hostile environment. However, despite these rulings, it continues to be difficult to win sexual harassment cases under the "reasonable person" standard established in the 1993 case because what may be perceived as a hostile work environment by the victim of harassment may not be viewed that way by a judge or a jury.[106]

The issues of sexual harassment exploded on the national scene in October 2017 when Ashley Judd, Angelina Jolie, Gwyneth Paltrow, and Rose McGowan alleged that Hollywood mogul Harvey Weinstein sexually assaulted them. Ten days later, actress Alyssa Milano encouraged other women to share their stories with the hashtag #MeToo, building on the movement started by activist Tarana Burke to raise awareness of sexual assault. Within 24 hours, the messages had been retweeted 500,000 times and shared in 12 million posts on Facebook. In 2020, Weinstein was convicted in a New York court and sentenced to 23 years in prison; he faces additional charges in California.[107] Allegations of sexual harassment or assault have ended the careers of Fox News anchor Bill O'Reilly, Senator Al Franken, comedian Bill Cosby, Representative John Conyers, Alabama Senate nominee Roy Moore, New York governor Andrew Cuomo, morning show anchors Matt Lauer and Charlie Rose, Olympic gymnast doctor Lawrence G. Nassar, public radio star Garrison Keillor, conductor James Levine, actor

At the fourth annual Washington, D.C., Women's March in 2020, demonstrators gathered to show their support for women's rights.

DID YOU KNOW?

Women working full-time earn

$0.81

compared with every dollar earned by men.

Source: payscale.com.

How it works: **in theory**

Civil Rights

Cases involving "suspect classification"
(race, ethnicity, religion, or national origin)

Strict Scrutiny Test

1. Is unequal treatment justified by a **"compelling state interest"**?

2. Is unequal treatment the **"least restrictive"** option?

Very few cases meet this standard.

Cases involving sex or gender equality

Intermediate Scrutiny Test

1. Is the discriminatory policy **"substantially related"** to an **"important government objective"**?

2. Is the discrimination **not substantially broader** than it needs to be to protect the important government interest?

Some discrimination based on gender is permitted, but this test is harder to pass than the rational basis test applied to gender cases in the past.

Cases involving age, economic status, or other criteria

Rational Basis Test

1. Is the law **rationally related to furthering** a legitimate government interest?

2. Does the policy avoid **"arbitrary, capricious, or deliberate"** discrimination?

This is the easiest hurdle for a law or policy to pass.

discrimination is legal

How it works: in practice

Evaluating Discrimination Cases

Strict Scrutiny Test

Case 1:

The University of Michigan Law School's "holistic" race-conscious admissions policy is designed to promote diversity.

Case 2:

The University of Michigan's more rigid race-conscious undergraduate admissions policy was designed to promote diversity.

The Court asked . . .

1. Is unequal treatment justified by a "compelling state interest"?
2. Is unequal treatment the "least restrictive" option?

The Court said . . .

In Case 1, discrimination is OK. In *Grutter v. Bollinger* (2003), the Court ruled that the state's interest in **racial diversity in higher education was compelling**, and that this specific admissions policy was narrowly tailored. This was affirmed in *Fisher v. Univ. of Texas* (2016).

In Case 2, discrimination is not OK. In *Gratz v. Bollinger* (2003), the Court **struck down Michigan's undergraduate admissions policy** for not being narrowly tailored.

Intermediate Scrutiny Test

Case 1:

A California state law says that men—but not women—can be guilty of statutory rape.

Case 2:

The Virginia Military Institute maintained a male-only admissions policy.

The Court asked . . .

1. Is the discriminatory policy "substantially related" to an "important government objective"?
2. Is the discrimination not substantially broader than it needs to be to protect the important government interest?

The Court said . . .

In Case 1, discrimination is OK. In *Michael M. v. Superior Court* (1981), the Court found that the state had a **strong interest in preventing illegitimate pregnancy** and in punishing only the participant, who, by nature, suffers few of the consequences of his conduct.

In Case 2, discrimination is not OK. In *United States v. Virginia* (1996), the Court **struck down the Virginia Military Institute's policy** as a violation of the equal protection clause of the Fourteenth Amendment.

Rational Basis Test

Case 1:

President Trump implemented a travel ban that focused primarily on Muslim-majority countries.

Case 2:

An Oklahoma law allowed 18- to 20-year-old women—but not men—to buy 3.2% ABV ("non-intoxicating") beer.

The Court asked . . .

1. Is the law rationally related to furthering a legitimate government interest?
2. Does the policy avoid "arbitrary, capricious, or deliberate" discrimination?

The Court said . . .

In Case 1, discrimination is OK. In *Trump v. Hawaii* (2018), the Court ruled that **the White House had shown a "sufficient national security justification" for the travel ban.** Dissenters argued that the Court should have applied the strict scrutiny standard rather than the rational basis test because the travel ban singled out Muslims.

In Case 2, discrimination is not OK. In *Craig v. Boren* (1976), the Court **struck down this law**, rejecting the rational basis that Oklahoma had claimed and instead applying intermediate scrutiny.

Critical Thinking

1. **Is it easier for the government to discriminate against** someone based on age or race? Why?
2. **What is the standard used by the Court if the state wants** to make distinctions between people based on race? Under what circumstances and in what scenarios is discrimination based on race legal?

Kevin Spacey, and many more. *Time* magazine named "The Silence Breakers" their "person of the year" for 2017 for their courage in bringing attention to this problem.[108]

While the court of public opinion and the actual courts have played a central role in bringing justice to the victims of sexual assault and harassment, the Supreme Court has been less sympathetic to plaintiffs in cases involving pay discrimination. Lilly Ledbetter sued Goodyear Tire & Rubber Company because she had received lower pay than men doing the same work over a 20-year period, which she claimed was gender discrimination. The Court rejected her claim, saying that she did not meet the time limit required by law, as the discrimination must have occurred within 180 days of the claim.[109] (This overturned the long-standing policy of the EEOC, which held that each new paycheck restarted the 180-day clock as a new act of discrimination.) Dissenters pointed out that pay discrimination usually occurs in small increments over long periods, so it would be impossible to recognize unequal pay within 180 days of an initial paycheck. Furthermore, workers do not have access to information about fellow workers' pay, so it would be almost impossible to meet the standard set by the Court. Congress restored the old standard in January 2009 by passing the Lilly Ledbetter Fair Pay Act. But as Figure 5.4 shows, significant pay disparities between men and women remain throughout much of the United States. Early in 2016, President Obama issued an executive order requiring companies with more than 100 employees to report to the federal government what they pay employees by race, gender, and ethnicity. He said, "Women are not getting the fair shot that we believe every single American deserves."[110] In 2017 President Trump overturned this order,[111] but then in 2021, President Biden issued an executive order establishing

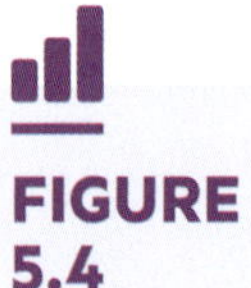

FIGURE 5.4

Lifetime Wage Gap for Women as Compared with Men

There is a substantial difference between women's and men's earnings in the United States. What could account for this variation? How much do you think it has to do with levels of discrimination, and how much with differences in the nature of the jobs that men and women hold?

Source: National Women's Law Center, "Lifetime Wage Gap Losses for Women: 2021 State Rankings," based on U.S. Census 2021 American Community Survey Data, March 2021, https://nwlc.org/wp-content/uploads/2021/03/Women-Overall-Lifetime-Losses-2021-v2.pdf (accessed 2/8/22).

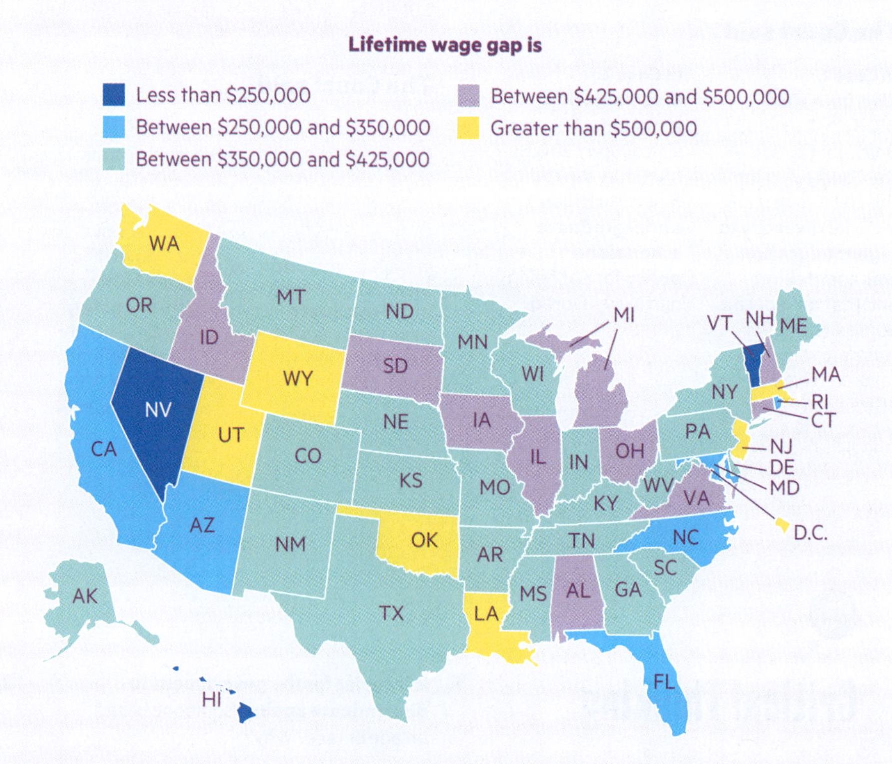

a White House Gender Policy Council and reaffirming a commitment to equal pay based on gender.[112]

The largest sexual discrimination lawsuit in the nation's history was filed in 2001 against Walmart on behalf of 1.5 million women who had worked at Walmart since 1998. Among other things, the plaintiffs alleged the following:

- Over objections from a female executive, senior management regularly referred to female store employees as "little Janie Qs" and "girls."
- A Sam's Club (Walmart's warehouse retail chain) manager in California told another woman that she should "doll up" to get promoted.
- Managers have repeatedly told female employees that men "need to be paid more than women because they have families to support."
- A male manager in South Carolina told a female employee that "God made Adam first, so women would always be second to men."
- A female personnel manager in Florida was told by her manager that men were paid more than women because "men are here to make a career and women aren't. Retail is for housewives who just need to earn extra money."[113]

But in 2011 the Court ruled that the class-action lawsuit was not valid because there was no "convincing proof of a companywide discriminatory pay and promotion policy." That is, women would have to prove discrimination individually, not as a group. Civil rights experts said this was the "death knell" for class-action lawsuits seeking monetary damages for discrimination.[114] However, the Court did not rule on the merits of the case, and in 2019 more than 100 current and former female Walmart employees sued for a persistent pattern of discrimination.[115] In 2020, Walmart paid $20 million to settle another nationwide gender discrimination suit.[116]

Gay Rights The Supreme Court has a similarly mixed record on gay rights. The Court's decisions in early cases were not supportive of gay rights. One of the first cases concerned Georgia's law banning sodomy. As we discussed in Chapter 4, the Supreme Court ruled in *Bowers v. Hardwick* (1986) that "homosexual behavior" was not protected by the Constitution and that state laws banning it could be justified under the most lenient rational basis test.[117]

After cases in which it sidestepped the issue, the Court first endorsed civil rights for gays in 1996. Here the Court struck down an amendment to the Colorado state constitution that would have prevented them from suing for discrimination in employment or housing. The Court said that the state amendment violated gay Americans' equal protection rights because it "withdrew from homosexuals, but no others, specific legal protection from the injuries caused by discrimination."[118] The Court rejected the state's "rational basis" arguments and came close to putting gays in the "suspect classification" that had been reserved for members of historically marginalized racial and ethnic groups.

An important ruling came in 2003 in a case involving two Houston men. As we discussed in Chapter 4, John Geddes Lawrence and Tyron Garner were prosecuted for same-sex sodomy (which was illegal in Texas) after police found them having sex in Lawrence's apartment. The Supreme Court ruled in a historic 6–3 decision that the due process clause of the Fourteenth Amendment guarantees freedom of not only thought, belief, and expression but also certain intimate conduct (including same-sex relations). This reasoning is rooted in the **substantive due process doctrine** that underlies constitutional protections for birth control, abortion, and decisions about how to raise one's children.

substantive due process doctrine
One interpretation of the due process clause of the Fourteenth Amendment; in this view the Supreme Court has the power to overturn laws that infringe on individual liberties.

The decision overturned *Bowers v. Hardwick*, and the majority opinion had harsh words for that decision, saying it "was not correct when it was decided, and it is not correct today." Five members of the majority signed on to the broad "due process" reasoning of the decision, rather than the narrower reasoning in Justice O'Connor's concurring opinion, in which she said that the decision should apply only to the four states that treated gays differently (that is, banning sodomy for homosexuals but not for heterosexuals). With the broader due process logic, a total of 13 state laws that banned sodomy were struck down. Justice Scalia wrote a strong dissent, saying that the decision was "the product of a court that has largely signed on to the so-called homosexual agenda" and warned that the ruling "will have far-reaching implications beyond this case." He predicted that the ruling would serve as the basis for constitutional protections for same-sex marriage.[119]

> ❞
>
> **The Constitution promises liberty to all within its reach . . . [and] extend[s] to certain personal choices central to individual dignity and autonomy, including intimate choices that define personal identity and beliefs.**
>
> **—Supreme Court's majority opinion in *Obergefell v. Hodges***

The Supreme Court issued two important rulings on same-sex marriage in 2013. The first case was a narrow ruling that reinstated same-sex marriage in California but did not affect any other state. The second case was a more far-reaching decision that struck down part of the Defense of Marriage Act (DOMA) as a violation of the Fifth Amendment's due process clause. The majority opinion said that the federal government cannot deny benefits to same-sex couples who are legally married under state law. The gradual movement toward endorsing same-sex marriage culminated in 2015 in the landmark ruling *Obergefell v. Hodges*, which legalized same-sex marriage in all 50 states.[120] The 5–4 ruling said that the fundamental right to marry is guaranteed by both the due process clause and the equal protection clause of the Fourteenth Amendment. When *Roe v. Wade* was overturned in 2022, some legal scholars predicted that same-sex marriage might be next (Justice Thomas urged this outcome in his concurring opinion in Dobbs, but the majority opinion said it only applied to abortion and should not be read more broadly to other rights that are grounded in substantive due process).[121]

In 2020, there was another landmark ruling in protection of the rights of gay and transgender people. In a 6–3 ruling on *Bostock v. Clayton County*, the Court said that the language of the Civil Rights Act of 1964 applies to discrimination based on sexual orientation and gender identity. As such, it protects gay and transgender individuals from discrimination in the workforce.[122] The plaintiff, Gerald Bostock, had been fired from his job for expressing interest in forming a gay softball league at work. The Supreme Court consolidated the case with two other similar cases of workplace discrimination: *Altitude Express Inc. v. Zarda* and *R.G. & G.R. Harris Funeral Homes Inc. v. Equal Employment Opportunity Commission*.[123] Writing for the majority, Justice Neil Gorsuch said, "An employer who fires an individual merely for being gay or transgender defies the law." Prior to this decision, it had been legal in almost half the states to fire an employee for being gay, bisexual, or transgender.

This section demonstrates that the courts can be both a strong advocate of and an impediment to civil rights. In general, however, the courts have a limited *independent* impact on policy. That is, as the school desegregation cases clearly demonstrate, the courts must rely on the other branches of government to carry out their decisions.

Congress

Congress has provided the basis for today's protection of civil rights through a series of laws that were enacted starting in the 1960s. Applying to historically marginalized racial and ethnic groups and to women, these laws attempted to ensure that there is a "level playing field" of equal opportunity.

Key Early Legislation The bedrock of equal protection that exists today stems from landmark legislation passed by Congress in the 1960s—the 1964 Civil Rights Act, the 1965 VRA, and the 1968 Fair Housing Act. President Kennedy was slow to seek civil rights legislation for fear of alienating southern Democrats. The events in Birmingham prompted him to act, but he was assassinated before the legislation was passed. President Lyndon Johnson, a former segregationist, helped push through the Civil Rights Act when he became president. The act barred discrimination in employment based on race, sex, religion, or national origin; banned segregation in public places; and established the EEOC as the enforcement agency for the legislation. One of the southern opponents of the legislation inserted the language referring to sex, thinking that it would defeat the bill (assuming, perhaps, that there would be a majority coalition of male chauvinists and segregationists), but it became law anyway.

The VRA of 1965 eliminated direct obstacles to voting for historically marginalized groups in the South, such as discriminatory literacy tests and other voter registration tests, and also provided the means to enforce the law: federal marshals were charged with overseeing elections in the South. After its passage, President Johnson hailed the VRA as a "triumph for freedom as huge as any ever won on any battlefield."[124] The VRA, which is often cited as one of the most significant pieces of civil rights legislation in our nation's history,[125] precipitated an explosion in Black political participation in the South. The most dramatic gains came in Mississippi, where Black registration increased from 6.7 percent before the VRA to 59.8 percent in 1967. As one political scientist noted, "The act simply overwhelmed the major bulwarks of the disenfranchising system. In the seven states originally covered, Black registration increased from 29.3 percent in March 1965, to 56.6 percent in 1971–1972; the gap between Black and White registration rates narrowed from 44.1 percentage points to 11.2."[126]

The last piece of landmark legislation, the Fair Housing Act of 1968, barred discrimination in the rental or sale of a home based on race, sex, religion, and national origin. Important amendments to the law enacted in 1988 added disability and familial status (having children under age 18) to the list of protected categories, provided new administrative enforcement mechanisms, and expanded Justice Department jurisdiction to bring suit on behalf of victims in federal district courts.[127]

There have been many other important amendments to civil rights laws since the 1960s. The 1975 amendments to the VRA extended coverage of many of the law's provisions to language minorities, guaranteeing that registration and voting materials are made available to voters in their native language in certain districts with large numbers of citizens who are not proficient in English. The 1982 VRA amendments extended important provisions of the law for 25 years and made it easier to bring a lawsuit under the act. The 1991 Civil Rights Act overruled or altered parts of 12 Supreme Court decisions that had eroded the initial intent of the 1964 civil rights legislation. It also expanded earlier legislation and increased the costs to employers for intentional, illegal discrimination. In 2006, Congress voted to extend the VRA for another 25 years. However, as we note above, Congress failed to reverse recent Supreme Court cases that curtailed that reach of the VRA.

Protections for Women Women have also received extensive protection through legislation. As noted, the section of the Civil Rights Act that bars discrimination based on gender, Title VII, was almost an accidental part of the bill (it was included by an opponent to the legislation). Indeed, the first executive director of the EEOC would not enforce the gender part of the law because it was a "fluke." In 1966, the National Organization for Women (NOW) was formed to push for enforcement of the law. Its members convinced President Johnson to sign an executive order that eliminated sex discrimination in federal agencies and among federal contractors, but the order was difficult to enforce. Finally, in 1970, the EEOC started enforcing the law. Before long, one-third of all civil rights cases involved sex discrimination, and those numbers have remained high in recent years (see Figure 5.5).

FIGURE 5.5

Discrimination Cases Filed with the Equal Employment Opportunity Commission, 2021

Discrimination based on race and color are the most frequently reported, but there is a significant amount of discrimination based on sex, age and disability as well. What types of discrimination do you think would be most likely to go unreported?

Note: Percentages do not sum to 100 because complaints may be filed in more than one category.

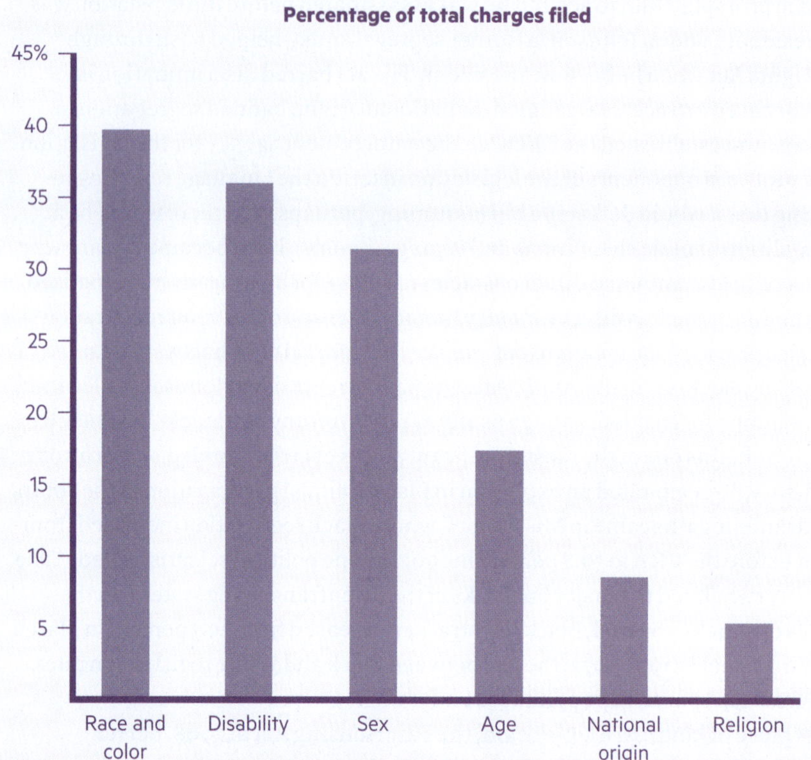

Source: "Charge Statistics, FY 1997 through FY 2023," U.S. Equal Employment Opportunity Commission, https://www.eeoc.gov/data/enforcement-and-litigation-statistics-0 (accessed 7/2/24).

Congress passed the next piece of important legislation for women in 1972: Title IX of the Education Amendments, which prohibits sex discrimination in institutions that receive federal funds. The law has had the greatest impact in women's sports. In the 1960s and 1970s, opportunities for women to play sports in college or high school were extremely limited. Very few women's scholarships were available at the college level, and budgets for women's sports were tiny compared with the budgets for men's sports. Although it took nearly 30 years to reach parity between men and women, most universities are now in compliance with Title IX. Nonetheless, the law has its critics. Many men's sports, such as baseball, tennis, wrestling, and gymnastics, were cut at universities that had to bring the number of male and female student athletes into rough parity. Critics argued that such cuts were unfair, especially given that the interest in women's sports was not as high. Defenders of the law argue that the gap in interest in women's and men's sports will not change until there is equal opportunity. There is some evidence to support that claim, as interest is increasing in professional women's soccer with the NWSL (National Women's Soccer League) and professional women's basketball with the WNBA (Women's National Basketball Association), as well as in well-established women's professional sports such as golf and tennis.

Another significant legislative effort during this period was the failed Equal Rights Amendment. The amendment was approved by Congress in 1972 and sent to the states for ratification. Its wording was simple: "Equality of rights under the law shall not be denied or abridged by the United States or any state on account of sex." Many states passed it within months, but the process lost momentum and after seven years (the deadline set by Congress for ratification by the states) the amendment fell 3 states short

While many people imagine Title IX as primarily affecting equal funding for college women's sports teams, it also provides important protections for survivors of sexual violence on college campuses. Here, students protest the Education Department's efforts to revise these provisions in February 2017.

of the 38 states required for adoption. The amendment received a three-year extension from Congress, but it still did not get the additional three states. Three more states have ratified the ERA since 2017, most recently Virginia in 2020, bringing the total to 38. Then, a few weeks after the Virginia vote, the House passed a bill nullifying the 1982 deadline for the ERA. After the Supreme Court overturned *Roe v. Wade*, supporters of abortion rights would like to provide constitutional protection.[128] However, five other states rescinded their ratifications back in the late 1970s (also North Dakota did in 2021) and the Senate is unlikely to take up the bill. Therefore, the only way to adopt the ERA would be to start the entire process over again.

In 1994, Congress passed the Violence against Women Act, which allowed women who were the victims of physical abuse and violence to sue in federal court and provided funding for investigating and prosecuting violent crimes against women, for helping the victims of such crimes, and for prevention programs. In 2000, part of the law was overturned by the Supreme Court, which ruled that Congress had exceeded its powers under the commerce clause.[129] Nonetheless, the funding provisions of the act were reauthorized and expanded by Congress , most recently in 2022.

No person in the United States shall, on the basis of sex, be excluded from participation in, be denied the benefits of, or be subjected to discrimination under any educational program or activity receiving Federal financial assistance.

—Full text of Title IX

Protections for Disabled People and for Gay Rights Yet another important piece of civil rights legislation was the 1990 Americans with Disabilities Act, which provided strong federal protections for the 45 million disabled Americans to prevent workplace discrimination and to provide access to public facilities. This law produced curb cuts in sidewalks, access for wheelchairs on public buses and trains, special seating in sports stadiums, and many other changes that make the daily lives of disabled people a little easier and that provide them with an opportunity to participate more fully in society.[130]

Congress's track record in protecting gay rights has not been as strong. In fact, most of the steps taken by Congress have been to restrict rather than expand gay rights. In 1996, Congress passed DOMA to avert the possibility that some liberal states such as Hawaii would allow gay marriage. This act defined marriage as only between a man and woman and barred couples in same-sex marriages from receiving federal insurance or Social Security spousal benefits and from filing joint federal tax returns. Nonetheless, as we have noted, the part of the law depriving same-sex spouses of federal benefits was struck down by the Supreme Court in 2013 and the entire law was overturned in 2015.

> You do not take a person who, for years, has been hobbled by chains and liberate him, bring him up to the starting line of a race and then say "you are free to compete with all the others," and still just believe that you have been completely fair.
>
> —**President Lyndon Johnson** on affirmative action

In what may represent a change of course, in October 2009 Congress passed the Matthew Shepard and James Byrd Jr. Hate Crimes Prevention Act. This legislation expanded the previous hate-crime laws based on race, color, religion, or national origin to include attacks based on a victim's sexual orientation, gender identity, or intellectual or physical disability. In signing the bill, President Obama said, "After more than a decade of opposition and delay, we've passed inclusive hate-crimes legislation to help protect our citizens from violence based on what they look like, who they love, how they pray or who they are."[131] The law commemorates the horrific murders of James Byrd Jr., a Black man who in 1998 was dragged behind a pickup truck by White supremacists for three miles until his head and right arm were severed, and Matthew Shepard, a gay teenager who in 1998 was beaten by two men, tied to a fence, and left to die. Also, the Employment Non-Discrimination Act, which would prohibit discrimination in employment based on sexual orientation, has been proposed in nearly every Congress since 1994. A more comprehensive version of the bill, the Equality Act, passed the House in 2021 but died in the Senate. However, Congress did pass the COVID-19 Hate Crimes Act in 2021 in response to the increase in hate crimes against Asian Americans and passed the Respect for Marriage Act in 2022, overturning DOMA and codifying *Obergefell*'s protection of same-sex marriage.[132]

The president

The mid-century civil rights movement benefited greatly from presidential action. President Truman integrated the armed services in 1948, and President Eisenhower used the National Guard to enforce a court order to integrate Central High School in Little Rock, Arkansas, in 1957. Executive orders by President Kennedy in 1961 and President Johnson in 1965 established affirmative action, and in 1969 Richard Nixon expanded the "goals and numerical ranges" for hiring members of historically marginalized groups in the federal government.

The most significant unilateral action taken by a president in the area of civil rights for gays and lesbians was President Clinton's effort to end the ban on gays in the military. Clinton was surprised by the strength of the opposition to his plan, so he ended up crafting a compromise policy of "don't ask, don't tell," which pleased no one. Under this policy, the military would stop actively searching for and discharging gays from the military ranks, and recruits would not need to reveal their sexual orientation. But if the military did find out (without conducting an investigation) that a person was gay, they still could be disciplined or discharged.

During the 2008 campaign, President Obama promised to repeal "don't ask, don't tell" and simply allow gays and lesbians to serve in the military. Republican filibusters stopped several attempts to change the policy in 2010, but Congress finally passed the Don't Ask, Don't Tell Repeal Act of 2010 (it went into effect on September 20, 2011). Minutes after the new policy was in place, navy lieutenant Gary Ross and his longtime partner were married in Vermont and Ross became the first openly gay married person in the military.[133] President Obama extended the policy to include transgender service members, but President Trump reversed that policy, tweeting that "the United States Government will not accept or allow transgender individuals to serve in any capacity in the U.S. Military."[134] President Biden overturned Trump's executive order in his first week in office, saying that "that gender identity should not be a bar to military service."[135]

In a landmark civil rights decision in 2020, the Supreme Court ruled that employers cannot discriminate against employees because of their sexual orientation or gender identity. President Trump rescinded the Obama-era policy of allowing transgender people to serve in the military in 2017, which was met with several court challenges. President Biden reversed this decision in 2021, once again allowing them to serve.

Recent presidential candidates have generally made civil rights policy a low priority, which means that it is less likely that significant and dramatic change will come from unilateral action by the president. Instead, attention to civil rights concerns in the executive branch in the past few decades has primarily been in two areas: racial diversity in presidential appointments and use of the bully pulpit to promote racial concerns and interests.

While the long-term impact of the Obama presidency on the civil rights movement remains to be seen, the historical significance of his successful campaign as a candidate from a historically marginalized group is clear. At the 2008 Democratic National Convention, some Black delegates openly wept as Obama accepted the party's nomination. Many delegates had not expected that they would live to see a Black American become a strong contender for the presidency. Obama's nominations for his cabinet and cabinet-level offices consisted of a diverse group of 14 men and 7 women, with 7 of them members of historically marginalized groups. Eric Holder was the first Black American to serve as attorney general, and Sonia Sotomayor is the first Latina on the Supreme Court. Obama also nominated Elena Kagan to the Supreme Court, putting three women on the Court for the first time. Obama's second-term team was similar, consisting of 14 men and 8 women, 6 of them from historically marginalized groups.

In his first term, Obama tried to downplay race and diversity concerns. Indeed, some observers argue that Obama's presidency signaled the beginning of a "post-racial politics" that places less emphasis on race and devotes more attention to issues that concern all Americans, such as the economy, education, and health care. However, Obama himself rejected this view. In Obama's second term, he used the bully pulpit to draw more attention to women's issues, such as rape on college campuses and equal pay; used executive action on immigration policy to limit deportations of young adults who were brought to the United States as children; called attention to racial disparities in the criminal justice system; and saw the Supreme Court recognize same-sex marriage as a fundamental right.

Donald Trump was elected with racially divisive positions, such as his promises to build a wall between the United States and Mexico and deport 12 million undocumented residents. In his election-night victory speech, he emphasized the importance of representing all Americans and uniting the country. As president, Trump has tended to express polarizing opinions on civil rights issues, rather than unifying themes. For example, he failed to condemn the attacks by White supremacists on counterprotesters in Charlottesville, Virginia, instead blaming "both sides" for the violence and saying that some of the White supremacists were "very fine people." As noted above, for many policies involving race, gender, and sexual orientation, President Biden has reversed many of the previous administration's policies, but much work remains to be done.[136]

"Why Should I Care?"

Why is it important for us to know who the key players are in civil rights? At various times in our history, different branches of government took the lead in promoting civil rights: Congress in the 1960s with the Civil Rights Act and the VRA, Presidents Clinton and Obama with promoting diversity in presidential appointments, and the Supreme Court in endorsing same-sex marriage. But in recent years, both the Supreme Court and President Trump have moved some civil rights policies in the other direction. If we want to see policies on these kinds of issues change, knowing who is involved and what impact these policies can have is critical.

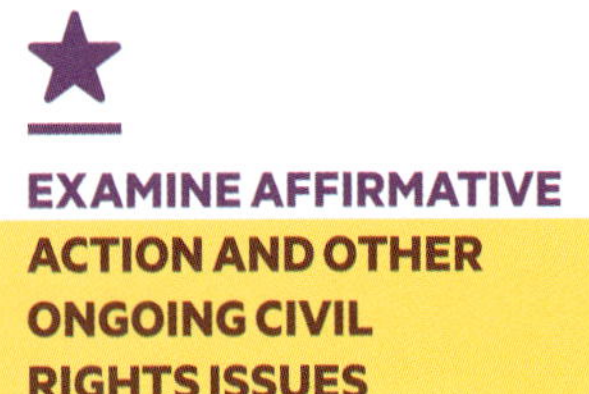

EXAMINE AFFIRMATIVE ACTION AND OTHER ONGOING CIVIL RIGHTS ISSUES

Civil rights issues today

Today, there is vigorous debate among proponents of three main perspectives on the likely direction of the civil rights movement in the twenty-first century. The first group, whose views are articulated by such scholars as Stephan Thernstrom of Harvard University and Abigail Thernstrom of the Manhattan Institute, has suggested that our nation must "move beyond race." This group argues that on many social and economic indicators the gap between Black Americans and White Americans has narrowed and that public opposition to race-based policies indicates the need for a new approach. The Supreme Court has largely endorsed this view by implementing a color-blind jurisprudence over a broad range of issues. The second group is represented by traditional civil rights activists and organizations such as the Congressional Black Caucus and the NAACP; it argues that the civil rights movement must continue to fight for equal opportunity by enforcing existing law and pushing for equality of outcomes through protecting and expanding affirmative action programs and other policies that address racial inequality. Black Lives Matter, while not a traditional civil rights organization because of its decentralized structure, fits into this category with its fight for racial equality in the criminal justice system. These first two groups share the goal of racial equality and integration but differ on how much progress we have made and how to make further progress. The third group does not support the goal of integration; instead, activists such as Louis Farrakhan and the Nation of Islam argue for Black self-sufficiency and separation. They believe that Black Americans can never gain equality within what they see as the repressive, White-dominated economic and political system.

Most civil rights advocates endorse the second view. They argue that it would be a mistake to conclude that the work of the civil rights movement is complete. They point to the resegregation of public schools, persistent gaps between White Americans and historically marginalized groups in health and economic status, racial profiling, hate crimes, a backlash against immigrant groups, and continuing discrimination in employment and housing. At the same time, this group rejects calls for racial separation as shortsighted and self-defeating.

The other two groups would argue that although the traditional civil rights agenda made important contributions to racial equality, further progress will require a different approach. Advocates of the color-blind approach prefer to stop making distinctions between people based on race. They want to use government policies to make sure there is no overt discrimination and to provide equal opportunity for all and then let merit decide outcomes. The segregationists have given up on the civil rights agenda and believe that historically marginalized groups can achieve success only on their own. Debates among advocates of these three views play out over a broad range of issues, several of which are outlined in the last section of this chapter.

Affirmative action

The Civil Rights Act of 1964 ensured that, at least on paper, all Americans would enjoy equality of opportunity. But even after the act was passed, Black Americans continued to lag behind White Americans in socioeconomic status; there was still a substantial gap between the equality of opportunity and the equality of outcomes. In an important speech at Howard University in 1965, President Johnson outlined his argument for affirmative action, saying, "This is the next and the more profound stage of the battle for civil rights. . . . We seek not just legal equity but human ability, not just equality as a right and a theory but equality as a fact and equality as a result. . . . To this end equal opportunity is essential, but not enough, not enough."[137] Later that year,

Johnson attempted to move closer to equality of outcomes by issuing an executive order requiring all federal agencies and government contractors to submit written proposals to provide an equal opportunity for employment of Black Americans, women, Asian Americans, and Native Americans within various job categories and to outline programs to achieve those goals. The policy was expanded under President Nixon, and throughout the 1970s and 1980s affirmative action programs grew in the private sector, higher education, and government contracting. Through such programs, employers and universities gave special opportunities to historically marginalized groups and women, either to make up for past discrimination or to pursue the general goals of diversity.

Affirmative action takes many forms. The most passive type involves extra effort to recruit women and members of historically marginalized groups for employment or college admission by placing ads in newspapers and magazines, visiting schools with diverse student populations, or sending out targeted mailings. A more active form involves including race or gender as a "plus factor" in admissions or hiring decisions. That is, in a pool of qualified candidates an applicant from a historically marginalized group may receive an advantage over White applicants. Women generally do not receive special consideration in admissions decisions, but gender may be a "plus factor" in some employment decisions, especially in professions in which women are underrepresented, such as engineering, architecture, the building trades, and computer programming. (In fact, many selective schools have been quietly applying affirmative action for men because more highly qualified women apply than men.) The strongest form of affirmative action is the use of quotas—strict numerical targets to hire or admit a specific number of applicants from underrepresented groups.

Affirmative action has been a controversial policy. Polls indicate that historically marginalized groups are more supportive of the practice than are White Americans. Many White Americans view it as "preferential treatment" and "reverse discrimination." Fifty-seven percent of White Americans support "affirmative action programs for racial minorities" compared with 69 percent of Black Americans and 79 percent of Latinos. But when asked specifically about race-based admissions, 78 percent of White Americans said that college admissions should not consider race as a factor in college admission decisions; 62 percent of Black respondents and 65 percent of Latino respondents said race should not be a factor.[138] This backlash has spilled over into state politics. California passed Proposition 209 in 1996, which banned the consideration of "race, sex, color, ethnicity or national origin" in public employment, public education, or public contracting.[139] Nine other states have similar laws.

The Supreme Court has helped define the boundaries of this policy debate. The earliest cases concerning affirmative action in employment upheld preferential treatment and rigid quotas when the policies were necessary to make up for past discrimination. The cases involved a worker training program that set aside 50 percent of the positions for Black Americans, a labor union that was required to hire enough members of historically marginalized communities to get its non-White membership to 29.23 percent, and a state police force that was required to promote one Black officer for every White even if there was a smaller pool of Black Americans who were eligible for promotion.[140] In each instance, there had been a previous pattern of discrimination and exclusion.

The Court moved in a more color-blind direction in an important reverse-discrimination employment case in 2009. In that case, 17 White firefighters and 1 Latino firefighter sued the city of New Haven, Connecticut, for throwing out the results of a test that would have been used to promote them. The city tried to ignore the results of the test because no Black firefighters would have qualified for promotion and the city feared a "disparate impact" lawsuit. However, the Court ruled that the exam did appear to be "job related and consistent with business necessity" (as required by Section VII of the Civil Rights Act) and that unless the city could provide a "strong basis in evidence" that it would have been sued, it had to consider the results of the exam.[141]

The landmark decision for affirmative action in higher education was *Regents of the University of California v. Bakke* (1978).[142] Allan Bakke, a White student, sued when he was denied admission to medical school at the University of California, Davis, in successive years. Bakke's test scores and GPA were significantly higher than those of some students from historically marginalized groups who were admitted under the school's affirmative action program. Under that program, 16 of the 100 slots in the entering class were reserved for disadvantaged students or students from historically marginalized groups. The Supreme Court agreed with Bakke that rigid racial quotas were unconstitutional, but the Court allowed race to be used in admissions decisions as a "plus factor" to promote diversity in the student body. This standard was largely unquestioned until 1996, when the Fifth Circuit Court of Appeals held that it was unconstitutional to consider race in law school admissions at the University of Texas.[143] In 2000, the Ninth Circuit Court of Appeals in Seattle, however, reached the opposite conclusion and ruled that race could be considered in admissions to promote educational diversity.[144]

In 2003, the Court affirmed *Bakke*, saying that the University of Michigan law school's "holistic approach," which considered race as one of the factors in the admission decision, was acceptable. However, the more rigid approach for undergraduate admissions at Michigan, which automatically gave students from historically marginalized groups 20 of the 100 points needed to guarantee admission, was unacceptable.[145] This was the first time that a majority of the Court clearly stated that "student body diversity is a compelling state interest that can justify the use of race in university admissions."[146] In 2006, voters in Michigan passed Proposal 2, an initiative to make it illegal for state bodies to consider race in admissions and hiring decisions; this policy was upheld by the Supreme Court in 2014.[147] Similar laws had previously been passed in California and Washington.

Demonstrators protested against an allegedly discriminatory affirmative action policy at Harvard University that disadvantages Asian-American students.

In 2008, a White student, Abigail Fisher, claimed she was a victim of reverse discrimination and sued the University of Texas at Austin. Texas had achieved a racially diverse student body by extending offers of admission to the top 6 percent of every graduating high school class in the state. This approach worked because most high schools in Texas were still fairly segregated. 75 percent of in-state students are admitted via the 6 percent plan. The remaining 25 percent of in-state students are admitted by a "holistic" program that evaluates their entire record and includes race as a "plus factor." It was this second part that Abigail Fisher challenged after being denied admission to the University of Texas. In June 2016, the Court upheld Texas's affirmative action policy by a 4–3 vote.[148] But in 2023, the Court struck down any consideration of race in college admissions when it said that the admissions process at Harvard University and the University of North Carolina violated the equal protection clause of the Fourteenth Amendment.[149] For more information on this case see the Take a Stand feature on page 207.

Multicultural issues and immigration policy

A host of issues involving the multicultural, multiracial nature of American society will become more important as White Americans cease to constitute the majority of the population by mid-century. At their cores, these issues are rooted in the fact that the United States is a nation of immigrants. Will that history continue, and if so, what shape will it take? Is our country a "melting pot," focused on the assimilation of new groups, or is it more like a "tossed salad," in which each immigrant group maintains its cultural identity but creates a new, better collective whole? Groups who favor one or the other of these conceptions of American society often clash over issues such as whether English should be our official language (32 states have such laws) and whether bilingual education should be offered in public schools. But the biggest area for debate on this topic in recent years concerns immigration reform and border security.

TAKE A STAND

Affirmative Action in College Admissions

From 1978 until 2023, the Supreme Court had endorsed the idea of race as a "plus factor" in college admissions while rejecting the idea of strict quotas or point systems. This approach was affirmed in a 2003 case involving the University of Michigan's law school, but many Court-watchers believed that affirmative action would be struck down in the 2016 case *Fisher v. University of Texas, Austin.*[a] Instead, swing vote Justice Kennedy sided with the liberal justices and the Court upheld the practice, ruling that the program could be justified as serving a "compelling state interest" under the strict scrutiny standard.

But in 2023, the Court reversed course and struck down the use of race in college admission. A group named Students for Fair Admissions sued Harvard University and the University of North Carolina (UNC), saying the race-based admissions violated the Fourteenth Amendment and discriminated against Asian American applicants (because they generally had higher test scores and grades than applicants who benefited from affirmative action). The majority opinion said applicants "must be treated based on his or her experiences as an individual—not on the basis of race"; in contrast, the Harvard and UNC policies "concluded, wrongly, that the touchstone of an individual's identity is not challenges bested, skills built, or lessons learned but the color of their skin. Our constitutional history does not tolerate that choice."[b]

Diversity deserves consideration. Advocates of affirmative action argue that a diverse student body promotes viewpoint diversity that is essential to learning. Having racial diversity in the student body is likely to produce more viewpoint diversity in classroom discussions than would occur with a mostly White student body. The majority opinion in the Texas case (and the dissenters in the Harvard/UNC case) also argued that a more diverse student body leads to "the destruction of stereotypes," promotes "cross-racial understanding," and prepares students "for an increasingly diverse work force and society." Stepping back from pursuing these goals will undermine the vision of a more equal and just society.

In her dissent in the Harvard/UNC case, Justice Sotomayor said, "The devastating impact" of the decision "cannot be overstated."[b] Justice Jackson pointed out the lingering effects of institutional discrimination: "Given the lengthy history of state-sponsored race-based preferences in America, to say that anyone is now victimized if a college considers whether that legacy of discrimination has unequally advantaged its applicants fails to acknowledge the well-documented 'intergenerational transmission of inequality' that still plagues our citizenry." Some proponents also argue that the courts are not the proper place to decide these issues. Instead, as with the complex and highly charged topic of racial redistricting, the political branches of government are where these decisions should be made. The Court endorsed this position of judicial restraint in a 2014 case involving a ban on affirmative action in Michigan.[c]

Affirmative action is just another kind of discrimination. Opponents reply that supporters of affirmative action have not provided convincing evidence that racial diversity in colleges has any beneficial effects. The majority opinion in the Harvard/UNC case said that while goals such as such as "training future leaders in the public and private sectors" and "promoting the robust exchange of ideas" are commendable, these outcomes are very hard to measure. Others argue that "viewpoint diversity" arguments assume that members of all historically marginalized groups think alike, drawing a comparison to racial profiling in law enforcement. It is just as offensive, they say, that an admissions committee thinks that one Black student has the same views as another Black student as it is that a police officer may pull over a Black teenage male just because he fits a certain criminal profile.

Opponents also argue that affirmative action amounts to "reverse discrimination" and that any racial classification is harmful. Justice Thomas's concurring opinion argued that affirmative action does not solve existing problems of discrimination and inequality, but creates divisions among students and leads to "increasing racial polarization and friction." Justice Thomas also argued that the policies do nothing to increase the overall number of Black and Hispanic students in college, but "simply redistribute individuals" among colleges and universities, "placing some into more competitive institutions than they otherwise would have attended" where they may not have as much chance for success.

If you had to rule on the Harvard/UNC case, how would you have decided? Take a stand.

Students protest outside the Supreme Court in support of diversity at the University of Texas.

take a stand

1. To what extent should race be used as a "plus factor" to promote racial diversity and viewpoint diversity, if at all?
2. Think of your own experiences in high school and college. Has racial diversity contributed to viewpoint diversity?

At first glance, it isn't clear why immigration would be considered a civil rights issue. After all, noncitizens don't have all the same legal rights as citizens—for example, only citizens can vote in federal elections and run for office. However, many parts of the Constitution, including the crucial Fourteenth Amendment, say "person," not citizen. And while the national government does have the ability to regulate who may enter the country, non-citizens have a right to payment for work performed, to a healthy and safe work environment, and even to a K–12 education (although some states are trying to change that). Even undocumented people who are being deported have the right to a hearing before an immigration judge, representation by a lawyer (but not at government expense), an opportunity to examine the evidence and the government's witnesses, services of an interpreter for non-English-speaking immigrants, and "clear and convincing proof that the government's grounds for deportation are valid."[150]

Following the September 11 terrorist attacks, some people saw immigration as a threat that must be curtailed. The government made it clear that it would not engage in racial profiling of Arab Americans—for example, subjecting them to stricter screening at airports—but many commentators argued that such profiling would be justified, and there was at least anecdotal evidence of an increase in discrimination against people of Middle Eastern descent. After the terrorist attacks in Paris and San Bernardino, California, in 2016, the debate in the presidential campaign shifted to a strongly anti-immigrant tone. During the campaign, Donald Trump proposed preventing all Muslims from entering the United States until the government could make sure they did not pose a terrorist threat. As president he issued an executive order narrowly targeting Muslim countries that was struck down by a federal court. A second version was also struck down, but in 2018 the Supreme Court upheld the third version of the travel ban. The Court deferred to the president's ability to define national security, saying that his executive power was not undermined by his political comments about the possible intent of the travel ban.[151] But once again, on his first day in office, President Biden reversed that executive order.[152]

Over the past two decades, immigration has been central in many political debates. The intensity of that debate increased in 2010 when Arizona enacted an anti-immigration law that requires local law-enforcement officials to check the immigration status of a person in a "lawful stop, detention, or arrest" if there is a "reasonable suspicion" that the person is an undocumented immigrant. The law also requires immigrants to always carry papers verifying their immigration status and bans people

When President Trump announced his original travel ban preventing individuals from select Muslim-majority countries from entering the United States, people flooded airports across the country in protest.

without proper documents from seeking work in public places. Many civil rights violations occurred when local law-enforcement officials started enforcing this law. States with similar laws include South Carolina, Alabama, Utah, Georgia, and Indiana. Arizona governor Jan Brewer said, "Decades of federal inaction and misguided policy have created a dangerous and unacceptable situation, and states deserve clarity from the Court in terms of what role they have in fighting illegal immigration."[153] Opponents of the law argue that it requires illegal racial profiling and that the federal government has the sole responsibility for deciding immigration law.

In 2012, the Supreme Court struck down three of the four main provisions of the law, citing the supremacy clause of the Constitution. This decision meant that Congress, not the states, determines immigration law when the two laws conflict. The Court upheld the controversial "show me your papers" part of the law, saying that the state was simply enforcing the federal law. However, the Court indicated that the law must be applied in a race-neutral way and could be struck down if there was clear evidence of racial profiling.[154] Several months later, a federal district court judge cleared the way for implementation of the "show me your papers" law, saying that the Supreme Court wanted to see actual evidence of discrimination rather than speculation that the law could have a discriminatory effect.[155]

The immigration system is widely viewed as broken and in need of reform, but neither President Bush nor President Obama was able to get Congress to approve his proposal to provide a "path to citizenship" for undocumented immigrants. In 2021, a poll showed strong support for reform, with 72 percent of those surveyed saying that "undocumented immigrants who entered the country as children, [should have] the ability to earn United States citizenship."[156] In 2015, President Obama used executive orders to implement part of his immigration policy (concerning the deportation of young adults who were brought to the United States without documentation by their parents and the deportation of the parents of children who are citizens). President Trump revoked Obama's executive order and, while Congress deadlocked on the issue, the courts allowed the program to continue for those already enrolled.[157] As you probably guessed by now, President Biden reversed that order and has pushed for comprehensive immigration reform (but without any success in Congress).[158]

The debates over affirmative action, English as the country's official language, and immigration reform clearly illustrate the conflictual nature of civil rights policy.

Hundreds of thousands of undocumented immigrants cross into the United States each year. They come seeking better economic opportunities or fleeing crime, war, or other life-threatening situations in their native country. Here, a border control agent detains migrants from Central America seeking asylum.

However, history has shown that when public opinion strongly supports a given application of civil rights—for example, the integration of Black Americans in the South in the 1960s and, more recently, allowing gays to openly serve in the military and recognizing same-sex marriage—public policy soon reflects those views. Although it is impossible to say when there will be comprehensive immigration reform that includes a path to citizenship, it is likely to eventually happen given the trends in public opinion.

Unpacking the Conflict

Considering all that we've discussed in this chapter, let's apply what we know about how civil rights work to the examples of profiling introduced at the beginning of this chapter. Is it ever acceptable to treat people differently based on the color of their skin, their ethnic background, their gender, or their sexual orientation, in a situation of racial profiling or otherwise?

Enforcing civil rights means providing equal protection of the law to individuals and groups that are discriminated against, which may include noncitizens and undocumented immigrants. But figuring out exactly when an individual's civil rights have been violated can be tricky. When does a routine traffic stop by a police officer turn into racial profiling?

To help figure that out, we now can answer the questions about possible civil rights violations that introduced this chapter:

- Scenario 1: On the one hand, the Black teenagers who were pulled over by the police may or may not have had their civil rights violated, depending on the laws in their state. In Massachusetts, for example, it is prohibited to consider the "race, gender, national or ethnic origin of members of the public in deciding to detain a person or stop a motor vehicle" except in "suspect specific incidents." (However, only 23 states have laws limiting racial profiling in law enforcement stops).[159] On the other hand, in the scenario in which the police pulled over White teenagers, the traffic stop would have been acceptable as long as there had been "probable cause" to justify the stop.
- Scenario 2: The Asian-American woman who did not get the job could certainly talk to a lawyer about filing a "disparate impact" discrimination suit. Under the 1991 Civil Rights Act, the employer would have the burden of proof to show that she was not a victim of the good ol' boy network.
- Scenario 3: The same-sex couple who could not rent the apartment because of their sexual orientation might have a basis for a civil rights lawsuit based on the Fourteenth Amendment. But this would depend on where they lived, given that there is no federal protection against discrimination against gay men and lesbians (and the Supreme Court has not applied the Fourteenth Amendment in this context). Only 19 states have the strongest protections against discrimination based on sexual orientation.[160]
- Scenario 4: Court decisions concerning affirmative action at the University of Michigan and the University of Texas show that the White student who was not admitted to the university of his choice would just have to take his lumps, as long as the affirmative action program considered race as a general "plus factor" rather than assigning more or fewer points for it (and the practice was allowed by his state).

This review of civil rights in the United States has highlighted only some of the most important issues, but a significant agenda remains. The civil rights movement will continue to use the multiple avenues of the legislative, executive, and judicial branches to secure equal rights for all Americans. Although this process may take many years, history demonstrates that when public opinion becomes more supportive of diversity and stronger civil rights, our political institutions eventually support the views of the people.

"What's Your Take?"

Should distinctions between people based on race, ethnic status, gender, or sexual orientation be uniformly prohibited?

Or are they OK under some circumstances?

CHECK YOUR UNDERSTANDING

"Why Should I Care?"

Civil rights in America is an evolving story of the continuous rebalancing of the rights of a minority and the power of a majority first established by our Constitution. That journey has progressed in fits and starts as our understanding of racial, ethnic, and gender identities has evolved. The early history of slavery and no political or economic rights for women gave way to the Fourteenth Amendment's promise of "equal protection of the laws" for all people. The next 150 years was the continual struggle to try to fulfill that promise by the women's rights, civil rights, and LGBTQ movements.

The evolution of our civil rights should be understood as this continual story rather than a discrete set of events. For example, the civil rights movement of the 1950s and 1960s was the culmination of multiple previous social movements and organizing efforts around civil rights. Furthermore, no group or movement's ideas or leaders stood in isolation; rather, all of them experienced transfers of knowledge, experiences, and skills through shared leadership and experiences. This continual evolution means the development of civil rights isn't stagnant. Instead, Supreme Court cases, legislation, and the resulting social and political structures are the product of the actions of political leaders and social movements of the time.

As individuals, each of us has overlapping character traits or identities making us part of different groups and communities. Some of these identities come with advantages, while others have disadvantages within American political and social structures. Organizing, activism, and engagement around civil rights are the direct result of individuals who share bonds of being disadvantaged seeking access to the protections and promises of the American system. It is a recent expectation that all Americans should be able to enter a coffee shop and receive service with a smile, or serve in the armed forces without worrying about whom they kiss goodbye when they deploy to serve their country. These evolving expectations didn't just happen but are the result of nearly 250 years of challenge and change.

1. **Most modern civil rights questions are rooted in the ____________ clause of the Fourteenth Amendment.**

a due process

b citizenship

c equal protection

d just compensation

2. **In the immediate aftermath of Reconstruction and ratification of the Thirteenth, Fourteenth, and Fifteenth Amendments, many southern states took advantage of which loophole in the amendments to disenfranchise Black citizens?**

a States could prevent citizens with criminal convictions from voting.

b The amendments did not explicitly guarantee a right to vote to Black citizens.

c Federal elections were the only ones in which Black citizens were guaranteed a right to vote.

d The Reconstruction Amendments allowed for states to petition the Supreme Court for exclusions to voting rights.

3. **Which fact do many Americans point to as evidence of institutional racism within the United States?**

a Black Americans are more likely to be convicted and serve longer sentences than White Americans accused of the same crimes.

b Black, Hispanic, and Asian Americans are more likely to have lower voter turnout when compared with White Americans.

c Nearly three-fifths of all hate crimes are race-based crimes of violence.

d The number of non-White public officials in the United States is significantly lower than the number of White officials.

4. **The 2013 ruling that declared part of the 1965 Voting Rights Act unconstitutional led most directly to which of the following?**

a Challenges to the Electoral College results by members of Congress

b Federal court challenges of state electoral maps and election laws

c Impeachment of the president and other high-ranking federal appointees

d Passage of laws increasing voter restrictions

5. **The Montgomery bus boycotts and the Seneca Falls Convention are illustrations of**

a collective action's power to keep issues on the policy agenda.

b the ability of individuals to spur national movements.

c electoral impacts of social justice movements.

d the power of legal challenges in effecting changes in civil rights.

6. **The nonviolent campaigns of civil disobedience led by Dr. Martin Luther King Jr. and the economic pressures of the strikes and boycotts led by individuals like Cesar Chavez and Dolores Huerta of the 1960s sought to accomplish which of the following?**

a Enforce federal laws and judicial rulings through coordinated actions in the absence of willingness of traditional police to implement the policies

b Deliver decisive electoral and legislative victories for marginalized communities through any means necessary

c Use conflict to bring public attention to injustices that would create political pressure for changing public policy

d Create unstable situations that would spill over into White communities that had largely been untouched by the inequalities of discriminatory policies

7. During the 1960s and 1970s the Supreme Court embraced a more expansive view of the federal government's role in creating equity for Americans from racially marginalized communities, while recent opinions of the Court indicate that a majority of justices are

- **a** willing to further expand the national government's influence in creating political and social equality.
- **b** embracing a color-blind approach when determining the constitutionality of civil rights policies.
- **c** rejecting claims of racial diversity as a compelling state interest in hiring and admissions.
- **d** encouraging growth of state-level affirmative action policies around race and sex.

8. The Supreme Court's willingness to continue President Obama's Deferred Action for Childhood Arrivals (DACA) program that protects individuals from deportation who were brought to the United States as children without documentation and President Trump's travel ban from predominantly Muslim nations reflects what truth about the American system?

- **a** In highly controversial issues, the Court is more likely to defer to one of the political branches.
- **b** Immigration policies are left to presidents to decide because of widespread public agreement on these issues.
- **c** Implementation of public policies with very different objectives that followed established rules of the political process is protected.
- **d** Presidential actions are more likely than congressional actions to receive support from the courts.

Use INQUIZITIVE *to help you study and master this material.*

6

Public Opinion

What do the people want? How should we measure opinion?

"In America, public opinion is the leader."
Frances Perkins, U.S. Secretary of Labor, 1933–1945

"You have to remember one thing about the will of the people: it wasn't that long ago that we were swept away by the Macarena."[1]
Jon Stewart, comedian

One of the foundations of democracy is the belief that public opinion matters: while in office, elected officials act in accordance with their constituents' demands or else face the possibility of being defeated in the next election. Every election season, candidates, political parties, journalists, and political scientists take thousands of polls to determine who is likely to vote, whom they are planning to vote for, and what sorts of arguments, slogans, and platforms might change their minds.

Political scientists also believe that public opinions have some basis in reality. According to political scientist V. O. Key, "in the large, the electorate behaves about as rationally and responsibly as we should expect, given the clarity and the alternatives presented to it and the character of the information available to it."[2] The expectation is that citizens' evaluations of what government does, their ideas of what they would like done differently, and their thoughts about what they like and don't like more broadly are all connected in some way to actual facts on the ground.

Significant percentages of Americans hold politically consequential beliefs that are factually untrue. This was apparent at many points during the pandemic. From disputes over shutdowns, mask mandates, and vaccination mandates, the public expressed opinions that had no data to back them up, demonstrating that other factors weighed heavily in their decision-making process. For example, debates over the legality of federal vaccine mandates went all the way to the Supreme Court.

However, a look at the results of some mass surveys might lead you to comedian and political commentator Jon Stewart's concern that public opinion is fickle and only loosely connected to reality. For example, in a July 2021 survey, 20 percent of Americans said they believed that the COVID-19 vaccines were being used to implant microchips in the population. In the same sample, 40 percent said that vaccines have been shown to cause autism.[3] (both claims are false.) Such responses raise a fundamental question about democracy: do we want, as Secretary Perkins put it, for "public opinion to be the leader" if a substantial number of Americans appear to believe things that have no basis in reality?

These concerns are magnified by recent polls that find some support for claims that elections are routinely stolen, that America is at risk of civil war, or that a military coup

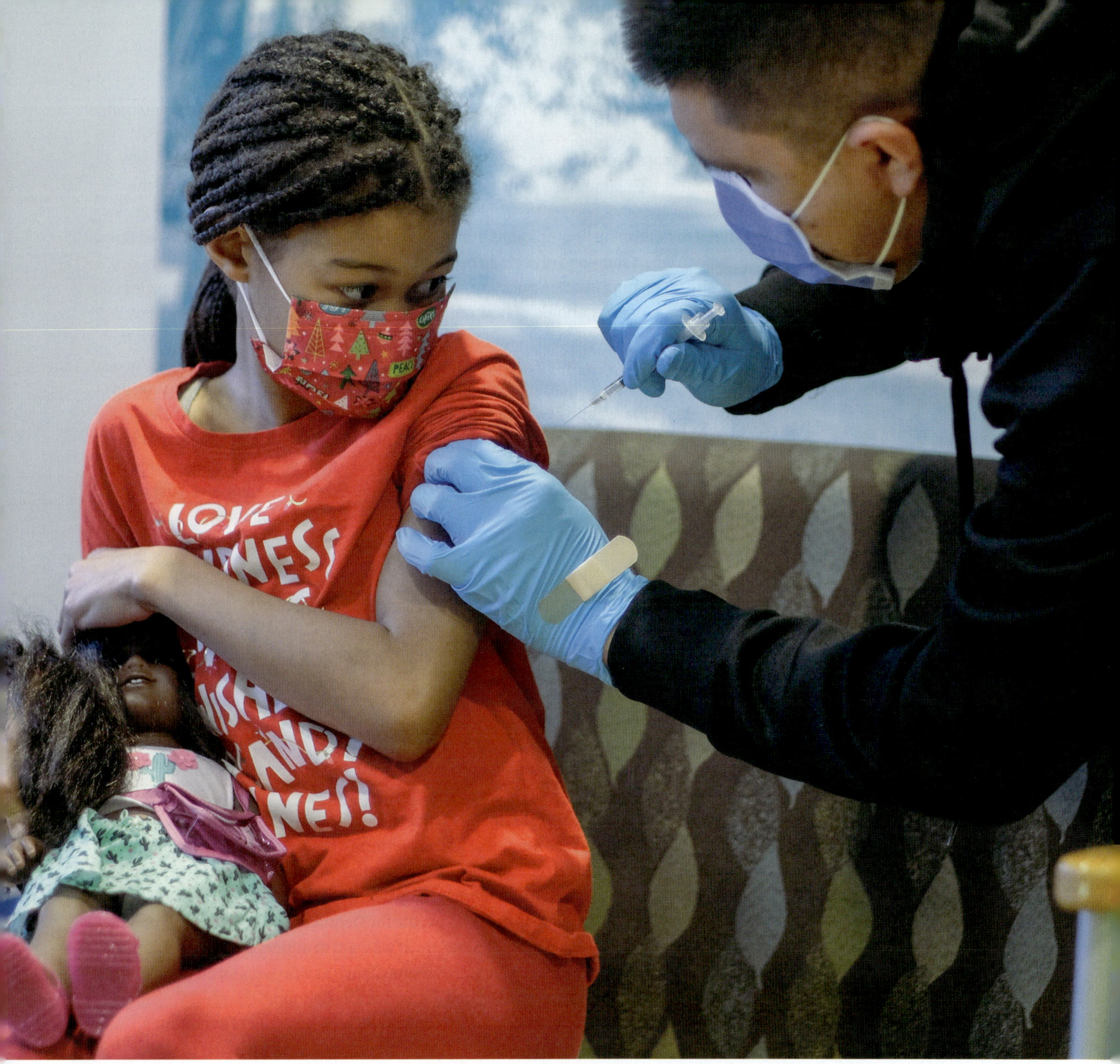

Define *public opinion* and explain why it matters in American politics (pp. 216–219)

Explain how people form political attitudes and opinions (pp. 219–228)

Describe basic survey methods and potential issues affecting accuracy (pp. 228–236)

Present findings on what Americans think about government and why it matters (pp. 236–247) is justified under some conditions. Some commentators see these results as evidence that American democracy itself is at risk—that the public no longer believes that elections are a good way to decide who gets to make policy choices.

Before we blame Americans for believing in conspiracy theories, question the viability of democracy, or take pollsters to task for mismeasuring public opinion, we need to determine how opinions are formed and how they are expressed. What does it mean when someone reveals an opinion, such as support for a conspiracy theory, a desire for change in some policy, or support for a president? Answering this question requires an understanding of how opinions are formed and what goes into them. We need to consider how Americans are reacting to changes in the amount and content of available political information, a topic we also discuss in Chapter 7 (Media). We also need to determine whether opinions are real, in the sense that they are considered judgments that shape behavior, and what problems arise when we ask people what they think about politics. Do Americans really hold the bizarre beliefs that are sometimes expressed in polling results? Can we take polls seriously if they produce results like these? Where does public opinion come from? Can politicians trust public opinion as a guide to what Americans want—and can we use opinions to measure the quality of American democracy?

DEFINE *PUBLIC OPINION* AND EXPLAIN WHY IT MATTERS IN AMERICAN POLITICS

What is public opinion?

public opinion
Citizens' views on politics and government actions.

Public opinion describes what the population thinks about politics and government—what government should be doing, evaluations of what government *is* doing, and judgments about elected officials and others who participate in the political process, as well as the wider set of beliefs that shape these opinions.

Public opinion matters for three reasons. First, citizens' political actions—including voting, contributing to campaigns, writing letters to senators, and other kinds of activism—are driven by their opinions.[4] For example, as we discuss in more detail in Chapter 8, party identification shapes voting decisions. A voter who thinks of himself or herself as a Democrat is more likely to vote for Democratic candidates than a voter who identifies as a Republican.[5] Therefore, if we want to understand an individual's behavior or analyze broader political outcomes, such as who wins an election or the fate of a legislative proposal, we need good data on public opinion.

Second, examining public opinion helps explain the behavior of candidates, political parties, and other political actors. Later chapters (particularly Chapters 9 and 10) show a strong link between citizens' opinions and candidates' campaign strategies and their actions in office. Politicians look to public opinion to determine what citizens want them to do and how satisfied citizens are with their behavior in office. For example, in Chapter 11 we see how congressional representatives are

Politicians read public-opinion polls closely to gauge whether their behavior will anger or please constituents. Few politicians always follow survey results—but virtually none would agree with Calvin's father that polls should be ignored entirely.

reluctant to cast votes that are inconsistent with their constituents' preferences (particularly those who share the representative's party identification), especially on issues that constituents consider important. Therefore, to explain a legislator's votes, you need to begin with some measurement of their constituents' opinions.

Third, because public opinion is a key to understanding what motivates both citizens and political officials, it can shed light on the reasons for specific policy outcomes. For example, changes in the policy mood—the public's demand for new policies—are linked to changes in government spending.[6] When people want government to do more, spending increases more rapidly; when people want government to do less, spending goes down (or increases more slowly).

"

Whoever can change public opinion can change the government.

—President Abraham Lincoln

Different kinds of opinion

Modern theories of public opinion distinguish between two types of opinions: opinions that are preformed and opinions that are formed on the spot as needed. The first kind of opinions are broad expressions, such as how people think about politics, what they want from government, or principles that apply across a range of issues. These kinds of beliefs typically form early in life and remain stable over time. Some of these beliefs are obviously political, such as party identification, **liberal or conservative ideology**, and judgments about society's responsibility to those in need. Liberal or conservative ideology is a good example of a stable opinion: the best way to predict an American's ideology at age 40 is to assume it will match their ideology at age 20. The same is true for party identification.

liberal or conservative ideology
A way of describing political beliefs in terms of a position on the spectrum running from liberal to moderate to conservative.

The most important thing to understand about public opinion is that although ideology and party identification are largely consistent over time, these opinions are exceptions to the rule.[7] The average person does not maintain a set of fully formed opinions on all political topics, such as evaluations of all the candidates for state or local office or assessments of the entire range of government programs. Instead, most Americans' political judgments are **latent opinions**: they are constructed only as needed, such as when answering a survey question or deciding on Election Day how to vote. For example, when most people are asked about the oppression of the Uyghur

latent opinion
An opinion formed on the spot, when it is needed (as distinct from a deeply held opinion that is stable over time).

A person's ideological perspective is relatively stable over time. People who subscribe to a conservative ideology generally support small government and decreased spending.

people in China, they probably do not have a specific response in mind simply because they have not thought much about the question. They might have, at best, some vague ideas about the situation and what should be done about it. Their opinions become concrete only when they are asked about them.

As we will show later, these bedrock beliefs serve another important purpose: they help people form opinions about other questions. Most importantly, in contemporary American politics, many people use party identification (their sense of affiliation with the Republican or Democratic parties) to decide about other matters. For example, when a citizen is asked about the state of the economy, most people don't stop and collect information about the stock market, inflation, or unemployment. Rather, they say things are good if the president is from their party and things are bad if not. (In fact, polling data show that when Democrat Joe Biden succeeded Republican Donald Trump in January 2021, Republican voters became much less positive about the economy, while Democratic voters became more positive.) Explaining why people resort to factors like partisanship to make judgments like these is one of the primary tasks of this chapter.

People who follow politics closely have more preformed opinions than the average American, whose interest in politics is relatively low. But very few people are so well informed that they have ready opinions on a wide range of political and policy questions. Moreover, even when people do form opinions in advance, they may not remember every factor that influenced their opinions. Thus, an individual may express opposition to vaccine mandates but may be unable to explain the reasons behind this opinion.[8]

Opinions also vary in intensity. For example, one individual might strongly favor policies that allow handgun ownership and open carry in public, while another might oppose both policies but with less intensity. Intensity matters because it shapes whether and how people act on their opinions. The strongly pro-gun individual would be more likely to consider a candidate's gun rights policy when deciding how to vote, while the individual who opposes gun ownership (but less intensely) would likely base their vote on other issues. Variation in intensity is one reason why government policies sometimes reflect minority opinions. In the case of gun rights, members of Congress are well aware of polls showing that a majority of people support restrictions on gun ownership. However, polls also show that most supporters of restrictions do not feel

Images of confrontation between pro-vaccine and anti-vaccine protesters may conceal the more nuanced considerations that underlie most Americans' opinions about the issue.

strongly about this issue, while people who oppose restrictions are more likely to be intense in their opposition. Thus, when responding to public opinion about gun control, members of Congress reflect the intense minority opinion, not the weaker opinions held by the majority.

"Why Should I Care?"

In a democracy, elected officials stay in office by keeping their constituents happy. As a result, knowing what public opinion looks like—what citizens believe, what they want government to do—helps us understand the choices elected officials make. New policy initiatives such as stricter gun control laws are unlikely to be enacted in the absence of strong, sustained public support. Conversely, even controversial proposals such as Obamacare can be enacted over strong opposition, as long as there are enough enthusiastic supporters. In both ways, public opinion both motivates and constrains elected officials.

Where do opinions come from?

★

EXPLAIN HOW PEOPLE FORM POLITICAL ATTITUDES AND OPINIONS

This section describes the sources that people draw from to inform their opinions and the ways that these different sources interact to determine both individual opinions and collective public opinions. Some opinions are influenced by early life experiences, such as exposure to the beliefs of parents, relatives, or teachers; others result from later life events or from informal conversations with friends. Politicians and other elites play a critical role in the opinion-formation process.

Socialization: families, communities, and networks

Theories of **political socialization** show that children develop a liberal or conservative ideology; a level of trust in others; their own class, racial, and ethnic identity; and other political opinions based on what they learn from their parents.[9] For example, one of the best predictors of a college student's party identification is the party ID of their parents. Opinions formed through socialization are not necessarily permanent; in fact, people often respond to events by modifying their opinions, even those developed early in life. Thus, an individual who originally identified as a Democrat because her parents were Democrats might move away from the party later in life because she did not like the party's candidates, because she thought Democrats did a poor job running the country, or because she disagreed with the party's platform. Even so, for many people, ideas learned during childhood continue to shape their political opinions throughout their lives.[10]

political socialization
The process by which an individual's political opinions are shaped by other people and the surrounding culture.

Beyond these influences, research finds broader aspects of socialization that shape political opinions. People are socialized by their communities, the people they interact with while growing up, such as neighbors, teachers, clergy, and others.[11] Support for democracy as a system of government and for American political institutions is higher for individuals who take a civics class in high school.[12] Growing up in a homogenous community, one where many people share the same cultural, ethnic, or political beliefs, increases adults' sense of civic duty—their belief that voting or other forms of political participation are important social obligations.[13]

Although events such as wars, economic upheavals, and major policy changes certainly influence public opinion, research shows that most Americans acquire some political opinions early in life from parents, friends, teachers, and others in their community.

Volunteering in community organizations as a child also shapes political beliefs and participation in later life.[14] Engaging in political activity as a teenager, such as volunteering in a presidential campaign, generates higher levels of political interest as an adult; it also strengthens the belief that people should care about politics and participate in political activities.[15]

Individuals' opinions are also shaped by random interactions—the people they meet each day.[16] Put another way, you might not think that meeting for coffee with a friend would affect your opinions about climate change, but suppose during the conversation your friend mentioned how much hotter this year had been compared with last year. While such casual conversations are unlikely to have a permanent impact, they might well influence your thinking in the short run—for example, if a week after having coffee, you have to decide how to vote in an election where climate change is an issue.

Events

Although socialization often influences individuals' fairly stable core beliefs, this does not mean that these beliefs or opinions are fixed. All kinds of events—from everyday interactions to traumatic, life-changing disasters—can capture people's attention and force them to revise their understanding of politics and the role of government.

Some events that shape beliefs are specific, individual experiences. For example, individuals' support for same-sex marriage is strongly influenced by the number of people they know who are gay or lesbian.[17] Major national or world events may also shape beliefs. For example, support for restrictions on gun ownership—such as background checks, bans on certain weapons, or confiscation of weapons from individuals with mental health issues—typically increases after a mass shooting event (although it generally returns to prior levels after a few weeks or months). And political scientists Bethany Albertson and Shana Kushner Gadarian show that feelings of anxiety generated by events (such as the COVID-19 pandemic) can also influence opinion formation by de-emphasizing considerations like partisanship and emphasizing others, such as the opinions of political elites.

Some events have a greater impact on public opinion than others, and some people are more likely than others to change their views. Opinion changes generated by an event or some other new information are more likely when an individual is unfamiliar with the event or information yet considers it to be important. In such cases, the individual does not have a set of preexisting principles or other considerations with which to interpret the event or information. People who do not have strong beliefs are also more likely to change their opinions than are people who hold strong opinions.[18]

Group identity

In the United States, opinions on many issues are correlated with the state or region where a person grew up or lives. For example, until the 1970s relatively few native White southerners identified with the Republican Party.[19] Even today, native White southerners tend to have different attitudes (such as less support for affirmative action) compared with similar people from other regions of the country.[20] People who live in the same area might have common beliefs because they experienced the same historical events at similar points in their lives or learned political viewpoints from one another. Political scientist Katherine Cramer has shown that rural resentment in contemporary American politics stems from the belief that elected officials at the state and national levels do not share the values held by rural residents and will thus shortchange rural communities in the policy process.

In some cases, group identity is a function of age. Changes in attitudes about same-sex marriage over the last decade illustrate this phenomenon (see Figure 6.1). The figure shows that overall support for allowing gay and lesbian couples to marry (or allowing civil unions) has more than doubled in the last 16 years. Moreover, while opinions have shifted in all age cohorts, younger Americans are much more likely to express support than are older Americans—in part because they are much more likely to know someone who is gay or lesbian and in part because they are likely to have other characteristics that predispose them to favor same-sex marriage, such as not being regular churchgoers.

Attitudes about Same-Sex Marriage

FIGURE 6.1

Over the last 16 years, support for same-sex marriage has grown. What do these graphs tell us about the influence of group identity on public opinion? Is support for same-sex marriage likely to increase or decrease in the future? Why?

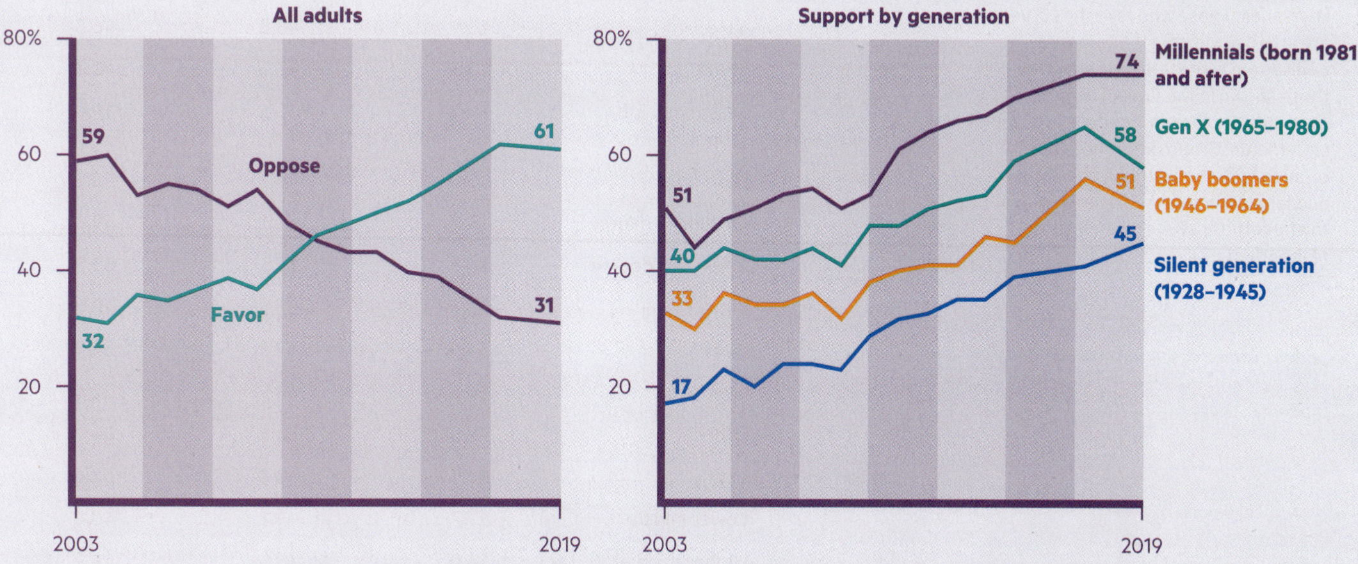

Source: Pew Research Center, "Majority of Public Favors Same-Sex Marriage, but Divisions Persist," May 14, 2019, www.people-press.org/2019/05/14/majority-of-public-favors-same-sex-marriage-but-divisions-persist/ (accessed 1/14/22).

Individuals also may rely on others who "look like" them as a source of opinions. Political scientists Donald Green, Bradley Palmquist, and Eric Schickler, for example, argue that group identities shape partisanship: when people are trying to decide between being a Republican or a Democrat, they think about which demographic groups are associated with each party and pick the party that has more members from the groups they identify with.[21]

It is important to examine group variations in public opinion because candidates and political consultants often formulate their campaign strategies in terms of groups. For example, analyses of the three previous presidential elections show that the electoral strategies of Democratic candidates are shaped by the goal of attracting support from young Americans, Black Americans, Latinos, and women. In contrast, Republican presidential candidates targeted regular churchgoers, as well as older voters and people living in rural areas.

Table 6.1 includes data on the variation in opinions across different groups of Americans, as measured in the General Social Survey (GSS). The table shows group differences on three broad questions: hiring preferences for Black Americans, access to abortions, and free speech. There are sharp differences among groups on some questions. For example, people of different education levels respond very differently to both questions about abortion and free speech—however, education has little to do with opinions about affirmative action.

TABLE 6.1

The Importance of Groups

The General Social Survey (GSS) has been conducted since 1972 to assess the opinions of Americans on certain key issues. Those who take the surveys are asked to indicate if they agree or disagree with statements such as those shown in the table. The percentages indicate those who agree with the statements. Group differences based on such factors as gender, age, race, and family income have been shown to affect the answers given by the respondents.

Source: 2022 data from General Social Survey 1972–2022, Cumulative Datafile, Survey Documentation and Analysis (SDA) at UC Berkeley, http://sda.berkeley.edu (accessed 9/15/24).

		"Favor preferences in hiring Blacks" (percentage who strongly support or support)	**"Abortions OK if woman wants one for any reason"** (percentage who agree)	**"OK to allow anti-American Muslim cleric to speak"** (percentage who agree)
Gender	Male	15.8%	50.3%	49.2%
	Female	15.6	49.6	37.7
Age	18–30	17.5	56.6	41.1
	31–40	17.8	53.5	44.6
	41–55	15.9	48.5	46.5
	56–89	13.8	43.2	40.3
Education	Less than high school	24.8	30.1	19.4
	High school	15.6	46.3	38.2
	Bachelor's degree	13.2	61.1	59.8
	Advanced degree	16.8	67.5	63.3
Race	White	10.7	51.4	48.8
	Black	34.9	47.0	34.9
	Latino	16.6	44.9	26.6
	Other	25.5	56.6	36.2
Family income	Low	18.7	43.0	32.6
	Lower middle	17.7	49.7	40.4
	Higher middle	14.0	47.0	44.9
	High	12.1	59.2	57.2

These data indicate that group characteristics can be important predictors of some of an individual's opinions, but they are not the whole story.[22] Because Americans' opinions are also a product of their socialization and life experiences, their group characteristics may tell us something about their opinions on some issues but reveal little about their thoughts on other issues.

Politicians and other political actors

Opinions and changes in opinion are also subject to influence by politicians and other political actors, including political parties and party leaders; interest groups; and leaders of religious, civic, and other large organizations. In part, this link exists because Americans look to these individuals for information based on their presumed expertise. For example, if you do not know what to think about immigration reform or gun control, you might seek out someone who appears to know more about the issues than you do. Insofar as the person's opinions seem reasonable, you might adopt them as your own.[23] Of course, people do not search haphazardly for advice; they take account of an expert's opinions only when they generally agree with the expert, perhaps because they are both conservatives or Democrats or because the individual has some other basis for thinking their preferences are alike. For example, former president Donald Trump's claims about a "deep state" of individuals in the federal bureaucracy who were working to thwart his policy agenda probably reinforced his supporters' high levels of distrust of government.

Politicians on both sides of the debate tried to influence public opinion about vaccine mandates. While Democrats sought to convince Americans that mandating vaccines was necessary, opponents played up the disadvantages, including the violation of individual freedoms.

Politicians and other political actors also actively work to shape public opinion. Political scientist Jane Mansbridge argues that representation involves tapping public opinion in ways that build support for policy initiatives.[24] That said, because politicians are generally seen as advocates for a particular point of view, it is relatively difficult for them to change opinions of people not already sympathetic to their views. For example, although President Biden and representatives from federal agencies such as the Centers for Disease Control expended much time and effort to convince Americans that COVID-19 vaccines are safe and effective, a substantial fraction of the population has disregarded this argument. If anything, the near-uniform support for vaccines among Democratic elected officials and members of the bureaucracy has probably hardened resistance among some groups, particularly supporters of former president Trump.

Considerations: the process of forming opinions

When people form opinions on the spot (which is true for most opinions), they are based on *considerations*: pieces of relevant information from sources like the ones we've just discussed—such as ideology, party identification, the influence of family and community members, personal and national events, group identification, or opinions and actions of politicians—that come to mind when the opinion is requested.[25] The process of forming an opinion usually is not thorough or systematic, since most people don't take into account everything they know about the issue in question.[26] Rather, they use only considerations that come to mind immediately.[27] Highly informed people who follow politics use this process, as do those with low levels of political interest and knowledge.[28]

In some cases, opinions are formed from very little information. For example, suppose right before the 2024 presidential election you were asked whether you approved of President Trump's performance in office from 2017 to 2020. There are many considerations you might have used, from your evaluations of Trump's response to COVID-19 or the Black Lives Matter protests, news coverage of Trump's tariff war with China or a profile of one of his staffers, or how Trump's tax reform affected your personal well-being (or that of your parents). Your opinions might have reflected things that have no connection to Trump, such as whether you just received a pay raise, whether you recently watched a video of politicians arguing with each other, or even whether you were just having a bad day. However, if you are like many Americans, your opinion would have centered on Trump's party affiliation: if you are a Republican, you approved, and if you're a Democrat, you disapproved. In fact, in modern American politics, party affiliation is used to form a wide range of political judgments, from evaluations of the economy, to the danger posed by the COVID-19 pandemic, to trust in government. There is also evidence that people use partisanship to form broader judgments about people from the other party: if, for example, you are a Republican, you may dislike Democrats simply because they are Democrats, not because of the policy positions you believe they hold.[29] We will discuss the important role of partisanship in American politics later in Chapter 8, Political Parties.

Basing decisions about presidential approval on party affiliation may seem simplistic, but in an era when the parties disagree on most things, a Republican voter is likely to agree with most decisions made by a Republican president and disagree with most decisions made by a Democrat. In that sense, considerations are a useful shortcut for people who need to make judgments about a president but don't want to spend too much time gathering or evaluating information. In other situations, considerations may lead to inaccurate judgments; this can happen, for example, when individuals decide what they think about the state of the economy based on the party affiliation of the president. The value of the shortcut is that it allows people to form a variety of opinions without expending much effort.

That said, as we discussed earlier, partisanship is not the only consideration people use to form political opinions. A generation ago, when differences between the parties were not as strong, evaluations of presidential performance were often shaped by perceptions of economic conditions, which in turn were based on some combination of personal financial well-being and judgments about the state of the economy. The impact of a candidate's personal characteristics has varied over time as well. For example, one of the author's parents reported that in her first presidential election (1952), she could not vote for the Democrat, Adlai Stevenson, because Stevenson was divorced. In the modern era, when the divorce rate is around 50 percent and many politicians are on their second or third marriage, absent unusual circumstances, divorce is unlikely to be a factor many voters think about when forming opinions about candidates. In the debate over Biden's performance in office, in which partisanship plays an important role, some citizens likely focus on economic conditions, the pandemic, or his affinity for chocolate-chip ice cream. So, if we look at individuals, opinions can sometimes be hard to predict or understand, because we don't know which considerations will come to mind when we ask them what they think.

Individual Considerations and Mass Public Opinion While public opinion may be difficult to predict on a person-to-person basis, at the aggregate level (where opinions are averaged across the population of a community, state, or nation) opinions are easier to understand. Over a large group of people, unique differences in how individuals form beliefs largely cancel each other out, leaving common factors that are important for most people.

As an example of how considerations work on an aggregate level, consider Figure 6.2, which shows the trend in presidential approval during the first two years of Joe Biden's presidency and the first four years of his two predecessors, Donald Trump and

FIGURE 6.2

First-Term Presidential Approval Ratings

Approval ratings for recent presidents have been relatively stable. What does this pattern say about the role of economic conditions or COVID-19 in shaping voter evaluations?

Source: FiveThirtyEight, "How Popular Is Joe Biden?," https://projects.fivethirtyeight.com/biden-approval-rating/ (accessed 9/15/24).

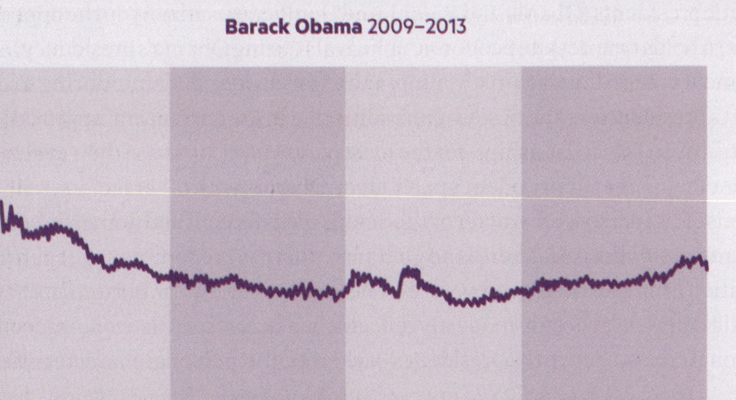

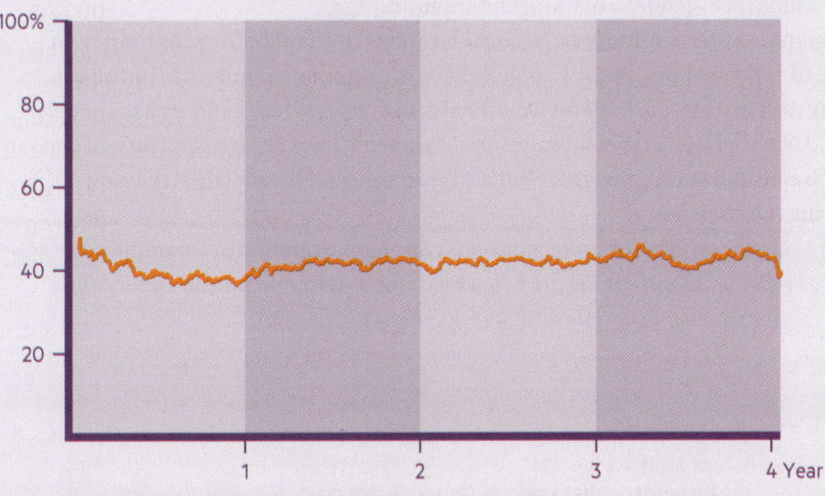

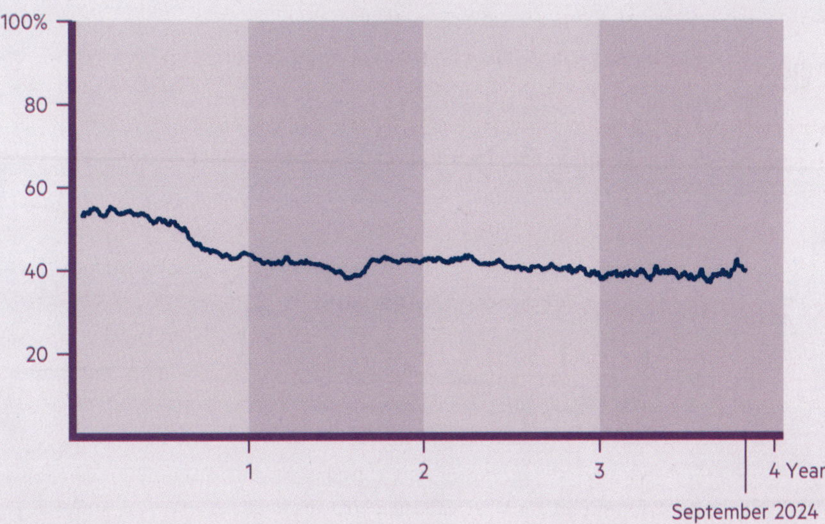

Barack Obama. For all three presidents, after a few months in office, the picture is one of stable approval ratings that reflect partisan divisions in the electorate—in the main, Republican citizens approve of Republican presidents (Trump) and disapprove of Democratic presidents (Obama and Biden), and Democratic citizens do the opposite. This pattern holds true despite economic upheavals during Obama's presidency, impeachment proceedings against Trump, and a worldwide pandemic during Trump's and Biden's presidencies. The best explanation is that in the current era, approval ratings are driven by partisanship—for the most part, Americans base their evaluations on whether they share the president's party identification, with other factors, such as evaluations of the person's character or the details of his foreign and domestic policy, playing a much smaller role. There is no guarantee that the predominance of party identification in presidential approval will continue into the future, but until it changes, presidential approval will only modestly reflect other factors such as economic conditions, international crises, or even the president's background or personal characteristics.

How Considerations Interact Considerations can also interact with each other in the opinion-formation process. Here again, partisanship currently plays a key role. As noted earlier, if you share the president's party affiliation, you are more likely to think that economic conditions are good and (assuming your judgments about the economy are constant) more likely to approve of the president's performance. Other potential filters include race, gender, sexual orientation, and age.

Opinions are often influenced by considerations that compete or contradict. In the case of abortion laws, many people believe in protecting human life but also in allowing women to make their own medical decisions.[30] When a survey asks people who hold both beliefs for their opinion about abortion laws, their response will depend on which consideration comes to mind and seems most relevant when they are answering the question.

When considerations compete, opinions can change rapidly for seemingly unrelated reasons. Consider Figure 6.3, which charts Republican and Democratic

FIGURE 6.3

Evaluations of Military Force in Iraq

The graph shows how Democratic and Republican evaluations of the war in Iraq changed over the last 15 years. What factors might have shaped the observed partisan differences? Why do you think beliefs have largely stayed the same in recent years?

Source: Pew Research Center, "The Iraq War Continues to Divide the U.S. Public, 15 Years after It Began," March 19, 2018, www.people-press.org (accessed 1/4/22).

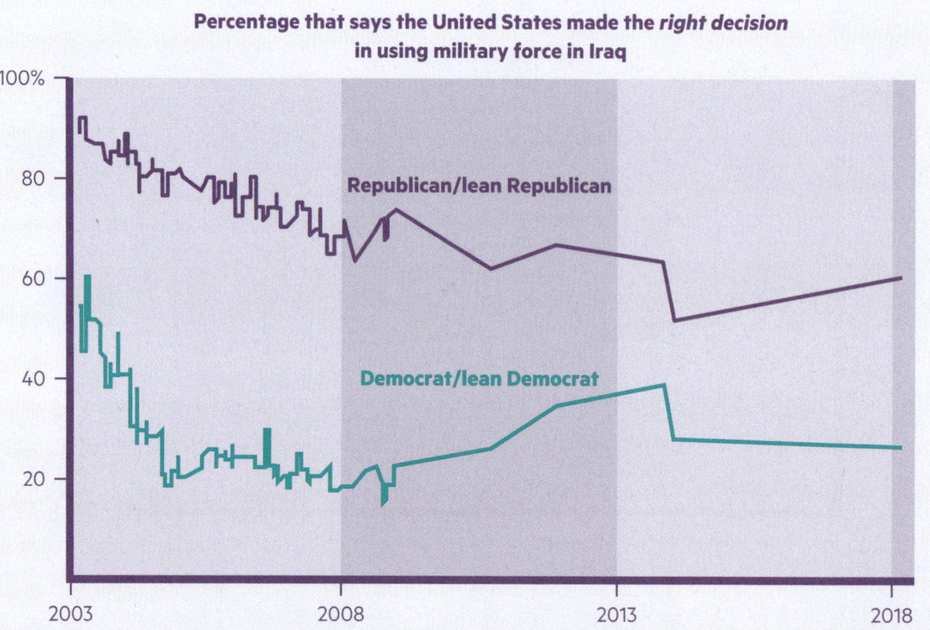

respondents' evaluations of whether the United States made the right decision to use force in Iraq. As you see, Republicans were always more likely to say that military action was the right choice, although the percentage declined for both parties as casualties mounted during 2003–2008. However, in 2009 a new trend emerged: Democrats became increasingly more likely to say that military force was the right choice, a shift that probably had more to do with Republican George Bush being replaced by Democrat Barack Obama.

Studies of public opinion confirm the opinion-formation strategies that we've just discussed: most people form the bulk of their opinions on the spot using a wide range of considerations. For example, attitudes about immigration are shaped by evaluations of the state of the economy.[31] Evaluations of affirmative action programs vary depending on whether the survey question reminds respondents that their own personal economic well-being may be hurt by these programs.[32] Issues related to race, including support for Black Lives Matter, as shown in Figure 6.4, and similar protests are linked to whether an individual grew up in an area where there were Civil Rights marches during the 1960s.[33] Finally, partisanship is a key consideration, even in policy areas seemingly far removed from politics: for example, support for childhood vaccinations is much lower among Republicans compared with Democrats, and evaluations of the severity of the COVID-19 pandemic differ significantly between the two groups as well.[34]

In sum, public opinion at the individual level is largely formed when needed and is driven by a variety of considerations. In the case of gun control, for example, beliefs are likely to depend on individuals' backgrounds—whether they own a gun, hunt, or know someone who does; their political beliefs, including their tolerance for government regulation of individual behavior and even their partisanship; and horrific events involving guns. Thus, although public opinion may shift somewhat in response to events such as a mass shooting or domestic terror attack, such events are only one factor that shapes opinion. As a result, even if an event is momentous, the shift in opinion may be quite small and transitory.

FIGURE 6.4

Support and Opposition to Black Lives Matter Movement, 2017–2021

The graph shows responses to the question of whether they strongly support or oppose the Black Lives Matters Movement. There was a sharp change in opinion after the shooting death of George Floyd, an unarmed Black man, by the police. What factors might shape respondents' opinions? What might account for the consistency in these opinions in the following year?

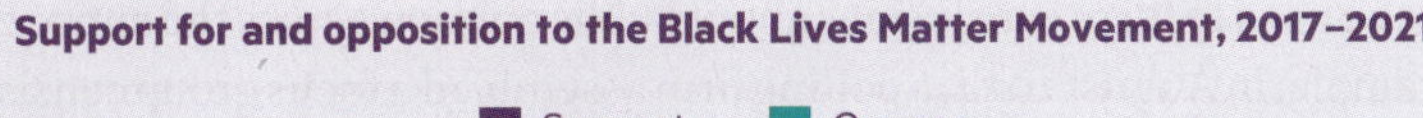

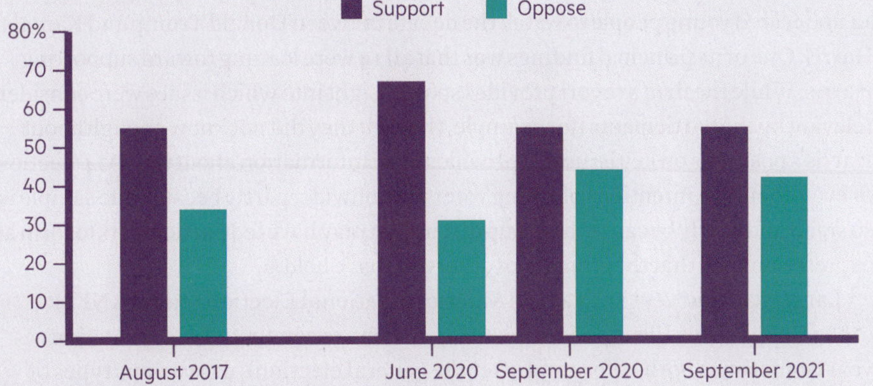

Source: Pew Research Center, "Support for Black Lives Matter Is Unchanged from a Year Ago," September 24, 2021, www.pewresearch.org/fact-tank/2021/09/27/support-for-black-lives-matter-declined-after-george-floyd-protests-but-has-remained-unchanged-since/ft_2021-09-27_blm_01/ (accessed 1/14/22).

"Why Should I Care?"

How people form opinions matters because understanding what people say about politics on the news, or in the classroom, or around the dinner table depends on where they are coming from. Perhaps an important event has shaped their opinion, maybe their parents or connection to a social or generational group has influenced them, or maybe a combination of all of these and more has affected them. Knowing what's behind someone's opinions and arguments on an issue can help you decide how you feel about that issue and whether or not the other person's argument carries weight.

DESCRIBE BASIC SURVEY METHODS AND POTENTIAL ISSUES AFFECTING ACCURACY

mass survey
A way to measure public opinion by interviewing a relatively small sample of a large population.

population
The group of people whom a researcher or pollster wants to study, such as evangelicals, senior citizens, or Americans.

sample
Within a population, the group of people surveyed in order to gauge the whole population's opinion. Researchers use samples because it would be impossible to interview the entire population.

Measuring public opinion

For the most part, information about public opinion comes from **mass surveys**—interviews (typically online) with a relatively small number of individuals that aim to measure the attitudes of a large **population** or group of people, such as the residents of a particular congressional district, evangelicals, senior citizens, or even the entire adult population in America (see the How It Works graphic on pp. 230–31). For large groups such as these, it would be impossible to survey everyone. So surveys typically involve **samples** of between a few hundred and several thousand individuals. One of the principal attractions of mass surveys is that they can, in theory, provide very accurate estimates of public opinion for a large population (such as a state or even the entire United States) using relatively small samples. This property of surveys is detailed in Nuts & Bolts 6.1. In fact, relatively small (1–5,000 respondents) random samples can provide much better insights into public opinion than much larger (hundreds of thousands of respondents) nonrandom samples.

An alternate technique for measuring public opinion uses focus groups, which are small groups of people interviewed in a group setting. Because focus groups allow respondents to answer questions in their own words rather than being restricted to a few options in a survey question, they can provide deep insights into why people hold the opinions they do. Candidates sometimes use focus groups to test campaign appeals or fine-tune their messages. However, because of their small size, focus groups cannot be used to form conclusions about public opinion across the entire country. For example, in August 2024, a polling firm assembled a focus group consisting of 14 undecided young people to watch the debate between Donald Trump and Kamala Harris. One of its principal findings was that all 14 were leaning toward supporting Harris. While the firm's report provides some insight into which issues were considered relevant by the participants (for example, they felt they did not know enough about Harris's positions on key issues), it provides little information about the 2024 election, or even about the intentions of young voters nationwide, partly because the sample is so small and partly because the group discussion may have led participants to form and express opinions that they might not otherwise have held.[35]

Large-scale surveys such as the American National Election Study (ANES) or the Cooperative Election Survey (CES), which are conducted every election year (sometimes both before and after the general election), use various types of questions to measure citizens' opinions. In presidential election years, participants in the ANES are first asked whether they voted for president. If they say they did, they are asked which candidate they voted for: a major-party candidate (for example, Donald Trump or Kamala Harris in 2024), an Independent candidate, or some other candidate.

DID YOU KNOW?

The probability that you will be contacted to participate in a typical national poll is

.00001

Source: Calculated by author.

NUTS & BOLTS 6.1

Sampling Error in Mass Surveys

The **sampling error** in a survey (the predicted difference between the average opinion expressed by survey respondents and the average opinion in the population, sometimes called the *margin of error*) using a random sample depends on the sample size. Sampling error is large for small samples of around 200 or fewer but decreases rapidly as sample size increases.

The graph shows how the sampling error for a random sample decreases as sample size increases. For example, in surveys with 1,000 respondents the sampling error is about 3 percent, meaning that 95 percent of the time the results of a 1,000-person survey will fall within the range of 3 percentage points above or below the actual percentage of the population who hold a particular opinion. If the sample size was increased to 5,000 people, the sampling error would decline to 1.4 percent. Mass surveys typically interview around 1,000 people. As the figure shows, this is the point where adding interviewees provides relatively little improvement in accuracy.

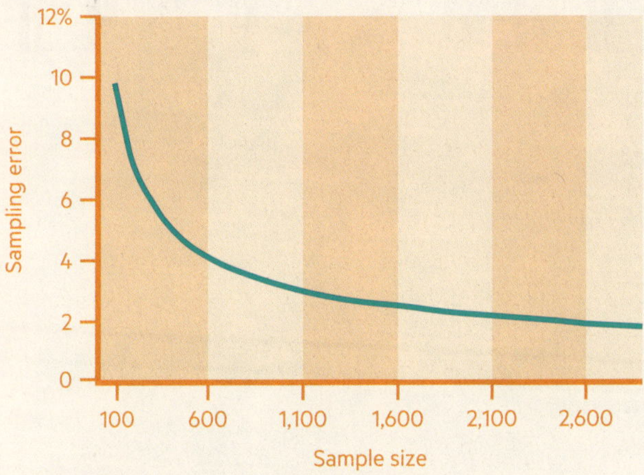

Sampling errors need to be taken into account when interpreting what a poll says about public opinion. For example, suppose a poll of 1,300 Americans found that 66 percent gave an unfavorable rating of Kamala Harris's performance in office and 33 percent rated her favorably. Because the difference between the percentages (33 points) exceeds the sampling error (about 2.5 points), it is reasonable to conclude that at the time the poll was conducted, more Americans saw Harris unfavorably than favorably.

In contrast, suppose the poll found a narrow 51–49 percent split slightly favoring approval. Because the difference in support is smaller than the sampling error, it would be a mistake to conclude that the majority of Americans had a favorable opinion of Harris. Even though more people in the sample expressed this opinion, there is a good chance that the opposite was true in the overall population.

You don't need to calculate sampling errors to make sense of political polls—just keep two things in mind. First, large samples (1,000 or more) are much more likely to provide accurate information about population opinions than small ones (fewer than 500). Second, be cautious when you read about small differences in survey responses, as these patterns are unlikely to hold true in the entire population.

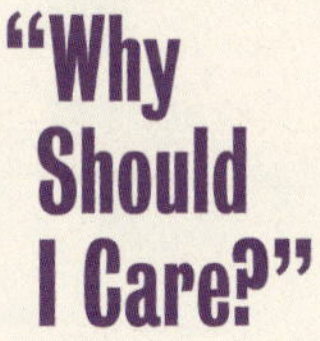

Not all data are equal! Statistical errors that occur when researchers don't select a sample that represents the entire population can significantly affect the accuracy of the conclusions they draw from that survey. When looking at survey data, you need to think critically about the size of the sample, as well as the small differences in results.

Another kind of survey question measures people's preferences using an *issue scale*. For a range of topics, two opposing statements are given and respondents are asked to pick the statement, or one of the choices between the two extremes, that comes closest to their views. As we discuss later, on questions such as these, most Americans pick positions in the middle of these scales.

sampling error
The predicted difference between the average opinion expressed by survey respondents and the average opinion in the population, sometimes called the *margin of error*. Increasing the number of respondents lowers the sampling error.

A typical survey like the GSS, ANES, or CES will ask several hundred questions related to issues and candidates, along with additional questions that elicit personal information such as a respondent's age, education, marital status, and other factors. Some surveys conducted by media sources, candidates, or political parties are shorter, focusing on voter evaluations of the candidates and the reasons for these evaluations.

How it works: in theory

Measuring What a Nation of 330 Million Thinks: A Checklist

A random sample:
Were the people who participated in the survey selected randomly, such that any member of the population had an equal chance of being selected?

Sample size:
How many people do researchers need to survey to know what 330 million Americans think? Major national surveys usually use a sample of 1,000–2,000 respondents.

Sampling error:
For a group of any size (even 330 million), 95 percent of the time a survey of 1,000 randomly selected respondents will measure the average opinion in a population within 3 percentage points. Reputable surveys will usually report this as the sampling error (sometimes also called "margin of error").

Question wording:
Did the way the question was worded influence the results? Scientific surveys try to phrase questions in a neutral way, but even in reputable polls, differences in question wording can influence answers.

Reliable respondents: Respondents often give socially acceptable answers rather than truthful ones—or invent opinions on the spot. Is there a reason to think people may not have answered a survey honestly and thoughtfully?

How it works: **in practice**

Surveying the 2022 Elections: Two Approaches

To illustrate how these requirements for good survey design play out in real life, we examine how two well-known polling organizations, the Pew Research Center and Rasmussen Reports, design polls to measure voter preference.

Rasmussen Reports

Use land lines . . . mostly.

A partially random sample: Contact people who have **land-line phones** and use a **nonrandom online panel** to sample groups that tend not to have land lines.

Respondent selection: Survey the **first person who answers the phone**.

Make robo-calls.

Computer-controlled: Use an automated script to survey respondents; do the survey in a **short time period (hours)**.

One-shot effort: **Don't call back** people whom you miss on the first try.

Adjust the results.

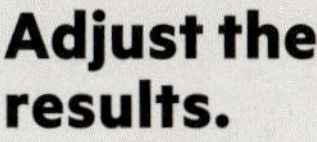

Weighting the responses: If there are more Democrats (or Republicans) in your sample than you expect, **adjust your results** to account for the difference.

Pew Research Center

Build a good sample.

A random sample: Contact **a random sample of all Americans**, including people with cell phones or no phones.

Oversamples: Use oversamples (extra respondents) to measure **opinions of groups that are a small percentage of the population**.

Use an online survey.

Online surveys: Put the survey online, and **give your sample an extended time to complete it**.

Survey access: If respondents don't have computers, **provide them with a tablet as well as Internet access**.

Don't adjust results.

Surprises are interesting: If the partisan divide in your sample is not what you expect, **treat it as a finding**—people may be changing their party ID.

Outcome

Rasmussen data are incomplete (at best) . . .

A random sample: **Rasmussen misses many people who use only cell phones** (many of whom are younger and are Democrats).

Sample size: Rasmussen is also **biased toward people who are likely to answer the phone**. These people tend to be older and include a higher proportion of men than in the population.

and assume nothing has changed.

Sampling error: Adjusting for partisanship **assumes that no changes in party ID have occurred** since the last election.

Reliable respondents: Rasmussen tactic **lowers response rate**. Rasmussen tactic makes poll results sensitive to short-term events.

Pew is more reliable.

Pew's results were generally regarded as more reliable than Rasmussen's—and generally **made more accurate predictions about results**. Furthermore, Rasmussen kept its data largely private, while Pew released its questionnaire and data. This made Pew's survey verifiable and provided an opportunity for further analysis.

Critical Thinking

1. **When evaluating these two polling organizations**, how would you respond to someone who said they still preferred Rasmussen's polls because they correctly predicted the outcome of a Senate race in their state in 2022?
2. **Which kinds of respondents are likely to be put off by polls** that the computer scripts? How might this affect the findings of the survey?

In the main, the length of a survey reflects the fact that people have limited attention spans, so there is a trade-off between learning more about each respondent's opinions and getting them to agree to be surveyed in the first place.

An important development in recent years is the use of techniques to combine individual surveys into a more powerful measure of public opinion. These techniques weigh data from different polls based on their accuracy in previous elections and combine state- and national-level results to generate predictions—thus, if a poll finds that candidate A is ahead in state 1 and polls have found that the winner in state 1 will also win state 2, then the results from state 1 will be used to help predict the result in state 2. These techniques generate powerful predictions of election returns. Even in 2020, when high voter turnout and large numbers of mail-in ballots complicated the prediction process, most pollsters correctly forecasted Joe Biden's victory. However, the technique missed in 2024, when polls failed to predict Trump's decisive victory.

Problems in measuring public opinion

On average, people should be more skeptical when they see numbers. They should be more willing to play around with the data themselves.

—Nate Silver, FiveThirtyEight.com

Polling is an imperfect science. Many pollsters failed to predict Trump's victory in 2016. While the same polls were largely correct in 2020, they missed badly in 2024, both for the presidential election and many Senate and House contests. Measuring public opinion is hard. The problems begin with gathering an appropriate, representative sample of subjects. Unfortunately, the percentage of people who agree to be surveyed when asked has been declining in recent years, so it is easy to create a situation of selection bias, where a sample designed to be random contains too many of some kinds of people and too few of others. One of the problems in 2016 was that opinion surveys contained too many college-educated voters and too few people with less education.

DID YOU KNOW?

90%

of people contacted by phone to participate in a political survey either don't answer or refuse to participate.

Source: Pew Research Center.

The difficulty of generating a good sample is compounded by issues pertaining to how people read and interpret survey questions. It is easy to create measurement error, where pollsters think they are asking about one thing, but respondents believe they are being asked about something else. For example, during the 2024 presidential campaign, a question about whether America is ready for a female president might be interpreted in terms of approval or disapproval for Kamala Harris's candidacy.

For these and other reasons, survey results must be read carefully, taking into account who is being surveyed, when they are being surveyed, what opinions are being asked about, and what mechanism is used to ask survey questions.

random sample
A subsection of a population chosen to participate in a survey through a selection process in which every member of the population has an equal chance of being chosen. This kind of sampling improves the accuracy of public-opinion data.

Issues with Survey Methods Building a **random sample** of individuals is not an easy task. Historically, pollsters chose households at random from census data and sent interviewers out for face-to-face meetings, or contacted people by telephone using random digit dialing, which allows surveyors to find people who have unlisted phone numbers or who use only a cell phone. In the modern era, pollsters contact people using phone calls, emails, or Internet advertising. Some organizations build large databases of respondents that can be sampled for multiple surveys over time. These techniques require careful weighting and analysis strategies to ensure that they come close to the ideal of a truly random survey. Sometimes these adjustments successfully predict results, and sometimes they don't.

For example, in the 2016 presidential race, pollsters did a relatively poor job (compared with recent elections) of predicting who was likely to vote. As a result of this error, polls taken close to the election predicted Clinton victories in Wisconsin,

Michigan, and Pennsylvania—states that were actually won by Trump. In the 2020 race, pollsters were unprepared for the sharp increase in turnout by both Republican and Democratic supporters. The net effect of these turnout assumptions was to underpredict support for Republican candidates by a few percentage points—enough to cause prediction errors in close races, including the Senate contests in Maine, Michigan, and South Carolina. The same thing happened in 2024, but with a larger magnitude.

To keep costs down, many organizations use a form of Internet polling, in which volunteer respondents log on to a website to participate in a survey, or robo-polls, in which an automated system phones people and interviews them. Although these techniques are less expensive, there are serious doubts about the quality of the samples they produce. (*Push polls*, in which a campaign uses biased survey questions as a way of driving support away from an opponent, are not legitimate polls because they are not designed to measure opinion—they are designed to shape it and are a form of negative campaigning; see Chapter 9.)

The wording of questions can also influence survey results. Table 6.2 shows different questions asked to measure opinions about former president Trump's 2017 executive order banning travel to the United States from seven predominantly Muslim countries. As you can see, support depends on how the question is asked: whether Trump's name is mentioned, the specific countries, and the rationale for the ban. These issues shouldn't make you suspicious that pollsters are trying to skew their findings—rather, they show just how hard it is to accurately measure opinions.

TABLE 6.2

The Impact of Question Wording on Opinions

How questions are worded can affect survey results. These surveys (all taken in January to February 2017) ask about President Trump's 2017 executive order banning citizens from certain countries from traveling to the United States, but differ in how they describe the details of the ban as well as the supposed goal. In light of how the responses to survey questions are shaped by the precise wording of these questions, what sort of question would you ask if your goal was to show that Americans favored the travel ban? What if you wanted to know the truth about what Americans really believed?

Percentage that supports or favors	Question	Pollster
57	Do you favor or oppose a temporary ban on refugees from Syria, Iraq, Iran, Libya, Somalia, Sudan, and Yemen **until the federal government improves its ability to screen out potential terrorists from coming here**?	Rasmussen
55	Do you approve or disapprove of [President Trump's] executive order prohibiting citizens from seven predominantly Muslim countries **from being able to enter the United States for 90 days and halting processing of refugees for 120 days**?	Politico
46	Do you support or oppose **suspending all travel by citizens of Iraq, Syria, Iran, Libya, Somalia, Sudan, and Yemen to the U.S. for 90 days**?	Quinnipiac
42	**Thinking now about some of the specific actions Donald Trump has taken since he has been in office**, would you say you approve or disapprove of ordering a temporary ban on entry into U.S. for most people from seven predominantly Muslim countries?	Gallup

Sources: Rasmussen Reports, "Most Support Temporary Ban on Newcomers from Terrorist Havens," January 30, 2017, www.rasmussenreports.com/public_content/politics/current_events/immigration/january_2017/most_support_temporary_ban_on_newcomers_from_terrorist_havens; Jake Sherman, "Poll: Democrats Want Leaders to Block Trump," Politico, February 7, 2017, www.politico.com/story/2017/02/trump-democrats-poll-234778; Quinnipiac Poll, "American Voters Oppose Trump Immigration Ban, Quinnipiac University National Poll Finds," February 7, 2017, https://poll.qu.edu/national/release-detail?ReleaseID=2427; Frank Newport, "About Half of Americans Say Trump Moving Too Fast," Gallup, February 7, 2017, https://news.gallup.com/poll/203264/half-americans-say-trump-moving-fast.aspx (all accessed 2/3/22).

Unreliable Respondents Another problem with surveys is that people are sometimes reluctant to reveal their opinions. Rather than speaking truthfully, they often give socially acceptable answers or answers that they believe the interviewers want to hear. In the case of voter turnout in elections, in most surveys up to one-third of respondents who say they voted when surveyed actually did not vote at all. Political scientists refer to this behavior as the social desirability bias, meaning that people answering survey questions are less willing to admit to actions or express opinions that they believe their neighbors or society at large would disapprove of, such as racial prejudice.[36]

Pollsters use various techniques to address this problem. One approach is to ask questions in multiple ways; another is to verify answers whenever possible, such as checking with county boards of elections to see if respondents who said they voted actually went to the polls. When there is concern that respondents will try to hide their prejudices, pollsters sometimes frame a question in terms of the entire country rather than the respondent's own beliefs. For example, during the 2008 and 2016 presidential primaries, rather than asking respondents whether they were willing to vote for a woman candidate (such as Democrat Hillary Clinton), some pollsters posed the question indirectly, asking whether a respondent believed that the country was ready for a woman president. Another tactic is to ask respondents for a different kind of evaluation—rather than asking whether they like or dislike candidates, pollsters ask whether they would sit down for a beer (or coffee) with them.

Of course, attempts to account for the social desirability bias by rephrasing a question can introduce new biases. For example, a survey question designed to ask about a sensitive topic might begin with "Some people have argued that . . ." However, in some cases adding this phrase to a question can produce higher levels of respondent agreement regardless of what is being asked. Again, the problem is not that pollsters are dishonest or inept—the problem is that public opinion is often difficult to measure.

The Accuracy of Public Opinion Because poll results play such an important role in media coverage and public discussions about politics, questions are often raised about the assumptions and corrections that pollsters use to account for the inevitable ambiguities related to poll results. During the 2020 presidential campaign, many Republican politicians and observers argued that polls showing a significant lead for Democrat Joe Biden over Republican Donald Trump were the product of inaccurate polling questions and assumptions about turnout. Some even argued that pollsters were deliberately skewing their findings to bolster support for Biden. Of course, Biden won the election, although it appears that pollsters did misestimate turnout of some groups. Overall, an analysis by FiveThirtyEight of a large number of polls for presidential, Senate, and House general elections, as well as presidential primaries, found that in 2020 the average poll was off by 6.3 percentage points, although the polls did correctly predict the winner about 80 percent of the time.[37] These numbers are typical for other recent elections. It's important to remember that the results include many close elections that are hard to predict and that some pollsters are consistently more accurate than others. In any case, the fact that polls aren't perfect highlights the difficulty of accurately surveying the American people and shows why we should be reluctant to overinterpret survey results.

In some cases, inaccurate or outlandish survey results are generated because some respondents don't take surveys seriously. They agree to participate but are not interested in explaining their beliefs to a stranger. Faced with a long list of questions, they give quick, thoughtless responses to end the interview as quickly as possible. Misperceptions may also result when respondents form opinions based on whatever considerations come to mind. And most importantly, people may reach for considerations that are easy to use but not very informative. Consider claims about foreign aid. Polls consistently find that the average American believes that about 25 percent of the federal budget is spent on foreign aid, even though the actual percentage is about 1 percent.[38]

How can these findings be squared with our earlier statement that Americans generally hold opinions that have some basis in reality? For one thing, many respondents probably had not thought about these questions in detail—and it's likely that only very few knew anything about the government's foreign aid budget in the first place. When asked for an opinion as part of a survey, respondents had no time to do research or think things through. The fact that estimates were so far from the truth suggests that many people are using considerations that do not provide much information about actual foreign aid spending.

Misinformation may also result from politicians making polarizing or extreme statements about an issue. Many politicians from both parties have criticized foreign aid spending as ineffective and wasteful. The Trump administration made numerous attempts to cut America's foreign aid spending. It's no wonder, then, that survey respondents overestimate foreign aid spending—after all, that's all they've been hearing from the political figures they listen to and generally agree with.

Finally, many supposed facts are actually "contested truths," meaning that even if people move beyond considerations and take into account multiple, nuanced sources of information, they may nevertheless arrive at different conclusions about complex questions.[39] For example, it is a fact that the unemployment rate declined slightly during the first three years of President Trump's term, then rose sharply in his final year in office. Do these changes mean that Biden was a better steward of the economy than Trump? Trump inherited a stable, growing economy that was thrown into turmoil by the COVID-19 pandemic, lockdowns, and difficulties in transporting goods to market. Biden took over just as the economy was recovering. People can easily arrive at different evaluations of Trump's and Biden's performance in office depending on how they account for these factors.

Such problems do not arise in all areas of public opinion. Studies show that respondents' ability to express specific opinions, as well as the accuracy of their opinions, rises if the survey questions have something to do with their everyday life.[40] Thus, average Americans would be more likely to have an accurate sense of the state of the economy or their personal economic condition than of the military situation in Afghanistan. Everyday life gives us information about the economy; we learn about Afghanistan only if we take time to gather information. These effects are magnified insofar as the respondent considers the economy the more salient issue of the two.

How useful are surveys?

As always, keep in mind that the poll does not, and cannot, predict the outcome of the election in November.

—Disclaimer on CNN preelection poll

By now, CNN's disclaimer about the limits of mass surveys should not be much of a surprise. Survey results are most likely to be accurate when they are based on a simple, easily understood question about a topic familiar to the people being surveyed—such as the choice between two candidates, measured close to an election—and when the survey designers have worked to account for all the problems discussed here. Under these conditions, with samples of 1,000 voters or more, poll results are generally within about 3 percentage points of the true population values.[41] You can be even more confident if multiple surveys addressing the same topic in different ways and at different times produce similar findings. However, if a single survey asks about a complex, unfamiliar topic—replacing the income tax with a national sales tax or determining whom to blame for a policy failure—then the results may not provide much insight into public opinion. (See the Take a Stand feature on p. 237 for a discussion of whether or not politicians should follow the polls, given the challenges in accurately assessing the public's opinion.)

The timing of surveys may also affect how useful the results are. Surveys taken immediately after an event—for example, a survey on gun control taken immediately after a school shooting—are generally not good guides to public opinion. The problem is not that people are being insincere or thoughtless. Rather, it is that respondents' opinions are colored by the recent tragedy—but only in the short term. Over the next days, weeks, or months, opinions are likely to return to what they were before the event. Thus, polls taken in the wake of a powerful event may not be a good guide to what people might demand from government in light of what has happened, nor may they reflect how people might react a year later. The same is true of polls taken well in advance of the time when the public actually has to act on their preferences—for example, a poll about the 2024 presidential election taken two years before the election, when most people know almost nothing about the candidates and have not even begun to think about their choice. Under these conditions, poll results tell us almost nothing about what people will ultimately do. On the other hand, polls taken right before an election are generally good predictors of election results.

Beyond all of these factors, the ability of preelection polls to predict election outcomes also depends on the closeness of the race. Many critiques of survey methods focus on the failure of most pollsters to predict Donald Trump's victory in 2024. This failure needs to be placed in context: most pollsters acknowledged that the race was close and that the outcome depended on who turned out to vote. In this sense, the polls got the underlying dynamic of the 2024 election right. Based on the polls, the best guess was a Harris victory, even though it would have been more accurate to add that the outcome was completely in doubt and that the result could change if assumptions about turnout were even slightly off (which they were). The problem was not how polls were taken but the media's desire to simplify a complex situation. We will discuss these issues further in Chapter 7.

"Why Should I Care?"

New technologies have made surveys cheaper and easier, allowing groups to poll more often and ask a much wider range of questions. However, polls are not infallible. Believing in survey results without some skepticism can lead to fundamental misunderstandings of public opinion, as exemplified by claims that pollsters failed to predict support for Trump and other Republicans in 2020.

PRESENT FINDINGS ON WHAT AMERICANS THINK ABOUT GOVERNMENT AND WHY IT MATTERS

What Americans think about politics

In this section, we describe American public opinion, including people's ideological beliefs and what they think of the federal government. These opinions drive overall support for government action and serve as the basis for opinions on more specific policy questions. To understand what America's national government does and why, we have to determine what Americans ask of it.

TAKE A STAND

Should Politicians Follow the Polls?

Elected officials in America work hard to cast votes and take other actions that their constituents will like. At first glance, this behavior seems easy. All a politician needs to do is take a poll, measure public opinion in their state or district, and comply with the demands expressed in the survey responses. The problem is, poll results need interpretation. As we saw for President Trump's travel ban in Table 6.2, small differences in question wording can produce very different responses, or public opinion can remain vague, despite the polls. As a result, even if representatives want to follow constituent opinion, they may decide that they don't really know enough about these opinions to decide what they should do.

Imagine that a survey on immigration was conducted in your congressional district, asking voters if they favored allowing undocumented immigrants to stay in the country or if people here without documentation should be deported as soon as possible. Suppose that the poll results indicate strong support for one of the two options and that you yourself have no strong feelings about undocumented immigrants. The decision you face is: Should you demand that Congress enact immigration reform consistent with the poll results, or should you quietly ask that immigration reform be kept off the agenda?

Follow the poll. Elected officials often have strong incentives to do what constituents demand—in this case, to push for immigration reform measures that are consistent with the demands expressed in the poll. By this logic, if most constituents want immigrants to gain legal status, then you'd ask for a reform proposal that made legal status possible. Conversely, if the poll indicated that most constituents favored deportation, you would push for legislation that funded a program to achieve this goal. Doing so would allow you to claim some credit for the specifics of the bill, as well as for your vote, which in theory would please most of your constituents and increase your chances of reelection.

Stay quiet. As we discuss throughout the chapter, poll results are highly sensitive to question wording, timing, and other factors, making it hard to interpret even seemingly clear findings. Suppose, for example, the poll indicates support for allowing undocumented immigrants to gain legal status. However, the survey did not ask about any of the details of legalization: whether legal status would require learning English, holding a stable job, paying back taxes, or other conditions. Even though none of these conditions were in the question, most of your constituents probably had some of them in mind when they thought about how they wanted to answer the question. In other words, your constituents' support of immigration reform depends on what the reforms look like. Even if you want to act in accordance with their demands, the survey may not tell you much about what exactly they want.

The situation is no easier if your poll indicates support for deportation. Would government officials search for undocumented immigrants to deport or just deport people they happen to find? What would happen to children whose parents entered the country without documentation but who were born in the United States and are therefore citizens? For some respondents, the solution is a nationwide house-to-house search, with children deported with their parents. But others would reject a deportation process that did either of these things. So here again, the poll results, one-sided as they are, don't provide you with foolproof guidance about how to vote.

Americans in both parties agree on the need for immigration reform but differ as to what they think the new immigration policies should be.

take a stand

1. Suppose you are a politician who feels that changes in immigration policy are needed but is faced with the quandary described above. Would you do nothing, so as to avoid alienating your constituency, or would you force a policy change and accept the political consequence—possible removal from office?

2. What poll questions would you use to get a clearer picture of public opinion on immigration?

Ideological polarization

ideological polarization
Sharp differences in Americans' overall ideas of the size and scope of government.

We begin by examining liberal and conservative ideology and party identification to see whether historical data show evidence of **ideological polarization**: sharp differences in Americans' overall ideas of the size and scope of government. Many commentators argue that government's inaction on issues like gun control or immigration reform, as well as continued conflict over issues like the Affordable Care Act (ACA), reflects increased polarization among the American public. The What Do the Facts Say? feature shows two kinds of survey data that can help us evaluate levels of polarization: responses to a question measuring ideology (liberal-moderate-conservative) and a question that taps a respondent's party identification (Republican-Independent-Democrat). The ideological data show no evidence of increased polarization; in the case of partisanship, a substantial percentage of Americans in 2022 described themselves as Independents. As we discuss in chapter 8, this stability in the size of the party coalitions masks changes over the last generation in the kinds of people who identify as Republicans and Democrats. For example, compared with the 1980s, contemporary liberals are more likely to be Democrats, and conservatives are more likely to be Republicans.

Looking more closely at opinion polarization, the third part of the What Do the Facts Say? feature divides the electorate into nine groups based on answers to questions that tap important principles, from foreign policy to domestic issues, civil liberties, and morality. Principles such as these are a kind of consideration—they form the basis for opinions that people express in surveys or act on when they vote or engage in other political behavior. The figure shows, first, that only about one-fifth of the electorate (Solid Liberals and Country-First Conservatives) hold consistent ideological beliefs—meaning that they generally give one kind of answer (conservative or liberal) when asked questions that tap their underlying principles. Moreover, a significant proportion of people fall into one of the intermediate groups, meaning that they express a mix of liberal and conservative issue positions, although they generally lean one way or the other.

Using similar data, political scientist Lilliana Mason and others have identified an increasingly high correlation in American public opinion between political attitudes like ideology and religious, racial, ethnic, and cultural identities.[42] In simple terms, compared with a generation ago, liberals are more likely to look like other liberals and to see differences in between themselves and conservatives. The result, they argue, is that political conflicts can become magnified because they are not just about policy questions—they also tap other differences. This development is a principal cause of the increasing amount of anger that people express when talking about politics.[43] It also likely contributes to the rise of negative (affective) partisanship in recent years, where people who have positive feelings for one party are increasingly likely to evaluate the other party in negative terms. We will discuss these beliefs in more detail in Chapter 8 (Political Parties).[44]

It is important to not overstate these differences. While the data confirm that Americans disagree on important policy questions, it is too simple to think in terms of a sharply polarized America, with a large group of secular liberal Democrats opposing another large group of religious Republican conservatives, and few people in the middle. For one thing, typologies like the one we've presented are designed to identify differences and disagreements—there are many other issues on which there is consensus among the American public.[45] And while there are large differences between extreme liberal and conservative positions on many issues, only a small fraction of the population holds these extreme positions.

Finally, even when people say they are liberals (or conservatives), this response does not mean that they hold liberal (or conservative) preferences on all issues.

Are the American People Polarized?

Many commentators describe politics in America as highly conflictual, with most Americans holding either liberal or conservative points of view and identifying with one of the two major parties. Is polarization as strong as these commentators think?

Liberal or conservative ideology in America

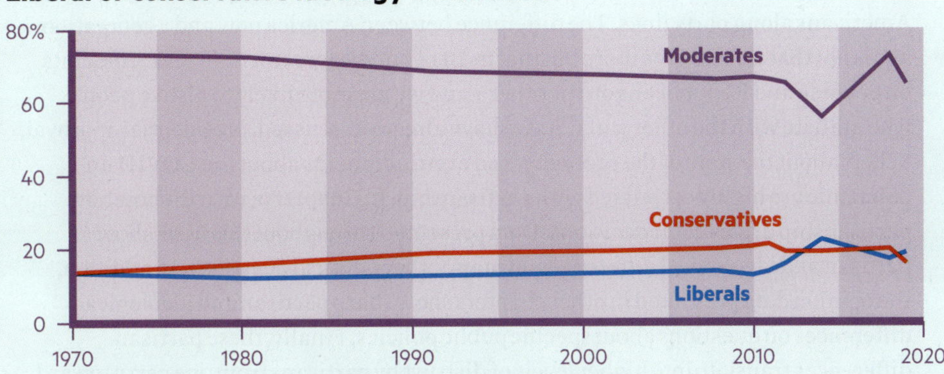

Party identification in America

Democrat	Independent	Republican	Other
31%	40%	25%	4%

Political typology in the general public

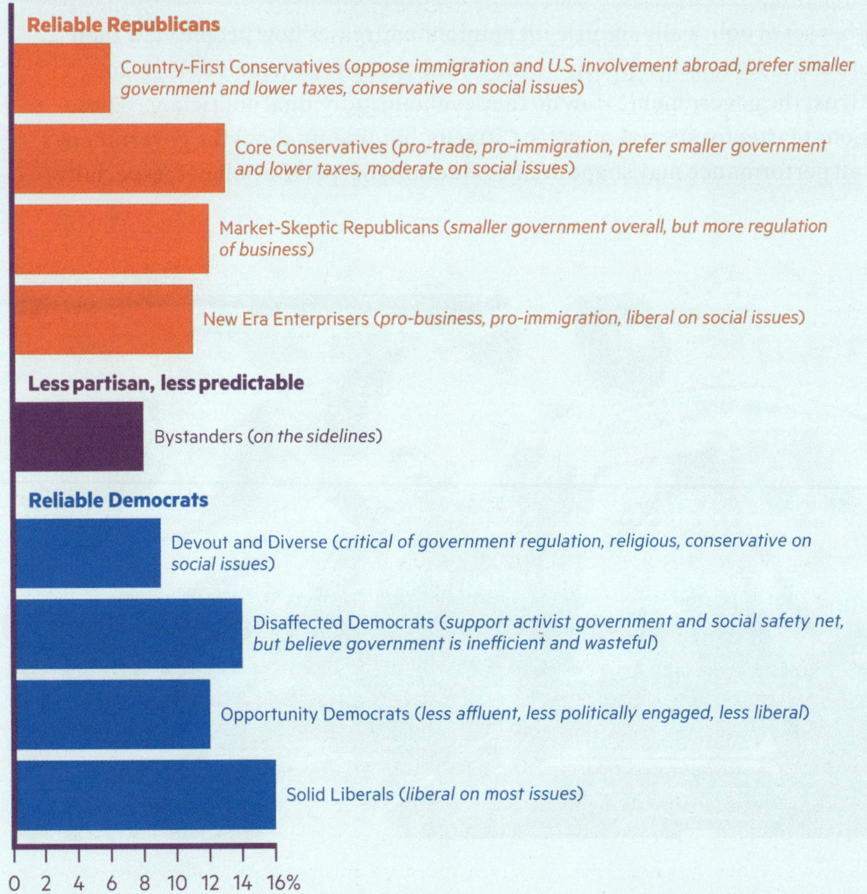

WHAT DO THE FACTS SAY?

Think about it

- **According to the top figure,** how have levels of polarization changed since the 1990s?
- **What does the political typology** reveal about divisions within each political party?

Sources: Data from General Social Survey 1972–2018, Cumulative Datafile, Survey Documentation and Analysis (SDA) at UC Berkeley, https://sda.berkeley.edu/sdaweb/analysis/;jsessionid=E9829C77CA98B226C5A8AEAFD3031D92?dataset=gss18; Gallup, "Party Affiliation," June 4, 2020, https://news.gallup.com/poll/15370/party-affiliation.aspx; Pew Research Center, "Political Typology Reveals Deep Fissures on the Right and Left," October 26, 2017, www.people-press.org/2017/10/24/political-typology-reveals-deep-fissures-on-the-right-and-left/ (all accessed 7/28/22).

Self-professed moderates may also hold relatively extreme preferences on certain policy questions. Thus, understanding what Americans think and what they want from government often requires data on specific policy questions rather than broad judgments about the liberal or conservative nature of American public opinion. (Whether elected officials themselves are more polarized than their constituents is a different story, which we will discuss in Chapter 11.)

Given these data, why do political scientists talk so much about high levels of polarization in contemporary America? For the most part, these comments refer to the fact that in contemporary American politics, most of the policy conflicts divide Americans along party lines. The difference between America now and a generation ago is not that we disagree more but that most of our disagreements have Democrats on one side and Republicans on the other—and we are more likely to dislike people who affiliate with the other party. As we have already discussed, presidential approval, beliefs about the state of the economy, and even judgments about the COVID-19 pandemic are highly correlated with partisanship. In Chapter 9, we will show how partisanship drives voter decisions. Data presented throughout this book show partisan and ideological differences on many other political questions. In addition, the opinion data presented in other chapters show sharp partisan and ideological differences on questions about specific public policies. Finally, these partisan differences translate into higher levels of distrust by partisans from one party toward politicians and citizens from the other.[46]

Evaluations of government and officeholders

Another set of politically significant opinions addresses how people view their government: How well or poorly do they think the government is doing? Do they trust the government? How do they evaluate individual politicians? These opinions matter for several reasons. Citizens' judgments about the government's overall performance may shape their evaluations of specific policies, especially

Trust in government reached a low point during the mid-1970s. The decline partly reflected the economic downturn and conflict over the Vietnam War, but opinions were also shaped by the discovery that President Richard Nixon had lied about the Watergate scandal. In this iconic image, Nixon departs the White House after resigning from office to avoid impeachment.

if they do not know much about the policies.[47] Evaluations of specific policies may also be shaped by how much a citizen trusts the government; greater trust brings more positive evaluations.[48] Trust in government and overall evaluations might also influence a citizen's willingness to vote for incumbent congressional representatives or for a president seeking reelection.[49]

The top graph in Figure 6.5 reveals that the average American is fairly disenchanted with the government. As of 2019, a majority believes that government is not run for the benefit of all the people and that government programs are usually wasteful and inefficient. These beliefs have not changed much over the last generation, nor in light of COVID-19.

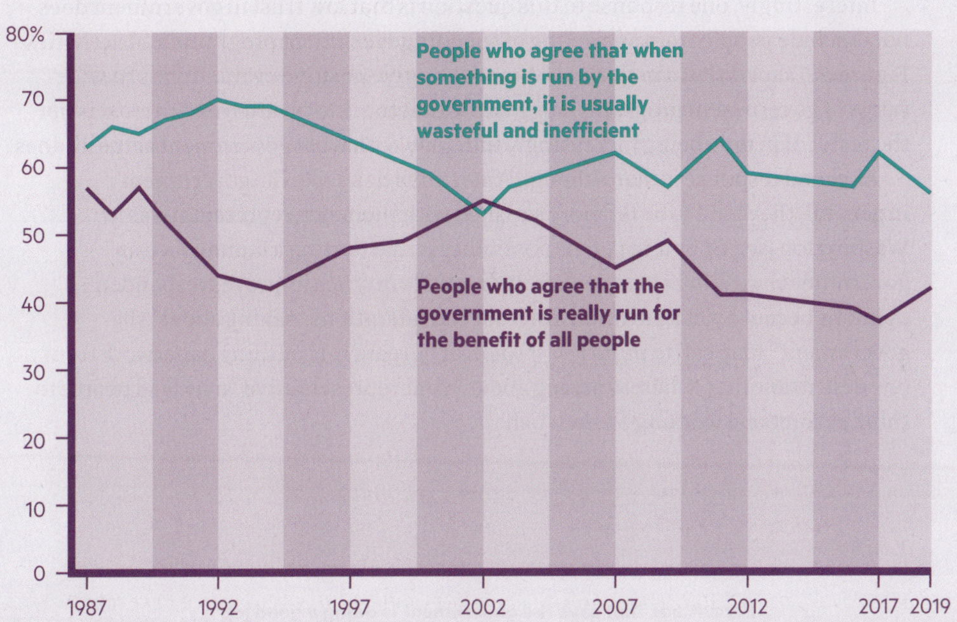

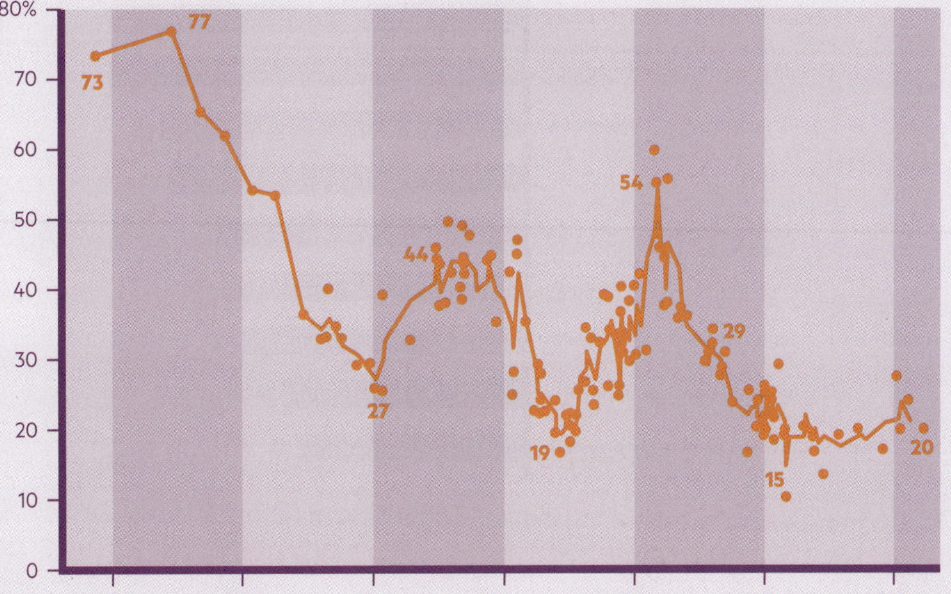

FIGURE 6.5

What Do Americans Think about Government?

A significant percentage of Americans have always been distrustful and disparaging of the federal government—and the percentage of people holding such views has increased markedly in the last generation. Does the perception that government is wasteful and inefficient make it easier or harder to enact new policies? How might the decline in trust explain the rise of candidates such as Donald Trump?

Sources: Pew Research Center, "Americans' Views of Government: Low Trust, but Some Positive Performance Ratings," Pew Research Center, September 14, 2020, www.pewresearch.org/politics/2020/09/14/americans-views-of-government-low-trust-but-some-positive-performance-ratings/ (accessed 1/10/22); Pew Research Center, "Americans' Views of Government: Decades of Distrust, Enduring Support for Its Role," June 6, 2022, www.pewresearch.org/politics/2022/06/06/americans-views-of-government-decades-of-distrust-enduring-support-for-its-role/ (accessed 11/7/22).

This impression of a disenchanted and disapproving public is reinforced by the second graph, which generally shows declining levels of trust in government since the 1960s. Within this overall trend, trust generally increases given a strong economy (the mid-1980s and late 1990s) and declines during times of economic or other hardship (the mid-2000s to now). As noted earlier, many scholars have argued that low levels of trust make it harder for elected officials to enact new policies, especially those that require large expenditures.[50] On a more profound level, some scholars argue that low levels of trust raise questions about the future of democracy in America.[51] How can we say that American democracy is a good or popular form of government when so many people are unhappy with the performance of elected officials and bureaucrats and so few people trust the government? Finally, trust in government also has a partisan cast—people are more likely to express trust in the government when someone from their party is serving as president.

Interestingly, one response to this question is that low trust in government does not preclude people from approving of specific government programs and activities. Figure 6.6 shows that a majority of Americans give positive evaluations of a wide range of government programs, suggesting that the downward trend in trust is not the result of people being increasingly unhappy with what government actually does.

A second response is that although Americans don't like the government in general, they tend to be far more satisfied with their own representatives in Washington (see Chapter 11). One possibility is that putting a human face on government by asking about specific individuals in office improves respondents' opinions because it calls to mind different considerations. Asking about "the government" may call to mind a vast room of bureaucrats pushing paperwork from one desk to another, whereas asking about "your representative" may lead people to think of someone working on their behalf.

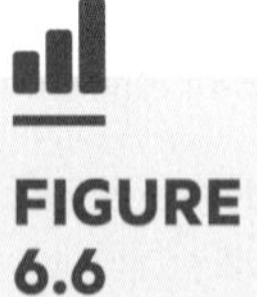

FIGURE 6.6

Measuring American Public Opinion: Is the Government Doing a Good Job?

How is it that Americans disapprove of government overall but give relatively high ratings in many specific areas?

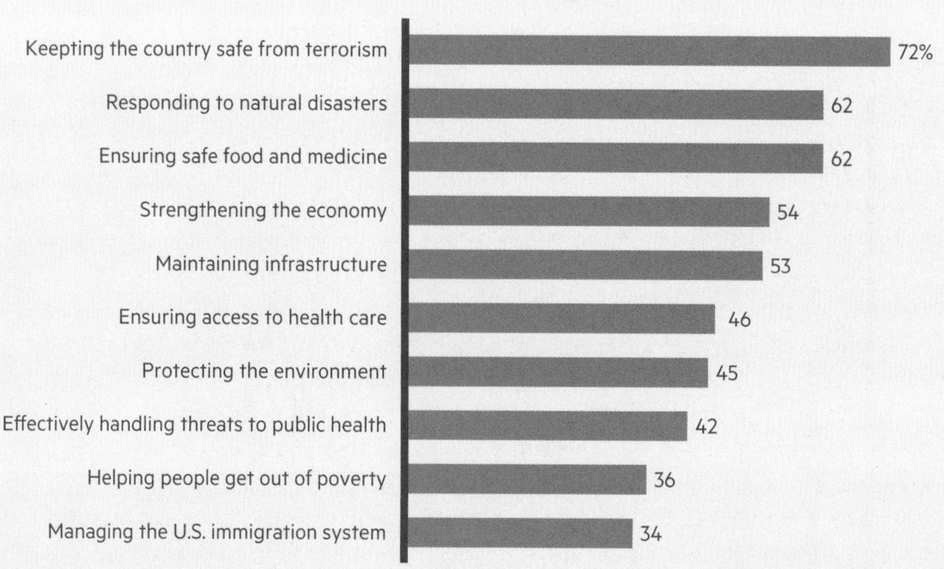

Source: Pew Research Center, "Americans' Views of Government: Low Trust, but Some Positive Performance Ratings," September 14, 2020, www.pewresearch.org/politics/2020/09/14/americans-views-of-government-low-trust-but-some-positive-performance-ratings/pp_09-14-20_views-of-government-00-0/ (accessed 1/10/22).

Survey respondents may also be responding to trust questions in ways we do not expect. In particular, in an era when citizens and political organizations are polarized to some degree, high levels of distrust are almost a given, as citizens whose partisan affiliation or leaning differs from the president's party ID are unlikely to report high levels of trust. Moreover, the data shown earlier suggest that even within the president's party, a significant percentage of people may report low trust because they disagree with the president's policy positions. If so, the decline in trust may say more about the nature of contemporary politics than it does about citizens' confidence in their government.

The same is likely true for polls that reveal seemingly dire findings about the public's belief about democracy. In a 2021 poll, political scientists Lane Cuthbert and Alexander Theodoridis found that a high percentage of Republicans believed that President Joe Biden's victory in 2020 was illegitimate. Moreover, these responses are not simply expressive responding, where a respondent's statements simply reflect disapproval of the outcome. Rather, many respondents could cite specific reasons for their judgment, including changes made to election rules by state and local officials, or decisions by local officials to destroy Trump ballots and count fraudulent votes cast for Biden. (As we discuss in Chapter 9, there is no evidence to support these claims.) On the other hand, many of these respondents are strong supporters of former president Trump, who has emphasized claims about having the 2020 election stolen from him. What we don't know yet is whether these survey findings reflect real skepticism about the conduct of the election or are due to Trump's enduring popularity among Republican voters. We will need additional surveys (and perhaps the rise of successors to Trump) to be sure.

Policy preferences

In a diverse country of more than 330 million, people care about a wide range of government policies. One useful measure of Americans' policy preferences is the **policy mood**, mentioned earlier, which captures the public's collective demands for government action on domestic policies.[52] Policy mood measures are constructed from surveys that ask about opinions on a wide range of policy questions.[53]

policy mood
The level of public support for expanding the government's role in society; whether the public wants government action on a specific issue.

Changes in the policy mood in America have led to changes in defense spending, environmental policy, and civil rights policies, among others—and have influenced elections (see Figure 6.7 on p. 244).[54] When the policy mood leans in an activist direction (Americans want government to do more, corresponding to lower values on the vertical axis), such as in the early 1960s, conditions are ripe for an expansion of the federal government involving more spending and new programs. In contrast, when the policy mood leans in the opposite direction (Americans want a smaller, less-active government, corresponding to higher values on the vertical axis), elected officials are likely to enact smaller increases in government spending and fewer new programs.

Political scientist Christopher Wlezien has shown that trends in policy mood also reflect a thermostatic model of public opinion, where policy changes in one direction tend to move opinion in the other.[55] For example, Democratic victories in the 2020 election reflect a more liberal, activist policy mood. But as Democrats used their political power to enact policies such as the American Rescue Plan, the policy mood shifted in a conservative direction—just like someone turning the heat on because their house is too cold, then switching to air conditioning because it has become too hot.

Regarding more specific policy preferences, everything we have said in this chapter reinforces the idea that public opinion is often a moving target. While some beliefs and

FIGURE 6.7

Policy Mood

Surveys assess the public's policy mood by asking questions about specific policy issues such as levels of taxation and government spending and the role of government. The level of conservatism (for example, support for smaller, less-active government) was at a high in 1952 and 1980. Could you have used the policy mood prior to the election to predict the outcomes of the 2020 elections?

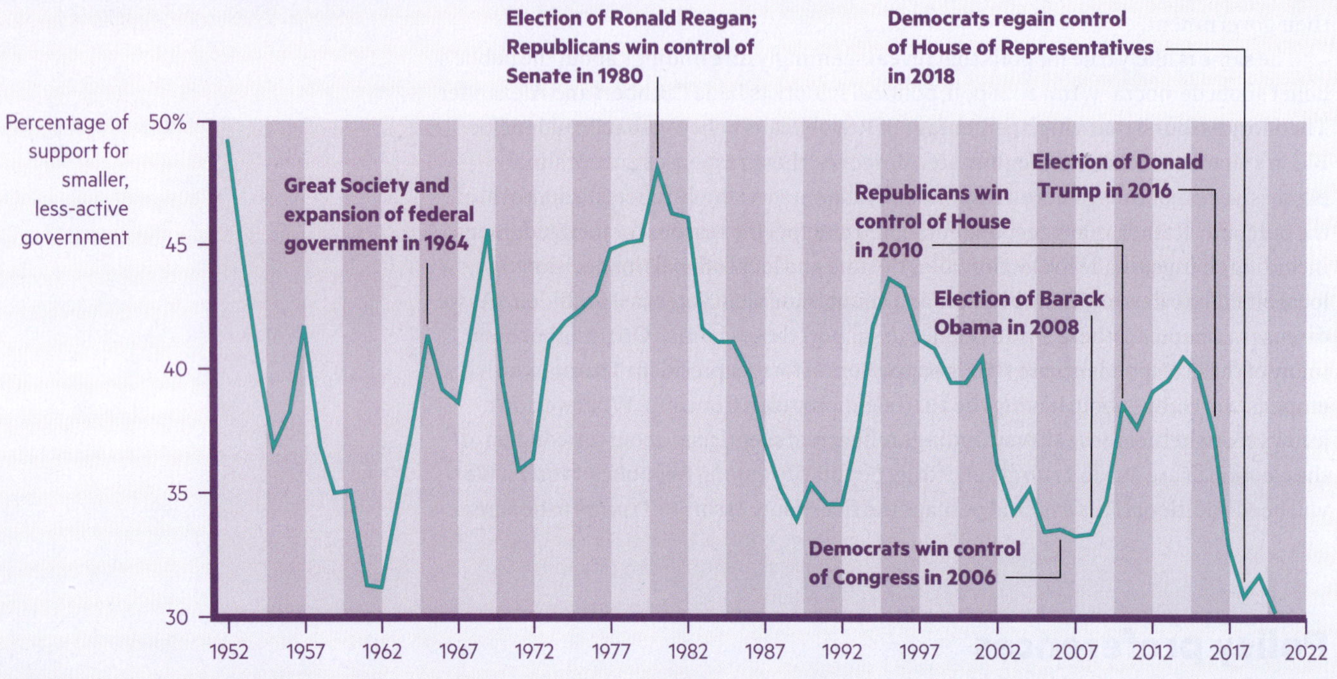

Source: Policy mood data available at http://stimson.web.unc.edu/data (accessed 11/7/22).

preferences are stable over time, opinions about specific policies can change from year to year, month to month, or even day to day. One of the best ways to take a snapshot of these beliefs is to ask citizens what they see as the top policy priorities facing the nation. Figure 6.8 shows responses to a 2021 survey.

Leaving aside the COVID-19 pandemic, the top priorities—the economy, terrorism, and health care—have not changed very much over the last several decades. It is no exaggeration to say that Americans are always worried about the economy. Even when other pressing issues, such as terrorism, surpass the economy as the most important problem to Americans, the economy is typically listed second or third. In general, as the state of the economy declines, more and more people rate the economy as their greatest concern. Moreover, the percentage of people who make reference to their personal economic concerns—for example, unemployment or worries about retirement—also increases. The notable change in the policy data for 2021 is increased concerns about political reform.

These policy priorities frame contemporary political debates and divide the political parties. Think about what Republicans and Democrats in Washington argue about: how best to fight terrorism and secure the United States from attack, how to increase economic growth and reduce the unemployment rate, and whether to change election laws and voting requirements. In fact, there are sharp partisan

FIGURE 6.8

The American Public's Policy Priorities, 2021

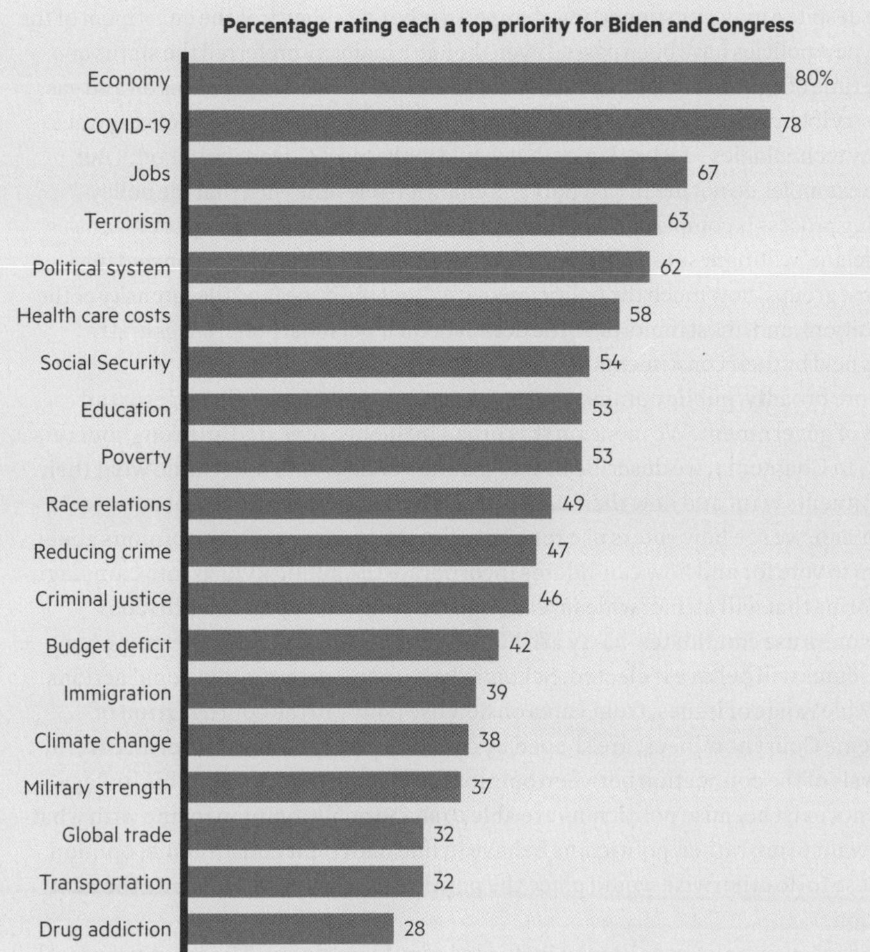

Given these data on policy priorities, what issues would you have expected to be prominent in the 2022 election campaign?

Source: Pew Research Center, "Public's Policy Priorities for 2021," January 28, 2021, www.pewresearch.org/politics/2021/01/28/economy-and-covid-19-top-the-publics-policy-agenda-for-2021/ (accessed 1/10/22).

disagreements on many of these issues; 59 percent of Democrats see climate change as an important problem, while only 14 percent of Republicans give the same response. Similar differences exist for economic inequality, racism, and immigration. However, in other areas, such as concerns over jobs and social security, responses do not vary much by party. Interestingly, there is little cross-party difference in the demand for political reform.

The list of policy priorities also explains government inaction on some issues. For example, gun control doesn't even appear on the list. Thus, the fact that Congress has not legislated on either of these issues in recent years is actually consistent with public opinion. For better or worse, the average American has other priorities for government action.[56]

Does public opinion matter?

We can say with confidence that public opinion remains highly relevant in American politics today. One key piece of evidence is the amount of time and effort politicians, journalists, and political scientists spend trying to find out what Americans think.

Of course, it is easy to find examples like gun control in which policy has stayed the same despite a majority supporting change. In other cases, such as the enactment of the ACA, new policies have been passed even though a majority preferred the status quo at the time of enactment. Political scientist Leah Stokes's work shows how oil and gas industry lobbyists were able to block policies designed to encourage use of renewable energy technologies—technologies that would make most citizens better off.[57] But these examples do not mean that public opinion is irrelevant—just that the policy-making process is complex. It is not always possible to please a majority of citizens. Politicians' willingness to do so depends on whether the majority is organized into interest groups, how much the politicians care about the issue (and the intensity of the opposition), and, most important, the details of their personal preferences and the views held by their constituents.

More broadly, public opinion exerts a conspicuous influence in widespread areas of government. We mention this broad influence repeatedly throughout this book. In Chapter 11, we describe how legislators endeavor to determine what their constituents want and how their constituents will respond to different actions. In Chapter 9, we see how voters use retrospective evaluations to form opinions about whom to vote for and how candidates incorporate the public's views into campaign platforms that will attract widespread support. And in Chapter 8, we discuss how voters use candidates' party affiliations like brand names to determine how candidates will behave if elected. Scholars have found that congressional actions on a wide range of issues, from votes on defense policy to the confirmation of Supreme Court nominees, are shaped by constituent opinion.[58] Moreover, careful analysis of the connection between opinions and actions shows that this linkage does not exist because politicians are able to shape public opinion in line with what they want to do; rather, politicians behave in line with their constituents' opinion because to do otherwise would place the politicians in jeopardy of losing the next election.[59]

Recent events also speak to the influence of public opinion. The massive federal assistance to individuals and businesses in the wake of COVID-19 were enacted in no small part because of public pressure for relief. On the other side, think about the failure of elected officials over the last few years to repeal Obamacare, enact immigration reform, or pass new limits on the ownership of handguns and assault rifles. In all of these cases, a significant portion of Americans wanted policy change, but a substantial percentage were opposed, and even the supporters disagreed on what kinds of changes were best. Congressional inaction on these measures

Public opinion influences government at election time when voters' opinions about incumbent politicians and the party in power affect their decisions at the polls. In 2020, voters' evaluations of President Trump were an important factor in the election outcome.

does not reflect a willful ignorance of public opinion. Rather, it reflects the lack of a public consensus about what government should do. Inaction on these issues is exactly what we should expect if public opinion is real and relevant to what happens in politics.

"Why Should I Care?"

Political scientists and pollsters spend so much time trying to measure public opinion because it shapes election outcomes and policy changes in Washington. If you want to know what the federal government is going to do (or why it's not doing what you think it should be doing), spend some time trying to determine where your own policy opinions fit in with the policy opinions of the country as a whole.

Unpacking the Conflict

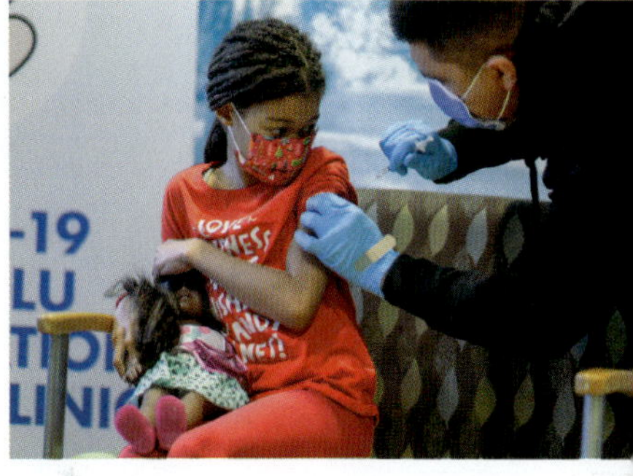

Considering all that we've discussed in this chapter, let's apply what we know about how public opinion works to the examples from the beginning of the chapter. Do Americans really hold the bizarre or extreme beliefs that are sometimes expressed in polling results? Can we take polls seriously, including those that suggest people believe elections were stolen or would support a military coup? Where does public opinion come from? Can politicians trust public opinion as a guide to what Americans want—and can we use opinions to measure the quality of American democracy?

Given how people form opinions, it's easy to see what Jon Stewart was talking about: at least some of the time, public opinion will be incomplete at best and wildly inaccurate at worst. But that's not surprising. For most people, politics is not the most important thing in their lives, and they don't spend much time worrying about it, learning the details, or forming judgments until they need to. This logic also explains why people are sometimes unable to answer seemingly easy questions.

When we ask how "good" opinions are, or whether the electorate acts "rationally and responsibly," as V. O. Key argued, the most important thing to remember is that there is no absolute standard of accuracy. As the quotation from Frances Perkins suggests, public opinion is the leader. One of the fundamental tenets of a democracy is that people are free to hold whatever opinions they want and to base these opinions on whatever factors they want to consider. If someone says they approve of Trump's performance in office, and we determine that their judgment is based on Trump's being a Republican, this opinion is as legitimate as that of someone whose evaluation is based on a detailed study of multiple factors.

Should we take polls seriously? Yes, but not too much. Given all the potential problems with mass surveys, we should be suspicious about surprising results. Respondents may not have taken the question seriously; they may have focused on subtle details of the question—or their reply may have been driven by considerations that have nothing to do with the question at hand. Right now, partisanship and feelings about President Trump appear to be driving a wide range of survey responses, from judgments about foreign policy and the state of the economy to questions about electoral fairness and the viability of democracy. These responses are concerning, but they probably are less significant than they appear at first glance.

More generally, we should take poll results seriously to the extent that they are based on multiple surveys, with differently worded questions; are conducted by reputable pollsters; and are conducted at a time when respondents are aware of the issues they are being asked about. One poll on its own or a series of polls taken at the same time doesn't tell us very much.

In sum, while you can't take every poll result you see at face value, public opinion is real, and it matters. Americans have ideas about what they want government to do, and they use these ideas to guide their political choices. Polls showing deep disagreement between Americans on some issues describe the policy landscape on which elections will be contested and the subsequent debates in Washington. While very few Americans are policy experts, their views on policy are the ultimate driver of our government's policy choices.

"What's Your Take?"

Is public opinion important enough that politicians should follow it? Or is public opinion too unreliable and unpredictable to trust?

And if public opinion cannot be trusted, whose wishes should government follow, if not the people's?

CHECK YOUR UNDERSTANDING

"Why Should I Care?"

Public opinion is at the heart of democracy. Our government is designed to be accountable to the public, and indeed one good measure of how well government is working is how satisfied people are. Because politicians are incentivized to care what their constituents think (because if they ignore us, we likely won't vote for them!), public opinion can help drive the actions of candidates and elected officials, and thus the direction in which policy moves. Public support is also a kind of political currency; when elected officials have public support on their side, it makes it much easier to get things done.

We should care, then, about public opinion because it strongly influences politics. But public opinion is not simply a "hotter, colder" lever that nudges politicians and policy. Rather, public opinion has many intertwined facets, can be hard to change, and can be even harder to measure.

Imagine being a policy maker trying to anticipate the next zig or zag in this complex landscape of public opinion. Ideally, you would want high-quality data to help you understand exactly which factors lead someone to vote Democrat versus Republican, to support versus oppose stricter gun control, and so on. Yet unfortunately for policy makers (and for pundits), in many ways public opinion has become harder to measure and predict, despite many advances in technology and statistical sophistication. Why? Among other reasons, because it's increasingly difficult to get a random, representative, and reliable sample of survey respondents in an age where most of us have cell phones but we block calls we don't recognize (and we can't be bothered to answer questions unless there's a promise of a gift card).

In short, we should care deeply about public opinion, because it fuels politics. And so, especially in today's era of challenging measurement issues, we should pay close attention to the details of every public opinion poll we see zoom across the screen: How was the sample collected (by phone, online survey, or another way)? What was the exact wording of the question? What was the sample size? What is the margin of error? (And were there gift cards involved?) Being astute consumers of public opinion data can help us stay informed about how the tide of public opinion is moving and where our own attitudes fall within it.

1. As a student of politics, being able to understand the results of public opinion polls means you

- **a** have tools to explain the behaviors of candidates and public officials.
- **b** can define the influences on the thinking of individual citizens.
- **c** better articulate arguments to change the minds of those who are surveyed.
- **d** may explain the considerations that determined the answers of the respondents.

2. The relationship between stable and latent opinions is best explained by which statement?

- **a** Latent opinions are more likely to affect intensity of belief than stable opinions.
- **b** Stable opinions are key in shaping the latent opinions that are developed on the spot.
- **c** Opinions, whether stable or latent, are equally likely to be influenced by situational considerations.
- **d** Fully formed sets of latent opinions developed through consistent experiences are even less likely to shift than stable opinions.

3. The consistent coherent sets of political attitudes and opinions held by Americans are most influenced by

- **a** dedicated study to policy issues and politics.
- **b** social factors like family, region, and peer groups.
- **c** mainstream media outlets and social media.
- **d** growing conflicts over culturally and politically divisive issues.

4. When conducting a survey on presidential approval, judging if the country is going in the right direction or wrong direction, or preferences on which group is most capable of handling particular policy issues, it is most likely that the responses of survey participants will be based on which factor?

- **a** Economic performance
- **b** Demographic characteristics
- **c** Partisanship
- **d** Complex interactions of information

5. A team of individuals seeking to find out what Americans believe about the state of the economy position themselves outside a large arena with the goal of gathering opinions from 1,000 attendees. Why can you immediately dismiss the findings of this survey without knowing the outcome?

- **a** Sample size problems
- **b** Question wording issues
- **c** Social desirability problems
- **d** Selection bias concerns

6. Which sample groups and selection methods have the greatest likelihood of discovering the accurate measure of Americans' feelings about the performance of Congress?

- **a** 1,200 registered voters chosen through digitally promoted online surveys and random-digit dialing
- **b** 1,124 college-educated eligible voters selected through information gathered by the U.S. Census Bureau
- **c** 150 citizens participating in professionally facilitated focus groups
- **d** 1,050 citizens picked randomly through the use of random-digit dialing

7. Scholars understand that popular portrayals of a sharply divided "red" and "blue" American electorate are misleading for which of the following reasons?

- **a** Less than one-quarter of Americans hold consistently liberal or conservative ideologies.
- **b** Partisan distrust has consistently fallen over the last generation.
- **c** Americans are still unified about their support for the effectiveness of democratic institutions.
- **d** Groups of liberals and conservatives have become more heterogeneous than in the past.

8. A great dichotomy about the distrust many Americans have toward our government and institutions is that

- **a** Americans generally reflect confidence in the ability of government to meet public expectations.
- **b** American attitudes toward government institutions have improved since the civil rights era.
- **c** Americans regularly show strong support for many individual government programs.
- **d** American positivity toward democracy and democratic practices remains consistently high.

Use INQUIZITIVE *to help you study and master this material.*

7

The Media

Do the media make us more informed?

"Fake news is like ice, once it comes in contact with the heat of the truth it melts quickly and suddenly evaporates."[1]
Oche Otorkpa, author

"Leaders who play by the rules are having trouble staying ahead of a relentless news cycle and must devote too much effort trying to disprove stories that seem to come out of nowhere and have been invented solely to do them in."[2]
Madeleine Albright, former secretary of state

For democracy to work well, citizens need information about what government is doing or could do. And they need information about the world around them, to make decisions about their own behavior and to form judgments about public policy. For most of us, becoming informed involves consulting a mix of media sources, from mainstream providers to posts on social media.

The COVID-19 pandemic has highlighted troubling features of this information-seeking process. On the one hand, major publications such as the *New York Times* have provided up-to-the minute reports on the spread of the pandemic. Scientists and front-line medical professionals have chronicled their efforts to treat patients as well as develop new medicines and vaccines. At the same time, other sources, some with larger audiences, have presented questionable or outright false information about the pandemic, pointing Americans to useless treatments, raising unfounded fears about vaccines, or even claiming that the pandemic is a hoax designed to justify the government's increased intrusion into everyday life.

After the 2020 election, many supporters of President Trump saw coverage in certain online news sources suggesting that there had been widespread election fraud, including ballot tampering and missing ballot boxes. As a result, they did not believe the election had been fair—many saying it had been stolen. Even after thorough nonpartisan investigations, many Trump voters refused to believe he had lost the election, demonstrating the power that these unvalidated sources can have in citizens' trust in government.

The experience of the pandemic raises three questions about the role of the media in contemporary society. A generation ago, proponents of the Internet and social media argued that the vast expansion of information sources and the availability of social media networks to drive the search for knowledge would lead to a better-informed society. However, while there is vastly more information available to the average citizen, these changes have not translated into higher levels of citizen knowledge. Why hasn't additional information made Americans smarter and more discerning?

Second, why have providers of questionable information survived and prospered, even when highly reputable sources carefully provide disconfirming information? For example, the QAnon website alleges that major political figures from both parties

CHAPTER GOALS

Describe the role of the media in American politics and how people get political information (pp. 254–262)

Explain how politicians use the media to achieve their goals (pp. 262–267)

Explain how the media influence how people think about politics (pp. 267–275)

Assess whether the media fulfill their role in American democracy (pp. 275–280) engaged in a satanic, pedophilic, cannibalistic plot against Donald Trump's presidency. Many mainstream media sources have documented the complete lack of evidence for any of these claims. Yet the website still exists, and some minor media sources cover the story as though it had some empirical support.[3]

The third question is one we've discussed throughout this book: who are the reliable sources for separating truth from fiction about COVID-19 or any other major policy issue? Regardless of where you think fake news comes from, there is a lot of it around. The problem is to become truly well-informed in the face of the fire hose of available facts and opinions.

To answer these questions, the first task is to understand the radically transformed media universe that exists in contemporary America, from major mainstream media providers to obscure websites that provide raw data, rumors, or other information about public policy. We also need to understand how Americans seek out information and what factors shape their choice of one source over another. Taken together, these data will help to explain the seeming paradox of the media in contemporary American politics: how has an increase in available information produced higher levels of confusion and misunderstanding?

DESCRIBE THE ROLE OF THE MEDIA IN AMERICAN POLITICS AND HOW PEOPLE GET POLITICAL INFORMATION

mass media
Sources that provide information to the average citizen, such as newspapers, television networks, radio stations, podcasts, and websites.

linking institution
An actor or a group of actors in American politics that informs citizens about government actions or helps them exercise control over policy.

Political media today

This section describes the **mass media**, the many sources of political information available to Americans, and how people use (or don't use) this information. The media are the first example in this book of a **linking institution**—an actor or group of actors in American politics that informs citizens about government actions or helps them exercise control over policy. The development of the Internet and the expansion of social media over the last generation have dramatically increased the number of media sources and the range of information available to the average American. As you will see, it has also increased the number of overtly ideological media sources—actors who are more interested in presenting a particular point of view than in providing a full and complete report about an issue, an event, or a policy question. Taken together, these trends mean that it is easier to become an expert on virtually any aspect of politics or public policy but also that there is a higher risk of incorporating biased or unreliable information into your beliefs.

To be clear, the points we make about media coverage of contemporary politics can be applied equally to all sides. It is easy to find left-leaning media coverage that is incomplete, simplistic, or even biased. The same is true on the conservative side. At the same time, there are multiple sources on both sides that offer useful perspectives on people and events in Washington. However, regardless of their motivations, very few sources provide complete, accurate coverage all the time. As a result, it is often difficult to stay well informed. One response to the problem is to throw your hands up and stay away from stories about politics—but this strategy leaves you ignorant about political events that can have a profound impact on your life. The alternative is to become a thoughtful consumer of political media, understanding where gaps or biases in coverage might arise and keeping in mind our media checklist presented here and elsewhere in the text. This chapter expands on the points made in our checklist so that you understand why we see them as crucial for evaluating media coverage.

Historical overview: how did we get here?

The role of the media as an information source and the controversy over how the media report about politics are nothing new. Since the Founding, politicians have understood that Americans learn about politics largely from the media, have complained about coverage, and have sought to influence both the stories the media select and the way they report on them.

The Media as Watchdog and Business From the beginnings of the United States, mass media has served as a reporter of political events and as a watchdog, keeping track of what politicians are doing and offering insight about their policy successes and failures. Many newspapers chronicled the conflicts of the Revolutionary War; after the war, while politicians negotiated over the size and scope of the new federal government, newspapers became a venue for debates over different plans.[4] While the media cover politics, politicians have always tried to shape this coverage to their advantage. During the ratification of the Constitution, for instance, Alexander Hamilton, John Jay, and James Madison supported pro-ratification forces in New York by publishing (under a pseudonym) a series of articles that came to be known as the *Federalist Papers* in local newspapers.[5] And in 1798 Congress and President John Adams enacted the Alien and Sedition Acts, which made it a crime to publish articles that criticized the president or Congress.[6] While these press restrictions were later repealed or allowed to expire, they serve as a reminder that the American media have never been free of government regulation or of the conflictual relationship between politicians and reporters.

Yellow journalism emphasized sensational stories and bold headlines but also made information about contemporary politics available to a wider audience.

Long before the Internet, changes in technology expanded the media's role as information provider, entertainment, and watchdog. In 1833, the *New York Sun* began selling papers for a penny a copy rather than the standard price of six cents. The price reduction, which was facilitated by cheaper, faster printing presses, made the newspaper available to the mass public for the first time, and this increase in circulation made it possible, even with the lower price, to hire more reporters.[7] The development of the telegraph also aided newspapers by enabling reporters on assignment throughout the country to quickly send stories back home for publication. Many of the new publications were unabashedly partisan. For example, the *New York Tribune* was strongly antislavery. By 1860, the *Tribune*'s circulation was larger than that of any other newspaper in the world and its articles "helped to add fuel to the fires of slavery and sectionalism that divided North and South."[8]

The media's role as a watchdog has always been constrained by the need to attract a paying audience in order to stay in business and turn a profit. The period after the Civil War saw the beginning of **yellow journalism**, reporting that drew in customers by using bold headlines, illustrations, and sensational stories (the name came from the yellow paper these newspapers were printed on).

yellow journalism
A style of newspaper reporting popular in the late 1800s that featured sensationalized stories, bold headlines, and illustrations to increase readership.

Yellow journalism also provides an early example of unreliable reporting. At the end of the nineteenth century, newspapers published by William Randolph Hearst and Joseph Pulitzer published articles advocating for a U.S. war with Spain and the capture of Cuba. After the sinking of the naval warship U.S.S. *Maine* in Havana Harbor in February 1898, Hearst and Pulitzer dispatched reporters to Cuba to write stories that the *Maine* was sunk by a Spanish mine. Although many naval experts at the time believed that the *Maine* was sunk by an internal explosion, Hearst was undeterred, telling one reporter, "You furnish the pictures, I'll furnish the war!"[9] At the other extreme, the *New York Times* was transformed in the 1800s into a nonpartisan paper with the goals of journalistic impartiality, accuracy, and complete coverage of events—its motto to the present day is, "All the News That's Fit to Print."[10]

During the 1920s hundreds of small, local radio stations appeared, along with some larger stations that could broadcast nationwide. The proliferation of stations eventually led to the development of networks, that is, groups of local radio (and, later, television) stations owned by one company that broadcast a common set of programs. While these new electronic sources made more information available to Americans, many of them were developed not as watchdogs but as highly profitable enterprises that delivered entertainment as well as news to citizens and monetized their audience by selling radio or television time to advertisers.

broadcast media
Communications technologies, such as television and radio, that transmit information over airwaves.

Federal Communications Commission (FCC)
A government agency created in 1934 to regulate American radio stations and later expanded to regulate television, wireless communications technologies, and other broadcast media.

equal time provision
An FCC regulation requiring broadcast media to provide equal air time on any non-news programming to all candidates running for an office.

Regulating the Media Until 1930 or so, there was only minimal federal regulation of the media, reflecting the Constitution's guarantee of freedom of the press—and the fact that newspapers were the only media source that existed. With the rise of the **broadcast media**, including radio and television, and the formation of the **Federal Communications Commission (FCC)** to allocate broadcast frequencies, a new position emerged: if broadcasters were going to make money off their use of the government's broadcast frequencies, the government could place conditions on how this business operated. In recent years, the emergence of new technologies (cable TV, the Internet) have changed the calculation; the emphasis is now on encouraging competition among media sources rather than regulating a few providers.

Federal regulation of broadcast media was driven by the concern that one company or organization might buy enough stations to dominate the airwaves in a given area and become a monopoly, offering only one set of programs or point of view. For many years, FCC regulations limited the number of radio and television stations a company could own in a community and the total nationwide audience that a company's television stations could reach. The FCC also created the **equal time provision**, which says that if a radio or television station gives air time to a candidate outside its routine news coverage—such as during an entertainment show or a cooking program—it has to give an equivalent amount of time to other candidates running for the same office. For example, when then-presidential candidate Kamala Harris appeared on *Saturday Night Live* in November 2024, NBC gave free television time to Donald Trump. He recorded an appeal for people to vote, which was aired during a NASCAR broadcast. The FCC also established a fairness doctrine, whereby broadcasters had to present opposing points of view as part of their coverage of important events; usually this was done by broadcasting editorials during news programs that presented both sides of an issue.

President Trump argued that he should receive "equal time" under the FCC's equal time regulations due to the negative coverage he often receives from late-night television hosts like Stephen Colbert (left) and Trevor Noah (right). Trump tweeted: "Late Night host are dealing with the Democrats for their very 'unfunny' & repetitive material, always anti-Trump! Should we get Equal Time?"

Deregulation The FCC's limits on ownership and content as well as the fairness doctrine have been eliminated because of the development of new communications technologies. The logic is that with so many sources of information, if one broadcaster ignores a candidate, an issue, or a viewpoint, citizens can still find out what they want to know from another source. Pressure for deregulation also came from the owners of media companies, who wanted to buy more television, radio, and cable stations, as well as from book and magazine publishers, Internet service providers, and newspapers.[11]

These regulatory changes have shaped the current media landscape in two ways. First, they have allowed for concentration: many media companies own multiple media sources in a town or community. For example,

NUTS & BOLTS 7.1

Holdings of the Walt Disney Company

The Walt Disney Company is an example of a media conglomerate, a company that controls a variety of media outlets throughout the world. It owns cable television networks, television and radio stations, cable channels, movie-production companies, subscription programming sites, and websites; this table provides just a few examples of its many holdings. This structure allows the company to rebroadcast or reprint stories in different outlets and thus operate more efficiently, but opponents are concerned that conglomerates might expand to control most—or even all—of the sources that are available to the average citizen, making it impossible to access alternate points of view.

Broadcast stations	Film companies
ABC broadcast network (owns 8 stations, over 200 affiliates)	20th Century Studios
KRDC-AM (Los Angeles)	Lucasfilm
Radio Disney (available through Internet platforms)	Marvel Studios
	Pixar
	20th Century Fox Television
	Walt Disney Studios

Cable channels		Other media
A&E	Lifetime	Vice Media
ESPN	National Geographic	FiveThirtyEight
Freeform	Four Disney-branded channels	Hulu
FX		Disney+

Source: Compiled by the authors.

"Why Should I Care?"

Think about where you get your news. If all your top sources for political information were owned by the same company, how might that affect the diversity of stories you see or the perspectives you hear? While conglomerates might help make the process of reporting and distributing the news more efficient, it's important to understand how the owners might influence what you ultimately read.

iHeartMedia owns over 850 AM and FM radio stations, including multiple stations in more than 30 cities. Similarly, Meta owns Facebook, which is a major source of news for many Americans, but also owns Instagram. Second, the changes have allowed for cross-ownership, in which one company owns several different kinds of media outlets, often in the same community. For example, Nexstar owns various Chicago media outlets, including the WGN radio station, the WGN television station, and the *Chicago Tribune* daily newspaper. These trends have given rise to **media conglomerates**, companies that control a wide range of news sources.[12] Nuts & Bolts 7.1 shows the diverse holdings of one such company, the Walt Disney Company. You may think of Disney in terms of theme parks, cruises, and *Avengers* or *Star Wars* movies and TV shows, but the company owns a wide range of media companies, including the ABC broadcast network, Hulu, ESPN, and the political information site FiveThirtyEight.

media conglomerates
Companies that control a large number of media sources across several types of media outlets.

Media sources in the twenty-first century

Over the last two decades, the Internet has become a primary conduit for information about American politics. Virtually all U.S. newspapers, magazines, television networks, radio stations, and cable stations offer free or (increasingly) paid access to their content via websites and mobile apps. Many Internet-only sites offer a combination of rumor, inside information, and deep analysis of American politics. Some, such as Axios, Politico, Vox, and FiveThirtyEight, have paid staff and report on a wide range of topics. Others have a narrower focus: the Monkey Cage (part of the *Washington Post* but run by

DID YOU KNOW?

Newspaper circulation per capita has declined

65%

since 1970.

Source: Pew Research Center.

political science professors) and the Mischiefs of Faction use political science research to explain contemporary American politics.[13] And many websites, run by ordinary citizens, activists and political insiders, or policy experts, provide their own insights and information about American politics. Finally, Facebook, Twitter, and other social media sites provide users with links to coverage written by others; people also use these sites to report and comment on political events themselves.

These changes have dramatically increased the amount of information about politics that is available to the average American. Imagine yourself in the late 1940s. Suppose you wanted to learn about President Truman's State of the Union address. If you couldn't go to Washington to hear it in person, where could you have gotten information about the speech? If you lived in a big city, the speech would probably be covered in the next day's newspaper. If you lived in a small town, your local paper might or might not run the story. If it didn't, you would need a subscription to either a big-city paper (which would arrive a week after the fact) or a weekly or monthly news magazine, or you would need a radio that could pick up a station broadcasting the speech.

Now consider the modern era, in which major political events saturate the media and a virtually unlimited amount of information is available on the Internet. Suppose you want to know about the president's State of the Union message. You can tune in to one of the major television broadcast networks, cable news channels, public television stations, or radio stations. Most television stations will feature pundits' commentaries on the speech and will interview prominent politicians and commentators. Jimmy Fallon and other late-night hosts will probably make jokes about it on television, and John Oliver will skewer the speech on his Sunday show. Tomorrow it will be front-page news and larger papers will publish the full text of the speech online. Countless websites will offer live streaming and analyses. Some of your friends (perhaps even you) might offer commentary on social media. The point is, there are many places to get information; you would have to work to avoid them.

Algorithms are not arbiters of objective truth and fairness simply because they're math.

—Zoë Quinn, author and video game developer

DID YOU KNOW?

67%

of American adults report they get at least some of their news from social media.

Source: Pew Research Center.

The Internet has also made new kinds of political information available to the average citizen. For example, the Center for Responsive Politics offers a searchable database of contributions to candidates and political organizations. Many sites such as FiveThirtyEight or RealClearPolitics collect and analyze public opinion surveys, including presidential election polls. Increasingly, podcasts such as the left-leaning *Pod Save America* or the right-leaning *Federalist Radio Hour* are used to deliver analysis and interviews. The Internet also creates new opportunities for interaction between citizens, reporters, and government officials. Many reporters host live online chat sessions, allowing people to ask follow-up questions about published stories, or interact with their audience through a variety of social media sites.

The Internet has also facilitated some entirely new kinds of media sources. People who know something about political events (or think they do) now have a variety of ways, from blogs to Twitter, to contribute to the commentary on political news stories and put information before a wide audience. During the COVID-19 pandemic, for example, many epidemiologists and public health experts used Twitter, Substack, and other venues to report on trends in caseloads and the effectiveness of new treatments and vaccines. Three good examples are the Substack page Your Local Epidemiologist, the Facebook page Friendly Neighborhood Epidemiologist, and the *Science* blog In the Pipeline.[14] The first two are written by PhD university professors; the third is written by a PhD who works in drug development. They exemplify the kind of detailed, reliable information that is readily available in the modern era that was all but inaccessible a generation ago.

At the same time, the rise of the Internet has exacerbated the trend toward shorter stories in major news sources, with fewer details and less background information. In theory, the elimination of space limitations should have produced longer, more in-depth reporting on the Internet, but in fact the opposite has occurred. Many popular Internet sources, such as Axios, are designed to present information in short,

easy-to-digest form. Similarly, news accounts that individuals may post on social media sites are often light on details—most notably, posts on Twitter are limited to 280 characters. Major news sources such as the *New York Times* and the *Washington Post* are also shifting both what they report and how they report in favor of stories that can gain the attention of an easily distracted public—and reporters are being evaluated in terms of the number of times their stories are viewed.

From protesters covering their marches to refugees filming their journeys, the Internet makes it easy for ordinary people to share political information and report on political events as they happen.

While there is much more information available today than there was a generation ago, media sources are constantly in flux. Websites and Web pages come and go. Individuals who post detailed analyses of one event may be too busy to comment on another. Even well-established media sources can quickly change. For example, in recent years companies that once owned newspapers in Chicago, Philadelphia, and Minneapolis have gone bankrupt, whereas several major U.S. cities, including Seattle, Birmingham, and New Orleans, have a hometown daily newspaper that appears only in digital form. Other newspapers have cut foreign bureaus, reduced their staff, and thinned the amount of news in every edition. (One exception is the *Washington Post*, which substantially expanded its newsroom under the ownership of Jeff Bezos, the founder of Amazon.) At the same time, the major television networks and cable television sources have seen declines in budgets and viewership.

The increase in sources has also led to a blurring of fact and opinion in some news coverage. Most mainstream media distinguish between news coverage, where the goal is to present facts and analysis without an ideological agenda, and opinion pieces, which have a clear point of view.[15] In print media, the latter stories are usually reserved for a special op-ed (opinions and editorials) section. Newer media sources, especially solo Web-only operations, may not follow these conventions, meaning that casual readers might assume they are reading a factual account when in fact they are not.

Don't believe everything you read on the Internet—quotes about media literacy have been humorously attributed to President Lincoln to satirize the prevalence of misinformation online.

Moreover, as we discussed earlier, the quality of information available on the Internet varies considerably—probably more than it did for the relatively small number of media sources that were available a generation ago. For example, it is easy to find fake photographs of all kinds on the Internet, including Barack Obama shaking hands with Osama bin Laden, former House Speaker Nancy Pelosi wearing a hijab (a headscarf worn by Muslim women that leaves only the face exposed), or Donald Trump carrying two cats to safety during hurricane relief operations. As the quote (falsely) attributed to Abraham Lincoln says, you can't believe something just because it's on the Internet. Even if fake Lincoln quotes are easy to spot, in a world where websites come and go and where citizens often do not take the time to investigate what they see or read, false information may easily be accepted as true, especially if it fits the preconceptions of whoever reads it.

While a great deal of false or inaccurate information is quickly identified as such, the process is nowhere near foolproof. This problem has been especially acute during the COVID-19 pandemic. For example, podcaster Joe Rogan promoted unproven

Joe Rogan, host of a popular podcast, regularly suggested that COVID-19 could be treated with unproven medicines, leading many of his listeners to not get the vaccine, demonstrating how fast misinformation can be spread.

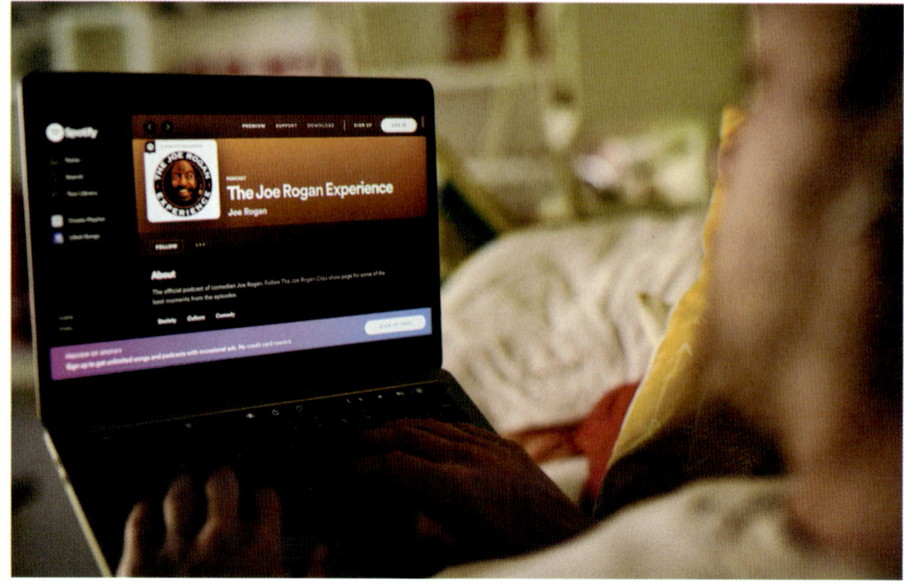

treatments for COVID-19 and questioned the usefulness of mask mandates and newly developed vaccines.[16] These claims do not survive even casual scrutiny: none of Rogan's proposed treatments have been shown to work (in fact, studies have shown they don't). The problem is, in a world where Rogan's podcast is one of the most popular in the country, some viewers may hear Rogan's claims but not seek out additional information.

A related problem is that the Internet has made it easier for partisan groups to publish stories that are labeled as investigative journalism but that are in no sense full, complete, or unbiased. For example, during 2017 and 2018, many blogs and media outlets reported on investigations of Russian efforts to help Donald Trump with the 2016 presidential election. One of the more extreme claims was that Trump knew about and approved of these efforts—as one 2017 article in the magazine *Mother Jones* put it, "We already know that Trump betrayed America."[17] The fact is, no one (not even Special Counsel Robert Mueller, who was named by the Justice Department to investigate these allegations and ran a large, multiyear investigation) found evidence that connected Trump to Russia. Put another way, an "investigation" can mean many things, and the fact that a magazine or blog labels an article as such does not mean it is true.

In general, legacy media is doing a fairly remarkable job keeping our democracy ship afloat in these uncharted waters, while social media is turning out to be a click-hungry sea monster.

—Amber Boydstun, political scientist

In sum, as the quote from political scientist Amber Boydstun illustrates, there is a sharp distinction between legacy media and the sources that have emerged with the development of the Internet and social media. While legacy media does not always get the story right, it faces strong incentives to be a reliable source of information, which generally leads it to do careful research and fact-checking, incorporating multiple perspectives, and issuing corrections when its stories turn out to be incorrect. Of course, legacy media also competes for attention, which sometimes can lead it away from reliability, but at least the pressure to be right the first time is there. For new media, the pressure to get attention and build an audience is more likely to trump an interest in reliability, which is problematic if people use these sites as their primary source of information.

Where do people get political information?

While there is a vast amount of information available about politics, very few Americans make it a priority to be well informed about politics—which would require them to systematically consult, evaluate, and integrate information from a range of different sources. Rather, most Americans acquire political information accidentally through a process known as the **by-product theory**.[18] As an example, in 2022 you may have logged in to Twitter or some other social media site to see what your friends were doing and happened to take a look at a political story that was posted in the sidebar. Perhaps the story was a profile of Florida Governor Ron DeSantis, a candidate for the 2024 Republican presidential nomination. Though you hadn't planned to read about DeSantis, you wound up doing so just because the story came up in your feed—perhaps you were a Florida resident, are a Republican voter, or were dissatisfied with President Biden's performance in office.

by-product theory
The idea that many Americans acquire political information unintentionally rather than by seeking it out.

This idea of learning about politics as a by-product of other activities also raises questions about the mechanisms that put information in front of people. For example, Facebook has a page that lists the top 10 posts based on reactions, comments, and how many people view the post in the first place. In recent years, this list has been dominated by posts about Republican politicians and conservative political causes.[19] The point is not that conservatives dominate Facebook or that Mark Zuckerberg is secretly trying to promote right-wing causes. Rather, a tool designed to flag widely read stories of all kinds is producing a politically colored collection.

When people receive information as a by-product, they don't evaluate it in the same way that they evaluate information gained through a careful search, such as the investigation you might have done if you wanted to check out DeSantis's background and issue positions. Suppose the story applauded DeSantis's policy on mask mandates. If you came upon this information after searching on your own, you would probably have thought about whether the source was credible or whether you think mandates are important. Because you are not consciously searching for information, you are much less likely to be skeptical when you acquire information as a by-product.[20]

When people seek out information consciously, research by political scientist Natalie Jomini Stroud shows evidence for partisan selective exposure—that is, people are more likely to use a source if they believe that the source's partisan lean matches their own.[21] Table 7.1 shows evidence for this phenomenon from an early-2022 survey on the news sources most trusted by Democrats and Republicans. By a large margin, the most trusted sources for Republicans were Fox News and the Weather Channel, while Democrats reported high trust for several sources, with CNN and PBS at the top. Notably, only the top two most trustworthy sources for Republicans garnered more than 50 percent support, while all ten of the top trustworthy sources for Democrats

Trust in News Sources among Democrats and Republicans

TABLE 7.1

Top 10 trustworthy news sources*							
Democrats				**Republicans**			
CNN	66%	Weather Channel	62%	Fox News	53%	*Wall Street Journal*	25%
PBS	66	*Washington Post*	61	Weather Channel	50	BBC	23
CBS	64	NPR	59	NewsMax	41	PBS	22
NBC	64	BBC	58	OAN	30	CBS	18
New York Times	63	Associated Press	54	Breitbart	27	*USA Today*	18

*Percentage saying each is very trustworthy or somewhat trustworthy
Source: Linley Sanders, "Trust in Media 2022: Where Americans Get Their News and Who They Trust for Information," YouGovAmerica, April 5, 2022, https://today.yougov.com/topics/politics/articles-reports/2022/04/05/trust-media-2022-where-americans-get-news-poll (accessed 9/9/22).

All I know is just what I read in the papers, and that's an alibi for my ignorance.

—Will Rogers, actor

DID YOU KNOW?

The weekly audience for Sean Hannity's program, the top conservative talk radio show, is

15 million.

The top liberal program has an audience of only 6 million.

Source: *TALKERS* magazine.

garnered more than 50 percent support, indicating significant partisan differences in trust in news media overall.

The question raised by Table 7.1 is whether the differences in issue positions and policy demands of Republicans and Democrats are driven by the differences in the media sources they consume. Do some people demand liberal policies because they listen to CNN, while others demand conservative policies because they listen to Fox News? The answer is almost surely no. As we discussed in Chapter 6, people aren't liberal or conservative because of the stories they listen to, watch, or read—their beliefs run much deeper than that. It's probably more accurate to say that ideological beliefs drive the selection of media sources, rather than media sources driving ideological beliefs.

The reality of partisan selective exposure has two implications for how people gather information and form beliefs about politics. On one hand, the fact that people seek out ideologically compatible sources means they are more likely to trust these sources and therefore take seriously the information they find. On the other, insofar as different sources report different information, the choice of which media to consume will shape what a person knows about politics—about the candidates, their policy proposals, and the government's performance overall. Focusing on a small set of ideologically compatible sources can strengthen preexisting beliefs. The danger is that Americans will learn only one side of a story (and perhaps not learn at all about some other stories), leaving them with an incomplete and perhaps misleading understanding of contemporary policy debates.

"Why Should I Care?"

It's important to have a clear and accurate understanding of today's media sources. If you're looking for someone to blame for Americans' lack of knowledge about politics, the mass media is not a good candidate. While most sources fall short in one way or another, there is a wealth of information available, most of it for free. But most people never search for political information and ignore much of what they encounter. Journalists can do the most effective reporting possible—providing in-depth, balanced coverage of critical events—but unless people take time to read or view that coverage, their knowledge of politics will be incomplete and possibly biased.

How do politicians use the media? How do the media use politicians?

While the media and politicians are often thought of as adversaries, with a watchdog press working to make sure the public knows what politicians are doing, the fact is that each side has something to offer the other. Reporters want to write stories that attract public attention, so they need information from politicians on what is happening inside the government, preferably information that is given only to them. Politicians in turn want media coverage that highlights their achievements, which ideally will build public support and secure their election (or reelection). Bureaucrats want favorable attention for their programs, and interest groups want publicity to further their causes. Thus, coverage of American politics reflects trade-offs between reporters who want compelling stories and sources who want favorable coverage.

Politicians' media strategies

Politicians and others in government try to influence coverage by providing select information to reporters. Sometimes they hold press conferences where they take questions from the media. Other times they speak to single reporters or to a group **on background or off the record**, meaning that reporters can use the information but cannot attribute it to the politician by name. These efforts are sometimes trial balloons, where politicians release details of a new proposal to gauge public reaction without committing themselves to anything. Other times politicians might reveal some details of a negotiation or conflict with the hope of producing media coverage that puts their contributions in a favorable light.

on background or off the record
Describes comments a politician makes to the press on the condition that they can be reported only if they are not attributed to that politician.

You don't tell us how to stage the news, and we won't tell you how to cover it.

—Larry Speakes, press secretary to President Ronald Reagan

Some scholars argue that elected officials try to use the media to shape public opinion in their favor by doling out information to reward reporters who write stories that support the officials' points of view.[22] To some extent this argument is true: much of the information reporters use to write their stories comes from political appointees, bureaucrats, elected officials, and party leaders.[23] Reporters who are known to be writing stories that are critical of a government program or a political leader may find that some people refuse to talk to them. However, while there is no doubt that elected officials would like to receive sympathetic media coverage and are sometimes successful, news reports on American politics reflect a multitude of sources and information. One politician's attempt to shape coverage by talking or remaining silent may be negated by another's efforts to promote a different point of view, with the same reporter or a different one.

All presidents use this media strategy. President Biden's staff invited the media to events that placed Biden in a favorable light, such as Biden's trips to communities that received infrastructure grants to rebuild highways and bridges or his visits with American troops. Biden held relatively few news conferences and granted fewer interviews than his predecessors, a strategy designed to limit opportunities for unfavorable coverage (although it created a new story, that Biden was avoiding the press). During press conferences, reporters who are likely to ask combative questions are less likely to be called on. Again, all presidents use these strategies. President Trump is unique in his willingness to speak directly to his supporters and the public at large using social media—with a guarantee that the press will report on his posts, simply because Trump is president.

Besides talking with the media, politicians also hold events specifically designed to secure favorable press coverage, or they appear at an event that the press is likely to cover. This strategy is particularly common among candidates campaigning for office. For example, during the summer of 2019, six months before the Iowa Caucuses met to begin selecting presidential nominees, Joe Biden and the other Democratic candidates for president in 2020 made a point of visiting the Iowa State Fair, where they shook hands, ate some local specialties (from pork chops on sticks to fried Snickers bars), and in general tried to attract as much media attention as they could. By attending the fair, candidates were trying to get their names and their pictures in local newspapers and on local television and thereby increase their name recognition. Such coverage might have also helped persuade Iowa voters that a candidate shared their views on the issues.

Another way politicians, especially candidates, try to shape citizen perceptions is to run campaign ads on television, in newspapers, and on websites. Candidates running for federal office generally spend about 80–90 percent of their budget on advertising. Candidates target these ads to reach groups of likely supporters. A conservative Republican might try to buy advertising slots during a broadcast of a NASCAR race, knowing that people who are interested in NASCAR tend to vote Republican. These ads are an example of the by-product theory in action; people don't watch NASCAR to learn about politicians, but watching the broadcast means they will be exposed to the candidate's messages.

Potential presidential candidates also often appear on television talk shows or allow reporters to shadow them on the campaign trail as a way of increasing name recognition and gaining some free advertising. Studies have shown that viewing a candidate in such a relaxed, nonconfrontational setting can help persuade opponents that a candidate is worth a second look.[24]

Like all campaign strategies, however, candidates' attempts to shape media coverage work only some of the time. Candidates have even lost support through misguided attempts to appreciate local cuisine, including biting into an unshucked tamale, asking for a glass of milk with a kosher hot dog, ordering Swiss on a Philly cheesesteak, asking for Dijon mustard on a cheeseburger, or eating pizza with a knife and fork. In the modern era, when everyone has a cell phone, these gaffes are captured on video and used to advantage by the opposition.

Campaign strategies can also backfire when their claims (particularly about opponents) are found to be questionable or outright falsehoods. During the 2020 presidential campaign, Republican politicians and operatives claimed that then-candidate Joe Biden's climate change policies would restrict Americans' meat consumption—as one Fox News reporter put it, "Americans are going to have to cut their red meat consumption by 90% in order to reduce emissions to hit Biden's target.

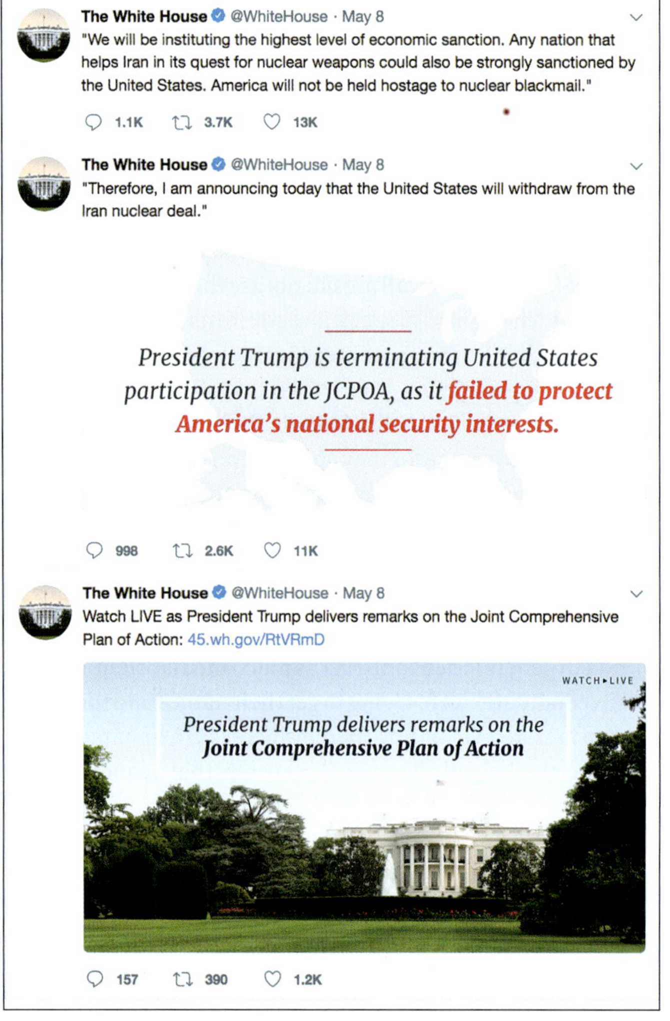

Information and coverage of important issues have become instantaneously available through Internet sources like Twitter feeds and blogs. While President Trump relied on Twitter to directly communicate his policy priorities, President Biden's administration hosted regular press briefings led by the press secretary to message policy positions and answer reporters' questions.

That means you're only allowed to eat four pounds of red meat a year. That adds up to a burger a month. That's it."[25] In fact, the Biden campaign had never said anything about beef consumption, and the four pounds per year limit came from an academic paper that assessed various ways of hitting carbon emissions targets. A British newspaper ran a story that connected Biden to the article. After it became clear that Republican claims were incorrect, the Biden campaign released some pictures of Biden cooking steaks on a barbeque and a quote from former president Obama about Biden's recommendation of a local Delaware diner known for its cheeseburgers. The result was a good day for the Biden campaign and a bad day for the Trump campaign.

The pressures and legal limits on reporters

The proliferation of media sources has increased competition among reporters to find and report on interesting stories. Reporters who refuse to use information that a politician has provided may find that the politician refuses to talk with them in the future, so reporters must carefully consider whether they want to use information provided, to keep their channel of communication with the politician open. Moreover, the Internet has increased the demand for new stories and updates of old ones. Even if reporters covering Congress think that nothing important is happening on a given day, they may be forced to write a story just to have something new on their newspaper's website. Similarly, an up-and-coming news or commentary site might use a politician's offerings as a way of building its audience.

Because of these demands, reporters rely heavily on their sources—people inside government who provide them with documents, inside information, and the details of negotiations—to supply them with material for new stories. When sources reveal information that is not supposed to be public knowledge, it is often referred to as **leaking**. Reporters covering important or controversial stories often promise their sources that they will remain anonymous in any coverage based on the information they provide. These assurances are an important factor in the decision to leak information, especially classified information. However, these assurances are not absolute. Reporters and their editors can, under certain circumstances, be compelled by a court to reveal the sources for their stories. Although some states have shield laws that allow reporters to refuse to name their sources, there is no such law at the federal level. As a result, federal prosecutors can ask a judge to force journalists to name their sources, on the grounds that the source's identity is fundamental to the prosecutor's case. If the judge agrees (which happens rarely), reporters can be jailed for contempt indefinitely unless they name their sources.

leaking
The practice in which someone in government provides nonpublic information to a reporter, with the aim of generating press coverage favorable to the leaker's aims.

To be clear, leaking or the publication of leaked information is not illegal as long as the information is not classified. For example, it was not illegal for former national security advisor John Bolton to disclose private conversations with President Trump. While these revelations were certainly embarrassing to Trump, Bolton did not break any law by writing a book about his experiences (in fact, as with other former National Security aides, he was required to—and did—submit the manuscript to the Justice Department for review prior to publication). During Trump's first term, lawyers in the Department of Justice tried to prevent publication of the book but lost their case.

Sometimes leaks are part of a larger strategy by the president and the president's administration. For example, in spring 2022, as concerns were raised about a Russian invasion of Ukraine, stories featuring anonymous American intelligence sources gave details about movements of Russian forces toward the border, provided estimates of civilian casualties from invasion, and detailed doubts within the Russian military about the prospects for success.[26] Besides suggesting that American intelligence

Leaks coming out of the Trump administration raised questions about what the role of the press should be in holding government accountable. In 2019, a senior official in the Trump administration anonymously published a tell-all book, titled *A Warning*, giving an inside look at the inner workings of the White House during Donald Trump's presidency. The author was later found to be Miles Taylor, who had worked in the Department of Homeland Security.

services were regularly intercepting Russian communications, these stories highlighted disagreements within the Russian government and raised the costs of any military action.

Notwithstanding the freedom of the press guaranteed in the Bill of Rights, reporters are subject to legal limitations that present hurdles as they research stories. If the government can convince a judge that publication of a particular story would lead to immediate harm to a person or persons, a judge can halt publication. But this test sets the bar extremely high for stopping publication of a story. As we discussed in Chapter 4, most attempts to prevent publication have been unsuccessful. In addition, it is not clear as a practical matter how the legal system could control the release of information via social media.

To appreciate the issues surrounding classified information and prior restraint, consider the case of Edward Snowden. While working as a contractor for the U.S. National Security Agency (NSA), Snowden downloaded files that documented the NSA's surveillance activities, including the collection of data on Americans' phone calls overseas and the monitoring of foreign politicians' cell phones. In 2012, Snowden approached several major publications across the world, including the *Washington Post*, to offer access to these documents. After several months of negotiation, the *Post* would not agree to all of Snowden's conditions—among other things, he wanted certain documents to be published in their entirety, while the *Post* wanted to hold back some classified information.[27] Snowden then came to an agreement with a British newspaper, the *Guardian*, which gradually made the documents public, although he also allowed the *Post* to publish some of the documents.

The *Post*'s refusal to accept Snowden's demands was the product of several months of discussions with the U.S. government over what information could be released without harming national security or placing confidential sources in jeopardy. Although some government officials mentioned the possibility of invoking the prior restraint prohibition, no attempts were made to do so. In any case, even if the *Post* could have been deterred from publication, the information would have soon appeared in stories published by other outlets.

The Snowden episode illustrates how government officials work to deter leaks or influence the media's coverage of a story without resorting to prior restraint. Laws prohibit government officials' disclosure of classified information in the first place, and recent administrations have been very aggressive about prosecuting leakers. Newspapers can also face prosecution for publishing classified information. In the case of the Snowden documents, the *Post* published its story only when it was rumored that the *Guardian* planned to release its own story. Even then, *Post* reporters and editors agreed to keep certain information out of their stories.

Why do reporters and publishers restrain their stories? Sometimes they agree with the government that keeping secrets is in the national interest. For example, when the president or other administration officials visit dangerous locations such as Iraq or Afghanistan, major media outlets voluntarily agree to not report on the trip until it is officially announced. Other times reporters are rewarded for cooperating—they may get information about another government policy or be promised future access to officials. Alternatively, reporters may be coerced to back down from a story through the threat of losing future access to people in government or even going to jail.

These constraints apply only to mainstream organizations and their reporters. Groups that are anonymous or that operate outside the United States can violate these laws and norms with impunity. For example, when the international WikiLeaks group released emails and documents during the 2016 campaign that had been stolen by hackers from the Democratic National Committee, the Clinton campaign, and the Gmail account of Clinton campaign chair John Podesta, there was no way for the affected groups (or the government) to initiate legal action or otherwise prevent publication.

Thus, both legal constraints and government officials' efforts to shape the news can affect the way that the media report about politics. Politicians will try to depict their opponents as ill-advised and scandal ridden and to shape media coverage in ways that show them winning and their opponents losing. Given the multitude of media sources, it is not hard for a politician to find a reporter who is willing to write exactly what that politician wants. And that reporter may file a story whether or not they believe that the information the politician provides is true or important—the reporter may be motivated by other factors, like attracting an audience, gaining the politician's trust, or hitting a deadline.

"Why Should I Care?"

Understanding the relationship between politicians and the media is critical for evaluating the quality and accuracy of the political news you see and read. Because journalists are constrained in what they can learn about and what they can report and because politicians may try to influence what reporters say, there is no guarantee that any one media source will be able to publish a full and complete account of a political event or outcome. Under these conditions, the only way to be well informed about politics is to consult multiple sources and remember that politicians and media members both have agendas. Sometimes those agendas are similar, but often politicians and the media want different things.

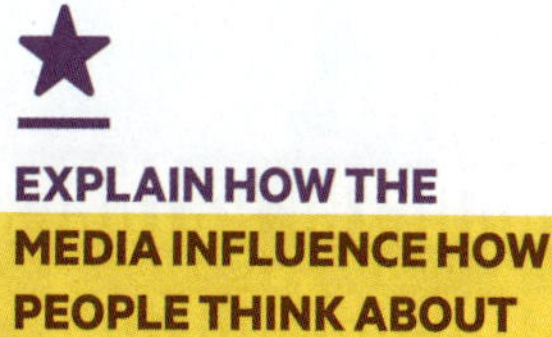

How do the media influence their audience?

The study of media effects explores whether exposure to media coverage of politics changes what people think or do (see the How It Works: graphic on pp. 268–69). There is considerable evidence that media coverage influences its audience—in simple terms, much of what Americans know about politics comes from stories they read, watch, or listen to. In part, **media effects** arise because people exposed to stories that describe a particular event learn new facts as a result of their exposure. However, some of the impact of media coverage stems not from what such stories contain but from how they present information or even whether a story is reported at all.[28]

media effects
The influence of media coverage on average citizens' opinions and actions.

Media bias and partisanship

Many studies have found that exposure to political coverage changes what citizens know: at the most basic level, people who watch, read, or listen to more coverage about politics know more than people who are exposed to less of this coverage.[29] What people learn from the media, in turn, can shape the demands they place on politicians.[30] However, at least part of the media's effect on people's knowledge level arises because of underlying interest: people who are interested in politics know more in the first place and, because of their interest, watch more media coverage of events as they happen. Moreover, because people can pick and choose which coverage to watch, read, or listen to, what they learn from the media tends to reinforce their preexisting beliefs.

How it works: in theory

How News Makes It to the Public

Editor assigns reporter to cover a particular story or event.

Filtering
Editor decides which stories are important and will attract an audience.

Reporter gathers information and prepares a story.

Framing: argument and tone
Reporter's story includes the overall argument and other information that shapes what the audience learns.

Framing: details
By describing events using some words or phrases and omitting others, the reporter has additional influence over what the audience learns.

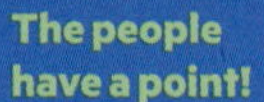

The people have a point!

Chaos in the streets!

Editor revises story, decides on length, content, and placement.

Filtering and framing
Decision about where, when, and how to carry the story gives an additional opportunity for filtering. In addition, the editor can make changes to a story that involve framing.

How it works: **in practice**

The Media's Coverage of the Build Back Better Proposal

During 2020 and 2021, many news outlets reported on candidate (and later President) Joe Biden's Build Back Better (BBB) proposal, a combination of spending on climate change mitigation, assistance to families with children, free community college tuition, and increases in other domestic spending programs. The proposal first attracted attention as a campaign promise, then as a test of Biden's ability to enact his domestic policy priorities.

Filtering
It's a story . . .

Coverage of the 2020 Biden campaign included stories on his campaign promises to **expand the child tax credit, provide free community college, and fight climate change.**

Framing
Or is it?

Other coverage of the campaign noted that even if Biden won, **he would face difficulty getting these proposals through Congress.**

Filtering
It's a call to action.

Interviews with Biden administration officials described the promises (now combined into BBB) as **helping the country recover from the COVID-19 pandemic.**

Framing
Maybe not.

Additional stories on BBB confirmed that **Republicans and moderate Democrats were strongly opposed to BBB.**

Filtering
It's impossible.

After it became clear that no **Senate Republican would vote for BBB,** media attention waned.

Framing
No, there's hope.

Coverage of BBB focused on how **Democrats could enact the program using the reconciliation process,** which required only a simple majority.

Filtering and framing
An unsuccessful bargain

Ultimately, Biden was unable to persuade moderate Democrats to support Build Back Better and the proposal died. The media emphasized the political consequences (would Biden be reelected?) rather than the policy consequences (such as the end of the child tax credit), but quickly moved on to other stories such as spread of the omicron variant of COVID-19.

Critical Thinking

1. **Of the two media effects** (filtering and framing), which is the easiest one for citizens to detect? Which one is the hardest?
2. **Do a Web search** for "Build Back Better." In the first two articles you see, find all the instances of filtering and framing. Do you think these articles provide a balanced picture of the proposal? Why or why not?

That is, a conservative might listen to Sean Hannity or watch Tucker Carlson or a program on One American News, while a liberal might watch MSNBC or listen to National Public Radio. Both people may learn something from the coverage, but the most likely result is that they will only grow more certain in the opinions that they already have.[31]

Given this evidence on media effects, one of the central questions is whether reporters and editors have a discernable bias: That is, do their decisions about which events to report on and how they report on them reflect a conscious effort to shape public opinion in a liberal, conservative, or other direction? Surveys of the American electorate have found a **hostile media effect**: regardless of respondents' partisan leanings, they believe that the media favor candidates and ideas from the other party.[32] Conservative critics of the media point to surveys that show that most reporters identify themselves as liberals. Liberal critics respond that most pundits, especially on talk radio, offer conservative points of view—and that many media sources are owned by large corporations, which could lead to underreporting of some stories, such as those offering a favorable portrayal of labor unions.[33]

hostile media effect
The tendency of people to see neutral media coverage of an event as biased against their point of view.

Questions about media bias have become more urgent since the election of Donald Trump, who criticized the media for reporting what he termed "fake news." Trump often claimed that the press was "the enemy of the American people."[34] Sometimes Trump used the "fake news" label for stories he found misleading or inaccurate, such as polls that show public disapproval of his actions in office. The deeper message of the "fake news" label is that Trump believed that media coverage of his presidency could not be trusted because reporters and their editors simply dislike him and his supporters.

It is easy to find examples of outright mistakes by reporters and their editors that suggest some sort of overt bias in coverage. For example, in December 2017 the *Washington Post* reporter Dave Weigel posted pictures on Twitter showing large numbers of empty seats at a Trump rally. However, the pictures were taken before the start of the rally; by the time it actually began, the stadium was full. After Trump complained on Twitter, Weigel apologized and published pictures showing that all the seats were taken. Similarly, as we describe in Chapter 9, most polls taken during the 2020 campaign understated support for then-president Trump. However, while

Regular White House press briefings give members of the media an opportunity to directly interact with the administration, asking questions and pressing for additional information about the president's policy agenda and priorities.

Trump and others may have seen this as evidence of a bias against him, the discussion in Chapter 6 shows how these errors reflect difficulties in determining whom citizens support and whether they plan to vote—and, moreover, that pollsters sometimes make the same mistakes when trying to assess the chances of liberal or Democratic candidates. There is no evidence that pollsters were biasing their results to hurt Trump or any other candidate. If anything, each pollster had a strong interest in accuracy—any pollster would have been gratified to have been the only one to correctly predict the 2020 results.

Many journalists and commentators admit that they take an ideological or partisan perspective. Recall the magazine *Mother Jones* discussed earlier. It's not hard to discern that its authors are writing about politics from a strongly liberal point of view. Talk show hosts Sean Hannity and Dan Bongino, for example, describe themselves as strong conservatives. And many commentators on Fox News make no secret of their conservative viewpoint—just as commentators on MSNBC make no secret of their liberal leanings.

It is also no surprise that politicians complain that media coverage is biased against them: the stakes for them are very high. For example, during the final weeks of the 2020 election, Donald Trump's campaign wanted more coverage of its claims that Joe Biden was a corrupt politician whose son and other family members had used connections to enrich themselves and less attention paid to the COVID-19 pandemic and the weak American economy. The Biden campaign in turn complained that the media were focusing too much on rumors about Biden's age and health or conflicts within the Democratic Party and not enough on Trump's missteps. Thus, while both campaigns complained about bias, the simple explanation for their complaints is that they wanted to win the election and therefore wanted media coverage that exposed their opponent's flaws rather than their candidate's flaws.

In fact, while it is easy to find media coverage of politics that is incomplete or sloppily reported, cases in which reporters made predictions that later turned out to be false, or stories that candidates wish had not been reported, it is hard to find cases of systematic bias in media coverage. President Trump often complains that reporters spend too much time searching for inconsistencies and exaggerations in his descriptions of past events, arguing that they did not scrutinize President Biden or other Democrats in the same way. Yet it is easy to find exhaustive media coverage of Biden's decision to withdraw American forces from Afghanistan, his administration's mistakes in managing the omicron variant of COVID-19, or their failure to convince moderate Democratic senators to support new spending programs.

Moreover, while some academic studies have found some evidence of press coverage favoring one type of candidate or issue position over another, an equally large body of work has produced important critiques of these studies. For one thing, a finding that most reporters are liberal (or Democrats) and few are conservative (Republicans) does not imply that political coverage must necessarily favor liberal positions or Democratic candidates. Reporters may prioritize being as objective as possible, fear that favoring one side will lose their audience, or be subject to review by editors who are on guard against bias. Similarly, the fact that a reporter criticizes a politician or party is not evidence of their lack of objectivity. Critiques do not in themselves suggest that a reporter is being unfair—the question is, what would a fair analysis look like? Many analyses of President Trump's first term (before COVID-19) acknowledged the strong American economy but gave little credit to Trump for this outcome. Were these reporters biased against Trump, or had they read the literature on political control of the economy, which shows that presidential actions have little impact on economic conditions? Untangling these effects is difficult, and if media bias were as pronounced as some critics claim, it would likely be easier to measure.

Filtering and framing

filtering
The influence on public opinion that results from journalists' and editors' decisions about which of many potential news stories to report.

framing
The influence on public opinion caused by the way a story is presented or covered, including the details, explanations, and context offered in the report.

Compared with overt bias, filtering and framing may produce subtler but stronger impacts on public opinion. **Filtering** (also called *agenda-setting*) refers to the ways in which journalists' and editors' decisions about which stories to report influence which stories people think about. **Framing** refers to how the description or presentation of a story, including the details, explanations, and context, changes the ways people react to and interpret the information. Space and time limitations mean that some filtering is inevitable as reporters and editors decide which of many potential news stories to cover. Framing can involve decisions about what to report and how to present the information. Media scholars believe that filtering and framing prime individuals—they shape the conclusions people draw both about which issues are important and how they think about them. Even if everyone in the political media adhered to the highest standards of accuracy, filtering and framing would still occur.

The concept of filtering is illustrated by Project Censored's annual list of Top Censored Stories. The group's list for 2020 and 2021 includes stories about the dangers of factory farming, threats to the Amazon rainforest, and new sources of pollution in the world's oceans.[35] The group's point is not that the government forces reporters to keep quiet; rather, it claims that reporters and their editors decide against covering these stories, sometimes for self-serving reasons, such as beliefs about what their audience wants to see or read.

The impact of filtering is also apparent in cases of government inaction. Figure 7.1 shows media coverage (as a percentage of total stories from 63,000 publications) of gun control–related stories following the 2018 shooting at Marjory Stoneman Douglas High School in Parkland, Florida. As you can see, the percentage of gun-related stories spiked upward initially, with additional spikes following student walkouts and protests, but returned to its former low level after 12 weeks. The pattern in the graph illustrates what happens when an event grabs public attention: media coverage increases in the days afterward, but the effect soon fades. Put another way, as Americans move on from thinking about a mass shooting or other event, media attention shifts with them. Whether sustained media attention would have galvanized public opinion behind stricter gun control laws is an open question. But if one effect of media coverage is to raise public awareness of an issue, people are not going to be aware of an issue the media ignore.

Reporting on violent crime in America shows clear framing effects. Over the last few years, sharp increases in homicide rates in cities such as Chicago, St. Louis, and Baltimore led to stories about lawless cities and a nationwide crime wave.[36] Notably, these stories overlooked the fact that many other cities saw homicide rates decline over the same time, and that rates of violent crime had been declining for two decades. In 2020, however, nationwide homicide rates jumped over 20 percent. How was this change framed? One set of stories attributed the rise to stresses from the COVID-19 pandemic.[37] Others focused on factors such as the need for more effective border control, the rise of drug gangs, and the need for churches to be more involved in community affairs.[38]

While the change in the murder rate is not in dispute, these examples illustrate how framing can change the inferences that people draw from a story. Depending on which story you encounter, you might think of the increased murder rate as an unwelcome

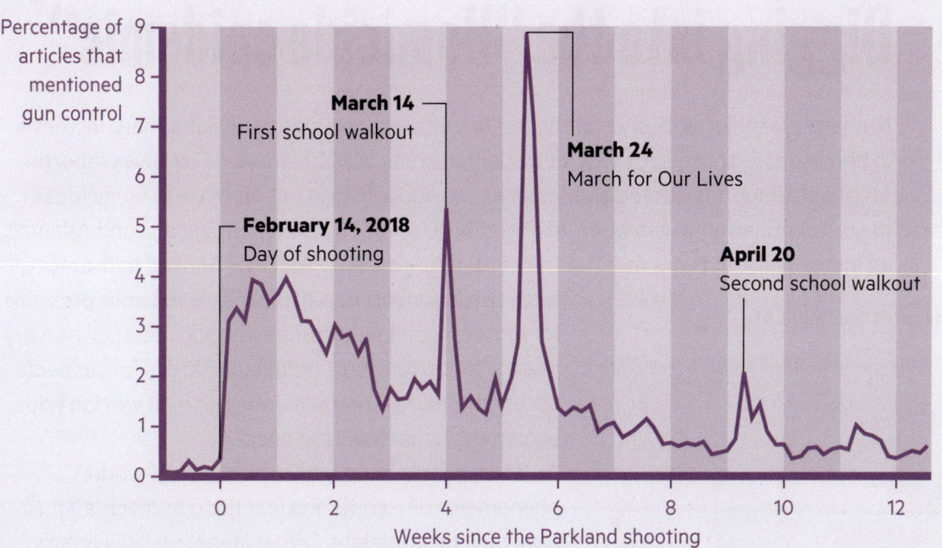

Source: Daniel Nass, "Parkland Generated Dramatically More News Coverage than Most Mass Shootings," The Trace, May 17, 2018, www.thetrace.org/2018/05/parkland-media-coverage-analysis-mass-shooting /(accessed 2/15/22).

FIGURE 7.1

Gun Control Stories per Week, February 2018 to May 2018

Press attention to gun control spikes upward after a mass shooting, then fades as reporters move on to other stories. How does this pattern help opponents of gun control legislation preserve the status quo?

consequence of COVID-19 or see it as a sign of deeper problems that require attention. Which frame is more accurate? As we discuss in the What Do The Fact Say? feature on page 274, the answer requires looking at a wider range of crime statistics.

In sum, reporting on politics requires reporters to move beyond "just the facts." They must choose what to report on, how to describe the news, whether to reveal secrets, and which sources to rely on. Moreover, events do not always speak for themselves—they require interpretation. The fact that Democrats and Republicans consult very different

The way a story is reported—which information is included in an article or which images are used—makes a big difference in what people learn from it. Stories that focus on cases of violent crime suggest an epidemic of murders, rapes, and assault, but actual data on crime rates paint a very different picture. The Black Lives Matters marches represent a prime example. Although the majority of these were peaceful protests, bad actors not connected to the movement took advantage of the crowds to loot and damage property.

WHAT DO THE FACTS SAY?

Digging into the "Homicide epidemic"

Numerous articles published in the last few years raised alarms about a sharp increase in homicides in some large U.S. metropolitan areas. A 2021 story by Fox News reporter Stephanie Pagones quoted a report that showed a 30 percent increase in homicides in major American cities between 2019 and 2020 (over 50 percent in Chicago and Atlanta), an increase the authors said "has no modern precedent."[a] In a video linked to the story, local officials attributed the increase to public pressure for more lenient law enforcement policies, such as early release for prisoners or reducing charges for suspects accused of minor crimes. As one put it, "If we don't do something, crime will take over."

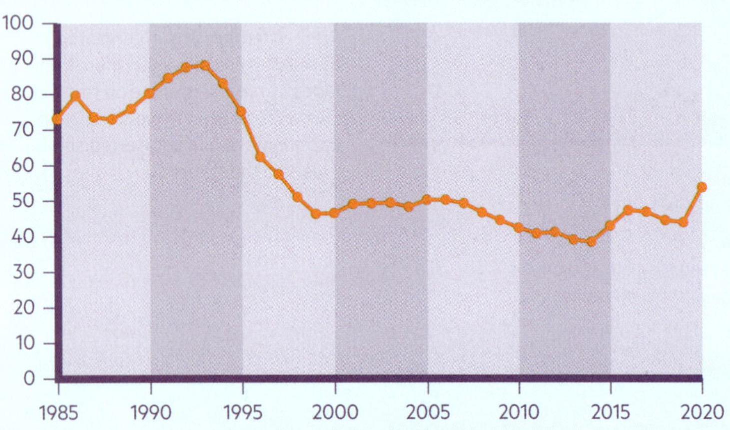

Nationwide robbery rates (per million)

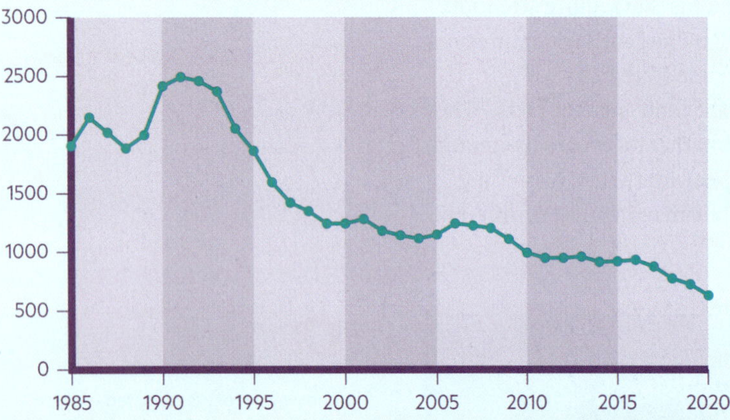

Source: Federal Bureau of Investigation Crime Data Explorer, "Expanded Homicide Offense Counts" and "Expanded Property Crime Offense Counts," September 2021, https://crime-data-explorer.app.cloud.gov/pages/explorer/crime/shr (accessed 3/23/22).

When people make a claim about a real-world phenomenon like crime, the first thing to check is if they have their facts straight. Crime rates are relatively easy to analyze because the police and medical examiners in most areas report annual statistics about crime to the FBI, which publishes national statistics. The figure to the left combines these data with Census population estimates to show the number of murders in the United States per million citizens over the last 35 years.

The nationwide data confirm part of the analysis: homicide rates were up 22.4 percent from 2019 to 2020. (The difference is because homicide rates are higher in the major urban areas discussed in the Fox story.) However, looking across 35 years of data, murder rates are on the decline, from a peak of 90 per million in the early 1990s to about 50 per million in 2020. The fact that the spike occurred in 2020, the first year of the COVID-19 pandemic, is a sign that the change may have had more to do with the stresses of the pandemic than anything else.

Support for this argument comes from looking at FBI data on robberies over time, as shown in the second figure. The data show that robberies have declined even more sharply than homicides, from 2,500 per million in the early 1990s to about 600 per million in 2020. More importantly, the robbery data show no spike in 2020. This finding is important—if lenient law enforcement policies were driving the murder spike, we would see a similar effect for robberies, and we don't.

In the end, these data do not tell us why murder rates were so high in 2020 and 2021. The authors of the study cited by Fox point to the possibility that the pandemic had a disproportionate effect on vulnerable populations. They discount the possibility that the increase was driven by protests against police brutality that occurred in summer 2020, concluding that "no simple connection exists" between crime rates and civil unrest.

The Fox story fails one of the key criteria we discussed in Chapter 1: it makes strong claims that are not confirmed by the data. In this case, even the analysis cited in the story does not support the tone or the conclusion of the Fox report. Identifying an increase in crime is one thing; explaining why crime increased is another. Always try to corroborate a story before you accept its conclusions.

Think about it

- **What additional information** might help put the change in homicide rates into context? Can you think of any comparative data points that might help make better sense of the numbers?
- **What are the dangers** of spreading misleading or incorrect information about public safety? How might these errors lead people to make uninformed decisions?

media sources (as shown in Table 7.1 on p. 261) suggests that people see different media sources as trustworthy based on their partisanship and that they are well aware of framing, filtering, and potential bias and choose their media sources accordingly. Given the vast array of political coverage in modern America, even if we take potential biases as well as filtering and framing into account, virtually all of us can find several sources that we consider reliable, if we take the time to search for those sources.[39]

"Why Should I Care?"

Americans often demand that journalists give "just the facts and all the facts" about politics and public policy. Most of the time, however, what looks like biased reporting is a journalist trying to make sense of a complex world. The act of reporting requires decisions on which stories matter, which facts deserve mention, and how events should be interpreted. To say that you don't like how a journalist resolves these decisions doesn't mean that they are pushing a particular political agenda.

ASSESS WHETHER THE MEDIA FULFILL THEIR ROLE IN AMERICAN DEMOCRACY

Do the media work?

In a democracy, the media's role is to provide citizens with information about politicians, government actions, and policy debates. It is easy to argue that the media are falling down on the job: surveys taken in recent years show that substantial percentages of Americans believe that voter fraud is a major problem, that a third of the federal budget is spent on foreign aid, that America is no longer the preeminent military power, and that undocumented immigration is on the rise. In fact, all four statements are false (actually, foreign aid spending is only about 2 percent of the federal budget).

Claims of ideological bias by mainstream media sources do not explain these shortcomings. The central finding of the political science literature on media effects is that systematic bias is hard to find. During President Trump's first term, the press gave considerable attention to anonymous sources that highlighted the president's supposed inattention to detail and unwillingness to spend time studying briefing documents. But these stories did not appear because reporters and editors are hard-core liberals (or Democrats) who wanted to destroy Trump's chances of getting reelected. Rather, coverage was driven by leaks from administration officials and by reporters' belief that Trump's work habits have a measurable effect on the quality of decisions made in the administration. The media have been similarly critical of President Biden, noting his inability to close bargains with members of Congress and his verbal gaffes during public remarks.[40]

You also have to recognize the difficulty of the task being assigned to the media. It's easy to say that the media should be objective, should give us "just the facts," and should report on both sides of an issue. But what if one side makes no sense? Some of the more bizarre QAnon theories posit that the world is being ruled by a small international cabal (led by former president John F. Kennedy, who allegedly faked his death) and that the Black Lives Matter movement and the COVID-19 pandemic were carefully orchestrated to ensure Trump's defeat in the 2020 election. Clearly, these theories do not deserve much attention—but what should reporters do when they believe that elected officials are misrepresenting the truth? Being objective may require them to advise readers that the truth lies on one side rather than in between. As the adage goes, "fair is not equal."

Lack of citizen interest

In part, the media's apparent failure to create a well-informed citizenry is driven by a lack of citizen interest. As we discussed in Chapter 6, the average American is only marginally interested in politics. Only a small percentage of Americans care enough to take the time and effort to become well informed. Everyone else learns about politics as a by-product of other things they do throughout the day.

The lack of citizen interest is one reason why the increased amount of information available on the Internet has not produced a better-informed citizenry: while information is available, average Americans make little attempt to find and understand it. As political scientist Markus Prior noted, the expansion of the Internet has increased the availability of all kinds of information, not just information about politics.[41] Not surprisingly, people gravitate to the topics they are interested in, which for most people is not politics. As a result, putting more information about politics on the Web does not make everyone better informed; rather, it widens the gap between the small percentage of Americans who care about politics and the vast majority whose interest level is much lower.

Even for people who are motivated to learn more about politics, finding information, sifting through conflicting sources, and assessing the credibility of different accounts is a difficult task, even for experts. Surveys by the Pew Research Center show that even highly interested, well-informed individuals can find it difficult to distinguish between factual and opinion statements in the news.[42] Even finding sources in the first place can be difficult. For example, suppose you want to learn more about the Black Lives Matter movement. A Google search in late 2022 of the term returned millions of Web pages, including press reports and blog entries by participants in the protests as well as by supporters and opponents. Thus, the problem is not finding information but deciding which of the millions of pages available will help you learn about the movement.

In short, despite the Internet's wealth of information, there is no guarantee that people will sit down, search for what they want or need to know, distinguish truth from falsehood, and assemble their findings into coherent conclusions. In fact, rather than creating a uniformly well-informed citizenry, the availability of information on the Internet may exacerbate the pattern we saw in Chapter 6, in which a small percentage of Americans are extremely well informed about politics, while the vast majority of the public may simply throw up their hands and make no attempt to become better informed—or focus on a relatively few sources of dubious reliability.[43]

Market forces

Another influence on media coverage is competition for an audience. Mass media sources have always tried to get as large an audience as possible in order to generate profits and stay in business, but the expansion of the Internet and the increased availability of free information have increased competitive pressures.[44] In part, these pressures have had positive effects for consumers: newspapers, for example, have put their content online and moved from publishing once per day to continually producing new stories and updates. Television stations have placed their video content online as well, including footage that was never used in broadcasts, so that people can watch at any time.

Many Americans, attracted by clickbait headlines and dramatic storylines, now get the bulk of their political news from nontraditional online sources like BuzzFeed.

One downside of audience pressures is that they lead reporters to search for stories—any stories—to have something new to offer their audience, who otherwise might get its news from somewhere else. For example, although most theories of elections show that polls taken during the early days of a political campaign are almost irrelevant, the media still cover poll results. Early on, most people know very little about the candidates, so a well-known figure, such as Donald Trump, may attract support simply because people know their name. Because reporters need something to write about, they may focus on a new poll even though they are well aware that the poll's findings are almost meaningless. The mere fact that reporters focus so much on each new poll may lead some readers to pay more attention to the findings than those findings actually deserve.

This quest for an audience also favors coverage of new, breaking issues, particularly if they involve some sort of controversy and feature well-known individuals. Political scientist Amber Boydstun has shown that this practice often leads reporters to sideline important issues in favor of newer, fresher events.[45] For example, while Afghanistan is still a place of untold human misery and political turmoil, the story has disappeared from major news outlets after the departure of American forces in summer 2021 in favor of stories on climate change, the economy, coronavirus, and whatever else happened yesterday. Afghanistan will not reappear on the front page unless something major happens, such as a terrorist attack from groups headquartered there. In the meantime, only a few Americans will even be aware of developments in the country.

More generally, audience pressures lead reporters to focus on making their stories simple and dramatic in order to catch the attention of a distracted audience. Stories that say "the state of the economy is hard to determine" or "today's events are hard to explain but almost surely will not affect who wins the election" will lose out to reports that cast events in simple, life-and-death terms. Consider media coverage of the early stages of the Democratic presidential nomination campaign, particularly the Iowa Caucuses held in February 2020. In the months before the caucuses, each debate or campaign appearance was framed in a way that made it seem significant, and thus more interesting to media audiences, as though it would provide deep insights about the candidates and their chances of winning the nomination and defeating Donald Trump. The fact is that a candidate's success in Iowa, a largely rural, racially homogenous state, does not tell us much about their prospects in other states—Joe Biden, who ultimately won the nomination, came in fourth place in this contest.

News right now is like a flock of speeded-up sheep running off the side of a cliff.

—Ali Smith, author

attack journalism
A type of increasingly popular media coverage focused on political scandals and controversies, which causes a negative public opinion of political figures.

horse race
A description of the type of election coverage that focuses more on poll results and speculation about a likely winner than on substantive differences between the candidates.

soft news
Media coverage that aims to entertain or shock, often through sensationalized reporting or by focusing on a candidate or politician's personality.

hard news
Media coverage focused on facts and important issues surrounding a campaign.

The media's efforts to spin a story to attract an audience are nothing new.[46] For decades, scholars have documented the rise of **attack journalism**, in which journalists focus on scandal, government failures, and politicians' personal failings.[47] Other researchers have argued that campaign coverage overemphasizes the **horse race** aspects, such as which candidates are ahead and which are falling behind, rather than offering a complete description of each candidate's promises and an analysis of how they are likely to behave in office.[48] Similarly, coverage of debates over public policy often focuses on personalities and predictions about who is likely to achieve their goals, not the details of what the policies include. Media coverage of politics also emphasizes **soft news** (stories that are sensational or entertaining) over **hard news** (stories that focus on important issues and emphasize facts and figures).[49] The media also often give disproportionate coverage to events that are more likely to be recognized by the average American. For example, media coverage of Hurricane Harvey, which hit land in Texas in 2017, was much more extensive than coverage of Hurricane Maria, which devastated Puerto Rico only a month later—and both of these disasters were covered far more aggressively than the far more deadly monsoon storms in Bangladesh that occurred at the same time.[50]

The pressure on journalists to publish as quickly as possible can also lead to major mistakes—in January 2019, initial stories on a confrontation involving high school students who attended an anti-abortion rally in Washington, D.C., and a Native American elder who was a counterprotester at the event alleged that the students had harassed the elder and used racial slurs. After several days of coverage, video of the incident showed that these claims were false. Some major outlets (including the *Washington Post*) had to issue major clarifications of their reporting, and at least one outlet (CNN) settled a lawsuit brought by one of the students.

Why do journalists ignore details and emphasize scandal? Describing the media as an information source for citizens makes sense in terms of how American politics works, but this description does not capture the sometimes-contradictory incentives that journalists face. They may feel the need to demonstrate their independence from politicians and government interests and perhaps counter or prevent claims of media bias. And this may lead to aggressive questioning of elected officials and cynical stories about the political process.[51] But again, reporters and their editors are in a competitive business to attract a paying audience.[52] Most American media outlets are for-profit enterprises. Because they need to produce coverage that attracts an audience, they often seek to create stories that consumers want. So if the media focus on something that seems frivolous, like Joe Biden's favorite food (ice cream) or First Lady Jill Biden's fashion choices (masks coordinated with her outfit), it is because these stories find a ready audience.

Even if reporters for major news outlets tried to explain how our democratic government works or the complexity of most policy questions, it is unlikely that citizens would respond favorably. There are sources available that work this way. The nightly television program *PBS NewsHour* has a reputation for producing thoughtful, in-depth stories about politics and policy. The magazine *Congressional Quarterly* is well-known among Congress scholars for its analysis of House and Senate proceedings. But the audience for these sources is minuscule, which is another indication that most people would prefer soft news, cynicism, and scandals to hard news, policy details, and sober analysis (see the Take a Stand feature on p. 279 for the debate over Facebook's plan to allow users to "grade" the news).

Thus, complaints about how the media cover American politics are to a large extent misdirected. The media give Americans the coverage they want. If the average citizen wants to become an expert on politics and public policy, the necessary information is surely available. But few people are interested in seeking that degree

TAKE
A STAND

Should Facebook Grade the News?

As we have discussed in this chapter, most Americans are exposed to only a small fraction of the media's coverage of American politics. Because people read or watch only a limited number of stories, it is especially important for them to judge the reliability of the sources they consult. Do the stories include the right facts? Are the facts being presented fairly? Is the coverage shaped by the authors' conscious or unconscious biases? These are not easy questions to resolve, especially for the typical American who is not highly interested in politics and who has other demands on their time.

Facebook, one of the most common channels through which people get their news, has suggested a solution to this problem. It proposes to ask a sample of Facebook users two questions: Do you recognize a particular media source, and how trustworthy do you rate that source? Facebook would use the results of the survey to determine which stories are promoted in News Feeds. Users looking at their News Feeds would then be able to focus on stories from sources that were rated as highly trustworthy and would not be exposed to stories from sources that received low trust scores. Facebook hopes that by filtering the news stories it promotes in this way, it can help users become more informed about politics.

It's a great idea. By asking a random sample of users, Facebook is letting the mass public express its feelings about which information sources it would like to see. While some people might be biased in favor of one source or another, the hope is that these biases will average out over a large sample, ultimately highlighting more neutral sources. Presumably, the survey results would also favor sources that produce simple, easy-to-understand stories. Conversely, if a panel of experts were consulted to pick the "best" sources for news, it might choose sources that generate overly complicated political analyses that the average Facebook user might ignore entirely or misinterpret. Thus, the mass survey is more likely to identify a set of sources that people will actually use if put in front of them. Of course, it would be great if seeing a political story on Facebook prompted a user to investigate further by going to other sites that offer more details and deeper analysis. But Facebook's trustworthiness surveys will increase the chances that people receive accurate information about politics, even if the amount is relatively small.

Many people have blamed Facebook for facilitating the circulation of "fake news" from untrustworthy sources.

It could make things worse. Facebook's survey strategy assumes that the biggest problem with individuals' assessments of media sources is that they favor sources that support their preferred candidates or policy proposals. Its hope is that these biases will cancel each other out in a large survey. However, the average American's media consumption is shaped by a variety of conscious and unconscious biases. People tend to trust the sources they regularly consult and distrust sources they have never heard of or have only seen a few times. They favor sources that simplify complex stories and deliver information in easy-to-read graphics. And most fundamentally, people like sources that reinforce their beliefs and dislike sources that challenge what they think or force them to learn new ways of thinking about an issue. Facebook's solution may not account for all of these additional biases. Rating sources by their perceived trustworthiness might well lead to a situation in which people think they are better informed, when in fact they are just as uninformed as they were before Facebook's efforts.

take a stand

1. Why do you think Americans are uninformed about political events? Will Facebook's trustworthiness ratings address this problem?
2. Suppose Facebook chose you to participate in its survey. Which media sources would you rate as trustworthy? Which would you rate as untrustworthy? How many would you have no opinion about?
3. What do you think motivated Facebook to begin its media evaluation initiative? Do you think Facebook is likely to succeed?

of understanding. For most Americans, the media's coverage of politics as a sports event is enough to keep them satisfied, even as they complain about a lack of details and an emphasis on scandal.

"Why Should I Care?"

Reporters compete for an audience—that's how they stay in business. That means that stories you consider important (or that really are important) may not get media attention because they're too hard to explain or because people aren't interested. The only way to get more detailed, thoughtful political coverage is for Americans to start demanding it.

Unpacking the Conflict

How hard is it to find accurate information about the state of the COVID-19 pandemic, a list of effective treatments, or the pros and cons of vaccines? How has an increase in available information produced higher levels of confusion and misunderstanding? All this information can be found with a little searching, including current caseloads, hospitalizations, and deaths, as well as evidence-based findings about vaccines and medications. But if you are like most in terms of how much time you spend following the media, you could be forgiven for ending your search more confused than when you started. The transformation of modern media was supposed to increase citizen knowledge and reduce the power of conspiracy theories—what went wrong?

The idea that the rise of the Internet would help create a better-informed population assumed that people would gravitate to reliable mainstream media sources and take the time needed to assimilate the fire-hose of new information generated each day. The producers of media content, from mainstream sources like the *New York Times* to anonymous Twitter users who post insider information about government agency decisions, should all work toward the goal of empowering the American public. The reality is that the media are businesses, in which the goal of attracting an audience often conflicts with the more idealistic goals of telling people what they need to know to make good decisions and acting as a watchdog to monitor government actions. Americans might be better informed if the media ignored sensational stories and focused on the details of public policy, but lurid stories help attract and keep an audience that media companies need to stay in business. Americans will get different media coverage only if they value sources that emphasize details and complexity over scandals and drama.

Social media advocates were right about the ways the media would change—but they were wrong about how citizens would react. Even now, most Americans behave as they always have, consulting a few trusted sources for information about politics. The fact that much more information is available now has not changed our consumption habits. The value of gathering additional information is simply not worth the trouble, especially given the need to reconcile different sources.

For all of these reasons, America's news media often fall short of the goal of acting as a watchdog, making sure people have the information they need to bring government policy in line with their interests. Though social media has changed many aspects of our lives, it has not changed this fundamental truth about American politics: we cannot blame people for refusing to take advantage of what the media offer them, but at the same time we cannot blame the media for citizens' ignorance and misinformation.

"What's Your Take?"

Should the media be judged based on the wealth of information it provides or on its failure to increase citizens' political knowledge?

Should Americans put more trust in the media?

CHECK YOUR UNDERSTANDING

"Why Should I Care?"

It is easy to make a case for why we should care about the media. When an important event or political development happens across the country or on the other side of the globe, the media are our best bet for hearing about it in the first place, understanding what it means, and tracking the situation as it unfolds. Without the media, our worlds would be much smaller, limited to only those pieces of information we experience directly or that we hear from friends. And without the media serving their particular role of watchdog, many policy problems would go unnoticed, and many corrupt politicians would go unchecked.

Yet our familiarity with the media might also make us take for granted how very powerful this "fourth branch" of government is and how much the shifting media landscape matters for politics and society. The media have the power to shine a spotlight on issues and social developments that deserve our attention. Under the right circumstances, they have the power to influence which events, issues, and politicians we think about and even *how* we think about them. The media have, in other words, the power to move hearts, minds, and nations.

How media employ this power, however, is determined in large part by the rules that do (or do not) govern them and by the incentives at play. The media's role in American politics is much different today, for example, than it was during the time of the Alien and Sedition Acts, or when the Federal Communications Commission still had the fairness doctrine and limits on media conglomerates in place. Today, media sources compete for our attention in a much more crowded field, against the backdrop of fast-paced social media, and in an increasingly partisan political climate. The result is that news reporting is getting shorter, less detailed, and more "clickbait-y"; the line between fact and opinion is increasingly blurry; and misinformation is all too easy to find.

These traits of the modern media system help explain why so few Americans trust the media. But we would argue that the answer isn't to give up on the news and recede to watching only YouTube and TikTok—where political information is still likely to sneak through! Instead, we'd recommend a diverse informational diet, including adorable cats on TikTok but also traditional news (and subscribing to your local newspaper if you can afford it). But wherever you get your news, pay attention to the political and informational preferences of each outlet's audience, which in turn likely influence the content. The media do an excellent job giving us what we want, so we can encourage them to give us better content by voting with our clicks.

1. As an institution, the professional media have both promoted and restrained government agendas by

- **a** highlighting wrongdoing by public officials and shortfalls in public services.
- **b** including both liberal and conservative perspectives among their guest personalities.
- **c** promoting controversial and entertaining topics related to policy making and political figures.
- **d** making space for the voicing of public opinion in letters to the editor and opinion-editorial pieces.

2. Americans have greater political exposure in all aspects of their life than ever before in history, but the primary impact of the Internet has been to

- **a** increase the overall knowledge and understanding citizens have about the role of government in their daily lives.
- **b** blur the lines between political fact and fiction because of the overwhelming availability of information without standards for posting.
- **c** expand major television and newspaper organizations due to increases in readers and viewers from large Internet followings.
- **d** lessen the ideological divisions between groups of American voters.

3. The decision of House members to hold public committee hearings during prime-time television viewing hours would best reflect which of the following?

- **a** Internet availability has driven Congress and mass media to try to create more specialized programming.
- **b** The media are willing to work collaboratively with the government in determining whether to release leaked classified information.
- **c** Elected officials may sometimes leak information to reporters to judge the public's reaction.
- **d** Political leaders seek to influence media narratives by creating carefully structured events.

4. Many political candidates run for office by portraying the professional media as an "enemy" driven by political bias. However, the reality is that

- **a** the Internet has made the mass media more equitable to all political ideologies.
- **b** reporters at media companies are critical of politicians of both parties.
- **c** professional journalists generally portray political leaders as positive figures.
- **d** public officials are increasingly returning to traditional media outlets for coverage rather than social media.

5. A person reading through the top international story on the Web page of a major national newspaper is given information that helps the person understand the context of the events as well as potential impacts on American diplomacy and international trade. The person has experienced which of the following effects of the media's need to determine how to use space and time limitations efficiently?

- **a** Hostile media effect
- **b** By-product theory
- **c** Framing
- **d** Yellow journalism

6. Conflict between groups with differing political ideologies is unlikely to decline because

- **a** the increasing number of information sources allows people to choose sources that reinforce their existing beliefs.
- **b** media consolidation has pushed more Americans into one of the two main ideological groups.
- **c** filtering of news stories is increasing American frustration with the one-sided reporting in the media.
- **d** citizen journalism has increased the number of reliable politically diverse sources of news.

7. According to researchers, the mass media in the United States have a bias that favors ___________ rather than ___________.

- **a** Democrats; Republicans
- **b** individuality; communalism
- **c** economic interests; political interests
- **d** editorial opinions; journalistic objectivity

8. The ability of Americans to make sense of political conflict, understand the processes of government, and see how politics shapes their daily lives increased remarkably with the expansive educational media resources online. What did this ultimately result in?

- **a** A growing gap between people who are interested and average Americans
- **b** Greater distribution of knowledge across the American population
- **c** Increased partisan polarization and tribalism among ideological groups
- **d** Expansion of voter participation in primary and general elections

Use INQUIZITIVE *to help you study and master this material.*

8

Political Parties

How do political parties organize American politics?

"Our diversity is our strength, our unity is our power."[1]
Speaker of the House Nancy Pelosi (D-CA)

"I've got news for the Republican establishment. I've got news for the Democratic establishment. They can't stop us."[2]
Senator Bernie Sanders (I-VT)

The power and limits of American political parties are best illustrated by the 2024 Democratic presidential nomination contest. The incumbent, Joe Biden, ran for reelection with only token opposition, receiving over 85% of the votes cast. Biden even won the New Hampshire primary running as a write-in candidate. Biden dominated the contest even though some groups within the Democratic party disagreed with some of his policy choices, such as support for Israel's strikes in Gaza, which killed more than 40,000 people, in retaliation for Hamas's October 7, 2023 attacks on the country. There were also real questions about Biden's age (81) and his ability to govern effectively for another term.

Democratic doubts increased exponentially after Biden performed poorly in a June 2024 debate with former President Trump. Over the next three weeks, an increasing but small number of Democratic politicians called for Biden to step aside—and many more made similar calls in private. But it was ultimately Biden's decision to make. No one in the party had the power to force him to end his reelection campaign—which he did, stepping aside and endorsing his Vice President, Kamala Harris.

Joe Biden's experience is an example of what political scientist Julia Azari calls "strong partisanship, weak parties."[3] On the one hand, decades of research have shown that most Americans have a long-term attachment to one of the major parties and that this attachment shapes their political behavior—even if they say they are voting for the better candidate rather than according to their party identification. Parties organize elections: although President Trump campaigned in 2016 as a political outsider, he won the presidency as the candidate of the Republican Party. And once candidates are elected to office, parties are also players in the legislative process. Congressional party leaders, such as Senate Majority Leader Chuck Schumer or House Speaker Nancy Pelosi during the 117th Congress, are important spokespeople and dealmakers. In these ways, parties unify and

During the 2020 Democratic primary, the field was initially crowded with several candidates from a variety of backgrounds. Ultimately, Joe Biden won the nomination and defeated incumbent president Donald Trump.

CHAPTER GOALS

Define *political parties* and show how American political parties and party systems have evolved over time (pp. 286–291)

Describe the main characteristics of American parties as organizations, in the government, and in the electorate (pp. 291–302)

Explain the important functions that parties perform in the political system (pp. 302–315)

Evaluate whether the American party system enhances or hinders democracy (pp. 315–318) mobilize disparate groups, simplify the choices that voters face, and bring efficiency and coherence to government policy making.

On the other hand, American political parties often seem powerless. With President Biden, Democratic party leaders could hint and signal and express doubts to the media, but because Biden was the presumptive Democratic nominee, there was no way for the party to take the seat away from him. Biden had won all of the convention delegates at stake in the nomination contests, so it was truly his decision to make.

Even after getting elected, presidents have often had conflictual relationships with their parties. President Biden had to change many of his legislative proposals to win support from moderate Democrats. And even though Donald Trump won in 2016 on promises to fully repeal Obamacare, build a wall at the Mexican border, and reform federal welfare programs, he was largely unsuccessful—even with Republican control of the presidency and both houses of Congress after his election in 2016. Over the past two years, Democratic party leaders in the House and Senate have faced a daunting task in trying to build winning coalitions given extraordinarily small majorities, with Republicans working to frustrate these efforts. Democrats succeeded in some areas, although many of their victories were far more modest than what was originally proposed, and most were enacted with only Democratic votes. The narrow partisan split in the upcoming Congress means that legislative victories in Congress will look much the same, with little bipartisan support and extensive negotiation required to produce winning coalitions.

Our task in this chapter is to understand that American political parties can simultaneously be strong and weak, or influential yet disliked and irrelevant. Why is it impossible to describe American politics without talking about Republicans and Democrats? At the same time, why do the parties seem like bystanders as nominees are chosen and policies are debated?

DEFINE *POLITICAL PARTIES* AND SHOW HOW AMERICAN POLITICAL PARTIES AND PARTY SYSTEMS HAVE EVOLVED OVER TIME

What are political parties and where did today's parties come from?

Political parties are organizations that run candidates for political office and coordinate the actions of officials elected under the party banner.[4] Looking around the world, we see, as political scientist David Karol says, "where there is democracy, there are political parties."[5] However, the structure and function of these parties vary. In many western European countries, the major political parties have millions of dues-paying members and party leaders control what their elected officials do. These countries typically have several major parties competing for office. In contrast, candidates in many new democracies run as representatives of a party, but party leaders have no control over what candidates say during the campaign or how they act in office.

America's two major political parties, the Republican Party and the Democratic Party, lie somewhere between these extremes. Rather than being unified organizations with party leaders at the top, candidates and party workers in the middle, and citizen-members at the bottom, American political parties are decentralized, each one a loose network of organizations, groups, and individuals who share a party label but are under no obligation to work together.[6] The **party organization** is the structure of national, state, and local parties, including party leaders and workers. The **party in government** is made up of the politicians who are elected as candidates of the party. And the **party in the electorate**

party organization
A specific political party's leaders and workers at the national, state, and local levels.

party in government
The group of officeholders who belong to a specific political party and were elected as candidates of that party.

party in the electorate
The group of citizens who identify with a specific political party.

includes all the citizens who identify with the party. For example, the Republican Party's national organization, the Republican National Committee (RNC), functions independently of Republican leaders in government like Senate Minority Leader Mitch McConnell during the 118th Congress; neither one is in charge of the other. In fact, many Republican politicians refused to endorse former President Trump in the 2024 election. Yet, although McConnell is the leader of Republican senators, he cannot tell them what to do. While McConnell's colleagues may be somewhat sympathetic to his arguments, there is no political compulsion to do what he asks. For example, McConnell was unable to prevent Republican senator Rick Scott in March 2022 from proposing an alternate policy agenda for Senate Republicans to run on in the 2022 midterms, which was a direct challenge to McConnell's strategy of deferring discussions about an agenda until after the election. Moreover, while many Americans think of themselves as members of a political party, someone who identifies with the Republican Party is not obligated to work for or give money to the party or to vote for its candidates. As you will see, organization matters: the fact that American political parties are split into three parts has important implications for what they do and for their impact on the nation's politics.

American political parties have three largely separate components: the party organization, represented here by Ronna Romney McDaniel, chair of the RNC; the party in government, represented here by Speaker of the House Nancy Pelosi and Senate Majority Leader Chuck Schumer during the 117th Congress; and the party in the electorate, exemplified here by the crowd, led by Bernie Sanders, at a rally for congressional candidate Nina Turner in Ohio.

History of American political parties

The Republican and Democratic parties have existed for a long time—the Republicans since 1854 and the Democrats since the early 1800s. Over this time, the parties have been transformed in every respect except their names. These changes are the first important clue about the nature of American political parties: there is nothing inevitable about what the parties stand for, the types of candidates who run under each party's banner, and the groups that support each party. The sharply polarized parties in today's America did not exist a generation ago. American political parties may look very different in the future.

The Republican and Democratic parties have survived throughout most of American history even though they often have not been very popular, even among their supporters. Their survival is partly due to state and local laws that make it easier for candidates to get on the ballot if they run as a major-party candidate. Both parties also work to find good candidates and raise money for their campaigns. In addition, as we discuss later, the fact that America elects officeholders from states or geographic districts makes it harder for new parties to form, keeping the two existing parties in place, a result known as Duverger's Law.[7]

Political scientists use the term **party system** to describe periods of time when the major parties' names, their groups of supporters, and the issues dividing them have all been constant (the beginning and end years that we use throughout this section are approximate). As Table 8.1 on page 288 shows, there have been six party systems in America.[8] For each party system, the table gives the names of the two major parties, indicates which party dominated (won the most presidential elections or controlled Congress), and describes the principal issues dividing the parties.

party system
Periods in which the names of the major political parties, their supporters, and the issues dividing them have remained relatively stable.

TABLE 8.1

American Party Systems

There have been six party systems in the United States since 1789.

Party system	Major parties (dominant party in boldface)	Key issues
First (1789–1828)	Federalists, Democratic-Republicans (neither party was dominant)	Location of the capital, financial issues (e.g., national bank)
Second (1829–1856)	**Democrats**, Whigs	Tariffs (farmers vs. merchants), slavery
Third (1857–1896)	Democrats, **Republicans**	Slavery (pre–Civil War), Reconstruction (post–Civil War), industrialization
Fourth (1897–1932)	Democrats, **Republicans**	Industrialization, immigration
Fifth (1933–1968)	**Democrats**, Republicans	Size and scope of the federal government
Sixth (1969–present)	Democrats, Republicans (neither party is dominant)	Size and scope of the federal government, civil rights, social issues, foreign policy

Source: Compiled by the authors.

There's no evidence from decades of Pew Research surveys that public opinion, in the aggregate, is more extreme now than in the past. But what has changed—and pretty dramatically—is the growing tendency of people to sort themselves into political parties based on their ideological differences.

—Pew Research Center

The Evolution of American Political Parties While most of the Founders held a dim view of political parties, many of them participated in the formation of such parties soon after the Founding of the United States. The Federalists and the Democratic-Republicans were primarily parties in government that consisted of like-minded legislators: Federalists wanted a strong central government and a national bank; Democratic-Republicans took the opposite positions. These political parties were quite different from their modern counterparts. There were no national party organizations, few citizens thought of themselves as party members, and candidates for office did not campaign as representatives of a party. Even so, the goals of those who developed these parties were similar to those of party leaders today: like-minded individuals banded together to help enact their preferred policies and defeat their opponents.

For two decades, the two parties were more or less evenly matched in Congress, although the Federalists did not win a presidential contest after 1800. However, in the 1814 elections Federalist legislators, who had opposed the War of 1812 and supported a politically unpopular pay raise for members of Congress, lost most of their congressional seats.[9] These defeats led to the demise of the Federalist Party and the start of the Era of Good Feelings, when there was only one political party: the Democratic-Republican Party. Following the election of President Andrew Jackson in 1828, this party became known as the Democratic Party. At the same time, another new party, the Whig Party, was formed in opposition to Democratic policy priorities, beginning the second party system.

The new Democratic Party cultivated electoral support by building organizations to mobilize citizens and bind them to the party. The operations of the party reflected two new concepts: the **party principle**, the idea that a party is not just a group of elected officials but an organization that exists apart from its candidates, and the **spoils system**, whereby party workers were rewarded with benefits such as federal jobs.[10]

party principle
The idea that a political party exists as an organization distinct from its elected officials or party leaders.

spoils system
The practice of rewarding party supporters with benefits like federal government positions.

In the 1840s, the issue of slavery split the second party system. Most Democratic politicians either supported slavery outright or wanted to avoid debating the issue.[11] The Whig Party was split between abolitionists, who wanted to end slavery, and politicians who agreed with the Democrats. Ultimately, antislavery Whigs left the party and formed the Republican Party, which also attracted antislavery Democrats, and the Whig Party soon ceased to exist. These changes initiated the third party system, in which the country was divided into a largely Republican Northeast, a largely Democratic South, and politically split midwestern and border states.[12] These developments illustrate that political parties exist not because the Constitution or laws say they must, but because elites, politicians, party leaders, and activists want them to. The Republican Party was created by people who wanted to abolish slavery, and many other politicians subsequently joined the party because of their ambition: these politicians believed that their chances of winning political office were higher as Republicans than as Whigs or Democrats.

After the Civil War, the Republicans and Democrats remained the two prominent national parties. They were divided over whether the federal government should help farmers and rural residents or inhabitants of rapidly expanding cities and whether it should regulate America's rapidly growing industrial base. Democrats built a coalition of rural and urban voters by proposing a larger, more active federal government, as well as other policies that would help both groups.

This strategy is one example of how American political parties have adapted their issue positions to societal changes and consequently reflect the basic political divisions between Americans. A similar shift occurred during the transition to the fourth party system, in which the parties were divided on the government's response to industrialization and restrictions on immigration. In part, this shift reflected the formation of two short-lived political parties, the Progressives and the Populists. As these parties began to gather support, Democratic and Republican candidates modified their campaign platforms to accommodate the new party's issue positions, thereby preserving their position as the two main political parties. There were also significant moves during this time in expanding who was eligible to vote, although women did not gain this right until the early twentieth century, and other historically marginalized groups were generally barred by a combination of laws and practices until the 1960s.[13]

"THAT'S WHAT'S THE MATTER."
Boss Tweed. "As long as I count the Votes, what are you going to do about it? say?"

The Tammany Hall political machine, depicted here as a rotund version of one of its leaders, William "Boss" Tweed, controlled New York City politics for most of the nineteenth and early twentieth centuries. Its strategy was "honest graft," rewarding party workers, contributors, and voters for their efforts to keep the machine's candidates in office.

The fifth party system was born out of the Great Depression: the worldwide economic collapse that led to the unemployment of millions of people. Many Republicans argued that conditions would improve over time and that government intervention would do little good, whereas Democrats proposed new programs that would help people in need and spur economic growth. The Democratic landslide in the 1932 election led to the New Deal, a series of federal programs proposed by President Franklin Delano Roosevelt and enacted by Congress to stimulate the national economy, help needy people, and impose a variety of new regulations on businesses. Debate over the New Deal brought together the New Deal coalition of Black Americans, Catholics, Jews, union members, and White southerners, who became strong supporters of Democratic candidates over the next generation.[14] This transformation established one of the basic divisions between the parties that exists to the present day: Democrats generally favor a large federal government that takes an active role in managing the economy and regulating behavior, and Republicans generally believe that many such programs should be provided by state and local governments or not provided at all.

The move from the fifth to the sixth party system was marked by the introduction of new political questions and debates that divided the parties.[15] Beginning in the late 1940s, many Democratic candidates and party leaders, particularly outside the South, came out against the "separate but equal" system of racial discrimination in southern states and in favor of programs designed to ensure equal opportunity for historically marginalized citizens. Then, during the 1960s, many Democratic politicians argued for expanding the role of the federal government in health care, antipoverty programs, and education. Most Republicans opposed such initiatives, although a significant portion did not.

At the same time, these new issues also began to divide American citizens and organized groups, leading to a gradual but significant shift in the groups that identified with each party.[16] White southerners and some Catholics moved to the Republican

Debate over Roosevelt's New Deal programs established the basic divide between Democrats and Republicans that continues to this day: in the main, Democrats favor a larger federal government that takes an active role in managing the economy; Republicans prefer a smaller federal government and fewer programs and regulations.

realignment
A change in the size or composition of the party coalitions or in the nature of the issues that divide the parties. Realignments typically occur within an election cycle or two, but they can also occur gradually over the course of a decade or longer.

Party, and members of historically marginalized groups, particularly Black Americans, started identifying more strongly as Democrats. Democrats also gained supporters in New England and West Coast states. By the late 1980s, all three elements of the Republican and Democratic parties (organization, government, and electorate) were much more like-minded than they had been a generation earlier, a trend that continues to the present day.

Broadly speaking, Democrats tend to favor a larger government that provides more benefits to citizens and regulates corporate and individual behavior, while Republicans advocate for a small government that does less. However, there are exceptions to these rules. On many social issues such as abortion and LGBTQIA+ rights, most Democrats favor individual choice and equality, while most Republicans favor limits on abortion and oppose equality for same-sex couples on issues such as marriage and adoption.[17] Moreover, as the 2020 Democratic presidential nomination contest demonstrates, issues such as expanding government-provided health care divide candidates and their supporters within each party.

The sixth party system also brought changes in party organizations. Both the Republican and Democratic parties increased their involvement in recruiting, training, conducting fund-raising, and campaigning for their party's congressional and presidential candidates in an effort to elect like-minded colleagues who would vote with them to enact their preferred policies.[18] At the same time, disagreements between congressional Republicans and Democrats increased, making it harder to find common ground in many policy areas.

Realignments Each party system is separated from the next by a **realignment**, a change in one or more of the factors that define a party system, including the issues that divide the parties, the nature and function of the party organizations, the composition of the party coalitions, and the specifics of government policy. Early work on realignments argued that realignments began with the emergence of a new question or issue debate that captured the attention of large numbers of ordinary citizens, activists, and politicians.[19] To spur a realignment, the issue had to be *crosscutting*, meaning that within each party coalition there were people who disagreed on what government should do about this new issue. These pressures culminated in a high-turnout election in which the parties took clear stands on the new issues (or a new party emerged) and voters switched parties based on which stand they liked best. Scholars also believed that realignments developed about a generation apart, as citizens who came of age as a past realignment occurred were replaced by new voters.

More recent work, particularly by political scientist David Mayhew, has shown that none of these conditions are necessary for a realignment.[20] Realignments don't happen once in a generation like clockwork, don't always involve a single crosscutting issue, and don't always occur all at once. It may be impossible to know that a realignment is happening until it has already occurred. A good example of what Mayhew is talking about is the change between the fifth (1933–1968) and the sixth (1969–present) party system.[21] Parties in the fifth party system were primarily divided by their positions on the appropriate size of the federal government. In the sixth party system, new issues such as civil rights and social issues as well as gender equality and abortion became more important markers of division between the parties and their supporters.[22] However, these changes only became apparent in the 1990s, as Republicans gained House and Senate seats in southern states, and Democrats gained seats in the Northeast, West, and Southwest.[23] After the 2022 elections, Republicans controlled no Senate seats in New England, while there were only a handful of Democratic senators in the South (two in Virginia).

Trump's election in 2016 and Joe Biden's victory in 2020 and Kamala Harris's in 2024 suggest that America may be beginning to develop a new party system. Other evidence for this possibility includes emerging Democratic support in coastal states and the Southwest, Republican gains in the Midwest, and new splits within each party coalition on issues such as trade, immigration, and a more aggressive role for government in providing health care and other benefits to citizens. It is too soon to tell, however, whether these changes will be significant enough to realign the parties, or even to replace one party with a new organization, particularly given the large and unexpected role that the COVID-19 pandemic played in the 2020 and 2022 elections.

"Why Should I Care?"

Looking at American political parties today, you might think that Democratic and Republican parties have been around forever, that they are evenly split in party identifiers and officeholders, and that their main disagreement has always concerned the size and scope of government. None of these ideas is true. Moreover, the changes over time in the Republican and Democratic parties illustrate how these organizations adapt to shifts in public opinion. Thus, American political parties may look very different 10 years from now than they do today.

DESCRIBE THE MAIN CHARACTERISTICS OF AMERICAN PARTIES AS ORGANIZATIONS, IN THE GOVERNMENT, AND IN THE ELECTORATE

American political parties today

We've seen that, almost from the beginning, political parties have been a central feature of American politics. The next steps are to examine the different aspects (the party organization, the party in government, and the party in the electorate) of American political parties, describe the role they play in elections and in government, and understand how their organization and operations shape American democracy.

The party organization

The principal body in each party organization is the **national committee** (the Democratic National Committee or the Republican National Committee), which consists of representatives from state party organizations, usually one man and one woman per state. The state party organizations in turn are made up of professional staff plus thousands of party organizations at the county, city, and town levels. The job of these organizations is to run the party's day-to-day operations, recruit candidates and supporters, raise money for future campaigns, and work to build a consensus on major issues. (Of course, other groups in the party, as well as individual politicians, carry out similar tasks at the same time and not always in agreement with the national or state committees.)

national committee
An American political party's principal organization, comprising party representatives from each state.

Both national party committees include several *constituency groups* (the Democrats' term) or *teams* (the Republicans' term). These organizations within the party work to attract the support of demographic groups or organizations—such as Black Americans, Latinos, people with strong religious beliefs, labor unions, senior citizens, women, and many others—who are considered likely to share the party's issue concerns and to assist in fund-raising.[24] In some cases, these organizations also attempt to win over groups typically identified with the other party. For example, Black Americans have long been strong supporters of Democratic candidates. Accordingly, the Democratic Party has a constituency group that informs Black Americans about the party's candidates and works to convince these citizens to vote on Election Day. The group also gives Black leaders a formal voice in party deliberations.

Each party organization also includes groups designed to build support for, or coordinate the efforts of, individuals or politicians. These groups include the Democratic and the Republican Governors' Associations, the Young Democrats, the Young Republicans, and more specialized groups such as the Republican Lawyers' Organization or the Democratic Leadership Council (DLC), an organization of moderate Democratic politicians.[25] The parties use their college and youth organizations to motivate politically minded students to work for the party and its candidates. Groups such as the Governors' Associations and the DLC hold meetings where elected officials discuss solutions to common problems and try to formulate joint strategies. People who work for a party organization perform a wide range of tasks, from recruiting candidates and formulating political strategies to mobilizing citizens, conducting fund-raising, filling out campaign finance reports, researching opposing candidates and parties, and developing websites for the party and its candidates.

political action committee (PAC)
An interest group or a division of an interest group that can raise money to contribute to campaigns or to spend on ads in support of candidates. The amount a PAC can receive from each of its donors and the amount it can spend on federal electioneering are strictly limited.

527 organization
A tax-exempt group formed primarily to influence elections through voter mobilization efforts and to issue ads that do not directly endorse or oppose a candidate. Unlike PACs, 527 organizations are not subject to contribution limits and spending caps.

Other Allied Groups Many other groups, such as **political action committees (PACs)** or **527 organizations**, labor unions, and other interest groups and organizations, are loosely affiliated with one of the major parties. For example, the organization MoveOn.org typically supports Democratic candidates. Similar organizations on the Republican side include the Club for Growth, Americans for Prosperity, Crossroads GPS, and many evangelical groups. Many of these organizations take advantage of a loophole in a provision of the IRS code to legally solicit large, anonymous donations from corporate and individual contributors. Although these groups often favor one party over the other, they are not part of the party organization and do not always agree with the party's positions or support its candidates—in fact, many have to operate independently of the parties and their candidates to preserve their tax-exempt status. (For more details on campaign finance, see Chapters 9 and 10.)

As this description suggests, the party organization has a fluid structure rather than a rigid hierarchy.[26] Individuals and groups work with a party's leaders and candidates when they share the same goals, but unless they are paid party employees, they are under no obligation to do so. (Even paid party workers can, of course, quit rather than

Both parties include internal organizations that attempt to attract the support of certain demographic groups, even ones that are typically identified with the opposite party. Women, for example, tend to vote more for Democrats on average. However, this isn't an absolute rule. No group votes as a monolith.

work for a candidate or a cause they oppose. The continued strong support for former President Trump from within the Republican party organization was partly due to departures—both voluntary and forced—of party workers and officials who opposed Trump's nomination and his policies.) Throughout the 2024 elections, Trump loyalists dominated the Republican party organization.

Party organizations at the local level, such as the Ohio county Democratic Party meeting shown here, coordinate support for the party's candidates, but they don't necessarily have to follow the lead of the national party organization.

Party Brand Names The Republican and Democratic party organizations have well-established "brand names." Because the parties stand for different things, in terms of both their preferred government policies and their ideological leanings, the party names themselves become a shorthand way of providing information to voters about the parties' candidates.[27] Hearing the term "Democrat" or "Republican" calls to mind ideas about what kinds of positions the members of each party support, what kinds of candidates each party runs, and how these candidates will probably vote if they are elected to office. Citizens can use these brand names as a cue to decide whom to vote for in an election. (See Chapter 9 for more information on voting cues.)

Differences in the details of party brand names also create opportunities for **issue ownership**: candidates from a party tend to concentrate their campaigns on issues that are part of their party's brand name and ignore issues that belong to the other party. Figure 8.1 on page 294 shows one way to measure issue ownership: by surveying citizens who identify with each party about their policy priorities.

issue ownership
The theory that voters associate certain issues or issue positions with certain parties (like Democrats and support for government-provided health insurance).

Limits of the Party Organization The critical thing to understand about the Democratic and Republican party organizations is that they are not hierarchies. No one person or group in charge determines what either organization does—which often makes them look disorganized. Because the RNC and DNC are organized in the same way, we can consider the example of Jaime Harrison, the chair of the DNC. He has some influence over who works at the DNC. However, the party organization's issue positions are set not by Harrison's employees but by DNC members from all 50 states. The individual committee members are appointed by their state party organizations, so they do not owe their jobs to Harrison—in fact, they can remove *him* from office if they like. If Harrison and the committee disagree, he can't force the committee members to do what he wants.

The national party organization is also unable to force state and local parties to share its positions on issues or comply with other requests. State and local parties make their own decisions about state- and local-level candidates and issue positions.[28] The national committee can ask nicely, cajole, or even threaten to withhold funds. But if a state party organization, an independent group, or even an individual candidate disagrees with the national committee, there's little the national committee can do to force compliance.

The one exception to this rule is former president Trump. While in office, he and his advisers worked to staff the national and state party committees with supporters. In addition, Trump departed from usual practice in endorsing supporters running in Republican primaries for Congress, state, and local offices. The result is that even as a former president, Trump is the closest thing we have seen to a powerful party leader, both because his endorsement can attract votes and because party officials are loyal to him. For example, in line with Trump's criticisms of the House special committee investigating the January 6, 2021 insurrection at the Capitol, the RNC in early 2022 censured Republican Representatives Liz Cheney (R-WY) and Adam Kinzinger (R-IL) for serving on the committee. Kinzinger ultimately retired from Congress and Cheney

I am not a member of an organized political party. I am a Democrat.

—Will Rogers, American actor

FIGURE 8.1

Democrats' and Republicans' Top Priorities, 2024

The Republican and Democratic party coalitions have different priorities on many issues, ranging from environmental protection to fighting the COVID-19 pandemic—and their differences are small on a few issues, such as securing Social Security. Do these differences make sense in light of each party's "brand name"?

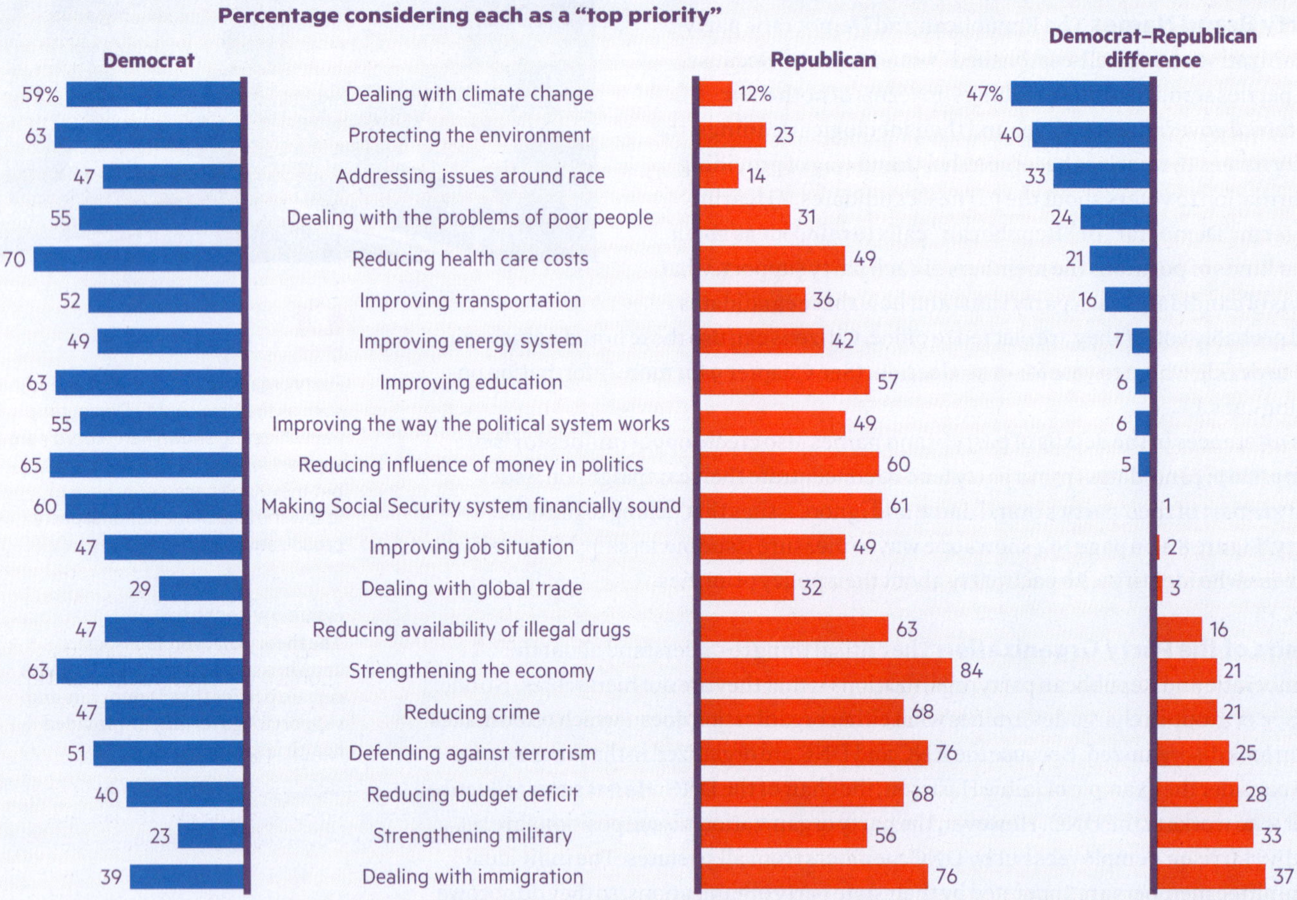

Percentage considering each as a "top priority"

	Democrat	Republican	Democrat–Republican difference
Dealing with climate change	59%	12%	47%
Protecting the environment	63	23	40
Addressing issues around race	47	14	33
Dealing with the problems of poor people	55	31	24
Reducing health care costs	70	49	21
Improving transportation	52	36	16
Improving energy system	49	42	7
Improving education	63	57	6
Improving the way the political system works	55	49	6
Reducing influence of money in politics	65	60	5
Making Social Security system financially sound	60	61	1
Improving job situation	47	49	2
Dealing with global trade	29	32	3
Reducing availability of illegal drugs	47	63	16
Strengthening the economy	63	84	21
Reducing crime	47	68	21
Defending against terrorism	51	76	25
Reducing budget deficit	40	68	28
Strengthening military	23	56	33
Dealing with immigration	39	76	37

Pew Research Center, "Americans' Top Policy Priority for 2024: Strengthening the Economy," February 29, 2024, available at https://www.pewresearch.org/politics/2024/02/29/americans-top-policy-priority-for-2024-strengthening-the-economy/ (accessed 8/29/24).

was defeated in a primary by a candidate Trump endorsed. However, Trump's control of the party is nowhere near absolute. For example, his criticisms of Senate Minority Leader McConnell have not led Senate Republicans to replace McConnell. Nor have House Republicans expelled Cheney and Kinzinger from their conference or canceled their committee assignments.

The party in government

The party in government consists of elected officials holding national, state, and local offices who took office as candidates of a particular party. They are the public face of the party, somewhat like the players on a sports team. Although players are only one part of a sports franchise—along with owners, coaches, trainers, and support staff—the players' identities are what most people call to mind when they think of the team.

President Trump continues to have a significant influence over the Republican Party, endorsing candidates, policy positions, and current Congress members. His influence could be seen in action during the hearings on the January 6, 2021, insurrection on the Capitol. As punishment for their participation on the committee investigating the events, Republican Representatives Lynn Cheney (R-WY) and Adam Kinzinger (R-IL) were censured by the RNC, meaning they were effectively expelled from the party. Kinzinger chose not to run for reelection, and Cheney lost her primary in 2022.

Because the party in government is made up of officeholders, it has a direct impact on government policy. Members of the party organization can recruit candidates, write platforms, and pay for campaign ads, but only those who win elections—the party in government—serve as members of Congress or as executive officials and propose, debate, vote on, and sign the legislation that determines what government does.

Caucuses and Conferences In the House and Senate, the Democratic and Republican parties are organized around working groups called a **caucus** (Democrats) and a **conference** (Republicans). The party caucus or conference serves as a forum for debate, compromise, and strategizing among a party's elected officials. Under **unified government** (in which the same party controls Congress and the presidency) these discussions focus on finding common ground within the party, as in the negotiations that led to the American Rescue Plan (COVID-19-related assistance) and the Infrastructure Investment and Jobs Act enacted by Congress in 2021. Under **divided government** (in which one party controls at least one house of Congress and the other party controls the presidency, as in 2023–2024), the focus changes to finding opportunities to work with the other party or strategizing on how to block the other party's initiatives. Divided government was relatively rare before the 1960s but has become increasingly common since then. Particularly when control is divided, partisan differences can yield policy gridlock, as neither side is willing to compromise and neither side has the votes to push its preferred package through. Measures such as the assistance legislation enacted by a bipartisan majority in response to the COVID-19 pandemic in March 2020 are very much the exception to the rule.

caucus (congressional)
The organization of Democrats within the House and Senate that meets to discuss and debate the party's positions on various issues in order to reach a consensus and to assign leadership positions.

conference
The organization of Republicans within the House and Senate that meets to discuss and debate the party's positions on various issues in order to reach a consensus and to assign leadership positions.

unified government
A situation in which one party holds a majority of seats in the House and Senate and the president is a member of that same party.

divided government
A situation in which the House, Senate, and presidency are not controlled by the same party—for example, when Democrats hold the majority of House and Senate seats and the president is a Republican.

Each party's caucus or conference meets to decide on legislative committee assignments, leadership positions on committees, and leadership positions within the caucus or conference.[29] Caucus or conference leaders also serve as spokespeople for their respective parties, particularly when the president is from the other party. The party in government also contains groups that recruit and support candidates for political office: the Democratic Congressional Campaign Committee (DCCC), the Democratic Senatorial Campaign Committee (DSCC), the National Republican Congressional Committee (NRCC), and the National Republican Senatorial Committee (NRSC).

Polarization and Ideological Diversity The modern Congress is polarized: in both the House and the Senate, Republicans and Democrats hold different views on government policy.[30] The graph in the What Do the Facts Say? feature on page 296 tells us that over the last 60 years the magnitude of ideological differences between the parties in Congress has increased. Until the 1980s there was some overlap between

WHAT DO THE FACTS SAY?

Are the Parties More Polarized Than Ever?

For the last 20 years, it seems as though all the news about political parties has been about conflict and stalemate. It seems like political campaigns are increasingly negative, bipartisan compromise is rare, and Republicans and Democrats have divided into camps that never agree on anything. Is this trend new? What do the facts say?

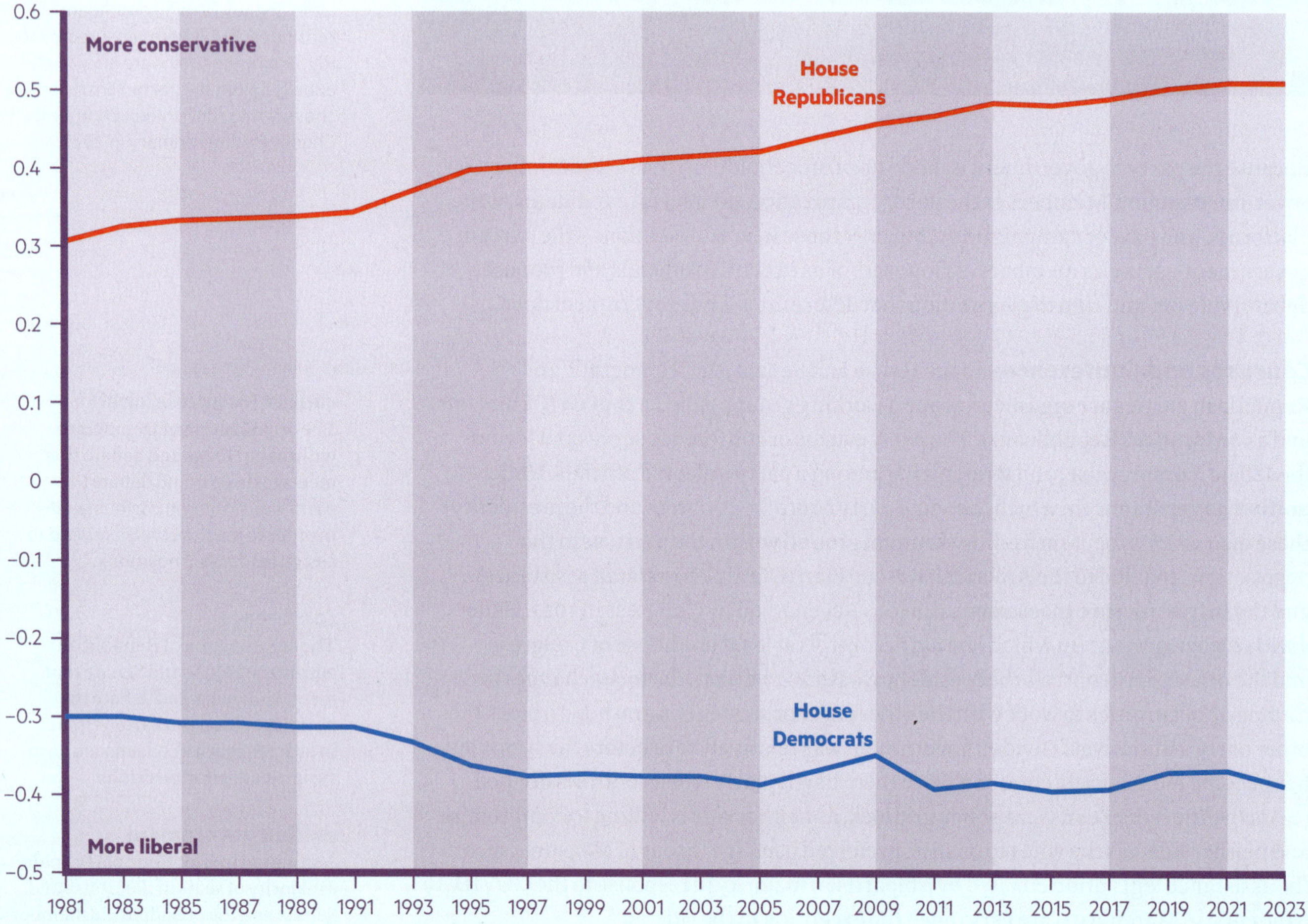

Source: Jeffrey B. Lewis et al., Voteview (congressional roll call votes database), https://voteview.com/ (accessed 8/29/24).

Think about it

- **This graph uses voting behavior to measure** the average ideology (liberal–conservative) of House Democrats and Republicans. Scores near 1 indicate a conservative ideology, while scores near −1 indicate a liberal ideology. Since the 1980s, have Republicans gotten more conservative, have Democrats become more liberal, or both? Has one party moved more than the other?
- **How might these changes make it harder** for members of the contemporary Congress to enact major changes in government policy? What is more likely: compromise or gridlock?

the positions of Democrats and Republicans, but this overlap has disappeared in recent years. However, if we expanded the figure to look at the ideologies of individual members, we'd find a mixture of ideologies, not a uniform consensus opinion. In the contemporary Congress, Democrats vary from the relatively liberal left end of the axis to the moderate (middle) and even slightly conservative right side. The same is true for Republican members of Congress: while most are conservative, there are some moderates, as well as a range of conservative opinions.

The ideological diversity within each party in government can create situations in which a caucus or conference is divided on a policy question. Compromise within a party's working group is not inevitable—even though legislators share a party label, they may not be able to find common ground. In the last few years, congressional Democrats have been divided on domestic spending, while divisions on the Republican side arose on issues of immigration policy as well as health care, taxation and spending levels, and the federal budget deficit. One issue that united both parties, at least in the beginning, was opposition to Russia's invasion of Ukraine.

The party in the electorate

The party in the electorate consists of citizens who identify with a particular political party. Most Americans say they are either Democrats or Republicans, although the percentage has declined slightly over the last two generations. **Party identification (party ID)** is a critical variable in understanding votes and other forms of political participation.

party identification (party ID) A citizen's loyalty to a specific political party.

Party ID To say you identify with a party is a personal orientation or decision that does not commit you to anything, nor does it give you any control over a party's actions. Although the Republicans and the Democrats have websites where people can sign up to receive email alerts and to contribute online to party causes, joining a party does not give a citizen any direct influence over what the party does. Rather, the party leaders and the candidates themselves make the day-to-day decisions. These individuals often heed citizens' demands, but there is no requirement that they do so. Real participation in party operations is open to citizens who become activists by working for a party

In a unique show of unity, both parties gave Ukrainian president Volodymyr Zelensky a standing ovation during his address to Congress. Later in 2023, emerging Republican opposition to Ukraine assistance again divided parties.

organization or one of its candidates. Activists' contributions vary widely and may include stuffing envelopes, helping out with a phone bank, being a delegate to a party convention, attending campaign rallies, or campaigning door-to-door.

Early theories of party ID described it as a deep attachment to a party that was acquired early in life from parents, friends, and political events and was generally unaffected by subsequent events.[31] Further work showed that party ID does not necessarily remain the same but rather involves continuing evaluation that takes account of new information.[32] Thus, when people say they identify with the Republican Party, they are saying that, based on what they have seen in American politics, they prefer the positions suggested by the Republicans' brand name and how Republicans behave in office. At the same time, party ID shapes how people think about politics and react to new information. Thus, when Republicans argue for managing the entry of undocumented individuals by building a border wall, while Democrats support expanding guest worker programs and providing a path to citizenship, the difference is not what they know but how they react to the same pieces of information—a response that is shaped by their party affiliation. Strong partisans are also more likely to use looser standards to evaluate members or officeholders from their own party, avoid contact with those who identify with the other party, and want preferential treatment for members of their party.[33]

negative partisanship
Identification with a political party that is based on dislike of the other party rather than positive feelings about the party identified with.

As we discussed in Chapter 6 (Public Opinion), there is also some evidence in recent years of **negative partisanship** (also called affective partisanship), in which party identification is based less on what you like about a party and more about what you dislike about the other party.[34] For example, voters might identify as Democrats even though they disapprove of President Biden and Democrats in Congress, because their feelings about the Republican Party and its supporters are even more negative. Such negative partisanship could drive lower evaluations of policy debates in Washington—regardless of who wins, someone motivated by negative partisanship will be disappointed by the outcome.

Figure 8.2 gives data on party ID in America from 1992 to 2019, measured when respondents were given the option to say whether they were a Democrat,

FIGURE 8.2

Party ID Trends among American Voters, 1992–2024

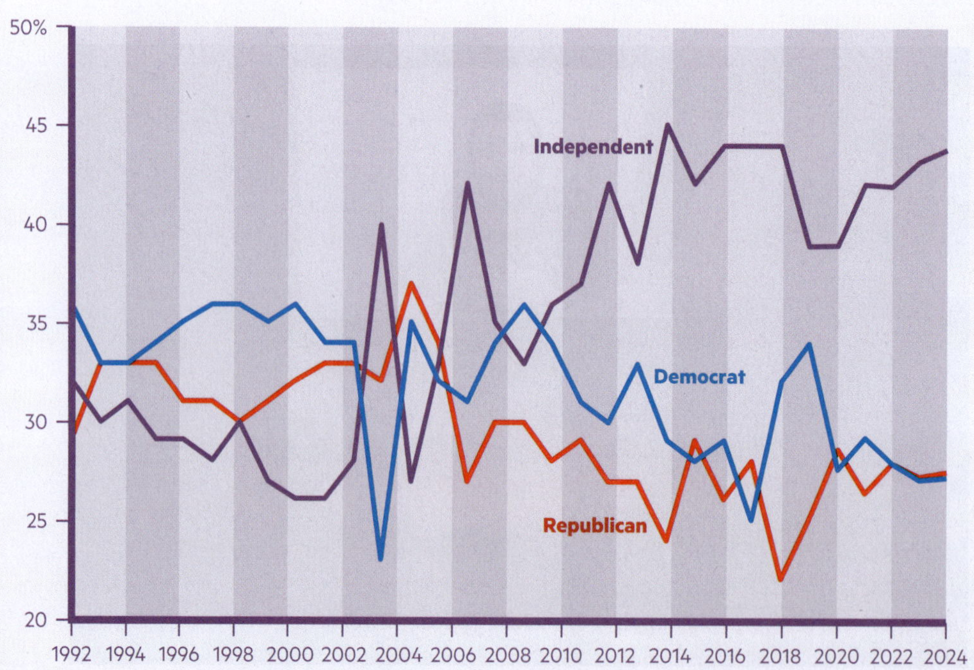

In terms of party ID, the parties have moved from rough parity in the 1990s to a slight Democratic advantage in the early twenty-first century, although this change has eroded in recent years. What events might have caused these changes in party ID?

Sources: 1992–2003 data from Pew Research Center, "Party Identification Trends, 1992–2017," March 20, 2018, www.people-press.org (accessed 6/15/20); 2004–2024 data from Gallup, "Party Affiliation," https://news.gallup.com/poll/15370/party-affiliation.aspx (accessed 8/30/24).

Activist volunteers, such as these two canvassing in the crucial swing state of Ohio, undertake most of the one-on-one efforts to mobilize support for a party and its candidates.

a Republican, or an Independent. Over this period, the parties have been nearly evenly split. At various times in the past, one party has opened some advantage over the other (as the Democrats did in the early 2000s), but there is no consistent trend.

Independents Some early analyses concluded that Independents were unaffiliated with a party because they were in the process of shifting their identification from one party to the other.[35] Others saw Independents as evidence that more and more people regarded the parties as irrelevant to their view of politics and their voting decisions.[36] The rise in the number of Independents was also seen as an indication that Americans were becoming more politically savvy—learning more about candidates and not always blindly voting for the same party.[37]

More recent work has modified these findings. Most Independents actually have some attachment to one of the major political parties—in fact, some scholars refer to Independents as "closet partisans": people who have party ties but who simply don't admit that they do.[38] In Figure 8.2, for example, more than 40 percent of the electorate says it does not identify with a party. However, the percentage of true Independents is much smaller: if we asked these so-called Independents if they leaned toward one party or the other, about two-thirds would claim they do have a slight affiliation, and they would be split evenly between Republicans and Democrats. Independents are not necessarily better informed about candidates, parties, or government policy than are party identifiers. However, they are much less likely to get involved in political activity beyond voting, such as contributing to or working for a candidate or party.[39]

With a closer look at voting decisions, Figure 8.3 shows how Democrats, Republicans, and Independents voted in the 2022 midterms ("closet partisan" Independents are grouped with the party they actually affiliate with). This figure shows that if you are trying to predict how someone will vote, the most important thing to know is their party ID.[40] Over 90 percent of Democrats voted for a Democratic House candidate, and about the same percentage of Republicans voted for a Republican House candidate.

DID YOU KNOW?

5%

of Americans say they worked for a political candidate or issue campaign during the last presidential election.

Source: Pew Research Center.

FIGURE 8.3

The Impact of Party ID on Voting Decisions in the 2022 Midterm Elections

Americans are much more likely to vote for candidates who share their party affiliation. What does this relationship tell us about the impact of campaign events (including speeches, debates, and gaffes) on voting decisions?

Source: 2022 CNN Exit Polls, www.cnn.com/election/2022/exit-polls/national-results/house/ (accessed 11/10/22).

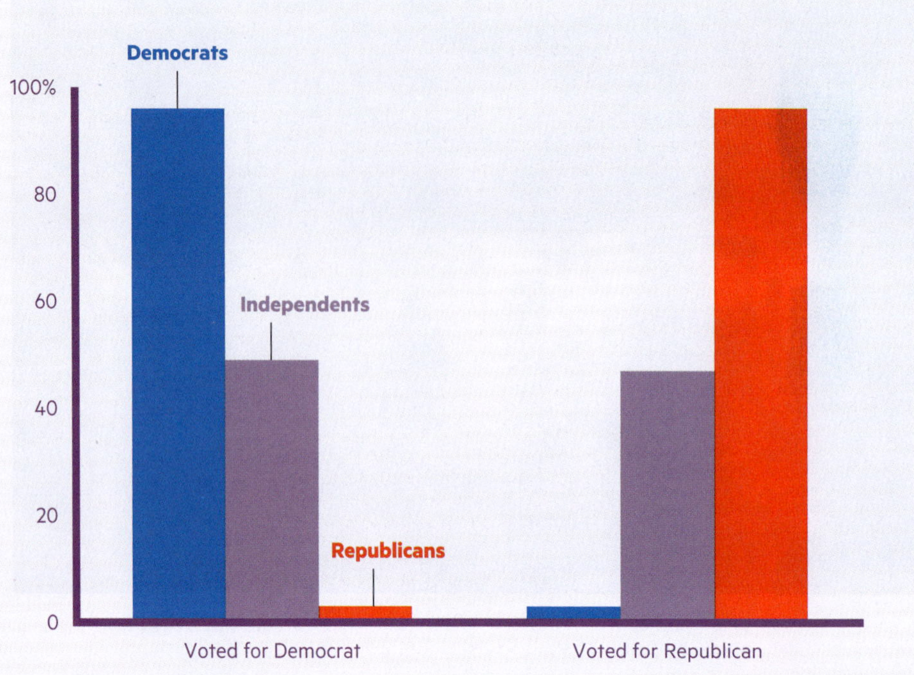

party coalitions
The groups that identify with a political party, usually described in demographic terms such as Black Democrats or evangelical Republicans.

Party Coalitions Data on party ID enable scholars to study **party coalitions**—that is, groups of citizens who identify with each party. Figure 8.4 shows the contemporary Democratic and Republican party coalitions. As you can see, some groups are disproportionately likely to identify as Democrats (Black women) and some are disproportionately likely to identify as Republicans (White evangelicals).[41] Again, these coalitions have shifted over time, often evolving during periods of realignment and changing from one party system to the next. For example, the Republican advantage among White southerners and White evangelical Protestants has existed only since the 1980s.[42] Additional analysis of these data shows that Republican identifiers are somewhat more united in terms of their ideological beliefs, while the Democratic party coalition is more a group of groups with distinct policy preferences.[43]

The Republican and Democratic party coalitions differ systematically in terms of their policy preferences—what they want government to do—as shown in Figure 8.1 on page 294. This indicates the extent to which they disagree about the relative importance of issues like providing health insurance to the uninsured, dealing with global warming, and strengthening the military. On only a few issues—for example, fighting drug addiction or dealing with crime—are the percentages of those in both parties who consider the matter a priority nearly the same. These data demonstrate that party labels are meaningful: if you know someone is a Republican (or a Democrat), this information tells you something about what that person probably wants government to do, and how they will likely vote in the next election.

Figure 8.5 on page 302 shows the most fundamental difference in Democratic and Republican identifiers: variation in political ideology. As you can see, the Democratic Party distribution is dominated by liberal identifiers, while the Republican distribution is dominated by conservatives—although there is still some overlap in the middle,

FIGURE 8.4

The Party Coalitions

Many groups, such as Black women and White evangelicals, are much more likely to affiliate with one party than the other. What are the implications of these differences for the positions taken by each party's candidates?

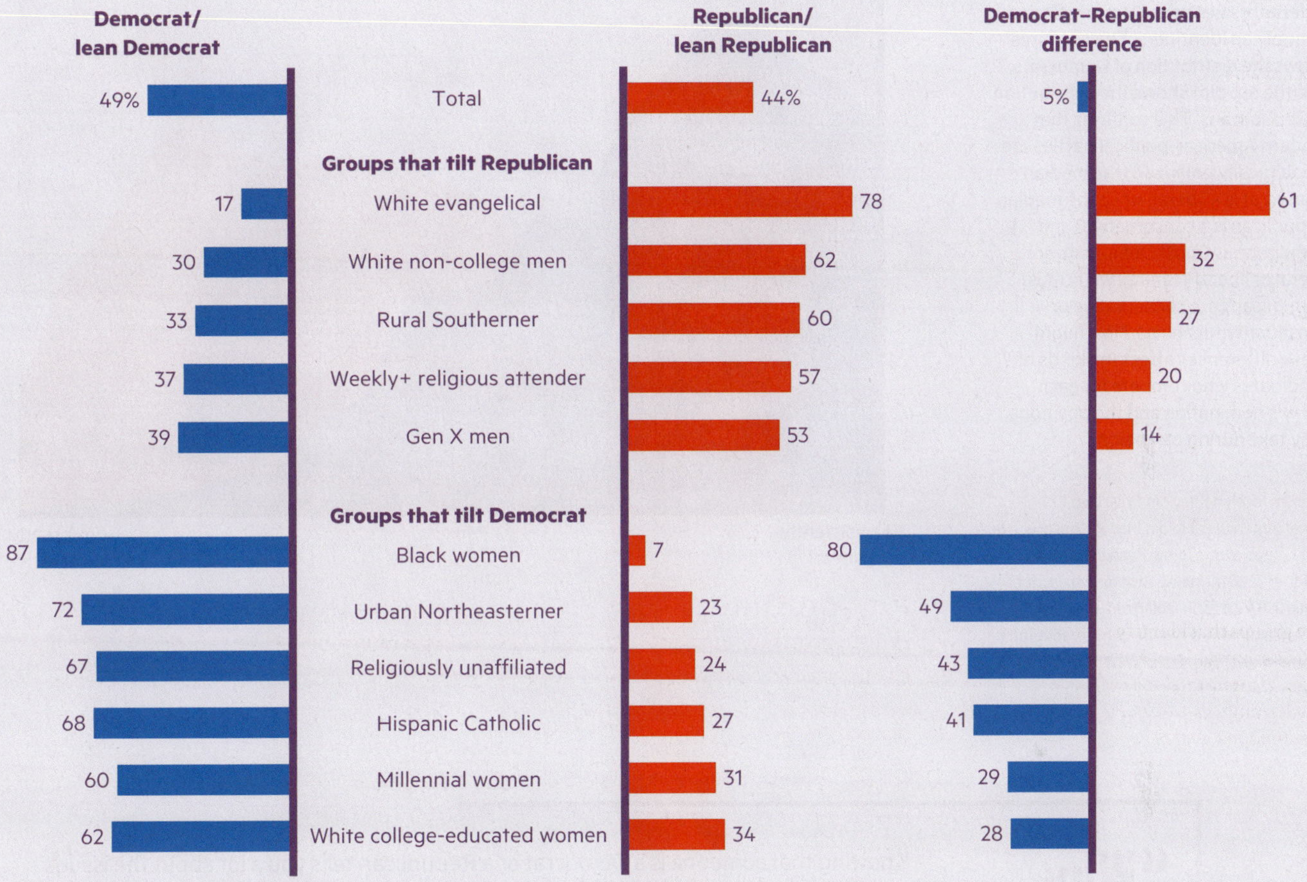

	Democrat/ lean Democrat	Republican/ lean Republican	Democrat–Republican difference
Total	49%	44%	5%
Groups that tilt Republican			
White evangelical	17	78	61
White non-college men	30	62	32
Rural Southerner	33	60	27
Weekly+ religious attender	37	57	20
Gen X men	39	53	14
Groups that tilt Democrat			
Black women	87	7	80
Urban Northeasterner	72	23	49
Religiously unaffiliated	67	24	43
Hispanic Catholic	68	27	41
Millennial women	60	31	29
White college-educated women	62	34	28

Source: Pew Research Center, "In Changing U.S. Electorate, Race and Education Remain Stark Dividing Lines," June 2, 2020, www.people-press.org (accessed 3/10/22).

meaning that both parties claim some moderates. Moreover, the current parties are much more homogenous than a generation ago, with liberals much more likely to be Democrats and conservatives more likely to be Republicans.[44]

Reflecting our discussion of public opinion in Chapter 6, Americans tend not to have a good sense of the party coalitions. For example, political scientists Douglas Ahler and Gaurav Sood have found that on average Americans believe that 32 percent of Democrats are LGBTQIA+ (the true percentage is 6 percent) and that 38 percent of Republicans have annual incomes above $200,000 (versus 2 percent in reality).[45] These misperceptions appear to be real, rather than people making something up for a survey. As such, they may provide a basis for the phenomena of affective partisanship discussed elsewhere in this chapter.

FIGURE 8.5

The Parties in the Electorate

This graph shows the ideological differences between Democratic and Republican identifiers. The blue area shows the distribution of Democrats, and the red plot shows the distribution of Republicans. This confirms that modern American political parties are ideologically polarized (the median Democrat is a liberal, while the median Republican is a conservative) and homogenous (most Democrats are liberal or liberal-leaning, while most Republicans are conservative or conservative-leaning). How might these differences affect the kinds of candidates who compete for each party's nomination and the positions they take during campaigns?

Source: Jocelyn Kiley, "In Polarized Era, Fewer Americans Hold a Mix of Conservative and Liberal Views," Pew Research Center, October 3, 2017, www.pewresearch.org/fact-tank/2017/10/23/in-polarized-era-fewer-americans-hold-a-mix-of-conservative-and-liberal-views/ (accessed 3/12/22).

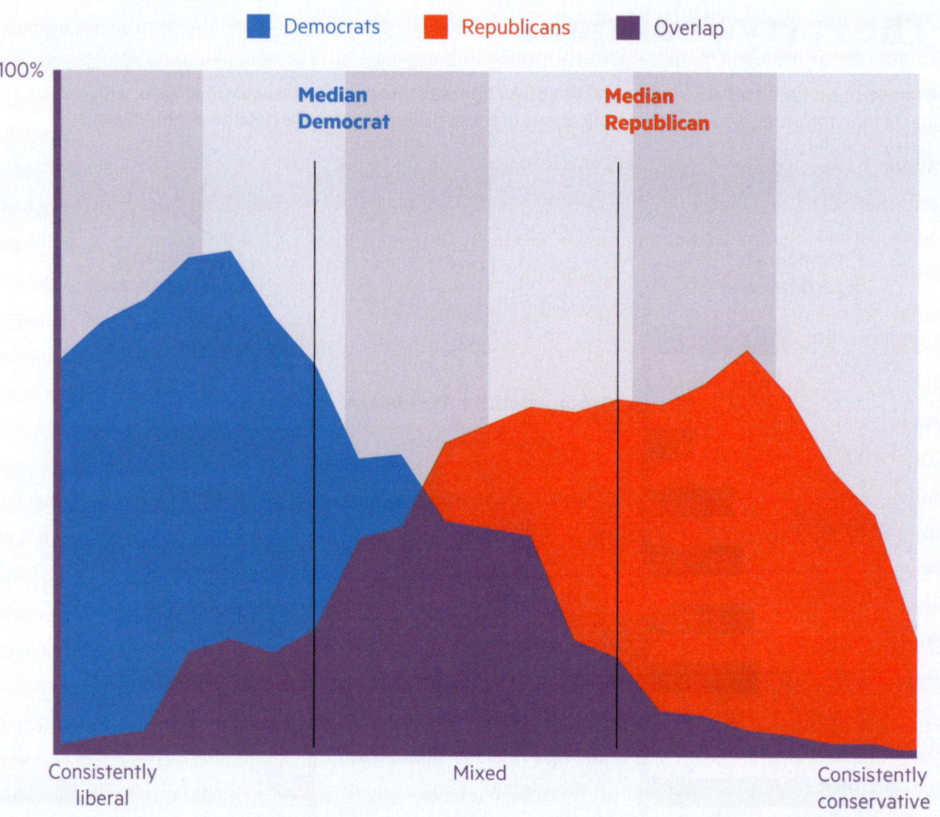

"Why Should I Care?"

Knowing that someone is a Democrat or a Republican tells you a lot about the issues that person cares about, whether they will like or dislike different candidates, and whom they will vote for in an election. Taken together, information about the kinds of people who identify with each party tells you a lot about the kinds of candidates who will run under the party banner and the platforms they will campaign on.

EXPLAIN THE IMPORTANT FUNCTIONS THAT PARTIES PERFORM IN THE POLITICAL SYSTEM

The role of political parties in American politics

Political parties play an important role in American politics, from helping to organize elections to building consensus across branches of government. But these activities are not necessarily coordinated. Candidates and groups at different levels of a party organization may work together, refuse to cooperate, or even actively oppose one another's efforts.

Organizing elections

In modern American politics, virtually everyone elected to a state or national political office is either a Republican or a Democrat. In the 119th Congress, elected in 2024, there are two Independent senators and no Independent House members. Similarly, the governors of all 50 states are either Democrats or Republicans, and of more than 7,300 state legislators very few are Independents or minor-party candidates. Even then, most Independent elected officials associate with one of the major parties—one of the Independent U.S. senators, Bernie Sanders, ran for the Democratic Party presidential nomination in 2016 and 2020, and the other, Angus King, gets his committee assignments from the Senate Democratic Caucus.

Recruiting and Nominating Candidates Historically, the recruitment of candidates was left up to local party organizations. But the process has become much more systematic, with state and national party leaders playing a central role in recruiting, endorsing, and funding candidates—and often promising those candidates help in assembling a staff, organizing a campaign, and raising more money. Actions like these can have a profound impact on congressional elections; years in which one party gains significant congressional seats (such as Republicans in 2010 or Democrats in 2018) are in part the result of one party's disproportionate success in its recruiting efforts.

In fact, one of the most well-known theories of presidential nomination contests argues that endorsements by party leaders and elected officials play a key role in determining which candidate emerges as the nominee.[46] Endorsements enhance a candidate's name recognition and help persuade undecided voters and contributors about candidates' electability and their ability to deliver on campaign promises. In all recent presidential nomination contests except 2016, the winning candidate was the one who gathered the most endorsements from party leaders, elected officials, and other notables. This theory was one of the main reasons why most political scientists thought that Donald Trump was unlikely to be the Republican nominee in 2016. While he led in the polls for several months, he received almost no endorsements from party leaders or elected officials. Conversely, one reason why Joe Biden was seen as the inevitable Democratic nominee in 2020 (as was Harris in 2024) was the relatively large number of endorsements they garnered from Democratic Party leaders.

Party leaders also play an active role in recruiting candidates for House and Senate seats. When a Senate seat opened up in Utah in 2018 because of Senator Orrin Hatch's retirement, many Republican national and state leaders encouraged former Republican presidential nominee Mitt Romney to enter the race and discouraged other potential candidates. These decisions reflected a simple political logic: party leaders believed that Romney would have a good chance of winning the general election given his reputation (including running the 2002 Winter Olympics in Utah) and Utah's large Mormon population.

Despite all of these efforts, however, parties and their leaders do not control who runs in House, Senate, or presidential races (see the Take a Stand feature on p. 304). In most states, candidates for these offices are selected in a **primary election** or a **caucus**, in which they compete for a particular party's spot on the ballot. Most of the states use some type of primary election; in 2020, only three states (Iowa, Nevada, and Wyoming) used caucuses. (see Nuts & Bolts 8.1 on p. 305). Most notably, Donald Trump won the 2016 Republican presidential nomination by virtue of his victories in the party's primaries and caucuses over the objections of many party leaders. Trump's victory demonstrates that party endorsements, while significant, are not the only factor in shaping nomination contests.[47]

primary election
A ballot vote in which citizens select a party's nominee for the general election.

caucus (electoral)
A local meeting in which party members select a party's nominee for the general election.

TAKE A STAND

Should Parties Choose Their Candidates?

One of the facts of life for the leaders of the Democratic and Republican parties is that they cannot determine who runs as their party's candidate for political office. They can encourage some candidates to run and attempt to discourage others by endorsing their favorites and funneling money, staff support, and other forms of assistance to the candidates they prefer. But in the end, congressional candidates get on the ballot by winning a primary or a vote at a state party convention; presidential candidates compete in a series of primaries and caucuses. Is this system a good one?

Let the party decide. Many scholars have argued that letting parties choose their candidates increases the chances of getting experienced, talented candidates on the ballot.[a] After all, party leaders probably know more than the average voter about who would make a good candidate or elected official. Plus, party leaders have a strong incentive to find good candidates and convince them to run: their party's influence over government policy increases with the number of people they can elect to political office. And finally, in states that have no party registration or day-of-election registration, giving the nomination power to party leaders would ensure that a group of outsiders could not hijack a party primary to nominate a candidate who disagreed with a party's platform or who was unqualified to serve in office.

While cases of outright hijacking of party nominations are fairly rare, political parties don't always get the nominees their leaders want and party leaders cannot force candidates out of a race. In the 2016 and 2024 election cycles, for example, many Republican Party leaders believed that Donald Trump was not the party's strongest nominee. Trump gained the nomination over their objections by winning the party's caucus and primary contests. You can judge whether his performance in office refuted or justified their concerns.

Let the people decide. One argument in favor of giving the nomination power to the people is that party leaders have not always shown good judgment in picking either electable or qualified candidates. Many of the same Republican leaders who opposed Trump had supported party nominees John McCain in 2008 and Mitt Romney in 2012, both of whom went on to lose their general-election contest. This track record suggests that party leaders are far from infallible. In 2020, most Democratic leaders believed that Joe Biden was more electable than the alternatives. While the COVID-19 pandemic complicates judgments about the 2020 election, the party leaders were probably right: Biden was best suited to win back White, less educated, midwestern voters who had defected to Trump in 2016.

The second argument for letting the people decide hinges on a judgment about whose wishes should prevail in nomination contests: the people who make up the party in the electorate or the people in the party organization. What right does the party organization have to select nominees, given that support for the party from the electorate (its contributions and votes in elections) is essential for electoral success? Moreover, shouldn't voters have a say in determining what their electoral choices look like? If party leaders choose, voters may not like any of the options put before them.

Why, then, do voters in America get to pick party nominees in primaries? Direct primaries were introduced in American politics during the late 1800s and early 1900s.[b] The goal was explicit: reform-minded party activists wanted to take the choice of nominees out of the hands of party leaders and give it to the electorate, with the assumption that voters should be able to influence the choice of candidates for the general election. Moreover, reformers believed that this goal outweighed the expertise held by party leaders.

Here is the trade-off: If party leaders select nominees, they will likely (but not inevitably) choose electable candidates who share the policy goals held by party leaders. If voters choose nominees, they can pick whomever they want, using whatever criteria they like—but there is no guarantee that these candidates will be skilled general-election campaigners or effective in office.

In the end, some groups must be given control over the selection of a party's nominees. Should this power be given to party leaders or to the people?

Both political parties organize a series of candidate debates during their presidential contests, giving candidates a chance to present themselves before a national audience.

take a stand

1. One reform proposal would increase the importance of the parties as sources of campaign funds. Would this change have made much of a difference in the 2020 Democratic presidential contest?
2. What kind of nomination procedure would be favored by insurgent groups?

NUTS & BOLTS 8.1

Types of Primaries and Caucuses

Primary election	An election in which voters choose the major-party nominees for political office, who subsequently compete in a general election.
Closed primary	A primary election system in which only registered party members can vote in their party's primary.
Nonpartisan primary	A primary election system in which candidates from both parties are listed on the same primary ballot. Following a nonpartisan primary, the two candidates who receive the most votes in the primary compete in the general election, even if they are from the same party.
Open primary	A primary election system in which any registered voter can participate in either party's primary, regardless of the voter's party affiliation.
Semi-closed primary	A primary election system in which voters registered as party members must vote in their party's primary, but registered Independents can vote in either party's primary.
Caucus election	A series of local meetings at which registered voters select a particular candidate's supporters as delegates who will vote for the candidate in a later, state-level convention. (In national elections, the state-convention delegates select delegates to the national convention.) Caucuses are used in some states to select delegates to the major parties' presidential nominating conventions. Some states' caucuses are open to members of any party, while others are closed.

Source: Compiled by the authors.

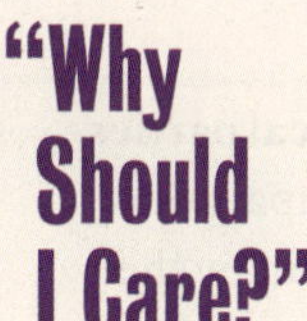

People often wonder if their vote really counts. Primaries give citizens the opportunity to select the candidates who will run in the upcoming election, but each format has its own advantages and disadvantages. Even the time of the year in which a primary occurs can matter. We saw this in play during the 2020 Democratic primary. Voters in states with primaries earlier in the year had many candidates on the ballot to choose from, while those whose primaries fell later in the year had far fewer options, as many of the original candidates had long since dropped out.

Running as a major party's nominee, as opposed to running as an Independent, is almost always the easiest way to get on the general-election ballot. Even Vermont senator Bernie Sanders, who won his Senate seat by running as an Independent, ran for the Democratic presidential nomination in 2016 and 2020. Some states give the Republican and Democratic nominees an automatic spot on the ballot. Even in states that don't automatically allocate ballot slots this way, the requirements for the major parties to get a candidate on the ballot are much less onerous than those for minor parties and Independents. For example, in California a party and its candidates automatically qualify for a position on the ballot if any of the party's candidates for statewide office received more than 2 percent of the vote in the previous election. In contrast, Independent candidates need to file petitions with more than 150,000 signatures to get on the ballot without a major-party label—an expensive, time-consuming task.[48] These advantages help explain why virtually all prominent candidates for Congress and the presidency run as Democrats or Republicans. Even billionaires Mike Bloomberg and Tom Steyer, who could have easily self-financed Independent campaigns for the presidency, chose to run as Democrats in 2020.

National parties also manage the nomination process for presidential candidates. This process involves a series of primaries and caucuses held over a six-month period beginning in January of a presidential election year. The type of election (primary or caucus) and its date are determined by state legislatures, although national party committees can limit the allowable dates, using their control over seating delegates at the party conventions to motivate compliance. Voters in these primaries and caucuses don't directly select the parties' nominees. Instead, citizens' votes are used to determine how many of each candidate's supporters become delegates to the party's national **nominating convention**, where delegates vote to choose the party's presidential and vice-presidential nominees. The national party organizations determine how many delegates each state sends to the convention based on factors such as state population, the number of votes the party's candidate received in each state in the last presidential election, and the number of House members and senators from the party that each state elected (see the How It Works graphic on pp. 308–9).

nominating convention
A meeting held by each party every four years at which states' delegates select the party's presidential and vice-presidential nominees and approve the party platform.

Minor parties sometimes have a significant impact on the major party organizations. As noted earlier, the major parties took note of the rise of the Populist and Progressive parties in the late 1800s, shifting their policy platforms to add some of the positions advocated by these new organizations. More recently, while the various Tea Party organizations that formed in 2009–2010 never coalesced into one party organization, Republican candidates and party leaders adopted many Tea Party positions to attract supporters.

Campaign Assistance One of the most visible ways that the political parties support candidates is by contributing to and spending money on campaign activities. By and large, federal law mandates that these funds be spent by the organization that raised them—the national party, for example, is limited in the amount of money it can directly contribute to congressional and presidential candidates or to state party organizations. As we will discuss in Chapter 10, however, party organizations can use the campaign funds they raise to help candidates in other ways, for example, through independent expenditures—running their own ads in a candidate's district or state.

Figure 8.6 shows the amount of money raised by the top groups within the Republican and Democratic parties for the 2024 election (through November 8). The final figures show that the parties and their various committees raised over $1.5 billion. The DNC and RNC raised the most money, but the congressional campaign committees also raised significant sums. Congressional Democratic committees outraised their Republican counterparts. And congressional leaders raised nearly $60 million for the campaigns of their colleagues.[49]

Along with supplying campaign funds, party organizations give candidates other assistance, ranging from offering campaign advice (including which issues to emphasize, how to deal with the press, and the like) to conducting polls. Party organizations at all levels also undertake get-out-the-vote activities, encouraging supporters to get to the polls. In the 2020 election, both campaigns had much less direct contact with voters because of COVID-19, relying more on social media, phone banks, and advertising. Things moved back toward normal in 2022, where both parties held mass campaign rallies and organized volunteers to go door-to-door to increase support for their candidates and encourage people to vote. Social media

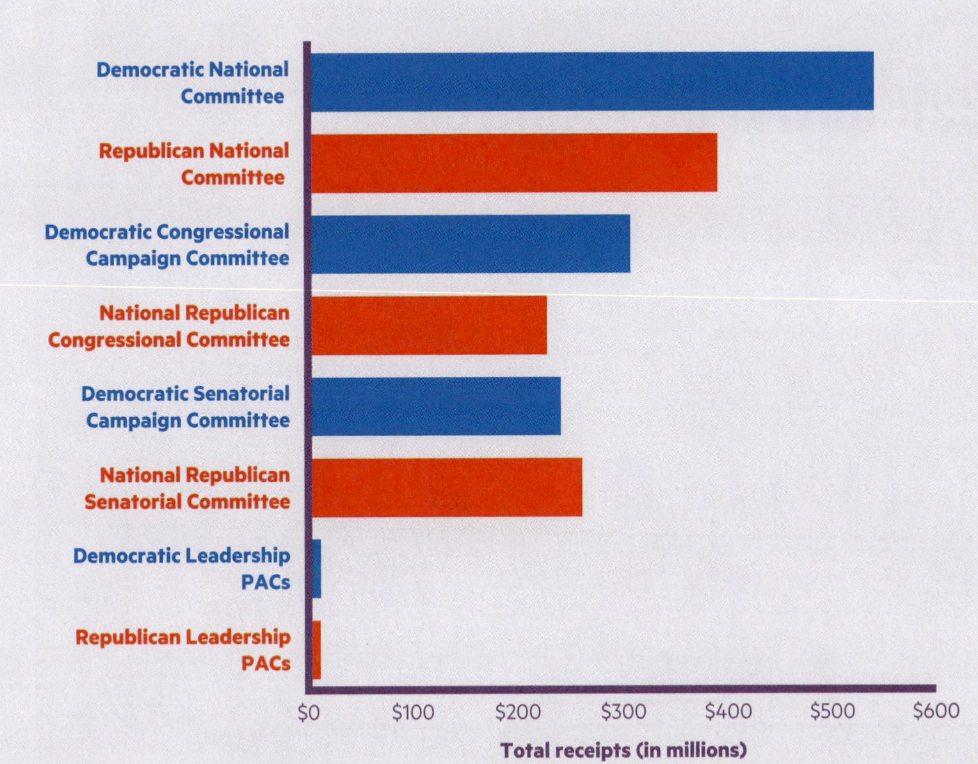

FIGURE 8.6

Democratic and Republican Fund-Raising in the 2023–2024 Election Cycle

In the 2023–2024 election cycle, party and leadership committees raised more than $1.9 billion in campaign funds. Although most of this money was raised by the national committees, the state, local, and candidate committees also raised significant sums. To what extent might these funds allow the national committees to force candidates to run on the party platform?

Source: The Center for Responsive Politics, www.opensecrets.org (accessed 11/8/24).

usage also increased, with many candidates posting frequently on X (formerly known as Twitter), TikTok, and, for some Republican candidates, Truth Social and Gab.

Party Platforms The **party platform** is a set of promises explaining what candidates from the party will do if elected. The most visible party platform is the one approved at each party's presidential nominating convention, but the party organizations in the House and Senate also release platforms, as do other major-party groups. Party platforms generally reflect the brand name differences between the parties. For example, the 2020 Democratic presidential platform expressed support for a woman's right to choose, meaning that abortion would be legal under a wide range of conditions. In contrast, the 2024 Republican platform was a series of short policy bullet points, including allowing states to set their own abortion restrictions.

party platform
A set of objectives outlining the party's issue positions and priorities. Candidates are not required to support their party's platform.

In theory, party platforms describe differences between the major parties, capture each party's diagnosis of the problems facing the country, and give the party's plan for solving those problems. In this way, party platforms give citizens an easy way to evaluate candidates. However, candidates are not obligated to support their party's platform and many take divergent stances on some issues. For example, notwithstanding the consistently strong pro-choice position on abortion in the Democratic Party's presidential platforms over the last generation, some Democratic members of Congress, such as Senator Bob Casey of Pennsylvania, have favored restrictions on abortion. For some of these candidates, their position reflects personal or religious beliefs; for others, it is driven by the desire to reflect the opinion of voters in their district or state.

Despite these exceptions, party platforms are important documents and it is unlikely that future parties will emulate the Republicans' 2020 strategy where they

How it works: in theory

Nominating Presidential Candidates

Primaries and caucuses . . .

Closed primaries
Only voters registered with party vote

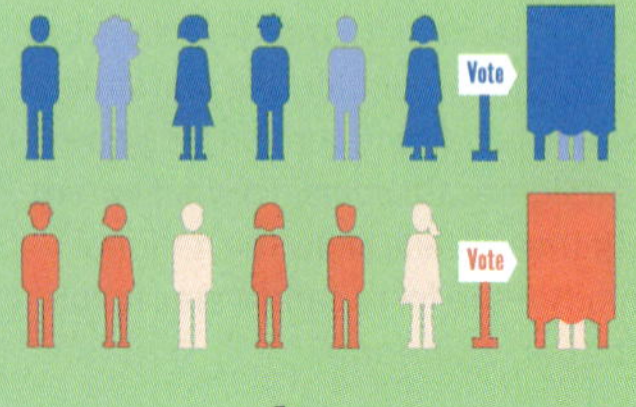

Open primaries
Open to voters from any political party and Independents

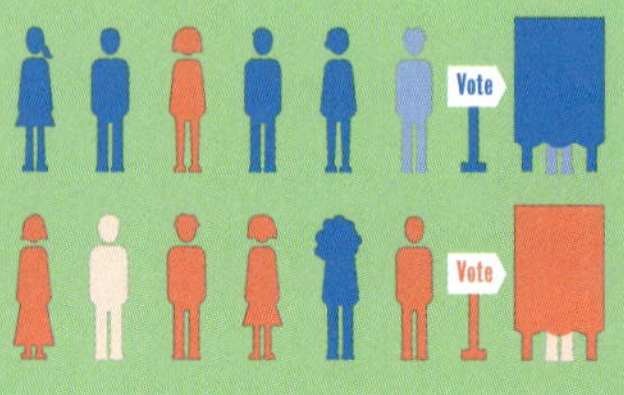

Caucus or local convention
Party members meet in groups to select delegates

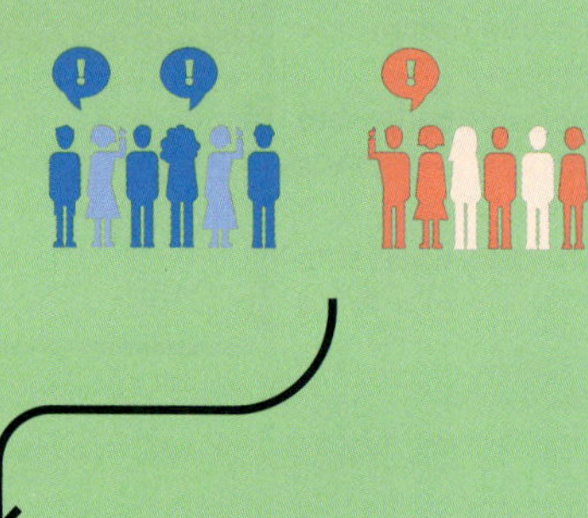

are used to select delegates . . .

Republican Party
States can award all delegates to the winning candidate

or award delegates proportionally.

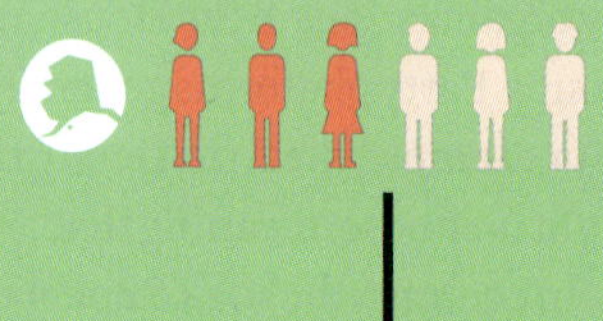

Democratic Party
The state's delegates are divided proportionally. A candidate must receive at least 15 percent of the vote either statewide or in a congressional district to receive delegates.

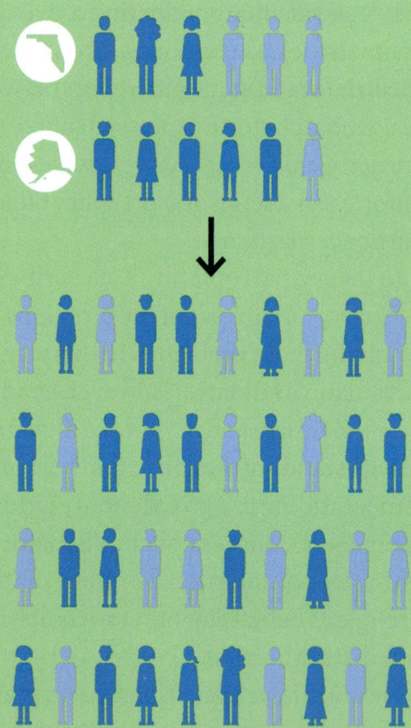

who attend national nominating conventions.

Delegates from all states attend the national convention, where they vote for the party's presidential and vice-presidential nominees based on the primary and caucus results. Superdelegates—important party leaders—also vote at the convention.

How it works: in practice

The Nomination of Joe Biden for President, 2020

While Joe Biden was the clear winner in the 2020 Democratic presidential nomination contest, his campaign benefited from the 15 percent threshold rule and the fact that many of the early contests were in states with high percentages of Black voters, who were strong Biden supporters.

% Percentage of popular vote won
Delegates allocated
† Caucus

Note: For the contests in which allocated delegates do not add up to the number available or for which the popular vote percentages do not total 100 percent, other candidates omitted here also received delegates or votes. If a candidate drops out of the race before the national convention, any delegates they have earned may be reallocated.

Source: Table compiled by the authors from press accounts and U.S. Census data.

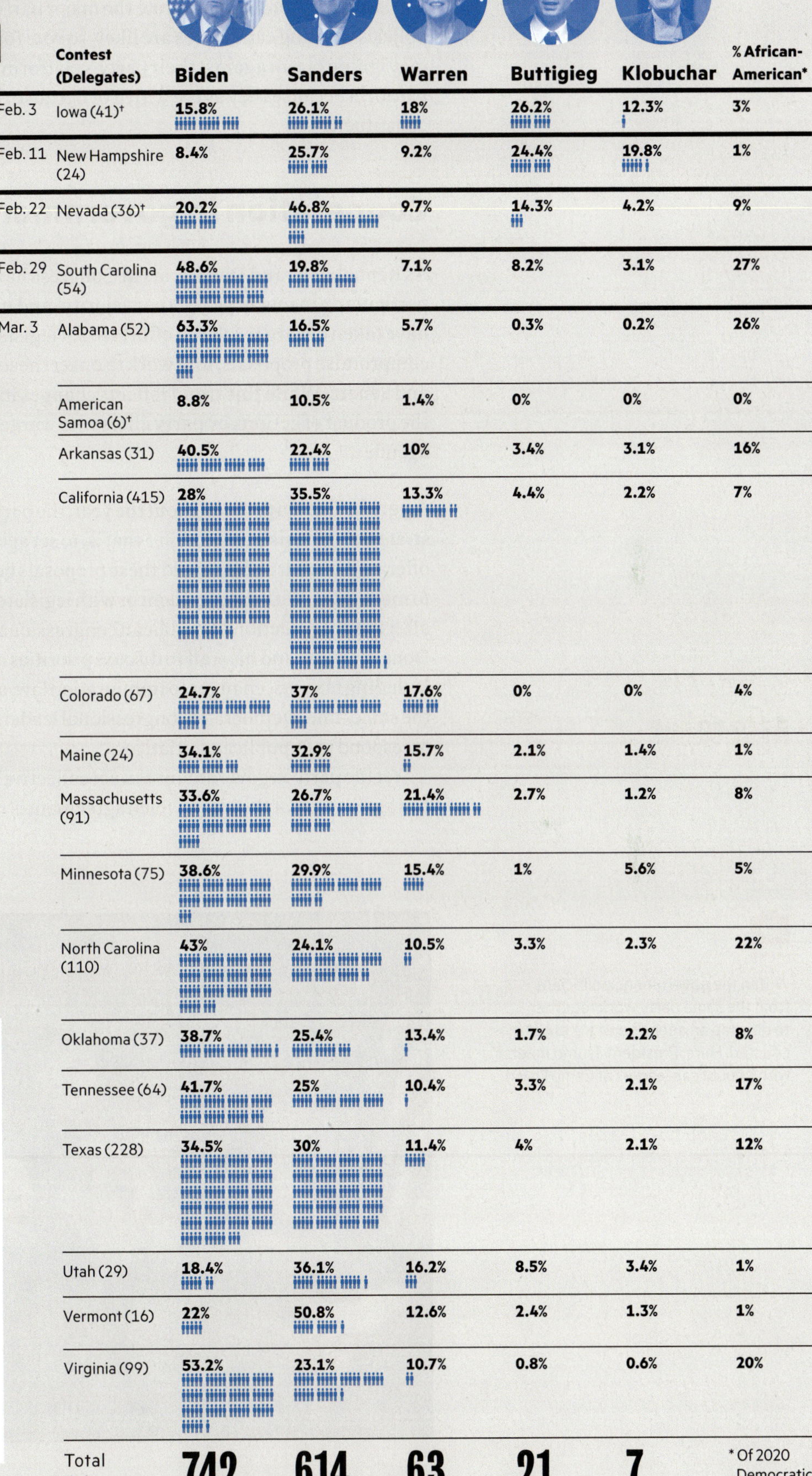

	Contest (Delegates)	Biden	Sanders	Warren	Buttigieg	Klobuchar	% African-American*
Feb. 3	Iowa (41)†	15.8%	26.1%	18%	26.2%	12.3%	3%
Feb. 11	New Hampshire (24)	8.4%	25.7%	9.2%	24.4%	19.8%	1%
Feb. 22	Nevada (36)†	20.2%	46.8%	9.7%	14.3%	4.2%	9%
Feb. 29	South Carolina (54)	48.6%	19.8%	7.1%	8.2%	3.1%	27%
Mar. 3	Alabama (52)	63.3%	16.5%	5.7%	0.3%	0.2%	26%
	American Samoa (6)†	8.8%	10.5%	1.4%	0%	0%	0%
	Arkansas (31)	40.5%	22.4%	10%	3.4%	3.1%	16%
	California (415)	28%	35.5%	13.3%	4.4%	2.2%	7%
	Colorado (67)	24.7%	37%	17.6%	0%	0%	4%
	Maine (24)	34.1%	32.9%	15.7%	2.1%	1.4%	1%
	Massachusetts (91)	33.6%	26.7%	21.4%	2.7%	1.2%	8%
	Minnesota (75)	38.6%	29.9%	15.4%	1%	5.6%	5%
	North Carolina (110)	43%	24.1%	10.5%	3.3%	2.3%	22%
	Oklahoma (37)	38.7%	25.4%	13.4%	1.7%	2.2%	8%
	Tennessee (64)	41.7%	25%	10.4%	3.3%	2.1%	17%
	Texas (228)	34.5%	30%	11.4%	4%	2.1%	12%
	Utah (29)	18.4%	36.1%	16.2%	8.5%	3.4%	1%
	Vermont (16)	22%	50.8%	12.6%	2.4%	1.3%	1%
	Virginia (99)	53.2%	23.1%	10.7%	0.8%	0.6%	20%
	Total delegates	742	614	63	21	7	

* Of 2020 Democratic primary and caucus voters

Critical Thinking

1. **What would have happened to Biden's candidacy** if more of the early states had lower percentages of Black voters?
2. **One argument about caucuses is that they allow** lesser-known candidates to build support. Did this work for any candidates in 2020?

simply promised to support then-President Trump. Political scientist John Gerring's research shows that platforms provide a general guide for voters about the issues and issue positions that separate the major parties. Platforms indicate what sorts of policies winning candidates are likely to vote for if elected. While some candidates may ignore or run against their party's platform, most candidates will support the platform because they agree with it or because they believe it is popular with their constituents.[50]

Cooperation in government

As Republicans and Democrats in Congress have become more polarized, particularly in recent years, the majority- and minority-party legislative caucuses have taken on larger roles in efforts to set legislative priorities, formulate compromise proposals, and work to enact these proposals on the floor of the House and Senate. While this trend reflects changes in American public opinion, it is also the product of actions by party elites who wanted to build party unity around policy agendas.[51]

Agenda-Setting Throughout the year, the parties in government meet to devise strategies for legislative action—that is, to set agendas. What proposals should they offer, and in what order should these proposals be considered? Should the parties try to make a deal with the president or with legislators from the other party? For example, after the 2024 election, Republican congressional leaders met with President-elect Donald Trump and his staff to discuss priorities for the 2025–2026 legislative term, including tax cuts, changes to immigration law, and changes to health care policies. At the same time, Democratic congressional leaders made their own plans, including how to respond to Republican initiatives.

Yet the party in government can act collectively this way only when its members can agree on what they want. Such agreement is not always possible or may require

Within the government, politicians from the same party work together to develop an agenda and try to get it enacted. Here, President Trump meets with Republican leaders at Camp David.

extensive negotiation and compromise. In theory, the 2024 elections gave Republicans control of the House, the Senate, and the presidency. Even so, the narrow majorities in both chambers meant that Republicans needed unanimity in their caucus to enact legislation.

Coordination Political parties play an important role in coordinating the actions taken in different branches of government. Such coordination is extremely important for enacting new laws, because, unless supporters in Congress can amass a two-thirds majority to override a veto, they need the president's support. Similarly, the president needs congressional support to enact the proposals they favor. To these ends, the president routinely meets with congressional leaders from their own party and occasionally meets with the entire caucus or conference. Various members of the president's staff also meet with House and Senate members to present the president's proposals and to hear what members of Congress from both parties want to enact.

During 2019 and 2020, President Trump held many meetings with Republican members of Congress to lobby them to support his policy proposals and to persuade them to oppose efforts to impeach him. Trump was successful on impeachment, in that virtually all Republicans voted against impeachment. But in other areas, including cuts to some federal programs and a plan to enact substantial reductions in legal immigration to the United States, Trump had little success. These two examples illustrate the limits of presidential persuasion: presidential victories have more to do with proposing something that members of Congress are inclined to support than with pressuring them to support a proposal they oppose.

Coordination can also occur between caucuses or conferences in the House and Senate. During the COVID-19 pandemic in 2020, for example, unified Democratic opposition to Republican-proposed economic stimulus legislation forced Senate Republicans to include many Democratic provisions in the final version. Similarly, the need for party unity partly explains Trump's September 2020 nomination of Amy Coney Barrett to the Supreme Court, as other short-listed candidates raised

Parties don't exert total control over their members. Democratic Party leaders could not stop Senator Joe Manchin (D-WV) from opposing President Biden's Build Back Better bill, effectively killing it.

more opposition among Senate Republicans. Such coordination efforts require real compromise, since party leaders in Congress do not have authority over each other or the elected members of their party. Nor can the president order a House member or senator to do anything, even if the legislator is from the president's own party. In 2017, for example, President Trump and congressional leaders needed the votes of several moderate Republicans, including Senator Susan Collins of Maine, to pass tax cut legislation in the Senate. The congressional leaders and the president held repeated meetings with Collins and her allies, offering various promises and enticements to secure their votes. Ultimately, these legislators voted for the proposal, but neither the president nor party leaders could have forced them to support it.

Accountability One of the most important functions political parties play in a democracy is to give citizens identifiable groups to reward or punish for government action or inaction. Using the ballot box, voters will reward and punish elected officials, often based on their party affiliation and on the behavior of that party's members in office. In this way, the party system gives the electorate a mechanism that can be used to hold officials accountable for outcomes such as the state of the economy or America's relations with other nations. This mechanism is most clear during periods of unified government, when one party holds majorities in both the House and the Senate *and* controls the presidency, meaning that party has enough votes to enact policies in Congress and a good chance of having them signed into law by the president. Arguments along these lines were one of the central themes of the Democratic campaigns during the 2018 midterms—that majority control of the House or Senate would enable Democratic legislators to limit the regulatory changes, judicial appointments, and budget cuts favored by congressional Republicans and the Trump administration. Democrats made a similar argument in 2022—that unified control would enable them to continue acting on Democratic priorities, including abortion rights and climate change.

In contrast, during times of divided government, when one party controls Congress but not the presidency or when different parties control the House and Senate (such as during the second half of Biden's presidency), it is not clear which party should be held accountable for the state of the nation. Republicans successfully argued in 2024 that Democrats should be punished for the high inflation during 2022 and 2023 as well as large numbers of unauthorized individuals entering the U.S. at its southern border. Analyses of the 2024 election show that many voters responded by supporting Republican candidates across the board.

Focusing on parties makes it easy for citizens to issue rewards and punishments. For example, if the economy is doing well, people can reward the party in power by voting for its candidates. But if the economy is doing poorly, or if people feel that government is wasting tax money or enacting bad policies, voters can punish the party in power by supporting candidates from the party that is currently out of power. When citizens behave this way, they strengthen the incentive for elected officials from the party in power to work together to develop policies that address voters' concerns—on the premise that if they do, voters will reward them with another term in office. Consider the 2020 elections. Although Democrats lost some seats in the House of Representatives, most of their incumbents were reelected. Why? Some were elected from states or districts dominated by Democratic identifiers. But many others were reelected because they campaigned on a platform of promoting Democratic party ideals or because of their efforts to help local constituents; in effect, these candidates said, "Instead of punishing me for my party affiliation, reward me for working on your behalf."

In the end, reelecting members of the party in power despite a poor economy or other troubles makes sense given how American political parties are organized and their lack of control over individual officeholders. Of course, insofar as incumbent members of the party in power present themselves as loyal party members and cast votes in accordance with the wishes of party leaders, they will increase the chances that their constituents will take account of their party label when casting their votes—which will help them get reelected in good times but will increase their chances of defeat when conditions turn against their party.

Minor parties

So far, this chapter has focused on the major American political parties, the Republicans and the Democrats, and paid less attention to other party organizations. The reason is that minor political parties in America are *so* minor that they are generally not significant players on the political stage. Many such parties exist, but few run candidates in more than a handful of races and very few minor-party candidates win political office. Few Americans identify with minor parties, and most of these parties exist for only a relatively short period.

Even so, you may think we are giving minor parties too little attention. Consider Jill Stein and Chase Oliver, who ran as the Green and Libertarian party candidates for president in 2024. If the votes they received had gone to Kamala Harris instead, she might have prevailed in close states and thereby won the election. In this sense, you might think of minor parties and their supporters as the kingmakers in modern American politics. However, the size of the minor-party vote in 2024 doesn't so much highlight the importance of minor parties as it illustrates the closeness of elections in some states. If Stein and Oliver had not run, Harris might have received enough additional support to win. But given that Trump's margin of victory in several states was so small, any number of seemingly minor events (rain in some areas and sunshine in others, or some small number of additional pro-Harris ads) could have had the same effect.

Minor-party presidential candidates, such as Libertarian Jo Jorgensen in 2020, sometimes attract considerable press attention because of their distinctive policy preferences, but they rarely affect election outcomes.

Even in terms of lower offices, minor-party candidates typically attract only meager support. While the Libertarian Party claims to have over 200 officeholders, many of these officials hold unelected positions such as seats on county planning boards or ran unopposed for relatively minor offices.[52] In 2020, Justin Amash, who was elected as a Republican representative for the state of Michigan, changed his party affiliation to become a Libertarian and in doing so became the party's first member to serve in Congress, though he chose not to seek reelection.

Looking back in history, we see that some minor-party candidates for president have attracted a substantial percentage of citizens' votes. George Wallace (governor of Alabama at the time) ran as the candidate of the American Independent Party in 1968, receiving about 13 percent of the popular vote nationwide. Texas millionaire Ross Perot, the Reform Party candidate for president in 1996, won 8.4 percent of the popular vote. Perot also ran as an Independent in 1992, winning 18.2 percent of the popular vote. And environmental and consumer activist Ralph Nader received about 5 percent of the popular vote in 2000.

Unique Issues Facing Minor Parties The differences between major and minor political parties in contemporary American politics grow even more substantial when considered in terms other than election outcomes. For most minor parties, the party in government does not exist, as few of their candidates win office. Many minor parties have virtually no organization beyond a small party headquarters and a website. Some minor parties, such as the Green Party and the Libertarian Party, have local chapters and an annual convention. But these modest efforts pale in comparison with the nationwide network of offices, thousands of workers, and hundreds of millions of dollars deployed by Republican and Democratic party organizations.

The most significant factor working against minor parties is the basic structure of the American political system. This principle is summed up by **Duverger's Law**, which states that in a democracy that has **single-member districts** and **plurality voting**, there will be only two political parties that are able to elect a significant number of candidates to political office. Given these electoral institutions (see Chapter 9), many people consider a vote for a minor-party candidate to be a wasted vote, as there is no chance that the candidate will win office. As a result, well-qualified candidates are driven to affiliate with one of the major political parties because they know that running as a minor-party nominee will put them at a considerable disadvantage. These decisions reinforce citizens' expectations that minor-party candidates have no chance of winning elections and that a vote for them is a wasted vote. Although there is no evidence that the Founders wanted to choose electoral institutions that made it hard for minor parties and their candidates, there is no doubt that the rules of the American electoral game have these effects.

Duverger's Law
The principle that in a democracy with single-member districts and plurality voting, only two parties' candidates will have a realistic chance of winning political office, as in the United States.

single-member district
An electoral system in which every elected official represents a geographically defined area, such as a state or congressional district, and each area elects one representative.

plurality voting
A voting system in which the candidate who receives the most votes within a geographic area wins the election, regardless of whether that candidate wins a majority (more than half) of the votes.

A second problem is that the issues and issue positions taken by minor parties and their candidates are almost always very different from those espoused by the major parties. The Constitution Party, for example, advocates ending government civil service regulations; banning compulsory school attendance laws; withdrawing from the UN and all international trade agreements; abolishing foreign aid, the income tax, the Internal Revenue Service, and all federal welfare programs; and repealing all campaign finance legislation, the Endangered Species Act, and federal firearms regulations. These positions are extreme, not in the sense of being silly or dangerous but in the sense that relatively few Americans agree with them. Even in the 2024 presidential contest, Libertarian Chase Oliver proposed major cuts in defense spending and domestic programs—positions that attract support from only a relatively small minority of Americans.

Some political scientists have proposed reforms that would likely increase the number of major political parties in America, most notably Lee Drutman, who advocates moving to a system of proportional representation, where citizens would vote for parties, not candidates, and a party's share of seats in Congress would depend on how many votes they received.[53] Most democracies that use proportional representation have additional parties—typically from three to even nine or ten, although usually some are small. Drutman's argument is that increasing the number of parties would ensure that all voters could find a party that matched their preferences (at least on important issues), as well as encourage bargaining and compromise in Congress. On the other side, moving to proportional representation would be a profound shift in American politics, and it is difficult to be sure how this change would affect parties or the policy process.

"Why Should I Care?"

You may dislike political parties or party leaders in Congress, but the fact is, the parties are key players in congressional policy making and in negotiations between Congress and the president. If you are trying to decide whether a new program (or nominee) has a chance of being approved, one of the first things you need to consider is whether the party caucuses in the House and Senate (particularly the majority-party caucuses) are in favor or opposed.

How well do parties operate?

EVALUATE WHETHER THE AMERICAN PARTY SYSTEM ENHANCES OR HINDERS DEMOCRACY

We have argued throughout this chapter that political parties can make democracy operate more smoothly by simplifying and improving the choices that citizens face in elections and by providing mechanisms that make it easier for elected officials to formulate and enact compromise proposals. However, these arguments are about what parties *can* do, not what they *actually* do. There is no assurance that party leaders, activists, candidates, and citizens who identify with parties will take the actions needed to turn these possibilities into reality. The problem is that the people who make up American political parties are not primarily interested in democracy; they are interested in their own careers, policy goals, and winning political office. These goals often lead them away from actions that would improve American democracy. In this section, we consider when and why American political parties might fall short of our highest expectations for them.

Recruiting good candidates

One of the most important things that American political parties can do for democracy is to recruit candidates who can run effective campaigns and uphold their elected positions. After all, a voter's choices are limited to the people on the ballot. If good candidates decide against running or are prevented from doing so, citizens will be dissatisfied no matter who wins the election.

However, parties have limited influence over candidacy decisions: the potential candidates have to decide for themselves whether their chances of winning justify the enormous investment of time and money needed to run a campaign. When a party is unpopular, the best potential candidates may decide to wait until the next election to run, leaving the already disadvantaged party with a less competitive set of candidates. Even when recruitment is not a problem, party leaders have only limited control over the nomination process—in some states, they cannot even restrict voting in primaries to citizens who are registered with the party. As Donald Trump's 2016 candidacy illustrates, party leaders cannot always prevent a candidate they do not favor from running; from dominating press coverage at the expense of other, more viable candidates; and from saying things that drive some important groups away from the party and its candidates. Of course, Trump won the 2016 election, indicating that party leaders underestimated his electability. Even so, insofar as party leaders are experienced politicians with deep knowledge of public opinion and political institutions, their lack of control over the nomination process can lead to unfavorable outcomes.

Working together in campaigns

Parties can improve the working of democracy by simplifying the choices voters face, most notably by getting their candidates to emphasize the same issues or to take similar issue positions. That way, citizens know that when they vote for, say, a Democrat, they are getting someone whose policy positions are likely to differ from those held by a Republican. As we've noted, however, even in modern America, where the differences between the parties are quite large, there are often disagreements within the party, either among elected officials or in the party organization. Suppose, for example, you want to vote in an election for the candidate who comes closest to your position on immigration policy. It's relatively easy to place Democratic candidates on the spectrum of positions on immigration, as most favor current limits on legal immigration and some form of legal status for undocumented individuals in the United States. It's much harder to determine a Republican candidate's position, as candidates from that party have a wide range of opinions and preferred immigration policies. Some favor policies close to the Democratic Party norm, while others advocate sharp reductions in legal immigration and aggressive deportation efforts against the undocumented. Moreover, immigration is not the exception. The simple fact is that on most issues, political parties in America speak with many voices, not one.

Why don't party leaders simply order their candidates to support the party platform or to work together in campaigns? As we have discussed, party leaders actually have very little power over candidates.[54] They can't kick a candidate off the ballot, because candidates win the nomination in a primary election or caucus, not through party appointment. Even though parties have a lot of campaign money to dispense, their contributions typically make up only a fraction of what a candidate spends on a campaign. And incumbent candidates, who generally hold an advantage over challengers when seeking reelection, are even less beholden to party leaders. Even if party leaders could somehow prevent an incumbent from running for reelection, they would have to find another candidate to take the incumbent's place, which would mean losing the incumbent's popularity and reputation and reducing the party's chances of holding the seat.

Working together in office

After the election, political parties can improve democracy by helping officeholders to find compromise policy proposals that attract broad support, and to select debate and voting procedures that speed enactment of these proposals. Sometimes, finding consensus both within and between parties is easy: for example, congressional Republicans and Democrats united in March 2020 to pass economic stimulus legislation in response to the COVID-19 pandemic. However, there are also many examples of issues that can split a party wide open, such as immigration reform for Republicans or Build Back Better for Democrats. Sometimes party members can compromise their differences, but there is no guarantee. And of course, even if the members of a party can find common ground, they may fail at building the bipartisan coalitions that are often necessary to enact major legislation, as was the case for many proposals considered during Joe Biden's years in office, including reform of federal sentencing guidelines and immigration. Even when compromise is reached, such as the enactment of clarifications to how electoral votes in presidential elections are counted and certified, the time spent negotiating means that members have less time to scrutinize the details of budgets and policy proposals. For this reason, one recent study argued that the party caucuses are "too weak to govern."[55] Party leaders may do a good job in determining what their colleagues want but be unable to persuade them to support a proposal that they are inclined to oppose.

The most important part of a Senate majority leader's education is over by the third grade, when he has learned to count.

—Howard Baker, former Senate Majority Leader

The fact that American political parties are ideologically diverse means that elected members of the party may not agree on spending, policy, or anything else. And even when senators and House members from a party find a way to bridge their differences, there is no guarantee that the president, even if they are from the same party, will agree to the compromise. In that sense, voters can't expect that putting one party in power will result in specific policy changes. Instead, policy outcomes depend on how (and whether) individual officeholders from the party can resolve their differences. Institutions such as the party caucuses or conferences provide a forum in which elected officials can meet and seek common ground, but there is no guarantee that they will find acceptable compromises.

Moreover, concerted action by members of a party in government may be aimed at political rather than policy goals. In recent years, both Democrats and Republicans have decided against bipartisan compromises, believing that standing their ground would help them gain seats in the next elections. As a result, many issues, from immigration reform to legalizing cannabis, have remained unresolved because of their value as campaign issues. In this way, the electoral imperatives faced by American political parties can work against the enactment of effective responses to public problems and increase, rather than decrease, the amount of conflict in American politics.

Providing accountability

Finally, parties can improve American democracy by acting as an accountability mechanism that gives citizens an identifiable group to reward when policies work well and to punish when policies fail. However, while individual legislators are happy to take advantage of party labels when being held accountable works in their favor, they will do everything they can to avoid being tied to an unpopular party. Republican legislators, for example, highlighted their party label in the 2010 election, as the party was much more popular than the Democratic Party at that time.[56] But in 2018, when the party brand was much less popular, many Republican incumbents emphasized their work as individual members of Congress on behalf of constituents and tried to stay as far away as possible from their party's unpopular image. Similarly, some Democratic House members in 2022 avoided talking about

Primary elections are an important opportunity for voters to assess the performance of their current representatives, as well as alternative candidates who might better support their ideological or policy priorities. Liz Cheney (R-WY), who faced Republican backlash for her leadership role on the January 6 Committee to investigate President Trump's involvement in the Capitol insurrection, was defeated in her primary by a candidate endorsed by President Trump.

President Biden or the Democratic Party, instead emphasizing their own efforts to help constituents.

When politicians work to secure their own political future by de-emphasizing their party affiliation, they make it harder for voters to use party labels to decide who should be rewarded and who should be punished for government performance. The result is that legislators are held accountable for their own performance in office, such as how they voted—but no one in Congress is accountable for large-scale outcomes such as the state of the economy or for foreign policy. Of course, attempts by officeholders to disassociate themselves from their party are not always successful, which is why Republicans lost their House majority in 2018. Even so, most Republicans and Democrats in Congress managed to survive these elections, suggesting that party-based accountability is rather weak in contemporary American politics.

Unpacking the Conflict

Considering all that we've discussed in this chapter, let's apply what we know about how political parties work to the examples of party dysfunction from the beginning of this chapter. Why is it impossible to describe American politics without talking about Republicans and Democrats? At the same time, why do the parties seem like bystanders as nominees are chosen and policies are debated?

The answer is that we have strong partisanship but weak parties. Party identification organizes how we think about politics as well as our political behavior as much as or more than it ever has in the past. However, at the same time Americans generally dislike political parties, even the one they identify with. And the laws governing elections allow candidates to claim a party label without having to support or even talk about their party's platform.

As a result, while America's political system gives enormous opportunities to political parties, from organizing elections to working inside Congress to build coalitions behind policy proposals, the fact that these opportunities exist does not ensure that political parties will be able to follow through on them. As we have seen, American political parties are often beset by internal conflicts over who should run for office and what their campaign platforms should look like. The party organization has little control over the party in government (or vice versa). And neither group can order party members in the electorate to work for the party, support its candidates, or do anything they don't want to do.

As a result of these organizational features, there is no guarantee that officeholders and election winners of the same party affiliation will have the same policy priorities or be able to compromise over their differences. This has been true even in recent years, when differences between Republicans and Democrats have been as large as ever. It will be just as hard for Democrats to agree among themselves about policy priorities as it will be to gain support for these proposals from Republicans. Republicans will face the same problem even if they gain unified control of government in the future. At the same time, while Americans may not approve of these outcomes, they show no signs of totally abandoning the Republicans or the Democrats in favor of new party organizations.

"What's Your Take?"

Are American political parties too dysfunctional to be useful?

Or do the benefits they provide outweigh their drawbacks?

CHECK YOUR UNDERSTANDING

"Why Should I Care?"

Political parties in contemporary America are best described as a case of "strong partisanship, weak parties." Most Americans have a strong connection to one party or the other: their party identification. Party ID is a strong determinant of how people vote, where they look for political information, and their judgments about political matters such as the state of the economy or whether they approve of the president's performance.

At the same time, party organizations are relatively weak. Party leaders have little control over who runs under the party banner. Similarly, party leaders in Congress cannot force elected representatives to vote in accordance with the strategies developed within the party caucus or conference. Even presidents are forced to bargain and compromise with their party's elected officials rather than simply telling them what to do.

The fact that partisanship is strong while parties are weak explains many important features of American politics circa 2025. It explains why Republican and Democrat voters hold such different views of the world, why they draw on different media sources, and why their perceptions of the economy or the state of the country change so radically when a president from one party is replaced by someone from the other. It explains the focus on mobilization over conversion in electoral campaigns—since partisanship has so much influence on vote decisions, candidates focus on getting co-partisans to the polls rather than trying to change the minds of voters from the other party.

The weakness of party organizations also has profound implications for how politics works. As the 2022 Senate elections illustrate, candidates who win primaries may well fail in the general election, even in states where a party has many supporters. A more powerful party would be able to determine which candidates ran under the party banner, and capitalize on opportunities such as a weak economy. Similarly, the weakness of parties in government explains why newly elected majorities often fail to enact their policy priorities. The high levels of party unity in Congress mask disagreements within each caucus. Party leaders must persuade members to go along with their plans rather than demanding they do so.

These examples also illustrate how changes in beliefs and institutions can change election outcomes and policy outcomes. The fact that we have strong partisanship and weak parties right now is no guarantee that this situation will continue. A weakening of partisan ties, for example, could transform campaigns. And if parties were allowed to select primary election candidates, that would help them to capitalize on whatever opportunities the elections provide.

1. Party systems across the history of politics in the United States are most defined by

- **a** foreign policy and economic policy changes that occur between presidential administrations.
- **b** shifts in major issues and supporting groups that characterize parties and political conflicts.
- **c** the activism or restraint of the Supreme Court and lower federal courts during a historic era.
- **d** changes in the relationship between the national government and state governments.

2. For a new party system to emerge in the United States, it generally involves the existence of which factors?

- **a** Public dissatisfaction with government and economic downturn
- **b** Crosscutting issues and a high-turnout election
- **c** Decline of one of the major parties and new groups added to the electorate
- **d** National crisis and culture war divisions

3. What is the best way to describe political party organizations so that an average American would understand?

- **a** Parties are highly structured groups that effectively leverage their membership to achieve specific goals.
- **b** Parties are carefully managed environments that function through clear hierarchy structures.
- **c** Parties are loosely connected organizations at multiple levels connected by shared ideology.
- **d** Parties are institutions that provide a brand under which people organize but have no control over what happens under that brand.

4. How do parties in government help the government function?

- **a** They develop policy priorities among members, select leadership, and seek areas of compromise.
- **b** They conduct public opinion surveys, communicate their agenda through the media, and offer political alternatives to majority proposals.
- **c** They demonstrate unwavering stands on principle, promote ideological frameworks, and screen the president's appointees.
- **d** They increase debate around proposed policies, promote diverse voices, and encourage strong partisan alignments.

5. Though the election rules and dates for holding primary elections or caucuses are decided by state legislatures, the allocation of delegates to presidential candidates at the nominating convention is controlled by which entity?

- **a** State political parties
- **b** Congress
- **c** National political parties
- **d** State constitutions

6. Policy making, economic activities, and policy implementation are complex activities for many Americans to understand, but the presence of political parties within government

- **a** even further complicates the ability of Americans to make sure that they achieve their preferred policy goals.
- **b** encourages clear positions of American voters to be taken on these complex issues through their representatives.
- **c** helps to clarify these issues by promoting various spokespeople to represent the issues and party positions to the people.
- **d** allows Americans to hold policymakers responsible for what they believe to be positive or negative effects of government.

7. Many Americans view the conflictual nature of parties in government as a reason to disengage from the political process, but what is a positive effect of political parties on American democracy?

- **a** Parties improve democracy by acting as gatekeepers preventing radical candidates from obtaining office.
- **b** Parties in government help to incentivize public officials to achieve policy rather than political victory.
- **c** Party caucuses in government can achieve policies by pushing ideological hardliners in the party to compromise.
- **d** Parties can provide clear policy positions that allow voters to make decisions more easily.

8. Which effect of American political parties has become destructive to our form of government?

- **a** Parties are unable to make incumbents follow the party platform and policy objectives set by the party leadership.
- **b** Parties increasingly ignore their voters to influence which candidates ultimately become the party nominees.
- **c** Voters are decreasingly likely to think of political parties as a way to hold officeholders accountable in elections for policies they like or dislike.
- **d** Partisans in government and in the electorate are less concerned with the success of democracy than their own careers and policy goals.

9

Elections

Who gets to represent the people?

"I won the election, got 71,000,000 legal votes. Bad things happened which our observers were not allowed to see. Never happened before. Millions of mail-in ballots were sent to people who never asked for them!"[1]
President Donald Trump, November 7, 2020

"I've worked extensively with the election officials in the city of Detroit, and they take it very seriously. . . . Are there errors that happen? Sure. But that's not fraud. . . . It never happens. Because you can't get away with it. It's way easier to just try and win the election."[2]
Josh Venable, Michigan Republican political operative

Every two years, Americans elect 435 House members and 33 or so senators; every four years (as in 2024), we also elect a president. The outcomes of these elections are scrutinized because they provide insights into what voters are thinking, because they reveal the usefulness of different campaign strategies, or because of what's at stake.

The 2024 presidential election met all these conditions. Voters faced the choice of returning to four more years of Donald Trump's version of Republican policies or electing a Democrat, Vice President Kamala Harris. The stakes included spending on America's military, domestic priorities, judicial appointments, and America's foreign policy. Looking over Joe Biden's four years in office, there is little doubt that things would look very different if Donald Trump had won reelection in 2020. It is unlikely that President Trump would have prioritized enactment of a trillion-dollar infrastructure package or sent massive military assistance to Ukraine as Russia threatened invasion. President Trump would have nominated very different judges to federal courts, further restricted immigration and admission of refugees, kept the United States out of the Paris Climate Change Accords, and made many other policy choices that are very different from those implemented by President Biden.

Our task is to understand the forces driving election outcomes. For example, in 2024, what led voters to return Donald Trump to the presidency and give Republicans control of the House and Senate? Was it the economy? Disapproval of border policies? Was Trump's personal behavior (including his extensive use of social media)

The two presidential candidates had two very different visions for the United States. One of the ways they got out their message was during a televised debate held two months before the election.

CHAPTER GOALS

Present the major rules and procedures of American elections (pp. 324–336)

Describe the features, strategies, and funding of campaigns for federal office (pp. 336–353)

Explain the key factors that influence voters' choices (pp. 354–358)

Analyze the issues and outcomes in the 2022 and 2024 elections (pp. 359–363) a factor, and did it help or hurt him? Are the 2024 results an indication of a new direction in American politics, or were they just about the candidates and issues that voters faced?

The 2024 presidential election is also a good example of the central themes of this text. Elections matter: no one watching the race would think that Harris and Trump would support the same policies if elected. Candidates competing for political office offer the people distinct, competing visions of what the federal government should do—from what the tax code should look like to what regulations the government should impose on individuals and corporations. In a very real sense, elections are how Americans resolve conflict over whose vision of government policy should prevail—at least until the next election.

Elections are also a good illustration of this book's focus on rules. For example, we elect presidents using a complex system where citizens' votes are tallied at the local and then state level to select slates of electors, whose votes are then counted and certified by a joint session of Congress. These rules and procedures can have a profound effect. For example, Donald Trump was elected president in 2016 despite winning a minority of citizens' votes. Similarly, Democratic victories in the 2020 U.S. Senate races in Georgia (which gave them control of the Senate and the ability to enact some of President Biden's policy priorities) were possible only because Georgia uses a two-step runoff system where if no candidate receives a majority on Election Day, a subsequent runoff is held between the top two candidates. (Both Democratic Senate candidates came in second place in the first-round election.)

Our analysis will focus on the interplay between rules and outcomes in American elections. Along the way, we will address concerns about the conduct of elections, such as the role of money in determining who wins and who loses and the claims by President Trump and his supporters that elections are marked by significant voter fraud. These issues bear on our ultimate question about American elections: How meaningful are they? What do election results tell us about why some candidates win and others lose? Why do these outcomes matter in American politics?

How do American elections work?

The American political system is a representative democracy: Americans do not make policy choices themselves, but they vote for individuals who make these choices on their behalf. This section describes the rules and procedures that define American national elections.

DID YOU KNOW?

There are a total of **510,000** federal, state, and local elected offices in the United States.

Source: Jennifer Lawless, *Becoming a Candidate*.

Functions of elections

Our working assumption for explaining the rules and processes of elections as well as the behavior of candidates and voters is that they are tied directly to what elections do: select representatives, give citizens the ability to influence the direction of government policy, and provide citizens with the opportunity to reward and punish officeholders seeking reelection.

Selecting Representatives The most visible function of American elections is the selection of officeholders, including, at the national level, members of the House and Senate and the president and vice president. Candidates can be **incumbents**, running for reelection to their current office, or challengers, running for the office for the first time. Because America is a representative democracy, by voting in elections, Americans have an indirect effect on government policy. Although citizens do not make policy choices themselves, they determine which individuals get to make these choices. In this way, elections are supposed to connect citizen preferences and government actions.

incumbent
A politician running for reelection to the office they currently hold.

Shaping Policy Although the fundamental choice in an election is between two or more candidates running for some political office, elections also involve a choice between candidates' policy platforms: the set of things they promise to do if elected. By investigating candidates' platforms, citizens learn about the range of options for government policy. Moreover, their voting decisions determine who gets to make choices about future government policy, and thereby shape government policy itself. For example, in the 2024 elections, Democrats wanted to ensure they kept their Senate majority, elected Kamala Harris, and regained control of the House, which would allow them to enact their policy priorities. Republicans in turn wanted to retain control of at least one chamber, which would allow them to block these initiatives. Optimally, they wanted to hold on to the House, and capture the presidency and the Senate, giving them unified government and the opportunity to enact their preferred policies.

Democrats controlled the Senate by a thin margin after the 2022 elections. Though incumbents generally fare well in elections, inflation, debates over the lingering effects of the pandemic, and social issues put this majority at risk in the 2024 races. As a result, senators such as Sherrod Brown (D-OH) lost their bid for reelection, as voters signaled they wanted to go in a different direction.

Promoting Accountability The election process also creates a way to hold incumbents accountable. When citizens choose between voting for an incumbent or a challenger, they can make a retrospective evaluation. They consider the incumbent's performance over the previous term(s) in office and ask, "Have they done a good job on the issues I care about?"[3] Citizens who answer yes typically vote for the incumbent, and those who answer no typically vote for the challenger. (Of course, as we discussed in Chapters 6 and 8, these judgments are often shaped by party affiliation, so in the case of the 2024 election, most Democrats concluded that Biden and Harris had done a good job in office, while most Republicans made the opposite judgment.)

Retrospective evaluations are significant because they make incumbents responsive to their constituents' demands.[4] If elected officials anticipate that some constituents will make retrospective evaluations objectively (rather than simply reflecting their partisanship), they will try to take actions that these constituents will look back upon favorably when they're in the voting booth. If incumbents ignore the possibility of voters' retrospective evaluations, they run the risk of being voted out of office in the next election. Retrospective evaluations can also form the basis for prospective judgments: voters' beliefs about how the country will fare if different candidates win. This provides an additional reason for incumbents to be responsive to citizens' demands.

Two stages of elections

Candidates running for federal office (House, Senate, or president) face a two-step procedure. First, if the prospective candidates want to run on behalf of a political party, they must win the party's nomination in a **primary** election. If the would-be candidates want to run as Independents, they need to gather signatures on a petition to secure a spot on the ballot. Different states hold **open primaries**, **semi-closed primaries**, or **closed primaries**, and state law sets the timing of these elections. For House and

primary
A ballot vote in which citizens select a party's nominee for the general election.

open primary
A primary election in which any registered voter can participate in the contest, regardless of party affiliation.

semi-closed primary
A primary in which anyone who is a registered member of the party or registered as an Independent can vote.

closed primary
A primary election in which only registered members of a particular political party can vote.

A voter wearing a protective mask checks in before voting during the primary election at a polling location in a high school in Washington, D.C. Americans vote in all sorts of places, including libraries, fire stations, schools, and private homes, all of which had to be configured to protect voters and volunteers throughout the COVID-19 pandemic.

Senate seats, a few states hold single primaries, in which there is one election involving candidates from both parties, with the top two finalists (regardless of party) receiving nominations to the general election.

general election
The election in which voters cast ballots for House members, senators, and (every four years) a president and vice president.

The second step in the election process is the **general election**, which is held throughout the nation on the first Tuesday after the first Monday in November. Federal law designates this day as Election Day. General elections determine who wins elected positions in government. The offices at stake vary depending on the year. Presidential elections occur every four years (2016, 2020, 2024, . . .). In a presidential election year, Americans elect the entire House of Representatives, one-third of the Senate, and a president and vice president. During midterm elections (2014, 2018, 2022, . . .), there is no presidential contest, but the entire House and a third of the Senate are up for election.

One implication of this two-step process of primary and general elections is that sometimes the winner of a primary is not a party's best candidate for the general election. For example, in the 2024 presidential race, one of the principal arguments for choosing someone other than Donald Trump as the Republican nominee (such as former South Carolina governor Nikki Haley) was that this candidate would have had a better chance of winning the general election. While Trump had many enthusiastic supporters, he was also strongly disliked by a sizable fraction of the American electorate. In the end, Trump's disapproval ratings did not carry the day, as he won a clear majority of the popular vote. It is unclear whether Haley would have done as well.

Mechanics of elections

The Constitution limits voting rights to American citizens who are at least 18 years old. There are also numerous restrictions on voter eligibility that vary across states, including residency requirements (usually 30 days) and prohibitions for people convicted of a major crime. A recent development in American elections is an increase in the practice of automatic absentee voting, in which someone can request an absentee ballot without having to provide a reason, such as being out of town on Election Day. Most states also allow early voting in the weeks prior to Election Day, and some allow voters to send in ballots by mail.[5] In 2020, the COVID-19 pandemic led additional states to allow voting by mail to minimize large crowds at polling stations. This decision was one reason why turnout was noticeably higher in 2020 than in recent years. Early and mail-in voting became even more popular in 2024. In some states, over half the ballots were cast before Election Day.

The most fundamental feature of American elections is that officeholders are elected in single-member constituencies in which only the winner of the most votes takes office. (Although both of each state's senators represent the whole state, they are elected separately, usually in different years.) Senate candidates compete statewide; House candidates compete in congressional districts. In most states, congressional district lines are drawn by state legislatures. In some states, nonpartisan commissions perform this function. Redistricting can happen at any time, but in general, district lines are revised after each census to make sure the boundary lines reflect shifts in population across and within states. (For details on redistricting, refer to Chapter 11.)

Because members of the House and Senate are elected from specific geographic areas, they often represent very different kinds of people. Their constituents differ in terms of age, race, income level, occupation, and political leaning, including party affiliation and ideology. Therefore, legislators from different areas of the country face highly diverse demands from their constituents, which often leads them to pursue very dissimilar kinds of policies.

For example, Democratic senator Charles Schumer represents the fairly liberal state of New York, where most people take some sort of pro-choice position on abortion rights, while Republican senator Tommy Tuberville represents the conservative state of Alabama, where most voters have long been opposed to abortion. Suppose the Senate votes on a measure to establish federal protections for abortion rights. Tuberville knows that most of his constituents would probably want him to vote against the proposal, and Schumer knows that most of his constituents would probably want him to vote for it. This example illustrates that congressional conflicts over policy often reflect differences in constituents' demands. Schumer and Tuberville themselves likely hold different views on abortion rights, but even if they agreed, their constituents' distinct demands would make it likely that as legislators they would vote differently.

Most House and Senate contests involve **plurality voting**: the candidate who gets the most votes wins. However, some states use **majority voting**, meaning that a candidate needs a majority (more than 50 percent of the vote) to win. If no candidate has a majority, a **runoff election** takes place between the top two finishers.

plurality voting
A voting system in which the candidate who receives the most votes within a geographic area wins the election, regardless of whether that candidate wins a majority (more than half) of the votes.

majority voting
A voting system in which a candidate must win more than 50 percent of votes to win the election. If no candidate wins enough votes to take office, a runoff election is held between the top two vote-getters.

runoff election
Under a majority voting system, a second election is held only if no candidate wins a majority of the votes in the first general election. Only the top two vote-getters in the first election compete in the runoff.

Ballots and Vote Counting Americans vote using a variety of machines and ballot structures based on where they live. States either use electronic touch screen voting machines, usually with some sort of paper receipt so voters can verify their choices, or have voters fill out paper ballots that are then scanned and recorded. When the polls close, workers transcribe vote totals from the various machines, then hand-carry the totals and individual ballots or receipts to county boards of election, where totals are aggregated and sent to state agencies, which certify the results. The process is largely run by volunteers, with both major parties having participants or observers at all stages.

Most states have laws that allow vote recounts if a race is sufficiently close (typically within 1 percent or less). Even when a recount occurs, it may be impossible to definitively determine who won a particular election, as the rules that determine which ballots are valid are often open to interpretation. More significant is that when an election is close the question of which candidate wins may depend on how ballots are structured and votes are counted. The problem is not that election officials are dishonest; rather, close elections inherently tend to produce ambiguous outcomes.

Claims are often made that officials manipulate election rules to guarantee wins for their favored candidates. Some states have laws that require voters to verify their identity with an official form of identification such as a driver's license or a passport. The purported goal is to prevent voter fraud—one person voting under another's name,

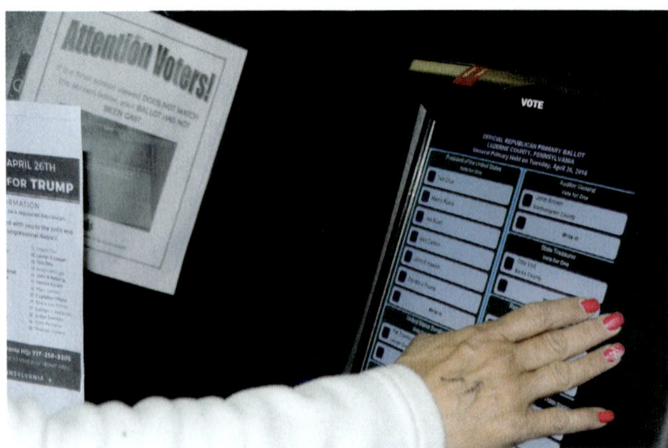

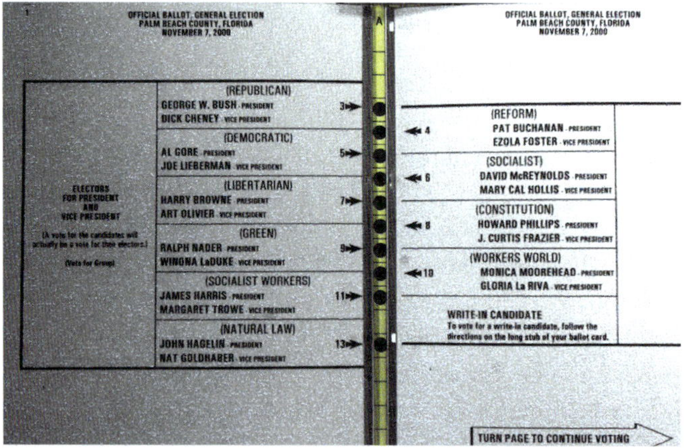
OFFICIAL BALLOT, GENERAL ELECTION
PALM BEACH COUNTY, FLORIDA
NOVEMBER 7, 2000

ELECTORS FOR PRESIDENT AND VICE PRESIDENT

(REPUBLICAN) GEORGE W. BUSH - PRESIDENT, DICK CHENEY - VICE PRESIDENT 3
(DEMOCRATIC) AL GORE - PRESIDENT, JOE LIEBERMAN - VICE PRESIDENT 5
(LIBERTARIAN) HARRY BROWNE - PRESIDENT, ART OLIVIER - VICE PRESIDENT 7
(GREEN) RALPH NADER - PRESIDENT, WINONA LaDUKE - VICE PRESIDENT 9
(SOCIALIST WORKERS) JAMES HARRIS - PRESIDENT, MARGARET TROWE - VICE PRESIDENT 11
(NATURAL LAW) JOHN HAGELIN - PRESIDENT, NAT GOLDHABER - VICE PRESIDENT 13

OFFICIAL BALLOT, GENERAL ELECTION
PALM BEACH COUNTY, FLORIDA
NOVEMBER 7, 2000

4 (REFORM) PAT BUCHANAN - PRESIDENT, EZOLA FOSTER - VICE PRESIDENT
6 (SOCIALIST) DAVID McREYNOLDS - PRESIDENT, MARY CAL HOLLIS - VICE PRESIDENT
8 (CONSTITUTION) HOWARD PHILLIPS - PRESIDENT, J. CURTIS FRAZIER - VICE PRESIDENT
10 (WORKERS WORLD) MONICA MOOREHEAD - PRESIDENT, GLORIA La RIVA - VICE PRESIDENT
WRITE-IN CANDIDATE

TURN PAGE TO CONTINUE VOTING

Many different mechanisms are used to record votes in American elections, including touch screens *(left)* and paper keypunch ballots. The design of the infamous butterfly ballot *(right)*, which was used in the 2000 presidential election in Palm Beach County, Florida, led some people who intended to vote for Democrat Al Gore to inadvertently select Reform Party candidate Patrick Buchanan.

casting multiple votes for the same candidate, voting in multiple places at once, voting in a district where the voter is not a resident, or voting as a noncitizen. However, no reputable study has found significant voter fraud. Many claims are based on simplistic ideas of what constitutes evidence of it. For example, an investigation of possible voter fraud conducted by the New Hampshire Secretary of State initially identified several thousand possible fraudulent votes, including cases in which an individual who voted in New Hampshire had the same name and birthdate as a voter in another state. Additionally, Republican candidates had claimed that Massachusetts residents had been bused to New Hampshire to vote. However, virtually all the cross-state matches turned out to be separate people, and the alleged Massachusetts voters were young adults who were attending school in New Hampshire and had legally registered to vote. No cases of actual vote fraud were identified.[6] Donald Trump and his supporters made similar allegations about the 2024 elections. They never had evidence to back up these claims, which were dismissed by state and federal courts. There were no significant vote fraud court cases in 2024.

These examples are consistent with a broader argument: voter ID laws solve a problem that does not exist. Moreover, voter ID laws create barriers to voting for individuals who lack an official ID—these individuals are generally poor, young, and from historically marginalized communities. While some supporters of voter ID laws may be sincerely concerned about preventing fraud, research shows that enacting these laws hurts Democratic candidates by lowering turnout from groups that are likely to support them.[7]

A related argument is that allowing vote-by-mail, extending poll hours, or similar measures somehow makes voting too easy. It is true that these measures reduce the costs and hassles of voting for some people, which probably increases the likelihood that they will vote. Why prioritize voting when budget shortfalls force cuts in other services? The counterargument is that holding elections is more important; it's arguably the most important thing local governments do. Moreover, much of the real-world debate over voting provisions is not about governmental priorities; it's about people trying to shape turnout and who votes in order to ensure election of their preferred candidates.

Presidential elections

Many of the rules governing elections, such as who is eligible to vote, are the same for both presidential and congressional elections. But presidential contests have several unique rules regarding how nominees are determined and how votes are counted.

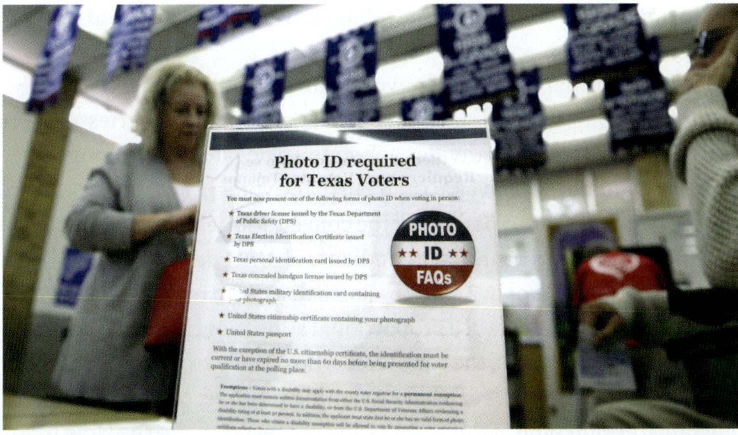

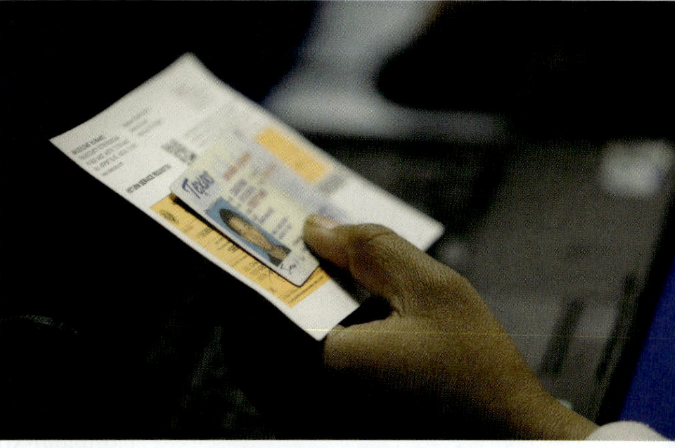

Currently 35 states require some form of ID as proof of identification for voters. While some argue this requirement prevents election fraud, others argue voter ID laws are a form of voter suppression. Texas provided several identification options.

Moreover, the constitutional requirements for presidential candidates are also somewhat stricter than those for congressional candidates (refer to Nuts & Bolts 9.1).

The Nomination: Primaries and Caucuses Presidential nominees from the Democratic and Republican parties are determined by the outcomes of state-level primaries and **caucuses** held over a five-month period beginning in January of an election year.[8] Primary and caucus voters select a candidate, but their votes do not count directly toward the election of that candidate; their votes instead count toward the selection of delegates who have pledged to support the candidate, who then go on to attend the party nominating conventions. There, the delegates cast votes that determine their party's presidential and vice-presidential nominees. The format of these elections, including their timing and the number of delegates selected per state, is determined on a state-by-state basis by the state and national party organizations.[9] In some states, each candidate preselects a list of delegates who will attend the convention if the candidate wins sufficient votes in the primary or caucus. In other states, delegates are chosen by party leaders after the actual primary or caucus takes place. In both cases, a candidate's principal goal is to win as many delegates as possible—and to select delegates who will be reliable supporters at the convention. Some states require delegates to vote for the candidate they are pledged to—at least for the first ballot at the

caucus
A local meeting in which party members select a party's nominee for the general election.

NUTS & BOLTS 9.1

Constitutional Requirements for Candidates

Office	Minimum age	Residency requirement
President	35	Natural-born citizen (born in the United States or on U.S. territory, or child of citizen parent)
Senator	30	Resident of state; U.S. citizen for at least nine years
Representative	25	Resident of state; U.S. citizen for at least seven years

Source: U.S. Constitution.

"Why Should I Care?" These age and citizenship requirements are the most fundamental limits on who can run for political office. They are one explanation for why there are no college-age people elected to Congress—they are prevented from running in the first place.

party nominating convention. However, these laws have never been tested, and it is not clear that they are enforceable.

proportional allocation
During the presidential primaries, the practice of determining the number of convention delegates allotted to each candidate based on the percentage of the popular vote cast for each candidate. All Democratic primaries and caucuses use this system, as do some states' Republican primaries and caucuses.

winner-take-all
During the presidential primaries, the practice of assigning all of a given state's delegates to the candidate who receives the most popular votes. Some states' Republican primaries and caucuses use this system.

The details of translating primary and caucus votes into convention delegates vary from state to state, but some general rules apply. All Democratic primaries and caucuses use **proportional allocation** to divide each state's delegate seats among the candidates; thus, if a candidate receives 40 percent of the votes in a state's primary, the candidate gets roughly 40 percent of the convention delegates from that state. (In the Democratic 2024 primaries, a candidate also needed to gain at least 15 percent of the vote statewide or in a congressional district to receive a share of delegates.) Some Republican contests use proportional allocation, but others use a **winner-take-all** system. In these states, the candidate who receives the most votes gets all the convention delegates. These rules can have a significant effect on candidates' campaign strategies and the outcome of the nomination process (refer to the How It Works graphic in Chapter 8).

The order in which the primaries and caucuses in different states take place is important because many candidacies do not survive beyond the early contests.[10] Most presidential candidates pour everything they have into the first few elections. Candidates who do well attract financial contributions, campaign workers, endorsements, and additional media coverage, all of which enable them to move on to subsequent primaries or caucuses. For candidates who do poorly in the first contests, contributions and coverage dry up, leaving these candidates with no alternative but to drop out of the race. For example, more than 20 candidates entered the race for the 2024 Republican presidential nomination. Several withdrew before any convention delegates were selected. By early-March, two months into the process and five months before the convention where the nominee would be selected, the race was down to only two serious candidates, Trump and Haley. After losing almost all of the contests on Super Tuesday, Haley suspended her campaign. Thus, the candidate who leads after the first several primaries and caucuses generally wins the nomination.[11] However, when the first few contests do not yield a clear favorite, the race can continue until the last states have voted or even until the convention.

Campaigns don't end—they run out of money.

—Richard Gephardt, former House Majority and Minority Leader and presidential candidate

When a sitting president runs for reelection, as Joe Biden initially did in 2024, they typically face little opposition for the party's general-election nomination—not because challengers defer to the president but because most presidents are popular enough among their own party's faithful supporters that they can win the nomination without too much trouble.

Biden's withdrawal from the race in July 2024 created a unique situation. Vice President Kamala Harris immediately announced her candidacy and, in only a few days, secured enough delegate votes to win the nomination.

Among the states, the presidential nomination process is always changing. In 2024, many states held their primaries on the same day in early March (Super Tuesday). Others moved the date of their primary, changed from a primary to a caucus, or changed rules about how delegates are won. For many years, Iowa and New Hampshire have held the first presidential nomination contests, with the Iowa Caucuses held a week before the New Hampshire primary. Democrats changed their ordering in 2023 to prioritize states such as South Carolina and Georgia and to demote Iowa, a state that has been trending Republican in recent elections. Regardless of who goes first, state party officials from other states often complain about the media attention given to these contests and their disproportionate influence in winnowing the candidate pool.

One rule that distinguishes the parties' candidate selection processes is that about one-fifth of the delegates to the Democratic convention are not supporters of a particular candidate, nor have they been chosen to attend the convention based on primary and caucus results. Rather, they are superdelegates, elected officials, and party officials whom their colleagues select to participate in the convention. Most are automatically seated at the convention regardless of primary and caucus results, and they are free to support any candidate for the nomination, although for the 2024 contest, they were forbidden from participating in the first round of voting at the convention. By forcing candidates to court support from superdelegates, the party aims to ensure that the nominee is someone who these officials believe can win the general election and whom they can work with if the nominee is elected.[12] Republicans give state party leaders automatic delegate slots at their convention, but the number of such delegates is a much smaller percentage than for Democrats.

Campaign appearances almost always involve extensive print and electronic media coverage. Here, Elise Stefanik, a representative from New York who ran for reelection in 2024, speaks to the media. The media helped get out Stefanik's message and policy agenda, and as a result, she won her reelection contest.

The National Convention Presidential nominating conventions happen late in the summer of an election year. Their main task is to select the party's presidential nominee, although usually the vote at the convention is a formality; in most recent presidential contests, one candidate has emerged from the nomination process leading up to the convention with a clear majority of delegates and has been able to win the nomination on the first ballot. To get the nomination, a candidate needs the support of a majority of the delegates. If no candidate receives a majority after the first round of voting at the convention, the voting continues until someone does.

After the convention delegates nominate a presidential candidate, they nominate a vice-presidential candidate. The presidential nominee gets to choose their running mate (generally shortly before the convention), and the delegates almost always ratify this choice without much debate. Delegates also vote on the party platform, which describes what the party stands for and what kinds of policies the party wants the candidate to enact if they are elected.

You win some, you lose some. And then there's that little-known third category.

—Al Gore, who lost the 2000 presidential vote in the Electoral College despite winning the most votes on Election Day

The final purpose of a convention is to attract public attention to the party and its nominees. Public figures give speeches during the evening sessions when all major television networks have live coverage. At some recent conventions, both parties have drawn press attention by recruiting speakers who support their political goals despite being associated with the opposing party. At the 2024 Democratic convention, Republicans Adam Kinzinger (former member of the House of Representatives) and Stephanie Grisham (former Press Secretary to Donald Trump) gave televised speeches voicing their support for Harris.

Once presidential candidates are nominated, the general-election campaign officially begins—although it often unofficially starts much earlier, as soon as the presumptive nominees are known. We will say more about presidential campaigns in a later section.

Counting Presidential Votes Let's assume for a moment that the campaigning is over and that Election Day has arrived. Even though in the voting booth people choose between the candidates by name, a choice that constitutes the **popular vote**, this vote is not directly for a presidential candidate. Rather, when you select your preferred candidate's name, you are choosing that person's slate of pledged supporters from your state to serve as electors, who will then vote to elect the president.

The number of electors for each state equals the state's number of House members (which varies by state population) plus the state's number of senators (two per state). Altogether, the electors chosen by the citizens of each state constitute the **Electoral College**, the body that casts **electoral votes** to formally select the president. Small-population states, therefore, have few electoral votes—Delaware and Montana, for example, each have only 3—while the highest-population state, California, has 55 (refer to the How It Works graphic on pp. 332–333). In most states, electoral votes are allocated on a winner-take-all basis: the candidate who receives the most votes from

popular vote
The votes cast by citizens in an election.

Electoral College
The body that votes to select America's president and vice president based on the popular vote in each state. Each candidate nominates a slate of electors who are selected to attend the meeting of the college if their candidate wins the most votes in a state or district.

electoral votes
Votes cast by members of the Electoral College; after a presidential candidate wins the popular vote in a given state, that candidate's slate of electors casts electoral votes for the candidate on behalf of that state.

How it works: in theory

The Electoral College

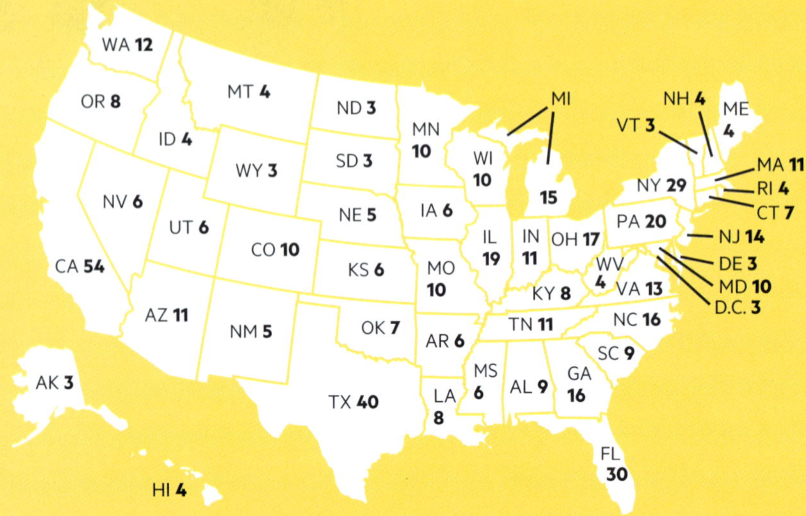

Electoral votes per state
The number of electors from each state equals the state's number of House members (which varies based on state population) plus the number of senators (two per state). Each elector has one vote in the Electoral College.

Who are the electors?
Candidates to be electors are nominated by their political parties. They pledge to support a certain candidate if they are elected to the Electoral College. When you cast your vote for a presidential candidate, you are in fact voting for the slate of potential electors who support that candidate.

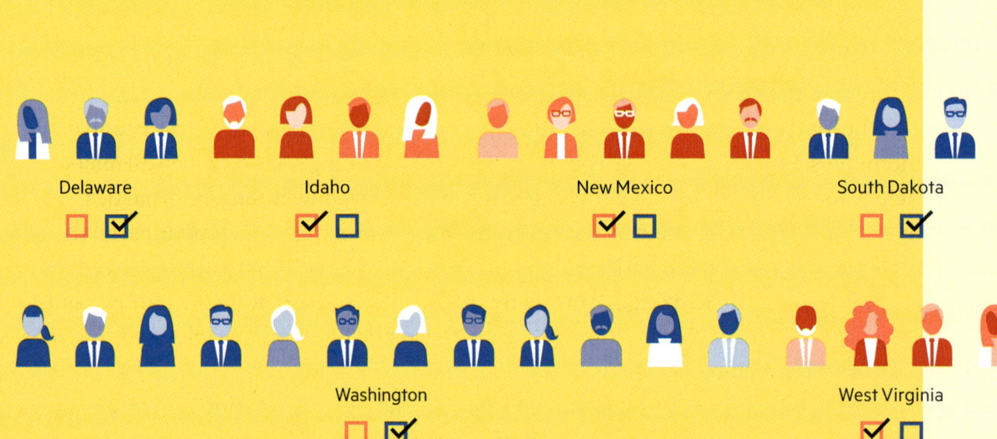

California popular vote

40%

60%

California electoral votes (54)

100%

100%
of electoral votes go to winner

Winning a state
Most states give all of their Electoral College votes to the candidate who wins the most votes in that state. So, even if a candidate only gets 51 percent of the vote in the state, the candidate's entire slate of electors is elected, and they get all of the state's votes in the Electoral College.

How it works: in practice

Donald Trump's Electoral College Strategy, 2024

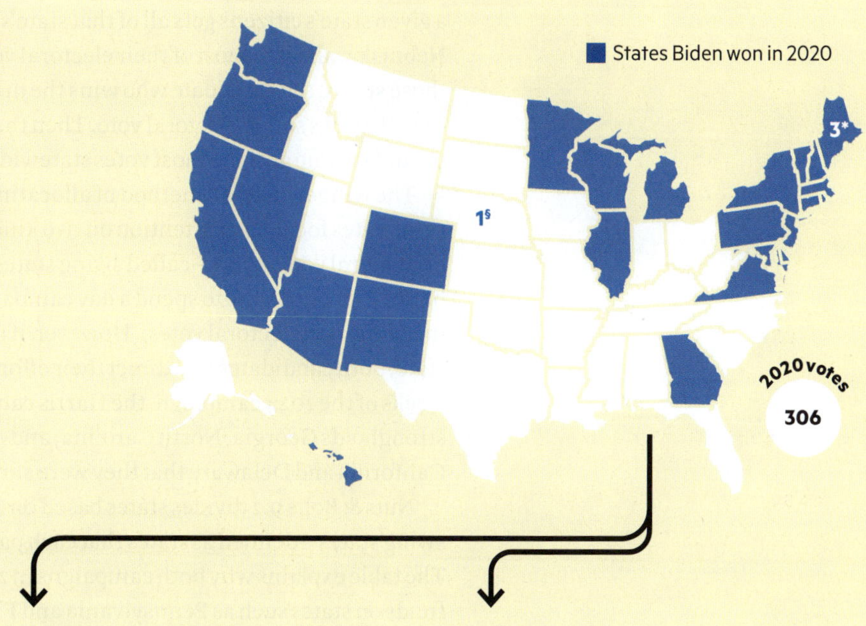

Trump's campaign started with the electoral map that resulted in his defeat in 2020. They focused on two groups of states—Rust Belt states where Joe Biden won narrow victories (Michigan, Pennsylvania, and Wisconsin) and Sun Belt states where Republicans were strong (Arizona, Georgia, North Carolina, and Nevada)—in an attempt to amass at least 270 electoral votes, the threshold required to win the election.

Win back the Rust Belt:
Michigan, Pennsylvania, and Wisconsin
Biden won these states by small margins in 2020.

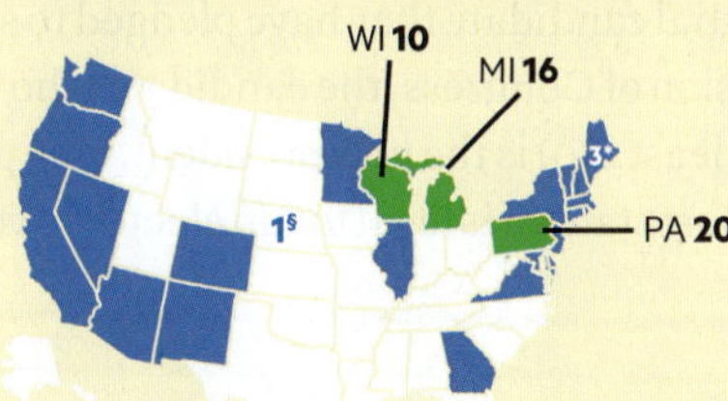

Hold the Sun Belt:
Arizona, Georgia, North Carolina, Nevada
Some recent Republican candidates had won statewide in these states.

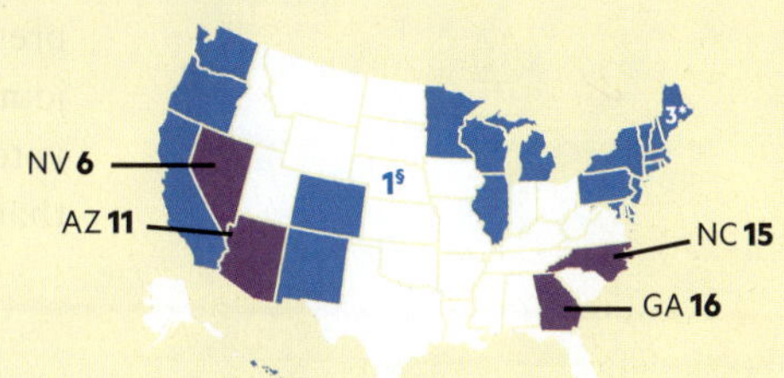

1*
4§
Total votes
312

2024 results

Trump's strategy succeeded. Republicans captured all of the seven states mentioned above, and the Harris campaign did not win any of the states that had voted for Trump in 2020.

Trump's final Electoral College map

AL – **9**	IA – **6**	MT – **4**	SC – **9**
AK – **3**	KS – **6**	NE – **4**	SD – **3**
AZ – **11**	KY – **8**	NV – **6**	TN – **11**
AR – **6**	LA – **8**	NC – **16**	TX – **40**
FL – **30**	ME – **1**	ND – **3**	UT – **6**
GA – **16**	MI – **15**	OH – **17**	WV – **4**
ID – **4**	MS – **6**	OK – **7**	WI – **10**
IN – **11**	MO – **10**	PA – **19**	WY – **3**

Critical Thinking

1. **Why didn't the Trump campaign** focus more time and energy on delegate-rich states like California and New York?

2. **In what states do you think the Trump campaign** spent the most money? Where do you think Trump made the most personal appearances? Why?

* Maine splits its electoral votes: in 2020, Trump received 1, Biden 3; in 2024, Trump received 1, Harris 3.

§ Nebraska splits its electoral votes: in 2020, Trump received 4, Biden 1; in 2024, Trump received 4, Harris 1.

a given state's citizens gets all of that state's electoral votes. But two states, Maine and Nebraska, allocate most of their electoral votes at the congressional district level: in those states, the candidate who wins the most votes in each congressional district wins that district's single electoral vote. Then the remaining two electoral votes go to the candidate who gets the most votes statewide.[13]

The winner-take-all method of allocating most states' electoral votes makes candidates focus their attention on two kinds of states: high-population states with lots of electoral votes and so-called swing states where the contest is relatively close. It's better for a candidate to spend a day campaigning in California (55 electoral votes) than in Montana (3 electoral votes). However, if one candidate is sure to win a particular state, both candidates will direct their efforts elsewhere. For example, during the final weeks of the 2024 campaign, the Harris campaign was targeting former Republican strongholds Georgia, North Carolina, and Arizona and ignoring states such as California and Delaware that they were sure to win.

Nuts & Bolts 9.2 divides states based on their electoral vote and whether they are swing states—defined as states that each party won at least once in recent elections. The table explains why both campaigns in 2024 spent so much time and campaign funds on states such as Pennsylvania and Florida (swing states with a large number of electoral votes)—and why they largely ignored states such as Delaware (small state, one-party-dominates category).

After citizens' votes are counted, each state's slate of electors meets in December in their state's capital. At their meeting, the electors almost always vote for the presidential candidate they have pledged to support. After the votes are certified by a joint session of Congress, the candidate who wins a majority of the nation's electoral votes (at least 270) is the new president. One peculiarity of the Electoral College is that in most states it is legal for an elector to vote for a candidate they are not pledged

NUTS & BOLTS 9.2

Electoral Votes and Swing States

Presidential campaigns focus their attention on states with high electoral votes and swing states where each candidate has a good chance of winning. In this box, we group states into categories based on their number of electoral votes and whether one party has consistently won the state in recent presidential elections.

Source: Compiled by the authors.

One party dominates in recent elections?

Number of electoral votes	Yes (Not a swing state)	No (Swing state)
3–5	D.C., Delaware, Alaska, Montana, North Dakota, South Dakota, Vermont, Wyoming, Hawaii, Maine, Rhode Island, Idaho, Nebraska, West Virginia, New Mexico	New Hampshire
6–10	Arkansas, Kansas, Utah, Connecticut, Oregon, Oklahoma, Iowa, Kentucky, Louisiana, Alabama, South Carolina, Maryland, Mississippi, Missouri, Minnesota, Colorado	Nevada, Wisconsin
More than 10	Massachusetts, Indiana, Tennessee, Washington, New Jersey, Illinois, New York, Texas, California, Ohio, Virginia, Florida	Arizona, North Carolina, Michigan, Pennsylvania, Georgia

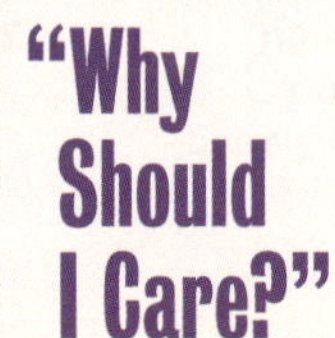

Data on a state's electoral votes and status as a swing state tell us why presidential candidates campaign in some states more than in others. For the most part, the crucial factor is whether both presidential candidates see a state as winnable—if they do, they will campaign there aggressively.

to support or to abstain from voting.[14] Such events are uncommon for the simple reason that electors are selected by the presidential candidates with an eye toward reliable support.

If no candidate receives a majority of the Electoral College votes, the members of the House of Representatives choose the winner. They follow a procedure in which the members from each state decide which candidate to support and then cast one collective vote per state, with the winner needing a majority of these state-level votes to win. This procedure has not been used since 1824, although it might be required if a third-party candidate wins a significant number of electoral votes or if a state's electors refuse to cast their votes.[15]

A presidential candidate can win the Electoral College vote, and thus the election, without receiving a majority of the votes cast by citizens (refer to Figure 9.1). In 2016, Democrat Hillary Clinton received several million more votes than Donald Trump because of large majorities in states such as California and New York, but Trump won a majority in the Electoral College because of narrow victories in states such as Wisconsin and Pennsylvania. A similar outcome occurred in 2000, leading to Republican George W. Bush's victory over Democrat Al Gore. Other presidents who won the Electoral College vote but lost the popular vote were John Quincy Adams in 1824, Rutherford B. Hayes in 1876, and Benjamin Harrison in 1888.

In the days leading up to congressional certification of the 2020 presidential election, some Republican-affiliated lawyers offered theories that Vice President Pence,

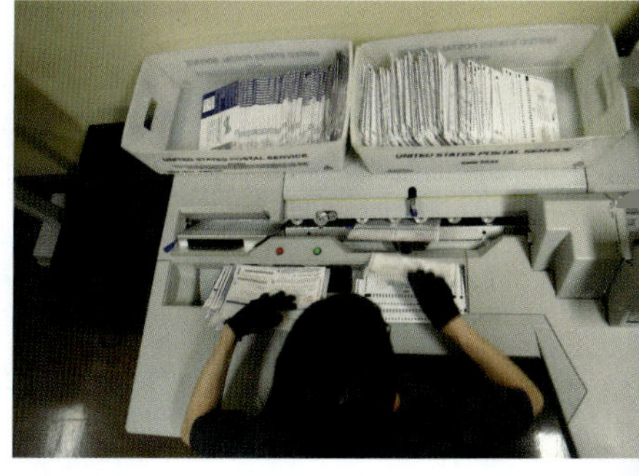

After the 2020 presidential election, President Trump's campaign demanded recounts in several states, including Wisconsin, Michigan, Georgia, and Pennsylvania. The recounts yielded only small changes in vote totals, and there was no evidence of the fraud the campaign repeatedly alleged had occurred.

FIGURE 9.1

Popular Vote versus Electoral Vote Percentages, 2000–2024

Political scientists argue that the Electoral College system tends to magnify the winning candidate's margin of victory. Do the data presented here support this view?

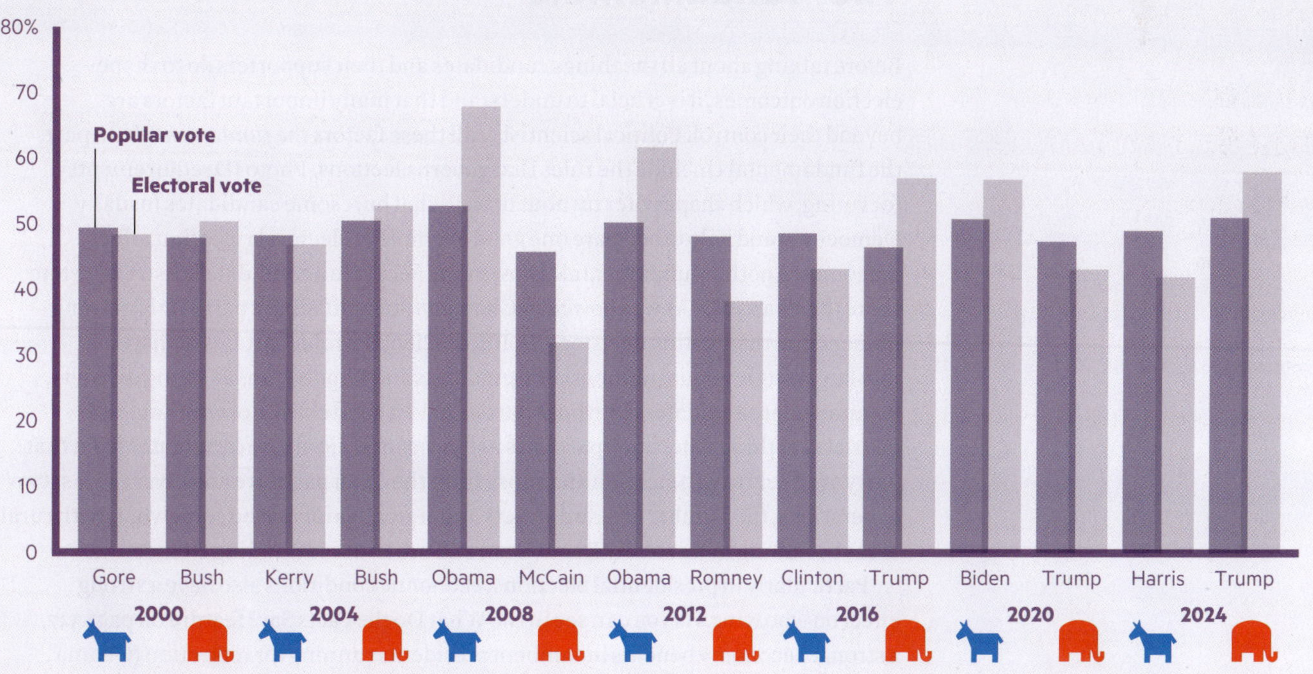

Source: 2000–2016 data from U.S. National Archives and Records Administration, https://www.archives.gov/electoral-college/results (accessed 4/19/22); 2020 data calculated by the authors from election results.

who presided over the certification, could decide to delay the process to allow states to investigate claims of voter fraud, certify alternate delegate slates rather than the ones named by state governments, or use parliamentary procedures to allow the House of Representatives to select the president. In all cases, these theories were offered by supporters of President Trump and were clearly aimed at overthrowing the results of the 2020 election. Pence rejected these theories and allowed members of Congress to certify the electoral vote results that had been sent to Congress. Congress later passed legislation clarifying that the Vice President's role is purely ceremonial.

"Why Should I Care?"

American elections incorporate a complex set of laws, rules, and procedures. And these rules matter—the candidates who win under current rules might lose given other reasonable ways to conduct elections. For example, in 2016, Democrat Hillary Clinton won the popular vote but lost the electoral vote (and the election) due to close losses in Florida, Michigan, Pennsylvania, and Wisconsin. Even small changes in voter registration, voter ID regulations, and other laws in these states might have given Clinton victories in these states—and the presidency.

DESCRIBE THE FEATURES, STRATEGIES, AND FUNDING OF CAMPAIGNS FOR FEDERAL OFFICE

Electoral campaigns

This section explores the campaign process and what candidates do to convince people to vote for them on Election Day. Our emphasis is on things that candidates do, regardless of the office they are running for, across the entire **election cycle**: the two-year period between general elections.

election cycle
The two-year period between general elections.

The "fundamentals"

Before talking about all the things candidates and their supporters do to shape election outcomes, it is crucial to understand that many important factors are beyond their control. Political scientists call these factors the *fundamentals*. In part, the fundamentals include the rules that govern elections. Photo ID requirements for voting, which shape voter turnout in ways that hurt some candidates (usually Democrats) and help others, are one good example of electoral rules that affect outcomes. Another fundamental is how many people in a candidate's district or state share their party ID. As we showed in Chapter 8, an individual's party ID is a strong influence on their voting decisions. Political scientists refer to states or districts that have roughly equal numbers of Democrats and Republicans as swing districts, meaning that candidates from both parties have a good chance of winning. Safe districts are those where one party has a significant majority, so candidates from that party are likely to win election and those from the other party are not. Over the last two generations, the number of safe districts and states has increased somewhat, with rural areas becoming more solidly Republican and urban areas trending Democratic.

Particularly in presidential elections, economic conditions also have a strong effect on who wins. As you can see in the What Do the Facts Say? feature on page 337, a stronger economy benefits incumbent presidents running for reelection (Obama in 2012), while a weak economy hurts incumbents (Jimmy Carter in 1980) and their successors (John McCain in 2008). Of course, fundamentals must be taken in context.

"The Fundamentals" and Presidential Elections

Political scientists argue that "the fundamentals" play a key role in American elections. For example, the state of the economy is thought to influence voter decisions in presidential elections—a strong economy benefits incumbent presidents or their successors. However, most candidates (and journalists) argue that the things candidates say and do during the campaign determine who wins and who loses. What do the facts say?

To answer this question, let's examine this figure, which shows the relationship between presidential election outcomes (vote share for the incumbent president or the candidate from the president's party) and economic conditions (the growth in real gross domestic product [GDP] in the year before the election). The blue line gives the predicted relationship between economic conditions and the popular vote, showing that on average, as economic conditions improve, the president or candidate from the president's party receives more votes.

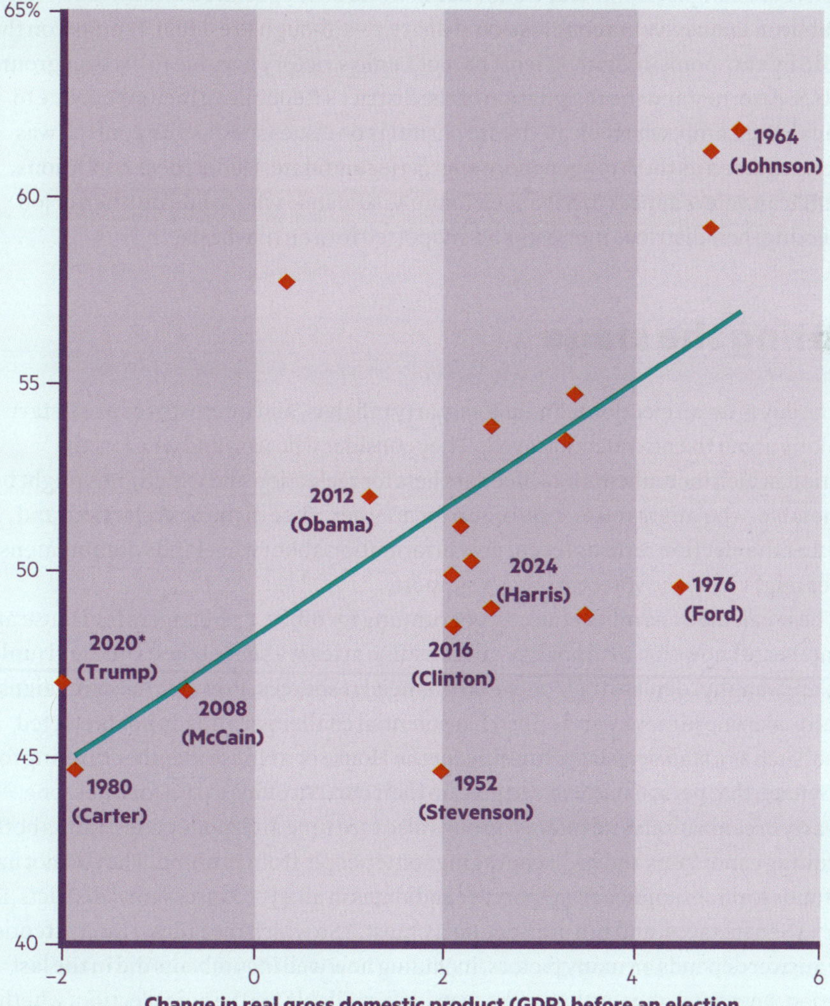

*In 2020, the change in real GDP was −31.4 percent due to the COVID-19 pandemic.
Source: Data calculated by the authors.

WHAT DO THE FACTS SAY?

Think about it

- **Why do incumbent presidents do better** when the economy is strong than when it is weak?
- **Candidates who lose, such as Clinton in 2016 or Romney in 2012, are criticized** for running poor campaigns. Look at the data points that describe economic conditions in these elections and the percentage of the popular vote received by Obama in 2012 and Clinton in 2016. Given the state of the economy in these years, is there any evidence that Romney or Clinton did worse than you would expect?
- **What signs are there in the graph** that other factors besides "the fundamentals" might influence presidential election outcomes?

Big onetime shocks have unique effects. For example, the COVID-19 pandemic caused a drop in second-quarter GDP that was so big we can't even include it in the figure (that's why there's an asterisk next to the 2020 data point). And in 2024, Harris inherited a growing economy, but faced problems because economic dislocations from the COVID-19 pandemic had caused significant price inflation in 2022 and 2023. That said, other factors contributed to Harris's loss in 2024, which we discuss later.

Candidates might like to think that they can convince people to vote for them regardless of circumstances. But the fundamentals like party ID and economic conditions tell us which candidates face an uphill fight and which an easy ride—either because voters are well aware of these factors before the campaign begins or because campaigns are mechanisms by which voters become informed about them.[16] It may not be fair to reward or blame candidates for the state of the economy, as even presidents have only limited control over economic growth or unemployment levels. For better or worse, however, a significant fraction of American voters behaves this way.[17] Similarly, for some challengers, defeat is a foregone conclusion because they are running in a state or district that is safe for the other party—no matter what they do, most of the electorate is unlikely to support them.

It's important to remember, though, that the fundamentals are not the final word in an election. The backgrounds of the candidates, their qualifications for office, and the decisions they make about their campaigns sometimes have significant, even decisive effects. For example, Democrat Conor Lamb won a 2018 special election in a strongly Republican Pennsylvania congressional district—although President Trump won there in 2016 by a 20-point margin. At least part of Lamb's victory was due to his background as a U.S. Attorney and the resignation of the district's Republican incumbent due to scandal. But Lamb, who took moderate positions on issues such as gun control, was widely regarded as the stronger, more energetic candidate. Under these conditions, Republican voters appear to have seen Lamb as someone who would do a better job protecting their district's interests and supported him on that basis.

Setting the stage

On the day after an election, candidates, party officials, and interest groups all start thinking about the next election cycle. They consider who won and who lost the election, which incumbents look like safe bets for reelection and which ones might be vulnerable, who might retire soon or run for another office in the next election, and whether the election returns reveal new information about what kinds of campaigns or issues might increase voter turnout or support.

These calculations reflect the costs of running for office. Challengers for House and Senate seats know that a campaign will consume at least a year of their time and (unless they are wealthy) deplete their personal financial resources. Presidential campaigns require even more money and effort. If a potential challenger already holds elected office, such as a state legislator running for the House or a House member running for the Senate, that person may have to give up their current office to run for a new one.[18]

Party organizations and interest groups also face time and money constraints both in recruiting candidates and in discouraging some people from running. They do not have the funds to offer significant support to candidates in all 435 congressional districts, in 33 or 34 Senate races, and in a presidential contest.[19] So which races draw their attention? The answer depends on many factors, including how well incumbents did in the last election, how much money those who won have available for the next election, whether party affiliation in the state or district favors Republicans or Democrats (and by how much), and whether the newly elected officeholders are likely to run for reelection.

Each term, members of Congress decide whether or not to run for another term. Sometimes they retire because of their age; sometimes it's a scandal or other factors that force their hand. In 2024, Mitt Romney (R-UT), who in 2012 was the Republican presidential candidate, announced his retirement citing his age and explaining he wanted to make way for the next generation of leaders.

Party committees and candidates also consider the likelihood that incumbents might retire, thereby creating an **open seat**. In the run-up to the 2024 elections, some senior citizen legislators such as Senator Mitt Romney (R-UT, 77 years old) announced their retirement, as did younger incumbents who planned to run for another office, became embroiled in a scandal, or had another reason to leave. Some Republican House members who resigned in mid-2024 claimed they were doing so because they were tired of not accomplishing anything. Open seats are of special interest to potential candidates and other political actors because incumbents generally hold an election advantage.[20] When a seat opens up, candidates from the party that does not control the seat know that they may have a better chance to win because they will not have to run against an incumbent. The incumbent's party leaders, in turn, have to recruit an especially strong candidate in order to hold the seat. Thus, in an election in which a relatively large number of members of Congress choose to retire (as was the case for Republicans in 2018), the party with fewer retirements is in the better position because it has fewer open seats to defend.

open seat
An elected position for which there is no incumbent.

Presidential campaigns also take incumbency into account. Virtually all first-term presidents run for reelection. Potential challengers in the opposing party study the results of the last election to see how many votes the president received and how this support was distributed across the states to determine their own chances of winning against the incumbent. Candidates in the president's party make the same calculations, although no sitting president in the twentieth century was denied renomination. Nonetheless, some presidents (Harry Truman in 1952, Lyndon Johnson in 1968) retired because their chances of being renominated were not good, while others (Gerald Ford in 1976, Jimmy Carter in 1980) barely won tough primary contests.[21]

Before the campaign

While in Office Most sitting House members, senators, and presidents work throughout the election cycle to secure their reelection. Political scientists describe this activity as the permanent campaign.[22] To stay in office, incumbents have to do two things: keep their constituents happy and raise money for their campaign. As we will see in Chapter 11, congressional incumbents pursue the first goal by taking actions that reflect the demands of their constituents. This, in turn, boosts voters' retrospective evaluations of the incumbents at election time.[23] Incumbent presidents make the same kinds of calculations. For example, during the COVID-19 pandemic, Donald Trump faced the decision of when to relax social distancing advisories and allow the economy to reopen. Part of Trump's calculation was to balance safety (preventing the spread of the virus) with the goal of preventing a prolonged economic downturn. But Trump's calculations undoubtedly included the goal of ensuring that voters would remember his actions in a positive way when they went to the polls in November 2020. Of course, many presidential actions are taken in response to events rather than initiated to gain voter support. Particularly in the case of wars and pandemics, it is far-fetched to say that presidents take actions only for political gain. Even so, presidents, just like other politicians, are keenly aware of the political consequences of their actions and the need to build a record they can run on in the next election.

Presidents can also use the federal bureaucracy both to their own advantage and to help members of their party. For example, some scholars have argued that presidents take measures to try to increase economic growth in the months prior to elections, with the aim of increasing support for their own candidacies (if they are eligible to run for reelection) and for their party's candidates.[24] Given the size and complexity of the U.S. economy and the fact that the independent Federal Reserve System controls monetary policy, it is unlikely that such efforts could have much success. Even so, it seems clear that out of a desire to stay in office and help their party's candidates, presidents would want to be seen as having a positive impact on the economy.

Fund-Raising Candidates for all offices, incumbents and challengers alike, also devote considerable time before the campaign to raising campaign funds. Fund-raising helps an incumbent in two ways.[25] First, it ensures that if they face a strong opponent, the incumbent will have enough money to run an aggressive campaign. Second, successful fund-raising deters opposition. Potential challengers are less likely to run against an incumbent if that individual is well funded with a sizable campaign war chest.[26] We'll discuss campaign fund-raising in more detail later in the chapter.

Promises and Party Positions Candidates also spend time before (and sometimes during) a campaign developing or refining their campaign platform, which includes stances on issues and promises about how the candidate will act in office. Given that few voters are well informed about public policy and aren't inclined to learn, candidates do not win elections by trying to educate the electorate or making complex promises. What works is making promises and taking positions that are simple and consistent with what the average voter believes, even if these beliefs are inconsistent with reality. For example, many people believe that interest groups have too much power in Washington, although their influence is far less powerful than most Americans think (refer to Chapter 10). Even so, many candidates accuse their opponents of being beholden to interest groups. These claims may be far-fetched, but they work well politically because they play into citizens' perceptions.

In writing their platforms, candidates may be constrained by positions they have taken in the past or by their party affiliation. For one thing, candidates whose positions vary from one election to another or between the primary and general elections often lose support from voters who see the changes as a sign of manipulation.[27] Also, as we saw in Chapter 8, the parties have strong brand identities (issue ownership) that lead many citizens to associate Democrats with liberal policies and Republicans with conservative ones. As a result, candidates often find it difficult to make campaign promises that contradict these perceptions. For example, during the 2024 presidential campaign, Donald Trump pledged to preserve Medicare and Social Security benefits. However, considering past attempts by Republican officeholders to cut these programs, voters might have doubted that Trump—the Republican nominee—would carry out this pledge if elected. A candidate's positions are also influenced by demands from potential supporters. In a state or district with many conservative or Republican voters, opposition to Obamacare or to amnesty for undocumented immigrants might be a winning electoral strategy—just as support for these proposals would generally be helpful for candidates running in states or districts where most voters are moderate to liberal or Democrats.

The two-step electoral process in American elections also influences candidate positions. To win office, candidates have to campaign three times: first to build a staff and gain contributors and volunteers (the so-called silent primary or money primary), then in a primary to get on the ballot, and then in a general election. This process gives candidates an incentive to take relatively extreme policy positions—and encourages the entry of relatively extreme candidates—because party activists, contributors, and primary voters (the people whose support candidates need to attract in the first two steps above) hold more extreme positions than voters in the general election. Thus, in the typical congressional district, Republican candidates win primaries by taking conservative positions, while Democratic candidates win primaries by upholding liberal views.

However, a position or promise that attracts votes in a primary election might not work so well in the general election, or vice versa. For example, during the 2024 Republican presidential nomination campaign, challenger Vivek Ramaswamy attracted some support by taking unusual positions, such as abolishing abortion, raising the voting age to 25, and firing 75 percent of federal civil service employees. While these positions were popular among some Republican activists and primary voters and helped distinguish Ramaswamy from his competitors, they would have been disastrous in the general election.

Table 9.1 lists part of the campaign platforms of the 2024 presidential candidates and shows their similarities and differences in eight issue areas that received

TABLE 9.1

Presidential Candidates' Issue Positions (Selected), 2024

The table indicates where Kamala Harris and Donald Trump stood on eight key issues in 2024 as the presidential election approached in November: immigration, health care, gun control, trade, climate change, Iran, international relations, and LGBTQIA+ rights.

Source: Compiled by the authors from news coverage and candidate websites.

Issue	Kamala Harris	Donald Trump
Immigration	Comprehensive reform with path to citizenship for undocumented immigrants	Build wall between United States and Mexico, increase deportations, ban refugees
Health care	Improve Obamacare	Repeal Obamacare
Gun control	Expand background check system	Repeal limits on gun ownership
Trade	Generally supportive of free trade	Renegotiate agreements, limit trade
Climate change	Address climate change, stress renewable energy	Repeal Biden-era clean energy tax credits, withdraw from the Paris Agreement on climate change
Iran	Re-implement Iran nuclear agreement	Increase sanctions on Iran
Relations with international allies	Prioritize consultation and cooperation with allies	Demand allies expand defense spending and defer to United States
LGBTQIA+ rights	End discrimination against LGBTQIA+ individuals	Support law giving businesses right to refuse service to LGBTQIA+ individuals

considerable attention during the campaign. In all these areas, Harris and Trump offered sharply different ideas of what government should do, although in some cases one or both platforms did not offer policy details. The sharp differences between the platforms on most of the issues are somewhat uncommon—in most elections, there are a few areas where parties offer similar proposals, differing only in details.

A candidate's issue positions as described in their platform help mobilize supporters and attract volunteers, activists, interest-group endorsements, and contributions. Issue positions also define what government will do differently depending on who gets elected. And as we will see later in this chapter, some people vote based on candidates' issue positions. Even so, there is considerable evidence that many voters do not know much about candidates' issue positions, particularly in House and Senate races. As a result, when a candidate wins a race or a party wins seats across the country, it is risky to read the outcome as a sign that the winners had the most popular set of issue positions.

Campaign Staff Finally, candidates spend time before the campaign building their organization. As with fund-raising, the success or failure of these efforts is a signal of a candidate's prospects. If experienced, well-respected people agree to work for a candidate's campaign, observers conclude that the candidate's prospects for being elected are probably good.

Skilled campaign consultants are among the most sought-after campaign staff. These consultants plan strategies, run public-opinion polls, assemble ads and buy television time, and talk with members of the media on the candidate's behalf, among other things. For many consultants, electioneering is a full-time, year-round position. Many concentrate on electing candidates from one party, although some work for whoever will hire them.

Almost all campaigns have paid and volunteer staff, ranging from the dozen or so people who work for a typical House candidate to the thousands needed to run a major-party candidate's presidential campaign. Some campaign staff work full-time for an incumbent's campaign committee or are on the incumbent's congressional or presidential staff. With some exceptions for senior presidential staff, federal law prohibits government employees from engaging in campaign activities during work hours or with congressional resources.[28] As a result, many congressional or presidential staffers take a leave of absence from their government jobs to work on their

Most officeholders are always campaigning—traveling around their states or districts, talking with constituents, and explaining their actions in office—all in the hope of winning and keeping support for the next election. Here, Lauren Underwood (D-IL) meets with constituents.

bosses' reelection campaigns during the last few months of the election cycle, then return to working for the government after the election—assuming the incumbent is reelected.

It's hard to separate what candidates do at election time from what they do between elections—incumbents are *always* campaigning, always making promises and taking positions, and always raising campaign funds—which is part of the reason they are so likely to win reelection. In many cases, incumbent House members and senators wind up running against poorly funded, inexperienced candidates because stronger challengers—seeing that the incumbent has been working hard to solidify a hold on the constituency—decide to wait until the incumbent retires, when they can run for the open seat. Thus, though incumbents are not automatically favored for reelection, they often win by large margins because of all the things they do while holding office in between elections.[29]

Primaries and the general election

Congressional primary elections occur throughout the spring and summer. For congressional candidates, winning the primary allows them to plan for the general election in November and gives them access to party resources including contributions, workers, and assistance with polling and other logistics. As we discussed earlier, presidential primaries and caucuses begin in early January and extend into June, culminating in the party nominating conventions held during the summer. Officially, the general-election campaigns begin in early September. By then, both parties have had their conventions and have chosen their presidential nominees and their congressional candidates. Interest groups, candidates, and party committees have raised most of the funds they will use or donate in the campaign. The race is on.

For presidential candidates, the move from primaries to the general election involves a sharp shift in campaign strategies. Unlike in the early primary states, where candidates engage in "retail politics" by meeting more directly with voters on a small, individual scale, the presidential general-election campaigns emphasize "wholesale politics," a style of campaigning in which candidates contact voters indirectly, such as through media coverage and campaign advertising. At this point, presidential campaign events generally involve large numbers of citizens, and if they are smaller events or one-on-one encounters, they are designed to generate media coverage and thereby reach a larger audience.

In contrast, some general-election campaigns for the House and even a few Senate races are more likely to practice retail politics, stressing direct contact with voters. Even so, the start of these general-election campaigns is usually when congressional candidates and groups supporting and opposing them go "on the air" with campaign advertising. (In contrast, all presidential campaigns run ads throughout the primary and general-election campaigns.)

Name Recognition One of the most fundamental campaign strategies, particularly in congressional campaigns, is to build name recognition. Since many citizens know fairly little about congressional candidates, efforts to increase a candidate's name recognition in these races can deliver a few extra percentage points of support—enough to turn a close defeat into a victory. Of course, many citizens vote for the candidate who shares their partisanship—but if the only thing a citizen knows is the name of one of the candidates, the citizen will almost surely vote for that candidate on Election Day. The importance of name recognition is one reason why campaigns invest in

Candidates may gain media attention and (if they are not incumbents) name recognition by hosting campaign events. During the 2024 presidential race, Trump faced multiple felony charges that required time in the courtroom, taking him away from the campaign trail. But Trump used these opportunities to stay in touch with his supporters, drawing parallels between his struggle for justice against what he said were false charges, and the bureaucracy, or Deep State, which he promised to cut.

GOTV ("get out the vote") or the **ground game**
A campaign's efforts to "get out the vote" or make sure its supporters vote on Election Day.

buttons, bumper stickers, and yard signs—all of which help ensure that voters know a candidate's name.

Getting Out the Vote A second basic strategy is mobilization. Turnout is not automatic: just because a citizen supports a candidate does not mean that the citizen will actually vote. Candidates have to make sure that their supporters go to the polls on Election Day. Moreover, focusing on getting supporters to the polls (or making sure they have an absentee ballot) is a relatively efficient use of candidates' resources. Given the importance of partisanship and the fact that most people don't pay much attention to politics, it's much easier to get a supporter to go to the polls than it is to convert an opponent into a supporter.

Campaign professionals refer to voter mobilization efforts as **GOTV ("get out the vote")** or the **ground game**.[30] Many campaigns for Congress or the presidency use extensive door-to-door canvassing, in which volunteers knock on doors and present their candidate's message to voters one at a time. Campaigns also use phone banks, email campaigns, and social media to reach out to potential supporters. To determine how best to contact these people and convince them to vote, both Republican and Democratic campaigns use sophisticated databases, combining voter registration data with demographics.[31]

Sometimes campaigns work to decrease support and turnout for their opponent. One tactic is push polling, in which a candidate or a group that supports a candidate conducts a voter "survey," typically by phone, that isn't actually designed to measure opinions so much as to influence them. Campaigns use these so-called polls to spread false or misleading information about another candidate by including this (mis) information in questions posed to large numbers of citizens.

Going Positive or Negative? Candidates and other organizations also need to determine the tenor of their campaign—whether they emphasize their own (or their preferred candidates') qualifications and platform (positive campaigning) or focus on criticizing their opponent's positions, experience, and lack of qualifications (negative campaigning). For example, when Kamala Harris talked about life lessons she had learned from her mother or her experience as a teenager working at McDonald's, that was an example of positive campaigning. But when Harris criticized Donald Trump's proposals to increase import tariffs or his efforts to restrict abortion access, that was negative campaigning. Candidates and their supporters often try to raise doubts about their opponents by citing politically damaging statements or unpopular past behavior. In conducting opposition research, candidates and interest groups dig into an opponent's past for embarrassing incidents or personal indiscretions, either by the candidate or by a member of the candidate's family or staff.

The positive or negative tone of a campaign may not be driven completely by the candidates themselves. The Internet, for example, facilitates efforts to popularize damaging information. During the 2024 campaign, many social media sites offered videos of candidates tripping on stairs, saying embarrassing things at campaign events, or trying to connect with voters who largely ignored them. Most of the time, these videos do not have a significant impact on election outcomes. They only reach a limited audience, and most voters have their minds made up before the campaign begins. Campaign gaffes matter only when they resonate with beliefs voters already have about a candidate.

Candidates who are behind in the polls (or the organizations that support them) sometimes resort to attack ads: campaign ads that criticize the opponent. While all critical ads are categorized as negative campaigning, campaign experts distinguish between ads that criticize a candidate but at the same time accurately describe their action or position, and ads that stretch the truth (or break it outright). In this sense, Harris's criticisms of Trump were negative but factually correct. On the other hand, an ad run during the 2017 special House election in Georgia falsely suggested that the Democratic candidate had ties to terrorist organizations, simply because the Middle Eastern news service Al Jazeera had run a story about the candidate and the race. Of course, attack ads often fail because they are too outlandish. However, some succeed in changing votes, while others force the opposing candidate to spend time and money denying the ads' claims.

At the beginning of 2024, the ages of the two candidates—Biden, 81, and Trump, 77—was a contentious issue. After their first debate, Biden struggled to articulate his thoughts, accomplishments, and ideas, so much so that party leaders began to question his ability to be competitive in the race, and the public openly expressed skepticism. In late summer, heeding these concerns, Biden stepped back and endorsed his vice president, Kamala Harris, to run at the top of the ticket.

Debates Candidates often contrast their own records or positions with those of opposing candidates or make claims designed to lower citizens' opinions of their opponents. Sometimes these interactions occur during a formal debate. Most congressional campaigns involve debates in front of an audience of likely voters, a group of reporters, or the editorial board of a local newspaper. Typically, candidates take questions from reporters or a debate moderator, although sometimes candidates question each other or answer questions from the audience.

Presidential campaigns involve multiple debates during the primary and caucus season. Throughout the months before the first primaries and caucuses, each party's candidates gather for many single-party debates using a variety of formats. During the general election, the Republican and Democratic nominees meet for several debates. One exception was Donald Trump, who refused to debate his opponents during the 2024 Republican nomination contest. The number and format are negotiated by the campaigns and the Commission on Presidential Debates, a nonpartisan organization that coordinates the debates.[32] The 2024 presidential campaign featured two debates between the presidential nominees (one time with Harris, the other with Biden) and one between the vice-presidential nominees. The debates not only give candidates a chance to present themselves to the electorate but also offer valuable free exposure. Given a relatively uninterested electorate, candidates must figure out how to present themselves to voters in a way that captures their attention and gains their support. Thus, during the 2024 presidential election debates, Republican Donald Trump positioned himself as a successful businessman who had managed the economy, international relations, and the COVID-19 pandemic—a good fit for Trump's status as a political outsider (despite being a former president), a good match to voters' concerns about Kamala Harris, and a good way to turn his personal wealth into a campaign asset.

Campaign advertising: Getting the word out

One of the realities of modern American electoral campaigns is that they are, for the most part, conducted indirectly—through social media, through news coverage of events, and (most importantly) through paid campaign advertising. Candidates, party committees, and interest groups spend more than several billion dollars during each election cycle on campaign-related activities by all candidates for federal office. Most of that money is spent on 30-second television spots. Campaign advertising is critical because, as we discussed in Chapter 7, candidates cannot assume that citizens will take the time to learn from other sources about the candidates, their qualifications, and their issue positions.

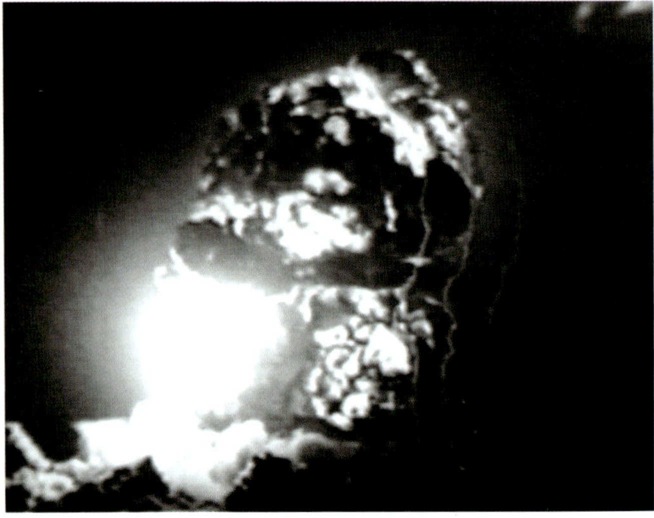

The "Daisy" ad from the 1964 presidential campaign interspersed images of a child in a field of flowers and footage of a nuclear detonation. It was broadcast only once but caused much controversy—and helped crystallize doubts about Republican candidate Barry Goldwater.

What Do the Ads Involve? Campaign advertising has evolved considerably over the last generation.[33] During the early years of television, many campaign ads consisted of speeches by candidates or endorsements from supporters and they ran several minutes in length. In the 1964 presidential race, Lyndon Johnson's campaign ran a five-minute ad titled "Confessions of a Republican" that featured an actor talking about why he didn't want to vote for Republican presidential candidate Barry Goldwater.[34] Johnson's campaign also ran a one-minute ad titled "Peace Little Girl" (nicknamed "Daisy"), which featured a child holding a daisy and pulling its petals off as she counted them aloud one by one. In the background, a voice provided a parallel countdown to the detonation of a nuclear bomb. The ad ended as the television screen filled with the image of the mushroom cloud produced by the nuclear explosion.[35] The implication was that electing Goldwater would increase the chances of a future conflict

TABLE 9.2

Campaign Advertising by Major Spenders in the 2024 Presidential Election

The table shows total spending and the total number of ads, as well as the tone of those ads, as paid for directly by the candidates, Republican PACs, and Democratic PACs.

	Organization	Spending (millions)	Number of ads	Slant of ads
Candidates	Harris campaign	$221.1	292,444	Mixed
	Trump campaign	165.8	266,018	Mostly negative
Republican Groups	Make America Great Again	148.1	102,160	Mostly negative
	Preserve America PAC	63.6	30,786	Mostly negative
	Others	226.6	291,198	Mostly negative
Democratic Groups	Future Forward USA	213.73	103,454	Mostly negative
	Others	280.93	310,690	Mostly negative

Source: Calculated by the authors from data available at Wesleyan Media Project, mediaproject.wesleyan.edu (accessed 11/10/24). Spending and ad data for Future Forward USA includes ads run in collaboration with Climate Action and the League of Conservation Voters Victory Fund.

involving nuclear weapons. The ad remains one of the most iconic pieces of campaign advertising.

Much like the "Daisy" ad, modern campaign ads are short, with arresting images that often use photomontages and bold text to engage a distracted citizenry. Content varies depending on who is running the ads. Table 9.2 provides data from campaign ads in the 2024 presidential general-election campaign from candidates and interest groups. These data show that the Harris campaign had a sizable financial advantage over the Trump campaign. The table also shows a striking difference in ad content: while the candidates ran a mix of positive and negative ads, ads run by interest groups were uniformly negative. Another new development in 2024 was that the party national committees did not run presidential ads.

Do Campaign Ads Work? One critical question about campaign advertising is whether the ads work—whether they shape what people know or influence their voting decisions or other forms of participation. Some observers have complained that campaign ads (particularly negative ads) depress voter turnout and reinforce citizens' negative perceptions of government, although political science research has uncovered no evidence for either effect.[36] Many of these arguments focus on attack ads or negative campaigning. Ads have portrayed candidates as evil blimps hovering over Washington, D.C., or even "demon sheep."[37]

In the 2020 presidential race, many of the ads aired by the Trump campaign and Republican groups criticized Joe Biden for his son Hunter's business dealings in Ukraine. As you can see in this ad, these groups questioned whether the Bidens asked for money in return for political favors—a quid pro quo arrangement.

Whether positive or negative, and regardless of whether they feature evil blimps or something else, campaign ads seek to catch voters' attention, to get them to focus on a race long enough to consider the candidates and their real messages. Nonetheless, studies of campaign advertising have shown that most of the time campaign ads fail at this task. Most citizens ignore the ads or remain unconvinced of their messages. For example, during the 2020 presidential nomination campaign, billionaires Tom Steyer and Mike Bloomberg spent hundreds of millions of dollars on campaign ads in Democratic primaries, only to find that citizens simply did not want to vote for them regardless of how many ads their campaigns ran.

Insofar as ads matter and Americans pay attention to politics, studies of campaign advertising suggest that Americans are reasonably thoughtful when assessing campaign ads. Evidence suggests that campaign advertising has several beneficial effects. Researchers have found that people who are exposed to campaign ads tend to be more interested in the campaign and to know more about the candidates.[38] Moreover, many campaign ads highlight real differences between the candidates and the parties.[39] Nonetheless, average citizens know that they cannot believe everything they see on television, so campaign advertising, if it does anything at all, captures their attention without necessarily changing their minds.[40] (Refer to the What Do the Facts Say? feature on p. 348 for more on evaluating facts in the media.) This is particularly true for negative campaign ads, which sometimes drive support away from the candidate running them. As a result, candidates often rely on party committees and interest groups to run negative ads. Then the candidates themselves can run more positive ads (recall Table 9.2) and can try to disassociate themselves from the negative ads run by others.

In the end, despite all the money and effort poured into campaign advertising, these messages must be designed to capture the attention of citizens whose interest in politics is minimal, delivering a message that can be understood without too much interpretation. In this way, campaign advertising reflects an old political belief, that most things candidates do in campaigns are wasted efforts that have little impact on the election—this is why political scientists stress the importance of the fundamentals when trying to predict election outcomes.

WHAT DO THE FACTS SAY?

Think about it

- **What techniques could you use** to check a map or figure to ensure the data presented represent "just the facts" and not the author's opinions?
- **What are several sources** of reliable political information or data?

Do Maps Offer "Just the Facts"?

When reading media coverage of politics, it's important to consider the source—the author of the story. In many cases, stories that ostensibly offer "just the facts" are cherry-picking data to support a particular point of view. When a story is written by an overtly partisan individual or publication, a closer look often reveals that the story's facts have been misreported or interpreted in an incorrect or limited way.

One example is the "try to impeach this" map that was featured on former Fox News host Sean Hannity's Web page and other conservative, pro-Trump media outlets in fall 2019 during the House impeachment hearings.[a] Counties where Trump received a majority of votes in 2016 were shown in red, while counties Hillary Clinton won were shown in blue. As you see, most of the country is red, with some blue counties on the coasts—supporting Hannity's argument that the Democratic move to impeach Trump amounted to undoing Trump's 2016 electoral victory.

Should we take this map as a serious, fair depiction of political reality? One reason to be suspicious is that Hannity makes no secret of his conservative ideology or the fact that his audience consists mostly of conservative Republicans. This is not to say that Hannity intentionally lies or misrepresents the facts, but simply to point out that his website is hardly the place to look for dispassionate analysis. In fact, the Fox TV network, which broadcasts Hannity's show, classifies it as opinion rather than news.

It also turns out that the map is both incorrect and misleading.[b] For one thing, it mistakenly classifies some counties in the middle of the country as red that should be blue. The bigger problem is that the red/blue classification doesn't consider population density—most of Trump's wins were in low-population rural counties, while Clinton won many high-population urban centers. Even though Trump won more counties than Clinton, Clinton received over 3 million more votes.

Campaign finance

"Campaign finance" refers to money collected for and spent on campaigns and elections by candidates, political parties, and other organizations and individuals. The **Federal Election Commission** administers election laws, including the complex regulations pertaining to how campaigns can spend money. Changes in campaign finance rules, which were passed as the Bipartisan Campaign Reform Act (BCRA), took effect after the 2002 elections and have been modified by subsequent Supreme Court decisions.

Federal Election Commission
The government agency that enforces and regulates election laws; made up of six presidential appointees, of whom no more than three can be members of the same party.

While campaign finance law is complex, most Americans believe the effects of campaign finance are simple: candidates cannot win without spending money, victory goes to the candidate with the larger budget, and, as a result, candidates listen to large donors and ignore average citizens. They also believe that elections cost too much. The reality is more complex. Candidates need money to run effective campaigns (particularly to pay for campaign ads), but spending does not guarantee victory. And while candidates court large donors, they are even more obsessed with winning the support of ordinary citizens, because in the end elections are about votes, not money.

Types of Contributions and Funding Organizations The limits on campaign contributions in the BCRA—also known as the McCain-Feingold Act—vary depending on whether contributions are made by an individual or a group and by the type of group, as shown in Table 9.3. These limits were modified in April 2014 by *McCutcheon v. Federal Election Commission*, in which the Supreme Court struck down limits on overall campaign contributions to candidates and PACs. A second Supreme Court decision, *Citizens United v. Federal Election Commission*, also eliminated restrictions on campaign advertising by corporations, organizations, and labor unions within 30 days

TABLE 9.3

Contribution Limits in the 2024 Elections

The BCRA of 2002 put into effect limits on how much individuals, organizations, and corporations could contribute to candidates' primary and general-election campaigns. The limits were changed based on Supreme Court decisions in 2010 and 2014. At present, although there are still limits on contributions that individuals and PACs can make to each individual candidate, there are no limits on total overall contributions to multiple candidates by individuals and PACs.

	Individual candidates	National party committees	State, district, and local parties	PACs	Limit on total contributions
Individuals	$3,300	$41,300	$10,000 (combined limit)	$5,000	No limit
PACs	$5,000	$15,000	$5,000 (combined limit)	$5,000	No limit
National party committees	$5,000	No limit	No limit	$5,000	$49,600 to Senate candidate per campaign
State, district, and local party committees	$5,000 (combined limit)	No limit	No limit	$5,000 (combined limit)	No limit

Source: Federal Election Commission, "Contribution Limits," https://www.fec.gov/help-candidates-and-committees/candidate-taking-receipts/contribution-limits/ (accessed 4/1/24).

of a primary or 60 days of a general election, which led to large increases in spending by these groups.

Current law distinguishes between independent expenditures, in which a party or group spends money to advocate for a candidate but the candidate or the campaign does not control, direct, or approve the activity, and coordinated expenditures, in which the candidate has some control. Independent expenditures are not limited, but coordinated expenditures are. For example, in Senate races, there is a cap on coordinated expenditures by political parties, ranging from several hundred thousand dollars in small states like Delaware to several million dollars in California.

hard money
Donations that are used to help elect or defeat a specific candidate.

soft money
Contributions that can be used for voter mobilization or to promote a policy proposal or point of view as long as these efforts are not tied to supporting or opposing a particular candidate.

A second distinction in campaign finance laws is between **hard money**, meaning contributions to a candidate, party organization, or other group that are intended to help elect or defeat a specific candidate, and **soft money**, meaning funds that are used for other activities and are not subject to the limits imposed on hard money. Groups defined by IRS regulations as 527 organizations, for example, can raise unlimited soft money from individuals or corporations for voter mobilization and for issue advocacy, but these expenditures must not be coordinated with a candidate or a party. Ads by 527s cannot advocate the election or defeat of a particular candidate or political party. Another type of organization, again described using the IRS code, is the 501(c)(4), which often collects and spends soft money. The principal difference between 527s and 501(c)(4)s is that the latter type of organization does not have to disclose the names of its contributors.

DID YOU KNOW?

Candidates, parties, and organizations spent a total of

$9.5 billion

during the 2023–2024 election cycle.

Source: OpenSecrets.org.

A third type of organization, the political action committee (PAC), is a group that aims to elect or defeat particular candidates or a particular political party. A company or an organization can form a PAC and solicit contributions from employees or group members. As Table 9.3 shows, the amount PACs can give to each candidate in an election is limited, but these limits pertain only to hard money. PACs can also form 527s, which can then accept unlimited amounts of soft money. So-called Super PACs are PACs that do not donate to candidates but use soft money to make unlimited independent expenditures in campaigns. Chapter 10 looks more closely at PACs, 527s, and 501(c)(4)s.

As discussed in Chapter 8, political party committees are entities within the Republican and Democratic parties. Both major parties have a national committee and a campaign committee in each house of Congress. Party committees are limited in the amount of hard money they can give to any given candidate's campaign and in the amount they can spend on behalf of the candidate as a coordinated expenditure. But a party committee (and, after *Citizens United*, organizations, corporations, and labor unions) can spend an unlimited amount in independent expenditures to elect a candidate or candidates.

Political action committees spend millions on campaign advertising. Often, their ads are highly negative. This one attacks Donald Trump for being homophobic in his rhetoric.

Current law gives presidential candidates the ability to receive federal campaign funds for the primary and general-election campaign (in the primary, these are matching funds; in the general election, they are a block grant). These federal funds are generated, in part, by money that taxpayers voluntarily allocate out of the taxes they pay to the federal government by checking off a particular box on their federal tax return form. Funds are also given to minor political parties if their candidate received more than 5 percent of the vote in the previous election. However, in order to accept federal funds, presidential candidates must abide by overall spending limits (and, during the nomination process, by state-by-state spending caps). During the last two presidential campaigns, all the major candidates decided against accepting these funds during the nomination and general-election campaign, which meant that they were not bound by the spending caps (although individual contributors were still limited to the amounts shown in Table 9.3).

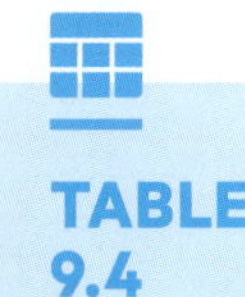

TABLE 9.4

Candidate, Party, and Interest-Group Election Fund-Raising, 2022–2024

Candidates and political parties raise and spend a great deal of money in their campaigns. Do these numbers help explain the high reelection rates for members of Congress?

Source: Calculated by the authors from data at www.opensecrets.org and fec.gov (accessed 11/4/24). 2024 data is incomplete.

	2022	2024
Presidential candidates		
Republican	—	$381,300,000
Democrat	—	$1,003,700,000
Congressional candidates		
House incumbents	$1,087,248,621	$1,081,800,000
House challengers	$353,649,153	$275,100,000
House open-seat candidates	$361,038,989	$239,800,000
Senate incumbents	$698,789,105	$522,300,000
Senate challengers	$319,999,125	$190,400,000
Senate open-seat candidates	$378,402,630	$320,200,000
Political parties		
Republicans	$364,183,817	$506,200,000
Democrats	$307,902,761	$772,500,000
Independent expenditures	$1,253,425,777	$4,190,500,000
Totals	$5,124,639,978	$9,483,800,000

The Effects of Money in Politics Campaign finance regulations reflect two simple truths. First, any limits on campaign activities involve balancing the right to free speech about candidates and issues with the idea that rich people or well-funded organizations should not be allowed to dominate what voters hear during the campaign. Second, an enormous amount of money is spent on American elections. Table 9.4 shows the amounts raised by candidates, political parties, and others in 2022 and 2024. More than $5 billion was raised for the 2022 midterms, and more than $9 billion was raised during 2024, a presidential election year. Moreover, campaign spending is concentrated among a relatively small number of organizations with sizable electioneering budgets. In each of the last several election cycles, the largest organizations have spent hundreds of millions of dollars on contesting the election.

The principal concern about all this campaign cash is that the amount of money spent on candidates' campaigns might matter more than the candidates' qualifications or issue positions. That is, candidates—in particular, wealthy candidates who could self-fund their campaigns—could get elected regardless of how good a job they would do, simply because they had more money than competing candidates to pay for campaign ads, polls, a large staff, and mobilization efforts. Another concern is that individuals and organizations or corporations that can afford to make large contributions (or to fund their own electioneering efforts) might be able to dictate election outcomes or, by funding certain candidates' campaigns, garner a disproportionate amount of influence over the subsequent behavior of elected officials. In the main, these concerns affect soft money contributions and independent

TAKE A STAND

Is There Too Much Money in Politics?

Campaign finance regulations place restrictions on what Americans can do to influence election outcomes—but should they? Suppose you are a wealthy individual who wants to help elect candidates who agree with your worldview. Under current law, you can make relatively small direct contributions to these candidates, but you can also form one of several types of organizations that can spend unlimited money to run campaign ads, or you can donate to an existing organization that will do the same thing. Clearly, having money gives you options for participation in American elections that are not open to the average citizen. (This is the chief criticism of the *Citizens United* decision that struck down limits on independent spending.) Is that a good thing?

It's a free country, and spending money on politics is part of that freedom. Limits on campaign spending conflict with fundamental tenets of American democracy. The Bill of Rights states that Congress cannot abridge "freedom of speech, or of the press; or the right of the people peaceably to assemble, and to petition the Government for a redress of grievances." One interpretation of the First Amendment that has shaped recent Supreme Court decisions on campaign finance is that people should be free to spend whatever they want on contesting elections.

Another argument for eliminating limits on political activities is that with one exception—donations to 501(c)(4) organizations—donors and political activists are required to file quarterly reports on their campaign activities. Therefore, other activists and even ordinary citizens would quickly learn of any large-scale attempts to manipulate election outcomes and could decide to work for the other side or simply vote against a big donor's preferred candidates.

And ultimately, given that campaign spending is no guarantee of electoral success, it is not clear that eliminating spending limits would give big donors control over election outcomes.

Campaign contributions need to be constrained. Even if there's no evidence that money buys elections, there is also no guarantee that under the right circumstances a big donation or ad campaign would not make the difference for one or more candidates. Because money for ads is a necessary component of a political campaign, the possibility remains that a rich donor could change election outcomes by giving large sums to challengers in congressional elections. And in close races, giving a candidate extra funds to increase his or her GOTV efforts or to run additional campaign ads might be enough to change the outcome.

With this possibility in mind, it makes sense to place broad limits on campaign contributions and independent expenditures to level the playing field between ordinary citizens and political activists with deep pockets. The fact that someone is rich shouldn't give them additional ways to influence election outcomes.

Moreover, while it is true that limiting campaign activities requires imposing limits on speech rights, limitations on civil liberties are nothing new. All the individual rights set out in the Bill of Rights are limited in one way or another. Even freedom of speech is limited in areas such as hate speech and statements that pose a clear and present danger. Imposing limits on campaign activities could be justified on the grounds that maintaining free and fair elections is important enough to justify a modest limitation on what individuals and organizations can do to influence election outcomes.

Does money equal speech, or should campaign contributions be limited?

Does the risk of allowing rich donors disproportionate power over elections outweigh the dangers associated with restricting their speech rights?

take a stand

1. Limits on individual campaign contributions guard against allowing wealthy people to dominate elections. What are some of the possible drawbacks of such regulations?

2. Under current law, corporations and unions (not just individuals) are allowed unlimited political expenditures as long as they are independent of a candidate's campaign organization. Why do you think independent expenditures are less regulated than direct contributions to campaigns?

expenditures because the current law places no limits on how much soft money a party can collect or on the size of a group's independent expenditures (refer to the Take a Stand feature on p. 352).

When you look at campaign finance data, the first thing you will see is that it is easy to find who gave money to a candidate, a political party, or another organization.[41] Thus, if you are worried that a particular organization is using campaign contributions to influence elected officials, you can learn which officeholders have received the group's donations. In fact, campaign finance records are so readily available that it is generally easy to identify fraudulent organizations.

However, the raw data do not always tell the whole story. For example, while total spending is often quite high, it is important to remember that a large percentage of campaign expenditures are for advertising. A 30-second ad on a major television network can cost tens or hundreds of thousands of dollars.[42] Given that even House campaigns may run hundreds of ads and presidential campaigns generally run tens of thousands of ads, it is easy to see why campaign costs pile up so quickly.

There is little evidence that campaign contributions alter legislators' behavior or that contributors are rewarded with votes supporting their causes or favorable policies. Research suggests that most contributions are intended to help elect politicians whom contributors already like, with no expectation that these officials will do anything differently because they received a contribution.[43] On the other hand, contributions may help with access, getting the donor an appointment to present arguments to a politician or their staff.[44] And yet people and organizations that generally contribute are already friendly with the politicians they support, so the politicians would likely hear their arguments in any case.

It's also clear that having a lot of campaign cash doesn't make a candidate a winner—and winners don't always outspend their opponents. The poster children for this argument are billionaires Tom Steyer and Mike Bloomberg, who both ran for the Democratic presidential nomination in 2020. Both candidates spent hundreds of millions on their campaigns, running thousands of ads, opening field offices, and hiring large staffs. Even so, both failed to attract much support. And in the 2016 general election, Hillary Clinton's campaign outspent Trump's by nearly $200 million. The Democratic Party and allied outside groups also outspent the Republican Party and its groups. The same was true for Harris in 2024. Even so, Trump won both times. Of course, Trump entered both campaigns with high levels of name recognition and a campaign message that resonated with large segments of the population. But that is exactly the point: victories aren't bought with campaign cash. Candidates need a base level of funding to hire staff, travel, and run some campaign ads. Beyond that point, success is a function of what candidates say and do, not the dollar amount of contributions they receive or the number of ads run on their behalf.[45]

"Why Should I Care?"

When you follow the news about political campaigns, pay attention to the money candidates raise (and spend), where they campaign (and to whom they appeal), the tone and message of their campaigns, and larger fundamentals, such as the strength of the economy. These factors can provide strong clues about who is likely to win (or lose). Remember, though, that politicians don't win elections just by spending a lot of money. Sometimes candidates win despite lower budgets. The other factors listed here and examined in this chapter often have stronger effects on the outcome than money alone.

EXPLAIN THE KEY FACTORS THAT INFLUENCE VOTERS' CHOICES

How do voters decide?

All the electoral activities we have considered so far are directed at citizens: making sure they are registered to vote, influencing their voting decisions, and getting them to the polls. In this section, we examine how citizens respond to these influences. The first thing to understand is that the high level of attention, commitment, and energy exhibited by candidates and other campaign actors is not matched by ordinary citizens. We have seen throughout this chapter and others that although politics is everywhere and elections are the primary mechanism citizens have to control the federal government, only a minority of citizens report high levels of interest in campaigns, many people know little about the candidates or the issues, and many people do not vote.[46]

After registering and informing themselves about the election, voters have to take the time to go to the polls and possibly wait in line. Voting is costly in terms of time and effort. In 2020, during the coronavirus pandemic, it became a calculated health risk too, as people struggled to socially distance while waiting.

Who votes, and why?

Politics is everywhere, but getting involved is your choice. Voting and other forms of political participation are optional. Surprisingly, even a strong preference between two candidates may not drive citizens to the polls. They may lack motivation to vote because they feel that their vote is just one of many.[47] And it's true that the only time a vote "counts," in the sense that it changes the outcome, is when the other votes are split evenly so that one vote breaks the tie. Moreover, voting involves costs. Even if citizens don't learn about the candidates but want to vote anyway, they still have to get to the polls. Thus, the **paradox of voting** is this: Why does anyone vote, given that voting is costly and the chances of affecting the outcome are small?

paradox of voting
The question of why citizens vote even though their individual votes stand little chance of changing the election outcome.

Figure 9.2 shows that among Americans the percentage of registered voters who actually voted in recent presidential elections has been around 60 percent, although actual turnout (votes as a percentage of the total adult population) has been closer to 50 percent.[48] Turnout is significantly higher in presidential elections than in midterms—in 2020, turnout hit new highs despite the pandemic, largely due to widespread mail-in

FIGURE 9.2

Turnout in Presidential and Midterm Elections, 2000–2024

The figure shows how turnout of registered voters varies both over time and between presidential and midterm elections. Why don't more people vote in midterm election years? Why don't more people vote in any given year?

Source: United States Election Project, www.electproject.org (accessed 11/9/24).

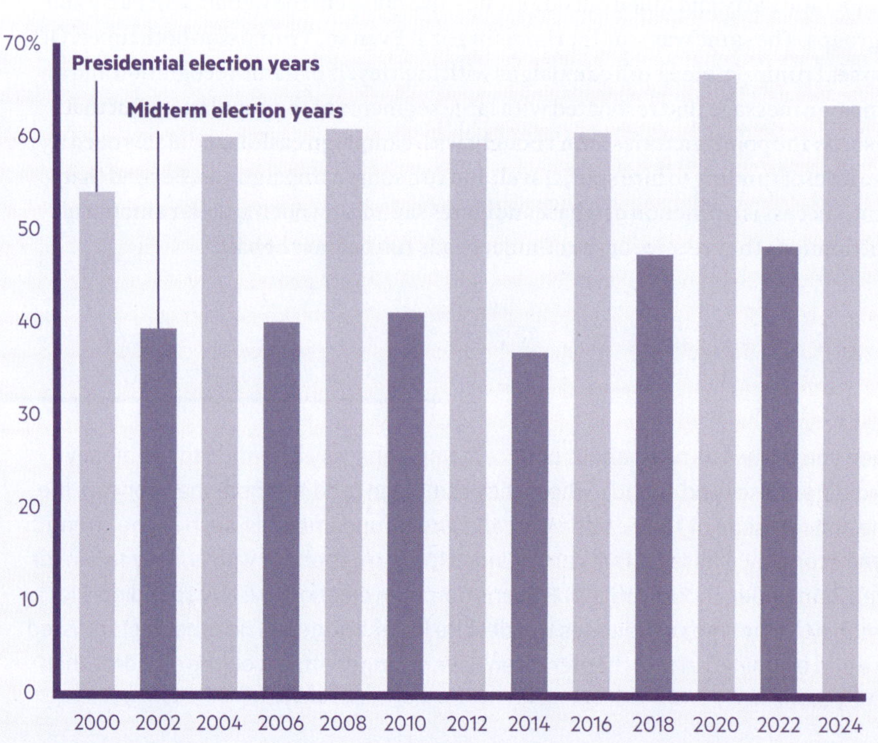

voting. Turnout is much lower in primaries and caucuses: in the 2020 presidential primaries, some states reported unusually high turnout exceeding 30 percent, although in cases like the Wisconsin primary held in April 2020 during the COVID-19 lockdown, most of the voters cast absentee ballots. Turnout for caucuses is generally only a few percentage points.

In the main, turnout is higher for White Americans than for non-White Americans (Black Americans were an exception in 2008 and 2012, when Barack Obama was on the ballot), for older Americans than for younger Americans, and for college graduates than for people with a high school education or less. Men and women, however, say they vote at roughly the same rate. Many factors explain variation in turnout. Turnout is also affected by structural factors, such as state laws that prohibit convicted felons from voting, laws that require citizens to be registered to vote a set number of days before an election, variation in early-voting and voting-by-mail laws, laws requiring a photo ID to vote, and laws that make it easier or harder to obtain an absentee ballot. (This is why ID requirements and efforts to curb voting by mail and polling hours are so controversial—they have significant effects on who votes.)

However, turnout is far below 100 percent, even in areas of the country where all these factors are set to make it easy for people to vote. Analysis shows that turnout is much higher among people who consider going to the polls an obligation of citizenship, feel guilty when they do not vote, or think that the elections matter. Turnout is much lower among those who are angry with the government, think that government actions do not affect them, or think that voting will have no impact on government policy. Citizens who hold these beliefs are unlikely to care about the outcome of the election, are unlikely to feel guilty for abstaining, and are unlikely to see voting as an obligation.[49] Thus, while it is possible to increase turnout somewhat by changing laws, the biggest gains come from convincing individual Americans that voting is something they should feel obligated to do.

These findings demonstrate the importance of mobilization in elections. As we discussed earlier, many candidates for political office spend at least as much time trying to convince their supporters to vote as they do trying to persuade others to become supporters in the first place. Because many Americans either do not vote or vote only sporadically, mobilization is a vital strategy for winning elections.

DID YOU KNOW?

Voter turnout was

59.6%

for Black Americans in the 2024 presidential election.

Source: Calculated by the authors from exit polls and historical data.

During campaigns, candidates often seek to strengthen the perception that they share (or at least are sympathetic to) average Americans' beliefs and interests. Here, Senator Kamala Harris (D-CA, *center*), who became vice president in 2021, meets with constituents at the Martin Luther King Jr. Kingdom Day Parade in Los Angeles.

How do people vote?

Some people are highly interested in politics, collect all the information they can about the candidates, and vote based on this information; they are known as **issue voters**.[50] But most citizens are not interested enough in politics to spend their time that way, and they don't care enough about the details of politics to find out which candidates come closest to their preferences. Reliable information about candidates is also often difficult to find. Although candidates, parties, and other organizations produce a blizzard of endorsements, reports, and press releases throughout the campaign, much of this information may be difficult to interpret. It is a daunting task, even for the rare highly motivated voter.

issue voters
People who are well informed about their own policy preferences and knowledgeable about the candidates, and who use all of this information when they decide how to vote.

Voting Cues This combination of a lack of interest and the relatively complex task of seeking information leads the majority of American voters to base their voting decision on easily interpretable pieces of information, or **voting cues**.[51] Voters in American national elections use many kinds of cues, most notably party ID (voting for the candidate who shares your party identification, as we discussed in Chapter 8), but also the personal vote (voting for a candidate who has helped you get assistance from a government agency or has helped your community benefit from desirable government

voting cues
Pieces of information about a candidate that are readily available, are easy to interpret, and lead a citizen to decide to vote for a particular candidate.

Are you better off than you were four years ago?

—**Ronald Reagan,** running for president against incumbent Jimmy Carter

projects), personal characteristics (voting for the candidate whose personal characteristics such as age, race, gender, ethnicity, religious beliefs, or background match your own), or pocketbook voting (voting for the incumbent if the economy is strong and for the challenger otherwise). Voters can also use multiple cues. Cues give people a low-cost way to cast what political scientist and campaign consultant Samuel Popkin called a reasonable vote—a vote that, more likely than not, is consistent with the voter's true preference among candidates.[52] Studies have found that citizens who use cues and are politically well informed are more likely to cast a reasonable vote than those who use cues but are otherwise relatively politically ignorant. In essence, knowing something about the candidates and the issues at stake in an election helps people select the right cue on which to base their vote.[53]

On the one hand, the role that cues play in voting decisions is one reason why "the fundamentals matter" in American elections. Because some people vote based on the state of the economy, incumbent presidents are good bets to win reelection when economic conditions are good and poor bets when the economy is in trouble. Similarly, because party ID is often used as a cue, candidates are more likely to win if their party affiliation is shared by the bulk of voters in their state or district. On the other hand, the use of cues is another way that candidates (and campaigns) matter. For example, citizens may use a candidate's record in office to guide their vote decision, especially if the candidate makes this record a central theme in their campaign speeches and advertising. In fact, many campaign events and communications are designed to reinforce the impression that candidates share voters' concerns and values. For example, at several points during his campaigns, Donald Trump tweeted pictures of his fast-food dinner on the campaign plane.

Moreover, because personal characteristics are used as a cue, some candidates have a better chance of winning than others, because they have one or more cues that citizens see as desirable. For example, some people voted for Kamala Harris in 2024 because of her perceived ideological moderation, or simply because she was a Democrat. Equally, some people voted for Donald Trump because of his career as a businessman or because he was a Republican. Table 9.5 offers some details on what

TABLE 9.5

Candidate Traits and Voter Choice

Many Americans cast votes based on candidates' personal characteristics and background. What sorts of candidates are advantaged by this practice—and what sorts are disadvantaged?

Willingness to vote for a candidate who is . . .	Percent
Black	96%
Hispanic	94
Female	93
Gay/Lesbian	78
Catholic	95
Jewish	93
Evangelical Christian	80
Muslim	66
Atheist	60
Under 40 years old	70
Over 70 years old	69

Source: L. Saad, 2020. Socialism and Atheism Still U. S. Political Liabilities, https://news.gallup.com/poll/285563/socialism-atheism-political-liabilities.aspx (accessed 4/1/24).

kind of candidate characteristics attract voter support. Almost all voters say they would vote for a Black, female, or Hispanic candidate. However, the percentages are significantly lower for other categories, such as Muslim, evangelical, or atheist candidates. It is also interesting to notice the lower percentages for candidates over 70, which show that the commentary over Biden and Trump's age was something deeper than support or opposition for these candidates.

Who (usually) wins?

All the strategies discussed so far are used to some extent in every election. In normal elections, when congressional reelection rates are high, voters generally use cues that focus on the candidates themselves, such as incumbency, partisanship, a personal connection to a candidate, the candidate's personal characteristics, or retrospective evaluations. This behavior is consistent with what Tip O'Neill, Speaker of the House from 1977 to 1987, meant when he said that "all politics is local": many congressional elections are independent, local contests in which a candidate's chances of winning depend on what voters think of the candidate in particular—not the president, Congress, or national issues. It also explains why electoral **coattails** are typically very weak in American elections and why some Americans cast **split tickets** rather than **straight tickets**. In the main, voting decisions in presidential and congressional elections are made independently of each other.

coattails
The ability of a popular president to generate additional support for candidates affiliated with their party. Coattails are weak or nonexistent in most American elections.

split ticket
A ballot on which a voter selects candidates from more than one political party.

straight ticket
A ballot on which a voter selects candidates from only one political party.

"Wave" elections generally occur when a large number of voters vote against incumbents because of poor economic conditions, political scandal, or a costly, unpopular war. In 2010, many Americans were concerned about the state of the economy, the size of corporate bailouts, the apparent ineffectiveness of economic stimulus legislation, and the enactment of health care reform, and they blamed the party in power (Democrats) for all of these outcomes. As a result, a significant percentage of Americans voted against Democratic congressional candidates either as a protest vote, because they disapproved of their performance, or as an effort to put different individuals in charge in the hope that new members would bring about improved conditions. Ultimately, Republicans gained several seats in the Senate and regained majority control of the House with a nearly 80-seat gain. In contrast, 2024 was not a wave election: while Republicans won the presidency and both houses of Congress, Trump won only a narrow majority of the popular vote, and only a few seats shifted in the House and Senate.

Even in wave elections, reelection rates for members of Congress (the percentage of incumbents who successfully run for reelection) are generally high, as Figure 9.3 shows. Over the last generation, neither party has had a House reelection rate less than 80 percent; even in 2006, when 100 percent of Democratic House incumbents running for reelection won, the reelection rate for House Republican incumbents was almost 90 percent. In wave elections such as the one in 2010, one party's House reelection rate is significantly higher than that of the other party's; in normal elections such as the one in 2020, the House reelection rates are similar and approach 100 percent. Reelection rates for Senate incumbents are somewhat lower but show the same patterns.

Reelection rates for members of Congress are so high because the members work to insulate themselves from electoral challenges through tactics we discussed in this chapter and will discuss further in Chapter 11. They raise large sums of campaign cash well in advance of upcoming elections, use redistricting to give themselves a safe district populated by supporters, and enact pork-barrel legislation that provides government benefits and programs to their constituents. Even so, congressional incumbents are not necessarily safe from electoral defeat. Rather, their high reelection

FIGURE 9.3

Percentage of House Incumbents Reelected, 2000–2024

The figure shows that despite public dissatisfaction with Congress, incumbents still tend to be reelected in their respective districts. According to the chart, which congressional elections were wave elections? Which were normal elections?

Source: Calculated by the authors from election results.

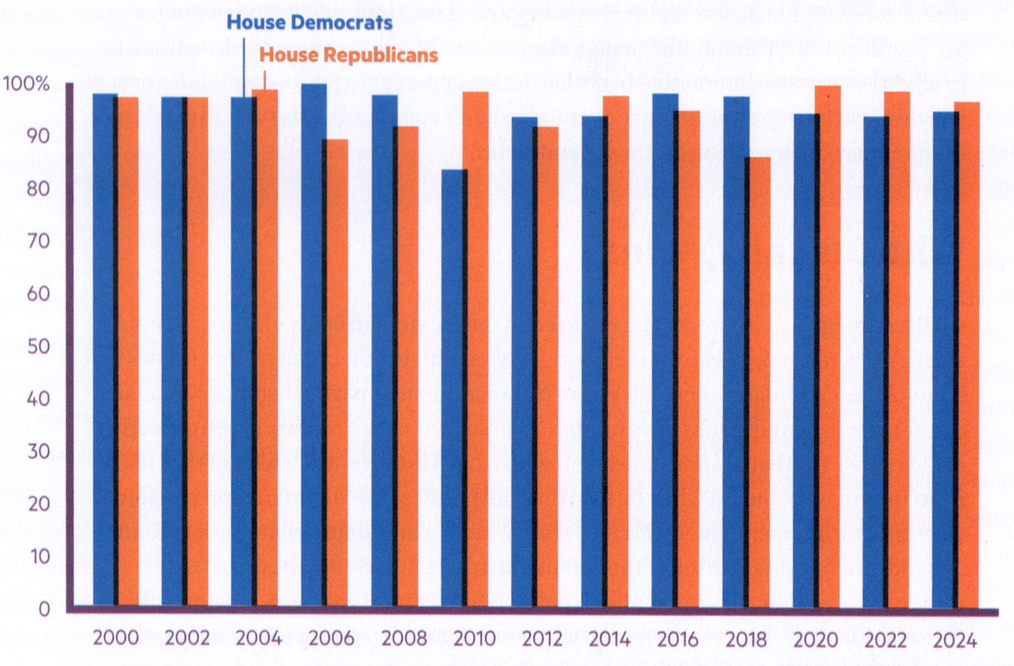

rates result from the actions they take every day, which are calculated to win favor with their constituents. In normal elections, these strategies are generally enough to ensure reelection. In nationalized elections, however, they are not enough to guarantee reelection for some legislators from the disadvantaged party, such as Democrats in 2010.

Wave elections are somewhat rare—once a decade or less. Most of the time, not many citizens are highly concerned about national issues or hold strong opinions about the president, Congress, or the overall state of the nation. Congressional incumbents also work hard to focus attention during their campaigns on the good things they have done for their constituents. Plus, they generally run in states or districts where the majority shares their partisanship. And it is important to remember that even in wave elections some voters still use the incumbent-centered cues described earlier. In a wave election, voters don't suddenly become better informed about politics. Rather, some of them just switch to a different set of voting cues depending on the circumstances of the election.

"Why Should I Care?"

After each election, people look at the results and try to figure out what the election was about—why some candidates won and others lost. Before each election, would-be candidates wonder whether this is "the year" to run for office (you may be one of these candidates someday). The most important thing to understand is that there are no easy explanations and no guarantees. The problem is not that voters are fickle or clueless or that the rules are too complex. Rather, elections boil down to voters and the many different ways they decide how to vote. Knowing what is likely to influence voters can help you make predictions about who will win elections and thus what policies and issues government will tackle.

Understanding the 2022 and 2024 elections

ANALYZE THE ISSUES AND OUTCOMES IN THE 2022 AND 2024 ELECTIONS

In recent years, every election has been described as "the most important election in American history." And in truth, elections always matter because they determine who exercises power in Washington—who sets government policy. In 2024, there were two crucial questions. First, whether voters would elect Democratic candidate Kamala Harris or return Republican former president Trump to office. Second, would Democrats retain control of the Senate—and would Republicans stay in charge of the House. President Biden had succeeded in enacting infrastructure legislation, COVID-19 assistance, and several other legislative accomplishments, which Kamala Harris could tout as her own successes as part of the adminstration. However, many voters blamed Biden for high inflation in 2022, lowering his popularity, and with it, Harris's. On the Republican side, the goal was to exploit the sour mood of the American public to gain unified control of government.

The path to 2024: The 2022 midterm election

The 2022 midterms were a good example of a normal congressional election. There was no overarching issue that framed campaigns and vote decisions. For the most part, election outcomes were driven by fundamentals such as the strength of the Republican and Democratic parties in local communities, candidate quality, variation in turnout across groups in each party, and voter perceptions of the state of the economy and party issue positions.

This is not to say that the election was inconsequential. Since gaining unified control of the federal government in the 2020 elections, President Biden and congressional Democrats had succeeded in enacting several important pieces of legislation, including a large COVID-19 assistance package, a billion dollars in infrastructure funding, and a similar-sized package to address climate change. Senate Democrats had also approved Biden's Supreme Court nominee, Justice Ketanji Brown Jackson.

Losing even a few seats in either chamber in 2022 would give Republicans majority control and allow them to block any further Democratic initiatives.

The Campaign At the beginning of the 2022 election cycle, Republicans had good reason to be optimistic. As we've discussed, the president's party typically loses congressional seats in midterm elections. Republicans also had unified control of more than 20 states, allowing them to manage redistricting efforts in favor of their candidates. The only advantage for Democrats was that Republicans had more Senate seats to defend, 21 versus 14, including vulnerable open Senate seats in Pennsylvania and North Carolina. However, Democrats had equally vulnerable incumbents in Arizona and Georgia. In House elections, attention focused on a small number of seats where the incumbents had won in districts that favored the other party, such as Democrat Abigail Spanberger in Virginia's 7th District.

Republicans were also given an advantage by the state of the economy. As the country exited the COVID pandemic, the annual rate of inflation had increased to about 8 to 10 percent, levels that had not been seen in a generation. Reflecting these conditions, less than 25 percent of Americans reported believing that the country was on the right track. Polls measuring voter intentions to cast a ballot also showed that the

Republican Party had a narrow but consistent advantage in turnout. All these factors together with President Biden's approval rating, about 40 percent, suggested that Republican gains could be significant.

Through most of the campaign, analyses of polling data gave Republicans a good chance of recapturing the House and a significant (although less than 50 percent) chance of gaining a Senate majority. While the Democrats' Senate majority was even narrower than in the House, they had only a few vulnerable incumbents. So it would take a significant Republican win to produce a Senate majority.

As the campaign proceeded, four developments favored Democrats. First, in some states, Republican primary voters selected political novices over experienced candidates, including J. D. Vance in Ohio, Blake Masters in Arizona, Herschel Walker in Georgia, Don Bolduc in New Hampshire, and Mehmet Oz in Pennsylvania. While these candidates had some advantages (for example, Walker was a well-known football star and businessman), their inexperience and other disadvantages (Oz, for example, became a Pennsylvania resident just before announcing his candidacy) raised hopes that Democrats could prevail in the general election.

Second, Democrats hoped that the Supreme Court's *Dobbs* decision, which repealed *Roe v. Wade* and ended federal abortion rights, would motivate turnout among women and younger voters, both key constituencies for the party. Third, Democrats believed that favorable economic developments, such as a significant drop in energy prices during summer 2022, would rebut Republican claims that Democrats had mismanaged the economy. Fourth, Republican gains from redistricting were smaller than expected, as Democrats worked equally hard to redistrict states where they controlled state governments, such as California.

Reflecting all these developments, polls at the end of summer 2022 showed Republicans' chances of winning the Senate were down to about 20 percent, although they remained the favorites to capture the House.

But the tides quickly turned. In the last weeks of the campaign, Democrats focused attention on saving incumbents in unexpectedly close elections, such as Sean Maloney (NY-17), chair of the Democratic Congressional Campaign Committee, and bolstering John Fetterman's Senate campaign in Pennsylvania. Republicans in turn boosted support to Masters in Arizona, Bolduc in New Hampshire, Vance in Ohio, and candidates in other states, hoping to expand their gains. Even so, polls showed that the Democrats' majorities could be maintained given high turnout from their core constituencies, including historically marginalized communities and young voters.

The Election In the end, the 2022 campaign results were somewhat surprising. Democrats maintained their Senate majority, suffering no incumbent losses and gaining a seat in Pennsylvania. Republican hopes that Bolduc, Masters, and others could flip Democratic-held seats were not realized. In the House, Republicans gained enough seats for a very narrow majority. Some vulnerable Democrats lost their seats (such as Representative Maloney), but many others were reelected (such as Representative Spanberger).

The 2024 elections

The Nomination Process At the beginning of the 2024 election cycle, many observers predicted a rematch between incumbent Joe Biden and former President Donald Trump. While some Democrats had concerns over Biden's age (he was

81 in 2024), he faced only token opposition. In contrast, Trump faced significant opposition—including former South Carolina governor Nikki Haley, Florida governor Ron DeSantis, and South Carolina senator Tim Scott—but won the nomination early in the process.

The race changed dramatically that summer. During a televised debate with Trump, Biden appeared meandering, confused, and unfocused. Afterward, several Democratic officials called for Biden to step aside. At the same time, polls showed that Trump had opened a significant lead over Biden, as well as weakening support for Democratic congressional candidates. Some organizations that normally supported Democratic candidates suggested they would stay out of the race unless Biden dropped out. Two weeks later, Biden ended his campaign and endorsed his vice president, Kamala Harris. In a matter of days, Harris won the support of most Democratic convention delegates, ensuring that she would win the nomination. Harris picked Minnesota governor Tim Walz as her vice-presidential candidate, while Trump selected Ohio senator J. D. Vance.

The General Election Campaign The substitution of Harris for Biden scrambled the race. Republicans were now unable to focus attention on Biden's age and stamina. Harris also brought unique advantages to the table. She was much younger than Biden and Trump, enough so that she could make an issue of Trump's age (78). She was only the second woman to be a general election nominee and the second minority candidate, with the potential to increase turnout among key Democratic voting groups. In fact, throughout the campaign, surveys found a sizable gender gap, with women (and especially young women) more likely to support Harris over Trump. What was unclear was whether these supporters would turn out to vote.

Issues such as the economy and immigration remained at the top of voters' minds throughout the race. Trump pointed to steady economic growth during most of his presidency (until the pandemic) and promised to improve the economy by imposing tariffs on imports from other nations, a strategy that was rejected by economists as being ineffective. Trump also made immigration a central issue, promising to close America's borders and deport people living in the United States without documentation.

Harris's campaign addressed the same issues, but with a different platform of proposed solutions. She promised tax credits to address high home prices and other credits to increase the formation of new small businesses. On immigration, Harris supported the Biden administration's efforts to reduce migrant entries but rejected calls for mass deportation. On both counts, Harris's problem was that even though inflation had moderated and border crossings were down, voters could easily remember that both issues were major concerns in 2022 and 2023. While Harris was not the president, voters saw her as a key member of the Biden administration, and thus a continuation of these problems.

Access to abortion was a third major issue in the campaign. As we discuss elsewhere, the Supreme Court's *Dobbs* decision allowed several states to enact very strong limits on abortions. While Trump claimed that most voters supported making the states responsible for abortion policy, this argument was not supported by poll data or by the success of state referenda that reversed legislative restrictions in some Republican states.

The sole debate between Harris and Trump was contentious, bringing these two different platforms into focus. Trump made claims that the Biden administration had destroyed the country, that the annual inflation rate was over 70 percent, and that Harris was a Marxist. Trump also repeated discredited rumors that Haitian immigrants in Ohio were causing economic dislocation, overburdening schools, and eating residents' cats and dogs. Polling for Trump didn't change much after the debate, nor in the wake of two assassination attempts just weeks apart.

One sharp difference between the campaigns was their get-out-the-vote efforts. The Harris campaign built a network of field offices in all swing states and assembled a large group of volunteers and paid workers to go door-to-door to contact would-be supporters. The campaign also ran a series of well-publicized rallies featuring celebrities such as Beyoncé, Cardi B, Willie Nelson, and Bruce Springsteen, as well as politicians such as former presidents Clinton and Obama. Trump's rallies were also central to his campaign. Elon Musk, the entrepreneur and owner of Tesla and X, as well as celebrities including Kid Rock, joined him on stage across battleground states. These events culminated in a rally a week before the election at Madison Square Garden that was attended by more than 20,000 people.

A final consideration during the presidential campaign was the state of congressional races. At the start of the campaign, each party controlled one chamber: Democrats had a lead in the Senate, and Republicans had a lead in the House. However, each party's majority was very slim, and Democrats had to defend 23 Senate seats, including several in Republican strongholds such as Montana, Ohio, and West Virginia. Even so, both sides could see a path to the trifecta: winning the presidency and majorities in the House and Senate, thereby producing unified government that would provide a path to enact significant policy change.

The General Election Polls showed a very close race throughout the general election campaign. With most states firmly in the Harris or Trump camps, the election would be decided by votes in seven swing states: Arizona, Georgia, Michigan, Nevada, North Carolina, Pennsylvania, and Wisconsin (refer to the How It Works graphic on pp. 332–333). While early voting in these states reached unprecedented levels (in Georgia, over half of the vote was cast early), the results did not unambiguously favor either candidate. Even days before the election, the best pollsters and political scientists could say was that the election could go either way.

Unlike in 2020, the winner came into focus on election night. With Donald Trump in the lead in both the popular vote and the Electoral College, the race was called for Trump after he secured a win in the crucial battleground state of Wisconsin. Trump delivered a victory speech in Palm Beach, supported by his family, key campaign figures, and his vice president, J. D. Vance.

But the results came into focus on election night, indicating a solid Trump lead. Trump won just over half of the popular vote, 312 electoral votes, and all seven swing states. In contrast to 2020, the results were decisive the morning after the elections. The difference between 2020 and 2024 was stronger momentum for Trump—an average of three percentage points across all areas of the country.

Congressional races mirrored the presidential result. Republicans gained a Senate majority, as Democrats lost Senate seats in Montana and West Virginia as expected, but also lost Ohio. The outcome in the House took several weeks to decide, but in the end, Republicans held on to their small majority in the chamber. With both chambers controlled by Republicans, Trump entered the White House with unified government.

What led to this resounding Republican victory? Early election analyses focused on economic and border concerns as strong drivers of voters' decisions. Harris could not convince swing voters that inflation under the Biden administration was the result of COVID-era disruptions. Nor was she able to avoid being held responsible for high numbers of undocumented migrants in the United States. Concerns about abortion rights did not appear to change many presidential votes, although referenda restoring abortion access were successful in five out of six states with state-level ballot initiatives.

The 2024 elections are a good example of one of our central themes, that politics is conflictual. Table 9.6 shows clear policy differences between Democrats and Republicans. These differences had policy consequences. Issues such as immigration

TABLE 9.6

Exit Polls and the 2024 Elections

		Harris	Trump
Approval of President Biden	Approve (41%)	96%	3%
	Disapprove (56%)	16	82
Most important issue	Immigration (11%)	9	90
	Abortion (14%)	74	25
	Economy (32%)	19	80
	Democracy (34%)	80	18
Gender	Male (47%)	42	55
	Female (53%)	53	45
Race	White (73%)	41	57
	Black (11%)	85	12
	Latino (12%)	52	46
Education	College graduate (43%)	55	42
	Not college graduate (57%)	42	56
Partisanship	Democrats (33%)	95	5
	Republicans (36%)	5	94
	Independents (31%)	49	46

Source: 2024 CNN Exit Polls, www.cnn.com/election/2024/exit-polls/national-results (accessed 11/10/24).

and economic concerns moved voters to Trump. The data also show a sizable shift of Latino voters to the Republican ticket.

The New Administration Donald Trump's victory will lead to significant policy changes. He has majorities in the House and Senate, has experience from prior service as president, and has articulated a bold agenda for policy change in many areas. Even so, Trump does not have enough Republican votes to overcome a Senate filibuster—although Senate Republicans have enough votes to remove this constraint if they wish. In the House, the Republican majority is small enough that any defections will make it impossible to legislate.

Trump faces significant policy constraints, including a large budget deficit and the expiration of tax credits, which will restrict new spending. Many of his proposals do not have support from the majority of the public. And while many of his proposals can be implemented without legislation, their feasibility is open to question. For example, Trump campaigned on a promise to begin mass deportation of the 15 million undocumented migrants currently living in America. Finding these individuals, detaining them, processing them for deportation, and physically transporting them to another country are all massive tasks. Accomplishing them will require new policies, additional personnel, and funding.

It is also important to remember that Trump leads a country as divided as ever. Even with Trump's clear victory in the 2024 election, Harris received over 70 million votes. Democrats also have significant strength in the House and Senate, and there are divisions among Republicans elected to both chambers. There is no sign of a broad national consensus on most important issues, and achieving policy victories under these conditions is certainly not guaranteed. We know that politics matters, so the fight to win elections and shape government policy will continue unabated.

Unpacking the Conflict

Considering all that we've discussed in this chapter, let's apply what we know about how elections work to the 2024 presidential election discussed throughout this chapter. How meaningful are elections? What do election results tell us about why some candidates win and others lose? Why do these outcomes matter in American politics?

Candidates in American national elections compete for different offices using a variety of rules that determine who can run for office, who can vote, and how ballots are counted and winners determined. Election outcomes are shaped not only by who runs for office and how they campaign, who decides to vote, and how they decide whom to support but also by the rules that govern electoral competition. By taking these factors into account for the 2024 election, we can explain why Donald Trump defeated Kamala Harris—and why Republicans will control both houses of Congress.

It is easy to complain about American elections. Citizens are not experts on public policy. They often know little about the candidates running for office. Candidates sensationalize, attack, and dissemble rather than giving details about what they would do if elected. Even so, however candidates campaign and voters vote, elections matter: there are clear, systematic differences between Democratic and Republican candidates that translate into different government policies depending on who holds office. Biden's first two years in office were marked by significant domestic and international policy accomplishments. Now, with a very narrow Republican House majority (or perhaps no party clearly in charge), opportunities for legislative action are severely limited.

Campaigns and election outcomes would surely be different if more Americans were well informed about candidates and campaign platforms, if turnout were higher, if campaigns always focused on important issues facing the country, and if attack ads never worked. Even so, despite all their limitations, elections are how we decide who gets to run the government. And as we have discussed, election outcomes are somewhat predictable—they are the product of national and local rules and regulations, the fundamentals of district factors and national forces, candidates' campaign strategies, and citizens' decisions about whether to vote and whom to vote for. The outcome of every election is the result of all these individual-level choices added together. In that sense, election outcomes reflect the preferences of the American people.

"What's Your Take?"

Do the campaigns that candidates run significantly affect election outcomes, or are the outcomes out of the candidates' control?

Are individual election outcomes representative of larger trends?

CHECK YOUR UNDERSTANDING

"Why Should I Care?"

Elections are the most fundamental element of modern democracy. In an election, citizens select representatives who will act on their behalf, choosing policies that will be imposed on the citizenry. Then, to stay in office, representatives must again appear before their constituents, who can replace them or keep them in office. This process is intended to link the demands held by citizens to the actions taken by their representatives.

Most of the things we study in elections are aimed at understanding the nature of this linkage. How do citizens make decisions about whom to vote for? To what extent do economic upsets, wars, and other events shape voters' decisions and election outcomes? What is the role of money in elections—does the richest candidate always win? Does a candidate's race, gender, age, occupation, or record in office matter—or do voters simply choose the candidate who shares their party ID?

What we know about contemporary American elections is that they are driven in large part by partisan factors such as party ID. But sometimes events matter. Donald Trump's defeat in 2020 was in part related to perceptions that his administration had mismanaged the response to the COVID pandemic. Democratic candidates in the 2022 midterms were helped by the relatively high turnout of voters who were mobilized in opposition to the Supreme Court's *Dobbs* decision that gave states the power to regulate access to abortions. And campaigns sometimes turn on one candidate's popularity or unpopularity.

Elections are also a good example of how rules shape outcomes. In presidential elections, for example, the fact that we use an Electoral College rather than the popular vote to decide the outcome has meant that in the last 25 years, two candidates (Al Gore in 2000 and Hillary Clinton in 2016) have lost despite winning a majority of votes. But this is just the most obvious example. How we divide up the country into congressional districts, the location of polling sites and the hours they are open, whether a state uses mail-in voting or encourages absentee ballots, the requirement for photo IDs—all of these factors determine the choices put before voters and affect the likelihood that different people cast ballots. Put another way, these features of our electoral process are controversial precisely because they can affect who wins and who loses political office.

It is easy to complain about American elections—that campaigns last too long, that candidates don't talk about the right issues, that some citizens use decidedly peculiar logic for deciding whom to vote for—and there are always complaints about the result. Even with all that, the amazing thing about elections is that we use them to determine who makes the rules for the rest of us, and that despite everything that is at stake, these events are generally conducted peacefully and fairly.

1. In 2016, the Fifth U.S. Circuit Court of Appeals ruled that a 2011 Texas voter ID law, defended by the state's governor and attorney general as necessary for preventing voter fraud, was unconstitutional because the legislature had deliberately favored some identification methods more common to White voters while disenfranchising voters of color. If courts like the Fifth U.S. Circuit Court of Appeals find a voter ID law does not increase security but does prevent certain groups from voting, it is logical to conclude that the authors of the law had which intention?

a Securing the vote from fraudulently cast ballots

b Increasing the state's role in electing national officials

c Affecting voter turnout to favor preferred candidates

d Improving opportunities to uphold gerrymandered districts

2. Out of the three Republican presidential victories between 2000 and 2020, two were achieved by winning the Electoral College while at the same time losing the popular vote. What reality about the American process for electing presidents can be credited with causing this phenomenon?

a Small-population rural states are overrepresented in the Electoral College.

b Populist trends have given greater sway to candidates who campaign in urban areas.

c Campaigns with more advertising dollars are better able to win elections.

d Certification of the presidential vote in close elections gives the House control over picking the president.

3. How does the American electoral structure encourage candidates to take more extreme positions on issues?

a Stronger positions at opposite ends of the ideological spectrum offer voters a clearer difference between candidates, which can be helpful in making voting decisions.

b Primary elections give outsized power to a small portion of the overall electorate who are more ideologically extreme in their views than the voters in the general election.

c Supreme Court decisions mandating that electoral districts be roughly equal in population and that considerations about representation of communities of color be made have polarized candidates.

d In the general election, the most extreme candidates usually have a late-breaking surge in popularity because voters are most likely to vote for whom they've seen in the news recently.

4. Which of the following is arguably the most significant impact of the Supreme Court ruling in *Citizens United v. Federal Election Commission*?

a Striking down preclearance requirements in Section 5 of the Civil Rights Act

b Upholding individual restrictions on cumulative campaign contributions

c Explosion in general election campaign spending

d Ending the use of soft money in elections

5. Because Rochelle and her spouse lost their business as a result of economic collapse associated with the COVID-19 pandemic, they voted against their incumbent U.S. senator and the sitting president in the 2020 election. The reasoning Rochelle and her spouse used in making their decision about which candidate they should vote for in the election is commonly referred to as what kind of voting?

- a Pocketbook voting
- b Personal characteristic
- c Issue voting
- d Retrospective voting

6. Extreme partisan gerrymandering during the redistricting process can be credited with what effect in congressional elections?

- a Higher voter turnout in general elections
- b Greater party polarization in the public
- c Increased number of safe seats in the House of Representatives
- d Declining numbers of women and people of color in Congress

7. What is the most important impact of our election process on our political system?

- a Extreme polarization of the American public
- b Undermining public trust of our public institutions
- c Increasing diversity of ideas and individuals in our political system
- d Allocation of control of government and policy making

8. In competitive states during the 2020 election, the large number of mail-in ballots being counted after the ballots cast on Election Day were counted and the constant messaging from President Trump in days leading up to and following the election had what significant impact?

- a Courts issued conflicting rulings on which ballots should be recounted or removed from the official count of state election returns.
- b Impassioned but wrong beliefs that there had been widespread voter fraud in the election were created.
- c Vice President Mike Pence was left to determine who the winner of the 2020 election would be.
- d President Trump was impeached for a second time.

Use INQUIZITIVE to help you study and master this material.

10

Interest Groups

Do interest groups serve the needs of the many, or the privileged few?

» **"This provision isn't about coronavirus, working families or small businesses struggling to stay afloat. It is just more insider politics to get millions to those who have millions, especially real estate investors and hedge fund managers."[1]**
Representative Lloyd Doggett (D-TX)

« **"The attempt to paint this tax provision as a boon for real estate and hedge fund investors completely misses the mark. . . . This misleading talking point ignores the unimaginable economic losses that are painfully occurring across my state of Iowa and the rest of America."[2]**
Senator Chuck Grassley (R-IA)

When a staggering number of Americans lost their jobs in 2020 as the coronavirus pandemic crossed the United States, it was clear Congress needed to act. In quick succession, it passed four relief bills that pumped trillions of dollars into the economy. The largest of these, the Coronavirus Aid, Relief, and Economic Security (CARES) Act, provided $2.2 trillion for direct payments to individuals, forgivable loans to small businesses, and assistance to state and local governments and hospitals. There were huge logistical problems with quickly distributing that much money, and there were some significant glitches: millions of people didn't receive their $1,200 checks for several months, and more than 200 large businesses engaged in the time-honored tradition of "feeding at the public trough" by taking billions of dollars that were intended for small businesses. Chastened by the public scrutiny and a stern warning from then–Treasury secretary Steven Mnuchin that large companies would face "severe consequences" if they took money they weren't entitled to, dozens of businesses returned the taxpayers' money, including Potbelly, Shake Shack, Ruth's Chris Steak House, and the Los Angeles Lakers basketball team.[3]

Donald Trump signed the CARES Act into law on March 27, 2020. The historic $2.2 trillion bill was passed as part of the emergency response to the 2020 COVID-19 pandemic.

While these problems made headlines, a much more significant misuse of taxpayers' funds initially slid through with little attention: a set of changes to the 2017 tax cuts,

CHAPTER GOALS

Define *interest groups* and describe the characteristics of different types of groups (pp. 370–382)

Explain how successful interest groups overcome collective action problems (pp. 382–384)

Explore the ways interest groups try to influence government policies (pp. 384–396)

Evaluate interest group influence (pp. 396–401)

which had been a key legislative success of the Trump administration and a fulfillment of a campaign promise to reduce the tax burden on businesses. These changes, when integrated into the COVID-19 legislation, illustrate the power of interest groups in the political system. In the 2017 tax cut legislation, Congress placed income limits on some of the more generous tax cuts to reduce the loss of revenue, but in the CARES Act it repealed those limits, which could result in a staggering loss of $135 billion in tax revenue over the next 10 years. The details get a little complicated, which is probably why this didn't get as much attention. After all, it is easier for people to understand why the L.A. Lakers, one of the most highly valued teams in the world (at $3.7 billion), shouldn't get a $4.6 million loan that was intended for small businesses than it is to understand arcane details of tax policy.

We don't need to get into the details here to understand the broad issues at play.[4] These income limit rollbacks affect how business owners can use losses from their businesses to cancel out other nonbusiness income. Another provision rolls back the restrictions on how much debt some companies can deduct from their taxes. How did this happen? Well, large corporations had lobbied hard to change these restrictions since they were enacted in 2017, and in an example that illustrates the power of these corporations' lobbying efforts, Congress snuck the provisions into the "must pass" massive bill.

Once these changes in the tax law came to light shortly after the CARES bill was signed, an analysis by the nonpartisan Joint Committee on Taxation revealed that 80 percent of the tax cuts included in the bill went to business owners making more than $1 million (because only couples with $500,000 of nonbusiness income benefited from the policy change). And 43,000 business owners received a tax cut of an average of $1.6 million each, which means they received more total dollars than the 47 *million* people earning less than $20,000, who got $1,200 each. The $135 billion for the tax credits is three times more than the CARES Act spent on safety-net programs like food and housing aid ($42 billion) and is more than was spent on hospitals and other public health services ($100 billion).[5] Perhaps the most outrageous part of the policy is that wealthy business owners can exploit losses unrelated to the pandemic because the law allows them to retroactively write off losses from 2018 and 2019, well before we even knew about the virus.

This chapter surveys the wide range of interest groups in American politics—from large, powerful groups such as the National Rifle Association (NRA) to small organizations that lobby on issues that concern only a few Americans. Our aim is to get to the bottom of examples in which the lobbyists lose and understand examples in which it seems like the lobbyists always win, as with the CARES Act tax cuts. Some people, such as Senator Chuck Grassley, argue that such policies are good for the overall economy and *are* in the public's interest. However, many others always root for lobbyists, with their perceived insider connections and undue influence, to lose their battles. Is it fair to characterize all interest groups as self-interested organizations that undermine the public good? Are interest groups really too-powerful manipulators of the American policy process?

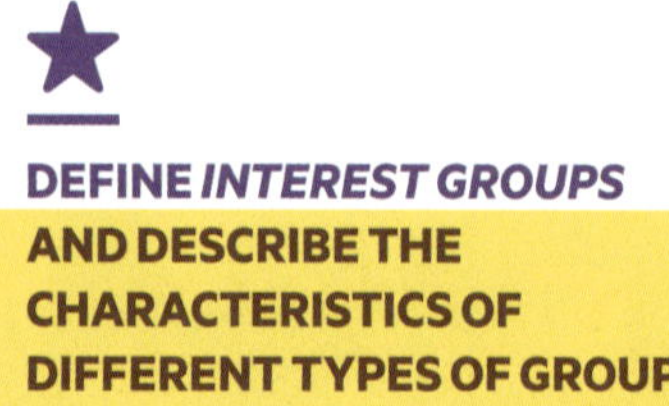
DEFINE *INTEREST GROUPS* AND DESCRIBE THE CHARACTERISTICS OF DIFFERENT TYPES OF GROUPS

What are interest groups?

Interest groups are organizations in society that seek to influence government policy. They represent groups in society that share common interests, which may be related occupational interests (such as teachers, business owners, or doctors), values (such as police reform or the environment), or specific issues (such as abortion or gun rights). Interest groups have been present in the United States since our founding, and the right to "petition the government for a redress of grievances" is guaranteed by the First Amendment. Alexis de Tocqueville notes in his two-volume work *Democracy in America* that in the 1830s, America was a nation of joiners and that "the freedom to associate for political goals is unlimited."[6] As we discussed in Chapter 2, James Madison saw "factions" (what we call interest groups today) as an inherent result of human self-interest: people will organize to try to influence policy they support. While Madison was concerned about the "evils of faction" that needed to be controlled by our system of checks and balances, the concern can be overstated. Virtually everyone has some interest that is represented by an organized interest group, whether you are a member of that group or not.

interest group
An organization of people who share common political interests and aim to influence public policy by electioneering and lobbying.

Interest groups may represent very specific or more general interests, and they use a variety of tactics, such as lobbying elected officials and bureaucrats, helping to draft legislation, mobilizing members and the public to apply pressure on and work with legislators and government agencies, and helping to elect candidates who support the organizations' policy goals. In its most basic form, **lobbying** involves persuasion and monitoring policy development by using reports, protests, informal meetings, or other techniques to convince an elected official or bureaucrat to help enact a law, craft a regulation, or do something else that a group wants. In this way, interest groups serve as a **linkage institution** between the people and their elected representatives. The members of an interest group can be individual citizens, local governments, businesses, foundations or nonprofit organizations, churches, or virtually any other entity. An interest group's employees or members may lobby on the group's behalf, or a group may hire a lobbyist or lobbying firm to do the work for it. Groups may lobby on their own or work with other groups to enact compromise proposals. Many organizations also have lobbying operations or hire lobbyists to work on their behalf. (See Nuts & Bolts 10.1 on p. 372 for some examples of the types of interest groups found in contemporary American politics.)

lobbying
Efforts to influence public policy through contact with public officials on behalf of an interest group.

linkage institutions
Institutions such as political parties, interest groups, the media, and elections that are channels through which individuals can communicate their preferences to policy makers.

Single-issue groups, ideological groups, and protest movements form with the goal of influencing society and government policy. One such group is Public Citizen, which conducts research projects, lobbies legislators and bureaucrats, and tries to rally public opinion on a range of environmental, health, and energy issues. In other cases, lobbying is only one part of what an organization does. The NRA, for example, endorses candidates, contributes to campaigns, and lobbies elected officials, but it also runs gun safety classes, holds competitions, and sells gun accessories to its members. Interest group activity is almost hidden within other organizations. For example, most drivers know that AAA (formerly the American Automobile Association) provides emergency roadside service and maps, but many people are not aware that AAA is also an interest group that lobbies for policies such as limiting new drivers to daylight-only hours.

As these descriptions suggest, interest groups and lobbying are ubiquitous in American politics. You may think that you don't belong to a group that lobbies the federal government, but the odds are that you do. In fact, one important view of American politics, *pluralism*, identifies interest groups as America's fundamental political actors.[7] Pluralists argue that most Americans participate in politics through their membership in interest groups like Public Citizen, the NRA, or even AAA. These groups lobby, try to elect candidates who share their views, and negotiate among themselves to encourage legislators to pursue policies that benefit their members. Pluralists see interest groups as important and appropriate participants in the democratic process. Others see interest groups in a more negative light, describing America as an **interest group state**, meaning that these groups are involved whenever policy is made, but in a self-interested way that can undermine the collective good.[8] More recent perspectives on interest group pluralism, such as Frank Baumgartner and coauthors' study of lobbying,[9] note that interest groups' influence is contextual and depends on a number of factors, but their importance in the political system is clear.

interest group state
A government in which most policy decisions are determined by the influence of interest groups.

NUTS
& BOLTS
10.1

Types of Interest Groups

Scholars often divide interest groups into categories based on who their members are or the number or kinds of things they lobby for. In addition to single-issue groups, ideological groups, and protest movements, which are described below, here are some of the most important types.

- ***Institutional interest groups*** are formed by nonprofits such as universities, think tanks, or museums. For example, the Big Ten Academic Alliance is a group of universities that prepares research to help individual universities make the case for continued federal support. Think tanks may also provide other support for interest groups, such as research.
- ***Businesses*** are for-profit enterprises that aim to influence policy in ways that will increase profits or satisfy other goals. Many corporations, such as Google, ExxonMobil, Boeing, Facebook, Citibank, and Sallie Mae, have lobbying operations that petition government for contracts or favorable regulations of their firm or industry.
- ***Trade or peak associations*** are groups of businesses (often in the same industry) that band together to lobby for policies that benefit all of them. For example, the National Beer Wholesalers Association, a nationwide group of local businesses that buy beer from brewers and resell it to stores and restaurants, lobbies to require intermediaries between beer producers and the stores, bars, and restaurants that sell beer to consumers.
- ***Professional associations*** represent individuals who have a common interest in a profession; examples include the American Society of Civil Engineers, National Education Association, American Medical Association, and American Bar Association.
- ***Labor organizations*** lobby for regulations that make it easy for workers to form labor unions, as well as for a range of other policies. The largest of these is the American Federation of Labor and Congress of Industrial Organizations (AFL-CIO).
- ***Citizen groups*** range from those with mass membership (such as the Sierra Club) to those that have no members but claim to speak for particular segments of the population. One such group is the Family Research Council (FRC), which describes itself as "promoting the Judeo-Christian worldview as the basis for a just, free, and stable society." FRC Action (the lobbying arm of the organization) promotes a range of policies, from legislation that defines marriage as between a man and a woman to legislation that would eliminate estate taxes.

Source: Compiled by the authors.

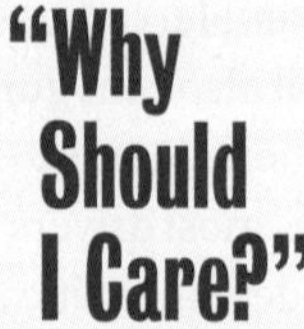

Categorizing interest groups can help you see which groups are working for collective interests and which groups are working for more particular or special interests. Which of the types above do you think fall into each category?

The business of lobbying

Interest group lobbying is regulated. Lobbying firms must file quarterly reports identifying their clients, specifying how much each client paid and the issues that the firms lobbied on. Similarly, interest groups and corporations must file reports listing staff members who spent more than 20 percent of their time lobbying Congress and listing the total expenditures to lobbying firms.[10] Also, most executive or legislative branch employees who take lobbying jobs are legally required to refrain from lobbying people in their former office or agency for one year; elected officials who become lobbyists must wait two years.

Today lobbying involves billions of dollars a year. Figure 10.1 (top) presents annual lobbying expenditures for 2000 through 2023. As the figure shows, a total of

FIGURE 10.1

Growth in Spending on Lobbying and Total Federal Spending, 2000–2023

These data show that in recent years interest groups have spent several billion dollars lobbying the federal government. Does this amount seem surprisingly large or surprisingly small, given what lobbyists do and given the total federal outlays of money?

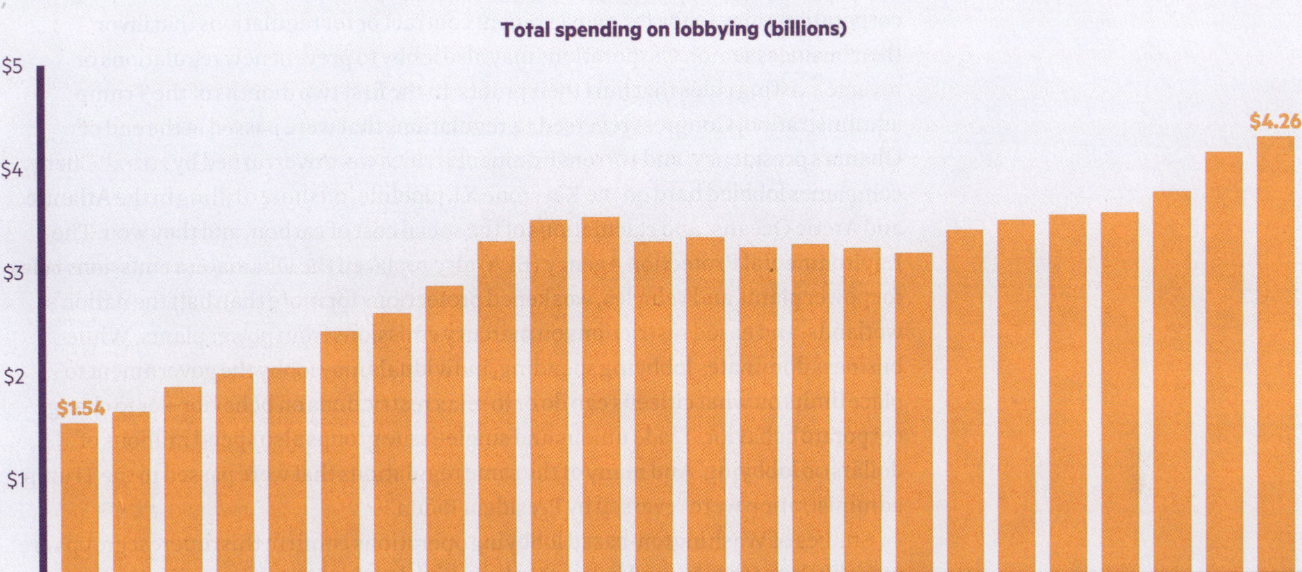

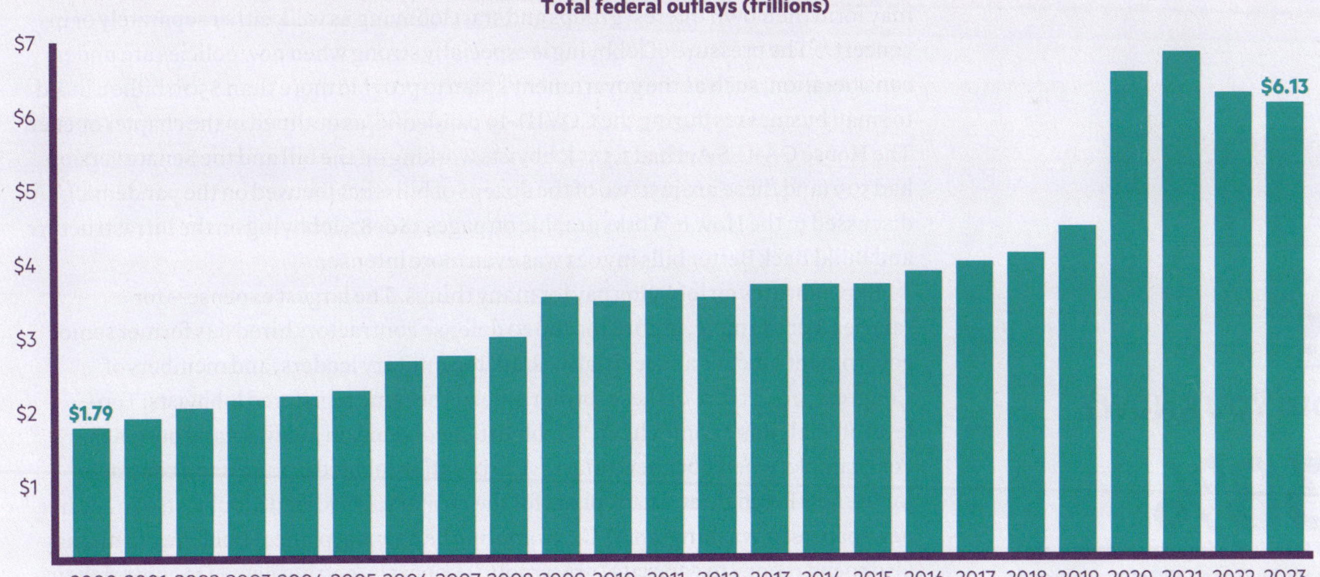

Sources: Lobbying data available at OpenSecrets, "Lobbying Database," www.opensecrets.org/federal-lobbying; federal spending from Congressional Budget Office, Historical Budget Data, February 2024, https://www.cbo.gov/system/files/2024-02/51134-2024-02-Historical-Budget-Data.xlsx (both accessed 8/1/24).

$4.26 billion was spent on lobbying in 2023. The amount spent, as well as the number of groups lobbying government, increased significantly from 2000 to 2010 and has held steady since then (although it has risen again in the past few years).

Why are there so many interest groups and registered lobbyists, and why are their numbers increasing? Figure 10.1 (bottom) suggests that this proliferation is related to the large size and widespread influence of the federal government. Simply put, the federal government does so many things and spends so much money that many individuals, organizations, and corporations have strong incentives for lobbying: corporations may lobby for a government contract or for regulations that favor their business sector. Corporations may also lobby to prevent new regulations or reverse existing rules that hurt their profits: in the first two months of the Trump administration, Congress reversed 14 regulations that were passed at the end of Obama's presidency, and 100 environmental rules were overturned by 2020.[11] Energy companies lobbied hard on the Keystone XL pipeline, offshore drilling in the Atlantic and Arctic Oceans, and calculations of the social cost of carbon, and they won. The Environmental Protection Agency (EPA) also replaced the Obama-era emissions rules for power plants and vehicles, weakened protections for more than half the nation's wetlands, and eased restrictions on mercury emissions from power plants. While business dominates lobbying spending, individuals may lobby the government to place limits on what citizens can do or to relax restrictions on behavior—or to change corporate behavior. Trade unions and single-issue groups also spend millions of dollars on lobbying. And many of the same regulations that were passed in the Trump administration were reversed by President Biden.[12]

Studies of Washington-based lobbying operations confirm this: interest groups are more likely to form around issues that have high levels of government involvement or when new programs or changes in government policy are likely.[13] Moreover, as groups form on one side of a policy question and start to lobby, people who oppose them may form their own interest groups and start lobbying as well, either separately or in concert.[14] The pressure of lobbying is especially strong when new policies are under consideration, such as the government's plan to provide more than $500 billion in aid to small businesses during the COVID-19 pandemic, as outlined in the chapter opener. The House CARES Act had 1,545 lobbyists working on the bill and the Senate version had 599 (and these are just two of the dozens of bills that focused on the pandemic).[15] As discussed in the How It Works graphic on pages 386–87, lobbying on the infrastructure and Build Back Better bills in 2021 was even more intense.

Expenditures on lobbying pay for many things. The largest expense is for salaries. For example, in 2018 the top 20 defense contractors hired 645 former senior government officials and legislative staff, top military leaders, and members of Congress; 90 percent of these former officials became registered lobbyists. Top-level officials don't come cheap.[16] Lobbyists also spend on publicity and outreach. For example, when Lockheed Martin Corporation lobbied Congress on contracts for the new F-35 fighter-attack plane for the military, Lockheed's lobbyists ran ads in newspapers in Washington, D.C., promoting its new warplane.[17] Lobbying firms may also spend money to generate "grassroots" support by getting people to contact their members of Congress, as we discuss later in the chapter.

DID YOU KNOW?

38%

of total lobbying expenditures are made by the top 100 interest groups.

Source: OpenSecrets.org.

Figure 10.2 shows lobbying expenditures for several different firms and associations for two years (2022–2023). Three associations and one policy center were the highest spenders on lobbying during this time. It's not hard to imagine why each group devotes so much effort to lobbying: realtors, for example, might be concerned about maintaining government policies that make it almost essential to hire a realtor to help buy or sell a home. While the $134 million the National Association of Realtors spent on lobbying may sound like a lot, it really isn't that

FIGURE 10.2

Variation in Lobbying Expenditures, 2022–2023

Lobbying expenditures vary widely. Some influential groups (such as the U.S. Chamber of Commerce) spend $70 to 80 million a year, but many other influential groups (such as NARAL Pro-Choice America and the Family Research Council) spend relatively little. How can groups have influence over government policy despite spending almost nothing on lobbying?

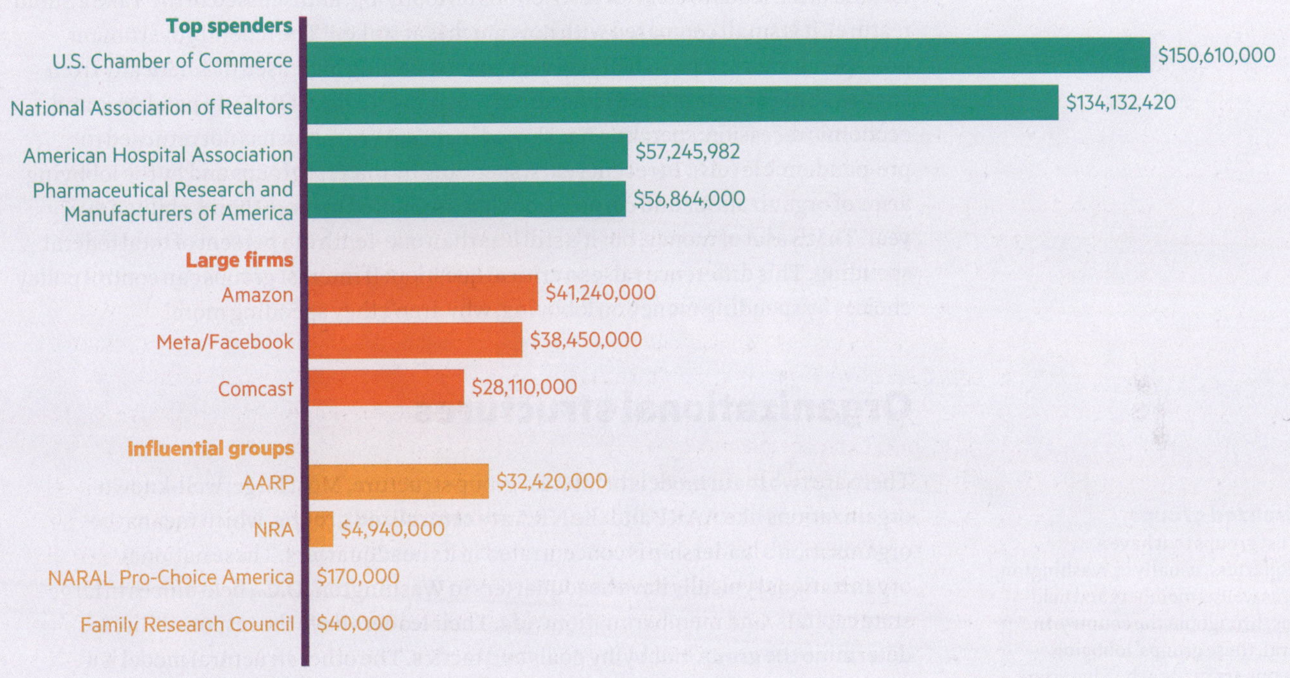

Source: Data available at OpenSecrets, "Lobbying Data Summary," www.opensecrets.org/federal-lobbying (accessed 8/1/24).

much.[18] After all, over a million people work in real estate, generating billions of dollars in profits every year. The surprise is that real estate brokers are willing to spend only a tiny fraction of their profits to keep their near monopoly in place. The same is true for the large firms listed in Figure 10.2. Apple, for example, one of the largest firms in the United States, didn't even crack the top 20 spenders on lobbying in the last two years, at $19.2 million. Meta, Amazon, and Comcast were the top three large firms in spending on lobbying, with defense contractors Raytheon, Lockheed Martin, and Boeing among other top spenders. And only one of the influential interest groups in Figure 10.2 (AARP) spends more than $10 million per year on lobbying. Clearly, the big spenders on lobbying are exceptions to the rule, and most interest groups and firms spend relatively little on lobbying.[19] For example, the group that sends a turkey to the White House for a ceremonial pardon every year at Thanksgiving, the National Turkey Federation, spends $140,000 a year to lobby the federal government on a relatively small range of issues. Many other groups spend even less, barely scraping together enough cash to send someone to plead their case in Washington. In fact, a few groups account for a substantial fraction of total lobbying expenditures.

That concentration of spending is evident in another way as well: a large proportion of lobbying is done by the business sector and relatively little by political or public interests. According to the Center for Responsive Politics, the top five sectors in 2022–2023 were all business interests (health, finance, communications, miscellaneous business, and energy/natural resources), with 79 percent of the total spending on lobbying, while education, nonprofits, clergy, and public officials (categorized as "Other") and ideological/single-issue political groups came in seventh and eighth, spending 7.6 and 4.9 percent, respectively.[20]

Although the amount of money spent on lobbying by interest groups may seem like a lot (and often leads to calls for restrictions on lobbying, as discussed in the Take a Stand feature), it is small compared with how much is at stake.[21] The federal government now spends more than $6 trillion every year (spending increased dramatically from 2020 to 2022 because of the extraordinary response to the COVID-19 pandemic and economic recession; spending has slowed in recent years, but has not returned to pre-pandemic levels). In recent years, spending by interest groups and by the lobbying arms of organizations and corporations has amounted to more than $4 billion every year. That's a lot of money, but it's still less than one-tenth of 1 percent of total federal spending. This difference raises a critical question: If interest groups can control policy choices by spending money on lobbying, why aren't they spending more?

Organizational structures

centralized groups
Interest groups that have a headquarters, usually in Washington, D.C., as well as members and field offices throughout the country. In general, these groups' lobbying decisions are made at headquarters by the group leaders.

confederations
Interest groups made up of several independent, local organizations that provide much of their funding and hold most of the power.

There are two main models of interest group structure. Most large, well-known organizations like AARP and the NRA are **centralized groups**, which means the organization's leadership is concentrated in its headquarters. These national organizations typically have headquarters in Washington, D.C., field offices in large state capitals, and members nationwide. Their leaders have the responsibility to determine the group's lobbying goals and tactics. The other structural model is a **confederation**, which is composed of largely independent, local organizations. For example, the National Independent Automobile Dealers Association (NIADA) is made up of 50 state-level organizations that provide membership benefits to car dealers who join the organization and that raise much of the money that NIADA contributes to candidates running for political office (several million dollars in recent elections).

Both organizational structures have advantages and disadvantages. A centralized organization controls all of the group's resources and can deploy them efficiently, but it can be challenging for these groups to find out what their members want. Confederations have the advantage of maintaining independent chapters at the state and local levels, so it is easier for the national headquarters to learn what the members want—all the national headquarters has to do is contact its local groups. But this strength is closely related to a weakness: confederated groups are often beset with conflict. Since state and local chapters attract members and raise money largely on their own, they mostly function independently of the national headquarters. However, the national headquarters depends on the local organizations for funds to pay its staff and make campaign contributions. In return, it allows the locals to direct contributions to their preferred candidates, and different local chapters may disagree over what to lobby for and which candidates to support.

Some organizations are hard to categorize, such as Black Lives Matter (BLM) that started in 2013 in reaction to the murder of Trayvon Martin, an unarmed Black teenager. The organization is similar to a confederation, in that it is composed of hundreds of local chapters, but the structure is not as well defined as an organization like NIADA. BLM is anchored by its focus on racial justice,[22] but there is great variation

TAKE A STAND

Restrictions on Interest Group Lobbying

Under current rules, members of Congress and their staffs are severely limited in the size of gifts they can receive from lobbyists. These restrictions were tightened in the mid-2000s after it was revealed that former-congressional-staffer-turned-lobbyist Jack Abramoff had used "golf junkets, free meals at the restaurant he owned, seats at sporting events, and, in some cases, old-fashioned cash" to lobby members of Congress.[a] The current restrictions limit members and their staffs to accepting gifts only if they are valued at less than $50—moreover, the total worth of the gifts that any lobbyist can give to a particular member of Congress or staffer is limited to $100 per year. In addition, "cooling off" rules, which prevent staffers and former members of Congress from lobbying for one year after leaving their government job, were instituted in an attempt to limit the revolving door between government and lobbying firms. President Trump vowed to "drain the swamp" of lobbyist influence in Washington, but lobbyists gained even more access in his administration. Are current restrictions fair? Do they help or hurt the political process? Are even stronger limitations needed?

Keep the rules, and maybe tighten them. Supporting this option seems like a no-brainer. These regulations are based on a sensible intuition that laws are needed to prevent well-funded, unscrupulous lobbyists from offering inducements to members of Congress and their staffs in return for policy change. Simply put, groups that can send people to Washington to wine and dine members of Congress, congressional staff, and bureaucrats might gain a significant advantage over those who are unable to do so. Even if a fancy lunch doesn't buy a legislator's vote, it might help with access—that is, it might give the group a chance to make its arguments and perhaps change some minds. In this way, rules that allow even small gifts create an advantage for interest groups that have a Washington office or hire lobbyists and a disadvantage for those that do not. As a result, many reform proposals should go further, preventing lobbyists from giving anything to a member of Congress, legislative staffer, or bureaucrat—even a cup of coffee.

Relax the rules (a little). Some argue that worries about interest group influence seem a little overstated. Congressional staff and the legislators they work for are going to support a group's proposals only if they help the member's constituents or if they move policy in a way the member favors, not just because of an interest group's free lunch.

When scandals surrounding Jack Abramoff came to light in 2005, many Americans considered him a typical lobbyist. Abramoff's actions were illegal, but the question remains: Are his tactics common in Washington, or was he a rare exception?

There are also downsides to tight controls on these gifts and perks. The current rules on lobbyists' gifts create a lot of paperwork for members and their staffs, who have to file reports on just about anything they receive from a lobbyist, even if that individual is a former colleague, neighbor, or friend. The rules are also extremely complicated—for example, legislators are allowed to eat the hors d'oeuvres provided at a reception, but they cannot sit down to a full meal without violating the gift restrictions. The disclosure requirements are also a burden to smaller interest groups and firms, which have to document everything they do on complex forms. As a result, members of Congress, their staff, interest groups, and lobbying firms spend considerable time and effort on documenting small gifts that are unlikely to have any effect on policy outcomes.

Do both. Another approach would be to relax some of the rules and strengthen others. For example, one suggestion is to get rid of the "cooling off" periods but have better disclosure of who is lobbying so constituents will be able to hold their elected officials accountable. Many lobbyists skirt current disclosure rules by generously interpreting the 20 percent rule (explained later in the chapter) to exclude what most would consider lobbying activity. These "shadow lobbyists" would be exposed by stricter disclosure rules.[b]

take a stand

1. To what extent do you think current congressional rules limiting the size of gifts that members of Congress and their staffers can receive from lobbyists have curbed illegal behavior by interest groups?
2. Are these rules aimed at exceptional cases or average interest groups?

Centralized interest groups typically have headquarters close to Washington, D.C., such as the NRA's offices shown here in Fairfax, Virginia. These offices serve as a hub for the organization's leaders, and the close proximity to the Capitol facilitates their lobbying goals.

in the activity of the chapters. Some hold meetings or public protests, some endorse candidates, some lobby local leaders on racial justice issues, some simply consist of a website run by one or two people, and others fight for more inclusive public art.[23]

Staff

Interest group staff fall into two categories: experts on the group's main policy areas and people with useful government connections and knowledge of procedures. The first group includes scientists, engineers, and others with advanced degrees; the second is dominated by people who have worked inside government as elected officials, bureaucrats, or legislative staff.[24] Sometimes these former members of government are also policy experts, but their unique contribution is their knowledge of how government works and their relationships with officeholders and other former coworkers in government.

revolving door
The movement of individuals from government positions to jobs with interest groups or lobbying firms, and vice versa.

The practice of moving from a government position to a job with an interest group or a lobbying firm, or of transitioning from a lobbyist to an officeholder, is often called the **revolving door**.[25] For example, as of 2020, more than half the members of Congress who retired at the end of the 115th Congress and were employed had moved to lobbying jobs.[26] The percentages are similar for congressional staff and bureaucrats. Many observers view this dynamic as potentially sowing seeds of corruption; they fear that past government employees might capitalize on personal ties with their former colleagues to negotiate favorable deals for their interest groups—or that people working in government may give special treatment to a corporation or an interest group that might hire them as a lobbyist in the future. These concerns have led to proposed restrictions on the revolving door, including banning former elected officials, staff, and bureaucrats from working as lobbyists for some time period after they have left government service, as well as banning former lobbyists in government positions from administering programs that they previously lobbied for.

President Trump's vow to "drain the swamp" was centered on these proposals to limit the revolving door. Of the five specific promises to tighten restrictions on lobbying that he made during the 2016 campaign, only one has been fulfilled (an executive order that bans executive branch officials from lobbying for foreign governments and overseas political parties after they leave the administration).[27] In fact, Trump quickly filled the swamp. In his first three years in office, one out of every 14 political appointees was a former lobbyist, with a total of 281 former lobbyists, including Secretary of Defense Mark Esper (former top lobbyist for Raytheon, one of the leading defense contractors), Secretary of the Interior David Bernhardt (a former oil industry lobbyist), and Trump's second head of the Environmental Protection Agency, Andrew Wheeler (a former coal industry lobbyist). In comparison, President Obama had only 65 former lobbyists among his political appointees in his first *five* years. The Trump administration weakened lobbying restrictions, including removing an Obama-era policy that prevented registered lobbyists from seeking or accepting employment with any executive agency that they lobbied the two years prior.[28] The Pentagon has recently attempted to undo a law authored by the late senator John McCain (R-AZ) that required retired Defense Department officials to wait for two years before lobbying on behalf of defense contractors.[29] On President Biden's first day in office, he issued an executive order that bans his political appointees from lobbying for two years after they leave the administration.[30]

DID YOU KNOW?

452

former members of Congress had been registered lobbyists as of 2022.

Source: OpenSecrets.org.

Such restrictions have costs as well as benefits. On the one hand, people who have worked in an industry or as lobbyists know a particular field and the relevant laws very well, making them well qualified to work in the corresponding area of the executive branch. Thus, a ban on hiring lobbyists may lead to a shortage of experienced candidates for government positions. Similarly, former officeholders, congressional staff, and bureaucrats are attractive candidates for lobbying jobs because they have firsthand knowledge of how policies are made and enjoy established relationships with people in government. On the other hand, these restrictions would help lower the potential for corruption mentioned earlier. It is very hard to craft restrictions that avoid these problems.

The revolving door also contributes to another feature of interest group lobbying, **iron triangles**, which refers to informal alliances between elected officials and their staff, bureaucrats, and interest groups. These alliances help these individuals dominate policy making on a set of issues, shutting everyone else out of the process. For example, the agriculture iron triangle would include representatives from farm states, bureaucrats from the Department of Agriculture, and interest groups representing farmers and companies that sell products for farmers. The revolving door helps iron triangles to form, as people in different organizations are likely to know each other because of their prior service. Some see "iron triangles" as an overly restrictive term for these relationships and prefer to use the term "issue networks" to characterize a more fluid set of issue-based relationships that may include the same actors in the iron triangle but also may include the media, think tanks, policy experts, and social media.

iron triangle
Informal alliance of elected officials, bureaucrats, and interest groups designed to let these groups and individuals dominate the policy-making process in a given area.

Membership

Interest groups can be categorized in terms of the size of their membership and the members' role in the group's activities. **Mass associations**, with many dues-paying members, tend to be citizens' groups and labor organizations. One example is the Sierra Club, which has 3.8 million members. Besides keeping its members informed about the implementation of environmental policy in Washington, D.C., the Sierra Club endorses judicial nominees and candidates for elected positions, files lawsuits to increase environmental protection on government projects, and works with members of Congress to develop legislative proposals. The group's members elect the organization's board of directors.

mass associations
Interest groups that have a large number of dues-paying individuals as members.

Many interest groups speak for large numbers of Americans, while others lobby for changes that would benefit only a few people. Mass associations, such as the Sierra Club, have large numbers of dues-paying members. Here, members in Michigan gather at the Detroit March for Justice to promote environmental issues.

peak associations
Interest groups whose members are businesses or other organizations rather than individuals.

Yet not all mass associations give members a say in selecting their leaders or determining their mission. To join AARP, which has 38 million members, one must be at least 50 years old and pay dues of $16 per year. Members get discounts on insurance, car rentals, and hotels, as well as driver safety courses and help doing their taxes. AARP claims to lobby for policies its members favor, but members actually have no control over which legislative causes the group chooses. Moreover, AARP does not poll members to determine its issue positions, nor do members elect AARP leadership.

The members of **peak associations** are businesses or other organizations rather than individuals.[31] Individuals cannot join peak associations—they may work for member companies or organizations, but they cannot become dues-paying members on their own. The Business–Industry Political Action Committee (BIPAC), an association of several hundred businesses and trade associations that aims to elect "pro-business individuals" to Congress, is a good example of a peak association.[32]

Resources and challenges

Interest groups use three key resources to support their lobbying efforts: people, money, and expertise. The resources that a group has at its disposal significantly influence its available lobbying strategies. (We will examine some of these strategies in more detail in a later section.) Some large groups have sufficient funding and staff to pursue a wide range of strategies, whereas some smaller groups with fewer resources face more significant challenges when it comes to the lobbying options they have at their disposal.

People A crucial resource for most interest groups is their membership. Group members can write to or meet with elected officials, travel to Washington for demonstrations, and even offer expertise or advice to their leaders. When the "members" of a group are corporations, as is the case with trade associations, CEOs and other corporate staff can help with the group's lobbying efforts.

Many mass organizations try to get their members involved in the lobbying process through links on their website that encourage members to contact their members of Congress. Mass membership organizations are also successful at using social media to mobilize their members to promote petition drives and spread their message. For example, Greenpeace, one of the largest, most active environmental groups, with more than 2.8 million supporters, mobilized its members for its "Save the Arctic" campaign. One study analyzed more than 8,000 Facebook posts by Greenpeace members to see the impact of posts on willingness to sign a petition to save the Arctic, finding that comments were very effective, while "shares" and emojis were less effective.[33]

Interest groups' ability to use people as a resource faces two major challenges. The first challenge is that interest groups must have members in the first place, and recruiting new members can be difficult and expensive. The second challenge is motivating members to participate. As we discuss later, although some interest groups have managed to change government policy by persuading their members to write to and visit elected officials, interest groups more often receive little response when they ask for members' help.[34]

Money Virtually everything interest groups do can be purchased as services: groups can spend money on hiring people to meet with elected officials and to fight for what they want in court. Money can also go toward campaign contributions or developing and running campaign ads. And, of course, money is necessary to fund interest groups' everyday operations. The importance of money for interest group operations is evident in their funding appeals to members. For example, the donations page from the Sierra

Interest groups use a variety of tactics to draw attention to their concerns, including events designed to generate media coverage. Members of People for the Ethical Treatment of Animals (PETA) dressed as monkeys outside a Los Angeles supermarket to protest the company selling a coconut milk brand that allegedly forces monkeys to climb trees to collect the coconuts, then keeps them in cruel conditions. Campaigns such as this are credited with raising the public's awareness of animal rights issues.

Club's website shows that supporters can give a membership as a gift, join as a life member, or pay dues monthly. They can make commemorative or memorial gifts, set up a planned giving scheme, or donate stock. The group even offers gift-giving plans for non-U.S. residents and a Spanish-language version of its donations page.

Well-funded interest groups and firms have a considerable advantage in the lobbying process. If they need an expert, a lobbyist, or a lawyer, they can simply hire one or open a Washington office to increase contacts with legislators and bureaucrats. They can pay for campaign ads and make contributions to candidates and parties. Groups with less cash, however, cannot use these strategies. Smaller firms might join a trade association that will lobby for policies that benefit all of the association's members.

Still, groups can be effective without spending much. They can rely on members to lobby for them, hire staff willing to work for low pay because they share the group's goals, or cite published research rather than funding their own studies to bolster their case for policy change. Moreover, the fact that a group spends the most money is no guarantee that its lobbying efforts will succeed. For example, in the third quarter of 2019 Amazon spent $4 million on heavy lobbying efforts for a $10 billion cloud computing contract that the Pentagon ended up awarding to Microsoft (which spent $2.3 million lobbying for the contract).[35]

Expertise Expertise takes many forms. Groups can employ staff (or can hire experts) to conduct research or develop policy proposals related to their interests. A firm's in-house lobbyists can provide information about how a change in government policy will affect the firm's profits and employment. Some lobbying firms (especially those that employ former members of Congress or congressional staff) may also have inside information on the kinds of policies that are likely to be enacted in the House or Senate. Interest groups with dues-paying members (such as the Sierra Club) can poll them to find out what they would like government to do. All of this information can be deployed to persuade elected officials or bureaucrats about the merits of a group's or a firm's demands (as well as the political consequences of inaction) and offer ready-made policy solutions to the problems the group has identified.

Consider AARP, whose website offers a vast array of research and analyses, including information about seniors' part-time employment, how people invest their

401(k) retirement accounts, age discrimination, and dealing with the COVID-19 pandemic.[36] AARP's lobbyists use this research when arguing for policy changes in their public testimony and in private meetings with members of Congress and congressional staff. And they hire former members of Congress and bureaucrats so they are well informed about the preferences of those inside government. However, only a few interest groups can match the wealth of expertise and resources of AARP.

Individual lobbyists also vary in what they offer to a group or corporation. Former members of Congress might know a lot about policy options and the preferences of their former colleagues but be less informed about public opinion or the business challenges faced by the firm that hires them to lobby. In-house lobbyists might know a lot about the firm they work for but much less about congressional preferences. And an interest group's policy expert might know everything there is to know about current government policies in some areas but know nothing about how to sell new proposals to a skeptical member of Congress.

"Why Should I Care?"

When you think of a lobbyist, don't imagine a person in an expensive suit carrying a briefcase of cash (or a campaign contribution). More often, people become lobbyists because they believe in the goals of the group they represent. And they generally don't wear expensive suits. Understanding who lobbyists really are, and the boundaries of what they can really do, is key to evaluating whether or not they have too much influence in American politics.

EXPLAIN HOW SUCCESSFUL INTEREST GROUPS OVERCOME COLLECTIVE ACTION PROBLEMS

Getting organized

A new interest group's first priority is to get organized, which involves formulating policy goals and a lobbying strategy and raising the money needed to hire staff, rent an office, and set up a website. In some cases, a lobbying firm is hired to perform these jobs. Once organized, the group must continue to attract funds for ongoing operations. These tasks are not easy. Even if a group of people (or corporations) shares the same goals, it may be challenging to persuade them to donate time or money to the lobbying operation.

The logic of collective action

collective action problem
A situation in which the members of a group would benefit by working together to produce some outcome, but each individual is better off refusing to cooperate and reaping benefits from those who do the work.

free riding
Relying on others to contribute to a collective effort while failing to participate on one's own behalf, yet still benefiting from the group's successes.

Research has found that **collective action problems** arise when a group of individuals (or corporations) has an opportunity to make itself better off through the cooperative provision of public goods. For interest groups, the public good in question would be a change in government policy desired by group members. Scholars refer to these situations as involving collective action. Even when all members of a group agree on the desirability of a public good and the costs of producing the good are negligible, cooperation is neither easy nor automatic (see Nuts & Bolts 10.2).

The logic of collective action provides insights into how interest groups are organized and how they make lobbying decisions. First, the logic of collective action tells us that group formation is not automatic. Even when a number of citizens want the same things from government, their common interest may not lead them to organize.

NUTS & BOLTS 10.2

Collective Action Problems

What is collective action?

"Collective action" refers to situations in which a group of individuals can work together to provide public goods. For example, working to help change certain government policies can result in public goods: if the government changes policy, such as strengthening environmental laws, everyone benefits from the cleaner air and water.

What are the problems?

Situations like those described above make it hard to motivate people to contribute to collective efforts to change a law, because each would-be group member can see that their contribution would be only a minuscule portion of what the group needs to succeed. Regardless of how many other people join, an individual is better off free riding—refusing to join but still being able to enjoy the benefits of any successes the group might have.

Why are collective action problems important?

Groups of like-minded citizens who seek changes in government policy may be unable to lobby effectively because they cannot solve their collective action problem. And organization matters. Groups that remain unorganized are less likely to get what they want from government.

How do interest groups solve collective action problems?

Interest groups solve collective action problems in three ways: (1) like some labor unions, they force people to join; (2) they are small enough so that every member's voice matters and free rider problems are lessened; and (3) they encourage a larger, engaged membership by offering incentives for people to join and participate.

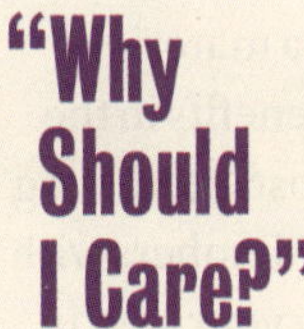

Collective action problems explain why it is difficult to provide public goods. They explain the tendency for the dirty dishes to pile up in the kitchen: in this case, the public good is a clean kitchen, but each roommate's self-interest is to free ride and let someone else wash the dishes. They also help explain the difficulty of interest group formation.

Society is full of groups of like-minded people who do not organize to lobby or who choose to engage in **free riding** and thus enjoy the benefits of organizations without participating. This tendency explains why certain debates in Washington feature well-organized groups on one side of the issue but few on the other.

Unless people can easily see benefits from participating, which does not happen often, group leaders must worry about finding the right strategies to get people to join. Thus, given the logic of collective action, motivating people to join and participate is just as important for a group's success as its lobbying strategy. Most organizations develop mechanisms to make cooperation and participation in an interest group's efforts worthwhile. These **selective incentives** fall into three categories: benefits from participation, coercion, and material goods.

Studies of political parties and interest groups find that some individuals volunteer out of a sense of duty or because they enjoy working together toward a common goal. Scholars refer to these benefits of participation as either **solidary benefits**, which come from working with like-minded people, or **purposive benefits**, which come from working to achieve a desired policy goal.[37] If most people were spurred to political action because of participation benefits, the free rider problem wouldn't exist.

When solidary or purposive benefits are not enough to solve the free rider problem, groups may require participation through **coercion**. Consider labor unions. They provide public goods to workers by negotiating with management on behalf of worker-members over pay and work requirements. Why don't union members free ride?

selective incentives
Benefits that can motivate participation in a group effort because they are available only to those who participate, such as member services offered by interest groups.

solidary benefits
Satisfaction derived from the experience of working with like-minded people, even if the group's efforts do not achieve the desired impact.

purposive benefits
Satisfaction derived from the experience of working toward a desired policy goal, even if the goal is not achieved.

coercion
A method of eliminating nonparticipation or free riding by potential group members by requiring participation, as in many labor unions.

AAA (formerly the American Automobile Association) is a well-known provider of emergency road service, yet few people are aware of its role as an interest group that lobbies for a wide range of policy changes and builds awareness of key transportation issues.

Because in many cases they have to join the union: union shop laws require them to pay union dues as a condition of their employment. These laws are critical to unions; states with laws that make union membership optional typically have weak unions—if any.

material benefits
Benefits that are provided to individuals for joining a group, such as a coffee mug or a T-shirt, that are distinct from the collective benefits provided by the group.

Finally, **material benefits** are benefits given only to the members of an interest group. These incentives are not public goods; an individual can receive a material benefit only by joining the group. Thus, interest groups offer material benefits in the hope of providing people with new reasons to participate. One of the most interesting cases of material benefits provided by an interest group involves AAA. Members with car trouble can call AAA at any time for emergency service (like locking your keys in the car which, ahem, one of the authors has done a few times). AAA also provides its 61 million members with annotated maps and travel guides, a travel agency, a car-buying service, discounts at hotels and restaurants, and other benefits. These services mask the interest group role of AAA. For example, its Foundation for Traffic Safety delivers research reports to legislators on topics ranging from lowering the blood alcohol level threshold that legally defines drunk driving to increasing the restrictions on driving for senior citizens.[38] It's unlikely that many AAA members—who join for the selective incentives—are aware of the organization's lobbying efforts. The incentives drive membership, which funds the organization's lobbying operation.

"Why Should I Care?"

The logic of collective action says that organization is neither automatic nor easy. Rather than complaining about how many lobbyists there are or how much they spend, we should consider whether some groups in society are ignored because they are never able to organize themselves and lobby for their concerns. Are you free riding off of any groups' efforts right now? What would it take to get you involved?

EXPLORE THE WAYS INTEREST GROUPS TRY TO INFLUENCE GOVERNMENT POLICIES

Interest group strategies

Once a group has organized and determined its goals, the next step is to decide how to lobby. There are two types of possible tactics: **inside strategies**, which are actions taken inside government (whether federal, state, or local), and **outside strategies** (also called indirect strategies), which are actions taken outside government (see the How It Works graphic on pp. 386–87).[39] The type of strategy is sometimes dictated by the policy in question. In the example of the tax breaks for wealthy individuals and companies hidden in the CARES Act discussed in the chapter opener, an insider strategy was essential because the public would have been opposed had it known about these tax breaks. In other cases, such as the lobbying effort of AARP to help save the Affordable Care Act, an outside strategy is effective to help put pressure on members of Congress. In general, these strategies are undertaken by a single group working on its own, sometimes in opposition to another group or groups. However, as we discuss later, interest groups sometimes work together toward common legislative goals.

inside strategies
The tactics employed within Washington, D.C., by interest groups seeking to achieve their policy goals.

outside strategies
The tactics employed outside Washington, D.C., by interest groups seeking to achieve their policy goals.

Inside strategies

Inside strategies involve some form of contact with elected officials or bureaucrats. Thus, inside strategies require a group to establish an office in Washington, D.C., or to hire a lobbying firm to act on its behalf.

Direct Lobbying When interest group staff meet with officeholders or bureaucrats, they plead their case through **direct lobbying**, asking government officials to change policy in line with the group's goals.[40] Such contacts are very common—on any given day, each congressional or administrative office gets phone calls, visits, or emails from dozens of lobbyists.

direct lobbying
Attempts by interest group staff to influence policy by speaking with elected officials or bureaucrats.

Direct lobbying is generally aimed at officials and bureaucrats who are sympathetic to the group's goals.[41] Through these efforts, interest groups and their representatives do not try to convert opponents into supporters; rather, these efforts are a way of helping legislators enact policies that they already prefer—and that the group prefers as well.[42] Groups can assist in a number of ways, from sharing information about proposed changes, to providing lists of other legislators who might be persuadable, to drafting legislative proposals or regulations. These efforts usually do not involve a trade in which the group expects legislative action in return for its help. In fact, legislators and their staff are often happy to meet with a like-minded group's representatives, as the information the group can provide may be vital to the legislators' efforts to enact legislation, manage the bureaucracy, or keep the support of constituents back home in their districts.[43] For example, corporations that stood to lose business if the government moved to direct student loans lobbied legislators whose districts included the companies' call centers and headquarters. For these legislators, helping these companies might have been good public policy, but it was also a way of preserving their constituents' jobs.

Interest groups also contact "fence-sitters" who neither support nor oppose them, with the goal of converting them into supporters. These efforts are less extensive than the lobbying of supporters, however, because opponents are unlikely to change their minds unless a group can provide new information that causes them to rethink their position. However, lobbying opponents may be useful if it forces opposing interest groups to counterlobby, using their limited resources to make sure that their allied legislators do not change their positions.[44]

As these descriptions indicate, interest groups place a high priority on maintaining access to their lobbying targets and being able to present their arguments, regardless of whether they expect to get what they want. Of course, interest groups want to achieve their policy goals, but access is the necessary first step that makes persuasion possible. Therefore, many interest groups try to keep their efforts low-key, providing information to friends and opponents alike and avoiding threats or harsh words, in the hope that they will leave a favorable impression and be able to gain access the next

How it works: in theory

Lobbying the Federal Government: Inside and Outside Strategies

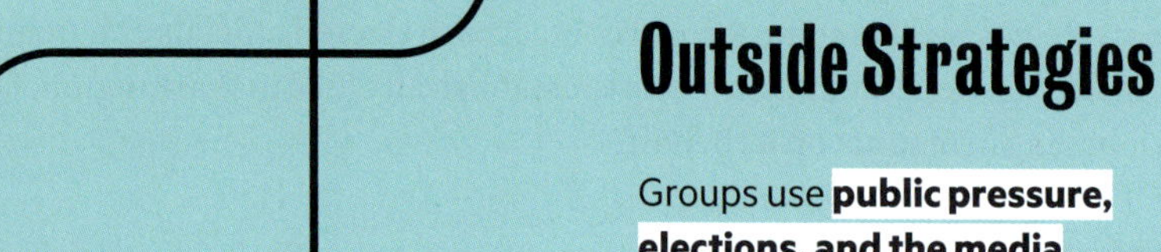

Inside Strategies

Groups **lobby government officials directly** in Washington, D.C.

Examples:

meeting with lawmakers

drafting legislation

providing research and testimony

taking the government to court

Outside Strategies

Groups use **public pressure, elections, and the media** to influence government.

Examples:

grassroots email, letter, social media, or phone campaigns

contributing to election campaigns

getting media coverage of their cause

How it works: in practice

Lobbying on Infrastructure and Build Back Better

The cornerstones of President Biden's domestic policy agenda were the American Jobs Plan and the American Families Plan. The former became the $1.2 trillion Infrastructure Investment and Jobs Act and was signed into law on November 15, 2021. The latter morphed into the Build Back Better (BBB) bill. Despite being pared back from its original $3.5 trillion price tag to just over half of that, it died a quiet death early in 2022.

Business, labor, and environmental interest groups lobbied and campaigned vigorously to shape the direction of the bills, crucially decoupling them, which paved the way for the more popular infrastructure bill to pass and the bigger bill to fail. Interest groups also used a broad range of insider and outsider tactics to help determine how the infrastructure bill would be funded, how the money would be spent, and to kill the bigger bill.

 Inside strategies

 Outside strategies

Critical Thinking

1. **How do the success of the infrastructure bill** and the failure of the Build Back Better bill illustrate the influence of interest groups?
2. **Imagine a world in which there was no lobbying** of members of Congress, phone calls, social media, or ad campaigns by groups. Do you think the fates of these two bills would have been any different?

Infrastructure Bill

Let's build some highways.

Businesses such as FedEx and Uber hire lobbyists and interest groups such as the U.S. Chamber of Commerce and the RATE Coalition and gear up to urge Congress to pass an infrastructure bill.

We are the experts!

February 2021
Dozens of businesses, labor groups, and environmental groups that would be impacted by the bills provide **testimony at committee and subcommittee hearings**.

Outreach.

May 2021
The Chamber of Commerce leads a wildly successful **social media day of action**, getting its message in front of hundreds of influential decision makers.

Let's get this done!

June 2021
Nearly 2,000 companies and organizations lobby Congress on the infrastructure bill, spending more than $450 million. The Chamber of Commerce organizes 330+ **meetings with members of Congress and their staff**.

Ad blast!

August 2021
Citizens for Responsible Energy Solutions launches a **$1.5 million TV, radio, and digital ad campaign** to build GOP support for the bipartisan infrastructure bill.

Tweaking the details.

November 2021
The digital advocacy group Fight for the Future lobbies to change language in the bill requiring disclosure of cryptocurrency transactions to the IRS. The group **generates thousands of grassroots calls** to senators.

Success! Now to divide the pie.

February 2022
Once the bill becomes law, more than 1,000 municipalities want their share of the "mother lode." They spend another $50 million lobbying in the second half of 2021, much of it on **personal meetings with members of Congress** to steer funds to specific projects.

Build Back Better Bill

At what cost?

These same businesses and groups also work to block any effort to roll back the corporate tax cuts enacted under President Trump and push for separating the traditional infrastructure bill from the larger social and environmental spending bill. Other groups mobilize to pass BBB.

Divide and conquer!

September 2021
Business interests successfully push to decouple the two bills. They then move on to Phase 2: trying to kill BBB. The Chamber of Commerce runs a **multi-pronged ad blitz** aimed at Senators Joe Manchin (D-WV) and Kyrsten Sinema (D-AZ), two moderate Democrats whose votes could stop it from passing.

Fight pressure with (more!) pressure.

October 2021
93 organizations, led by the Economic Policy Institute and the Institute for Policy Studies, **delivered a letter** urging Congress to stand up to pressure from lobby groups representing big corporations and pass BBB.

Let's do both!

October 2021
Building Back Together **spends $150 million on advertising** to support the infrastructure bill and BBB's allocated spending for the care economy, lowering health care costs, and climate change.

Manchin and Sinema pull the plug.

December 2021
Saying that BBB costs too much, **Sens. Manchin and Sinema declare the bill is dead**. Liberal groups say they are tools of the pharmaceutical and banking industries, while conservative groups applaud their independence.

time they want to lobby their opponents. After all, people who are opposed to a group's current priorities one day may agree with the group on some future issue.

Whom do these groups contact for direct lobbying? Analysis of lobbyists' annual disclosure forms shows that they contact people throughout the federal government, including elected officials, members of the president's staff, and bureaucrats in the executive branch. They seek this wide range of contacts because different officials play distinct roles in the policy-making process and thus have various types of influence. Members of Congress shape legislation and budgets; members of the president's staff influence the formation of new policies and obtain presidential consent for new laws; and executive branch bureaucrats change the ways regulations are written and policies are implemented.

Drafting Legislation and Regulations Interest groups sometimes draft legislative proposals and regulations, which they deliver to legislators and bureaucrats as part of their lobbying efforts. For example, in 2020, the Broadband Data Act closely followed the proposal from the broadband association USTelecom.[45] Surveys of interest groups found that more than three-quarters reported drafting proposals for members of Congress.[46] In recent years, the role of lobbyists in drafting legislation has become more prominent because Congress has less internal capacity to write the laws due to cuts in committee staff.[47]

While the practice is common in Congress, it has gotten out of control in state legislatures. A recent study used a computer algorithm to detect similar language in nearly one million bills in all 50 state legislatures and Congress introduced over an eight-year period. The search used hundreds of cloud computers that ran nonstop for months to compare known "model legislation" written by lobbyists with bills introduced by lawmakers. The analysis found 10,163 introduced bills that were nearly identical to the model legislation and 2,121 were passed into law. Forty-two percent of the bills were from industry (27 percent of which were passed), 40 percent from conservative groups (20 percent became law), and 16 percent from liberal groups (9 percent became law). The study concludes, "In all, these copycat bills amount to the nation's largest, unreported special-interest campaign, driving agendas in every statehouse and touching nearly every area of public policy."[48]

Legislators often didn't know the source of the legislation, and bills typically used misleading titles, such as the "Asbestos Transparency Act," which was written by corporations to make it more difficult for victims to sue for damages. The "HOPE Act" was written by a conservative advocacy group to restrict access to food stamps. The "Campus Free Speech Act" prevented universities from blocking controversial speakers and imposed penalties, up to expulsion, on students who disrupted such events.[49]

One reason that lobbyists are successful at getting their "model legislation" passed is that they do not give proposals to just anyone: they seek out legislators who already support their cause and who have significant influence within Congress (and state legislatures). A lobbying effort aimed at cutting interest rates on student loans would target supporters of this change who are also members of the congressional committee with jurisdiction over student loan programs—preferably someone who chairs the committee or one of its subcommittees.[50] Interest groups also lobby bureaucrats to influence the details of new regulations.[51] If the types of regulations involved can go into effect without congressional approval, then lobbying the bureaucracy can result in groups' getting exactly what they want. But even if new regulations require approval by Congress or White House staff, interest groups can increase their chances of success by getting involved in the initial drafting of policy.

Research Interest groups often prepare research reports on topics of interest to the group. For example, Public Citizen features on its website a series of research reports on topics such as protecting democracy, making government work, consumer and worker safety, globalization and trade, climate and energy, health care, and justice and the courts.[52] Such reports serve multiple purposes. They may sway public opinion, help persuade elected officials or bureaucrats, or directly influence the industry that is the subject of the report. They also help interest group staff claim expertise on some aspect of public policy. Members of Congress are more likely to accept a group's legislative proposal if they think that the group's staff has research to back up its claims. Journalists are also more likely to respond to an interest group's requests for publicity if they think that the group's staff has supporting evidence.

Hearings Interest group staff often testify before congressional committees. In part, this activity is aimed at informing members of Congress about issues that matter to the interest group. For example, the Chamber of Commerce's website shows that its staff has testified in congressional hearings in favor of the infrastructure bill, arguing that modernizing our transportation systems would "bolster inclusive economic growth." However, as we noted in the How It Works feature, the Chamber also testified against the Build Back Better bill.[53]

Litigation Another inside strategy involves taking the government to court. In bringing their case, interest groups can argue that the government's actions are not consistent with the Constitution or that the government has misinterpreted existing law.[54] Interest groups can bring these actions via lawyers on their staff, a hired law firm, or lawyers who will work for no fees. Interest groups can also become involved in an existing case by filing amicus curiae ("friend of the court") briefs, documents that offer judges the group's rationale for how the case should be decided. The drawback of litigation is that it is costly and time-consuming—cases can take years to work through the federal court system. At a minimum, groups that use the litigation strategy generally combine it with direct lobbying or other strategies. The litigation strategy has been especially important for public interest law advocacy groups that use the courts to enforce environmental, consumer, and product safety laws. Starting in the 1960s with groups such as Ralph Nader's Center for the Study of Responsive Law and the Natural Resources Defense Council, and continuing through today with groups such as the Southern Poverty Law Center, public interest law groups have played a key role in many important Supreme Court cases on these topics in the past fifty years.[55] Business groups also are quite successful in using this strategy to protect their interests.

The American Civil Liberties Union is an interest group that often uses litigation strategies in its efforts to change government policy. Here, members of the ACLU chapter in Washington State announce their filing of an abortion rights lawsuit against several local hospitals.

Working Together To increase their chances for success, interest groups can work together in their lobbying efforts, formulating a common strategy and future plans. In general, these coalitions of groups are short-term efforts focused on achieving a specific outcome, like supporting or opposing the confirmation of judicial and cabinet nominees.[56] The tax giveaway discussed in the chapter opener had unlikely allies such as Coca-Cola, Hewlett Packard Enterprise, Morgan Stanley, and the National Association of Manufacturers (whose members include companies such as ExxonMobil, Raytheon, and Caterpillar), which would all gain billions of dollars from the change in the tax law.[57]

Why do groups work together? The most obvious reason lies in the power of large numbers: legislators are more likely to respond, or at least provide access, when many groups with large or diverse memberships are all asking for the same thing.[58]

The problem with working together is that groups may agree on general goals but disagree on specifics, thereby requiring negotiation. If differences cannot be bridged, groups may undertake separate and possibly conflicting lobbying efforts or decide against lobbying entirely. For example, although there are many groups pressing for climate change legislation, they have not developed a unified lobbying effort. The problem? The groups disagree on which policies should be implemented, who should pay for them, and whether the government should aid companies that would be forced to purchase new antipollution equipment. In the absence of agreement, working alone seems a better strategy.[59]

grassroots lobbying
A lobbying strategy that relies on participation by group members, such as a protest or a letter-writing campaign.

Outside strategies

Outside strategies involve things that groups do across the country rather than in Washington. Again, these activities can be orchestrated by the group or be organized by a firm hired by the group.

Grassroots Lobbying Directly involving interest group members in lobbying efforts is called **grassroots lobbying**. Members may send letters, make telephone calls, participate in a protest, or express their demands in other ways. Many groups encourage grassroots lobbying. For example, AARP's website has a page where members can watch a webinar to get "tips and tools for engaging elected officials virtually."[60] Other links allow members to email or to fax their representatives letters that are prewritten by AARP to express the group's positions on various proposals, such as pension protection legislation and proposals to curb identity theft. AARP also organizes district meetings with elected officials and encourages its members to attend.

Mass protests are another form of grassroots lobbying. In addition to trying to capture the attention of government officials, mass protests also seek to draw media attention, with the idea of publicizing the group's goals and perhaps gaining new members or financial support. For example, after the election of Donald Trump, hundreds of groups partnered with the organizers of the Women's March on January 21, 2017, in 673 marches on all seven continents, including 408 marches in the United States. There were more than 5 million participants worldwide (the estimates for the United States range from 3.3 to 5.2 million).[61] The marches were aimed at drawing attention to a range of progressive issues connected with women's rights. The lead sponsors were Planned Parenthood and the Natural

The Black Lives Matter movement, formed in 2013 in support of issues of racial justice and police reform, utilizes protests for grassroots lobbying. In 2020, after the killing by police of George Floyd, an unarmed Black man in Minneapolis, Minnesota, mass protests across the country brought increased attention to and support for the group's goals, including ending police brutality and systemic racism.

Resources Defense Council; more than 550 organizations were listed as "partners" on the Women's March website.[62]

Grassroots strategies are useful because elected officials are loath to act against a large group of citizens who care enough about an issue to express their position.[63] These officials may not agree with the group's goals, but they are likely to at least arrange a meeting with its staff, so that they appear willing to learn about their constituents' demands.[64] However, these member-based strategies work only for a small set of interest groups. To take advantage of these strategies, groups first need a large number of members. Legislators begin to pay attention to a letter-writing campaign only when they receive several thousand pieces of mail.

In addition, for grassroots lobbying to be effective, the letters or other efforts have to come from a Congress member's own constituents. The effectiveness of grassroots lobbying also depends on perceptions of how much a group has done to motivate participation. Suppose a representative gets 10,000 emails demanding an increase in federal student aid. However, virtually all the messages contain the same appeal because they were generated and sent from a group's website. Congressional staff refer to these efforts as **Astroturf lobbying**.[65] Given the similarity of the letters, the representative may discount the effort, believing that it says more about the group's ability to make campaign participation accessible than it does about the number of district residents who strongly support an increase in federal student aid. Even so, politicians are sometimes reluctant to completely dismiss Astroturf efforts—the fact that so many people participated, even with facilitation by an interest group, means that their demands must at least be considered.

Astroturf lobbying
Any lobbying method initiated by an interest group that is designed to look like the spontaneous, independent participation of many individuals.

In recent years, these Astroturf efforts have evolved into a practice that is *truly* fake grassroots: organizations that claim to represent grassroots entities but in reality advocate for big industry. For example, Amazon and Google created Connected Commerce Council (3C) to lobby Congress on issues that are important to Big Tech. They know that Big Tech has had image problems lately, so they attempted to create the impression that their issues were important to thousands of small businesses. An investigation revealed that many of the thousands of listed "members," including a hair salon, a towing company, a barbershop, and a blacksmith, had never heard of 3C. The blacksmith, who makes hand-forged metal works and grilling tools, said,

Amazon, Google, and other large technology companies responded to negative press around worker rights and customer privacy, among other issues, by setting up an interest group called Connected Commerce Council. The group lobbied Congress on issues important to Big Tech under the guise of a grassroots interest group.

"Technology is not exactly my forte." After the story was published, the website took down the names of several thousand small businesses. While some of the businesses reported that they had signed up on the website, Amazon and Google provide all of the funding for the group.[66] Airbnb and Uber have used similar tactics.[67]

Mobilizing Public Opinion One strategy related to grassroots lobbying involves trying to change what the public thinks about an issue in the hope that elected officials will see this change and respond by enacting (or opposing) new laws or regulations to keep their constituents happy.

Virtually all groups try to influence opinion. Most maintain a website that presents their message, and they write press releases to get media coverage. Most groups are also very active on social media, using Facebook, Twitter, and Instagram to keep in touch with members and let them know about issues that the group is working on. Any contact with citizens, whether to encourage them to join the group, contribute money, or engage in grassroots lobbying, also involves elements of persuasion—trying to transform citizens into supporters and supporters into true believers and even activists. For example, the Sierra Club's Climate Emergency Mobilization Team mobilizes its members to contact their elected officials and to express their opinions on a broad range of issues related to climate change.[68]

A focused mobilization effort involves contacting large numbers of potential supporters (beyond just members) through email, phone calls, direct mail, television advertising, print media, social media, and websites. In order to get legislators to respond, a group has to persuade large numbers of people to get involved. One example of mobilization occurs during congressional hearings on nominees to the Supreme Court or other federal judgeships. One study found that about one-third of the groups that lobbied for or against these nominees also deployed direct mail and leaflets and ran phone banks as a way to influence public opinion.[69] Most recently, interest groups mobilized their members for and against the nomination of Ketanji Brown Jackson to the Supreme Court.[70]

Electioneering Interest groups get involved in elections by making contributions to candidates, mobilizing people (including their own staff) to help in a campaign, endorsing candidates, funding campaign ads, or mobilizing a candidate's or party's supporters. All these efforts seek to influence who gets elected, with the expectation that changing who gets elected will affect what government does.

Federal laws limit groups' electioneering and lobbying efforts (see Nuts & Bolts 10.3). For example, most private organizations and associations in America are organized as 501(c)(3) organizations, a designation based on their Internal Revenue Service classification, which means that donations to the group are tax deductible. However, 501(c)(3) organizations are not allowed to advocate for or against political candidates, and lobbying must not constitute more than 20 percent of the group's total expenditures (certain public-education programs or voter-registration drives that are conducted in a nonpartisan manner do not count toward that 20 percent), although some groups are always looking for loopholes in these restrictions. Groups that want to engage in lobbying or electioneering without looking for exceptions can incorporate under other IRS designations and operate as a **political action committee (PAC)**, a **527 organization**, or a 501(c)(4). Although contributions to these organizations are not tax deductible, such organizations have fewer restrictions on the size of the contributions they can make and on how their money is spent—for example, 527 organizations have no contribution or spending limits.

Two new options for electioneering by interest groups emerged in recent elections: Super PACs and 501(c)(4) organizations. The former was a consequence of the *Citizens*

political action committee (PAC)
An interest group or a division of an interest group that can raise money to contribute to campaigns or to spend on ads in support of candidates. The amount a PAC can receive from each of its donors and the amount it can spend on federal electioneering are strictly limited.

527 organization
A tax-exempt group formed primarily to influence elections through voter mobilization efforts and issue ads that do not directly endorse or oppose a candidate. Unlike PACs, 527s are not subject to contribution limits and spending caps.

NUTS & BOLTS 10.3

Interest Groups and Electioneering: Types of Organizations

An interest group's ability to engage in electioneering depends on how it is organized—specifically, what section of the IRS code applies to the organization. The following table gives details on four common organizations: 501(c) organizations, 527 organizations, PACs, and so-called Super PACs. Many individuals choose to contribute money to nonprofits organized as 501(c)(4) groups, which can lobby and engage in electioneering as long as their "primary activity" (at least half of their overall activity) is not political.

Type of organization	Advantages	Disadvantages
501(c)(3)	Contributions tax deductible	Cannot engage in political activities, and lobbying can be no more than 20 percent of spending (but voter education and mobilization are permitted)
527	Can spend unlimited amounts on issue advocacy and voter mobilization	Cannot make contributions to candidates or coordinate efforts with candidates or parties
501(c)(4)	Can spend unlimited amounts on electioneering; does not have to disclose contributors	At least half of its activities must be nonpolitical; cannot coordinate efforts with candidates or parties
PACs	Can contribute directly to candidates and parties	Strict limits on direct contributions
Super PACs	Can spend unlimited amounts on electioneering; can support or oppose specific candidates	Cannot make contributions to candidates or coordinate efforts with candidates or parties

Source: Compiled by the authors.

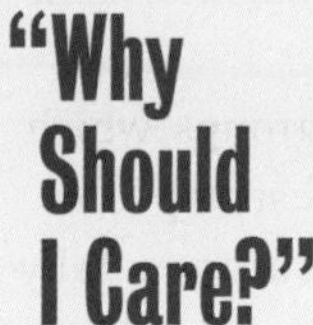

This may seem a little deep in the weeds, but understanding the different types of interest groups is important for understanding how they influence elections. Some types of groups have to disclose their donors and others don't. It is more difficult for voters to hold their leaders accountable if voters don't know who is supporting candidates' campaigns.

United Supreme Court decision that authorized unlimited independent spending by corporations and labor unions in federal elections.[71] Many groups set up new PACs to take advantage of these latest rules—the "Super" label reflects the fact that these groups take in and spend much more money than the typical PAC. All the major 2020 presidential candidates had an independent Super PAC running ad campaigns on their behalf.

In 2020, federally focused PACs and Super PACS spent more than $7 billion for electioneering and contributions to candidates and parties, of which ActBlue raised a staggering $3.45 billion and WinRed raised $1.35 billion (ActBlue and WinRed are the political parties' online platforms for raising money from groups and individuals for congressional campaigns).[72] However, these large numbers mask some important details. To begin with, some of the largest firms in America (Google, Walmart, and ExxonMobil, for example) have PACs that spend only a million or so on contributions. Another large firm, Apple, has no PAC. The PAC for the Pharmaceutical Research and Manufacturers of America is also small, and the other influential interest groups mentioned earlier in Figure 10.2 (AARP, NARAL Pro-Choice America, and the Family

Research Council) spend even less or don't have a PAC or a 527. These numbers suggest that money doesn't buy elections or policy outcomes—if it did, these organizations would probably spend a lot more on campaign donations and television ads.

Spending totals can also be deceptive. The National Association of Realtors, for example, made about $4 million in contributions in 2020 election cycles—but spread out the funds over 500 candidates, with slightly more going to Democrats than Republicans.[73] The PAC for EMILY's List collected $480.6 million, but only $18.4 million went to contributions to candidates and parties, with the rest for fund-raising and overhead. Another large spender, NextGen Climate Action, was funded largely by a single wealthy donor (83 percent of the $56.3 million raised) but did not make any contributions to federal candidates in the 2020 cycle—their spending was on issue ads. (The founder, billionaire entrepreneur Tom Steyer, ran as a candidate for president during the 2020 Democratic primary.) And some groups used most of their money against candidates they opposed: the conservative Super PAC America First Action spent almost all of its $149 million against Democratic contenders.[74]

Finally, while the $7 billion that these groups raised together seems large, only about two-thirds was spent on behalf of or as contributions to candidates. Most PACs contributed to only a few candidates. And while more than a thousand Super PACs were active in the 2020 election, most were small, and the average group spent just over $500,000. These data highlight a sharp difference in electioneering strategies between the very few large, well-funded interest groups and everyone else. A few 527s, Super PACs, 501(c)(4)s, and PACs have the money to deploy massive advertising and mobilization efforts for candidates or issues they like or against those they don't like. There are also some very large associations that can persuade large numbers of members to work for and vote for candidates whom the group supports or against candidates whom the group wants to defeat. And just a few rich individuals can make outsized contributions to a candidate they favor.

But these strategies are not available to the vast majority of interest groups, which simply don't have the resources. Most interest groups hope to give modest help to a few candidates who are sympathetic to their goals. These contributions are generally made in the hope that, once elected, the officeholder will remember their contribution when their group asks for a meeting. It is important to remember that electioneering is only one strategy available to interest groups. Some groups do no electioneering at all, possibly because they lack sufficient funds, because they want to avoid making enemies based on whom they support or don't support, or because other strategies are more promising given the resources that are available to them. Many groups opt for quiet lobbying efforts that use their expertise, or they undertake grassroots efforts to build public support for their policy goals. Massive electioneering operations by interest groups are relatively rare.

Conservative Super PACs, such as the Conservative Political Action Conference (CPAC), hold conventions that give candidates a venue to present themselves to conservative activists and donors.

Cultivating Media Contacts Media coverage helps a group publicize its concerns without spending any money. Thus, most interest group leaders talk often with journalists to pursue favorable coverage of news stories that pertain to the group's issues. Such attention may mobilize public opinion indirectly, by getting people to join the group, contribute money, or urge elected officials to support the group's agenda. Favorable media coverage also helps a group's leaders assure members that they are actively working on members' concerns.

Journalists listen when interest groups call if they feel that the group's story will catch their readers' attention or address their concerns. Smart interest group leaders make it easy for journalists to cover their cause, holding events that produce intriguing news stories. These stories may not change anyone's mind, but the media coverage provides free publicity for the groups' policy agendas.

Bypassing Government: The Initiative Process A final outside strategy for interest groups bypasses government entirely: a group can work to get its proposed policy change voted on by the public in a general election through an initiative or a referendum. Referenda and initiatives allow citizens to vote on specific proposed changes in policy. The difference between these procedures lies in the source of the proposal. In a **referendum** the legislature or another government body proposes the question that is put to a vote, whereas in an **initiative** citizens put questions on the ballot, typically after gathering signatures of registered voters on a petition.

referendum
A direct vote by citizens on a policy change proposed by a legislature or another government body. Referenda are common in state and local elections, but there is no mechanism for a national-level referendum.

initiative
A direct vote by citizens on a policy change proposed by fellow citizens or organized groups outside government. Getting a question on the ballot typically requires collecting a set number of signatures from registered voters in support of the proposal. There is no mechanism for a national-level initiative.

Initiatives can occur only in states and municipalities that have the appropriate procedures in place; there is no mechanism for a nationwide vote on an interest group's proposal. So if a group wants to use this process to effect national change, it has to get its measure on the ballot in one state at a time. Moreover, only some states allow initiatives, and some permit this kind of vote only on a narrow range of issues. The champion state for initiatives is California, whose citizens often vote on dozens of initiatives in each general election, ranging from funding for stem-cell research to limits on taxation and spending.[75]

There are many examples of groups using the initiative process to change government policy. Most notably, advocates of term limits for state legislators have used the initiative process to establish such limits in 21 states, although in 6 states the limits have since been overturned by legislative action or subsequent initiatives (so 15 states currently have term limits for state legislators).[76] Also, 33 states have approved legal use of marijuana in some form through statewide ballot measures.[77] Five of those states legalized its use, to varying degrees, in 2020, two in 2022, and one in 2023.[78] Research shows that states with more active interest groups have more initiatives on the ballot, so groups are taking advantage of this mechanism for influencing policy.[79]

One of the principal concerns about the initiative process is that it favors well-funded groups that can advertise heavily in support of their proposals and can mobilize their supporters to vote on Election Day.[80] But spending a lot of money often is not enough: even groups with substantial resources have sometimes been unable to reform policy or stop policy change through the initiative process.[81] For example, in 2016 large tobacco companies spent $71.3 million dollars to try to defeat Proposition 56 in California, which increased the tax on a pack of cigarettes by $2. Supporters of the proposition spent only half that amount ($35.5 million), but voters approved the measure 64–36 percent.[82]

Choosing strategies

Most groups give testimony, do research, contact elected officials and bureaucrats, talk with journalists, and develop legislative and regulatory proposals.[83] A particular group's decisions about which strategies to use depend partly on its resources and partly on what approach the group believes will be most effective in promoting its particular issues. Some strategies that work well for one group's agenda might not be appropriate for another's. The Humane Society of the United States is an organization that lobbies to prevent the abuse and neglect of animals. It spent $180 million in 2021 but has only a small Washington office. Its lobbying expenses for 2021 were $650,000.[84] Rather than lobbying members of Congress, the group's focus is on investigations and grassroots organizing, highlighting situations in which corporations and countries are not behaving according to existing laws against animal cruelty.

Other interest groups advance their causes in ways that don't look like lobbying. For example, as NASA begins to formulate plans for sending humans to Mars in the 2030s, the Boeing Company has released a series of films and videos about these plans. At one level, Boeing's efforts are all about highlighting the many important discoveries that a voyage to Mars might generate—but they are also a way to increase the chances that NASA's plans will attract public support and be funded by Congress, which, if it happens, will likely generate a series of very lucrative contracts for Boeing to build and help operate exploration hardware.

At first glance, lobbying victories should go to the groups that can spend a lot on contributions to candidates or on direct lobbying. But there are many other ways to succeed in the battle to shape public policy, from organizing American citizens to preparing new proposals or doing background research. Policy influence isn't as much about the size of a group's budget as it is about factors such as the size of the group's membership or the perception of its expertise. Even poorly funded groups can find ways to win. If there's an issue that you believe in, you can find a group that supports it, large or small, and get involved in any number of ways.

EVALUATE INTEREST GROUP INFLUENCE

How much power do interest groups have?

I will Make Our Government Honest Again—believe me. But First, I'm going to have to #DrainTheSwamp in DC.

—President Donald Trump

Two 2020 presidential candidates, Democrats Bernie Sanders and Elizabeth Warren, focused much of their campaigns on the need to reduce the power of large corporations and special interests over policy making in Washington. While neither Sanders nor Warren gained the nomination, their campaigns spoke for the widely held belief about how Washington works: that interest groups have too much power and something drastic must be done to end their domination over policy making in Washington. Donald Trump capitalized on this same sentiment with his pledge to "drain the swamp" in 2016.

As we discuss in the What Do the Facts Say? feature, some studies of interest group influence support Sanders and Warren's claims—but others tell a very different story, one in which a group's chances of getting what it wants depend on whether there is organized opposition to their demand. In other words, as one analysis put it, "the solution to lobbying is more lobbying."[85]

Scholarly research also reveals four reasons why it is so hard to measure interest group influence. First, we know that interest groups usually lobby their friends in government rather than their enemies and moderate their demands in the face of resistance.[86] As a result, what looks like success may in fact be a signal of something else. For example, the NRA leadership would probably favor a new federal law that made it legal to carry a concealed handgun throughout the nation. Why doesn't the NRA demand enactment of this legislation? Because there is no sign that Congress would comply. A more limited proposal that would force states to honor concealed carry permits issued by other states passed the House late in 2017 with the strong support of the NRA,[87] but the bill died in the Senate. Thus, the NRA's decision to not push for national concealed carry legislation and its inability to get the more limited bill through the Senate show the limits of the organization's power.

Interest Group Power

Conventional wisdom says that business interest groups have too much power over policy outcomes in Washington. But what do the facts say?

To address this question, a group of political scientists tracked a series of issues through years of lobbying, congressional debate, legislative action, and implementation by the bureaucracy. Their goal was to determine whether business groups were successful in getting what they want from Congress, particularly when their efforts were opposed by citizen groups or government officials. This figure shows what they found.

WHAT DO THE FACTS SAY?

Think about it

- **Many people believe that business groups** always succeed in their lobbying efforts. Does this figure confirm or deny these suspicions?
- **After looking at these data,** do you think business groups have too much power? How do these data help us understand the winners and losers in the tax benefits in the CARES Act discussed at the beginning of this chapter?

Which interest groups win . . . and when?

After four years . . .

Business groups win | Other side wins | Both/neither win

Business groups vs. citizen groups or unions

Business groups vs. government (executive branch, members of Congress)

Business groups unopposed

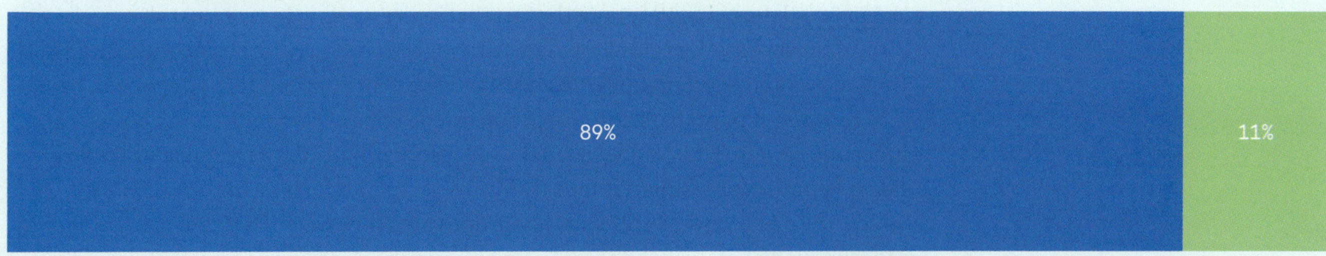

Source: Marie Hojnacki, Kathleen Marchetti, Frank Baumgartner, Jeffrey M. Berry, David C. Kimball, and Beth L. Leech, "Assessing Business Advantage in Washington Lobbying," *Interest Groups and Advocacy* 4 (2015): 206–24.

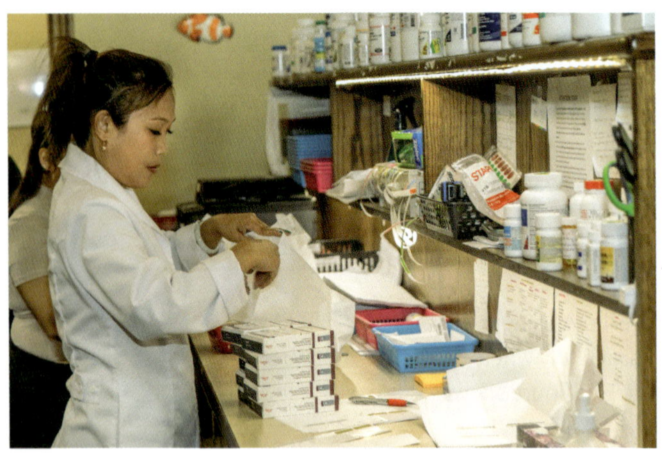

While many observers credit lobbying by the pharmaceutical industry for policies such as the Medicare Prescription Drug Benefit (and its ban on importing medicines), favorable public opinion, the efforts of AARP, and bureaucrats' independent judgments probably had greater influence on passing the Drug Benefit Act.

Second, some complaints about the power of interest groups come from the losing side in the political process. Consider the "net neutrality" rule that was recently overturned by the Federal Communications Commission. The rule "prohibited internet service providers (ISPs) from blocking, slowing or speeding up web content or charging customers additional fees to access certain web services," so corporations like AT&T, Verizon, and Comcast were strongly in favor of eliminating the regulation. The losing side of this debate, which included Microsoft, Google, and Netflix, complained that the large ISPs influenced the outcome with tens of millions of dollars in lobbying and contributions. However, lobbying was intense on both sides.[88]

Third, many interest groups claim responsibility for policies and election outcomes regardless of whether their lobbying made the difference. Consider the hotly contested election to fill the Senate seat of President Trump's first attorney general, Jeff Sessions, in Alabama. In the campaign for or against the two candidates, 45 outside groups spent about $13.7 million, which surpassed the $13.5 million spent by the candidates themselves. With nearly $10.3 million of the outside money being spent on behalf of the winning Democratic candidate, Doug Jones, it is not surprising that interest groups would take some credit for the win. However, the losing Republican candidate, Roy Moore, was a deeply flawed candidate who was shunned by the Republican leadership in the Senate (but endorsed by Donald Trump). He was accused of sexually assaulting a 14-year-old when he was an attorney in his 30s, said that the United States was better off under slavery, and had been kicked off the state supreme court for refusing to follow the order of a federal court. Clearly these factors were central in Moore's defeat.[89] Yet the leaders of interest groups have a considerable incentive to make strong claims about their group's influence and impact, as these claims help them attract members and keep their jobs.[90]

> **But this is the great danger America faces. That we will cease to be one nation and become instead a collection of interest groups: city against suburb, region against region, individual against individual. Each seeking to satisfy private wants.**
>
> —**Barbara Jordan,** civil rights leader and former member of Congress

Fourth, arguments about the impact of interest groups on election outcomes, such as Moore's defeat in 2017, ignore the fact that interest groups are almost always active on both sides of an election campaign. Although Moore was the target of attack ads funded by interest groups and many groups gave contributions to his opponent, he also received support from interest groups in the form of campaign contributions and independent ads. Thus, it doesn't make sense to attribute Moore's defeat to actions taken by one set of groups without asking why similar efforts on his behalf had no effect. You can't conclude that interest groups are all-powerful without explaining why Moore's supporters were unable to help him win the election in an overwhelmingly Republican state.

In sum, dire claims about the overwhelming influence of interest groups and lobbying on Washington policy making are probably wrong. Rather than making a blanket claim about interest group influence, a better response is to ask, What are the conditions that enhance a group's influence over policy, and what are the conditions that reduce it? That is, what determines when interest groups succeed?

What determines when interest groups succeed?

Three factors shape interest group influence. The first is the group's goal: Does it want to change a policy (including enacting a new policy) or to prevent change? The second is salience: How many Americans care about what a group is trying to do? The third is conflict: To what extent do other groups or the public oppose the policy change?

Change versus Preventing Change In general, groups are going to have an easier time preventing a change than working to implement one. As we discuss in Chapter 2, enacting a new policy requires the approval of both houses of Congress, the president's signature (or a veto override), and implementation from the appropriate bureaucratic agency. Each of these steps provides an opportunity for interest groups to lobby members of government to do nothing. So if the groups are successful, change will not occur. Studies show that groups are much more likely to be successful when their goals involve this kind of negative lobbying that seeks to block changes in policy.[91] The NRA has successfully lobbied against a new ban on assault weapons and reforms to the system of national background checks for handgun purchases. However, following mass shootings in a Buffalo supermarket and a Texas elementary school, Congress passed a law in 2022 that expanded background checks for 18- to 21-year-olds, gave incentives to states to pass red flag laws, and prevented dating partners who had been convicted of domestic abuse from owning a gun.

While the success of the NRA's negative lobbying attracts considerable attention, its failures in lobbying for policy change do not. Consider the NRA's advocacy of concealed carry laws. As noted earlier, there is little doubt that the NRA's leaders and most of its members favor the passage of such laws nationwide, but efforts to lobby Congress in favor of such laws are unlikely to be successful given public opposition and well-funded interest groups that are against concealed carry. These groups could respond with negative lobbying against any effort the NRA might make. As a result, while the NRA lobbies for concealed carry, it has failed to help enact national legislation; the limits on its power over legislation do not get much publicity.

Salience Interest groups are more likely to succeed when their request has low **salience** or attracts little public attention.[92] When the average voter does not know or care about a group's request, legislators and bureaucrats do not have to worry about the political consequences of giving the group what it wants. The only question is whether the officials themselves favor the request or can be convinced that the group's desired change is worthwhile. In contrast, when salience is high, legislators' response to lobbying will hinge on their judgment of constituent opinion: Do voters favor what the group wants? After all, the average legislator has a strong interest in reelection and is unlikely to act against their constituents' wishes. As a result, lobbying may count for nothing in the face of public opposition or may be superfluous when the group's position already has public support.[93]

salience
The level of familiarity with an interest group's goals in the general population.

If you have ever heard of the National Turkey Federation, it's probably because of its participation in the annual presidential "pardoning" of a turkey before Thanksgiving. The federation's relative anonymity has been beneficial: its effort to increase the amount of turkey served in federally funded school lunches was aided by most Americans' lack of awareness of the proposal.

While the idea of interest group lobbying probably brings to mind titanic struggles on controversial issues, such as gun control, abortion rights, or judicial nominations, low-salience issues are surprisingly common. Many groups are indeed active for or against these high-profile issues and try to capture public attention as a way of pressuring people in government. However, the typical issue attracts much less activity. One analysis of lobbying disclosure forms found that 5 percent of issues attracted more than 50 percent of lobbying activity and 50 percent of issues attracted less than 3 percent.[94] Thus, the typical issue debated by members of Congress may involve relatively little interest group activity, and a group's request may generate little or no opposition from other groups. Remember the National Turkey Federation—the people who give the president a turkey every Thanksgiving? In the winter of 2014, the federation successfully lobbied federal bureaucrats to increase propane supplies to Midwest states facing record cold temperatures, including areas where the federation's members use propane to heat their barns. The policy change resulting from the federation's lobbying efforts attracted no publicity, which is precisely the point. When few people know or care about a policy change, interest groups are able to dominate the policy-making process. Sometimes the public *would* care about an issue, as with the $135 billion in tax credits in the CARES Act, but people don't find out about the issue until it is too late. Then when opponents of the move try to undo it, they fail, illustrating the principle that preventing change is easier than change.

Conflict Interest group influence is much less apparent on conflictual issues—those for which public opinion is split and groups are typically active on both sides of the issue. Consider a high-salience issue such as gun control. The ongoing debate over gun control attracts many well-funded interest groups and coalitions, which support different versions of gun control or want no change to current policy. There is no consensus among members of Congress, interest groups, or the American public about which policy changes are needed. Under these conditions, access doesn't count for very much; legislators have a keen sense of the political costs of accommodating a group's demands. As a result, stalemate or incremental policy change is the likely outcome, which is exactly what has happened over the last few years: no major gun control laws were passed from 1994 until 2022, but there have not been many significant changes in the other direction, either. Examples of incremental change include the response to the 2017 massacre in Las Vegas, in which 58 people were killed and 546 injured, when the NRA said it would favor additional regulation of "bump stocks," which allow 90 rounds to be fired in 10 seconds. President Trump banned bump stocks in 2018, but the Supreme Court struck down that ban in 2024.[95] The 2022 gun control law mentioned previously was the most significant in almost 30 years but fell short of what activists wanted. Thus, if policy change occurs at all, it is likely to reflect a complex process of bargaining and compromise, with no groups getting exactly what they want. In such cases, it is hard to say whether a particular group has won or lost or to attribute any aspect of the final bargain to a particular group's efforts.

The case of gun control illustrates that the fact that a group is large or well funded does not mean government officials will always comply with its requests. As mentioned earlier, many people worry that well-funded interest groups will use their financial resources to dominate the policy-making process, even if public opinion is against them, but this holds only under certain conditions. More often, the conditions that are ripe for well-funded interest groups to become involved in a policy debate typically ensure that there will be well-funded groups on all sides of a question. Under these conditions, no group is likely to get everything it wants and no group's lobbying efforts are likely to be decisive. Some groups may not get anything.

However, gun control is not a typical case. Most cases of interest group influence look a lot like the Turkey Federation's request for more propane: a group asks for something, there is relatively little opposition, and Congress or the bureaucracy responds with appropriate policy changes. The situation might have been very different if another group had lobbied on the other side against the Turkey Federation. If so, satisfying one group would have required displeasing at least one other group. Faced with this no-win situation, bureaucrats or legislators would be less likely to give the group what it wanted. At a minimum, they would have had to measure the Turkey Federation's arguments against those made by the other groups.

"Why Should I Care?"

Suppose you want to change some federal government policy—you want more funding for a program or an end to some regulation. Does having enough money guarantee a win? Generally speaking, the answer is no. What matters more is the salience of the policy or regulation you're trying to change and whether there is organized opposition on the other side. If your group is the only one lobbying, chances are good that you'll win. But if the issue is highly salient and you have opposition, your prospects aren't good, regardless of the size of your bankroll.

Unpacking the Conflict

Considering all that we've discussed in this chapter, let's apply what we know about how interest groups work to the example of the tax credits discussed at the beginning of this chapter. Is it fair to characterize all interest groups as self-interested organizations that undermine the public good? Are interest groups really too-powerful manipulators of the American policy process?

Many Americans think that interest groups are powerful manipulators of the American policy process and that they are able to get what they want regardless of the impact on everyone else. Sometimes it seems like "Heads they win. Tails we lose." While the chapter opener's example of income limit repeals in the CARES Act would support this view, there are countless counterexamples of laws that have been passed over the objections of corporations, including environmental protections, worker safety laws, consumer product and food safety regulations, and minimum wage laws.

So the truth is much more complex. Interest groups represent many different Americans, many of whom are unaware that lobbying occurs on their behalf. Moreover, for many groups the challenge is to get organized in the first place or to scrape together enough resources to start lobbying. These efforts don't always succeed because of the collective action problem. Interest groups are more likely to get what they want when their demands attract little public attention and no opposition from other groups. When a group asks for a large or controversial policy change, it stands little chance of success, even if the group has many members, a large lobbying budget, or an influential leader directing its operation.

The CARES Act also reflects this complexity. While lobbyists were able to sneak in the tax provisions that benefited their clients to the tune of $135 billion over 10 years, the bill also did a lot of good for millions of Americans who were in desperate need. Small businesses, hospitals, state and local governments, and researchers rushing to make a vaccine all received necessary aid. Most Americans received a $1,200 check just in time to help them make their next rent payment, and millions of people who lost their jobs benefited from the extension of unemployment compensation. So the special interests had their big chunk of the pie, but the American people received more of what they needed to try to get back on their feet.

In sum, while individual lobbying efforts often reflect the efforts of small groups to achieve favored policy outcomes at the expense of the majority, when we look across the entire range of interest group activities, a different picture emerges: in the main, interest groups reflect the conflictual nature of American politics and the resulting drive of individuals, groups, and corporations to shape American public policy in line with their policy goals. The average citizen benefits as well as loses from lobbying activities.

"What's Your Take?"

Are interest groups really too-powerful manipulators of the American policy process?

Or do groups play an important role in helping all citizens' voices be heard?

CHECK YOUR UNDERSTANDING

"Why Should I Care?"

Interest group activities represent a multitude of viewpoints and have helped produce many of the improvements in our society, like safe and efficient automobiles, strengthening our civil rights and civil liberties, greater access to health care and education, and the safety of our food and medicines. But the public is right to be skeptical of groups of people who are organized around their own interests. The Founders shared this concern.

In *Federalist 10*, James Madison articulated his concern about the selfish nature of people who would organize for their own interests and impose them on others. The Founders' solution was to prevent the absolute control of government by any single group by making factions compete with each other and compromise in order to achieve their outcomes. Political parties, similar to interest groups in that they seek to create and implement policies that benefit their members, complicated the plan for competition almost immediately by consolidating numerous groups of voters and their interests into two large factions that sought to win control of government through elections and the institutions that create election rules. However, even with this reality, the structures and institutions of American government and politics that divide power among branches, levels of government, and agencies create exceptionally large numbers of access points through which groups seek to influence public policies by leveraging their resources like membership, information, financial support, litigation, and public appeals.

As the nation and its systems of government have become more complex, so too have the organizations seeking to influence public policy. By creating access by hiring former public officials, reinforcing networks that make up so-called iron triangles, and effectively using financial vehicles to mobilize support for candidates and issues, like PACs, Super PACs, 527 groups, and others, interest groups are well prepared and highly motivated to achieve policy outcomes that benefit their members and supporters. Social media and deepened ideological divisions have spurred a rapid increase in the number of groups and their ability to organize effectively and with greater speed but without clear public consensus or reliably salient issues.

1. Interest group membership and the activities associated with group advocacy efforts are guaranteed by which clauses?

- **a** Free speech and free press
- **b** Assembly and petition
- **c** Free exercise and establishment
- **d** Due process and equal protection

2. In his 1996 State of the Union address, President Bill Clinton declared, "The era of big government is over." Yet the total of government spending and the number of people employed by the government have continued to grow. What role do interest groups play in preventing significant reforms to policies and government structures?

- **a** Groups create confusion about what it is that the public wants.
- **b** Competing interest groups create contradictory policies that enlarge the size of government.
- **c** Most members of Congress are elected having made promises that will enlarge the size of government.
- **d** Close networks among elected officials, bureaucrats, and interest groups are difficult to break.

3. The activities of an organization representing about 10 percent of a state's professional educators include lobbying, testifying in committee hearings, and providing data to legislators on relevant committees. These activities led to a raise in the base pay of all classroom teachers in the state. This scenario illustrates what issue that groups have in achieving their policy goals?

- **a** Collective action problem
- **b** Iron triangle
- **c** Astroturfing
- **d** Electioneering

4. When someone joins a professional association because of the liability insurance the organization provides for its members, that person was induced to join for which of the following benefits?

- **a** Solidary
- **b** Material
- **c** Purposive
- **d** Coercive

5. A political scientist who has spent their career studying the work of 527 groups, 501(c)(4) and 501(c)(3) organizations, and political action committees has most likely developed an expertise in which subject?

- **a** The effect of groups on legislative agendas
- **b** Impacts of the prevalence of the revolving door effect on group activism
- **c** The influences of money on campaign activities and outcomes
- **d** Legislative and judicial responses to public outreach campaigns

6. Consider this scenario: the American Legislative Exchange Council (ALEC), a conservative organization that boasts a membership made up of more than a quarter of state legislators from across all fifty states, hosts an annual convention bringing together ideologically similar legislators from across the nation. Activities include presenting legislators with so-called model bills that between 2010 and 2018 were presented in state legislatures as proposed bills over 600 times.[96] The activities in which ALEC is engaging in this real-world scenario can best be classified as which of the following?

- **a** Grassroots lobbying
- **b** Electioneering
- **c** Inside strategy
- **d** Initiative

7. One of the biggest factors improving the likelihood of an interest group's success is

- **a** limited public interest and engagement on an issue.
- **b** unclear public opinion on an issue.
- **c** outspoken public activism.
- **d** clear public consensus.

8. What is one reason it is difficult to measure interest group influence?

- **a** Most lobbying occurs behind closed doors, and it is difficult to know whom lobbyists are attempting to influence.
- **b** Many interest groups claim responsibility for policies and election outcomes regardless of whether their lobbying made a difference.
- **c** Interest groups largely support only Democratic candidates, so measuring the negative impact on Republican candidates is tricky.
- **d** Usually, interest groups lobby their enemies in government and push for their agenda despite any resistance they may meet.

Use INQUIZITIVE *to help you study and master this material.*

11

Congress

Whom does Congress represent?

"I do not believe we should be granting a path to citizenship to anybody here illegally."[1]

Senator Ted Cruz (R-TX)

"We can't allow these young people to continue to live in fear, to be at risk."[2]

Representative Joe Neguse (D-CO)

"Only Congress can ensure a permanent solution by granting a path to citizenship for Dreamers that will provide the certainty and stability that these young people need and deserve."[3]

President Joe Biden

For more than a decade, between 625,000 and 850,000 young people have been stuck in legal limbo. Frustrated with congressional deadlock on comprehensive immigration reform, in 2012 President Barack Obama started the Deferred Action for Childhood Arrivals (DACA) program that allowed residents who were brought as children to the United States without proper documentation to remain in the country if they had graduated from high school, were currently in school or had served in the military, and had not committed a felony. President Trump initially expressed strong support for the program, calling the 700,000 people enrolled "incredible kids." However, Trump believed that President Obama had overstepped his authority by creating the program through executive action, so Trump asked Congress to create a legislative solution.[4] In a meeting with congressional leaders early in 2018, President Trump said that he would sign whatever compromise on DACA Congress could agree to. Polls showed that between 73 and 87 percent of Americans favored allowing the Dreamers, as program participants are called, to stay and have a path to citizenship.[5]

One would think that enacting a policy that is supported by more than three-fourths of Americans, the president, and both parties in Congress would be a no-brainer. But shortly before the March 5 deadline, the wheels came off. Democrats initially tried to attach the DACA bill to a must-pass budget bill, but this effort failed after a three-day government shutdown. Democrats agreed to a two-year budget bill three weeks later, but without a resolution to the DACA issue. In a reversal of his earlier position that he would sign any DACA bill that Congress put forward, President Trump linked DACA

While both parties in Congress agree that undocumented children brought to the United States deserve a path to citizenship, since 2012 Congress has been deadlocked on a permanent solution. As a result, hundreds of thousands of young people are stuck in legal limbo. Most recent bills brought forward by the Biden administration met a fate similar to earlier bills—they died in the Senate.

CHAPTER GOALS

Explain how members of Congress represent their constituents and how elections hold members accountable (pp. 409–428)

Examine how parties, the committee system, and staffers enable Congress to function (pp. 428–439)

Trace the steps in the legislative process (pp. 440–448)

Describe how Congress ensures that the bureaucracy implements policies correctly (pp. 449–450) with $25 billion in funding for the border wall with Mexico. Critics on the right, such as Senator Ted Cruz, called it amnesty for illegal immigrants, while those on the left wanted a "clean bill" that addressed only the Dreamers and not funding for the wall. After Democrats took control of the House in 2019, they passed a bill that would have provided a path to citizenship for 2.3 million undocumented immigrants, including the Dreamers, but the bill was not taken up in the Senate.

After President Biden was elected, that same bill passed the House but died in the Senate again. Plan B was to try to attach the Dreamers' legislation to a reconciliation bill that could pass the Senate on a simple majority vote rather than the 60 votes needed to stop a filibuster. But the Senate parliamentarian ruled that it did not have significant budget implications and therefore could not be included in the reconciliation bill.[6] The Dreamers weren't even included in a bipartisan immigration reform early in 2024 that Senator James Lankford (R-OK) called "by far the most conservative border security bill in four decades." That bill was killed by a Senate filibuster when former President Trump said it wasn't strong enough.[7]

Given Congress's inability to solve the problem, DACA supporters turned to the courts, which stopped the deportation of the Dreamers. Then, in June 2020 the Supreme Court ruled in a 5–4 decision that President Trump had not provided legal justification for ending the program, and as a result he could not disassemble it. The ruling granted a reprieve to the close to 650,000 people in the program who had been brought to the United States as children. But then in 2021, a federal court ruled that President Biden's executive order reinstating DACA could not be implemented because the program was "created in violation of the law" and "illegally implemented." While no more applications are being accepted for the program, those currently protected by the program may keep their status while the case is being appealed.[8] Thus the legal limbo for more than 600,000 young people in this country.

On a basic level, this appears to be an example of congressional incompetence and dysfunction. How could a policy with such broad support and positive consequences for the economy not be passed? It is even more surprising because it is not unusual for congressional leaders to use a consensual policy such as DACA to help pass more controversial legislation such as building the wall with Mexico or generally strengthening border security. Some would argue that this type of deal-making is an essential feature of the legislative process.

The essential nature of conflict and compromise in the legislative process is not very well understood by the general public. Americans often view the type of wheeling and dealing that is necessary to reach compromises as improper and wonder why there is so much conflict. A typical sentiment is "Why does there have to be so much partisan bickering? Can't they just implement the best solutions to our problems?"

In this chapter, we argue that Congress members' behavior is driven by their desire to respond to constituent interests (and the closely related goal of reelection) and constrained by the institutional structures within which they operate (such as the committee system, parties, and leadership). At the same time, members try to be responsible for broader national interests, which are often at odds with their constituents' interests and, consequently, the goal of reelection.

This tension between being responsible and responsive is a source of conflict and requires members of Congress to make tough decisions, often involving political trade-offs and compromises. Should a House member vote for dairy price supports for local farmers even if it means higher milk prices for families around the nation? Should a senator from an oil-producing state vote to support alternative "clean energy," even if it may compete with the local carbon-based energy businesses? Should a member vote to close a military base, as requested by the Pentagon, even if it means the loss of thousands of jobs back home? These are difficult questions. On a complex issue, such as immigration, there is no obvious "responsible" solution and fair-minded people can disagree. These disagreements take on a partisan edge, as most Republicans favor building a stronger border with more limits on legal immigration while most Democrats do not, which obviously leads to conflict. Why is it so hard for Congress to compromise on issues that appear to be consensual, like protecting the Dreamers? How can members of Congress best serve the collective interests of the nation while also representing their local constituents?

Congress and the people

EXPLAIN HOW MEMBERS OF CONGRESS REPRESENT THEIR CONSTITUENTS AND HOW ELECTIONS HOLD MEMBERS ACCOUNTABLE

Congress and the Constitution

Congress was the "first branch" in the early decades of our nation's history. The Constitution specified for Congress a vast array of enumerated powers, including regulating commerce, coining money, raising and supporting armies, creating the courts, establishing post offices and roads, declaring war, and levying taxes (refer to Article I, Section 8, of the Constitution in the appendix). In contrast, the president was given few explicit powers and played a much less prominent role early in our history. Furthermore, much of Congress's authority came from its implicit powers, which were rooted in the elastic clause of Article I of the Constitution, which gives Congress the power "to make all Laws which shall be necessary and proper for carrying into Execution the foregoing Powers."

bicameralism
The system of having two chambers within one legislative body, like the House and Senate in the U.S. Congress.

As noted in Chapter 2, the compromises that gave rise to Congress's initial structure reflected an attempt to reconcile the competing interests of the day (large versus small states, northern versus southern interests, and proponents of strong national power versus state power). These compromises included establishing a system of **bicameralism**, that is, a bicameral (two-chambered) institution made up of a popularly elected House reflecting the relative populations of the states and a Senate chosen by state legislatures, representing each state equally; allowing each enslaved person to count as three-fifths of a person for purposes of apportionment for the House; and setting longer terms for senators (six years) than for House members (two years).

But these compromises also laid the foundation for the split loyalties that members of Congress have: they must respond to both their local constituencies and the nation's interests. Although the Founders hoped that Congress would pass legislation that emphasized the national good over local interests, they also recognized the importance of local constituencies. Thus, the relatively short two-year House term was intended to tie legislators to public sentiment.

The Founders viewed the House as more passionate than the Senate, or as the "hot coffee" that needed to be cooled in the "saucer" of the Senate. This perception probably did not include coming to blows over differences in policy as Congressmen Albert G. Brown and John A. Wilcox did in 1851 about whether Mississippi should secede from the Union.

At the same time, the *Federalist Papers* made it clear that the new government was by no means a direct democracy that would put all policy questions to the public. In *Federalist 57*, Madison asserted that "the aim of every political constitution is, or ought to be, first to obtain for rulers men who possess most wisdom to discern, and most virtue to pursue, the common good of the society." This common good may often conflict with local concerns, such that members are expected to both "refine and enlarge the debate" to encompass the common good *and* represent their local constituents.

In general, the Founders viewed the Senate as the more likely institution to enlarge the debate and speak for the national interests; it was intended to check the more responsive and passionate House. Because senators were indirectly elected and served longer terms than

House members, the Senate was more insulated from the people. A famous (although perhaps fictional) story of an argument between George Washington and Thomas Jefferson points out the differences between the House and Senate. Jefferson did not think the Senate was necessary, while Washington supported having two chambers. During the argument, Jefferson poured some coffee he was drinking into his saucer. Washington asked him why he had done so. "To cool it," replied Jefferson. "Even so," said Washington, "we pour legislation into the senatorial saucer to cool it." This idea of a more responsible Senate survived well into the twentieth century, even after the Seventeenth Amendment in 1913 allowed the direct, popular election of senators.

Today the Senate is still more insulated than the House. Because of the six-year terms of senators, only one-third of the 100 Senate seats are contested in each election, while all 435 House members are elected every two years. However, differences between the representational roles of the House and the Senate have become muted as senators seem to campaign for reelection 365 days a year, every year, just like House members.[9] This "**permanent campaign**" means that senators are now less insulated from electoral forces than they were in the past.

permanent campaign
The continual quest for reelection that is rooted in high-cost professional campaigns that are increasingly reliant on consultants and expensive media campaigns.

The relationship between the president and Congress has also evolved significantly. In the nineteenth century, Congress's roots in geographic constituencies made it well suited for the politics of the time. Although several great presidents left their mark on national politics early in U.S. history (George Washington and Abraham Lincoln, among others), Congress dominated much of the day-to-day politics, which revolved around issues such as the tariff (taxes on imported or exported goods), slavery, and internal improvements such as building roads and canals. Given the tendency to address these issues with patronage and the **pork barrel**—that is, jobs and policies targeted to benefit specific constituents—Congress was better suited for the daily task of governing than the president was.

pork barrel
Legislative appropriations that benefit specific constituents, created with the aim of helping local representatives win reelection.

Beginning around the turn of the twentieth century and accelerating with the New Deal of the 1930s (which established modern social welfare and regulatory policies), the scope of national policy expanded and politics became more centered in Washington. With this nationalization of politics and the increasing importance of national security issues from World War II through the War on Terror, the president has assumed a more central policy-making role. Nonetheless, the central tensions between representing local and national interests remain essential in understanding the legislative process and the relationship between members of Congress and their constituents.

Congress represents the people (or tries to)

Americans have a love–hate relationship with Congress; that is, we generally love our own member of Congress, but we hate Congress as a whole. Well, "hate" is a strong word, but as we show later in this section, individual members of Congress routinely have approval ratings 30 to 40 points higher than the institution's. One poll found that members of Congress landed third from the bottom in a ranking of 22 professions in terms of perceived honesty and ethical standards, narrowly ahead of car salespeople and lobbyists (nurses and military officers were at the top).[10] A more whimsical poll by Public Policy Polling asked respondents questions such as "What do you have a higher opinion of, Congress or root canals?" Root canals won handily, 56 percent to 32 percent. Congress was also less popular than head lice, traffic jams, and cockroaches but narrowly beat out telemarketers and had a comfortable margin over North Korea, the Kardashians, and meth labs.[11] Why is Congress so unpopular? How do members of Congress try to represent their constituents? And how do elections influence this important dynamic?

The American Republic will endure until the day Congress discovers that it can bribe the public with the public's money.

—Alexis de Tocqueville,
French diplomat and author

Types of Representation The relationships between constituents and their member of Congress can be characterized in two basic ways: as both descriptive and substantive. **Descriptive representation** occurs when members of Congress "look like" their constituents in demographic or socioeconomic terms. For example, are members Black, Latino, or White; male or female; Catholic, Protestant, or some other religion; middle-class or upper-class? Many people believe that this kind of representation is a distinct value in itself. Having positive role models for various demographic groups helps create greater trust in the system. Moreover, constituents benefit from being represented by someone who shares something as basic as their skin color.

descriptive representation
Representation in which a member of Congress shares the characteristics (such as gender, race, religion, or ethnicity) of their constituents.

Suppose you were an idiot. And suppose you were a member of Congress. But I repeat myself.

—Mark Twain, author

Descriptive representation is also related to the perceived responsiveness of a member of Congress. In general, constituents report higher levels of satisfaction with representatives who are of their same racial or ethnic background. Thus, descriptively represented constituents are more likely than those who are not to assume that their interests are being represented.[12] If you doubt that descriptive representation makes a difference, ask yourself whether it would be fair if all 435 House members and 100 senators were White male Protestants. Although the demographics of Congress are considerably more diverse than this, the legislature does not come close to "looking like us" on a nationwide scale (refer to the What Do the Facts Say? feature on p. 412). This is especially true in the Senate, where only eleven Black Americans and eleven Latinos have served in the history of the institution (in the 118th Congress, 2023–2025, there were four Black Americans and six Latinos in the Senate).[13] However, this is the most diverse Congress in U.S. history.

DID YOU KNOW?

was the median net worth of the 116th Congress (2019–2021). More than half of all members of Congress are millionaires.

Source: Center for Responsive Politics.

Although descriptive representation is important, it goes only so far. More important than a member's race, gender, or religion, many argue, is the *substance* of what that person does. The fact that a representative shares some characteristics with you does not necessarily mean that they will represent your interests. However, extensive research demonstrates a link between descriptive representation and how our elected leaders represent us: members of Congress from historically marginalized groups are more likely to pay attention to racial issues than White members are, and female members are more committed to women's issues than male members are. For example, political scientist Michele Swers finds that women senators are more active than male senators on women's issues, playing a key role on fair pay, abortion, women's rights, and representation on the Supreme Court.[14]

Substantive representation involves *how* the member serves constituents' interests. Two long-standing models of this kind of representation are (1) the **trustee**, who represents the interests of constituents from a distance, weighing numerous national, collective, local, and moral concerns; and (2) the **delegate**, who carries out the direct desires of the voters. In a sense, trustees are more concerned with being responsible and delegates are more interested in being responsive.

substantive representation
Representation in which a member of Congress serves constituents' interests and shares their policy concerns.

trustee
A member of Congress who represents constituents' interests while also taking into account national, collective, and moral concerns that sometimes cause the member to vote against the preference of a majority of constituents.

delegate
A member of Congress who loyally represents constituents' direct interests.

One of the most famous examples of a representative acting as a trustee was Marjorie Margolies-Mezvinsky (D-PA) in a crucial 1993 vote on President Clinton's budget, which included controversial tax increases and spending cuts to balance the budget. Hours before the vote, she told reporters that she would vote against the budget, in accordance with her constituents' wishes. But she had also promised Clinton she would support the bill if her vote was needed. As she cast the critical vote in the 218–216 cliff-hanger (in which she fulfilled her promise to the president), she did what she thought was in the best long-term interests of her constituents and the nation, even though it meant voting against their wishes, which led to her defeat in the next election. More recently, in 2008 bipartisan majorities in the House and Senate voted for the hugely unpopular Troubled Asset Relief Program (TARP or, as its critics called it, the Wall Street bailout) because President Bush and congressional leaders convinced them it was necessary to prevent a complete economic meltdown. In 2017, Senators John McCain (R-AZ), Susan Collins (R-ME), and Lisa Murkowski (R-AK) voted against the repeal of Obamacare, even

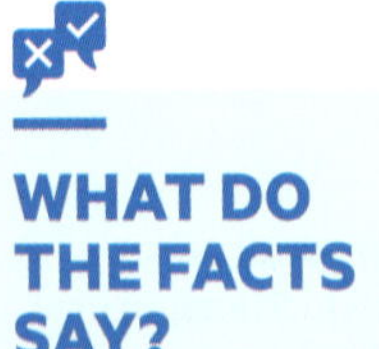

WHAT DO THE FACTS SAY?

Descriptive Representation in the 118th Congress

Compared with a generation ago, the number of women and members of historically marginalized groups in Congress has increased. But on these dimensions, how representative of the people is Congress? How close does Congress come to "looking like us"? What do the facts say?

Gender in Congress

Racial and ethnic composition of Congress

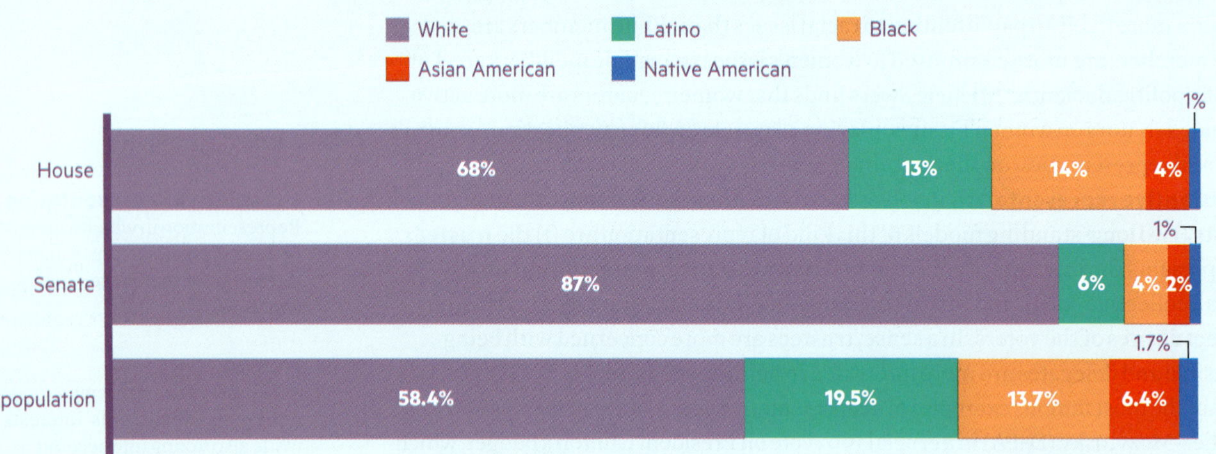

Sources: Congressional data from Jennifer Manning, "Membership of the 118th Congress: A Profile," Congressional Research Service, April 29, 2024, pp. 7–8, https://crsreports.congress.gov/product/pdf/R/R47470; population data from U.S. Census Bureau, "Quick Facts: United States," July 1, 2023, www.census.gov/quickfacts (both accessed 4/30/24).

Think about it

- **Which comes closer to "looking like us,"** the House or the Senate?
- **How could having more women or members of historically marginalized groups** in Congress affect legislation and policy decisions?
- **Latinos now make up the largest historically marginalized ethnic group** in the United States, yet they still lag behind Black Americans in terms of representation in the House. Why do you think this is?

Members of Congress spend a good deal of time in their districts, developing relationships with constituents, listening to their concerns, and raising funds for reelection. Here, Representative Byron Donalds (R-FL) speaks with constituents at a community open house at Fort Myers's Riverside Park. (Andrea Melendez—USA TODAY NETWORK.)

though Obamacare was very unpopular in their party. Then in 2024, House Speaker Mike Johnson (R-LA) worked with Democrats to get $66 billion in military aid for Ukraine, Israel, and Taiwan over the objections of his constituents and large majorities in his party.

In contrast, a delegate does not have to worry about angering voters, because a delegate simply does what voters want. Examples are so numerous it is pointless to single out one member for attention: when it comes to tax cuts, agricultural subsidies, increases in Medicare payments, or new highway projects, hundreds of representatives act as delegates for their districts' interests.

Truth be told, nearly all members act like trustees in some circumstances and like delegates in others. The third model of representation captures this reality: the **politico** is more likely to act as a delegate on issues that are highly salient to their constituency (such as immigration reform or farm subsidies) but as a trustee on less salient or very complex issues (such as some foreign policies). Therefore, the crucial component of representation is the nature of the constituency and how the member of Congress attempts to balance and represent constituents' conflicting needs and desires.

politico
A member of Congress who acts as a delegate on issues that constituents care about (such as immigration reform) and as a trustee on more complex or less salient issues (such as some foreign policy or regulatory matters).

The Role of the Constituency Most voters do not monitor their representatives' behavior closely. Can representation work if voters are not paying attention?

Members of Congress behave as if voters were paying attention, even when constituents are inattentive. Incumbents know that at election time challengers may raise issues that become salient after the public thinks about them, so they try to deter challengers by anticipating what the constituents would want *if* they were fully informed.[15] For example, the public hadn't thought much about voting by mail, but it became an issue in the 2020 elections when the COVID-19 pandemic forced many states to cut down on in-person voting. President Trump claimed that voting by mail was an effort by Democrats to steal the election, while many states argued that it was a way to protect voters from being exposed to the virus. Savvy incumbents would have tried to stake out a position consistent with what the voters would want *before* a strong challenger raised the issue in a campaign. Richard F. Fenno, one of the leading congressional scholars of the twentieth century, points out that some segments of the constituency are more attentive and more important for a member's reelection than

FIGURE 11.1

How Do Representatives See Their Constituents?

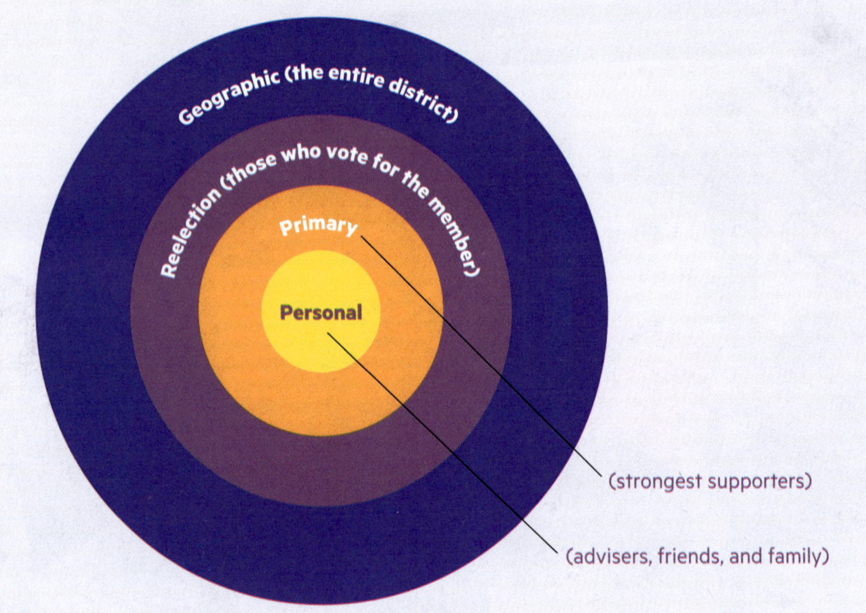

The concentric circles of a congressional constituency illustrate the various parts of a district that a member represents. Can you think of an issue on which House members would be more responsive to their reelection constituency than to their geographic constituency?

Source: Based on Richard F. Fenno, *Home Style: House Members in Their Districts* (Boston: Little, Brown, 1978).

others (refer to Figure 11.1).[16] For example, the "primary constituency" probably had a well-formed view about voting by mail early in the election season because they are more politically engaged, while many in the "geographic constituency" may have become aware of the issue only when it was raised by a challenger.

Another way to examine the representative–constituency relationship is to look at differences across districts. How do districts vary? First, they differ in size: Senate "districts" (that is, states) vary in terms of area and population. House districts all have about 770,000 people, but they vary tremendously in geographic size, from Alaska's 663,000 square miles to New York's 13th District with 10.25 square miles. Second, districts differ in terms of who lives there and what they want from government. Some districts are located in poor neighborhoods, where voters' concerns are economic development, crime control, antipoverty programs, and looser immigration regulations. Some are wealthy and urban, where citizens are more supportive of foreign aid and higher taxes to support social programs. Some are suburban, where funding for education and transportation is critical. Some are conservative and rural, where agricultural policies, gun rights, and support for tax cuts dominate. Some consider government a force for good, while others argue that government should get off people's backs. And some districts are a mixture of all these things.

Because districts are so multifaceted, the legislators they elect differ from one another as well. Regardless of the office, most voters want to elect someone whose policy positions are close to theirs. As a result, legislators tend to reflect the central tendencies of their districts. At one level, electing a legislature that "thinks like America" sounds good: if legislators act and think like their districts, then the legislature will contain a good mixture of the interests representing the country or state. But this often makes finding compromise difficult. We elect legislators to get things done, but they may be unable to agree on anything because their disagreements are too fundamental to bridge. Consider abortion rights. The country is sharply divided on this issue, as are the House, the Senate, and most state legislatures, which is no surprise: just as citizens disagree, so do their elected representatives. After the Supreme Court overturned *Roe v. Wade*, the House passed the Women's Health Protection Act of 2022 on a nearly

What Do People Want from Congress?

FIGURE 11.2

Members of Congress are often criticized for being out of touch with their constituents. Based on a *USA Today* poll, Americans seem to want their congressional members to vote in line with their constituents' views, to work across party lines, and to spend more time in the district rather than Washington, D.C. But what happens if these goals conflict? What if the member represents a very partisan district where the majority does not want them to work with the other party? Also, is there no room for trustees who follow their conscience and stick to their principles?

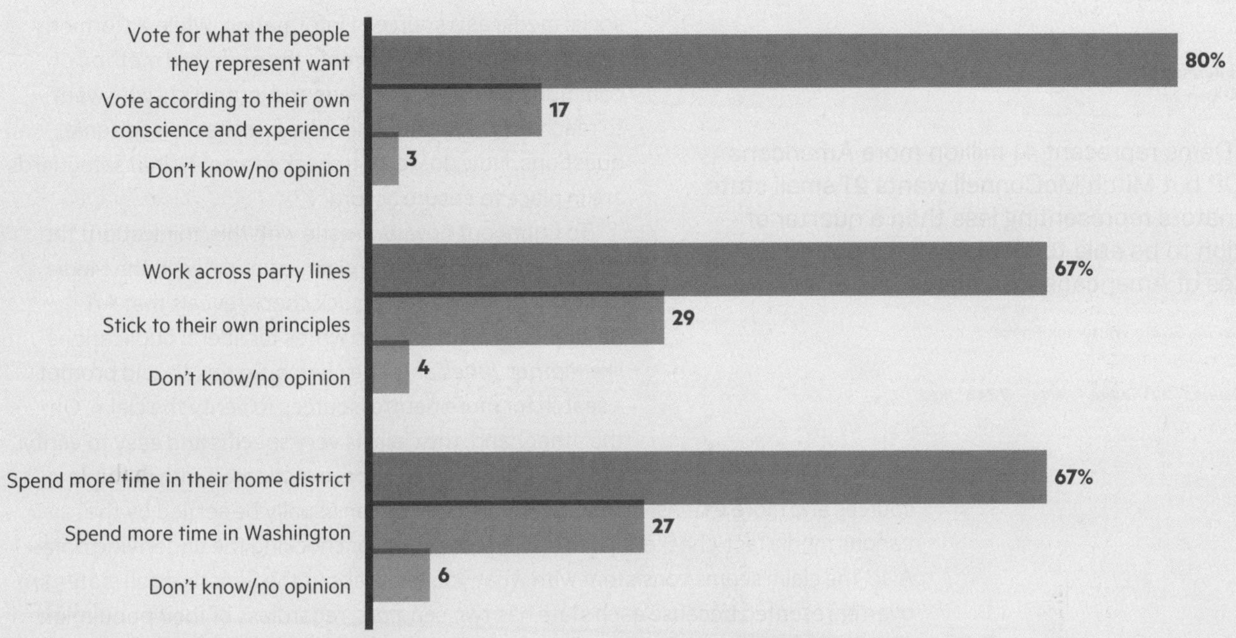

Source: Susan Page and Kendall Breitman, "Divided We Still Stand—and Getting Used to It," *USA Today*, March 23, 2014, www.usatoday.com/story/news/politics/2014/03/23/congress-divided-poll/6792585/ (accessed 3/15/22).

party-line vote that would preserve access to abortion at the federal level. However, it did not become law because the bill had previously been voted down in the Senate 49–51.

Despite the vast differences between congressional constituencies, voters want many of the same things: a healthy economy, a safe country (in terms of national defense and local crime), good schools, and effective health care. Figure 11.2 reports responses to a survey about how citizens feel legislators should do their jobs. The survey shows tensions between being a delegate and a trustee. Respondents want their representatives to "vote for what the people they represent want" and "spend more time at home," and they show little interest in having the representatives "spend more time in Washington." Thus, responsibilities for national interests may be more difficult for members of Congress to explain to their constituents. (Refer to What Do the Facts Say? on p. 416.)

Members of Congress want to keep their jobs

Members' relationships to their constituents also must be understood within the context of their desire to be reelected. Political scientist David R. Mayhew argues in *Congress: The Electoral Connection* that members of Congress are "single-minded seekers of reelection."[17] Members certainly hold multiple goals, including making good policy, but if they cannot maintain their seats, then they cannot attain other goals in office.

Is the Senate Unrepresentative?

Many have long questioned if the Senate can truly be considered a representative institution, given the fact that each state, regardless of its size, has just two senators. This issue came to the fore during the Biden administration as key bills like Build Back Better passed the House but died in the Senate. The tweet from journalist Ari Berman presents an opinion on the issue, as well as a question about the reliability of social media as a source of information. While X (formerly known as Twitter) has become the preferred method of communication for politicians and journalists who want to reach a broader audience, the form has raised some questions. How do we fact-check a tweet? What safeguards are in place to ensure accuracy?

Senate Dems represent 41 million more Americans than GOP but Mitch McConnell wants 21 small state GOP senators representing less than a quarter of population to be able to block laws supported by huge majorities of Americans with filibuster

9:22 AM · Jan 22, 2021 · Twitter for iPhone

3,593 Retweets **321** Quote Tweets **7,748** Likes

To figure out how to wrestle with this, think about the source and the size of the claim, as outlined in the Media Checklist in Chapter 1. A quick check reveals that Ari Berman is a journalist who writes for liberal publications like *Mother Jones* and *The Nation*. So this should prompt a search for more neutral sources to verify the claim. On the other hand, the claim is very specific and easy to verify. While big claims need to be investigated with multiple sources and more extensive reading, smaller claims can usually be settled by the various media fact-checkers, such as FactCheck.org, or checking the underlying data. Also, the claim seems consistent with what you know about the Senate: small states are overrepresented because each state has two senators, regardless of their population.

Yet 41 million seems like a big number given that Democrats and Republicans both had 50 senators at the time of the tweet.

A search reveals the underlying spreadsheet for the claim and the calculation used: each state with two senators of the same party is allocated all of those residents of the state in the running tally; if the state has one senator from each party, the population is split between the two parties. The numbers check out: the 50 Democratic senators represent 41,549,808 more people than the 50 Republican senators.[a]

What about the claim that the Republicans in the 21 smallest states with less than 25 percent of the population are able to stop a bill? Well, you recall that 41 senators can sustain a filibuster, but it doesn't seem likely that Republicans would control all of the smallest states. A quick check of the same spreadsheet shows that Democrats have 17 senators in the 21 smallest states and Republicans have 25. However, the 41 Republican senators representing only 21.3 percent of the voters *can* sustain a filibuster. So the claim about the 21 smallest states was *not* true, but the essential point about the unrepresentativeness of the Senate is.

One final point—liberal reformers often call for amending the Constitution to address this issue. However, the likelihood that this will happen is very slim, as altering representation in the Senate would require the approval of all 50 states: Article V says, "No state, without its Consent, shall be deprived of its equal Suffrage in the Senate." The smaller states, with the outsized say in the Senate, would not want to give up that power.

Think about it

- **When you read something** in a news story or in a tweet, do you have a favorite fact-checker you consult? This can be a very useful tool for being a good consumer of the news.
- **How do you decide** about the size of the claim that is being made? When would you need to consult more sources to get to the bottom of a story?

After assuming that reelection is central, Mayhew asks this question: "Members of Congress may be electorally motivated, but are they in a position to do anything about it?"[18] Although individual members of Congress cannot do much to alter national economic or political forces that may affect voters' choices, they can control their own activities in the House or Senate. The importance of the **electoral connection** in explaining the behavior of members of Congress seems especially clear for marginal incumbents who are constantly trying to shore up their electoral base. But for those from safe districts, why should they worry?

electoral connection
The idea that congressional behavior is centrally motivated by members' desire for reelection.

Incumbents Work toward Reelection While objectively it looks as though about 90 percent of House members (and a large proportion of senators) are absolutely safe (refer to Figure 11.3 on p. 419), incumbents realize that this security is not guaranteed. Even in elections with relatively low turnover overall, many incumbents are "running scared"; in every election, a few supposedly safe incumbents are unexpectedly defeated, and members tend to think that it could happen to them the next time around. Mayhew warns: "When we say 'Congressman Smith is unbeatable,' we do not mean that there is nothing he could do that would lose him his seat." This actually means: "Congressman Smith is unbeatable as long as he continues to do the things that he is doing."[19] Members recognize that becoming inattentive to their district, being on the wrong side of a key string of votes, or failing to bring home the district's share of federal benefits could cost them their seats. A potential challenger is always waiting in the wings.

Mayhew outlines three ways that members promote their chances for reelection: advertising, credit claiming, and position taking. Each approach shapes the way members relate to their constituents. "Advertising" in this context refers to appeals or appearances without issue content that get the member's name in front of the public in a favorable way. Advertising includes activities associated with "working the district," such as attending town meetings; appearing in a parade; going to a local Rotary Club lunch; or sending letters of congratulation for graduations, birthdays, or anniversaries. Members of Congress also spend a fair amount of time meeting with their constituents in Washington, D.C., including seeing school groups, tourists, and interest groups from their districts.

In "credit claiming," the member of Congress takes credit for something of value to voters—most commonly, pork-barrel policies targeted to benefit specific constituents or the district as a whole. The goods must be specific and small enough in scale that the member of Congress may believably claim credit. In other words, it is far less credible to take credit for a national drop in violent crime or an increase in SAT scores than for the renovations at a local veterans' hospital or a highway improvement grant. The other main source of credit claiming is **casework** for individual constituents who request help with tasks such as tracking down a lost Social Security check or expediting the processing of a passport. This activity, like advertising, has both district-based and Washington-based components.

casework
Assistance provided by members of Congress to their constituents in solving problems with the federal bureaucracy or addressing other specific concerns.

"Position taking" refers to any public statement—such as a roll call vote, a speech, an editorial, or a position paper—about a topic of interest to constituents or interest groups. This may be the toughest aspect of a member's job, because, on many issues, the member is likely to alienate a certain segment of the population no matter what position they take. Members try to appeal to specific audiences within their district. For example, while speaking to the Veterans of Foreign Wars, members might emphasize their support for a particular new weapons program, but in meetings with college students they might highlight their opposition to the National Security Agency's collection of millions of phone records.

Representatives' focus on reelection has some costs. We'll identify five common ones here: (1) There is a perception that Congress has granted itself too many special privileges aimed at securing reelection (such as funding for large staffs and the franking privilege, which allows congressmembers to send mail, including updates

Representative Lauren Underwood (D-IL, center) speaks to constituents at the Fox Valley Women's March in Geneva, Illinois. "Position taking," such as in this speech, is an important way representatives show they are responsive to their constituents' interests.

on their accomplishments in office, at no cost). (2) Evidence suggests that some voters question the value of pork-barrel spending, even when it is targeted to their district.[20] (3) Members' desire to please means that Congress has a difficult time refusing any group's demands, which may lead to passage of contradictory policies. (4) Given that most members are experts at getting reelected, they achieve a certain level of independence from the party leadership—that is, they do not depend on party leaders for their reelection. This fact contributes to the fragmentation of Congress and creates difficulties for congressional leaders as they attempt to shepherd policies through the legislative maze. (5) Time spent actively campaigning takes time away from the responsibilities of enacting laws and overseeing their implementation.

The desire to be reelected influences House members' and senators' behavior both in their districts and in Congress. Consider the early career of Senator Tammy Baldwin (D-WI), who served as the representative of Wisconsin's 2nd congressional district from 1999 to 2013. Initially elected in 1998, she was Wisconsin's first female representative and the first openly gay person ever elected to a freshman term in Congress.[21] In her first two elections, she won with the overwhelming support of liberal voters in Madison, but she lost the surrounding rural areas and suburbs, narrowly winning districtwide. Baldwin recognized that she needed to shore up support outside Madison, and she spent time over the next several years meeting with constituents in the rural and suburban parts of her district. She also explored issues important to these voters, such as the dairy price support program and the problem of chronic wasting disease in Wisconsin deer. Having built up her electoral base (and having benefited from favorable redistricting in 2002), she cruised to victories in her next two elections, winning nearly two-thirds of the vote. After winning reelection to the House four more times, she became the first lesbian elected to the Senate in 2012 and was reelected in 2018 and 2024.

The Incumbency Advantage Members' success at pleasing constituents produces large election rewards. As Figure 11.3 shows, very few members are defeated in their reelection races. One way that political scientists have documented the growth of the **incumbency advantage** is to examine the electoral margins in House elections. If a member is elected with less than 55 percent of the vote, they are said to hold a marginal seat. Since the late 1960s, the number of marginal districts has been declining. Having fewer marginal districts does not necessarily translate into fewer incumbent defeats, but in the past two decades incumbent reelection rates have been near record high levels, with 95–98 percent of House incumbents winning in many years.[22]

incumbency advantage
The relative infrequency with which members of Congress are defeated in their attempts for reelection.

House and Senate Reelection Rates, 1956–2024

FIGURE 11.3

The whole House is up for reelection every two years, so the line showing the reelection of House members in a given election year represents the percentage of the entire House. Since senators are up for reelection every six years, only one-third of the members are seeking reelection every two years. The line for the Senate represents the percentage of those who won who were up for reelection in that election year. Why do you think that House members have an easier time getting reelected than senators?

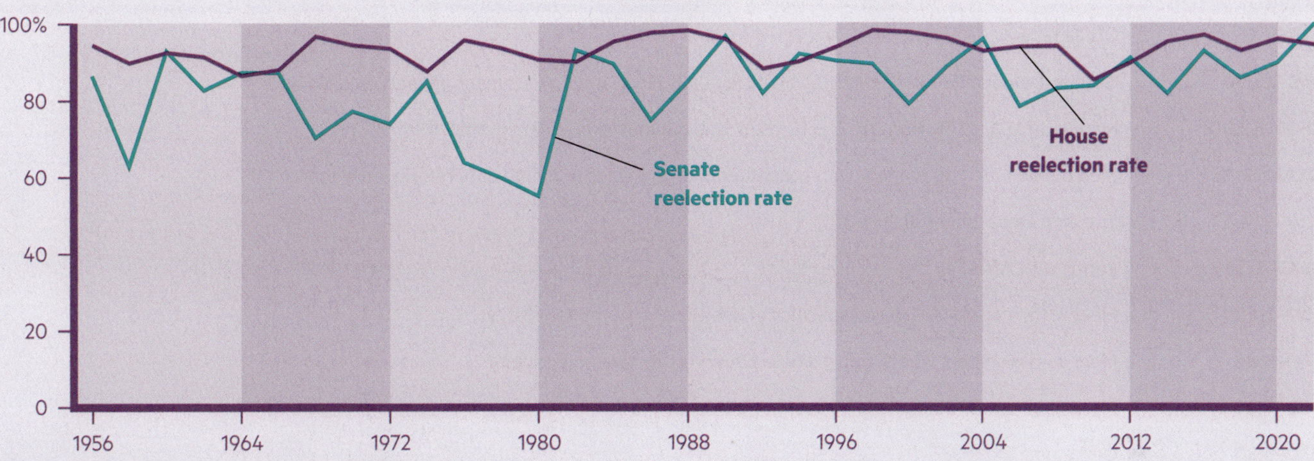

Sources: 1956–2012 percentages were compiled from Norman J. Ornstein, Thomas E. Mann, Michael J. Malbin, and Andrew Rugg, "Vital Statistics on Congress," www.brookings.edu/vitalstats, pp. 49–50 (accessed 7/26/20); 2014–2022 percentages were calculated from OpenSecrets.org (accessed 4/30/24).

In 2008, in an election that many called transformational, 94 percent of House incumbents were still reelected. Even in the "tsunami" election of 2010, in which Republicans made the largest gains in the House since 1948, picking up 63 seats, 86 percent of all incumbents were reelected. In the 2022 midterms, despite an electorate that was very concerned about inflation and unhappy with President Biden, 94.5 percent of House incumbents were reelected and no Senate incumbent lost. Why are incumbents so successful? Scholars have offered several reasons for this increase in incumbency advantage.

In the District: Home Style One explanation for the increasing incumbency advantage is rooted in the diversity of congressional districts and states. Members typically respond to the diversity in their districts by developing an appropriate home style: a way of relating to the district.[23] A home style shapes the way members allocate resources, the way incumbents present themselves to their district, and the way they explain their policy positions.

Given the variation among districts, members' home styles vary as well. In some rural districts it is important for representatives to have local roots and voters expect extensive contact with members. Urban districts expect a different kind of style. They have a more mobile population, so it is not crucial to be homegrown. Voters expect less direct contact and place more emphasis on how members explain their policy positions. Incumbency advantage may be explained in part by the skill with which members have cultivated their individual home styles in the last two decades. Members are spending more time at home and less time in Washington than was true a generation ago. This familiarity with the voters has helped them remain in office.

Table 11.1 on page 420 shows how one member, Senator Tammy Baldwin, spent her time in Washington and in her district as a House member. In general, a legislator's workday in the Capitol is split among committee meetings, briefings, staff meetings,

TABLE 11.1

Typical Workdays for a Congressional Representative

Members of Congress are generally busy from morning until late at night, both in Washington, D.C., and in their districts, attending meetings and events. This is the actual schedule for Tammy Baldwin when she represented Wisconsin's 2nd congressional district in the House.

In Washington, D.C. (votes scheduled throughout the day)	
9:15–9:45	Office time
9:45–10:00	Caucus, Democratic members, Subcommittee on Energy and Environment on markup legislation
10:00–12:00	Markup of H.R. 3276, H.R. 3258, H.R. 2868, Subcommittee on Energy and Environment
11:30–11:45	Step outside markup to meet with constituents on specifics of health care reform legislation
12:00–12:15	Travel to Department of Justice
12:15–1:15	Lunch with Attorney General Eric Holder
1:30–1:45	Meet with health care CEO on specifics of health care reform legislation
2:00–3:00	Meet with members who support single-payer health care amendment
3:00–4:30	Markup of H.R. 3792, Subcommittee on Health
4:30–5:30	Office time
5:30–6:00	Caucus, Democratic members, Energy and Commerce Committee on financial services bill
6:00–6:30	Meet with legislative staff
6:30–7:00	Meet with chief of staff
7:00–7:50	Office time
8:00–10:00	Dinner with chief of staff and political adviser
In the District	
7:00 ET–8:00 CT	Fly from Washington, D.C., to Madison, WI
8:15–10:30	Free time at home
10:30–10:40	Phone interview with area radio station on constituent survey, health care reform, and upcoming listening session
12:15–12:25	Travel to office
12:25–1:00	Office time, edit/sign correspondence
1:00–1:20	Travel to Madison West High School
1:30–1:55	Remarks at school plaza dedication ceremony
2:00–2:30	Travel to Stoughton, WI
2:45–5:00	Listening session (originally scheduled for one hour but continued until all present could speak)
5:00–5:40	Travel home
5:15–5:20	Phone interview with University of Wisconsin student radio station
6:15–6:45	Travel to Middleton, WI
7:00–8:00	Attend and give brief remarks at NAACP annual banquet
8:05–8:25	Travel home

Note: The authors would like to thank then-representative Tammy Baldwin and her press secretary, Jerilyn Goodman, for sharing this information. Ms. Goodman emphasized that there really isn't a "typical day" for a member but said that these two days illustrate the workload. Baldwin was reelected to the U.S. Senate in 2024 (having won her first Senate term in 2012).

meetings with constituents, and various dinners and fund-raisers with interest groups and other organizations, punctuated by dashes to the floor of the House or Senate to vote. Days in the district are spent meeting with constituents to explain what is happening in Washington and to listen to voters' concerns.

DID YOU KNOW?

On average, House incumbents raised

$2,823,053

for their campaigns in 2024. The average Senate incumbent raised $21,801,522. This is compared with $1,309,984 and $8,599,980 for the average House and Senate challengers (including candidates for open seats).

Source: OpenSecrets.org.

Campaign Fund-Raising Raising money is also key to staying in office. Incumbents need money to pay for campaign staff, travel, and advertising. It takes at least $1 million to make a credible challenge to an incumbent in most districts, and in many areas with expensive media markets the minimum price tag is $2 million or more. Few challengers can raise that much money. The gap between incumbent and challenger spending has grown dramatically in the past decade, and incumbents now spend about two to three times as much, on average, as challengers.[24] However, Senate challengers outspent incumbents in 2020, but only five of them won. In 2024, the incumbent advantage returned to the norm. (For more on campaign finance, refer to Chapters 9 and 10.)

Money also functions as a deterrent to potential challengers. A sizable reelection fund signals that an incumbent knows how to raise money and will run a strong campaign. The aim is to convince would-be challengers that they have only a slim chance of beating the incumbent—and to convince contributors and party organizations that there's no point in trying to find or support a challenger. This last point is crucial in explaining incumbency advantage, because it is nearly impossible for a weak challenger to beat an incumbent. Consider that only 10–15 percent of challengers in a typical election year have any previous elective experience; when such a high proportion of challengers are amateurs, it is not surprising that so many incumbents win.

Constituency Service Another thing incumbents do to get reelected is "work their districts," taking every opportunity to meet with constituents, listen to their concerns, and perform casework (helping constituents interact with government programs or agencies). Most legislators travel around their districts or states with several staffers whose job is to follow up with people who meet the incumbent, write down their contact information, and note what the incumbent has promised to do for them. High levels of constituency service may help explain why some incumbents have become electorally secure.

Members of Congress love doing constituency service because it is an easy way to make voters happy. If a member can help a constituent solve a problem, that person will be more likely to support the member in the future.[25] Many voters might give the incumbent some credit simply for being willing to listen. Therefore, most members devote a significant portion of their staff to constituency service, publish newsletters that tout their good deeds on behalf of constituents, and solicit citizens' requests for help through their newsletters and websites. Most House members have a "How can I help?" type of link on their home page that connects to information on government agencies, grants, internships, service academies, and visiting Washington, D.C.

Most House members work their districts to an extreme; they are said to be in the "Tuesday to Thursday Club," meaning they are in Washington only during the middle of the week and spend the rest of their time at home in their districts. These members go to diners and coffee shops on Saturday mornings to chat, spend the day at public events in their "Meet Your Representative" RV, then hit the bowling alleys at night to meet a few more people. One member has even joked that his wife has given up sending him out for groceries because he spends three hours talking with people while getting a loaf of bread.

This combination of factors gives incumbents substantial advantages over candidates who might run against them. By virtue of their position, they can help constituents who have problems with an agency or a program. They attract media attention because of their actions in office; small local newspapers will even reprint members' press releases verbatim. Members can use the money and other resources associated with their position for casework and contact with voters (trips home to their district and the salaries of their staffers who do constituency service are taxpayer funded). And they use their official position as a platform for raising campaign cash. A contributor who donates as a way to gain access to the policy-making process will be inclined to give to someone already in office. Finally, most incumbents represent states or districts whose partisan balance (the number of likely supporters of their party versus the number likely to prefer the other party) is skewed in their favor—if it weren't, they probably wouldn't have won the seat in the first place.

National Forces in Congressional Elections There is also another consequence of the electoral connection. Because congressional politics tends to be local, voters generally are not strongly influenced by the president or the national parties. Because most incumbents can insulate themselves from national forces, it is more difficult to hold members of Congress accountable. For example, in the 2022 elections 68 percent of voters believed the nation was "on the wrong track." Yet 94.5 percent of House incumbents won reelection.

Many House and Senate candidates distance themselves from the national party. For example, in 2022 when President Biden's approval numbers were not strong, the Democratic nominee for U.S. Senate in Ohio, Representative Tim Ryan, declined to campaign with Biden. Several Republican candidates also tried to distance themselves from Donald Trump's claims about the 2020 election.[26] Some elections, like 2018, are examples of nationalized "wave" elections in which national issues overwhelmed incumbents' attempts to insulate themselves. As Democrats regained control of the House, 29 Republican incumbents were defeated but no Democratic incumbents were. In the 2010 midterms, the same thing happened to moderate Democrats, who were ousted by voters who believed the government had gone too far in responding to the recession and providing access to health care. These national forces led the Democrats to lose 63 House seats (and 6 Senate seats), with the result that the Republicans regained control of the House. National forces were more muted in 2022, as Democrats did better than expected, losing fewer than 10 seats in the House and hanging on to control of the Senate.

National forces in congressional elections also may be evident in presidential years. In 2008, Republicans faced a backlash against Bush, and avoided being seen with him. Democrats highlighted their opponents' earlier support for him, and ultimately gained unified control of government. The 2016 presidential election featured two nominees, Hillary Clinton and Donald Trump, who had the highest negative ratings of any pair of major-party candidates. Republican congressional candidates were especially likely to distance themselves from their party's nominee. President Trump won a tight race, but Democrats picked up two seats in the Senate and six in the House (but Republicans retained majorities in both chambers). In 2020, Joe Biden defeated Trump, but it was a status quo election, rather than the blue wave Democrats were hoping for. Democrats picked up three Senate seats, giving them majority control with the 50–50 split (Vice President Harris breaks ties votes) and Republicans gained 12 House seats.

In 2024, Democrats were likely to lose control of the Senate (which they held 51–49), given that they were defending seven of the eight most competitive seats. When Donald Trump surged to victory at the top of the ticket, he helped Republican challengers beat incumbents in West Virginia, Ohio, Montana, and Pennsylvania, giving them a 53–47 majority. Democrats were hoping to flip control of the House, but as this text goes to press, it looks like the most likely outcome will be no net change, with Republicans holding their same 221–214 margin.

Overall, the localized nature of congressional elections and the incumbency advantage promote congressional stability in the face of presidential change. This dynamic has profound implications for governance because it increases the likelihood that different parties will control the presidency and Congress. Divided government complicates accountability. Because the president and Congress have become adept at blaming each other when things go wrong, voters do not always know whom to vote out of office when they're unhappy with the status quo.

Redistricting connects representation and elections

The shape and makeup of congressional districts are critical to understanding representation in Congress and the electoral connection. District boundaries determine who is eligible to vote in any given congressional race, and these boundaries are re-drawn every 10 years, after each national census. **Redistricting** is usually the task of state legislatures. Its official purpose is to ensure that districts are roughly equal in population, which in turn ensures that every vote counts equally in determining the composition of the legislature. This decennial process placed additional significance on state elections in 2020, as control over redistricting was at stake. Republicans picked up control of several state legislative chambers and three governorships in the 2020 and 2021 elections and had unified control in 23 states. Democrats controlled 14 state governments, and 13 states had split control heading into the redistricting process.

redistricting
Re-drawing the geographic boundaries of legislative districts. This happens every 10 years to ensure that districts remain roughly equal in population.

District populations vary over time as people move from state to state or from one part of a state to another. At the national level, states gain or lose legislative seats after each census through **apportionment**, which is the process of dividing the fixed number of House seats (435) among the states based on increases and decreases in state populations. After the 2020 census, Texas picked up two seats, five states gained one seat, and seven states lost a single seat. Overall, states that Trump carried in 2020 picked up three seats, and states that Biden carried lost three seats.[27]

apportionment
The process of assigning the 435 seats in the House to the states based on increases or decreases in state population.

House reelection rates have been upwards of 90 percent for decades, but incumbents still campaign vigorously. Congressman Kurt Schrader (D-OR), a seven-term incumbent, lost his 2022 primary bid to progressive challenger Jamie McLeod-Skinner after district lines were redrawn following the 2020 Census.

The one legislature in America that is not redistricted is the U.S. Senate, which has two legislators elected per state. Voters in small states thus have proportionally more influence than those in large states when it comes to the Senate.

In theory, redistricting proceeds from a set of principles that define what districts should look like. One criterion is that districts should be roughly equal in population based on the principles of "one-person, one-vote" established by the Supreme Court with *Baker v. Carr* in the 1960s.[28] They should also reflect "communities of interest," grouping like-minded voters into the same district. There are also technical criteria, including compactness (districts should not have extremely bizarre shapes) and contiguity (one part of a district cannot be completely separated from the rest of the district). Mapmakers also try to respect traditional natural boundaries, avoid splitting municipalities, preserve existing districts, and avoid diluting the voting power of historically marginalized communities.

Partisan Redistricting Although the preceding principles are important, they are not the driving force in the redistricting process. Suppose a Democrat holds a House seat from an urban district populated mainly by citizens with strong Democratic Party ties. After a census, the Republican-dominated state legislature develops a new plan that extends the representative's district into the suburbs, claiming that the change counteracts population declines within the city by adding suburban voters. However, these suburban voters will likely be Republicans, increasing the chance that the Democrat will face strong opposition in future elections and lose their seat. Such changes have an important impact on voters as well. Voters who are "shifted" to a new district by a change in boundaries may be unable to vote for the incumbent they have supported for years and may instead get a representative who doesn't share their views.

In congressional redistricting, a reduction in the number of seats allocated to a state can lead to districting plans that put two incumbents in the same district, forcing them to run against each other. Incumbents from one party use these opportunities to defeat incumbents from the other party. Both parties use this technique and other tools of creative cartography to gain partisan advantage.

These attempts to use the redistricting process for political advantage are called **gerrymandering**. The term is named after Elbridge Gerry, a Massachusetts House member and governor, vice president under James Madison, and author of the original partisan redistricting plan in 1812 (including a district with a thin, winding shape resembling a salamander). While partisan motivations have produced some funny-looking districts (refer to Nuts & Bolts 11.1 for examples of a partisan gerrymander and redistricting strategies), the courts have allowed the practice to continue until recently. More than 30 years ago, the Supreme Court ruled that partisan gerrymandering *may* be unconstitutional, but over the next three decades the Court struggled to find a standard that allowed it to distinguish between partisan bias so extreme that it violated the Constitution and normal partisan politics.[29]

gerrymandering
Attempting to use the process of re-drawing district boundaries to benefit a political party, protect incumbents, or change the proportion of minority voters in a district.

Then, from 2016 through 2018, a flood of litigation in federal and state courts showed judges' increasing willingness to rule that parties had gone too far in their redistricting plans. Increasingly sophisticated mapping programs and access to detailed political data allowed parties to slice and dice districts with increasing precision, yielding partisan maps that were no longer acceptable to the courts. In Wisconsin, North Carolina, Maryland, and Pennsylvania, federal and state courts struck down state legislative and congressional maps that they ruled to be unfairly partisan (refer to the Take a Stand feature on p. 429 for more on the debate on this topic). However, in June 2019 the Supreme Court took up cases from North Carolina and Maryland and concluded that "partisan gerrymandering claims

Types of Gerrymanders

NUTS & BOLTS 11.1

We have learned that the redistricting process is a powerful tool politicians can use to help their party, or individual members, win and maintain seats in Congress. Let's look at two key types of gerrymandering.

Partisan gerrymanders
Elected officials from one party draw district lines that benefit candidates from their party and hurt candidates from other parties. This usually occurs when one party has majorities in both houses of the state legislature and occupies the governorship and can therefore enact redistricting legislation without input from the minority party.

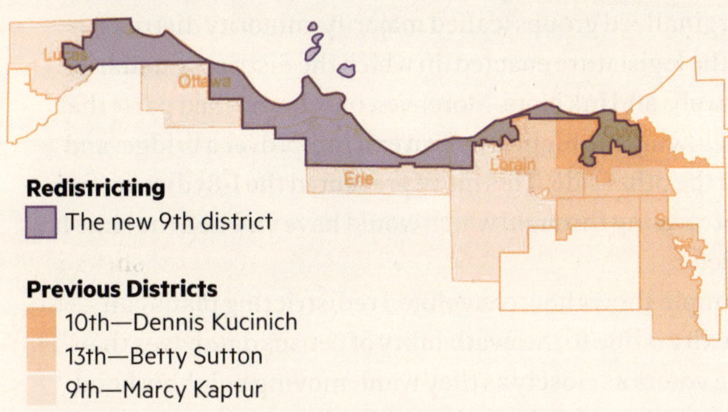

After the 2010 census, Ohio lost two seats in Congress (refer to our discussion of apportionment on p. 423). Republicans controlled the redistricting process and wanted the loss of seats to come from the Democrats. So the Republicans drew a new 9th congressional district that cut across the districts of three existing Democratic members of Congress. Obviously only one could win the Democratic primary—that happened to be Marcy Kaptur. Democrats Kucinich and Sutton had to leave Congress.

Racial gerrymanders
Redistricting is used to help or hurt the chances of minority legislative candidates. The Voting Rights Act (VRA) of 1965 mandated that districting plans for many parts of the South be approved by the U.S. Department of Justice or a Washington, D.C., district court. Subsequent interpretations of the 1982 VRA amendments and Supreme Court decisions led to the creation of districts in which racial minorities are in the majority. The aim of these majority-minority districts was to raise the percentage of Black and Latino elected officials.

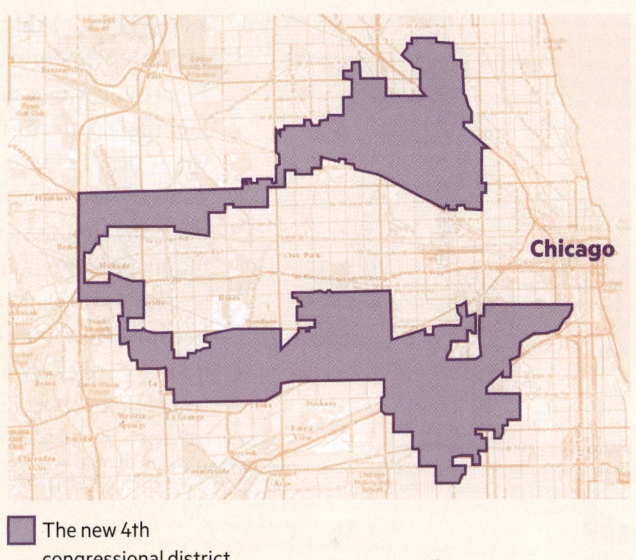

The new 4th congressional district

Illinois's 4th congressional district is a clear example of racial gerrymandering. The district has a very odd shape, but it incorporates two heavily Latino areas. (The northern part has a high Puerto Rican population and the southern part is largely Mexican; both areas are heavily Democratic.) This district was a stronghold of Democrat Luis Gutiérrez, who is of Puerto Rican descent, and is currently held by Chuy García, who is of Mexican descent. It is seen as a safe district for Democrats.

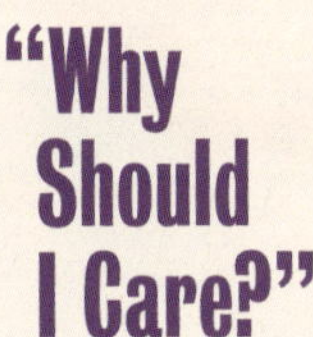

Many people question whether or not their vote "counts." While all votes count, actions like gerrymandering are attempts to manipulate the results to ensure particular geographic areas are overwhelmingly Republican or Democratic, thus diluting the influence of minority-party voters in those regions.

present political questions beyond the reach of the federal courts" because they lacked a "limited and precise standard" for evaluating the extent of partisan bias. While recognizing that partisan gerrymandering may "reasonably seem unjust" and is "incompatible with democratic principles," the Court left it up to states to resolve this problem. Justice Kagan issued a scathing dissent, writing, "For the first time ever, this Court refuses to remedy a constitutional violation because it thinks the task beyond judicial capabilities. . . . Part of the Court's role in that system is to defend its foundations. None is more important than free and fair elections." While the effects of the 2021–2022 redistricting won't be known for a few election cycles, one analysis calculated that there are 10 more "strong Trump" districts, one more "strong Biden" district, and 11 fewer competitive districts in 2022 when compared with 2020.[30]

Racial Redistricting Redistricting may yield boundaries that look highly unusual. During the 1992 redistricting process in North Carolina, the Justice Department told state legislators that they needed to create two districts with majority populations of voters of historically marginalized groups (called majority-minority districts). Figure 11.4 shows the plan the legislature enacted, in which the district boundaries look like a pattern of spiderwebs and ink blots. Moreover, one district had parts that were only as wide as I-85, following the highway off an exit ramp, over a bridge, and down the entrance ramp on the other side. This move prevented the I-85 district from bisecting the district it was traveling through, which would have violated the state law requiring contiguous districts.

The North Carolina example shows how convoluted redistricting plans can become. Part of the complexity is due to the availability of census databases that allow line drawers to divide voters as closely as they want, moving neighborhood by neighborhood, even house by house. Why bother with this level of detail?

FIGURE 11.4

North Carolina Redistricting, 1992

This set of House districts was the subject of the landmark Supreme Court ruling *Shaw v. Reno* (1993), in which the Court said that "appearances matter" when drawing district lines. Do you agree? Should other factors such as race, party, and competitiveness play a greater role than district shape?

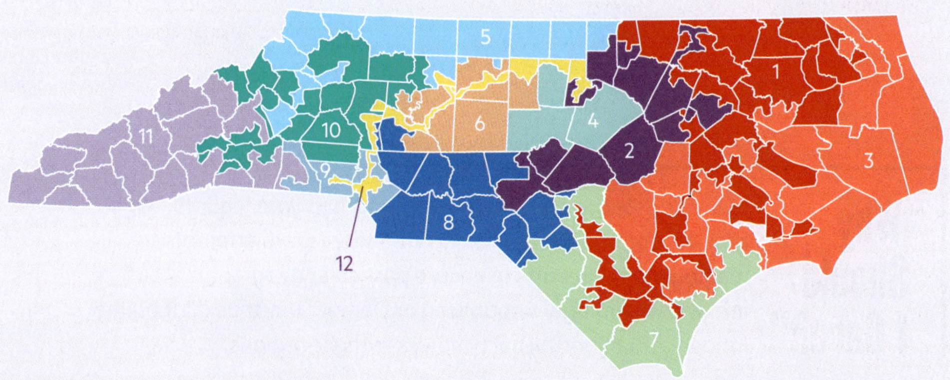

Source: North Carolina General Assembly, 1992 Congressional Base Plan No. 10, www.ncleg.gov/Files/GIS/ReferenceDocs/2011/NC%20Congressional%20Districts%20-%20Historical%20Plans%20-%201941-1992.pdf (accessed 3/15/22).

Because redistricting influences who gets elected. It is active politicking in its most fundamental form. The North Carolina plan was ultimately declared unconstitutional by the U.S. Supreme Court in *Shaw v. Reno*—a ruling that opened the door for dozens of lawsuits about racial redistricting. (Refer to the discussion in Chapter 5 of the Voting Rights Act of 1965 and more recent Supreme Court rulings on racial redistricting, especially the 2013 case in which the Court struck down the part of the law that identified states that needed to have their redistricting plans preapproved by the Justice Department.[31]) The current legal standard is that race cannot be the *predominant* factor in drawing congressional district lines, but it can be one of the factors. However, in a surprise decision in 2023, Justices Roberts and Kavanaugh ruled with the three liberals on the Court that Section 2 of the Voting Rights Act required the creation of a second Black majority district in Alabama.[32] But then a three-judge panel ruled in 2024 that the new district that was drawn to comply with that ruling violated the "equal protection" clause of the Fourteenth Amendment for the white voters in the district.[33]

The obvious political implications of redistricting often lead to demands that district plans be prepared or approved by nonpartisan committees or by a state agency (as in Iowa) who are theoretically immune from political pressure. Such a process, as used in 18 states, often produces more competitive districts. Political support for a nonpartisan process has surged in recent years, with voters in four states approving redistricting commissions in 2018 and three more in 2020.[34]

The responsibility–responsiveness dilemma

As mentioned earlier, polls show that despite generally approving of their own member of Congress, people hold Congress itself in very low esteem. This is rooted in the conflicts that arise from Congress's dual roles: responsibility for national policy making and responsiveness to local constituencies.[35] This duality may make members of Congress appear to be simultaneously great leaders who debate important issues and locally oriented representatives who work hard to deliver benefits for the district (which may not be good for the country as a whole). Part of the national frustration with Congress arises because we want our representatives to be responsible *and* responsive; we want them to be great national leaders *and* to take care of our local and, at times, personal concerns.

Difficult choices have to be made between being responsive and being responsible. Rather than understanding these issues as inherent in the legislative process, we often accuse members of **gridlock** and partisan bickering when our conflicting demands are not met. For example, public-opinion polls routinely show that the public wants lower taxes; more spending on education, the environment, and health care; and balanced budgets. But those three things cannot happen simultaneously. We often expect the impossible from Congress and then are frustrated when it doesn't happen.

gridlock
An inability to enact legislation because of partisan conflict within Congress or between Congress and the president.

The responsibility–responsiveness dilemma brings us back to the puzzle we posed at the beginning of this section: Why is there a persistent 30–40 percent gap between approval ratings for individual members and for the institution? As Richard Fenno put it, "If Congress is the 'broken branch,' how come we love our congressman so much?"[36] The answer may simply be that members of Congress tend to respond more to their constituents' demands than to take on the responsibility of solving national problems. And when Congress becomes embroiled in debates about constituencies' conflicting demands, the institution may appear ineffectual. But as long as members keep the "folks back home" happy, their individual popularity will remain high.

"Why Should I Care?"

How would you like your member of Congress to represent you? Should members represent the interests of just their district or the broader nation? Should they be responsive or responsible? Constituents have an interest in holding their members accountable, yet most congressional elections are not very competitive. So if you don't like how your member is representing you, what can you do about it? Understanding the nature of representation and the incumbency advantage can help answer these important questions.

EXAMINE HOW PARTIES, THE COMMITTEE SYSTEM, AND STAFFERS ENABLE CONGRESS TO FUNCTION

The structure of Congress

As we have seen, the goal of getting reelected greatly influences the behavior of members of Congress. The reelection goal also has a strong influence on the way that Congress is structured, both formally (staff, the committee system, parties, and leadership roles) and informally (norms). Despite the importance of the electoral connection, the goal of being reelected cannot explain everything about members' behavior and the congressional structure. This section examines some other explanations that underlie the informal and formal structures of Congress: the policy motivations of members, the partisan basis for congressional institutions, and the importance of the committee system.

By 2021, politics had become so polarized in Congress that the massive $1 trillion infrastructure bill discussed in the previous chapter passed the House on a largely party-line vote (the Senate was more bipartisan in its support, with a 69–30 margin). However, many Republicans who voted against the bill still claimed credit for the projects as they started construction.

Informal structures

Various norms provide an informal structure for the way Congress works. *Universalism* is the norm that when benefits are divided up, they should be awarded to as many districts and states as possible. Thus, when it comes to handing out federal highway dollars or expenditures for the Pentagon's weapons programs, the benefits are broadly distributed across the entire country, which means that votes in support of these bills tend to be very lopsided (as some areas of the country need the federal funds more urgently than others). For example, the $86.2 billion 2020 transportation bill contained some spending in every part of the country and passed by strong bipartisan votes, even though it was introduced in the middle of the contentious impeachment process.[37]

Another norm, **logrolling**, reinforces universalism with the idea that "if you scratch my back, I'll scratch yours." This norm leads members of Congress to support bills that they otherwise might not vote for in exchange for other members' votes on bills that are very important to them. For example, House members from a dairy state might vote for tobacco price supports even if their state has no tobacco farmers, and in return they would expect a member from the tobacco state to vote for the dairy price support bill. This norm can produce wasteful pork-barrel spending. For example, in the 2011 budget a $1.1 trillion omnibus appropriations bill contained more than 6,488 **earmarks** worth $8.3 billion, so nearly everyone gained something by passing it. The $1.4 trillion 2020 omnibus appropriations bill did not include any traditional earmarks (or "pork," as they

TAKE A STAND

Partisan Redistricting

Partisan redistricting is the re-drawing of legislative district lines in a way that gives one party an advantage. As we have noted, until recently the courts allowed the practice as a normal part of politics: of course, the majority party that controls the redistricting process has tried to stack the deck in its favor. When combined with the reluctance of the Supreme Court to address "political questions"—those that are better left to the elected branches—there was a powerful incentive to stay out of the "political thicket."[78] But as mapping software and "big data" political tools became readily available, the extent of partisan bias in redistricting became more pronounced. In Pennsylvania, a Republican gerrymander gave the party 13 of the state's 18 U.S. House seats, despite the Republicans' failure to win a majority of the statewide vote in the House races. In Maryland, a Democratic gerrymander turned a safe Republican House seat into a Democratic seat. Should this practice be reined in by the Court? Is it fair that some votes seem to count more than others?

Redistricting is always partisan. Those who say that the courts should stay out of redistricting argue that the practice is inherently partisan. The majority party will always try to solidify or expand its power when it has the opportunity. This has been true since the earliest years of our nation. Furthermore, those on this side of the argument say that courts are not well suited to draw legislative maps; this responsibility should remain with the state legislatures.

A second line of argument concedes that the process has gotten a little out of hand, but contends that the standard for redistricting should be partisan *neutrality* rather than partisan *fairness*. That is, rather than trying to make sure that the votes for candidates of one party have the same collective impact on the outcome of elections as the votes for the other party (fairness), the redistricting process should simply ignore partisanship (neutrality). Another perspective, adopted by the Supreme Court when it deemed partisan gerrymandering to be a political question, is that there are no objective standards to identify partisan fairness, so the problem cannot be resolved by the courts.

Partisan redistricting undermines democracy. The other side of the debate counters that just because we have always had partisan gerrymandering doesn't make it right. Indeed, democracy means that voters should be able to choose their representatives, not the other way around. Because politicians have a self-interest in maintaining their political power and will work to further this self-interest through redistricting, unfairly drawn districts undermine democratic accountability.

The strategy of emphasizing neutrality instead of fairness in redistricting is plausible but does not convince those who support this side of the argument. While it is true that Republicans would continue to have some advantage in most states if districts were neutrally drawn, it is possible to draw maps that follow traditional districting principles but also promote partisan fairness.

take a stand

1. If you were a Supreme Court justice, how would you have ruled in the Pennsylvania and Maryland cases? Should partisan redistricting be limited?
2. Is the appropriate standard for evaluating a legislative map partisan neutrality or partisan fairness? Or should the courts stay out of redistricting entirely?

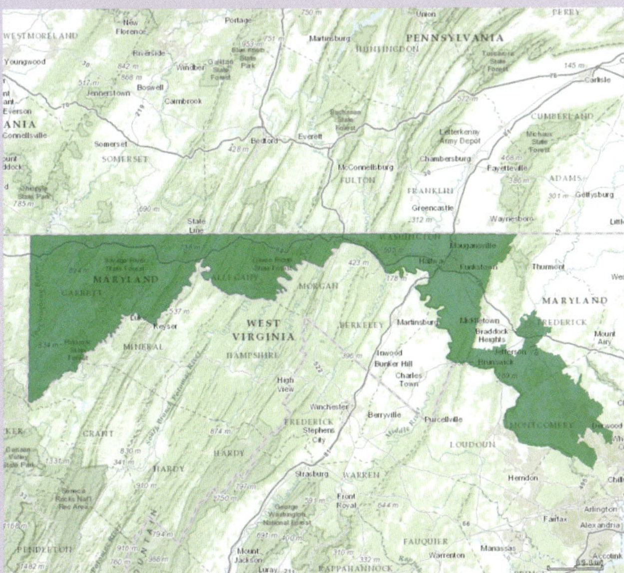

Maryland's 6th congressional district from 2011 map.

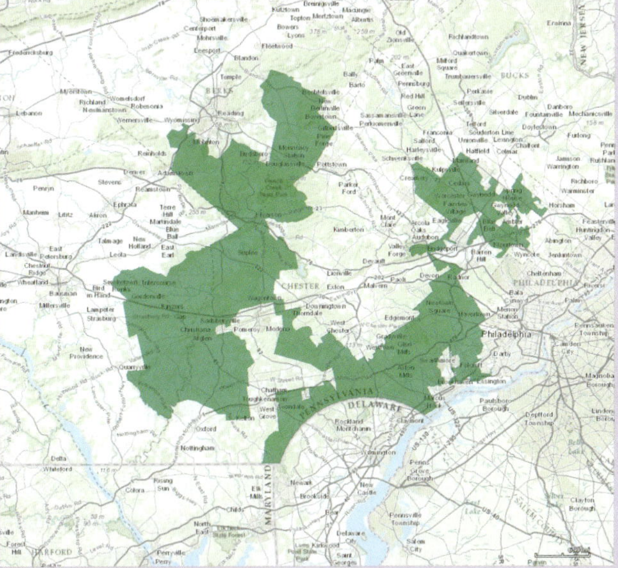

Pennsylvania's 7th congressional district from 2011 map.

Representative Bill Flores (R-TX) poses with Faye, a potbellied pig, after a news conference held by Citizens Against Government Waste at the Phoenix Park Hotel to release the "2017 Congressional Pig Book," which identifies pork-barrel spending in Congress.

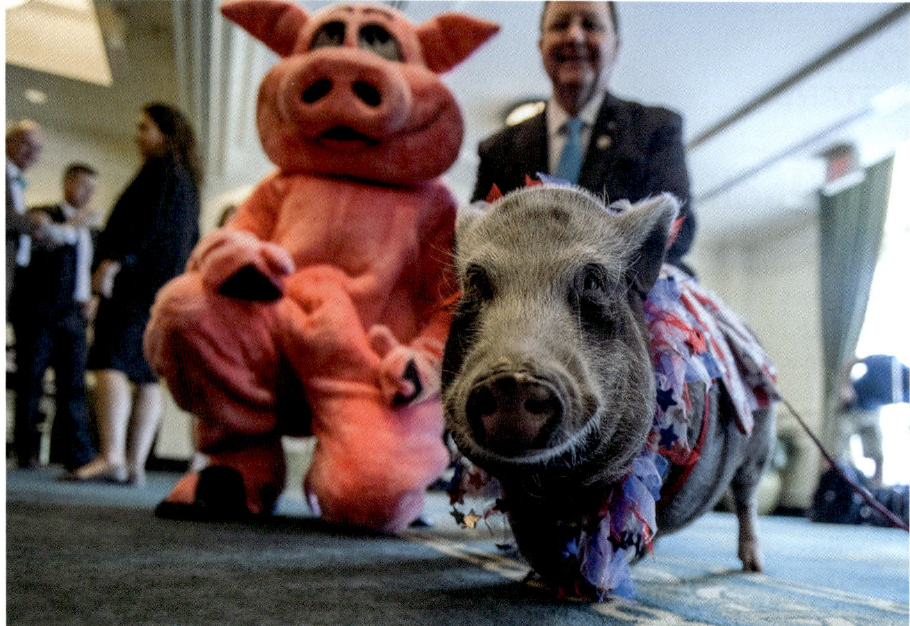

are informally known), following the ban on formal earmarks in both the House and Senate in 2011, but there were still billions of dollars in targeted spending as members of Congress found ways to secure funding for their district or state. Representative Jim Banks (R-IN) complained about the wasteful spending in the sprawling bill, saying, "Like 'mystery meat,' you don't want to know what's in it. Also like 'mystery meat'—you can bet at least one ingredient is a whole lot of pork."[38]

logrolling
A form of reciprocity in which members of Congress support bills that they otherwise might not vote for in exchange for other members' votes on bills that are very important to them.

earmarks
Federally funded local projects attached to bills passed through Congress.

In 2021, Congress brought back earmarks, but with new labels: the House calls them "community project funding" and the Senate "congressionally directed spending." The practice also comes with new restrictions: total spending on earmarks must be less than 1 percent of the budget, members must publicly swear that they had no personal financial connection to the requests, projects must have support in the local communities, and each House member is limited to 10 earmark requests (there is no limit in the Senate). Democratic leaders hoped that having earmarks would help break gridlock in Congress and bring more transparency to how public dollars are spent on projects.[39]

The norm of *specialization* is also important, both for the efficient operation of Congress and for members' reelection. By specializing and becoming an expert on a given issue, members provide valuable information to the institution as a whole and also create a basis for credit claiming. This norm is stronger in the House, where members often develop a few areas of expertise, whereas senators tend to be policy generalists. For example, Representative John Lewis (D-GA), who passed away in 2020 after serving 17 terms, dedicated much of his decades-long House career to the issue of civil rights, while Senator Lisa Murkowski (R-AK) has her hand in a variety of issues, especially energy and public lands but also Native American issues, health care, and women's issues.

seniority
The informal congressional norm of choosing the member who has served the longest on a particular committee to be the committee chair.

The **seniority** norm also serves individual and institutional purposes. This norm holds that the member with the longest service on a given committee will chair that committee. Although there have been numerous violations of this norm in the past 30 years, whereby the most senior member has been passed over for someone whom the party leaders favored, the norm benefits the institution by ensuring orderly succession in committee leadership.[40] The norm also benefits members by providing a tangible reason why voters should return them to Congress year after year. Many members of Congress make this point when campaigning, and the issue is more than just posturing. Committee chairs *are* better able to "bring home the bacon" than a junior member who is still learning the ropes.

Formal structures

Formal structures also shape members' behavior in Congress. Political parties, party leadership, the committee system, and staff provide the context within which members of Congress make policy and represent their constituents (refer to Nuts & Bolts 11.2 on p. 432).

Parties and Party Leaders Political parties are important for allocating power in Congress. Party leaders are always elected on straight party-line votes, with the majority party determining committee leadership, the division of seats on committees, and the allocation of committee resources. Parties in Congress also become more important when opposing parties control the two chambers. This was the case in 1981–1986 and in 2019–2020, when Republicans controlled the Senate and Democrats controlled the House, and in part of 2001 and 2002, 2011–2014, and 2023–2024 when the opposite was true.

A leading theory of congressional organization points to the importance of parties in solving collective action problems in Congress. Without parties, the legislative process would be much more fractured and decentralized because members would be autonomous agents in battle with one another. Parties provide a team framework that allows members to work together for broadly beneficial goals. Just think how difficult it would be for a member of Congress to get a bill passed if they had to build a coalition from scratch every time. Instead, parties provide a solid base from which coalition building may begin. As discussed in Chapter 8, political parties provide brand name recognition for members.

The top party leader in the House—and the only House leader mentioned in the Constitution—is the **Speaker of the House**, who is the head of the majority party and influences the legislative agenda, committee assignments, scheduling, and overall party strategy. The Democratic Party made history in January 2007 when its representatives elected Nancy Pelosi (D-CA) as the first woman to serve as Speaker. John Boehner was elected Speaker in 2011 after Republicans regained control of the House and was replaced by Paul Ryan in 2015. Ryan, who was only 48 years old and at the peak of his career, shocked the Washington establishment when he retired in 2018. Nancy Pelosi then reassumed the role in 2019 when the Democrats took control of the House. Kevin McCarthy (R-CA) became Speaker after Republicans regained control of the House in 2022.

However, nine months later, McCarthy was removed as Speaker by a "motion to vacate," led by eight conservative House Republicans who were upset that he had worked with Democrats on passing a budget to keep the government open.[41] Without a Speaker, the House devolved into a "three-week civil war . . . that paralyzed the chamber" (under House rules, no legislative activity can take place without a Speaker). Representative Patrick McHenry (R-NC) served as Speaker pro tempore, a position created after the terrorist attacks of 9/11, but his only job was to facilitate the election of a Speaker. After passing on the Majority Leader, Steve Scalise (R-LA), Representative Jim Jordan (R-OH), and Majority Whip, Tom Emmer (R-MN), the House elected Mike Johnson (R-LA), ending the deadlock.[42] Speaker Johnson survived a challenge to his leadership in May, 2024 (again, for working with Democrats to pass a budget and an aid package for Israel, Taiwan, and Ukraine) when 3 Democrats voted to support him (it is extremely rare to cross party lines on a vote for Speaker).[43]

The Speaker is aided by the **Majority Leader**, the Majority Whip, and the conference or caucus chair (in addition to many others in lower-level party positions). The Majority Leader is one of the national spokespersons for the party and also helps with the day-to-day operation of the legislative process. The Majority Whip oversees the extensive **whip system**, which has three functions: information gathering, information

Speaker of the House
The elected leader of the House of Representatives.

Majority Leader
The elected head of the party holding the majority of seats in the House or Senate.

whip system
An organization of House leaders who work to disseminate information and promote party unity in voting on legislation.

NUTS & BOLTS 11.2

Majority-Party Structure in the House of Representatives and the Senate

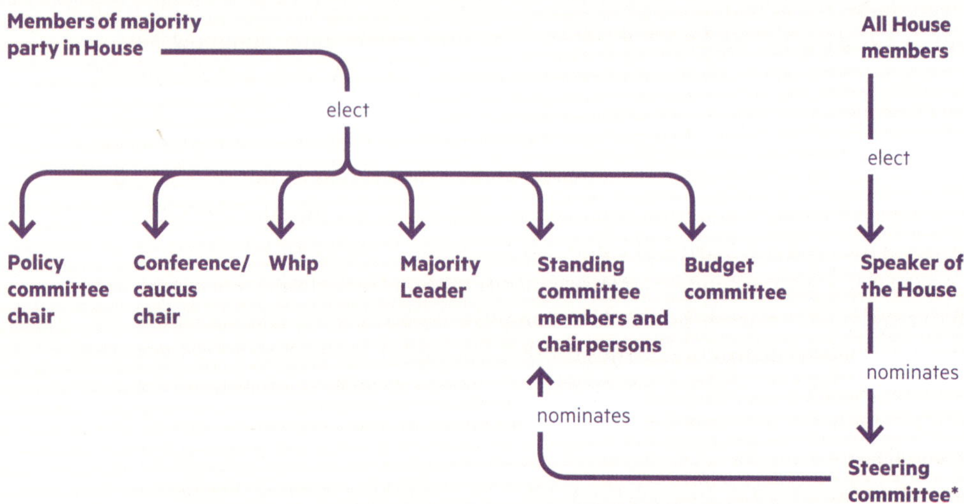

*Steering committee includes the Speaker, Majority Leader, and whip, and some members who are appointed by the Speaker and some who are elected by the conference.

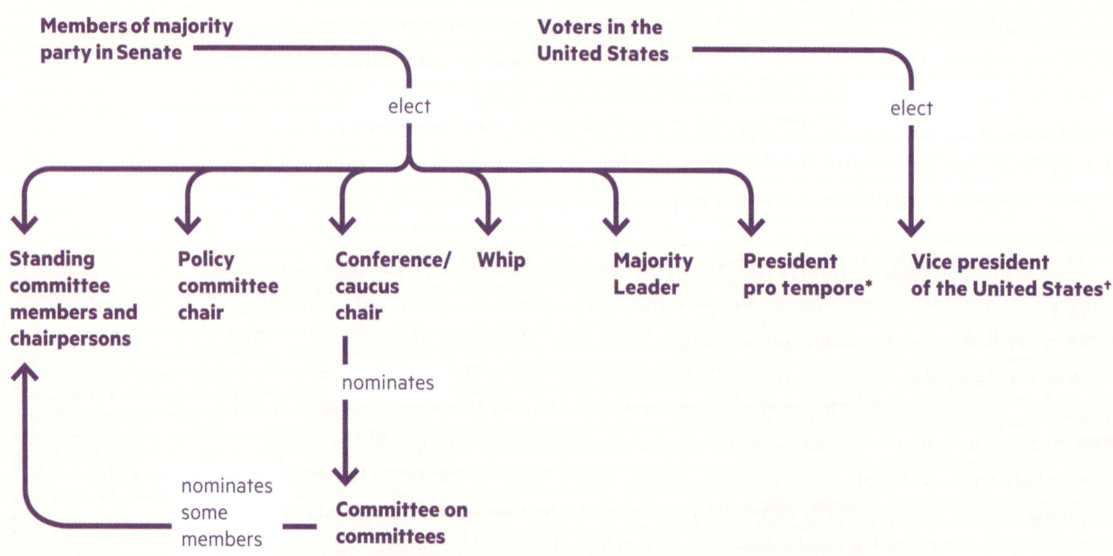

*The president pro tempore is elected by the majority-party members, but by custom is the most senior member of the majority party.
†The vice president of the United States is the president of the Senate, but rarely presides over the floor. The vice president's most important role is to break tie votes.

Source: Compiled by the authors.

dissemination, and coalition building. The whips meet regularly to discuss legislative strategy and scheduling. The whips then pass along this information to colleagues in their respective parties and indicate the party's position on a given bill. Whips also take a head count of party members in the House on specific votes and communicate this information to the party leaders. If a vote looks close, whips try to persuade members to support the party's position ("whip" comes from the fox-hunting term "whipper-in," meaning the person who keeps the hounds from wandering too far from the pack; similarly, party whips try to ensure that members do not stray too far from party positions). The conference chair for the Republicans, or caucus chair for the Democrats, runs the party meetings to elect floor leaders, to make committee assignments, and to set legislative agendas. The minority party in the House has a parallel structure: its leader is the **Minority Leader**, and the second in command is the Minority Whip.[44]

Minority Leader
The elected head of the party holding the minority of seats in the House or Senate.

The Senate leadership does not have as much power as the House leadership, mostly because individual senators have more power than individual House members due to the Senate's rule of unlimited debate, as we will discuss later. The Majority Leader and Minority Leader are the leaders of their respective parties, and second in command to them are the Assistant Majority and Minority Leaders. The Senate also has a whip system, but it is not as developed as the House system. Republicans have a separate position for the conference chair, while the Democratic leader also serves as the caucus chair. Officially, the country's vice president is also the president of the Senate but appears in the chamber only when needed to cast a tie-breaking vote. After three years in office, Vice President Kamala Harris broke 33 ties, which broke the all-time record.[45] The Constitution also mentions the **president pro tempore** of the Senate, whose formal duties involve presiding over the Senate when the vice president is not there. This is typically the member of the majority party with the greatest seniority, and the position does not have any real power. In fact, the actual president pro tempore often delegates the role to a more junior senator.

president pro tempore
A largely symbolic position usually held by the most senior member of the majority party in the Senate.

The Role of Parties and Conditional Party Government Parties in Congress also reflect the individualism of the institution. Compared with parties in parliamentary systems, U.S. congressional parties are very weak. They do not impose a party line or penalize members who vote against the party and have virtually no ability to impose electoral restrictions (such as denying the party's nomination) on renegade members.

Party leadership is central in the legislative process. During the 118th Congress, in 2023 and 2024, Speaker of the House Mike Johnson (R-LA), Senate Majority Leader Chuck Schumer (D-NY), Senate Minority Leader Mitch McConnell (R-KY), and House Minority Leader Hakeem Jeffries (D-NY) had to work together and with other members of Congress to pass legislation.

roll call vote
A recorded vote on legislation; members may vote "yes," "no," or "present," or they may abstain.

party vote
A vote in which the majority of one party opposes the position of the majority of the other party.

Although still weaker than their overseas counterparts, parties in Congress have greatly strengthened since the 1960s (refer to Figure 11.5). Partisanship—evident when party members stick together in opposition to the other party—reached its highest levels of the post–World War II era in recent years. About 70 percent of all **roll call votes** were **party votes**, in which a majority of one party opposed a majority of the other party. The proportion of party votes fell to between 50 and 60 percent between 1996 and 2008 but recently has hit new highs. The highest proportions were 79 percent in the Senate in 2021 and 76 percent in the House in 2017; the level was down a bit in the House

FIGURE 11.5

Party Votes and Unity in Congress, 1962–2021

Party votes are said to occur when a majority of one party opposes a majority of the other party, and party unity refers to the percentage of the party members who vote together on party votes. These two graphs make two important points. First, partisanship has increased in the last two decades, in terms of both the proportion of party votes and the level of party unity. Second, despite these increased levels of partisanship, only about two-thirds of all votes in the House and Senate divide the two parties. Given these potentially conflicting observations, how would you assess the argument that partisanship in Congress is far too intense?

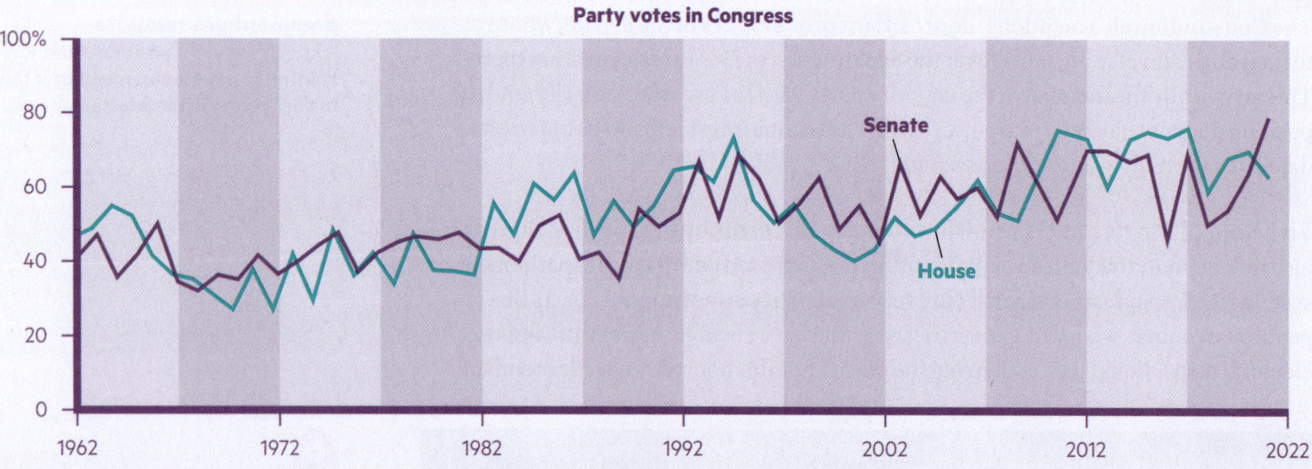

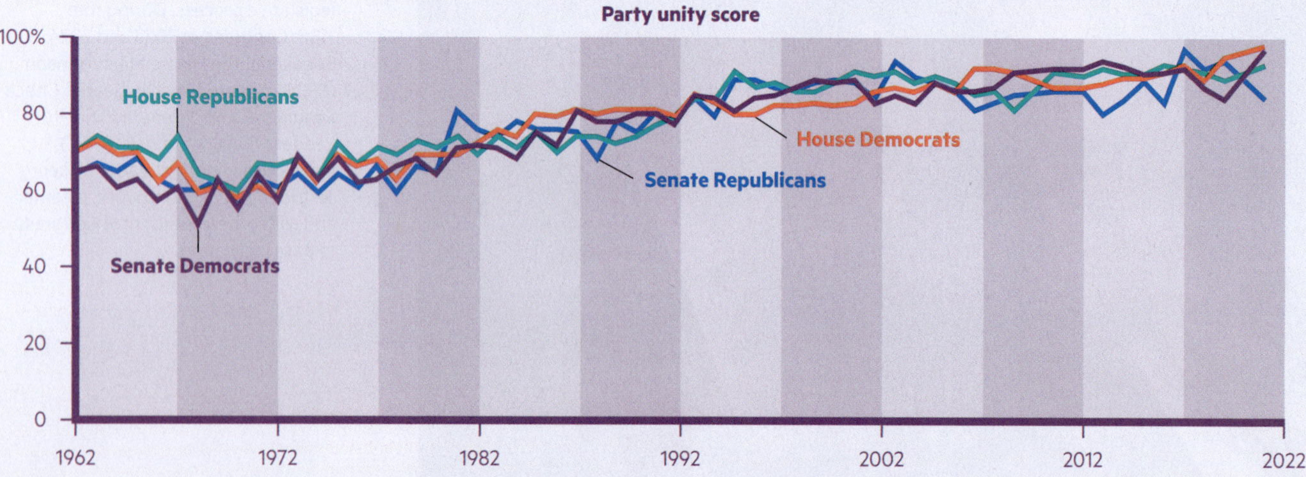

Source: Congressional Quarterly, "CQ Federal Congressional Bill Tracker," https://info.cq.com/legislative-tracking/cq-federal/ (accessed 9/26/22).

in 2021 to 63 percent. **Party unity**, the percentage of party members voting together on party votes, soared during this period as well, especially in the House. Party unity hit an all-time high for House Democrats in 2021, with 98 percent of them voting together on party votes. House Republicans were almost as unified at 93 percent. With the chamber split 50–50, Senate Democrats voted together a record 97 percent of the time, while Republicans were at 84 percent unity.[46]

party unity
The extent to which members of Congress in the same party vote together on party votes.

Party-line votes have become more common as the Democratic Party has become more cohesive: southern Democrats now vote more like their northern counterparts, partly because of the importance of Black voters, who tend to vote for Democrats in the South. Moreover, increasing Republican strength in the South means that the remaining Democratic districts are more liberal, because Republicans defeat the more moderate Democrats. Similarly, there are fewer moderates within the Republican Party, as most regions of the country that used to elect moderate Republicans are now electing Democrats.[47]

If you want to get along, go along.

—Sam Rayburn, former Speaker of the House

Another way to examine changes in the composition of the parties is to examine the ideological distribution of members of Congress (refer to Figure 11.6). The parties in Congress are now more polarized than they have been at any point in U.S. history. In the 1970s, there was considerable overlap between the Democratic and Republican parties. But recently, the two parties are completely separated—that is, the most conservative Democrat is to the left of the most liberal Republican. At the same time, the parties are growing farther apart, which makes it even harder for the Republicans and the Democrats to work together and compromise to pass legislation.

FIGURE 11.6

Ideological Polarization in Congress, 1879–2023

Although party polarization in Congress has been high in the past, it lessened in the early twentieth century. Polarization has increased steadily in the last 70 years, and today's Congress is more polarized than ever. What do you think causes this extreme polarization?

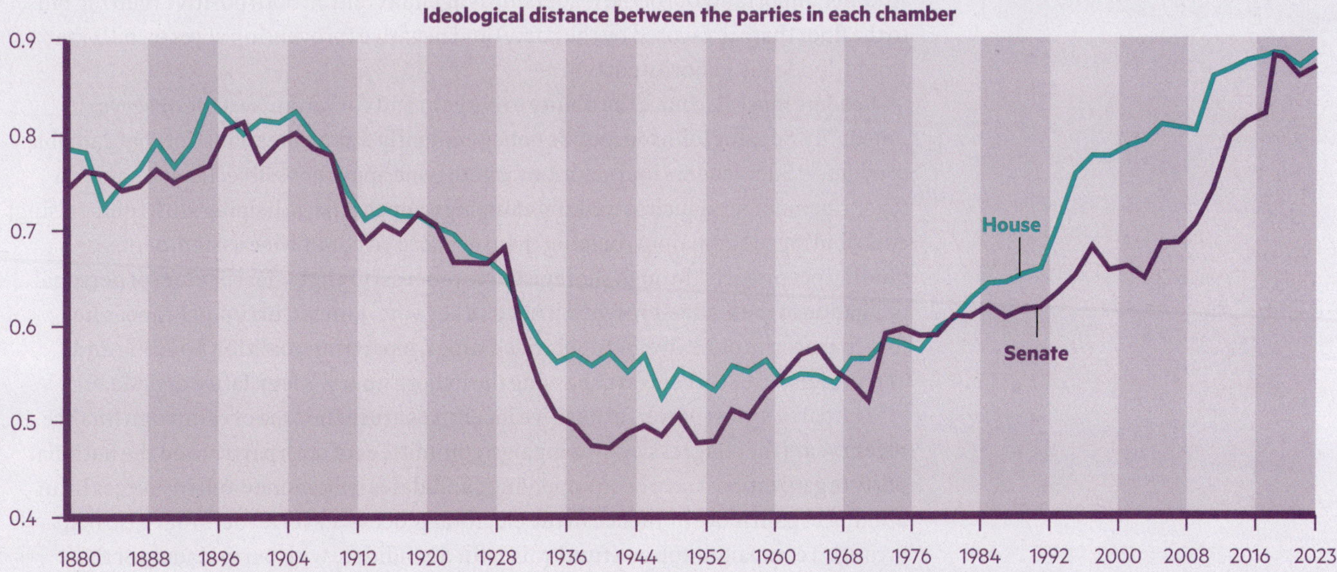

Source: Polarization in Congress, "Liberal-Conservative Partisan Polarization by Chamber," Jeff Lewis, March 11, 2018, https://voteview.com/articles/party_polarization (accessed 7/29/20); updated with Realtime NOMINATE Ideology and Related Data, which track the ideological distance between each party's average vote, voteview.com (accessed 5/6/24).

Senate Majority Leader Mitch McConnell (R-KY) was joined by several Republican senators at a press conference in December 2019 regarding the impeachment proceedings against President Donald Trump, which they argued were fueled by partisan politics rather than legitimate concerns.

This greater cohesiveness within parties and separation across parties means that conditional party government may be in play—that is, strong party leadership is possible in Congress, but it is conditional on the consent of party members.[48] That consent is more likely if there are strong differences between the parties but unity within parties. Leaders' chief responsibility is to get their party's legislative agenda through Congress, but they primarily have to rely on persuasion and control over the timing of when bills come up for a vote rather than telling members what to do. Leaders' success largely depends on their personal skills, communicative abilities, and trustworthiness. Some of the most successful leaders, such as Lyndon Johnson (D-TX), Majority Leader of the Senate from 1955 to 1961, and Sam Rayburn (D-TX), Speaker of the House for more than 17 years, kept in touch with key members on a daily basis. Another important tool of the leadership is agenda control: both positive (getting bills to the floor that are favored by the party) and negative (preventing votes on bills that would divide the majority party).

Leaders must also have the ability to bargain and compromise. One observer noted, "To Senator Johnson, public policy evidently was an inexhaustibly bargainable product."[49] Such leaders find solutions where none appear possible. Leaders also do favors for members (such as making campaign appearances, helping with fund-raising, contributing to campaigns, helping them get desired committee assignments, or guiding pet projects through the legislative process) to engender a feeling of personal obligation to the leadership when it needs a key vote. James Curry and Frances Lee find that even in our extremely polarized times, bipartisan coalition building and compromise are still central in passing the majority party's legislative agenda.[50]

The party's most powerful positive incentives are in the area of campaign finance. In recent years the congressional campaign committees of both parties and the national party organizations have been supplying candidates with money and resources in an attempt to gain more influence in the electoral process. Party leaders may also help arrange a campaign stop or a fund-raiser for a candidate with party leaders or the president. For example, President Obama held dozens of fund-raisers for Democrats in 2014, earning him the label of "Fundraiser-in-Chief" from CNN.[51] President Trump campaigned actively for congressional Republicans during the 2018 midterms.

Despite headlining a record-breaking fund-raiser, he held fewer for other candidates than any president since Ronald Reagan. President Biden reverted to the norm, raising $7.3 million for Democrats at five events early in 2022.[52]

Despite these positive reinforcements, members' desire for reelection always comes before party concerns, and leadership rarely tries to force a member to vote against their constituents' interests. For example, Democrats from rural areas, where most constituents support gun ownership, would not be expected to vote the party line favoring a gun control bill. But if a member of Congress did something much more extreme that crossed the party's leadership—for example, supporting the opposing party's candidate for Speaker or passing strategic information to the opposition—the member could expect to be disciplined by the party's leaders.

The most difficult challenge for party leadership in recent years has been the confrontational behavior of junior members who ignore the norms of institutional behavior. Marjorie Taylor Greene (R-GA), for example, was stripped of her committee assignments for expressing support for killing Speaker Pelosi, threatening other House members, and endorsing various conspiracy theories linked to QAnon.[53] Representative Paul Gosar (R-AZ) was censured by the House for posting an animated video showing him killing Representative Alexandria Ocasio-Cortez (D-NY), and attacking President Joe Biden. Gosar was only the 22nd House member in U.S. history and the 8th in nearly 150 years to be censured. Representatives Lauren Boebert (R-CO) and Taylor Greene were widely criticized for disrupting President Biden's 2022 State of the Union message. Matt Gaetz (R-FL) is being investigated by the House Ethics Committee for having sex with a minor,[54] and several other Republican House members were being investigated for possibly having a role in the January 6, 2021, attack on the Capitol.[55] While all of these members have created headaches for House Republican leaders, they have largely stood by them. Liz Cheney (R-WY) was removed from House leadership for her criticism of President Trump and his role in the January 6 insurrection.

When Republicans regained control of the House in 2023, they censured three Democratic members: Adam Schiff (D-CA) for leading investigations of President Donald Trump, Rashida Tlaib (D-MI) for her comments about the Israel-Hamas war, and Jamaal Bowman (D-NY) for pulling a fire alarm in a House office building when there was no emergency. While these censure votes were largely along party lines, the expulsion of George Santos (R-NY) was strongly bipartisan, with 105 Republicans joining most Democrats to kick him out for seeking to "fraudulently exploit every aspect of his House candidacy for his own personal financial profit." Representative Santos was only the sixth House member to be expelled in U.S. history.[56]

Party leadership sometimes struggles to ensure that newer members of Congress adhere to the norms of the institution. In recent years, Republican representatives, including Lauren Boebert (R-CO) and Marjorie Taylor Greene (R-GA), were reprimanded by leadership for yelling during President Biden's State of the Union speech, and members of the so-called Democratic Squad, which includes Alexandria Ocasio-Cortez, were reprimanded for not staying on message.

The Committee System The committee system in the House and Senate is another crucial part of the legislative structure. There are four types of committees: standing, select, joint, and conference. **Standing committees**, which have ongoing membership and jurisdictions, are where most of Congress's work gets done. These committees draft legislation and oversee the implementation of the laws they pass. For example, the Agriculture Committees in the House and Senate have jurisdiction over farm programs such as commodity price supports, crop insurance, and soil conservation. But they also create and oversee policy for rural electrification and development; nutrition programs like the Supplemental Nutrition Assistance Program (SNAP); and the inspection of livestock, poultry, seafood, and meat products. Many committees share jurisdiction on policy—for example, the House Natural Resources Committee oversees the U.S. Forest Service and forests on federally owned lands, and the Agriculture Committee oversees policy for forests on privately owned lands. There are 21 standing committees in the House and 18 in the Senate.[57]

standing committees
Committees that are a permanent part of the House or Senate structure, holding more importance and authority than other committees.

Select committees typically address a specific topic for one or two terms, such as the House Select Committee on the Climate Crisis or the Select Committee to Investigate the January 6th Attack on the United States Capitol. These committees do not have the same legislative authority as standing committees; rather, they mostly serve to collect information, provide policy options, and draw attention to a given issue.

select committees
Committees in the House or Senate created to address a specific issue for one or two terms.

There are four **joint committees** made up of members of both the House and the Senate, and they rarely have legislative authority. The Joint Committee on Taxation, for example, does not have authority to send legislation concerning tax policy to the floor of the House or Senate. Instead, it gathers information and provides estimates of the consequences of proposed tax legislation. Joint committees may also be temporary, such as the "Supercommittee" (officially the Joint Select Committee on Deficit Reduction) that was formed in 2011 to try to reach bipartisan agreement on a deficit reduction plan. The committee failed to reach agreement and was disbanded in 2012.

joint committees
Committees that contain members of both the House and Senate but have limited authority.

Conference committees are formed as needed to resolve specific differences between House and Senate versions of legislation that are passed in each chamber. These committees mostly comprise standing committee members from each chamber who worked on the bill in question.

conference committees
Temporary committees created to negotiate differences between the House and Senate versions of a piece of legislation that has passed through both chambers.

The committee system creates a division of labor that helps members get reelected by facilitating specialization and credit claiming. For example, a chair of the Agriculture Committee or of a key agricultural subcommittee may reasonably take credit for passing an important bill for the farmers back home, such as the Cottonseed Payment Program that provides assistance to cottonseed farmers who lost crops due to hurricanes.[58] The number of members who could make these credible claims expanded dramatically in the 1970s with the proliferation of subcommittees (there are 104 in the House and 70 in the Senate). Speaking about the House, one observer said, with some exaggeration, that if you ever forget a member's name, you can simply refer to them as "Mr. or Ms. Chairman" and you will be right about half the time.

This view of congressional committees is based on the **distributive theory**, which is rooted in the norm of reciprocity and representatives' incentives to provide benefits for their districts. The theory holds that members will seek committee assignments to best serve their district's interests, the leadership will accommodate those requests, and the floor will respect the views of the committees in a big institution-level logroll—that is, committee members will support one another's legislation. This means that members tend to have an interest in and to support the policies produced by the committees they serve on. For example, members from farm states would want to serve on the Agriculture Committee, and members with a lot of military bases or defense contractors in their districts would want to be on the Armed Services Committee.

distributive theory
The idea that members of Congress will join committees that best serve the interests of their district and that committee members will support one another's legislation.

Nonetheless, the committee system does not exist simply to further members' electoral goals. According to **informational theory**, it also provides collective benefits to the rest of the members through committee members' expertise on policy, which helps reduce uncertainty about policy outcomes.[59] By deferring to expert committees, members are able to achieve beneficial outcomes while using their time more efficiently. This informational theory is also consistent with the argument made by Richard Fenno 50 years ago that members will serve on committees for reasons other than simply trying to achieve reelection (which is implied by the distributive theory). Fenno argued that members also were interested in achieving power within the institution and in making good policy.[60] Others argue that goals vary from bill to bill and all members pursue reelection advantage, institutional power, and effective policy in different circumstances.[61] Thus, the committee system does not exist only to further members' electoral goals, but it often serves that purpose.

informational theory
The idea that having committees in Congress made up of experts on specific policy areas helps ensure well-informed policy decisions.

Committees also serve the policy needs of the majority party, largely because the party in power controls a majority of seats on every committee. The party ratios on each committee generally reflect the partisan distribution in the overall chamber, but the majority party gives itself somewhat larger majorities on the important committees such as Ways and Means (which controls tax policy), Appropriations, and Rules. This is especially true for the Rules Committee (in which the majority party controls 9 of the 13 seats). The Rules Committee is important to the majority party because it structures the nature of debate in the House: it sets the length of debate and the type and number of amendments to a bill that will be allowed. These decisions are called *rules* and must be approved by a majority of the House members. The Rules Committee has become an arm of the majority-party leadership, and in many instances it provides rules that support the party's policy agenda or that protect its members from having to take controversial positions. For example, the Rules Committee prevented amendments on the articles of impeachment brought against President Trump in December 2019, fearing that amendments could have divided the Democratic Party.[62] Majority members are expected to support their party on votes on rules, even if they end up voting against the related legislation.

Congressional Staff The final component of the formal structure of Congress is congressional staff. The size of personal and committee staff exploded in the 1970s and 1980s but has since leveled off. The total number of congressional staff is more than four times as large as it was 50 years ago. Part of the motivation for this growth was to reduce the gap between the policy-making capability of Congress and the president, especially with regard to fiscal policy. The other primary motivation was electoral. By increasing the size of their personal staff, members were able to open multiple district offices and expand opportunities for helping constituents. When the Republicans took control of Congress in 1994, they vowed to cut the waste in the internal operation of the institution, in part by cutting committee staff. However, although they reduced committee staff by nearly a third, they made no cuts in personal staff.

The Constitution says very little about the internal structure of Congress, so the institution is largely the creation of its members. The norms of the institution and its formal structure facilitate members' electoral and policy goals, so if they don't like the way something works, they can change it. While this may sound very self-serving, members of Congress also work to serve broader collective and policy goals—or else they would be booted out of office. Understanding this fundamental point provides great insight into why Congress is structured the way that it is.

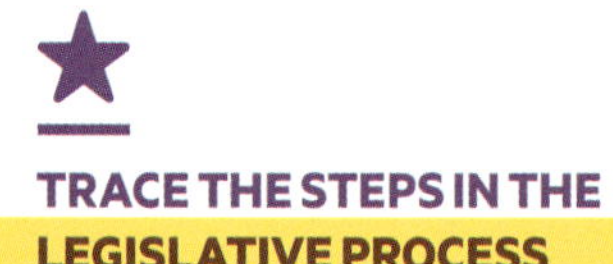

TRACE THE STEPS IN THE LEGISLATIVE PROCESS

How a bill becomes a law

Every introductory textbook on American politics has an obligatory section including a neat little diagram that describes how a bill becomes a law (refer to the How It Works graphic on pp. 442–443). But we provide an important truth-in-advertising disclosure: many important laws do not follow this orderly path. In fact, Barbara Sinclair's book *Unorthodox Lawmaking* argues that "the legislative process for major legislation is now less likely to conform to the textbook model than to unorthodox lawmaking."[63] After presenting the standard view, we describe the most important deviations from that path.

The conventional process

The details of the legislative process can be incredibly complex, but its basic aspects are fairly simple. The most important thing to understand about the process is that before a piece of legislation can become a law it must be passed *in identical form* by both the House and the Senate and signed by the president. If the president vetoes the bill, it can still be passed with a two-thirds vote in each chamber. Note, however, that all legislation that is signed by the president (or for which Congress overrides a veto) carries the weight of law; legislation that is not signed by the president has only internal legislative or symbolic purposes (refer to Nuts & Bolts 11.3 for a description of different types of legislation). Here are the basic steps of the process to pass a bill:

1. A member of Congress introduces the bill.
2. A subcommittee and committee craft the bill.
3. Floor action on the bill takes place in the first chamber (House or Senate).
4. Committee and floor action takes place in the second chamber.
5. The conference committee works out any differences between the House and Senate versions of the bill. (If the two chambers pass the same version, steps 5 and 6 are not necessary.)
6. The conference committee version is given final approval on the floor of each chamber.

NUTS & BOLTS 11.3

Types of Legislation

- **Bill:** A legislative proposal that becomes law if it is passed by both the House and the Senate in identical form and approved by the president. Each is assigned a bill number, with "H.R." indicating bills that originated in the House and "S.R." denoting bills that originated in the Senate. Private bills are concerned with a specific individual or organization and often address immigration or naturalization issues. Public bills affect the general public if enacted into law.
- **Simple resolution:** Legislation used to express the sense of the House or Senate, designated by "H.Res." or "S.Res." Simple resolutions affect only the chamber passing the resolution, are not signed by the president, and cannot become public law. Resolutions are often used for symbolic legislation, such as congratulating sports teams or naming a post office after a famous person (refer to Figure 11.7).
- **Concurrent resolution:** Legislation used to express the position of both chambers on a nonlegislative matter to set the annual budget or to fix adjournment dates, designated by "H.Con.Res." or "S.Con.Res." Concurrent resolutions are not signed by the president and therefore do not carry the weight of law.
- **Joint resolution:** Legislation that has few practical differences from a bill (passes both chambers in identical form, signed by the president) unless it proposes a constitutional amendment. In that case, a two-thirds majority of those present and voting in both the House and the Senate and ratification by three-fourths of the states are required for the amendment to be adopted, and it does not require the president's signature.

7. The president either signs or vetoes the final version.
8. If the bill is vetoed, both chambers can attempt to override the veto with a two-thirds vote in both chambers.

The first part of the process, unchanged from the earliest Congresses, is the introduction of the bill. Only members of Congress can introduce the bill, either by dropping it into the "hopper," a wooden box at the front of the chamber in the House, or by presenting it to one of the clerks at the presiding officer's desk in the Senate. Even the president would need to have a House member or senator introduce a bill. Each bill has one or more sponsors and often many co-sponsors. Members may introduce bills on any topic they choose, but often the bills are related to a specific constituency interest. For example, Senator Josh Hawley (R-MO) introduced Senate Resolution 578, "Congratulating the Kansas City Chiefs on their victory in Super Bowl LVIII" (refer to Figure 11.7). Obviously, most legislation is more substantive, but members of Congress are always attentive to issues their constituents care about.

Taking Care of the Fans

FIGURE 11.7

The congratulatory resolution here is symbolic and commends the Kansas City Chiefs for winning the Super Bowl in 2024. Why do you think members of Congress spend time passing seemingly trivial resolutions like this?

S. RES. 578

In the Senate of the United States
March 6, 2024

Congratulating the Kansas City Chiefs on their victory in Super Bowl LVIII in the successful 104th season of the National Football League.

Whereas, on Sunday, February 11, 2024, the Kansas City Chiefs defeated the San Francisco 49ers by a score of 25 to 22 to win Super Bowl LVIII in Las Vegas, Nevada;

Whereas the Chiefs made their fourth Super Bowl appearance and third Super Bowl win in 5 years . . .

Whereas quarterback Patrick Mahomes completed 34 of 46 pass attempts for 333 yards and 2 touchdowns, rushed 9 times for 66 yards, and was named Super Bowl Most Valuable Player, making him the third player to have won the award 3 times;

Whereas kicker Harrison Butker completed a perfect postseason in field goal attempts, set a new Super Bowl record with a 57-yard field goal, scored more than half of the Chiefs' total points . . .

Whereas tight end Travis Kelce led the team in receiving with 9 receptions for 93 yards;

Whereas running back Isiah Pacheco rushed 18 times for 59 yards and had 6 receptions for 33 yards . . .

Whereas Arrowhead Stadium, home of the Chiefs, holds the world record for loudest crowd roar at a sporting event with 142.2 decibels;

Whereas the victory of the Kansas City Chiefs in Super Bowl LVIII instills a sense of pride for Chiefs fans in the State of Missouri, the State of Kansas, and across the Midwest;

and

Whereas people all over the world are asking, "How 'bout those Chiefs?":

Now, therefore, be it *Resolved*, That the Senate—

(1) congratulates the Kansas City Chiefs and their entire staff, Mayor of Kansas City Quinton Lucas, Governor of Missouri Mike Parson, and fans everywhere of the Kansas City Chiefs for their victory in Super Bowl LVIII . . .

Source: Congress.gov, https://www.congress.gov/bill/118th-congress/senate-resolution/578/text (accessed 8/6/24).

How it works: in theory

Passing Legislation

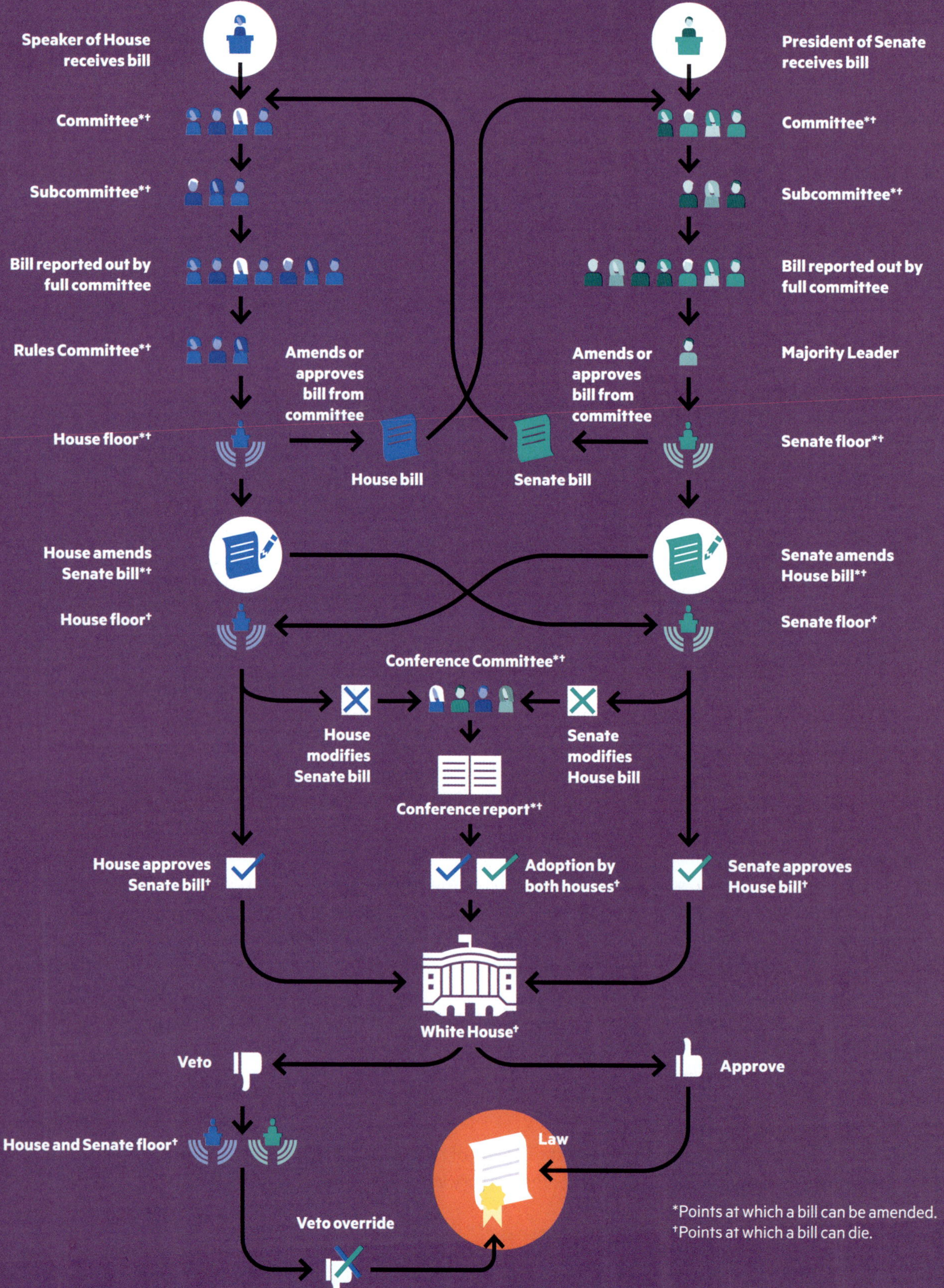

How it works: in practice

Passing the American Rescue Plan Act of 2021

The 2021 American Rescue Plan Act, which provided $1.9 trillion in relief for the COVID-19 pandemic, is an example of how passing legislation often deviates from the conventional method. This may be one of the most unconventional ever, with 251 distinct steps in the process! We have distilled that down to the key moments. With no Republican senators supporting the bill, 60 votes were needed to stop a filibuster, so Democrats used the reconciliation process (which only requires a simple majority). Passing the budget resolution with reconciliation in the House and Senate took 130 of the 251 steps.

In the House . . .

Six committees tackle different parts of the bill.

Let's make this more complicated.

The Senate parliamentarian rules that a **$15 minimum wage cannot be included** in the reconciliation bill.

Let's speed this up . . .

The House Budget Committee **consolidates the work of the six committees** and sends the bill to the floor.

Passed!

House passes the bill by a 219–212 vote.

In the Senate . . .

A vote on the motion to proceed to debate **passes on a party-line** vote with Vice President Kamala Harris breaking the 50–50 tie.

Vote-a-rama!

Senators stock up on energy drinks and snacks for a **marathon session of voting on amendments**.

But first!

Senator Ron Johnson (R-WI) **forces the Senate to read the entire text** of the 628-page bill, which takes more than 11 hours.

Is this going to work?

It looks like Democratic unity could break as **Senator Joe Manchin (D-WV) wavers** on the extension of unemployment benefits.

Buy some time!

Senator Bernie Sanders's amendment to raise the minimum wage to $15 is voted down. To give time to bring Senator Manchin back into the fold, **Senator Chuck Schumer holds the vote open for 11 hours and 50 minutes**, a new record for the longest roll call vote.

Whew!

Senator Manchin is on board and the vote-a-rama continues. Thirty-five amendments are rejected and two are approved, one on veterans' education and one on aiding homeless children.

Passed!

Senate passes the bill by a 50–49 vote

Passed!

House passes the Senate version by a 220–211 vote.

Signed into law.

President Biden **signs the bill into law** on March 11, 2021.

Critical Thinking

1. **What are the most significant ways in which** the process to pass the 2021 American Rescue Plan Act deviated from the conventional method?
2. **Do you think the 2021 American Rescue Plan Act could have been** passed without this unconventional process? Why or why not?

The next step is to send the bill to the relevant committee. House and Senate rules specify committee jurisdictions (there are more than 200 categories), and the bill is matched with the committee that best fits its subject matter. In the House, major legislation may be sent to more than one committee in a practice known as multiple referral, but one of the committees is designated the primary committee and the bill is reviewed by the other committees sequentially or in parts. The practice is less common in the Senate, partly because senators have more opportunities to amend legislation on the floor. However, there were three committees in the House and five in the Senate that simultaneously worked on health care reform in 2009.

Once the bill goes to a committee, the chair refers it to the relevant subcommittee, where much of the legislative work is done. One important point: 80–90 percent of bills die at this stage of the process; they never make it out of the subcommittee or committee. For bills that see some action, the subcommittee holds hearings, calls witnesses, and gathers the information necessary to rewrite, amend, and edit the bill. The final language of the bill is determined in a collaborative process known as the **markup**. During this meeting, members debate aspects of the issue and offer amendments to change the language or content of the bill. After all amendments have been considered, a final vote is taken on whether to send the bill to the full committee. If it is sent, the full committee then considers whether to pass it along to the floor. This committee also has the option of amending the bill, passing it as is, or tabling it (which kills the bill). Every bill sent to the floor by a committee is accompanied by a report and full documentation of all the hearings. These documents constitute the bill's legislative history, which the courts, executive departments, and the public use to determine the purpose and meaning of the law.

markup
One of the steps through which a bill becomes a law, in which the final wording of the bill is determined.

When the bill makes it to the floor, it is placed on one of the various legislative calendars. Bills are removed from the calendar to be considered by the floor under a broad range of possible rules. When the bill reaches the floor, the majority party and minority party each designate a bill manager who is responsible for guiding the debate on the floor. In the House, debate proceeds according to tight time limits and rules governing the nature of amendments. Senate debate is much more open and unlimited in most circumstances (unless all the senators agree to a limit). If you have ever watched C-SPAN, you know that often there are very few people on the floor during debates. Typically only the small number of people who are most interested in the bill (usually members of the committee that produced it) actively participate and offer amendments.

When debate is completed and all amendments have been considered, the presiding officer calls for a voice vote, with those in favor saying "aye" and those opposed "no." If it is unclear which side has won, any member may call for a "division vote," which requires members on each side to stand and be counted. At that point, any member may call for a recorded vote (there is no way of recording members' positions on voice votes and division votes). If at least 25 members agree that a recorded vote is desired, buzzers go off in the office buildings and committee rooms, calling members to the floor for the vote. Once they reach the floor, members vote by an electronic system in which they insert ATM-like cards into slots and each vote is recorded on a big board at the front of the House or Senate chamber.

If the bill passes the House and the Senate in different forms, the discrepancies have to be resolved. On many minor bills, one chamber may simply accept the other chamber's version to solve the problem. On other minor bills and some major bills, differences are resolved through a process known as amendments between the chambers. In this case, one chamber modifies a bill passed by the other chamber and sends it back. These modifications can go back and forth several times before both houses agree on an identical bill. A complicated version of this approach was used to pass health care reform in 2010.

The most common way to resolve differences on major legislation is through a conference committee made up of key players in the House and the Senate. A majority of major bills go to a conference committee, but minor bills rarely do.[64] Sometimes the conferees split the difference between the House and Senate versions, but at other times the House and Senate approaches are so different that one must be chosen—an especially tricky prospect when different parties control the two chambers. Sometimes the conference cannot resolve differences and the bill dies. If the conference committee can agree on changes, each chamber must pass the final version, the conference report, by a majority vote and neither chamber is allowed to amend it.

The bill is then sent to the president. If the president approves and signs the measure within 10 days (not counting Sundays), it becomes law. If the president objects to the bill, they may **veto** it within 10 days, sending it back to the chamber where it originated, along with a statement of objections. Unless both the House and the Senate vote to override the veto by a two-thirds majority, the bill dies. If the president does not act within 10 days and Congress is in session, the bill becomes law without the president's approval. If Congress is not in session, the measure dies through what is known as a **pocket veto**.

veto
The president's rejection of a bill that has been passed by Congress. A veto can be overridden by a two-thirds vote in both the House and Senate.

pocket veto
The automatic death of a bill passed by the House and Senate when the president fails to sign the bill in the last 10 days of a legislative session.

One final point on how a bill becomes a law is important: any bill that appropriates money must pass through the two-step process of authorization and appropriation. In the authorization process, members debate the merits of the bill, determine its language, and limit the amount that can be spent on the bill. The appropriations process involves the Budget Committees in both the House and the Senate, which set the overall guidelines for the national budget, and the Appropriations Committees in the two chambers, which determine the actual amounts of money that will be spent. In recent years, Congress has been unable to pass its appropriations bills in time for the start of the new fiscal year, so it ends up having to pass "continuing resolutions" that spend money at the last year's levels in order to keep the government open. Congress passed five continuing resolutions for the 2021 fiscal year and three in 2023. That may sound like a lot, but the record is 21 for the 2001 fiscal year.[65]

Deviations from the conventional process

There are many ways in which legislation may not follow the typical path. First, in some Congresses up to 20 percent of *major* bills bypass the committee system. This may be done by a discharge petition, in which a majority of the members force a bill out of its assigned committee, or by a special rule in the House. In some cases, a bill may go to the relevant committee, but then party leadership may impose its version of the bill later in the process. For example, in the wake of the terrorist attacks of September 11, the House Judiciary Committee, after hard bipartisan work, quickly approved a version of the Patriot Act to be considered by the full House to give the government stronger surveillance powers. But a few days later, according to committee member Representative Jerrold Nadler (D-NY), "then the bill just disappeared. And we had a new several hundred-page bill revealed from the Rules Committee" that had to be voted on the next day. Most members of Congress did not have a chance to read it.[66] The Affordable Care Act (ACA) also deviated from the standard path.

Second, about one-third of major bills are adjusted post-committee and before the legislation reaches the floor by supporters of the bills to increase their chances of passage. Sometimes the bill goes back to the committee after these changes, and sometimes it does not. One good example of this approach was the ACA, which was altered by House and Senate leadership after the committees deadlocked on different versions of the bill. The legislation also bypassed the conference committee; party leadership worked out the differences between the House and Senate versions directly. Thus, although most of the legislative work is accomplished in committees, a significant amount of legislation bypasses committee review.

Third, summit meetings between the president and congressional leaders may bypass or jump-start the normal legislative process. For example, rather than going through the Budget Committees to set budgetary targets, the president may meet with top leaders from both parties and hammer out a compromise that is presented to Congress as a done deal. This technique is especially important on delicate budget negotiations or when the president is threatening to use the veto. Often the congressional rank and file go along with the end product of the summit meeting, but occasionally they reject it—as happened in November 2021, when Speaker Pelosi had to postpone a vote on the infrastructure bill when liberals in her party balked at separating it from the larger social spending bill.[67]

omnibus legislation
Large bills that often cover several topics and may contain extraneous, or pork-barrel, projects.

Fourth, **omnibus legislation**—massive bills that run hundreds of pages long and cover many different subjects and programs—often requires creative approaches by the leadership to guide the bill through the legislative maze. In addition, the massive legislation often carries riders—extraneous legislation attached to the "must pass" bill to secure approval for pet projects that would otherwise fail. This is a form of pork-barrel legislation and another mechanism used in the quest for reelection. One example was the 1,012-page 2024 omnibus bill that provided $1.2 trillion for the Defense, Financial Services, Homeland Security, Labor-HHS-Education, Legislative Branch and State-Foreign Operations appropriation bills (about 70 percent of discretionary funding). Republicans complained that the bill contained wasteful spending, including $200 million for a new FBI headquarters, a $1 million earmark for an organization that provides services to LGBTQ elders, and a $1.8 million project for the midwifery unit at a hospital in Providence, R.I., that also provides abortion and related services. "Here we are again. The swamp is back," said Representative Chip Roy (R-TX).[68]

Differences in the House and Senate legislative processes

There are three central differences in the legislative processes of the House and the Senate: (1) the continuity of the membership and the impact this has on the rules, (2) the way in which bills get to the floor, and (3) the structure of the floor process, including debate and amendments. As discussed earlier, the Senate is a continuing body, with two-thirds of its members returning to the next session without facing reelection (because of the six-year term), whereas all House members are up for reelection every two years. This has an important impact on the rules of the two chambers: there has been much greater stability in the rules of the Senate than in those of the House. Whereas the House adopts its rules anew at the start of each new session (sometimes with major changes, sometimes with only minor modifications), the Senate has not had a general reaffirmation of its rules since 1789. However, the Senate rules can be changed at the beginning of a session to meet the needs of the new members.

The floor process is much simpler and less structured in the Senate than in the House. In part, this is due to the relative size of the two chambers: the House with its 435 members needs to have more rules than the Senate with its 100 members. Ironically, however, the floor process is actually much easier to navigate in the House because of its structure. Since the adoption of Reed's Rules in 1890, the House has been a very majoritarian body—that is, a majority of House members can almost always have their way. Named after Speaker Thomas Reed, the rules were an implementation of his view that "the best system is to have one party govern and the other party watch."[69]

In contrast, the Senate has always been a much more individualistic body. Former Majority Leader Howard Baker compared leading the Senate to "herding cats," saying it was difficult "trying to make ninety-nine independent souls act in concert under rules that encourage polite anarchy and embolden people who find majority rule a dubious proposition at best."[70]

The Filibuster Part of the challenge in getting the Senate to act collectively is rooted in the Senate's unlimited debate and very open amendment process. Unless restricted by a unanimous consent agreement, senators can speak as long as they want and offer any amendment to a bill, even if it isn't directly related to the underlying bill. Debate may be cut off only if a supermajority of 60 senators agree in a process known as invoking **cloture**. Therefore, one senator can stop any bill by threatening to talk the bill to death if 40 of their colleagues agree. This practice is known as a **filibuster**. The filibuster strengthens the hand of the minority party in the Senate, giving it veto power over legislation unless the majority party has 60 senators who support a bill.

cloture
A procedure through which the Senate can limit the amount of time spent debating a bill (cutting off a filibuster) if a supermajority of 60 senators agree.

filibuster
A tactic used by senators to block a bill by continuing to hold the floor and speak—under the Senate rule of unlimited debate—until the bill's supporters back down.

Before the 1960s, senators really did hold the floor for hours by reading from the phone book or reciting recipes. The late senator Strom Thurmond of South Carolina holds the record of 24 hours and 18 minutes of continuous talking. Today it is rare for a filibuster to tie up Senate business, since a senator's threat to filibuster a bill is usually enough to take the bill off the legislative agenda. If the bill is actually filibustered, it goes on a separate legislative track so that it does not bring the rest of the business of the Senate to a halt. Alternatively, if supporters of the bill think they have enough votes, they can invoke cloture to stop the filibuster and bring the bill to the floor for a vote. Frustrated over repeated Republican filibusters on President Obama's nominations to federal courts and agencies, Senate Democrats in November 2013 removed the filibuster for all presidential nominations, except those to the Supreme Court.[71] When Democrats filibustered Trump's nomination of Neil Gorsuch to the Supreme Court in April 2017, the Senate changed the rules again to allow Supreme Court nominees to be confirmed by a simple majority vote.[72]

Because of the practice of unlimited debate in the Senate, much of its business is conducted under unanimous consent agreements by which senators agree to adhere to time limits on debate and amendments. However, because these are literally *unanimous*

Calls for the Senate to change the rules and allow regular legislation to be passed by a simple majority have increased in recent years. Opponents of the filibuster argue that its consistent use has made the Senate less representative of Americans' political beliefs and policy priorities.

hold
An objection to considering a measure on the Senate floor.

reconciliation
Reconciliation allows for expedited consideration of certain tax, spending, and debt limit legislation. The main advantage of the procedure is that reconciliation legislation is not subject to filibusters in the Senate and therefore may be passed with simple majorities in the House and Senate.

agreements, a single senator can obstruct the business of the chamber by issuing a **hold** on the bill or presidential nomination. This practice is often a bargaining tool to extract concessions from the bill's supporters, but sometimes, especially late in a session when time gets tight, a hold can actually kill a bill by removing it from the active agenda.

One way that the Senate has circumvented the filibuster is through the **reconciliation** process, which was established in 1974 to make the budget process more efficient. If reconciliation legislation is related to budget matters and does not increase the deficit outside the specified time period (and satisfies several other rules), it may be passed with a simple majority vote in the House and Senate. The process was initially used for budget items, but in recent years it has been used to pass other controversial bills that threatened to be derailed by a filibuster. For example, the Affordable Care Act (ACA) was passed in 2010 through reconciliation, and the process was also used for various attempts to repeal the ACA (the most recent attempt, in 2017, failed in the Senate by a single vote). It was also used to pass the 2017 Tax Cuts and Jobs Act, the 2021 COVID Relief bill, and the 2022 Inflation Reduction Act (that provided $370 billion for clean energy and carbon reduction). However, reconciliation may only be used once every fiscal year, so party leaders must be strategic in how they use it.

closed rules
Conditions placed on a legislative debate by the House Rules Committee prohibiting amendments to a bill.

open rules
Conditions placed on a legislative debate by the House Rules Committee allowing relevant amendments to a bill.

modified rules
Conditions placed on a legislative debate by the House Rules Committee allowing certain amendments to a bill while barring others.

House Rules In contrast to the Senate, the House is a more orderly, although complex, institution. The Rules Committee exerts great control over the legislative process, especially on major legislation, through special rules that govern the nature of debate on a bill. There are three general types of rules: **closed rules** do not allow any amendments to the bill, **open rules** allow any germane amendments, and **modified rules** allow some specific amendments but not others. House leadership has used closed and modified rules much more aggressively in recent years. Twenty-five years ago, as many as two-thirds of bills would come to the floor under an open rule. From May 2016 through January 2023, there has not been a single bill considered under an open rule. While the current Republican leadership has allowed some amendments to be offered from the floor, open rules are still rare.[73] Once a special rule is adopted, general debate is tightly controlled by the floor managers. Amendments are considered under a five-minute rule, but this rule is routinely bent as members offer phantom "pro forma" amendments to, for example, "strike the last word" or "strike the requisite number of words." This means that the member is not really offering an amendment but simply going through the formal procedure of offering one in order to get an additional five minutes to talk about the amendment.

These descriptions of the two chambers show that although the Senate is formally committed to unlimited debate, senators often voluntarily place limits on themselves through unanimous consent, which makes the Senate operate much more like the House. Similarly, although the House has very strict rules concerning debate and amendments, there are ways of bending those rules to make the House operate a bit more like the potentially freewheeling Senate.

"Why Should I Care?"

Otto von Bismarck, the Prussian statesman of the late nineteenth century, famously said, "Laws are like sausages; it is better not to see them being made." Indeed, the legislative process may be messy, but knowledge of how laws are made is important both for being an effective legislator and for being a good democratic citizen. Understanding how a bill becomes a law, seeing the various stages of the process, and recognizing the various veto points at which a bill may die all help put into context the simplistic complaints about gridlock and conflict. Now that you have a better understanding of the legislative process, you should have a stronger basis for evaluating what Congress is doing.

Oversight

DESCRIBE HOW CONGRESS ENSURES THAT THE BUREAUCRACY IMPLEMENTS POLICIES CORRECTLY

Once a bill becomes a law, Congress plays another crucial role by overseeing the implementation of the law to make sure the bureaucracy interprets it as Congress intended. Other motivations drive the oversight process as well, such as the desire to gain publicity that may help in the reelection quest or to embarrass a president of the opposite party. For example, in 2015 Republicans used their oversight powers to call attention to Hillary Clinton's use of private servers for her work-related email as secretary of state and the way that she handled the attack on the U.S. embassy in Benghazi. Similarly, when Democrats investigated (and eventually impeached) President Trump for withholding of funds to Ukraine until its president promised to investigate the Bidens (refer to Chapter 2), there were serious concerns about an abuse of executive power that undermined national security.[74] While these hearings were, at least in part, politically motivated, the most important motivation for oversight is to ensure that laws are implemented properly.

There are several mechanisms that Congress may use to accomplish this goal (also refer to Chapter 13). First, the bluntest instrument is the power of the purse. If members of Congress think an agency is not properly implementing their programs, they can simply cut off the funds to that agency. However, this approach to punishment is rarely used because it often eliminates good aspects of the agency along with the bad.

Second, Congress can hold hearings and investigations. By summoning administration officials and agency heads to a public hearing, Congress can use the media spotlight to focus attention on problems within the bureaucracy or on issues that have been overlooked. For example, the House Oversight Committee has investigated Russian interference in the 2016 election, violations of the emoluments clause by President Trump (with a focus on the hotel he owned in Washington, D.C.), the process for providing security clearances, immigration policy, and voting rights.[75] That same committee called Hunter Biden to testify, in hopes of finding incriminating evidence involving his father.[76] This type of oversight is known as "fire alarm oversight"—that is, members wait until there is a crisis before they spring to action.[77] It is in contrast to "police patrol" oversight, which involves constant vigilance in overseeing the bureaucracy. For example, House Democrats were very concerned about the executive branch interfering with the Justice Department, dating back to President Trump's firing of FBI director James Comey in 2017 and Attorney General William Barr's handling of the Mueller report, which documented Russian interference in the 2016 election and possible obstruction of justice by the White House. Tensions between Democrats in Congress and the Justice Department continued throughout Trump's impeachment trial into the summer of 2020, with congressional hearings on prosecutorial independence.[78] The Select Committee to Investigate the January 6th Attack is another example of this type of oversight.[79] Of the two, fire alarm oversight is far more common because Congress does not have the resources to constantly monitor the entire bureaucracy.

Finally, the Senate exercises specific control over other executive functions through its constitutional responsibilities to provide "advice and consent" on presidential appointments and approval of treaties. The Senate typically defers to the president on these matters, but it may assert its power, especially when constituent interests are involved. Two current examples would be the Senate's increasing skepticism about free-trade agreements negotiated by the president's trade representatives and the Senate's holds on presidential nominations. President Biden had hundreds of his nominees held up by the Senate in his first year, giving him an overall confirmation rate of only 41 percent, the lowest in decades. However, by 2024, 91 percent of his nominees had been confirmed.[80]

The ultimate in congressional oversight is the process of removing the president, vice president, other civil officers, or federal judges through impeachment. The House and Senate share this power: the House issues articles of impeachment, which outline the charges against the official, and the Senate conducts the trial of the impeached officials. Three presidents have been impeached: Andrew Johnson in the controversy over Reconstruction after the Civil War, Bill Clinton over the scandal involving White House intern Monica Lewinsky, and Donald Trump twice, first for the abuse of power and obstruction of Congress concerning his interactions with Ukraine and then for his role in the January 6 insurrection. However, none of them were convicted and removed by the Senate. When Republicans took control of the House in 2023, they initiated investigations of Homeland Security Secretary Alejandro Mayorkas (then eventually impeached him, but the Senate killed the articles of impeachment)[81] and President Biden.[82]

As should be clear from this summary, one important aspect of congressional oversight is to serve as a check on the executive branch. The boundaries of the system of checks and balances could have been fundamentally altered during the Trump presidency because of his unprecedented claims of absolute executive immunity from congressional subpoenas. There were three sets of cases involving Trump's taxes and financial records, White House Counsel Donald McGahn's testimony in the first impeachment inquiry, and access to White House communication concerning the January 6 insurrection. In June 2020, the Supreme Court ruled 7–2 against the president in both financial cases (one concerned subpoenas from House committees for Trump's tax records and the other from the Manhattan district attorney for financial and tax records). Chief Justice John Roberts wrote the majority opinions, concluding, "In our system, the public has a right to every man's evidence. . . . Since the founding of the Republic, every man has included the President of the United States."[83] In the McGahn case, the White House was able to run out the clock until after the election, so the issue was never resolved.[84] The most significant ruling was the Supreme Court's 8–1 decision early in 2022 to uphold an appeals court ruling and allow the National Archive to turn over White House communications that Trump had been trying to keep from the House Select Committee to Investigate the January 6th Attack.[85] While the limits of claims of executive privilege still have not been defined by the Supreme Court, it is clear that that balance has tipped toward Congress in the last two years.

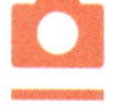

Four Capitol officers testified before Congress about the January 6, 2021, insurrection, during which the building was stormed and many officers were attacked by a mob trying to stop the certification of Biden's election. They described being beaten, shocked with their own tasers, and sprayed with wasp repellent.

Unpacking the Conflict

Considering all that we've learned in this chapter about how Congress works, let's return to our discussion of DACA. Why is it so hard for Congress to compromise on issues that appear to be consensual, like protecting the Dreamers? How can members of Congress best serve the collective interests of the nation while also representing their local constituents?

Although the details of the legislative process and the institutions of Congress can be complicated, the basic explanations for members' behavior are quite straightforward when viewed in terms of the trade-off between responsiveness and responsibility. Members of Congress want to be reelected, so they are generally quite responsive to constituents' interests. They spend considerable time on casework—meeting with people in their district and delivering benefits for their district. At the same time, members are motivated to be responsible—to rise above local interests and attend to the nation's best interests. The conflict between these two impulses can create contradictory policies that contribute to Congress's image problem. For example, the chapter opener discussed the difficulty of reaching a compromise on DACA. Both parties and the president appeared to want to help the Dreamers, but conservatives in the Republican Party were strongly opposed to providing any path to citizenship. Clearly, the country as a whole benefits from the economic and social contributions of the Dreamers, but some members of Congress responded to their political base by opposing a compromise. The tension between responsible lawmaking and responsiveness to constituents is evident on many issues.

Considering members' motivations is crucial to understanding how Congress functions, but their behavior is also constrained by the institutions in which they operate. When moderate House Republicans were on the verge of forcing a vote on the Dreamers during the Trump presidency, the Senate Republican Leader stood firm in his opposition, saying he would not bring a bill to a vote in the Senate that did not have President Trump's approval. So ultimately, it did not matter that the House was able to find a compromise solution. In this instance, party leadership served as a constraint. Then when Democrats regained unified control of government in 2021, they were stymied on the issue by the filibuster in the Senate (recall, the Senate parliamentarian ruled that Democrats couldn't use the reconciliation process with the Dreamers, which would have required only 50 votes to pass instead of 60, because it wasn't centrally related to the budget).

On the more positive side, when they aren't obstructing legislation, parties in Congress can provide coherence to the legislative agenda and help structure voting patterns on bills. The committee system can provide a positive vehicle for lawmaking as an important source of expertise and information, and it provides a platform from which members can take positions and claim credit. Rules and norms constrain the nature of debate and the legislative process. Although these institutions shape members' behavior, it is important to remember that members can also change those rules and institutions. Therefore, Congress has the ability to evolve with changing national conditions and demands from voters, groups, and the president. For example, in 2022, Congress managed to pass the first major gun control law in 28 years, the largest spending bill ever to fight climate change, a major infrastructure bill, protection for same-sex marriage, and a bill that provides cheaper drug prescriptions despite the narrow party margins in both chambers. However, with the return of divided government in 2023, Congress was on pace to pass the fewest bills since at least the 1920s (as of this writing, only 51 laws have been enacted; the previous low was 284 in 2011–2013).[86]

In this context, much of what Congress does can be understood in terms of the conflicts inherent in politics. As we have seen, even on consensual issues like DACA, conflict and political strategy may doom the common ground that is within reach. The extremes on the right and left did not want to compromise on DACA: the former viewed any path to citizenship as amnesty, and the latter wanted a "clean bill" with no money for the wall or other changes to immigration policy. There was a huge majority in the middle that could have passed a DACA bill with some money for border security and the wall, but President Trump and Republicans wanted to leverage the consensual issue of DACA to enact the broader immigration policies they favored. Their approach did not work, and we got deadlock instead. Congress does not always live up to the expectations of being the "first branch" of government, but it tries to do the best it can to balance the conflicting pressures it faces.

"What's Your Take?"

Does Congress do a reasonable job of representing both national and local interests?

If not, how should Congress change?

CHECK YOUR UNDERSTANDING

"Why Should I Care?"

Congressional legislation affects our lives in countless ways. But the lawmaking process can be mystifying to the uninitiated. Bills go through committees to be amended and discussed by members of Congress with expertise on the issue, but not all bills make it out of committee to be voted on. Then differences between House and Senate versions have to be worked out. Then bills successfully voted on in both chambers are subject to the president's veto. If a bill does become law, Congress has to make sure that the bureaucracy is implementing it the way that it intended.

Keeping all of that in mind, whom is Congress representing with its lawmaking? Should members of Congress be responsive to their constituency or be responsible lawmakers who vote against their voters' desires on policies that may be necessary (such as raising taxes or cutting spending on a popular program)? These negotiations can result in gridlock, especially on bills that have practical and partisan implications. In addition, disagreement on proposed legislation becomes even more likely when we consider that members of Congress are more polarized now than ever. Consider your members of Congress: Would you say they are liberal or conservative? Would you consider yourself to be liberal or conservative? Does your member represent you?

Since members of Congress are concerned with reelection, their stances have to be defensible to their constituency whether they are being responsive to their constituents or the nation as a whole. It is no wonder why people love their members of Congress and hate Congress as an institution. Members of Congress try to be responsive to the needs and demands of their constituency even at the expense of passing laws. Take a look at the voting records of your members of Congress. Would you say that you "like" how they have voted on legislation that is important to you? Are they being responsive to your needs and demands as a voter?

While voting on bills and sitting on committees are important parts of the work that members of Congress do, it is not all that they do. Members of Congress maintain a connection to their district or state in a number of ways. Considering these questions might help you think about your elected representatives in a different way. Incumbents are usually reelected, but not always. It is up to voters like you to keep them accountable for their decision-making.

1. Why does partisan gerrymandering contribute to the public distrust and disapproval of Congress?

a It reflects the partisan-driven appropriations process of Congress.

b Gerrymandering reflects the significant undercounts of historically marginalized groups.

c Technology has created the ability to draw boundaries with remarkably specific detail.

d Voters are drawn into districts where the outcome is often predetermined.

2. What is one result of descriptive representation in Congress?

a Constituents report higher levels of satisfaction with representatives who are of their same racial or ethnic background.

b Representatives focus purely on the interests of others who share their racial or ethnic background.

c As descriptive representation increases, so does the portion of representatives acting primarily as trustees.

d Trust in government has declined.

3. In the eyes of the Founders, the U.S. House of Representatives was more __________ than the U.S. Senate.

a homogenous and deliberative

b responsive and passionate

c partisan and professional

d equitable and collaborative

4. Someone arguing that Congress has become more responsive to the public might try to support their argument with which claim?

a Members of Congress are more likely to make time for local media stations than for national networks.

b Modern congressional members are more likely to stand on their principles than seek compromise with members from other parties.

c The number of personal staff members in congressional offices has grown significantly over the last 50 years.

d Congressional committees have become more open to receiving testimony from members of the public.

5. In December 2020, President Trump threatened to veto a defense spending bill being considered by Congress if the bill didn't include a repeal of protections for social media companies from being sued for the content posted on their platforms. What is it about his veto threat that makes it an important consideration in the legislative process?

- **a** Presidents only use veto threats to force negotiations when members of the opposite party control one or both chambers of Congress.
- **b** Congress must achieve a supermajority in support of legislation in order to overcome presidential vetoes.
- **c** Veto threats are a formal structure through which presidents propose legislation or legislative amendments.
- **d** Congressional leaders use veto threats as an opportunity to rally support behind a piece of legislation.

6. The overwhelming majority of the critical work in the legislative process, including the filtering of most proposed bills, occurs at what point?

- **a** Assignment to committee by leader of the chamber
- **b** Consideration in committee
- **c** Floor debate
- **d** Referral to the president

7. Which of the following is the best real-world example of how Congress carries out its oversight function in relation to the other branches?

- **a** The Joint Committee on Taxation assisted the House Ways and Means Committee in drafting the 2017 Tax Cuts and Jobs Act.
- **b** The Senate Environment and Public Works Committee questioned ecologists about the benefits and costs of potentially adding new animals to the Endangered Species List.
- **c** The House Appropriations Committee heard testimony from the Joint Chiefs of Staff about budgetary needs of the armed forces.
- **d** The Select Committee to Investigate the January 6 attack on the Capitol was convened.

8. Which of the following best describes the process of impeachment?

- **a** The president nominates senators to be removed through a two-thirds vote in the House.
- **b** The Senate and House collaborate to remove low-level appointed bureaucrats.
- **c** The House issues articles of impeachment, and the Senate conducts the trial of the impeached official.
- **d** Federal judges issue articles of impeachment, and Congress votes to remove the impeached official.

Use INQUIZITIVE to help you study and master this material.

12

The Presidency

Are there limits on presidential power?

» **"This is when somebody is the President of the United States, the authority is total and that's the way it's got to be. It's total, it's total—and that's the way it's got to be. And the governors know that."[1]**
President Donald Trump, in a COVID-19 briefing, April 13, 2020

« **"I will be speaking to all 50 governors very shortly and I will then be authorizing each individual governor of each individual state to implement a reopening and a very powerful reopening plan of their state at a time and in a manner as most appropriate."[2]**
President Donald Trump, in a COVID-19 briefing, April 14, 2020

Is the power of the president "total"? What powers does the Constitution grant the president? The COVID-19 pandemic raised many questions about the power of the presidency, during both the Trump and Biden administrations, and can explain why President Biden's approval rating has declined in the face of inaction on key policy issues he spoke about while campaigning and during his first two State of the Union addresses, including inflation, rising gasoline costs, and new domestic programs.

Outlining the major achievements of Donald Trump's and Joe Biden's years in office illustrates the immense power of the presidency. Trump commanded the most powerful military forces on Earth—and pushed through budget increases that will make them even stronger. Working with Republicans in Congress, Trump enacted the largest tax cut in American history. His directives transformed federal policy in areas such as immigration, the environment, and federal regulations.[3] Similarly, Biden enacted a large infrastructure package, COVID-19 assistance, and a package of climate change and renewable energy programs. Biden also provided massive defense and reconstruction funds to Ukraine. His appointees in the bureaucracy revised regulations on power plant emissions and many other areas. And both men were the symbol of the United States, and the lead representative of the nation to other countries.

At the same time, both Trump's and Biden's presidencies illustrate the limits of presidential power. As the quotes above illustrate, Trump was forced to acknowledge that he could not order state governors to do whatever he wanted. Although Trump campaigned on promises to repeal Obamacare and build a wall on the Mexican border, he did not succeed. During 2022 and 2023, Joe Biden could do little to reduce price inflation. Biden also had to wait six months in 2023–2024 for members of Congress to enact a large aid package for Ukraine, Israel, and Taiwan.

Just like the other 44 presidents before them, Biden and Trump have often been constrained by factors out of their control, from disagreements with other members

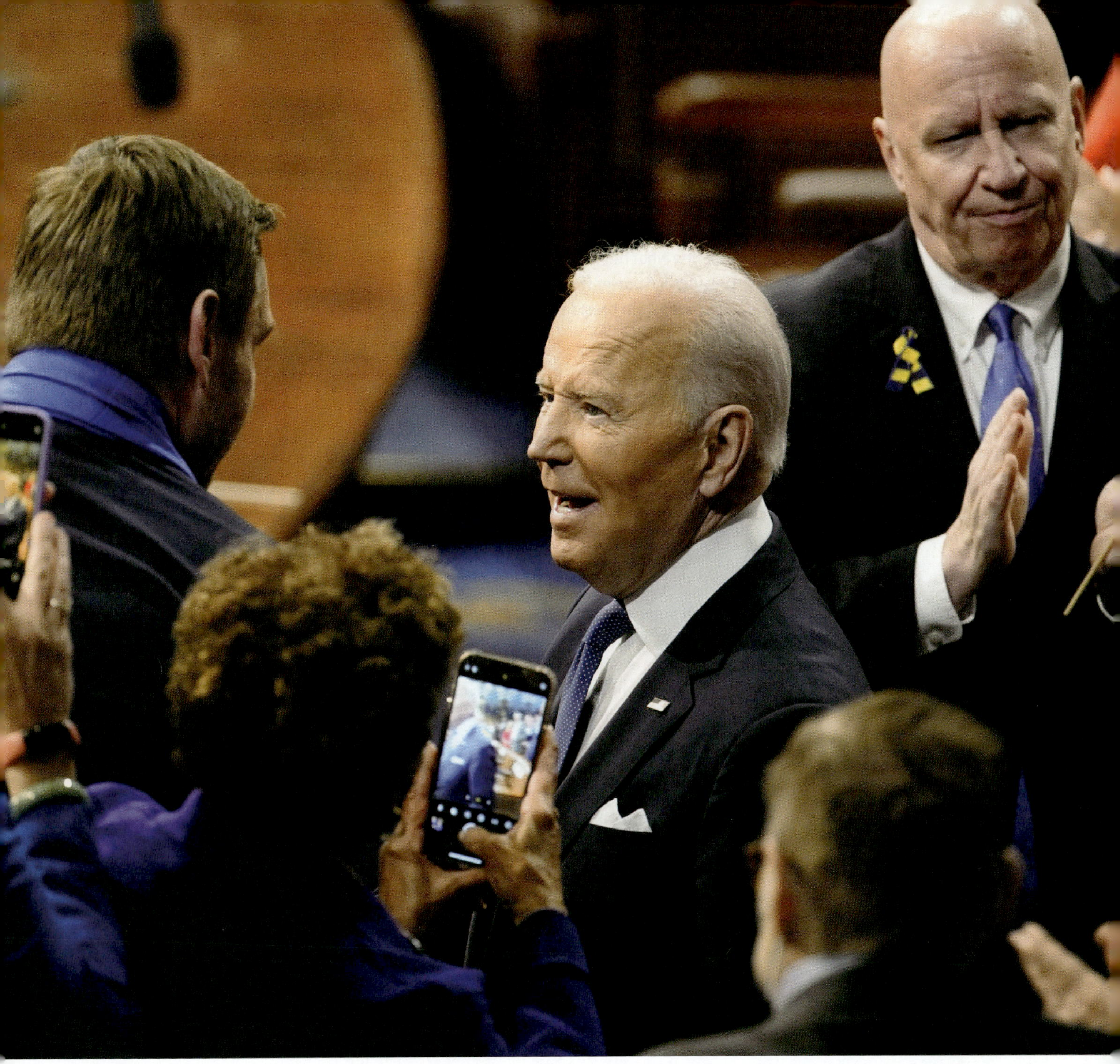

CHAPTER GOALS

Trace the evolution of presidential power (pp. 458–461)

Describe the constitutional and statutory powers of the president today (pp. 462–475)

Explain how the Executive Office of the President, the vice president, and the Cabinet help the president (pp. 476–479)

Explain how modern presidents have become even more powerful (pp. 479–488) of the federal government to the sometimes-fickle opinions of the American public. The fact is that the president is but one actor in a complex political system tasked with achieving often-impossible goals. This truth has constrained all presidents, not just Biden and Trump. And it will likely be true in Trump's second term, as well.

The examples of Biden and Trump raise important questions about where presidential power comes from and what limits there are on its exercise. Did Trump redefine what makes a successful president—or a failed one? What can we learn about presidential power from Biden's time in office? What factors distinguish presidential successes from presidential failures?

The development of presidential power

As we consider the history of America's 46 presidents, four facts stand out: (1) Presidents matter. Their actions have had profound consequences for the nation, in both domestic and foreign policy. (2) Presidents get their power from a variety of sources, from provisions of the Constitution to their management of the actions taken by the executive branch of government. (3) Presidential power has increased over time, not because of changes in the Constitution but because of America's growth as a nation, its emergence as a dominant actor in international politics, the expansion of the federal government, and various acts of legislation that have given new authority to the president. (4) There are sharp limits to presidential power. Presidents are often forced to compromise or abandon their plans in the face of public, congressional, or foreign opposition. It is also important to note that while all 46 presidents have been men, and almost all of them have been White, breaking this regularity is only a matter of time. In recent years, in addition to the election of Barack Obama in 2008 and 2012, the groundbreaking presidential campaign of Hillary Clinton in 2016, and the election of Kamala Harris as vice president in 2020, more women as well as members of historically marginalized communities—including Senators Cory Booker (D-NJ), Elizabeth Warren (D-MA), Amy Klobuchar (D-MN), and Tim Scott (R-SC), and former South Carolina governor Nikki Haley—have been credible contenders for their party's presidential nominations.[4] In 2020, Pete Buttigieg, then the mayor of South Bend, Indiana, and now the secretary of Transportation, became the first openly gay presidential candidate.

These lessons are particularly important as we consider the presidencies of Joe Biden and Donald Trump. Trump's background and behavior in office were often described as being radically different from those of past presidents. Even so, Trump has had to contend with the same limits on presidential power faced by his predecessors, including voters' high expectations; unexpected events such as pandemics, natural disasters, or military actions by other countries; conflicts within his own party as well as between Republicans and Democrats in Congress; and differences between his goals and those held by federal bureaucrats who implement his decisions. Joe Biden faced the same constraints. Understanding how the accomplishments of past presidents were shaped by these constraints can help us begin to analyze and understand these two individuals and their presidencies.

Early years through World War I

George Washington remains, for many Americans, the presidential ideal—a leader whose crucial domestic and foreign policy decisions shaped the growth of America's democracy.

Since the early years of the Republic, presidents' actions have had profound consequences for the nation. Presidents George Washington, John Adams, and Thomas Jefferson forged compromises on domestic issues such as choosing a permanent location for the nation's capital, establishing the federal courts, and financing the government. Presidents Andrew Jackson and Martin Van Buren were instrumental in forming the Democratic Party and its local party organizations.[5]

In addition, early presidents made important foreign policy decisions. For example, the Monroe Doctrine issued by President James Monroe in 1823 stated that America would remain neutral in wars involving European nations and that these nations must cease attempts to colonize or occupy areas in North and South America.[6] Presidents John Tyler and James Polk oversaw the admission of the huge territory of Texas into the Union following the Mexican-American War, as well as the acquisition of land that later became Oregon, Washington, Idaho, and parts of Montana and Wyoming.[7]

Presidents also played key roles in the conflict over slavery. President Millard Fillmore's support helped enact the Compromise of 1850, which limited slavery in California, and Franklin Pierce supported the Kansas-Nebraska Act, which regulated slavery in those territories. And, of course, Abraham Lincoln, who helped form the Republican Party in the 1850s, played a transformative role during the Civil War. His orders raised the huge Union army, and as commander in chief he directed the conduct of the bloody war that ultimately ended slavery and brought the southern states back into the Union.[8]

During the late 1800s and early 1900s, presidents were instrumental in federal responses to the nation's rapid expansion and industrialization.[9] The country's growing size and economy generated conflict over which services the federal government should provide to citizens and the extent to which the government should regulate individual and corporate behavior.[10] Presidents advocated for legislation that created new federal agencies as well as new presidential powers and responsibilities. For example, Republican president Theodore Roosevelt used the Sherman Antitrust Act to break up the Northern Securities Company, a mammoth nationwide railroad trust. Roosevelt also expanded federal conservation programs and increased the power of the Interstate Commerce Commission to regulate businesses. Democratic president Woodrow Wilson further increased the government's role in managing the economy through his support of the Clayton Antitrust Act, the Federal Reserve Act, the first federal income tax, and legislation banning child labor.[11]

As these examples illustrate, presidential power has grown over time as the federal government has expanded. The president and members of the executive branch have obtained new regulatory powers over corporations and individual Americans. Presidents have also proposed new policies in response to shifts in public opinion. Moreover, the power of the presidency grew around the turn of the century and thereafter due to the actions of presidents, particularly Roosevelt and Wilson, who firmly believed that the presidency was the most important federal office.

Yet the limits of presidential power were also evident during this era—for example, in Wilson's foreign policy initiatives. Although he campaigned in the 1916 election on a promise to keep America out of World War I, Wilson ultimately ordered American troops to fight on the side of the Allies. After the war, Wilson offered a peace plan that proposed (1) reshaping the borders of European countries in order to mitigate future conflicts; (2) creating an international organization, the League of Nations, to prevent future conflicts; and (3) taking other measures to encourage free trade and democracy.[12] However, America's allies rejected most of Wilson's proposals and the Senate refused to allow American participation in the League of Nations.

The Great Depression through the present

Presidential actions defined the government's response to the Great Depression—the worldwide economic collapse in the late 1920s and 1930s marked by high unemployment, huge stock market declines, and many bank failures. After winning the 1932 presidential election, Democrat Franklin Roosevelt and his staff began reshaping American government to pull the country out of the Depression. Roosevelt's New Deal reforms created many federal agencies that helped individual Americans and imposed many new corporate regulations.[13] This expansion continued under Roosevelt's successors. Even Republican Dwight Eisenhower, whose party had initially opposed many New Deal reforms, preserved these changes, created new agencies, and initiated the building of the interstate highway system.[14]

Presidential power also grew as the United States became more involved in the international arena. America was a key player in the Allied coalition against Germany and Japan in World War II, with President Roosevelt leading the negotiation of key agreements with American allies over war aims and the establishment of the United Nations. After the war, through the beginning of the Cold War with the Soviet Union, America's military might, dominant nuclear forces, and overwhelming economic power made it the leader of the free world. Because of this position, postwar presidents such as Harry Truman had enormous influence over the lives of people everywhere.

Presidents were instrumental in the civil rights reforms and expansion of the federal government in the 1960s. With congressional approval, President Lyndon Johnson's administration created a wide range of domestic programs, such as the Department of Housing and Urban Development, Medicare, Medicaid, and federal funding for schools. The job of enacting voting rights and civil rights legislation also took place during Johnson's presidency.

Both Johnson and his successor, Richard Nixon, directed America's involvement in the Vietnam War, with the goal of forcing the North Vietnamese to abandon their plans to unify North and South Vietnam. But presidential efforts in Vietnam did not meet with success. Despite enormous deployments of American forces and the deaths

Presidents throughout the twentieth century expanded the power of the office in terms of both domestic and foreign policy making. President Franklin Delano Roosevelt *(left)* called on the public to support his New Deal social programs through his signature "fireside chat" radio broadcasts. President Ronald Reagan *(right)* was instrumental in negotiating and executing numerous arms reduction agreements with the Soviet Union, then led by Mikhail Gorbachev.

of more than 58,000 American soldiers, Nixon eventually signed an agreement that allowed American troops to leave but did not end the conflict, which concluded only after a North Vietnamese victory in 1975.

The two presidents immediately after Nixon, Republican Gerald Ford and Democrat Jimmy Carter, faced the worst economic conditions since the Great Depression, largely due to increased energy prices. Both presidents offered plans to reduce unemployment and inflation, restore economic growth, and enhance domestic energy sources. However, their efforts were largely unsuccessful, which became a critical factor in their failed reelection bids. The experiences of Ford and Carter highlight that presidents often face situations for which there are no good solutions. Given the realities of the American economy in the 1970s, it is hard to imagine policies that would have improved on Ford and Carter's performance.

The political and policy importance of presidential actions continued to increase during the presidency of Republican Ronald Reagan, despite the fact that he ran on a platform of tax cuts, fewer regulations, and smaller government. Reagan and his staff also negotiated important arms control agreements with the Soviet Union. Reagan's successor, Republican George H. W. Bush, led American and international participation in the Persian Gulf War during 1990 and 1991, which succeeded in removing Iraqi forces from Kuwait with minimal American casualties.

Democrat Bill Clinton's presidency was marked by passage of the North American Free Trade Agreement, welfare reform, arms control agreements, and successful peacekeeping efforts by U.S. troops in Haiti and the Balkans. His presidency also was distinguished by having one of the longest periods of economic growth in U.S. history and the first balanced budgets since the 1960s. President George W. Bush won congressional approval of his tax cuts and education reforms, but he is remembered for managing America's response to the September 11 attacks, including the wars in Iraq and Afghanistan.

President Obama secured several notable changes in domestic and foreign policy, including the enactment of health care reform, economic stimulus legislation, and new financial regulations. However, Obama had to compromise on many of these policies, and in areas such as immigration reform and gun control he was largely unsuccessful. Obama's experience highlights a fundamental limit on presidential power: in many areas, presidents require congressional support to achieve their policy goals.

In his first term, Donald Trump had considerable success in forcing policy and regulatory changes through administrative actions. However, in many cases (and particularly after Democrats regained a House majority in 2019), his plans were blocked by lack of public support and the failure to build majorities in the House and Senate. In many ways, the same phrases can be used to describe the first four years of Joe Biden's presidency—notable successes, but also notable failures. No one would think these two individuals have much in common—why are their presidencies so similar?

After presidents leave office, their performance is often evaluated as though their powers and foresight during their term had been unlimited. The history of presidential successes and failures reminds us that, in fact, presidents are often constrained by circumstances. Many of the problems past presidents have faced were totally unanticipated or had no good solutions. Other times, attempts to address national needs failed because of congressional resistance. Thus, before we make judgments about presidential performance, we need to understand the president's job and the resources available to accomplish it.

DESCRIBE THE CONSTITUTIONAL AND STATUTORY POWERS OF THE PRESIDENT TODAY

constitutional authority (presidential)
Powers derived from the provisions of the Constitution that outline the president's role in government.

The president's job description

This section describes the president's **constitutional authority** (powers derived from the provisions of the Constitution) and **statutory authority** (powers that come from laws), as well as the additional capabilities that presidents derive from their position as the head of the executive branch of government. Nuts & Bolts 12.1 summarizes the president's constitutional and statutory powers. As the box indicates, some presidential powers arise from the Constitution only, and others derive from a combination of constitutional and statutory authority. Questions about the sources and limits of presidential authority have bedeviled political scientists for several generations. In fact, political scientist Richard Neustadt in his book *Presidential Power* argued that the main source was a president's power to persuade people to do what the president wanted.[15] Building on more recent research, our aim is to show how the provisions that define presidential authority operate in modern-day American politics: what kinds of opportunities and constraints they create for the current president and future holders of the office.

NUTS & BOLTS 12.1

Presidential Powers

Power	Source of power
Head of government, head of state (vesting clause)	Constitutional authority
Implementation of laws ("faithful execution")	Constitutional and statutory authority
Executive orders and similar directives (rare)	Constitutional and statutory authority
Administration of executive branch	Constitutional authority
Nominations and appointments to executive branch and judiciary	Constitutional and statutory authority
Commander in chief of armed forces	Constitutional authority
Negotiation of treaties and executive agreements	Constitutional and statutory authority
Veto of congressional actions	Constitutional authority
Presidential pardons	Constitutional authority
Other ceremonial powers	Constitutional authority
Executive privilege	Other
Recommendation of spending levels and other legislative initiatives	Other

Source: Compiled by the authors.

"Why Should I Care?"

The question of where a president's power comes from matters because it affects the extent of the power, and whether it can be taken away or blocked by other actors in American politics.

Head of the executive branch

A president's responsibilities and the source of presidential power begin with the constitutional responsibilities of the office. The Constitution's **vesting clause**—"The executive Power shall be vested in a President of the United States of America"—makes the president the **head of government**, or the leader of the executive branch, as well as the **head of state**, or the symbolic and political representative of the country. The precise meaning of the vesting clause has been debated for more than 200 years. Presidents and their supporters argue for an expansive meaning, while their opponents counter that the clause is so vague as to be meaningless. These debates are an important clue that presidential power is only partially due to specific constitutional grants of authority—some of it comes from how each president interprets less concrete statements such as the vesting clause.

The Constitution also places the president in charge of the implementation of laws, saying "he shall take Care that the Laws be faithfully executed." Sometimes the implementation of a law is nearly automatic, as was the case with the 2020 and 2021 COVID-19 assistance packages that provided direct cash payments to most Americans. In this case, all the president needed to do to implement the directive was to ask Treasury bureaucrats to send the payments, either by direct deposit or by mail.

statutory authority (presidential)
Powers derived from laws enacted by Congress that add to the powers given to the president in the Constitution.

vesting clause
Article II, Section 1, of the Constitution, which states: "The executive Power shall be vested in a President of the United States of America," making the president both the head of government and the head of state.

head of government
One role of the president, through which the president has authority over the executive branch.

head of state
One role of the president, through which the president represents the country symbolically and politically.

More commonly, the president's authority to implement the law requires using judgment to translate legislative goals into programs, budgets, and regulations. For example, the assistance packages for Ukraine enacted in 2022, 2023, and 2024 allocated funding but did not specify the precise types or numbers of weapons that were to be sent to Ukraine. All of these provisions were left up to the Department of Defense, giving them and the president considerable discretion to determine what the Ukrainians received. President Biden and senior Defense officials also negotiated with America's allies to determine what they would send, as well, giving the President another way to shape Ukrainian assistance.

Millions of Americans found themselves unemployed in the wake of the COVID-19 pandemic, and small businesses especially suffered, scrambling to find loans and grants to stay open throughout the crisis. As a temporary solution, Presidents Trump and Biden approved stimulus packages that provided cash payments to most Americans, and the secretary of the Treasury made grants and loans to firms to prevent additional layoffs and bankruptcies.

Appointments

The president appoints ambassadors, senior bureaucrats, and members of the federal judiciary, including Supreme Court justices.[16] As the head of the executive branch, the president can appoint individuals to about 8,000 positions, ranging from high-profile jobs such as secretary of state to mundane administrative and secretarial positions. About 1,200 of these appointments—generally high-level positions such as cabinet secretaries—require Senate confirmation. These individuals "serve at the pleasure of the president," meaning that presidents can remove them from their positions whenever they like. Thus, when Donald Trump fired National Security Advisor John Bolton in November 2019, this action was a legitimate exercise of presidential authority, as was Trump's nomination of Robert O'Brien to succeed Bolton.

The president also nominates individuals to fill federal judgeships, including Supreme Court justices, although these nominations require Senate approval in order to take effect. Because these positions are lifetime appointments, they enable the president to put people into positions of power who will remain after the president leaves office. For example, President Biden nominated many justices to federal judgeships during the first two years of his presidency, including Supreme Court associate justice Ketanji Brown Jackson. The full effects of these and future judicial appointments by Biden will not be completely apparent for years to come.

The need for Senate confirmation of the president's appointments is one of the fundamental limits on presidential power. Historically, the Senate has approved virtually all nominees without much debate or controversy, although in recent years senators (particularly Republicans during Obama's presidency) have blocked votes on judicial and agency nominees. In the first two years of Biden's presidency, some of his appointees to executive branch positions were approved only because Vice President Kamala Harris (who is the president of the Senate under the Constitution) voted to break a tie. (After the 2022 midterms, Democrats gained an additional Senate seat, giving them a narrow 51–49 majority.) Presidents can also name individuals to serve as acting cabinet secretaries; these positions do not require Senate confirmation, but the officeholders can serve only for a limited time.[17]

If the Senate is in recess (adjourned for more than three days), the president can make a **recess appointment**, whereby an appointee is temporarily given a position without a Senate vote and holds the office until the beginning of the next congressional session. All presidents make recess appointments, but typically for relatively minor offices and for noncontroversial nominees. For example, when the Republican-controlled Senate refused to vote on President Obama's 2016 Supreme Court nominee, Merrick Garland, it would have been highly unusual (and perhaps unconstitutional) for President Obama to appoint Garland to the Supreme Court via a recess appointment. In any case, the Senate can (and sometimes does) eliminate the possibility of recess appointments by holding brief working sessions as often as needed to ensure that no recess lasts more than three days.

recess appointment
Selection by the president of a person to be an ambassador or the head of a department while the Senate is not in session, thereby bypassing Senate approval. Unless approved by a subsequent Senate vote, recess appointees serve only to the end of the congressional term.

Executive orders

Presidents have the power to issue **executive orders**—that is, proclamations that unilaterally change government policy without subsequent congressional consent[18]—as well as other kinds of orders that change policy, such as National Security Presidential Directives and Presidential Findings (see the How It Works graphic on pp. 466–67). For example, one of President Biden's orders reversed a Trump-era travel ban on citizens from five predominantly Muslim nations. Another imposed a COVID-19 vaccination mandate on employees working for large American corporations. (This mandate was later reversed by a Supreme Court decision.)

executive orders
Proclamations made by the president that change government policy without congressional approval.

The public sees presidents as speechmakers, but it's mostly butt-in-seat work, a continuous cycle of meetings, decisions, and preparation for meetings and decisions. Governing is a lot harder than tweeting.

—Michael Grunwald, Politico reporter

As the What Do the Facts Say? feature on page 465 shows, all presidents issue many executive orders. Most are not consequential, like the annual order that gives federal employees an early dismissal on the last working day before Christmas. But some executive orders implement large changes in federal policy. Lincoln's Emancipation Proclamation was issued as an executive order. Similarly, President Trump issued a series of executive orders that have reduced the number of refugees admitted to the United States each year, from about 70,000 per year during the Obama administration to only about 18,000 in 2019. (This policy was also reversed by the Biden administration, although refugee admissions have not returned to the Obama-era levels and are likely to decline in Trump's second term.)

Executive orders may appear to give the president authority to do whatever the president wants, even in the face of strong opposition from Congress. However, particularly during the first Trump administration, executive orders have been used to signal intentions rather than directly change policy. For example, one of Trump's executive orders directed the Border Patrol to end its "catch and release" policy whereby people caught trying to enter the United States from Mexico illegally were simply escorted back to a border checkpoint and set free. However, the order did not

WHAT DO THE FACTS SAY?

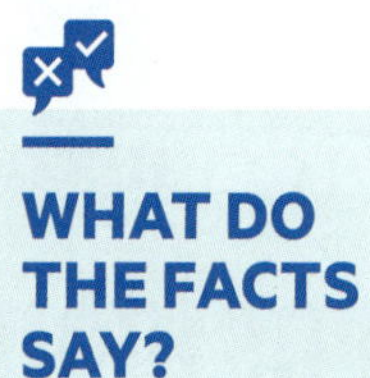

Executive Orders

Many critics (including then–presidential candidate Donald Trump) argued that President Obama issued an unprecedented number of executive orders in order to bypass a Republican Congress that was unsympathetic to his policy proposals. Was Obama an outlier? How did Trump behave in office?

Executive orders issued by recent presidents

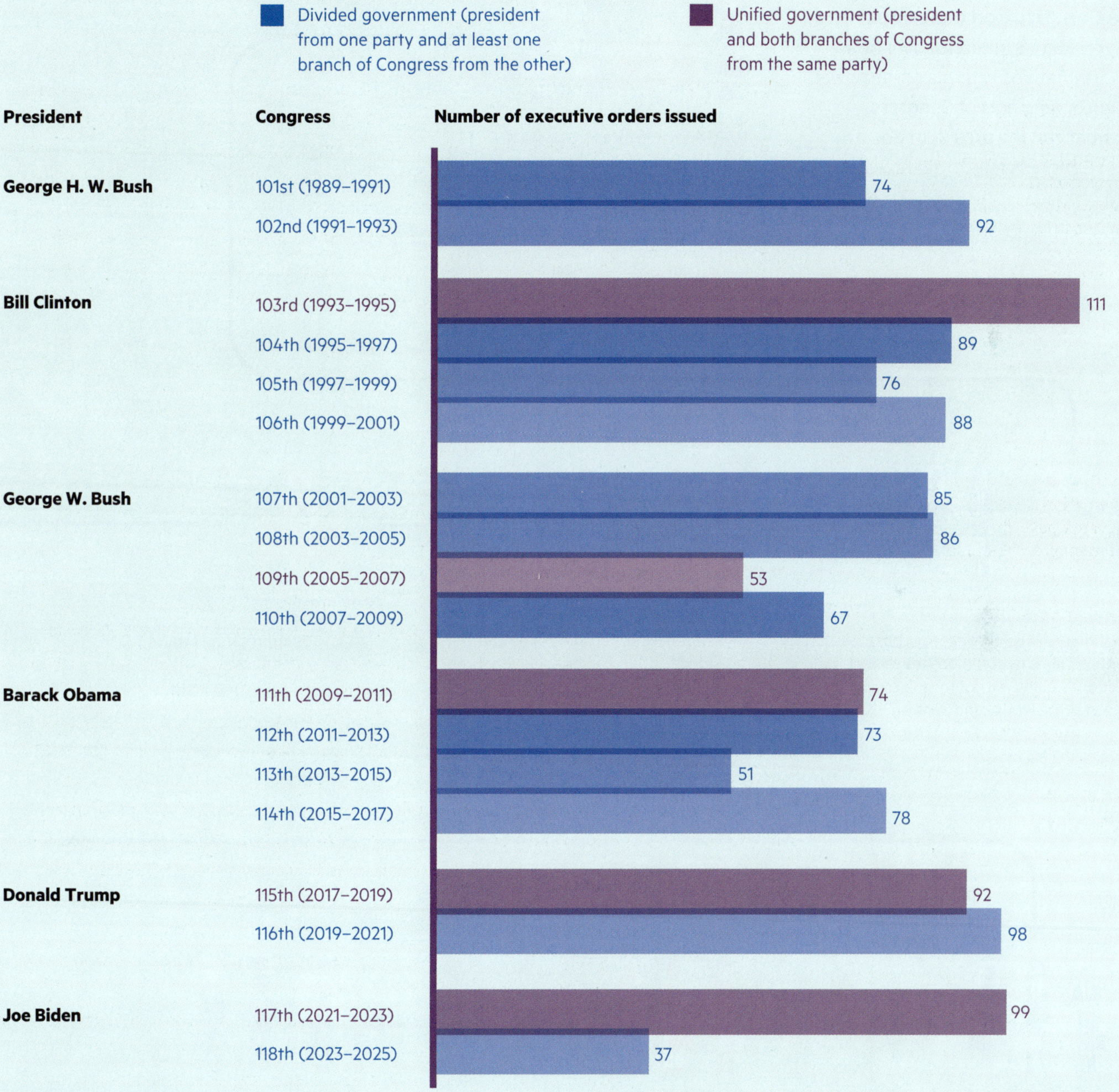

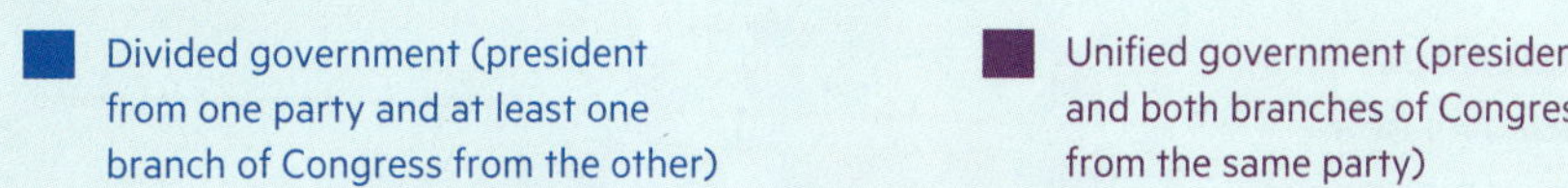

Divided government (president from one party and at least one branch of Congress from the other)
Unified government (president and both branches of Congress from the same party)
President
Congress
Number of executive orders issued
George H. W. Bush
101st (1989–1991)
74
102nd (1991–1993)
92
Bill Clinton
103rd (1993–1995)
111
104th (1995–1997)
89
105th (1997–1999)
76
106th (1999–2001)
88
George W. Bush
107th (2001–2003)
85
108th (2003–2005)
86
109th (2005–2007)
53
110th (2007–2009)
67
Barack Obama
111th (2009–2011)
74
112th (2011–2013)
73
113th (2013–2015)
51
114th (2015–2017)
78
Donald Trump
115th (2017–2019)
92
116th (2019–2021)
98
Joe Biden
117th (2021–2023)
99
118th (2023–2025)
37

Think about it

- **Is there any evidence** that Biden issued more executive orders than his predecessors?
- **Do presidents issue** more executive orders under divided government compared to unified government?

Note: Data current as of November 10, 2024.

Source: "Executive Orders Disposition Tables Index," *Federal Register*, www.federalregister.gov/presidential-documents/executive-orders (accessed 11/10/24).

How it works: in theory

How Presidents Make Policy Outside the Legislative Process

The Constitution describes the president's influence over new policy initiatives in terms of the power to sign or veto acts of Congress. But what can the president do when Congress fails to act how they want?

President + White House staff develop proposals—they talk to the public, members of Congress, interest groups, union and corporation heads, party leaders, and others. Some of these groups initiate contact and submit their own ideas or even fully drafted plans.

President + Congress sometimes find compromise proposals—but other times negotiations reveal that the president's plans will not receive majority support in the House and Senate.

President + White House staff investigate whether some or all of the president's goals can be achieved through executive order or other means.

President issues appropriate orders and directives.

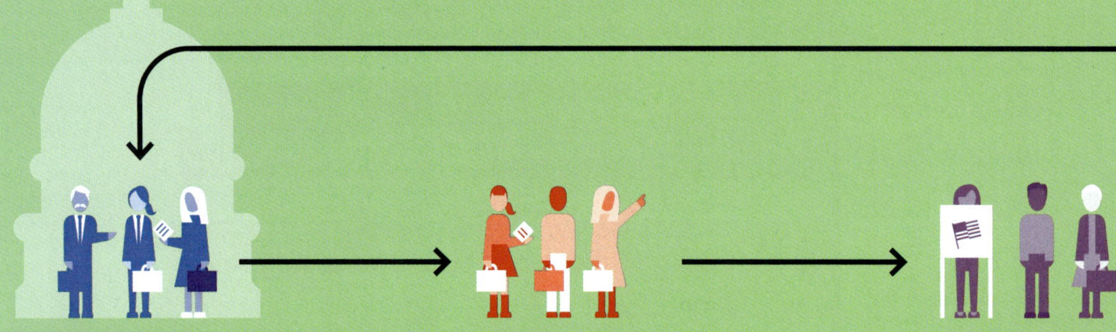

Congress decides whether to enact legislation reversing the president's actions. They need a two-thirds majority in both houses to override an expected presidential veto.

Presidential appointees, assuming congressional attempts to reverse the new policies are unsuccessful, administer implementation of the new policies.

A future president can revise or overturn these new policies because they aren't enacted into law or part of a ratified treaty.

How it works: in practice

Presidential Action and the Paris Agreement on Climate Change

The United States' involvement in the Paris Agreement on Climate Change illustrates how presidents can bypass Congress and initiate meaningful policy change. Members of President Obama's executive branch participated in negotiations to develop the accord. However, facing opposition from a Republican Senate, Obama announced that the United States would comply with the provisions of the agreement without submitting it for ratification. But there were repercussions to this shortcut that left it vulnerable to the policy preferences of other presidents.

President + Outside Organizations

This is important.

During President Obama's second term, **American diplomats were deeply involved in negotiating** the United Nations Framework Convention on Climate Change.

We have a deal.

Representatives from 196 nations **developed the Paris Agreement on climate change**. U.S. Secretary of State John Kerry signed the accord in November 2015.

It's a big deal.

American compliance with the Paris Agreement would transform the economy, **requiring massive increases in production and distribution**, as well as reducing the value of oil and gas deposits owned by American firms.

President + Congress

We want a say!

Many Republican senators (especially those from states with large energy industries) **demanded that President Obama submit the agreement** for ratification as a treaty.

You don't get one.

The Obama administration announced it would implement the accord as an executive agreement, so a **congressional vote was not required**.

Taking a risk.

But making the accord an executive agreement meant that **any future president could end the United States' participation** without further action by Congress.

New Presidents

We're out!

And that's what happened. Obama's successor, Donald Trump, who had campaigned against the Paris Agreement, **withdrew from the agreement in November 2019**.

Not so fast.

Then it happened again. After Joe Biden defeated Trump in the 2020 election, one of his first actions in office was to **rejoin the Paris Agreement and begin discussing additional measures** to mitigate climate change.

Nothing is set in stone.

When does this end? **Biden's actions could be reversed** if Republicans win the presidency in 2024.

Critical Thinking

1. **Why do you think Presidents Obama and Biden decided to treat the agreement** as an executive agreement rather than a treaty? Would the situation be different if Democrats had a large majority in the Senate?
2. **Candidate Trump campaigned against the Paris Agreement—** but President Trump did show some willingness to remain in a renegotiated accord. Why might he have reconsidered his initial position once he was in office?

command the Border Patrol to hold all undocumented immigrants for trial; rather, it instructed the agency to determine what changes would be needed to implement this practice.

On the whole, when the president issues an order that makes real policy changes and Congress does not respond, it means that congressional majorities agree with the president's actions or there is already a law giving the president the authority that the president is exercising in the order. That said, presidents often turn to executive orders and other directives when they know they cannot secure congressional support for the policy changes they want to implement—as was likely the case for Biden's mask mandate executive order. While members of Congress can overrule the president, they may be too busy with other matters to do so, or simply not care enough about the change to take the steps needed to undo it.

Commander in chief

The Constitution makes the president the commander in chief of America's military forces but gives Congress the power to declare war. These provisions are potentially contradictory, and the Constitution leaves open the broader question of who controls the military.[19] In practice, however, the president controls day-to-day military operations through the Department of Defense and has the power to order troops into action without explicit congressional approval. For example, both the Trump and Obama administrations joined over a dozen other nations to aid rebel forces in the Syrian civil war. They provided arms and training to rebel fighters and conducted air strikes against ISIS and Syrian government forces. Even today, some American group forces remain in Syrian territory, and limited air strikes continue. Similarly, the 2011 attack on Osama bin Laden's compound and the 2020 drone strike that killed Iranian general Qasem Soleimani were carried out without prior congressional approval. In fact, even though the United States has been involved in hundreds of military conflicts, there have been only five declarations of war: the War of 1812, the Mexican-American War (1846), the Spanish-American War (1898), World War I (1917), and World War II (1941).

As a way of restraining presidential war-making power, Congress enacted the War Powers Resolution of 1973 (Nuts & Bolts 12.2 lists the specific provisions of the resolution). However, a 2019 study found that the War Powers Resolution has been formally used by Congress to limit presidential authority only once, to limit the duration of a deployment of Marines in Lebanon on a peacekeeping mission.[20] Moreover, although it has been in effect for nearly 50 years, it has never faced Supreme Court review. Some scholars have even argued that the resolution actually expands presidential power because it gives the president essentially unlimited control for the first 90 days of a military operation—and in many cases, 90 days is more than enough time to complete military action without getting Congress involved.[21]

Even with its limitations, the War Powers Resolution has had some impact on presidential decisions regarding the use of force. Threats by members of Congress to invoke the War Powers Resolution were one factor in President Obama's 2011 decision to curtail American involvement in the NATO-led mission to end the Libyan civil war. The impact of the War Powers Resolution is also evident in the fact that presidents often consult with congressional leaders or try to gain congressional approval in some form before committing troops to battle. It is important to remember, too, that the act is not the only tool available to members of Congress who disagree with a president's policy: they can curb a president's war-making powers through budget restrictions, legislative prohibitions, public appeals, and, ultimately, impeachment.[22]

NUTS
& BOLTS
12.2

The War Powers Resolution of 1973

1. The president is required to report to Congress any introduction of U.S. forces into hostilities or imminent hostilities.
2. The use of force must be terminated within 60 days unless Congress approves of the deployment. The time limit can be extended to 90 days if the president certifies that additional time is needed to safely withdraw American forces.
3. The president is required whenever possible to consult with Congress before introducing American forces into hostilities or imminent hostilities.
4. Any congressional resolution authorizing the continued deployment of American forces will be considered under expedited procedures.

Source: Richard F. Grimmett, "The War Powers Resolution: After Thirty Years," Congressional Research Service Report RL32267, March 11, 2004, www.hsdl.org/?view&did=446200 (accessed 5/12/22).

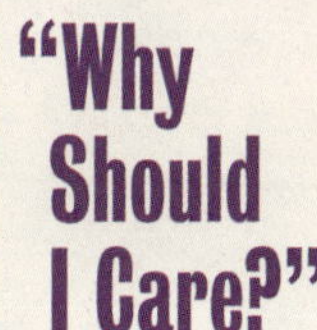

"Why Should I Care?" While the War Powers Resolution is often described as a way for Congress to limit the president's control over America's armed forces, the reality is that the procedures do not address the vast majority of military operations.

Treaty making and foreign policy

Treaty-making power is shared between Congress and the president: presidents and their staff negotiate treaties, which are then sent to the Senate for approval. (Many need the support of a two-thirds majority of senators to be approved, but some need only a simple majority.) However, the president has a first-mover advantage in the treaty-making process. Congress considers treaties only after negotiations have ended; there is no way for members of Congress to force the president to negotiate a treaty or limit its scope. That said, the need for congressional approval often leads presidents to take account of senators' preferences when negotiating treaties, which often results in significant compromise between the two branches.

Presidents have two strategies for avoiding a congressional treaty vote. One is to announce that the United States will voluntarily abide by a treaty without ratifying it. In the case of the 2015 Paris Agreement on climate change, one of the reasons why President Obama supported voluntary targets for reductions in greenhouse gases was that such an agreement did not require Senate approval. Of course, this strategy allowed Obama's successor, Donald Trump, to unilaterally withdraw from the agreement in 2017—although one of President Biden's early executive orders was to resume compliance with the Paris Agreement.

It is also possible to structure a deal as an **executive agreement** between the executive branch and a foreign government, which does not require Senate approval. This strategy was followed in the case of the deal between the United States, its allies, and the Iranian government to curtail Iran's nuclear weapons research program. In this case, Congress passed (and President Obama signed) a law giving members 30 days to review the deal and the opportunity to pass a resolution rejecting it. The deal ultimately went into effect, although Donald Trump ended U.S. participation in early 2018.

executive agreement
An agreement between the executive branch and a foreign government, which acts as a treaty but does not require Senate approval.

The president also serves as the principal representative of the United States in foreign affairs other than treaty negotiations. Presidential duties include communicating with foreign leaders, nongovernmental organizations, and even ordinary citizens to persuade them to act in ways that the president believes are in the best interest of the United States.

The president often meets with foreign leaders in both formal and informal settings. For example, in December 2021, President Biden met with Russian president Vladimir Putin to discuss concerns, including the Russian buildup of forces along the Ukrainian border. Such meetings provide a venue for the president not only to present American views and mediate disagreements but also to act as a visible symbol of America's position as a world superpower.

For example, in February 2022 President Biden met with European allies to coordinate the response to Russia's invasion of Ukraine, including arrangements with some countries whereby the United States would replace weapons sent to Ukrainian forces. Biden also gave several speeches reiterating the U.S. commitment to defend members of the North Atlantic Treaty Organization (including several nations bordering Russia) against all attacks. Similar efforts have continued to the present day.

The amount of time the administration devotes to foreign policy is subject to domestic and world events and therefore not entirely under presidential control. When President Biden took office, for example, few observers expected an all-out Russian invasion of Ukraine. The U.S. response to the invasion involved a combination of political and economic sanctions against Russia, deliveries of billions of dollars in military hardware to Ukraine, and efforts to convince European allies to implement similar measures. Implementing these measures required time and attention from senior White House officials and President Biden himself. There is little doubt that Biden and his aides would have preferred to concentrate on other priorities, such as devising a strategy to lower inflation or directing media attention to Senate confirmation of the first Black female Supreme Court Justice, Ketanji Brown Jackson. But events focused their attention on international politics.

Legislative power

The Constitution establishes lawmaking as a shared power between the president and Congress, and compromise between the two branches is fundamental to passing laws that satisfy both.[23] The president recommends policies and legislative priorities to Congress, notably in the annual **State of the Union** address. Presidents and their legislative staff also work with Congress to develop legislative proposals: they spend considerable time lobbying members of Congress to support their proposals and negotiating with legislative leaders over policy details. Although the president cannot formally introduce legislation, it is typically easy to find a member of Congress willing to sponsor a presidential proposal.[24]

State of the Union
An annual speech in which the president addresses Congress to report on the condition of the country and to recommend policies.

The president's legislative power also stems from the ability to veto legislation (see Nuts & Bolts 12.3). Once both chambers of Congress have passed a bill by simple majority, the president must decide within two weeks of congressional action whether to sign it or issue

NUTS & BOLTS 12.3

The Veto Process

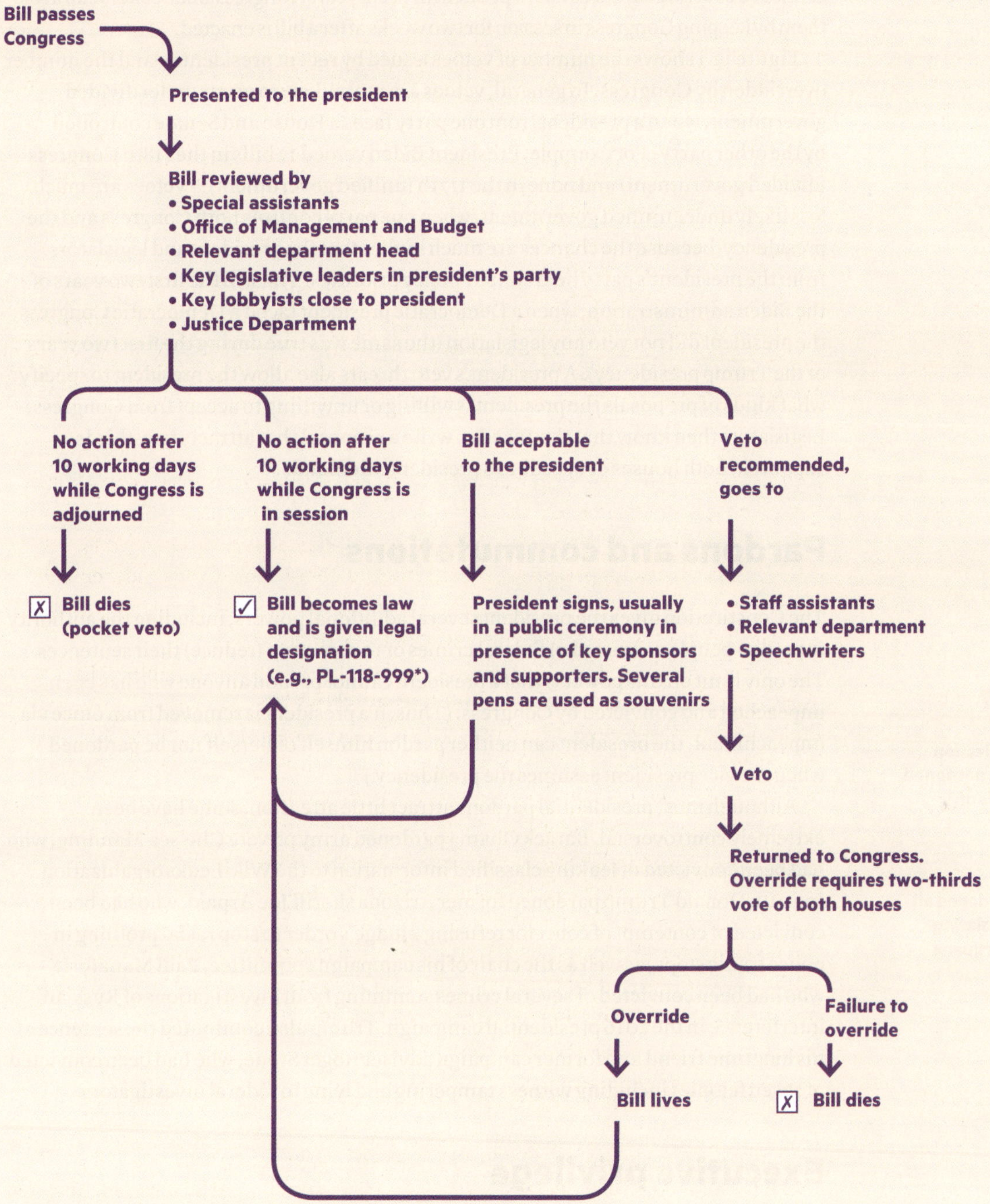

Bill passes Congress → Presented to the president

Bill reviewed by
- Special assistants
- Office of Management and Budget
- Relevant department head
- Key legislative leaders in president's party
- Key lobbyists close to president
- Justice Department

No action after 10 working days while Congress is adjourned → ☒ Bill dies (pocket veto)

No action after 10 working days while Congress is in session → ☑ Bill becomes law and is given legal designation (e.g., PL-118-999*)

Bill acceptable to the president → President signs, usually in a public ceremony in presence of key sponsors and supporters. Several pens are used as souvenirs → Bill becomes law

Veto recommended, goes to
- Staff assistants
- Relevant department
- Speechwriters

→ Veto → Returned to Congress. Override requires two-thirds vote of both houses

- Override → Bill lives → Bill becomes law
- Failure to override → ☒ Bill dies

*PL = public law; 118 = number of Congress (118th is 2023–2025); 999 = number of the law.

Source: Compiled by the authors.

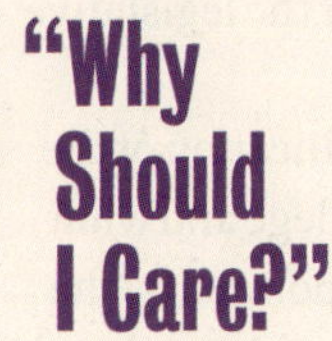

All presidents can veto legislation—but some do it more than others, typically when they face a Congress controlled by the other party.

a veto. Signed bills become law, but vetoed bills return to the House and Senate for a vote to override the veto. If both chambers enact the bill again with at least two-thirds majorities, the bill becomes law; otherwise, it is defeated. If Congress adjourns before the president has decided, the president can *pocket veto* the proposal by not responding to it. Pocket vetoes cannot be overridden, but as has happened in recent years, congressional leaders can avoid them by keeping Congress in session for two weeks after a bill is enacted.

Figure 12.1 shows the number of vetoes issued by recent presidents—and the number overridden by Congress. In general, vetoes are most likely to occur under divided government, when a president from one party faces a House and Senate controlled by the other party. For example, President Biden vetoed 12 bills in the 118th Congress (divided government) and none in the 117th (unified government).[25] Vetoes are much less likely under unified government, when one party controls both Congress and the presidency, because the chances are much higher that the president and legislators from the president's party hold similar policy priorities. Thus, in the first two years of the Biden administration, when a Democratic president faced a Democratic Congress, the president did not veto any legislation (the same was true during the first two years of the Trump presidency). A president's veto threats also allow the president to specify what kinds of proposals the president is willing or unwilling to accept from Congress. Legislators then know that they need to write a proposal that attracts two-thirds support in both houses or accede to a president's demands.

Pardons and commutations

DID YOU KNOW?

From his inauguration to Election Day 2024, President Biden pardoned or commuted the sentences of

25

individuals. Biden also pardoned all individuals convicted of violating federal laws regarding marijuana possession and use.

Source: U.S. Department of Justice.

The Constitution gives the president several additional powers, including the authority to pardon people convicted of federal crimes or to commute (reduce) their sentences. The only limit on this power is that a president cannot pardon anyone who has been impeached and convicted by Congress. (Thus, if a president is removed from office via impeachment, the president can neither pardon himself or herself nor be pardoned when the vice president assumes the presidency.)

Although most presidential pardons attract little attention, some have been extremely controversial. Barack Obama pardoned army private Chelsea Manning, who had been convicted of leaking classified information to the WikiLeaks organization. In 2020, Donald Trump pardoned former Arizona sheriff Joe Arpaio, who had been convicted of contempt of court for refusing a judge's order to stop racial profiling in police traffic stops, as well as the chair of his campaign committee, Paul Manafort, who had been convicted of several crimes stemming from investigations of Russian interference in the 2016 presidential campaign. Trump also commuted the sentence of his longtime friend and former campaign adviser Roger Stone, who had been convicted of seven felonies including witness tampering and lying to federal investigators.

Executive privilege

executive privilege
The right of the president to keep executive branch conversations and correspondence confidential from the legislative and judicial branches.

Finally, although this power is not formally set out in the Constitution or a statute, all presidents have claimed to hold the power of **executive privilege**. This refers to the ability to shield themselves and their subordinates from revealing White House discussions, decisions, or documents (including emails) to members of the legislative or judicial branches of government.[26]

Although claims of executive privilege have been made since the ratification of the Constitution in 1789, it is still not clear exactly what falls under the privilege and what does not. In the 1974 case *United States v. Nixon*, a special prosecutor appointed by the Justice Department to investigate the Watergate scandal challenged President Nixon's

FIGURE 12.1

Presidential Vetoes from H. W. Bush to Biden

The figure shows the number of vetoes issued by recent presidents in each congressional term they held office, along with whether the term involved unified or divided government. Do the data support the argument that vetoes are less likely given unified government? Compared with other presidents, did Presidents Biden and Trump issue an inordinately high or low number of vetoes?

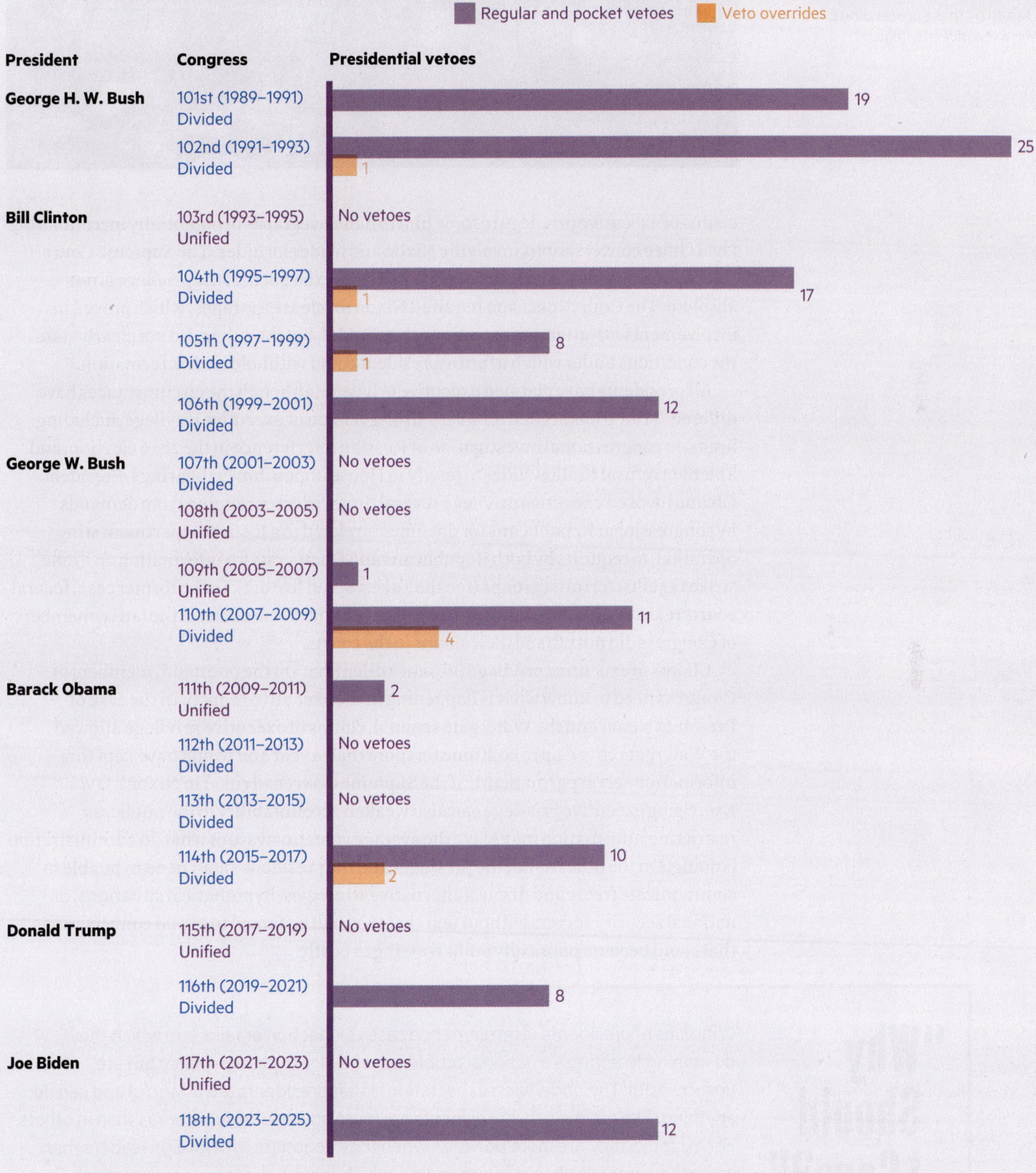

Note: Data current as of November 10, 2024.

Source: United States House of Representatives, History, Art, & Archives, "Presidential Vetoes," https://history.house.gov/Institution/Presidential-Vetoes/Presidential-Vetoes (accessed 11/10/24); data aggregated by the authors.

During the congressional impeachment hearings, Trump claimed executive privilege in order to prevent his aides from testifying in the Ukraine investigation. Numerous expert witnesses, as seen being sworn in here, testified on constitutional issues raised by these proceedings, including executive privilege.

claims of executive privilege to force him to hand over tapes of potentially incriminating Oval Office conversations involving Nixon and his senior aides. The Supreme Court ruled unanimously that executive privilege does exist but that the privilege is not absolute. The Court's decision required Nixon to release the tapes, which proved his involvement with attempts to cover up the scandal, but the ruling did not clearly state the conditions under which a future president could withhold such information.[27]

All presidents have claimed executive privilege, although the circumstances have differed. Trump has argued for a very strong version of executive privilege, including limits on congressional investigation of Russian interference in the 2016 election, and a blanket refusal to allow aides to testify in House impeachment hearings. President Obama invoked executive privilege several times, in cases ranging from demands by congressional Republicans for documents related to a Justice Department sting operation, to requests by both Republicans and Democrats for information on drone strikes against terrorist groups (see the Take a Stand feature). In the former case, federal courts rejected Obama's claim, forcing release of the documents; in the latter, members of Congress did not pursue their claims in the courts.

Claims of executive privilege present a dilemma. On the one hand, members of Congress need to know what is happening in the executive branch. In the case of President Nixon and the Watergate scandal, claims of executive privilege allowed the Watergate cover-up to continue for more than a year and would have kept this information secret permanently if the Supreme Court had ruled in Nixon's favor.[28] Exercising executive privilege can also weaken accountability to the public, as restricting information may leave the average voter unaware of what an administration is doing. On the other hand, the president and the president's staff need to be able to communicate freely and discuss alternative strategies, hypothetical situations, or national security secrets without fear that they will be forced to reveal conversations that could become politically embarrassing or costly.

"Why Should I Care?"

Criticisms of presidents often center on cases of inaction or failure, in which they do nothing to address a national problem or they try to change policy but are unsuccessful. The underlying expectation is that presidents are powerful and can do anything. The reality is that presidents are more powerful in some areas than in others. For example, they are more powerful when they negotiate with foreign leaders than when they propose changes in spending, which require congressional approval. Thus, when we judge presidents' performance, we must consider whether achieving their goals required the assistance of others to make their proposals a reality.

TAKE A STAND

The Limits of Executive Privilege

Deciding what information a president can be compelled to release to the public or to other branches of government and what information can be kept confidential requires confronting fundamentally political questions. There are no right answers, and the limits of executive privilege remain unclear. On the one hand, members of Congress need facts, predictions, and estimates from the executive branch to make good public policy. On the other hand, the president and the president's staff have a right to keep their deliberations confidential, as well as a practical need to keep some things secret.

Consider the controversy over the practice (begun during the Bush administration and continued under recent presidents) of targeting terrorists using attacks by unmanned drone aircraft. Compared with deployments of other military forces, drone attacks have the advantages of surprise (drones are small and fly high enough to be invisible), low cost (drones are cheaper than fighters or bombers), and lower risk (the drones can be controlled from anywhere, so there is no risk of American casualties in an attack). Nonetheless, drone attacks carry the risk of collateral damage—an attack may also hurt or kill innocent civilians. Moreover, because drone attacks are conducted in secret, there is little to no congressional oversight of who gets targeted by drone strikes or the potential for collateral damage. Should drone attacks fall under executive privilege?

Keep the attacks secret. Clearly, revealing the targets of drone strikes in advance of the actual attacks would destroy the secrecy that makes these strikes so effective—terrorists could stop using cell phones, stay indoors as much as possible, travel only at night, and take other actions to make themselves hard to spot from the air. But there would be danger even in forcing an administration to release information after an attack, as such documents would reveal the criteria used to decide which terrorists to target, the limits of the drone technology, and what factors made it easier to carry out a successful attack. All of this information would help terror targets evade future drone attacks and perhaps require a return to using Special Forces to attack terror targets, which would place American lives at risk.

Reveal the information. The problem with imposing a high level of secrecy on drone attacks is that it is an exception to the rule of keeping Congress informed about the use of military force. In the end, a drone is simply a different way of attacking terrorists or their organization. While the need for secrecy in advance of an attack makes sense, it is not obvious why it should continue after an attack has been carried out. In general, presidents are required to give Congress (in the case of secret operations, the chairs and ranking members of the Intelligence Committees) "prompt notification" of all secret operations. This rule was intended to govern reporting of all covert operations. Should drone attacks be given a higher level of secrecy, or should presidents be forced to keep members of Congress informed?

The president's role as commander in chief of America's armed forces gives the president a tremendous amount of power—power that often can be exercised secretly. What should be the limits on presidential secrecy?

take a stand

1. One argument for using drones to attack terrorist targets highlights their greater effectiveness and lower costs than other options. But drone attacks also involve lower political risks to the president. Explain why this is so.
2. Under current law, the president has to inform only a few members of Congress about covert operations and can wait until an operation is in progress before releasing information. Why would members of Congress want expanded notification requirements, such as informing more members or requiring disclosure during the planning of an operation?

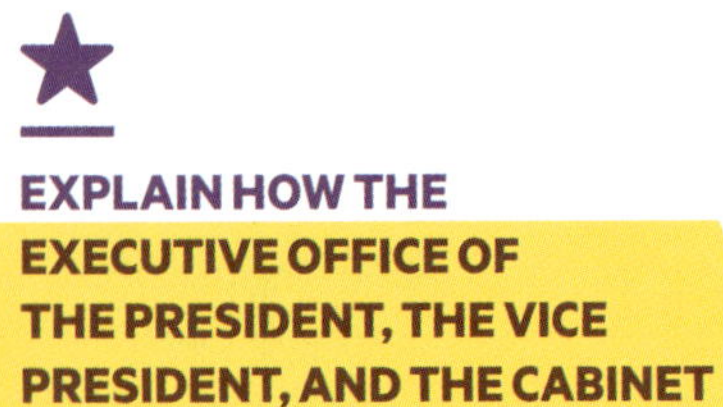

The presidency as an institution

As head of the executive branch, the president runs a huge, complex organization with hundreds of thousands of employees. We describe this organization as an "institution" to emphasize that both the *structure* of the executive branch (the division of responsibilities across different agencies and offices) and the *individuals* who serve in different positions (their experience, skills, and ideological leanings) can have a profound impact on government policies. This section describes the organizations and staff who help the president exercise the president's vast responsibilities, from managing disaster-response efforts to implementing policy changes. Among these employees are appointees who hold senior positions in the government. These individuals serve as the president's eyes and ears in the bureaucracy, making sure that bureaucrats are following presidential directives.

The Executive Office of the President

Executive Office of the President (EOP)
The group of policy-related offices that serve as support staff to the president.

The executive branch's organizational chart begins with the **Executive Office of the President (EOP)**, which has employed several thousand people in recent administrations, divided between policy-making positions and administrating personnel. About a third of these employees are concentrated in two offices: the Office of Management and Budget, which develops the president's budget proposals and monitors spending by government agencies, and the Office of the United States Trade Representative, which negotiates trade agreements with other nations. Nuts & Bolts 12.4 lists the organizations that make up the EOP.

NUTS & BOLTS 12.4

The Executive Office of the President

- Council of Economic Advisers
- Council on Environmental Quality
- Domestic Policy Council
- Homeland Security Council
- National Economic Council
- National Security Council
- Office of Administration
- Office of Faith-Based and Community Initiatives
- Office of Management and Budget
- Office of National AIDS Policy
- Office of National Drug Control Policy
- Office of Science and Technology Policy
- Office of the First Lady
- Office of the United States Trade Representative
- President's Foreign Intelligence Advisory Board
- Privacy and Civil Liberties Oversight Board
- White House Fellows Office
- White House Military Office
- White House Office

Source: Compiled by the authors from whitehouse.gov.

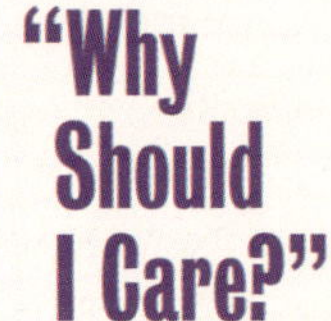

Organizations in the EOP play a major role in bringing information to the president and executing the president's directives. They reflect presidential priorities and policy goals.

One of the most important duties of EOP staff is helping presidents achieve their policy goals and get reelected. In the Biden White House, for example, Senior Adviser Susan Rice focused on domestic policy (especially health and immigration policy). Another senior adviser, Mike Donilon, was Biden's chief strategist during the 2020 presidential campaign. These individuals, as well as other influential EOP staff, occupy offices in the West Wing of the White House. The West Wing contains the president's office, known as the Oval Office, and space for the president's chief aide and personal secretary, as well as the vice president, the president's press secretary, and the chief of staff (for Trump, Susan Wiles), who manages all aspects of White House operations—including, as former Reagan chief of staff James Baker put it, who gets to play tennis on the White House courts. Some recent chiefs of staff have been central in the development of policy proposals and negotiations with members of Congress. However, the chief of staff serves as the agent of the president—what matters is what the president wants, not a chief of staff's policy preferences.

You don't need to know who's playing on the White House tennis court to be a good president.

—James Baker, former White House chief of staff

Most EOP staff members are presidential appointees who retain their positions only as long as the president who appointed them remains in office. These individuals are often drawn to government service out of loyalty to the president or because they share the president's policy goals.[29] However, most leave their positions after two or three years to escape the pressures of the job, the long hours, and the relatively low government salaries.[30] Some EOP offices—such as the Office of Management and Budget, the Office of the United States Trade Representative, and the National Security Council (NSC)—also have a significant number of permanent staff analysts and experts.[31] The emphasis on loyalty in presidential appointments has obvious drawbacks: appointees may not know much about the jobs they are given, and they may not be very effective at managing the agencies they are supposed to control. For example, during President Trump's first term, his son-in-law, Jared Kushner, was given responsibility for American efforts to negotiate a peace deal between Israel and the Palestinian Authority, even though his prior experience was as a real estate developer and he had never served in government.

The president's closest advisers are chosen for their loyalty to the president and their policy goals. President Biden's closest advisers include colleagues from his time as vice president. For example, Biden's first chief of staff, Ron Klain, was also his chief of staff during the Obama administration when he served as vice president. Here they meet with other cabinet members and immigration advisers at the White House.

The vice president

As set out in the Constitution, the vice president's job is to preside over Senate proceedings. This largely ceremonial job is, in practice, usually delegated to the president pro tempore of the Senate, who in turn typically gives the duty to a more junior member. The vice president also has the power to cast tie-breaking votes in the Senate. The vice president's other formal responsibility is to become president if the current president dies, becomes incapacitated, resigns, or is impeached, convicted, and ultimately removed from office. Of the nation's 46 presidents, 9 were vice presidents who became president in midterm.

These rather limited official duties of the vice president pale in comparison with the influential role played by recent vice presidents. Vice President Dick Cheney, who served with President George W. Bush, exerted a significant influence over many policy areas, including the rights of terror suspects, tax and spending policy, environmental

While many people perceive the vice president's position to be ceremonial and relatively powerless, recently the vice president's role has expanded significantly. For example, Kamala Harris took a very active role as president of the Senate, casting numerous tie-breaking votes that confirmed nominations to key administrative positions. She also spread awareness about the Biden administration's legislative priorities, including the Infrastructure Investment and Jobs Act, by speaking with key groups such as small business owners about how the act would benefit them.

decisions, and the writing of new government regulations.[32] Although Cheney's level of influence was unique, other recent vice presidents have also had real power. And, as Vice President Harris' 2024 campaign illustrates, many vice presidents become presidential candidates.

The president's Cabinet

Cabinet
The group of 15 executive department heads who implement the president's agenda in their respective positions.

The president's **Cabinet** is composed of the heads of the 15 executive departments in the federal government, along with other appointees given cabinet rank by the president. Nuts & Bolts 12.5 lists the Cabinet and cabinet-level positions. The cabinet members' principal job is to be the frontline implementers of the president's agenda in their executive departments. As we discuss in Chapter 13, these appointees monitor the actions of the lower-level bureaucrats who retain their jobs regardless of who is president and are not necessarily sympathetic to the president's priorities.

Like other presidential appointees, cabinet members are chosen for a combination of loyalty to the president and expertise. Biden's secretary of state, Antony Blinken, was a career State Department official who served as senior adviser to Biden during the Obama administration. Biden's secretary of the Treasury, Janet Yellen, was an economics professor who held senior positions in the Federal Reserve, including chair from 2014 to 2018.

As secretary of the Treasury, Janet Yellen played a central role in the Biden cabinet during the COVID-19 pandemic in making monetary policy changes to control inflation and monitor the economy.

NUTS & BOLTS 12.5

Cabinet and Cabinet-Level Positions

The president's Cabinet is composed of the heads of the 15 executive departments along with other appointees given cabinet rank by the president.

Secretary of Agriculture	Secretary of Transportation
Secretary of Commerce	Secretary of the Treasury
Secretary of Defense	Secretary of Veterans Affairs
Secretary of Education	Vice President
Secretary of Energy	White House Chief of Staff
Secretary of Health and Human Services	Attorney General
Secretary of Homeland Security	Director of the Environmental Protection Agency
Secretary of Housing and Urban Development	Director of the Office of Management and Budget
Secretary of the Interior	United States Trade Representative
Secretary of Labor	Director of National Intelligence
Secretary of State	Administrator of the Small Business Administration
Director of the Office of Science and Technology Policy	Ambassador to the United Nations
Chair of the Council of Economic Advisers	

Source: Compiled by the authors from whitehouse.gov.

"Why Should I Care?"

Cabinet secretaries are the president's eyes and ears in the executive branch, carrying out the president's wishes and serving as the public faces of the departments they lead.

Having read the job description for America's president, you might reasonably ask, How does any one person handle all of these responsibilities? The answer is that presidents have help: trusted advisers and people chosen for policy knowledge, political skills, and loyalty. Put another way, if you want to know whether someone will make a good president, don't look at the president's experience or campaign promises—look at the people the president picks to help run the government.

Presidential power today

EXPLAIN HOW MODERN PRESIDENTS HAVE BECOME EVEN MORE POWERFUL

As we have discussed, presidential authority comes from two sources, on paper: the limited powers granted by the Constitution, and laws that have expanded the president's power. Even so, assessing presidential power requires expanding our notions of where this power actually comes from. Saying that presidents have become more powerful over time because of the expansion of the United States or the increased size of the federal budget or bureaucracy tells only part of the story. What about these circumstances made presidents more powerful?

One important clue about where presidential power comes from is that, after more than two centuries, many of the limits to these powers are not well defined. It is unclear, for example, which executive actions require congressional approval and which ones can be reversed by Congress. The very ambiguity of the Constitution and most statutes also creates opportunities for the exercise of presidential power. As we have seen, the Constitution makes the president military commander in chief but gives Congress the power to declare war and to raise and support armies, without specifying which branch of government is in charge of the military. Thus, at least part of presidential authority must be derived or assumed from what the Constitution and statutes *do not say*—the ways in which they fail to define or to delineate presidential power—and how presidents use this ambiguity to pursue their goals.

In addition to these ambiguities, presidents also gain real power from other, more informal aspects of their office. Recall our discussion of the president's ability to influence the legislative process. In the Constitution, the president's powers in this realm are limited to advising Congress on the state of the Union and to vetoing legislation (subject to congressional override). But presidents often have very real influence at all points in the legislative process: they can offer a variety of small inducements, such as visits to the Oval Office and campaign assistance, and they can draw on the natural respect that most people (including members of Congress) feel for the presidency regardless of who holds the office, thereby securing compromises that achieve the president's policy goals.[33]

Donald Trump made no secret of his willingness to push the boundaries of presidential authority in areas such as executive privilege, to keep key executive branch positions open or rely on acting appointments, and to build relationships with the leaders of nondemocratic regimes such as Vladimir Putin of Russia, Xi Jinping of China, and Kim Jong-un of North Korea. Regardless of whether or not you support these moves, they are not in violation of the Constitution or established law. Moreover, all presidents take similar actions. Both Presidents Biden and Obama initiated a policy known as DACA (deferred action for childhood arrivals) that provided employment authorization and a path to citizenship for undocumented individuals living in the United States who were brought to America while children. In both cases, these policies were invalidated by the federal courts.

Presidents, unilateral action, and policy making

unilateral action (presidential)
Any policy decision made and acted upon by the president and presidential staff without the explicit approval or consent of Congress.

Political scientists Terry M. Moe and William G. Howell argue that constitutional and statutory ambiguities in some cases enable presidents to take **unilateral action**, changing policy on their own without consulting Congress or anyone else.[34] Although Congress can, in theory, undo unilateral actions through legislation, court proceedings, or impeachment, Moe and Howell maintain that the costs of doing so, in terms of time, effort, and public perceptions, are often prohibitive. The result is that presidents can take unilateral action despite congressional opposition, knowing that their actions stand little chance of being reversed.

The 2022 debate over U.S. aid to Ukraine provides a good example of how constitutional ambiguities create opportunities for unilateral action. In the weeks before Russia's invasion, some Republicans argued that the United States had only a minimal interest in what happened in Ukraine—Senator Josh Hawley, for example, argued that America should focus on the increasing military and economic power of China.[35] Notwithstanding these concerns, the Biden administration sent massive amounts of military assistance to Ukraine (including training missions staffed by American troops). After the invasion, the administration stepped up arms deliveries but stopped short of putting U.S. forces in places where they might encounter Russian troops. In both cases, President Biden was taking unilateral actions—actions that could be overturned by congressional majorities. While some members of Congress (particularly Republicans) publicly advocated alternate strategies, no such vote was ever taken. More recently, while members of Congress debated further arms transfers, U.S. military officials gave Ukraine intelligence on the location of Russian forces.

This example is far from the first time that Congress has complained about presidential actions but done nothing to counter them. During the Iraq War, when some Democrats in Congress wanted to cut off war funding to force the withdrawal of American forces, supporters of the Bush administration cited the **unitary executive theory** to argue that the Constitution's description of the president as commander in chief of America's armed forces meant that even if Congress refused to appropriate funds for the war, the president could (1) order American forces to stay in Iraq and (2) order the Department of the Treasury to spend any funds necessary to continue operations. Ultimately, members of Congress approved a funding resolution. (The unitary executive theory was also cited during the investigation of possible collusion between the Russian government and the 2016 Trump presidential campaign, when President Trump's lawyers used it to justify their claim that since the Constitution made Trump the head of the executive branch, including the Justice Department, he could not be indicted for committing a crime.)

unitary executive theory
The idea that the vesting clause of the Constitution gives the president the authority to issue orders and policy directives that cannot be undone by Congress.

The Bush administration's position left members of Congress with a single unattractive option: invoking the War Powers Resolution to force the end of combat operations. This option would take time, as it would require building majority support in the House and the Senate for the resolution. It would also trigger Supreme Court review of the War Powers Resolution, which is a significant risk—if the Court were to rule in favor of the president and to hold that the resolution was unconstitutional, it would sharply reduce Congress's control over future military operations.

In addition to asking Congress for funds to support Ukraine's defense against the Russian invasion, President Biden met with key members of the Ukrainian government, including Foreign Minister Dmytro Kuleb, to reaffirm the United States' support for the Ukrainian people.

Presidents act unilaterally to make domestic policy as well. During President Obama's second term in office, Obama gave several directives to the Justice Department that limited deportations of undocumented immigrants. President Biden used an executive order to have the United States rejoin the Paris Climate Change Accord—reversing President Trump's executive order to leave the Accord. Of course, none of these policies continued after Donald Trump began his second term of office in January 2025.

It is important to understand that throughout the nation's history, there have been many other examples of unilateral presidential actions, such as the annexation of Texas, the freeing of enslaved people in the Emancipation Proclamation, the desegregation of the U.S. military, the initiation of affirmative action programs, and the creation of agencies such as the Peace Corps.[36] In part, unilateral actions are the product of the president's constitutional and statutory authority, which gives the president the right to act on the president's own under some circumstances. Additional opportunities are created by the ambiguities in the president's authority that we discussed earlier. Finally, because no one becomes president without a strong, broad vision of what they would like government to do, it should be no surprise that presidents are continually testing the bounds of their authority by taking unilateral actions as a way of translating their policy ideas into reality.

Control over the interpretation and implementation of laws

By virtue of their control over the executive branch, presidents can sometimes shape policy outcomes by influencing how a law is implemented. For example, after Congress passed a law in 2017 that mandated sanctions on Russians who had participated in efforts to interfere in the 2016 American presidential election, the Trump administration took over six months to identify which individuals would be subject to sanctions. Besides missing a deadline laid out in the bill, the administration's actions targeted only a small number of individuals—significantly fewer than supporters of the law had expected. However, because the law did not specify how extensive the sanctions had to be, the administration's actions, while unilateral, were in fact legal.

Other presidents have found and exploited loopholes in laws that were initially designed to restrict presidential power. For example, current law requires the president to give congressional leaders "timely notification" of secret intelligence operations. However, during the Reagan administration, senior officials did not reveal the existence of ongoing operations for several months. When these operations were eventually discovered, officials claimed they were within the letter of the law because it did not specify a time limit within which Congress must be notified.[37]

signing statement
A document issued by the president when signing a bill into law explaining the president's interpretation of the law, which often differs from the interpretation of Congress, in an attempt to influence how the law will be implemented.

Most presidents have tried to control the implementation of laws by issuing **signing statements** when signing bills into law. These documents, which explain the president's interpretation of a new law, are issued most often when the president wishes to approve a bill but disagrees with the way that supporters of the bill in Congress interpret the legislation. Presidents issue signing statements so that if the courts have to resolve uncertainties about the bill's intent, judges can take into account not only the views expressed during congressional debates about the bill but also the president's interpretation of it.[38]

Congressional responses to unilateral action

In theory, members of Congress can undo a president's unilateral action by enacting a law to overturn it, but this is harder than it may sound.[39] Some members of Congress may approve of what the president has done or be indifferent to it, or they may give a higher priority to enacting other laws, making it hard to assemble a majority of legislators who are motivated enough to pass a law overturning the president's action. For example, the Trump administration went far enough on its implementation of the Russia sanctions that only a minority of House members and senators were willing to invest the time to enact a new bill that went further. Still, reversals do happen: Congress enacted a Russia sanctions bill over the objections of then-president Trump in his first term. And the first impeachment of Donald Trump can be seen as a response to claims that Trump had pressured the government of Ukraine to investigate his 2020 political rival, Democrat Joe Biden.

Members of Congress can also write laws in a way that limits the president's authority over their implementation.[40] However, this strategy has drawbacks. The problem is that members of Congress delegate authority to the president or the executive branch bureaucracy for good reasons—either because it is difficult for legislators to predict how a policy should be implemented or because they cannot agree among themselves on an implementation plan.[41] In the case of Russia sanctions, for example, members of Congress may have been unsure of whom to sanction or what appropriate punishments would look like. Members of Congress from the president's party may also want to grant authority to the president because they hold policy goals similar to the president's and would therefore benefit from the exercise of unilateral power.

Aside from legislation, the only option for members of Congress to overturn a president's unilateral action is to take the president to court (probably all the way to the Supreme Court) to demonstrate that the president overstepped the president's authority. In the case of the Biden administration's imposition of a COVID-19 vaccination mandate on large employers, some members of Congress were involved

President Biden entered office promising to put science first to control the pandemic. One of the key levers of that plan was vaccination requirements for large employers. However, this was a controversial issue, with many people and companies saying a vaccine requirement infringed on their civil liberties. The mandate was eventually overturned by the Court, demonstrating the way in which the courts can check the power of the president.

in court cases intended to suspend or reverse the mandate. The problem with pursuing this option is the time required for judicial proceedings—and the fact that the courts may uphold the president's right to act unilaterally. In the case of the vaccine mandate, for example, many people were vaccinated before a federal court overturned the mandate.

Congress also has the power to remove the president or vice president from office through the impeachment process. However, removing a president is much more difficult than passing a law to undo a unilateral action. First, House members must impeach (indict) the president by majority vote, which accuses the president of a crime or breach of the president's sworn duties. Then senators hold a trial, followed by a vote in which a two-thirds majority is required to remove the president from office. Only three presidents have faced an impeachment vote: Andrew Johnson in 1866, Bill Clinton in 1999, and Donald Trump in 2019 and 2021 (a fourth president, Richard Nixon, resigned from office to prevent an impeachment vote). Johnson was involved in a political dispute over administration of the southern states after the Civil War; Clinton was alleged to have lied under oath in a sexual harassment lawsuit. Although both were impeached by the House, they were not convicted by the Senate, so they stayed in office.

The first set of impeachment proceedings for Donald Trump focused on Trump's request to the prime minister of Ukraine to open an investigation into Democratic presidential candidate Joe Biden's son, Hunter Biden, who had been appointed as a director of Burisma, a Ukrainian energy company. At about the same time, the Trump administration had suspended military aid to Ukraine. A whistleblower working for the National Security Council, Army Lieutenant Colonel Alexander Vindman, used established procedures to reveal these developments to senior Inspector General staff in the National Security Council, who then forwarded the complaint to Congress, as they were obligated to do under the law. The key question was whether Trump's actions constituted a quid pro quo—whether Trump was trying to encourage the investigation to damage Biden's chances in 2020. Ultimately, the House of Representatives voted to impeach Trump in December 2019 almost completely along party lines. The Senate held an abbreviated trial; it voted on largely partisan lines against calling witnesses and acquitted Trump by majority vote, with only one Republican, Senator Mitt Romney (R-UT), voting to convict on one of the articles of impeachment.

The second impeachment proceeding against Trump centered on whether he had incited protesters to storm the U.S. Capitol on January 6, 2021, just as members of Congress were beginning the process of certifying the results of the 2020 presidential election. After a brief debate, the House again impeached Trump, this time with ten Republican supporters. A Senate trial ended with Trump's acquittal, although a majority of the Senate (including seven Republicans) voted to remove Trump from office.

The Trump impeachments illustrate how impeachment is of limited use in curbing unilateral action by a president. Particularly in an era of high partisan polarization, members of Congress who are upset about presidential actions might nevertheless oppose removing the president from office—this was exactly the argument used by several Republican senators and House members in both proceedings. They might approve of the president's other initiatives, want to prevent the vice president from becoming president, have concerns about the political backlash that impeachment could generate against them or their party, or believe that the president's actions did not rise to the level needed to remove the president from office.

In sum, ambiguities in the Constitution create opportunities for unilateral presidential action. These actions are subject to reversal through legislation, court decisions, and impeachment, but members of Congress face significant costs if they undertake any of these options. As long as presidents are careful to limit their exercise of unilateral power to actions that do not generate intense opposition in Congress, they can implement a wide range of policy goals without official congressional consent—provided that bureaucrats go along with the president's wishes, a question we take up in the next chapter.

Presidents as politicians

He'll sit here, and he'll say, "Do this! Do that!" And nothing will happen. Poor Ike—it won't be a bit like the Army. He'll find it very frustrating.

—President Harry Truman, describing incoming president Dwight Eisenhower

Aside from situations in which the president has (or has been given) the authority to act unilaterally, the reality of presidential power is that much of what presidents do (or want to do) requires support from others, including legislators, bureaucrats, and citizens. As a result, the presidency is an inherently political office—something that all presidents learn is true, regardless of their expectations when they take office.[42] Presidents have to take into account the political consequences of their decisions: the effects on their political support, reelection prospects, and party. A president must also contend with the reality that achieving the president's personal policy goals often requires bargaining and compromising with others, both inside and outside government.

presidential approval rating The percentage of Americans who think that the president is doing a good job in office.

In part, presidents must keep their eyes on the political implications of their actions in office because they want to be reelected to a second term. One important indicator of presidential performance is the **presidential approval rating**, the percentage of the public who think the president is doing a good job in office. Figure 12.2, which shows the presidential approval ratings for the last ten presidents who ran for reelection, reveals that first-term presidents with less than 50 percent approval are in real trouble. No recent president (including Trump) has been reelected with less than a 50 percent approval rating. A low approval rating was one reason why President Biden ended his reelection campaign in July 2024 and endorsed Vice President Kamala Harris.

Of course, it would be wrong to say that presidents are single-mindedly focused on keeping their approval rating as high as possible. For one thing, as we discussed in Chapter 6, presidential approval is shaped by factors that they have only limited control over, such as the state of the economy. And all presidents have taken actions that were politically costly because they believed that the policies were worthwhile. For example, President Biden's revisions to border control procedures were opposed by a majority of Americans. Even so, presidents and their advisers are keenly aware of the political

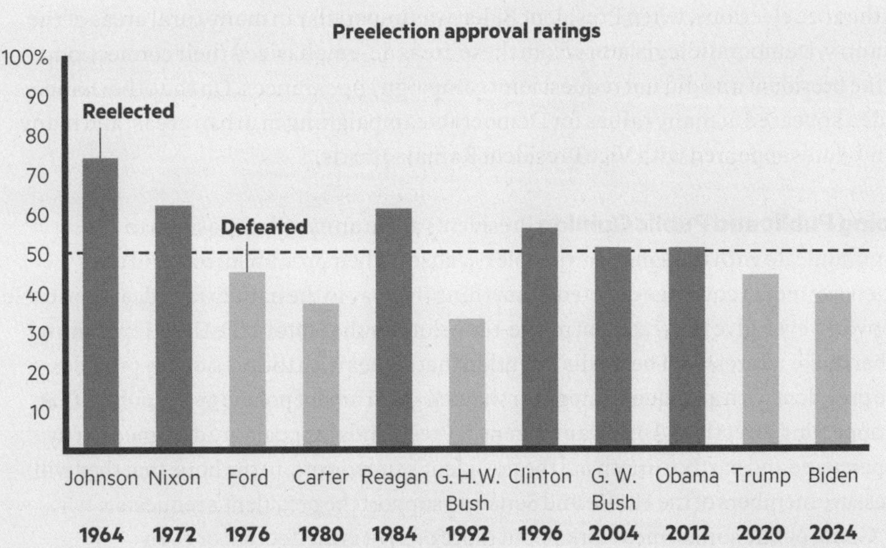

Source: Approval data from the Roper Center for Public Opinion Research, Cornell University, "Presidential Approval," https://presidential.roper.center (accessed 9/15/24).

FIGURE 12.2

Presidential Popularity and Reelection

This figure shows the preelection-year average approval ratings for recent presidents who ran for reelection. It shows that a president's chances of winning reelection are related to that president's popularity. At what level of approval would you say that an incumbent president is likely to be reelected?

consequences of their actions, and there is no doubt that these consequences shape both their decisions and how they explain these actions to American citizens.

The President as Party Leader The president is the unofficial head of the president's political party and generally picks the party's day-to-day leaders (or at least has considerable influence over their selection). This process begins when a presidential candidate captures the party's nomination and continues through the president's time in office. For example, while many members of the Republican National Committee (RNC) opposed Donald Trump's nomination in 2016, the party organized to help Trump get elected and ran countless campaign ads on his behalf. After the election, Trump supporters moved into positions within the party organization. Even while out of office, Trump continues to be a strong influence on the party organization. His daughter-in-law, Lara Trump, was named party co-chair in 2024.

The connection between the president and the party reflects their intertwining interests. The president needs support from members of the president's party in Congress to enact legislation, and the party and its candidates need the president to compile a record of policy achievements that reflect well on the organization and to help raise the funds needed for the next election. Therefore, party leaders generally defer to a presidential candidate's (or a president's) staffing requests, and most presidents and presidential candidates take time to meet with national party leaders and the congressional leadership from their party to plan legislative strategies, make joint campaign appearances, and raise funds for the party's candidates. This is not to say that members of the president's party always agree with the president's behavior and issue positions: President Biden, for example, was unable to convince moderate Democratic senators to support his Build Back Better initiative, and settled for a more modest proposal, the Inflation Reduction Act, in 2022.

Presidents' value to the party also depends on their popularity. When presidential approval ratings drop to low levels, most members of Congress see no political advantage in campaigning with the president or supporting White House proposals, and they may become increasingly reluctant to comply with the president's requests. In the 2022 elections, when President Biden was unpopular in many rural areas of the country, Democratic legislators from these areas de-emphasized their connection to the president and did not request joint campaign appearances. On the other hand, Biden appeared at many rallies for Democrats campaigning in urban areas, and many candidates appeared with Vice President Kamala Harris.

Going Public and Public Opinion Presidents are in an excellent position to communicate with the American people because of their prominent role and the extensive media coverage devoted to anything they say to the nation. Broadcast and cable networks even give the president prime-time slots for the State of the Union speech and other major addresses. The media attention that comes with the presidency provides the president with a unique strategy for shaping government policy: **going public**, that is, appealing directly to American citizens.[43] Presidential appeals are designed partly to persuade and partly to motivate the president's supporters, in the hope that they will pressure members of the House and Senate to support the president's requests.

going public
A president's use of speeches and other public communications to appeal directly to citizens about issues the president would like the House and Senate to act on.

Going public sometimes works—but more often it is ineffectual or even counterproductive. A president's appeals may energize supporters, but they may also have a similar effect on opponents. Thus, rather than facilitating compromise (or a wholesale presidential victory), publicizing an issue may deepen existing conflicts. More generally, studies suggest that most Americans ignore or reject a president's attempts to go public. As presidency scholar George C. Edwards III notes, people who disapprove of a president's time in office are not going to change their minds just because of a presidential speech.[44] Other times, presidential efforts to shape opinion fail spectacularly, such as President Trump's use of a Sharpie to alter a National Oceanographic and Atmospheric Administration (NOAA) hurricane prediction map to justify his tweeted assertion that the storm might hit Alabama.[45]

George C. Edwards's findings explain why most recent presidents have had little success with their efforts to go public. While President Barack Obama gave many speeches in an effort to enact gun control legislation, these efforts had little effect.

After mistakenly tweeting that Alabama was under threat from Hurricane Dorian in September 2019, President Donald Trump appeared during a briefing by federal agencies with a map that seems to have been updated with a Sharpie marker to extend the range of at-risk areas into Alabama. The National Weather Service never included Alabama in its projected path for Dorian, leaving many Americans confused about whom to trust.

And while President Trump used a broader range of media outlets compared with his predecessors (most notably, Twitter and his campaign rallies), his efforts to shape public opinion on issues such as the travel ban, the border wall, or immigration reform have not significantly changed public opinion (see Figure 12.3). President Biden had little success in speeches to highlight favorable economic conditions. Thus, while presidents have a unique platform from which to deliver their arguments directly to the American people, in practice they are often frustrated in their ability to shape public opinion.

The difficulty presidents have in shaping public opinion is another reason why some presidents seem to accomplish more than others. Political scientist Stephen Skowronek argues that presidents are constrained by the era in which they govern.[46] Some presidents (such as Ronald Reagan in 1981) take office when public opinion is strongly behind their policy agenda, making it easier for them to persuade Congress and bureaucrats to comply with their requests. Other presidents have the misfortune to hold office when public opinion is not supportive of significant policy change in the form of new laws or changes in regulations. Under these conditions, presidents are limited in what they can do, even with all their powers and capability for unilateral action. Even though President Trump held office with unified Republican control of the House and Senate, there was only modest public support for many of his initiatives, such as free community college, cutting entitlement programs, or curtailing government regulations. The same is true for some of President Biden's proposals, such as immigration reform or ending tuition for community college.

Public opinion is difficult to shape, and it explains why many presidents fail to see their key policy priorities succeed once in office. For example, despite a lot of momentum behind free community college, Biden did not see substantial legislation supporting these goals of his administration. It was also a priority of First Lady Dr. Jill Biden, who teaches English composition at Northern Virginia Community College.

FIGURE 12.3

Presidential Approval Ratings for Joe Biden

Joe Biden began his first term with an approval rating above 50 percent, which slowly declined through 2021 and 2022 before increasing somewhat in the months before the 2022 midterm. What developments in domestic or international affairs might have contributed to these trends?

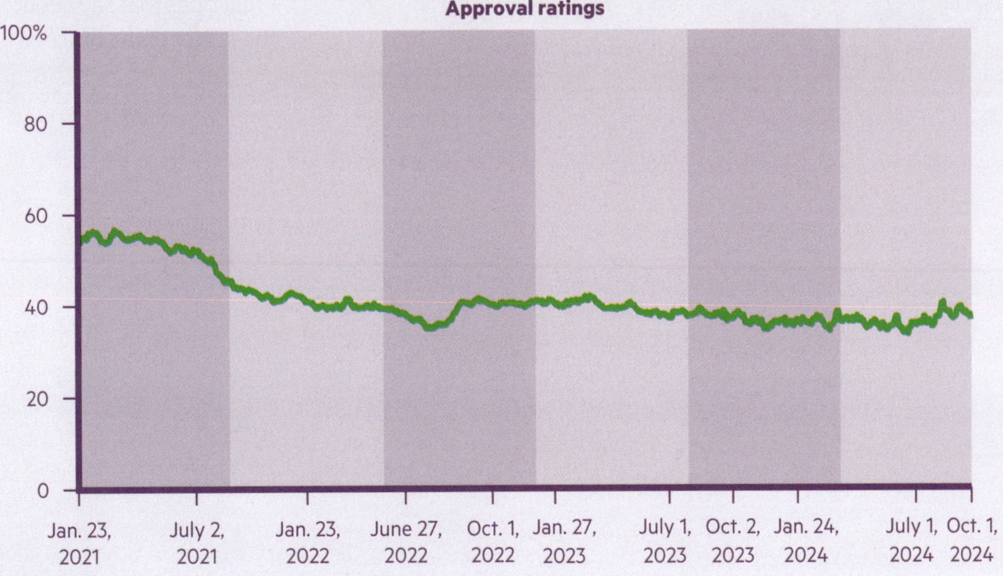

Source: FiveThirtyEight, "How Popular Is Joe Biden?," https://projects.fivethirtyeight.com/biden-approval-rating/ (accessed 11/10/24).

Unpacking the Conflict

Considering all that we've discussed in this chapter, let's apply what we know about how the office of the president works to the questions we presented at the beginning of this chapter. Will Trump redefine what makes a successful president? Was Biden's relatively low-key approach to the presidency a good idea? What factors distinguish presidential successes from presidential failures?

The president occupies an office whose power is derived from constitutional authority, statutory authority, and ambiguities that enable unilateral action. While both Biden and Trump promised to transform America, their presidencies highlight the difficulties that any president would face in trying to deliver on this promise. Although presidents are given considerable powers, big policy changes generally require congressional consent and strong support from citizens. And as we have seen, even with unified government, neither president was completely successful at persuading members of Congress to accept their policy plans. Both presidents also faced opposition from within the bureaucracy and from citizens pursuing their claims through the federal judicial system.

Even so, both presidents had some notable successes, particularly in areas where they could act unilaterally using executive orders or directives, as well as in shaping American foreign policy. Both presidents' appointees made significant progress in the form of regulatory changes and new interpretations of existing laws. Considering these successes along with the failures that we've noted, we should not conclude that either president had some special powers that his predecessors lacked or that he was deficient in some crucial talent. Their day-to-day behavior and overall performance were not surprising. Rather, they illustrate both the possibilities and the limitations of the presidency in contemporary American politics.

"What's Your Take?"

Did Trump's presidency represent a departure from the norm?

How do the results Biden has thus far achieved in office compare with those of previous presidents? What does that say about the power of the office?

CHECK YOUR UNDERSTANDING

"Why Should I Care?"

America's identity and national public policy, whether we like it or not, are deeply tied to the person who occupies the Oval Office. The president's role as head of state sends a message to other countries and international organizations about how we view our place in the world. Moreover, as a president is America's chief diplomat, the president's priorities shape our alliances and agreements with other nations. As head of government, the president uses control over the executive branch and applies pressure to Congress to adopt and implement the president's policy priorities. The presidency matters more than just as a job because it shapes who America is and what government does for the length of time a president serves; that is the true power of the American presidency.

How do we as citizens influence presidential actions? Being active in the political process gives us the opportunity to help shape our country in a meaningful way by selecting presidents and members of Congress. Even if our preferred candidates lose, our votes can send a message to our government about how we want our country to look and act. For example, what do you think should be our priorities when it comes to the president's role as head of state? Should we get involved in the affairs of other countries, or focus our attention and resources on domestic issues? How about issues pertaining to the president's job as head of government? What policy issues do you think are most pressing? To a very large extent, policy decisions in government are shaped by who shows up to vote on Election Day. Staying home is a real choice; but if you do so, you increase the chances that other voices (ones you may disagree with) will be heard.

While the issues the president manages, as discussed in this chapter, can seem removed from our daily lives, they have very real implications. Consider the Trump and Biden administrations. When President Trump was elected in 2016, he campaigned with a mandate to put America first. Domestically, he selected Supreme Court justices—a record three—whose conservative leanings will influence the Court for decades to come. His international policies emphasized America's economic interests over long-term security concerns. While President Biden focused on many of the same domestic issues President Trump emphasized, including building a strong economy and investing in infrastructure, he has chosen very different policy instruments to achieve these goals. Moreover, some of Biden's priorities, including a focus on expanding and protecting voter rights and strong support from citizens, were almost the opposite of what Trump tried to do. These two presidencies highlight just how consequential elections can be, as well as the need to appreciate the vast differences between how Democratic and Republican candidates behave in office.

1. Unquestionably, presidential power has grown significantly since the eighteenth century, with most of the remarkable growth finding its root in which cause?

- **a** Constitutional amendments changing the balance of power
- **b** Executive orders that have gone unchecked by Congress
- **c** Congressional increases in size and responsibilities of the executive branch
- **d** Changes in the public desire for a growth in government and regulation

2. Expansions in the size of government and the executive branch have often been associated with what events in American history?

- **a** State efforts to increase the amount of money being spent in cooperative programs
- **b** Intense lobbying efforts by business and labor interest groups
- **c** Discovery of wrongdoing and corruption in the government
- **d** The rise of national and international crises

3. The president's State of the Union address has the greatest importance for which of the following reasons?

- **a** It provides members of Congress an opportunity to directly address congressional priorities with the president.
- **b** It is required by the Constitution that the president report to Congress every year on the state of affairs.
- **c** It allows the president to communicate his or her legislative priorities for the next year to the nation and Congress.
- **d** It enumerates for the nation the areas of agreed compromise between the president and congressional leaders.

4. Presidents favor executive orders and executive agreements because they allow them to avoid the conflicts and uncertainties in seeking the consent of the Senate. But, by governing with these tools, presidents face which risk?

- **a** Executive orders and agreements can be simply repealed by a subsequent president.
- **b** Executive orders and agreements are often overridden by congressional actions.
- **c** There are difficulties in changing the executive orders and agreements once they are implemented.
- **d** Presidents will likely encounter resistance from leadership of departments and agencies.

5. Though most Americans are unaware of the Executive Office of the President and its functions, it would be helpful for them to understand that the offices in this organization carry out which important function?

- **a** Development and implementation of the president's policy agenda
- **b** Oversight of the activities and spending of the legislative and executive branches
- **c** Coordination of efforts with presidential campaigns
- **d** Interpretation and implementation of statutes that have been passed by Congress

6. The Cabinet is both professional and political in nature, being made up of the fifteen heads of the major government departments. The political nature of the Cabinet is established by which reality?

- **a** Significant numbers of Cabinet members have been removed by Congress after losing favor.
- **b** Cabinet members serve only while they have the favor of the president.
- **c** Most Cabinet members are individuals who previously served as popular elected officials.
- **d** Cabinet members can be removed by a consensus of the other members.

7. Which statement best exemplifies the position of a person who supports the Unitary Executive Theory?[47]

- **a** "I would say that law is precedent and history is anecdote—nice stories. Elaborating on how 'this President did this' and 'that President did that' is interesting, but it doesn't tell us much about the proper constitutional scope of executive power."
- **b** "Federal agencies now regulate almost every aspect of American life. If the president has near-total control over them, he or she has much greater power than originally granted."
- **c** "In response to the threat of fascism, the architects of executive control of the administrative state embraced separation of powers, especially internal to the executive branch."
- **d** "The Constitution provides: 'The executive Power shall be vested in a President of the United States.' This does not mean *some* of the executive power, but *all* of the executive power."

8. What best describes the importance of presidential signing statements?

- **a** Signing statements consist of a planned media event in which the president directly addresses the nation to express his or her view about the impact of the legislation.
- **b** The president issues a memo when signing a law that reflects his or her view of how the legislation should be implemented by the executive branch agencies.
- **c** Congressional leaders issue the statement jointly with the president to make clear the intent of the legislation and its outcomes.
- **d** Signing statements are an opportunity for the president to recognize the congressional leadership and public figures who were integral in the passage of legislation.

Use INQUIZITIVE to help you study and master this material.

13

The Bureaucracy

What's with all this red tape?

"Government! Three fourths parasitic and the other fourth stupid fumbling."[1]

Robert A. Heinlein, American writer

"Bureaucracy is not an obstacle to democracy but an inevitable complement to it."[2]

Joseph A. Schumpeter, American economist

Throughout the COVID-19 pandemic, one of the most important pieces of information was the number of people who died each day from the disease. Death statistics captured not only changes in how many people were suffering from the virus but also our success at treating these cases. At the same time, death statistics were politically significant, as they were a visible indicator of the government's ability (or inability) to deal with the pandemic. As waves of COVID-19 infections rose and fell, sharp increases in the number of daily COVID-related deaths highlighted gaps in state and local government preparedness, differences in local reopening and mask-wearing policies, variation in vaccine supply and distribution policies, and the willingness or unwillingness of local government officials to take the problem seriously.

The political significance of death statistics was one reason for an ongoing debate within the federal government over measuring COVID-related deaths. For example, if a patient with a compromised immune system caught the virus and died, was the death due to COVID-19 or the underlying condition that increased that person's vulnerability? During the Trump presidency, scientists at the federal Centers for Disease Control and Prevention (CDC) wanted to ignore underlying conditions, while members of President Trump's staff favored excluding cases from the pandemic's mortality statistics if an underlying condition could be identified. Later, the Biden administration allowed the CDC to make its own decisions about case and death counts as well as data on vaccination rates.

In the midst of the COVID-19 outbreak, the White House Coronavirus Task Force held daily television briefings to disseminate information to the public. Here, Dr. Anthony Fauci, director of the National Institute of Allergy and Infectious Diseases, can be seen placing his hand over his face in dismay as President Trump made a comment about "deep state" conspiracies during a briefing, demonstrating the often-contentious relationship between President Trump and the federal bureaucracy.

This example highlights three essential features of the federal bureaucracy. First, bureaucrats are often engaged in highly technical tasks that require expertise and judgment. Second, these tasks have political consequences—for President Trump, a reduction in death statistics would have helped him argue during the 2020 election campaign that his administration had responded effectively to the pandemic. Third, while Trump and Biden wield considerable power as presidents, they cannot simply order bureaucrats to do whatever they want. Even President Trump, who often

CHAPTER GOALS

Define *bureaucracy* and explain its major functions (pp. 494–503)

Trace the expansion of the federal bureaucracy over time (pp. 504–507)

Describe the size and structure of the executive branch today (pp. 508–514)

Describe who bureaucrats are and the regulations that govern their employment (pp. 514–517)

Explain how Congress and the president oversee the executive branch (pp. 517–523) described bureaucrats as an autonomous "deep state," was nevertheless forced to defer to their procedures and, in some cases, their policy decisions.

Up to now, we've described the policy-making process in terms of three steps: (1) citizens elect representatives, (2) these representatives go to Washington and enact laws, and (3) bureaucrats are given these laws to implement. The reality is that the responsibility for implementing laws conveys policy-making power. When bureaucrats write regulations, sign contracts with private corporations, deliver services to citizens, or make judgments about how to measure things like COVID-19 deaths, they are translating often-vague statutes into concrete decisions. Moreover, because of their training and experience, bureaucrats are often better informed than elected officials about the details of government policy. Bureaucratic expertise creates a new problem for elected officials: if they ignore what bureaucrats tell them or force bureaucrats to implement laws and directives as written, the result may be policy failures. However, if elected officials acknowledge bureaucratic expertise and allow them to make as well as implement government policy, elected officials give up significant power to the bureaucracy—something that the Trump administration was unwilling to risk. Were bureaucrats really obstructing the Trump agenda, or were they just doing their jobs? How do elected officials control a bureaucracy of experts, in the midst of a pandemic or in more routine times?

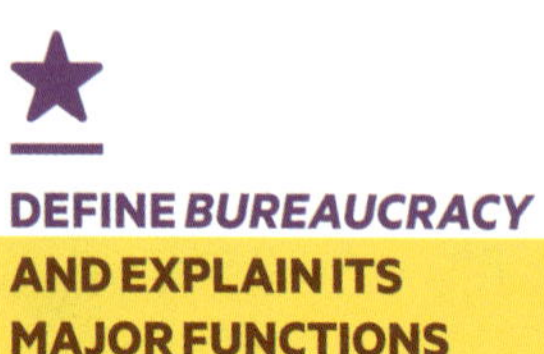

What is the federal bureaucracy?

bureaucracy
The system of civil servants and political appointees who implement congressional or presidential decisions; also known as the *administrative state*.

civil servants
Employees of bureaucratic agencies within the government.

political appointees
People selected by an elected leader, such as the president, to hold a government position.

The federal **bureaucracy** is the vast network of agencies that makes up the government's executive branch. It is composed of millions of **civil servants**, who work for the government in permanent positions, and thousands of **political appointees**, who hold short-term, usually senior positions and are appointed by the president. Another name for the bureaucracy is the *administrative state*, which refers to the role bureaucrats play in administering government policies.[3] Most constitutional scholars agree that the president is nominally in charge of the bureaucracy—although generally the president shares this power with members of Congress.

In general, the job of the federal bureaucracy includes a wide range of tasks, from regulating the behavior of individuals and corporations to buying pencils, jet fighters, vaccines, and everything in between. At one level, these actions implement policy decisions made by others, including presidential directives or legislation enacted by Congress. But as we will see, implementation often involves giving bureaucrats considerable discretion over the details of policy decisions. Moreover, these activities are inherently political and often conflictual: ordinary citizens, elected officials, and bureaucrats themselves often disagree about aspects of these activities, and they work to influence bureaucratic actions to suit their policy goals.

The key thing to understand about bureaucrats is that they have their own ideas about government policy. Rather than being mindless paper-pushers, they often push back against presidential or congressional directives. As a very influential political scientist, Theda Skocpol, once wrote, "Autonomous state actions will regularly take forms that attempt to reinforce the authority, political longevity, and social control of the state"—meaning we should expect bureaucrats to do things that increase their control over government policy.[4] What bureaucrats do with this power is an open question. They might have their own policy goals, might simply want to block presidential or congressional initiatives, or are working to secure a well-paying job after retirement from government service. But if we are trying to understand what government does, we need to include bureaucrats in our analysis.

What do bureaucrats do?

The task of the bureaucracy is to develop and implement policies established by congressional acts or presidential decisions. Sometimes the tasks associated with putting these laws and resolutions into effect are very specific. For example, in the appropriations bill for fiscal year 2024, Congress appropriated $5.2 billion for the purchase of 48 F-35 attack jets from defense contractor Lockheed Martin. This provision required no discretion on the part of the bureaucrats tasked to implement it—all they needed to do was sign the contract, make sure the jets were delivered, and pay Lockheed Martin.

More commonly, however, legislation provides only general guidelines for meeting governmental goals. Bureaucrats thus have considerable latitude to develop particular policies and programs. For example, the 1938 Federal Food, Drug, and Cosmetic Act gave the Food and Drug Administration (FDA) the job of determining which drugs are safe and effective (including drugs to treat COVID-19 symptoms and vaccines to prevent people from getting the disease), but it allowed FDA bureaucrats to develop their own procedures for making these determinations.[5] Currently, the FDA requires that drug manufacturers first test new drugs for safety and then conduct further trials to determine their effectiveness. An FDA advisory board of scientists and doctors reviews the results of these tests, and FDA bureaucrats decide whether to allow the manufacturer to market the drug. (The so-called Right to Try exception allows patients to bypass this procedure, but only if they have a terminal illness, if they have exhausted other treatments, and if medicine is available and has been proven safe.) While members of Congress and the president created these procedures (including Right to Try), they have no way to intervene except by enacting a new bill that sets out a new process.

Developing Regulations A **regulation** is a rule that allows the government to exercise control over individuals and corporations by allowing or prohibiting behavior, setting out the conditions under which certain behaviors can occur, or assessing costs or granting benefits based on behavior. Bureaucrats gain the authority to write regulations from acts passed by Congress, either through the statute that initially set up their agency or through subsequent laws. For example, the Environmental

regulation
A rule that allows the government to exercise control over individuals and corporations by restricting certain behaviors.

Although the term "bureaucracy" may suggest workers shuffling papers and answering emails in cubicles, the agencies of the federal bureaucracy perform a wide range of tasks. The Centers for Disease Control and Prevention—a federal agency—contributed in many ways during the COVID-19 pandemic, including tracking the spread of the virus, launching campaigns to educate people on how to protect themselves from the virus, and helping distribute lifesaving equipment to affected areas, including vaccines and medicines to mitigate the virus's effects.

Protection Agency (EPA) has many regulations that limit the amount of pollutants emitted from factories, automobiles, and electrical power plants. (for more details, see the How It Works graphic on pp. 498–99).

notice-and-comment procedure
A step in the rule-making process in which proposed rules are published in the *Federal Register* and made available for debate by the general public.

Regulations are developed according to the **notice-and-comment procedure**.[6] Before most proposed regulations can take effect, they are published in the *Federal Register*, an official journal that includes rules, proposed rules, and other types of government documents. Individuals and companies potentially affected by the regulation can then comment, or respond to the agency that proposed it, either supporting or opposing the regulation or offering different versions for consideration. They can also appeal to members of Congress or to the president's staff for help in lobbying bureaucrats to revise the proposal. The agency then issues a final regulation that incorporates changes based on the comments. This final regulation is also published in the *Federal Register* and then put into effect. The process is time-consuming. For example, an ongoing effort of the Federal Aviation Administration (FAA) to develop regulations on the use of drone aircraft began with a congressional mandate issued in 2012. Current regulations limit the size and weight of drones that can be flown without registering with the agency, but as of 2024 the FAA is still developing rules to govern larger package-delivery drones that fly over populated areas. Many regulations can take even longer to craft from beginning to end.

This process of devising or modifying regulations is highly political. Members of Congress and the president usually have strong opinions about how new regulations should look—and even when they don't, they may still get involved on behalf of a constituent or an interest group. Bureaucrats take account of these pressures from elected officials for two reasons: (1) the bureaucrats' policy-making power may derive from a statute that members of Congress could overturn, and (2) bureaucrats need congressional support to get larger budgets and to expand their agency's mission. Thus, despite bureaucrats' power to develop and implement policies, their agencies' budgets, appointed leaders, and overall missions are subject to elected officials' oversight.

Many regulations are issued each year, contained in thousands of pages of the *Federal Register*. For example, the *Register* for September 13, 2024, contained 2 proposed regulations, 5 new regulations, and 127 notices from agencies at various milestones in the regulatory process.[7] Although nearly all government agencies issue regulations, most come from a few agencies, including the Federal Trade Commission (FTC),

Federal regulations influence many aspects of everyday life that would seem unlikely to be affected by government actions. The increase in the number of women's intercollegiate athletic teams is partly due to regulations that require equal funding for men's and women's teams. Pictured here is the University of South Carolina's 2022 NCAA women's basketball championship team.

which regulates commerce; the Federal Communications Commission (FCC), which regulates media companies that create content as well as telecommunications companies that transmit information; and the Food and Drug Administration (FDA), which regulates drugs, medical products, food, and cosmetics.

Federal regulations affect most aspects of everyday life. They influence the gas mileage of cars sold in the United States, the materials used to build roads, and the price of gasoline. They determine the amounts that doctors can charge senior citizens for medical procedures; the hours that medical residents can work; the criteria used to determine who gets a heart, lung, or kidney transplant; and the allowable emissions from power plants. Regulations set the eligibility criteria for student loans, limit how the military can recruit on college campuses, determine who can get a home mortgage and what the interest rate will be, and describe what constitutes equal funding for men's and women's college sports teams. Regulations also shape contribution limits and spending decisions in political campaigns.

Regulations are often controversial because they involve trade-offs between incompatible goals, as well as decisions made under uncertain circumstances. For example, the regulations that guide the FDA drug-approval process prioritize the goal of preventing harmful drugs from coming to market.[8] As a result, patients sometimes cannot get access to experimental treatments, even with the Right to Try exception. Some experimental drugs may be in short supply, while others may be available only as part of a small clinical trial. The FDA can accelerate the approval process in emergency cases, a process used during the COVID-19 pandemic to speed availability of vaccines and medicines that had been tested for safety and approved for treatment of other diseases.

The nine most terrifying words in the English language are: I'm from the government, and I'm here to help.

—President Ronald Reagan

President Trump campaigned on a platform of reducing government regulations, and he issued many directives to bureaucrats to reduce the number and scope of regulations. You may wonder if the number of regulations was, in fact, reduced during the first Trump administration. The short answer is no. Though federal agencies issued fewer new regulations during the Trump administration, much of this decline can be attributed to the delay or cancellation of proposed rules that Trump inherited from the Obama administration. In 2017, Republican majorities in Congress also took advantage of a law that allows the House and Senate to repeal regulations issued during the last months of a presidential term. However, Trump had only limited success in eliminating regulations that were already in force when he entered office. The problem is that once regulations are in place, changing or repealing them is a lengthy process that often requires Congress to pass new laws. For example, while Trump and his appointees at the EPA proposed repealing some environmental regulations (including the Clean Power Plan described in the How It Works graphic), the process was delayed by court challenges and congressionally mandated hearings and other procedures and was nowhere near finished at the end of Trump's term of office. Trump's successor, Joe Biden, suspended these proceedings and in fact initiated the process of establishing stronger regulations.

Bringing Expertise to Policy Making Bureaucrats are also an important source of new government policies. For example, Congress and the president give civilian and military personnel in the Department of Defense the job of revising military doctrines—broad directives on how our armed forces should go about accomplishing specific tasks such as protecting civilian freighters from attacks by Somali pirates, deploying troops to rescue American civilians in hostile territory, or sending military assistance to countries such as Ukraine. While military doctrines reflect input from members of Congress, the State Department and the president's appointees, and groups outside government (including lobbyists, think tanks, and defense contractors), they also reflect the preferences of the bureaucrats assigned to the task. Thus, as in the case of regulations, when it comes to government policy, bureaucrats are not just implementers: they have a significant influence on what government does and does not do.

How it works: in theory

Bureaucracy and Legislation

After Congress passes legislation and the president signs it, the transition from legislation to regulation begins. Input from local government officials, interest groups, and others helps to refine the regulations as they are developed and has a strong influence on how regulations will affect people "on the ground."

Congress passes legislation.

↓

The president signs the bill into law.

↓

Bureaucrats interpret the law and design appropriate regulations.

↓

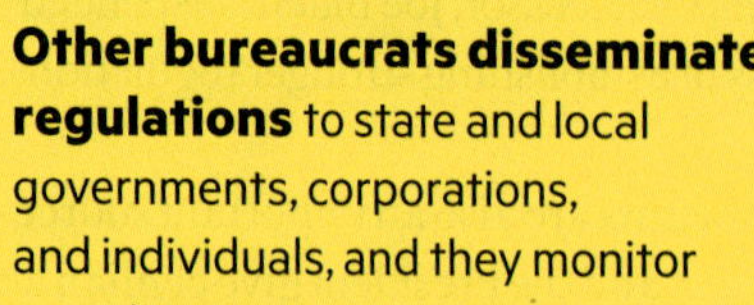

Other bureaucrats disseminate regulations to state and local governments, corporations, and individuals, and they monitor compliance.

↓

Regulations can be revised in light of changing circumstances, different political climates, or unanticipated consequences.

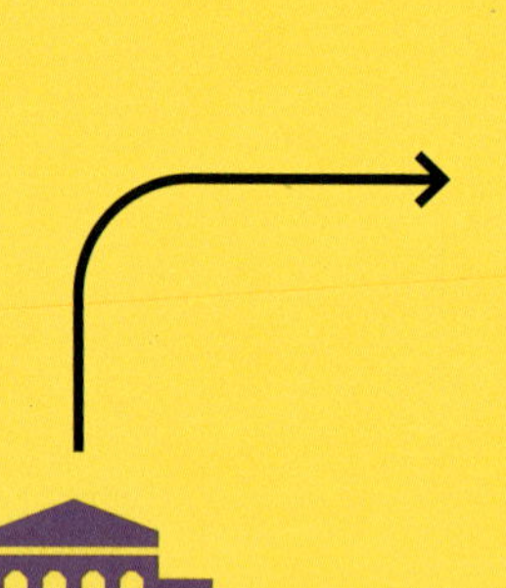

Courts respond to challenges to the law, and they can provide guidelines for implementation.

Citizens and interest groups provide information and proposals to bureaucrats, and they lobby for their preferred implementation of the legislation.

How it works: in practice

Regulating Greenhouse Gas Emissions

Current efforts by the Biden Administration to limit CO_2 emissions from fossil fuel power plants are some of the latest steps in a 60-year process of court cases, congressional enactments, presidential directives, and actions by Environmental Protection Agency (EPA) bureaucrats.

New Acts!

Congressional Action: Congress enacts two Clean Air Acts, in 1963 and 1970, respectively, with amendments in 1977 and 1990, authorizing the government to monitor and limit emissions of harmful chemicals into the atmosphere.

Although . . . maybe not?

Bureaucratic Action (2003): The EPA announces that the **Clean Air Act does not give it the authority to regulate CO_2** and other greenhouse gases.

Actually . . . yes.

Judicial Action (2007): In response to a case brought by 12 states, the Supreme Court rules that **greenhouse gases are covered by the Clean Air Act**.

Obama weighs in.

Presidential Directive (June 2013): President Obama **directs the EPA to develop additional regulations** for limiting CO_2 emissions from new and existing power plants.

Results?

September 2013: The EPA modifies its draft regulations to place **CO_2 standards** on new power plants and issues a revised proposal.

June 2014: The EPA proposes an additional rule that aims **to cut CO_2 emissions from existing power plants**.

Third try!

New Regulations Finalized (August 2015): After receiving over 6 million comments, the EPA **announces its Clean Power Plan**, which will regulate CO_2 emissions from both new and existing power plants.

Rollback?

November 2017: Under the Trump administration, **the EPA announces a plan to repeal and replace the Clean Power Plan**.

A new effort.

March 2021: The Biden Administration declines to reverse Trump's repeal only because they are developing more aggressive limits on CO_2 emissions.

Stand by.

June 2022: SCOTUS holds that the Clean Power Plan does not empower the federal government to regulate CO_2 emissions, forcing the Biden Administration to find a new justification for its planned regulations.

Critical Thinking

1. **Critics of the regulatory process complain that unelected** bureaucrats make most of the decisions while elected officials sit on the sidelines. Is this complaint supported by the case of the Clean Power Plan?
2. **The Clean Power Plan illustrates how acts of legislation are often** reinterpreted years after their passage. Why don't members of Congress write legislation in ways that prevent this from happening?

Delivering Services Some bureaucrats are the face of the federal government, interacting directly with citizens to provide services and other benefits. People working in the Department of Agriculture assist farmers by processing crop loans and providing advice on new technologies and techniques. Members of the Park Service operate the network of national parks and wilderness areas. The Transportation Security Administration staffs the security checkpoints at American airports. And during the COVID-19 pandemic, National Guard troops helped staff facilities that provided medical care and vaccinations in hard-hit areas. These and other jobs are a reminder of how intertwined the federal government is with the lives of ordinary Americans. We may like to think of the federal government as something that exists only in Washington, D.C., but the reality is that bureaucrats are spread out across the country and are deeply involved with all elements of American society.

Bureaucratic expertise and its consequences

Bureaucrats are experts. Even compared with most members of Congress or presidential appointees, the average bureaucrat is a specialist in a certain policy area (often holding an advanced degree), with a good grasp of their agency's mission. For example, people who hold scientific or management positions in the FDA usually know more about the benefits and risks of new drugs than people outside the agency do. Their decision to deny unapproved drugs to seriously ill patients may seem cruel, but it may also reflect a balancing of two incompatible goals: preventing harmful drugs from reaching the market and allowing people who have exhausted all other treatments access to risky, experimental products. A bureaucracy of experts is an important part of what political scientists call **state capacity**—the knowledge, personnel, and institutions needed to effectively implement policies.[9] It is an important check on elected officials, helping to ensure that government policies are effective and efficient.

DID YOU KNOW?

28%

of federal bureaucrats have an advanced degree (post-bachelor). The corresponding percentage for large private businesses is about 11 percent.

Source: U.S. Census.

state capacity
The knowledge, personnel, and institutions that the government requires to effectively implement policies.

While having an expert bureaucracy seems like an obvious good idea, it creates a new problem for elected officials. Bureaucrats can bring expertise to their policy choices only if elected officials stop ordering bureaucrats around and instead allow them to act as they think best. But when elected officials allow such discretion, they risk losing control over the policy-making process and having to live with policy choices that serve bureaucratic interests without satisfying the elected officials or their constituents.

The Problem of Control: Principals and Agents Political scientists refer to the difficulty that elected officials and their staff face when they try to interpret or influence bureaucratic actions as the **problem of control**.[10] A classic illustration of this situation is the **principal–agent game**. The principal–agent game describes an interaction in which an individual or a group (an "agent") acts on behalf of another (the "principal"). In the federal government, the president and Congress are principals and bureaucrats are agents. An agent in the bureaucracy may not want to work because they are lazy or, more commonly, because they prefer outcomes that the principal does not like. Moreover, because the agent is an expert at the task they have been given, the agent has additional knowledge and experience that are inaccessible to the principal. The conundrum for the principal, then, is this: giving the agent very specific orders prevents the agent from acting based on expertise, but if the principal gives the agent the freedom to make decisions based on expertise, the principal has less control over the agent's actions.

problem of control
A difficulty faced by elected officials in ensuring that when bureaucrats implement policies they follow these officials' intentions but still have enough discretion to use their expertise.

principal–agent game
The interaction between a principal (such as the president or Congress), who needs something done, and an agent (such as a bureaucrat), who is responsible for carrying out the principal's orders.

For example, suppose Congress and the president directed the FDA to shorten its drug-approval process to approve new drugs or vaccines to fight a future pandemic. FDA officials might have mandated a lengthy process based on their expert assessment of the best way to screen out harmful drugs. By giving orders that superseded the

FDA officials' screening process, elected officials would be sacrificing the valuable bureaucratic expertise behind the policy and risking the hasty approval of unsafe drugs. On the other hand, if Congress and the president allowed FDA bureaucrats to devise their own procedures and regulations, there would be a chance that the FDA could use this freedom to pursue goals that have nothing to do with drug safety. For example, some critics of the FDA's procedures have asserted that a drawn-out approval process is designed to favor large companies that already have drugs on the market over smaller companies trying to get approval for drugs that would compete with existing products.

The principal–agent game can also be framed in terms of citizens. Figure 13.1 shows that a majority of survey respondents agreed that the federal government is typically inefficient and wasteful—although the percentage agreeing with this assessment declined from its peak in 1994 until more recent years, when it again increased. Such opinions give citizens a strong motivation to demand that elected officials control the bureaucracy—to reduce the waste and inefficiency or, as the earlier quote from Ronald Reagan suggests, to prevent bureaucrats from overly intruding into American society.

Members of Congress and citizens are sometimes right to question the motives of members of the bureaucracy. Sometimes bureaucratic actions are the result of **regulatory capture**, which occurs when bureaucrats cater to a small group of individuals or corporations, regardless of the impact of these actions on public welfare. For example, in 2015 the FCC allowed telecommunications companies to charge very high rates for phone calls made by individuals in federal prisons to their families, friends, or legal counsel. The companies have long argued to the FCC that these rates were justified by the cost of special hardware needed to monitor prison calls—but no one was lobbying the FCC in favor of federal prisoners, who have no alternative but to pay what the companies charge. Ultimately, the FCC put new limits in place, but the companies managed to get the new regulations thrown out in court on grounds that the FCC could not regulate intrastate (within state) calls, which is where the situation stands today. Research by political scientists Susan Webb Yackee and Jason Webb Yackee show that this pro-business tilt in regulations and rule-making is very common.[11]

regulatory capture
A situation in which bureaucrats favor the interests of the groups or corporations they are supposed to regulate at the expense of the general public.

FIGURE 13.1

How Americans View the Federal Bureaucracy

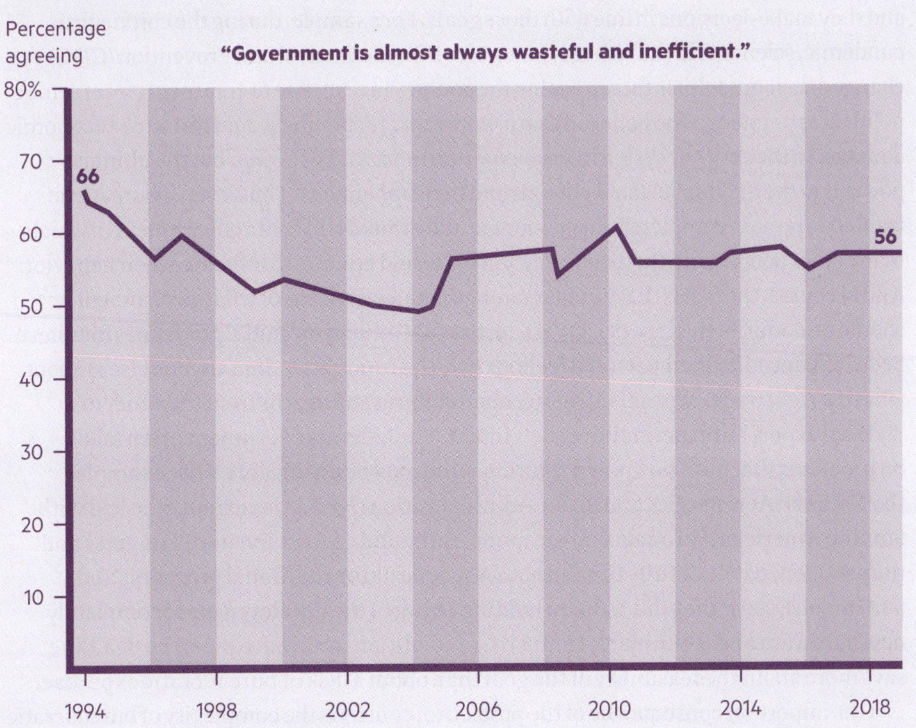

Many Americans believe the bureaucracy is wasteful and inefficient. Note, however, that the magnitude of negative feelings varies over time. Consider the time frame represented in the graph. What happened during these years that might explain the changes in citizens' opinions about the government?

Source: Pew Research Center, "In a Politically Polarized Era, Sharp Divides in Both Partisan Coalitions," December 17, 2019, www.pewresearch.org/politics/2019/12/17/views-of-government-and-the-nation/ (accessed 5/20/22).

During the COVID-19 pandemic, government was divided on the best way to get the country back to work and reopen the economy after the shutdown. John Howard, MD, the director of the National Institute for Occupational Safety and Health, testified on how to protect workers from COVID-19 at a U.S. House Committee on Education and Labor Subcommittee on Workforce Protections hearing.

One mechanism for capture occurs when short-term political appointees come from (and will return to) the very industries they are supposed to regulate, a phenomenon known as the revolving door (as discussed in Chapter 10). In the case of the FDA, one argument for the agency's alleged favoritism toward big companies is that agency bureaucrats hope to gain well-paid positions with these companies after retirement from government service. There are instances of bureaucrats behaving in this way, particularly political appointees who only serve for short periods. For example, in 2019 an appointee in the Department of the Interior who had pushed for expanded oil drilling in Alaska left the government to work for one of the companies that would benefit from this expansion.[12]

You might think that the problem of control isn't too difficult to solve as long as bureaucrats act as impartial experts and set aside their own policy goals. Many studies of bureaucracies, beginning with the work of the early political theorist Max Weber, argue that bureaucrats should provide information and expertise and avoid taking sides on policy questions or being swayed by elected officials, people outside government, or their own policy goals.[13] However, bureaucrats' behavior doesn't always fit Weber's vision. Many enter the bureaucracy with their own ideas about what government should do, and they make decisions in line with those goals. For example, during the coronavirus pandemic, scientists in the federal Centers for Disease Control and Prevention (CDC) changed their guidelines for reopening the country in response to comments from senior political appointees, who believed that a more rapid reopening would minimize economic damage. In the end, our system places experts in positions of power, but the ultimate power is in the hands of elected officials and their appointees. Thus, even if bureaucrats wanted to remain completely dispassionate, they would still face a government in which many other people with their own policy goals would attempt to influence their behavior.[14] And of course, the fact is that bureaucrats have their own ideas of what government should be doing. In the case of COVID-19, the CDC scientists' initial guidelines may have been influenced by their personal feelings (which are no better than anyone else's) about what the right trade-off was between economic harm and deaths from the pandemic.

Even expert bureaucrats have their limits. The federal government often takes on problems that have no known solution—and may be unsolvable.[15] For example, the National Aeronautics and Space Administration (NASA) is currently tasked with landing American astronauts on the moon by the end of 2027. Even so, Congress and the president have not fully funded NASA's requests for additional programs and personnel. Even if they did, a moon landing requires the development of completely new hardware and techniques. Under these conditions, failing to meet the deadline says more about the feasibility of the goal than about a lack of bureaucratic expertise.

One important consequence of the problem of control is the complexity of bureaucratic organizations and procedures. Despite bureaucrats' policy expertise, their decisions

red tape
Excessive or unnecessarily complex regulations imposed by the bureaucracy.

standard operating procedures (SOPs)
Rules that lower-level bureaucrats must follow when implementing policies.

often appear to take too much time, rely on arbitrary judgments of what is important, and have unintended consequences—to the point that actions designed to solve one problem may create worse ones. Examples include **red tape**, which refers to excessive or unnecessarily complex regulations, and **standard operating procedures (SOPs)**, which are the rules that lower-level bureaucrats must follow, regardless of whether they actually apply, when implementing policies.

In part, red tape and SOPs are inevitable given the complexity of the tasks bureaucrats are given to do. For example, the U.S. Tax Code takes up thousands of pages—but in a country as large as the United States, where people have many different sources of income and there are many distinct kinds of corporate activity, a tax code that treats people and companies fairly while raising enough revenue to run the government is inevitably going to be complicated.

Despite their policy expertise, bureaucrats still make mistakes. When the Small Business Administration (SBA) initiated the Paycheck Protection Program in 2020 to provide assistance to small businesses during the COVID-19 pandemic, it developed a website with detailed information on the application process—only to find that many small business owners were not familiar with navigating the internet. The SBA had to engage community organizations in outreach efforts to bring these businesses into the program.

However, sometimes red tape and SOPs are the result of elected officials' attempts to mitigate the problem of control. For example, some of the complexity of the American tax code is due to congressional mandates that create tax breaks for favored corporations and constituencies. In the abstract, elected officials might prefer that the tax code be determined by expert bureaucrats, who can predict the long-term consequences of changes to the code. In reality, however, members of Congress want to make sure their state or district is treated fairly—as well as provide tax breaks in order to increase their chances of getting reelected—and are willing to sacrifice expertise in favor of these other benefits, even if it makes the tax code more complex.

In other ways, such as the notice-and-comment procedure described earlier, elected officials require bureaucrats to inform them in advance about proposed policy decisions before they are implemented. Other congressional mandates define who can work in different jobs at an agency, where agency offices are located, and many other specifics of agency structure and process. While few of these mandates contribute to bureaucratic nimbleness, that is not their intent. What they are designed to do is give elected officials ways to mitigate problems of control.

The problem of control has existed throughout the history of the federal government. It affects both the kinds of policies that bureaucrats implement and the structure of the federal bureaucracy, including the number of agencies and their missions, staff, and tasks. Moreover, elected officials use a variety of methods to solve the problem of control, including making it easier for people outside government to learn about agency actions before they take effect. However, all these tactics are, at best, partial solutions to the problem of control. The trade-off between expertise and control remains.

"Why Should I Care?"

Bureaucrats aren't mindless paper pushers. Rather, they are experts who have considerable power to shape what government does. The way many elected officials talk, it's easy to think that once they pass a piece of legislation or issue an executive order, government policy automatically changes. In most cases, however, these directives are only the first step. To bring these changes to life, bureaucrats must step in to translate often-vague goals into concrete regulations, budgets, and actions. In other words, while you might not think much about bureaucrats, they can have a profound effect on your daily life.

TRACE THE EXPANSION OF THE FEDERAL BUREAUCRACY OVER TIME

How has the American bureaucracy grown?

The evolution of America's federal bureaucracy was not steady or smooth. Most of its important developments occurred during three short periods: the late 1890s and early 1900s, the 1930s, and the 1960s.[16] In all three, the driving force was a combination of citizens' demands for enhanced government services and elected and government officials' desires to either respond to these demands or increase the size and scope of the federal government to be more in line with their own policy goals.

The beginning of America's bureaucracy

From the Founding of the United States until the election of Andrew Jackson in 1828, federal bureaucrats numbered at most in the thousands. The small size of the federal government during these years reflected Americans' deep suspicion of government, especially unelected officials. In the Declaration of Independence, in fact, one of the charges against George III was that he had "erected a multitude of new offices and sent hither swarms of officers to harass our people and eat out their substance."[17]

In these early years, there were only three executive departments (State, Treasury, and War), along with a postmaster general, and executive branch offices were formed only when absolutely necessary. This small bureaucracy performed a very narrow range of tasks, such as collecting taxes on imports and exports and delivering the mail. The national army consisted of a small Corps of Engineers and a few frontier patrols. The attorney general was a private attorney who had the federal government as one of his clients. Members of Congress outnumbered civil servants in Washington, and the president had very little staff at all.[18]

This cartoon of a monument depicting President Andrew Jackson riding a pig decries his involvement in the spoils system, which allowed politicians to dole out government service jobs in return for political support.

Despite its small size, conflicts soon arose around control of the bureaucracy. The legislation that established the departments of State, Treasury, and War allowed the president to nominate the people in charge of these departments but made these appointments subject to Senate approval. The same is true today for the heads of all executive departments and many other presidential appointments.

The election of Andrew Jackson in 1828 brought the first large-scale use of the spoils system: people who had worked for Jackson's campaign were rewarded with new positions in the federal government (usually as local postmasters).[19] The spoils system was extremely useful to party organizations, as it gave them a powerful incentive with which to convince people to work for the party, and it was a particularly important tool for Jackson. His campaign organization was at that time the largest ever organized.

The challenge facing the spoils system was ensuring that these party-loyalists-turned-government-employees, who often lacked experience in their new fields, could actually carry out their jobs. The solution was to develop procedures for these employees that guided them on exactly what to do even if they had little or no experience or training.[20] These instructions became one of the earliest uses of standard operating procedures. They ensured that the government could function even if large numbers of employees had been hired in reward for political work rather than because of their qualifications.[21]

As America expanded in size, so did the federal government, which saw an almost eightfold increase in the bureaucracy between 1816 and the beginning of the Civil War in 1861. This growth did not reflect fundamental changes in what the government did; in fact, much of the increase came in areas such as the Post Office, which needed to serve a geographically larger nation—and, of course, to provide additional "spoils" for party workers in the form of government jobs.[22] Even by the end of the Civil War, the federal government still had very little involvement in the lives of ordinary Americans. State and local governments provided services such as education, public works, and welfare benefits, if they were provided at all. The federal government's role in daily life was limited to mail delivery, the collection of import and export taxes, and work in a few other sectors.

Building a new American state: the Progressive Era

Political developments in the second half of the nineteenth century transformed America's bureaucracy.[23] While the transformation began after the Civil War, the most significant changes occurred during the Progressive Era, from 1890 to 1920. Many laws and executive actions increased the government's regulatory power during this period, including the Sherman Antitrust Act of 1890, the Pure Food and Drug Act of 1906, the Federal Meat Inspection Act of 1906, expansion of the Interstate Commerce Commission, and various conservation measures.[24] Now the federal government was no longer simply a deliverer of mail and a defender of borders; rather, it began to have a direct impact on everyday life. When Americans bought food or other products, went to work, or traveled on vacation, the choices available to them were shaped by the actions of federal bureaucrats in Washington and elsewhere.

These developments were matched by a fundamental change in the federal bureaucracy following passage of the 1883 Pendleton Civil Service Act. This measure created the **federal civil service**, in which the merit system (qualifications, not political connections) would be the basis for hiring and promoting bureaucrats.[25] In other words, when new presidents took office they could not replace government workers with their own campaign workers. Initially, only about 13,000 federal jobs acquired civil service protections, but over the next two decades many additional positions were incorporated into the civil service. In some cases, presidents gave civil service protections to people who had been hired under the spoils system to prevent the next president from replacing these bureaucrats with the president's own loyalists. Over time, these reforms created a bureaucracy in which people were hired for their expertise and allowed to build a career in government without having to fear being fired when a new president or Congress took office.[26] In the modern era, virtually all full-time, permanent government employees other than senior political appointees have civil service protections.

federal civil service
A system created by the 1883 Pendleton Civil Service Act in which bureaucrats are hired on the basis of merit rather than political connections.

The New Deal, the Great Society, and the Reagan Revolution

Dramatic expansion of the federal bureaucracy occurred during the New Deal period in the 1930s and during the mid-1960s Great Society era. In both cases, the changes were driven by a combination of citizen demands and the preferences of elected officials who favored an increased role of government in society. These expansion trends were only marginally curtailed during the Reagan Revolution of the 1980s.

The New Deal "The New Deal" refers to the government programs implemented during Franklin Roosevelt's first term as president in the 1930s. At one level, these programs were a response to the Great Depression and the inability of local governments and private charities to provide adequate support to Americans during this economic crisis. Many advocates of the New Deal also favored an expanded role for government in American society, regardless of the immediate need for intervention.[27] Roosevelt's programs included reforms to the financial industry as well as efforts to help people directly, including the stimulation of employment and economic growth,

Franklin Roosevelt's New Deal programs greatly expanded the power of the federal government and the bureaucracy. As this cartoon shows, these changes were controversial, with some seeing them as moving too much power from Congress to the president and bureaucracy.

and the formation of labor unions. The Social Security Act, the first federally funded pension program for all Americans, was also passed as part of the New Deal.

These reforms resulted in a vast increase in the size, responsibilities, and capacity of the bureaucracy, as well as a large transfer of power to bureaucrats and to the president.[28] While the Progressive Era reforms created an independent bureaucracy and state capacity, the New Deal reforms broadened the range of policy areas in which this capacity could be applied. Before the New Deal, the federal government influenced citizens' choices through activities such as regulating industries and workplace conditions. After the New Deal, the federal government took on the role of directly delivering a wide range of benefits and services to its citizens—from jobs to electricity. It also increased regulations on many industries, most notably the banking and financial sectors.

The expansion of the federal government during the New Deal and the subsequent delegation of power to bureaucrats and to the president were controversial changes, both when they were enacted and as they were implemented in subsequent years.[29] Many Republicans and some Democrats opposed New Deal reforms because they believed that the federal government could not deliver services efficiently, that an expanded federal bureaucracy would create a modern spoils system, or that establishing a broad social safety net would erode freedom and personal responsibility. Many southerners worried that the federal government's increased involvement in everyday life would endanger the system of racial segregation in southern states.[30] Even so, Democratic supporters of the New Deal, aided by public support in northern cities and some rural areas, carried the day.

The Great Society The Great Society was a series of federal programs enacted during Lyndon Johnson's presidency (1963–1969) that further expanded the size, capacity, and activities of the bureaucracy. During these years, Johnson proposed and Congress passed programs that funded bilingual education, loans and grants for college students, special education, preschools, construction of elementary and secondary schools, mass-transit programs in many cities, health care for seniors and poor people, housing in urban and rural areas, job training, enhanced voting rights and civil rights for minorities, environmental protection, funding for the arts and cultural activities, and space exploration.[31]

The Great Society programs had mixed success. Voting rights and civil rights reforms ended the "separate but equal" system of social order in southern states and dramatically increased political participation by Black Americans.[32] But many of the antipoverty programs were dismal failures. During the 1960s and 1970s, poverty rates among most groups remained relatively constant, and some actually increased. In retrospect, the people who designed and implemented these programs did not realize the complexities of the problems they were trying to address.[33] For example, many antipoverty programs were built on the assumption that most people receiving welfare needed job training programs in order to transition from welfare to permanent, paid employment. However, additional data that became available a decade after these laws were passed showed that most people receiving welfare do so for short periods because of medical or family crises—problems that the Great Society programs did not address.[34] Despite these shortcomings, the expansion of the federal government during the New Deal and Great Society has remained in place well into the twenty-first century.

The Reagan Revolution and Afterward The election of Ronald Reagan to the presidency in 1980, along with a Republican takeover of the Senate and Republican gains in the House of Representatives, created an opportunity for conservatives to roll back the size and scope of the federal government. These efforts were largely unsuccessful. In the years since Reagan, members of Congress and presidents from both parties have fought for large expansions in government policy. For example, while Democrat Barack Obama's administration issued many new environmental regulations and profoundly changed the American health care system, these changes are not too different in magnitude from the reforms championed by Republican George W. Bush, including education policies that increased federal control over local school districts, new drug financing benefits for seniors, and changes to financial regulations that increased financial reporting requirements for corporations. After four years in office, the Trump administration had little success in cutting overall federal spending or in reducing the size of specific agencies. For example, the administration initially proposed several cuts in the budget of the State Department for fiscal year 2018, only to ultimately accept a congressional budget that kept spending levels constant. And while Trump campaigned in 2024 on a promise to end civil service protections for about 50,000 senior policy makers, it is unclear whether he will be able to fully implement his plans.

Under President George W. Bush, the federal bureaucracy continued to expand. Programs like No Child Left Behind increased the role of government in society.

"Why Should I Care?"

Though sometimes their rhetoric seems to tell a different story, the difference between Republicans' and Democrats' philosophies about the bureaucracy is not over the size of the federal government but over what government should do. While Republicans often argue for making government smaller and Democrats respond by highlighting the consequences of even a small cut in services, the truth is that most people on both sides accept the fact that a large federal government is here to stay. Knowing how the federal bureaucracy has grown, as well as evaluating whether this growth has caused problems or created benefits, is central to building your own ideas about what government should do.

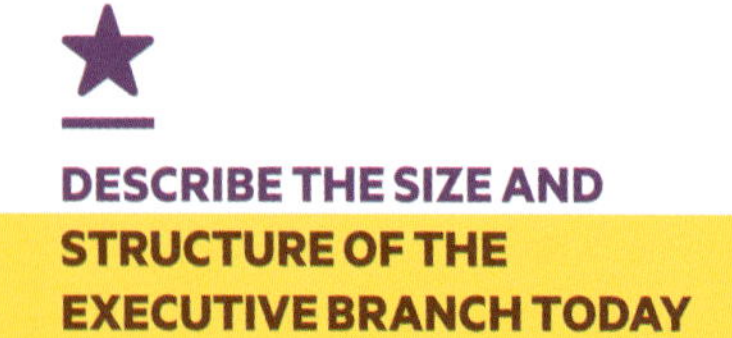

DESCRIBE THE SIZE AND STRUCTURE OF THE EXECUTIVE BRANCH TODAY

The modern federal bureaucracy

The size and scope of the modern federal bureaucracy reflect the expansion of the federal government over the last half century and its increased role in the lives of everyday Americans. The structure of the bureaucracy also reflects ongoing attempts by presidents, members of Congress, and others to control bureaucratic actions in line with their policy goals.

The structure of the federal government

Office of Management and Budget
An office within the EOP that is responsible for creating the president's annual budget proposal to Congress, reviewing proposed rules, and performing other budget-related tasks.

independent agencies
Government offices or organizations that provide government services and are not part of an executive department.

Nuts & Bolts 13.1 shows the structure of the executive branch of the federal government. As discussed in Chapter 12, the Executive Office of the President (EOP) contains organizations that support the president and implement presidential policy initiatives. Individuals working in these organizations aim to ensure that bureaucrats (agents) act appropriately to implement the president's (principal's) policy priorities and preferences.[35] Among its many offices, the EOP contains the **Office of Management and Budget**, which prepares the president's annual budget proposal to Congress and monitors government spending and the development of new regulations. Below the EOP are the 15 executive departments, from the Department of Agriculture to the Department of Veterans Affairs, which constitute the major divisions within the executive branch. The heads of these 15 organizations (plus others added by presidential order) make up the president's Cabinet. One thing to remember: while the diagram places the EOP above the cabinet departments and all other government agencies, the president's authority to direct agency decisions is not absolute, as it is limited by statute, regulations, and the Constitution, as well as by the pressure of business and a lack of information. These limits are discussed later in this chapter as well as in Chapter 12.

Each executive department contains many smaller, sometimes diverse organizations. Nuts & Bolts 13.2 shows the organizational chart for the Department of Agriculture, for example (see p. 510). As you can see, the Department of Agriculture includes offices that help farmers produce and sell their crops and offices that ensure food safety, but it also houses the Forest Service and offices that manage issues related to housing and utilities in rural areas. The Department of Agriculture also administers the Supplemental Nutritional Assistance Program (SNAP; formerly known as food stamps), even though the program has no direct connection to farming or food safety.

In addition to executive departments, the government contains a group of agencies, commissions, and government corporations that are called **independent agencies** to highlight that they are not part of an executive department. Most of these agencies carry out specialized functions, such as regulating a particular activity (these are called independent regulatory agencies) or carrying out policy in a narrow area. The Federal Reserve System, for example, manages the money supply, banking system, and interest rates, while NASA directs aviation research and space exploration. Nuts & Bolts 13.1 includes only noteworthy or well-known agencies; there are many more.

There are two important lessons to draw from these charts. First, the federal government handles an enormous range of functions. Second, the division of activities among executive departments and independent agencies does not always have an obvious logic. Why, for example, does the Department of Agriculture administer rural utilities programs and SNAP? Similarly, it is not always clear why certain tasks are handled by an independent agency whereas others fall within the scope of an executive department.[36]

The Executive Branch of the Federal Government

The executive branch includes the 15 cabinet offices, as well as several independent agencies, commissions, and government corporations.

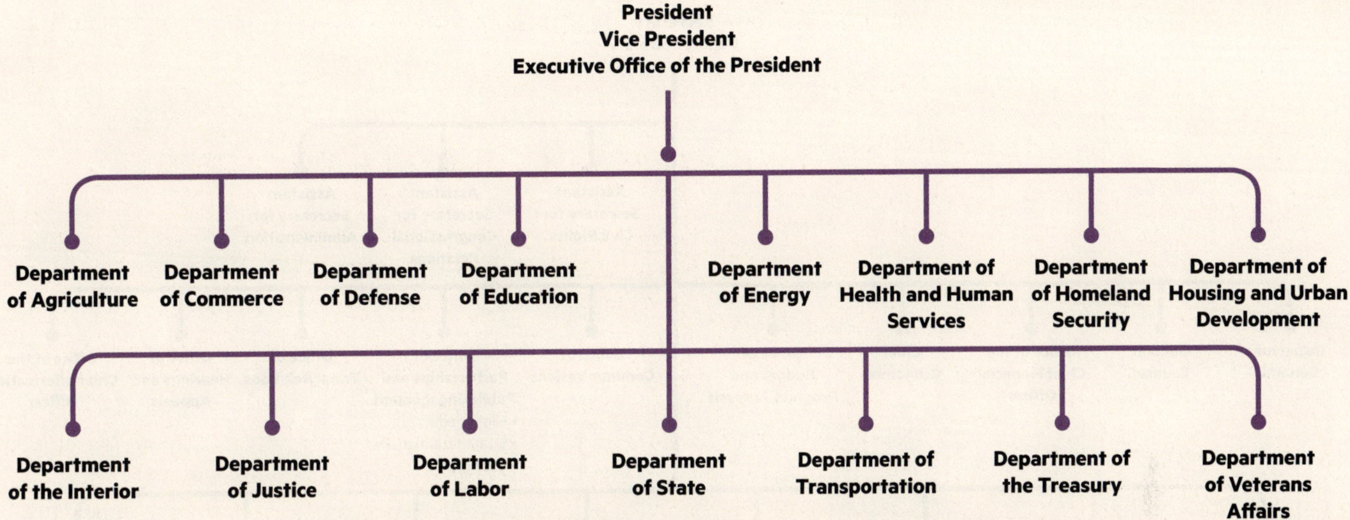

Selected independent establishments and government corporations

Central Intelligence Agency
Consumer Financial Protection Bureau
Consumer Product Safety Commission
Environmental Protection Agency
Equal Employment Opportunity Commission
Federal Communications Commission
Federal Deposit Insurance Corporation
Federal Election Commission
Federal Reserve System
Federal Trade Commission
General Services Administration
National Aeronautics and Space Administration
National Foundation on the Arts and the Humanities
National Labor Relations Board
National Railroad Passenger Corporation (Amtrak)
National Science Foundation
Occupational Safety and Health Review Commission
Peace Corps
Securities and Exchange Commission
Selective Service System
Small Business Administration
Social Security Administration
U.S. Agency for International Development
U.S. Postal Service

Source: United States General Services Administration, "Government Organizational Chart," www.usgovernmentmanual.gov/ReadLibraryItem.ashx?SFN=Myz95sTyO4rJRM/nhlRwSw==&SF=VHhnJrOeEAnGaa/rtk/JOg== (accessed 5/20/22).

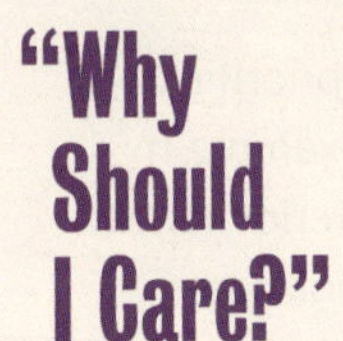

The list of cabinet departments and agencies illustrates the priorities of the federal government—the issues that are a high enough priority to be given an agency to address them.

Why is the Food and Drug Administration (FDA) an independent agency rather than part of the Department of Commerce—and why is the Federal Aviation Administration (FAA) located within the Department of Transportation rather than being independent?

Organizational decisions like these often reflect elected officials' attempts to shape agency behavior—and the extent to which political process matters. Part of the difference between independent agencies and the organizations contained within executive departments has to do with the president's ability to control these organizations' activities. Organizations that fall within an executive department, such as the FAA or the Federal

NUTS & BOLTS 13.2

The Structure of the Department of Agriculture

The Department of Agriculture is headed by the secretary of agriculture and the deputy secretary of agriculture and includes various assistant secretaries and undersecretaries for specific areas, such as natural resources and the environment, farm services, rural development, and food safety.

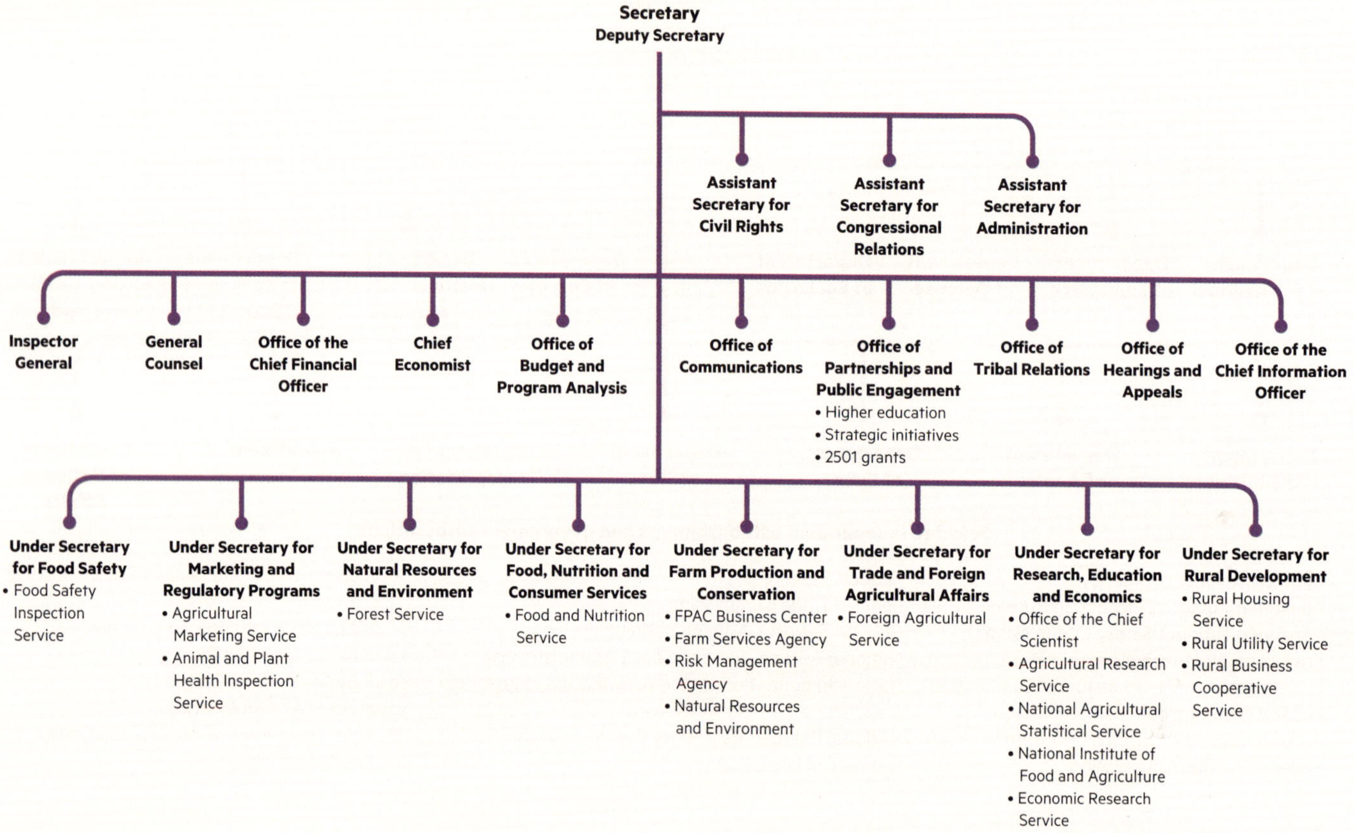

Secretary
Deputy Secretary

- **Assistant Secretary for Civil Rights**
- **Assistant Secretary for Congressional Relations**
- **Assistant Secretary for Administration**

- **Inspector General**
- **General Counsel**
- **Office of the Chief Financial Officer**
- **Chief Economist**
- **Office of Budget and Program Analysis**
- **Office of Communications**
- **Office of Partnerships and Public Engagement**
  - Higher education
  - Strategic initiatives
  - 2501 grants
- **Office of Tribal Relations**
- **Office of Hearings and Appeals**
- **Office of the Chief Information Officer**

- **Under Secretary for Food Safety**
  - Food Safety Inspection Service
- **Under Secretary for Marketing and Regulatory Programs**
  - Agricultural Marketing Service
  - Animal and Plant Health Inspection Service
- **Under Secretary for Natural Resources and Environment**
  - Forest Service
- **Under Secretary for Food, Nutrition and Consumer Services**
  - Food and Nutrition Service
- **Under Secretary for Farm Production and Conservation**
  - FPAC Business Center
  - Farm Services Agency
  - Risk Management Agency
  - Natural Resources and Environment
- **Under Secretary for Trade and Foreign Agricultural Affairs**
  - Foreign Agricultural Service
- **Under Secretary for Research, Education and Economics**
  - Office of the Chief Scientist
  - Agricultural Research Service
  - National Agricultural Statistical Service
  - National Institute of Food and Agriculture
  - Economic Research Service
- **Under Secretary for Rural Development**
  - Rural Housing Service
  - Rural Utility Service
  - Rural Business Cooperative Service

Source: U.S. Department of Agriculture, "USDA Organization Chart," www.usda.gov/sites/default/files/documents/usda-organization-chart.pdf (accessed 5/20/22).

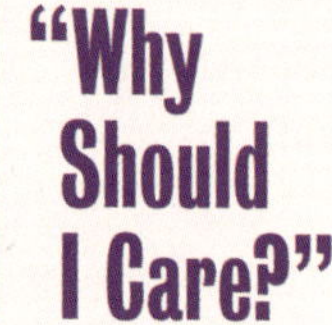

Organizational charts illustrate both governmental priorities and which agencies are subordinate to others. For example, if the Forest Service were in the Department of the Interior instead of Agriculture, America would likely have different policies concerning the management of forests and timber.

Highway Administration (FHA) (both within the Department of Transportation), can be controlled by the president (to some extent) through the president's appointees.[37] In contrast, independent agencies are often designed to have more freedom from oversight and control by the president and Congress. For example, governors of the Federal Reserve, though nominated by the president and confirmed by the Senate, serve for 14 years—outlasting the administration that nominated them. Outside the nomination and confirmation process, the president and Congress have very little control over the Federal

Reserve's policies; the organization is self-financing, and its governors can be removed from office only if Congress takes the extreme step of impeaching them.

In contrast, appointees to executive departments and the EOP serve "at the pleasure of the president," meaning the president can remove them from office at any time. Such removals happen in all presidential administrations because of scandal, complaints about performance, or concerns about leaks to the media or disloyalty to the president. President Trump placed a high priority on loyalty and prioritized having bureaucrats who would execute his directives without question. For example, in April 2020 Trump removed Dr. Rick Bright from his position as head of the Department of Health and Human Services' Biomedical Advanced Research and Development Authority. Bright had pressed for further review of the drug hydroxychloroquine before allowing it to be used to treat COVID-19 patients and had continued to raise objections even after President Trump made strong statements in favor of prescribing the drug.[38] Whether it was ethical and politically wise to fire Bright is a good question—but there is no doubt that Trump had the authority to remove him from office.

These details about the hiring and firing of bureaucrats and the location of agencies in the structure of the federal government matter because they determine the amount of political control that other parts of the government can exercise over an agency, as well as which individuals (the president or members of Congress) get to exercise this power. As political scientist Terry M. Moe puts it, "The bureaucracy rises out of politics, and its design reflects the interests, strategies, and compromises of those who exercise political power."[39]

The size of the federal government

The federal government employs millions of people. Table 13.1 shows the number of employees in each executive department. The Department of Defense is the largest cabinet department, with more than 700,000 civilian employees. The Department of Education is the smallest, with only 4,000 employees. Many departments are on the small side: four cabinet departments have fewer than 20,000 employees. The same is

TABLE 13.1

Employment in Cabinet Departments

Organization	Total employees
Defense (civilian only)	738,200
Veterans Affairs	406,900
Homeland Security	201,600
Justice	116,600
Treasury	96,300
Agriculture	83,700
Health and Human Services	81,600
Interior	63,400
Transportation	54,500
Commerce	46,500
State	25,400
Labor	14,700
Energy	14,400
Housing and Urban Development	7,900
Education	4,000

Source: Office of Management and Budget, "Analytical Perspectives," www.whitehouse.gov/omb/budget/analytical-perspectives/ (accessed 5/20/22).

true for many independent agencies and organizations within the EOP. The General Services Administration (GSA), for example, has only about 12,000 employees. Millions of additional people work for the government as members of the armed forces, as employees of the Postal Service, as employees of civilian companies that contract with the government, or as recipients of federal grant money.

The What Do the Facts Say? feature on page 513 shows the number of civilian federal employees from 1961 to 2022. Clearly, the federal workforce increased steadily in the early years, although it has declined from its peak in the 1990s and remained steady in recent years. The steady growth of the bureaucracy in the 1960s and 1970s led some scholars to argue that bureaucrats are **budget maximizers** who never pass up a chance to increase the size of their organization regardless of whether the increase is worthwhile.[40] Of course, the fact that federal employment has remained steady in recent years suggests that something besides budget maximization is at work. The best explanation for the overall size of the federal government is the size of America itself—nearly 330 million people spread out over an area more than twice the size of the European Union—combined with America's position as the most powerful nation in the world with the largest military, and the increased costs associated with some government services, such as health care.

budget maximizers
Bureaucrats who seek to increase funding for their agency whether or not that additional spending is worthwhile.

DID YOU KNOW?

In the first two years of the Trump presidency, 12 of 15 cabinet departments reduced their number of employees, some by almost

10%

Source: Office of Personnel Management.

Those who blame bureaucrats for the increasing size of the federal government miss some important points. First, the increase in total federal spending masks the fact that many agencies see their budgets shrink.[41] Particularly in recent administrations, one of the principal missions of presidential appointees, both in agencies and in the EOP, has been to scrutinize budget requests with an eye to cutting spending as much as possible.[42] And in most years, some government agencies are eliminated (in fact, most of the department head counts in Table 13.1 have grown smaller in recent editions of this text).[43]

Public-opinion data also provide an explanation for the overall growth in government: the American public's demand for services.[44] Despite complaints about the federal bureaucracy, polls find little evidence of demands for less government. When the Pew Research Center asked people in 2019 to name programs that should have their spending cut as a way of reducing the budget deficit, the only program that was named by more than a quarter of respondents was foreign aid (see Figure 13.2). Far fewer people favored

FIGURE 13.2

Public Opinion on Spending Cuts

Many Americans complain about the size of the federal government. However, their complaints do not translate into support for reductions in policy areas or cuts in specific programs that could significantly reduce spending. Based on these data, are there any kinds of proposals for significantly reducing the size of the federal government that might attract widespread support?

Source: Pew Research Center, "Little Public Support for Reductions in Federal Spending," April 11, 2019, www.people-press.org/2019/04/11/little-public-support-for-reductions-in-federal-spending/ (accessed 5/22/22).

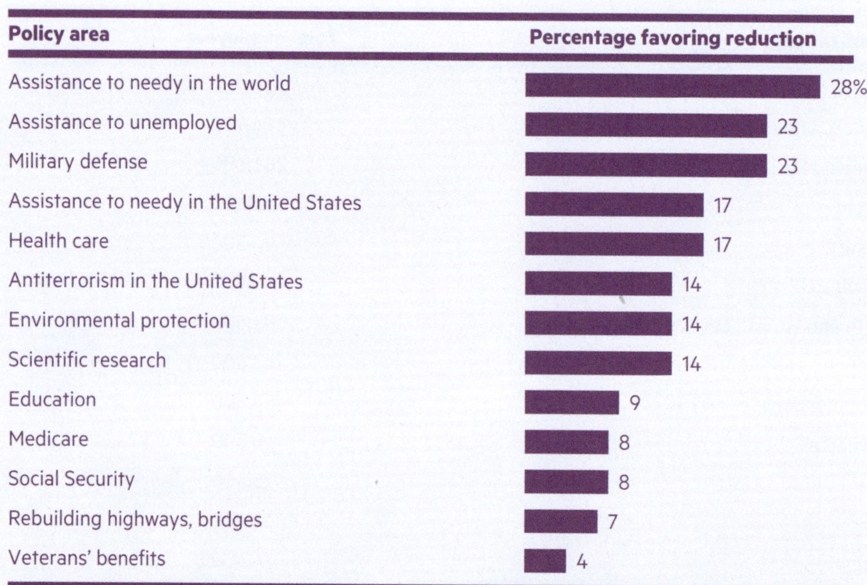

Is the Federal Bureaucracy Too Big?

One of the most intense conflicts in American political life is over the size of the federal government. Generally, Republicans say that the size of the federal bureaucracy should be reduced, while Democrats tend to favor increasing the size of government programs, including adding more employees if needed. Has the size of government increased over time?

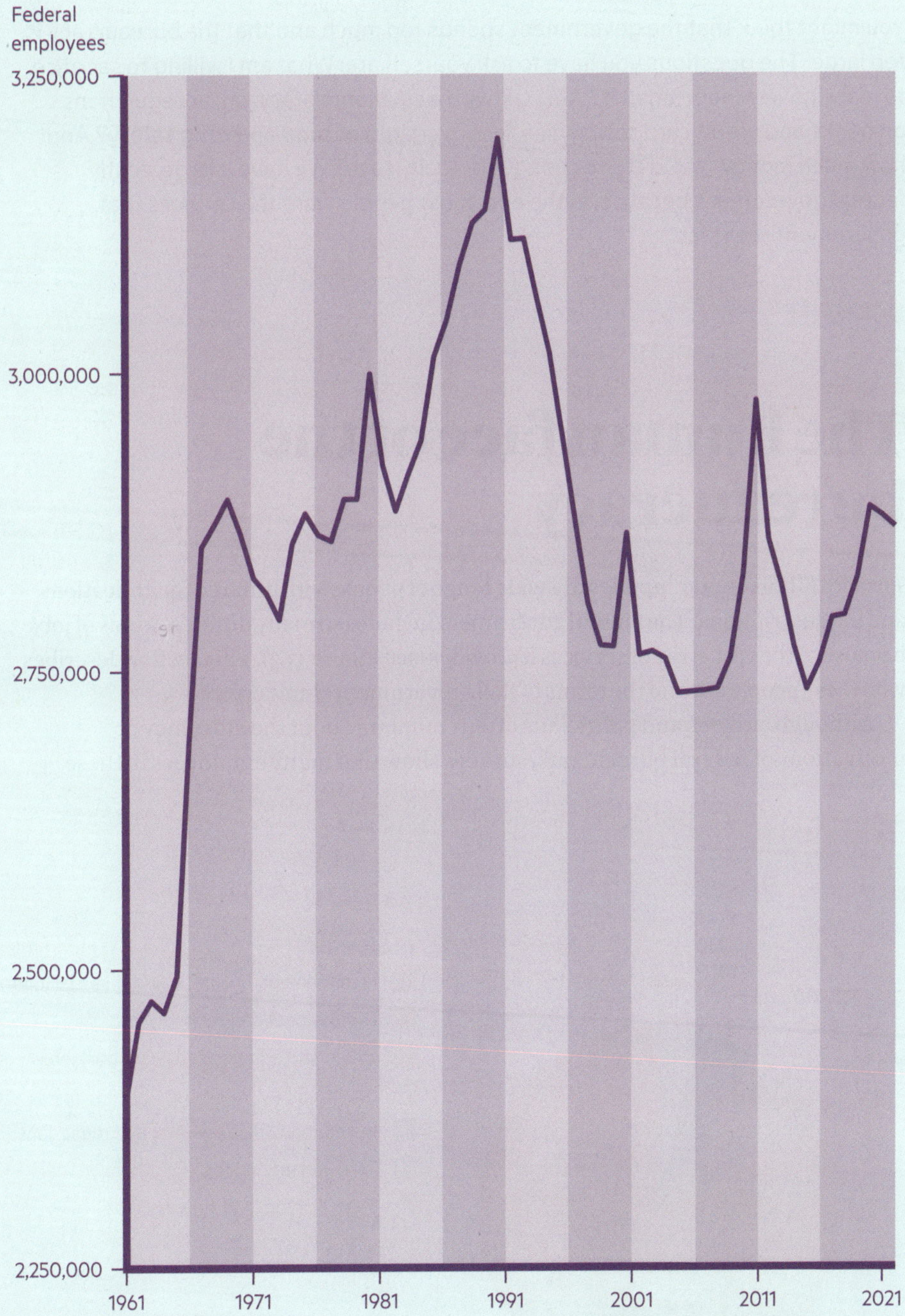

Federal employees

3,250,000

3,000,000

2,750,000

2,500,000

2,250,000

1961 1971 1981 1991 2001 2011 2021

Source: Based on Federal Reserve Bank, St. Louis, "All Employees: Government: Federal," https://fred.stlouisfed.org/series/CES9091000001#0 (accessed 5/21/22).

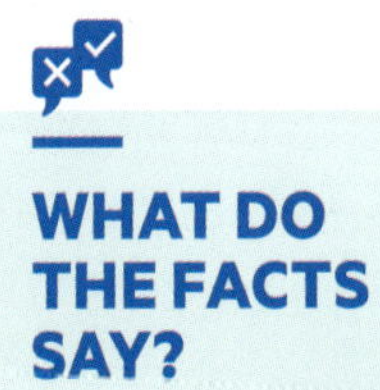

WHAT DO THE FACTS SAY?

Think about it

- **During the 2020 presidential campaign,** candidate Donald Trump claimed that the total size of the federal bureaucracy had significantly increased under President Obama and decreased during his presidency. Do the data support this assertion?
- **The size of the federal bureaucracy** increased significantly during the 1960s and 1970s, then declined after about 1990. What political or historical events explain these changes?

cuts in the programs that account for much of federal spending: defense, health care spending, and Social Security. In other words, while in the abstract Americans might want a smaller government that is less involved in everyday life, they do not support the large-scale budget cuts that would be necessary to achieve this goal. The public's desire for more government services is often encouraged by elected officials, who create new government programs (and expand existing ones in response to constituent demands) as a way of building support and improving their chances of reelection.

You might think that the government spends too much and that the bureaucracy is too large. The questions you have to ask yourself are: What am I willing to sacrifice to make government smaller? Am I OK with a smaller military, fewer regulations on banks and credit card companies, less oversight of food and drug safety? And how much money would these changes actually save? We have a large, costly federal government because, in the end, most people want the services that government provides.

DESCRIBE WHO BUREAUCRATS ARE AND THE REGULATIONS THAT GOVERN THEIR EMPLOYMENT

The human face of the bureaucracy

The term "bureaucrat" applies to a wide range of people with different qualifications and job descriptions. The federal government includes so many different kinds of jobs because of the vast array of services it provides (see Figure 13.3). This section describes who these people are and the terms of their government employment.

Although citizens and politicians often complain about the efficiency or motivations of federal bureaucrats, surveys show that many employees in these

FIGURE 13.3

Types of Federal Workers

Note: Data may not total 100 percent due to rounding.

Source: Bureau of Labor Statistics, "Occupational Employment Statistics," www.bls.gov/oes/current/naics4_999100.htm#00-0000 (accessed 5/22/22).

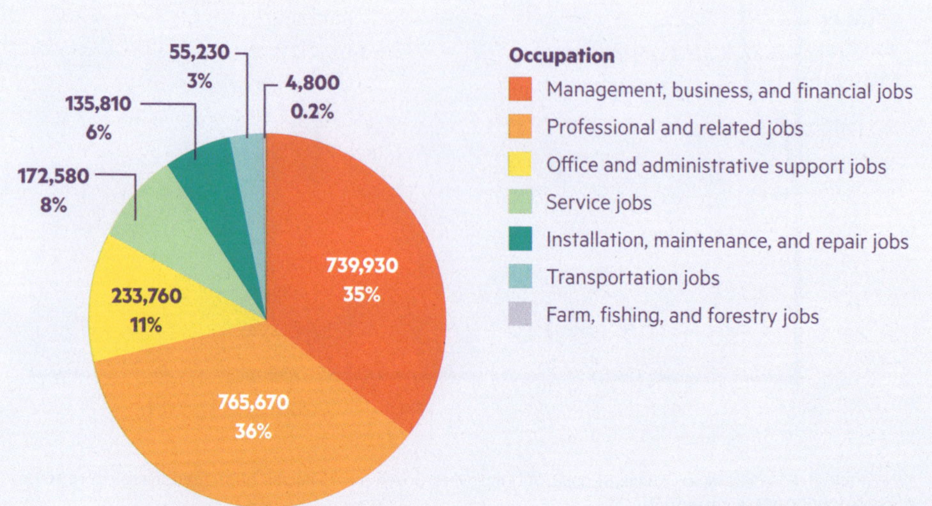

positions have a strong interest in public service or the implementation of good public policy. In fact, these motivations are often strong enough that scholars such as James L. Perry have argued against attempts to motivate federal workers with monetary incentives—bureaucrats who work hard because they feel it is the right thing to do may resent incentive schemes that presume they are lazy or only interested in money.[45]

Civil service regulations

Most jobs in the federal bureaucracy are subject to the civil service regulations that we described earlier.[46] The current civil service system sets out job descriptions and pay ranges for all federal jobs. The system also establishes tests that determine who is hired for low-level clerical and secretarial positions. People with less than a college degree are generally eligible for entry-level jobs, and, as in the private sector, a college degree or an advanced degree and work experience qualify an individual for higher-level positions. Federal salaries are supposed to be comparable to what people earn in similar, private-sector positions, and salaries are somewhat higher for federal employees who work in areas with a high cost of living.

Civil service regulations provide job security. After three years of satisfactory performance, employees cannot be fired except "for cause," meaning that their superiors must cite a reason. Civil service regulations set out a multistep procedure for firing someone, beginning with low performance evaluations, then warning letters, followed by a lengthy appeals process before a firing takes place.[47] As a result, rather than being fired, a subpar performer may be assigned other duties, transferred to another office, or even given nothing to do in the hope that the person will leave voluntarily out of boredom or embarrassment. It is hard to get exact data, but most estimates are that about 10,000 federal employees are fired every year—out of a total civilian workforce of over 2 million.

If you think civil service regulations seem cumbersome, you're right.[48] The hiring criteria remove a manager's discretion to hire someone who would do an excellent job but lacks the education or work experience that the regulations specify as necessary for the position. The firing requirements make it extremely difficult to remove poor performers. The salary and promotion restrictions create problems with rewarding excellent performance or promoting the best employees rather than those with the most seniority.

Why do these requirements exist? Recall that the aim of civil service regulations was to separate politics from policy. The mechanism for achieving this goal was a set of rules and requirements that made it hard for elected officials to control the hiring and firing of government employees to further their own political goals. In effect, even though civil service regulations have obvious drawbacks, they also provide this less apparent but very important benefit. For example, without civil service protections, members of Congress might pressure employees in the Office of Personnel Management to hire their constituents or increase pensions for retiring federal workers who support them.

Although loyalty to the president is a widely accepted criterion for hiring agency heads and other presidential appointees, professionals with permanent civil service positions are supposed to be hired based on their qualifications, not their political beliefs. In fact, it is illegal to bring politics into these hiring decisions. However, there is no doubt that all presidential administrations worry about the political loyalties of midlevel bureaucrats because of the problem of control, as we discussed earlier.

Limits on political activity

Legislation places limits on the political activities that federal employees can undertake. The Hatch Act, enacted in 1939 and amended in 1940, prohibited federal employees from engaging in organized political activities.[49] Under the act, employees could vote and contribute to candidates but could not work for candidates or for political parties. These restrictions were modified in the 1993 Federal Employees Political Activities Act, which allows federal employees to participate in a wider range of political activities, including fund-raising and serving as an officer of a political party. Senior members of the president's White House staff and political appointees are exempt from most of these restrictions, although they cannot use government resources for political activities.

While the Hatch Act is often invoked when government employees express controversial views, it technically restricts only activities that directly help a particular political candidate. For example, in 2019 a Department of Energy (DOE) employee was disciplined for giving a tour of the Hanford Nuclear Waste Site to a congressional candidate and allowing the candidate to take pictures that would be used in the candidate's campaign. (The DOE employee had been warned that giving the tour would constitute a violation.)[50]

The Hatch Act makes life especially difficult for presidential appointees whose job duties, such as helping the president they work for get reelected, often mix government service with politics. To comply with Hatch Act restrictions, these officials need to carry separate cell phones to make calls related to their political activities and maintain separate e-mail accounts—usually provided by the party or campaign committee—for their political communications.

Federal employees must be careful that their comments to the media comply with Hatch Act restrictions. Kellyanne Conway, former counselor to President Trump, violated the Hatch Act when she advocated for and against candidates in the 2017 Senate special election in Alabama on CNN and Fox News programs.

Political appointees and the Senior Executive Service

Not every federal employee is a member of the civil service. About 3,000 senior positions in the executive branch—such as the upper-level members of executive departments and independent agencies like NASA, as well as members of the EOP—are not subject to civil service regulations. The president appoints individuals to these positions, and, in some cases, the Senate must confirm them. The majority of a president's appointees act as the president's eyes, ears, and hands throughout the executive branch—mitigating but not eliminating the problem of control. Their jobs involve finding out what the president wants from their agency and ordering, persuading, or cajoling their subordinates to implement presidential directives.

Some appointees get their jobs as a reward for working on the president's campaign staff, contributing substantial funds to the campaign, or raising money from other donors. These individuals are not always given positions with real decision-making power. Some government agencies have the reputation of being **turkey farms**, places where campaign stalwarts can be appointed without the risk that their lack of experience will lead to bad policy.[51]

turkey farms
Agencies to which campaign workers and donors can be appointed in reward for their service because it is unlikely that their lack of qualifications will lead to bad policy.

In many agencies, people in the top positions are members of the Senior Executive Service (SES), who are also exempt from civil service restrictions.[52] As of 2020, there were about 8,000 SES members, most of whom were career government employees who held relatively high-level agency positions before moving to the SES. This change of employment status costs them their civil service protections but allows them to apply for senior leadership positions in the bureaucracy. Some political appointees are also given SES positions, although most do not have the experience or expertise held by career bureaucrats who typically move to the SES.

President Trump's use of political appointments raises a puzzle. In both of his presidential campaigns, his promise to undertake large-scale changes in government policy suggested that Trump would make appointments as rapidly as possible, so that he would have people in each agency who were loyal to him and would implement his reform efforts. However, in Trump's first term, the pace of his appointments was slow compared with that of previous presidents, and even after four years in office many senior-level positions in the bureaucracy were vacant or filled by a series of acting appointees.[53] In part, appointments were slowed by Senate Democrats who opposed Trump's nominees. Some potential appointees did not want to work in a Trump-led administration. Others were dropped from consideration because they had opposed Trump during the 2016 campaign or had spoken publicly against Trump's actions in office.

Perhaps because of the difficulties in appointing senior-level officials, many relatively young individuals who had worked for the Trump campaign and thereafter were appointed to positions in various executive departments and independent agencies.[54] These individuals were chosen for their loyalty to Trump rather than their knowledge of the agency they were assigned to—some of them were even finishing their college degrees while working in the executive branch. Their primary job seemed to be monitoring agency operations and reporting how agency staff were responding to Trump's directives. However, because these individuals knew little about their agencies and because they had no authority to issue policy directives on their own, they were relatively ineffective in implementing the Trump agenda.

President Biden's appointment practices returned to the norms of his predecessors, balancing expertise and loyalty.[55] Of course, because Biden appears to have fewer policy conflicts with career bureaucrats than Trump did, it is easier for him to find compatible civil servants for SES positions and to recruit former political appointees from the Obama administration to return for another term of government service.

"Why Should I Care?"

The problem of control shapes the kinds of people who are hired as bureaucrats as well as their job protections. Political appointees and members of the SES are supposed to ride herd on the rest of the bureaucracy. Civil service protections exist to ensure that bureaucrats' decisions reflect expertise rather than political considerations.

Controlling the bureaucracy

EXPLAIN HOW CONGRESS AND THE PRESIDENT OVERSEE THE EXECUTIVE BRANCH

As the expert implementers of legislation and presidential directives, bureaucrats hold significant power to influence government policy. This situation creates the problem of control illustrated by the principal–agent game, as we discussed earlier: elected officials must figure out how to reap the benefits of bureaucratic expertise without simply giving bureaucrats free rein to do whatever they want.

One strategy is to take away discretion entirely and give bureaucrats simple, direct orders. For example, from 1996 to 2015 a law passed by Congress forbade the CDC from conducting research that would "advocate or promote gun control"—which was interpreted by the CDC as limiting all gun-related research by agency scientists or by outside researchers who received agency funds.[56] (The ban was repealed after a series of mass shootings in 2013, although to this day the CDC conducts very little gun-related research.) Similarly, the Trump administration banned the use of the words "climate change" and "global warming" from the EPA's websites and documents and abolished scientific advisory panels dealing with this topic.[57] These practices were reversed during the early days of the Biden administration.

The problem with eliminating bureaucrats' discretion in this way is that it limits the positive influence of their expertise. Particularly when new policies are being developed, taking away bureaucratic discretion is costly for legislators or presidential appointees because it forces them to work out the policy details themselves—and may produce less effective policies than those constructed by bureaucrats with specialized knowledge.[58] Moreover, preventing bureaucrats from using their judgment makes it impossible for them to craft policies that take into account new developments or unforeseen circumstances.[59]

bureaucratic drift
Bureaucrats' tendency to implement policies in a way that favors their own political objectives rather than following the original intentions of the legislation.

For all these reasons, elected officials must find other ways to reduce or eliminate **bureaucratic drift**—that is, bureaucrats' pursuit of their own goals rather than their assignments from officeholders or appointees—while still reaping the benefits of bureaucratic expertise. This section describes two common strategies: changing the way agencies are organized and staffed and using standardized procedures for monitoring agency actions. In both cases, the aim is to set up agencies so that bureaucrats can use their expertise, while making sure their actions are consistent with elected officials' wishes.[60] These measures mitigate—but do not eliminate—the problem of control (see the Take a Stand feature).

Agency organization

Over the last 20 years, political scientists have shown how agencies can be organized to minimize bureaucratic drift.[61] Specifically, when an agency is set up or given new responsibilities, the officials who initiate the change don't simply tell the new agency what to do. To make sure that the agency pursues the policies officials want, they also determine where the agency is located within the federal government structure and who runs it. These efforts may occur solely within Congress, may involve both Congress and the president, or may be arranged by presidential actions.[62]

For example, one of the Obama administration's responses to the 2008 financial crisis was to form a new agency, the Consumer Financial Protection Bureau (CFPB), which would help enforce new bank regulations and investigate consumer complaints about financial firms. However, Republican senators opposed Obama's initial nominee to run the agency, Elizabeth Warren, believing she would encourage her subordinates to be excessively pro-consumer. (Warren later became a senator from Massachusetts and ran for the 2020 Democratic presidential nomination.) Similarly, in 2017 President Trump appointed Michael Mulvaney (a former Republican congressman and the head of the Office of Management and Budget and chief of staff in the Trump administration) to run the agency, even though Mulvaney was a longtime opponent of the CFPB who as a member of Congress had sought to abolish the agency. Both Trump and Obama's appointments were intended to shape agency operations by appointing an individual who was expected to act in line with the then-president's preferences.

TAKE A STAND

Is Political Control of the Bureaucracy Beneficial?

When working with bureaucrats, elected officials (the president or members of Congress) face the problem of political control: Should they allow bureaucrats to exercise judgment when implementing policies or give them specific, narrow directives? Compounding this problem is the fact that most bureaucrats are civil service employees, meaning they cannot be fired except under very extreme circumstances. As a result, even when elected officials give very specific directives to an agency, they may find that bureaucrats essentially ignore the directives and that very little can be done to force compliance. After all, regardless of what bureaucrats do or don't do, they will still have a job—and they can wait for a new administration or a change in congressional majorities who may reverse the directive. Civil service protections also mean that members of Congress or a new presidential administration cannot clean house in an agency, replacing untrustworthy bureaucrats with individuals who will do what they are told. Should civil service protections be abolished?

Get rid of civil service protections. The civil service system began in an era when few government jobs required specialized knowledge, expertise, or an advanced degree.

The modern federal bureaucracy is exactly the opposite: most jobs, particularly those that involve real policy-making power, require expertise to be done effectively. Under these conditions, civil service protections are to some extent unnecessary, as bureaucrats have considerable job security because of their expertise and experience. Getting rid of recalcitrant bureaucrats involves significant costs: by removing their knowledge of the policies being decided and the procedures by which decisions are made, it may become impossible for an agency to function at all. Moreover, a bureaucrat's reluctance to behave as ordered may be a sign that something is wrong—that the directive makes no sense or that there are easier ways of accomplishing the task.

Consider the U.S. Environmental Protection Agency. There is little doubt that most EPA scientists believe that climate change is real and that it is the result of human actions. Both of these views were in opposition to President Trump's stated positions. Were civil service protections the only thing preventing Trump from firing these scientists? Firing the scientists would have decimated the EPA and made it impossible for the agency to carry out many of its functions, some of which (like cleaning up Superfund sites) were things Trump favored. Trump may not have liked having EPA scientists who disagree with him, but he would probably have liked the consequences of a mass firing even less. Moreover, the replacements would have operated within existing resource, regulatory, and legal constraints, so their actions might not have looked different from those of their predecessors.

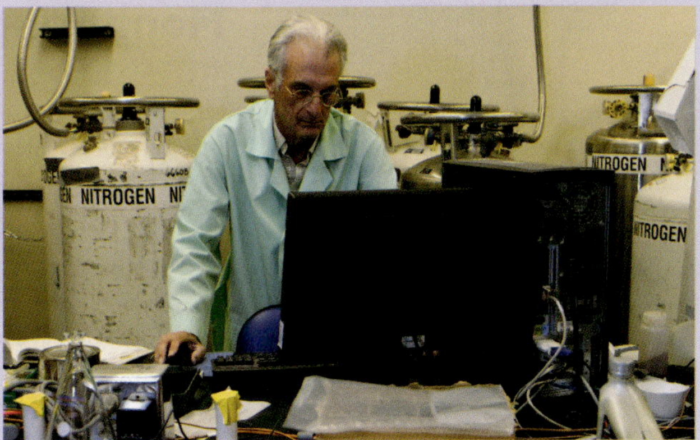

Civil service protections help ensure that agency scientists will continue to do cutting-edge research and report their findings, even if their conclusions conflict with the views of their political superiors.

Civil service protections are still needed. The fact that firing bureaucrats costs the government the benefit of their experience and expertise does not mean that elected officials will never threaten to do so, or even carry out their threats. Removing civil service protections—making bureaucrats vulnerable to threats about their future employment—could easily lead to bad policy outcomes. Eliminating civil service protections would also change the kinds of people who undertake careers in government service. Civil service protections enable policy experts to work for the government without fearing that they will be fired for simply voicing their concerns or because a new administration places a high value on loyalty. Without the protections afforded by civil service regulations, these individuals might choose a different career, depriving the federal government (and the American people) of the benefits of their knowledge and training.

In the case of the EPA, civil service protections helped ensure that agency scientists continued to do cutting-edge research and report their findings—even if their conclusions conflicted with the views of their political superiors—and that these scientists work for the agency in the first place.

take a stand

1. Compared with former President Trump, President Biden has had a much lower level of conflict with the permanent civil service. What factors are behind this change in relations between the president and Congress?
2. Not all jobs in the federal bureaucracy require specialized knowledge and expertise. Would it make sense to abandon civil service protections for low-level jobs such as clerical positions? Why or why not?

Monitoring

oversight
Congressional efforts to make sure that laws are implemented correctly by the bureaucracy after they have been passed.

One of the most important ways elected officials prevent bureaucratic drift is by keeping an eye on what bureaucrats are doing or planning to do. Information gathering by members of Congress about bureaucratic actions is termed **oversight**. Congressional committees often hold hearings to question agency heads, secretaries of executive departments, or senior agency staff. Similarly, one of the primary responsibilities of presidential appointees is to monitor how lower-level bureaucrats are responding to presidential directives. The problem is that appointees may be unable to fulfill this role. Because they are chosen for their loyalty to the president, they may lack the experience needed to fully understand what bureaucrats in their agency are doing. Moreover, given that appointees typically hold their position for only a year or two, they have little time to learn the details of agency operations.

Advance Warning Members of Congress, the president, and the president's staff gain advance knowledge of planned bureaucratic actions through the notice-and-comment procedure described earlier in the chapter, which requires bureaucrats to disclose proposed regulations before they take effect.[63] This delay gives opponents the opportunity to register complaints with their congressional representatives, and it allows these legislators time either to pressure the agency to revise the regulation or to even enact another law undoing or modifying the agency action. Members of Congress also pressure bureaucrats to release memos, working drafts, and other documents as a way of keeping track of what bureaucrats are doing. For example, in 2020 members of Congress requested documents from the State Department in the wake of the removal of Inspector General Steve Linick—the concern was that Linick was fired because he was investigating complaints that Secretary of State Mike Pompeo had used State Department staff to run personal errands.[64]

Investigations: Police Patrols and Fire Alarms Congress, legislative staff, or presidential appointees may initiate investigations of government programs or offices to scrutinize the organizations, their expenditures, and their activities. There are two types of investigation: police patrol oversight and fire alarm oversight. Ideally, every agency would be investigated on a consistent basis, with agencies that have large budgets or carry out important functions being investigated more frequently. These investigations may involve fact-finding trips to local offices,

The Senate's power over the confirmation of senior agency officials is often used as a tool to shape agency policy and operations. Richard Cordray *(left)*, the first head of the Consumer Financial Protection Bureau, was nominated after some senators objected to President Obama's first nominee, Elizabeth Warren, who was a Harvard law professor at the time. The current head of the CFPB, Rohit Chopra *(right)*, was approved after Vice President Kamala Harris cast a tie-breaking Senate vote in September 2021.

interviews with senior personnel, audits of agency accounts, and calls to the agency to see how it responds to citizens' requests. This method of investigation is called **police patrol oversight**.[65] Think of a police officer walking the beat, rattling doors to see if they are locked, checking out broken windows, and looking down alleys for suspicious behavior.

police patrol oversight
A method of oversight in which members of Congress constantly monitor the bureaucracy to make sure that laws are implemented correctly.

The disadvantage of police patrol oversight is that it is costly in terms of money and staff time. Moreover, these investigations often find that agencies are doing what they should be doing. Because of these problems, Congress and the president often follow a different strategy. Rather than undertaking a series of investigations, they wait until they receive a complaint about bureaucratic actions, then focus investigative efforts on those cases. This practice is labeled **fire alarm oversight**.[66]

fire alarm oversight
A method of oversight in which members of Congress respond to complaints about the bureaucracy or problems of implementation only as they arise rather than exercising constant vigilance.

The so-called fire alarm that sets off an investigation can take many different forms. Constituents may let their congressional representatives or their staff know of a problem with the bureaucracy. Similarly, lobbyists, corporate executives, and ordinary citizens often contact the president and the president's staff with complaints. Newspaper reporters and bloggers also provide information on what bureaucrats are doing. Most agencies have advisory committees that not only help make agency decisions but also keep Congress and the president informed about their agencies' actions.[67]

The case of the COVID-19 death statistics mentioned at the beginning of this chapter is a clear example of fire alarm oversight. After major media outlets reported on the debate between the Trump White House and the CDC over which deaths should be included (and some members of Congress then came out in support of the CDC), the White House quietly ended its effort to intervene in the CDC's reporting process. These fire alarms provide exactly the sort of information that Congress and the president often lack about how bureaucrats are implementing laws and directives, including cases in which bureaucrats are doing (or planning to do) something that contradicts their mandate. Such communications tell Congress and the president where to focus their efforts to monitor the bureaucracy, drawing their attention to agencies or programs in which problems have been reported and removing the need to try to oversee the entire government at once.

While we have talked a lot in this chapter about the efforts of President Trump to control the bureaucracy, an interest in bureaucratic actions is a bipartisan phenomenon in Washington. Democratic elected officials may prefer a larger, more active government, but they are just as unwilling as Republicans to remove all checks on bureaucratic actions. Democrats often take the position of protecting bureaucrats against executive branch interference. At the same time, though, Democratic elected officials use their control over budgets to push bureaucrats toward decisions they prefer. For example, in the case of NASA's moon landing plans discussed earlier, Texas Democrats have worked to ensure that the project is controlled by the Johnson Space Center in Houston rather than another NASA center located elsewhere.

Correcting violations

When the president or members of Congress find a case of bureaucratic drift, they can take steps to influence the bureaucrats' actions. Many tactics can be used to bring a wayward agency into line. Legislation or an executive order can send a clear directive to an agency or remove its discretion, tasks and programs can be moved to an agency that is more closely aligned with elected officials' goals, political appointees at an agency can be replaced, and agencies can be reorganized. For example, one consequence of the Trump administration's slow process of making political appointments and its reliance

One reason that attempts to pass legislation forcing the FDA to alter its drug-approval process have had little success is that the FDA's process is considered to have worked mostly as intended, approving new drugs that are safe and effective and keeping ineffective or unsafe drugs off the market. This was especially important as drug manufacturers raced to find vaccines and other treatments for COVID-19.

on acting positions, particularly for the State Department, was a shift in policy-making power to individuals in the White House, as these positions were staffed while those in the State Department were vacant.

One of the most significant difficulties in dealing with bureaucratic drift is disagreement between members of Congress and the president about whether an agency is doing the right thing—regardless of whether the agency is following its original orders. Many strategies for influencing an agency's behavior require joint action by the president and congressional majorities. Without presidential support, members of Congress need a two-thirds majority to impose corrections. Without congressional support, the president can only threaten to cut an agency's proposed budget, change its home within the federal bureaucracy, or set up a new agency to do what the errant agency refuses to do. However, carrying out these threats requires congressional approval. As a result, disagreements between the president and Congress can give an agency significant freedom, as long as it retains the support of at least one branch of government.

An agency may also be able to fend off elected officials' attempts to take political control if it has a reputation for expertise. For example, one reason that attempts to pass legislation forcing the FDA to alter its drug-approval process have had little success is that the FDA's process is thought to have worked mostly as intended, approving new drugs that are safe and effective and keeping ineffective or unsafe drugs off the market. At the same time, the FDA has responded to pressure from Congress and the president to revise some rules on its own, such as the Right to Try program.

Finally, agencies can sometimes combat attempts to control their behavior by appealing to groups that benefit from agency actions.[68] For example, since the 1980s the Occupational Safety and Health Administration (OSHA) has resisted attempts by Republican presidents and Republican members of Congress to eliminate the agency or limit its operations.[69] One element of its strategy has been to build strong ties to labor unions. As a result, OSHA is much more likely to receive complaints about workplace safety from companies with strong unions. The second prong of the strategy has involved building cooperative arrangements with large companies to prevent workplace accidents, an approach that not only protects workers but can save companies a lot of money over the long term. Moreover, when OSHA levies fines against companies that violate safety regulations, the fines are generally much less than the maximum fines that would be allowed by law. As a result, when proposals to limit or eliminate OSHA are debated in Congress, members hear from unions as well as many large corporations in support of keeping the agency in place. Over time, this strategy has generated support for the agency from Democrats and Republicans in the House and Senate.

The consequences of control

Elected officials' competing desires to both control what bureaucrats do and tap their expertise explain many of the seemingly dysfunctional aspects of the bureaucracy. Part of the problem is the nature of the tasks given to bureaucrats. Even when members of Congress and the president agree on which problems deserve attention, bureaucrats often face the much harder task of translating these officials' lofty problem-solving goals into concrete policies. Given the magnitude of this job, it is no surprise that even the best efforts of government agencies do not always succeed.

Most important, the use of standard operating procedures is rooted partly in the complexity of bureaucrats' tasks—but also in the desire of agency heads and elected officials to control the actions of lower-level staff. In some disaster relief efforts, government agencies have found that preset plans and procedures worked against the need to respond quickly to alleviate human suffering. And while the FDA's drug-approval process succeeds for the most part at preventing harmful drugs from coming to market, the delays imposed by the process do prevent some patients from receiving lifesaving treatments. However, in all these cases the decisions do not reflect incompetence or malice. Rules and procedures are needed in any organization to ensure that decisions are made fairly and that they reflect the goals of the organization. But it is impossible to find procedures that will work well in all cases, particularly for the kinds of policy decisions made by bureaucrats.

"Why Should I Care?"

Cases of bureaucratic failure (poorly conceived policies or regulations, inaction, red tape) are often cited to "prove" that bureaucrats are incompetent, lazy, or dumb. The real story is that bureaucrats are often given nearly impossible tasks or political mandates that limit their authority. In this sense, complaints about bureaucrats have more to do with what we want them to do than with their unwillingness or inability to execute these missions.

Unpacking the Conflict

Considering all that we've discussed in this chapter, let's return to President Trump's often-contentious relationship with members of the federal bureaucracy. Were bureaucrats really obstructing the Trump agenda, or were they just doing their jobs? How do elected officials control a bureaucracy of experts, in the midst of a pandemic or in more normal times?

A deeper look shows that some of the time, conflicts between President Trump and bureaucratic officials reflected real disagreements. In the case of counting deaths from COVID-19, for example, it is not hard to see why Trump or his political advisers preferred a definition that minimized casualties. However, the fact that many bureaucrats are policy experts suggests an alternative explanation for their preference for a different accounting scheme. Rather than trying to embarrass Trump or ensure his defeat, bureaucrats may have been acting from expertise, working to account for the pandemic in a way that facilitated an effective governmental response.

Bureaucratic expertise and the resulting problem of control also explain the cumbersome procedures for hiring, firing, and decision making that are a feature of operations in many government agencies. Sometimes bureaucrats simply make mistakes, choosing the wrong policy because they—and, in some cases, all the people involved—lack information about the tasks they were given. Bureaucrats may drag their feet when they oppose their tasks on policy grounds. But in many cases, cumbersome procedures are the result of a fundamental trade-off faced by elected officials between wanting to exercise control over the bureaucracy and wanting to ensure that changes in policy produce their intended effect. Put another way, conflict over public policy often translates into conflicting ideas about what bureaucrats should do, resulting in complex, often-contradictory mandates and directions imposed on bureaucrats. In this way, politics shapes virtually all aspects of the bureaucracy and of the choices bureaucrats make, even in places where it is hard to discern political motivations.

"What's Your Take?"

Should elected officials defer to bureaucratic expertise?

Or should the president's agenda override other concerns?

CHECK YOUR UNDERSTANDING

"Why Should I Care?"

America's bureaucracy is an organization of experts. Bureaucrats translate legislation into policies, develop regulations, and deliver services to the population. By virtue of their training, position, and actions, they know more than the average citizen or even elected officials about which policies will effectively, efficiently reach different outcomes.

It is this expertise that on the one hand motivates elected officials to give up control to the bureaucracy and on the other makes them suspicious about what bureaucrats do with their power. Without bureaucrats, elected officials would be overwhelmed and would make mistakes. But by delegating responsibility, elected officials create the problem of control: how can they be sure that bureaucrats are doing what they are told? What prevents bureaucrats from ignoring policy directives, acting in line with their own ideas about good policy, and citing expertise as their justification for suspicious actions?

This dilemma is sharpened by the size and scope of the federal government. Politics is everywhere because government is everywhere. While many Americans say they support reductions in the size of government, what they generally mean is that they want to eliminate policies they dislike and spend the money on activities they support. Given these opinions, a large federal government that reaches into virtually all aspects of society is a fact of life. It is not going to go away.

Understanding this problem of control explains why elected officials are often suspicious of bureaucratic actions. It also explains why they place so many requirements and restrictions on the bureaucracy. Red tape doesn't happen because bureaucrats like to make things as complicated as possible—many times, it exists because elected officials are trying to solve the problem of control. It also explains why civil service protections are so controversial. By making it all but impossible to fire most bureaucrats, these protections remove one of the most potent tools for controlling government employees, the fear of losing their job.

In the end, the dilemma that elected officials (and, by extension, American citizens) face is that a bureaucracy of experts is both necessary and problematic. It would be impossible to run the federal government without delegating some responsibilities to bureaucrats. But it is equally impossible to delegate without making bureaucrats real players in the policy process whose goals shape what government does.

1. Standard operating procedures, which some view as another form of "red tape," are important to any bureaucratic structure. Why?

a They provide a necessary slowdown for the political process to make sure that the will of the majority does not override the rights of the minority.

b They are uniform structures across agencies that make sure all agencies follow the same practices in implementation of public policy.

c They consist of important detailed structures for implementation that are embedded in the legislation passed by Congress.

d They create a uniform set of practices to guarantee the reliable continuation of services regardless of which person or party holds office.

2. What is the function of a bureaucracy?

a To create structures and programs to dissuade the public from using various government resources or services

b To provide oversight structures for the executive and legislative branches and act as a check on the overall growth of government

c To develop regulations and policies to implement and enforce congressional actions and presidential directives

d To outline legislative goals and identify problems for Congress to address through public policy

3. What was a key development in the bureaucracy during the Progressive Era?

a The spoils system was put into effect.

b The welfare state was created.

c The size of the bureaucracy was dramatically reduced.

d The government began to have a direct impact on everyday life.

4. Which of the following best characterizes the reasons for the growth of the bureaucracy?

a Successive presidents have demanded Congress fund expansions of governmental agencies in order to deliver on campaign promises to the public.

b The bureaucracy has grown to meet the demands of the public for services and protections the public could not provide for itself.

c A small percentage of the payroll taxes received from Americans is designated to funding the federal bureaucracy, which increases as the overall amount paid in taxes increases.

d Bureaucratic structures and the numbers of employees within the bureaucracy have increased to meet the increasingly complex relationships that have developed from globalization.

5. What role has the American public played in making it nearly impossible for presidents and members of Congress to cut the federal budgets and the size of the bureaucracy?

a The public does not want a reduction in services that would correspond with cutting spending.

b Americans have alternated between voting for presidents who promise to cut and to grow the overall size of the government.

c The American public has consistently voted in support of cutting large spending programs like Social Security and Medicare that are protected categories of the budget that cannot be cut.

d Members of the American public have confused their message by voting for presidents who promise more government programs and members of Congress who promise less spending.

6. What counterargument can you make when a person promotes the idea that members of the federal bureaucracy are just interested in growing their numbers of employees and maximizing the amount of money available to spend each year?

a The number of federal employees has continued with steady growth, but it is proportionate to the percentage of overall population increase in the United States.

b The size of the federal bureaucratic system has grown and contracted depending on the president who was in office at the time.

c The size of the federal bureaucracy is significantly smaller than it was a generation ago and remains about the size that it was during the civil rights era.

d The budgets and numbers of employees have increased overall, but the pace of the growth has slowed since the Clinton administration of the 1990s.

7. For any president, high-level executive appointees within the departments, agencies, and bureaus of the federal bureaucracy serve what significant purpose?

a Monitoring and intervening in ways that ensure the president's agenda is being carried out through the structures of the government

b Reporting the most critical information from their respective areas to Congress and the president on a daily basis

c Maximizing the efficiency and efficacy of the federal government

d Continuing the efforts of modern presidents to make sure that the government agencies adopt more businesslike practices throughout the bureaucratic structures

8. What factual evidence exists that would disprove a belief that the bureaucracy is composed of unqualified individuals who draw government salaries while acting to implement their own political ideologies rather than acting in the public interest?

- a Qualifications for positions, hiring practices, and regulation of political behavior are all set in law.
- b Government employees are employed subject to the approval of the president and the Senate.
- c Because the public chooses presidents from different parties, it balances out which political agendas are being enacted by federal employees.
- d Regular elections that allow the public to choose members of Congress and presidents act as a check on which employees are in government and the actions they are able to take.

9. Many members of Congress run for office claiming that the federal bureaucracy acts to implement policies contrary to the public interests and in violation of the will of Congress. What is the reality about the relationship between Congress, the president, and the bureaucratic structures?

- a Congress has very little ability to affect the bureaucratic structures and regulatory powers of the federal bureaucracy.
- b The bureaucratic structures of government are subject to the oversight of Congress and must implement laws, directives, and policies.
- c The president prevents Congress from intervening in the activities of the federal bureaucracy without involvement from the judicial branch.
- d The bureaucracy largely acts on its own priorities because of the infighting between the legislative and executive branches of government.

10. Which statement best summarizes the challenge of translating laws and public policy directives into effective and efficient implementation by bureaucrats and bureaucratic agencies?

- a Federal agencies and their employees are very often resistant to the problem-solving priorities laid out in federal legislation passed by Congress.
- b Members of Congress lay out specific requirements and structures within legislation for solving problems that counter the desired outcomes and regulations of bureaucratic institutions.
- c Creating clear, specific, and actionable structures consists of complex tasks to achieve the often-broad goals of legislation passed by Congress.
- d Including public input and feedback from members of Congress on how to create the right structures for implementing public policy is often counter to the interests of the federal government.

Use INQUIZITIVE *to help you study and master this material.*

14

The Courts

What is the role of courts in our political system?

"The fact that [President Biden is] willing to make a promise at the outset, that it must be a Black woman, I got to say that's offensive. . . . He's saying, 'If you're a White guy, tough luck. If you're a White woman, tough luck. You don't qualify.'"[1]

Senator Ted Cruz (R-TX)

"This is a Jackie Robinson moment for our nation. For generations America has been blessed with extraordinary legal talent in people of all backgrounds, but for the first time in our history an extraordinarily talented Black woman will serve on the Supreme Court."[2]

Senator Cory Booker (D-NJ)

President Biden's nomination of Judge Ketanji Brown Jackson to the Supreme Court was historic. She was the first Black woman to be nominated to the highest court in the country. However, rather than embracing the historical moment, the Senate quickly divided into its partisan camps. Shortly before the hearings, Senate Minority Leader Mitch McConnell (R-KY) acknowledged her strong qualifications but raised concern about her liberal-leaning decisions: "She's clearly a sharp lawyer with an impressive resume. But when it comes to the Supreme Court, a core qualification is judicial philosophy."[3]

The Constitution dictates that the president gets to nominate Supreme Court justices but the Senate is to offer "advice and consent." As a result, these nominations can become political battles, as was demonstrated during the confirmation hearings for President Biden's first nomination, Ketanji Brown Jackson. The first Black woman to be nominated to the highest court in the land, she was subjected to questioning from the Republican Party. Jackson was ultimately confirmed in April 2022.

Justice Jackson faced aggressive questioning concerning her record in criminal cases (especially dealing with pedophiles) and her views on critical race theory and religion. She was asked if "child predators are misunderstood," if babies are racists, whether she could "fairly judge a Catholic," and to define a woman (to discern her views on transgender rights). Her defenders saw the questions as "cruel and unfair," while Republican senators said they were simply trying to understand her views.

The Senate confirmation process has become much more partisan and contentious in recent years. Ruth Bader Ginsburg, who was a strong liberal presence on the Court for 37 years, was confirmed in 1993 by a 96–3 vote. Justice Sonia Sotomayor, the first Latina to serve on the Court, was confirmed by a bipartisan 68–31 vote in 2009. But Justice Jackson squeaked through with a nearly party-line 53–47 vote in 2022. None of President Trump's three nominees to the Court received more than 54 votes.[4]

CHAPTER GOALS

Explain how the power of judicial review was established (pp. 531–535)

Outline the structure of the court system (pp. 535–546)

Describe how cases reach the Supreme Court (pp. 547–551)

Describe the Supreme Court's procedures for hearing a case (pp. 552–557)

Analyze the factors that influence Supreme Court decisions (pp. 558–563)

Assess the Supreme Court's power in the political system (pp. 564–569)

Senator Susan Collins (R-ME), in announcing her support for Justice Jackson, lamented this "disturbing trend" of a politicized confirmation process: "It used to be common for Senators to give the President, regardless of political party, considerable deference in the choice of a nominee. . . . This approach served the Senate, the Court, and the Country well. It instilled confidence in the independence and the integrity of the judiciary and helped keep the Court above the political fray." Collins also explicitly rejected Senator McConnell's view that judicial philosophy should be a "core qualification," saying the Senate's role is to determine the nominee's qualifications, "not to assess whether a nominee reflects the individual ideology of a senator or would vote exactly as an individual senator would want."[5]

Partisan warfare in the Senate confirmation process has led to a broader perception that justices are partisans rather than an independent branch of government. After President Trump complained about an "Obama judge" who ruled against him in a political asylum case, Chief Justice John G. Roberts Jr. rebuked him. "We do not have Obama judges or Trump judges, Bush judges or Clinton judges," Roberts said. "What we have is an extraordinary group of dedicated judges doing their level best to do equal right to those appearing before them. That independent judiciary is something we should all be thankful for."[6] Other justices have also felt compelled to weigh in on the independence of the Court. In a speech at the University of Louisville, Justice Amy Coney Barrett said, "My goal today is to convince you that this court is not comprised of a bunch of partisan hacks." In a speech at Harvard Law School, former Justice Stephen Breyer said justices should not be regarded as "junior-varsity politicians."[7] The Senate and the president clearly view the Court as another venue for partisan warfare, but the justices' defense of the independence of the Court taps into the powerful image of the blindfolded Lady Justice, holding the scales, neutrally applying the law rather than acting as a committed partisan. As Chief Justice Roberts famously said, justices are like baseball umpires, just calling the balls and strikes within the constitutional system. After all, the guiding principles of the "rule of law" in the American political system—embodied in the words carved above the entrance to the Supreme Court ("Equal Justice under Law") and the image of Lady Justice—seem to contradict the view of a political Supreme Court. We normally think of the courts as objectively applying the law and interpreting the Constitution for each case. Indeed, there is often consensus among the justices on how to rule in a given case. In the 2023–2024 term, 46 percent of the cases were unanimous (27 of 59, and 2 more had only one dissenting vote).[8]

The Supreme Court building features the words "Equal Justice under Law" across the facade, as well as a statue titled *The Contemplation of Justice*.

However, a massive body of political science research shows that the Supreme Court can be quite political and divided ideologically. In the most recent term, 22 cases split 6–3 and 5 were divided 5–4 (there are six conservative and three liberal justices), on important topics such as redistricting, property rights, deference to administrative expertise, gun rights, federalism, and executive immunity. As justices interpret the Constitution, they also play one of two roles in our political system: either asserting their own policy-making authority or deferring to the decisions of others (Congress, the president, or the people). The Court's decision about which path to take in a given case is often political, involving conflict, trade-offs, and compromise, much like decision-making in Congress.

For those who resist the view that the courts are a policy-making institution, the theme "political process matters" may not seem to apply in this chapter. However, the courts often *do* make policy, and the way they make decisions has an impact on outcomes. To see how political process matters for the courts, it is important to answer the following questions: What are the different roles of the courts and the structure of the judicial system? How do court decisions shape policy? In a nutshell, what is the nature of judicial decision-making? With this context in mind, we can reexamine the role of the Senate in the confirmation process. Should the Senate treat Court nominees as partisan politicians? What is the proper place of the courts within our political system? Should judges attempt to neutrally apply the law, or should their political views play a role?

The development of an independent and powerful federal judiciary

EXPLAIN HOW THE POWER OF JUDICIAL REVIEW WAS ESTABLISHED

The Constitution did not definitively establish the role of the courts in American politics or the Supreme Court's authority as the ultimate interpreter of the Constitution. The powers of the Supreme Court evolved over time, and debates about its proper role continue to this day.

The Founders' views of the courts: The weakest branch?

The Federalists and Antifederalists did not see eye to eye on much, and the judiciary was no exception. Alexander Hamilton, writing in *Federalist 78*, said that the Supreme Court would be "beyond comparison the weakest of the three departments of power." In contrast, one of the authors of the *Antifederalist Papers* wrote, "The supreme court under this constitution would be exalted above all other power in the government and subject to no control."[9] Hmmm, which is it, weakest or strongest? Although the framers could not agree on how powerful the Court was likely to be relative to the other branches of government, there was surprisingly little debate at the Constitutional Convention about the judiciary. Article III of the Constitution, which concerns the judicial branch of government, created one Supreme Court and gave the courts independence by providing federal judges with lifetime terms (assuming "good behavior").

The main disagreements about the judiciary had to do with how independent the courts should be vis-à-vis the other branches of government and how much power to give to the courts. Some of the framers feared a tyrannical Congress and wanted to create judicial and executive branches that could check this power. Others argued for making the executive and judicial branches more closely related so they would be better able to balance Congress. A central debate was whether to give the judiciary some "revisionary power" over Congress, similar to the president's veto power. This idea of judicial review would have given the Supreme Court the power to strike down laws passed by Congress that violated the Constitution. The framers could not agree on judicial review, so the Constitution remained silent on the matter.

While the Constitution clearly specified the kinds of cases over which the Court would have **original jurisdiction** (refer to Nuts & Bolts 14.1), many details about the Supreme Court were left up to Congress, including its size, the time and place it would meet, and its internal organization. These details, and the system of lower federal courts, were outlined in the **Judiciary Act of 1789**. This law set the number of justices at six (one chief justice and five associates). The number of justices gradually increased to ten by the end of the Civil War and was then restricted to seven under Reconstruction policies. In 1869 the number was set at nine, where it has remained ever since.[10] The 1789 act also created a system of federal courts, which included 13 **district courts** and 3 circuit courts—the intermediate-level courts with **appellate jurisdiction**. Since the circuit courts hear cases on appeal from lower courts, they are now more commonly called appeals courts. The district courts each had one judge, while the circuit courts were each staffed by two Supreme Court justices and one district judge. This odd arrangement in which Supreme Court justices had to preside over both cases in

original jurisdiction
The authority of a court to handle a case first, as in the Supreme Court's authority to initially hear disputes between two states. However, original jurisdiction for the Supreme Court is not exclusive; the Court may assign such a case to a lower court.

Judiciary Act of 1789
The law in which Congress laid out the organization of the federal judiciary. The law refined and clarified federal court jurisdiction and set the original number of justices at six. It also created the office of the attorney general and established the lower federal courts.

district courts
Lower-level trial courts of the federal judicial system that handle most U.S. federal cases.

appellate jurisdiction
The authority of a court to hear appeals from lower courts and change or uphold the decision.

NUTS & BOLTS 14.1

Jurisdiction of the Federal Courts

Jurisdiction of lower federal courts

- Cases involving the U.S. Constitution, federal laws, and treaties.
- Controversies between two or more states. (Congress passed a law giving the Supreme Court exclusive jurisdiction over these cases.)
- Controversies between citizens of different states.
- Controversies between a state and citizens of another state. (The Eleventh Amendment removed federal jurisdiction in these cases.)
- Controversies between a state or its citizens and any foreign states, citizens, or subjects.
- Cases affecting ambassadors, public ministers, and consuls.
- Cases of admiralty and maritime jurisdictions.
- Controversies between citizens of the same state claiming lands under grants of different states.

Jurisdiction of the Supreme Court

Original jurisdiction*

- Cases involving ambassadors, public ministers, and consuls.
- Cases that involve a state.

Appellate jurisdiction

- Cases falling under the jurisdiction of the lower federal courts, "with such exceptions, and under such Regulations as the Congress shall make."

* This does not imply exclusive jurisdiction. For example, the Supreme Court may refer to a district court for a case involving an ambassador (the more likely outcome).

Source: Lee Epstein and Thomas G. Walker, *Constitutional Law for a Changing America: Institutional Powers and Constraints*, 5th ed. (Washington, DC: CQ Press, 2004), p. 65.

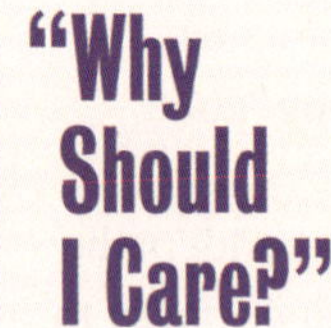

"Why Should I Care?"

Understanding the type of cases that are heard by the federal courts is essential for recognizing their role in the system of checks and balances. Congress has some power to limit the jurisdiction of the federal courts.

Washington and cases in their assigned circuit remained in place for more than 100 years, over the objections of the justices who resented having to "ride circuit" in difficult traveling conditions.[11] Today separate judges are appointed to fill the appeals courts.

The Supreme Court had a rough start. Indeed, it seemed determined to prove Alexander Hamilton right, that it was the weakest branch. Of the six original justices appointed by George Washington, one declined to serve and another never showed up for a formal session. The Court's first sessions lasted only a few days because it did not have much business. In fact, the Court did not decide a single case in 1791 or 1792. When Justice Rutledge resigned in 1791 to take a state court position, two potential appointees turned down the job in order to keep their positions in their state legislatures! Such career decisions would be unimaginable today, when serving on the Supreme Court is considered the pinnacle of a legal career.[12]

Judicial review and *Marbury v. Madison*

The Court started to gain more power when John Marshall was appointed chief justice in 1801. Marshall single-handedly transformed the Court into an equal partner in the system of checks and balances. The most important step was the decision

Marbury v. Madison (1803), which gave the Supreme Court the power of **judicial review**. As noted earlier, the framers were split on the wisdom of giving the Court the power to strike down laws passed by Congress, and the Constitution does not explicitly address the issue. However, historians have established that a majority of the framers, including the most influential ones, favored judicial review (Hamilton endorsed it in some detail in *Federalist 78*). Given that the Constitution did not address the issue of judicial review, Marshall simply asserted that the Supreme Court had the power to determine when a law was unconstitutional. As the power of judicial review has evolved, it has become a central part of the system of checks and balances (refer to Chapter 2).

judicial review
The Supreme Court's power to strike down a law or an executive branch action that it finds unconstitutional.

The facts and legal reasoning behind *Marbury* are worth explaining because it is one of the most important court cases in American history. The Federalists had just lost the election of 1800 to Thomas Jefferson and the Democratic-Republicans. In a last-minute power grab, the Federalist-controlled lame-duck Congress gave outgoing president John Adams an opportunity to appoint 42 new justices of the peace for the District of Columbia and Alexandria, Virginia. Adams made the appointments, and the Senate confirmed them, but not before time ran out and the new administration took over. The secretary of state, John Marshall (the same Marshall who had just been confirmed as chief justice before President Adams left office), failed to ensure that all the commissions for the new judges were delivered by midnight. When President Jefferson assumed office, he ordered his new secretary of state, James Madison, not to deliver the remaining commissions that had been issued by the outgoing Federalist administration. William Marbury was one of the people who did not receive his commission, and he asked the Supreme Court to issue an order giving him the position.

As leading figures in opposing parties, Chief Justice Marshall and President Jefferson did not like each other. This put Marshall in a difficult position. He was concerned that if he issued the order that Marbury wanted, giving Marbury his job, Jefferson probably would ignore it. (Though Secretary of State Madison was technically the other party in the lawsuit, Jefferson was calling the shots.) Given the weakness of the Court, having such an order disregarded by the president could have been a final blow to its position in the national government. However, if the Court did not issue the order, it would be giving in to Jefferson despite the merits of Marbury's case—he really had been cheated out of his job. It appeared that the Court would lose whether it issued the order or not.

Chief Justice John Marshall favored the idea of judicial review and claimed this power for the Court in the *Marbury v. Madison* decision.

To get out of the predicament, Marshall applied the idea of judicial review. Although the idea was not original to Marshall, the Court had never before exercised its authority to rule on the constitutionality of a federal law. Marshall's reasoning was quite clever: he agreed there was a wrong (the Court's opinion said that Marbury was due his commission), but the Court could not provide the remedy to the wrong (giving him his job) because the part of the Judiciary Act of 1789 that gave it the power to do so was unconstitutional! The portion of the act in question was Section 13, which gave the Court the power to issue orders (writs of mandamus) to anyone holding federal office. Because this section expanded the original jurisdiction of the Supreme Court, Marshall ruled that Congress had overstepped its bounds in passing it. The original jurisdiction of the Court is clearly specified in the Constitution, so any attempt by Congress to change that jurisdiction through legislation would be unconstitutional; the only way to change original jurisdiction would be through a constitutional amendment.[13] Marshall wrote, "It is emphatically the province and duty of the judicial department to say what the law is. . . . If two laws conflict with each other, the courts must decide on the operation of each. So if a law be in opposition to the Constitution . . . the court must determine which of these conflicting rules governs the case. This is of the very essence of judicial duty."[14]

Judicial review in practice

Chief Justice Marshall and the Federalists lost the battle—poor Mr. Marbury never did get his job, and Jefferson appointed the people he wanted to be justices of the peace—but the Supreme Court won the war. By asserting its power to review the constitutionality of laws passed by Congress, the Court became an equal partner in the institutional balance of power. Although it would be more than 50 years until the Court would use judicial review again to strike down a law passed by Congress (in the unfortunate 1857 *Dred Scott* case, which concerned slavery and effectively led to the Civil War), the reasoning behind *Marbury* has never been challenged by subsequent presidents or Congresses.[15]

Interpreting federal laws may seem like a logical responsibility for the Supreme Court, but what about state laws? Should the Supreme Court have final say over them as well? The Constitution does not answer this question. But the supremacy clause requires that the Constitution and national laws take precedence over state constitutions and state laws when they conflict. The Judiciary Act of 1789 made it clear that the Supreme Court would rule on these matters.

The contours of the relationship between the national government and the states have been largely defined by the Supreme Court's assertion of judicial review and its willingness to intervene in matters of state law. For much of the nineteenth century, the Court embraced dual federalism, in which the national government and the states operated on two separate levels (refer to Chapter 3). Later the Court involved itself more in state law as it moved toward a more active role for the national government in regulating interstate commerce and using the Fourteenth Amendment to selectively incorporate the amendments that constitute the Bill of Rights (refer to Chapter 4).

All in all, the Court has struck down more than 350 acts of Congress (and about 1,400 state laws).[16] This seems like a lot, but Congress passed more than 60,000 laws in its first 230 years. Over time, the Court has ruled on state laws in many important areas, including civil liberties, desegregation and civil rights, abortion, privacy, redistricting, labor laws, employment and discrimination, and business and environmental regulation.

constitutional interpretation
The process of determining whether a piece of legislation or governmental action is supported by the Constitution.

statutory interpretation
The various methods and tests used by the courts for determining the meaning of a law and applying it to specific situations. Congress may overturn the courts' interpretation by writing a new law; thus, it also engages in statutory interpretation.

When the Supreme Court strikes down a congressional or state law, it engages in **constitutional interpretation**—that is, it determines that the law is unconstitutional. But the Supreme Court also engages in **statutory interpretation**—that is, it applies national and state laws to particular cases (statutes are laws that are passed by legislatures). Often the language of a statute may be unclear and the Court must interpret how to apply the law. For example, should the protection of endangered species prevent economic development that may destroy the species' habitat? How does one determine if an employer is responsible for punishing sexual harassment in the workplace? How should the voting rights of historically marginalized communities be protected? In each case, the Court must interpret the relevant statutes to determine what Congress really meant. In addition, in the third main area of the law—administrative law—the Court is sometimes required to assess how federal agencies have interpreted and implemented laws passed by Congress. Often this involves the controversial practice of consulting legislative histories—floor debates, congressional hearings, and so on—to determine how the legislature intended the laws to be interpreted. But the late justice Antonin Scalia argued that such searches are inherently subjective and that justices should interpret only the actual text of the laws in question.

Although politicians and other political actors accept judicial review as a central part of the political system, critics are concerned about its antidemocratic nature. Why, for example, do we give nine unelected justices such extraordinary power over our elected representatives? Debates about the proper role for the Court will continue as long as it is involved in controversial decisions. We will take up this question later in the chapter when we address the concepts of judicial activism and judicial restraint.

Judicial review may seem like "inside baseball" that doesn't really matter for most Americans. However, the power to strike down laws and government actions means that the Court may act against political majorities to strike down unconstitutional actions such as segregating schools by race and discriminating against same-sex marriage. Judicial review may also be used, however, to frustrate popular majorities during times of political change, such as during the New Deal of the 1930s. Recently, the Court has done some of both—requiring the government to have a court order to search cell phone records (a popular decision) but also deciding that states must collect sales taxes on Internet sales, despite public opposition to the practice. In either case, judicial review is an awesome political power that puts the Supreme Court on an equal institutional footing with Congress and the president.

"Why Should I Care?"

The American legal and judicial system

Two sets of considerations are necessary to understand the overall nature of our judicial system: the fundamentals of the legal system that apply to all courts in the United States, and the structure of the court system within our system of federalism. You may have some understanding of the legal system from watching *Law and Order* or *Better Call Saul*, but a refresher on the basics never hurts.

Court fundamentals

The general characteristics of the court system begin with the people who are in the courtroom. The **plaintiff** brings the case, and the **defendant** is the person or party who is being sued or charged with a crime. If the case is appealed, the petitioner is the person bringing the appeal and the respondent is on the other side of the case. In a civil case, the plaintiff sues to determine who is right or wrong and to gain something of value, such as monetary damages, the right to vote, or admission to a university. For example, imagine that your neighbor accidentally backs his car into the fence that divides your property, destroying a large section of it. The neighbor does not have adequate insurance to cover the damages and refuses to pay for the repairs. You do not want to pay the $1,000 deductible on your insurance policy, so you (the plaintiff) sue your neighbor (the defendant) to see whether your neighbor has to pay for the repairs. In a criminal case, the plaintiff is the government and the prosecutor attempts to prove the guilt of the defendant (the person accused of the crime).

plaintiff
The person or party who brings a case to court.

defendant
The person or party against whom a case is brought.

Many, but not all, civil and criminal cases are heard before a jury that decides the outcome in the case, which is called the verdict. Often cases get settled before they go to trial (or even in the middle of the trial) in a process known as **plea bargaining**. In a civil case, this would mean that the plaintiff and the defendant agree on a monetary settlement and admission of guilt (or not; in some cases the defendant may agree to pay a fine or damages but not to admit guilt). In a criminal case, the defendant may agree to plead guilty in exchange for receiving a shorter sentence or being charged with a lesser crime. Almost 97 percent of federal felony cases that result in a conviction are settled in this way.[17] Plea bargaining is an excellent example of how legal conflict between two parties can be resolved through compromise.

plea bargaining
Negotiating an agreement between a plaintiff and a defendant to settle a case before it goes to trial or the verdict is decided. In a civil case, this usually involves an admission of guilt and an agreement on monetary damages; in a criminal case, this often involves an admission of guilt in return for a reduced charge or sentence.

In 2019, several celebrities were accused of participating in a college admissions scandal that involved using their wealth and influence to improve the odds of their children being admitted to selective colleges; the scheme included falsifying SAT scores and academic records. Actor and producer Lori Loughlin, center, was accused of bribing an athletic coach to get her two daughters admitted to the University of Southern California. She ultimately accepted a plea bargain to reduce her prison sentence and fine.

Differences between Civil and Criminal Cases There are important differences between civil and criminal cases. One is the standard of proof that serves to determine the outcome of the case. In civil cases, the jury has to determine whether the "preponderance of evidence"—that is, a majority of the evidence—proves that the plaintiff wins. In criminal cases, a much stiffer standard must be met: the defendant must be found guilty "beyond a reasonable doubt."

Another difference is where the burden of proof lies. In criminal cases, there is a presumption of "innocent until proven guilty"—that is, the state must prove the guilt of the defendant. However, in civil cases the burden of proof may be on either the plaintiff or the defendant, depending on the law that governs the case. Even more complicated, in civil cases the plaintiff may have to prove certain points and the defendant other points. For example, in certain race-based voting rights cases plaintiffs would have to prove that race was the predominant motivation for creating a Black-majority congressional district to support their complaint that their interests were not being served in the district. If that point is demonstrated, then the burden of proof shifts to the defendants to show that there was some "compelling state interest" to justify the use of race as a predominant factor.

class-action lawsuit
A case brought by a group of individuals on behalf of themselves and others in the general public who are in similar circumstances.

One type of civil suit is the **class-action lawsuit**, a case brought by a group of individuals on behalf of themselves and others in similar circumstances. Their target may be a corporation that produced hazardous or defective products or that harmed a particular group through illegal behavior, such as sexual harassment or racial discrimination. Suits are often filed on behalf of shareholders of companies that have lost value because of fraud committed by corporate leaders. Cases like these are an important mechanism for providing accountability and justice in our economic system. Federal regulators do not have the ability to ensure the complete safety of food, drugs, and consumer products or to continually monitor all potential business fraud. Therefore, consumers rely on the legal system and class-action lawsuits to ensure that businesses act fairly and produce safe products.

Common Elements of the Judicial System Several characteristics of the judicial system apply to all cases. First, ours is an adversarial system in which lawyers on both sides have an opportunity to present their case, challenge the testimony of the opposing side, and try to convince the court that their version of the events is true. The process of "discovery," in which both sides share the information that will be presented in court before the trial begins, ensures a fair process and few last-minute surprises. Second, 49 of the 50 states and the federal courts operate under a system of **common law**, which means that legal decisions build from precedents established in previous cases and apply commonly throughout the jurisdiction of the court. The alternative, which

common law
Law based on the precedent of previous court rulings rather than on legislation. It is used in all federal courts and 49 of the 50 state courts.

is practiced only in Louisiana, is the civil law tradition, which is based on a detailed codification of the law that is applied to each specific case.

The notion of **precedent** (or stare decisis: "let the decision stand") deserves special attention. Precedent is a previously decided case or set of cases that serves as a guide for future cases on the same topic. Lower courts are bound by Supreme Court decisions when there is a clear precedent that is relevant for a given case. In many cases, following precedent is not clear-cut because several precedents may seem relevant. The lower courts have considerable discretion in sorting out which precedents are the most important. The Supreme Court tries to follow its own precedents, but in the past 70 years justices have been willing to deviate from earlier decisions when they think that the precedent is flawed. The Court has overruled more than five times as many decisions since 1950 as it overturned in the previous 161 years.[18] Part of this can be explained by the relatively small number of precedents that *could* have been overturned in the first few decades of our nation's history. But even when accounting for the natural accumulation of more precedents to potentially overturn, recent Courts have been much more willing to deviate from precedent than previous Courts. The Court has developed four factors that it uses to decide if a case should be overturned: the quality of the past decision's reasoning, its consistency with related decisions, legal developments since the past decision, and reliance on the decision throughout the legal system and society. But in some cases, the Court overturns a precedent simply because the ideological composition of the Court has changed. For example, in a case concerning states' immunity from lawsuits in another state's courts, the Court overturned a 40-year precedent even though none of the four factors were met.[19] As this record indicates, precedent is not a rule the Court must follow but a norm that constrains its behavior.

precedent
A legal norm established in court cases that is then applied to future cases dealing with the same legal questions.

Another characteristic common to all cases is that the person bringing the case must have **standing** to sue in a civil case, which means that the person has a legitimate basis for bringing the case. This usually means that the individual has suffered some direct and personal harm from the action addressed in the court case. Standing is easy to establish for private parties; in our earlier example, if your neighbor destroys your fence, you have been harmed. However, determining who has standing gets more interesting when the government is the one being sued. For example, when an environmental group challenged the Interior Department's interpretation of the Endangered Species Act, the Supreme Court ruled that the group did not have standing to sue because it had not demonstrated that the government's policy would cause it "imminent" injury.[20] In 2024, the Court ruled that doctors opposed to the abortion medication, mifepristone, did not have standing because they were not harmed by the Food and Drug Administration's rules that expanded access to the drug because they could simply not prescribe it.[21] Similarly, federal courts have ruled that 10 members of Congress did not have standing to challenge American bombing in Libya and that taxpayers do not have standing to sue the government if they disagree with a specific policy.[22] Depending on your politics, you may not want your hard-earned cash going to buy school lunches for children from under-resourced communities or to fund various wars. However, your status as a taxpayer does not give you enough of a personal stake in these policies to challenge them in court, so you do not have standing. Later, in the section discussing how cases get to the Supreme Court, we will see that justices have some leeway in defining standing.

standing
Legitimate justification for bringing a civil case to court.

The final general characteristic of the legal system is the **jurisdiction** of the court. When bringing a case before the court, you must choose a court that actually has the power to hear your case. For example, if you wanted to contest a speeding ticket, you would not file your case in the state supreme court or in the federal district court; you would file it in your local traffic court. What if you believed you were the victim of discrimination in the workplace? Would you sue in state or federal court? You probably could do either, but the decision would be based on which set of laws would provide you with more protection from discrimination. This varies by state, so the proper

jurisdiction
The sphere of a court's legal authority to hear and decide cases.

jurisdiction for a given case is often a judgment call based on specific legal questions. (This practice of seeking the best court for your case is called *venue shopping*.)

Structure of the court system and federalism

The structure of the court system is like the rest of the political system: it is divided within and across levels of government. Across the levels of government, the court system operates on two parallel tracks within (1) the state and local courts and (2) the federal courts. Within each level of government, both tracks include courts of original jurisdiction, appeals courts, and courts of special jurisdiction.

State Courts As shown in the How It Works graphic on pages 540–541, the state courts are entirely separate from the federal courts, with the exception of the small number of cases that are appealed from a state supreme court to the U.S. Supreme Court. There is much variation between the states in terms of how they structure their court systems. However, they all follow the same general pattern of trial courts with limited and general original jurisdiction and appeals courts (either one or two levels, depending on the state).

Most Americans are much more likely to have experience with state courts rather than federal courts given that more than 83 million cases a year are filed in state courts and only about 300,000 in federal courts. Just over half of the cases in state courts (42 million) were in traffic courts, but an overwhelming proportion of criminal cases, juvenile and family cases (such as divorce), and small claims will be in state and local courts.[23]

District Courts Workhorses of the federal system, the district courts handle more than a quarter of a million filings a year. There are 89 districts in the 50 states, with at least one district court for each state. There are also district courts in Puerto Rico, the Virgin Islands, the District of Columbia, Guam, and the Northern Mariana Islands to bring the total to 94 districts with 677 judges.[24] There are two limited-jurisdiction district courts: the Court of International Trade, which addresses cases involving international trade and customs issues, and the U.S. Court of Federal Claims, which handles most claims for money damages against the United States, disputes over federal contracts, unlawful "takings" of private property by the federal government, and other claims against the United States.

appeals courts
The intermediate level of federal courts that hear appeals from district courts. More generally, an appeals court is any court with appellate jurisdiction.

Appeals Courts The **appeals courts** (officially called circuit courts until 1948)[25] are the intermediate courts of appeal, but in practice they are the final court for most federal cases that are appealed from the district courts. The losing side in a federal case can appeal to the Supreme Court, but given that the highest court in the land hears so few cases, the appeals courts usually get the final word. Appeals courts did not always have this much power; in fact, through much of the nineteenth century they had very limited appellate jurisdiction and did not hear many significant cases.

The number of appeals courts in the nation slowly expanded as the workload of these courts grew. Currently, there are 12 regional courts and the Court of Appeals for the Federal Circuit, which handles specialized cases from all over the country. The smallest of the regional appeals courts is the First Circuit, which has six judges, and the largest is the Ninth Circuit, which has 29 judges. In 2023, there were 179 appeals court judges and about 85 "senior judges" (these numbers include the appeals court for the federal circuit).[26] Senior judges are semi-retired judges who hear certain cases to help out with the overall federal court system workload; they typically handle about 20–25 percent of the workload for the federal court system (there are also about 400 senior judges in the district courts who handle about a quarter of the workload).[27]

The Supreme Court The Supreme Court sits at the top of the federal court system. The Supreme Court is the "court of last resort" for cases coming from both the state and the federal courts. One important function of the Court is to ensure that the application and interpretation of the Constitution are consistent nationwide by resolving conflicts between lower courts, or between state law and federal law, or between laws in different states. A district court or appeals court ruling is applicable only within the specific region of that court, whereas Supreme Court rulings apply to the entire country.

Although the Supreme Court is the most important interpreter of the Constitution, the president and Congress also interpret the Constitution on a regular basis. This means that the Supreme Court does not always have the final say. For example, if the Court strikes down a federal law for being overly vague, Congress can rewrite the law to clarify the offending passage. Thus, in cases involving statutory interpretation, Congress may have the final word. For example, Congress overturned *Ledbetter v. Goodyear Tire & Rubber Co.* (2007) when it passed the Lilly Ledbetter Fair Pay Act in 2009. The law explicitly states that the Supreme Court had misinterpreted the 1964 Civil Rights Act when it ruled in 2007 that Ledbetter would have had to file her pay discrimination suit within 180 days of being hired.[28]

Even on matters of constitutional interpretation rather than statutory interpretation, Congress can fight back by passing a constitutional amendment. However, this is a difficult and time-consuming process (refer to Chapter 2). Nevertheless, that option is available as a way of overturning an unpopular Court decision. Perhaps the best example of this is the very first major case ever decided by the Supreme Court—*Chisholm v. Georgia* (1793). This case upheld the right of a citizen of one state to sue another state in federal court. The states were shocked by this challenge to their sovereignty, and a constitutional amendment to overturn the decision quickly made its way through Congress. By 1795, the Eleventh Amendment had been ratified and citizens could no longer sue a state (in federal court) in which they did not live.[29]

How judges are selected

State Courts One summary of how judges are selected for state courts described it as a "dizzying assortment of methods."[30] Indeed, there is great variation across states and within states for different types of courts. The biggest difference between state and federal courts in the selection process is that 39 states elect at least some of their judges, whereas all federal judges are appointed by the president and confirmed by the Senate. In 16 states, the governor appoints judges to the state supreme court and then after serving their terms (which vary in length), judges are reselected in unopposed retention elections. Fourteen states have contested nonpartisan elections and eight have partisan elections for the highest court. Overall, there are five methods of picking state judges: commission-based appointment by the governor (or merit selection), appointment by the governor, partisan election, nonpartisan election, and legislative election.[31]

Federal Courts Although the Constitution provides detailed stipulations for serving in Congress and as president, it does not specify requirements for serving on the federal courts. Federal judges don't even have to have a law degree! (This is probably due to the limited number of law schools at the time of the Founding; when the Constitution was written, someone who wanted to be a lawyer generally would serve as an apprentice in a law office to learn the trade.) The president appoints federal judges with the "advice and consent" of the Senate, which in practice means that the Senate must approve the nominees with a majority vote. As noted in the chapter opener, nomination battles for federal judges can be intense, because the stakes are high: the Supreme Court plays a central role in the policy process, and because justices have life tenure, a justice's impact can outlive the president and Senate that put the justice on the Court. Justices often serve for decades, much longer than the people who appoint them.

DID YOU KNOW?

50

of the 116 people to serve on the Supreme Court have had law degrees. However, all since 1957 have had law degrees, and all but one of the current Court justices attended either Harvard or Yale law school (Amy Coney Barrett attended Notre Dame).

Source: SupremeCourt.gov.

How it works: in theory

The Court System

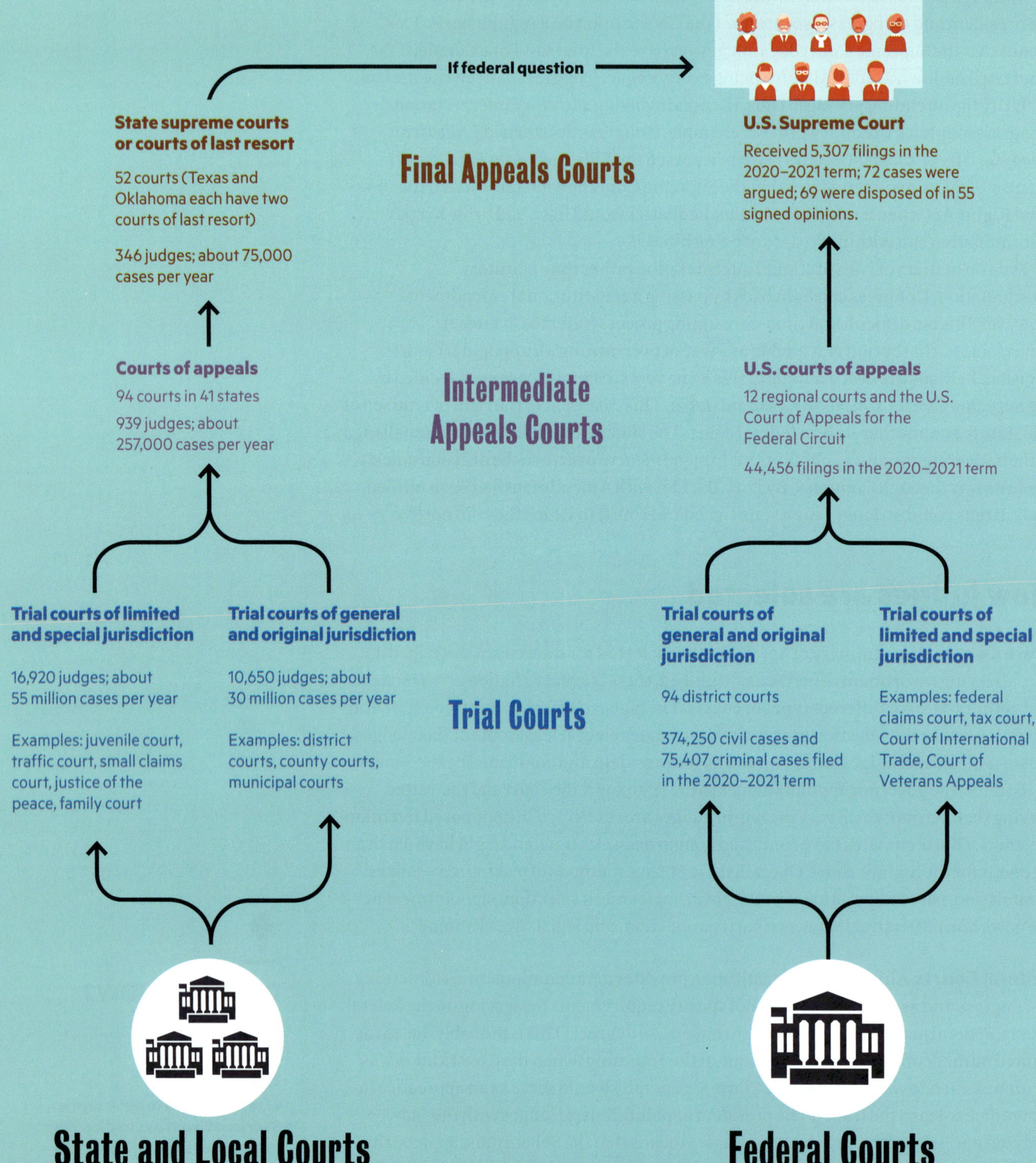

Sources: Data on federal courts are from U.S. Supreme Court, "2021 Year-End Report on the Federal Judiciary," www.supremecourt.gov/publicinfo/year-end/2021year-endreport.pdf (accessed 2/17/22). Data on state courts are from National Center for State Courts, www.ncsc.org; Ballotpedia.org, "Intermediate Appellate Courts," https://ballotpedia.org/Intermediate_appellate_courts; and Ron Malega and Thomas H. Cohen, "State Court Organization, 2011," U.S. Department of Justice, Bureau of Justice Statistics, www.bjs.gov/content/pub/pdf/sco11.pdf (all accessed 5/3/22).

How it works: **in practice**

Partisan Gerrymandering through the Court System

Partisan gerrymandering has been addressed in dozens of state and federal court cases in the past 30 years. A landmark case decided in June 2019 illustrates how cases make their way through the court system and how the Supreme Court may decide *not* to resolve a conflict.

It's okay to do this, right?

State and federal trial courts:
From 1986 to 2004, the Supreme Court **upheld partisan gerrymanders but left the door open for proving they were unconstitutional** if the right evidence was presented.

Well, maybe, maybe not . . .

Over the next decade, state and federal courts struggled with various issues concerning redistricting, but **conflicting decisions left the issue unresolved**.

It's unconstitutional.

Federal courts:
In Ohio, North Carolina, Maryland, and Wisconsin, federal courts **struck down state legislative or congressional maps as unconstitutional**.

Hang on, don't get too excited . . .

In June 2018, the Court punted in cases from Wisconsin and Maryland, **sending the cases back to the lower courts**.

We *still* don't like it!

North Carolina and Maryland stuck to their guns and **struck down their maps again**. Michigan and Ohio agreed.

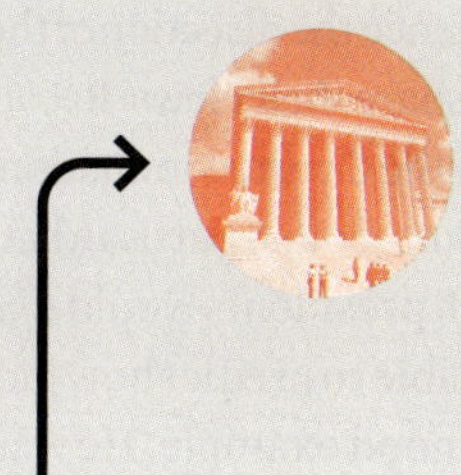

Okay, let's resolve this—or not!

Supreme Court:
In a landmark ruling in June 2019, the Supreme Court got out of the partisan gerrymandering business, saying it is a "nonjusticiable political question." The majority opinion **recognized it as a problem but said the Court does not have a measure to determine when a set of districts is unconstitutional**. The dissenters feared for the future of democracy.

The states don't like it either!

State courts:
In Pennsylvania and Florida, state courts **struck down partisan gerrymanders, and voters in more than a dozen states took the control over redistricting out of the hands of politicians** and gave it to nonpartisan commissions.

We will just leave this sticky problem to the states.

The majority opinion noted that **states would still be free to address partisan gerrymandering**, but this path is not open to states where politicians don't want to reform the process and voters don't have the initiative and referendum process to impose the change. The 2021–2022 round of redistricting produced Republican gerrymanders in Ohio, Texas, Utah, and North Carolina and Democratic gerrymanders in Illinois, Oregon, Massachusetts, and New York.

Critical Thinking

1. **What are the advantages and disadvantages** of having such a complex court system?
2. **When is it appropriate for the Supreme Court to decide** an issue is a "political question"? Do you think it was appropriate in this case? Can you think of an issue other than partisan gerrymandering for which this is likely to occur?

The Role of the President Given the Constitution's silence on the qualifications of federal judges, presidents have broad discretion over whom to nominate. Presidents have always tried to influence the direction of the federal courts, especially the Supreme Court, by picking people who share their views. Because the Senate often has different ideas about the proper direction for the Court, nomination disputes end up being a combination of debates over the merit of a nominee and partisan battles about the ideological composition of the Court.

Although presidents would *like* to influence the direction of the Court, it is not always possible to predict how judges will behave once they are on the bench. Earl Warren is a good example. He was appointed by Republican president Dwight Eisenhower and had been the Republican governor of California, yet he turned out to be one of the most liberal chief justices of the last century. Eisenhower called Warren's nomination the biggest mistake he ever made.[32]

Nonetheless, the president can make a good guess about how a justice is likely to vote based on the nominee's party affiliation and the nature of their legal writings and decisions (if the nominee has prior judicial experience). Not surprisingly, 106 of the 116 justices who have served on the Court have shared the nominating president's party (91 percent). Overall, more than 90 percent of the lower-court judges appointed by presidents in the twentieth and twenty-first centuries have also belonged to the same party as the president.

The most partisan move to influence the Court was President Franklin Delano Roosevelt's infamous plan to pack the Court. FDR was frustrated because the Court had struck down several pieces of important New Deal legislation, so to get a more sympathetic Court, he proposed nominating a new justice for every justice who was over 70 years old. At the time, six justices were over 70, so this would have increased the size of the Court to 15 justices. Roosevelt's effort to disguise the partisan power play as a humanitarian gesture (to help the old-timers with their workload) didn't fool anyone. The plan to pack the Court ran into opposition, but once the Court started ruling in favor of the New Deal legislation, the plan was dropped.

In addition to the ideological considerations about whom to nominate, the president also considers their relationship to the candidate and the candidate's reputation as a legal scholar. Further considerations are the candidate's ethical standards, religion, gender, and race (refer to Figure 14.1). The religion of justices has undergone a complete transformation: for the nation's first 125 years, nearly all justices were Protestants. Now there are six Catholic justices, one Jewish justice, one Protestant, and one unknown (Gorsuch was raised Catholic but most recently attended an Episcopal church).[33] Over time, the federal courts have steadily become more diverse in terms of race and gender.

President Trump nominated Amy Coney Barrett to the Supreme Court. While the Supreme Court is a nonpartisan body, presidents nominate justices whose party affiliation or legal writings align with their own political leanings. For example, Amy Coney Barrett, one of President Trump's nominees, had been a clerk for the conservative Supreme Court justice Clarence Thomas, suggesting that she too would represent conservative interests.

However, Donald Trump reversed this trend. Only 4 percent of the judges he appointed were Black and 4 percent were Hispanic, the lowest percentages since Ronald Reagan in the 1980s. In contrast, Biden's judges were the most racially diverse in history with 37 percent White, 27 percent Black, and 15 percent Hispanic. In one term, Biden appointed more non-White judges (127) than any other president in two terms (Obama had the second highest, 115). Just under a quarter of Trump's nominees were women, compared with 42 percent for President Obama and 64 percent for Biden (refer to Figure 14.1).

Race and Gender on Federal Courts

FIGURE 14.1

Since the 1980s, the proportion of women appointed to the federal bench by the president has gone up eightfold, while the percentage of White men has plummeted by more than half. Do you think that descriptive representation in the judicial branch is important?

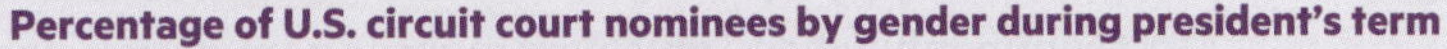

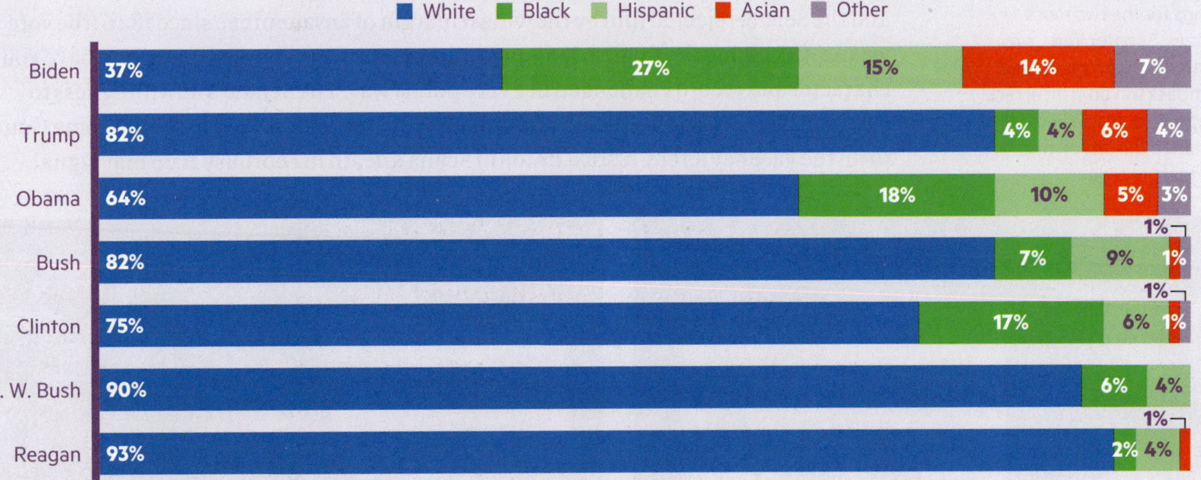

Sources: Nick Mourtoupalas, "Biden has installed the most non-White judges of any president," Washington Post, May 17, 2024, https://www.washingtonpost.com/politics/2024/05/17/biden-trump-judges-diversity/; John Gramlich, "How Trump compares with other recent presidents in appointing federal judges," Pew Research Center, January 13, 2021, https://www.pewresearch.org/short-reads/2021/01/13/how-trump-compares-with-other-recent-presidents-in-appointing-federal-judges/ (accessed 5/29/24). Data may not add up to 100 percent due to rounding.

The Role of the Senate The Senate is the other half of the equation that determines the composition of the federal courts. The Senate has shifted from a very active role in providing "advice and consent" on court appointments to a passive role and then back to an active role. One constant is that the Senate rarely rejects nominees because of their qualifications; rather, it tends to reject them for political reasons. Of 28 Supreme Court nominees rejected by the Senate in the history of the United States, only two were turned down because they were seen as unqualified. Serious questions were also raised about a third justice, Clarence Thomas, who had served for only 18 months as a federal judge before being nominated to the Court. Thomas also was accused of sexual harassment by former colleague Anita Hill. Hill's testimony in 1991 predates the #MeToo movement by 26 years and brought sexual harassment into the public limelight for the first time. There were only two women in the Senate at the time and the unsympathetic hearing she received before the all-male Senate Judiciary Committee helped produce the "Year of the Woman" in House and Senate races the next year (as of 2020, there are now 26 women in the Senate, an all-time high). Nonetheless, Thomas ultimately won confirmation by a 52–48 vote. The other 26 nominees were rejected for political reasons. Most commonly, when a president makes a nomination close to an election and the Senate is controlled by the opposing party, the Senate will kill the nomination, hoping that its party will win the presidency and nominate a justice more to its liking.

Throughout the nineteenth century, the Senate was very willing to turn down Court nominations for political reasons. In fact, between 1793 and 1894 the Senate did not confirm 21 nominees to the Court, which was about a third of the total number nominated. In contrast, between 1894 and 1968 the Senate did not even require nominees to testify, and during that period only 4 nominees were rejected.

A rethinking of this passive role occurred in the late 1960s. President Nixon vowed to pull the Court back from the "liberal excesses" of the Warren Court, but the Senate stiffened its spine and rejected two conservative nominees in a row: Clement Haynsworth (in 1969) and G. Harrold Carswell (in 1970). With Haynsworth, there were ethical problems involving his participation in cases in which he had a financial interest. Carswell had a mediocre judicial record, and civil rights groups raised questions about his commitment to enforcing antidiscrimination laws. Nixon must have thought that the Senate wouldn't reject his choice twice in a row! The most recent Senate rejection took place in 1987. Judge Robert Bork was a brilliant, very conservative, and controversial figure. Liberal interest groups mobilized against him, and the Senate rejected him by the widest margin of any nominee since 1846 (the vote was 42–58), giving the English language a new verb: to get "borked" means to have your character and record challenged in a very public way. The Senate's unwillingness to even consider President Obama's nomination of Merrick Garland to the Supreme Court to fill the vacancy left by Justice Antonin Scalia's death in February 2016 may signal

As with most Supreme Court hearings, partisan tensions were on display during hearings for the two most recent nominees. Senator Ted Cruz (R-TX) questioned Biden's nominee Ketanji Brown Jackson on critical race theory, while Senator Mazie Hirono (D-HI) questioned Barrett on her opinions on legal precedent.

a return to the more politicized era of Supreme Court nominations in the nineteenth century, especially given that the strategy worked: Trump won the presidency and nominated Neil Gorsuch, who was approved by a 54–45 vote in the Senate. Brett Kavanaugh, whose confirmation was more contentious due to sexual assault allegations, was ultimately confirmed in a 50–48 vote, the second-closest positive vote in history. Partisan tensions were even higher when liberal icon Ruth Bader Ginsburg passed away in September 2020 and the Senate rushed through confirmation of Amy Coney Barrett by a 52–48 vote. The 46 days between Ginsburg's death and Election Day marked the shortest period in U.S. history during which a justice was confirmed before a presidential election (the second shortest span between a vacancy and the election was 149 days in 1916). Those partisan tensions were on display in Justice Jackson's confirmation hearings, as noted in the chapter opener.

Yet not all recent Supreme Court nominations have been controversial. President Bill Clinton's two Supreme Court picks were overwhelmingly confirmed—Ginsburg by a 96–3 vote and Stephen Breyer by an 87–9 vote. George W. Bush's nominees, John G. Roberts Jr. and Samuel Alito Jr., were confirmed by comfortable margins. President Obama appointed the first Latina to serve on the Supreme Court, Sonia Sotomayor, who was confirmed by a 68–31 vote. Elena Kagan's confirmation by a 63–37 vote in 2010 meant that three women were serving on the Court for the first time (and there were then four in 2023, with Barrett replacing the late Ginsburg in 2020 and Jackson replacing Breyer in 2022).

Battles over Lower-Court Judges The contentious battles between the president and the Senate over nominees to the federal bench and the Supreme Court have recently expanded to include nominees to the district and appeals courts. For much of the nation's history, the president did not play a very active role in the nomination process for district courts, instead deferring to the home-state senators of the president's party to suggest candidates—a norm called **senatorial courtesy**. If neither senator from the state was from the president's party, he would consult House members from his party and other high-ranking party members from the state for district court nominees. The president typically has shown more interest in appeals court nominations. The Justice Department plays a key role in screening candidates, but the local senators of the president's party remain active as well through the "blue slip" process: home-state senators record their support or opposition to nominees on blue slips of paper. Some committee chairs have allowed a single home-state senator to use the blue slip to veto a nominee, but others have not followed the process so strictly (in the current Senate, blue slips are generally used for district court, but not appeals court, nominations).

senatorial courtesy
A norm in the nomination of district court judges in which the president consults with their party's senators from the relevant state in choosing the nominee.

Recently the process has become much more contentious. While the confirmation rate for federal judges has been relatively stable in the past 35 years (between 80 and 90 percent), the average time to confirm nominees has increased dramatically. The average length of delay from nomination to confirmation has increased from a little over 50 days in the 1980s to over 200 days in recent years (refer to Figure 14.2 on p. 546), and the situation has intensified. Democrats blocked 39 of President Bush's nominees between 2001 and 2009,[34] and Republicans returned the favor during Obama's presidency by blocking dozens of his nominees, which included employing a record number of filibusters of lower-court nominees. After the Senate blocked three nominees to the D.C. Court of Appeals, the second-most-important court in the nation, Democrats responded in November 2013 by eliminating the filibuster on lower-court and executive branch nominations but not Supreme Court nominations.[35] This move was originally labeled the "nuclear option" by Democrats who had threatened to shut down the Senate if the Republican leadership got rid of the filibuster during the George W. Bush presidency. In response to the detonation of the nuclear option, the confirmation process slowed to a trickle in President Obama's last year, which produced

FIGURE 14.2

Average Confirmation Delay for Federal Court Nominations, 1981–2022

Since the 1980s, the length of time needed to confirm federal court nominations has increased dramatically. Why do you think this happened? Why does it matter?

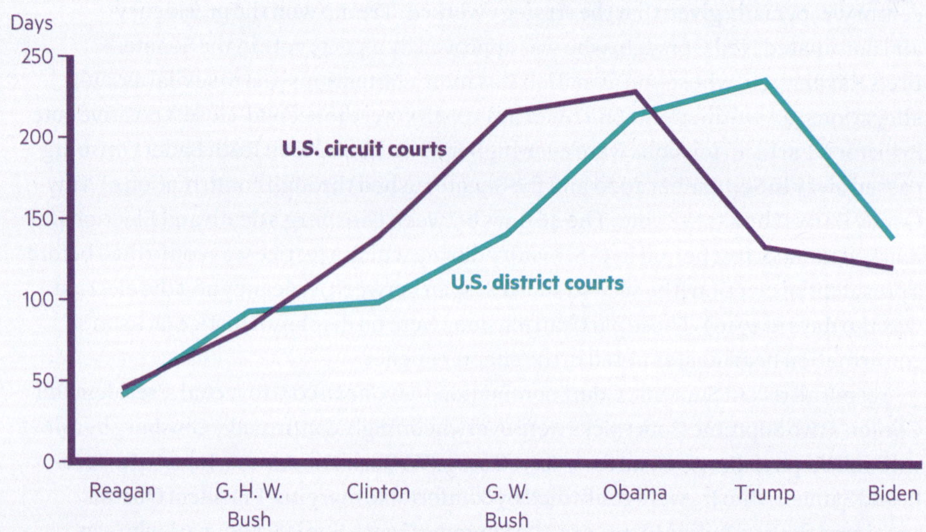

Source: Barry J. McMillion, "Judicial Nomination Statistics and Analysis: U.S. Circuit and District Courts, 1977–2022," Congressional Research Service, April 3, 2023, https://crsreports.congress.gov/product/pdf/R/R45622 (accessed 5/29/24).

a near-record level of vacancies (more than 10 percent of all federal judgeships). With unified control of government for the first time since 2009, Republicans moved quickly to fill many of those vacancies and approve Trump's nominations. To approve Neil Gorsuch's nomination, Senate Republicans eliminated the filibuster on Supreme Court nominations. With the process still not moving as quickly as it wanted, the Senate also changed Senate rules to limit floor debate on nominations to 2 hours instead of 30 hours. The Senate also approved a record number of appeals court nominees in Trump's term (54, which was almost as many as the 55 Obama picked in his eight years). President Biden has been a bit of an outlier with both the lowest confirmation rate (68 percent) of any president since Jimmy Carter, but shorter delays than recent presidents.

Although there is no definitive answer as to how active the Senate should be in giving "advice and consent," it is clear that the Founders intended the Senate to play an active role. The first draft of the Constitution gave the Senate the sole power to appoint Supreme Court justices. However, the final version made appointment a shared power with the president. It was not expected that the Senate would compete with the president over whom to nominate, but it *was* assumed that the Senate would exercise independent judgment as to the suitability of the president's nominees.

"Why Should I Care?"

It is safe to assume that most Americans do not follow the details of battles over court nominations. However, these battles are every bit as important as the elections that *do* capture much attention. Unelected judges often serve for 20 or 30 years, much longer than the average member of Congress, and have the power to strike down laws that Congress passes. Confirmation battles also support our argument that politics is conflictual and that we should expect it to be that way. The Founders certainly did not expect that the process would be free of politics or that the Senate would be an essentially passive and subordinate player in a nominally joint enterprise. Even George Washington had two of his nominations turned down by the Senate for political reasons. Therefore, politics will continue to play an important role in deciding who serves on the federal bench.

Access to the Supreme Court

DESCRIBE HOW CASES REACH THE SUPREME COURT

It is extremely difficult to get a case heard by the Supreme Court. Currently the Court hears just over 1 percent of the cases submitted (72 of 5,307 cases in the most recent completed term).[36] This section explains how the Court decides which cases to hear. When a case is submitted, the clerk of the Court assigns it a number and places it on the docket, which is the schedule of cases.

The Court's workload

Statistics on the Supreme Court's workload initially suggest that the size of the docket has increased dramatically since 1980 through the early 2000s, only to decline again (refer to Figure 14.3). However, a majority of cases are frivolous and are dismissed after limited review. The Court has become increasingly impatient with these frivolous petitions and has moved to prevent "frequent filers" from harassing the Court. One often-cited case involved Michael Sindram, who asked the Court to order the Maryland courts to remove a $35 traffic ticket from his record. Our favorite example concerned a wealthy drug dealer, Frederick W. Bauer, who was convicted on 10 counts of dealing drugs and petitioned the Court 12 times on various issues. The justices finally had enough and directed "the Clerk not to accept any further petitions for *certiorari* or petitions for extraordinary writs from Bauer in noncriminal matters" unless he paid his docketing fees. They concluded that the order would allow the Court to focus on "petitioners who have not abused our processes."[37]

FIGURE 14.3

The Court Sees More Opportunities . . . but Hears Fewer Cases

The Supreme Court's workload appears to be headed in two directions: the Court receives far more cases than it actually hears. What are the implications of having the Supreme Court hear so few cases, relative to the number they receive? Should something be done to try to get the Court to hear more cases?

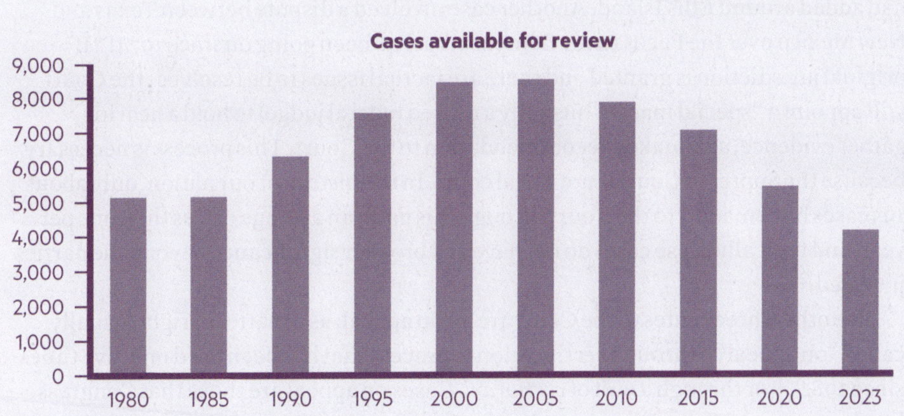

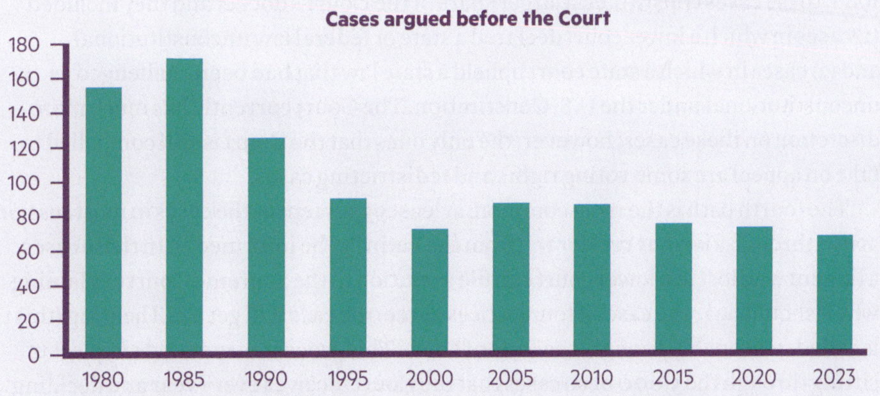

Source: Data compiled from John Roberts, "2023 Year-End Reports on the Federal Judiciary," U.S. Supreme Court, December 31, 2023, www.supremecourt.gov/publicinfo/year-end/2023year-endreport.pdf (accessed 5/30/24).

Although the increase in workload is not as significant as it appears due to the high number of frivolous cases, another change is more important: the number of opinions issued by the Court has fallen by more than half in the past 45 years. The Court heard roughly 150 cases a year through the 1980s, but this number has fallen to only 65 to 75 cases in recent years (refer to Figure 14.3).[38] The change is even more dramatic when one considers that the Court has reduced the number of "summary decisions" it issues (cases that do not receive a full hearing but on which the Court issues a decision anyway) from 150 a year in the 1970s to a handful today. The number of summary judgments declined when Congress gave the Court more control over its docket and dramatically reduced the number of cases that it was *required* to hear on appeal. However, there is no good explanation for why the Court issues half as many opinions as it used to, other than that the chief justices have decided that the Court shouldn't issue so many opinions.

Rules of access

On rare occasions the Supreme Court serves as a court of original jurisdiction. One of those unusual times is when there is a dispute between two states, such as when the Court had to settle a disagreement between Texas and New Mexico over the Pecos River.

With the smaller number of cases being heard, it is even more important to understand how the Court decides which cases to consider. There are four paths that a case may take to get to the Supreme Court.

First, Article III of the Constitution specifies that the Court has original jurisdiction in cases involving a foreign ambassador or foreign countries or cases in which a state is a party. As a practical matter, the Court shares jurisdiction with the lower courts on these issues. In recent years, the Court has invoked original jurisdiction only in cases involving disputes between two or more states over territory, water rights, or natural resource issues. For example, New Jersey and New York had a disagreement about which state should control 24 acres of filled land that the federal government had added around Ellis Island. Another case involved a dispute between Texas and New Mexico over the Pecos River Compact that has been going on since 1974![39] If original jurisdiction is granted and there are factual issues to be resolved, the Court will appoint a "special master" (usually a retired federal judge) to hold a hearing, gather evidence, and make a recommendation to the Court. This process is necessary because the Supreme Court is not a trial court. In the history of our nation, only about 195 cases have made it to the Court through this path, an average of less than one per year, and typically these cases do not have any broader significance beyond the parties involved.[40]

The other three routes to the Court are all on appeal: as a matter of right (usually called "on appeal"), through certification (a process that has been used only five times since 1982),[41] or through a writ of *certiorari*. Cases on appeal are those that Congress has determined to be so important that the Supreme Court must hear them. Before 1988, these cases constituted a larger share of the Court's docket and they included (1) cases in which a lower court declared a state or federal law unconstitutional and (2) cases in which a state court upheld a state law that had been challenged as unconstitutional under the U.S. Constitution. The Court currently has much more discretion on these cases, however; the only ones that the Court is still compelled to take on appeal are some voting rights and redistricting cases.

writ of *certiorari*
The most common way for a case to reach the Supreme Court, in which at least four of the nine justices agree to hear a case that has reached them via an appeal from the losing party in a lower court's ruling.

The fourth path is the most common: at least 95 percent of the cases in most sessions arrive through a **writ of *certiorari*** (from the Latin "to be informed"). In these cases, a litigant who lost in a lower court can file a petition to the Supreme Court explaining why it should hear the case. If four justices agree, the case will get a full hearing (this is called, reasonably enough, the Rule of Four). This process may sound simple, but sifting through the 5,000 or so cases that the Court receives every year and deciding which 70 to 75 of them will be heard is daunting. Former justice William O. Douglas said that this winnowing process is "in many respects the most important and interesting of all our functions."[42]

The Court's criteria

How does the Court decide which cases to hear? Several factors come into play, including the specific characteristics of the case and the broader politics surrounding it. Although several criteria generally must be met before the Court will hear the case, justices still have leeway in defining the boundaries of these conditions.

Collusion, Standing, and Mootness First, there are the constitutional guidelines, which are sparse. The Constitution limits the Court to hearing actual "cases and controversies," which has been interpreted to mean that the Court cannot offer advisory opinions about hypothetical situations but must deal with actual cases. The term "actual controversy" also includes several other concepts that limit whether a case will be heard: collusion, standing, and mootness. *Collusion* simply means that the litigants in the case cannot want the same outcome and cannot be testing the law without an actual dispute between the two parties.[43]

Standing, as we noted earlier, means that the party bringing the case must have a personal stake in the outcome. The Court has discretion in defining standing: it may hear cases that it thinks are important even when the plaintiff may not have standing as traditionally understood, or it may avoid hearing cases that may be politically sensitive on the grounds that there is no standing. In an example of the former, the Court decided several important racial redistricting cases even when the White plaintiffs had not suffered any personal harm by being in the Black-majority districts.[44] In an example of the latter, the Court decided not to hear a politically sensitive case involving the Pledge of Allegiance and the First Amendment, saying that the father of the student who brought the case did not have standing because he did not have sufficient custody over his daughter (he was divorced and the mother had primary custody).[45] Clearly, the Court was more eager to voice its views on redistricting than on the Pledge of Allegiance, because it could have just as easily avoided hearing the former case by saying the plaintiffs did not have standing and taken up the latter case despite the concern over custody (it was his daughter after all, which should have given him some stake!). This is an important point to consider: the Court often avoids hearing a controversial case based on a "threshold" issue like standing and then does not have to decide on the merits of the case.

A significant case the Court decided not to hear because of standing was the suit brought by Texas seeking to overturn the 2020 presidential election results in Georgia, Michigan, Pennsylvania, and Wisconsin, saying, "Texas has not demonstrated a judicially cognizable interest in the manner in which another State conducts its elections."[46] Because this case was brought to the Court under original jurisdiction (because it involved a dispute between states), Justices Alito and Thomas believed that the Court was compelled to hear the case.

A controversy must still be relevant when the Court hears the case; **mootness** occurs when a case is irrelevant by the time it is brought before a federal court. Nonetheless, there are exceptions to this principle, because some types of cases are necessarily moot by the time they get to the Supreme Court. For example, exceptions have been made for abortion cases because a pregnancy lasts only nine months, and it always takes longer than that for a case to get from district court to the appeals court to the Supreme Court.

mootness
The irrelevance of a case by the time it is received by a federal court, causing the Supreme Court to decline to hear the case.

Protesters gathered outside the Supreme Court building while the justices deliberated over whether or not to hear a suit brought by Texas challenging the presidential election results in Georgia, Michigan, Pennsylvania, and Wisconsin. After the election, there were concerns, which were never proven, that there had been widespread voter fraud that led to President Trump's defeat. Ultimately, the justices decided not to hear it.

Also, the Court may decide to hear a case even when it may not seem relevant. For example, in the recent case concerning the EPA's ability to regulate carbon emissions, the Obama-era rule in question had never been in effect and was later withdrawn by the Trump administration. While conceding that the Court had the right to hear the case, Justice Kagan pointed out in her dissent, "because no one is now subject to the Clean Power Plan's terms, there was no reason to reach out to decide this case. . . . But this Court could not wait—even to see what the new rule says—to constrain EPA's efforts to address climate change."[47]

Thousands of cases every year meet these basic criteria. One very simple guideline eliminates the largest number of cases: if a case does not involve a "substantial federal question," it will not be heard. This essentially means that the Court does not have to hear a case if the justices do not think it is important enough. Of course, the "federal" part of this standard is also important: if a case is governed by state law rather than federal law, the Court will decline to hear the case unless there are constitutional implications. The "political question doctrine" is another basis upon which the Court may decide not to hear a case (as we'll discuss in more detail later, these are cases that the Court thinks are better handled by the elected branches of government). After considering all of these criteria, 20–30 percent of the cases originally submitted for the Court's consideration are left. These cases are then winnowed to the final list with the more specific guidance of Rule 10 in the Supreme Court rules (refer to Nuts & Bolts 14.2). Of the criteria listed in Rule 10, conflict between appeals court decisions is most likely to produce a Supreme Court hearing.

Internal politics

cert pool
A system initiated in the Supreme Court in the 1970s in which law clerks screen cases that come to the Supreme Court and recommend to the justices which cases should be heard.

Not much is known about the actual discussions that determine which cases will be heard by the Court. The justices meet in conference with no staff or clerks. Leaks are rare, but a few insider accounts and the papers of retired justices provide some insights to the process. First, since the late 1970s most justices have used a **cert pool**, whereby their law clerks take a first cut at the cases. Law clerks to the justices

NUTS & BOLTS 14.2

Deciding to Hear a Case in the Supreme Court

Rule 10 of the *Rules of the Supreme Court of the United States* says that a case is more likely to be heard when

- there is conflict between appeals court opinions or between a state supreme court opinion and another state supreme court on an important federal question,
- there is conflict between a federal appeals court and a state supreme court on an important federal question,
- a lower-court decision has "departed from the accepted and usual course of judicial proceedings,"
- a state supreme court or appeals court has ruled on a substantial federal question that has not yet been addressed by the Court, or
- a state supreme court or appeals court ruling conflicts with Supreme Court precedent.

Rule 10 also states that *certiorari* is unlikely to be granted when "the asserted error consists of erroneous factual findings or the misapplication of a properly stated rule of law."

Source: U.S. Supreme Court, *Rules of the Supreme Court of the United States*, adopted April 8, 2019, effective July 1, 2019, www.supremecourt.gov/ctrules/2019RulesoftheCourt.pdf (accessed 8/15/22).

"Why Should I Care?"

Rule 10 helps explain how the Supreme Court decides which cases it will hear of the 6,500 it receives every year. However, the Court still has great discretion, with the only firm rule being that four justices have to agree to hear a case to put it on the docket.

are top graduates of elite law schools who help justices with background research at several stages of the process. Clerks write joint memos about groups of cases, providing their recommendations about which cases should be heard. The ultimate decisions are up to the justices, but clerks have significant power to help shape the agenda.

Second, the chief justice has an important agenda-setting power: they decide the "discuss list" for a given day. Any justice can add a case to the list, but there is no systematic evidence on how often this happens. Only 20–30 percent of the cases are discussed in conference, which means that about three-quarters of the cases that are submitted to the Supreme Court are never even discussed by the justices. The decision not to discuss certain cases is often justified because of the high proportion of frivolous suits submitted to the Court.[48]

Many factors outside the legal requirements or internal processes of the Court influence access to the Court and which cases will be heard. Cases that have generated a lot of activity from interest groups or other governmental parties, such as the solicitor general, are more likely to be heard. The **solicitor general** is a presidential appointee who works in the Justice Department and supervises the litigation of the executive branch. In cases in which the federal government is a party, the solicitor general or someone else from that office will represent the government in court. The Court accepts about 70–80 percent of cases in which the U.S. government is a party, compared with about 1 percent overall.[49]

Even with these influences, the Court has a great deal of discretion as to which cases it hears. Well-established practices such as standing and mootness may be ignored (or modified) if the Court wants to hear a specific case. However, one final point is important: although the justices may pick and choose their cases, they cannot completely set their own agenda. They can select only from the cases that come to them.

Law clerks, such as those seen here with Justice Clarence Thomas, often take a first cut at the cases and help justices with background research.

solicitor general
A presidential appointee in the Justice Department who conducts all litigation on behalf of the federal government before the Supreme Court and supervises litigation in the federal appellate courts.

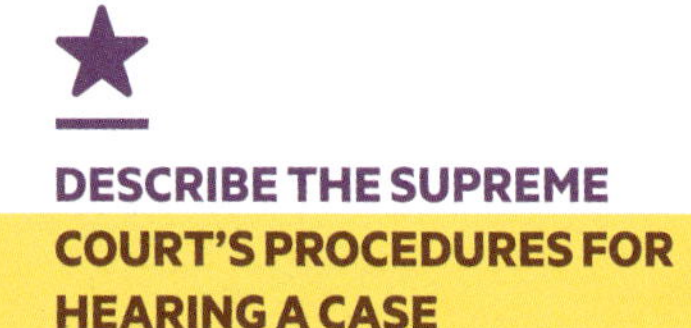

DESCRIBE THE SUPREME COURT'S PROCEDURES FOR HEARING A CASE

Hearing cases before the Supreme Court

A surprisingly small proportion of the Court's time—only about 37 days per term—is actually spent hearing cases. The Court's term extends from the first Monday in October through the end of June. It hears cases on Mondays through Wednesdays in alternating two-week cycles in which it is in session from 10 a.m. to 3 p.m., with a one-hour break for lunch. In the two weeks of the cycle when it is not in session, justices review briefs, write opinions, and sift through the next batch of petitions. On most Fridays during the Court's term, the justices meet in conference to discuss cases that have been argued and to decide which cases they will hear. Opinions are released throughout the term, but the bulk of them come in May and June.[50]

The Court is in recess from July through September. Justices may take some vacation, but they mostly use the time for studying, reading, writing, and preparing for the next term. During the summer, the Court also considers emergency petitions (such as stays of execution) and occasionally hears important cases. For example, on September 9, 2009 (nearly a month before the fall session started), the Court heard a challenge to the Bipartisan Campaign Reform Act, more commonly known as the McCain-Feingold Act after its two principal sponsors. Congress urged the Court to give the law a speedy review, given its importance for the upcoming 2010 elections. In the blockbuster case *Citizens United v. Federal Election Commission*, the Supreme Court decided that independent spending in campaigns by corporations and labor unions is protected by the First Amendment.

Briefs

During its regular sessions, the Court follows rigidly set routines. The justices prepare for a case by reading the briefs submitted by both parties. Because the Supreme Court hears only appeals (except in cases of original jurisdiction), it does not call witnesses or gather new evidence. Instead, in structured briefs of no more than 50 pages the parties present their arguments about why they either support the lower-court decision or believe the case was improperly decided. Interest groups often submit **amicus curiae** ("friend of the court") briefs that convey their opinions to the Court; in fact, 85 percent of cases before the Supreme Court have at least one amicus brief.[51] The federal government also files amicus briefs on important issues such as school busing, school prayer, abortion, reapportionment of legislative districts, job discrimination against women and minorities, and affirmative action in higher education.

amicus curiae
Latin for "friend of the court," referring to an interested group or person who shares relevant information about a case to help the Court reach a decision.

It is difficult to determine the impact of amicus briefs on the outcome of a case, but those that are filed early in the process increase the chances that the case will be heard.[52] Given the limited information that justices have about any given case, interest group involvement can be a strong signal about the importance of a case. There is also some evidence that briefs from the solicitor general have an impact on the outcome of a case.[53]

Oral argument

Once the briefs are filed and have been reviewed by the justices, cases are scheduled for **oral arguments**. Except in unusual circumstances, each case gets one hour, which is divided evenly between the two parties. In especially important cases,

oral arguments
Spoken presentations made in person by the lawyers of each party to a judge or an appellate court outlining the legal reasons their side should prevail.

Cameras are not allowed in the Supreme Court, so artists' sketches are the only available images of oral arguments. As such, they provide details of these important hearings. In 2021, the Court heard arguments in *Dobbs v. Jackson Women's Health Organization,* in which Mississippi asked the Supreme Court to reverse all its prior abortion decisions and return the abortion question to the states.

extra time may be granted (for example, the case challenging Obamacare had six hours of oral argument, which was the most since a Voting Rights Act case in 1966).[54] Usually there is only one lawyer for each side who presents the case, but parties who have filed amicus briefs may participate if their arguments "would provide assistance to the Court not otherwise available." Given the tight time pressures, the Court is usually unwilling to extend the allotted time to allow "friends of the court" to testify.[55]

The Court is strict about its time limits and uses a system of three lights to show the lawyers how much of their allotted 30 minutes is left. A green light goes on when the speaker's time begins, a white light provides a five-minute warning, and a red light means to stop. Most textbooks cite well-known examples of justices cutting people off in midsentence or walking out of the courtroom as the lawyer drones on. One source implies that these anecdotes are generally revealing of Court procedure, saying, "Anecdotes probably tell as much about the proceeding of the Court during oral argument as does any careful study of the rules and procedures."[56]

However, having a preference for "careful study" over anecdotes, we were curious about how common it was for justices to strictly impose the time limits. Initially, we examined 42 cases from the 2004–2005 term, using the online transcripts on the Court's website.[57] We found that most lawyers did not use all their allotted time, with 62 percent of the cases coming in under 60 minutes, 17 percent at exactly an hour, and 21 percent at over an hour. One-sixth of the lawyers still had at least five minutes left on the clock. We found only two instances in which a justice cut someone off in midsentence after the person had gone over the half-hour limit. We updated the analysis for the Roberts Court, examining all 61 cases argued in the 2019–2020 term. Roberts was not much of a stickler for adhering to the time limits: nearly 60 percent of oral arguments went past their allotted time (most by only a minute or two), 16 percent were exactly one hour, and 25 percent were under an hour. However, things changed dramatically when the Court moved to teleconference on May 3, 2020, because of the COVID-19 pandemic. All 10 of the oral arguments went over time, most of them substantially so. However, even with the new format, only 2 of the 10 oral arguments

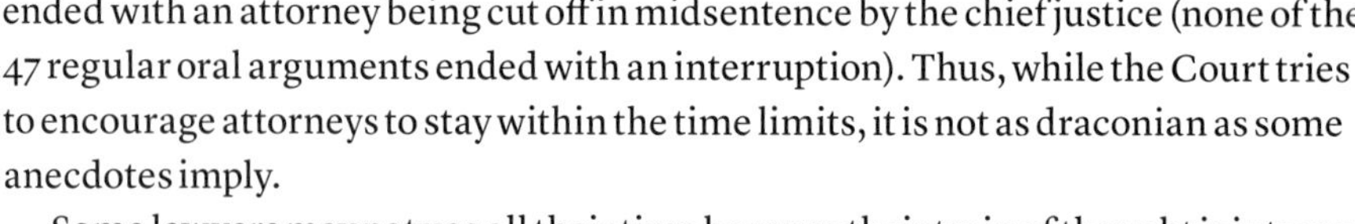

ended with an attorney being cut off in midsentence by the chief justice (none of the 47 regular oral arguments ended with an interruption). Thus, while the Court tries to encourage attorneys to stay within the time limits, it is not as draconian as some anecdotes imply.

Some lawyers may not use all their time because their train of thought is interrupted by aggressive questioning. Transcripts reveal that justices jump in with questions almost immediately and some attorneys never regain their footing. The frequency and pointedness of the questions vary by justice, with Justice Jackson the most frequent speaker and Gorsuch and Kagan far behind.[58] Justice Thomas went more than 10 years without asking a single question but broke his streak in 2016, perhaps feeling the need to fill the void created by the death of Justice Scalia.[59]

DID YOU KNOW?

The late Justice Scalia was the funniest justice. According to one study, he holds the record, prompting

77

rounds of laughter in the 2004–2005 term, which made him 19 times funnier than his friend Justice Ginsburg.

Source: thedailybeast.com.

The new teleconference format was much more structured, with the questions being asked in order of seniority and the chief justice serving as a timekeeper to allocate time more evenly.[60] Once the Court was back in-person, the justices returned to the more free-wheeling format. However, one element of the remote sessions has been retained: justices are allowed a final round of questions to tie up loose ends. This has produced many oral arguments that go well beyond the allotted one hour.[61] Cameras are not allowed in the courtroom, so most Americans have never seen the Court in action—although a small live audience is admitted every morning the Court is in session, and live audio was streamed online for the first time ever as a result of the Supreme Court's move to teleconferencing in the midst of the COVID-19 pandemic. If you are curious about oral arguments, audio recordings of every case since 1995 are available at www.oyez.org.

Conference

After oral arguments, the justices meet in conference to discuss and then vote on the cases. As with the initial conferences, these meetings are conducted in secret. We know, based on notes in the personal papers of retired justices, that the conferences are orderly and structured but can become quite heated. The justices take turns discussing the cases and outlining the reasons for their positions. Justice Thurgood Marshall described the decision-making process in conference as

> *a continuing conversation among nine distinct individuals on dozens of issues simultaneously. The exchanges are serious, sometimes scholarly, occasionally brash and personalized, but generally well-reasoned and most often cast in understated, genteel language. . . . In other cases, a majority of justices start down one path, only to reverse direction.*[62]

Opinion writing

After the justices indicate how they are likely to vote on a case, if the chief justice is in the majority (which is most of the time), the chief justice decides who will write the majority opinion. Otherwise, the most senior justice in the majority assigns the opinion. Several considerations determine how an opinion will be assigned. First, the chief justice will try to ensure the smooth operation of the Court by trying to equalize the number of cases across the nine justices. John Roberts has been especially careful to spread out the workload evenly.[63] A second factor is the justices' individual areas of expertise. For example, Justice Harry Blackmun had developed expertise in medical law when he was in private practice. This experience played a role in Chief Justice Burger's decision to assign Blackmun the majority opinion in the landmark abortion decision *Roe v. Wade* (1973). Likewise, Justice Sandra Day O'Connor developed expertise in racial redistricting cases and authored most of those decisions in the 1990s, while Justice Samuel Alito has specialized in criminal justice cases.[64]

Strategy on the Court Other factors in how opinions are assigned are more strategic, taking into account the Court's external relations, internal relations, and the personal policy goals of the opinion assigner. The Court must be sensitive to how others might respond to its decisions because it must rely on the other branches of government to enforce them. One famous example of this consideration in an opinion assignment came in a case from the 1940s that struck down a practice that had prevented Black Americans from voting in Democratic primaries.[65] Originally, the opinion was assigned to Justice Felix Frankfurter, but Justice Robert Jackson wrote a memo suggesting that it might be unwise to have a liberal, politically independent Jew from the Northeast write an opinion that was sure to be controversial in the South. Chief Justice Harlan Fiske Stone agreed and reassigned the opinion to Justice Stanley Reed, a Protestant and Democrat from Kentucky.[66] It may not seem that the Court is sensitive to public opinion, but these kinds of considerations happen fairly frequently in important cases. Internal considerations occasionally cause justices to vote strategically—differently from their sincere preferences—so they can put themselves in the majority. If they are the most senior justice in the majority, they then have the power to assign the opinion, and they often assign it to themselves.

Justices may also assign opinions to further their own personal policy goals. The most obvious strategy is for the chief justice to consider their own position and assign opinions to justices who are closest to it. This practice is constrained by the chief justice's responsibility to ensure the smooth operation of the Court. If the chief justice assigned all the opinions based on their own ideology, then justices with other ideological leanings would get a chance to write opinions only in the 15–20 percent of cases in which the chief justice is in the minority. However, Chief Justice Roberts has allocated the most important cases to his ideological allies and has taken about

Chief Justice John Roberts *(lower left)* stands with Associate Justices Amy Coney Barrett, Brett Kavanaugh, and Elena Kagan as retiring Justice Breyer is recognized by President Biden during Biden's 2022 State of the Union address.

twice as many of the most important cases for himself (compared with what would have been expected by chance).[67] Charles Hughes, chief justice from 1930 to 1941, sometimes assigned opinions on liberal decisions to conservative justices and cases with conservative outcomes to liberal justices in order to downplay the importance of ideology on the Court.[68]

After the opinions are assigned, the justices work on writing a draft opinion. Law clerks typically help with this process. Some justices insist on writing all of their opinions, whereas others allow a clerk to write the first draft. The drafts are circulated to the other justices for comments and reactions. Some bargaining may occur, in which a justice says they will withdraw support unless a provision of the opinion is changed. Justices may join the majority opinion, may write a separate concurring opinion, or may dissent (refer to Nuts & Bolts 14.3 for details on the types of opinions).

So that's the dissenter's hope: that they are writing not for today but for tomorrow.

—Justice Ruth Bader Ginsburg

Dissents Two final points about the process of writing and issuing opinions are important. First, until 1940, there was a premium placed on unanimous decisions. John Marshall, who was chief justice from 1800 to 1835, started this practice. Through the 1930s, about 80–90 percent of decisions were unanimous. This changed dramatically in the 1940s, when most cases had at least one dissent. In recent decades, about two-thirds of cases have had a dissent.[69] However, in the 2013–2014 term two-thirds of the cases were unanimous, the highest proportion since at least 1946. That proportion fell to 48 percent in the 2023–2024 term.[70] Second, dissents serve an important purpose. Not only do they allow the minority view to be expressed, but they also often provide the basis later on for reversing a poorly reasoned case. When justices

Types of Supreme Court Decisions

- **Majority opinion:** The core decision of the Court that must be agreed upon by at least five justices. The majority opinion presents the legal reasoning for the Court's decision.
- **Concurring opinion:** Written by a justice who agrees with the outcome of the case but not with part of the legal reasoning. Concurring opinions may be joined by other justices. A justice may sign on to the majority opinion and write a separate concurring opinion.
- **Plurality opinion:** Occurs when a majority cannot agree on the legal reasoning in a case. The plurality opinion is the one that has the most agreement (usually three or four justices). Because of the fractured nature of these opinions, they typically are not viewed as having as much clout as majority opinions.
- **Dissent:** Submitted by a justice who disagrees with the outcome of the case. Other justices can sign on to a dissent or write their own, so there can be as many as four dissents. Justices can also sign on to part of a dissent but not the entire opinion.
- **Per curiam (Latin for "by the court") opinion:** An unsigned opinion of the Court or a decision written by the entire Court. However, this is not the same as a unanimous decision that is signed by the entire Court. Per curiam opinions are usually very short opinions on noncontroversial issues, but not always. For example, *Bush v. Gore*, which decided the outcome of the 2000 presidential election, was a per curiam opinion. Per curiam decisions may also have dissents.

Source: Compiled by the authors.

The type of decision influences how to interpret the impact of the decision. Majority opinions generally carry more weight than plurality opinions, concurring opinions are important for developing some of the nuances on the winning side, and dissent may lay the groundwork for future shifts in the opinions of the Court.

strongly oppose the majority opinion, they may take the unusual step of reading a portion of the dissent from the bench.

The Shadow Docket There is an alternative path to the Supreme Court that has been increasingly important in recent years: emergency appeals to the Court that sidestep the lengthy process of cert petitions, briefs, conference discussions, oral arguments, and opinion writing that can take up to a year (or more). The "**shadow docket**" follows none of these procedures and can result in rulings that are made in weeks or even days, often with unsigned opinions that provide limited rationale. While the decisions are supposed to not carry the full weight of precedent and only be binding on the parties in the immediate case, they often *are* treated as precedent by the lower courts and may signal the direction the Court will go when it does have a full hearing on the case.[71]

shadow docket
The alternative path to the Supreme Court that involves emergency appeals of lower-court decisions. The cases do not involve a full briefing and oral arguments and often are unsigned opinions.

These emergency rulings have existed since 1790 for urgent situations such as stays of execution, but both the range of topics and frequency of the cases have grown in recent years. President Trump's Justice Department asked the Court to stay or overturn a lower-court ruling 41 times in four years, compared with a total of eight such requests in the 16 years of the Bush and Obama presidencies (the Court granted the requests 28 times for Trump and 4 times for Bush and Obama).[72] Cases involved Trump's travel ban, funding for the wall with Mexico, various COVID-19 policies (religious freedom, rental evictions, and vaccinations), voting rights, redistricting, and abortion. The practice continued in the Biden administration with about 40 requests and eight granted emergency petitions per year. More than a third of the requests were death penalty cases (which were mostly denied), but there were many important cases such as attempts to keep Donald Trump off the 2024 ballot under the Fourteenth Amendment's insurrection clause, abortion, racial redistricting, and bans on gender affirming care for minors.[73]

Part of the increase in the number of cases is because of the increase in the number of lower-court nationwide injunctions that stopped various executive actions in the Trump administration, but other cases appear to be driven by the Court's policy goals. For example, the Court could have allowed the lower courts to deal with a Texas abortion case and a Wisconsin redistricting case rather than intervening. In dissenting in the Texas case, Chief Justice John Roberts wrote, "We are at this point asked to resolve these novel questions—at least preliminarily—in the first instance, in the course of two days, without the benefit of consideration by the District Court or Court of Appeals. We are also asked to do so without ordinary merits briefing and without oral argument."[74] The practice has raised questions about the independence and political nature of the Court, leading to congressional hearings to determine if reforms are necessary.[75] Senate Democrats introduced a bill in 2024 that would require the Court disclose their votes and provide an explanation of their shadow docket decisions.[76]

The process of hearing cases before the Court, including the written briefs, oral arguments, discussions in conference, and opinion assignment, is a very political one. As discussed in the chapter opener, it may be disturbing to think of the Court as a political institution that bargains and considers external forces like public opinion. Although justices do not have to answer to voters, they are still sensitive to a broad range of considerations in hearing cases.

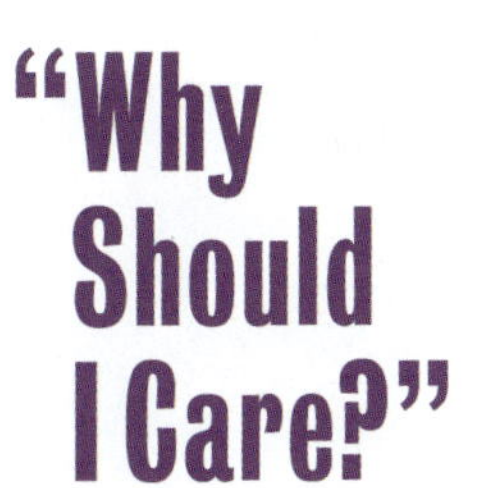

ANALYZE THE FACTORS THAT INFLUENCE SUPREME COURT DECISIONS

Supreme Court decision-making

Judicial decision-making is influenced by many different factors, but the two main categories are *legal* and *political*. Legal factors include the precedents of earlier cases and the norm that justices must follow the language of the Constitution. Political influences include the justices' preferences or ideologies, their stances on whether the Court should take a restrained or activist role with respect to the elected branches, and external factors such as public opinion and interest group involvement. Most observers of the Court recognize that both legal and political factors are important in explaining judicial decision-making, but some stake out a view more strongly on one side or the other. Some scholars argue, for example, that all Court behavior is political and that the use of legal factors is just a smoke screen for hiding personal preferences. The fact that there are differences of opinion as to which factors are most important can often make empirical arguments (those that describe the way decisions are made) evolve into normative arguments (those about the way that justices *should* behave). These different perspectives about how justices make decisions may also lead to arguments about the proper role of the Court within our political system, which we will explore in the next section.

The words of the Constitution . . . are so unrestricted by their intrinsic meaning or by their history or by tradition or by prior decisions that they leave the individual Justice free, if indeed they do not compel him, to gather meaning not from reading the Constitution but from reading life.

—Felix Frankfurter, former Supreme Court justice

Legal factors

Legal factors embody the image we cited at the beginning of the chapter of Lady Justice neutrally applying the law while fairly balancing various interests. While this ideal image is incomplete, legal factors do independently influence judicial decision-making on a broad range of cases.

Precedent The most basic legal factor is precedent, discussed earlier. Precedent does not determine the outcome of any given case, because every case has a range of precedents that can serve to justify a justice's decision. The "easy" cases, in which settled law makes the outcome obvious, are less likely to be heard by the Court because of the justices' desire to focus on the more controversial areas of unsettled law or cases in which there is conflict between lower courts' decisions. However, as shown by research on the "legal model," in some areas of the law—such as free speech, the death penalty, and search and seizure—precedent is an important explanation for how the justices decide a case.[77]

The Language of the Constitution The Constitution is the obvious starting point for any Supreme Court case that involves a constitutional right.[78] However, there are various perspectives on exactly how, and to what degree, the language of the Constitution can and should influence judicial decision-making today.

People in one camp argue that the *language* used in the Constitution is the most important guiding factor. Their perspectives fall under the heading of **strict construction**. The most basic of these is the literalist view of the Constitution. Sometimes this view is called a textualist position because it sees the text of the document as determining the outcome of any given case. Literalists argue that justices need to look no further than the actual words of the Constitution.

strict construction
A way of interpreting the Constitution based on its language alone.

Justice Hugo Black was one of the most famous advocates of the literalist position. When the First Amendment says that "Congress shall make no law . . . abridging the freedom of speech," that literally means *no* law. Justice Black said, "My view is, without deviation, without exception, without any ifs, buts, or whereases, that freedom of speech means that government shall not do anything to people . . . either for the views they have or the views they express or the words they speak or write."[79] While that may be clear enough with regard to political speech, how about pornography, Internet speech, or symbolic speech, such as burning an American flag or wearing an armband to protest the Vietnam War? A literal interpretation of the Constitution does not necessarily help determine whether these forms of speech should be restricted. (Indeed, Black was one of the two dissenters in a case that upheld students' right to wear armbands as a form of symbolic speech. Black believed that school officials should be allowed to decide whether a symbolic protest would be too disruptive in the classroom and argued that only spoken and written speech should be afforded the strongest protection of the First Amendment. So much for "without deviation, without exception" concerning restricting expression of the "views . . . [people] have"!)

Mary Beth Tinker and two other students in the Des Moines, Iowa, public schools were suspended for wearing armbands to protest the Vietnam War. The Supreme Court ruled in *Tinker v. Des Moines Independent Community School District* (1969) that the First Amendment protected symbolic political speech, even in public schools. Mary Beth is shown here with her mother and brother.

On the current Court, Neil Gorsuch is the most well-known for the textualist position. A recent example involves statutory rather than constitutional interpretation, but the concept is the same: justices should follow the plain language of the law. When the Court in 2020 ruled that Title VII of the 1964 Civil Rights Act prohibits employers from discriminating based on sexual orientation (gays and lesbians) or gender identity (transgender people), Gorsuch wrote, "When the express terms of a statute give us one answer and extratextual considerations suggest another, it's no contest. Only the written word is the law, and all persons are entitled to benefit."[80]

Critics of strict construction also point out that the Constitution is silent on many important points (such as a right to privacy) and could not have anticipated the many legal implications of changes in technology in the twentieth and twenty-first centuries, such as eavesdropping devices, cloning, and the Internet. Also, although the language of the First Amendment is relatively clear when it comes to political speech, other equally important words of the Constitution such as "necessary and proper," "executive power," "equal protection," and "due process" are open-ended and vague.

Some strict constructionists respond by arguing that if the words of the Constitution are not clear, the justices should be guided by what the Founders *intended* by the words, a perspective called the **original intent** or originalist perspective. Clarence Thomas is the current justice who is most influenced by this view, especially on issues of federalism. Note that the textualist and originalist perspectives can lead to different outcomes, as in the LGBTQ case noted above: Justice Gorsuch interpreted the law barring discrimination "because of sex" to apply to gay and trans people because of the plain meaning of the words; Justice Thomas said they are not protected from discrimination because the authors of the law in 1964 did not intend that interpretation. Justice Alito's position as a "practical originalist" is gaining traction among the conservative justices with the "history and tradition" test that was first employed in the 2022 New York gun control case discussed in Chapter 4. This test was employed in the *Dobbs* decision that returned abortion policy to the states and has been used by lower courts on decisions concerning drag shows and gender affirming care for minors.[81] However, a 2024 case showed that the Court is not willing to push this test to its logical limits when it ruled that states do have the right to prevent convicted domestic abusers from owning guns, even if the Founders who wrote the Second Amendment would not have thought of such an exception.[82]

original intent
The theory that justices should surmise the intentions of the Founders when the language of the Constitution is unclear.

Those in the other camp are often described as supporting a **living Constitution** perspective on the document (refer to Chapter 2). They argue that originalism or other versions of strict construction can "make a nation the prisoner of its past, and reject any constitutional development save constitutional amendment."[83] If the justices are bound to follow the literal words of the Constitution, *with the meaning they had when*

living Constitution
A way of interpreting the Constitution that takes into account evolving national attitudes and circumstances rather than the text alone.

the document was written, we certainly could be legally frozen in time. The option of amending the Constitution is a long and difficult process, so that is not always a viable way for the Constitution to reflect changing norms and values. Justice William Brennan, a critic of originalism, also argued it was "arrogance cloaked in humility" to presume to know what the framers intended. According to this view, interpreting the Constitution is always somewhat subjective and it is misleading to claim otherwise.[84]

Political factors

The living Constitution perspective points to the second set of influences on Supreme Court decision-making: political factors. Indeed, many people are uncomfortable thinking about the Court in political terms and prefer to think of the image of "blind justice," in which constitutional principles are fairly applied. However, political influences are clearly evident in the Court—maybe less than in Congress or the presidency, but they are certainly present. This means that the courts respond to and shape politics in ways that often involve compromise, both within the courts themselves and in the broader political system.

attitudinalist approach
A way of understanding decisions of the Supreme Court based on the political ideologies of the justices.

Political Ideology and Attitudes There is evidence that justices' ideology or attitudes about various issues influence their decisions. Those who argue that this is the most important factor in understanding Supreme Court decision-making are said to take an **attitudinalist approach**. Liberal judges are strong defenders of individual civil liberties (including defendants' rights), tend to be pro-choice on abortion, support regulatory policy to protect the environment and workers, support national intervention in the states, and favor race-conscious policies such as affirmative action. Conservative judges favor state regulation of private conduct (especially on moral issues), support prosecutors over defendants, tend to be pro-life on abortion, and support the free market and property rights over the environment and workers, states' rights over national intervention, and a color-blind policy on race. Refer to the What Do the Facts Say? feature on page 561 for more on how the balance between liberal and conservative judges has shifted.

These are, of course, just general tendencies. However, they do provide a strong basis for explaining patterns of decisions, especially on some types of cases. For example, there were dramatic differences in the chief justices' rulings on civil liberties cases from 1953 to 2001: Earl Warren took the liberal position on 79 percent of the 771 cases he participated in, Warren Burger took the liberal position on 30 percent of 1,429 cases, and William Rehnquist took the liberal position on only 22 percent of his 2,127 cases.[85] If justices were neutrally applying the law, there would not be such dramatic differences. While there are plenty of deviations from ideological consistency, there are substantial differences in the behavior of Democrat- and Republican-appointed judges.

Proponents of the attitudinalist view also argue that justices who *claim* to be strict constructionists or originalists are really driven by ideology because they selectively use the text of the Constitution. For example, Justice Thomas voted against the University of Michigan's affirmative action program without considering whether the authors of the Fourteenth Amendment supported the practice (the historical record shows that they supported similar policies for newly freed enslaved people). Therefore, if Justice Thomas had been true to his originalist perspective, he would have supported affirmative action, but his ideology led him to oppose the policy. The example of Hugo Black's contradictory position on free speech rights cited earlier demonstrates that a liberal textualist view may also be inconsistently applied.

Other Justices' and Politicians' Preferences Another approach to understanding Supreme Court decision-making, known as the strategic model,

The Shifting Ideological Balance of the Court

After Justice Antonin Scalia died in early 2016, the open seat on the Supreme Court became a major issue in the presidential election. Why? As this figure shows, when justices are replaced, the ideological shifts can be quite large (as when Thurgood Marshall, a very liberal justice, was replaced by a strong conservative, Clarence Thomas) or nonexistent (as when Sonia Sotomayor replaced David Souter—they both were moderate liberals). Many people said that replacing Scalia with Merrick Garland would have drastically altered the ideological makeup of the Court, given the 4–4 split on the Court between liberal and conservative justices. When Scalia was replaced by Neil Gorsuch instead of Garland, what happened to the ideological balance of the Court? Then, when Anthony Kennedy retired in 2018, he was replaced by conservative Brett Kavanaugh and the center of the Court was kept in about the same place. In 2022, Ketanji Brown Jackson replaced Stephen Breyer following his retirement. What happened when Amy Coney Barrett replaced Ruth Bader Ginsburg? Will Justice Jackson's replacing Justice Breyer affect the median voter? What do the facts say?

WHAT DO THE FACTS SAY?

Think about it

- **Look at where Scalia is on the ideological scale.** If the Democratic candidate, Hillary Clinton, had been elected in 2016 and all but ensured Garland's joining the Court, where would Scalia's dot have likely moved?
- **Did the median justice change** with the addition of Neil Gorsuch and Brett Kavanaugh to the Court?
- **What happened when John Roberts replaced Kennedy** as the median justice for the 2018 term?

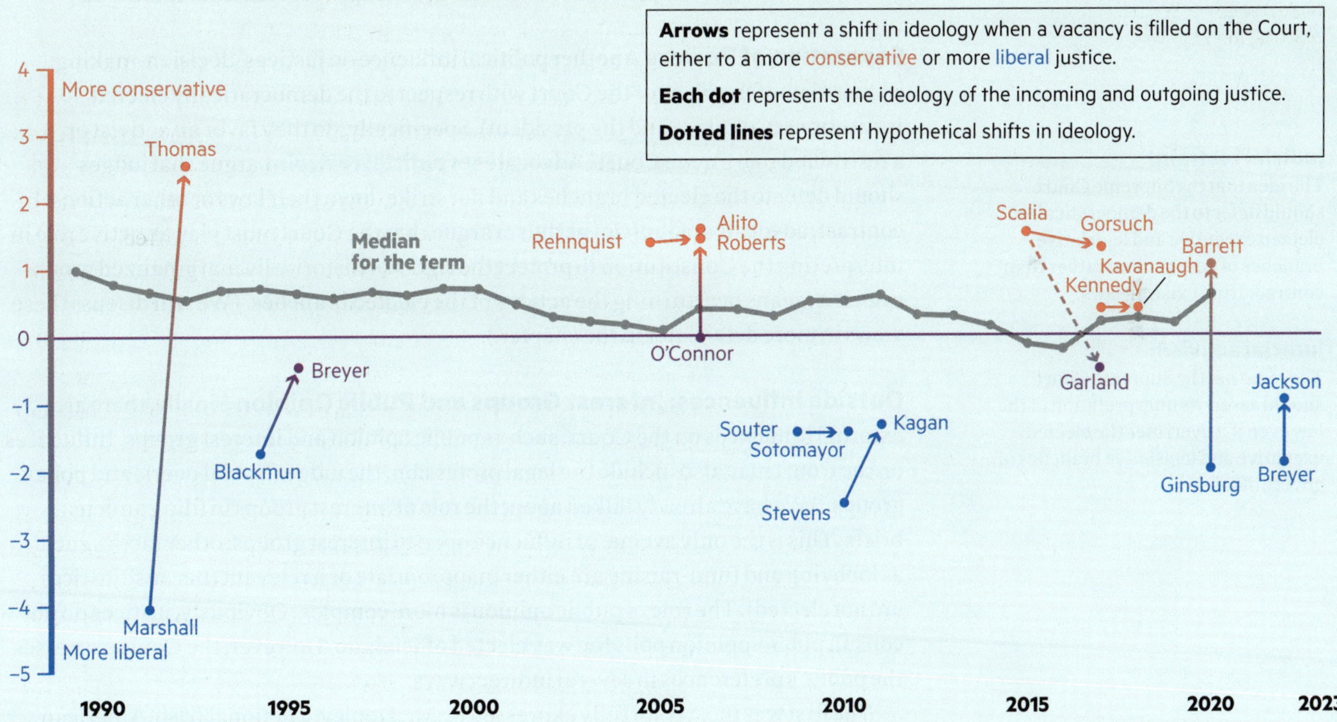

Sources: Alicia Parlapiano and Margot Sanger-Katz, "A Supreme Court with Merrick Garland Would Be the Most Liberal in Decades," *New York Times*, March 16, 2016, www.nytimes.com/interactive/2016/02/18/upshot/potential-for-the-most-liberal-supreme-court-in-decades.html; data for Scalia, Gorsuch, Kennedy, Kavanaugh, and Breyer are from Martin Quinn Scores, "Measures," http://mqscores.lsa.umich.edu/measures.php; estimate for Garland is from Adam Bonica et al., "New Data Show How Liberal Merrick Garland Really Is," *Washington Post*, March 30, 2016, www.washingtonpost.com/news/monkey-cage/wp/2016/03/30/new-data-show-how-liberal-merrick-garland-really-is / (all accessed 6/24/20); estimate for Barrett is from "The Supreme Court May Be About to Take a Hard Right Turn," *The Economist*, September 21, 2020, www.economist.com/graphic-detail/2020/09/21/the-supreme-court-may-be-about-to-take-a-hard-right-turn (accessed 11/10/20); estimate for Jackson based on the "judicial common space" scores from her decisions on the DC Court of Appeals, Amelia Thomson-DeVeaux, "How Ketanji Brown Jackson Could Change The Supreme Court," February 25, 2022, https://fivethirtyeight.com/features/how-ketanji-brown-jackson-could-change-the-supreme-court/ (accessed 7/1/22).

focuses on justices' calculations about the preferences of the other justices, the president, and Congress; the choices that other justices are likely to make; and the institutional context within which they operate. After all, justices do not operate alone: at a minimum, they need the votes of four of their colleagues if they want their position to prevail. Therefore, it makes sense to focus on the strategic interactions that take place to build coalitions.

The median voter on the Court—the one in the middle when the justices are arrayed from the most liberal to the most conservative—has an especially influential role in the strategic model. For many years, the median justice was Anthony M. Kennedy. The four conservatives to his right (Thomas, Scalia, Roberts, and Alito) and the four liberals to his left (Breyer, Ginsburg, Souter, and Stevens) all wanted to attract his vote. When Justice Sotomayor replaced Justice Souter, Justice Kagan replaced Justice Stevens, and Justice Gorsuch replaced Justice Scalia, Kennedy remained the median voter on the Court (because Souter, Sotomayor, Stevens, and Kagan were all to his left and Gorsuch and Scalia were both to his right). When Kennedy retired and Brett Kavanaugh took his place, Roberts became the median and the center of the Court stayed in roughly the same place. With Justice Barrett replacing Ginsburg, Kavanaugh is the new median, with the center moving slightly to the right, and he remained the median after Justice Jackson replaced Justice Breyer. Research shows that at least one justice switches their vote at some stage in the process (from the initial conference to oral arguments to the final vote) on at least half the cases, so strategic bargaining appears to be fairly common.[86] Our earlier discussion of opinion assignment and writing opinions to attract the support of a specific justice is more evidence in support of the strategic model.

> **The Supreme Court, of course, has the responsibility of ensuring that our government never oversteps its proper bounds or violates the rights of individuals. But the Court must also recognize the limits on itself and respect the choices made by the American people.**
>
> **—Justice Elena Kagan**

Separation of Powers Another political influence on justices' decision-making is their view of the place of the Court with respect to the democratically elected institutions (Congress and the president). Specifically, do they favor an activist or a restrained role for the Court? Advocates of **judicial restraint** argue that judges should defer to the elected branches and not strike down their laws or other actions. In contrast, advocates of **judicial activism** argue that the Court must play an active role in interpreting the Constitution to protect the rights of historically marginalized groups even if it means overturning the actions of the elected branches. (We will discuss these views in more detail later in the chapter.)

judicial restraint
The idea that the Supreme Court should defer to the democratically elected executive and legislative branches of government rather than contradicting existing laws.

judicial activism
The idea that the Supreme Court should assert its interpretation of the law even if it overrules the elected executive and legislative branches of government.

Outside Influences: Interest Groups and Public Opinion Finally, there are external influences on the Court, such as public opinion and interest groups. Influences on the Court may also include the legal profession, the judges' social peers, and policy groups.[87] We have already talked about the role of interest groups in filing amicus briefs. This is the only avenue of influence open to interest groups; other tactics such as lobbying and fund-raising are either inappropriate or irrelevant (because justices are not elected). The role of public opinion is more complex. Obviously, justices do not consult public-opinion polls the way elected officials do. However, the Court expresses the public's preferences in several indirect ways.

The first was most colorfully expressed by Mr. Dooley, a fictional Irish-American bartender whom newspaper satirist Finley Peter Dunne created in 1898. Mr. Dooley offered keen insights on politics and general social criticism, including this gem on the relationship between the Supreme Court and the public: "th' supreme coort always follows th' iliction returns."[88] That is, the public elects the president and the Senate, who nominate and confirm the justices. Therefore, sooner or later, the Court should reflect the views of the public. Subsequent work by political scientists has confirmed this to be largely the case,[89] especially in recent years, when Supreme Court nominations have become more political and more important to the public.[90]

The second mechanism through which public opinion may influence the Court is somewhat more direct: when the public has a clear position on an issue that is before the Court, the Court tends to agree with the public. One study found that the "public mood" and Court opinions correlated very highly between 1956 and 1981, but their association was weaker through the rest of the 1980s.[91] One scholar found that three-fifths to two-thirds of Supreme Court decisions are consistent with public opinion when the public has a clear preference on an issue.[92] More recent work demonstrates that the Court is constrained by public opinion, in part because it may fear resistance to implementing an unpopular decision.[93]

Several high-profile examples support the idea that the Court is sensitive to public opinion: the Court switched during the New Deal in the 1930s to support Roosevelt's policy agenda after standing in the way for four years, gave in to wartime opinion to support the internment of Japanese Americans during World War II, limited an accused child molester's right to confront their accuser in a courtroom, and supported same-sex marriage. In each of these cases, the justices reflected the current public opinion of the nation rather than a strict reading of the Constitution or the Founders' intent. On the other hand, there are plenty of decisions in which the Court has stood up for unpopular views, such as banning prayer in schools, allowing flag burning, and protecting criminal defendants' rights.

Sometimes the Court may shift its views to reflect *international* opinion. The most recent example struck down the death penalty for minors in 12 states. Ruling by a 5–4 vote that the execution of 16- or 17-year-olds violated the Eighth Amendment's prohibition against "cruel and unusual punishments," the majority opinion overturned a 1989 case and said that the new decision was necessary to reflect the "evolving standards of decency" concerning the definition of "cruel and unusual punishments." Justice Kennedy, who had voted on the other side of this issue 16 years earlier, wrote, "It is fair to say that the United States now stands alone in a world that has turned its face against the juvenile death penalty." Justice Kennedy said that although the Court was not obligated to follow foreign developments, "it is proper that we acknowledge the overwhelming weight of international opinion" for its "respected and significant confirmation for our own conclusions."[94] This explicit recognition of the role of public opinion firmly placed a majority of the Court on the side of the "living Constitution" perspective on this issue, while rejecting the strict constructionist view of the dissenters.

Another way that the Court may consider the public mood is to shift the timing of a decision. The best example here is the landmark school desegregation case, *Brown v. Board of Education* (1954), that the Court sat on for more than two years—until after the 1952 presidential election—because it didn't think the public was ready for its bombshell ruling.[95] Others have argued that the Court rarely *changes* its views to reflect public opinion,[96] but at a minimum the evidence supports the notion that the Court is usually in step with the public.[97]

"Why Should I Care?"

Shouldn't the Court be neutrally applying the words of the Constitution to the cases it hears? While a normatively appealing view, this textualist view ignores many of the realities of how the Court actually operates. Justices often let their own political views shape their decisions, but more neutral forces such as precedent and deferring to the elected branches also play important roles. A realistic perception of the various factors that go into a justice's decision can help you understand why the Court strikes down some laws and upholds others.

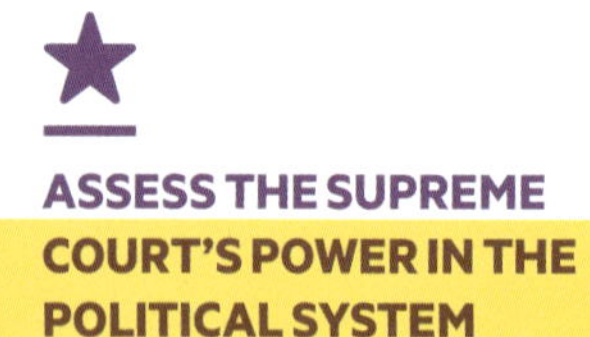

ASSESS THE SUPREME COURT'S POWER IN THE POLITICAL SYSTEM

The role of the Court in our political system

We conclude with the topic addressed early in the chapter—the place of the Court within the political system. Is the Court the "weakest branch"? As Alexander Hamilton pointed out, the Court has "neither the power of the purse nor the sword." Therefore, it is not clear how it can enforce decisions. In some instances, the Court can force its views on the other branches; in other cases, it needs their support to enforce its decisions.

Compliance and implementation

To gain compliance with its decisions, the Court can rely only on its reputation and on the actions of Congress and the president to back it up. If the other branches don't support the Court, there isn't much it can do. The Court's lack of enforcement power is especially evident when a ruling applies broadly to millions of people who care deeply about the issue. Consider school prayer, which still exists in hundreds of public schools nationwide despite having been ruled unconstitutional nearly 60 years ago. It is impossible to enforce the ban unless someone in a school complains and is willing to bring a lawsuit.

In most cases that involve a broad policy, the Court depends on the president for enforcement. After *Brown v. Board of Education* (1954), the landmark school desegregation case, Presidents Eisenhower and Kennedy had to send in federal troops to desegregate public schools and universities. However, presidential foot-dragging can have a big impact on how the law is enforced. President Nixon attempted to lessen the impact of a school busing decision in 1971 that forced the integration of public schools by interpreting it very narrowly. The Court must rely on its reputation and prestige to compel the president and Congress not to stray too far from its decisions.

Students at a middle school in Alton, Illinois, gather around a flagpole for prayers before the start of the school day. Unless someone complains, it is difficult to enforce the ban on prayer in public schools.

Relations with the other branches

Relations with the other branches of government may become strained when the Court rules on fundamental questions about institutional power. In some cases, the other branches may fight back; in others, the Court may exercise self-restraint and not get involved.

Judicial Activism and Restraint A central question concerning the role of the Court within our political system revolves around judicial review: Should the Court strike down laws passed by Congress and actions of the executive (activism) or defer to the elected branches (restraint)? Often the answer to this question varies when considered in light of specific lines of cases. A political conservative may favor activist decisions striking down environmental laws or workplace regulations but oppose activist decisions that defend flag burning or defendants' rights. Political liberals may do the opposite—calling for judicial restraint on the first set of cases but for judicial activism to protect civil liberties.

The term "activist judges" often appears in the media. Sometimes the media mistakenly assert that liberal justices are more activist than conservative justices. In fact, though, that is not always the case. The current Court is quite conservative, but it is also activist.[98] Two conservative justices, Roberts and Thomas, have voted to overturn laws passed by Congress 71 percent and 76 percent of the time, respectively, whereas two of the most liberal justices in the 2020 session, Breyer and Ginsburg, took the activist position in only 58 percent and 56 percent of the cases.[99] The 1930s Court that struck down much of the New Deal legislation was also conservative and activist, but the Warren Court of the late 1950s and early 1960s was liberal and activist. Also note that activism is different from overturning precedent. For example, while overturning *Roe v. Wade* was a momentous decision, it was not activist because it returned policy-making authority on abortion to the elected branches of the states.

A prominent legal journalist observed that the way the popular media describe activism and restraint typically boils down to ideology: if you like a decision, it is restrained; if you do not like a decision, it is activist. For example, *Bush v. Gore*, the decision that decided the outcome of the 2000 presidential election, shows that "most conservatives tie themselves in knots to defend judicial activism when they like the results and to denounce it when they do not. As the reactions to *Lawrence* [the gay sodomy case discussed in Chapter 4] and, earlier, *Roe* [the landmark abortion case] have shown, liberals have been no less selective in their outrage at judicial adventurousness."[100] However, there are instances in which restraint reflects more than ideology and preferences. Justice O'Connor, for example, took restrained positions on abortion and affirmative action, despite her personal views against these policies. Another prominent example of judicial restraint being more important than ideology is Chief Justice Roberts's position in the health care reform case; he said that some decisions "are entrusted to our nation's elected leaders, who can be thrown out of office if the people disagree with them." However, despite providing the pivotal vote to uphold central provisions of the law, he made his personal views against the law clear. "It is not our job," he said, "to protect the people from the consequences of their political choices."[101]

It is important to define activism and restraint in terms of the Court's role in our nation's system of separated powers: Does the Court check the elected branches by overturning their decisions through judicial review? If so, the Court has taken an activist position.

TAKE A STAND

The Independence of the Courts

Many presidents have been frustrated by federal court decisions that they perceived to be unreasonable. Some have responded by lashing out at the courts—an action that never fails to stir controversy. Recently, both Presidents Obama and Trump have criticized high-profile Court decisions. In Obama's 2010 State of the Union address, he noted his disagreement with the Court's ruling in *Citizens United v. Federal Election Commission* (2010) and stated that he believed the decision had opened the floodgates for corporate spending—including by foreign corporations—in elections. Justice Alito was caught on camera mouthing the words "not true" in response. Washington was abuzz for days about whether the president's comment or Alito's response was out of line.[a] President Trump, for his part, was incensed with the Supreme Court's "horrible and politically charged decisions" on LGBTQ rights and the Dreamers, calling them "shotgun blasts into the face of people that are proud to call themselves Republicans or Conservatives."[b] Though it is not very common for presidents to openly criticize the federal courts, they routinely try to influence the courts through nominations to the federal bench. As we discussed earlier, all presidents try to pick justices who share their political views. Is this kind of influence different from that of presidents who directly express their opinions on Court decisions? Is either kind of influence acceptable?

Presidents should be able to influence the courts. Some argue that whether it is President Obama criticizing the Court's ruling on campaign finance or President Trump expressing his views on its decisions on LGBTQ rights and DACA, presidents should be able to express their views on the important issues of the day. Furthermore, presidents are not obligated to nominate centrist judges. If a Republican president can nominate conservative judges, that is certainly their right. Trump exercised this right, to the dismay of some observers who believe that he picked extremely conservative judges to push his policy agenda.

Trump's appointees, like those of any other president, had to be confirmed by the Senate. If people don't like the ideological makeup of the judges the president selects, they can vote out the president and their senator in the next election. Besides, the president speaks for the people they were elected by, while the courts are less democratic because they are not elected.

President Barack Obama was criticized during his 2010 State of the Union address for his comments on *Citizens United v. Federal Election Commission*, a federal court decision that he perceived to be unreasonable.

The independence of the courts is crucial: the president needs to back off. Others argue that while it is fine for presidents to express their policy views on issues that come before the Court, they should refrain from direct criticism of specific cases or judges.

And though it is true that all presidents try to influence the Court through their nominations, moderation here would also serve the long-term interests of the country better than wild swings between ideological extremes.

The ballot box is the ultimate recourse for accountability, but even the mighty power of the vote is limited when it comes to holding judges responsible: many judges will serve on the bench for 25 years or more, much longer than the president or most senators.

take a stand

1. Where would you draw the line on presidents' criticizing the courts?
2. Does it bother you that courts are not accountable to the people and yet make important policy decisions? If so, how should presidents be able to influence the courts?
3. Should presidents be able to nominate whomever they want to the courts (subject to Senate approval, of course), or should the process be less partisan and less ideological?

In a survey taken about the judicial branch, most respondents were unable to name any Supreme Court justices. Just so you are not in danger of falling into that category, as of fall 2022 the justices are *(front row, left to right)* Sonia Sotomayor, Clarence Thomas, John G. Roberts Jr. (chief justice), Samuel Alito Jr., Elena Kagan *(standing, left to right)* Amy Coney Barrett, Neil Gorsuch, Brett Kavanaugh, and Ketanji Brown Jackson.

Resistance from the Other Branches The president and Congress often fight back when they think the Court is exerting too much influence, which can limit the Court's power as a policy-making institution. For the president, this can escalate to open conflict. In the Take a Stand feature, we discuss President Obama's criticism of the Court's ruling in *Citizens United v. Federal Election Commission* (2010) in his State of the Union message and President Trump's conflict with the federal courts over their decisions on LGBTQIA+ rights and the status of DACA recipients. Such open conflict with the Court is often criticized as inappropriate. For example, during his confirmation process, Neil Gorsuch told Senator Richard Blumenthal (D-CT) that Trump's criticisms were "disheartening" and "demoralizing" to independent federal courts.[102] The president can counter the Court's influence in a more restrained way by failing to enforce a decision vigorously.

Congress can try to control the Court by blocking appointments it disagrees with (however, this often involves a disagreement with the president more than the Court), limiting the jurisdiction of the federal courts, changing the size of the Court, or even impeaching a judge. The latter three options are rarely used, but Congress often threatens to take these drastic steps. The most common way for Congress to respond to a Court decision that it disagrees with is simply to pass legislation that overturns the decision (if the case concerns the interpretation of a law).

Recent concerns about justices' behavior that raised questions about their impartiality—including accepting luxury travel from people who had business before the Court and Justice Thomas's wife involvement with the effort to provide bogus slates of electors in the 2020 presidential election—led the Senate to introduce an ethics code for the Court.[103] Justices Kagan and Alito publicly disagreed as to whether Congress has the power to impose such a code.[104] Bending to the public pressure, the Court adopted its own ethics code, but critics argued that it did not resolve any of the difficult issues concerning conflicts of interest and recusal.[105] Questions about the impartiality of the Court and recusal surfaced again in 2024 when Justice Alito was criticized for flying flags that were associated with the January 6 insurrection at his home and vacation house. He declined to recuse himself from cases related to the events of January 6.[106]

Self-Imposed Restraint In general, the Court avoids stepping on the toes of the other branches unless it deems it to be absolutely necessary. The Court often exercises self-imposed restraint and refuses to act on "political questions"—issues that are outside the judicial domain and should be decided by elected officials. The practice dates back to an 1804 dispute over whether a piece of land next to the Mississippi River belonged to Spain or the United States. The Court observed, "A question like this, respecting the boundaries of nations, is . . . more a political than a legal question, and in its discussion, the courts of every country must respect the pronounced will of the legislature."[107]

A more recent application of the doctrine came when the Washington, D.C., district court dismissed a lawsuit from Representative Charles Rangel (D-NY) against former Speaker John A. Boehner (R-OH) concerning the House of Representatives' censure of Rangel for tax evasion and other unethical behavior. The district court dismissed the suit, in part on the grounds that this was a political question that should be decided by Congress, not the Court: "The House has wide discretion to discipline its Members under the Discipline Clause, and this Court may not lightly intrude upon that discretion."[108] The Court is generally reluctant to get involved in internal congressional disputes.

Although this self-imposed limitation on judicial power is important, one must also recognize that the Court reserves the right to decide what a political question is. Therefore, one could argue that this is not much of a limit on judicial power after all. For example, for many decades the Court avoided the topic of legislative redistricting, saying that it did not want to enter that "political thicket." However, it changed its position in the 1960s in a series of cases that imposed the idea of "one-person, one-vote" on the redistricting process, and it has been intimately involved in redistricting ever since. The Court's ability to define the boundaries of political questions is an important source of its policy-making power.

However, in some cases the Court cannot duck important political questions and define the boundaries of the separation of powers. One important example was from the summer of 2024 when the election interference case against Donald Trump was getting ready to go to trial, Trump attorneys claimed that the president's actions leading up to January 6 (and on that day) were covered by absolute executive immunity. In *Donald Trump v. United States* the Court rejected that claim, but returned the case to district court to define which presidential actions were official acts covered by immunity (that is, criminal charges could not be brought against the president for these acts) and which were illegal private actions for which the president could be convicted. The Court has never clearly defined the boundaries of executive immunity and was aware, as Justice Gorsuch said, that they were "writing a rule for the ages." Gorsuch continued, he was "not concerned about this case as much as future ones."[109]

The Court's Multifaceted Role This "big picture" question about the relationship of the Court to the other branches boils down to this: Does the judiciary constrain the other branches, or does it defer to their wishes? Given the responsiveness of the elected branches to the will of the people, this question can alternatively be stated: Does the Court operate against the political majority to protect minority interests, or does it defer to the popular will? The evidence on this is mixed.

The judicial branch as a whole contains a basic paradox: it may be simultaneously seen as the least democratic and most democratic branch.[110] The least democratic part is obvious: federal judges and many state and local judges are unelected and are not accountable to the voters (except indirectly through the elected leaders who appoint them). But the judiciary can also be seen as the most democratic branch. Cases that are brought to the courts come from the people and, as long as the legal criteria for bringing a case are met, the courts must hear those cases. Although people have the right to petition "the government for a redress of grievances," there is no guarantee that Congress or the executive branch will listen to them. Of course, only a small fraction of the cases brought to the Supreme Court are heard, so the antidemocratic charge carries

The Court has been an important protector of the rights of historically marginalized groups, including in the civil rights era. This picture from 1953 shows people waiting in line at the Supreme Court to hear oral arguments in *Brown v. Board of Education*. But at other times, the Court has supported the will of the majority.

more weight at the top. However, the court system as a whole may be seen as providing an important outlet for participation in our political system.

Whether the Supreme Court goes against our elected leaders—that is, is the Court a countermajoritarian force in our political system?—is also a complicated question to sort out. The Court is activist on many issues, exercising judicial review, but on many other issues it defers to the elected institutions. Sometimes an activist Court defends minority interests on issues such as criminal defendants' rights, school prayer, gay rights (which initially were not supported by the majority but are now), and flag burning, but that is not always the case. Is the Court acting undemocratically when it exercises its power of judicial review (or, as critics would say, "legislates from the bench")? Or is it playing its vital role in our constitutional system as a check on the other branches, as with some of its recent cases concerning the legal rights of enemy combatants in the War on Terror and the attempts by President Trump to end DACA and challenge the outcome of the 2020 election?

The answers depend somewhat on one's political views. Conservatives would generally applaud the activism of the Rehnquist and Roberts Courts, while liberals would see it as an unwarranted check on the elected branches, but it depends on the issue (such as the 2020 election!). Moreover, the Court's role has varied throughout history: in some instances, it defended unpopular views and strongly protected the rights of historically marginalized groups; in other cases, it followed majority opinion and declined to play that important role. But clearly, the Court has the *potential* to play an important policy-making role in our system of checks and balances; whether it actually plays that role depends on the political, personal, and legal factors outlined in this chapter.

Our system of checks and balances is based on the complex relationship between the branches of government. Some of the most heated interbranch skirmishes involve the Supreme Court's use of judicial review to strike down Congress's laws and the president's actions. Is the Court antidemocratic, or does it stick up for unpopular views that are not represented elsewhere in the political system? How can Congress and the president check the Court's views if they disagree?

Unpacking the Conflict

Considering all that we've discussed in this chapter, let's apply what we know about how the courts work to the events introduced at the beginning of this chapter: the politicization of the Supreme Court nomination process and the independence of the courts. Was the Senate playing its proper role with the aggressive questioning of Justice Jackson, or is Senator Collins correct that this just supports the perception of a politicized Court and undermines its independence? Was Justice Roberts overreacting to Trump's comments about political judges, or is it necessary for justices to defend the independence of the Court? What is the proper place of the courts within our political system? Should judges attempt to neutrally apply the law, or should their political views play a role?

The chapter-opening examples demonstrate that we often have a difficult time coming to grips with the political nature of the Supreme Court and prefer the comforting image of the neutral and fair Lady Justice: that is why there was such a strong reaction to partisan battles over the Court. We *want* our courts to be politically neutral, but the reality is very different.

Politics is indeed everywhere, even in the courts, where you would least expect to see it. Politics affects everything from the selection of judges to the decisions they make. Some characteristics of the federal courts (the most important of which is judges' lifetime tenure) insulate the system from politics. However, courts are subject to influence by judges' ideologies, interest groups, and the president and Senate, who try to shape the courts' composition through the nomination process.

While many recoil from a politicized Court, we also value its independence and don't want the president and Congress stepping on its toes. Thus, if the federal courts are allowed to play their proper role, they can serve as a referee between the other branches of government, and between the national and state governments, by defining the boundaries of permissible conduct as when federal and state courts protected the outcome of the 2020 elections.

The courts demonstrate that politics is conflictual. And many conflicts demonstrate that the courts are political. Although plenty of unanimous Supreme Court decisions do not involve much conflict among the justices, many landmark cases deeply divide the Court on constitutional interpretation and how to balance those competing interpretations against other values and interests. These conflicts in the Court often reveal deeper fault lines in the broader political system.

"What's Your Take?"

What should the proper place of the courts be in our political system?

How much influence should the executive and legislative branches have over the courts, and vice versa?

CHECK YOUR UNDERSTANDING

"Why Should I Care?"

Our constitution can be maddening in its vagueness, but that vagueness is also where it draws its strength from. Countries that govern themselves under constitutions made up of very narrowly drawn, minutiae-laden clauses find themselves faced with limited options to amend their norms to keep up with changes in the way their citizens see the world around them. In the American system of separation of powers, the constitutionally called-for Supreme Court and the inferior courts of the federal court system, created by the Federal Judiciary Act of 1789, step into the breach, to allow the United States to enact policies that breathe into the space created by all that vagueness.

Constitutional interpretation is the main focus of the Court's power of judicial review, giving the Supreme Court the venue to flesh out its own identity based on the cases within its jurisdiction that it chooses to take. The judicial philosophies espoused by each of the justices on the Court is based on their perception of the position of the Court relative to the other branches in government.

The unelected nature, as well as the term lengths, of the justices raises the question, to whom is this branch responsive? As you learned in the chapters on Congress and the presidency, American voters communicate their satisfaction or displeasure for the people holding these roles at the ballot box, but Supreme Court justices are protected from electoral consequences.

In recent years, we have seen large-scale protests outside the Supreme Court building to attempt to communicate the preferences of the people related to the cases the justices are hearing arguments on. In 2022, a draft opinion written by Justice Samuel Alito communicating the overturning of *Roe v. Wade* (1973) was leaked, sparking large-scale, vehement protests to try to communicate to the justices just how much of the American population does not want to see the overturning of the right to access abortion care. What this case does, in addition to limiting access to abortion and other reproductive health services across the country, is to continue on the path set out by the Court to return the power of lawmaking to the states, in the cases where the subject of the law should be taken on by Congress but has not been. The next decade will be about reasserting the balance of the national government with that of state governments, and the Supreme Court will be the pivot point on which that balance hinges.

1. Judicial review, as envisioned by Chief Justice John Marshall, can best be defined in what way?

- **a** Ability of the Supreme Court to determine the validity of a challenged statute or other public act
- **b** Authority of the federal courts to preempt the activities of the legislative and executive branches
- **c** Inclusion of federal judges as a part of a council of revision that could veto legislation
- **d** Practicing respect of precedent in questions of the constitutionality of laws and executive acts

2. When the Supreme Court is asked to review whether an administrative law is constitutional, many justices turn to what source to understand the intentions and applications of the law in question?

- **a** The Constitution
- **b** Hearings and floor debate involved in creating the legislation
- **c** Major newspapers and journalistic institutions of the time period
- **d** Works of American historians

3. Over 95 percent of federal felony cases that result in a conviction are a result of

- **a** jury selection bias.
- **b** the quality of federal prosecutors.
- **c** the necessity of courts to move quickly.
- **d** plea bargains.

4. What is the most important difference between courts with original jurisdiction and courts with appellate jurisdiction?

- **a** Appellate courts can hear both new cases and cases on appeal.
- **b** Courts with original jurisdiction hear both civil and criminal cases, while appeals courts do not.
- **c** Original jurisdiction is rooted in the constitutional debates.
- **d** Appellate courts hear appeals from lower courts and change or uphold the decision.

5. Of all the factors that increase the likelihood of the Supreme Court to hear a case, which is thought to be given the greatest weight by the justices?

- **a** Clearly defined public divisions
- **b** Involvement of the solicitor general
- **c** Alleged state violations of civil rights
- **d** Cases that involve unique constitutional questions

6. In what scenario would the Supreme Court have original jurisdiction?

- **a** New Jersey and New York disagree over which state should control the 24 acres of land around Ellis Island.
- **b** A woman sues her employer for discrimination based on gender.
- **c** A person is charged with racially motivated murder.
- **d** Orange County argues that its border with Los Angeles needs to be redrawn.

7. What is the best way to describe amicus curiae briefs to a beginning student of political science?

- **a** A summary document created by clerks of the justices about a particular case to help them decide whether the justices should grant a hearing
- **b** A document issued when at least four justices agree that the Court should grant a writ of *certiorari*
- **c** A draft opinion circulated among the justices to build support for the majority position in the outcome of a case
- **d** A document expressing the views, legal reasoning, and desired outcome of a case with the intention of influencing the outcome of the Court's decision

8. When considering the so-called shadow docket, perhaps the most important argument that it is bad for American government may be which of the following?

- **a** The shadow docket is used to promote political agendas of an increasingly polarized Court without identifying authors of the opinions.
- **b** The Court's so-called shadow docket has become an avenue through which special interests have increased access and influence over the Court.
- **c** It creates precedent for lower courts without the benefits of establishing legal reasoning or legitimizing the legal outcome.
- **d** Increasing use of the shadow docket further diminishes the number of cases on important constitutional questions that the Court hears during a year.

9. Conservative justice Neil Gorsuch has promoted a judicial perspective that suggests that the Court should use the understandings of the text in policies to determine their constitutionality. Meanwhile, fellow conservative justice Clarence Thomas argues that when deciding a case, justices must use the original intent of the authors at the time the policy was written. What conclusion can students of political science reach considering the perspectives of these two justices?

- **a** Liberal members of the Court have abandoned the practice of trying to understand the historic meanings and contexts of the language in the Constitution or statutes being considered by the Court.
- **b** Conservative members of the Court have a more comprehensively constructed view of how to analyze and apply the language of statutes and the Constitution when in question.
- **c** Conservative justices who have endorsed using text for decision-making do not have a uniform belief in how this is to be done in determining constitutionality of a statute or executive action.
- **d** The liberal and conservative members of the Court are highly fragmented when it comes to the way that they consider issues being considered by the Court.

10. For the Supreme Court, what is the benefit of a significant majority of their case opinions falling in line with public opinion?

- **a** It suggests that the Court has reached the correct outcome in consideration of the issue.
- **b** The public is more likely to see the Court as legitimate, and therefore is more willing to follow along with the decision.
- **c** The Court is less likely to face retaliation by the executive and legislative branches.
- **d** It decreases the likelihood of further controversies on the same issue reaching the Court in the future.

11. Because the Supreme Court does not have any enforcement mechanism, what does it rely on to make sure that the public and other government institutions follow its decisions?

- **a** Its reputation as legitimate in the decision-making process
- **b** Popular agreement with the decision that was reached by the Court
- **c** Appointment and confirmation of highly qualified individuals to the Court
- **d** Successful coordination of public outreach efforts

12. One way the Court protects itself from being viewed by the public and other branches as overstepping its constitutional authority is to remove itself from issues involving what kinds of problems?

- **a** Civil rights questions
- **b** Political questions
- **c** Interstate questions
- **d** Foreign ambassador questions

Use INQUIZITIVE to help you study and master this material.

15

Economic Policy

How does the government help promote a strong economy?

"Forget about this $3 trillion left-wing wish list that even House Democrats are criticizing. It ain't gonna happen."[1]
Senate Majority Leader Mitch McConnell (R-KY), 2020

"Sen. McConnell's months-long refusal to engage in bipartisan talks on the next phase of federal relief legislation has created needless uncertainty and pain for millions of families who are still reeling from the public health and economic crises."[2]
Senate Minority Leader Chuck Schumer (D-NY), 2020

As the COVID-19 pandemic swept the country early in 2020, most state governments responded by ordering all nonessential businesses to close and recommending or requiring that people stay home to slow the spread of the virus. Schools and universities closed and went online (to the extent that was possible); airlines and the service industry, especially hotels and restaurants, were hard-hit; sports, entertainment, and the arts were completely shut down. As a result, the economy shed 20.5 million jobs in April, leaving nearly 24 million people out of work and increasing the unemployment rate to 14.7 percent—the highest since the Great Depression in the 1930s. By June 20, nearly 33 million people had claimed unemployment benefits.[3]

Congress responded with four bills, totaling nearly $3 trillion in spending, with the centerpiece the $2.2 trillion Coronavirus Aid, Relief, and Economic Security Act, or CARES Act, which passed with unanimous support in the Senate (96–0) and by a voice vote in the House. The bills provided $600 billion in payments to individuals ($1,200 each for people making less than $75,000), $600 billion to small businesses, $500 billion to large corporations (such as airlines), $154 billion to health care, $340 billion to state and local governments, and $44 billion to education.[4]

Lawmakers have passed several bills that soften the blow of the COVID-19 pandemic, including the American Rescue Plan Act in 2021, which provided $1.9 trillion in economic stimulus spending.

The Federal Reserve also moved aggressively to ensure stability in the financial sector by pumping nearly $3 trillion into the economy. In addition to buying federal treasuries, state and municipal bonds, and (for the first time) corporate debt, the Fed dropped its target interest rate to 0.25 percent, eliminated the reserve requirement for banks, relaxed regulations on capital requirements to encourage more lending,

CHAPTER GOALS

Explain the main purposes of government involvement in the economy (pp. 577–584)

Describe the roles played by each of the branches of government in shaping economic policy (pp. 584–594)

Examine how fiscal, monetary, regulatory, and trade policies influence the economy (pp. 594–614)

A major feature of the March 2020 CARES Act legislation was the $1,200 stimulus check paid out to Americans as a means to offset the negative effects of the COVID-19 recession.

backstopped money market mutual funds, and supported loans to medium-sized businesses that were too big to qualify for congressionally funded aid.[5]

The bipartisan response was unprecedented in its scope and size, but by the middle of the summer it became clear that more action was needed. The House moved first, passing the $3 trillion Health and Economic Recovery Omnibus Emergency Solutions Act (the HEROES Act). However, as the chapter-opening quotes indicate, this bill was "dead on arrival" in the Senate because the majority leader dismissed it as a "left-wing wish list." The bipartisan harmony that existed in the first part of the crisis gave way to the familiar partisan conflict in Washington, and that conflict only intensified after Democrats regained unified control of the federal government in 2021. Democrats passed the $1.8 trillion (over ten years) American Rescue Plan Act early in 2021 on straight party-line votes, arguing that more stimulus was needed for the recovering economy. The legislation included more money for vaccinations, funding to safely reopen schools, $1,400 per person in relief payments, extending unemployment benefits, increasing the child tax credit, and expanding childcare assistance.[6]

Conflict over economic policy goes beyond emergency responses to the economic downturn caused by the COVID-19 pandemic. Many of America's political debates concern economic policy: Should we try to protect domestic industries from foreign competition or promote free trade? Should we have a largely unregulated free market—or regulations for things like pollution and health care? Should we spend more money to create "green jobs" and promote alternative energy, or subsidize offshore oil drilling and build more natural gas pipelines? Democrats tend to favor a more activist government that supports a broader range of redistributive programs and regulates the economy to ensure a range of public goods, such as rebuilding the infrastructure. Republicans tend to favor a more limited approach to government that promotes lower taxes and less regulation and allows the free market to determine more social and economic decisions, such as allowing greater development of domestic energy sources.

As our political leaders debate how best to support a growing economy, it becomes increasingly important to understand the economic policy–making process. How much should the government do to get us out of a recession? Does too much economic stimulus overheat the economy and contribute to inflation? Which side is right about trade policy or environmental policy? More generally, what is the proper role of the government in a free market economy? How do political players deal with the conflict that is inherent in economic policy making?

Goals of economic policy

EXPLAIN THE MAIN PURPOSES OF GOVERNMENT INVOLVEMENT IN THE ECONOMY

Public policy is a course of action pursued by government to address a specific problem. Economic policy makers thus attempt to influence the economy with specific goals in mind. This section will examine those goals, and later in the chapter we will look at the tools used to pursue the goals. The most important tools are **fiscal policy**—tax and spending policy that is created by Congress and the president—and **monetary policy**—control of the money supply and interest rates, which is primarily the domain of the Federal Reserve System, or "the Fed."

Many economic policy goals seem obvious, such as full employment (clearly, it is better to have more people working than not working). However, it may be less obvious why other goals, such as promoting stable prices and market growth, are important for the economy. These varied goals are often difficult for policy makers to pursue simultaneously because there are trade-offs among some of them.

public policy
A course of action pursued by government to address a specific problem.

fiscal policy
Government decisions about how to influence the economy by taxing and spending.

monetary policy
Government decisions about how to influence the economy using control of the money supply and interest rates.

Full employment

Employment seems like a good starting point for a healthy economy. If people have jobs, they pay taxes and do not depend directly on the government for support. Despite this, **full employment** was not an explicit goal of economic policy until 1946, when Congress passed the Employment Act. Leaders were concerned that with millions of World War II veterans returning and the wartime economy gearing down, the nation might slide back into the **economic depression** that had created so much hardship in the 1930s. Although the act was largely symbolic (it did not create a guaranteed right to employment); it did create the **Council of Economic Advisers (CEA)**, which provides the president with economic information and advice. A more concrete effort to ensure that returning veterans could find jobs was the 1944 Servicemen's Readjustment Act (the GI Bill). By the time this law expired in 1956, it had provided low-interest home mortgages for 2.4 million veterans and higher education assistance to 7.8 million veterans. Today the government seeks to support the creation of as many jobs as possible by maintaining a strong economy. With the massive $5 trillion in spending to confront the COVID recession discussed in the chapter opener, levels of employment almost matched their pre-recession levels in only two years, compared with six years for the 2008–2009 recession.[7]

On a technical level, "full employment" does not literally mean that everyone is working. Instead, economists consider a 4.0–4.5 percent unemployment rate to be the level of full employment, or the "natural rate of unemployment." This accounts for the substantial portion of potential workers who are not looking for a job and a certain amount of "frictional unemployment" when people are between jobs.

full employment
The theoretical point at which all citizens who want to be employed have a job.

economic depression
A deep, widespread downturn in the economy, like the Great Depression of the 1930s.

Council of Economic Advisers (CEA)
A group of economic advisers, created by the Employment Act of 1946, that provides objective data on the state of the economy and makes economic policy recommendations to the president.

Stable prices

The economy saw the highest inflation rates in 40 years, which impacted the cost of gas and food and made home mortgages more expensive.

The importance of having stable prices is not as obvious as the need for jobs. Why are rising prices—**inflation**—a problem? This is a common question during periods of low inflation. Especially for workers who have automatic raises (cost-of-living adjustments, or COLAs) as part of their basic pay package, moderate inflation isn't much of a problem. For example, if your rent goes up 4 percent, the price of groceries goes up 3 percent, and the cost of entertainment goes up 3 percent, and you get a 4 percent raise, you will likely be at least as well-off as you were in the previous year. However, it's possible for inflation to be much higher: from 1979 to 1980 inflation was running at 12–14 percent rather than the 2–3 percent that policy makers aim for. In early 2022, the inflation rate hit 8.5 percent—the highest in 40 years—because of tight labor markets (when unemployment is low, wages go up, which drives up the cost of goods and services), global and domestic supply chain problems, the war in Ukraine (which contributed to increase food and energy costs), and the fiscal and monetary stimulus.[8]

Double-digit inflation can have serious effects on the economy. First, because the entire economy is not indexed to inflation (that is, protected from inflation by automatic pay or benefit increases that are pegged to the rate of inflation), some people will experience an erosion of their purchasing power. If your rent goes up 10 percent and groceries go up 15 percent, but your pay goes up by only 4 percent, you are substantially worse off. Second, high inflation penalizes savers as inflation outstrips savings interest rates (so savings are actually worth *less* over time). On the other hand, inflation may benefit debtors, because people can repay their debts with dollars that are worth less in the future. Finally, long-term economic planning by businesses becomes more difficult when inflation is high: investors will demand high interest rates to compensate for the added risk of future inflation, and businesses will be reluctant to accept loans at these rates. In 1979 and 1980, for example, short-term interest rates spiked as high as 18 percent. Very few businesses were willing to take on additional debt at that rate of interest rather than the more typical 5–8 percent for long-term loans, so the economy headed into a recession. Inflation remained a major concern in the 2024 elections despite falling to just over two percent by October 2024.

It's a recession when your neighbor loses his job; it's a depression when you lose your own.

—President Harry Truman

As counterintuitive as it may sound, *falling* prices, or **deflation**, may be equally as devastating for an economy as prices that are rising too quickly. During the Great Depression, prices fell by 10 percent each year from 1930 to 1933. This trend exacerbated the depression as businesses made less money, wages fell (for those who were still working), production fell, and real debt increased (that is, when wages were falling by 30 percent, it was much harder to pay off debts, because they couldn't be repaid with cheaper dollars). American policy makers were concerned about possible deflation after the Great Recession of 2008–2009, but those fears subsided as inflation remained at a low level until 2021–2022.[9]

Typically, unemployment and inflation are not high at the same time. The unusual period of relatively high unemployment and inflation in the 1970s generated two new economic terms to describe this phenomenon: "stagflation" (a stagnant economy with inflation) and the "Misery Index" (the sum of the inflation rate and the unemployment rate; see Figure 15.1). The Misery Index started to creep up in 1970–1971, and policy makers were desperate to do something about it. President Nixon wanted to halt inflation in its tracks, in part to help his reelection chances in 1972. He announced a 90-day wage freeze in 1971, followed by wage and price controls after his reelection. The experiment was abandoned in 1974 when it became obvious that interfering with market forces in these ways was not working.[10] From that point on, fighting inflation has largely been left to the Federal Reserve, which raises interest rates to cool down the economy. We will discuss this process later in the chapter.

inflation
The increase in the price of consumer goods over time.

deflation
A decrease in the general prices of goods and services.

FIGURE 15.1

Inflation and Unemployment, 1960–2024

The Misery Index is the sum of the unemployment rate and the inflation rate. Which periods have had the highest misery rate since 1960? Were there any external explanations for the high misery rate? How did the government respond to the high levels of unemployment and inflation?

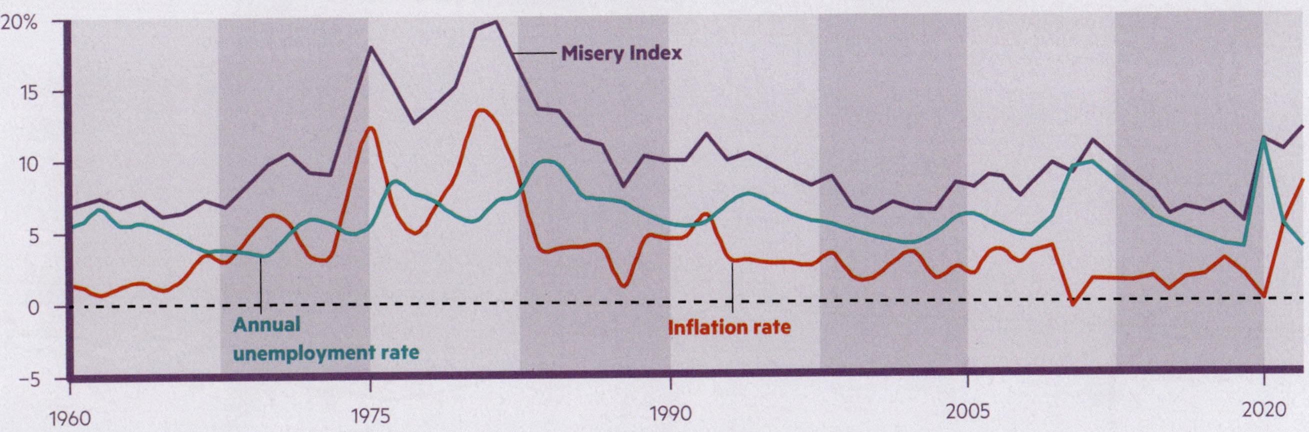

Source: Data from the U.S. Department of Labor, Bureau of Labor Statistics, www.bls.gov (accessed 8/2/24).

Promotion of the free market and growth

The American economy is a capitalist system, which means that most economic decisions are voluntarily made between individuals and firms for their mutual benefit. The government generally stays out of most economic activity, except to regulate the market when it produces too much of something that is not in the public's interest, such as pollution or unsafe products. Economists tout the advantage of the free market as promoting the most efficient use of resources. Economic growth is also a central goal. Growth is seen in an increase in **gross domestic product (GDP)**, a measure of the nation's overall economic output and activity. A growing economy provides a better standard of living for each generation.

gross domestic product (GDP) The value of a country's economic output taken as a whole.

Though government does not get directly involved in most economic transactions, it can provide the foundation for a strong free market and economic growth. The government protects property rights so that businesses that invest in the growth of their company know that another firm or the government cannot appropriate their property. Property rights also cover intellectual property, which is protected by patent and copyright laws. If entrepreneurs know that they will benefit from their own discoveries and labor, they are more likely to put in the countless hours required for innovative breakthroughs in science, technology, and medicine. The government also guarantees the security and transparency of capital markets through the oversight of the Securities and Exchange Commission and provides a secure banking system through the Federal Deposit Insurance Corporation and the Federal Reserve System.

Critics of the government's focus on the market and growth claim that the free market often produces inequality and that growth doesn't measure well-being. This was a big issue in the 2020 presidential campaign, especially given the racial inequalities in income, wealth, and health care that became more evident during the COVID-19

FIGURE 15.2

Wealth Inequality across the World

Economic inequality was higher in Europe than in the United States until the late twentieth century. Today the United States has a higher income inequality than Europe and China. What are the factors that have led to increased economic inequality in the United States?

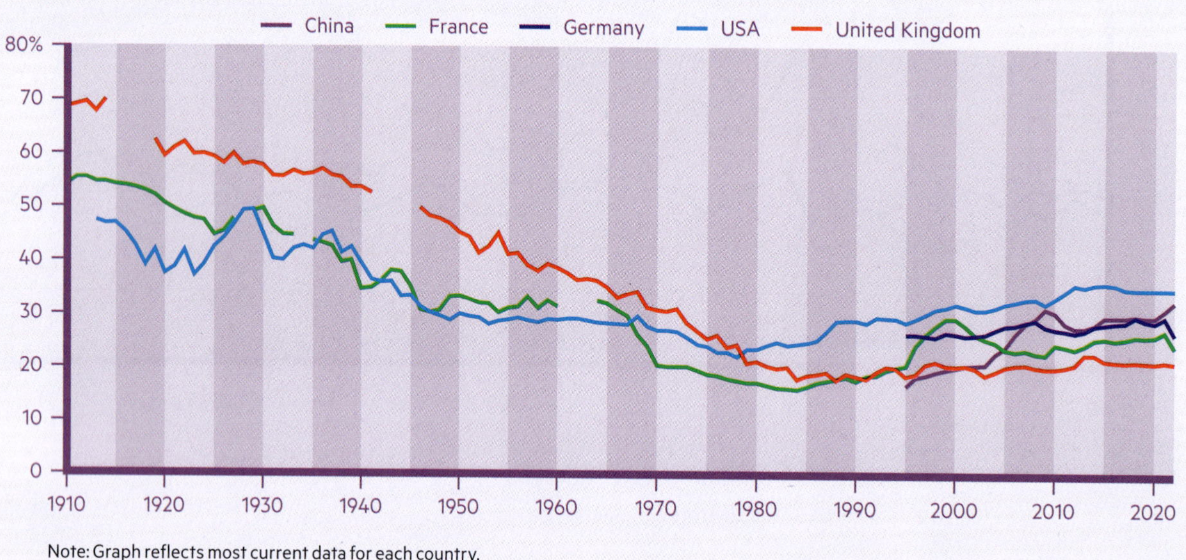

Note: Graph reflects most current data for each country.

Source: World Inequality Database, "Wealth Inequality: Top 1% Share," https://wid.world/data/ (accessed 4/21/22).

pandemic (and became part of the discussion of how to address the nation's systemic racism in the wake of the George Floyd protests). But historically, the United States has not focused as much on this economic policy goal as many other Western nations have. As a consequence, the United States ranks 111th in the world (out of 167 nations in the study) in income equality, just behind nations such as Uruguay, Turkey, Kenya, and Chad and just ahead of Haiti, and it has become less equal than other major countries in the distribution of wealth (see Figure 15.2).[11] Other critics of the focus on growth include environmentalists who advocate a "small is beautiful"[12] approach and point out the environmental costs of economic growth. In addition, there are economists who question the traditional interpretations of economic growth measurements—in particular, the increase in GDP. These critics argue that a significant part of GDP actually captures a decline in well-being. For example, if we have to spend billions of dollars putting alarms in our homes and cars to warn against intruders, this does not signal an improvement in the standard of living from the time when such alarms were unnecessary. Yet the purchase of such crime-fighting tools adds to GDP. An ideal measure of economic growth would distinguish between positive and negative forms of economic activity.[13]

balanced budget
A spending plan in which the government's expenditures are equal to its revenue.

budget deficit
The amount by which a government's spending in a given fiscal year exceeds its revenue.

Balanced budgets

Maintaining a **balanced budget** has been what can be best characterized as an aspirational goal since the 1980s, when **budget deficits** skyrocketed (see Nuts & Bolts 15.1). That is, both parties give lip-service to wanting a balanced budget (especially when they are the party out

Deficits and Debt

NUTS & BOLTS 15.1

Budget deficits and the federal debt are related concepts that are easily confused.

- A *budget deficit* occurs when tax revenue is not sufficient to cover government spending in a given year. If tax revenue is higher than spending, then there is a budget surplus.
- The *federal debt* is the total accumulation of all outstanding borrowing by the government.
- The concepts of deficit and debt are related because when the government runs a deficit it must borrow money to cover the gap. This borrowing then builds up the federal debt.

Source: Compiled by the authors.

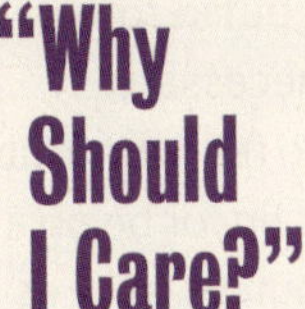

"Why Should I Care?"

You can think of this in terms of your own spending habits. Any time you spend more money in a given month than you earn, you are running a deficit. You must borrow money to make up that deficit from a bank, from your parents, or by running up the balance on your credit card. The accumulated sum of your monthly deficits is the total debt that you owe. However, there is one obvious point that should be made: you cannot print your own money, unlike the government!

of power!), but because of the need to address the deepest recessions since the 1930s, first the 2008–2009 recession and then the 2020 COVID-19 recession, this has been more of a theoretical goal than a practical one.

Yet, in the long term, large deficits (the deficit for fiscal year 2024 was $1.9 trillion) are a concern for several reasons. First, the debt accumulated over years of running budget deficits takes a big bite out of current spending. About $892 billion, or 13 percent, of the 2024 fiscal year budget was for financing the federal debt.[14] These dollars went to people and financial institutions that earn interest on the money that they loaned to the federal government; this money did not pay for a single uniform for a soldier, highway exit ramp, or student loan. Second, the total federal debt is a burden on future generations. Each man, woman, and child in the United States in effect carries more than $104,000 of federal (total debt has grown steadily; see What Do the Facts Say? on p. 582). This means that future generations will either have fewer government services and less generous benefits from programs like Social Security or pay higher taxes (or a mix of the two). Third, borrowing by the government "crowds out" private borrowing in the overall economy, because there is a finite pool of dollars that people can invest. Let's say you have $1,000 to invest. You could invest it privately and buy stocks or corporate bonds that provide businesses the money they need to expand, or you could invest it publicly and buy government bonds that allow the government to spend your $1,000 with the promise to pay it back later with interest. In the aggregate, this means that if the government is borrowing $1.9 trillion in a given year (like 2024), then that $1.9 trillion is not available for private borrowing that could go directly to creating more jobs and generating economic growth. People may obviously choose to invest in private debt, but U.S. government bonds are a very attractive investment option. They are seen as the most secure investment in the world, so especially during times of economic uncertainty, investors around the world buy U.S. bonds even if they pay a lower interest rate than private debt.

WHAT DO THE FACTS SAY?

Are Deficits and the National Debt out of Control?

Economic policy is difficult for most Americans to understand. Even something as basic as the implications of the size of the federal debt can be difficult to grasp, especially when dueling headlines say, "National Debt: Will It Destroy America's Economy?"[a] and "Debt? What Debt? At $22 Trillion, Here's the Argument the National Debt Doesn't Matter."[b]

Being a good consumer of media can help you sort out the dueling headlines. Is the claim too simple? Will national debt really destroy our economy? Does it really not matter at all? In both of those cases, the claims are too extreme and therefore too simple. If an explanation is too simple, it means that it is ignoring the complexity of the issue. Too much debt can create certain problems for the economy, but in some circumstances, such as a deep recession, taking on more debt may be necessary.

Often this type of over-the-top headline can be clickbait to get you to read the article. You should read such pieces with a healthy dose of skepticism. Another tip for being a good consumer of economic news is to seek out trusted government sources, such as the Congressional Budget Office, or bipartisan organizations, such as the Committee for a Responsible Federal Budget (see its recent article "Why Should We Worry about the National Debt?").[c] These sources are less likely to rely on simple arguments and will provide reliable facts to support an argument. For example, look at the two figures below. The first shows the budget deficit, which can look extreme out of context. The second figure shows the percentage of the GDP that that deficit represents (especially notice the difference between the two figures for 1945, with the extreme deficit spending during World War II). What do the facts say? Which headline is right?

Budget deficits

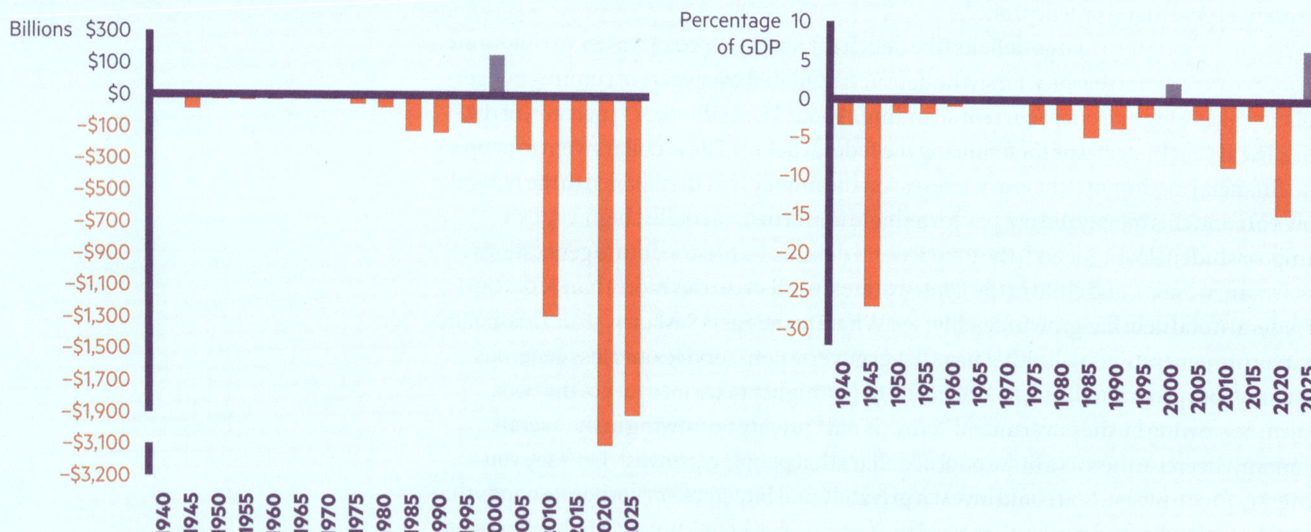

Note: Deficits include the Social Security Trust Fund. Data for 2025 are estimates.

Source: Congressional Budget Office, Budget Projections, various documents from www.cbo.gov/topics/budget (accessed 8/2/24).

Think about it

- **Economists argue that debt** becomes a potentially serious problem when it is as big as the overall economy. Have we ever hit that level since 1940?
- **After examining these data,** do you think the United States' budget deficits are out of control? Why or why not?

However, as we discuss below in the section on fiscal policy, deficit spending is sometimes necessary to stimulate the economy during a recession. When there is slack in the economy, the negative effects of too much government borrowing, such as the crowding out effect, will not be as significant, especially if the debt is funded by foreign investors or the Federal Reserve (Modern Monetary Theory suggests that the latter approach can be pursued with no negative consequences in an economic downturn, as long as there is enough slack in the economy).[15]

Balance of payments, or the current account

The balance of payments may sound like balanced budgets, but the two are completely different: the latter has to do with the federal budget that we just discussed, while the balance of payments concerns international monetary transactions. The broadest measure of a nation's balance of payments with the rest of the world is the **current account**: the difference between a nation's receipts (exports and money that Americans earn on foreign investments) and its payments (imports and money that foreigners earn on American investments). The aspect of the current account that gets the most political attention is the **trade deficit**, the difference between imports and exports. The American appetite for foreign goods is huge, and in recent years the United States has gone from being the world's largest creditor nation to being the world's largest debtor nation.

current account
The balance of a country's receipts and its payments in international trade and investment.

trade deficit
A measure of how much more a nation imports than it exports.

There are differences of opinion over whether the United States' debtor status with respect to other countries is a problem. Most economists agree that if the current account deficit is driven by more foreign investment in America than America has invested overseas, there is no great cause for concern. Although some economists worry about the increasing share of U.S. businesses and real estate owned by foreign investors, overall this is simply evidence of the strength of the U.S. economy—that is, investors think they can get a greater return on their investments in America than in other countries. However, if the current account deficit is driven by the trade deficit, which is based on consumption rather than investment, unsustainable longer-term economic problems may be created. We discuss this topic more in the section on trade policy.[16]

Trade-offs between economic goals

One challenge facing economic policy makers is that it is difficult to "have it all." Though the United States enjoyed low unemployment, low inflation, economic growth, falling budget deficits (and a surplus by the end of the decade), and a healthy current account throughout most of the 1990s, this was relatively unusual. Typically, at least part of the economy is not performing well and some goals are not being met. For example, if inflation starts to increase, the Federal Reserve will attempt to bring it down by increasing interest rates, as it did by raising the federal funds rate eleven times from 2.5 percent in March 2022 to 5.5 percent in July 2023. When interest rates go up, the economy slows because businesses are less willing to expand when the cost of borrowing increases. As a result, unemployment increases. Therefore, there is a trade-off, at least in the short run, between stable prices and full employment and economic growth.

Steps to address the trade deficit also conflict with other goals. Politicians are often under pressure to protect American jobs and prevent them from going overseas. For example, the $1 trillion infrastructure bill passed late in 2021 requires that all the material used to build the highway, bridges, water systems, or broadband internet have to be made in the United States.[17] But if policy makers impose barriers to free trade to protect domestic products and jobs, this action violates the goal of promoting an efficient free market. That is, political goals and economic goals may come into conflict.

The current administration and the past Trump administration both prioritized keeping jobs in the United States. Most recently, the Infrastructure and Jobs Act that passed in 2021 allows for $1 trillion in spending toward crucial digital and transportation infrastructure but stipulates that all materials used to build these structures must be made in the United States.

Another example would be budget deficits: politicians have a strong political incentive to keep budget deficits high (because, even though people don't like paying taxes, they support keeping spending the same or increasing it for most policies), but this may not be the best economic policy in some situations. Policy makers must tread carefully when addressing economic problems to ensure that they are not making some other problem worse. The next section explores who these policy makers are.

"Why Should I Care?"

Understanding the goals of economic policy is essential for making sense of much of what happens in Washington and in political campaigns. If a presidential candidate promises to cut your taxes and increase spending on education and national defense, without increasing budget deficits, your truth-o-meter should be buzzing. If the president talks about slapping punitive tariffs on China, you should be concerned about the impact of a trade war on the economy. Having a realistic set of goals is an important first step for sound economic policy.

DESCRIBE THE ROLES PLAYED BY EACH OF THE BRANCHES OF GOVERNMENT IN SHAPING ECONOMIC POLICY

The key players in economic policy making

Now that we know the goals of economic policy, we need to answer these questions: Who are the key policy makers? What role do they play in shaping American economic policy?

Congress

The Constitution places Congress at the center of economic policy making by giving legislators the "power of the purse"—that is, power over the nation's fiscal policy of taxing and spending. In a way, everything Congress does has an impact on the economy, whether it is providing money for an interstate highway or a student loan, regulating the level of air pollutants, or funding the Social Security system. Some committees are more directly related than others to economic policy. Budget Committees, Appropriations Committees, and tax committees (Ways and Means in the House and Finance in the Senate; see Chapter 11) direct fiscal policy, while the Banking Committees have a hand in overseeing aspects of monetary policy. The Commerce Committees, especially in the House, also have their hand in a range of economic policies. Because it is the most important of Congress's economic policy-making responsibilities, we focus our discussion on the budget-making process.

Budget making in Congress was decentralized through much of its history, with no real way to coordinate activity among the various committees and subcommittees involved in the process. The Appropriations Committees had a difficult time keeping spending requests from other committees in line with overall budgetary expectations because of the two-step process Congress uses to approve any spending: the authorizing committee writes the law that authorizes the spending, and then the Appropriations Committee approves the level of spending.[18] As a result, budgetary power shifted from Congress to the president, starting with the Budget and Accounting Act of 1921. From that point on, presidents have played a central role in the budget process by submitting their budgets to Congress. The president's budget often serves as the starting point for the congressional budget.

budget making
The processes carried out in Congress to determine how government money will be spent and revenue will be raised.

Congress revamped the budget process in 1974 with the Budget and Impoundment Control Act. This law created the Budget Committees in the House and Senate, set up the budget process (see the How It Works graphic on pp. 586–87), and established the Congressional Budget Office (CBO). This office gave Congress independent expertise and advice on budgetary matters so it did not have to rely on the president's numbers. For the first time, Congress had the institutional capacity on budgetary matters to deal with the president on an equal footing.

However, the new process and institutions did not guarantee smooth sailing. In fact, Congress has continued to have a difficult time meeting the various deadlines, and the process has not helped eliminate budget deficits. **Budget reconciliation**, a powerful tool in the 1974 Budget Act, was first used in 1980 to bring spending levels into line with the budget resolution. (This obviously requires that there *be* a budget resolution—15 times in the past 25 years Congress has failed to adopt the overall budget blueprint, most recently with the 2024 fiscal year budget.)[19] A former Budget Committee staffer observed, "The budget rules that are supposed to guide what the president and Congress do about the budget each year have died an ignominious death because of a combination of abject abuse and atrocious neglect."[20]

budget reconciliation
The process by which congressional committees are held to the spending targets specified in the budget resolution. During this process, the House and Senate Budget Committees combine the budgetary changes from all the legislative committees into an omnibus reconciliation bill to be approved by Congress.

Although the budget process is often ignored, committees are supposed to meet specific spending targets laid out in the budget resolution, and then any necessary changes to individual committees' budgets are supposed to be combined into one omnibus reconciliation bill. In terms of adopting budget cuts—which are always difficult to pass because most programs have strong advocates who oppose the cuts—this procedure has two advantages. First, having everything in a single huge bill makes it much more difficult for members to vote against it, because to do so would mean turning down the entire package, including elements of the bill that individual members of Congress like. Depending on the timing, failure to pass an omnibus spending bill may mean shutting down the government. Second, the Senate treats reconciliation bills differently from other bills or amendments. Most important, in the Senate these bills cannot be filibustered—and anything unrelated to deficit reduction can be struck down, which makes reconciliation an important tool in deficit reduction.[21] Overall, reconciliation has been used in about two-thirds of the budgets since 1980 and has been responsible for cutting hundreds of billions of dollars of

How it works: in theory

The Budget Process

First Monday in February: The president submits budget request to Congress.

February 15: Congressional Budget Office (CBO) issues budget and economic outlook report.

Within six weeks of president's submission: Other committees with budgetary responsibilities submit "views and estimates" to Budget Committees.

Early April: House Budget Committee creates its budget resolution and the House votes on it.

Early April: Senate Budget Committee creates its budget resolution and the Senate votes on it.

Early April: Budget Conference Committee reconciles the House and Senate versions of the budget resolution.

By April 15: House votes on conference version. Senate votes on conference version.

Appropriations: After both houses approve the budget resolution, Appropriations Committees draft legislation authorizing expenditures to the relevant agencies. Each appropriations bill must be passed by both houses and signed into law by the president. If this process is not completed by October 1 and no temporary measure (a "continuing resolution") is in place, the government will shut down.

October 1: Start of the fiscal year.

How it works: **in practice**

The 2022 Budget Process

Although there is a "textbook" path that politicians try to follow when passing a budget, they almost always deviate wildly from it. In fact, it has been 26 years since Congress passed all 12 appropriations bills using the regular process. In 2022, the budget resolution was four months late, so Congress resorted to continuing resolutions (CRs).

Fixing last year's mess.

December 2020–March 2021: Congress doesn't pass a budget; **instead it passes 5 CRs and an omnibus spending bill** in December (three months late).

Tricky!

Democrats use the FY2021 budget resolution **to pass the $1.9 trillion COVID-19 relief bill under reconciliation.**

Starting a little late.

May 28: President Biden submits his budget for the 2022 fiscal year—**116 days late**.

CBO does its thing.

July 30: CBO submits a partial analysis of the president's budget, saying it didn't have time for a comprehensive analysis—**165 days late**. (But who's counting? Oh, I guess we are.)

Whatever . . .

Over the summer, the Budget Committees **fail to pass a budget resolution**. This should have been passed by April 15.

Wait, can they do that?

June–August: The House Appropriations Committee **forges ahead without a budget resolution**. (Yes, they can do that, through a procedure called "deeming.")

Making some progress . . .

July: The House **passes 9 of its 12 appropriations bills**, but things grind to a halt in the Senate.

Better late than never.

August 11 and 24: The Senate passes the FY 2022 budget resolution after an all-night vote-a-rama session. The resolution includes reconciliation, which Dems. hope to use to pass Biden's Build Back Better agenda. **The House passes the resolution.**

Um, we have a deadline . . .

September 30: On the last day of the old fiscal year, **the House and Senate pass** a CR, extending government funding through December 3.

Shutdown, anyone?

December 2: With one day to spare, the House and Senate pass another CR, **keeping the government open through December 20.**

Once more, with feeling.

February 7, 2022: Congress passes a third continuing resolution, **funding the government through March 11.**

Again, better late than never!

March 11–15: Biden signs the $1.5 trillion budget bill after it passed the Senate, 68–31, and the House, 361–69 (security portion) and 260–171 (nonsecurity portion). Congress also passed a four-day CR to give the president time to sign the bill. The process wasn't completed until nearly halfway through the fiscal year!

?

Critical Thinking

1. **How might the type of "brinkmanship" budgeting** described here—that is, using the threat of a government shutdown to achieve policy goals—affect the economy?
2. **If you were a businessperson trying to decide** whether or not to expand, would the uncertainty created by a threatened shutdown affect your decision?

proposed spending. As we discussed in Chapter 11, reconciliation was crucial in passing the Tax Cuts and Jobs Act in 2017 because it allowed Republicans to avoid a Democratic filibuster. As noted in the How it Works feature, Democrats used reconciliation to pass the $1.9 trillion COVID relief bill in 2021 because the previous Congress has not bothered to even pass a budget resolution.

In response to exploding budget deficits in the early to mid-1980s, which even reconciliation was inadequate to address, an additional mechanism was employed in 1990 to give Congress more traction in managing the deficits: a zero-sum, pay-as-you-go (PAYGO) process whereby any new tax cut or spending increase had to be paid for by raising another tax or cutting spending in some other program. The PAYGO procedure, along with the tax increases in President Clinton's 1993 budget, put the nation on the path for the first budget surpluses since the 1960s. By 1999 the budget was balanced, and in 2000 there was a substantial surplus ($86.3 billion) for the first time in nearly 50 years.[22]

However, the surpluses soon evaporated and massive budget deficits returned in 2002. One major contribution to this explosion in the deficits was that PAYGO was allowed to lapse for the 2002 budget—in part to enable Congress to fund the war in Iraq and the war on terrorism but also to make it politically easier to pass additional tax cuts. Congress reinstated the PAYGO rule in 2007 and made it permanent in 2010. However, there are exemptions in the statutory PAYGO rule for Social Security, interest on the debt, and at least 12 other programs.[23] The rule also has been routinely suspended whenever Congress wants to extend a popular tax cut or pay for emergency spending, such as drought relief, extension of unemployment benefits, or expansion of Medicare and the Children's Health Insurance Program (CHIP).[24] Without the need to pay for tax cuts or spending increases, it has proved too tempting to let the deficits increase to unsustainable levels.

Increased partisan polarization in Congress and differences between Democrats and Republicans in their view of tax and spending policy have made it difficult to pass a budget in a timely fashion. In recent years, Congress has relied on "continuing resolutions," which keep spending at the level of last year's budget, when members cannot agree on a new budget. Even traditionally noncontroversial aspects of fiscal policy, such as increasing the debt ceiling to authorize government borrowing, have become opportunities for partisan politics. And even unified control of government for the first time since 2010 did not make the budget process work more smoothly from 2017 to 2019 for the Republicans or from 2021 to 2023 for the Democrats.

Things really went off the rails at the end of 2018. A continuing resolution provided funding through December 15, so a few days before the deadline the Senate unanimously passed a spending bill. However, it did not include the $5.7 billion President Trump had requested for building the border wall. Facing a veto threat if the bill did not include wall funding, the House did not take up the Senate bill and the government closed all nonessential services on December 15, 2018. When Democrats took control of the House on January 3, 2019, they passed the Senate bill, but the Senate now refused to take up the bill they had passed a few weeks earlier (they had to vote on it again because it was a new session of Congress). The impasse continued until January 25, making it the longest government shutdown in U.S. history. The nonpartisan Congressional Budget Office estimated that the shutdown cost $11 billion in reduced economic growth.[25] Congress eventually passed a spending bill that did not include funding for the wall, but the president declared a national emergency so he could shift spending from other programs, mostly military construction projects, to pay for the wall. This was challenged as a violation of Congress's "power of the purse" under Article I of the Constitution, which says, "No Money shall be drawn from the Treasury but in Consequence of Appropriations made by law." One commentator said this was the most brazen of Trump's norm violations, "the constitutional equivalent of stealing a car parked in front of a police station."[26] Lower courts ruled that Trump's emergency spending was unconstitutional. However, the Supreme Court ruled twice that the president could go ahead and spend the money while the issue was being litigated, without ruling on the underlying constitutional question.[27]

When President Biden took office, he rescinded Trump's $6 billion in emergency spending and restored the spending that Congress had authorized. Given this change in policy, the Supreme Court ruled that the case was moot and canceled a hearing that had been scheduled for March 2021.[28] The Court also ruled that a subsequent lawsuit brought by House Democrats was moot.[29] Supreme Court justices probably breathed a sigh of relief that they wouldn't have to rule on the case, but ultimately they may need to resolve the question of Congress's power of the purse because some Democrats were urging Biden to declare an emergency to be able to spend more money to fight COVID-19 when Congress cut back his $22.5 billion request for additional funds to $10 billion.[30] If the precedent of the president's unilateral power to spend is not explicitly rejected by the Court, other presidents may try the move.

The president

Once they are in office, presidents quickly realize that the public expects them to promote a healthy economy. Indeed, the state of the economy has a big impact on the public's assessment of presidential performance, and it also influences election outcomes. President Obama focused on the economy in his first months in office, pushing through a massive stimulus bill; later, in the face of major unemployment, Obama also signed legislation aimed at creating more jobs. The signature achievement of President Trump's first two years was enacting the $1.5 trillion tax cut, which gave a short-term boost to the economy.[31] The Tax Cuts and Jobs Act of 2017 reduced individual income taxes by more than $1.1 trillion over 10 years, reducing the top marginal rate from 39.6 percent to 37 percent, nearly doubling the standard deduction, and doubling the child tax credit. The law also limited the deductions for state and local income tax, sales tax, and property taxes to $10,000, which raised taxes for some people in states with high taxes. The corporate tax rate was lowered from 35 percent to 21 percent, and a 20 percent deduction on "pass-through income" benefited many small business owners. The law also doubled the value of assets that were exempt from the estate tax.

The impact of the tax cuts was mixed. While analysis of the impact varies, the consensus view is that they had a modest impact on economic growth (about 0.5 percent additional growth in GDP per year from 2018 to 2020) and real disposable income, a strong stock market, and the continued strength of the job market (until the bottom fell out because of the pandemic). However, other effects included a drop in tax revenue from 17.3 percent of GDP in 2017 to 16.2 percent in 2019 (led by a 40 percent drop in corporate tax revenue), which contributed to a trillion-dollar deficit in fiscal year 2019 (before the COVID-19 spending); an increase in income inequality as a disproportionate share of tax benefits went to upper-income people; and most significantly, a substantial drop in business investment, which was counter to the expectations for changes in the tax law that benefited businesses.[32] The last result occurred partly because the trade war created uncertainty but also because large publicly traded corporations chose to repurchase their shares rather than making new investments.[33]

As we discussed in Chapter 12, the president is unable to accomplish much single-handedly on the economic front: Congress, the Fed, and broader domestic and international economic forces all exert an equal or greater influence on the health of

In late 2018, President Trump renegotiated NAFTA, now known as the United States–Mexico–Canada–Agreement (USMCA). President Trump *(center)* signed the agreement alongside President Enrique Peña Nieto of Mexico *(left)* and Prime Minister Justin Trudeau of Canada *(right)*. It went into effect in 2020.

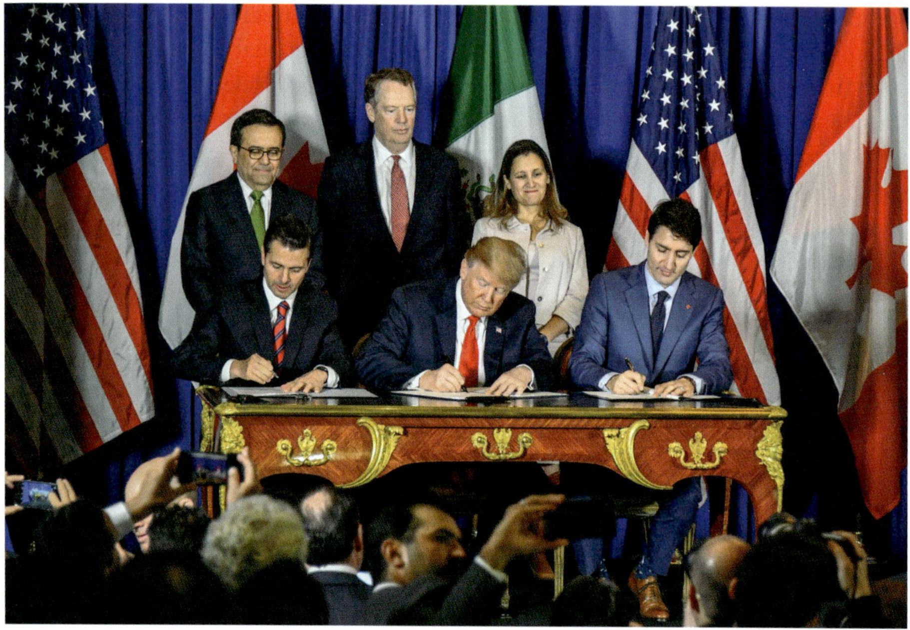

United States Trade Representative (USTR)
An agency founded in 1962 to negotiate with foreign governments to create trade agreements, resolve disputes, and participate in global trade-policy organizations. Treaties negotiated by the USTR must be ratified by the Senate.

National Economic Council (NEC)
A group of economic advisers created in 1993 to work with the president to coordinate economic policy.

the economy. However, the executive branch has a large advising structure that helps the president formulate economic policy. The Office of Management and Budget (OMB), the Council of Economic Advisers (CEA), the Office of the **United States Trade Representative (USTR)**, and the **National Economic Council (NEC)** all provide important economic advice.

The department with the longest track record is the OMB. It plays a central role in creating the budget by soliciting spending requests from all federal agencies, suggesting additional cuts, and then coordinating these requests with presidential priorities. It is ultimately responsible for putting together the president's budget, which is then submitted to Congress. The OMB also oversees government reorganization plans and recommends improvements in departmental operations.

The CEA was created by the Employment Act of 1946. Its central function is to provide the president with objective data on the state of the economy and expert advice on economic policy. The agency is responsible for creating the *Annual Economic Report of the President*, which has a wealth of data on various aspects of the economy and an overview of the president's policies. Presidents have varied in how closely they work with the CEA or the other parts of their economic team. Some prominent CEA members have been influential in shaping and promoting the administration's tax policy and jobs program. Others have had a more secondary role.

The USTR is responsible for developing and coordinating U.S. international trade, commodity, and direct investment policy and for overseeing negotiations on trade policy with other countries.[34] With the increasing importance of globalization and international trade, and Congress's deference to the executive branch on trade issues through the fast-track authority, the USTR is an important player in economic policy making. The fast-track process gives the USTR wide latitude to negotiate trade deals that have to be approved by Congress but cannot be amended or filibustered.

The NEC was established in 1993 to fulfill a campaign promise by President Clinton to elevate economic policy to the level of national security and foreign policy. It has four principal functions: "to coordinate policy-making for domestic and international economic issues, to coordinate economic policy advice for the President, to ensure that policy decisions and programs are consistent with the President's economic goals, and to monitor implementation of the President's economic policy agenda."[35] The NEC coordinates policy by bringing together cabinet secretaries who work on economic issues, such as the Treasury secretary, budget director, Commerce secretary, CEA chairman, and Labor secretary. The NEC initially appeared to challenge the CEA's turf, but a division of labor has preserved an important role for each: the NEC is the political arm that coordinates economic policy, and the CEA is the technical arm that provides information about the economy.

Though we have described the roles of Congress and the president separately, understanding the interactions between these government branches is central to understanding economic policy. If the president's party controls Congress, then the president's budget becomes the starting point for congressional negotiations over the budget. If the opposing party controls Congress, then the president's budget is usually considered "dead on arrival" and Congress creates its own document. But even in 2018, Trump's budget was ignored by congressional leadership, although the president and the leadership belonged to the same party. Biden had better luck in 2021 getting his major priorities of COVID relief and the infrastructure bill passed, but then his Build Back Better bill died early in 2022 (but a scaled-back version of the bill, the Inflation Reduction Act, passed later that year). Of course, the president can use the veto threat to try to move Congress, but when the budget is contained in one large package that must be signed or vetoed in its entirety, it is difficult to carry out such threats.[36]

The bureaucracy

All the departments explained so far could be considered part of the larger bureaucracy, but they are included within the Executive Office of the President and therefore are usually considered in conjunction with the president. Here, we will focus on two bureaucratic agencies that are key in creating monetary policy: the **Federal Reserve System** (an independent agency, commonly known as "the Fed") and the **Treasury Department** (a cabinet-level department). While the Fed and the Treasury are the most important agencies for economic policy making, many other agencies are important for both making regulatory policy (which we discuss later) and implementing spending on a broad range of policies, from agricultural subsidies to building highways to defense spending. All of these bureaucratic decisions have an impact on the economy.

Federal Reserve System
An independent agency that serves as the central bank of the United States to bring stability to the nation's banking system.

Treasury Department
A cabinet-level agency that is responsible for managing the federal government's revenue. It prints currency, collects taxes, and sells government bonds.

The Federal Reserve System The Federal Reserve Act of 1913 established the Federal Reserve System to bring stability and continuity to the nation's banking system. The Federal Reserve Reform Act of 1977 gave the Fed a dual mandate of pursuing stable prices and maximum employment. The chair, vice-chair, and five other governors serve on the **Federal Reserve Board**. The governors have 14-year overlapping terms and are appointed by the president and approved by the Senate. The president selects the chair and vice-chair from the sitting governors for 4-year terms; they may be renominated for additional terms as chair or vice-chair until their terms on the Board of Governors expire. The board is responsible for establishing monetary policy for the nation, which includes influencing interest rates and the money supply, and regulating the lending activity of member banks (discussed in more detail later in the chapter). There are 12 regional Federal Reserve Banks, more than 3,000 member banks, and about 17,000 other depository institutions (which include nonmember commercial banks, savings and loan associations, savings banks, and credit unions).[37]

Federal Reserve Board
The group of seven presidential appointees who govern the Federal Reserve System.

U.S. Federal Reserve chair Jerome Powell testifies before a congressional panel in the midst of the COVID-19 pandemic in 2020, offering insight into how long it will take the U.S. economy to recover from the pandemic-induced recession.

We examine the Fed's operations in the section on monetary policy, but briefly, the regional banks lend money to banks, hold reserves for them, supply currency and coins, buy and sell government securities, and report on the state of the economy in their respective regions.

One crucial characteristic of the Fed is its political independence, which has three primary sources. First, the Fed is an independent agency: though the president and Senate determine who sits on the board of the Fed, its decisions are not subject to presidential or congressional review. Second, the 14-year terms for the governors and the 4-year terms for the chair and vice-chair purposefully do not overlap with the federal election calendar. One strong indication of the Fed's independence is that presidents typically reappoint chairs who were initially appointed by presidents of the other party. For example, Ben Bernanke was nominated by Bush and renominated by Obama for one term.[38] However, Trump broke that tradition by replacing Janet Yellen with Jerome Powell, but then Biden renominated Powell in 2021.[39] Unlike other presidential appointees in the bureaucracy, members of the Federal Reserve Board can be removed only "for cause," the precise definition of which has never been tested. This largely insulates the Fed from the political process.

Third, the Fed does not depend on Congress for its operating budget because it can literally create its own money (as we will discuss later). Congress's control of the bureaucracy is rooted in the power of the purse (see Chapter 13), but because Congress does not provide the Fed's budget, Congress has much less leverage over it. The Fed's primary source of income is interest on the Treasury securities it owns. Typically, the Fed returns a surplus to the Treasury, but in 2023 the Fed had a deficit for the first time ever ($116 billion). Overall, in 2023 the Fed employed 20,790 people with total salaries of $2.9 billion.[40] The employees are not subject to civil service rules or pay grades; thus, the Fed can offer top salaries and hire some of the best people in finance and economics.

Is the Fed's independence a good thing or a bad thing? Supporters point out that the Fed's central goal is shared by nearly all politicians and Americans: a stable economy and slow, steady growth (as mentioned earlier, the Fed has a dual mandate of pursuing stable prices and maximum employment). Therefore, the argument goes, we should leave the Fed alone, let it do its job, and keep politics out of monetary policy. However,

Though the Fed's monetary policy is always aimed at stabilizing the economy and fostering steady growth, markets can still have adverse reactions. When the Fed announced that it would cut interest rates to nearly 0 percent in March 2020 to try to avoid a deepening recession, the S&P 500 index declined 8 percent shortly after the opening bell, triggering a key circuit breaker that halted trading for 15 minutes in an attempt to slow the market's decline.

critics argue that the Fed's lack of accountability means that it can do things that hurt the economy—and voters have no recourse. For example, during Jerome Powell's confirmation hearing in 2017, senators grilled the nominee about the impact of the Fed's policies on the economy. Senator Sherrod Brown (D-OH) worried that the Fed would ease up on enforcing regulations on big banks, saying, "Americans are still struggling because of low wages, underemployment or unemployment and lack of opportunities. And loosening the rules for some of the country's largest banks isn't the way to solve these problems."[41] If the Fed moved in that direction, voters could do nothing about it.

But the Fed is not immune to political influence. In fact, one line of research argues that the Fed tries to help presidents during reelection years by encouraging a pro-growth economy.[42] Evidence on this point is mixed, but at a minimum presidents do have the ability to make it clear when they disagree with the Fed's policies. Presidents also have the opportunity to appoint the chair and vice-chair of the Fed, but presidents usually go for continuity over change because they do not want to upset the financial markets. Other research has shown that the Fed is at least somewhat sensitive to the preferences of the president and Congress, who may publicly criticize the Fed when they disagree with its policies.[43] For example, in the early days of the pandemic, President Trump threatened to demote Powell, saying he was "not happy with the Fed" because it was "following" and "we should be leading."[44] Shortly after these comments, the Fed took more aggressive action to address the economic downturn.

The Fed's ultimate accountability is to Congress, because if things really got out of hand—for example, if the Fed decided to increase interest rates to 20 percent without good reason—Congress could amend the Federal Reserve Act and remove the Fed's responsibility or autonomy in specific areas. The Fed must report to Congress annually on its activities and to the Banking Committees of Congress twice a year on its plans for monetary policy. The Fed's annual report is subject to an outside audit. Fed officials also frequently testify before Congress on a broad range of issues.

The Treasury Department The Treasury Department is another part of the bureaucracy that plays an important role in economic policy making. According to its website, the mission of the Treasury "is to promote the conditions for prosperity and stability in the United States and encourage prosperity and stability in the rest of the world." Specifically, the range of its responsibilities related to economic policy making includes:

- managing federal finances;
- collecting taxes, duties, and monies paid to and due to the United States and paying all bills of the United States;
- producing currency and coinage;
- managing government accounts and the public debt;
- supervising national banks and thrift institutions;
- advising on domestic and international financial, monetary, economic, trade, and tax policy;
- enforcing federal finance and tax laws; and
- investigating and prosecuting tax evaders, counterfeiters, and forgers.[45]

Some of these responsibilities overlap with the Fed's, especially supervising banks and managing the public debt. In most instances the responsibilities are complementary rather than competing, such as the management of currency and coins: the Treasury produces currency at the Bureau of Engraving and Printing (about 3.3 billion bills were printed in 2023) and coins at the U.S. Mint (which made just over 11.4 billion coins in 2023), and the Fed distributes them to member banks.[46] Financing federal debt is another matter. The Treasury generally prefers lower interest rates to keep down the cost of financing the debt and to promote economic growth, whereas the Fed is concerned about keeping rates high enough to avoid inflation. Therefore, the Fed and Treasury must often coordinate their policies to avoid working at cross-purposes. One unanticipated consequence of the COVID-19 recession was an extreme shortage of coins and bills as people stopped circulating cash. The Fed was unable to meet the requests for coins and bills from retailers and banks through much of the summer of 2020, but the situation has largely resolved by 2021.[47]

"Why Should I Care?"

The president, Congress, and the Fed all play an important role in making economic policy. As a citizen and voter, you want our elected leaders to be responsive to our preferences. Yet in the area of economic policy, one of the central players—the Fed—is largely independent from political influence. The Fed is designed this way to make sure that it can make unpopular decisions that may be important for the health of the economy, such as helping to bail out Wall Street during an economic crisis. Political goals and economic goals may not always align, so is the Fed necessary to save us from ourselves, or should there be more democratic control of monetary policy?

EXAMINE HOW FISCAL, MONETARY, REGULATORY, AND TRADE POLICIES INFLUENCE THE ECONOMY

Tools and theories of economic policy

Now that we know the key players in economic policy and their goals, it is time to examine the tools those policy makers use to accomplish those goals. Policy makers cannot pull levers and push buttons to achieve desired outcomes, nor are they immune from external forces that can sink the economy despite their best efforts. However, there are certain things that leaders can do to move the massive U.S. economy in the right direction.

Fiscal policy

Fiscal policy is the use of the government's tax and spending power to influence the direction of the economy. Developed by economist John Maynard Keynes in the 1930s, **Keynesian economics** argues that policy makers can soften the effects of a recession by stimulating the economy when overall demand is low—during a recession, when people aren't spending as much—through tax cuts or increased government spending. Tax cuts put more money in people's pockets, allowing them to spend more than they otherwise would. The government can also inject money into the economy by purchasing various goods, such as highways or military equipment, or by issuing direct payments to individuals, such as unemployment compensation. From this perspective, it is acceptable to run budget deficits to increase employment and national income, which in turn gives a short-term boost to the economy. Keynes also pointed out that if overall demand is too high, which might result in inflation, policy makers should cool off the economy by cutting spending or raising taxes.[48]

Perhaps the best example of a Keynesian tax cut used to stimulate the economy was the Revenue Act of 1964. The tax cut, one of the largest in the twentieth century, helped lay the foundation for unprecedented economic expansion in the 1960s.[49]

A competing theory of fiscal policy was the basis for Ronald Reagan's tax cuts in 1981 and has been the centerpiece of economic policy for many Republicans since then. **Supply-side economics** focuses on the effects of tax policy and regulations on the labor supply (how much people work) rather than their effects on overall demand (how much people spend). The idea is based on the relationship between the top **marginal tax rate** and total tax revenue, a measure of how much people are working (as more people work, more tax revenue is generated), as shown in the Laffer curve, named for economist Arthur Laffer (see Figure 15.3). The basic shape of the curve is intuitive, and the end points are noncontroversial: if the tax rate is zero, there will be no tax revenue; if the tax rate is 100 percent, nobody will work because they won't get to keep any of their money, so total tax revenue at that end of the curve is also zero.[50] Laffer argued that if tax rates are too high (to the right of the peak in the graph), people will work less because a large percentage of their income is going to the government. In this situation, the government should cut taxes in order to raise total government revenue—a claim that seems counterintuitive.[51]

Keynesian economics
The theory that governments should use economic policy, like taxing and spending, to maintain stability in the economy.

supply-side economics
The theory that lower tax rates will stimulate the economy by encouraging people to save, invest, and produce more goods and services.

marginal tax rate
The tax rate paid on income up to some threshold. For example, in 2020 single people paid no income tax on their first $12,200 of income (because of the $12,200 standard deduction). After deductions, they paid 10 percent on the first $9,875 of taxable income; 12 percent on income between $9,876 and $40,125; 22 percent on income between $40,126 and $85,525; and so on, all the way up to 37 percent on income over $518,400.

No nation has ever taxed itself into prosperity.

—Rush Limbaugh, conservative radio host

FIGURE 15.3

The Laffer Curve

The Laffer curve shows the theoretical relationship between the tax rate and total tax revenue. How did this curve contribute to the budget deficits of the 1980s?

Total tax revenue (trillions)
$6
$5
$4
$3
$2
$1
$0
0
25
50
75
100
Tax rate (%)

In practice, this theory was too good to be true. When the Reagan administration cut taxes in 1981, with the top marginal rate going from 70 percent to 50 percent, revenue fell and budget deficits exploded. Supporters of the supply-side theory argued that the problem was on the spending side of the equation rather than on the tax revenue side. That is, deficits went up because the Democratic Congress spent too much, not because of Reagan's tax cuts. However, both tax revenue and government spending as a share of the overall economy fell during the Reagan presidency, which suggests that spending was not the source of the budget deficits in the 1980s.[52] A similar relationship between a cut in tax rates and a decline in revenue was observed after Bush's tax cuts in 2001 and Trump's tax cuts in 2017.[53] The latter are a good example of supply-side thinking because clearly the tax cuts could not be justified on Keynesian grounds, given that the economy was moderately growing and at full employment at the time of the tax cuts.

How Much Can Fiscal Policy Really Affect the Economy? Economists continue to debate the extent to which fiscal policy can influence the economy. Two factors have limited the effectiveness of fiscal policy. First, fiscal policies often cannot be implemented quickly enough to have the intended impact on the **business cycle**—the normal expansion and contraction of the economy. This is especially true when one party controls Congress and the other controls the presidency, but it can also be the case even during unified government.

business cycle
The normal pattern of expansion and contraction of the economy.

The $787 billion American Recovery and Reinvestment Act of 2009, designed to stimulate the economy and create jobs after the 2008 economic crisis, ran into problems along these lines. Although the legislation had a limited immediate impact on the economy, it is impossible to spend that much money (or implement tax cuts) without some time lag. Of the $787 billion total, tax cuts constituted $288 billion; contracts, grants, and loans were $275 billion; and onetime payments to Social Security recipients were $224 billion. One year after the recovery bill was enacted, the government reported that nearly 600,000 jobs had been saved, but only 34.6 percent of the money ($272.2 billion) had been spent. Austerity policies at the state level also blunted the impact of the stimulus; that is, at the same time that the national government was trying to stimulate the economy, states were cutting spending and raising taxes to balance their budgets. Republicans criticized the Democrats, who controlled Congress and the presidency at the time, for spending too much money and not enacting policies that would have had a more immediate effect (such as payroll tax cuts). Critics on the left, meanwhile, argued that the stimulus wasn't big enough. A payroll tax cut was implemented for 2011–2012 that reduced the rate from 6.2 percent to 4.2 percent, putting an additional $1,000 in the pocket of the average American household for each of those years. As discussed in the chapter opener, there was strong bipartisan support for the fiscal stimulus needed to address the economic fallout of the COVID-19 pandemic in March 2020, but then, as the effects of the slowdown lingered, the parties diverged on the direction of additional government spending.

Second, on the other side of the Keynesian coin, tax increases or spending cuts during good economic times are much more difficult to implement than tax cuts or spending increases, which are more politically popular. Although the latter are limited by the difficulty of timing these fiscal policies to have a maximum economic impact, the former are limited by politics: politicians do not like to raise taxes or cut spending. Furthermore, even if politicians *wanted* to cut spending to influence the economy or to reduce the federal deficit, it is becoming increasingly difficult to do so because a growing portion of the federal budget is devoted to **mandatory spending**—that is, entitlements such as Social Security, which must be spent by law, and interest on the federal debt, which must be paid (if the United States defaulted on its debt, there would be an international economic meltdown).

mandatory spending
Expenditures that are required by law, such as the funding for Social Security.

In order for Congress to balance the budget and eliminate the deficit ($1.9 trillion in 2024), it could cut all **discretionary spending**—spending that can be cut from the budget without changing the underlying law—and still be in the hole! Discretionary spending, currently $948 billion in non-defense spending and $849 billion in defense spending, accounts for everything other than entitlements and interest on the debt.[54] This would literally mean shutting down most of the operations of the State Department; Homeland Security; the Department of Defense; the Justice Department, which includes the FBI and all federal law enforcement; and the Interior Department, which includes the National Park Service and the U.S. Forest Service; and eliminating all spending on science, including the National Science Foundation and NASA; transportation; the arts and public broadcasting; student loans; and the SNAP (food stamps) and child nutrition programs. The share of the budget allotted to discretionary spending is projected to fall from 12 percent of GDP in 1970 to only 5.5 percent by 2034 (see Figure 15.4).[55] This has clear implications for efforts to balance the budget in the future: it cannot be done through cutting discretionary spending alone and will have to include cuts in mandatory spending (such as Social Security and Medicare) and tax increases. Indeed, balancing the federal budget is not possible in the near future without causing significant damage to the economy, given the spending cuts and tax increases that would be required.

discretionary spending
Expenditures that can be cut from the budget without changing the underlying law, which is everything other than defense, entitlements, and interest on the debt.

Given the tenuous relationship between fiscal policy and the state of the economy, critics have suggested an alternative rationale to justify large budget deficits in relatively good economic times. (Recall that a Keynesian perspective says that the government should run surpluses during good times, and supply-siders argue that tax cuts should produce surpluses rather than deficits.) Instead of being primarily an effort to stimulate the economy, large tax cuts and budget deficits like those of the 1980s and early 2000s

FIGURE 15.4

Mandatory and Discretionary Spending, 1974–2034

The percentage of the budget allocated for discretionary spending has been shrinking since the 1970s. What implications does this have for members of Congress and the president as they try to reduce the federal deficits?

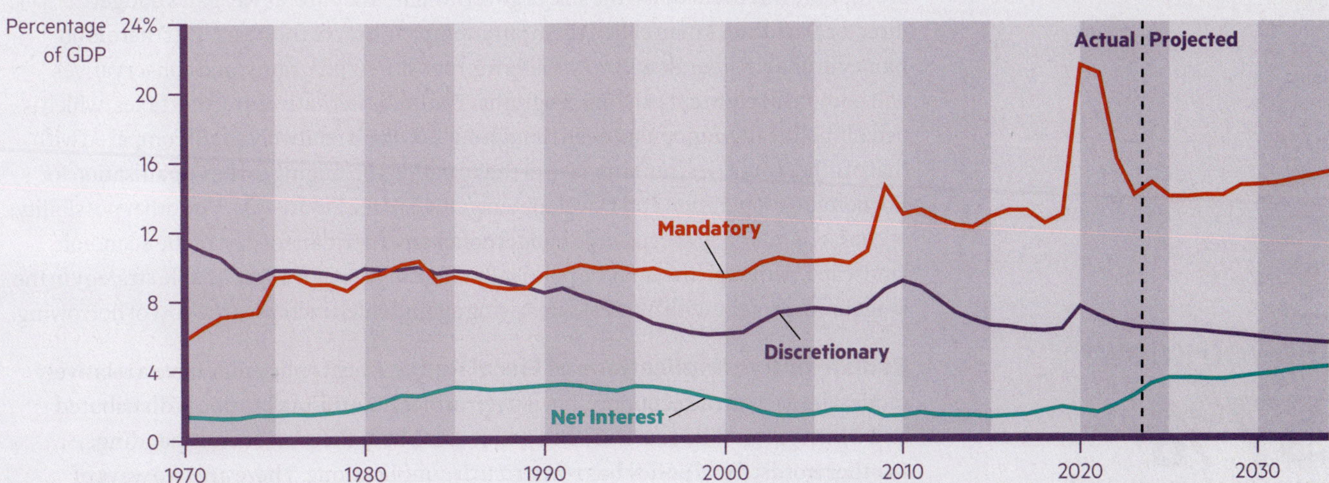

Source: Congressional Budget Office, "An Update to the Budget and Economic Outlook: 2024 to 2034," June 2024, www.cbo.gov/publication/60419 (accessed 8/2/24).

FIGURE
15.5

Comparing Global Tax Rates

Tax rates vary considerably around the world. Given the data in the graph, do you feel that taxes in the United States are too low or too high?

Source: Organisation for Economic Co-operation and Development, "Tax Revenue," 2022, https://data.oecd.org/tax/tax-revenue.htm (accessed 4/22/22).

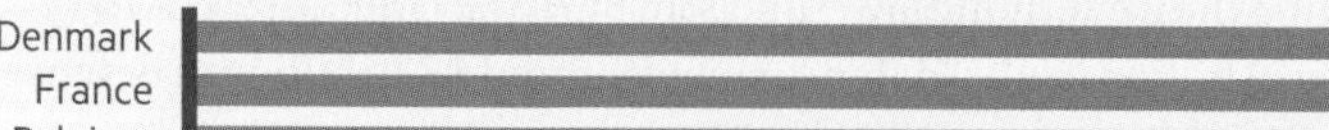

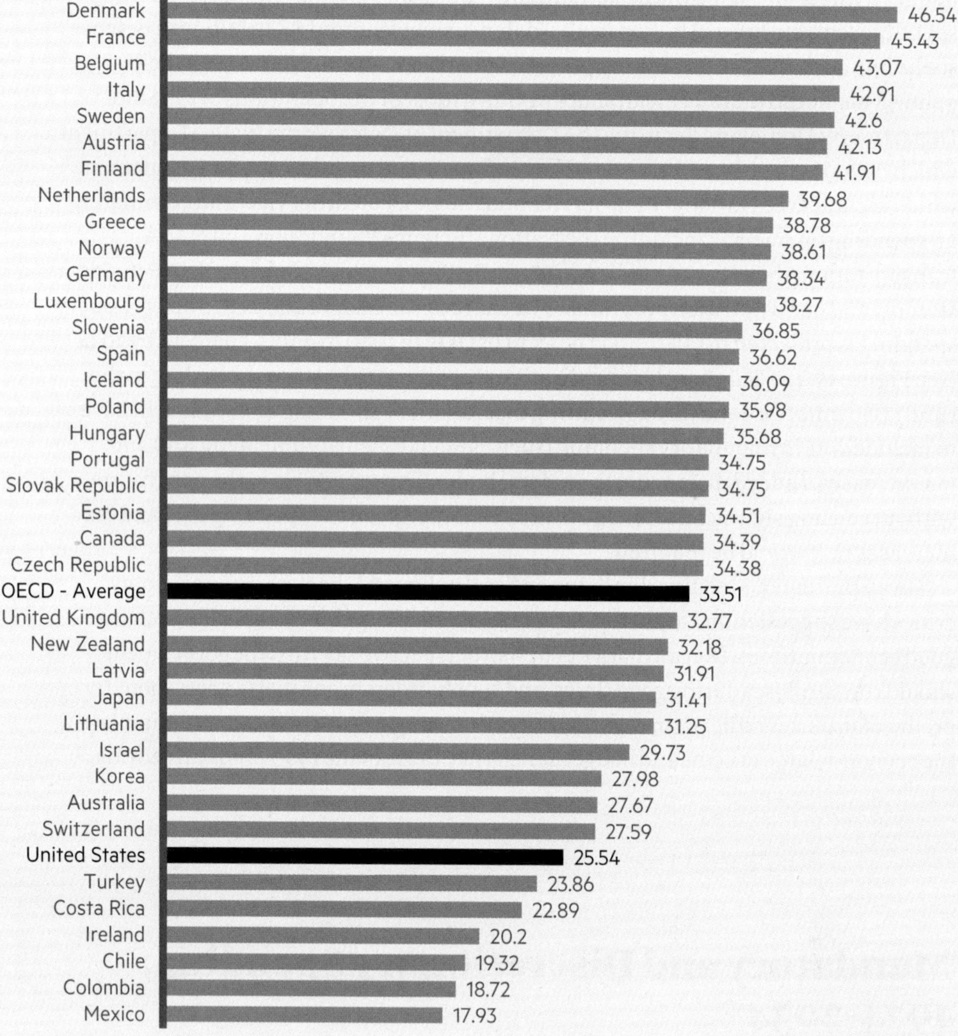

are the only way to cut down the size of government—they are, as Reagan's budget director David Stockman called them, an attempt to "starve the beast."[56] If there is no money available, liberals will not be able to propose new programs, and conservatives will be more likely to cut existing programs. The only alternative is raising taxes, which is usually politically unpopular, even though our tax bite is relatively small compared with that of other countries, ranking 34th of the 39 nations belonging to the Organisation for Economic Co-operation and Development (OECD) (see Figure 15.5). The other possibility, of course, is to simply accept large budget deficits as a permanent part of the economic landscape. Although that may be politically tempting, it is not a sustainable strategy in the long run, especially with interest rates rising again, which increases the cost of borrowing.

Redistributive Implications of Fiscal Policy Fiscal policy may have a relatively modest impact on the economy, but it determines how the tax burden is distributed and which parts of the economy and policy areas benefit from federal spending. In other words, fiscal policy has *redistributive* implications. There are two ways of thinking about the characteristics of federal taxes: (1) the different types of taxes and (2) their redistributive nature—that is, whether a specific tax is regressive, neutral,

DID YOU KNOW?

57%

of Americans pay no federal income tax.

Source: Tax Policy Center.

or progressive. There are four major types of federal taxes: personal income taxes, corporate taxes, payroll taxes (for Social Security and Medicare), and excise taxes (such as taxes on cigarettes, alcohol, gasoline, air travel, and telephone lines). The pie charts in Figure 15.6 show how the distribution of tax revenue changed between 1962 and 2024. The proportion of personal income taxes held relatively steady, but excise taxes and corporate taxes fell and payroll taxes doubled.

FIGURE 15.6

Federal Revenues and Spending, 1962 and 2024

A much larger share of tax revenue comes from payroll taxes than was true in the 1960s. What implications does this have for the redistributive nature of federal taxes? What have been the biggest changes since the 1960s in the way the federal tax dollar is spent? Are these trends likely to reverse or continue in the next 30 years?

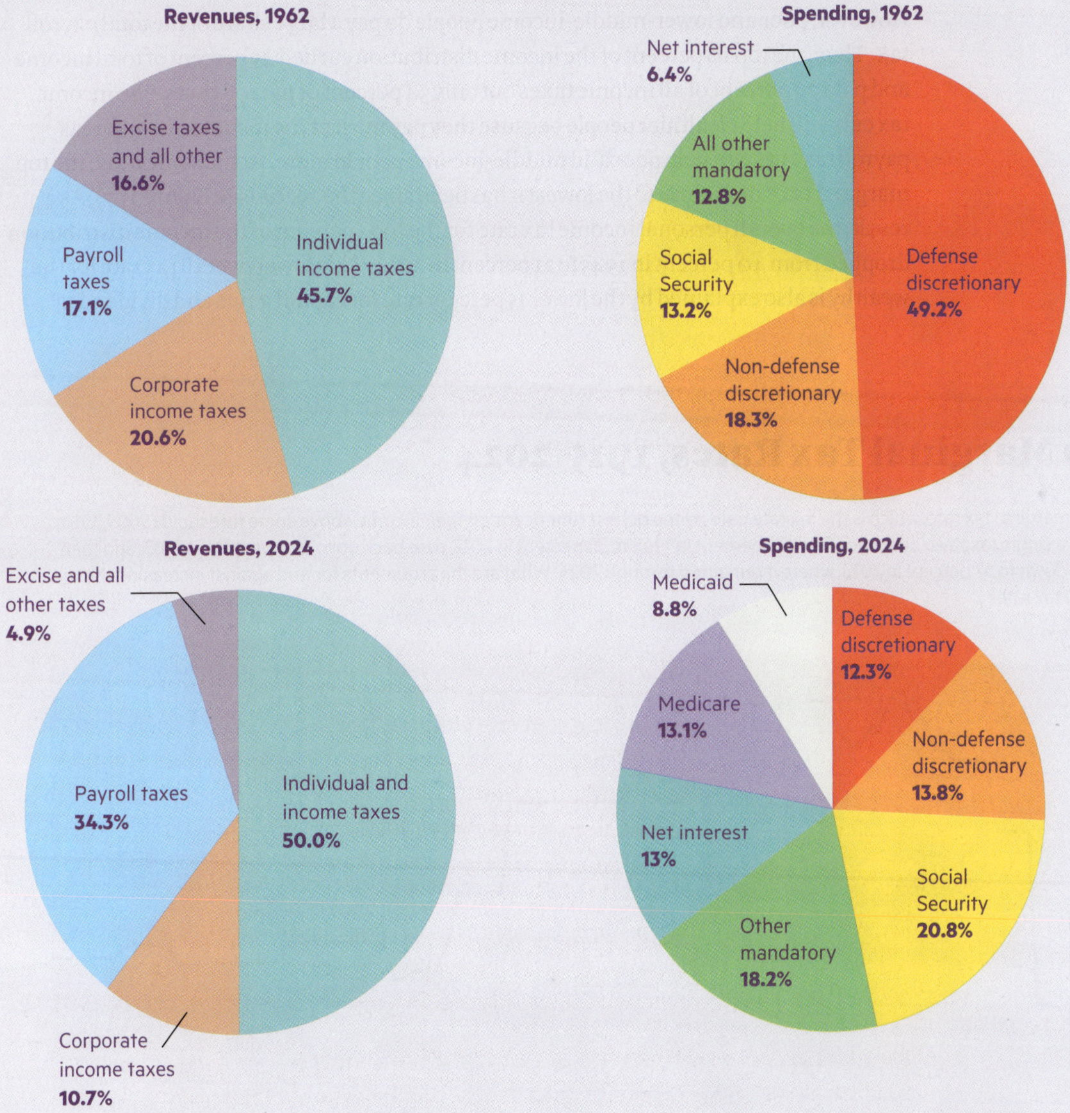

Sources: The Tax Foundation, "Federal Tax Revenue by Source, 1934–2018," Table 2, https://taxfoundation.org/federal-tax-revenue-source-1934-2018/#per; Mindy R. Levit, D. Andrew Austin, and Jeffrey M. Stupak, "Mandatory Spending since 1962," Congressional Research Service, March 18, 2015, https://fas.org/sgp/crs/misc/RL33074.pdf; Congressional Budget Office, "An Update to the Budget and Economic Outlook: 2024 to 2034," June 2024, www.cbo.gov/publication/60419 (accessed 8/2/24).

regressive
Describes taxes that take a larger share of poor people's income than wealthy people's income, such as sales taxes and payroll taxes.

progressive
Describes taxes that require upper-income people to pay a higher tax rate than lower-income people, such as income taxes.

The increasing share of tax revenue that comes from the payroll tax has important implications for the redistributive nature of taxes. Payroll taxes are **regressive** because everyone who works pays the same rate of 6.2 percent, up to a certain income level ($168,600 in 2024; also, all workers pay an additional 1.45 percent on all income to support Medicare). Thus, someone who earns $168,600 pays the same *amount* of Social Security tax ($10,543) as a wealthy individual such as Elon Musk does, but the tax represents a much larger share of the lesser-paid person's income than it does of Musk's. Excise taxes are also regressive—poor people spend a larger portion of their income on cigarettes, alcohol, and gas than wealthier people do. Income taxes, in contrast, are **progressive**: upper-income people pay a larger share of their income in taxes than poorer people do.

One criticism of Donald Trump's tax cut was that a disproportionate share of the cuts went to the wealthiest people in the country, making taxes less progressive. This may make sense from one perspective, given that the bottom 57 percent of taxpayers do not pay any personal income tax because of the standard deduction (which was $29,200 for married couples and $14,600 for individuals in 2024) and the Earned Income Tax Credit. However, poor and lower-middle-income people do pay a large share of the total payroll tax. Thus, the top 10 percent of the income distribution earned 45 percent of total income and paid 79 percent of all income taxes but only 34 percent of payroll taxes.[57] So income tax cuts will help wealthier people because they pay most of the income tax, whereas payroll tax cuts will help poor and middle-income people more. At the same time, the top marginal tax rate is close to the lowest it has been since the 1920s (see Figure 15.7). As a result, the overall personal income tax rate for the top 1 percent of the income distribution dropped from 40 percent in 1945 to 21 percent in 2024. This lower overall tax rate for the wealthy is also explained by the lower 15 percent rate for capital gains and dividends.[58]

FIGURE 15.7

Top Marginal Tax Rates, 1915–2024

The top marginal tax rate, which is the tax rate paid by the richest Americans on their income above some threshold ($609,351 in 2024 for a single taxpayer), declined from 94 percent in 1945 to 35 percent in 2012, rose back up to 39.6 percent in 2013, and then fell back down to 37 percent in 2018, where it remained through 2024. What are the arguments for and against increasing the top marginal tax rate?

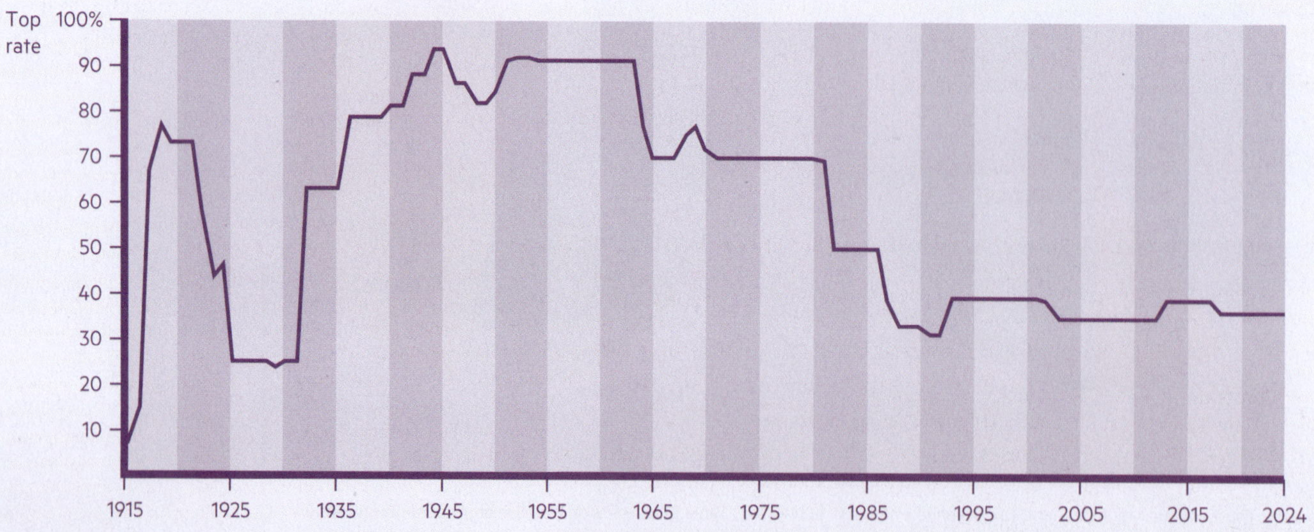

Sources: Data from the Internal Revenue Service, "SOI Tax Stats–Historical Table 23," www.irs.gov/statistics/soi-tax-stats-historical-table-23 (accessed 7/5/22); 2008–2024 rates from www.irs.gov (accessed 08/5/24).

Monetary policy

What is money? You probably think that you know what the green stuff in your wallet is. You may wish you had more of it, but you know what it is. But money is much more than bills and coins. You probably pay for more things with plastic (debit and credit cards) than with coins and currency. Are those cards "money" as well? Economists categorize debit cards as money because debit cards represent the money you already have in your checking account—which *is* the same as cash. Credit cards are not considered money because when you use a credit card you are, in essence, getting a short-term loan. Broader definitions of money also include savings accounts and certificates of deposit. So far, so good. The tricky part involves understanding where money comes from. The answer may seem simple: the government prints it. But what about the banking part? If you've never thought this through, it can be confusing or even unsettling.

It is well enough that people of the nation do not understand our banking and monetary system, for if they did, I believe there would be a revolution before tomorrow morning.

—Henry Ford, founder of Ford Motor Company

Consider this example: You have just graduated from college and you want to start your own business as a political consultant. You have volunteered on several campaigns and have even run a few statewide campaigns. Two candidates want to hire you for the next election cycle, but you need to rent an office and buy computers, phones, and other office equipment. This will obviously take some money. So you go to a bank with your business proposal and show them your contracts for the coming election and your plan for repaying the $100,000 loan that you are requesting. To your surprise, the loan officer says yes and you leave the bank with a checkbook and debit card $100,000 strong! The bank just created $100,000, seemingly out of thin air.[59] How can that be? Doesn't money have to be something more tangible? Doesn't it have to be based on gold or other real assets rather than just a contractual promise to repay the money? No—at least not in this country. In 1933, the United States nationalized privately held gold and said that contracts must be paid in dollars, not gold; then, in 1971 the country completely abandoned the gold standard. Why doesn't the whole system fall apart? Because it is based on trust and confidence in the banking system. After you receive your loan from the bank, you could go directly to the computer store and purchase $10,000 worth of computers with your new debit card. And because your debit card purchase will be electronically authorized at the cash register, the sales staff will have no reason to ask where your money came from. They would just give you the computers.

Most people rarely think about how the banking system works, simply assuming that their money is safe. But now that we have gotten you thinking about where money comes from, we will provide more details about the banking system by examining the targets and tools of monetary policy.

In the late nineteenth century, presidential candidate William Jennings Bryan railed against the burdensome "cross of gold" and argued for a silver-backed currency. But since 1971, the value of the U.S. dollar depends not on gold or silver but on the banking system and international currency markets.

Targets of Monetary Policy The Fed monitors levels of bank lending, the money supply, and interest rates and tries to meet specific targets in each of these three categories set at its monthly meetings. Bank lending is important to monitor and regulate because it is the source of most new money in the economy. It is crucial for economic growth because businesses borrow money to expand, and as they grow they add jobs. If credit is tight and businesses cannot borrow money, economic growth will suffer, as became painfully evident in late 2008 and 2009. Large public corporations can raise money to expand by selling shares of their company in the stock market, but small businesses do not have this option.

The money supply is also central to economic growth and directly related to levels of lending activity. The Fed can influence the amount of money in the system by making

monetarist theory
The idea that the amount of money in circulation (the money supply) is the primary influence on economic activity and inflation.

it easier or harder for banks to lend money. According to the **monetarist theory** of macroeconomic policy, the amount of money in circulation is the most important determinant of economic activity and inflation. If there is too much money chasing too few goods, there could be inflationary pressure on the economy and prices might rise too quickly.[60] In contrast, if there isn't enough money available, a recession could occur.

Perhaps the most obvious targets of monetary policy are interest rates. Changing interest rates affects the economy by making borrowing money either cheaper or more expensive. Businesses and consumers are more likely to borrow if the interest rate is 5 percent than if it is 10 percent. Consumer purchases of big-ticket items—things that are financed by borrowing rather than being purchased with cash—also increase when interest rates are low. These purchases dry up when interest rates are high. That is why so many appliance stores and car dealers advertise: "Zero dollars down, and zero percent interest until next January!" Entire sectors of the economy, such as housing, construction, consumer durables (such as appliances), and cars, are very sensitive to interest rates.

reserve requirement
The minimum amount of money that a bank is required to have on hand to back up its assets.

Tools of Monetary Policy What can the Fed do to meet targets it sets on credit availability, the money supply, and interest rates? It uses three central tools of monetary policy. The first tool, the **reserve requirement**, is the most obvious and potentially powerful tool for affecting the availability of credit, but it isn't used as often as the other two tools. Banks are required to have a certain amount of money in reserve to make sure they have cash on hand to cover withdrawals. By simply changing the amount of money that banks are required to hold for every deposit, the Fed can have a big impact on the amount of money that banks can lend. For example, requiring banks to hold 15 percent of all deposits in reserve instead of 10 percent would contract the amount of money those institutions could lend, whereas dropping the requirement to 5 percent would have the opposite effect. However, because changing the reserve requirement has such a powerful impact on the economy, the Fed has rarely used this tool.[61] But in March 2020, in response to the massive unemployment caused by the COVID-19 pandemic, the Fed dropped the reserve requirement to zero for the first time in the nation's history. The rate had been unchanged since 1992, when it was reduced from 12 percent to 10 percent. *Forbes* published an article headlined "The Fed Fires 'the Big One,'" along with a picture of a mushroom cloud, indicating the dramatic nature of the move.[62] As of late fall 2024, the requirement was still at zero.

discount rate
The interest rate that a bank must pay on a short-term loan from the Federal Reserve Bank.

federal funds rate (FFR)
The interest rate that a bank must pay on an overnight loan from another bank.

The second monetary-policy tool, interest rates, is more difficult to manage than the reserve requirement. With the reserve requirement, the Fed simply announces the change in the rate. With interest rates, there is only one rate—the **discount rate**—that the Fed sets directly. This is the rate that the Fed charges member banks for short-term loans. However, it is far less important as a policy tool than the **federal funds rate (FFR)**, the rate that member banks charge one another on overnight loans, which are short-term loans that banks use to meet their reserve requirements. Beginning in 1995, the FFR has been the central interest rate target for the Fed.[63] The FFR is set by the demand for overnight loans that are necessary to settle accounts, but the Fed greatly affects those rates.

To make this process clearer, let's go back to our example of the enterprising campaign consultant who got the $100,000 loan. If the bank that provided the loan also had some unexpected withdrawals during that business day, its "vault cash" at the end of the day may have been short of the 10 percent reserve requirement (or in the current extremely unusual environment, the amount of cash necessary to meet the needs of regular withdrawals). The bank would have to go to the federal funds market and borrow money from a bank that had excess reserves on that given day. This process of borrowing and lending allows money to flow smoothly throughout the banking system. If reserves are tight all around the country, the FFR will rise. If this happens, the Fed can inject more reserves into the system to keep the FFR at its target (we will explain how in the next section). The FFR has a broad impact on the economy because many short-term interest rates track the FFR quite closely. Despite the Fed's ability to influence short-term interest rates, it has only an indirect impact on long-term interest rates, including consumer rates such as mortgages, car loans, and student loans. Long-term rates are set by the market—specifically by the expectations of the bond market for inflation. If an investor thinks that inflation will increase from 8 percent to 10 percent over the next five years, the investor will demand a higher interest rate for lending their money to the government or a corporation than if the investor thinks inflation will hold steady at about 8 percent or fall to a more normal level of 3 or 4 percent. For example, the interest rate for a 30-year home mortgage increased from about 3 percent at the end of 2021 to almost 8 percent by late 2023, as the markets anticipated that the Fed would raise interest rates to cool down the economy and fight inflation. Over that same time the FFR increased from 0.08 percent to 5.3 percent.[64]

The third tool that the Fed uses to meet its monetary targets is **open market operations**—the buying and selling of securities. This is the Fed's most important tool because it influences the FFR and the level of bank reserves and thus the money supply. If the Fed wants to increase the money supply and put downward pressure on the FFR, it will purchase securities such as government bonds from a bank. The bank gives the Fed its bonds, and the Fed deposits the appropriate amount of money into the bank's account at the Fed. The bank can use this money to support new loans.

open market operations
The process by which the Federal Reserve System buys and sells securities to influence the money supply.

Where does the Fed get its money to buy the bonds from the bank? Well, the Fed simply creates the money. You probably have heard the claim that if the government wanted to, it could just "print money" to pay for its programs and policies. That claim is literally true, but it would be completely irresponsible. Any government that would run the printing presses to pay for its programs, rather than raising the money through taxes, fees, and borrowing, would soon find itself with hyperinflation, as experienced in Germany, Poland, Austria, and Hungary after World War I. (The worst inflation ever recorded was in Hungary after World War II: between July 1945 and August 1946, prices rose by a factor of 30,000,000,000,000,000,000,000,000,000!)[65] Our government prints money only to meet the demand for currency from its member banks. However, the Fed's purchase of a government security is like "printing money" and has the same potential inflationary impact, so this powerful tool must be used only when new money is needed in the system. The tool may also be used to contract the money supply or raise interest rates; if this is the desired outcome, the Fed will sell government securities. The member bank will give the Fed money to cover the cost of the bond and therefore take money out of circulation.

Hyperinflation in Germany, Hungary, and other parts of Europe between the two world wars was so high that some countries' currency became essentially worthless. In Germany in 1923, it was cheaper to burn money than to buy wood, as this woman demonstrates—using several million deutsche marks as kindling.

In 2008, the supply of new money in the economy was significantly limited as a result of the subprime mortgage market meltdown and related problems in the bond markets. Fed chair Ben Bernanke responded to this "credit crunch" by "flooding the street with money," just as the famous banker Benjamin Strong had advocated as the appropriate response to the Great Depression.[66] The Fed increased its assets from $927 billion on September 10, 2008, to what seemed like an eye-popping $2.26 trillion by November 11, 2008. Assets held by the Fed, mostly government securities and mortgage-backed securities, peaked at $4.5 trillion in October 2015 and then fell a bit until the record-breaking purchase of assets starting in March 2020. The Fed's balance sheet increased another *$4.5 trillion* to just under $9 trillion on April 13, 2022![67] Starting in June, the Fed started to shrink its balance sheet by selling some assets at a rate of 47.5 billion a month. These unprecedented interventions in the financial sector clearly prevented more serious crises and deeper recessions, but as noted, critics argue that the Fed has become a too powerful, unaccountable player in economic policy making.

Regulatory policy

DID YOU KNOW?

The Fed owns

$4.4 trillion

in U.S. Treasury securities, which is 2.3 times as much as the U.S. debt owned by China and Japan combined.

Source: FederalReserve.gov.

Government regulation has a huge impact on the economy. For example, the federal government regulates the quality of food and water, the safety of workplaces and airspaces, and the integrity of the banking and finance system. In general, regulations address market failures such as monopolies, imperfect information, and negative externalities (which we'll discuss later in the chapter). There are two main types of regulation: economic and social. Economic regulation sets prices or conditions for entry of firms into an industry, whereas social regulation addresses issues of quality and safety.[68]

Economic and Social Regulation A common type of economic regulation concerns price regulation of monopolies. A monopoly occurs when a single firm controls the entire market for a product and thus is not subject to competition. In this situation, the firm with the monopoly could charge extremely high prices if the government did not regulate it. Sometimes a "natural monopoly" occurs because getting into a specific business is so costly that it makes sense to have only one company. For example, to have more than one water company in a given town or city would not make sense because it costs so much to install water pipes and other necessary infrastructure. Though in this instance there is only one company, the government regulates the prices that the company can charge; alternatively, the water system may be owned by the local government.

When the competitive situation is not a natural monopoly, a large firm may act in a monopolistic way to restrict competition—for example, by slashing prices to drive the competition out of business. As soon as all competitors go out of business, the monopoly is free to raise prices again. Concern about this type of behavior led to the first two significant laws aimed at economic regulation: the Interstate Commerce Act (1887), which created the Interstate Commerce Commission to regulate railroad rates, and the Sherman Antitrust Act (1890), which served to break up Standard Oil in 1910, among other monopolies.

More common than a true monopoly is a firm that controls most but not all of a market and thus starts acting like a monopoly. In such cases, the government will try to make sure that free market forces continue to operate and the monopoly-like companies cannot jack up prices. For example, in 1998 Microsoft was sued by the Justice Department and 19 states for trying to quash its competition in the rapidly growing area of Internet browsers. After the case bounced around in the federal courts for six years, Microsoft agreed to share its application programming interfaces

Government regulation affects many aspects of our lives. Regulations may be aimed at producing a cleaner environment *(left)* or preventing monopolies. In 2020, executives from large technology firms Meta (formerly Facebook), Apple, Google, and Amazon testified before Congress (virtually, during the COVID-19 pandemic) about their market power. At right, Amazon founder Jeff Bezos testifies about possible antitrust violations.

with third-party companies to make sure it did not have an unfair advantage in the software market.[69] In a more recent similar case, the European Union fined Google three different times: first, $2.7 billion in 2017 for illegally steering users toward its comparative shopping site; then, $5 billion in 2018 for forcing Android phones to install the Google search app and the Chrome Web browser; and finally, $1.7 billion in 2019 for using its online advertising to limit its rivals from working with companies that had deals with Google.[70]

The Microsoft and Google examples offer two lessons. First, regulation affects our daily lives in ways that may not be obvious. The extent to which a company can dominate the software industry is determined, in part, by the extent to which the government regulates the company's behavior. Second, politics plays a key role in this process. An important event in the Microsoft case was the election of a president who took a less aggressive stance on regulating potential monopolies than his predecessor had. Recall that Republicans tend to favor a strong role for the free market and advocate a pro-business perspective, which both require a smaller role for government regulation, whereas Democrats generally favor more government regulation to protect the interests of consumers (in the Microsoft case, these interests would have led to a broader range of options for Internet browsers), the environment, and workers.

The most common market failures that lead to social regulation are negative externalities: they occur when the costs of a firm's behavior are not entirely borne by the firm and are passed on to other people. When this happens, the firm produces more of an unwanted good than is socially desirable. The classic example is pollution. In a free market, the owners of a coal-fired power plant do not bear the cost of the pollution spewing out of its smokestacks. The people who live downwind from the plant bear the cost. Therefore, the power plant owners have little incentive to curb pollution unless a government agency, like the Environmental Protection Agency (EPA), regulates it. Other examples of agencies that set social regulations are those that promote safety, such as the National Highway Traffic Safety Administration, the Consumer Product Safety Commission, and the Occupational Safety and Health Administration. Carbon emissions are another good example of a product (carbon) that would be overproduced by the market if there were no regulations.

Externalities may also be positive. For example, firms invest in research and development, but the knowledge and products that come from that R&D may have broader social benefits (such as developing a new drug that cures a disease). Goods with positive externalities may be *under*-produced by the free market unless firms are given economic incentives to invest in them. One important policy tool to address positive externalities is a patent. Patents are exclusive "property rights" that are given for a specific period of time to an inventor or company that develops a new product. The money to be gained from holding these rights provides an incentive to invest in developing innovative technology and ideas. In 2021, the U.S. Patent Office granted 327,798 patents in response to the 650,654 applications it received.[71]

The Politics of Regulation Regulatory policy also involves interbranch politics between Congress and the bureaucracy. Even when members of Congress agree on some general policy goal—for example, limiting air pollution—they often cannot agree on the precise mechanisms for achieving that goal, so they delegate authority to a regulatory agency. As discussed in Chapter 13, this produces a "principal–agent problem" in which Congress (the principal) cannot be sure that the bureaucracy (the agent) will implement policy according to its legislative goals. A related concern is that the regulatory agency will not be responsive to the wishes of Congress because it has been "captured" by the interests it is supposed to regulate (see Chapter 13). The Food and Drug Administration, the Federal Aviation Administration, and the

U.S. Department of Agriculture, among others, have been accused of serving the very industries they are supposed to regulate, rather than protecting American consumers.[72]

Another area in which regulatory policy has generated some political heat concerns the trade-off between regulation and economic growth. Regulations impose costs on the free market, which may limit job growth. The Trump administration moved aggressively to limit regulations and allow the free market to make more decisions. Some of the significant actions to reduce regulation included pulling out of the Paris Agreement on climate change, revising the fuel-efficiency regulations for cars and light trucks, weakening Obama-era limits on planet-warming carbon dioxide emissions from power plants, repealing the Clean Power Plan, opening the Arctic National Wildlife Refuge for oil production, dismantling parts of the Dodd-Frank Act in order to impose fewer regulations on smaller banks, and dropping the Clinton-era policy of "once in, always in" that aimed to lock in reductions of hazardous air pollution from industrial sources. More than one-third of all rules issued by non-independent agencies were reviewed, even when they did not have an economic impact (which is a significant departure from previous administrations). At least 100 regulations were eliminated or revised. According to the former head of the EPA, Scott Pruitt, these actions have saved businesses over $1 billion, but critics are concerned about the long-term damage to the environment.[73] Joe Biden has reinstated many of these rules in 2021–2022.[74]

Despite these recent moves to tackle the trade-off between regulation and economic growth by favoring free market policies, in recent years another approach to economic policy has attempted to address the trade-off by using the free market to further environmental goals. First, economists have long argued for introducing more market incentives and reducing government regulation to achieve environmental goals. Under cap and trade, the government sets an overall cap on carbon emissions, and then companies buy permits that allow them to emit a certain amount of carbon. Companies that reduce their carbon emissions can sell their permits to companies that want to emit more carbon. The benefit of this approach is that it uses market forces, rather than regulations, to find the best way to reduce carbon emissions. Launched in 2013, California's cap-and-trade program has been called "the best-designed program in the world" and is expected to reduce carbon emissions by more than 16 percent between 2013 and 2020, and by an additional 40 percent by 2030.[75] In cases like this, environmentalists have learned that using market principles can work to their advantage; another example, involving grazing rights in the West, is discussed in the Take a Stand feature.

Second, rather than simply regulating old sources of dirtier energy, an alternative is to promote a clean-energy economy or "green jobs" focused on biofuels, hybrid and electric cars, hydrogen fuel cells, and renewable energy sources such as solar and wind. Barack Obama promised to create 5 million green jobs and laid out a plan to invest $150 billion over 10 years. Those goals were not fully funded, nor was the target reached, but green jobs are a growth area. The Bureau of Labor Statistics (BLS) provided the first count of green jobs in 2009: 2.2 million jobs. By 2011 that had grown to 3.4 million jobs, but the BLS stopped collecting this information because of budget cuts.[76] However, other estimates reveal that green jobs continue to grow. One study found that the U.S. green economy generates $1.3 trillion in annual revenue and creates 9.5 million full-time jobs. Another study estimated that 67 million new jobs would be created in the world's green economy by 2030.[77]

So while political debates over regulatory policy may still be quite intense, common ground may be found in pursuing market solutions to regulatory problems. In general, the public interest is often served by regulations that protect the environment, ensure

TAKE A STAND

Fighting Climate Change with Market Forces or Regulation

There is no serious scientific dispute today that climate change is real and that global warming must be limited or the planet is in serious trouble. However, there are intense policy debates over the best path to reduce global warming. The 2021 UN Climate Change Conference of the Parties (COP26), involving 120 world leaders and 40,000 participants, set goals of keeping average temperatures no more than 2°C above preindustrial levels (with 1.5°C "within reach") and net-zero carbon emissions by 2050.[a]

Significant policy changes would be required in the United States to meet those goals. President Biden pledged to cut carbon emissions by 50 percent below 2005 levels by 2030 and included $550 billion in his Build Back Better bill for clean energy tax incentives and spending for recharging stations for electric cars. But that legislation was killed in the Senate. In addition to these policies, market forces and/or new regulations will be required.

Using market forces to fight climate change The easiest way to reach the COP26 goals is to make carbon-based energy more expensive and let market forces do the rest. There are two main methods of carbon pricing: "cap and trade" and a carbon tax. The former, described in more detail in the text, pushes utilities toward alternative energy and away from coal and natural gas in the production of electricity. A carbon tax is just what it sounds like—a tax on any carbon-based energy. More than 40 nations have some form of carbon pricing. However, the average increase in the price of carbon from these policies has only been $2 a ton, well short of the estimated $75 a ton (in 2030) that would be needed to reach the 2°C warming target.

Of course, the problem with this approach is that nobody likes tax increases and a $75 per ton carbon tax would double the price of electricity generated by coal, while natural gas (used for heating and cooking in many homes, in addition to electricity production) would go up by about 70 percent, and the price of gasoline would go up by 5 to 15 percent.[b] Supporters of this approach point out that some of the revenue raised from the carbon tax could be returned to people as tax rebates, while encouraging consumers and producers of energy to shift to green sources.

President Biden was among 120 world leaders at COP26 tackling the issue of global warming.

Regulatory approach The other main approach to reduce carbon emissions is through regulation. COP26 focused on regulations to limit deforestation, methane emissions, car emissions, and coal production. In the United States, there are a broad range of laws that regulate vehicle fuel economy, oil and natural gas systems, solid waste landfills, and greenhouse gas standards and promote increased energy efficiency in homes, schools, and federal buildings (for example, banning incandescent lightbulbs and adopting LED or compact fluorescent bulbs and installing more energy-efficient windows, and better insulation).[c]

In 2007, the Supreme Court explicitly recognized the Environmental Protection Agency's power to regulate greenhouse gases as air pollutants under the Clean Air Act. But in 2022, that power was questioned when the Supreme Court ruled that the Environmental Protection Agency cannot put state-level caps on carbon emissions, stating in its decision that such authority would steer states away from coal and toward other types of power sources that emit less carbon.[d]

take a stand

1. Do you think the market-based approach or a regulatory approach to reduce carbon emissions would be more effective? Why?
2. Opposition to either approach will be intense from the stakeholders impacted by the changes. What approaches could political leaders take to overcome the opposition?

the safety of the food supply, and regulate the dumping of hazardous chemicals, whether it is through traditional economic regulations or market approaches. In each instance, *politics* ends up defining how the public interest is served through regulation.

Trade policy and the balance of payments

Many of the factors that shape trade policy are beyond policy makers' control. It is extremely difficult for the U.S. government to influence the strength of the dollar relative to other currencies, consumer tastes, the low cost of labor in developing nations (especially China and India), and economic conditions worldwide—all issues that influence the trade balance. As such, strategies aimed at influencing trade can be considered the most difficult area of economic policy making.

Exchange Rates, Consumer Tastes, and Labor Costs The first factor influencing trade and the balance of payment is the relative value of currencies. However, there isn't much the government can do about the value of the dollar because that value is determined by international currency markets. When the dollar is strong, imports are relatively cheap to consumers in the United States and U.S. exports are expensive to consumers in other countries. Therefore, if the United States is running a trade deficit—importing more than it is exporting—it would like the value of the dollar to fall in the hopes that this would increase the sales of U.S. products abroad.

How does the value of the dollar affect the trade deficit? Consider the following example. As of August 2024, a dollar was worth 0.92 euro. Therefore, a BMW 330i that would sell for 40,000 euros in Germany would go for about $43,478 in the United States, whereas a Cadillac XT4 that would retail in America for $45,000 would sell for 41,400 euros in Europe—although this example doesn't factor in shipping costs, dealer incentives, higher taxes in Europe, and so on.

Next, see what happens if the dollar falls in value: now you can only get 0.70 euro for a dollar instead of 0.92. Now that Cadillac could be purchased in Germany for 31,500 euros and the BMW would still cost 40,000 euros, while the BMW would cost an American consumer $57,143 and the Cadillac would still cost $45,000. Nothing has changed except the value of the dollar, but suddenly the car buyer's choices have changed dramatically. In both countries, the Cadillac has become a much better bargain, and therefore, theoretically, Cadillac sales (and sales of other GM models, as well as those of Chrysler, Tesla, and Ford) should increase and BMW (and Mercedes, Volkswagen, Fiat, MINI Cooper, and so on) sales should fall.

We say "theoretically" because in the real world, car manufacturers do not pass along every price change based on currency fluctuations to consumers. But over time, changes in the value of the dollar will affect the prices of imports and exports. Also, the second factor that influences trade—consumer tastes—can blunt the impact of a weaker dollar. If consumers are willing to pay an increasing premium for foreign goods, then a weaker dollar may not help the trade deficit. There isn't much policy makers can do about consumer tastes, despite the ongoing campaign urging citizens to "buy American." Even with President Trump's campaign pledges to "Make America Great Again" and the focus on restoring American jobs, there is little evidence that this political talk has influenced consumer tastes or broad market forces.

The low cost of labor is a third factor affecting the trade balance that policy makers cannot do much to influence. If a foreign firm pays its workers a daily wage that is equal to what American workers earn in a single hour for the same job, the foreign firm has a huge competitive advantage. Consequently, the United States has been flooded with cheap consumer goods from nations where labor is very cheap. Low prices are good for American consumers, but they come at the price of large trade deficits and lost American jobs. The final factor—the strength of foreign economies—is also outside the control of American policy makers. If foreign economies are weak, consumers abroad do not have the income to purchase U.S. exports.

Trade Policy and Trade Deficits Although it is difficult to control trade outcomes because exchange rates, consumer tastes, and labor costs in other countries are all largely outside the control of policy makers, Congress and the president still try by altering trade policies. The main target of trade policy is the trade balance, which is defined as the difference between the total value of our exports and imports of goods. In recent years, the balances have reached record deficits, exceeding $830 billion a year in 2008 and reaching just over $1 trillion in 2021 to 2023. At the same time, the United States has consistently run a trade surplus in services of between $250 billion and $300 billion in recent years (see Figure 15.8). The current account deficit, the broadest measure of the balance of payments including investments, has also been running at record levels. Economists have warned that deficits of this level are not sustainable. There is increasing consensus that something must change—either we need to stop buying as many imports and sell more exports or the value of the dollar must fall to help make this happen.

The trade deficits have to be financed with borrowing from overseas. In the past, these loans came largely from foreign investment by private individuals who saw greater returns on their investments in the United States than in other countries.

DID YOU KNOW?

The United States exported

$354 billion

in goods to Canada in 2023 (more than any other country) and imported the most from Mexico ($475 billion, with China second at $427 billion, and Canada third at $419 billion).

Source: United States Census Bureau.

FIGURE 15.8

Trade Deficits, 1990–2023

The trade deficit remains high. Which groups are most likely to support policies aimed at reducing the trade deficit, and which groups would oppose these policies?

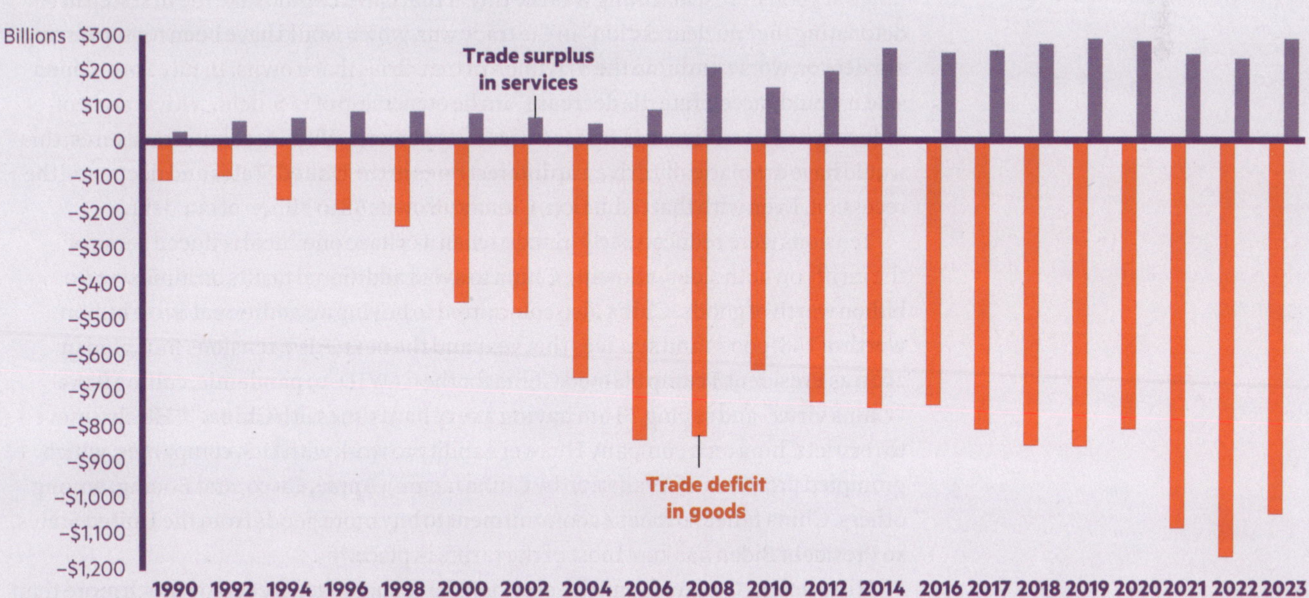

Note: Totals are calculated on a balance of payment basis.

Source: Data from Bureau of Economic Analysis, "International Trade in Goods and Services," www.bea.gov/data/intl-trade-investment/international-trade-goods-and-services (accessed 8/5/24).

The net international investment position in August 2024 was –$21.3 trillion (that is, the value of foreign investments in the United States exceeded the value of U.S. investments abroad).[78] Foreign investors now own about 29 percent of our publicly owned government debt, with Japan and China owning about a quarter of that foreign debt.[79] Why does this matter? If foreign governments decide to stop investing in treasury securities or to start selling them, interest rates will have to rise, perhaps dramatically, to attract buyers for our debt.

To reduce the trade deficit, people in government may support protectionist policies such as trade sanctions, tariffs, and quotas, or attempt to reduce the value of the dollar. Advocates for protectionist policies argue that "free trade" is a myth and we are being taken advantage of by nations that engage in unfair trade practices while selling goods in our open markets. The late senator Ernest F. Hollings once said, "We hear those in the national Congress running around saying, 'Free trade, free trade, I am for free trade,' when they know free trade is like dry water. There is no such thing."[80] Donald Trump focused on this issue in the 2016 campaign, arguing that the United States is getting "ripped off," "absolutely crushed," and "killed" on trade with China, Japan, and Mexico and continued to make it a central issue throughout his presidency.[81] It is only fair, protectionist proponents argue, that we set up trade barriers or impose quotas to support our own goods and protect American jobs. Although broadly based protectionist policies have been rare in the past couple of decades, U.S. policy makers have applied protection in selected markets. For example, in September 2009 President Obama imposed a 35 percent tariff on Chinese tires. And President Trump imposed steel and aluminum tariffs in 2017, battled with European allies over everything from cheese to cars, and kept tensions high with Mexico and Canada over renegotiating the North American Free Trade Agreement (NAFTA). The latter was successfully resolved with a new United States-Mexico-Canada Agreement (USMCA) that received some concessions from Mexico and Canada (especially for the auto and dairy industries) and was generally viewed as a pro-free-trade deal. However, the trade war with China deepened in 2018, with three new rounds of tariffs on more than $500 billion worth of goods from China. The trade war intensified through 2019 as both sides slapped steeper tariffs on a broader range of goods. Most alarming was the threat that China would take the first step in detonating the "nuclear option" in the trade war, which would have been to stop buying our debt or, worse, to dump the $1 trillion in treasuries that it owns. In July 2019, China said it would "accelerate the decrease" in the ownership of U.S. debt, with a target of reducing its $1.1 trillion in U.S. treasuries by 25 percent. Without countermeasures, this would have dramatically driven up interest rates in the United States and deepened the recession. Even with that reduction, China still owns $810 billion of our debt.

Tensions were reduced early in 2020 when a "phase one" deal reduced some of the tariffs on both sides, allowing China to avoid additional tariffs on almost $160 billion worth of goods. China also committed to buying an additional $200 billion worth of U.S. goods and services that year and the next. Also, tensions mounted in 2020 as President Trump blamed China for the COVID-19 pandemic, calling it the "China virus" and saying, "I am having a very hard time with China."[82] He also moved to restrict China tech company Huawei's ability to work with U.S. companies, which prompted promises of retaliation by China (again), Apple, Cisco, and Boeing, among others. China failed to meet its commitment to buy more goods from the United States, so President Biden has kept most of the tariffs in place.[83]

Historically, Congress and the president have supported free trade much more than protectionism. Economists have long touted the virtues of exploiting "comparative advantage" through free trade. In 1817 David Ricardo was the first to develop this notion with the example of the production of wine and cloth in Portugal and Britain.[84] According to the argument, Portugal should produce excess wine and export it to

Britain because that is where Portugal's greatest *relative* advantage lies. Even if it seems counterintuitive, Britain should produce excess cloth and export it in exchange for the wine, even if Portugal can produce cloth more cheaply than Britain. By focusing on this comparative advantage, free trade maximizes wealth in both countries.[85]

Congress has pursued free-trade policies through NAFTA (1993), the Uruguay round of the General Agreement on Tariffs and Trade (1994), fast-track authorization for the USTR to negotiate trade agreements with minimal congressional interference (2002), most-favored-nation trading status for China (2000), and the Central American Free Trade Agreement (CAFTA, 2005), which reduced barriers and opened markets. The Trans-Pacific Partnership (TPP) with 11 nations in the Asia-Pacific region was signed on February 4, 2016, but President Trump pulled out of TPP early in 2017. As noted earlier, Trump also renegotiated NAFTA to gain concession from Mexico and Canada in important areas for trade, such as the auto and dairy industries. Critics of the free-trade laws say that they do not provide adequate protections for workers and the environment, promoting a "race to the bottom" to cut costs while putting additional pressure on American jobs and wages.

The impact of free-trade agreements on American jobs and wages varies widely, with estimates ranging from 1 million to 4 million jobs lost in the past 20 years. Supporters of the law point out that even when some jobs have been lost, the overall economy has benefited; one study found that for every job lost because of NAFTA, $450,000 was added to the economy in the form of higher productivity and lower consumer prices.[86] Also, some of these jobs would have been lost even without the trade agreements, even in areas in which the United States was thought to have a comparative advantage, such as computer programming. When programmers or computer customer support staff in India earn about one-tenth of what they make in the United States, it is difficult for American firms to compete in international markets unless they employ cheaper labor.[87] This downward pressure on wages has contributed to income inequality in the United States, and competitive pressures have led to the virtual extinction of some U.S. industries, such as the manufacturing of consumer electronics, textiles, shoes, and, increasingly, clothing. Thus, while free trade generally enhances worldwide economic growth, there can be significant consequences for specific industries. However, as has become increasing clear from the lengthy trade war with China, protectionist policies have even higher costs—disrupted supply chains, slower economic growth, and the devastating impact on affected sectors such as farm commodities.[88]

The Politics of Trade Policy With stakes this high, it is not surprising that politics often plays a central role in trade policy. There are two main explanations for the nature of political influence on trade policy: constituency and ideology.[89] The constituency explanation sees the two major parties as representing different groups—Democrats representing labor, Republicans representing capital—which tends to make the Democrats more protectionist and the Republicans more supportive of free trade. Though the constituency explanation is generally true, there are divisions within each constituency. For example, autoworkers' and steelworkers' unions are much more protectionist than dockworkers' unions because any industry with strong exports will support free trade, whereas those that have relatively few exports but are vulnerable to cheap imports are more likely to be protectionist. The ideological explanation focuses on the bipartisan consensus on trade that emerged after the Great Depression, which was seen as having been caused in part by the protective tariffs of the 1930 Smoot-Hawley Act.[90] As with the theories of regulation, both perspectives explain part of the truth. Our political leaders largely support a free-trade ideology (with the obvious exception of the Trump presidency), but there are divisions along constituency lines on some legislation.

Putting it all together: the 2008–2009 economic crisis and the 2020 COVID-19 recession

The Economic Crisis One example of dramatic intervention in the economy is the 2008 economic crisis. Problems in the subprime, or high-risk, mortgage market; the collapse of housing prices; and the tightening of credit markets had been putting pressure on the economy through the spring and summer of 2008. The first sign of serious trouble came in March, when the New York Federal Reserve loaned $30 billion to JPMorgan Chase to facilitate the buyout of Bear Stearns, an investment bank that was going bankrupt because of its exposure to mortgage-backed securities. Over the next six months, several of the nation's largest financial institutions, such as investment bank Merrill Lynch and the world's largest insurance company, American International Group (AIG), had to be bailed out by the federal government. When investment bank Lehman Brothers went bankrupt and Washington Mutual, the nation's sixth-largest bank, failed, the markets panicked.

This series of disasters and near disasters led to around-the-clock meetings of Fed and Treasury leaders, who produced a plan for the government to buy mortgage-related assets from banks and other financial institutions. A month before the election, Congress passed the Troubled Asset Relief Program (TARP) to buy up to $700 billion in bad assets to help stabilize the banks. Despite this significant rescue plan, the crisis spiraled out of control in the following weeks. Stock markets plunged worldwide, with the U.S. stock market shedding 35 percent of its value in the two months after the crisis began. Credit markets remained frozen, and it became clear that an alternative approach was needed. European leaders swiftly agreed to an approach in which governments would directly invest in banks, providing them with desperately needed capital in return for equity stakes in the banks. The United States followed suit with an initial allocation of $250 billion to directly invest in banks, followed by an announcement that the Treasury would abandon its plan to buy toxic debt created by the subprime mortgage mess and use all the funds to directly invest in banks. By mid-November, the economic panic had eased, but the situation remained fragile.

During the financial crisis of 2008–2009, the government had to take unprecedented action to avoid an even deeper crisis. Here, then–Senate Majority Leader Harry Reid (D-NV, *center*) speaks to reporters. He is joined by other congressional leaders and Ben Bernanke *(far right)*, who was Federal Reserve chairman at the time.

When President Obama took office in 2009, things were still very grim. Congress acted quickly to pass the Recovery Act, which allocated $831 billion over 10 years, roughly split among tax cuts, federal spending, and support for state and local governments.[91] Stocks finally bottomed in March 2009 (down 56 percent from their October 2007 high), shortly after Treasury Secretary Timothy Geithner announced the administration's Financial Stability Plan. The plan focused on four problems: frozen credit markets, weakened bank capital, a backlog of troubled mortgage assets on bank balance sheets, and falling home prices. Working with the Fed to stabilize the financial markets, the Treasury had largely resolved three of those four problems one year later. Credit markets were operating, and banks were in much better shape, having raised more than $140 billion in capital and $60 billion in unsecured debt. Banks used these funds to repay the Treasury. The final expenditures for the TARP programs were $31.1 billion, which is only 4.3 percent of the originally authorized $700 billion.[92] The housing market has also stabilized, with sales up and prices slowly rising in most markets. Troubled mortgage assets remain on the balance sheets of many banks, but with their stronger base of capital and the strengthened housing market, these securities were not as great a concern as they had been.[93] In September 2012, the Fed announced a new policy to inject money into the economy, promising to buy $40 billion a month of mortgage-backed securities. Three months later, this policy was increased to $85 billion a month. This was an open-ended commitment and was seen as the boldest move yet by the Fed to revive the economy. Overall, the Fed increased its balance sheet from just over $900 billion when the crisis began to just over $4.5 trillion when the balance sheet peaked in October 2015 (see Figure 15.9). Thus, the Fed injected more than $3.6 trillion into the economy.[94]

Despite the broad success of the financial rescue, it remained a political liability. The rescue was widely perceived as a bailout of Wall Street. Many citizens were outraged

The Fed Balance Sheet

FIGURE 15.9

The amount of assets held by the Fed in mortgage-backed securities expanded after the 2008 financial crisis and then again with the COVID-19 pandemic. What effect does increasing the balance sheet have on the circulation of the dollar?

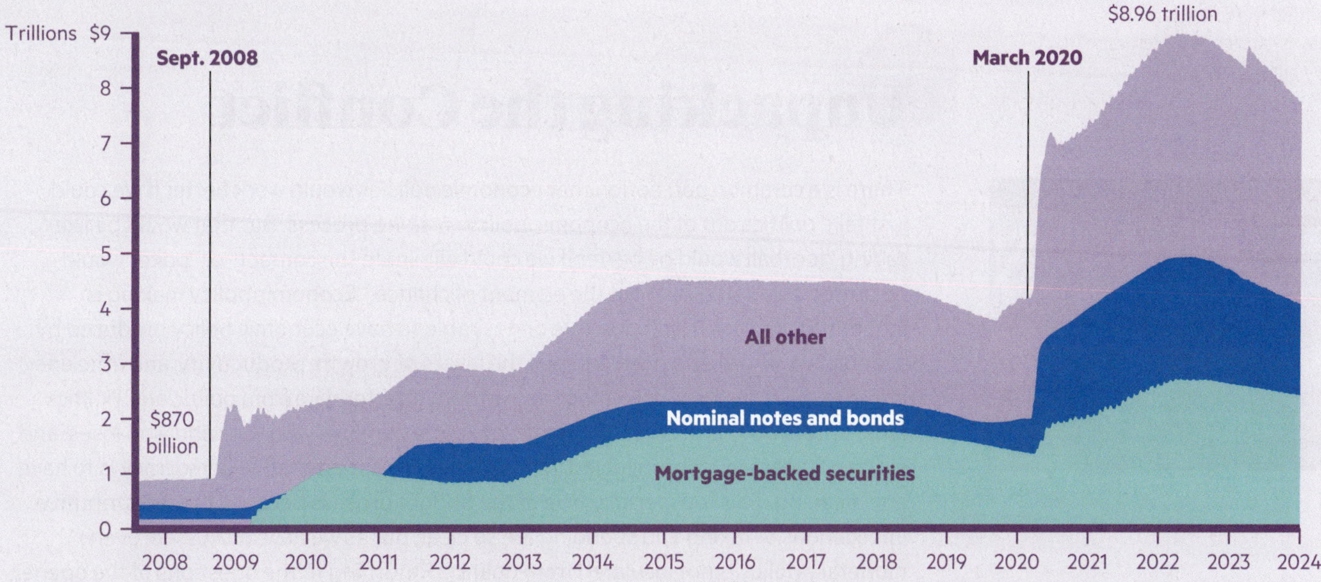

Source: Federal Reserve (U.S.), "Economic Data," Federal Reserve of St. Louis, https://fred.stlouisfed.org/graph/?g=D4ft#0 (accessed 10/5/22).

Protesters at a rally against government bailouts for Wall Street called for the resignation of the chief executive of Goldman Sachs and cancellation of bonuses for all Goldman employees. Huge profits and bonuses on Wall Street in 2009–2010 were very controversial, as the national unemployment rate held at nearly 10 percent.

over corporate salaries and bonuses, the government bailouts, and the perception that not enough was being done to help average Americans. While these are legitimate concerns, the overall response of the Bush and Obama administrations was a textbook example of the use of fiscal policy (the 2008 TARP law and the 2009 Recovery Act) and monetary policy (the various actions by the Fed and Treasury to stabilize the banks) to address an economic crisis.

The COVID-19 Recession The CARES Act and the American Rescue Plan Act discussed in the chapter opener are other great examples of fiscal stimulus: when businesses were shutting down, workers were laid off, and millions of people were having a hard time paying their bills, Congress pumped trillions of dollars into the economy. But as with the 2008–2009 recession, Congress needed help from the Treasury and Fed to provide the needed stimulus. For example, the Paycheck Protection Program provided forgivable loans to small businesses to maintain their payroll and hire back employees, and this was supported by a lending facility from the Fed.[95]

Despite this fiscal stimulus, financial markets were disrupted due to economic uncertainty. The Fed responded with aggressive action to buy Treasury securities (increasing their balance sheet to an eye-popping $9 trillion by April 2022), stabilizing financial markets, and supporting the flow of credit in the economy while keeping the federal funds rate close to zero.[96] As we noted above, the Fed is now starting to unwind its balance sheet and raise interest rates, recognizing that the economy has heated up too much with unemployment at record lows and inflation at the highest levels in 40 years.

"Why Should I Care?"

Tax and spending policy, monetary policy, regulatory policy, and trade have more effect on your everyday life than anything else the government does. From the taxes you pay, to the interest rate on your student loan, to the quality of the air you breathe and the water you drink, to the cheap consumer goods that you are able to buy, decisions by policy makers have a tremendous effect on your economic world.

Unpacking the Conflict

There is a common perception that economic policies would work better if we could just take politics out of the economic policy–making process. But that would be like saying "football would be better if we could eliminate the contact" or "poker would be better if we could take out the element of chance." Economic policy making is inherently political. It isn't possible or desirable to have economic policy produced by economists who would push and pull the levers of growth, productivity, and efficiency, implementing their economic theories without interference from politicians. Politics must enter into this process. Economic policy determines who wins and who loses, and elected leaders must be involved in this process if representative democracy is to have any meaning. This is especially true of the budget process because the redistributive implications of taxing and spending are so clear, but as we have discussed, even monetary policy is not insulated from politics. Returning to the questions of the opener, how much should the government do to support the economy during an economic crisis, like that brought on by the coronavirus pandemic in 2020? More generally, what is the proper role of the government in a free market economy? How do political players deal with the conflict that is inherent in economic policy making?

Both economic theory and history tell us that we are better off with free markets than with an economy in which politicians pick the winners and losers. However, there is still clearly a role for the government in the economy through regulations, tax and spending policy, and monetary policy, especially during times of economic crisis. Having the government in the economy means that politics must have a role in economic policy making. In fact, this is guaranteed by our system of checks and balances: Congress, the president, and to some extent the courts all have a hand in shaping economic policy. The clash between politics and economic theory and the conflicted nature of economic policy making can be illustrated with a few examples.

We discussed earlier the limitation of implementing Keynesian economic theories in fiscal policy. Often political considerations make it impossible to implement the swift, targeted action called for in the theory. That is because the budget inherently involves debates over some central political questions: How large should the government be? How progressive should the income tax be? Should we impose tariffs on our trading partners to try to get them to change their trade policies? Should budget deficits be allowed to expand to put pressure on government spending, rather than to stimulate the economy? These are not purely economic questions but also political ones that must be answered through debate and conflict between the opposing parties and branches of government.

These questions have been central in the disputes over how the government responds to an economic downturn, as discussed with respect to the COVID-19 recession in the chapter opener. There was a strong bipartisan consensus that a robust response was needed to both the 2008 crisis and the COVID-19 recession: the 2008 TARP bill passed with a centrist bipartisan coalition, and the CARES Act had nearly unanimous support. However, the 2009 Recovery Act had no Republican support in the House, and only three Republican senators voted for it. Additional funding to battle the COVID-19 recession in 2021 and 2022 divided along partisan lines.

These examples are not intended to suggest that politics shouldn't enter into the economic policy–making process. Indeed, just the opposite. They are excellent illustrations of the themes that politics is everywhere and politics is conflictual. It shouldn't be surprising when politics enters the economic policy debate. Elected leaders should be responsive to what their constituents think about the central questions concerning the direction of the economy.

"What's Your Take?"

How often should the government intervene in the economy, if ever?

Do the complexity and fragility of the economy make intervention here and there necessary?

CHECK YOUR UNDERSTANDING

"Why Should I Care?"

Compared with many topics in American government, it probably won't take too much to convince you that you should care about economic policy making. The state of the economy almost always ranks as the number one concern in election-year polls. And as the saying goes, "nothing is certain except death and taxes"—everyone has to help pay for our government programs, whether it is through income, sales, payroll, or property taxes. As you head toward graduation in a few years, you almost certainly would like to have a strong economy in which to conduct your job search.

While it may be self-evident that you should care about the state of the economy, it may not be as obvious how government policy influences the direction of the economy. This chapter has provided you with a basic understanding of the goals of economic policy making, the players who make the policy, and the tools they use. As you hear stories about the Fed increasing interest rates, understand these issues, while seeming remote, impact your daily life, from the health of the job market to the interest you'll pay on a mortgage if you want to purchase a house.

But the crucial point in the context of a class on American government is that the decisions about economic policy are inherently *political*. Economic policies are redistributive, determining winners and losers, so those decisions should be controlled by politics. Making sure that your voice is heard in the political process is more likely if you have a good understanding of how that process works, which includes the formation of fiscal, monetary, regulatory, and trade policy.

1. What is one of the greatest drivers of the persistent budget deficits and borrowing by the national government?

- **a** The dichotomy of Americans wanting low taxes and sustained or increasing programs and benefits
- **b** Government shutdowns and the use of continuing resolutions to fund the government
- **c** Disproportionate funding of foreign aid compared with other government spending items
- **d** Decreased value of the dollar due to inflation and foreign competition which have made repayment of debt more problematic

2. The United States consistently ranks as one of the nations with the highest levels of income inequality in the world, primarily because of which characteristic of the American economic structure?

- **a** Redistributive tax policies enacted in the New Deal and Great Society programs of Presidents Franklin Roosevelt and Lyndon Johnson
- **b** Limited government regulation of the free market system
- **c** The incentives among states to provide the fewest services for the public
- **d** Tools used by international organizations to measure inequity that do not capture the diversity income levels in the American population

3. Congress is charged with setting taxes and creating the national budget but has faced persistent problems in achieving these goals in recent history. What is the best way to explain why the U.S. Senate has increasingly used the budget reconciliation process to pass fiscal policy priorities like the Tax Cuts and Jobs Act of 2017 and the 2022 Inflation Reduction Act?

- **a** Congress granted presidents the power to annually propose fiscal policies to Congress using the budget reconciliation process during annual budget considerations.
- **b** The Supreme Court ruled that the budget reconciliation process is a specialized power covered by the taxing and spending powers of Congress in the Constitution.
- **c** Budget reconciliation does not require senators to have 60 votes to overcome a minority party filibuster to pass legislation.
- **d** Congress may use the budget reconciliation process to reallocate funds to meet needs at the end of the year when bureaucratic agencies have unspent balances left in their budgets.

4. The president relies on many people and groups, like the U.S. trade representative, the Council of Economic Advisors, the National Economic Council, and the Office of Management and Budget, for advice and policy proposals when considering what economic policies should be given priority by the administration. If a president was considering creating a trade agreement with the African Economic Community, which advisory groups would the president need to involve in structuring the deal and calculating the likely costs and benefits of such an agreement for the U.S. economy?

- **a** U.S. trade representative and the Office of Management and Budget
- **b** U.S. ambassador to the United Nations and the Council of Economic Advisors
- **c** Office of Management and Budget and the National Economic Council
- **d** Congressional Budget Office and the U.S. trade representative

5. Which of the following is an example of using Keynesian economic theory to deal with a recession or a slowing economy?

- **a** In a slowing economy, the government will raise interest rates to try to encourage the public to save and slow down the rate of spending.
- **b** Government spending increases, even if it grows the deficit, to make more money available to the public and encourage consumer demand.
- **c** During a recession, the Federal Reserve and Department of the Treasury encourage Congress to cut discretionary spending to decrease budget deficits and stabilize the economy.
- **d** The government is most likely to make decisions that devalue the dollar in order to increase the costs of goods and services to require that more money be spent by consumers.

6. While cutting the spending of the national government is a much more popular idea with the public than raising taxes to deal with budget deficits, it is increasingly more difficult to make cuts that would have any significant impact. Why?

- **a** The growing influence of interest groups has made it nearly impossible for public officials to cut any spending in the government.
- **b** Falling wages and increased income inequality have created less revenue for the government, making it more difficult to argue for increasing taxes or cutting services.
- **c** Increased spending on foreign aid, the military, and border security have created new mandatory spending obligations.
- **d** The growing number of Americans entitled to Social Security and Medicare along with the increasing cost of interest on the national debt are areas that cannot be cut.

Use INQUIZITIVE to help you study and master this material.

16

Social Policy

What should be the role of the government in providing the social safety net?

"We essentially repealed Obamacare because we got rid of the individual mandate . . . and that was a primary source of funding of Obamacare."[1]
President Donald Trump

"Overall, this change will be disruptive, but not terminal. It certainly does not 'essentially repeal' Obamacare. We rate Trump's claim False."[2]
PolitiFact

President Obama signed the Patient Protection and Affordable Care Act ("Obamacare") into law on March 30, 2010. This comprehensive and historic health care reform legislation was the culmination of a 15-month partisan struggle in Congress. The law provides subsidized health insurance to most Americans who don't have insurance, while preventing health insurance companies from dropping sick policy holders or refusing to cover people with preexisting conditions.

Health care reform was controversial from the start. As public opposition grew, it became clear that the votes for health care reform would have to come from within the Democratic Party. Indeed, the final version of the bill passed without any Republican support. Republicans cried foul because Democratic leaders used the reconciliation process in an unorthodox way to avoid a filibuster in the Senate (the process is typically used for budget-related issues, not for passing substantive policy).

The day after the law went into effect, House Republicans introduced a bill to repeal it. After regaining control of the House in the 2010 midterms, House Republicans voted 62 times over the next six years to repeal or change part of Obamacare, including 6 times to repeal the entire law.[3] Of course, Senate Democrats were having none of it and ignored the House's efforts. These conflicting views came to a head in the fall of 2013 when House Republicans tied approval of the annual budget to repealing Obamacare. Democrats viewed this as blackmail and refused to negotiate, while Republicans argued that the public was on their side as polls showed that most Americans did not approve of Obamacare. This disagreement led to a shutdown of all nonessential federal government services from October 1

Social policies can be complicated, conflictual, and personal, though few issues have been as contentious as health care reform. The political process used to tackle these conflicts is often tedious, complex, and time-consuming.

CHAPTER GOALS

Explain what we mean by social policy and how the national government's role in social policy has evolved (pp. 621–625)

Examine the problem of poverty as a target of social policies (pp. 625–629)

Describe the roles played by each branch of the national government and by the states in making and implementing social policy (pp. 629–633)

Trace the steps through which problems are addressed by social policies (pp. 634–639)

Analyze the current major areas of social policy (pp. 639–658) to 16, 2013. The White House estimated that the shutdown cost the economy about 120,000 jobs and between $2 and $6 billion.[4] While Obamacare remained unpopular, most Americans rejected the confrontational tactics and blamed House Republicans for the shutdown.[5]

When Donald Trump was elected in 2016 and Republicans had unified control of the government, they had the opportunity to repeal and replace Obamacare. However, with no agreed-upon plan to replace the law, repeal failed by a single vote in the Senate in 2017. While Republicans were unable to repeal the law, they enacted several measures weakening the law, hoping to slowly kill it off. They eliminated the unpopular individual mandate tax penalty for individuals who do not have health insurance, cut the ACA's advertising budget by 90 percent, shortened the open-enrollment period from three months to six weeks a year, and reduced funds for personal enrollment assistance by 41 percent.[6]

Despite these efforts, and contrary to President Trump's claim that his administration had "essentially repealed" Obamacare, by the end of Trump's presidency more than 27 million Americans had gained health insurance coverage because of the law (an increase of about 700,000 between 2016 and 2020). Perhaps most surprising was that enrollment in the health care exchanges only dropped by 442,000 during Trump's presidency, despite the 50 percent shorter enrollment period and the lack of advertising promoting the enrollment.[7] While the number of people with insurance because of Obamacare increased slightly during Trump's presidency, the percentage of uninsured increased from 8.6 percent in early 2016 to 10.3 percent by the end of 2020 (this was down to 8 percent in 2023).[8]

The ACA is proving to be resilient as enrollments in the health care exchanges and overall coverage of the law hit record highs early in 2024 at 21.4 million and 45 million, respectively, dropping the uninsured rate to a near record low of 8.8 percent.[9] The gains were driven by President Biden's reversing several of Trump's executive orders aimed at limiting the ACA[10] and increased subsidies provided by the American Rescue Plan Act of 2021 for insurance purchased in 2021 and 2022 on the health insurance exchanges.[11] While Americans have had a more favorable than unfavorable view of the ACA since 2017 (in May 2024, 62 percent had a favorable view and 37 percent unfavorable), a deep partisan divide remains: 87 percent of Democrats view the law favorably, while 66 percent of Republicans view it unfavorably (Independents were 65 percent favorable).[12]

Is this how social policy works? A contentious battle in which neither side is satisfied with the outcome (many Democrats wanted even broader health care coverage, while most Republicans wanted to repeal Obamacare)? Although the level of conflict around the ACA is unusual in American politics, trade-offs between social policy and other government priorities often produce political conflict. More money for health insurance subsidies, Social Security, Medicare, nutritional assistance programs, and welfare means less money for highways, the military, or development of alternative energy. These trade-offs become especially acute as the population ages, requiring an increasing share of federal spending to go to Social Security and Medicare. The trade-offs must be resolved through a political process filled with conflict and compromise.

One of the biggest challenges Americans face today is how to make sense of all the claims they hear about public policy. Is Social Security going bankrupt, and will it therefore not pay the current generation of young Americans any benefits when they retire? Does the government spend too much money on nutritional assistance programs and welfare, or are these important tools for reducing inequality? More fundamentally, does the government have a responsibility to provide a "social safety net" for its citizens, or should more of that be left to the private sector and charitable organizations? This chapter will help answer these important questions by discussing the evolution of social policy in the United States, outlining the conditions that create

The disagreements over social policy run deep. Conflicts over "Trumpcare," the proposed replacement to Obamacare, led to the legislative failure of any repeal or replacement of the ACA.

the need for social policies, describing the key players in the social policy–making process, and explaining the status of key social policies today and the efforts to reform them. We begin with the historical background of social policy.

The roots and goals of social policy

EXPLAIN WHAT WE MEAN BY SOCIAL POLICY AND HOW THE NATIONAL GOVERNMENT'S ROLE IN SOCIAL POLICY HAS EVOLVED

Social policy is generally defined in terms of the "social safety net," or **welfare**, which is financial or other assistance provided to individuals by the government, usually based on need. A broader conception of social policy includes government programs aimed at achieving some general social goal, such as programs that support public education, the income tax deduction for interest paid on home mortgages (to encourage home ownership), or policies designed to promote job creation and growth. This chapter will address both types of social policies and discuss how some traditional social welfare programs, such as Social Security, are not based on need. First, we'll outline the evolution of social policy in the United States and describe various types of social policy (see Nuts & Bolts 16.1 on p. 622).

social policy
An area of public policy related to maintaining or enhancing the well-being of individuals.

welfare
Financial or other assistance provided to individuals by the government, usually based on need.

Early social-policy efforts

Early in our nation's history, the federal government took little responsibility for social welfare. Private charities, churches, and families largely took care of the poor and disadvantaged. The first significant social policy appeared in the nineteenth century in the form of federal financial support for Civil War veterans and their families. Between 1880 and 1910, the national government spent more than a quarter of its budget on Civil War pensions and support for veterans' widows. Other than interest on the debt, this was a larger share of the budget than any other single item and a greater percentage of federal spending than today's expenditure on Social Security.[13] (Today we spend more than one-fifth of our budget on Social Security, but, of course, the overall budget was

NUTS & BOLTS 16.1

Types of Social Policy

1. **Contributory** (or social insurance) programs include Social Security, Medicare, disability insurance, and unemployment compensation.
   - Programs are similar to insurance programs in that people pay a specified amount of money to cover some future benefit (either expected, as with the programs related to retirement, or unexpected, as with disability and unemployment).
   - Programs are not means-tested; that is, all people may participate in the program regardless of their income.

2. **Noncontributory** (or public-assistance) programs include Medicaid, SNAP, housing assistance, welfare, and school lunches.
   - Recipients are not expected to pay for the programs, which are means-tested, meaning that they are aimed at helping poor people.

Source: Compiled by the authors.

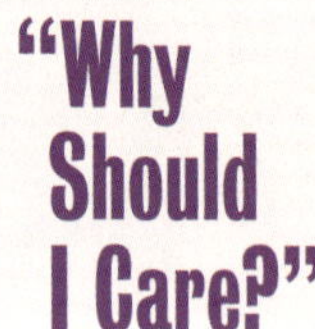

The ACA ("Obamacare") has elements of both contributory and noncontributory programs. People who are required to buy health insurance are "contributing" to their own insurance. However, those who cannot afford to pay for their insurance receive government subsidies (and thus are participating in a noncontributory program).

much smaller then.) During the recession of the mid-1890s, populist and progressive reformers sought a national system of unemployment compensation, but such broad-scale policies were several decades ahead of their time.

The New Deal

The stock market crash in 1929 and the ensuing Great Depression created a desperate economic situation for millions of Americans. The value of the stock market shrank by 80 percent, the gross national product decreased by 25 percent, and unemployment climbed to at least 25 percent in the depth of the depression in 1933. Yet, during the presidential campaign of 1932, the Republican incumbent, Herbert Hoover, upheld the administration's policy of limited government intervention in the economy and in social welfare policies. In contrast, the Democratic candidate, Franklin Delano Roosevelt, pledged "a new deal for the American people" in which the federal government would actively confront the problems of the depression. FDR won a sweeping victory. Democrats also gained control of both houses of Congress, which paved the way for the enactment of FDR's policies.

The test of our progress is not whether we add more to the abundance of those who have much; it is whether we provide enough for those who have too little.

—President Franklin D. Roosevelt

An immediate concern was to alleviate the suffering caused by unemployment. As FDR argued, "No country, however rich, can afford the waste of its human resources. Demoralization caused by vast unemployment is our greatest extravagance. Morally, it is the greatest menace to our social order."[14] FDR also wanted to implement a broader "preventative social policy" as outlined by social scientists at the University of Wisconsin, including John R. Commons, who was a significant force in the creation of unemployment compensation policies, and Edwin Witte, the architect of Social Security.[15] The **New Deal** included a number of policies enacted between 1933 and 1935:

New Deal
The set of policies proposed by President Franklin Roosevelt and enacted by Congress between 1933 and 1935 to promote economic recovery and social welfare during the Great Depression.

- The Agricultural Adjustment Administration provided farmers with much-needed assistance. Farmers were hit hard in the depression when plummeting commodity prices forced many family farms into bankruptcy.

Before the New Deal programs in the 1930s, poverty relief was provided mainly by private charities. Here, future First Lady Eleanor Roosevelt serves meals to unemployed women and their children in a New York restaurant.

- The National Recovery Administration and Public Works Administration reinvigorated the business sector.
- The Federal Emergency Relief Administration provided $500 million in emergency aid for the poor (about $12 billion in today's dollars).
- Jobs programs such as the Civil Works Administration and Civilian Conservation Corps put more than 2 million people to work. Later the Works Progress Administration, a broader program, employed at least one-third of the nation's unemployed.
- Social Security, including the familiar retirement policy, also supported the states with funds to spend on unemployment compensation, disability programs, and support for dependent children of single mothers. This New Deal–era program was the precursor of the central welfare program, Aid to Families with Dependent Children (AFDC), which existed until 1996.
- The National Labor Relations Act guaranteed the right to organize a union and set regulations for collective bargaining between management and labor.[16]

The role of the federal government in social policy was forever changed. Although some aspects of the New Deal, such as the jobs programs, were never repeated on such a broad scale, most of its other programs became the cornerstone of social policy for subsequent generations.

The Great Society

The next major expansion of social policy came during the **Great Society** of President Lyndon Johnson in the mid-1960s. In Chapter 5, we discussed one pillar of this social agenda: the civil rights movement, which culminated with the passage of the Civil Rights Act in 1964 and the Voting Rights Act in 1965. The other important aspect of Johnson's Great Society included the War on Poverty and programs concerning health, education, urban redevelopment, and housing. Johnson's "unconditional" War on Poverty brought economic development and jobs to depressed regions, especially densely populated urban areas, by creating the Office of Economic Opportunity, the Jobs Corps, the Neighborhood Youth Corps, Volunteers in Service to America (VISTA, a domestic counterpart to the Peace Corps), and the Model Cities program. Other

Great Society
The wide-ranging social agenda promoted by President Lyndon Johnson in the mid-1960s that aimed to improve Americans' quality of life through governmental social programs.

programs focused on helping children, including Head Start, which provided preschool education and enrichment for poor children; the Child Nutrition Act of 1966; and an expanded school lunch program. Johnson's administration also greatly expanded the food stamp program; developed more public housing; created the new cabinet-level department of Housing and Urban Development; and got more involved in an area that typically had been left to the states in the Elementary and Secondary Education Act of 1965. Perhaps the most significant legislation was in health care, with the creation of Medicare, the national program that funds medical care for the elderly, and Medicaid, which funds health care for the poor.[17]

Over the following decades, Johnson's Great Society suffered some setbacks. The mounting costs of the Vietnam War in the late 1960s and early 1970s created a trade-off: it wasn't possible to continue funding both ambitious social programs and the war without causing inflation. In addition, there was some conservative backlash against the "welfare state," especially during the Reagan years (1981–1989), as spending on social programs was cut and some programs were eliminated. However, with some exceptions, the Great Society programs remain core components of today's social safety net.[18]

ownership society
The term used to describe the social-policy vision of President George W. Bush, in which citizens take responsibility for their own social welfare and the free market plays a greater role in social policy.

President George W. Bush maintained most existing programs with some cuts and one major expansion, the addition of a prescription benefit to Medicare. As a "compassionate conservative," Bush attempted to place his stamp on American social policy with the idea of an **ownership society**, in which people take more responsibility for their own social welfare. Bush proposed privatizing part of Social Security and creating private savings accounts to cover more out-of-pocket medical expenses, in combination with more free market forces and a bigger role for private and religious charity. President Obama favored an approach that emphasized the market and community while preserving an important role for government. As the 2008–2009 recession and natural disasters such as Superstorm Sandy demonstrated, crises can overwhelm even the most aggressive and sustained community responses. Market forces cannot adequately address the needs of the unemployed and very poor, especially in times of economic recession.

President Trump and the Republican Congress attempted to scale back social policies, most significantly Obamacare, as noted in the chapter introduction. By eliminating the individual mandate, giving employers the freedom to provide policies with less coverage, cutting back on the open enrollment period, and reducing subsidies to buy insurance,

Many families in the United States rely on social policies, including the Supplemental Nutrition Assistance Program (SNAP), which subsidizes the cost of healthy food. SNAP benefits can easily be used at a range of stores and local farmers' markets. While there is debate over who should receive these types of subsidies, recipients have to demonstrate that they are working or trying to obtain a job.

the opponents of Obamacare were trying to create a "death spiral" in which the health insurance program would become more expensive and therefore less attractive. Trump was also attempting to reshape welfare programs; he issued an executive order in 2018 directing federal agencies to review their social programs, with the goal of getting more people to work and off welfare. The most significant change would have tightened work requirements for recipients of the Supplemental Nutrition Assistance Program (SNAP), formerly known as food stamps (to qualify for SNAP, able-bodied adults without dependents must work at least 80 hours a month, with a three-month grace period every three years if you lose your job). This proposed rule limited the criteria states could use to apply for waivers to the work requirement and would have eliminated benefits for about 700,000 Americans and affected up to 1.3 million others. However, shortly before the rule was to go into effect, a federal judge stopped the rule, saying it was "arbitrary and capricious." Five days later, one of the COVID-19 relief bills suspended the rule until after the national coronavirus emergency is declared over.[19] Early in 2021, an appeals court upheld the district court ruling, killing the proposed change.[20]

"Why Should I Care?"

Historical context is always important for understanding current policy, but this is especially true for social policy. Most of our important social policies today, such as Social Security, Medicare, and Medicaid, date back to the New Deal or Great Society periods. All Americans will be touched by the "social safety net" at some point in their lives. Some of this may seem remote—you may feel that you don't have to think about it until you are closer to retirement. However, most of you will be affected in the next few years by an important change in social policy: the ACA allows you to stay on your parents' health insurance until you are 26 years old.

Poverty and income inequality

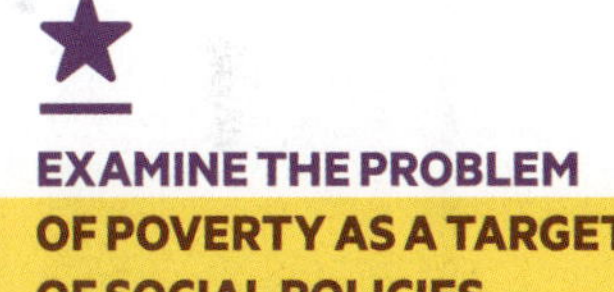

EXAMINE THE PROBLEM OF POVERTY AS A TARGET OF SOCIAL POLICIES

The economic dislocation and poverty of the Great Depression and the desire to eliminate poverty in the 1960s were the two central stimuli for social policies. Although these policies had some success in reducing poverty, the persistence of poverty remains the primary motivator for most social policy. In 2024, the poverty line for a family of four was an annual income of $31,200; for a single person it was $15,060.[21] In 2023, official estimates determined that 36.8 million Americans were living in poverty—11.1 percent of the population. Even the social programs that do not directly help the poor and disadvantaged, such as Social Security and Medicare, affect poverty. As the What Do the Facts Say? feature on page 626 shows, the percentage of the elderly population living in poverty plummeted from more than 35 percent in 1959 to 9.7 percent in 2023. Official statistics on poverty were not collected before 1959, but the rate was certainly much higher in the 1930s, before Social Security was established.[22] Given that more than half of the elderly rely on Social Security as their primary income, the poverty rate for the elderly would be much higher if Social Security and Medicare did not exist.

Another source of concern for some policy advocates is the growing income and wealth inequality in the United States. Indeed, people in the top income levels in the nation are benefiting disproportionately from income increases. From 1976 to 2023, for the top 1 percent of the income distribution (with an average household income of

WHAT DO THE FACTS SAY?

Poverty Rates by Age

Children today are in poverty at a rate 50 percent higher than that of the elderly, whereas 50 years ago the poverty rate among the elderly was twice that of children. What changes in social policies in the past 80 years could help explain this change? What do the facts say?

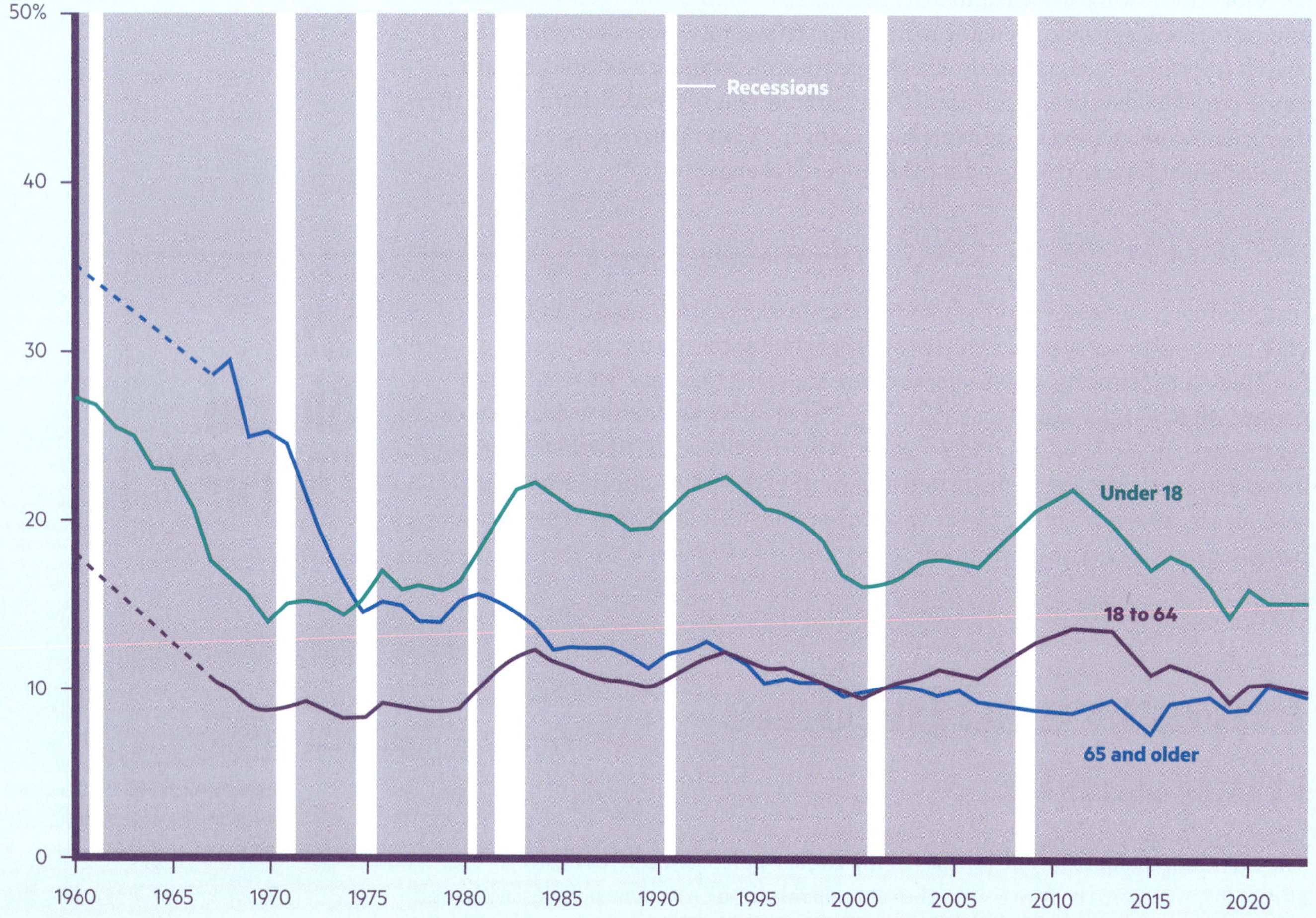

50%
40
30
20
10
0
1960 1965 1970 1975 1980 1985 1990 1995 2000 2005 2010 2015 2020
Recessions
Under 18
18 to 64
65 and older

Note: The data for 2013 and beyond reflect the implementation of the redesigned income questions. The data points are placed at the midpoints of the respective years. Data for people aged 18 to 64 and aged 65 and older are not available from 1960 to 1965. For information on recessions, see p. 82 of source. For information on confidentiality protection, sampling error, nonsampling error, and definitions, see www2.census.gov/programs-surveys/cps/techdocs/cpsmar17.pdf (accessed 7/5/22).

Source: Emily A. Shrider, U.S. Census Bureau, Current Population Reports, P60–283, *Poverty in the United States: 2023*, U.S. Government Publishing Office, Washington, DC, September 2024, p. 5, www2.census.gov/library/publications/2024/demo/p60-283.pdf (accessed 10/3/24).

Think about it

- **The white shaded areas** show economic recessions, when economic activity shrinks. What do you notice about the poverty rate in those years?
- **What are the most important things** that the government can do to address poverty?
- **Would it be better** to leave support for the social safety net up to private charities and more personal funding of health care and retirement benefits? Why or why not?

$2.8 million in 2023), real income grew by 252 percent compared with a 13.8 percent gain for the bottom half (who had an average income of $19,000) and a 33.5 percent increase for the middle 40 percent (average income $188,100).[23] These trends have produced a growing concentration of income at the top. In 2023, the top 10 percent of households—those earning an average of $641,000 a year—earned more than half the nation's income (53.1 percent), which was just below the highest proportion since 1917 (see Figure 16.1); and the top 1 percent of households earned 22.9 percent of the nation's income.[24]

There's class warfare, all right, but it's my class, the rich class, that's making war, and we're winning.

—Warren Buffett, America's fourth-wealthiest person

The wealth gap is far greater. The median (meaning that half are above this level and half are below) net worth of U.S. households in 2022 was $192,900, but the median wealth for the top 10 percent was nearly $3.8 million, and this group held 71 percent of the nation's wealth. Racial wealth inequality received extensive attention in 2020 with the renewed focus on racial justice: in 2022, the median wealth of a White family was $285,000, while the median wealth of a Black family was just 16 percent of that amount: $44,900.[25] Even within the top 10 percent, the wealth is concentrated at the top. *Forbes* publishes a list of the wealthiest Americans every year. Elon Musk topped the 2023 list with a net worth of $251 billion, and the person at the bottom of the "Forbes 400" was worth $2.9 billion. The collective net worth of the nation's wealthiest 400 people in 2023 was $4.5 trillion, which is a more than 48-fold increase since 1982, when *Forbes* first calculated their net worth at $93 billion.[26] This is four times the total wealth held by the bottom 50 percent of Americans.[27]

One important point to recognize when considering social policy as a tool to address income inequality is that government policies help middle-income people and even the wealthy, in addition to the poor. Consider federal housing policy: in fiscal year 2021, poor people received $425.1 billion a year from the federal government in direct subsidies for their rent (with another $23.7 billion spent on all housing programs for

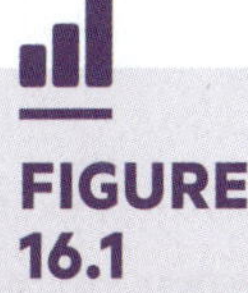

FIGURE 16.1

Percentage of All Income Earned by the Top 10 Percent of Earners, 1917–2023

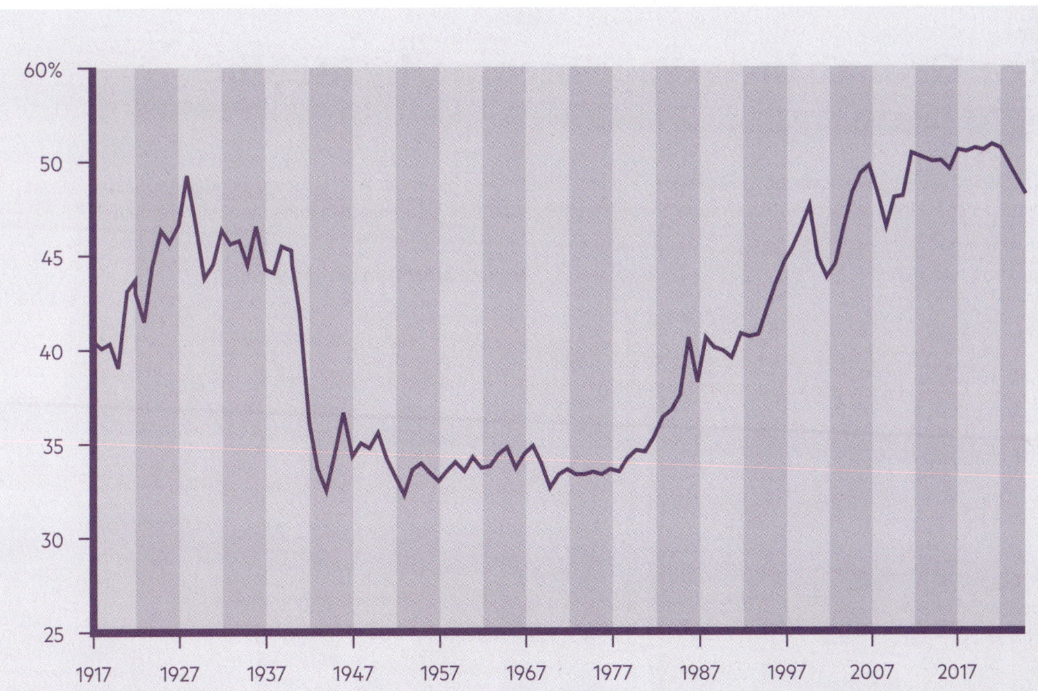

Income inequality in the United States today is higher than ever. The wealthiest 10 percent of Americans now receive 48.2 percent of all U.S. income. How will this inequality affect the outcomes of social policy?

Note: Includes capital gains. This figure shows the most recent data available.

Source: Historic data from Thomas Piketty and Emmanuel Saez, "Income Inequality in the United States, 1913–1998," *Quarterly Journal of Economics*, 118:1 (2003): 1–39. Recent data are from https://realtimeinequality.org/ (accessed 8/10/24).

the poor). However, this number is much smaller than the $80.1 billion spent on tax expenditures for housing in 2022, for the mortgage interest deduction, property tax deduction, and capital gains tax exclusions. Most of this money went to relatively wealthy people; for example, 73 percent of the tax savings from deducting mortgage interest goes to people in the top 20 percent.[28] Other government policies that help the wealthy include patent and copyright law, bankruptcy law, bailouts of the financial sector, immigration policy, enforcement of tax law, and monetary policy.[29]

Government programs that help the wealthy not only target individuals but also benefit corporations. These policies, often called "corporate welfare," are defined by the Cato Institute, a libertarian think tank, as "any government spending program that provides unique benefits or advantages to specific companies or industries. That includes programs that provide direct grants to businesses, programs that provide research and other services for industries, and programs that provide subsidized loans or insurance to companies." The Cato Institute estimates that there are more than 100 corporate welfare programs in the federal budget, including crop subsidies to large corporate farmers and tax deductions for oil companies to encourage exploration and drilling, with annual expenditures of more than $100 billion.[30] Another study found that state and local governments provide $95 billion in tax incentives to businesses every year.[31] Liberal groups such as the Tax Justice Network estimate levels of corporate welfare at nearly three times that amount.[32] Clearly, there is much more to welfare policies than programs for the poor.

Nonetheless, the social programs described in this chapter are very important for reducing income inequality. The nonpartisan Congressional Budget Office shows that means-tested transfers, such as Medicaid, SNAP, and Supplemental Security Income (SSI), and federal taxes cause household incomes to be more evenly distributed. In 2020, the most recent year included in its 2023 study, transfers and taxes increased average income for the bottom quintile by $21,900 to $45,800 while they decreased the income of the highest quintile by $82,100 to $275,700.[33] Figure 16.2 shows how the

FIGURE 16.2

Cumulative Growth in Average Income, by Income Group, 1979–2020

Social policies such as Social Security, Medicare, and progressive income taxes have a big impact on reducing income inequality. How much greater would income inequality be today without those transfers and taxes? How much income inequality remains?

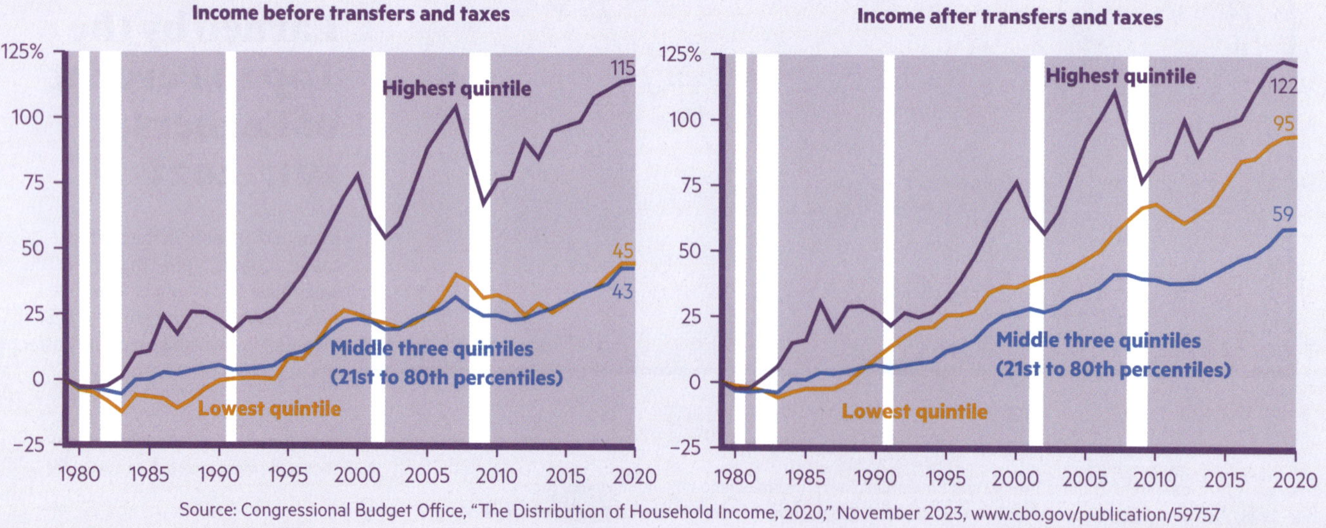

Source: Congressional Budget Office, "The Distribution of Household Income, 2020," November 2023, www.cbo.gov/publication/59757 (accessed 8/1/24).

income of the bottom quintile, and to some extent the second through fourth quintiles, has increased much more than it would have without our social policies and progressive taxes. This is especially evident with the trillions of dollars in spending on COVID-19 relief efforts that prevented millions of people from falling into poverty.

Partisanship and income inequality

These statistics generate different reactions among politicians and are a good reminder that politics is conflictual. Republicans, on the one hand, argue that the best way to address poverty is through supply-side tax cuts that promote the creation of capital, investment, and jobs, and thus ensure a healthy economy (see Chapter 15). From this perspective, income inequality may in fact be a necessary condition for bringing people out of poverty, because wealthy people are the only ones who have enough money to invest to create jobs.

Democrats, on the other hand, argue that making the wealthy pay a larger share of their income in taxes could fund programs to help the poor directly and would be more efficient than waiting for the trickle-down effect of tax cuts for the wealthy. From this perspective, a direct trade-off exists between income inequality and reducing poverty, and progressive taxes are needed to help the poor. Several Democratic presidential primary candidates in 2020, including Bernie Sanders and Elizabeth Warren, endorsed the idea of a wealth tax for the extremely wealthy (starting at $32 million in net worth for Sanders and $50 million for Warren), but President Biden has not supported the idea.[34]

"Why Should I Care?"

Income inequality is one of the central issues of the past decade. It emerged as an important issue in the 2020 elections. Democrats and Republicans alike agree that steps need to be taken to address inequality, although obviously they differ in their approaches. Democrats emphasize increasing the minimum wage and improving the affordability of health care and housing, while Republicans tout the benefits of the 2017 tax cuts and the low unemployment rate. However, the social safety net has become much more important with the increase in inflation as millions of Americans have difficulty paying their rent and bills. A recent survey showed that 34 percent of Americans couldn't come up with $400 in cash to pay for a car repair or health care emergency, while one in five say they have more credit card debt than emergency savings.[35] If you were in this category, whom would you turn to for help?

DESCRIBE THE ROLES PLAYED BY EACH BRANCH OF THE NATIONAL GOVERNMENT AND BY THE STATES IN MAKING AND IMPLEMENTING SOCIAL POLICY

The key players in social policy making

Congress, the president, and the bureaucracy all play key roles in shaping social policy. State governments also play a central role in some policy areas such as education and welfare policy, while interest groups are especially important for policies that affect the elderly.

Congress and the president

Given the differences between how the Democratic and Republican parties approach social policy as a tool for reducing income inequality, it may not be surprising that the poverty rate is more likely to fall during Democratic presidencies than Republican. This is exactly what Figure 16.3 shows. Between 1960 and 2023, Democrats controlled the White House for 31 years and Republicans for 33 years. During Democratic presidencies, the poverty rate fell from the previous year in 24 of those 31 years and for 2 years remained the same as in the previous year. During Republican presidencies, the poverty rate fell in only 17 of the 32 years and remained the same in 2 years. Overall, the poverty rate went down by 0.44 percent in Democratic years and it went up by 0.04 percent in Republican years. These differences may not sound like much, but given that each percentage point change in the poverty rate represents more than 3 million people today, the differences are significant. In 2008, political scientist Larry M. Bartels found that in the previous six decades the inflation-adjusted incomes of working-poor families increased six times faster under Democratic presidents than under Republican presidents.[36] This makes some sense given the political base of the two parties: Democrats win large percentages of the votes of poor people, and Republicans usually do better among wealthier voters.

The data on changes in the poverty rate during different presidential administrations by party ignored one important point: Democratic presidents were more likely than Republican presidents to have a Congress controlled by their party. From 1960 to 2023, Democrats controlled the presidency for 31 years and Republicans for 33 years. But Democrats had unified control of government for 18 years and Republicans had control for only 7 years. This means that Democratic presidents had more opportunity to implement their agendas, whereas Republican presidents had to do more negotiating with the other party. You might argue that this divided control only prevented Republican presidents from making even deeper cuts in social programs, which could have driven the poverty rate even higher, because Democrats in Congress would not have been supporting those cuts. Although this is a possibility, especially during the

FIGURE 16.3

Changes in Poverty Rates by Party

The poverty rate tends to decrease under Democratic presidents and to go up by about the same margin under Republican presidents. What could explain this difference?

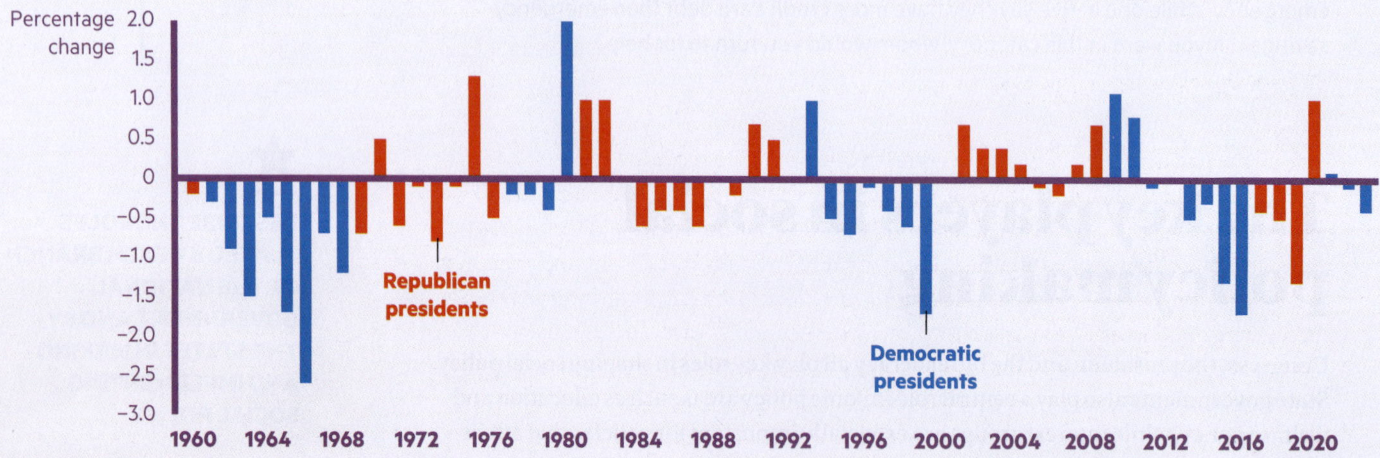

Source: Data from the U.S. Census Bureau, Poverty: Historical Tables, www.census.gov (accessed 10/6/22).

When Biden was elected in 2020, he was committed to funding programs that would create jobs and provide child care support as well as continual funding to support issues related to COVID-19. While the Infrastructure Investment and Jobs Act passed into law, the Build Back Better plan was sidelined by centrist democrats including Kyrsten Sinema (D-AZ) and Joe Manchin (D-WV), who were concerned about the costs. The president met with each of them to try to find a compromise but was ultimately unsuccessful, demonstrating the necessity of cooperation and collaboration in order to pass social policy legislation.

Reagan years, divided control may also have prevented Republican presidents from implementing their alternative visions of the best way to address poverty.

This discussion underlies the more basic point that Congress and the president both play central roles in shaping social policy. In some instances, the president may take the lead, as with FDR and the New Deal or Lyndon Johnson and the Great Society. In other instances, Congress plays a central role, as with health care reform in 2009–2010. In all cases, the president and Congress must find some common ground. This may be especially difficult under divided government, but even when the president and Congress are of the same party, Congress may be obstructionist: in 2017 a Republican-controlled Congress failed to deliver on one of President Trump's key campaign promises to "repeal and replace" Obamacare, and in 2021–2022, Democrats did not pass President Biden's signature Build Back Better plan when Democratic senators Joe Manchin (D-WV) and Kyrsten Sinema (D-AZ) balked at the high price tag. However, in August 2022, Congress passed a scaled-back version of the plan, the Inflation Reduction Act, which spends $386 billion on energy and climate change (including things like building charging stations for electric cars and economic incentives for alternative energy, such as wind and solar) and $98 billion for health care over 10 years. It also raised $790 billion in taxes and savings over 10 years, providing $305 billion in net deficit reduction.

The bureaucracy

You might assume that the bureaucracy itself makes little difference in social policy because it simply implements the policies determined by Congress and the president. For some policies, that is fairly close to what happens. For example, in the case of Social Security and other programs that have levels of benefits determined by law, implementing policy largely involves determining that the proper amount of money is going to the right people and making sure that these people receive the money. However, as we discussed in Chapter 13, the "on-the-ground" public employees responsible for executing many other social policies have a great deal of discretion. Welfare offices in general tend not to be very welcoming places. People often have to wait for hours, and welfare office workers are sometimes rude and ask their clients personal questions that are not required by law.

Some potential welfare recipients are so alienated by the process that they give up. This is not true of all welfare offices, but there are general differences in how recipients are treated in different types of social welfare programs. One study found that welfare agencies that handed out AFDC benefits had a more "hostile and punitive" attitude toward their clients than those that administered the disability program under Social Security.[37]

Sometimes problems of bureaucratic implementation may be at the top, as when problems concerning Veterans Affairs (VA) hospitals came to light in 2014. Thousands of veterans had long waits for services that were covered up by VA hospital administrators. Veterans Affairs secretary Eric Shinseki was forced to resign for his failure to address the problem.[38] These problems persisted into the Trump presidency as veterans faced longer wait times and had less overall satisfaction than patients at non-VA hospitals.[39] Finally, problems may also arise when the government tries to respond quickly to a problem and provides insufficient oversight to make sure that money is being properly spent. The most dramatic example of this was the early response to mitigate the economic consequences of the COVID pandemic. Congressional investigations revealed that $84 billion in potentially fraudulent loans and grants were distributed through the Paycheck Protection Program (PPP) and Economic Injury Disaster Loan (EIDL) programs.[40]

Bureaucratic discretion may also serve more positive ends. Political scientist Daniel P. Carpenter reported that many bureaucratic agencies in the late nineteenth and early twentieth centuries developed political autonomy and strong reputations that allowed them to analyze and solve problems, create new programs, and plan and administer programs efficiently.[41] Many of the same insights apply to agencies that deliver social policies today, such as the Social Security Administration, which has a very strong base of popular and political support.

The states

Social policy has always been strongly influenced by our system of federalism. As long as welfare has existed in the United States, it has been administered at the state and local levels, with varying degrees of national control. The 1996 welfare reform bill, Temporary Assistance to Needy Families (TANF), gave more power to the states and eliminated all national guarantees. Medicaid is administered at the state level (with federal assistance), and education is almost completely controlled by local and state governments. One sticking point with health care reform in 2009–2010 was the extent to which policy would be centered in the states or have a stronger national component. Many Democrats argued for a national "public option," while Republicans favored a more limited approach in which insurance companies would be allowed to compete across state lines. The stronger national approach failed, but the new law clearly signaled a shift to a more national role in health care. Education policy is another area where the trend has been toward more involvement of the national government rather than more power returning to the states. But even with the national accountability mechanisms and testing requirements established by President Bush's No Child Left Behind Act and the incentives provided by President Obama's Race to the Top program, education policy remains largely a state and local

Sometimes, problems in social service administration can stem from poor management. Veterans Affairs (VA) hospitals have been plagued by long wait times in recent years, forcing veterans to wait much longer for care than patients at non-VA hospitals.

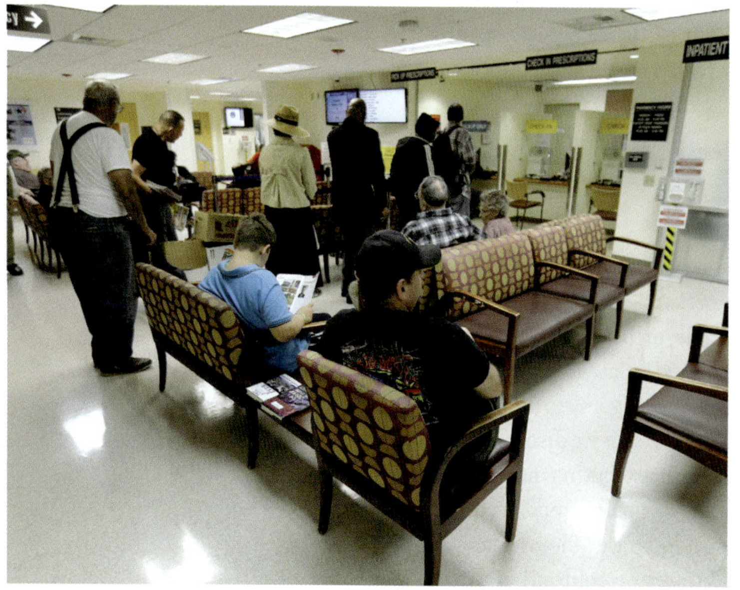

affair. President Trump's education policy was consistent with maintaining the central role for state and local government, calling for cuts in many federal programs but big increases in spending for public and private school choice programs.[42]

The importance of the states has been extremely clear in the response to the COVID-19 pandemic. Early in the pandemic the national government took a hands-off approach, leaving it to the states to determine the best way to respond. This state flexibility makes sense because what would be appropriate for New York City would not be useful in rural North Dakota. Also, it probably would not be constitutional for the president to either order everyone to stay home for six months or open up states' economies. These decisions ultimately reside with governors and state legislatures.[43] Some states responded with strict stay-at-home orders and very slowly opened up their economies, and others never implemented strict orders and opened up their economies while the virus was still spreading. As a result, early in the pandemic, infection rates in some states were 50 times higher than in others.[44] By the third wave of the pandemic in 2022, those differences started to even out, but the overall age-adjusted COVID death rate remained five times as high in Mississippi as Hawaii.[45] Of course, some of the difference in death rates is explained by factors other than the policy response by state and national governments—most significantly, the vaccination rate. After courts struck down most vaccines mandates, this became a matter of individual choice.

Interest groups

In general, interest groups that advocate for social policy are not as influential as business or labor groups, many other professional associations, or even other public interest groups that focus on specific issues such as gun ownership or protection of the environment. A major exception is AARP, one of the most powerful lobbies in the United States (see Chapter 10). AARP has long had a strong voice on behalf of Social Security and Medicare. For example, when President George W. Bush proposed "personal savings accounts" to replace part of the Social Security system, AARP mobilized its significant political muscle to crush the idea before it could receive serious debate in Congress. Similarly, when Medicaid and Medicare were targeted for deep cuts in the 2019 fiscal year budget, AARP was a powerful voice for protecting those programs (while Medicaid is based on financial need rather than age, many seniors in nursing homes receive assistance from the program).[46]

Many interest groups and think tanks work on behalf of the poor, the homeless, and other disadvantaged people, but decision makers in Washington, D.C., generally are less responsive to their concerns because these groups and the people they are aligned with are not politically powerful. The poor tend not to vote or donate money to political campaigns. Many politicians in Washington care deeply about issues concerning poverty, homelessness, and other social-policy problems, but the interest groups and think tanks that try to focus politicians' attention on these issues face a particularly difficult task because of the relatively disadvantaged position of the people they represent.

Understanding the role of the "key players" is obviously important for understanding how social policy is made. However, it is also important for a reason more directly linked to this class: the policy section of the book allows you to pull together all the material that you learned earlier in the semester. Now that you understand the role of Congress, the president, the bureaucracy, parties, and interest groups, this discussion of how these key players influence the policy-making process should make sense to you.

TRACE THE STEPS THROUGH WHICH PROBLEMS ARE ADDRESSED BY SOCIAL POLICIES

The policy-making process

Another way to understand the role of key players in making policy is to examine the various stages of the process. The How It Works graphic on pages 636–37 shows the stages by which Social Security was conceived and enacted, but all policies go through similar steps. The first stage is to define a problem as an issue that requires the federal government's attention. Of the thousands of possible issues, Congress acts on a relatively small number. Consider a social policy such as SNAP. Poor and hungry people have been part of American society since the arrival of the first settlers, but this was not seen as a problem requiring government intervention until the twentieth century. What causes a society to change its assumptions about whether and how government should address social problems?

Sometimes there is a triggering event: the assassination of President John F. Kennedy led to the passage of gun control legislation, the energy crisis of the early 1970s led to the first comprehensive discussions of energy policy, and Hurricane Katrina and the COVID-19 pandemic led to a reexamination of our readiness for emergencies and our social safety net. Sometimes redefining an issue can move the policy to the next step of the process. For example, the estate tax has been part of our tax system since 1917, but when Republican leaders in Congress redefined it as the "death tax" in the late 1990s, they transformed the politics of the debate and made it a problem that needed a solution. After all, who could support a tax on dead people? (Of course, dead people don't pay taxes—the estate's heirs do—but that nuance was lost in the redefinition of the problem.)

policy agenda
The set of desired policies that political leaders view as their top priorities.

Recognizing and defining a problem is just the first step; it still needs to come to the attention of political leaders and then get on the **policy agenda**. The basic idea is that when conditions are right, with the appropriate national political mood and participation from key interest groups and government actors, an issue can reach the agenda. Once the issue is on the active agenda, alternatives are proposed and debated and the final version of the policy is formulated in Congress (if it is a bill) or the executive branch (if it is an administrative action). Enactment involves a roll call vote in the House and the Senate and then a signature by the president, a regulatory decision or administrative action by the bureaucracy, or unilateral action by the president (such as an executive order or agreement).

Many factors determine whether or not the finalized policy is implemented successfully. First, the problem the policy is designed to fix has to be solvable. Second, the policy must be clear and consistent in its objectives. It wouldn't make sense for Congress to pass a law telling the Department of Health and Human Services to "make sure everyone has health care," because such a law would not indicate how this should be done. Third, the policy must be funded adequately and administered by competent bureaucrats who have the required expertise. Finally, external support from the public and relevant interest groups may be critical to the policy's success. For example, AARP's support is critical for the success of any social policy that affects older people. Its support helped pass the Prescription Drug Benefit that was added to Medicare in 2003 and comprehensive health care reform in 2010.[47]

Implementation of a policy is an ongoing process. To ensure that the desires of Congress and the president are being followed, policy evaluation is a critical stage of the policy-making process. (See Chapter 13 for a discussion of attempts by Congress and the president to control the bureaucracy.) Evaluation has become more visible since passage of the Government Performance and Results Act of 1993. Under the law, agencies are required to publish strategic plans and performance measures. Though these efforts sound impressive, it is incredibly difficult to assess whether a government program is achieving its aims. The law also improved policy implementation by focusing on performance. A review of this effort to "reinvent government" on its 25th anniversary noted improvements in the areas of procurement, acquisition of IT systems, and category management, which involves leveraging government's buying power to get discounts for large volumes. The Trump administration was enthusiastic in applying and expanding these market-oriented practices through the Office of American Innovation (with leadership from Trump's son-in-law, Jared Kushner).[48] Biden's approach emphasized empowering federal workers to attract the most qualified people, rather than attempting to make the government mirror the private sector.[49]

Political scientist James Q. Wilson explains the difference between measuring success in the private and public sectors—specifically, he compares McDonald's with the Department of Motor Vehicles (DMV).[50] It is relatively easy to know whether McDonald's is doing a good job: simply look at the profits being generated and compare them with those of the previous period. If profits are going up at a reasonable pace, the burger flippers and fry cooks are doing their jobs. The DMV's performance is much more difficult to assess because there is no simple measure, such as profit, to look at. Maybe you could review the number of people served per hour or the average length of time people have to wait to get their driver's license. But that would ignore many other considerations, such as how well the DMV serves disadvantaged populations or people for whom English is a second language. We wouldn't expect a DMV office where 50 percent of its applicants don't speak English to be as efficient as one at which all applicants speak English.

Evaluating a public agency such as the State Department is even more difficult. How do we know if diplomacy is being conducted in a manner consistent with congressional and presidential preferences? Would success be defined as staying out of war? Increasing economic activity or cultural exchanges between countries? Strengthening democratic institutions in emerging democracies? Getting cooperation in the war on terrorism? Measuring the achievement of objectives like these is very difficult even if those goals can be clearly defined.

Despite these limitations, extensive efforts to evaluate policy do provide decision makers with some basis for deciding whether to modify, expand, or terminate a policy. Programs are notoriously difficult to cut or eliminate. Examples abound, such as wool and mohair subsidies implemented after World War II and the Korean War. More than half the wool needed to make uniforms during these wars was imported, so the Pentagon wanted to increase domestic production of wool. The National Wool Act in 1954 provided direct subsidies to farmers. By 1994 the program was spending nearly $240 million a year, despite the fact that the Pentagon removed wool from its "strategic materials" list in 1960! The subsidies were finally killed in 1994, but the 2002 Farm Act added wool and mohair to the list of commodities eligible for marketing assistance loans and the subsidy persists today.[51] Some policies are like the zombies in *The Walking Dead*—unless you kill them in just the right way, they keep coming back.

Alternative perspectives on the policy-making process

The "stages model" of policy making described earlier is a pretty basic description of the process. Several elaborations and extensions provide a more nuanced understanding of the process.[52] For example, the first two steps, problem recognition and agenda setting, were conceptualized by John Kingdon as multiple streams of problems, politics, and policies. These three streams are independent and may or may

How it works: in theory

The Social Policy-Making Process

Problem recognition

Attention is drawn to an existing problem. This can be triggered by an event or a disaster, such as the emergency response to the COVID-19 pandemic, the impact of an economic recession on the jobless and the poor, or global warming.

Agenda setting

Public awareness of the problem increases as the media, relevant interest groups, and political leaders talk about the problem. The problem becomes a priority for the government.

Deliberation and formulation

Different policy proposals are suggested to address the problem; input is provided by interested parties, relevant executive agencies, and congressional committees.

Enactment

Congress passes the legislation and the president signs it into law.

Implementation

The relevant bureaucratic agencies put the law into effect, writing specific regulations when needed, distributing benefits, and handling government contracts and procurement.

Evaluation

Policy analysts, inside and outside government, determine whether the policy is working as intended.

Possible modification, expansion, or termination of policy

Based on the policy evaluations and public reaction to the policy, political leaders tweak the law to improve it, expand the scope of the law if it is working well, or sometimes repeal the law.

How it works: **in practice**

The Enactment and Evolution of Social Security

Social Security, the federal government's social insurance program to provide financial support to retired people, provides a good example of the various stages of the policy-making process.

There is a problem.

A large proportion of elderly people were living in poverty.

We need to fix this.

As poverty among the elderly worsened during the Great Depression, **solving the problem became a priority within FDR's New Deal agenda**.

We have an idea.

The proposal for **Social Security came from FDR's President's Committee on Economic Security**.

Signed into law.

Social Security was passed by Congress and **signed into law by the president in 1935**.

Moving forward . . .

The Social Security Administration **implements the policy**.

Let's look at that again.

Social Security has been **evaluated at various times**, most recently by presidential commissions on reform.

Updated.

Social Security has been modified and expanded several times, most recently in 1983 and 2000.

More change?

With the Social Security Trust Fund **expected to run out in 2033**, only 79 percent of benefits would be covered by existing taxes. This shortfall has led to more calls to shore up this popular program.

Critical Thinking

1. **Social Security is one of our** most popular social programs. Under what conditions would it be modified or changed?
2. **What groups are most likely to oppose reductions** in Social Security benefits? Which are most likely to support them? Do you think these groups should have influence on Social Security policy? Why or why not?

Both Trump and Biden made funding to curb the opioid epidemic a priority, demonstrating that the issue has bipartisan support. In 2019, representative Mikie Sherrill (D-NJ), along with Representatives David Trone (D-MD) and Denver Riggleman (R-VA), announced over $1.5 billion in funding to the issue in the 2020 federal budget.

not intersect. Objective conditions may or may not turn into problems. For example, the abuse of opioid painkillers has been evident for many years. But the death of the musician Prince called attention to this condition and turned it into a *problem* that policy makers felt more pressure to address. This changed the *politics* of the problem as people were more likely to see the problem as something that required government action. Congress responded in July 2016 by passing the Comprehensive Addiction and Recovery Act (CARA), which changed the government's *policy* related to the opioid problem. The Trump administration made it a priority as well, allocating $1.8 billion in 2019 to combat the problem.[53] In 2022, President Biden announced the State Opioid Response (SOR) grant funding opportunity that will provide nearly $1.5 billion to states to help address the opioid addiction and overdose epidemic.[54] With 188 Americans dying every day from opioid overdoses, politicians from both parties have recognized it as a crisis that needed further government action.[55]

There typically are various policy options available to address any given problem, but whether or not policy makers act on them depends on either the presence of a policy entrepreneur who pushes for change or, more broadly, the occurrence of a political change that creates a "policy window"—an opportunity to implement the policy. Political change may occur thanks to a change in the national mood, interest group pressure, or an administrative or legislative change in control.[56] All this is to say that agenda setting and eventually passing a law are not as linear and static as implied by the basic stages model.

Frank R. Baumgartner and Bryan D. Jones provide additional insight into *how* policy change happens with their "punctuated equilibrium" model. They argue that the policy process features long periods of incremental change punctuated by brief periods of major policy change. Change comes about when an alternative "policy image" can expand an issue beyond the control of the policy specialists who resist change. For example, the ACA overcame decades of resistance to major change in health insurance by emphasizing a policy image that focused on the millions of Americans who did not have insurance.[57]

One final question about the policy-making process concerns policy diffusion: Why do some policies quickly spread across the country while others are adopted in only a few states? The idea that states are "laboratories of democracy" is an invitation to explore that variation. One comprehensive study took up the challenge and examined 130 policy innovations, explaining the relative rates of diffusion by the type of policy, the involvement of interest groups, and the level of government attention. For example, the Amber Alert child abduction notification system that was adopted in more than 30 states in less than six years is an example of a "policy outbreak" that quickly spread across the states (and now exists in all 50 states).[58] And an analysis of anti-smoking policy found that learning from early adopters, economic competition between proximate cities, imitation of larger cities, and coercion from state governments all explained whether or not a city adopted an anti-smoking policy.[59]

Understanding the policy-making process and the key actors in that process is important for seeing why policies are adopted. Why do some policies, such as a 21-year-old drinking age and anti-smoking policies, spread quickly across the country, while others, such as marijuana legalization and some environmental regulations, are adopted in a few states and spread more slowly? If Congress gets involved, as with health care reform, or the Supreme Court decides an issue, as with same-sex marriage, then policy change can happen in big, nonincremental steps.

"Why Should I Care?"

ANALYZE THE CURRENT MAJOR AREAS OF SOCIAL POLICY

Social policy today

As of the 2024 fiscal year, Social Security, Medicare, and Medicaid make up nearly half of all federal spending ($3.2 trillion out of $6.8). With an aging population and health care costs that continue to grow as a percentage of the economy, these policies will take an even greater share of the budget in the future. Given other spending priorities, political pressure is mounting to put spending for social programs on a more sustainable path. This section will explain the nature of these important programs and discuss recent efforts to reform them.

Social Security

Social Security is the most popular social program in the United States. Consequently, it has developed a reputation as the "third rail" of politics (like the dangerous, power-conducting rail on electrified train tracks) because a politician who dares to touch Social Security risks political death. Despite serious problems concerning its long-term solvency, Social Security has proven remarkably immune to any steps that could be taken to shore up its financial health, such as cutting benefits, raising taxes, or privatizing part of the program. Why is Social Security so popular, what long-term challenges does it face, and what are the possible solutions to ensure the program's long-term viability?

Social Security
A federal social insurance program that provides cash benefits to retirees based on payroll taxes they have paid over the course of their careers. It is a "pay as you go" program in which working Americans pay taxes to support today's retirees, with a promise that when today's workers retire their benefits will be paid by the next generation.

One reason that Social Security is so popular is its universal quality—that is, nearly every working American participates in the program, from Jeff Bezos to the teenager flipping burgers at McDonald's. Once people reach a certain age, they are all entitled to Social Security checks without regard to how much income they have from other sources, such as dividends, interest, or other pensions. So, unlike many social programs that help only a subset of the population and thus may foster an "us against them" mentality (taxpayers may ask, "Why should we have to support other people?"), Social Security does not pit citizens from different classes or ethnic groups against each other. Social Security is also popular because it works. It is more efficient than most privately managed pensions and retirement funds, with about 0.6 percent going to administrative expenses, compared with the average mutual fund that spends about

1 percent.[60] More important, Social Security has accomplished its central goal of helping most Americans have an adequate retirement income: around 10 percent of the elderly are in poverty today (9.7 percent), which is a lower rate than for the general public (see What Do the Facts Say? on p. 626) and significantly lower than the 35 percent of the elderly who were in poverty in 1960. Census data also show that 38 percent of the elderly would be in poverty today without their Social Security payments.[61]

How Social Security Works Before we examine the various proposals to change Social Security, it is important to understand how the program works. Social Security is funded by a payroll tax of 6.2 percent on income up to $168,600 (in 2024), with an equal 6.2 percent that is paid by employers. (The self-employed pay both halves.) The payroll tax has an additional 1.45 percent on all income for Medicare (which we will discuss later). This is considered a regressive tax because poor and middle-income people put a higher percentage of their income toward the Social Security tax than wealthy people do. The maximum Social Security tax you can pay is $10,453 a year, which is 6.2 percent of $168,600. So someone making a million dollars would pay 1 percent of their income in the Social Security payroll tax compared with the 6.2 percent that everyone earning less than $168,600 pays. Although the taxes are regressive, the benefits are progressive; that is, poorer people receive back in benefits a larger share of their lifetime payroll taxes (71 percent) than wealthy people (25 percent) receive (because the maximum benefit amounts are fixed, as shown in Nuts & Bolts 16.2).

NUTS & BOLTS 16.2

Social Security

Number of recipients for old-age, survivors, and disability insurance	
Old-age insurance (the basic retirement program)	53,758,000
Survivors insurance (retirement program for widows, widowers, and the children of deceased primary wage earners)	5,800,000
Disability insurance (payments for people and their families who cannot work because of a disability and are not yet retired)	8,312,000

Monthly retirement benefits		
Individual	Average: $2,482	Maximum: $4,011
Couple	Average: $3,723	Maximum: $6,016

Note: The maximum benefit for the couple is based on the spousal benefit; if both people worked at least 35 years at or above the contribution base, the couple's benefit would be simply twice the individual benefit.

Sources: Figures on the number of recipients are from the U.S. Social Security Administration Office of Policy, "Monthly Statistical Snapshot, June 2024," Table 2, www.ssa.gov/policy/docs/quickfacts/stat_snapshot/; figures on monthly benefits are from Social Security Administration, *2024 OASDI Trustees Report*, May 7, 2024, Table V.C7, p. 156, www.ssa.gov/OACT/TR/2024/tr2024.pdf (both accessed 8/10/24).

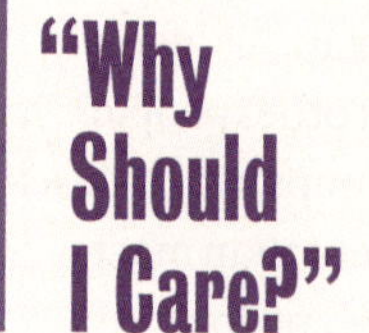

Social Security is the main source of financial support for many retired people in the United States.

In 1983 several changes were made to Social Security to strengthen its long-term finances. One significant change was a gradual increase in the retirement age from 65 to 67. People born in 1937 or earlier could retire in 2002 at age 65 and receive full benefits. Between 2003 and 2027 the retirement age increases gradually to 67 for full benefits. Early retirement at 62 is an option, if the retiree is willing to accept a permanently reduced benefit level. Delaying retirement until age 70 permanently increases the retiree's Social Security benefits.

Social Security's Long-Term Challenges Despite its successes and overall popularity, Social Security faces long-term problems. Unless certain fundamental issues are tackled, the program will be unable to cover its obligations. The longer we wait to address the shortfall, the more difficult solving the problem will be.

Basic changes in the nation's demographic profile are driving the projected shortfall. The **baby-boom generation**, people born between 1946 and 1964, is retiring at an increasing rate. The COVID pandemic produced the "Great Resignation," especially for those in the peak earning years of 55–65. Of course, those early retirees cannot receive full benefits, but they also are not paying Social Security taxes if they are not working.[62] Between 2000 and 2030 the number of Americans over the age of 65 will more than double, whereas the number of working-age Americans (20–64) will grow by only 19 percent.[63] This trend means that there will be fewer workers to support the increasing number of retirees. In fact, the number of workers per Social Security recipient fell from 16.5 in 1950 to 2.7 in 2023; by 2040 it will be only 2.3.[64] See Figure 16.4 for evidence of the aging population.

"Wait a minute," you may be saying. "Why does it matter how many workers there are for each retiree? I thought that Social Security was a pension program that you pay into while you're working and then get the benefits when you retire." Not exactly. Social Security is not a self-funded pension but a "pay as you go" system in which today's workers support today's retirees through the payroll tax discussed earlier. Therefore,

baby-boom generation
Americans born between 1946 and 1964, who are retiring in large numbers over the next 20 years.

DID YOU KNOW?

22.4%

of women and 31.5 percent of men between 65 and 74 are working full-time.

Source: Bureau of Labor Statistics.

FIGURE 16.4

People 65 and Older as a Share of the U.S. Population

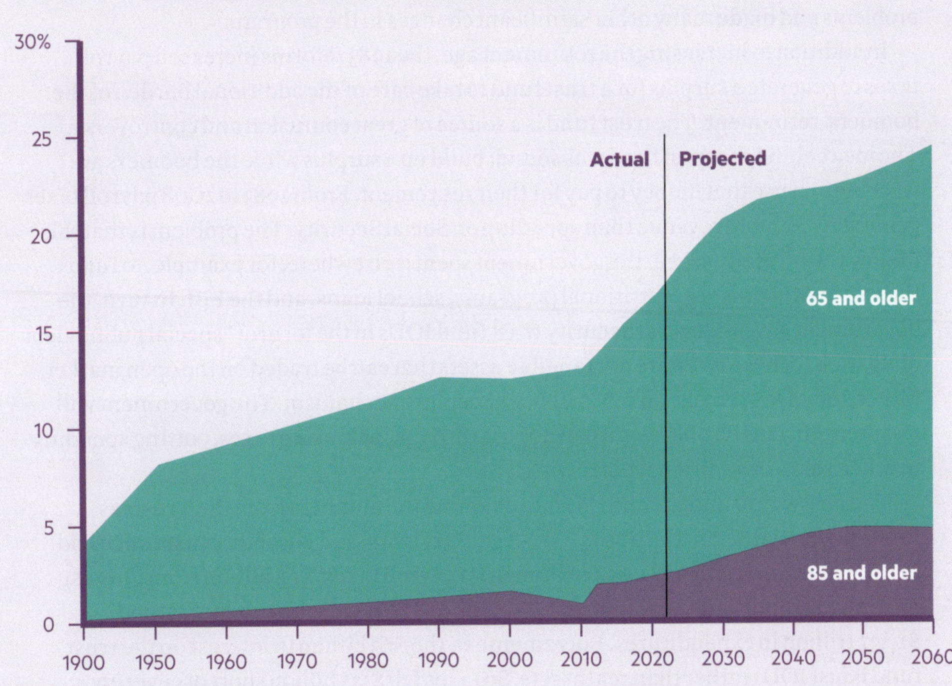

Elderly people will constitute a much larger share of the U.S. population in 2060 than they do today. How might the aging population affect social policy—both in terms of the politics of policy making and in terms of the fiscal implications of this trend?

Source: United States Census Bureau, "2023 National Population Projections Tables: Main Series," Table 2, www.census.gov/data/tables/2023/demo/popproj/2023-summary-tables.html (accessed 8/10/24).

the huge increase in the number of retirees (or Boomers retiring early!) will strain the system because each worker will have to pay higher taxes to maintain the same level of Social Security benefits. Of course, benefits could be cut, but the third-rail status of the program has prevented that, at least up to now.

Another problem with the pay-as-you-go nature of Social Security is the intergenerational transfer of wealth. The flip side of Social Security's success in reducing the poverty rate for seniors is that more children and working poor are in poverty today (15.3 percent of those under 18 are in poverty, compared with only 9.7 percent of those over 65 and 10 percent of those between 18 and 65).[65] Some critics have wondered if it makes sense, for example, for single mothers working for the minimum wage or recent college graduates who are starting their careers and paying off student loans to pay 6.2 percent of their income in taxes to support the benefits of some people who are living comfortably in retirement. This critique also points out that current retirees will receive far more in benefits than they paid in Social Security taxes, while many current workers won't get back as much as they paid in (if interest on the taxes paid is considered). For example, the average worker who retired in 1990 got back all their Social Security taxes, plus interest, by 1999. It is difficult to project the rate of return for current workers because we do not know what future benefits or taxes will be.[66] However, it is safe to bet that taxes will be higher and benefits will not maintain the same rate of increase that they have had for the past several decades. Therefore, today's retirees are reaping a windfall that strikes some critics as unfair, especially given that these retirees are better off, on average, than the workers who are currently paying taxes. Now you can start to see why reforming Social Security is so controversial. Debate over Social Security reform exposes highly charged class-based and intergenerational tensions.

Policy makers have known since the early 1960s about the eventual wave of retiring baby boomers, so why haven't they remedied the boomers' effect on Social Security? Actually, Social Security faced its first real crisis in the early 1980s, well before the boomers started retiring. Benefits had increased faster than payroll taxes throughout the 1970s, and the Social Security Administration estimated that it would not be able to meet its obligations as early as 1983. As a result, President Reagan and Congress passed the 1983 Social Security Amendments, which solved Social Security's short-term problems and made many other significant changes in the program.

In addition to increasing the retirement age, the 1983 reforms increased payroll taxes to generate a surplus for a trust fund to take care of the additional burden of the boomers' retirement. The trust fund is a source of great confusion and controversy. The idea behind the trust fund was sound: build up a surplus while the boomers are working and use that money to pay for their retirement. From 1983 to 2008 payroll taxes generated far more revenue than spending on Social Security. The problem is that this money wasn't really saved: the government spent it elsewhere, for example, to fund the war in Afghanistan, nutritional programs, school loans, and the FBI. In turn, the government gave the Social Security trust fund IOUs in the form of "special public-debt obligation." These IOUs are not tangible assets that can be traded on the open market; rather, they are used like an internal bookkeeping mechanism. The government will pay them off, but the only way it can do so is through increasing taxes, cutting spending in other areas, or additional borrowing.

The best way to understand this is to examine the numbers from the Trustees Report on Social Security. In 2023, Old-Age, Survivors, and Disability Insurance had \$1.167 trillion in income (\$1.054 trillion from payroll taxes, \$63 billion from interest on the trust fund, and \$50 billion from taxation of Social Security benefits) and \$1.237 trillion in expenditures. But remember, the \$63 billion in interest on the trust fund is just IOUs rather than real assets. So taxes fell \$133 billion short of covering

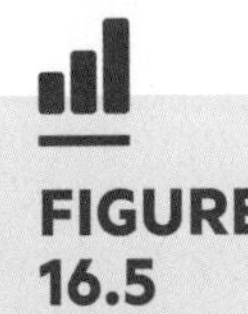

FIGURE 16.5

Social Security Trust Fund

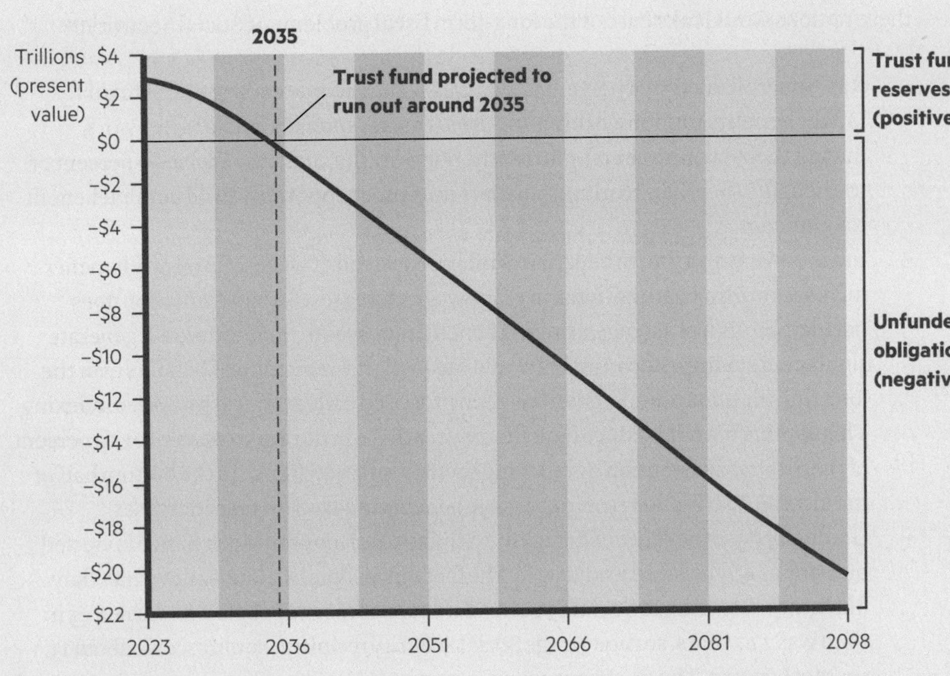

Since 2010, the cost of the Social Security program has exceeded Social Security payroll taxes, so taxes will need to be raised to cover the trust fund's obligations and the program's ongoing expenses. What do you think are the best solutions to address the long-term future of Social Security? What are the politically viable solutions?

Source: Social Security Administration, "The 2024 Annual Report of the Board of Trustees of the Federal Old-Age and Survivors Insurance and Federal Disability Insurance Trust Funds," May 7, 2024, Figure II.D5, www.ssa.gov/OACT/TR/2024/tr2024.pdf (accessed 8/10/24).

expenses ([$1,054 + $50] – $1,237). This means that the shortfall had to be made up with general tax revenue. The present value of the trust fund peaked at $2.9 trillion in 2019 and has moved downward since then as promised benefits exceed payroll tax revenue. The trust fund runs out in 2035, at which point the Social Security system will be able to fund only about 79 percent of its obligations.[67]

Democrats and Republicans alike have misused this issue for political purposes. Democrats criticize Republicans any time they try to reform Social Security, claiming that the program is on strong fiscal ground—while ignoring that the need for $2.24 trillion from general taxes over an 11-year period (from 2024 to 2035) will further strain the system and that a huge shortfall remains, even after generating that additional money. Republicans argue that the system is in crisis and that privatization is the only way out. Some Republicans suggest that Social Security will be "bankrupt" in 2035, which is incorrect given that the system would still be able to pay 79 percent of its obligations. Although both sides have used the issue as demagoguery, both parties do raise important points. Republicans are correct that the sooner we act, the better. The system may not be in crisis today, but it *will* be if we don't do anything about it soon. Democrats are correct that the problems can be solved with relatively small changes to benefits and taxes (the most recent Trustees Report estimates that the 75-year projected shortfall amounts to 3.89 percent of taxable payroll), but the required changes won't be small if we wait much longer.[68]

Social Security Reform So what is to be done? Dozens of plans to reform Social Security and make it fiscally sound for coming generations have been suggested. There is a surprising amount of agreement among all the serious plans that saving Social Security requires a mixture of benefit cuts and tax increases. The calculations get very complicated in terms of the projected fiscal impact of various reforms, but a mixture of these options would take care of the long-term fiscal problems of Social Security:[69]

- Raise payroll taxes by 1 percent and increase the income ceiling that is taxable.
- Lower benefits for nonworking spouses (that is, spouses who did not work during their earning years). Currently, nonworking spouses receive 50 percent of the benefits that their working partners do. Some proposals would cut that benefit to 33 percent.
- Index current and future benefits to inflation instead of wages. Currently benefit increases are linked to national average wage increases. Because inflation does not increase as fast as wages, linking benefit increases to inflation would generate significant savings. Because this would mean a large reduction of benefits over the long run, a less extreme version has been proposed called progressive price indexing. This approach would reduce benefits only for those in the top 50 percent or 70 percent of the income distribution by indexing them to inflation (those in the bottom half of the income distribution would still have benefits indexed to wage increases).
- Gradually raise the retirement age to 70 (by 2030). This proposed change is viewed by many as fair because it adjusts for the fact that people live longer now than they did in the early years of Social Security. Life expectancy of people who turned 65 in 1940 was 77.7 years, so the average Social Security recipient would receive about 13 years of benefits. Those who turned 65 in 2023 could expect to live 19.2 more years, and life expectancy is expected to increase by about six months per decade. Therefore, by 2035 the average life expectancy for those who reach 65 will be 85.3 years (it is 86.6 for women and 84.1 for men). To bring the expected stream of benefits back in line with where it was in 1940, the retirement age would have to be increased to 73.9.[70] Changing the retirement age to 70 would save $620 billion by 2040.

More controversial proposals include the following:

- Lower benefits for wealthier recipients. The strongest argument in favor of this approach is that Jeff Bezos doesn't need the measly couple of thousand dollars he will receive each month from Social Security. In fact, he wouldn't even notice if that money was used to reduce Social Security's deficit. More broadly, if benefits are phased out for those in the top third of income levels, it will save billions of dollars a year. The main argument against this proposal is that it would end the universal nature of Social Security and possibly turn it into another welfare program.
- Eliminate the $147,000 taxable maximum or raise the limit to $350,000.

A bipartisan commission established by President Obama to examine the long-term viability of Social Security favored increasing the retirement age to keep up with longevity; increasing the amount of income subject to the payroll tax to 90 percent of all income; and making benefits more progressive, which would reduce benefits for wealthier people while increasing them for poorer people. The commission said that these changes would place Social Security on a secure long-term foundation.[71] However, despite the bipartisan nature of the recommendations, Congress ignored the report.

privatization
The process of transferring the management of a government program (like Social Security) from the public sector to the private sector.

The most controversial plans concern partial or full **privatization** of Social Security. This is the main issue that divides Democrats and Republicans: Democrats favor maintaining the basic structure of Social Security's public social insurance system, and Republicans favor moving part or all of the "pay as you go" system to private accounts. The central argument in favor of private accounts is that over the long term investing in the stock market has historically provided returns higher in value than the Social Security checks that people can expect to receive. Also, with private accounts, all assets in the account

As the baby-boom generation retires, additional stress will be placed on the Social Security system unless significant reform takes place. Some proposals for reform include raising the retirement age or lowering benefits, which could disadvantage some retirees in the short term but would help ensure that the Social Security trust fund could still meet its obligations to younger Americans as they retire in the decades to come.

are owned by the individual and that person's heirs, whereas with Social Security, when an individual dies, their heirs do not receive any additional benefits from the individual's lifetime contributions to Social Security (but a surviving spouse continues to receive benefits from those contributions that will vary depending on the couple's work histories). Advocates argue that if all workers were able to take their 6.2 percent payroll tax and put that in a retirement account, they would have a modest nest egg by the time they retired.

Democrats point out the problems with this approach—most important, the transition costs. Because the current system is "pay as you go," if we stopped taking payroll taxes and allowed people to put the money into private accounts, there wouldn't be any money to pay for today's retirees and everyone else who has paid into the system for a substantial number of years. These transition costs are estimated to be $7 to $8 *trillion*!

A second criticism of privatization is that Social Security should be a part of everyone's retirement plan that they can count on. Investing in the stock market is fine as a supplement to Social Security, but it is too risky to be counted on as a sole source of retirement income. Although it is true that the stock market outperforms other investments over the long haul, there have been periods as long as 20 years when stock market returns have been flat. So if you happened to retire at the end of one of those slumps, you could find yourself with a much smaller nest egg than you had counted on. Finally, critics point out that the administrative overhead costs of these private accounts would eat up much of the additional returns that they might earn.

These issues are not likely to be resolved any time soon, which illustrates that politics is conflictual. Social Security reform can pit one generation against another or wealthy people against poor people. The stakes in Social Security are extremely high because it is the most popular and visible social program, which makes it all the more difficult to handle.

Health care

Health care policy seemed as difficult to reform as Social Security. Every president since Theodore Roosevelt who attempted comprehensive reform failed until President Obama's success in 2010 with the ACA. In order to understand the law, we have to understand how health care is provided in the United States and the factors that the ACA has been designed to address: the nation's aging population, health care costs that are rising faster than inflation, and the lack of health insurance among a significant number of Americans before the implementation of the law. The United States spends more on health care than any other nation in the world—$4.8 trillion, or 17.6 percent of GDP, compared with 9.9 percent for other developed countries (for example, Germany 11.8 percent, France 11.9 percent, and Italy 8.4 percent.[72] All these countries have government-funded universal health care; thus, we spend at least 50 percent more than they do (in relative terms) but leave 25 million people without coverage.[73] This illustrates the issue with the two-tier system of health care in the United States, in which those who have access to health care get some of the best carein the world and those without access are much less likely to get the health care they need.

DID YOU KNOW?

62.6 million

people received benefits from Medicare in 2021.

Source: Centers for Medicare and Medicaid Services.

Medicare and Medicaid As Figure 16.6 shows, our current system combines government spending (Medicare and Medicaid), private insurance, and out-of-pocket payments. Medicare and Medicaid, the two pillars of federally provided health care that predate the ACA, are administered by the Department of Health and Human Services.

FIGURE 16.6

The Health Care Dollar: Where It Comes from and Where It Goes, 2020

Funding for our current health care system comes from a variety of sources and is spent on many types of care. In an effort to slow the increases in health care costs, which areas should receive the most attention?

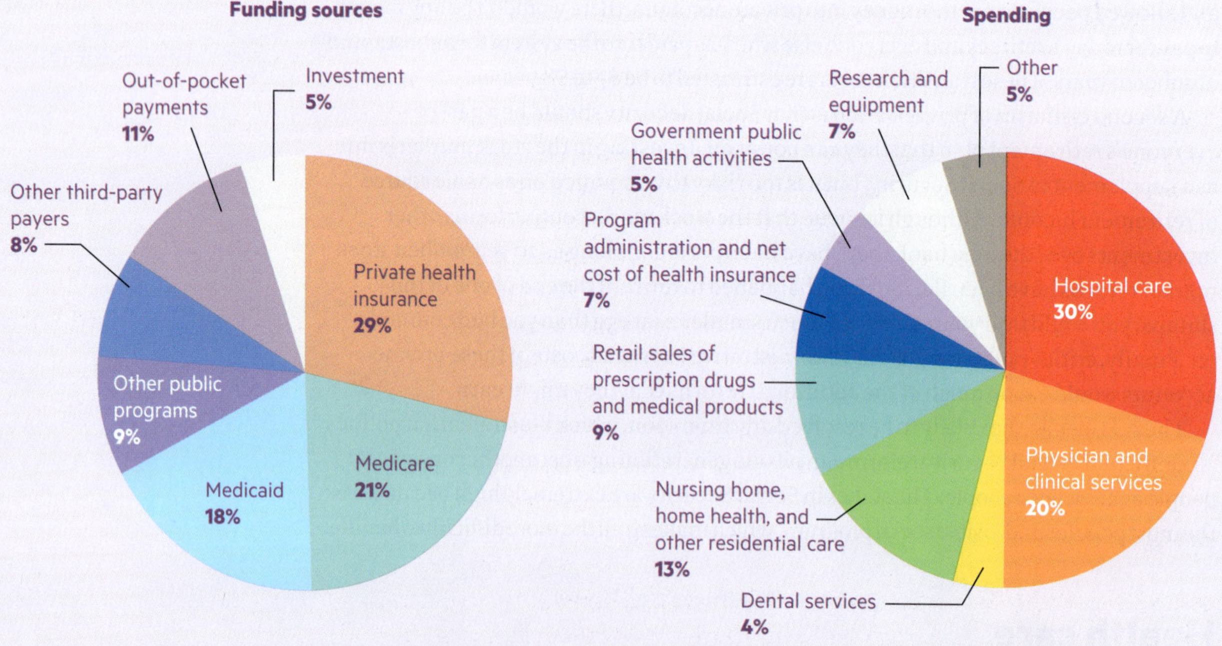

Note: Percentages shown may not add up to 100 percent due to rounding.

Source: "The Nation's Health Dollar ($4.5 Trillion), Calendar Year 2022," Center for Medicare and Medicaid Services, www.cms.gov/files/document/nations-health-dollar-where-it-came-where-it-went.pdf (accessed 8/11/24).

Medicare, the federal health care program for retired people, has three main parts. Part A automatically applies to retirees when they qualify for Social Security; it covers inpatient care in hospitals and skilled nursing facilities, hospice care, and some home health care. Medicare Part B helps cover doctors' services; outpatient hospital care; some other medical services that Part A does not cover, such as some physical and occupational therapy; and other types of home health care. In 2003, Congress passed an important new benefit, the Medicare Prescription Drug, Improvement, and Modernization Act (Part D). The plan covers about 75 percent of the cost of prescription drugs for anyone who is enrolled in Part A or Part B of Medicare, up to a certain level of expenses.

Medicare
The federal health care plan created in 1965 that provides coverage for retired Americans for hospital care (Part A), medical care (Part B), and prescription drugs (Part D).

The other government health care program, **Medicaid**, serves poor people who otherwise would have no health care. Medicaid is administered through the states with substantial funding from the federal government. Although Medicaid is an **entitlement**, states have considerable discretion over the program. As the government's website on Medicaid explains, each state

Medicaid
An entitlement program funded by the federal and state governments that provides health care coverage for low-income Americans who would otherwise be unable to afford health care.

entitlement
Any federal government program that provides benefits to Americans who meet requirements specified by law.

establishes its own eligibility standards; determines the type, amount, duration, and scope of services; sets the rate of payment for services; and administers its own program. Medicaid policies for eligibility, services, and payment are complex and vary considerably, even among states of similar size or geographic proximity. Thus, a person who is eligible for Medicaid in one state may not be eligible in another state, and the services provided may differ considerably in amount, duration, or scope from services provided in a similar or neighboring State.[74]

This variation in state coverage means that some states cover virtually all poor people and others cover as few as one-third of those in need. Overall, 89.9 million Americans receive health care through Medicaid at a cost of $803 billion. The federal government reimburses the states for 60 percent of the costs ($482 billion in 2022), but this percentage varies by state income level and whether or not a state accepted the expansion of Medicaid under Obamacare, as we will discuss below.[75] The federal government paid all the costs associated with expanding Medicaid for the 12 poorest states in fiscal year 2019 under the enhanced reimbursements from the ACA, and 88 percent of the costs for the 14 wealthiest states, which is the minimum level set by law.[76] The American Rescue Plan Act of 2021 also covered the costs of providing COVID-19 vaccines for Medicaid enrollees.[77] Like Medicare, Medicaid faces growing budgetary pressures in the coming years. An increasing share of Medicaid's costs is for long-term nursing home care for the indigent elderly, and the need for this service continues to grow as the population ages. At the other end of the age spectrum, Medicaid was expanded in 1997 to provide health care for children in families that make too much to qualify for Medicaid but not enough to buy private insurance for their children (incomes that are no more than double the poverty level). By 2022, the Children's Health Insurance Program (CHIP) covered 6.8 million children, and 33.8 million additional children were covered by Medicaid.[78] This popular program had always received strong bipartisan support until 2017, when House Republicans attempted to tie cuts in Obamacare to reauthorization of CHIP. A deadlock left the program unfunded for nearly four months, until Congress reauthorized it for six more years early in 2018.[79]

Federally Provided Health Care's Long-Term Challenges The long-term fiscal problems of Medicare and Medicaid are severe. In fact, they dwarf Social Security's problems. The 2024 *Medicare Trustees Report* estimates that Social Security's unfunded liabilities through 2099, or the amount of additional money (beyond the current payroll tax) required to fund all the program's commitments, are $24.9 trillion,

FIGURE 16.7

Projected National Spending on Health Care (Percentage of GDP)

If current spending patterns hold, an increasing percentage of federal spending will be devoted to health care, crowding out other programs. Clearly, such trends are not sustainable. What changes do you support to reduce health care spending in the long run?

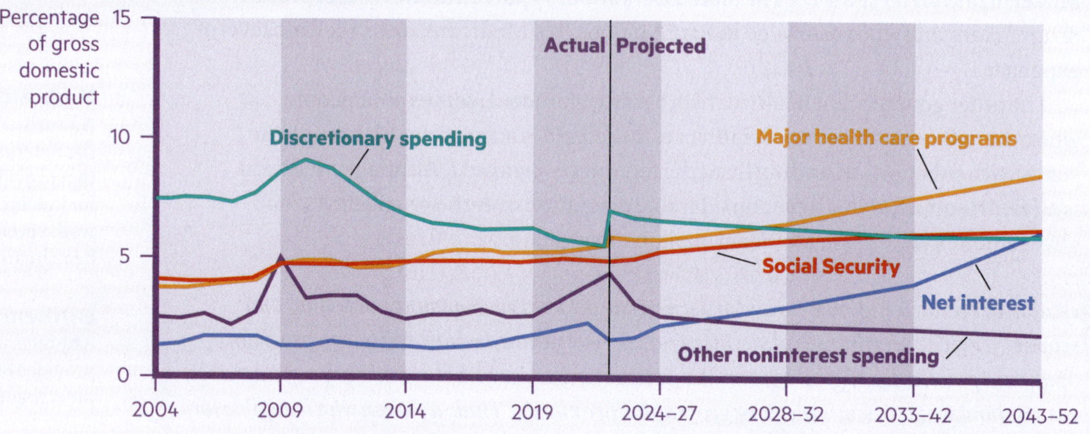

Source: Historic data are from Congressional Budget Office, "The 2019 Long-Term Budget Outlook," p. 3, www.cbo.gov/system/files/2019-06/55331-LTBO-2.pdf; projections are from "The Budget and Economic Outlook: 2022 to 2032," Congressional Budget Office, May 2022, p. 18, www.cbo.gov/system/files/2022-05/57950-Outlook.pdf (both accessed 6/17/22).

and Medicare has unfunded liabilities of $50.2 trillion.[80] Even though such projections depend on assumptions about future economic performance, demographic trends, and other uncertain variables, the *relative* difference between the two programs is significant. Medicare's troubles are more than twice as serious as Social Security's! Although the long-term Medicare deficit is huge, the projected unfunded liabilities were cut in half by the ACA. However, the trustees noted that their projections assume that cuts in Medicare reimbursements mandated in the new health care law will stick. The report expressed skepticism that this would happen.[81]

Another study by the nonpartisan Congressional Budget Office (CBO) shows that federal spending on health care (including Medicare, Medicaid, and subsidies for the new health insurance exchanges) will continue to grow through 2052 (see Figure 16.7). The CBO estimates that by 2052 federal spending on health care, Social Security, and interest on the debt will reach 21.1 percent of GDP. That is, if the size of the federal government stays around its historic average of 20.8 percent of GDP, the two major social-policy programs plus interest on the debt constitute all of federal spending by 2052. The choices are clear: everything else must be cut from the budget (defense, education, transportation), health care costs and Social Security must be reined in, or the size of government must grow. Clearly, the current trends are not sustainable.

DID YOU KNOW?

Twenty-eight percent of Americans who buy insurance on the health care exchange get coverage for

$10

or less per month, 85 percent of those with a marketplace account get some assistance. The average cost for premiums is $133 per month.

Source: ObamacareFacts.com and MorningConsult.com.

Health Care Reform Central to President Obama's 2008 campaign platform was reforming America's health care system. Upon election in 2009, he outlined several goals: controlling health care costs, providing health insurance for more Americans (as close to universal coverage as possible), and paying for the program without adding to the deficit. He then urged Congress to hammer out the details.

In formulating the legislation, Congress sifted through hundreds of options that represent three main types of systems: (1) national single-payer plans, (2) state-regulated health insurance networks combined with public subsidies to help pay for insurance for those who cannot afford it, and (3) market-based solutions based on tax credits and flexible spending accounts. The first of these was quickly rejected by Congress and is not likely to be implemented in the United States, despite being the program of choice for nearly all other Western developed nations. Critics dismiss single-payer plans as "socialized medicine" and point to the rationing of care that often occurs under such programs. However, the single-payer plan received a boost in the 2020 Democratic presidential primary when it was recast as "Medicare for All." Ten of the 27 candidates, most prominently Bernie Sanders and Elizabeth Warren, endorsed some form of the idea, while Joe Biden did not.

Similarly, market-based solutions, which most Republicans supported, were rejected by Democratic leaders who believed the approach would leave too many Americans uninsured. This approach has the greatest potential for addressing the inflation of health care costs, but some health care professionals argued that many people would lack the knowledge base necessary to make the appropriate decisions concerning their own health care, because buying health care is much more difficult than shopping for food, clothing, or other consumer goods.

This left the middle ground between a single-payer plan and market-based approaches. In the introduction to this chapter, we discussed the politics of how reform passed. Here we summarize the main provisions, as it is impossible to discuss all the details of the voluminous, more-than-2,000-page law that one reporter described as "twice as long, and half as intelligible, as Tolstoy's masterwork *War and Peace*."[82]

Understanding the ACA ("Obamacare") President Obama's first goal—comprehensive coverage—was essential. The problem had to be tackled as a whole. If the law were to require insurance companies to cover people with preexisting conditions without mandating that everyone have insurance, people would avoid personal expense and wait until they were seriously ill before they purchased any health insurance. To spread the costs of expensive care needed by those with

Proposed budgetary solutions to Medicare and Social Security's unfunded liabilities involve politically unpopular benefit cuts and tax increases. Similarly, public support for Medicare for All, a proposed program that would extend government-funded health care benefits to all Americans, has increased significantly in recent years and gained further traction during the 2020 Democratic presidential primary, with candidates Elizabeth Warren, Kirsten Gillibrand, Kamala Harris, and Bernie Sanders voicing their support for the proposal.

preexisting conditions and others, the law needed to mandate coverage for all, thus "pooling" healthy people and young people with older and sick people. Comprehensive coverage was achieved by requiring businesses with more than 50 employees to provide coverage and by requiring all individuals without employer coverage to purchase insurance through new state-regulated private health insurance exchanges, which were implemented in 2014. Businesses and individuals who did not comply with the mandate would face government fines. However, individuals who could not afford to purchase their own insurance would receive federal tax credit subsidies on a sliding scale (using a complicated formula that would provide the biggest subsidies to the poorest people and some support to people with incomes all the way up to four times the federal poverty rate). The individual mandate was one of the most controversial parts of the bill, but it was repealed, effective in 2019. During the formulation of the law, it was stated that most people who were pleased with their current health insurance through their employer would not have to change anything. However, people with policies that did not meet the minimum standards of the law would be required to get new insurance policies. This became a sticky issue for President Obama once the ACA was rolled out.

Other features of the law included incentives to computerize medical records, seen as a way to reduce medical mistakes, facilitate medical evaluations, and, as a result, improve the overall quality of care. Integration of technology into medical processes and record keeping was one of the law's central cost-control mechanisms. In addition, a new nonprofit organization, the Patient-Centered Outcomes Research Institute, would be authorized to engage in "comparative effectiveness research" to identify the best practices in health care. It would research such questions as which health care procedures work to make people healthier and which are a waste of money, and why some parts of the country spend more than twice as much on treating the same conditions. The ACA would encourage health care providers to adopt identified best practices. The law was also designed to focus more resources on preventive care to keep people healthy, so that, theoretically, people would be less likely to get sick and need further, expensive treatment.

One other goal was that health care had to pay for itself. Obama vowed that the bill would not "add one dime to the deficit." With a price tag of just under $1 trillion over the first 10 years, the bill was a challenge to finance. However, a combination of higher Medicare taxes, a new investment tax for the wealthy, an excise tax on insurers for expensive "Cadillac" health care plans, new fees for drug companies and health insurers, and cuts in Medicare reimbursement meant that the law would actually reduce the federal deficit by $143 billion over the first decade.[83] While some of those taxes were never fully implemented (such as the "Cadillac tax"), the law actually did a better job of cutting costs than initial estimates predicted. One study estimated that the Affordable Care Act saved $2.3 trillion in health care costs over 10 years.[84]

Nonetheless, the political battle over health care reform was not over when Obama signed the bill into law. House Republicans repeatedly attempted to repeal the law. As discussed in the chapter opener, although these efforts were not successful, the rollout of the law was very rocky. The national health care insurance exchange, HealthCare.gov, was supposed to be operational on October 1, 2013, but the system repeatedly crashed during the first several months of operation, leading to substantial delays and great frustration for Americans attempting to enroll. Millions of poor Americans were not able to get coverage when the states they lived in declined the option to expand Medicaid to cover everyone whose income was 138 percent of the poverty line (see Chapter 3 for a discussion of this conflictual issue). Because of the bumpy start, President Obama granted about a dozen extensions of various deadlines, including enrollment deadlines for the individual mandate, the employer mandate to cover all employees for businesses with between 50 and 100 employees (which was extended until the end of 2016), the high-risk pool that was intended to be temporary, and the requirement that people who had previously been covered by a substandard insurance policy get insurance on the exchange (this, too, was extended until the end of 2016).[85] An additional problem is that not as many young healthy people have signed up on the exchanges as predicted. So some insurance companies, such as Aetna and United Health, have lost significant amounts of money and are pulling out of many states. This means less competition and rising rates.

The Future of "Obamacare" President Trump and the Republican leadership in Congress vowed to "repeal and replace" Obamacare. However, they faced many challenges. First, more than 27 million more Americans had health insurance because of the law: 10.5 million Americans who previously did not have health insurance successfully used the exchanges to sign up for insurance, and more than 6 million young adults were able to remain on their parents' health insurance until age 26.[86] Also, 12.3 million new enrollees were covered through the expansion of Medicaid.[87] Second, many popular parts of the law had been in effect since 2010—and these types of benefits are hard to repeal once the American public recognizes their value. These included a high-risk insurance pool for adults with preexisting conditions (which includes making it against the law for insurers of children under 19 years old with preexisting conditions to be dropped from their parents' policies); a fix for the Medicare prescription drug plan "donut hole" (previously, people who spent above a minimal level on drugs but below a high amount were not covered by the law); and coverage for young adults (up to age 26) on their parents' plans. Other popular parts of the law that went into effect in 2013 prohibited insurers from charging co-payments or deductibles for preventive care on all new insurance plans and prevented insurers from dropping policy holders when they get sick.

However, President Trump and congressional Republicans tried to keep the popular parts of Obamacare while getting rid of the unpopular parts (such as the individual mandate). The difficulty is that if insurance companies must provide coverage for people with preexisting conditions but people are not required to buy insurance, then people will wait until they have some serious condition before they sign up for insurance, while healthy people will opt out. This means that rates will go up for everyone, making it even more difficult to get coverage. This appears to have happened in some markets: premiums for health insurance on the state exchanges increased by double digits, while several million people dropped their coverage once they were no longer required to have it.[88] Although Republicans agreed on repealing Obamacare, no single Republican alternative had universal support within the party. Most Republicans argued for market-based reforms that would introduce more competition into the system to help keep costs down and for health savings accounts that would be tax deductible. But the basic problem was not resolved of how to maintain coverage for the 27 million people who had insurance under Obamacare at the time of the attempted repeal. Now more than 45 million have been covered by the law, so future attempts to change or repeal the law will be even more difficult.

Income support and welfare

When most people think of social policy aimed at helping the poor, they think of welfare. The earlier section on the history of social policy outlined the evolution of welfare from a limited policy aimed at helping dependent children of single mothers to a broader policy directed more generally to households headed by one person. Welfare

income support
Government programs that provide support to low-income Americans, such as welfare, food assistance, unemployment compensation, and the EITC.

is usually thought of as cash support for people who cannot support themselves. However, **income support** can take many forms, including nutritional support benefits, unemployment insurance, the Earned Income Tax Credit (EITC), and Supplemental Security Income (SSI). We will discuss each and then describe the major reform of welfare in 1996.

The Supplemental Nutrition Assistance Program (SNAP) provides nutritional support benefits, which today are government-issued debit cards that may be used as cash to buy groceries. Anyone who has an income that is less than 130 percent of the poverty level and has resources that do not exceed specific levels may qualify for SNAP. In 2024, the maximum monthly gross income for a family of four to qualify for SNAP was $3,250. As the effects of the 2008 economic crisis lingered through 2013, the number of people using SNAP peaked at a record of nearly 47.8 million in June 2013, with an average monthly benefit of $133 per person. With improvements in the economy, by May 2024 the numbers had dropped to 41.7 million and $212 per person (the average benefit was increased substantially during the COVID-19 pandemic).[89]

The Federal-State Unemployment Compensation Program was established in 1935 as part of the Social Security Act. The U.S. Department of Labor oversees the program, but it is administered by the states. The program provides temporary and partial wage replacement for people who have been laid off from their jobs and helps stabilize the economy during recessions. States set a broad range in benefit levels, minimum amount of income earned, and hours worked during the period leading up to unemployment. (For example, you do not qualify for unemployment insurance if you have worked only five hours a week in a minimum wage job.) Also, laid-off workers have to make themselves "available for work." About 97 percent of workers are covered by unemployment insurance, but only about half of the eligible unemployed make use of the benefit. The regular state programs provide up to 26 weeks of income support, and the Federal-State Extended Benefits Program temporarily provides up to 20 additional weeks in states with relatively high unemployment rates. The COVID-19 pandemic overwhelmed the unemployment compensation programs because 30 million people had claimed regular state unemployment insurance by mid-May 2020, up from an average of 2 million in a typical week. By August 2024, the number of people receiving unemployment compensation was down to 1.9 million as the unemployment rate remained at a relatively low level.[90]

The EITC is one of the most successful programs for providing income support for the working poor. Established in 1975, the program aims to help poor people move from welfare to work: it provides tax credits to people who do not earn enough to pay income taxes and are relatively poor. It is intended to offset the burden of Social Security taxes, which all workers pay as part of payroll taxes. In 2023, you could qualify for an EITC as a couple if you had two children and earned less than $59,478, one child and earned less than $53,120, or no children and earned less than $24,210; the figures were about $6,500 lower if you were single.[91] The federal government provided $57 billion in EITCs in 2019 to more than 23 million recipients, with an average annual benefit of $2,411;[92] Figure 16.8 shows average yearly individual recipient figures for other programs. Clearly, nobody is getting rich from this program, but it provides added assistance for the working poor.

Another source of income support for poor people is Supplemental Security Income (SSI), a program for aged, blind, and disabled individuals with limited income. The Social Security Administration runs the SSI program, but it is financed through general tax revenues, not Social Security taxes, and it is a means-tested program rather than a contributory program. Many states supplement the maximum monthly federal benefit of $943 for an individual and $1,415 for a couple (in 2024). More than 7.4 million people received SSI benefits in early 2024, and 84 percent of those recipients were disabled or blind.[93]

FIGURE 16.8

Average Yearly Benefits in Means-Tested Programs

Some types of social welfare benefits have increased in the past few decades, whereas others have decreased and some have remained the same. Identify examples from each category and try to provide a political explanation for why those benefits have increased, decreased, or been funded at about the same level.

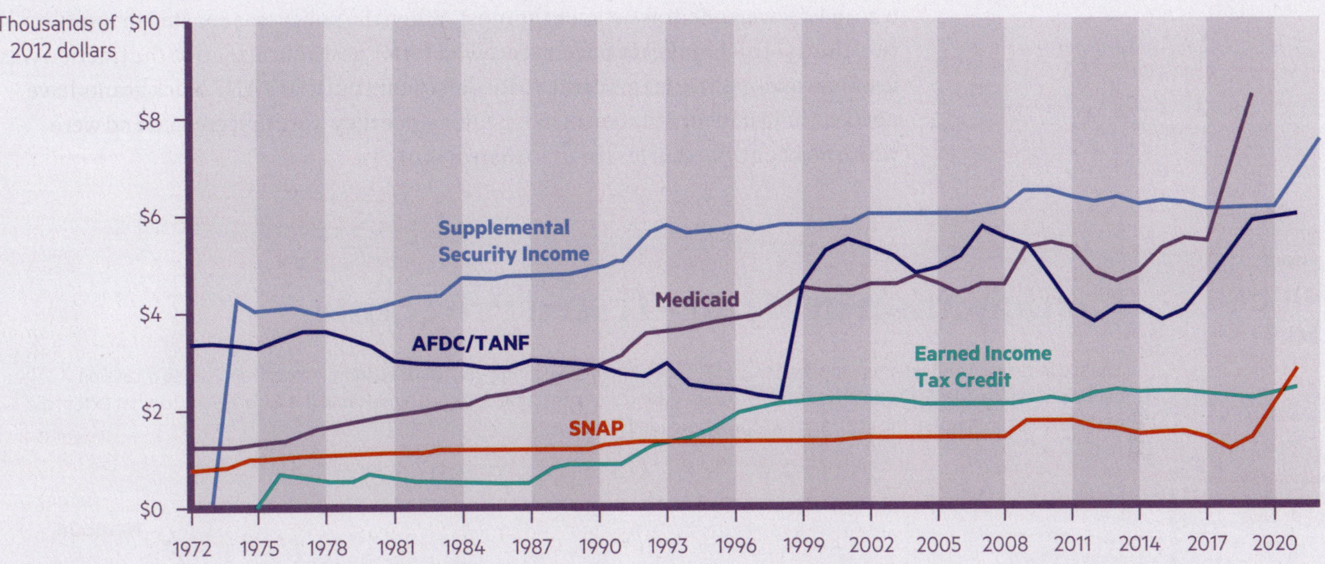

Note: Data from AFDC/TANF and the EITC cover people of all ages, including the elderly.

Source: Congressional Budget Office, "Growth in Means-Tested Programs and Tax Credits for Low-Income Households," February 11, 2013, www.cbo.gov/publication/43934 (accessed 7/5/22). Data for 2014–2019 collected from a variety of sources. Data for 2021: IRS, "EITC Fast Facts," www.eitc.irs.gov/partner-toolkit/basic-marketing-communication-materials/eitc-fast-facts/eitc-fast-facts; Center on Budget and Policy Priorities, "Policy Basics: The Supplemental Nutrition Assistance Program," www.cbpp.org/research/food-assistance/policy-basics-the-supplemental-nutrition-assistance-program-snap#:~:text=How%20Much%20Do%20Households%20Receive,meal)%20in%20fiscal%20year%202018.&text=A%20family%20with%20no%20net,size%20(see%20Table%201); Social Security Administration, "Monthly Statistical Snapshot, April 2022," www.ssa.gov/policy/docs/quickfacts/stat_snapshot/; Medicaid.gov, "How Much Do States Spend per Medicaid Enrollee?," www.medicaid.gov/state-overviews/scorecard/how-much-states-spend-per-medicaid-enrollee/index.html; Congressional Research Service, "The Temporary Assistance to Needy Families (TANF) Block Grant: Responses to Frequently Asked Questions," March 31, 2022, https://fas.org/sgp/crs/misc/RL32760.pdf (all accessed 6/17/22).

Welfare is straight cash assistance for people who are not working and do not qualify for unemployment compensation. The primary welfare program for the latter half of the twentieth century was **Aid to Families with Dependent Children (AFDC)**. This program became increasingly unpopular through the 1980s, and in 1992 Bill Clinton was the first Democratic presidential nominee to campaign against welfare, promising to "end welfare as we know it."[94] Clinton got the ball rolling on welfare reform in June 1993 by appointing a task force that submitted its bipartisan plan in January 1994; the president's plan was submitted to Congress in June. When the Republicans took over Congress in 1994, the momentum for reform grew. Clinton and Congress haggled over the issue for two years, with the president vetoing three versions of the bill that he believed were too harsh.

Finally, in 1996 Clinton and Congress agreed on a major reform called **Temporary Assistance for Needy Families (TANF)**. The new law set a five-year lifetime limit on welfare benefits, required single mothers with children above the age of five to find work after two years of receiving benefits, required unmarried mothers who were

Aid to Families with Dependent Children (AFDC)
The federal welfare program in place from 1935 until 1996, when it was replaced by TANF under President Clinton.

Temporary Assistance for Needy Families (TANF)
The welfare program that replaced AFDC in 1996, eliminating the entitlement status of welfare, shifting implementation of the policy to the states, and introducing several new restrictions on receiving aid. These changes led to a significant decrease in the number of welfare recipients.

younger than 18 years old to live with an adult and attend school to get full benefits, denied benefits to drug users who were convicted of a felony, and limited people who were not raising children and were between the ages of 18 and 50 to three months of food stamps in any three-year period in which they were not working. Perhaps most important, welfare lost its status as an entitlement and would be administered by the states with the assistance of federal block grants. In 2006, Congress reauthorized TANF and required that half of a state's caseload participate in work activities for at least 30 hours per week. Welfare reform significantly reduced the number of people on welfare, as Figure 16.9 shows, but it has been criticized for being too hard on the people who need government assistance the most. When the policy was enacted in 1996, two-thirds of all families in poverty received TANF assistance; in 2020 the fraction was less than one-quarter (21 percent). Critics also point out that TANF block grants have not been adjusted for inflation in most states since they were first created and were worth nearly 40 percent less in 2020 than in 1996.[95]

FIGURE 16.9

Participation in Means-Tested Programs

The social-policy "safety net" is supposed to protect poor Americans during periods of economic recession. A deep recession happened in the early 1980s, and the other recession during the time frame depicted here was in the early 1990s. To what extent did the safety net accomplish the goal for which it was intended?

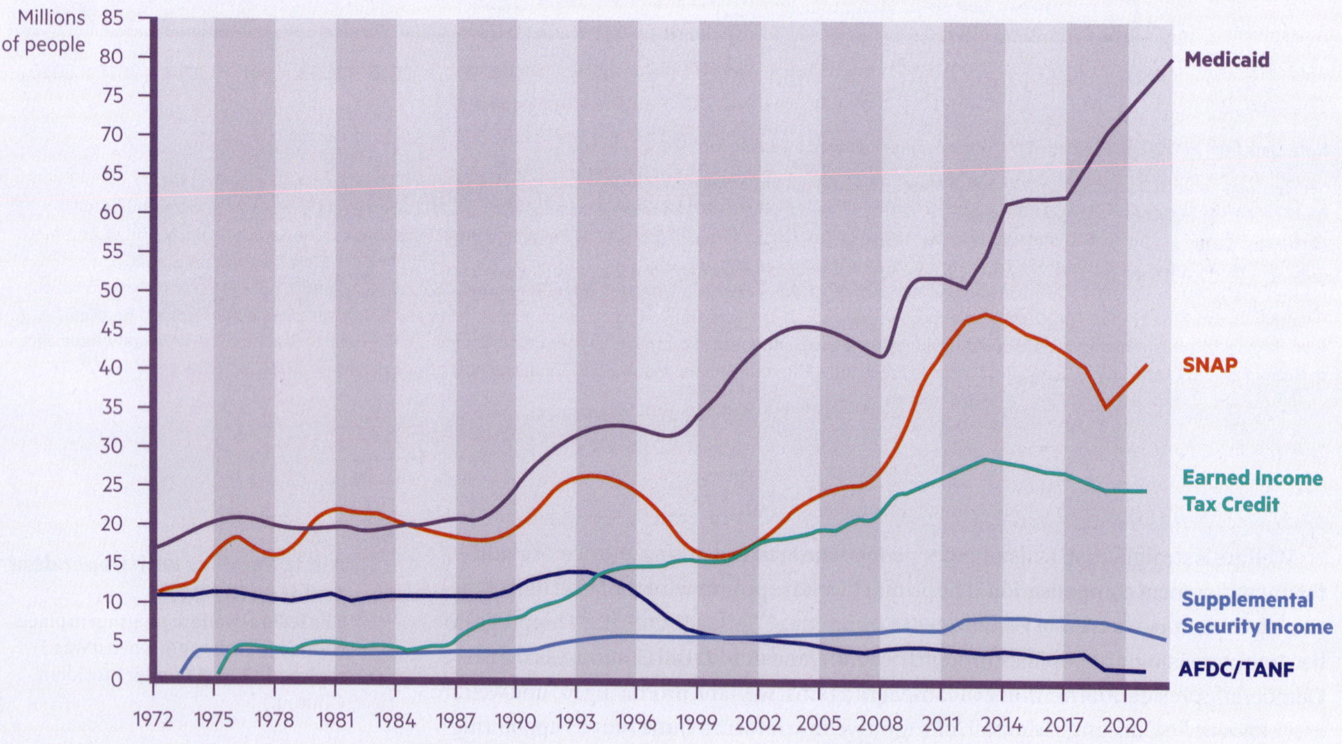

Sources: Data for 1972–2013 are from Congressional Research Service, based on data from the U.S. Department of Health and Human Services; and Congressional Budget Office, "Changes in Participation in Means-Tested Programs," February 2013, www.cbo.gov (both accessed 11/15/16). Data for 2014–2019 were collected by the author from various sources. Data for 2021 are from Medicaid.gov, "February 2022 Medicaid & CHIP Enrollment Data Highlights," www.medicaid.gov/medicaid/program-information/medicaid-and-chip-enrollment-data/report-highlights/index.html; U.S. Department of Agriculture, Food and Nutrition Service, "SNAP Data Tables," June 14, 2022, www.fns.usda.gov/pd/supplemental-nutrition-assistance-program-snap; U.S. Department of Health and Human Services, Administration for Children and Families, "TANF Total Number of Recipients," www.acf.hhs.gov/sites/default/files/documents/ofa/fy2021_tanf_caseload.pdf; IRS, "EITC Fast Facts," www.eitc.irs.gov/partner-toolkit/basic-marketing-communication-materials/eitc-fast-facts/eitc-fast-facts; and Center on Budget and Policy Priorities, "Policy Basics: Supplemental Security Income," March 2, 2022, www.cbpp.org/research/social-security/policy-basics-supplemental-security-income#:~:text=SSI%20recipients%20are%20limited%20to,and%20%241%2C157%20for%20a%20couple (all accessed 7/5/22).

Education

Education policy is largely the domain of state and local governments. For the first century of our nation's history, the national government played virtually no role in education. One important exception was the Morrill Act in 1862, also known as the Land Grant College Act. This law gave land to eligible states to establish colleges that would promote education in the practical professions such as agriculture and mechanical arts. More than 75 colleges and universities today are land grant institutions.

The next major forays by the federal government into education policy came with the GI Bill of Rights in 1944, which provided access to higher education for returning World War II veterans, and the Elementary and Secondary Education Act of 1965, which was part of President Johnson's War on Poverty. The Department of Education was created in 1980, signaling the national government's interest in playing an important role in education policy by the following:

- establishing and monitoring policies for distribution of federal financial aid for education,
- collecting data on America's schools and disseminating research,
- focusing national attention on key educational issues, and
- prohibiting discrimination and ensuring equal access to education.[96]

A more recent debate concerning the national government's role in education policy has focused on standards-based education reform: Should the national government establish standards and impose accountability as a way to improve public schools? The No Child Left Behind Act of 2001 required yearly statewide standardized testing in math and reading. If the test results showed that a school was not meeting annual academic benchmarks, it was labeled a "failing school," which meant that it lost some federal funding and its students could transfer to another public school. Critics argue that standardized test results are a poor measurement of progress because top-down standards incentivize schools to "teach to the test" and manipulate other aspects of the evaluation system. Responding to these concerns that one size does *not* fit all, Congress enacted the Every Student Succeeds Act in 2015. The new law maintains annual testing but gives states more control over setting student performance targets and school ratings.

The latest example of a nationwide, state-based effort to shape education is the Common Core standards that were developed by the National Governors Association in response to concerns that American schools were falling behind. This relatively modest set of standards in math and English was quickly adopted by 46 states between 2010 and 2015 but became a lightning rod for concern about national control of education. Conservative radio host Glenn Beck said that the standards "are breeding an entire new generation of slaves"; then–Louisiana governor Bobby Jindal compared the standards to central planning in the Soviet Union; and Florida state representative Charles Van Zant said the Common Core's goal is to "attract every one of your children to become as homosexual as they possibly can."[97] So far, the backlash has led six states to rescind their adoption of the Common Core standards, and repeal efforts are underway in at least 28 more states.[98] The assessment of the program after 10 years is that it did not do much to improve student learning, but it did lead states to raise their benchmarks and improve curricular materials.[99]

President Obama's Race to the Top grant program used a "carrot" rather than a "stick" approach to educational innovation, dedicating $4.35 billion to competitive grants from 2010 to 2013 to encourage schools to adopt more challenging standards and better tools of assessment, promote better leadership and methods for assessing and rewarding excellent teaching, create better data systems for tracking students' progress, and obtain stronger commitments for improving the worst-performing schools. These grants were aimed at strengthening the quality of public education while also improving accountability.[100] The emphasis on accountability was criticized by both the left and the right. The largest teachers' union, the National Education Association, called for Education Secretary Arne Duncan's resignation (he left the administration in early 2016). Many Republicans thought that Duncan was interfering too much in state education policy. There was more bipartisan support behind Obama's effort to expand programs to improve access to higher education, such as increasing the number of Pell Grant recipients to 9.3 million and, in 2016, launching a new online "college scorecard" to provide objective information about college costs and quality.

States and local school districts are also experimenting with various policies aimed at introducing more competition for public schools, including public school choice (allowing students to choose which public school they attend) and publicly funded vouchers for attending private schools. These approaches were strongly favored by the Trump administration's secretary of education, Betsy DeVos (see the Take a Stand feature). Private foundations have also gotten involved in education policy. The Gates Foundation has contributed more than $2.8 billion to create smaller schools, reduce class sizes, provide scholarships for higher education (most significantly, $1.5 billion to the United Negro College Fund), improve the use of data, and provide access to technology.[101]

In Virginia, citizens disagreed on whether or not the curriculum in their public schools should teach topics like systemic racism. Some argued it would make students more aware of the history of racism in this country and the work that still needs to be done to correct it, while others argued it would make students uncomfortable. Ultimately, the state legislature passed a ban on "divisive concepts," and Virginia's Republican governor Glenn Youngkin also signed a similar executive order banning certain topics.

Another significant development at the state level in 2021–2022 was the effort to define how topics such as race, sexuality, gender, and LGBTQ issues are taught. Since January 2021, 122 bills have been introduced in 33 states and ten states have enacted twelve laws.[102] For example, in Florida, a "Don't Say Gay" law prohibits any instruction about sexual orientation or gender identity between kindergarten and third grade. Other states have passed laws that prohibit the teaching of anything that would cause a student "discomfort, guilt, anguish or any other form of psychological distress on account of his or her race or sex." For example, if a student felt guilty about the legacy of slavery or anguish about the horrors of the Holocaust, a teacher could be prevented from teaching those subjects. One study found that 160 teachers were either fired or resigned their jobs in the past two academic years because of these culture wars, for being perceived as too liberal, but also for being too conservative.[103] The issue played a role in many midterm elections in 2022 and in the 2024 presidential election.

Housing

The lack of affordable housing is an increasing problem in the United States. With average rents increasing 30 percent from 2019 to 2023 (and more than 50 percent in many urban areas), the median rent for available apartments was nearly $2,000 early in 2024.[104] The United States needs more than 7 million affordable housing units for the 10.8 million families who are below the poverty line. Seventy percent of these low-income families spend more than half their income on rent.[105] The most visible consequence of the affordable housing shortage is the 326,000 Americans who are unhoused.[106]

Home ownership has been the engine of middle-class wealth creation, but that too is available to a shrinking share of the population as the median price of a home increased by 45 percent from 2019 to 2022 ($274,600 to $397,600). To qualify for a mortgage to buy a median-priced home requires an income of $82,416.[107] A recent poll showed that 49 percent of Americans say that the availability of affordable housing in their community is a major problem (and 36 percent said it is a minor problem). This is

TAKE A STAND

School Vouchers

One of the most controversial areas of education policy over the past 20 years has been school vouchers—the practice of providing taxpayers' money directly to families to allow them to send their children to private schools rather than public schools. The vouchers are similar to a scholarship and are used in 13 states, including Wisconsin, which implemented the first voucher program in 1999 in Milwaukee, and Indiana, which implemented the first statewide program in 2011.[a]

Vouchers establish needed competition between public and private schools. Supporters of the program say that it introduces competition into public education, which suffers from the inefficiencies that are typical of monopolies. They argue that many urban school systems have failed to educate their children and that poor minority students deserve a better education than the one they get in public schools. They say that students who are given the opportunity to leave public schools often improve their academic performance in private schools. Betsy DeVos, the secretary of education in the Trump administration, pushed a proposal that would provide private school vouchers for military families instead of the "impact aid" for public schools that the federal government has always provided for public schools near military bases.

Supporters of school vouchers are an unusual alliance between free market conservatives, who are typically Republicans, and minorities living in urban areas, who normally are strong Democrats. The former believe that school systems can benefit from introducing competitive market forces, and the latter are desperate for anything that will rescue their children from failing public schools. These supporters of vouchers are opposed by teachers' unions, most Democratic politicians, and those who favor strengthening the public schools by investing more money in them and trying new approaches, such as public magnet schools, charter schools, and public school choice.

Vouchers undermine an already challenged public school system. Opponents say that private schools engage in "cherry-picking," choosing the more motivated students and leaving the more difficult students to be educated in the public schools, contributing to a downward spiral in these institutions. Opponents also argue that standardized test scores do not improve for students who participate in voucher programs. Finally, they claim that voucher programs are an unconstitutional violation of the separation between church and state because an overwhelming proportion of the students in these programs attend Catholic parochial schools.

Evidence on voucher opponents' first two points is mixed, but the bulk of the evidence supports their views.

Most school vouchers go to private Catholic schools, like the one attended by the students shown here.

The most studied voucher program is the Milwaukee program mentioned earlier. In the most systematic analysis of that program, John F. Witte, political scientist and expert on education policy, argues that vouchers should be evaluated on a basic question of values, the clash between freedom of choice and equality of opportunity, rather than specific programmatic outcomes, because the effects are small to nonexistent.[b]

The Supreme Court has upheld voucher programs while asserting that they did not violate the separation of church and state. However, in a case upholding Cleveland's voucher program, the Court did not give vouchers a green light beyond the narrow facts of the case. Indeed, that 5–4 decision required a voucher program to, among other things,

- be a part of a much wider program of multiple educational options, such as magnet schools and after-school tutorial assistance;
- offer parents a real choice between religious and nonreligious education, perhaps even providing incentives for nonreligious education; and
- not only address private schools but also ensure that benefits go to schools regardless of whether they are public or private, religious or not.[c]

Meanwhile, the state supreme courts in Arizona and Colorado struck down school voucher programs as a violation of the separation of church and state, but a similar program was upheld in Alabama.

take a stand

1. What do you see as the advantages and disadvantages of providing vouchers to allow students to attend any school they want?
2. Should these programs be expanded, or would they undermine the quality of public schools?

Rising rates of homelessness have been caused by soaring housing and rent prices, housing shortages, and the COVID-19 pandemic. In reaction, Massachusetts residents gathered in front of the State House to demand the state government enact legislation to protect against a wave of evictions and foreclosures related to these pandemic-related issues.

a higher percentage than concern for crime (22 percent), COVID-19 (34 percent), and drug addiction (35 percent).[108]

While some of the conditions that have created the housing shortage are beyond the control of public policy (such as the COVID pandemic that reduced the rate of construction of new homes and rental units), existing policies do more to support housing for middle- and upper-income people than to provide affordable housing. As we discussed above, the federal government spent $80.1 billion on tax expenditures for housing in 2022, mostly for the mortgage interest deduction, property tax deduction, and capital gains tax exclusions (with almost none of that money going to affordable housing), while spending only $48.9 billion on the two most important federal programs for affordable housing: rent subsidies and public housing. The rent subsidy program (referred to as Section 8) is so underfunded that only one-quarter of the people who qualify receive subsidies. The program provides a subsidy for rent that exceeds more than 30 percent of income, but many landlords opt out of the program because of the bureaucratic red tape, and the wait for a rent voucher can be more than 10 years.[109]

Some cities, such as Minneapolis, are trying innovative solutions such as eliminating single-family zoning restrictions to try to encourage more construction of affordable housing (Oregon, California, and Maine have passed similar laws). Early analyses show that the policy has had some modest effects.[110] At the national level, the most important policy change would be to shift some of the dollars going to subsidize housing for the upper-middle income and the wealthy to affordable housing, but the tax subsidies are so popular, they would be very difficult to eliminate or reduce.

"Why Should I Care?"

Social Security and Medicare may seem like things you don't have to worry about for at least 40 years. However, 7.65 percent of every dollar you earn goes to pay for these programs. Also, given changes that will almost certainly be made to these programs in the next few years, it is important to understand what is at stake. Education policy is more obviously important for your life. While state and local politics are more central for shaping education policy, federal programs support both higher education and K–12 schools.

Unpacking the Conflict

The varying successes and failures of efforts to reform Social Security and health care reveal a great deal about the role of key players in the policy-making process. The interaction between the president and Congress is central to both stories. With Social Security reform, the president initiated a serious reform agenda, but Congress killed the proposal by failing to act. With health care reform, Congress and the president worked together to pass significant legislation, but then under different party leadership, Congress tried to undo that legislation. In both instances, interest groups played a key role. Doctors, other health care providers, insurance companies, and drug companies largely supported health care reform, which helped Congress pass the historic but controversial legislation. With Social Security reform, opposition from AARP and a tepid response from the public doomed the idea of private savings accounts, at least for now. But the last chapter on reform is yet to be written. Sooner or later, policy makers will have to confront the massive long-term deficits in these programs. Is Social Security going bankrupt, and will it therefore not pay the current generation of young Americans any benefits when they retire? Does the government spend too much money on nutritional assistance programs and welfare, or are these important tools for reducing inequality? More fundamentally, does the government have a responsibility to provide a "social safety net" for its citizens, or should more of that be left to the private sector and charitable organizations?

The experiences with social-policy reform also illustrate the themes of this book. First, health care reform is a perfect example of the conflictual nature of politics. From initial debates over health coverage for illegal immigrants and abortion to repeated efforts to repeal the ACA in the House, health care reform ignited many contentious debates. Substantive disagreements about the scope of coverage and how to pay for it also revealed deep fault lines across and within the parties. Despite this conflict, congressional leaders pieced together compromises that created an imperfect but historic law. However, conflict over social policy is far from resolved, as Republicans in Congress work to change Obamacare. The reform of Social Security and Medicare provides fertile ground for intergenerational struggle and class conflict. Clearly, resolving the long-term problems facing social policy in the United States will involve many intense debates.

Social policy, especially the recent legislative struggles over health care reform, demonstrates that political process matters. The filibuster in the Senate played an important role in the first stages of shaping health care reform, and the decision to use the reconciliation process late in the game ensured passage of the law. House Republicans' decision to shut down the government in an effort to repeal the law ended up backfiring, but it is yet another example of how the political process can be used in ways that have substantive impacts: the shutdown cost billions of dollars and slowed economic growth. Politicians' decisions have a key impact on policy outcomes, and the timing and politics of the policy-making process clearly drive the results. Had congressional leaders made different decisions, it is possible that health care reform would have failed. Finally, politics is everywhere. Social policies touch all Americans at some point in their lives, and the struggles over reforming these policies are at the core of contemporary American politics.

"What's Your Take?"

Has Obamacare been "essentially repealed"? Are Social Security and Medicare going bankrupt?

Should these social programs be strengthened or repealed?

CHECK YOUR UNDERSTANDING

"Why Should I Care?"

Social policy touches almost every aspect of our lives. It isn't just about "welfare" policy, but more so about the role of the government ensuring that Americans have their basic needs met, including health care and education, homeownership and housing, agriculture and business, employment and wages, as well as urban and rural revitalization.

The stakes are high, in part, because most Americans and their political representatives see politics and resources as a zero-sum game. And debates around these seem to hinge on three things: power—who has connections, the ability to mobilize, time, and/or financial resources to get involved in politics to speak up; deservingness—the extent to which a group that would largely benefit from a policy is generally well liked and well respected; and timing matters, too—which party is in control of the executive and legislative branches of government as well as the sway of public opinion.

If you ask a large number of Americans what are the most important issues of the day, the answers often converge and agree. This is especially true for Generation Z, who care a great deal about staying healthy, their financial well-being (due in part to the challenges presented by student loan debt), and matters of egalitarianism, including across categories of race, gender, and sexuality. These issues fall into the realm of social policy.

The answer is "politics," the constant struggle in power over who gets what, when, and how. To be sure, there is another element that might be lurking in the background. Today's Congress and president are among the oldest on record; in many ways, the U.S. government can be characterized as a "gerontocracy." Their views about political power and deservingness are likely to be quite different from the newest American voters, including readers of this book. Indeed, many younger Americans may not believe that Social Security and Medicare are relevant for their future, either because they don't think that those policies will be around when they retire or just because retirement seems so far in the future. Furthermore, the way political power is being wielded is also changing, as more people can leverage the power of social media to expand the scope of conflict and build new political coalitions.

As Millennials and Gen Z take the reins from an aging generation, will they run into the same problems, have the same debates, and view the problems from the same perspectives as the current generation of leaders? Or will they recognize the magnitude of the social policy problems at hand and leverage the tools of politics to solve some of the greatest problems the United States and the globe have ever faced?

1. What is it that makes the programs and policies of President Franklin Roosevelt's New Deal so significant in the evolution of American social policy?

- **a** The government intervened for the first time in the daily lives and economic activities of Americans.
- **b** Debt was used for the first time by the American government to deal with the global economic crisis.
- **c** The three branches of government and the states aligned in support of the administration's New Deal proposals.
- **d** The New Deal revived economic policies that had not been used by the government since the nation's founding.

2. In comparing the Great Society programs of President Lyndon Johnson with the New Deal Programs of President Franklin Roosevelt, an observer might conclude that Johnson's Great Society placed a more significant emphasis on what types of goals?

- **a** Economic and foreign policy
- **b** Economic equality and civil rights
- **c** States' rights and the free market
- **d** Balancing the budget and economic recovery

3. An evaluation of income growth among Americans from 1976 to 2022, where the top 1 percent saw growth in real income of 225 percent compared with a growth in real income for the bottom 50 percent of Americans of only 32.7 percent, suggests that which of the following is true about the structures of American social and economic policies?

- **a** Lower-income groups in the United States have less incentive to use the benefits of the capitalist economic structures because of benefits associated with programs that provide for the poor.
- **b** Income growth at the top of American economic groups reflects the monetary rewards in the American economic system for the upper classes who reinvest profits into the labor force.
- **c** Social and economic policy in the United States rewards innovation and ability similarly regardless of socioeconomic status.
- **d** Economic policy in the United States has a greater benefit for wealthy Americans than those in lower-income groups.

4. Liberal and conservative organizations alike have expressed dismay about policies that they label as "corporate welfare," a concept that can be best described in which way?

- **a** The growing influence of labor unions and corporate interest groups in steering government contracts to private industries that are favored by lawmakers
- **b** Programs that incentivize corporations to take on the management of welfare programs that were previously managed by national and state governments
- **c** Policies that provide funding or tax benefits to corporations or industries to stabilize or encourage economic activity
- **d** Programs providing skills training for workers from industries being affected by globalization to be equipped to find new jobs

5. The success or failure of public policies largely rests with how they are implemented by the federal bureaucracy and on-the-ground employees within government agencies. How might an "on-the-ground" public employee have a significant impact in the way public policy is implemented in American society?

- **a** Rejecting an applicant's eligibility for government aid based on the government employee's impression of the kinds of people seeking aid from the program
- **b** Creation of the processes through which government agencies determine how to carry out laws passed by Congress
- **c** Reorganizing the reporting structures of staff within an agency to better carry out public policy
- **d** Surveying recipients of services from government agencies to evaluate the effectiveness of an agency's work

6. Which statement best characterizes the relationship between the national and state governments in the development and implementation of health, education, and welfare policies in the United States?

- **a** States have significant flexibility in carrying out the numerous national mandates.
- **b** Public policy in health, education, and welfare is still dominated by states, though some national requirements have been applied.
- **c** Rapid growth of national policies in public health care, the national education system, and welfare programs is increasingly preempting state policy-making authority.
- **d** The modern trend in public policy has been a devolution of national powers to the states in education, welfare, and health care.

7. Of the four factors that determine whether social policy is implemented effectively, which one cannot be incorporated within the structures of the policy?

- **a** Problems that have identifiable solutions
- **b** Support from public and relevant interest groups
- **c** Funding and administration of policy that are adequate to the task
- **d** Objectives that are clearly related to the issue and achievable

8. Many Americans express the idea that government should be run like a business, with simple and clear metrics for defining success, effectiveness, and efficiency. Why is this perspective a critical misconception about the activities and implementation of public policy?

- **a** Many industries already use incentive and promotion structures that are very similar to those in use by government agencies.
- **b** Corporations operate more efficiently than government because of their emphasis on talent and promotions based on merit.
- **c** Government administration of public policy lacks the motivation and incentive to measure performance in the same way businesses do.
- **d** Implementation of social policies often involves objectives that are ongoing or have limited metrics to measure achievement and efficiency.

9. The most significant challenge to the financial security of the Social Security program is associated with which reality about American society?

- **a** The falling rate of educational attainment among the American population creating declining incomes
- **b** The growing number of Americans reaching retirement age compared with those in the workforce
- **c** Privatization of entitlements like Social Security creating a shortfall in program funding
- **d** Declining approval of Social Security and similar programs which has caused participation to fall

10. When considering welfare programs like the Supplemental Nutritional Assistance Program (SNAP) or the Temporary Assistance for Needy Families (TANF) that are managed by states but funded, at least partially, by the federal government, what conflicting interests were central to lawmakers in developing the programs?

- **a** Improving benefits and incentivizing people to leave the programs sooner
- **b** Increasing penalties for abuse of the programs and limiting access to welfare
- **c** Meeting the needs of those in poverty and cutting the costs of welfare programs
- **d** Allowing for greater state management and expanding implementation of national priorities

Use INQUIZITIVE *to help you study and master this material.*

17

Foreign Policy

What is America's role in the world?

»

"Presidents from Roosevelt to Obama have sought to help allies protect themselves and to engage in collective defense against common dangers. We did this not in a spirit of charity but because we had learned the hard way that problems abroad, if unaddressed, could, before long, imperil us."[1]
Madeleine Albright, former secretary of state

«

"Upon my inauguration, I announced that the United States would return to a simple principle: The first duty of our government is to serve its citizens, many of whom have been forgotten. But they are not forgotten any more. With every decision and every action, we are now putting America first."[2]
President Donald Trump

In a busy world, it is easy to put America's foreign policy in the category of things you don't need to worry about. After all, these decisions only affect people in other countries. Why should Americans care about what happens in the rest of the world?

Now think about Russia's February 2022 invasion of Ukraine. Because Ukraine is a major exporter of grain, the conflict raised the possibility of a major worldwide food shortage, which could increase flows of refugees to Europe and America. Sanctions on Russian exports of oil and gas caused energy prices to rise, increasing the chances of a global economic recession. And the decision by the United States and its allies to send military assistance to Ukraine put these nations on the verge of conflict with Russia, a major nuclear power. Food, refugees, energy, and nuclear weapons—it is hard to imagine a set of more consequential issues for Americans.

At the height of the conflict between Ukraine and Russia, Speaker of the House Nancy Pelosi met with the president of Ukraine to show support for the country's defense.

War in Ukraine is not an exception. Many decisions about America's foreign policy have a direct impact on our everyday lives. For example, continuing economic growth in America requires imports of raw materials from other nations and the ability to export products throughout the world—these in turn require a complex system of trade agreements to protect copyrights and patents held by American firms and set tariffs on imports and exports that protect domestic industries while preserving the incentives for people in other countries to buy American products. Even seemingly humanitarian

CHAPTER GOALS

Describe the major approaches to understanding foreign policy, and trace how America's role in the world has evolved (pp. 664–674)

Explain how the various branches of government shape foreign policy (pp. 674–686)

Examine the ways American foreign policy is implemented (pp. 686–691)

Analyze several major areas of foreign policy and why they are often controversial (pp. 691–698) policies often directly serve American interests: providing COVID-19 vaccines to third world nations may seem like a kind gesture, but doing so reduces the chances that the virus will mutate into a new vaccine-resistant variant that could spread throughout the world.

These examples also illustrate how foreign policy can be just as conflictual as domestic policy. Americans often see disagreement over foreign policy as somehow unpatriotic, citing the late senator Arthur Vandenberg, who is credited for the saying "Politics stops at the water's edge." But foreign policy choices create winners and losers, just as in the domestic arena. In the case of Ukraine, some Republicans argued that America had no reason to contest Russia's invasion because America's security would not be affected even if Russia conquered the entire country. Trade policies are controversial because some American firms cannot compete against cheaper imported products, so encouraging imports can cost American jobs. And by sending vaccines and other assistance throughout the world, America reduces the supplies available to its own citizens.

In contemporary American politics, these controversies cut across partisan lines. Many Republicans agree with President Trump, who imposed punitive tariffs on America's major trading partners, ordered the renegotiation of long-standing trade agreements, and made it clear that America expected to get more from these agreements than it had in the past. Trump also threatened to withdraw from international security arrangements such as the North Atlantic Treaty Organization's if other nations did not increase their defense spending. In contrast, Democrats such as former president Joe Biden champion free trade and continued international engagement by the United States. Indeed, one of the major issues in the 2024 presidential campaign was whether the U.S. should continue to support Ukraine's fight against Russia's invasion.

These examples illustrate that we should expect disagreement over foreign policy, including between the political parties, inside the executive branch, and even between civilians and military personnel. Although these debates often have political consequences, with lawmakers sometimes taking positions for political gain, in the main they reflect sincere differences of opinion about what role America should play in the modern world.

The reality of disagreement about foreign policy options raises the question of how these differences are resolved. What is at stake when foreign policy decisions are made? What is the role of Congress, the courts, and the bureaucracy in the making of foreign policy? Where does public opinion enter into this process? Who gets to decide America's foreign policy? How is foreign policy made?

DESCRIBE THE MAJOR APPROACHES TO UNDERSTANDING FOREIGN POLICY, AND TRACE HOW AMERICA'S ROLE IN THE WORLD HAS EVOLVED

What is foreign policy?

Foreign policy encompasses government actions involving countries, corporations, groups, and individuals that lie outside America's borders. Foreign policy includes military operations, economic interactions, human rights policies, environmental agreements, foreign aid, helping build or sustain democratic systems, interventions in civil wars and other conflicts, and international efforts to limit weapons of mass destruction (WMDs), including nuclear weapons.

Foreign policy principles and perspectives

Foreign policy actions are often rooted in general principles or rules that guide people or nations in their decision-making. These principles and rules capture the decision to act, whether America acts alone or with other nations, and the motivations for actions. (See Nuts & Bolts 17.1 on p. 666 for a summary of these guiding principles.)

foreign policy
Government actions that affect countries, corporations, groups, or individuals outside America's borders.

Should We Act Alone? There are three important distinctions in foreign policy. The first is between unilateral action and multilateral action. **Unilateral action** occurs when one country does something on its own, without coordinating with other countries. For example, some U.S. antiterrorism operations under recent presidents have been undertaken without any consultation with U.S. allies, such as the 2020 attack on Iranian general Qasem Soleimani in the Baghdad airport, which was carried out by U.S. forces without even informing the Iraqi government. Similarly, some of President Trump's actions during preparations for his June 2018 summit meeting with North Korean leader Kim Jong-un, such as the snap decision in May to cancel the summit entirely (a decision Trump later reversed), were made without first talking with U.S. allies.

unilateral action (national)
Independent acts of foreign policy undertaken by a nation without the assistance or coordination of other nations.

American foreign policy more commonly involves **multilateral action** by the United States alongside other countries or international organizations such as the UN. For example, in the run-up to Russia's invasion of Ukraine, the United States and many European nations sent weapons and training missions to improve Ukraine's armed forces. Arms transfers intensified after the invasion, including many cutting-edge technologies such as armed drones, and training continued outside Ukraine, in Poland, Slovakia, and other countries.

multilateral action
Foreign policy carried out by a nation in coordination with other nations or international organizations.

Should We Intervene? A second important distinction in foreign policy is between **isolationism** and **internationalism**. Isolationists believe that the United States should avoid making alliances and agreements with other nations, concentrate on defending America's borders, and let the people in other countries work out their problems for themselves. In the case of Ukraine, an isolationist might argue that U.S. intervention

isolationism
The idea that a country should refrain from involvement in international affairs.

internationalism
The idea that a country should be involved in the affairs of other nations, out of both self-interest and moral obligation.

When the United States acts multilaterally in foreign policy, it often works through organizations such as the UN. Here, President Biden addresses a session of the UN General Assembly, where he spoke about a new chapter of diplomacy after ending the two-decade Afghan war.

would be futile or potentially counterproductive, too costly, or simply inappropriate—that it is not America's problem to solve, or that keeping Russia out of Ukraine does not serve American interests.[3]

An internationalist, however, would argue that the United States should establish many agreements with other nations and intervene in international crises whenever it may be able to help, both because of possible economic and security gains and because intervening in civil wars and helping solve humanitarian crises are morally right. In the case of Ukraine, an internationalist argument would cite factors such as the civilian casualties caused by Russia's invasion, the potential for a humanitarian crisis caused by refugees leaving Ukraine, the need to curb Russia's ambitions to rebuild the Soviet Union, and the principle that international disputes should not be solved by violence.

realism
The idea that a country's foreign policy decisions are motivated by self-interest and the goal of gaining more power.

idealism
The idea that foreign policy decisions reflect normative goals such as justice, equality, and human rights.

nation building
The use of a country's resources, including the military, to help nondemocratic nations transform themselves into democracies.

Are We Only Out for Ourselves? The third major distinction in foreign policy making is between **realism** and **idealism** (also known as liberalism, although the term has a very different meaning than the liberal ideology in domestic politics).[4] Realists believe that countries pursue their own interests, seeking to increase their economic and military power and their international influence. In approaching a policy decision, a realist would choose the policy that maximizes American military and economic power relative to other states. Idealists, in contrast, believe that states' concerns extend beyond increasing their power and should include upholding principles such as freedom or democracy. For example, idealists generally believe in helping nondemocratic nations transform themselves into democracies with strong court systems (also called **nation building**).

To illustrate the differences between these explanations, consider the cases made by each side regarding intervention in the ongoing Syrian civil war. Realist scholar John Mearsheimer has argued that there was no need to intervene.[5] In his view, America has no compelling interest in the outcome of the civil war in Syria. Moreover, intervention would be costly, would put American lives at risk, and could produce a wider conflict involving America's allies in the Middle East. This position is close to that of President Trump, who argued that America's interest in the Syrian conflict should be limited to

NUTS & BOLTS 17.1

Theories of Foreign Policy

Realism	Foreign policy is driven by a state's national interest, as defined by its leaders.
Idealism	Foreign policy reflects the ideals held by a state's leaders, such as protection of human rights.
Internationalism	States should, whenever possible, pursue their foreign policy goals by working together with other nations.
Isolationism	States should, whenever possible, work alone to define and implement their foreign policy, working with other nations only when absolutely necessary.

Source: Compiled by the authors.

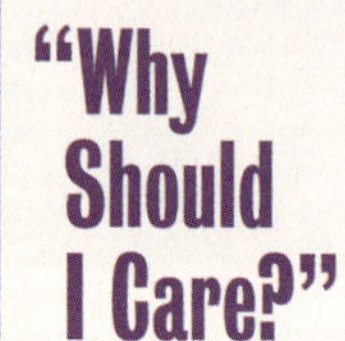

Foreign policy theories can help us understand why a president or Congress decides to take action or refrain from taking action.

destroying the ISIS terrorist organization that was an active participant in the conflict. In fact, Trump withdrew U.S. ground forces and many advisers from Syria after ISIS strongholds were eliminated. In contrast, the idea that America is morally obligated to help Syrian rebels fight against their brutal government—a position held by some Democrats and some Republicans in Congress—is a clear example of idealism. In the case of Ukraine, realists tended to argue against American intervention, while idealists favored a strong American response

Realism and idealism are used often in foreign policy debates because they offer convenient ways to summarize the motivations behind policy decisions. That is how we use the terms in this chapter, but in reality neither of them provides a fully accurate definition of what motivates nations or individuals. As the quote from President Barack Obama illustrates, no one is a realist or an idealist all the time. For example, some realists argued that aiding Ukraine was in America's self-interest, as it prevented Russia from reconstituting its control over the former Soviet states. Conversely, most idealists argued for limits on America's response, including no direct attacks on Russian aircraft and no American forces on the ground in Ukraine.

You take victories where you can. You make things a little bit better rather than a little bit worse. And that's in no way a concession to this idea that America is withdrawing or there's not much we can do. It's just a realistic assessment of how the world works.

—President Barack Obama

History of American foreign policy

American foreign policy has evolved throughout the country's history. Tracing the course of America's relations with other nations since the Founding allows us to illustrate the types of choices U.S. politicians have faced, how these policy options have changed over time, and the fact that politicians have always disagreed about how to resolve foreign policy issues.

The Founding to World War I Until America's entry into World War I in 1917, American foreign policy was largely isolationist. Most presidents and other elected officials behaved in accordance with George Washington's assertion that the United States should "avoid entangling alliances" with other nations.[6] Isolationism made sense during this period for several reasons. America's distance from Europe reduced the potential for international economic interactions, lowered the level of military

Internationalists argue that America is the only nation with the will and the resources needed to address humanitarian crises throughout the world, such as by providing food aid to people in Syrian refugee camps.

Monroe Doctrine
The American policy initiated under President James Monroe in 1823, stating that the United States would remain neutral in conflicts between European nations and that these nations should stop colonizing or occupying areas of North and South America.

threat, and gave early America room to expand without conflicting with European nations.[7] The **Monroe Doctrine**, established by President James Monroe in 1823, stated that America would remain neutral in wars involving European nations and that the United States expected these nations to stop trying to colonize or occupy areas in North and South America.[8]

America's foreign policy was never completely isolationist, however, even in the early years. The American navy was deployed on many occasions to protect U.S. ships and citizens, and America had several colonies far beyond its borders. Even in the early years, the United States expanded by purchasing land from other countries or from Native Americans—adding much of the Midwest through the Louisiana Purchase—and by annexing land after military conflicts, such as the large section of the Southwest acquired from Mexico following the Mexican-American War. Later, America built the Panama Canal, leasing land from Panama in the process, and sent troops into conflicts in Nicaragua and other Central American countries. America also maintained significant trading relationships with nations in Europe and elsewhere.

Still, America's involvement in World War I (1914–1918) marked a sharp departure in foreign policy, in terms of both the country's participation in an international alliance and the president's willingness to continue alliance membership after the conflict.[9] With the war almost over, President Woodrow Wilson offered a peace plan, the Fourteen Points, which proposed reshaping the borders of European countries to mitigate future conflict, creating measures to encourage free trade and democracy, and establishing an international organization that would prevent wars.[10] American diplomats participated in the negotiations that culminated in the Treaty of Versailles, which officially ended the war.[11] The treaty created the League of Nations, an organization similar to the modern UN, but the U.S. Senate rejected the treaty, which meant that the United States never joined the League of Nations.[12]

The Rise of Internationalism World War II (1939–1945) marked a great transition in American foreign policy. The United States became directly involved in the conflict on December 8, 1941, declaring war on Japan the day after the country carried out air attacks on Pearl Harbor in Hawaii and American bases in the Philippines. Germany subsequently declared war on the United States on December 11. However, even before the United States officially became involved, the U.S. military had been supplying Great Britain and its allies with arms, ships, and other supplies in return for payments and long-term leases on British military bases throughout the world—actions that only narrowly escaped a congressional vote to reverse. During the war, the Allied Powers—the United States, Great Britain, the Soviet Union, and other countries—fought as a formal alliance, making joint plans and sharing military hardware and intelligence.

After World War II, American politicians and scholars felt that the United States should be a central actor in world affairs. This new policy was justified by realist arguments, such as the need to deter future conflicts and the desire for economic benefits from trading with other nations.[13]

Idealists argued for the same policies on the grounds that America had a moral obligation to preserve world peace.[14] However, this shift toward internationalism only increased the amount of conflict in American foreign policy, as actors disagreed on where the United States should get involved; what its goals should be; whether intervention should involve military force, foreign aid, diplomacy, or some other policy tool; and whether the country should act alone or in concert with other nations.

Cold War
The period of tension and arms competition between the United States and the Soviet Union that lasted from 1945 until 1991.

The Cold War Soon after World War II ended, the **Cold War** (1945–1991) began, as the victorious Allies disagreed—with the United States and Great Britain on one

The Marshall Plan, which helped European nations rebuild their economies after World War II, was part of America's strategy to build alliances against the Soviet Union.

side and the Soviet Union on the other—over the reconstruction of Germany and the reformation of Eastern European countries that Germany had occupied during the war. In a 1946 speech, former British prime minister Winston Churchill referred to an "iron curtain" that had split Eastern and Western Europe, leaving the East under Soviet domination with few political freedoms.[15] American diplomat George F. Kennan argued that America should use diplomatic, economic, and military means to prevent the Soviet Union from expanding the set of countries that it controlled or was allied with—a strategy that he labeled "**containment**."[16] This idea served as a guiding principle for American foreign policy over the next generation.[17]

containment
An important feature of American Cold War policy in which the United States used diplomatic, economic, and military strategies in an effort to prevent the Soviet Union from expanding its influence.

During this period the United States implemented several measures to build and strengthen alliances against the Soviet threat. The first was the Marshall Plan, a series of aid and development programs enacted in the late 1940s to restore the economies of Western European countries devastated during World War II.[18] The United States was also instrumental in the formation of the World Bank and the International Monetary Fund (IMF), as well as international trade agreements such as the General Agreement on Tariffs and Trade (we will discuss some of these institutions in more detail later in this chapter).

The United States also formed alliances with other countries, including the North Atlantic Treaty Organization (NATO) in 1949. The goal of these organizations was the maintenance of collective security, based on the principle that "an attack against one is an attack against all."[19]

The aim was to deter Soviet attacks throughout the world by formalizing America's commitment to defend its allies. The Soviets formed their own alliances, most notably the Warsaw Pact, with nations in Eastern Europe.[20]

The United States was also a key player in the 1945 creation of the UN, an international organization with the aim of preventing wars by facilitating negotiations between combatants and, if necessary, sending military forces from member states to stop conflicts. The UN has also been instrumental in administering relief efforts for refugees, running development efforts, codifying international law, and publicizing and condemning human rights violations.

The goal of containment influenced every aspect of American foreign policy after World War II.[21] The Korean War, in which American troops defended South Korea against invasion by North Korea, was motivated largely by containment—North Korea's efforts had the strong support of the Soviet Union and China.[22] America also supported brutal dictators in other countries, such as the Shah of Iran during the 1970s, and overlooked these governments' dismal human rights records on the grounds that their leaders would be valuable allies against the Soviets.[23]

mutually assured destruction
The idea that two nations that possess large stores of nuclear weapons—like the United States and the Soviet Union during the Cold War—would both be annihilated in any nuclear exchange, thus making it unlikely that either country would launch a first attack.

America also maintained large military forces, beginning its first peacetime draft in the 1950s and building a large store of nuclear weapons. These weapons were intended to deter war with the Soviet Union through the threat of **mutually assured destruction**: the idea that even if the Soviet Union unleashed an all-out nuclear assault on U.S. forces, enough American weapons would remain intact to deliver a similarly devastating counterattack. The United States stationed hundreds of thousands of troops in Western Europe and elsewhere to deter the Soviet threat. War nearly broke out during the Cuban missile crisis, when the Soviets tried to place nuclear missiles in Cuba—within striking range of the United States. However, the issue was defused once the Soviets withdrew in the face of an American naval blockade of Cuba and a secret American promise to withdraw similar missiles from Turkey.

domino theory
An idea held by American foreign policy makers during the Cold War that the creation of one Soviet-backed communist nation would lead to the spread of communism in that nation's region.

In the early 1960s America became involved in the conflict in Vietnam, believing that North Vietnam's drive to take over South Vietnam was part of the Soviet Union's plan for world domination.[24] The **domino theory** held by many American policy-makers posited that if the United States did not prevent the fall of South Vietnam, the next step would be a Soviet-backed conflict in the Philippines, in Australia, or with some other American ally. The Vietnam War demonstrated that the domino theory was fundamentally inaccurate; the conflict between North and South Vietnam was a civil war rather than an international event.[25] Though the North Vietnamese accepted Soviet support, they did not take orders from the Soviets.

détente
An approach to foreign policy in which cultural exchanges and negotiations are used to reduce tensions between rival nations, such as between the United States and the Soviet Union during the 1970s.

Beginning in the early 1970s, President Richard Nixon began a process of **détente** with the Soviet Union, which involved a series of negotiations and cultural exchanges designed to reduce tensions and promote cooperation.[26] These efforts culminated in the 1972 Strategic Arms Limitation Treaty (SALT I), which limited the growth of U.S. and Soviet missile forces.[27] At the same time, the Arab nations' embargo prohibiting oil shipments to Western countries after the 1973 Arab-Israeli war served as a reminder that containment of the Soviet Union could not be America's only foreign policy priority. Tensions over oil increased again when the Organization of the Petroleum Exporting Countries (OPEC) raised prices in 1979. Both events contributed to a recession in America and the electoral defeats of two incumbent presidents: Gerald Ford in 1976 and Jimmy Carter in 1980. Carter's defeat was also, in part, the result of the Iran hostage crisis, in which Iranian students, with government backing, held American embassy staff hostage for more than 14 months.[28]

Tensions with the Soviets increased again with their support for the Sandinista rebellion in Nicaragua in the late 1970s and then with their invasion of Afghanistan in 1980.[29] In response to Soviet military actions in Afghanistan, President Carter withdrew the U.S. Olympic team from the 1980 games in Moscow, suspended sales of wheat to the Soviets, and increased defense spending. These increases steepened under Ronald Reagan, who vowed to put communism "on the ash heap of history." Notwithstanding this rhetoric, Reagan also worked to negotiate arms control agreements with the Soviet Union.[30]

The real change in U.S.-Soviet relations began with the selection of Mikhail Gorbachev as leader of the Soviet Union in 1985 and his policies of glasnost

In 1989, the fall of the Berlin Wall, which separated West Berlin from communist East Berlin, provided a powerful symbol of the end of the Cold War. With just one superpower—the United States—left, many predicted that democracy would spread and peace would prevail. However, new foreign policy challenges quickly emerged.

("openness") and perestroika ("restructuring"). The Warsaw Pact was dissolved in 1991, and most of its former members became democracies. The Soviet Union splintered into 15 countries in 1991, effectively ending the Cold War. Scholars still debate the reasons for these changes. Some argue that the costs of responding to America's military buildup bankrupted the Soviet state, while others point to disaffection of Soviet citizens with the communist ideology and the inability of the Soviet economy to provide goods and services.[31]

Since the end of the Cold War, the United States and Russia have continued to disagree over many policies, including the enlargement of NATO to include most former Warsaw Pact countries, the deployment of American anti-ballistic missile systems in Eastern Europe, the U.S. invasion of Iraq in 2003, the Russian invasion of Georgia in 2008, Russia's annexation of Crimea (a part of Ukraine) in 2013, Russia's intervention on the side of the Syrian government starting in 2015, Russia's efforts to influence citizen opinions and votes in the 2016 U.S. presidential election, and, most recently, Russia's invasion of Ukraine in 2022. While these conflicts have increased tensions, it is important to remember that only 30 years ago both countries had enough weapons aimed at each other to destroy the entire world. Today, however, there is little chance of direct conflict between the United States and Russia.

After the Cold War: Human Rights, Trade, and Terrorism The end of the Cold War, along with the growing number of democracies worldwide and the development of democratic peace theories (which argue that democracies will not fight other democracies), suggested to some observers that military conflicts would become much rarer and other concerns would emerge to influence America's foreign policy.[32] Events early in the post–Cold War era seemed to support this thesis. Human rights became a more important foreign policy topic.[33] The United States became involved in humanitarian relief and nation-building efforts in Somalia, Bosnia, and Kosovo. A series of agreements, including the North American Free Trade Agreement (NAFTA) in 1994 and the formation of the World Trade Organization (WTO) in 1995, lowered tariffs throughout the world. Technological advances in transportation also lowered the cost of shipping goods worldwide, and the industrialization of many developing countries made them low-cost suppliers of manufactured goods to the United

States, causing many domestic factories to close. The world's nations also began to negotiate over voluntary limits on carbon emissions to address climate change. These developments exemplify the concept of "soft power": that is, America's influence over other nations through increased economic interactions and cultural ties rather than the use of military force.[34] Soft power can also arise from the actions of individual citizens: the spring 2020 protests in the United States over Black Lives Matter and the killing of George Floyd at the hands of Minneapolis police officers triggered similar events in several European nations, partly in solidarity with U.S. protesters but also against discrimination against minority groups in those countries.[35]

However, it is important to understand that there is considerable disagreement about the usefulness of soft power. Some Republicans, including former president Trump, argue that military force remains the dominant factor in shaping international relations, meaning that America must remain the dominant military power to maintain its security and strong economy. The resolution of this ongoing debate shapes America's military spending and deployments of armed forces, its decisions about participation in international trade agreements and climate control agreements, its decisions about intervention in internal conflicts such as the Syrian civil war and the Israeli–Palestinian conflict, and many other areas.

> **We don't want the smoking gun to be a mushroom cloud.**
>
> —**Condoleezza Rice,** secretary of state under George W. Bush

Near the end of the twentieth century, new security threats emerged in the form of terrorist groups, most notably Al Qaeda, led by Osama bin Laden, who organized the September 11, 2001, attacks on the World Trade Center in New York and the Pentagon in Washington, D.C. Some analysts and politicians, including President George W. Bush, described these attacks as part of a worldwide "clash of civilizations," pitting the secular West against radical Islam.[36] After the attacks, President George W. Bush announced a new U.S. policy, the **Bush Doctrine**, or the doctrine of preemption, whereby the United States would not wait until after an attack to respond but would use military force to eliminate potential threats before they could be put in motion. This policy change was intended to prevent another September 11 attack, as the quote from Bush's National Security Advisor and Secretary of State Condoleezza Rice illustrates.

Bush Doctrine
The foreign policy of President George W. Bush, under which the United States would use military force preemptively against threats to its national security.

President Obama emphasized improving foreign perceptions of America and Americans, ending the ground war in Iraq, and avoiding unilateral action in favor of multilateral coalitions. However, many of Obama's policies in regard to the War on Terror, such as his emphasis on drone attacks (see the Take a Stand feature) and America's limited involvement in the Syrian civil war, were quite similar to those established by the Bush administration.

The Al Qaeda terrorist organization headed by Osama bin Laden was the driving force behind many terrorist attacks on Americans, including the 2001 attacks on the World Trade Center and the Pentagon. In 2011, American forces killed bin Laden, but the group, along with newer organizations such as ISIS, remains a significant threat.

On one level, Donald Trump's foreign policy, with its emphasis on "putting America first," was a sharp departure from that of his predecessors, particularly the imposition of trade tariffs on other countries such as China and the withdrawal from trade agreements with other nations; threats to use military force against countries such as North Korea; efforts to reduce admissions of refugees to the United States; and the emphasis on enhanced border security (including efforts to build a wall between the United States and Mexico). On another level, while all these changes were significant, major portions of America's foreign policy remained unchanged. For example, while Trump's rhetoric emphasized attacking ISIS forces in Syria rather than helping rebel forces fighting the Syrian government, America and its allies continued to give military aid and technical support to rebel forces.

Trump's second term is just as complex. American assistance to Ukraine in the face of Russia's invasion is the most visible foreign policy issue. However, Trump and his advisers (as well as members of Congress) must also determine how America should respond to ongoing crises, such as the need to curb carbon emissions to mitigate climate change. Here, as in other areas, Trump's foreign policy choices are likely to be a sharp departure from those of former president

TAKE A STAND

Should America Carry Out Drone Attacks against Terrorists?

One of the elements of America's strategy to fight terrorist groups is the increased use of drones—small, pilotless aircraft that fly into foreign airspace, monitor the activities of terror suspects on the ground, and launch missiles against these targets. Over the last 15 years, drone attacks in countries such as Syria, Afghanistan, Yemen, and Pakistan have decimated the leadership and infrastructure of terrorist groups and inflicted significant casualties on lower-level fighters. Drones also played a key role in identifying the safe house in Pakistan where Al Qaeda leader Osama bin Laden was located, making possible the attack that resulted in bin Laden's death in 2011. However, the use of drones by American forces continues to be highly controversial inside the United States and throughout the world.

Drones are an effective tool. Drone attacks allow the United States to combat terrorists throughout the world without putting American troops at risk. Drone attacks are also less expensive than conventional forces. For example, rather than sending a special operations unit across the world to attack a target in the Middle East, American crews working at a base in Nevada can remotely control drones launched from a secure base in the Middle East or a ship in the Persian Gulf. Because drones have no crew, they can be small and quiet and stay in the air for long periods of time, making a surprise attack more feasible. Even if an attack is not being planned, drones allow the United States to monitor suspected terrorists and collect intelligence.

Describing drones as a tool also highlights their similarity to other examples of military force. How different is it if a terrorist camp is attacked by a drone rather than U.S. ground troops? Any argument against drones (the danger of civilian casualties or that terrorists can publicize the attack as a way of galvanizing public opposition to the U.S. strategy) can be applied just as well to other ways the United States might attack terrorists.

Drones bring risks and negatively affect decision-making. Some people foresee that the very advantages ascribed to drones—that they are relatively inexpensive and require no human pilots or ground forces—could likely lead decision makers to use drones more quickly than they might use conventional weapons. In a similar vein, there are those

The use of drones is controversial. Here, a protester in Yemen holds a sign denouncing the practice.

who believe that drones remove the personal element from warfare, making it easier to disregard the moral implications of an attack.

Moreover, at least up to now, drone strikes have occurred with little congressional oversight or approval. As we discussed in Chapter 12, Congress has the power to limit military operations—but doing so in the case of drones would be difficult because most of these operations are carried out in secret. How could members stop an operation they didn't know about until after it occurred?

While mistakes are possible in any military operation, drone attacks involve special risks. Because drone operators view their targets through long-range cameras mounted on the drones, the chances of civilian casualties or other collateral damage are probably higher than with Special Forces units who carry out their attacks at short range.

The problem for decision makers is this: prohibiting drone attacks on suspected terrorists does not mean that these individuals and organizations will go scot-free; most of these operations will instead be carried out by American armed forces, with the risk that some of these troops will be wounded, killed, or taken hostage. Should decision makers use drones or send in the troops?

take a stand

1. If you were writing a letter to your member of Congress about the use of drones, what position would you take? What arguments would you use to support your position?

2. If you favor the use of drones, are there situations in which we shouldn't use them? If you oppose them, are there situations in which drones have advantages over traditional troops?

The reality is that we live in a global world, and even if we want to remain isolated and focused on our own domestic issues and policies, we need to address worldwide problems in order the prevent them from spreading or worsening in the United States. This was seen during the COVID-19 pandemic when both President Biden and President Trump pushed for distribution of vaccines abroad.

Biden. In the case of climate change, for example, Trump is unlikely to support international efforts to address the causes and consequences of global warming. Finally, American decision-makers must contend with many of the issues discussed earlier, including conflict between Israel and the Palestinians and North Korea's nuclear program.

"Why Should I Care?"

Maybe you don't care about foreign policy—although as we discuss throughout this chapter, you probably should. In the modern era, no nation can separate itself from the rest of the world. The same is true for individual citizens, even you. Your job, the cost of living, and even your personal safety are affected by America's foreign policy. Making sense of foreign policy (or deciding where you stand on foreign policy questions) requires you to know some history and some basic terminology. History helps you understand America's place in the world and how different issues came about. Knowing the basic terminology used in foreign affairs helps you understand what politicians and pundits are talking about when they discuss foreign policy issues.

EXPLAIN HOW THE VARIOUS BRANCHES OF GOVERNMENT SHAPE FOREIGN POLICY

Foreign policy makers

Who shapes the United States' relations with other nations, and what is the source of their influence? We begin with the president and the executive branch, then consider Congress, the courts, and, finally, other groups and individuals outside the government. Nuts & Bolts 17.2 summarizes the foreign policy powers of the two most important actors: the president and Congress.

Our discussion focuses on people and organizations in government whose primary job is foreign policy making, but virtually all executive branch departments and agencies have some responsibility for issues with international reach. For example, the Department of Education administers programs that fund undergraduate, graduate, and

NUTS & BOLTS 17.2

Foreign Policy Powers of the President and Congress

President	Congress
Commander in chief of armed forces	Can declare war
Nominates and appoints senior officials in Department of Defense	Senate must approve Defense nominees
Negotiates treaties and executive agreements with other nations	Treaties take effect only if approved by Senate
Changes policy with executive orders and findings	Can overturn orders and findings with legislation
Attempts to mobilize public opinion behind foreign policy goals	Makes policy using "power of the purse" (annual budget)

Source: Compiled by the authors.

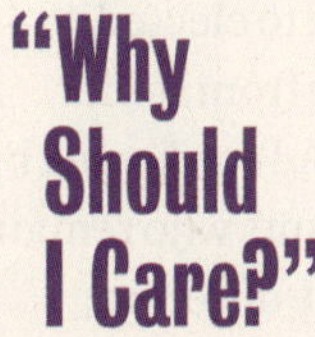

Foreign policy powers determine who can act, what they can do, and what process is necessary before they can move forward. Knowing about these powers helps us understand when and why the United States engages abroad.

scholarly study of the politics, history, and culture of other nations, as well as educational exchanges with universities abroad (in fact, both authors of this text are former Fulbright Scholars). The sharp increase in international students enrolled in American universities over the last 20 years is due in part to State Department visa policies that make it possible for these individuals to live in the United States for extended periods. Similarly, the Department of Agriculture oversees programs that encourage food exports to other nations and that protect Americans against unsafe imports.

The president and the executive branch

The president is the dominant actor in American foreign policy.[37] The president can negotiate treaties or executive agreements with other nations, change policy through executive orders or findings, mobilize public opinion to prompt action by Congress, and shape foreign policy by appointing people to agencies and departments that administer these policies (see Chapter 12). The president also serves as commander in chief of America's armed forces. Furthermore, the president is the first point of contact between America and other world leaders—in fact, one set of impeachment proceedings against President Trump began because of comments Trump made to the president of Ukraine in a routine phone conversation in 2019 about Russian aid to rebel groups in Eastern Ukraine.

While the president comes first in our discussion of how foreign policy gets made, presidents generally do not act on their own. So, for example, when President Biden announced he was sending military assistance to Ukraine in Spring 2022, , this was only the first step. Staff throughout the executive branch play key roles in defining as well as implementing policy options, including the specifics of what Ukraine would actually receive. Moreover, as we discuss here and in Chapter 12, presidential power is limited by the Constitution, by statutes, and by the ability of members of Congress and the courts to set policy or reverse presidential elections. For example, some of Biden's announcements about aid were actually requests for Congress to appropriate funds for assistance to Ukraine. Thus, a full accounting of the policy-making process (as well as the real effects of presidential initiatives) requires us to go beyond the president to consider all these other actors.

National Security Council (NSC)
An agency within the EOP that advises the president on matters of foreign policy.

Within the Executive Office of the President (EOP), the principal foreign policy agency is the **National Security Council (NSC)**, which develops foreign policy options and presents them to the president. The EOP also includes the Office of the United States Trade Representative, which focuses on tariffs and trade disputes; the president's Foreign Intelligence Advisory Board, a group of academics, politicians, and former government officials who advise the president; and the Office of Management and Budget, which prepares the president's annual budget proposals for federal agencies and departments, including those with foreign policy responsibilities.

The Department of State The principal foreign policy department in the executive branch is the Department of State. Its head, the secretary of state, acts as the official spokesperson for the United States in foreign relations and is an important adviser to the president. State Department officials operate U.S. embassies abroad and interact extensively with the leaders of other countries; they also offer expertise to elected officials on the politics, economics, and cultures of other nations. Aside from senior staff such as the secretary of state, who is nominated by the president and confirmed by the Senate, State Department personnel are generally career civil servants who remain in their positions even after a new president takes office. There are many different offices and working groups in the State Department, from people who deal with treaties to coordinators of international aid, arms control, or assistance for refugees.

The Department of Defense The Department of Defense carries out military actions as ordered by civilian authorities, ranging from large military operations (there are none at present) to smaller operations such as the ongoing drone attacks against Al Qaeda and ISIS forces throughout the Middle East or the deployment of troops, ships, and aircraft for training, humanitarian relief, and other purposes. For example, crewed and uncrewed navy ships and submarines routinely transit the South China Sea to contest China's sovereignty claims and to gather information on Chinese ships and military installations.

The secretary of state is the official spokesperson for the United States in foreign relations and is often one of the most powerful and influential members of the president's Cabinet. In 2022, the current secretary of state, Antony Blinken, met with Ukrainian president Volodymyr Zelensky to discuss the United States' supplying the country with military and humanitarian aid during the conflict with Russia.

The military's role in foreign policy is not limited to uses of force. Military personnel also deliver humanitarian aid or help American citizens evacuate from areas of conflict. For example, U.S. ships and helicopters deliver medical supplies and assist relief operations after natural disasters. In addition, some military planes were used to return citizens to the United States during the COVID-19 pandemic. And military personnel may also play a role in foreign policy making, with senior military officials serving as consultants during policy debates and midlevel officers serving in the NSC and on the staff of some congressional committees. For example, former generals James Mattis and Lloyd Austin served as secretaries of defense for presidents Trump and Biden, respectively.

The overriding principle of America's military is the concept of **civilian control**—the idea that military personnel do not formulate policy but rather implement directives from their civilian leaders in the executive branch (the president and senior leaders in the Defense Department) and Congress. Of course, just as in other areas of the executive branch, members of the military are experts who often know more than their civilian leaders about the feasibility of goals and the best ways to achieve them and are therefore often given leeway by civilians to develop and implement policies.

civilian control
The idea that military leaders do not formulate military policy but rather implement directives from civilian leaders.

DID YOU KNOW?

In 2022, American military personnel acted as advisers or trainers in over

150

countries.

Source: State Department report.

What should a president do when military leaders disagree with the president's policy goals? Their disagreement may reflect fundamental problems with the president's plans or simply indicate that military leaders would prefer a different policy. For example, many senior military officers apparently disagreed with the use of National Guard troops (as well as Trump's threats to deploy regular army forces) to clear protesters from Lafayette Square near the White House during the June 2020 protests against police brutality. As we discussed in Chapter 13, these dilemmas are inevitable in all areas of the bureaucracy, including the military, given the reality of bureaucratic expertise. In general, the norm is that military leaders are free to express their disagreement if they do so in private and are willing to carry out the orders they are ultimately given—or resign if they cannot do so.

The Department of Homeland Security The Department of Homeland Security was formed after the September 11 attacks by combining the Coast Guard, the Transportation Security Administration, the Border Patrol, and several other agencies. The department's responsibilities are to secure America's borders, prevent future terrorist attacks, and coordinate intelligence gathering. On the one hand, Homeland Security's record is exemplary: there has not been a major terrorist attack on American soil since September 11, 2001. On the other hand, there is concern that many Homeland Security policies (such as requiring extensive screening for all airline passengers, including removing jackets and shoes and unpacking electronics) impose large societal costs while having a marginal impact on safety.[38]

Intelligence Agencies Agencies such as the Central Intelligence Agency (CIA) and National Security Agency (NSA) are primarily responsible for government intelligence gathering. Most of their work consists of collecting information from public or semipublic sources, such as data on industrial outputs. However, these agencies also undertake covert operations to acquire intelligence, use satellites and other technology to monitor communications, or even attack individuals, other nations, or organizations. The Director of National Intelligence in the EOP leads and coordinates the activities of the various intelligence agencies.

How Much Foreign Policy Power Does the President Have? Some people argue that the broad powers of the modern presidency have allowed for "imperial presidents" who can implement their preferred foreign policies without the consent of Congress, the American people, or anyone else.[39] These complaints reflect a simple truth: presidents dominate the making of American foreign policy. Thus, in 2022, President Biden used existing grants of authority to impose sanctions on Russia after

Unilateral presidential powers in the foreign policy arena allow presidents to make foreign policy decisions as they see fit, although in many cases these decisions can be reversed by a successor. For example, President Trump elected to remove the United States from the Paris Agreement on climate change, although President Biden rejoined the agreement as one of his first actions in office.

it invaded Ukraine. Similarly, congressional consent was not required when President Trump withdrew the United States from the Paris Agreement on climate change—although if the accord had been initially voted on as a treaty, a two-thirds vote in the Senate would have been required for Trump's decision to take effect.

A deeper explanation for presidents' dominance of foreign policy lies in the ability of presidents to act unilaterally (see Chapter 12).[40] Although the Constitution grants the president only several specific foreign policy powers, it does not set explicit limits on what the chief executive can and cannot do. This ambiguity has given presidents considerable latitude to make foreign policy as they see fit. Members of Congress who disagree with the president must build veto-proof, two-thirds majorities in the House and Senate to overturn presidential foreign policy actions. For example, while some Democrats in Congress criticized Trump's decision to withdraw from the Paris Agreement, they could not build the two-thirds majority needed to prevent it. Moreover, the ability to carry out operations in secret using the military or intelligence agencies is a major presidential power that has been used (and sometimes abused) by many presidents.

Nonetheless, presidents sometimes pull back from a new foreign policy if they believe congressional support will not be forthcoming. For example, President Trump initially decided in 2019 to withdraw U.S. military forces from northern Syria, where they were aiding rebel forces, only to largely reverse the decision after criticism from senior advisers and members of Congress. Similarly, no president has ever submitted the 1996 Nuclear Test Ban Treaty for Senate ratification, although all presidents since Bill Clinton have implemented a voluntary moratorium on tests. And congressional opposition was one argument against the United States and its allies imposing a "no-fly zone" for Russian aircraft over Ukraine in 2022, although the primary concern was the danger of a direct conflict with Russia.

Clearly, the president dominates foreign policy—but Congress can reverse or thwart presidential initiatives. Thus, in most cases in which presidents appear to have acted without constraints, the reality is that members of Congress actually approved of the president's action, were unaware of the action, or were unwilling or unable to organize to overturn the president's policy.

Congress

Congress holds three types of influence over foreign policy. The first is the power of the purse. Since members of Congress write annual budgets for every government department and agency, one way for members to shape foreign policy is to forbid expenditures on activities that members want to prevent.

Second, the Senate has the power to approve treaties and confirm the appointments of senior members of the president's foreign policy team, including the secretaries of state and defense, the Director of National Intelligence, and America's ambassador to the UN. Although it is rare for senators to reject a treaty or nominee, sometimes they issue preemptive warnings about what kinds of treaties they will accept (in response, presidents often avoid asking for a vote on treaties they know will be rejected).

Third, the Constitution grants Congress the power to declare war on other nations. However, the Constitution does not say that this declaration must occur before hostilities can begin or whether the declaration is necessary at all. In fact, although the United States has been involved in hundreds of military conflicts since the Founding, there have been only five U.S. declarations of war: the War of 1812, the Mexican-American War (declared in 1846), the Spanish-American War (in 1898), and both world wars (declared in 1917 and 1941, respectively). In an attempt to codify war-making powers, in 1973 Congress adopted the War Powers Resolution. This legislation was designed to limit the president's war-making powers and to give members of Congress a way to reverse a president's decision to deploy American forces. Although the resolution has been in effect for nearly 50 years, the question of which branch of the government controls America's armed forces remains controversial. (See the How It Works graphic on pp. 680–81 for more details.)

Several groups within Congress participate in making foreign policy. The Committee on Foreign Affairs in the House and the Foreign Relations Committee in the Senate are responsible for writing legislation that deals with foreign policy, including setting the annual budget for agencies that carry out those policies. These committees also hold hearings in which they pose questions to foreign policy experts from inside and outside the government. While hearings do not necessarily lead to changes in policy, they can educate members of Congress on foreign policy matters, draw media and public attention to issues important to the committee, and force presidential nominees to make commitments about how they will perform in office. For example, during confirmation hearings in 2018, CIA Director Gina Haspel agreed that CIA operatives would conform to limitations on the use of torture when interrogating suspects.

The House and Senate each have an Intelligence Committee that oversees covert operations and the actions of the CIA, the NSA, and similar agencies. Under current law, the president is supposed to give Congress "timely notification" of covert intelligence operations (although there is some dispute over what "timely" means).[41] These arrangements help ensure that someone outside the executive branch knows about secret operations and can organize congressional opposition if these actions are deemed illegal, immoral, or unwise.

Of course, members of Congress always have the power to block a president's foreign policy initiatives, but doing so requires enacting a law with enough votes to override a presidential veto, which is often an impossible task. For example, after Congress passed a resolution in 2019 disapproving of a sale of U.S. military equipment to the United Arab Emirates, President Trump vetoed the measure and the Senate failed to override, meaning the sale went through. In other cases, such as during the debate over U.S. assistance to Ukraine, resolutions were offered to limit these efforts but were not passed by either house of Congress.

The federal courts

The federal courts, including the Supreme Court, weigh in on foreign policy questions through judicial review, determining whether laws, regulations, and presidential actions are consistent with the Constitution. For example, during the War on Terror, a series of lower-court and Supreme Court decisions forced the Bush administration to revise its policy of holding terror suspects indefinitely without charges; the rulings

How it works: in theory

War Powers: Who Controls the Armed Forces?

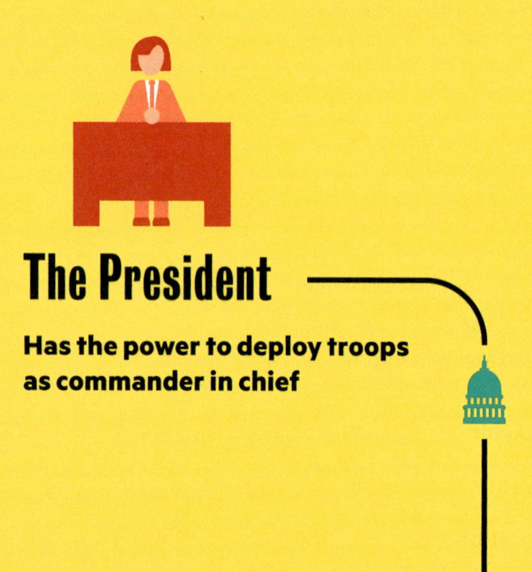

The President

Has the power to deploy troops as commander in chief

Under the War Powers Resolution, the president has to notify Congress, and the use of force must be terminated within 60 days if Congress does not approve. However, Congress has never voted to terminate military action, and most presidents have argued that the act is unconstitutional.

Armed Forces

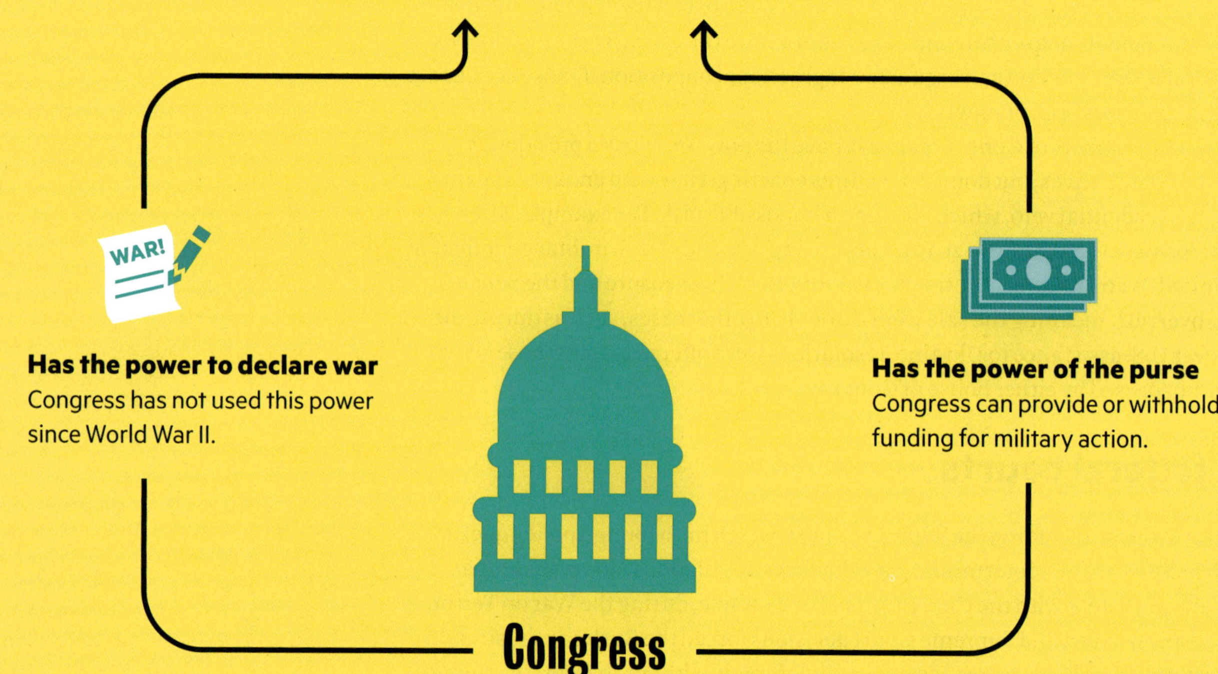

Has the power to declare war
Congress has not used this power since World War II.

Has the power of the purse
Congress can provide or withhold funding for military action.

Congress

How it works: in practice

America's Role in the Russian–Ukrainian War

America's intervention in the ongoing conflict between Russia and Ukraine illustrates how the constitutional allocation of war powers plays out in practice. Although Presidents Obama, Trump, and Biden had wide authority to deploy American forces and send supplies to Ukraine and neighboring countries, their actions reflected consultations with allies and were subject to congressional review and limitations.

Critical Thinking

1. **As you see in this example,** though the president is commander in chief, military action generally follows an extended process of consultation and negotiation with members of Congress and representatives from other nations. What are the benefits and costs of this deliberative process?
2. **At the beginning of this chapter,** we noted that some Americans believe that "politics stops at the water's edge." Do the United States' policies regarding the Ukrainian conflict support or disprove this statement?

Annexation!

In March 2014, **Russian forces take over the Crimean Peninsula**, territory that belongs to Ukraine. Russia also sends military assistance and some troops to aid separatist forces in Eastern Ukraine.

Taking sides.

The United States and its allies protest the annexation of Crimea and **implement a series of economic sanctions against Russia**. The United Nations passes a resolution describing the annexation as illegal.

An agreement.

In 2015, Ukraine, Russia, and representatives from the Organization for Security and Cooperation in Europe (including the United States) **negotiate a series of agreements** to end the conflict in Eastern Ukraine.

The conflict continues.

Despite the agreements, **Russia continues to send aid and troops to Eastern Ukraine** and implements cyberattacks against the Ukrainian government and Ukrainian businesses.

Should we assist?

President Trump **threatens to withhold military assistance appropriated by Congress** unless the Ukrainian government investigates Hunter Biden, the son of Trump's opponent in the 2020 election.

Congressional pressure.

Trump is impeached but not removed from office for his actions regarding Ukraine. The administration ultimately decides to send the assistance as approved by Congress.

More assistance.

During 2021, the Biden administration expands on the Trump effort, **sending over a billion dollars in military supplies to Ukraine** and neighboring countries, including advanced anti-tank missiles.

An international effort.

The United States' NATO allies contribute to the Ukrainian effort, join the United States in **sending military units to countries in eastern Europe**, and coordinate threats to impose economic sanctions on Russia.

Invasion!

Russian forces invade Ukraine on February 24, 2022.

Still more assistance.

Joined by other nations, the **Biden administration sends additional supplies to Ukraine**. Congress approves over $30 billion in defense and humanitarian assistance.

Ukraine wants more.

The Ukrainian government asks NATO to implement a no-fly zone over Ukraine and to send advanced fighter jets. **Both requests are rejected**.

required that the suspects be charged with crimes and tried on those charges. Although this example shows how the courts can reverse presidential actions, three points are key. First, the decisions were not a complete defeat for President Bush. While his policy was overturned, the courts acknowledged that similar policies would be constitutional. Second, court proceedings require time: adjudicating the terror suspect cases required several years, during which the administration's policy remained in place and the defendants were imprisoned without trial or any way to contest their imprisonment.[42] And third, in many cases, the courts have ultimately supported presidential orders.

Groups outside the federal government

A variety of individuals, groups, and forces outside government influence foreign policy. These include interest groups, the media, and public opinion, as well as intergovernmental, nongovernmental, and international organizations.

DID YOU KNOW?

Since 2016, foreign governments have spent over

$3.4 billion

to lobby the U.S. federal government.

Source: OpenSecrets.org.

Interest Groups Interest groups are organizations that work to convince elected officials and bureaucrats to implement policy changes in line with the group's goals. Diverse groups and organizations lobby government over foreign policy.[43] For example, during the congressional debate over the last decade over negotiations with Iran regarding limits on its nuclear weapons programs, the American-Israel Public Affairs Committee (AIPAC), one of the most powerful interest groups in Washington, has led opposition to any agreement. A coalition of smaller groups (including J Street, another pro-Israel lobbying organization that often opposes AIPAC on issues relating to Israel, as well as groups of scientists and the left-leaning organization MoveOn) have lobbied in favor of approval.

Lobbying efforts can even involve foreign governments. In these cases, lobbying efforts center on economic and military aid, trade deals, and more general efforts to improve a country's image among members of Congress and the bureaucracy. In the case of Russia's invasion of Ukraine, Ukraine's president, Volodymyr Zelensky, held a Zoom meeting with over a hundred senators and representatives, as well as numerous telephone calls and other interactions, to persuade members to send military assistance, sanction Russia, help Ukrainian refugees in Poland and other countries, and end Russia's blockade of Ukrainian exports.

U.S. politicians and government officials, including Speaker of the House Nancy Pelosi, regularly speak at AIPAC events. However, it would be a mistake to conclude that the attention paid to this or other interest groups automatically translates into U.S. government support for the groups' policy proposals.

Sometimes interest group lobbying pits business interests against other concerns, such as national security. For example, during both the Obama and Trump presidencies, the Chinese government and two of its major telecommunications technology firms, Huawei and ZTE, complained that the U.S. government had prevented these firms from expanding into U.S. markets. The United States had also discouraged its allies from purchasing equipment from these companies. U.S. technology firms argued that Huawei and ZTE should be kept out of the United States because their equipment could be used for spying or cyberattacks. Although the U.S. technology firms' claims likely had some truth to them (the evidence was classified), it was also the case that the U.S. firms had lost market share to Chinese firms in recent years. Raising national security concerns may have just been a way for the U.S. firms to force the federal government to keep Huawei and ZTE out of the lucrative American market.

Finally, some groups focus on publicizing international events in the hope of prompting citizens to demand government action. For example, in recent years religious groups met with elected officials and worked to gain press

During the conflict between Russia and the Ukraine, Ukrainian president Zelensky met with many high-ranking members of the U.S. government to advocate for measures to punish Russia for the invasion, such as economic sanctions, as well as increase funding for their defense. While the United States didn't take all of the actions Zelensky requested, his efforts went far to raise global awareness of the crisis.

coverage of the plight of refugees fleeing the civil war in Syria. At the same time, major American media outlets published photos of squalid refugee camps and refugee children who drowned after the boat they were traveling on sank in the Mediterranean. Similar efforts have been made to document the plight of refugees who have been forced to leave Ukraine as well as Russian atrocities inside the country.

As mentioned in Chapter 10, the impact of these lobbying efforts is hard to determine. As of fall 2024, the United States has sent over $150 billion in military and civilian assistance to Ukraine, with more on the way. However, it is likely that the individuals involved in these decisions (including, at the top, President Biden) were sympathetic to Ukraine and would have delivered much the same assistance without any lobbying. Also, U.S. assistance stopped short of satisfying all Ukrainian requests—the United States has rejected demands for a no-fly zone over Ukraine and has mandated that Ukraine not use some rocket systems to attack targets in Russia.

The Media Television, radio, print media, and the Internet all inform the public about events in America and elsewhere. As discussed in Chapter 7, although media coverage is a prime source of information about domestic and foreign policy for most Americans, one cannot say that evaluations of America's foreign policy are driven solely by the news media's decisions about what to cover and how to report it. The press informs individuals about events and may to some extent frame the criteria people use to judge America's foreign policy and consider alternatives, but as we have seen elsewhere, most of the time, media attention to a foreign policy question or problem has a limited impact on opinions and policy choices.

Public Opinion Foreign policy decisions are also sensitive to public opinion. As with many domestic issues, elected officials are aware of their constituents' views and are reluctant to support policies that conflict with opinions held by a majority of their constituents. On issues such as lowering tariffs with other countries, congressional voting is highly correlated with constituents' support of or opposition to these measures. However, public opinion is not a decisive influence on foreign policy. For example, in the case of Syrian refugees, American public opinion has consistently been opposed to allowing them to live in the United States. (This finding is not exceptional—in many other cases, Americans have opposed admission of refugees from political crises.)[44]

One reason that foreign policy does not always mirror public opinion was discussed in Chapter 11: most politicians have political goals other than winning reelection, including affecting some aspect of American relations with other nations. For example, President Obama favored admission of Syrian refugees and ordered American forces to intervene in the Syrian civil war with air strikes, arms shipments, and military assistance, although a strong majority of the American public favored different policies (some Americans wanted a more aggressive effort, while others favored disengagement). Given the public's opposition, it is hard to square Obama's policy choices with the goal of mirroring public opinion. A better explanation is that Obama acted in accord with his own conception of what America's foreign policy should look like. This is not to say that public opinion was irrelevant to Obama's choices (as in the case of Syrian refugees, for example), but it is not the only (or even the decisive) factor shaping policy choices. The same is true for Presidents Trump and Biden. Trump's decision to end admissions of Syrian refugees, as well as Biden's decisions to aid Ukraine's armed forces, reflected the opinions of these presidents and their advisers, not a shift in public opinion.

The final reason that American public opinion is not decisive is that many Americans know little about other countries. A case in point occurred after the 2020 attack that killed Iranian general Qasem Soleimani (a time when open conflict with Iran seemed possible if not likely), when a survey asked Americans to locate Iran on a map. Only 28 percent of respondents located Iran correctly (see Chapter 6). Most people knew Iran's location only approximately, and a significant percentage were wildly wrong.[45] More recent surveys confirm this impression. For example, a 2016 survey found that most college-educated adults incorrectly identified China as America's largest trading partner (the correct answer, Canada, was picked by only 10 percent of respondents),[46] and in 2014 only a small fraction could find Ukraine on a map (see Figure 17.1).

Americans are more likely to pay attention to foreign policy news or concerns following an important event. Thus, six months after the September 11 attacks, one poll found that Americans rated preventing future attacks a higher priority than any particular domestic policy, even though domestic policy as a general category took priority over foreign policy.[47] However, as the attacks receded into the past, the

FIGURE 17.1

Where's Ukraine?

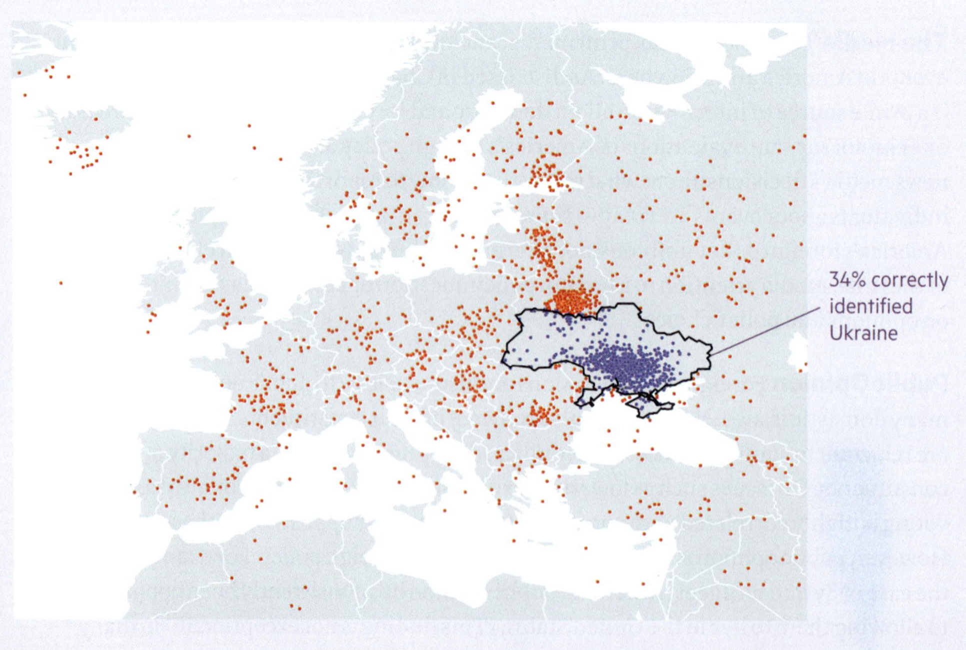

These data reveal a marked lack of geographic knowledge among Americans. Despite the considerable media attention given to Russia's invasion of Ukraine, in a 2022 survey only a small fraction could locate Ukraine on a map (accurate dots are blue; inaccurate dots are red). What might explain this lack of geographical knowledge?

Source: Matthew Kendrick, "34% of Americans Can Find Ukraine on a Map. They're More Likely to Support an Aggressive Posture against Russia," Morning Consult, February 9, 2022, https://morningconsult.com/2022/02/09/can-americans-find-ukraine-on-a-map/ (accessed 6/27/22).

intensity of public concern about preventing future attacks declined somewhat as well, and domestic issues such as economic growth became the paramount concern of most Americans. The same pattern is true for more recent terrorist attacks, as well as other major international events, such as the civil war in Syria or the threat of nuclear weapons use by North Korea. Even Russia's invasion of Ukraine, which dominated news coverage in February and March 2022, received much less attention as the conflict dragged on into 2023 and 2024.

Intergovernmental Organizations, Nongovernmental Organizations, and International Organizations America's relationship with the rest of the world is not just about government action. Members of **intergovernmental organizations (IGOs)** and **nongovernmental organizations (NGOs)** provide information and humanitarian assistance and carry out other activities that the U.S. government is unable or unwilling to undertake. IGOs are associations of sovereign states, while NGOs are private organizations. Thousands of IGOs and NGOs operate throughout the world.[48]

intergovernmental organizations (IGOs)
Organizations that seek to coordinate policy across member nations.

nongovernmental organizations (NGOs)
Groups operated by private institutions (rather than governments) to promote growth, economic development, and other agendas throughout the world.

A primary goal of NGOs and IGOs is promoting global economic development and growth. One of the largest IGOs, the **World Bank**, funds economic development projects throughout the world. Another IGO, the **International Monetary Fund (IMF)**, helps countries manage budget deficits and control the value of their currencies. Many NGOs, such as the Asia Foundation, focus on development in a particular region or on certain activities, such as microlending, in which banks or other institutions provide small loans to citizens in developing nations as a way of stimulating business growth and reducing poverty.

World Bank
An intergovernmental organization established in 1944 that provides financial support for economic development projects in developing nations.

International Monetary Fund (IMF)
An intergovernmental organization established in 1944 to help stabilize the international monetary system, improve economic growth, and aid developing nations.

A second role of NGOs is providing humanitarian relief. In the wake of a disaster such as an earthquake or a flood, or during a famine or a war, organizations such as Oxfam International supply populations in crisis. Other groups such as Doctors without Borders provide medical care to populations threatened by violence, epidemics, or natural disasters. These groups played a key role in the response to COVID-19 outbreaks in Africa and elsewhere. Some NGOs also promote human rights. Amnesty International spotlights international cases of people jailed for their political beliefs or held without trial, and the use of cruel punishments such as stoning. Amnesty's campaigns, as well as those of other NGOs, are not always supportive of U.S. policy. In recent years, for example, Amnesty has criticized the rendition of terror suspects by the United States.[49]

Finally, NGOs help build democracies. The Open Society Foundations fund efforts to increase mass political participation, strengthen political organizations, and verify the fairness of elections in new democracies throughout the world. The National Democratic Institute and the International Republican Institute (both funded by the federal government) conduct similar activities. Both organizations, for example, are working with groups in countries such as Myanmar and Pakistan to increase the transparency of electoral institutions, recruit candidates, and help citizens build political organizations.

The United States is also a member of many international organizations. Best known is the **United Nations (UN)**, an assembly of ambassadors representing almost all of the world's nations that addresses issues of worldwide concern. The UN is involved in economic development, environmental protection, humanitarian relief, and peacekeeping efforts. The UN has deployed peacekeeping forces to separate warring parties in Africa, the Middle East, and the former Yugoslavia. In fall 2022, nearly 100,000 UN peacekeeping troops, police, and other personnel were deployed in 12 different areas.[50]

United Nations (UN)
An international organization made up of representatives from nearly every nation, with a mission to promote peace and cooperation, uphold international law, and provide humanitarian aid.

Inside the UN, the Security Council, a group of 15 nations (permanent members Britain, China, France, Russia, and the United States, plus 10 rotating nations), makes the most important UN decisions, particularly those involving its military missions. The UN General Assembly, in which each nation has one vote, debates and votes on other concerns.

"Why Should I Care?"

It may look to you like foreign policy is all about what the president wants. However, for the most part, the same kinds of people (in many cases, the same people) who influence domestic policy choices also shape America's foreign policy—including elected officials, interest groups, and the public at large. The president is a key player in making foreign policy choices, but the president is far from being the only voice that matters.

EXAMINE THE WAYS AMERICAN FOREIGN POLICY IS IMPLEMENTED

The tools of foreign policy

Now that we know the key players in foreign policy making, what are the tools and methods these players use to implement policy?

Diplomacy

economic sanctions
Penalties applied by one country or group of countries on another, usually in the form of tariffs or other trade barriers.

Diplomacy has often been a limited but useful foreign policy tool. The process of diplomacy involves using personal contact and negotiations with national leaders and representatives to work out international agreements or persuade other nations to change their behavior. Sometimes these efforts involve the threat of military action or **economic sanctions**, or incentives such as economic assistance or other forms of aid. The United States may participate directly in such efforts or mediate between the parties in a dispute. When two countries refuse to meet face-to-face, U.S. diplomats may take part in shuttle diplomacy, in which they meet separately with each country's representatives to convey the other country's proposals and counterproposals. For example, the efforts of American and Russian diplomats were instrumental in establishing a brief cease-fire in Syria in 2016 and in getting both sides of the conflict to allow convoys carrying relief supplies to enter besieged areas of the country—although this agreement had little impact on the larger conflict.

Diplomacy has its limits. The various parties in a conflict have to be willing to make a deal and to accept American efforts to negotiate. In the case of Syria, attempts to build on the cease-fire deal were stalled by U.S.-Russia conflicts in other areas and by the Syrian government's belief that it could win the conflict on the battlefield (which it eventually did). In the case of the war in Ukraine, diplomatic efforts prior to the conflict by European nations and the UN were completely unsuccessful in persuading Russia not to attack.

Diplomacy often involves protracted negotiations and many participants. The Singapore Summit between North Korea and the United States, which yielded a promise for peaceful relations and denuclearization of the Korean Peninsula, required months of preparation and the cooperation of the Singaporean government.

The makers of foreign policy may also simply decide that diplomatic negotiations are not worth the effort. For example, by increasing the defense budget, keeping many senior State Department positions unfilled, pushing career diplomats to retire, and withdrawing from efforts to negotiate international agreements, the Trump administration signaled that it was less interested than its predecessors in diplomacy as a tool of foreign policy. The Biden administration's efforts to rebuild State Department cadres is a strong signal of the emphasis it places on diplomacy as a tool of foreign policy.

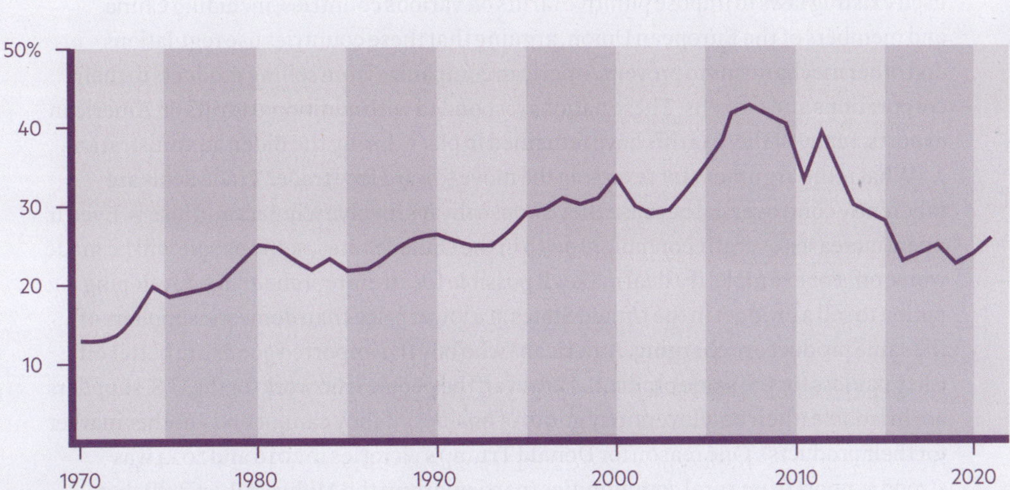

Source: Office of the United States Trade Representative, *2022 Trade Policy Agenda*, March 2022, https://ustr.gov (accessed 6/03/22).

FIGURE 17.2

U.S. Imports and Exports as a Percentage of GDP

This figure illustrates the importance of trade to the U.S. economy. In recent years imports and exports have accounted for almost 30 percent of U.S. economic activity. Based on these data, what arguments would you make for lowering or increasing barriers to trade?

Trade and economic policies

Trade and economic policies can be crucial instruments of foreign policy: they can sustain economic growth in the United States and elsewhere, as well as create foreign markets for the goods produced by America's domestic industries. Figure 17.2 shows total American trade (imports and exports) with other countries over the last 50 years, expressed as a percentage of U.S. gross domestic product (GDP), which measures the size of the U.S. economy. In recent years, imports and exports together have constituted almost 30 percent of GDP. Investment returns (profits from American-owned companies located abroad) are also becoming an ever-larger component of total trade. In dollar terms, the report cited in Figure 17.2 estimated that the total value of U.S. trade with other nations was over $5 trillion per year. Clearly, foreign trade is a critical component of the American economy.

The main tools of trade policy are tariffs and trade agreements. A **tariff** is a tax on the import or export of certain commodities, and a trade agreement sets tariff levels or limits the quantities of particular items that can be imported or exported. The United States International Trade Commission maintains a list of all tariffs in effect.[51] By adjusting tariff rates, the government can help or hurt domestic industries. High tariffs on imports help American producers charge lower prices than foreign competitors, and low tariffs on exports help American producers sell to overseas markets.

tariff
A tax levied on imported or exported goods.

Over the last two generations, the United States and most other nations have lowered tariffs and established free-trade zones, agreements to eliminate tariffs on all imports and exports among specific nations. Examples include a long-standing free trade agreement with Canada and Mexico, and the Central American Free Trade Agreement (CAFTA) among the United States, five Central American nations, and the Dominican Republic. Other organizations, such as the **World Trade Organization (WTO)**, facilitate negotiations over tariffs and provide a mechanism for adjudicating cases when one nation believes that another is using tariffs unfairly. Finally, the United States has granted many other countries **most-favored-nation status**: tariffs on imports to the United States from these nations are set at rates lower than those placed on any other nation.

World Trade Organization (WTO)
An international organization created in 1995 to oversee trade agreements between nations by facilitating negotiations and handling disputes.

most-favored-nation status
A standing awarded to countries with which a nation has good trade relations, providing the lowest possible tariff rate. WTO members must give one another this preferred status.

Donald Trump overturned many of these policies, claiming that many of these trade deals did not serve U.S. interests. He sought to renegotiate trade agreements and used existing laws to impose punitive tariffs on various countries, including China and members of the European Union, arguing that these countries use regulations and other mechanisms to prevent American companies from selling products to their corporations and citizens. These nations responded with additional tariffs on American exports. Many of these tariffs have remained in place during the Biden administration.

What is the argument for reversing the move toward free trade? Trade deals are inherently controversial because they almost always involve winners and losers. Even if a deal increases overall economic growth in the United States, some people will be made worse off. For example, if a deal makes it possible for an entrepreneur in a developing nation to sell a product in the United States at a lower price than domestic suppliers of the same product are charging, Americans who buy the imported goods are better off (they pay less for the same product). However, the people who work for the U.S. suppliers are in trouble (their employers may go out of business if they cannot find another market for their products). One reason for Donald Trump's victories in 2016 and 2024 was strong support from rural communities (particularly in the Midwest Rust Belt) that have lost manufacturing jobs because companies responded to lower tariffs by moving factories overseas and because companies face competition from foreign suppliers.

Trade is an important part of foreign policy. The United States has used free-trade agreements and tariffs to bargain with countries for concessions in noneconomic policy areas or to cement international alliances. For example, one of the incentives Trump offered to North Korea as part of a denuclearization deal was to reduce economic sanctions on the country, allowing increased trade and investment. Similarly, one of the reasons why America has played a central role in crafting trade agreements with Asian nations was that the government wanted to strengthen America's political and economic ties with these nations, as a counter to the increased regional economic and military power of China.

Economic policies are also used to threaten or sanction countries as a way of inducing them to change their behavior. After Russia's invasion of Ukraine, several countries including the United States, Canada, and other nations in Europe and throughout the world imposed trade and other sanctions on Russia, effectively banning imports and exports (except for Russian oil and natural gas sold to European nations) and cutting the country and its citizens off from the international financial

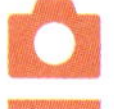

The West took swift action in an effort to stop Russia's assault on Ukraine. This involved cooperation between countries to approve economic sanctions, as well as bans on importing Russian oil.

system. These sanctions did not deter Russia from invading, but they inflicted severe damage on the Russian economy, and isolated Russia and its citizens from the world community. While sanctions have not ended the conflict thus far, they have increased the price paid by Russia for continuing the conflict.

Foreign aid

Foreign aid is money, products, or services given to other countries or the citizens of these countries. Sometimes aid reflects the desire to provide basic assistance to satisfy fundamental human needs. For example, American military ships and aircraft are often used to deliver food and medical supplies to the victims of earthquakes and other natural disasters. Foreign aid also serves to stimulate economic growth in other nations. For instance, funding from the United States helps build factories; pays for technical advisers who provide locals with training on the construction and operation of water, power, or sewage treatment plants; and buys hardware to support infrastructure such as Internet access or telephone networks. Foreign aid also facilitates international agreements. For example, the peace treaty between Egypt and Israel in 1979 was facilitated by America's agreement to provide substantial military and economic assistance to both countries.[52] Promises of continued American aid to Israel have also been one factor in discouraging Israel from attacking Iranian nuclear facilities in the last several years.

Figure 17.3 shows the level of American nonmilitary foreign aid in 2019 measured as a percentage of gross national income (GNI, which includes GDP as well as accounting for investment income from other countries) and total volume in U.S. dollars, compared with that of the six other countries that are members of the G7 group of major industrialized nations. Compared with these countries, America gives a relatively low percentage of GNI in foreign aid, although part of the explanation lies in the size of the U.S. economy: America's foreign aid contributions are the largest of any country when measured in total dollars, but it also has the largest GNI of any country.

DID YOU KNOW?

The United States spends

<1%

of its annual budget on foreign aid. According to one poll, Americans on average think the country spends 28 percent.

Source: Kaiser Family Foundation Poll.

FIGURE 17.3

U.S. Foreign Aid in Comparative Perspective

This figure shows foreign aid contributions expressed both in total volume and as a percentage of gross national income (GNI). Do these data imply that America is less generous with aid than other nations are? What other explanations are there for the differences across countries?

Note: Bars represent aid in volume and dots represent aid as percent of GNI. Data are from 2021.

Source: Organization for Economic Cooperation and Development, *Development Co-operation Report 2021*, www.oecd.org/ (accessed 6/3/22).

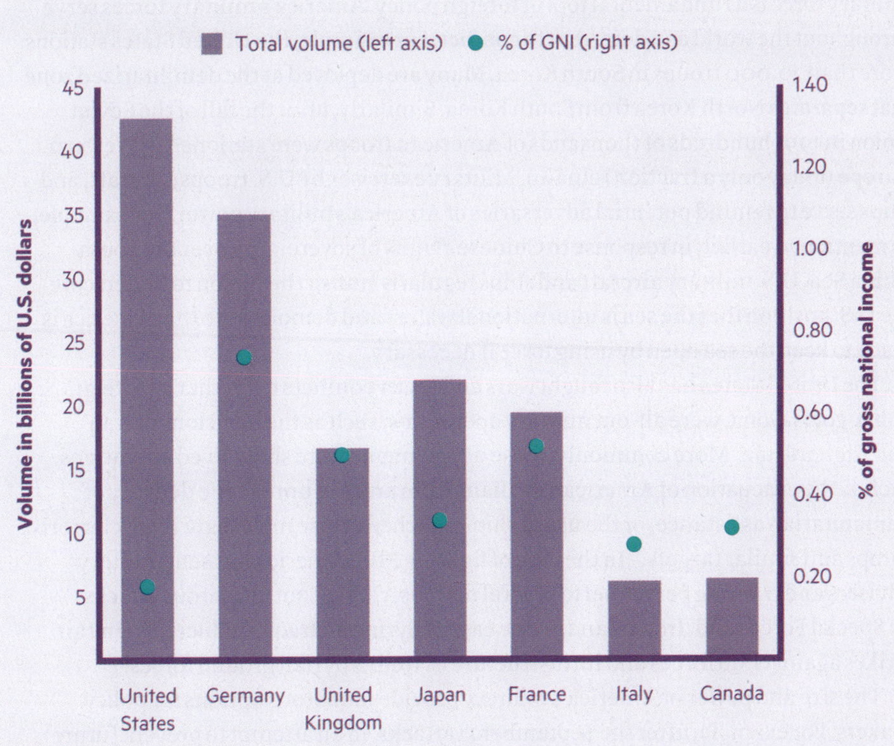

Alliances and treaties

A treaty is an agreement between nations to work together on economic or security issues. An alliance is an agreement that commits nations to security guarantees, which are assurances that one country will help another if it is attacked. America is a member of many international alliances, most notably NATO. This alliance was formed by the North Atlantic Treaty after World War II to provide collective security against the Soviet Union and Warsaw Pact countries. The organization's mission shifted after the Cold War to focus on coordinating military force toward common goals, with the organization's 2011 intervention in the Libyan civil war the first instance of operations outside Europe. Most NATO nations provided military and humanitarian assistance to Ukraine after Russia's invasion. Historically, the United States has paid a disproportionate share of the cost of NATO operations and devoted a larger share of GNI to defense spending. In recent years, the United States has successfully pressured its NATO allies to increase their spending on defense.

The United States is a party to treaties with many countries.[53] Several of these treaties implemented significant changes in both U.S. and other military forces, from capping the size of nuclear forces, to restricting the numbers of these forces, to banning some kinds of weapons. These agreements enable the United States to commit itself to a course of action or signal its intentions to other nations.[54] By helping form NATO and stationing troops in Europe, the United States guaranteed that if Warsaw Pact troops invaded the West, U.S. forces would be directly involved in the defense of Western Europe. More recently, after Russia's invasion of Ukraine, America and its NATO partners sent aircraft, troops, and ships to countries adjacent to Ukraine and other countries that were part of the former Soviet Union to signal their opposition to Russia's plans and their support for these governments. (Ukraine is not, however, a member of NATO.)

Military force

Military force is a fundamental tool of foreign policy. America's military forces serve throughout the world as a deterrent to conflict. For example, the United States stations more than 20,000 troops in South Korea. Many are deployed at the demilitarized zone that separates North Korea from South Korea. Similarly, until the fall of the Soviet Union in 1991 hundreds of thousands of American troops were stationed in Western Europe (today only a fraction remain). Military exercises by U.S. troops, aircraft, and ships serve to remind potential adversaries of America's military power. For example, as mentioned earlier, in response to Chinese claims of sovereignty over the South China Sea, U.S. military aircraft and ships regularly transit the region to underscore the U.S. position that the sea is international waters and demonstrate that America is ready to keep the sea open by using force if necessary.

The United States has also fought wars and lesser conflicts to further its foreign policy goals. Some were all-out military operations, such as the invasions of Iraq and Afghanistan. More commonly, these deployments were short-lived operations, such as the evacuation of American civilians from areas of unrest, the delivery of humanitarian assistance, or the use of ship-launched cruise missiles to attack terrorist camps and similar targets.[55] In the case of fighting ISIS, America has sent military advisers and training personnel to several nations, carried out numerous attacks by Special Forces and drones, and, in the case of Syria and Iraq, conducted many air strikes against ISIS forces and infrastructure as well as Syrian ground forces.

The size and power of America's military provide numerous options for policy makers. For example, after the September 11 attacks, in an attempt to prevent future terror attacks by Al Qaeda, U.S. forces invaded Afghanistan, which had been used as a base of operations for the organization.[56] It is highly unlikely that any other country would have been able to carry out such a large-scale operation so far from home. America's military also provided the majority of international forces in the attacks in Libya and Syria and against ISIS.

Nonetheless, military force is not all-powerful. For example, despite nearly two decades of combat operations in Afghanistan and large amounts of economic and military aid to the Afghan government, the U.S. armed forces were not able to prevent the Taliban (a religious-political organization) from overturning the Afghani government (American forces were finally withdrawn in summer 2021.). Similarly, while air strikes in Iraq and Syria have significantly reduced ISIS's military might, the organization remains able to plan future terror attacks throughout the world. Moreover, it is not clear whether any level of military force can remove this threat.

"Why Should I Care?"

It's easy to think that America can get what it wants from other nations by making threats involving military force—after all, America's military is the largest in the world by far. However, foreign policy isn't that simple. There are many other ways for America to achieve its foreign policy goals, from diplomacy to economic sanctions or even aid programs. The reason why these strategies are used is that they work—and often work better than force would.

The politics of foreign policy today

ANALYZE SEVERAL MAJOR AREAS OF FOREIGN POLICY AND WHY THEY ARE OFTEN CONTROVERSIAL

The making of foreign policy, like everything else in the federal government, is a political act—a contest involving elected officials, bureaucrats, interest groups, and other actors, all of whom have their own goals. In this sense, there are always conflicts over what America's foreign policy should look like, and compromise is fundamental to the making of it. This section describes three of the major foreign policy issues facing America in the contemporary era: trade, terrorism, and nuclear proliferation—and how all these issues raise human rights concerns. These issues demonstrate the complexity of America's foreign policy choices and how these decisions are shaped both by conflicts and by political processes.

In addition, this section argues against claims about the decline of American influence throughout the world. Although it is true that other countries such as China are increasing their economic and military power and that the United States faces many new and complex issues, the United States still continues to be an international power and in many respects is the strongest nation on the globe, with enormous influence over economic, social, and military events worldwide. How the issues described in this section will be resolved remains in question, but there is no doubt that the foreign policy choices of the United States will play a decisive role.

You should also realize that as with domestic policy, the rise and fall of foreign policy challenges is difficult to predict. Even in late 2021, it was difficult to imagine that Russia would invade Ukraine with the goal of overthrowing the government and incorporating the territory into Russia itself. It was almost as difficult to imagine that

Western nations would stand firm against the invasion, offering military support to Ukraine and accepting the economic impact of higher energy costs caused by sanctions on Russian oil. And yet here we are.

We face the same uncertainty looking to the future in today's world. For example, our plans to address climate risks may be upended by abrupt changes in temperature or precipitation; sea level rise; or technological innovations that reduce carbon dioxide emissions or remove this substance from the atmosphere. The only things we can be sure of are that Americans will face important foreign policy questions, that citizens and politicians will disagree about the answers, and that the way these questions are decided will affect all of our lives.

Managing international trade: China

For the United States, trade is a necessity. America imports a wide range of resources and manufactured goods from other countries, and increased trade can enhance the economic growth of the nation overall. Many economic analyses describe trade in terms of the theory of comparative advantage, which holds that nations export items they can produce cheaply, in return for imports that can be produced more efficiently elsewhere. Similarly, outsourcing jobs to foreign countries with lower labor costs makes American companies more efficient, which raises their profits and allows them to expand operations, which may result in new jobs.

globalization
The increase over the last generation in trade, travel, and the flow of ideas and beliefs between nations.

These practices are examples of **globalization**: the trend toward increasing interaction and connections among individuals, corporations, and nations (see Chapter 15). New technologies have leveled the global playing field, allowing suppliers of goods and services to sell their products throughout the world. Many American companies and their employees profit from this process. Reflecting this development, the last generation of American politics has been marked by international agreements to reduce or eliminate tariffs among nations, the growth of international organizations such as the WTO to regulate trade and adjudicate trade disputes, and increases in outsourcing of manufacturing jobs and services from developed countries to developing countries.[57] The trade policy of the Trump administration, which emphasized threats of higher tariffs and withdrawal from trade agreements, was a sharp departure from these trends, although the Biden administration has reversed some but not all of Trump's changes.

At the same time, even if trade deals increase economic growth in America as a whole, opening America's markets will hurt some individuals—those whose livelihoods are threatened by cheaper foreign imports. For example, in many midwestern towns, manufacturing plants have been closed because of competition from cheaper foreign imports. In theory, displaced workers could enter retraining programs and move on to new jobs with companies that are able to grow because of new opportunities to export to other countries. However, these workers may not be able to find, afford, or complete a retraining program and may not want to move to another state for a new job, particularly if it involves a significant pay cut. As a result, while trade deals attract significant political support, they also generate strong opposition from individuals and communities that correctly see the deals as a threat to their way of life. An additional complication is that even if countries reduce or eliminate tariffs, existing regulations create significant barriers to foreign companies that want to sell products there.

America's relations with China are a prime example of these developments. Many American companies have factories in China that produce a variety of products that are sold in America. China is a major producer of rare earth metals that are used to build computer chips. American corporations are also opening stores in China—the coffee chain Starbucks, for example, opens more than one store per day there.[58] In recent

Globalization has transformed economics and society in the United States and abroad. Brands such as Starbucks have spread around the world. Revenue growth for the company in China and Southeast Asia has been substantially higher than in the United States.

years, China has been one of America's largest trading partners, with over $600 billion in imports and exports during 2021.[59]

Although these moves toward increased trade with China generate significant benefits, the changes do not make everyone better off. American manufacturing jobs have been lost as factories that could not compete with cheaper foreign suppliers have either closed or moved to another country, leaving behind unemployed American workers.[60] Moreover, there have been numerous complaints that Chinese companies have stolen trade secrets from American corporations or violated American copyright laws—in some cases with the apparent support of the Chinese government. Moreover, China often requires technology companies to disclose trade secrets and source codes as a condition of being allowed to sell products there. America has also enacted restrictions, such as the ban discussed earlier on government purchases of telecommunications equipment from Chinese firms.

President Trump departed from previous administrations in his aggressive use of punitive tariffs to force China and other countries to change their trade practices. The problem is, in a global economy in which America is only one potential market, such threats may simply lead foreign companies to sell their goods elsewhere, raising the prices paid by American consumers. Trump's tariffs also triggered increased tariffs on American goods, which reduced American exports and hurt employees of affected companies. Most important, however, even if trade barriers disappear and global markets become completely open, American communities will still suffer because of increased foreign imports. While there are some federal programs to retrain workers whose jobs are eliminated because of new trade agreements, many workers who have lost their jobs due to globalization are not eligible for these programs, and others are unaware that they exist. Moreover, it is often extremely difficult to retrain people to compete for new jobs that will provide pay and benefits comparable to what they received in their former positions. In addition, there are no systematic American efforts to help citizens of other countries who are hurt by globalization.

Finally, globalization raises new human rights questions. For example, do U.S. companies such as Apple, which has outsourced the production of iPhones to factories

What I'm saying is this: I'm saying that we do it, but if they [China] don't start treating us fairly and stop devaluing and let their currency rise so that our companies can compete and we don't lose all of these millions of jobs that we're losing I would certainly start taxing goods that come in from China. Who the hell has to lose $505 billion a year?

—President Donald Trump

One of the effects of globalization is outsourcing—moving jobs to different countries, usually to take advantage of lower wages and looser restrictions on manufacturing practices. Here, workers in China assemble electronic products for a foreign company.

in China, have a responsibility to monitor conditions in these factories and ensure that workers there are paid a fair wage? More generally, should the United States increase its trade with a country such as China that restricts the political, religious, and social freedoms of its citizens in ways that most Americans would find objectionable? Or should it push for as much trade as possible, on the grounds that exposure to American commerce and culture will encourage the other country's citizens to press their government for reforms?

Trade is an example of a more general phenomenon: the state of each national economy is increasingly linked to economic conditions throughout the world. For example, China has an enormous trade surplus (more exports than imports) with America and holds hundreds of billions of dollars in American government bonds. Some observers believe these assets give the Chinese the ability to severely damage the American economy, either by withholding exports or by selling large quantities of American government bonds on international markets, thus raising the interest rate the United States would have to offer to finance its budget deficit. However, the Chinese economy is equally vulnerable. Eliminating the U.S. market for exports would leave Chinese factories without one of their major buyers. And selling bonds at below-market prices to increase American interest rates would likely damage the Chinese economy even more than the American economy.

One way to respond to these complications is to take a stand along the lines of Donald Trump's punitive tariffs—that the United States should renegotiate trade agreements to protect American workers and increase American exports, with the threat that America will impose high import tariffs on countries that refuse to comply with these demands. President Biden made less-severe threats as a way to push the Chinese into protecting intellectual property and forcing Chinese companies to improving working conditions in factories. These threats may work—but in past situations, they have led to tit-for-tat tariff increases and other measures that have left both countries worse off. The ongoing debate over trade with China illustrates a central truth: while U.S. policy can encourage or discourage trade, outsourcing, and other interactions that cross national borders, all these choices will make some people better off and some worse off. As in so many other areas of American politics, because of the wide range of interests that Americans bring to the table, there is no one trade policy that is clearly better than all the others.

Fighting terrorism: ISIS

There have been no major terrorist attacks on the United States since September 11, 2001, and Al Qaeda and ISIS have been decimated by U.S. counterattacks using drones, Special Forces troops, air strikes, and ground forces. Nevertheless, the potential for terrorism remains, and groups such as ISIS have continued to carry out smaller operations, such as attacks in various European cities. ISIS has also encouraged individuals to plan and execute their own attacks, such as the attacks by an American citizen in a Miami nightclub in June 2016 and by a New York City resident who drove a truck into a crowd of pedestrians in October 2017 (there have been none since).

The fight against global terror is different from a conventional war. In a conventional war, there are clear victory criteria: the losing nation's government capitulates. In contrast, terrorism involves multiple organizations with fluid memberships. Eliminating one individual or group may not reduce the danger of future attacks, because these victories do not address the factors that drive terrorism, including poverty and a deep-set anger that some individuals have against Western interests. For example, while the United States and its allies have recaptured land in Syria and Iraq that was controlled by ISIS and have killed or captured many ISIS fighters, offshoots of the organization still exist throughout the world, as do anti-American, anti-West sentiments among some groups.

The same is true for Al Qaeda. Over the last 20 years, the United States has invaded Afghanistan and removed the Afghan Taliban government that supported Al Qaeda, destroyed many camps and other centers in Afghanistan and elsewhere, and captured or killed many operatives and leaders of the organization. (The Taliban have since regained control of Afghanistan.) However, while Al Qaeda is far weaker than it was in 2001, the possibility of an attack on Americans in the United States or abroad by the remnants of Al Qaeda or some new organization remains very real (although, as we discuss in the What Do the Facts Say? feature on p. 696, many Americans overestimate the threat of terrorist attacks).

Political scientist John Mueller argues that terrorism is hard to deter because its primary purpose is to frighten people; as a result, the set of possible targets is very large.[61] We typically think of terrorists attacking big, visible targets such as the World Trade Center or the U.S. Capitol, but in fact, there are many public places, from malls to urban centers, where an attack could cause high casualties and public panic (the ISIS attacks in the United States in 2016 and 2017 are examples). This fact makes the job of preventing attacks virtually impossible. And given that the number of actual terrorists is quite small, they are extremely difficult to find, regardless of whether they are in Syria or in America.

Human rights concerns also shape antiterrorism efforts. American attacks against terror groups have the potential to cause civilian casualties—especially in places such as Afghanistan, where these groups have tried to hide among civilians to discourage such attacks. In addition, investigating terror groups may involve increased surveillance of Americans and their communications. American decision makers must also decide whether they will overlook problems in other countries to pursue terror suspects. For example, the government of Pakistan is routinely cited for human rights abuses, but Pakistani officials have allowed the United States to use Pakistani airspace to send drones into Iraq and Iran.

In sum, regardless of what happens in Syria, Afghanistan, and other areas where ISIS and other terrorist organizations operate, the fight against global terrorism will continue for the foreseeable future. It is easy to work backward from this conclusion to a critique of past policies—to conclude, for example, that things would be better if the United States had stayed in Afghanistan, had not invaded Iraq, or had refused to intervene in the Syrian civil war. However, because terror attacks can come from

WHAT DO THE FACTS SAY?

The Threat of Terrorism

As the Gallup poll here indicates, a substantial percentage of Americans worry that they or members of their family will be the victims of a terrorist attack—in fact, these concerns even predate the September 11 attacks. Are these fears justified? How great is the risk? What do the facts say?

How worried are you that you or someone in your family will become a victim of terrorism?

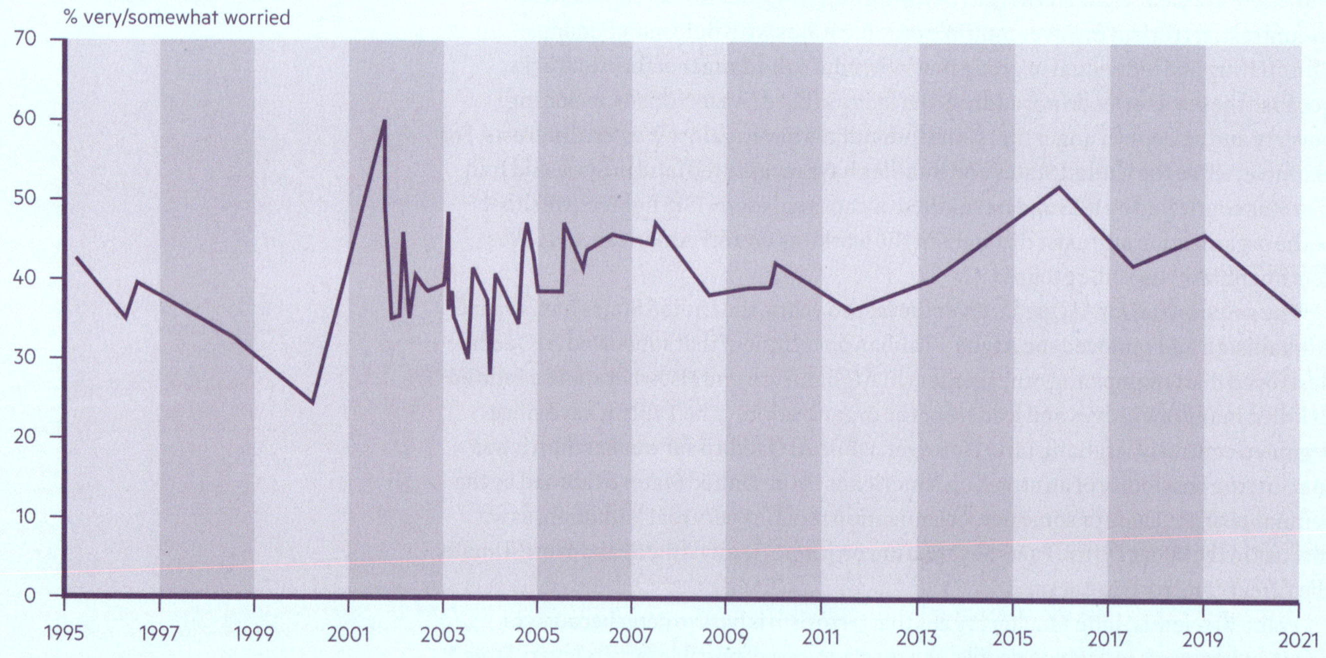

Think about it

- **Is the public's concern over the dangers of terrorist attacks** justified by the fatality data?
- **Suppose you are a bureaucrat from the Department of Homeland Security** who is testifying before Congress on the need to increase funding for antiterrorism programs. One of the members of Congress at the hearing argues that such funding is unnecessary because the likelihood of dying from a terrorist incident is so low. How would you respond?

Hazard	Annual fatality risk
Traffic accidents	1 in 8,200
Homicide	1 in 22,000
Industrial accidents	1 in 53,000
Natural disasters	1 in 480,000
Drowning in bathtub	1 in 950,000
Home appliances	1 in 1,500,000
Deer accidents	1 in 2,000,000
Commercial aviation	1 in 2,300,000
Peanut allergies	1 in 6,000,000
Lightning	1 in 7,000,000
Terrorist attack	1 in 110,000,000

Sources: Gallup Poll, "Terrorism," https://news.gallup.com/poll/4909/terrorism-united-states.aspx (accessed 6/27/22); John Mueller and Mark G. Stewart, *Chasing Ghosts: The Policing of Terrorism* (New York: Oxford University Press, 2015).

many sources, because the fight against these organizations touches on human rights concerns, and because it is not clear how to eliminate the threat, there is no clear best strategy in the War on Terror. As a result, the threat from terrorism, and the debate over how to respond, will persist.

Preventing the spread of WMDs: North Korea

The term "**weapons of mass destruction (WMDs)**" refers to nuclear bombs, chemical weapons such as nerve gas, and biological weapons such as anthrax. Given the potential for these weapons to inflict mass casualties, the United States has placed a high priority on (1) limiting the number of nations that have these weapons and (2) preventing terrorist organizations from obtaining or developing them. For example, North Korea's efforts to build a nuclear arsenal raise concerns that North Korea might use the weapons against South Korea or even the United States or that terrorist organizations could buy or steal the weapons to use themselves. (Similar concerns arise for other nuclear powers, including Pakistan and other countries that have had nuclear weapons research programs, such as Iran.)

weapons of mass destruction (WMDs)
Weapons that have the potential to cause large-scale loss of life, such as nuclear bombs and chemical or biological weapons.

The enduring problem for the United States is to determine how to respond to North Korea's nuclear capabilities. Military operations are problematic, as North Korea's weapons and the factories that manufacture them are buried deep underground and may not be destroyed even by a massive attack. An unsuccessful attack might goad the North Korean government to launch its remaining weapons against U.S., South Korean, or Japanese targets. Moreover, how should America respond to a nuclear attack against its citizens or its allies, particularly if it is unclear which nation or group is responsible?

Historically, America's policy toward North Korea as well as other near-nuclear powers has emphasized incentives as well as threats. Economic and military sanctions serve to pressure nations that continue to develop weapons, while offers of economic aid and even civilian nuclear reactors serve to persuade nations to give up their weapons programs.[62] Of course, because these agreements are voluntary, nations giving up their nuclear weapons programs get something in

North Korea has one of the world's least predictable and most isolated political regimes. Its nuclear capabilities and large military make North Korea a threat to the stability of the region. However, because of the poor state of the country's economy, economic sanctions are unlikely to foster movement toward democracy and openness.

return. In the case of the deal with Iran, the United States and its allies made crucial concessions—the lifting of economic sanctions and the return of Iranian assets held after the Iranian Revolution of 1979. These concessions were hugely valuable to the Iranian regime because of their importance in the Iranian economy, although most were later reimposed when President Trump withdrew the United States from the agreement.

The problem with America's carrots and sticks is that the North Korean economy is already in shambles and the country has relatively little trade with other nations. As a result, economic sanctions are not very threatening. The North Korean government has essentially isolated its citizens from the outside world and carried out a widespread program of indoctrination to reinforce beliefs that building nuclear weapons is an appropriate response to threats from the rest of the world. The government also imprisons dissidents and withholds basic resources from the North Korean people, focusing instead on building a strong military. Under these conditions, the offer to reopen commercial and cultural ties is not very attractive to the North Korean leadership.

The difficulty of the problem does not eliminate conflict in American politics over what policy to follow. The disagreement is in part over the potential for success of different tactics. Some believe that North Korea's weapons could be destroyed by a bombing attack, for example. Despite ongoing missile tests, it is also uncertain whether North Korea has the means to reliably launch nuclear weapons against American targets. Others see a wider range of motivations, agreeing that North Korea's nuclear capability must be eliminated but also arguing that it is America's responsibility to free the North Korean people from an oppressive dictatorship.

How this conflict is resolved will drive future policy choices. On the one hand, if human rights concerns dominate or if the threat is seen as imminent, it is likely that military operations will proceed. On the other hand, if North Korea is seen as making threats it cannot carry out and if the cost of conflict (including the suffering of the North and South Korean people following an attack) is seen as unacceptably high, then the status quo of diplomacy and the promise of economic aid is likely to continue, even as the threat posed by North Korean weapons remains.

Unpacking the Conflict

Foreign policy matters. National security is a top priority for many Americans. The state of the American economy, from home prices to the unemployment rate, is affected by economic conditions elsewhere. Trade agreements with other nations determine how much American companies are allowed to export and what taxes and fees they must pay to import raw materials and other goods. It is hard to find a domestic issue that does not have a foreign policy component. And the COVID-19 pandemic highlights that in an interconnected world, problems that start within one nation's borders can expand across the entire globe. Who gets to decide America's foreign policy? How is foreign policy made?

One significant difference between foreign and domestic policies is the preeminent role played by the president in determining America's relations with other nations and its role in the world. Even so, other actors, especially Congress, can block presidential initiatives or set policy on their own. In fact, many presidential foreign policy powers, such as the ability to change tariffs, have been delegated to the executive branch by Congress.

That the president is the dominant actor does not always mean that presidents get their way. President Trump and his supporters believed that demands for renegotiation of existing agreements would increase American exports and improve the American economy, only to find that foreign leaders responded with their own demands. Former president Biden and our European allies supported Ukraine in its fight against Russian invasion, but Russia refused to comply with demands to withdraw. The problem is that foreign policy outcomes are contingent on what other nations do—and they may not be inclined to act as the United States wants.

The most important thing to remember about foreign policy making is that it is conflictual. It is tempting to think that because foreign policy involves dealing with other countries, Americans should hold similar preferences and stand united. The reality is that disagreements among elected officials over what to do about terrorist groups, trade agreements, worldwide pandemics, or any other question of foreign policy are not just attempts to attract political support or get media attention. These differences of opinion reflect real dilemmas over what government should do and how it should do it.

In all these respects, the issues discussed in this chapter, including the fight against global terrorism, the Middle East, conflicts with China over trade policy, and persuading Iran and North Korea to curb their nuclear ambitions, are not exceptions to the rule; rather, they epitomize just how close to home foreign policy is. Ordinary Americans are finding their lives increasingly affected by actions taken outside U.S. borders—a trend that is likely to continue over the next generation. And the political process will determine how these pressing foreign policy questions will be resolved.

"What's Your Take?"

What should be America's foreign policy objectives? Should foreign policy makers focus on providing foreign aid to stimulate growth in other countries, as well as intervening to support foreign governments?

Or should the goal be to return to isolationism, focusing on domestic rather than international issues, as Trump proposed in his inauguration speech?

CHECK YOUR UNDERSTANDING

"Why Should I Care?"

You might want to ignore America's foreign policy on the grounds that it only affects people who live in other countries. You might want the federal government to focus its attention inside our borders. Or you might believe foreign policy to be outside of politics, since Americans should be united when dealing with the rest of the world. Everyday life is complicated enough; why worry about the rest of the world?

America's national security and economic well-being are affected by things that happen in other nations. Taking good care of America's citizens requires our government to engage other countries in areas such as trade, tourism, and collaborations in scientific research. These foreign policy issues are as conflictual as domestic policy. When Americans debate foreign policy, either in concrete terms such as assistance to Ukraine or in the abstract, such as idealism versus realism, they are arguing over issues that have very real consequences for their welfare, as well as for the welfare of other nations. Foreign policy isn't about other nationals and people; it is emphatically about us.

One crucial difference between foreign and domestic policy is the disproportionate influence of the president. The president is commander-in-chief of America's armed forces and, through their control of the executive branch, directs interactions with other nations through the State Department, the Department of Commerce, and other agencies. Explaining America's foreign policy must begin with the president and their policy goals. Congress also has a role in shaping foreign policy because of its control over budgets, senior executive-branch appointments, and the Senate's treaty-approval power.

Foreign policy is likely to become even more important and controversial in the future. Imports and exports are an increasing share of America's gross national product. As the COVID pandemic subsides, international travel by American citizens (and citizens of other nations to America) will resume their steady increase. And, as Russia's invasion of Ukraine illustrates, there is no sign that international conflicts are going away. You may want to ignore questions about foreign policy, but these issues can have profound consequences for your everyday life.

1. President Biden's economic and military support for Ukraine after the Russian invasion in 2022 and his order directing that the United States rejoin the Paris Climate Accords signal that which ideas may be key in his beliefs about the conduct of U.S. foreign policy?

a Unilateral action

b Isolationism

c Nation building

d Internationalism

2. Many Americans argue that the United States should cut foreign aid to increase spending on domestic policies and programs. Yet foreign aid programs like the Marshall Plan that funded much of the rebuilding of Western Europe after World War II, funding the International Monetary Fund to offer low-interest loans to developing nations, and the donation of vaccines to less wealthy nations during the COVID pandemic all provide a benefit to the United States. What is that benefit?

a Creation of good will to influence and promote American policy objectives

b Containment of Communism and the promotion of regime changes in Communist nations

c Creating financial obligations through which the United States may extract valuable resources

d Competition among nations that allows for the expansion of American commercial interests

3. As the authors of the Constitution considered the foreign policy structures of the United States, they intentionally placed which part of government as the central figure in conducting foreign relations?

a The U.S. State Department

b States

c The president

d Congress

4. The U.S. State Department primarily involves itself in the use of "soft power" by engaging in diplomatic negotiations and offering expertise to elected officials. Meanwhile, the military is used in more tense or serious situations that require force or large-scale coordination of aid. What is the most important constitutional principle connecting the two?

a American foreign policy remains under the control of a civilian government.

b The U.S. government has the ability to use force if necessary.

c American military might and diplomatic relations are rarely used without engaging other allies.

d High-ranking military officers, like appointees in the State Department, can be removed by Congress.

5. Which of the following statements best characterizes the idea behind using economic sanctions as a tool of conducting foreign policy by the United States?

a Sanctions have regularly proven to be the most effective tool in bringing other nations into negotiations during times of conflict.

b The size of the American economy, and access to it, creates a significant incentive for negotiating with the United States.

c Other allied nations regularly also apply sanctions to nations out of favor with the United States to avoid the potential of also being sanctioned by the United States.

d The decision to apply economic sanctions to another nation is largely dependent on the policy mood of the American public.

6. How does the World Trade Organization (WTO) play a significant role in balancing the conflictual nature of international relations?

a Implementing American-led sanctions on nations being targeted by the United States and allies

b Granting most-favored-nation status to member nations that have achieved economic stability and transparency goals

c Intervening in disputes between member nations and reviewing claims about unfair trade practices

d Providing military and humanitarian assistance to allied member nations

7. For the U.S. economy, the tradeoff of globalization to meet the demand of American consumers for more products, cheaper prices, and faster delivery times has meant that Americans must also face which kinds of challenges?

a Potentially widespread inflation related to the competition for raw materials and finished products in the United States

b Labor shortages resulting from the increased global demand for American products

c Increased demand for a greater variety of American-made products to compete with the wide variety of foreign-made imported goods

d Declining numbers of jobs in industries where international competition can provide goods and labor at lower cost

8. Which statement best characterizes the challenges to the United States in developing foreign policy involving Iran, North Korea, and other similar nations?

a The U.S. commitment to the principle of limiting engagement with violent or oppressive governments must be balanced with a commitment to limiting access to weapons that can cause widespread devastation.

b The decision regarding the potential preemptive use of nuclear weapons against aggressor nations seeking to develop their own nuclear weapons programs must be weighed against the likelihood of a nation achieving its nuclear ambitions.

c The potential economic damages to the United States of isolating nations like Iran and North Korea must be considered against the prospective harms of allowing them to continue to develop nuclear weapons programs.

d The widespread global support for nations developing new nuclear weapons programs to defend themselves against existing superpowers has to be balanced with the U.S. interests in protecting its status as the most powerful nation.

Use INQUIZITIVE to help you study and master this material.

APPENDIX

The Declaration of Independence

In Congress, July 4, 1776

The unanimous Declaration of the thirteen united States of America,

When in the Course of human events, it becomes necessary for one people to dissolve the political bands which have connected them with another, and to assume among the powers of the earth, the separate and equal station to which the Laws of Nature and of Nature's God entitle them, a decent respect to the opinions of mankind requires that they should declare the causes which impel them to the separation.

We hold these truths to be self-evident, that all men are created equal, that they are endowed by their Creator with certain unalienable Rights, that among these are Life, Liberty and the pursuit of Happiness.—That to secure these rights, Governments are instituted among Men, deriving their just powers from the consent of the governed. —That whenever any Form of Government becomes destructive of these ends, it is the Right of the People to alter or to abolish it, and to institute new Government, laying its foundation on such principles and organizing its powers in such form, as to them shall seem most likely to effect their Safety and Happiness. Prudence, indeed, will dictate that Governments long established should not be changed for light and transient causes; and accordingly all experience hath shewn, that mankind are more disposed to suffer, while evils are sufferable, than to right themselves by abolishing the forms to which they are accustomed. But when a long train of abuses and usurpations, pursuing invariably the same Object evinces a design to reduce them under absolute Despotism, it is their right, it is their duty, to throw off such Government, and to provide new Guards for their future security.—Such has been the patient sufferance of these Colonies; and such is now the necessity which constrains them to alter their former Systems of Government. The history of the present King of Great Britain is a history of repeated injuries and usurpations, all having in direct object the establishment of an absolute Tyranny over these States. To prove this, let Facts be submitted to a candid world.

He has refused his Assent to Laws, the most wholesome and necessary for the public good.

He has forbidden his Governors to pass Laws of immediate and pressing importance, unless suspended in their operation till his Assent should be obtained; and when so suspended, he has utterly neglected to attend to them.

He has refused to pass other Laws for the accommodation of large districts of people, unless those people would relinquish the right of Representation in the Legislature, a right inestimable to them and formidable to tyrants only.

He has called together legislative bodies at places unusual, uncomfortable, and distant from the depository of their public Records, for the sole purpose of fatiguing them into compliance with his measures.

He has dissolved Representative Houses repeatedly, for opposing with manly firmness his invasions on the rights of the people.

He has refused for a long time, after such dissolutions, to cause others to be elected; whereby the Legislative powers, incapable of Annihilation, have returned to the People at large for their exercise; the State remaining in the mean time exposed to all the dangers of invasion from without, and convulsions within.

He has endeavoured to prevent the population of these States; for that purpose obstructing the Laws for Naturalization of Foreigners; refusing to pass others to encourage their migrations hither, and raising the conditions of new Appropriations of Lands.

He has obstructed the Administration of Justice, by refusing his Assent to Laws for establishing Judiciary powers.

He has made Judges dependent on his Will alone, for the tenure of their offices, and the amount and payment of their salaries.

He has erected a multitude of New Offices, and sent hither swarms of Officers to harrass our people, and eat out their substance.

He has kept among us, in times of peace, Standing Armies without the Consent of our legislatures.

He has affected to render the Military independent of and superior to the Civil power.

He has combined with others to subject us to a jurisdiction foreign to our constitution, and unacknowledged by our laws; giving his Assent to their Acts of pretended Legislation:

For Quartering large bodies of armed troops among us:

For protecting them, by a mock Trial, from punishment for any Murders which they should commit on the Inhabitants of these States:

For cutting off our Trade with all parts of the world:

For imposing Taxes on us without our Consent:

For depriving us in many cases, of the benefits of Trial by Jury:

For transporting us beyond Seas to be tried for pretended offences:

For abolishing the free System of English Laws in a neighboring Province, establishing therein an Arbitrary government, and enlarging its Boundaries so as to render it at once an example and fit instrument for introducing the same absolute rule into these Colonies:

For taking away our Charters, abolishing our most valuable Laws, and altering fundamentally the Forms of our Governments:

For suspending our own Legislatures, and declaring themselves invested with power to legislate for us in all cases whatsoever.

He has abdicated Government here, by declaring us out of his Protection and waging War against us.

He has plundered our seas, ravaged our Coasts, burnt our towns, and destroyed the lives of our people.

He is at this time transporting large Armies of foreign Mercenaries to compleat the works of death, desolation and tyranny, already begun with circumstances of Cruelty & perfidy scarcely paralleled in the most barbarous ages, and totally unworthy the Head of a civilized nation.

He has constrained our fellow Citizens taken Captive on the high Seas to bear Arms against their Country, to become the executioners of their friends and Brethren, or to fall themselves by their Hands.

He has excited domestic insurrections amongst us, and has endeavoured to bring on the inhabitants of our frontiers, the merciless Indian Savages, whose known rule of warfare, is an undistinguished destruction of all ages, sexes and conditions.

In every stage of these Oppressions We have Petitioned for Redress in the most humble terms: Our repeated Petitions have been answered only by repeated injury. A Prince whose character is thus marked by every act which may define a Tyrant, is unfit to be the ruler of a free people.

Nor have We been wanting in attentions to our Brittish brethren. We have warned them from time to time of attempts by their legislature to extend an unwarrantable jurisdiction over us. We have reminded them of the circumstances of our emigration and settlement here. We have appealed to their native justice and magnanimity, and we have conjured them by the ties of our common kindred to disavow these usurpations, which, would inevitably interrupt our connections and correspondence. They too have been deaf to the voice of justice and of consanguinity. We must, therefore, acquiesce in the necessity, which denounces our Separation, and hold them, as we hold the rest of mankind, Enemies in War, in Peace Friends.

We, Therefore, the Representatives of the United States of America, in General Congress, Assembled, appealing to the Supreme Judge of the world for the rectitude of our intentions, do, in the Name, and by Authority of the good People of these Colonies, solemnly publish and declare, That these United Colonies are, and of Right ought to be Free and Independent States; that they are Absolved from all Allegiance to the British Crown, and that all political connection between them and the State of Great Britain, is and ought to be totally dissolved; and that as Free and Independent States, they have full Power to levy War, conclude Peace, contract Alliances, establish Commerce, and to do all other Acts and Things which Independent States may of right do. And for the support of this Declaration, with a firm reliance on the protection of divine Providence, we mutually pledge to each other our Lives, our Fortunes and our sacred Honor.

The foregoing Declaration was, by order of Congress, engrossed, and signed by the following members:

John Hancock

New Hampshire
Josiah Bartlett
William Whipple
Matthew Thornton

Massachusetts Bay
Samuel Adams
John Adams
Robert Treat Paine
Elbridge Gerry

Rhode Island
Stephen Hopkins
William Ellery

Connecticut
Roger Sherman
Samuel Huntington
William Williams
Oliver Wolcott

New York
William Floyd
Philip Livingston
Francis Lewis
Lewis Morris

New Jersey
Richard Stockton
John Witherspoon
Francis Hopkinson
John Hart
Abraham Clark

Pennsylvania
Robert Morris
Benjamin Rush
Benjamin Franklin
John Morton
George Clymer
James Smith
George Taylor
James Wilson
George Ross

Delaware
Caesar Rodney
George Read
Thomas M'Kean

Maryland
Samuel Chase
William Paca
Thomas Stone
Charles Carroll, of Carrollton

Virginia
George Wythe
Richard Henry Lee
Thomas Jefferson
Benjamin Harrison
Thomas Nelson, Jr.
Francis Lightfoot Lee
Carter Braxton

North Carolina
William Hooper
Joseph Hewes
John Penn

South Carolina
Edward Rutledge
Thomas Heyward, Jr.
Thomas Lynch, Jr.
Arthur Middleton

Georgia
Button Gwinnett
Lyman Hall
George Walton

Resolved, That copies of the Declaration be sent to the several assemblies, conventions, and committees, or councils of safety, and to the several commanding officers of the continental troops; that it be proclaimed in each of the United States, at the head of the army.

The Articles of Confederation

Agreed to by Congress November 15, 1777;
ratified and in force March 1, 1781

To all whom these Presents shall come, we the undersigned Delegates of the States affixed to our Names, send greeting. Whereas the Delegates of the United States of America, in Congress assembled, did, on the fifteenth day of November, in the Year of Our Lord One thousand Seven Hundred and Seventy seven, and in the Second Year of the Independence of America, agree to certain articles of Confederation and perpetual Union between the States of Newhampshire, Massachusetts-bay, Rhodeisland and Providence Plantations, Connecticut, New-York, New-Jersey, Pennsylvania, Delaware, Maryland, Virginia, North-Carolina, South-Carolina and Georgia in the words following, viz. "Articles of Confederation and perpetual Union between the states of Newhampshire, Massachusettsbay, Rhodeisland and Providence Plantations, Connecticut, New-York, New-Jersey, Pennsylvania, Delaware, Maryland, Virginia, North-Carolina, South-Carolina and Georgia.

Art. I. The Stile of this confederacy shall be "The United States of America."

Art. II. Each state retains its sovereignty, freedom and independence, and every Power, Jurisdiction and right, which is not by this confederation expressly delegated to the United States, in Congress assembled.

Art. III. The said states hereby severally enter into a firm league of friendship with each other, for their common defence, the security of their Liberties, and their mutual and general welfare, binding themselves to assist each other, against all force offered to, or attacks made upon them, or any of them, on account of religion, sovereignty, trade, or any other pretence whatever.

Art. IV. The better to secure and perpetuate mutual friendship and intercourse among the people of the different states in this union, the free inhabitants of each of these states, paupers, vagabonds and fugitives from Justice excepted, shall be entitled to all privileges and immunities of free citizens in the several states; and the people of each state shall have free ingress and regress to and from any other state, and shall enjoy therein all the privileges of trade and commerce, subject to the same duties, impositions and restrictions as the inhabitants thereof respectively, provided that such restriction shall not extend so far as to prevent the removal of property imported into any state, to any other state, of which the Owner is an inhabitant; provided also that no imposition, duties or restriction shall be laid by any state, on the property of the united states, or either of them.

If any Person guilty of, or charged with treason, felony, or other high misdemeanor in any state, shall flee from Justice, and be found in any of the united states, he shall, upon demand of the Governor or executive power, of the state from which he fled, be delivered up and removed to the state having jurisdiction of his offence.

Full faith and credit shall be given in each of these states to the records, acts and judicial proceedings of the courts and magistrates of every other state.

Art. V. For the more convenient management of the general interests of the united states, delegates shall be annually appointed in such manner as the legislature of each state shall direct, to meet in Congress on the first Monday in November, in every year, with a power reserved to each state, to recall its delegates, or any of them, at any time within the year, and to send others in their stead, for the remainder of the Year.

No state shall be represented in Congress by less than two, nor by more than seven Members; and no person shall be capable of being a delegate for more than three years in any term of six years; nor shall any person, being a delegate, be capable of holding any office under the united states, for which he, or another for his benefit receives any salary, fees or emolument of any kind.

Each state shall maintain its own delegates in a meeting of the states, and while they act as members of the committee of the states.

In determining questions in the united states, in Congress assembled, each state shall have one vote.

Freedom of speech and debate in Congress shall not be impeached or questioned in any Court, or place out of Congress, and the members of congress shall be protected in their persons from arrests and imprisonments, during the time of their going to and from, and attendance on congress, except for treason, felony, or breach of the peace.

Art. VI. No state without the Consent of the united states in congress assembled, shall send any embassy to, or receive any embassy from, or enter into any conference, agreement, or alliance or treaty with any King, prince or state; nor shall any person holding any office or profit or trust under the united states, or any of them, accept of any present, emolument, office or title of any kind whatever from any king, prince or foreign state; nor shall the united states in congress assembled, or any of them, grant any title of nobility.

No two or more states shall enter into any treaty, confederation or alliance whatever between them, without the consent of the united states in congress assembled, specifying accurately the purposes for which the same is to be entered into, and how long it shall continue.

No state shall lay any imposts or duties, which may interfere with any stipulations in treaties, entered into by the united states in congress assembled, with any king, prince or state, in pursuance of any treaties already proposed by congress, to the courts of France and Spain.

No vessels of war shall be kept up in time of peace by any state, except such number only, as shall be deemed necessary by the united states in congress assembled, for the defence of such state, or its trade; nor shall any body of forces be kept up by any state, in time of peace, except such number only, as in the judgment of the united states, in congress assembled, shall be deemed requisite to garrison the forts necessary for the defence of such state; but every state shall always keep up a well regulated and disciplined militia, sufficiently armed and accoutred, and shall provide and constantly have ready for use, in public stores, a due number of field pieces and tents, and a proper quantity of arms, ammunition and camp equipage.

No state shall engage in any war without the consent of the united states in congress assembled, unless such state be actually invaded by enemies, or shall have received certain advice of a resolution being formed by some nation of Indians to invade such state, and the danger is so imminent as not to admit of a delay, till the united states in congress asssembled can be consulted; nor shall any state grant commissions to any ships or vessels of war, nor letters of marque or reprisal, except it be after a declaration of war by the united states in congress assembled, and then only against the kingdom or state and the subjects thereof, against which war has been so declared, and under such regulations as shall be established by the united states in congress assembled, unless such state be infested by pirates; in which case vessels of war may be fitted out for that occasion, and kept so long as the danger shall continue, or until the united states in congress assembled shall determine otherwise.

Art. VII. When land-forces are raised by any state for the common defence, all officers of or under the rank of colonel, shall be appointed by the legislature of each state respectively, by whom such forces shall be raised, or in such manner as such state shall direct, and all vacancies shall be filled up by the state which first made the appointment.

Art. VIII. All charges of war, and all other expences that shall be incurred for the common defence or general welfare, and allowed by the united states in congress assembled, shall be defrayed out of a common treasury, which shall be supplied by the several states in proportion to the value of all land within each state, granted to or surveyed for any Person, as such land and the buildings and improvements thereon shall be estimated according to such mode as the united states in congress assembled, shall from time to time direct and appoint.

The taxes for paying that proportion shall be laid and levied by the authority and direction of the legislatures of the several states within the time agreed upon by the united states in congress assembled.

Art. IX. The united states in congress assembled, shall have the sole and exclusive right and power of determining on peace and war, except in the cases mentioned in the sixth article—of sending and receiving ambassadors—entering into treaties and alliances, provided that no treaty of commerce shall be made whereby the legislative power of the respective states shall be restrained from imposing such imposts and duties on foreigners, as their own people are subjected to, or from prohibiting the exportation of any species of goods or commodities whatsoever—of establishing rules for deciding in all cases, what captures on land or water shall be legal, and in what manner prizes taken by land or naval forces in the service of the united states shall be divided or appropriated—of granting letters of marque and reprisal in times of peace—appointing courts for the trial of piracies and felonies committed on the high seas and establishing courts for receiving and determining finally appeals in all cases of captures, provided that no member of congress shall be appointed a judge of any of the said courts.

The united states in congress assembled shall also be the last resort on appeal in all disputes and differences now subsisting or that hereafter may arise between two or more states concerning boundary, jurisdiction or any other cause whatever; which authority shall always be exercised in the manner following. Whenever the legislative or executive authority or lawful agent of any state in controversy with another shall present a petition to congress stating the matter in question and praying for a hearing, notice thereof shall be given by order of congress to the legislative or executive authority of the other state in controversy, and a day assigned for the appearance of the parties by their lawful agents, who shall then be directed to appoint by joint consent, commissioners or judges to constitute a court for hearing and determining the matter in question: but if they cannot agree, congress shall name three persons out of each of the united states, and from the list of such persons each party shall alternately strike out one, the petitioners beginning, until the number shall be reduced to thirteen; and from that number not less than seven, nor more than nine names as congress shall direct, shall in the presence of congress be drawn out by lot, and the persons whose names shall be so drawn or any five of them, shall be commissioners or judges, to hear and finally determine the controversy, so always as a major part of the judges who shall hear the cause shall agree in the determination: and if either party shall neglect to attend at the day appointed, without shewing reasons, which congress shall judge sufficient, or being present shall refuse to strike, the congress shall proceed to nominate three persons out of each state, and the secretary of congress shall strike in behalf of such party absent or refusing; and the judgment and sentence of the court to be appointed, in the manner before prescribed, shall be final and conclusive; and if any of the parties shall refuse to submit to the authority of such court, or to appear to defend their claim or cause, the court shall nevertheless proceed to pronounce sentence, or judgment, which shall in like manner be final and decisive, the judgment or sentence and other proceedings being in either case transmitted to congress, and lodged among the acts of congress for the security of the parties concerned: provided that every commissioner, before he sits in judgment, shall take an oath to be administered by one of the judges of the supreme or superior court of the state, where the cause shall be tried, "well and truly to hear and determine the matter in question, according to the best of his judgment, without favour, affection or hope of reward:" provided also, that no state shall be deprived of territory for the benefit of the united states.

All controversies concerning the private right of soil claimed under different grants of two or more states, whose jurisdictions as they may respect such lands, and the states which passed such grants are adjusted, the said grants or either of them being at the same time claimed to have originated antecedent to such settlement of jurisdiction, shall on the petition of either party to the congress of the united states, be finally determined as near as may be in the same manner as is before prescribed for deciding disputes respecting territorial jurisdiction between different states.

The united states in congress assembled shall also have the sole and exclusive right and power of regulating the alloy and value of coin struck by their own authority, or by that of the respective states—fixing the standard of weights and measures throughout the united states—regulating the trade and managing all affairs with the Indians, not members of any of the states, provided that the legislative right of any state within its own limits be not infringed or violated—establishing and regulating post-offices from one state to another, throughout all the united states, and exacting such postage on the papers passing thro' the same as may be requisite to defray the expences of the said office—appointing all officers of the land forces, in the service of the united states, excepting regimental officers—appointing all the officers of the naval forces, and commissioning all officers whatever in the service of the united states—making rules for the government and regulation of the said land and naval forces, and directing their operations.

The united states in congress assembled shall have authority to appoint a committee, to sit in the recess of congress, to be denominated "A Committee of the States," and to consist of one delegate from each state; and to appoint such other committees and civil officers as may be necessary for managing the general affairs of the united states under their direction—to appoint one of their number to preside, provided that no person be allowed to serve in the office of president more than one year in any term of three years; to ascertain the necessary sums of Money to be raised for the service of the united states, and to appropriate and apply the same for defraying the public expenses—to borrow money, or emit bills on the credit of the united states, transmitting every half year to the respective states an account of the sums of money so borrowed or emitted,—to build and equip a navy—to agree upon the number of land forces, and to make requisitions from each state for its quota, in proportion to the number of white inhabitants in such state; which requisition shall be binding, and thereupon the legislature of each state shall appoint the regimental officers, raise the men and cloath, arm and equip them in a soldier like manner, at the expense of the united states; and the officers and men so cloathed, armed and equipped shall march to the place appointed, and within the time agreed on by the united states in congress assembled: But if the united states in congress assembled shall, on consideration of circumstances judge proper that any state should not raise men, or should raise a smaller number than its quota, and that any other state should raise a greater number of men than the quota thereof, such extra number shall be raised, officered, cloathed, armed and equipped in the same manner as the quota of such state, unless the legislature of such state shall judge that such extra number cannot be safely spared out of the same, in which case they shall raise officer, cloath, arm and equip as many of such extra number as they judge can be safely spared. And the officers and men so cloathed, armed and equipped, shall march to the place appointed, and within the time agreed on by the united states in congress assembled.

The united states in congress assembled shall never engage in a war, nor grant letters of marque and reprisal in time of peace, nor enter into any treaties or alliances, nor coin money, nor regulate the value thereof, nor ascertain the sums and expenses necessary for the defence and welfare of the united states, or any of them, nor emit bills, nor borrow money on the credit of the united states, nor appropriate money, nor agree upon the number of vessels of war, to be built or purchased, or the number of land or sea forces to be raised, nor appoint a commander in chief of the army or navy, unless nine states assent to the same: nor shall a question on any other point, except for adjourning from day to day be determined, unless by the votes of a majority of the united states in congress assembled.

The congress of the united states shall have power to adjourn to any time within the year, and to any place within the united states, so that no period of adjournment be for a longer duration than the space of six Months, and shall publish the Journal of their proceedings monthly, except such parts thereof relating to treaties, alliances or military operations, as in their judgment require secrecy; and the yeas and nays of the delegates of each state on any question shall be entered on the Journal, when it is desired by any delegate; and the delegates of a state, or any of them, at his or their request shall be furnished with a transcript of the said Journal, except such parts as are above excepted, to lay before the legislatures of the several states.

Art. X. The committee of the states, or any nine of them, shall be authorised to execute, in the recess of congress, such of the powers of congress as the united states in congress assembled, by the consent of nine states, shall from time to time think expedient to vest them with; provided that no power be delegated to the said committee, for the exercise of which, by the articles of confederation, the voice of nine states in the congress of the united states assembled is requisite.

Art. XI. Canada acceding to this confederation, and joining in the measures of the united states, shall be admitted into, and entitled to all the advantages of this union: but no other colony shall be admitted into the same, unless such admission be agreed to by nine states.

Art. XII. All bills of credit emitted, monies borrowed and debts contracted by, or under the authority of congress, before the assembling of the united states, in pursuance of the present confederation, shall be deemed and considered as a charge against the united states, for payment and satisfaction whereof the said united states and the public faith are hereby solemnly pledged.

Art. XIII. Every state shall abide by the determinations of the united states in congress assembled, on all questions which by this confederation are submitted to them. And the Articles of this confederation shall be inviolably observed by every state, and the union shall be perpetual; nor shall any alteration at any time hereafter be made in any of them; unless such alteration be agreed to in a congress of the united states, and be afterwards confirmed by the legislatures of every state.

And Whereas it hath pleased the Great Governor of the World to incline the hearts of the legislatures we respectively represent in congress, to approve of, and to authorize us to ratify the said articles of confederation and perpetual union. Know Ye that we the undersigned delegates, by virtue of the power and authority to us given for that purpose, do by these presents, in the name and in behalf of our respective constituents, fully and entirely ratify and confirm each and every of the said articles of confederation and perpetual union, and all and singular the matters and things therein contained: And we do further solemnly plight and engage the faith of our respective constituents, that they shall abide by the determinations of the united states in congress assembled, on all questions, which by the said confederation are submitted to them. And that the articles thereof shall be inviolably observed by the states we respectively represent, and that the union shall be perpetual. In Witness whereof we have hereunto set our hands in Congress. Done at Philadelphia in the state of Pennsylvania the ninth day of July, in the Year of our Lord one Thousand seven Hundred and Seventy-eight, and in the third year of the independence of America.

The Constitution of the United States of America

[PREAMBLE]

We the People of the United States, in Order to form a more perfect Union, establish Justice, insure domestic Tranquility, provide for the common defence, promote the general Welfare, and secure the Blessings of Liberty to ourselves and our Posterity, do ordain and establish this Constitution for the United States of America.

Article I

SECTION 1

[LEGISLATIVE POWERS]

All legislative Powers herein granted shall be vested in a Congress of the United States, which shall consist of a Senate and House of Representatives.

SECTION 2

[HOUSE OF REPRESENTATIVES, HOW CONSTITUTED, POWER OF IMPEACHMENT]

The House of Representatives shall be composed of Members chosen every second Year by the People of the several States, and the Electors in each State shall have the Qualifications requisite for Electors of the most numerous Branch of the State Legislature.

No Person shall be a Representative who shall not have attained to the Age of twenty five Years, and been seven Years a Citizen of the United States, and who shall not, when elected, be an Inhabitant of that State in which he shall be chosen.

Representatives and *direct Taxes*[1] shall be apportioned among the several States which may be included within this Union, according to their respective Numbers, *which shall be determined by adding to the whole Number of free Persons, including those bound to Service for a Term of Years, and excluding Indians not taxed, three fifths of all other Persons.*[2] The actual Enumeration shall be made within three Years after the first Meeting of the Congress of the United States, and within every subsequent Term of ten Years, in such Manner as they shall by Law direct. The Number of Representatives shall not exceed one for every thirty Thousand, but each State shall have at Least one Representative; *and until such enumeration shall be made, the State of New Hampshire shall be entitled to chuse three, Massachusetts eight, Rhode-Island and Providence Plantations one, Connecticut five, New-York six, New Jersey four, Pennsylvania eight, Delaware one, Maryland six, Virginia ten, North Carolina five, South Carolina five, and Georgia three.*[3]

When vacancies happen in the Representation from any State, the Executive Authority thereof shall issue Writs of Election to fill such Vacancies.

The House of Representatives shall chuse their Speaker and other Officers; and shall have the sole Power of Impeachment.

SECTION 3

[THE SENATE, HOW CONSTITUTED, IMPEACHMENT TRIALS]

The Senate of the United States shall be composed of two Senators from each State, *chosen by the Legislature thereof,*[4] for six Years; and each Senator shall have one Vote.

Immediately after they shall be assembled in Consequence of the first Election, they shall be divided as equally as may be into three Classes. The Seats of the Senators of the first Class shall be vacated at the Expiration of the second Year, of the second Class at the Expiration of the fourth Year, and of the third Class at the Expiration of the sixth Year, so that one third may be chosen every second Year; *and if Vacancies happen by Resignation, or otherwise, during the Recess of the Legislature of any State, the Executive thereof may make temporary Appointments until the next Meeting of the Legislature, which shall then fill such Vacancies.*[5]

No Person shall be a Senator who shall not have attained to the Age of thirty Years, and been nine Years a Citizen of the United States, and who shall not, when elected, be an Inhabitant of that State for which he shall be chosen.

The Vice President of the United States shall be President of the Senate, but shall have no Vote, unless they be equally divided.

The Senate shall chuse their other Officers, and also a President pro tempore, in the Absence of the Vice President, or when he shall exercise the Office of President of the United States.

The Senate shall have the sole Power to try all Impeachments. When sitting for that Purpose, they shall be on Oath or Affirmation. When the President of the United States is tried, the Chief Justice shall preside: And no Person shall be convicted without the Concurrence of two thirds of the Members present.

Judgment in Cases of Impeachment shall not extend further than to removal from Office, and disqualification to hold and enjoy any Office of honor, Trust or Profit under the United States: but the Party convicted shall nevertheless be liable and subject to Indictment, Trial, Judgment and Punishment, according to Law.

SECTION 4

[ELECTION OF SENATORS AND REPRESENTATIVES]

The Times, Places and Manner of holding Elections for Senators and Representatives, shall be prescribed in each State by the Legislature thereof; but the Congress may at any time by Law make or alter such Regulations, except as to the Places of chusing Senators.

The Congress shall assemble at least once in every Year, and such Meeting shall be on the first Monday in December, unless they shall by Law appoint a different Day.[6]

SECTION 5

[QUORUM, JOURNALS, MEETINGS, ADJOURNMENTS]

Each House shall be the Judge of the Elections, Returns and Qualifications of its own Members, and a Majority of each shall constitute a Quorum to do Business; but a smaller Number may adjourn from day to day, and may be authorized to compel the

---

[1] Modified by Sixteenth Amendment.
[2] Modified by Fourteenth Amendment.
[3] Temporary provision.
[4] Modified by Seventeenth Amendment.
[5] Modified by Seventeenth Amendment.
[6] Modified by Twentieth Amendment.

Attendance of absent Members, in such Manner, and under such Penalties as each House may provide.

Each House may determine the Rules of its Proceedings, punish its Members for disorderly Behaviour, and, with the Concurrence of two thirds, expel a Member.

Each House shall keep a Journal of its Proceedings, and from time to time publish the same, excepting such Parts as may in their Judgment require Secrecy; and the Yeas and Nays of the Members of either House on any questions shall, at the Desire of one fifth of those Present, be entered on the Journal.

Neither House, during the Session of Congress, shall, without the Consent of the other, adjourn for more than three days, nor to any other Place than that in which the two Houses shall be sitting.

SECTION 6

[COMPENSATION, PRIVILEGES, DISABILITIES]

The Senators and Representatives shall receive a Compensation for their Services, to be ascertained by Law, and paid out of the Treasury of the United States. They shall in all Cases, except Treason, Felony and Breach of the Peace, be privileged from Arrest during their Attendance at the Session of their respective Houses, and in going to and returning from the same; and for any Speech or Debate in either House, they shall not be questioned in any other Place.

No Senator or Representative shall, during the Time for which he was elected, be appointed to any civil Office under the Authority of the United States, which shall have been created, or the Emoluments whereof shall have been encreased during such time; and no Person holding any Office under the United States, shall be a Member of either House during his Continuance in Office.

SECTION 7

[PROCEDURE IN PASSING BILLS AND RESOLUTIONS]

All Bills for raising Revenue shall originate in the House of Representatives; but the Senate may propose or concur with Amendments as on other Bills.

Every Bill which shall have passed the House of Representatives and the Senate, shall, before it become a Law, be presented to the President of the United States: If he approve he shall sign it, but if not he shall return it, with his Objections to that House in which it shall have originated, who shall enter the Objections at large on their Journal, and proceed to reconsider it. If after such Reconsideration two thirds of that House shall agree to pass the Bill, it shall be sent, together with the Objections, to the other House, by which it shall likewise be reconsidered, and if approved by two thirds of that House, it shall become a Law. But in all such Cases the Votes of both Houses shall be determined by yeas and Nays, and the Names of the Persons voting for and against the Bill shall be entered on the Journal of each House respectively. If any Bill shall not be returned by the President within ten Days (Sundays excepted) after it shall have been presented to him, the Same shall be a Law, in like Manner as if he had signed it, unless the Congress by their Adjournment prevent its Return, in which Case it shall not be a Law.

Every Order, Resolution, or Vote to which the Concurrence of the Senate and House of Representatives may be necessary (except on a question of Adjournment) shall be presented to the President of the United States; and before the Same shall take Effect, shall be approved by him, or being disapproved by him, shall be repassed by two thirds of the Senate and House of Representatives, according to the Rules and Limitations prescribed in the Case of a Bill.

SECTION 8

[POWERS OF CONGRESS]

The Congress shall have Power

To lay and collect Taxes, Duties, Imposts and Excises, to pay the Debts and provide for the common Defence and general Welfare of the United States; but all Duties, Imposts and Excises shall be uniform throughout the United States;

To borrow Money on the credit of the United States;

To regulate Commerce with foreign Nations, and among the several States, and with the Indian Tribes;

To establish an uniform Rule of Naturalization, and uniform Laws on the subject of Bankruptcies throughout the United States;

To coin Money, regulate the Value thereof, and of foreign Coin, and fix the Standard of Weights and Measures;

To provide for the Punishment of counterfeiting the Securities and current Coin of the United States;

To establish Post Offices and post Roads;

To promote the Progress of Science and useful Arts, by securing for limited Times to Authors and Inventors the exclusive Right to their respective Writings and Discoveries;

To constitute Tribunals inferior to the supreme Court;

To define and punish Piracies and Felonies committed on the high Seas, and Offences against the Law of Nations;

To declare War, grant Letters of Marque and Reprisal, and make Rules concerning Captures on Land and Water;

To raise and support Armies, but no Appropriation of Money to that Use shall be for a longer Term than two Years;

To provide and maintain a Navy;

To make Rules for the Government and Regulation of the land and naval Forces;

To provide for calling forth the Militia to execute the Laws of the Union, suppress Insurrections and repel Invasions;

To provide for organizing, arming, and disciplining, the Militia, and for governing such Part of them as may be employed in the Service of the United States, reserving to the States respectively, the Appointment of the Officers, and the Authority of training the Militia according to the discipline prescribed by Congress;

To exercise exclusive Legislation in all Cases whatsoever, over such District (not exceeding ten Miles square) as may, by Cession of particular States, and the Acceptance of Congress, become the Seat of the Government of the United States, and to exercise like Authority over all Places purchased by the Consent of the Legislature of the State in which the Same shall be, for the Erection of Forts, Magazines, Arsenals, dock-Yards, and other needful Buildings;—And

To make all Laws which shall be necessary and proper for carrying into Execution the foregoing Powers, and all other Powers vested by this Constitution in the Government of the United States, or in any Department or Officer thereof.

SECTION 9

[SOME RESTRICTIONS ON FEDERAL POWER]

The Migration or Importation of such Persons as any of the States now existing shall think proper to admit, shall not be prohibited by the Congress prior to the Year one thousand eight hundred and eight, but a Tax or duty may be imposed on such Importation, not exceeding ten dollars for each Person.[7]

[7] Temporary provision.

The Privilege of the Writ of Habeas Corpus shall not be suspended, unless when in Cases of Rebellion or Invasion the public Safety may require it.

No Bill of Attainder or ex post facto Law shall be passed.

No Capitation, or other direct, Tax shall be laid, unless in Proportion to the Census or Enumeration herein before directed to be taken.[8]

No Tax or Duty shall be laid on Articles exported from any State.

No Preference shall be given by any Regulation of Commerce or Revenue to the Ports of one State over those of another; nor shall Vessels bound to, or from, one State, be obliged to enter, clear, or pay Duties in another.

No Money shall be drawn from the Treasury, but in Consequence of Appropriations made by Law; and a regular Statement and Account of the Receipts and Expenditures of all public Money shall be published from time to time.

No Title of Nobility shall be granted by the United States: And no Person holding any Office of Profit or Trust under them, shall, without the Consent of the Congress, accept of any present, Emolument, Office, or Title, of any kind whatever, from any King, Prince, or foreign State.

SECTION 10

[RESTRICTIONS UPON POWERS OF STATES]

No State shall enter into any Treaty, Alliance, or Confederation; grant Letters of Marque and Reprisal; coin Money; emit Bills of Credit; make any Thing but gold and silver Coin a Tender in Payment of Debts; pass any Bill of Attainder, ex post facto Law, or Law impairing the Obligation of Contracts, or grant any Title of Nobility.

No State shall, without the Consent of the Congress, lay any Imposts or Duties on Imports or Exports, except what may be absolutely necessary for executing its inspection Laws: and the net Produce of all Duties and Imposts, laid by any State on Imports or Exports, shall be for the Use of the Treasury of the United States; and all such Laws shall be subject to the Revision and Control of the Congress.

No State shall, without the Consent of Congress, lay any Duty of Tonnage, keep Troops, or Ships of War in time of Peace, enter into any Agreement or Compact with another State, or with a foreign Power, or engage in War, unless actually invaded, or in such imminent Danger as will not admit of delay.

Article II

SECTION 1

[EXECUTIVE POWER, ELECTION, QUALIFICATIONS OF THE PRESIDENT]

The executive Power shall be vested in a President of the United States of America. *He shall hold his Office during the Term of four Years, and, together with the Vice President, chosen for the same Term, be elected, as follows*[9]

Each State shall appoint, in such Manner as the Legislature thereof may direct, a Number of Electors, equal to the whole Number of Senators and Representatives to which the State may be entitled in the Congress: but no Senator or Representative, or Person holding an Office of Trust or Profit under the United States, shall be appointed an Elector.

The electors shall meet in their respective States, and vote by ballot for two Persons, of whom one at least shall not be an Inhabitant of the same State with themselves. And they shall make a List of all the Persons voted for, and of the Number of Votes for each; which List they shall sign and certify, and transmit sealed to the Seat of the Government of the United States, directed to the President of the Senate. The President of the Senate shall, in the Presence of the Senate and House of Representatives, open all the Certificates, and the Votes shall then be counted. The Person having the greatest Number of Votes shall be the President, if such Number be a Majority of the whole Number of Electors appointed; and if there be more than one who have such Majority, and have an equal Number of Votes, then the House of Representatives shall immediately chuse by Ballot one of them for President; and if no Person have a Majority, then from the five highest on the List the said House shall in like Manner chuse the President. But in chusing the President, the Votes shall be taken by States, the Representation from each State having one Vote; A quorum for this Purpose shall consist of a Member or Members from two thirds of the States, and a Majority of all the States shall be necessary to a Choice. In every Case, after the Choice of the President, the person having the greatest Number of Votes of the Electors shall be the Vice President. But if there should remain two or more who have equal Votes, the Senate shall chuse from them by Ballot the Vice President.[10]

The Congress may determine the Time of chusing the Electors, and the Day on which they shall give their Votes; which Day shall be the same throughout the United States.

No Person except a natural born Citizen, or a Citizen of the United States, at the time of the Adoption of this Constitution, shall be eligible to the Office of President; neither shall any Person be eligible to that Office who shall not have attained to the Age of thirty five Years, and been fourteen Years a Resident within the United States.

In Case of the Removal of the President from Office, or his Death, Resignation, or Inability to discharge the Powers and Duties of the said Office, the Same shall devolve on the Vice President, and the Congress may by Law provide for the Case of Removal, Death, Resignation or Inability, both of the President and Vice President, declaring what Officer shall then act as President, and such Officer shall act accordingly, until the Disability be removed, or a President shall be elected.

The President shall, at stated Times, receive for his Services, a Compensation, which shall neither be increased nor diminished during the Period for which he shall have been elected, and he shall not receive within that Period any other Emolument from the United States, or any of them.

Before he enter on the Execution of his Office, he shall take the following Oath or Affirmation:—"I do solemnly swear (or affirm) that I will faithfully execute the Office of President of the United States, and will to the best of my Ability, preserve, protect and defend the Constitution of the United States."

SECTION 2

[POWERS OF THE PRESIDENT]

The President shall be Commander in Chief of the Army and Navy of the United States, and of the Militia of the several States, when called into the actual Service of the United States; he may require the Opinion, in writing, of the principal Officer in each of the executive Departments, upon any Subject relating to the Duties of their respective Offices, and he shall have Power to grant Reprieves and Pardons for Offences against the United States, except in Cases of Impeachment.

He shall have Power, by and with the Advice and Consent of the Senate, to make Treaties, provided two thirds of the Senators present concur; and he shall nominate, and by and with the Advice

---

[8] Modified by Sixteenth Amendment.

[9] Number of terms limited to two by Twenty-second Amendment.

[10] Modified by the Twelfth and Twentieth Amendments.

and Consent of the Senate, shall appoint Ambassadors, other public Ministers and Consuls, Judges of the supreme Court, and all other Officers of the United States, whose Appointments are not herein otherwise provided for, and which shall be established by Law: but the Congress may by Law vest the Appointment of such inferior Officers, as they think proper, in the President alone, in the Courts of Law, or in the Heads of Departments.

The President shall have Power to fill up all Vacancies that may happen during the Recess of the Senate, by granting Commissions which shall expire at the End of their next Session.

SECTION 3

[POWERS AND DUTIES OF THE PRESIDENT]

He shall from time to time give to the Congress Information of the State of the Union, and recommend to their Consideration such Measures as he shall judge necessary and expedient; he may, on extraordinary Occasions, convene both Houses, or either of them, and in Case of Disagreement between them, with Respect to the Time of Adjournment, he may adjourn them to such Time as he shall think proper; he shall receive Ambassadors and other public Ministers; he shall take Care that the Laws be faithfully executed, and shall Commission all the Officers of the United States.

SECTION 4

[IMPEACHMENT]

The President, Vice President and all civil Officers of the United States, shall be removed from Office on Impeachment for, and Conviction of, Treason, Bribery, or other high Crimes and Misdemeanors.

Article III

SECTION 1

[JUDICIAL POWER, TENURE OF OFFICE]

The judicial Power of the United States, shall be vested in one supreme Court, and in such inferior Courts as the Congress may from time to time ordain and establish. The Judges, both of the supreme and inferior Courts, shall hold their Offices during good Behaviour, and shall, at stated Times, receive for their Services, a Compensation, which shall not be diminished during their Continuance in Office.

SECTION 2

[JURISDICTION]

The judicial Power shall extend to all Cases, in Law and Equity, arising under this Constitution, the Laws of the United States, and Treaties made, or which shall be made, under their Authority;—to all Cases affecting Ambassadors, other public Ministers and Consuls;—to all Cases of admiralty and maritime Jurisdiction;—to Controversies to which the United States shall be a Party;—to Controversies between two or more States;—*between a State and Citizens of another State;*—between Citizens of different States,—between Citizens of the same State claiming Lands under Grants of different States, *and between a State,* or the Citizens thereof, *and foreign States, Citizens or Subjects.*[11]

In all Cases affecting Ambassadors, other public Ministers and Consuls, and those in which a State shall be Party, the supreme Court shall have original Jurisdiction. In all the other Cases before mentioned, the supreme Court shall have appellate Jurisdiction, both as to Law and Fact, with such Exceptions, and under such Regulations as the Congress shall make.

The Trial of all Crimes, except in Cases of Impeachment, shall be by Jury; and such Trial shall be held in the State where the said Crimes shall have been committed; but when not committed within any State, the Trial shall be at such Place or Places as the Congress may by Law have directed.

SECTION 3

[TREASON, PROOF, AND PUNISHMENT]

Treason against the United States, shall consist only in levying War against them, or in adhering to their Enemies, giving them Aid and Comfort. No Person shall be convicted of Treason unless on the Testimony of two Witnesses to the same overt Act, or on Confession in open Court.

The Congress shall have Power to declare the Punishment of Treason, but no Attainder of Treason shall work Corruption of Blood, or Forfeiture except during the Life of the Person attainted.

Article IV

SECTION 1

[FAITH AND CREDIT AMONG STATES]

Full Faith and Credit shall be given in each State to the public Acts, Records, and judicial Proceedings of every other State. And the Congress may by general Laws prescribe the Manner in which such Acts, Records and Proceedings shall be proved, and the Effect thereof.

SECTION 2

[PRIVILEGES AND IMMUNITIES, FUGITIVES]

The Citizens of each State shall be entitled to all Privileges and Immunities of Citizens in the several States.

A Person charged in any State with Treason, Felony or other Crime, who shall flee from Justice, and be found in another State, shall on Demand of the executive Authority of the State from which he fled, be delivered up, to be removed to the State having Jurisdiction of the Crime.

No person held to Service or Labour in one State, under the Laws thereof, escaping into another, shall, in Consequence of any Law or Regulation therein, be discharged from such Service or Labour, but shall be delivered up on Claim of the Party to whom such Service or Labour may be due.[12]

SECTION 3

[ADMISSION OF NEW STATES]

New States may be admitted by the Congress into this Union; but no new State shall be formed or erected within the Jurisdiction of any other State; nor any State be formed by the Junction of two or more States, or Parts of States, without the Consent of the Legislatures of the States concerned as well as of the Congress.

The Congress shall have Power to dispose of and make all needful Rules and Regulations respecting the Territory or other Property belonging to the United States; and nothing in this Constitution shall be so construed as to Prejudice any Claims of the United States, or of any particular State.

---

[11] Modified by the Eleventh Amendment.

[12] Repealed by the Thirteenth Amendment.

SECTION 4
[GUARANTEE OF REPUBLICAN GOVERNMENT]

The United States shall guarantee to every State in this Union a Republican Form of Government, and shall protect each of them against Invasion; and on Application of the Legislature, or of the Executive (when the Legislature cannot be convened), against domestic Violence.

Article V
[AMENDMENT OF THE CONSTITUTION]

The Congress, whenever two thirds of both Houses shall deem it necessary, shall propose Amendments to this Constitution, or, on the Application of the Legislatures of two thirds of the several States, shall call a Convention for proposing Amendments, which, in either Case, shall be valid to all Intents and Purposes, as Part of this Constitution, when ratified by the Legislatures of three fourths of the several States, or by Conventions in three fourths thereof, as the one or the other Mode of Ratification may be proposed by the Congress; *Provided that no Amendment which may be made prior to the Year One thousand eight hundred and eight shall in any Manner affect the first and fourth Clauses in the Ninth Section of the first Article;* and that no State, without its Consent, shall be deprived of its equal Suffrage in the Senate.

Article VI
[DEBTS, SUPREMACY, OATH]

All Debts contracted and Engagements entered into, before the Adoption of this Constitution, shall be as valid against the United States under this Constitution, as under the Confederation.

This Constitution, and the Laws of the United States which shall be made in Pursuance thereof; and all Treaties made, or which shall be made, under the Authority of the United States, shall be the supreme Law of the Land; and the Judges in every State shall be bound thereby, any Thing in the Constitution or Laws of any State to the Contrary notwithstanding.

The Senators and Representatives before mentioned, and the Members of the several State Legislatures, and all executive and judicial Officers, both of the United States and of the several States, shall be bound by Oath or Affirmation, to support this Constitution; but no religious Test shall be required as a Qualification to any Office or public Trust under the United States.

Article VII
[RATIFICATION AND ESTABLISHMENT]

The Ratification of the Conventions of nine States, shall be sufficient for the Establishment of this Constitution between the States so ratifying the Same.

Done in Convention by the Unanimous Consent of the States present the Seventeenth Day of September in the Year of our Lord one thousand seven hundred and Eighty seven and of the Independence of the United States of America the Twelfth. *In Witness* whereof We have hereunto subscribed our Names,

G:° WASHINGTON—
Presidt. and deputy from Virginia

New Hampshire
John Langdon
Nicholas Gilman

Massachusetts
Nathaniel Gorham
Rufus King

Connecticut
Wm. Saml. Johnson
Roger Sherman

New York
Alexander Hamilton

New Jersey
Wil: Livingston
David Brearley
Wm. Paterson
Jona: Dayton

Pennsylvania
B Franklin
Thomas Mifflin
Robt. Morris
Geo. Clymer
Thos. FitzSimons
Jared Ingersoll
James Wilson
Gouv Morris

Delaware
Geo: Read
Gunning Bedford jun
John Dickinson
Richard Bassett
Jaco: Broom

Maryland
James McHenry
Dan of St Thos. Jenifer
Danl. Carroll

Virginia
John Blair—
James Madison Jr.

North Carolina
Wm. Blount
Richd. Dobbs Spaight
Hu Williamson

South Carolina
J. Rutledge
Charles Cotesworth Pinckney
Charles Pinckney
Pierce Butler

Georgia
William Few
Abr Baldwin

Amendments to the Constitution

Proposed by Congress and Ratified by the Legislatures of the Several States, Pursuant to Article V of the Original Constitution.

Amendments I–X, known as the Bill of Rights, were proposed by Congress on September 25, 1789, and ratified on December 15, 1791.

Amendment I

[FREEDOM OF RELIGION, OF SPEECH, AND OF THE PRESS]

Congress shall make no law respecting an establishment of religion, or prohibiting the free exercise thereof; or abridging the freedom of speech, or of the press; or the right of the people peaceably to assemble, and to petition the Government for a redress of grievances.

Amendment II

[RIGHT TO KEEP AND BEAR ARMS]

A well regulated Militia, being necessary to the security of a free State, the right of the people to keep and bear Arms, shall not be infringed.

Amendment III

[QUARTERING OF SOLDIERS]

No Soldier shall, in time of peace be quartered in any house, without the consent of the Owner, nor in time of war, but in a manner to be prescribed by law.

Amendment IV

[SECURITY FROM UNWARRANTABLE SEARCH AND SEIZURE]

The right of the people to be secure in their persons, houses, papers, and effects, against unreasonable searches and seizures, shall not be violated, and no Warrants shall issue, but upon probable cause, supported by Oath or affirmation, and particularly describing the place to be searched, and the persons or things to be seized.

Amendment V

[RIGHTS OF ACCUSED PERSONS IN CRIMINAL PROCEEDINGS]

No person shall be held to answer for a capital, or otherwise infamous crime, unless on a presentment or indictment of a Grand Jury, except in cases arising in the land or naval forces, or in the Militia, when in actual service in time of War or in public danger; nor shall any person be subject for the same offence to be twice put in jeopardy of life or limb; nor shall be compelled in any criminal case to be a witness against himself, nor be deprived of life, liberty, or property, without due process of law; nor shall private property be taken for public use, without just compensation.

Amendment VI

[RIGHT TO SPEEDY TRIAL, WITNESSES, ETC.]

In all criminal prosecutions, the accused shall enjoy the right to a speedy and public trial, by an impartial jury of the State and district wherein the crime shall have been committed, which district shall have been previously ascertained by law, and to be informed of the nature and cause of the accusation; to be confronted with the witnesses against him; to have compulsory process for obtaining witnesses in his favor, and to have the Assistance of Counsel for his defence.

Amendment VII

[TRIAL BY JURY IN CIVIL CASES]

In suits at common law, where the value in controversy shall exceed twenty dollars, the right of trial by jury shall be preserved, and no fact tried by a jury, shall be otherwise reexamined in any Court of the United States, than according to the rules of the common law.

Amendment VIII

[BAILS, FINES, PUNISHMENTS]

Excessive bail shall not be required, nor excessive fines imposed, nor cruel and unusual punishments inflicted.

Amendment IX

[RESERVATION OF RIGHTS OF PEOPLE]

The enumeration in the Constitution, of certain rights, shall not be construed to deny or disparage others retained by the people.

Amendment X

[POWERS RESERVED TO STATES OR PEOPLE]

The powers not delegated to the United States by the Constitution, nor prohibited by it to the States, are reserved to the States respectively, or to the people.

Amendment XI

[*Proposed by Congress on March 4, 1794; declared ratified on January 8, 1798.*]

[RESTRICTION OF JUDICIAL POWER]

The Judicial power of the United States shall not be construed to extend to any suit in law or equity, commenced or prosecuted against one of the United States by Citizens of another State, or by Citizens or Subjects of any Foreign State.

Amendment XII

[*Proposed by Congress on December 9, 1803; declared ratified on September 25, 1804.*]

[ELECTION OF PRESIDENT AND VICE PRESIDENT]

The Electors shall meet in their respective states and vote by ballot for President and Vice-President, one of whom, at least, shall not be an inhabitant of the same state with themselves; they shall name in their ballots the person voted for as President, and in distinct ballots the person voted for as Vice-President, and they shall make distinct lists of all persons voted for as President, and of all persons voted for as Vice-President, and of the number of votes for each, which lists they shall sign and certify, and transmit sealed to the seat of the government of the United States, directed to the President of the Senate;—the President of the Senate shall, in presence of the Senate and House of Representatives, open all the certificates and the votes shall then be counted;—The person having the greatest number of votes for President, shall be the President, if such number be a majority of the whole number of Electors appointed; and if no person have such majority, then from the persons having the highest numbers not exceeding three on the list of those voted for as President, the House of Representatives shall choose immediately, by ballot, the President. But in choosing the President, the votes shall be taken by states, the representation from each state having one vote; a quorum for this purpose shall consist of a member or members from two-thirds of the states, and a majority of all the states shall be necessary to a choice. And if the House of Representatives shall not choose a President whenever the right of choice shall devolve upon them, before the fourth day of March next following, then the Vice-President shall act as President, as in the case of the death or other constitutional disability of the President.—The person having the greatest number of votes as Vice-President, shall be the Vice-President, if such number be a majority of the whole number of Electors appointed, and if no person have a majority, then from the two highest numbers on the list, the Senate shall choose the Vice-President; a quorum for the purpose shall consist of two-thirds of the whole number of Senators, and a majority of the whole number shall be necessary to a choice. But no person constitutionally ineligible to the office of President shall be eligible to that of Vice-President of the United States.

Amendment XIII

[Proposed by Congress on January 31, 1865; declared ratified on December 18, 1865.]

SECTION 1

[ABOLITION OF SLAVERY]

Neither slavery nor involuntary servitude, except as a punishment for crime whereof the party shall have been duly convicted, shall exist within the United States, or any place subject to their jurisdiction.

SECTION 2

[POWER TO ENFORCE THIS ARTICLE]

Congress shall have power to enforce this article by appropriate legislation.

Amendment XIV

[Proposed by Congress on June 13, 1866; declared ratified on July 28, 1868.]

SECTION 1

[CITIZENSHIP RIGHTS NOT TO BE ABRIDGED BY STATES]

All persons born or naturalized in the United States, and subject to the jurisdiction thereof, are citizens of the United States and of the State wherein they reside. No State shall make or enforce any law which shall abridge the privileges or immunities of citizens of the United States; nor shall any State deprive any person of life, liberty, or property, without due process of law; nor deny to any person within its jurisdiction the equal protection of the laws.

SECTION 2

[APPORTIONMENT OF REPRESENTATIVES IN CONGRESS]

Representatives shall be apportioned among the several States according to their respective numbers, counting the whole number of persons in each State, excluding Indians not taxed. But when the right to vote at any election for the choice of electors for President and Vice-President of the United States, Representatives in Congress, the Executive and Judicial officers of a State, or the members of the Legislature thereof, is denied to any of the male inhabitants of such State, being twenty-one years of age, and citizens of the United States, or in any way abridged, except for participation in rebellion, or other crime, the basis of representation therein shall be reduced in the proportion which the number of such male citizens shall bear to the whole number of male citizens twenty-one years of age in such State.

SECTION 3

[PERSONS DISQUALIFIED FROM HOLDING OFFICE]

No person shall be a Senator or Representative in Congress, or elector of President and Vice-President, or hold any office, civil or military, under the United States, or under any State, who, having previously taken an oath, as a member of Congress, or as an officer of the United States, or as a member of any State legislature, or as an executive or judicial officer of any State, to support the Constitution of the United States, shall have engaged in insurrection or rebellion against the same, or given aid or comfort to the enemies thereof. But Congress may by a vote of two-thirds of each House, remove such disability.

SECTION 4

[WHAT PUBLIC DEBTS ARE VALID]

The validity of the public debt of the United States, authorized by law, including debts incurred for payment of pensions and bounties for services in suppressing insurrection or rebellion, shall not be questioned. But neither the United States nor any State shall assume or pay any debt or obligation incurred in aid of insurrection or rebellion against the United States, or any claim for the loss or emancipation of any slave; but all such debts, obligations and claims shall be held illegal and void.

SECTION 5

[POWER TO ENFORCE THIS ARTICLE]

The Congress shall have power to enforce, by appropriate legislation, the provisions of this article.

Amendment XV

[Proposed by Congress on February 26, 1869; declared ratified on March 30, 1870.]

SECTION 1

[BLACK SUFFRAGE]

The right of citizens of the United States to vote shall not be denied or abridged by the United States or by any State on account of race, color, or previous condition of servitude.

SECTION 2

[POWER TO ENFORCE THIS ARTICLE]

The Congress shall have power to enforce this article by appropriate legislation.

Amendment XVI

[Proposed by Congress on July 2, 1909; declared ratified on February 25, 1913.]
[AUTHORIZING INCOME TAXES]

The Congress shall have power to lay and collect taxes on incomes, from whatever source derived, without apportionment among the several States, and without regard to any census or enumeration.

Amendment XVII

[Proposed by Congress on May 13, 1912; declared ratified on May 31, 1913.]
[POPULAR ELECTION OF SENATORS]

The Senate of the United States shall be composed of two Senators from each State, elected by the people thereof, for six years; and each Senator shall have one vote. The electors in each State shall have the qualifications requisite for electors of the most numerous branch of the State legislatures.

When vacancies happen in the representation of any State in the Senate, the executive authority of such State shall issue writs of election to fill such vacancies: *Provided,* That the legislature of any State may empower the executive thereof to make temporary appointments until the people fill the vacancies by election as the legislature may direct.

This amendment shall not be so construed as to affect the election or term of any Senator chosen before it becomes valid as part of the Constitution.

Amendment XVIII

[Proposed by Congress December 18, 1917; declared ratified on January 29, 1919.]

SECTION 1

[NATIONAL LIQUOR PROHIBITION]

After one year from the ratification of this article the manufacture, sale, or transportation of intoxicating liquors within, the importation thereof into, or the exportation thereof from the United States and all territory subject to the jurisdiction thereof for beverage purposes is hereby prohibited.

SECTION 2

[POWER TO ENFORCE THIS ARTICLE]

The Congress and the several States shall have concurrent power to enforce this article by appropriate legislation.

SECTION 3

[RATIFICATION WITHIN SEVEN YEARS]

This article shall be inoperative unless it shall have been ratified as an amendment to the Constitution by the legislatures of the several States, as provided in the Constitution, within seven years from the date of the submission hereof to the States by the Congress.[1]

Amendment XIX

[Proposed by Congress on June 4, 1919; declared ratified on August 26, 1920.]

[WOMAN SUFFRAGE]

The right of citizens of the United States to vote shall not be denied or abridged by the United States or by any State on account of sex.

Congress shall have power to enforce this article by appropriate legislation.

Amendment XX

[Proposed by Congress on March 2, 1932; declared ratified on February 6, 1933.]

SECTION 1

[TERMS OF OFFICE]

The terms of the President and Vice President shall end at noon on the 20th day of January, and the terms of Senators and Representatives at noon on the 3d day of January, of the years in which such terms would have ended if this article had not been ratified; and the terms of their successors shall then begin.

SECTION 2

[TIME OF CONVENING CONGRESS]

The Congress shall assemble at least once in every year, and such meeting shall begin at noon on the 3d day of January, unless they shall by law appoint a different day.

SECTION 3

[DEATH OF PRESIDENT-ELECT]

If, at the time fixed for the beginning of the term of the President, the President elect shall have died, the Vice President elect shall become President. If a President shall not have been chosen before the time fixed for the beginning of his term, or if the President elect shall have failed to qualify, then the Vice President elect shall act as President until a President shall have qualified; and the Congress may by law provide for the case wherein neither a President elect nor a Vice President elect shall have qualified, declaring who shall then act as President, or the manner in which one who is to act shall be selected, and such person shall act accordingly until a President or Vice President shall have qualified.

SECTION 4

[ELECTION OF THE PRESIDENT]

The Congress may by law provide for the case of the death of any of the persons from whom the House of Representatives may choose a President whenever the right of choice shall have devolved upon them, and for the case of the death of any of the persons from whom the Senate may choose a Vice President whenever the right of choice shall have devolved upon them.

SECTION 5

[AMENDMENT TAKES EFFECT]

Sections 1 and 2 shall take effect on the 15th day of October following the ratification of this article.

SECTION 6

[RATIFICATION WITHIN SEVEN YEARS]

This article shall be inoperative unless it shall have been ratified as an amendment to the Constitution by the legislatures of three-fourths of the several States within seven years from the date of its submission.

[1] Repealed by the Twenty-first Amendment.

Amendment XXI

[Proposed by Congress on February 20, 1933; declared ratified on December 5, 1933.]

SECTION 1

[NATIONAL LIQUOR PROHIBITION REPEALED]

The eighteenth article of amendment to the Constitution of the United States is hereby repealed.

SECTION 2

[TRANSPORTATION OF LIQUOR INTO "DRY" STATES]

The transportation or importation into any State, Territory, or Possession of the United States for delivery or use therein of intoxicating liquors, in violation of the laws thereof, is hereby prohibited.

SECTION 3

[RATIFICATION WITHIN SEVEN YEARS]

This article shall be inoperative unless it shall have been ratified as an amendment to the Constitution by conventions in the several States, as provided in the Constitution, within seven years from the date of the submission hereof to the States by the Congress.

Amendment XXII

[Proposed by Congress on March 21, 1947; declared ratified on February 27, 1951.]

SECTION 1

[TENURE OF PRESIDENT LIMITED]

No person shall be elected to the office of President more than twice, and no person who has held the office of President or acted as President, for more than two years of a term to which some other person was elected President shall be elected to the office of the President more than once. But this Article shall not apply to any person holding the office of President when this Article was proposed by the Congress, and shall not prevent any person who may be holding the office of President, or acting as President, during the term within which this Article becomes operative from holding the office of President or acting as President during the remainder of such term.

SECTION 2

[RATIFICATION WITHIN SEVEN YEARS]

This article shall be inoperative unless it shall have been ratified as an amendment to the Constitution by the legislatures of three-fourths of the several States within seven years from the date of its submission to the States by the Congress.

Amendment XXIII

[Proposed by Congress on June 16, 1960; declared ratified on March 29, 1961.]

SECTION 1

[ELECTORAL COLLEGE VOTES FOR THE DISTRICT OF COLUMBIA]

The District constituting the seat of Government of the United States shall appoint in such manner as the Congress may direct:

A number of electors of President and Vice President equal to the whole number of Senators and Representatives in Congress to which the District would be entitled if it were a State, but in no event more than the least populous State; they shall be in addition to those appointed by the States, but they shall be considered, for the purposes of the election of President and Vice President, to be electors appointed by a State; and they shall meet in the District and perform such duties as provided by the twelfth article of amendment.

SECTION 2

[POWER TO ENFORCE THIS ARTICLE]

The Congress shall have power to enforce this article by appropriate legislation.

Amendment XXIV

[Proposed by Congress on August 27, 1962; declared ratified on January 23, 1964.]

SECTION 1

[ANTI-POLL TAX]

The right of citizens of the United States to vote in any primary or other election for President or Vice President, for electors for President or Vice President, or for Senator or Representative of Congress, shall not be denied or abridged by the United States or any State by reason of failure to pay any poll tax or other tax.

SECTION 2

[POWER TO ENFORCE THIS ARTICLE]

The Congress shall have power to enforce this article by appropriate legislation.

Amendment XXV

[Proposed by Congress on July 6, 1965; declared ratified on February 10, 1967.]

SECTION 1

[VICE PRESIDENT TO BECOME PRESIDENT]

In case of the removal of the President from office or his death or resignation, the Vice President shall become President.

SECTION 2

[CHOICE OF A NEW VICE PRESIDENT]

Whenever there is a vacancy in the office of the Vice President, the President shall nominate a Vice President who shall take the office upon confirmation by a majority vote of both houses of Congress.

SECTION 3

[PRESIDENT MAY DECLARE OWN DISABILITY]

Whenever the President transmits to the President pro tempore of the Senate and the Speaker of the House of Representatives his written declaration that he is unable to discharge the powers and duties of his office, and until he transmits to them a written declaration to the contrary, such powers and duties shall be discharged by the Vice President as Acting President.

SECTION 4

[ALTERNATE PROCEDURES TO DECLARE AND TO END PRESIDENTIAL DISABILITY]

Whenever the Vice President and a majority of either the principal officers of the executive departments, or of such other body as Congress may by law provide, transmit to the President pro tempore of the Senate and the Speaker of the House of Representatives their written declaration that the President is unable to discharge the powers and duties of his office, the Vice President shall immediately assume the powers and duties of the office as Acting President.

Thereafter, when the President transmits to the President pro tempore of the Senate and the Speaker of the House of Representatives his written declaration that no inability exists, he shall resume the powers and duties of his office unless the Vice President and a majority of either the principal officers of the executive department, or of such other body as Congress may by law provide, transmit within four days to the President pro tempore of the Senate and the Speaker of the House of Representatives their written declaration that the President is unable to discharge the powers and duties of his office. Thereupon Congress shall decide the issue, assembling within forty eight hours for that purpose if not in session. If the Congress, within twenty one days after receipt of the latter written declaration, or, if Congress is not in session, within twenty one days after Congress is required to assemble, determines by two-thirds vote of both Houses that the President is unable to discharge the powers and duties of his office, the Vice President shall continue to discharge the same as Acting President; otherwise, the President shall resume the powers and duties of his office.

Amendment XXVI

[Proposed by Congress on March 23, 1971; declared ratified on July 1, 1971.]

SECTION 1

[EIGHTEEN-YEAR-OLD VOTE]

The right of citizens of the United States, who are eighteen years of age or older, to vote shall not be denied or abridged by the United States or by any State on account of age.

SECTION 2

[POWER TO ENFORCE THIS ARTICLE]

The Congress shall have power to enforce this article by appropriate legislation.

Amendment XXVII

[Proposed by Congress on September 25, 1789; declared ratified on May 8, 1992.]

[CONGRESS CANNOT RAISE ITS OWN PAY]

No law varying the compensation for the services of the Senators and Representatives, shall take effect, until an election of representatives shall have intervened.

The Federalist Papers

No. 10: Madison

The Same Subject Continued: The Utility of the Union as a Safeguard against Domestic Faction and Insurrection

Among the numerous advantages promised by a well constructed Union, none deserves to be more accurately developed than its tendency to break and control the violence of faction. The friend of popular governments never finds himself so much alarmed for their character and fate, as when he contemplates their propensity to this dangerous vice. He will not fail therefore to set a due value on any plan which, without violating the principles to which he is attached, provides a proper cure for it. The instability, injustice, and confusion introduced into the public councils have, in truth, been the mortal diseases under which popular governments have everywhere perished, as they continue to be the favorite and fruitful topics from which the adversaries to liberty derive their most specious declamations. The valuable improvements made by the American constitutions on the popular models, both ancient and modern, cannot certainly be too much admired; but it would be an unwarrantable partiality to contend that they have as effectually obviated the danger on this side, as was wished and expected. Complaints are everywhere heard from our most considerate and virtuous citizens, equally the friends of public and private faith and of public and personal liberty, that our governments are too unstable, that the public good is disregarded in the conflicts of rival parties, and that measures are too often decided, not according to the rules of justice and the rights of the minor party, but by the superior force of an interested and overbearing majority. However anxiously we may wish that these complaints had no foundation, the evidence of known facts will not permit us to deny that they are in some degree true. It will be found, indeed, on a candid review of our situation, that some of the distresses under which we labor have been erroneously charged on the operation of our governments; but it will be found, at the same time, that other causes will not alone account for many of our heaviest misfortunes; and, particularly, for that prevailing and increasing distrust of public engagements and alarm for private rights which are echoed from one end of the continent to the other. These must be chiefly, if not wholly, effects of the unsteadiness and injustice with which a factious spirit has tainted our public administration.

By a faction I understand a number of citizens, whether amounting to a majority or minority of the whole, who are united and actuated by some common impulse of passion, or of interest, adverse to the rights of other citizens, or to the permanent and aggregate interests of the community.

There are two methods of curing the mischiefs of faction: the one, by removing its causes; the other, by controlling its effects.

There are again two methods of removing the causes of faction: the one, by destroying the liberty which is essential to its existence; the other, by giving to every citizen the same opinions, the same passions, and the same interests.

It could never be more truly said than of the first remedy, that it is worse than the disease. Liberty is to faction what air is to fire, an aliment without which it instantly expires. But it could not be a less folly to abolish liberty, which is essential to political life, because it nourishes faction, than it would be to wish the annihilation of air, which is essential to animal life, because it imparts to fire its destructive agency.

The second expedient is as impracticable, as the first would be unwise. As long as the reason of man continues fallible, and he is at liberty to exercise it, different opinions will be formed. As long as the connection subsists between his reason and his self-love, his opinions and his passions will have a reciprocal influence on each other; and the former will be objects to which the latter will attach themselves. The diversity in the faculties of men, from which the rights of property originate, is not less an insuperable obstacle to a uniformity of interests. The protection of these faculties is the first object of Government. From the protection of different and unequal faculties of acquiring property, the possession of different degrees and kinds of property immediately results; and from the influence of these on the sentiments and views of the respective proprietors, ensues a division of the society into different interests and parties.

The latent causes of faction are thus sown in the nature of man; and we see them everywhere brought into different degrees of activity, according to the different circumstances of civil society. A zeal for different opinions concerning religion, concerning Government, and many other points, as well of speculation as of practice; an attachment to different leaders ambitiously contending for pre-eminence and power; or to persons of other descriptions whose fortunes have been interesting to the human passions, have in turn divided mankind into parties, inflamed them with mutual animosity, and rendered them much more disposed to vex and oppress each other, than to co-operate for their common good. So strong is this propensity of mankind to fall into mutual animosities, that where no substantial occasion presents itself, the most frivolous and fanciful distinctions have been sufficient to kindle their unfriendly passions, and excite their most violent conflicts. But the most common and durable source of factions has been the various and unequal distribution of property. Those who hold and those who are without property have ever formed distinct interests in society. Those who are creditors, and those who are debtors, fall under a like discrimination. A landed interest, a manufacturing interest, a mercantile interest, a moneyed interest, with many lesser interests, grow up of necessity in civilized nations, and divide them into different classes, actuated by different sentiments and views. The regulation of these various and interfering interests forms the principal task of modern Legislation, and involves the spirit of party and faction in the necessary and ordinary operations of Government.

No man is allowed to be judge in his own cause, because his interest would certainly bias his judgment and, not improbably, corrupt his integrity. With equal, nay with greater reason, a body of men are unfit to be both judges and parties at the same time; yet what are many of the most important acts of legislation but so many judicial determinations, not indeed concerning the rights of single persons, but concerning the rights of large bodies of citizens; and what are the different classes of legislators but advocates and parties to the causes which they determine? Is a law proposed concerning private debts? It is a question to which the creditors are parties on one side and the debtors on the other. Justice ought to hold the balance between them. Yet the parties are, and must be, themselves the judges; and the most numerous party, or in other words, the most powerful faction must be expected to prevail. Shall domestic manufacturers be encouraged, and in what degree, by restrictions on foreign manufacturers? are questions which would be differently decided by the landed and the manufacturing classes, and probably by neither with a sole regard to justice and the public good. The apportionment of taxes on the various descriptions of property is an act which seems to require the most exact impartiality; yet there is, perhaps, no legislative act in which greater opportunity and temptation are given to a predominant party to trample on the rules of justice. Every shilling with which they overburden the inferior number is a shilling saved to their own pockets.

It is in vain to say that enlightened statesmen will be able to adjust these clashing interests and render them all subservient to the public good. Enlightened statesmen will not always be at the helm. Nor, in many cases, can such an adjustment be made at all without taking into view indirect and remote considerations, which will rarely prevail over the immediate interest which one party may find in disregarding the rights of another or the good of the whole.

The inference to which we are brought is that the *causes* of faction cannot be removed and that relief is only to be sought in the means of controlling its *effects*.

If a faction consists of less than a majority, relief is supplied by the republican principle, which enables the majority to defeat its sinister views by regular vote. It may clog the administration, it may convulse the society; but it will be unable to execute and mask its violence under the forms of the Constitution. When a majority is included in a faction, the form of popular government, on the other hand, enables it to sacrifice to its ruling passion or interest both the public good and the rights of other citizens. To secure the public good and private rights against the danger of such a faction, and at the same time to preserve the spirit and the form of popular government, is then the great object to which our enquiries are directed. Let me add that it is the great desideratum by which alone this form of government can be rescued from the opprobrium under which it has so long labored and be recommended to the esteem and adoption of mankind.

By what means is this object attainable? Evidently by one of two only. Either the existence of the same passion or interest in a majority at the same time must be prevented, or the majority, having such co-existent passion or interest, must be rendered, by their number and local situation, unable to concert and carry into effect schemes of oppression. If the impulse and the opportunity be suffered to coincide, we well know that neither moral nor religious motives can be relied on as an adequate control. They are not found to be such on the injustice and violence of individuals, and lose their efficacy in proportion to the number combined together, that is, in proportion as their efficacy becomes needful.

From this view of the subject it may be concluded that a pure Democracy, by which I mean a Society consisting of a small number of citizens, who assemble and administer the Government in person, can admit of no cure for the mischiefs of faction. A common passion or interest will, in almost every case, be felt by a majority of the whole; a communication and concert results from the form of Government itself; and there is nothing to check the inducements to sacrifice the weaker party or an obnoxious individual. Hence it is that such Democracies have ever been spectacles of turbulence and contention; have ever been found incompatible with personal security or the rights of property; and have in general been as short in their lives as they have been violent in their deaths. Theoretic politicians, who have patronized this species of Government, have erroneously supposed that by reducing mankind to a perfect equality in their political rights, they would at the same time be perfectly equalized and assimilated in their possessions, their opinions, and their passions.

A Republic, by which I mean a Government in which the scheme of representation takes place, opens a different prospect and promises the cure for which we are seeking. Let us examine the points in which it varies from pure Democracy, and we shall comprehend both the nature of the cure and the efficacy which it must derive from the Union.

The two great points of difference between a Democracy and a Republic are: first, the delegation of the Government, in the latter, to a small number of citizens elected by the rest; secondly, the greater number of citizens and greater sphere of country over which the latter may be extended.

The effect of the first difference is, on the one hand, to refine and enlarge the public views by passing them through the medium of a chosen body of citizens, whose wisdom may best discern the true interest of their country and whose patriotism and love of justice will be least likely to sacrifice it to temporary or partial considerations. Under such a regulation it may well happen that the public voice, pronounced by the representatives of the people, will be more consonant to the public good than if pronounced by the people themselves, convened for the purpose. On the other hand, the effect may be inverted. Men of factious tempers, of local prejudices, or of sinister designs, may, by intrigue, by corruption, or by other means, first obtain the suffrages, and then betray the interests of the people. The question resulting is, whether small or extensive Republics are most favorable to the election of proper guardians of the public weal; and it is clearly decided in favor of the latter by two obvious considerations.

In the first place it is to be remarked that however small the Republic may be, the Representatives must be raised to a certain number in order to guard against the cabals of a few; and that however large it may be they must be limited to a certain number in order to guard against the confusion of a multitude. Hence, the number of Representatives in the two cases not being in proportion to that of the Constituents, and being proportionally greatest in the small Republic, it follows that if the proportion of fit characters be not less in the large than in the small Republic, the former will present a greater option, and consequently a greater probability of a fit choice.

In the next place, as each Representative will be chosen by a greater number of citizens in the large than in the small Republic, it will be more difficult for unworthy candidates to practise with success the vicious arts by which elections are too often carried; and the suffrages of the people being more free, will be more likely to centre on men who possess the most attractive merit and the most diffusive and established characters.

It must be confessed that in this, as in most other cases, there is a mean, on both sides of which inconveniencies will be found to lie. By enlarging too much the number of electors, you render the representative too little acquainted with all their local circumstances and lesser interests; as by reducing it too much, you render him unduly attached to these, and too little fit to comprehend and pursue great and national objects. The Federal Constitution forms a happy combination in this respect; the great and aggregate interests being referred to the national, the local and particular to the State legislatures.

The other point of difference is the greater number of citizens and extent of territory which may be brought within the compass of Republican than of Democratic Government; and it is this circumstance principally which renders factious combinations less to be dreaded in the former than in the latter. The smaller the society, the fewer probably will be the distinct parties and interests composing it; the fewer the distinct parties and interests, the more frequently will a majority be found of the same party; and the smaller the number of individuals composing a majority, and the smaller the compass within which they are placed, the more easily will they concert and execute their plans of oppression. Extend the sphere and you take in a greater variety of parties and interests; you make it less probable that a majority of the whole will have a common motive to invade the rights of other citizens; or if such a common motive exists, it will be more difficult for all who feel it to discover their own strength and to act in unison with each other. Besides other impediments, it may be remarked, that where there is a consciousness of unjust or dishonorable purposes, communication is always checked by distrust in proportion to the number whose concurrence is necessary.

Hence, it clearly appears that the same advantage which a Republic has over a Democracy in controlling the effects of faction is enjoyed by a large over a small republic—is enjoyed by the Union over the States composing it. Does this advantage consist in the substitution of representatives whose enlightened views and virtuous sentiments render them superior to local prejudices and to schemes of injustice? It will not be denied that the representation of the Union will be most likely to possess these requisite endowments. Does it consist in the greater security afforded by a greater variety of parties, against the event of any one party being able to outnumber and oppress the rest? In an equal degree does the increased variety of parties comprised within the Union increase this security? Does it, in fine, consist in the greater obstacles opposed to the concert and accomplishment of the secret wishes of an unjust and interested majority? Here again the extent of the Union gives it the most palpable advantage.

The influence of factious leaders may kindle a flame within their particular States but will be unable to spread a general conflagration through the other States: a religious sect may degenerate into a political faction in a part of the Confederacy; but the variety of sects dispersed over the entire face of it must secure the national Councils against any danger from that source: a rage for paper money, for an abolition of debts, for an equal division of property, or for any other improper or wicked project, will be less apt to pervade the whole body of the Union than a particular member of it; in the same proportion as such a malady is more likely to taint a particular county or district than an entire State.

In the extent and proper structure of the Union, therefore, we behold a republican remedy for the diseases most incident to Republican Government. And according to the degree of pleasure and pride we feel in being republicans ought to be our zeal in cherishing the spirit and supporting the character of Federalists.

PUBLIUS

No. 51: Madison

The Structure of the Government Must Furnish the Proper Checks and Balances between the Different Departments

To the People of the State of New York:

To what expedient, then, shall we finally resort, for maintaining in practice the necessary partition of power among the several departments as laid down in the constitution? The only answer that can be given is that as all these exterior provisions are found to be inadequate the defect must be supplied, by so contriving the interior structure of the government as that its several constituent parts may, by their mutual relations, be the means of keeping each other in their proper places. Without presuming to undertake a full development of this important idea I will hazard a few general observations which may perhaps place it in a clearer light, and enable us to form a more correct judgment of the principles and structure of the government planned by the convention.

In order to lay a due foundation for that separate and distinct exercise of the different powers of government, which to a certain extent is admitted on all hands to be essential to the preservation of liberty, it is evident that each department should have a will of its own; and consequently should be so constituted that the members of each should have as little agency as possible in the appointment of the members of the others. Were this principle rigorously adhered to, it would require that all the appointments for the supreme executive, legislative, and judiciary magistracies should be drawn from the same fountain of authority, the people, through channels having no communication whatever with one another. Perhaps such a plan of constructing the several departments would be less difficult in practice than it may in contemplation appear. Some difficulties, however, and some additional expense would attend the execution of it. Some deviations, therefore, from the principle must be admitted. In the constitution of the judiciary department in particular, it might be inexpedient to insist rigorously on the principle: first, because peculiar qualifications being essential in the members, the primary consideration ought to be to select that mode of choice which best secures these qualifications; second, because the permanent tenure by which the appointments are held in that department must soon destroy all sense of dependence on the authority conferring them.

It is equally evident that the members of each department should be as little dependent as possible on those of the others for the emoluments annexed to their offices. Were the executive magistrate, or the judges, not independent of the legislature in this particular, their independence in every other would be merely nominal.

But the great security against a gradual concentration of the several powers in the same department consists in giving to those who administer each department the necessary constitutional means and personal motives to resist encroachments of the others. The provision for defence must in this, as in all other cases, be made commensurate to the danger of attack. Ambition must be made to counteract ambition. The interest of the man must be connected with the constitutional rights of the place. It may be a reflection on human nature that such devices should be necessary to control the abuses of government. But what is government itself but the greatest of all reflections on human nature? If men were angels, no government would be necessary. If angels were to govern men, neither external nor internal controls on government would be necessary. In framing a government which is to be administered by men over men, the great difficulty lies in this: You must first enable the government to control the governed; and in the next place oblige it to control itself. A dependence on the people is, no doubt, the primary control on the government; but experience has taught mankind the necessity of auxiliary precautions.

This policy of supplying, by opposite and rival interests, the defect of better motives, might be traced through the whole system of human affairs, private as well as public. We see it particularly displayed in all the subordinate distributions of power, where the constant aim is to divide and arrange the several offices in such a manner as that each may be a check on the other; that the private interest of every individual may be a sentinel over the public rights. These inventions of prudence cannot be less requisite in the distribution of the supreme powers of the State.

But it is not possible to give to each department an equal power of self-defense. In republican government, the legislative authority necessarily predominates. The remedy for this inconveniency is to divide the legislature into different branches; and to render them, by different modes of election and different principles of action, as little connected with each other as the nature of their common functions and their common dependence on the society will admit. It may even be necessary to guard against dangerous encroachments by still further precautions. As the weight of the legislative authority requires that it should be thus divided, the weakness of the executive may require, on the other hand, that it should be fortified. An absolute negative on the legislature appears, at first view, to be the natural defense with which the executive magistrate should be armed. But perhaps it would be neither altogether safe nor alone sufficient. On ordinary occasions it might not be exerted with the requisite firmness, and on extraordinary occasions it might be perfidiously abused. May not this defect of an absolute negative be supplied by some qualified connection between this weaker branch of the stronger department, by which the latter may be led to support the constitutional rights of the former, without being too much detached from the rights of its own department?

If the principles on which these observations are founded be just, as I persuade myself they are, and they be applied as a criterion to the several State constitutions, and to the federal Constitution, it will be found that if the latter does not perfectly correspond with them, the former are infinitely less able to bear such a test.

There are, moreover, two considerations particularly applicable to the federal system of America, which place that system in a very interesting point of view.

First. In a single republic, all the power surrendered by the people is submitted to the administration of a single government; and usurpations are guarded against by a division of the government into distinct and separate departments. In the compound republic of America, the power surrendered by the people is first divided between two distinct governments, and then the portion allotted to each subdivided among distinct and separate departments. Hence a double security arises to the rights of the people. The different governments will control each other, at the same time that each will be controlled by itself.

Second. It is of great importance in a republic not only to guard the society against the oppression of its rulers, but to guard one part of the society against the injustice of the other part. Different interests necessarily exist in different classes of citizens. If a majority be united by a common interest, the rights of the minority will be insecure.

There are but two methods of providing against this evil: The one by creating a will in the community independent of the majority—that is, of the society itself; the other, by comprehending in the society so many separate descriptions of citizens as will render an unjust combination of a majority of the whole very improbable, if not impracticable. The first method prevails in all governments possessing an hereditary or self-appointed authority. This, at best, is but a precarious security; because a power independent of the society may as well espouse the unjust views of the major as the rightful interests of the minor party, and may possibly be turned against both parties. The second method will be exemplified in the federal republic of the United States. Whilst all authority in it will be derived from and dependent on the society, the society itself will be broken into so many parts, interests and classes of citizens, that the rights of individuals, or of the minority, will be in little danger from interested combinations of the majority.

In a free government the security for civil rights must be the same as that for religious rights. It consists in the one case in the multiplicity of interests, and in the other in the multiplicity of sects. The degree of security in both cases will depend on the number of interests and sects; and this may be presumed to depend on the extent of country and number of people comprehended under the same government. This view of the subject must particularly recommend a proper federal system to all the sincere and considerate friends of republican government: Since it shows that in exact proportion as the territory of the Union may be formed into more circumscribed Confederacies, or States, oppressive combinations of a majority will be facilitated; the best security, under the republican form, for the rights of every class of citizens, will be diminished; and consequently the stability and independence of some member of the government, the only other security, must be proportionally increased. Justice is the end of government. It is the end of civil society. It ever has been and ever will be pursued until it be obtained, or until liberty be lost in the pursuit. In a society under the forms of which the stronger faction can readily unite and oppress the weaker, anarchy may as truly be said to reign as in a state of nature, where the weaker individual is not secured against the violence of the stronger: And as, in the latter state, even the stronger individuals are prompted, by the uncertainty of their condition, to submit to a government which may protect the weak as well as themselves: So, in the former state, will the more powerful factions or parties be gradually induced, by a like motive, to wish for a government which will protect all parties, the weaker as well as the more powerful.

It can be little doubted that if the State of Rhode Island was separated from the Confederacy and left to itself, the insecurity of rights under the popular form of government within such narrow limits would be displayed by such reiterated oppressions of factious majorities that some power altogether independent of the people would soon be called for by the voice of the very factions whose misrule had proved the necessity of it. In the extended republic of the United States, and among the great variety of interests, parties, and sects which it embraces, a coalition of a majority of the whole society could seldom take place on any other principles than those of justice and the general good; and there being thus less danger to a minor from the will of the major party, there must be less pretext, also, to provide for the security of the former, by introducing into the government a will not dependent on the latter, or, in other words, a will independent of the society itself. It is no less certain than it is important, notwithstanding the contrary opinions which have been entertained, that the larger the society, provided it lie within a practicable sphere, the more duly capable it will be of self-government. And happily for the *republican cause,* practicable sphere may be carried to a very great extent by a judicious modification and mixture of the *federal principle.*

PUBLIUS

No. 78: Hamilton

To the People of the State of New York:

We proceed now to an examination of the judiciary department of the proposed government.

In unfolding the defects of the existing Confederation, the utility and necessity of a federal judicature have been clearly pointed out. It is the less necessary to recapitulate the considerations there urged, as the propriety of the institution in the abstract is not disputed; the only questions which have been raised being relative to the manner of constituting it, and to its extent. To these points, therefore, our observations shall be confined.

The manner of constituting it seems to embrace these several objects: 1st. The mode of appointing the judges. 2d. The tenure by which they are to hold their places. 3d. The partition of the judiciary authority between different courts, and their relations to each other.

First. As to the mode of appointing the judges; this is the same with that of appointing the officers of the Union in general, and has been so fully discussed in the two last numbers, that nothing can be said here which would not be useless repetition.

Second. As to the tenure by which the judges are to hold their places; this chiefly concerns their duration in office; the provisions for their support; the precautions for their responsibility.

According to the plan of the convention, all judges who may be appointed by the United States are to hold their offices DURING GOOD BEHAVIOR; which is conformable to the most approved of the State constitutions and among the rest, to that of this State. Its propriety having been drawn into question by the adversaries of that plan, is no light symptom of the rage for objection, which disorders their imaginations and judgments. The standard of good behavior for the continuance in office of the judicial magistracy, is certainly one of the most valuable of the modern improvements in the practice of government. In a monarchy it is an excellent barrier to the despotism of the prince; in a republic it is a no less excellent barrier to the encroachments and oppressions of the representative body. And it is the best expedient which can be devised in any government, to secure a steady, upright, and impartial administration of the laws.

Whoever attentively considers the different departments of power must perceive, that, in a government in which they are separated from each other, the judiciary, from the nature of its functions, will always be the least dangerous to the political rights of the Constitution; because it will be least in a capacity to annoy or injure them. The Executive not only dispenses the honors, but holds the sword of the community. The legislature not only commands the purse, but prescribes the rules by which the duties and rights of every citizen are to be regulated. The judiciary, on the contrary, has no influence over either the sword or the purse; no direction either of the strength or of the wealth of the society; and can take no active resolution whatever. It may truly be said to have neither FORCE nor WILL, but merely judgment; and must ultimately depend upon the aid of the executive arm even for the efficacy of its judgments.

This simple view of the matter suggests several important consequences. It proves incontestably, that the judiciary is beyond comparison the weakest of the three departments of power; that it can never attack with success either of the other two; and that all possible care is requisite to enable it to defend itself against their attacks. It equally proves, that though individual oppression may now and then proceed from the courts of justice, the general liberty of the people can never be endangered from that quarter; I mean so long as the judiciary remains truly distinct from both the legislature and the Executive. For I agree, that "there is no liberty, if the power of judging be not separated from the legislative and executive powers." And it proves, in the last place, that as liberty can have nothing to fear from the judiciary alone, but would have every thing to fear from its union with either of the other departments; that as all the effects of such a union must ensue from a dependence of the former on the latter, notwithstanding a nominal and apparent separation; that as, from the natural feebleness of the judiciary, it is in continual jeopardy of being overpowered, awed, or influenced by its co-ordinate branches; and that as nothing can contribute so much to its firmness and independence as permanency in office, this quality may therefore be justly regarded as an indispensable ingredient in its constitution, and, in a great measure, as the citadel of the public justice and the public security.

The complete independence of the courts of justice is peculiarly essential in a limited Constitution. By a limited Constitution, I understand one which contains certain specified exceptions to the legislative authority; such, for instance, as that it shall pass no bills of attainder, no ex-post-facto laws, and the like. Limitations of this kind can be preserved in practice no other way than through the medium of courts of justice, whose duty it must be to declare all acts contrary to the manifest tenor of the Constitution void. Without this, all the reservations of particular rights or privileges would amount to nothing.

Some perplexity respecting the rights of the courts to pronounce legislative acts void, because contrary to the Constitution, has arisen from an imagination that the doctrine would imply a superiority of the judiciary to the legislative power. It is urged that the authority which can declare the acts of another void, must necessarily be superior to the one whose acts may be declared void. As this doctrine is of great importance in all the American constitutions, a brief discussion of the ground on which it rests cannot be unacceptable.

There is no position which depends on clearer principles, than that every act of a delegated authority, contrary to the tenor of the commission under which it is exercised, is void. No legislative act, therefore, contrary to the Constitution, can be valid. To deny this, would be to affirm, that the deputy is greater than his principal; that the servant is above his master; that the representatives of the people are superior to the people themselves; that men acting by virtue of powers, may do not only what their powers do not authorize, but what they forbid.

If it be said that the legislative body are themselves the constitutional judges of their own powers, and that the construction they put upon them is conclusive upon the other departments, it may be answered, that this cannot be the natural presumption, where it is not to be collected from any particular provisions in the Constitution. It is not otherwise to be supposed, that the Constitution could intend to enable the representatives of the people to substitute their will to that of their constituents. It is far more rational to suppose, that the courts were designed to be an intermediate body between the people and the legislature, in order, among other things, to keep the latter within the limits assigned to their authority. The interpretation of the laws is the proper and peculiar province of the courts. A constitution is, in fact, and must be regarded by the judges, as a fundamental law. It therefore belongs to them to ascertain its meaning, as well as the meaning of any particular act proceeding from the legislative body. If there should happen to be an irreconcilable variance between the two, that which has the superior obligation and validity ought, of course, to be preferred; or, in other words, the Constitution ought to be preferred to the statute, the intention of the people to the intention of their agents.

Nor does this conclusion by any means suppose a superiority of the judicial to the legislative power. It only supposes that the power of the people is superior to both; and that where the will of the legislature, declared in its statutes, stands in opposition to that of the people, declared in the Constitution, the judges ought to be governed by the latter rather than the former. They ought to regulate their decisions by the fundamental laws, rather than by those which are not fundamental.

This exercise of judicial discretion, in determining between two contradictory laws, is exemplified in a familiar instance. It not uncommonly happens, that there are two statutes existing at one time, clashing in whole or in part with each other, and neither of them containing any repealing clause or expression. In such a case, it is the province of the courts to liquidate and fix their meaning and operation. So far as they can, by any fair construction, be reconciled to each other, reason and law conspire to dictate that this should be done; where this is impracticable, it becomes a matter of necessity to give effect to one, in exclusion of the other. The rule which has obtained in the courts for determining their relative validity is, that the last in order of time shall be preferred to the first. But this is a mere rule of construction, not derived from any positive law, but from the nature and reason of the thing. It is a rule not enjoined upon the courts by legislative provision, but adopted by themselves, as consonant to truth and propriety, for the direction of their conduct as interpreters of the law. They thought it reasonable, that between the interfering acts of an equal authority, that which was the last indication of its will should have the preference.

But in regard to the interfering acts of a superior and subordinate authority, of an original and derivative power, the nature and reason of the thing indicate the converse of that rule as proper to be followed. They teach us that the prior act of a superior ought to be preferred to the subsequent act of an inferior and subordinate authority; and that accordingly, whenever a particular statute contravenes the Constitution, it will be the duty of the judicial tribunals to adhere to the latter and disregard the former.

It can be of no weight to say that the courts, on the pretense of a repugnancy, may substitute their own pleasure to the constitutional intentions of the legislature. This might as well happen in the case of two contradictory statutes; or it might as well happen in every adjudication upon any single statute. The courts must declare the sense of the law; and if they should be disposed to exercise WILL instead of judgment, the consequence would equally be the substitution of their pleasure to that of the legislative body. The observation, if it prove any thing, would prove that there ought to be no judges distinct from that body.

If, then, the courts of justice are to be considered as the bulwarks of a limited Constitution against legislative encroachments, this consideration will afford a strong argument for the permanent tenure of judicial offices, since nothing will contribute so much as this to that independent spirit in the judges which must be essential to the faithful performance of so arduous a duty.

This independence of the judges is equally requisite to guard the Constitution and the rights of individuals from the effects of those ill humors, which the arts of designing men, or the influence of particular conjunctures, sometimes disseminate among the people themselves, and which, though they speedily give place to better information, and more deliberate reflection, have a tendency, in the meantime, to occasion dangerous innovations in the government, and serious oppressions of the minor party in the community. Though I trust the friends of the proposed Constitution will never concur with its enemies, in questioning that fundamental principle of republican government, which admits the right of the people to alter or abolish the established Constitution, whenever they find it inconsistent with their happiness, yet it is not to be inferred from this principle, that the representatives of the people, whenever a momentary inclination happens to lay hold of a majority of their constituents, incompatible with the provisions in the existing Constitution, would, on that account, be justifiable in a violation of those provisions; or that the courts would be under a greater obligation to connive at infractions in this shape, than when they had proceeded wholly from the cabals of the representative body. Until the people have, by some solemn and authoritative act, annulled or changed the established form, it is binding upon themselves collectively, as well as individually; and no presumption, or even knowledge, of their sentiments, can warrant their representatives in a departure from it, prior to such an act. But it is easy to see, that it would require an uncommon portion of fortitude in the judges to do their duty as faithful guardians of the Constitution, where legislative invasions of it had been instigated by the major voice of the community.

But it is not with a view to infractions of the Constitution only, that the independence of the judges may be an essential safeguard against the effects of occasional ill humors in the society. These sometimes extend no farther than to the injury of the private rights of particular classes of citizens, by unjust and partial laws. Here also the firmness of the judicial magistracy is of vast importance in mitigating the severity and confining the operation of such laws. It not only serves to moderate the immediate mischiefs of those which may have been passed, but it operates as a check upon the legislative body in passing them; who, perceiving that obstacles to the success of iniquitous intention are to be expected from the scruples of the courts, are in a manner compelled, by the very motives of the injustice they meditate, to qualify their attempts. This is a circumstance calculated to have more influence upon the character of our governments, than but few may be aware of. The benefits of the integrity and moderation of the judiciary have already been felt in more States than one; and though they may have displeased those whose sinister expectations they may have disappointed, they must have commanded the esteem and applause of all the virtuous and disinterested. Considerate men, of every description, ought to prize whatever will tend to beget or fortify that temper in the courts: as no man can be sure that he may not be to-morrow the victim of a spirit of injustice, by which he may be a gainer to-day. And every man must now feel, that the inevitable tendency of such a spirit is to sap the foundations of public and private confidence, and to introduce in its stead universal distrust and distress.

That inflexible and uniform adherence to the rights of the Constitution, and of individuals, which we perceive to be indispensable in the courts of justice, can certainly not be expected from judges who hold their offices by a temporary commission. Periodical appointments, however regulated, or by whomsoever made, would, in some way or other, be fatal to their necessary independence. If the power of making them was committed either to the Executive or legislature, there would be danger of an improper complaisance to the branch which possessed it; if to both, there would be an unwillingness to hazard the displeasure of either; if to the people, or to persons chosen by them for the special purpose, there would be too great a disposition to consult popularity, to justify a reliance that nothing would be consulted but the Constitution and the laws.

There is yet a further and a weightier reason for the permanency of the judicial offices, which is deducible from the nature of the qualifications they require. It has been frequently remarked, with great propriety, that a voluminous code of laws is one of the inconveniences necessarily connected with the advantages of a free government. To avoid an arbitrary discretion in the courts, it is indispensable that they should be bound down by strict rules and precedents, which serve to define and point out their duty in every particular case that comes before them; and it will readily be conceived from the variety of controversies which grow out of the folly and wickedness of mankind, that the records of those precedents must unavoidably swell to a very considerable bulk, and must demand long and laborious study to acquire a competent knowledge of them. Hence it is, that there can be but few men in the society who will have sufficient skill in the laws to qualify them for the stations of judges. And making the proper deductions for the ordinary depravity of human nature, the number must be still smaller of those who unite the requisite integrity with the requisite knowledge. These considerations apprise us, that the government can have no great option between fit character; and that a temporary duration in office, which would naturally discourage such characters from quitting a lucrative line of practice to accept a seat on the bench, would have a tendency to throw the administration of justice into hands less able, and less well qualified, to conduct it with utility and dignity. In the present circumstances of this country, and in those in which it is likely to be for a long time to come, the disadvantages on this score would be greater than they may at first sight appear; but it must be confessed, that they are far inferior to those which present themselves under the other aspects of the subject.

Upon the whole, there can be no room to doubt that the convention acted wisely in copying from the models of those constitutions which have established good behavior as the tenure of their judicial offices, in point of duration; and that so far from being blamable on this account, their plan would have been inexcusably defective, if it had wanted this important feature of good government. The experience of Great Britain affords an illustrious comment on the excellence of the institution.

PUBLIUS

Endnotes

Chapter 1

1. Joanna Walters, "Short and to the Point: Five Fauci Quotes to Get You through the Week," *Guardian*, July 19, 2020, www.theguardian.com/world/2020/jul/19/five-fauci-quotes-to-get-you-through-the-week (accessed 10/14/21).
2. Kevin McCarthy, Twitter post, July 27, 2021, 10:29 p.m., https://twitter.com/GOPLeader/status/1420209661735804934?ref_src=twsrc%5Egoogle%7Ctwcamp%5Eserp%7Ctwgr%5Etweet (accessed 7/15/22).
3. Thomas Hobbes, *Leviathan* (1651; repr., Indianapolis, IN: Bobbs, Merrill, 1958).
4. Alexander Hamilton, James Madison, and John Jay, *The Federalist Papers*, ed. Roy P. Fairfield, 2nd ed. (1788; repr., Baltimore, MD: Johns Hopkins University Press, 1981), p. 160.
5. Hamilton, Madison, and Jay, *Federalist Papers*, p. 18.
6. E. E. Schattschneider, *The Semisovereign People: A Realist's View of Democracy in America* (New York: Holt, Rinehart, and Winston, 1960).
7. Irving L. Janis, *Victims of Groupthink: A Psychological Study of Foreign-Policy Decisions and Fiascoes* (Boston: Houghton Mifflin, 1972).
8. Larry M. Bartels, *Unequal Democracy: The Political Economy of the New Gilded Age*, 2nd ed. (Princeton, NJ: Princeton University Press, 2016); Lawrence Baum, *Ideology in the Supreme Court* (Princeton, NJ: Princeton University Press, 2017).
9. Robert S. Erikson and Kent L. Tedin, *American Public Opinion*, 9th ed. (New York: Routledge, 2015).
10. John R. Hibbing and Elizabeth Theiss-Morse, *Stealth Democracy: Americans' Beliefs about How Government Should Work* (New York: Cambridge University Press, 2002), p. 147. See Diana E. Hess, *Controversy in the Classroom: The Democratic Power of Discussion* (New York: Routledge, 2009), for evidence that diverse viewpoints in the classroom have important effects on discussion.
11. For various surveys on abortion, see www.pollingreport.com/abortion.htm (accessed 11/1/21).
12. Donald Green, Bradley Palmquist, and Eric Schickler, *Partisan Hearts and Minds* (New Haven, CT: Yale University Press, 2004); Christopher Achen, "Parental Socialization and Rational Party Identification," *Political Behavior* 24:2 (2002): 151–70.
13. Robert S. Erikson, Michael B. MacKuen, and James A. Stimson, *The Macro Polity* (New York: Cambridge University Press, 2002); Christopher H. Achen and Larry M. Bartels, *Democracy for Realists: Why Elections Do Not Produce Responsive Government* (Princeton, NJ: Princeton University Press, 2016).
14. Office of Personnel Management, September 2019, www.fedscope.opm.gov/; Congressional Budget Office, November 2019, www.cbo.gov/topics/budget; Code of Federal Regulations, www.govinfo.gov/help/cfr#about (all accessed 11/1/21).
15. Andrew Heywood, *Political Theory: An Introduction*, 4th ed. (New York: Macmillan, 2015).
16. Morris P. Fiorina, with Samuel J. Abrams and Jeremy C. Pope, *Culture War: The Myth of a Polarized America*, 3rd ed. (New York: Pearson, Longman, 2010), pp. 46–47.
17. For more on political culture, see Pippa Norris, *Democratic Deficit: Critical Citizens Revisited* (New York: Cambridge University Press, 2011).
18. Frank M. Bryan, *Real Democracy: The New England Town Meeting and How It Works* (Chicago: University of Chicago Press, 2004).

Chapter 2

1. Donald J. Trump, June 16, 2023, remarks posted on X, https://x.com/TeamTrump/status/1669732758116024320 (accessed 6/12/24).
2. "Key Quotes From US President Biden's Jan. 6 Democracy Speech," Reuters, January 5, 2024, https://www.usnews.com/news/us/articles/2024-01-05/key-quotes-from-us-president-bidens-jan-6-democracy-speech (accessed 6/12/24).
3. "Widespread feeling that the 2024 presidential election carries serious stakes for the country," The Associated Press-NORC Center for Public Affairs Research, December 15, 2023, https://apnorc.org/projects/widespread-feeling-that-the-2024-presidential-election-carries-serious-stakes-for-the-country/ (accessed 6/12/24).
4. For a good overview of the political thought of the American Revolution, see Gordon S. Wood, *The Radicalism of the American Revolution* (New York: Vintage Books, 1993). For an excellent summary of the history, see Wood's *The American Revolution: A History* (New York: Modern Library, 2003).
5. David McCullough, *John Adams* (New York: Simon and Schuster, 2001), p. 90.
6. Thomas Slaughter, *Independence: The Tangled Roots of the American Revolution* (New York: Hill and Wang, 2015): 2; Paul H. Smith, "The American Loyalists: Notes on Their Organization and Numerical Strength," *William and Mary Quarterly* 25:2 (April 1968): 259–77; Maya Jasanoff, "The Other Side of Revolution: Loyalists in the British Empire," *William and Mary Quarterly* 65:2 (April 2008): 205–32.
7. A classic text on the Founding period is Gordon S. Wood, *The Creation of the American Republic* (New York: W. W. Norton, 1969).
8. J. W. Peltason, *Corwin and Peltason's Understanding the Constitution*, 7th ed. (Hinsdale, IL: Dryden, 1976), p. 12.
9. The pamphlet sold 120,000 copies within a few months of publication, a figure that would leave the Harry Potter books in the dust in terms of the proportion of the literate public that purchased the book.
10. Thomas Hobbes, *Leviathan* (1651; repr., Indianapolis, IN: Bobbs, Merrill, 1958).
11. John Locke, *Second Treatise of Government* (1690; repr., Indianapolis, IN: Bobbs, Merrill, 1952).
12. Robert A. Dahl, *How Democratic Is the American Constitution?* (New Haven, CT: Yale University Press, 2001), p. 12.

13. John Jay to Richard Price, September 27, 1785, in *The Founders' Constitution*, ed. Philip B. Kurland and Ralph Lerner (Chicago: University of Chicago Press, 1987), vol. 1, chap. 15, document 31, http://press-pubs.uchicago.edu/founders/documents/v1ch15s31.html (accessed 1/6/22).
14. Hamilton, Madison, and Jay, *Federalist Papers*, p. 22.
15. Locke, *Second Treatise of Government*, Section 160.
16. Many delegates probably assumed that the electors would reflect the wishes of the voters in their states, but there is no clear indication of this in Madison's notes. (Hamilton makes this argument in the *Federalist Papers*.) Until the 1820s, many electors were directly chosen by state legislatures rather than by the people. In the first presidential election, George Washington won the unanimous support of the electors, but in only five states were the electors chosen by the people.
17. Richard Beeman, *Plain, Honest Men: The Making of the American Constitution* (New York: Random House, 2009), pp. 66–67.
18. The actual language of the section avoids the term "slavery." Instead, it says: "The Migration or Importation of such Persons as any of the States now existing shall think proper to admit, shall not be prohibited by Congress prior to the Year one thousand eight hundred and eight." The ban on the importation of enslaved people was implemented on the earliest possible date, January 1, 1808.
19. Reid Wilson, "Conservatives Prepare New Push for Constitutional Convention," *The Hill*, December 8, 2021, https://thehill.com/homenews/state-watch/584835-conservatives-prepare-new-push-for-constitutional-convention (accessed 12/21/21).
20. Brutus 1, October 18, 1787, Teaching American History, https://teachingamericanhistory.org/document/brutus-i/ (accessed 1/6/22).
21. Patrick Henry, "Shall Liberty or Empire Be Sought?," in *America, 1761–1837*, vol. 8 of *The World's Famous Orations*, ed. William Jennings Bryan (New York: Funk and Wagnalls, 1906), pp. 73, 76.
22. Thomas Jefferson to John Adams, 1787, in *The Writings of Thomas Jefferson*, Memorial Edition, ed. Andrew A. Lipscomb and Albert Ellery Bergh (Washington, DC: Thomas Jefferson Memorial Association of the United States, 1903), vol. 6, p. 370.
23. "Proclamation on Ending Discriminatory Bans on Entry to the United States," The White House, January 20, 2021, www.whitehouse.gov/briefing-room/presidential-actions/2021/01/20/proclamation-ending-discriminatory-bans-on-entry-to-the-united-states/ and "President Biden Renews U.S. Leadership on World Stage at U.N. Climate Conference (COP26)," The White House, November 1, 2021, www.whitehouse.gov/briefing-room/statements-releases/2021/11/01/fact-sheet-president-biden-renews-u-s-leadership-on-world-stage-at-u-n-climate-conference-cop26/ (both accessed 12/21/21).
24. Michael D. Shear and Zolan Kanno-Youngs, "Biden Pardons Thousands Convicted of Marijuana Possession under Federal Law," *New York Times*, October 6, 2022, www.nytimes.com/2022/10/06/us/politics/biden-marijuana-pardon.html (accessed 11/11/22).
25. Associated Press, "House Overwhelmingly Votes Bipartisan Condemnation of Trump Withdrawal of U.S. Troops from Syria," October 16, 2019, www.nbcnews.com/politics/congress/house-overwhelmingly-votes-bipartisan-condemnation-trump-withdrawal-u-s-troops-n1067586 (accessed 1/6/22).
26. *Hamdi v. Rumsfeld*, 542 U.S. 507 (2004); *Rasul v. Bush*, 542 U.S. 466 (2004); *Hamdan v. Rumsfeld*, 548 U.S. 557 (2006); *Boumediene v. Bush*, 553 U.S. 723 (2008).
27. Charlie Savage, "Obama's War on Terror May Resemble Bush's in Some Areas," *New York Times*, February 17, 2009, p. A1.
28. Peter M. Shane, *Madison's Nightmare: How Executive Power Threatens American Democracy* (Chicago: University of Chicago Press, 2009).
29. The responses on the three branches are from "Americans' Knowledge of the Branches of Government Is Declining," Annenberg Public Policy Center, September 13, 2016, www.annenbergpublicpolicycenter.org/americans-knowledge-of-the-branches-of-government-is-declining (accessed 1/6/22); the responses on the right to own a pet or home are from "Is There a Constitutional Right to Own a Home or a Pet?," Annenberg Public Policy Center, September 16, 2015, www.annenbergpublicpolicycenter.org/is-there-a-constitutional-right-to-own-a-home-or-a-pet (accessed 1/6/22).
30. NCC staff, "What We Can Learn about the Constitution from *The Simpsons*," National Constitution Center, January 14, 2018, https://constitutioncenter.org/blog/what-we-can-learn-about-the-constitution-from-the-simpsons (accessed 1/6/22).
31. *United States v. Alfonso D. Lopez, Jr.*, 514 U.S. 549 (1995).
32. Alexander Hamilton, John Jay, and James Madison, *The Federalist Papers*, ed. Roy P. Fairfield, 2nd ed. (1788; repr., Baltimore, MD: Johns Hopkins University Press, 1981).
33. Thomas Jefferson to James Madison, in *Thomas Jefferson on Democracy*, ed. Saul Padover (New York: Mentor Books, 1953), p. 153.
34. Cass R. Sunstein, "Making Amends," *New Republic*, March 3, 1997, p. 42.
35. *Furman v. Georgia*, 408 U.S. 238 (1972).
36 The case concerning minors was *Roper v. Simmons*, 543 U.S. 551 (2005), and the case concerning the mentally impaired was *Atkins v. Virginia*, 536 U.S. 304 (2002).
37. Valerie Strauss, "In the Age of Trump, a New Surge of Interest in the Constitution," *Washington Post*, August 17, 2017, www.washingtonpost.com/news/answer-sheet/wp/2017/08/17/in-the-age-of-trump-a-new-surge-of-interest-in-the-u-s-constitution/?utm_term=.e3abb53b9976 (accessed 8/18/2017).
38. Walter F. Murphy, "The Nature of the American Constitution," The Edmund Janes James lecture, December 6, 1987 (Department of Political Science, University of Illinois at Urbana-Champaign, 1989), p. 8, http://babel.hathitrust.org/cgi/pt?id=mdp.39015078286518;view=1up;seq=12 (accessed 1/22/20).

Take a Stand

a. Kristen Bialik, "Growing Share of Americans Say Supreme Court Should Base Its Rulings on What Constitution Means Today," Pew Research Center, May 11, 2018, www.pewresearch.org/fact-tank/2018/05/11/growing-share-of-americans-say-supreme-court-should-base-its-rulings-on-what-constitution-means-today/ (accessed 1/6/22).
b. Clarence Thomas, "How to Read the Constitution," *Wall Street Journal*, October 20, 2008.
c. *State of Missouri v. Holland*, 252 U.S. 416 (1920), 252.
d. William Rehnquist, "The Notion of a Living Constitution," *Harvard Journal of Law and Public Policy* 29 (2006): 402.
e. Rehnquist, "Notion," p. 405.
f. Thurgood Marshall at the Annual Seminar of the San Francisco Patent and Trademark Law Association, Maui, Hawaii, May 6, 1987, www.thurgoodmarshall.com/speeches/constitutional_speech.htm (accessed 1/6/22).

Chapter 3

1. "Press Briefing by White House COVID-19 Response Team and Public Health Officials," October 20, 2021, www.whitehouse.gov/briefing-room/press-briefings/2021/10/20/press-briefing-by-white-house-covid-19-response-team-and-public-health-officials-62/ (accessed 11/11/21).
2. Renzo Downey, "Ron DeSantis Mocks Joe Biden 'Obsession' with Masking Kindergarteners amid Afghanistan Crisis," *Florida Politics*, August 19, 2021, https://floridapolitics.com/archives/451535-ron-desantis-calls-joe-biden-obsessed-with-masking-kindergarteners-amid-afghanistan-crisis/ (accessed 11/11/21).
3. "Could the President or Congress Enact a Nationwide Mask Mandate?" *Congressional Research Service*, August 2021, https://crsreports.congress.gov/product/pdf/LSB/LSB10530/2 (accessed 11/2/21).
4. Slaughterhouse Cases, 83 U.S. 36 (1873). See Ronald M. Labbe and Jonathan Lurie, *The Slaughterhouse Cases: Regulation, Reconstruction, and the Fourteenth Amendment* (Lawrence: University Press of Kansas, 2003).
5. Civil Rights Cases, 109 U.S. 3 (1883).
6. *United States v. E. C. Knight Co.*, 156 U.S. 1 (1895).
7. *Hammer v. Dagenhart*, 247 U.S. 251 (1918).
8. *Schechter Poultry Corporation v. United States*, 295 U.S. 495 (1935).
9. Four key cases are *West Coast Hotel Company v. Parrish* (1937), *Wright v. Vinton Branch* (1937), *Virginia Railway Company v. System Federation* (1937), and *National Labor Relations Board v. Jones and Laughlin Steel Corporation* (1937).
10. Martin Grodzins, *The American System* (New York: Rand McNally, 1966).
11. *Brown v. Board of Education*, 347 U.S. 483 (1954); *Swann v. Charlotte-Mecklenburg Board of Education*, 402 U.S. 1 (1971).
12. *Baker v. Carr*, 369 U.S. 186 (1962); *Reynolds v. Sims*, 377 U.S. 533 (1964); *Wesberry v. Sanders*, 376 U.S. 1 (1964); Martha Derthick, *Keeping the Compound Republic: Essays in American Federalism* (Washington, DC: Brookings Institution, 2001).
13. *Miranda v. Arizona*, 384 U.S. 436 (1966); *Mapp v. Ohio*, 367 U.S. 643 (1961).
14. Barry Rabe, "Environmental Policy and the Bush Era: The Collision between the Administrative Presidency and State Experimentation," *Publius* 37:3 (May 2007): 413–31.
15. Lois Beckett, "Nullification: How States Are Making It a Felony to Enforce Federal Gun Laws," *ProPublica*, May 2, 2013, www.propublica.org/article/nullification-how-states-are-making-it-a-felony-to-enforce-federal-gun-laws (accessed 11/15/13).
16. From a review of Michael S. Greve, *Real Federalism: Why It Matters, How It Could Happen* (Washington, DC: American Enterprise Institute Press, 1999), www.federalismproject.org/publications/books (accessed 10/10/07).
17. *Gregory v. Ashcroft*, 501 U.S. 452 (1991).
18. *City of Boerne v. Flores*, 521 U.S. 507 (1997), 520.
19. *Kimel et al. v. Florida Board of Regents*, 528 U.S. 62 (2000).
20. *United States v. Lopez*, 514 U.S. 549 (1995).
21. *United States v. Morrison*, 529 U.S. 598 (2000); Nia-Malika Henderson, "Obama Signs a Strengthened Violence Against Women Act," *Washington Post*, March 7, 2013, www.washingtonpost.com/politics/obama-signs-a-strengthened-violence-against-women-act/2013/03/07/e50d585e-8740-11e2-98a3-b3db6b9ac586_story.html (accessed 3/21/14).
22. *Romer v. Evans*, 517 U.S. 620 (1996).
23. *National Federation of Independent Business v. Sebelius*, 132 S. Ct. 2566 (2012).
24. *National Federation of Independent Business v. Sebelius*, p. 51.
25. Martha Derthick, *Keeping the Compound Republic: Essays on American Federalism* (Washington, DC: Brookings Institution, 2001), pp. 9–32.

What Do the Facts Say?

a. Hannah Bleau, "Florida's Coronavirus Case Average per Capita Lower Than All but Two States," Breitbart News, October 19, 2021, www.breitbart.com/politics/2021/10/19/floridas-coronavirus-case-average-per-capita-lower-than-all-but-two-states/ (accessed 12/22/21).
b. Philip Bump, "Ron DeSantis Can't Figure Out Who Made Covid All Political," *Washington Post*, October 28, 2021, www.washingtonpost.com/politics/2021/10/28/ron-desantis-cant-figure-out-who-made-covid-all-political/ (accessed 11/2/21).
c. Bump, "Ron DeSantis."

Chapter 4

1. *Kennedy v. Bremerton School District*, 597 U.S. ___ (2022).
2. *Kennedy v. Bremerton School District*, 597 U.S. ___ (2022), Justice Sotomayor dissent.
3. *Kennedy v. Bremerton School District*, 597 U.S. ___ (2022).
4. *Kennedy v. Bremerton School District*, 597 U.S. ___ (2022), Justice Sotomayor dissent.
5. *Arar v. Ashcroft et al.*, WL 346439 (E.D. N.Y. 2006). The case was dismissed because Arar, a Canadian citizen, did not have standing to sue the U.S. government. Supporters of this decision (and the practice more generally) say that it is an essential part of the War on Terror and that the enemy combatants who are arrested have no legal rights. Opponents say that the practice violates international law and our own standards of decency; furthermore, torture almost never produces useful information because people will say anything to get the torture to stop.
6. *State v. Massey et al.*, 51 S.E.2d 179 (N.C. 1949). The case was appealed to the Supreme Court, but the Court declined to hear the case, which means that the state decision stands (*Bunn v. North Carolina*, 336 U.S. 942 [1949]).
7. Alan Blinder, "Tennessee Pastor Disputes a Wildlife Possession Charge by State," *New York Times*, November 15, 2013, www.nytimes.com/2013/11/16/us/tennessee-pastor-disputes-wildlife-possession-charge-by-state.html?_r=0 (accessed 1/24/14).
8. *Pennsylvania v. Miller*, Court of Common Pleas, WL 31426193 (Penn. 2002). However, supreme courts in Minnesota, Wisconsin, and several other states have decided that requiring the Amish to use orange SMV triangles violates their free exercise of religion.
9. *Wisconsin v. Yoder*, 403 U.S. 205 (1972).
10. Jeffrey Rosen, "Lemon Law," *New Republic*, March 29, 1993, p. 17.
11. *Florida v. Jardines*, 569 U.S. 1 (2013), 6–7.
12. Max Farrand, ed., *The Records of the Federal Convention of 1787*, rev. ed. (New Haven, CT: Yale University Press, 1937), pp. 587–88, 617–18.
13. *The Papers of Thomas Jefferson*, ed. J. Boyd (Princeton, NJ: Princeton University Press, 1958), pp. 557–83, cited in Lester S. Jayson, ed., *The Constitution of the United States of*

America: Analysis and Interpretation (Washington, DC: U.S. Government Printing Office, 1973), p. 900.

14. Ralph Ketcham, *The Anti-Federalist Papers and the Constitutional Convention Debates* (New York: Signet Classics, Penguin Putnam, 2003), p. 247.
15. The two that were not ratified by the states were a complicated amendment on congressional apportionment and the pay raise amendment.
16. *Annals of Congress* 755 (August 17, 1789), cited in Lester S. Jayson, ed., *The Constitution of the United States of America* (Washington, DC: U.S. Government Printing Office, 1973), p. 898.
17. There is an intense scholarly debate on whether the authors of the Fourteenth Amendment intended for it to apply the Bill of Rights to the states. The strongest argument against this position is Raoul Berger's *The Fourteenth Amendment and the Bill of Rights* (Norman: University of Oklahoma Press, 1989), and a good book in support is Akhil Reed Amar's *The Bill of Rights* (New Haven, CT: Yale University Press, 1998).
18. *Barron v. Baltimore*, 32 U.S. 243 (1833), 250. The 1873 case was *Slaughter-House Cases*, 83 U.S. 36 (1873). The Supreme Court also declined to apply the Bill of Rights to the states in the *Civil Rights Cases*, 109 U.S. 3 (1883), in which the Court ruled that the Fourteenth Amendment did not give Congress the power to regulate the conduct of private business (thus the Civil Rights Act of 1875 was unconstitutional and private businesses could discriminate on the basis of race).
19. *Chicago, Burlington, and Quincy Railroad v. Chicago*, 166 U.S. 226 (1897); *Twining v. New Jersey*, 211 U.S. 78, 98 (1908).
20. *Gitlow v. New York*, 268 U.S. 652 (1925).
21. James Hutson, "'A Wall of Separation,'" *Library of Congress Information Bulletin* 57:6 (June 1998), www.loc.gov/loc/lcib/9806/danbury.html (accessed 3/3/08).
22. Henry J. Abraham and Barbara A. Perry, *Freedom and the Court: Civil Rights and Civil Liberties in the United States,* 8th ed. (Lawrence: University Press of Kansas, 2003), p. 300.
23. *Engel v. Vitale*, 370 U.S. 421 (1962).
24. *Wallace v. Jaffree*, 482 U.S. 38 (1985).
25. *Lee v. Weisman*, 505 U.S. 577 (1992); *Santa Fe Independent School District v. Doe*, 530 U.S. 290 (2000).
26. *Marsh v. Chambers*, 463 U.S. 783 (1983); *Jones v. Clear Creek Independent School*, 61 LW 3819 (1993); *Town of Greece, N.Y. v. Galloway*, 572 U.S. 565 (2014).
27. *Lemon v. Kurtzman*, 403 U.S. 602 (1971).
28. *Lynch v. Donnelly*, 465 U.S. 668 (1984), 672–73.
29. Jeffrey Rosen, "Big Ten," *New Republic*, March 14, 2004, p. 11.
30. *American Legion v. American Humanist Association*, 588 U.S. (2019).
31. *Kennedy v. Bremerton School District,* 597 U.S. ____ (2022), p. 23.
32. *Zelman v. Simmons-Harris*, 536 U.S. 639 (2002).
33. *Arizona Christian School Tuition Organization v. Winn*, U.S. Supreme Court slip. op. 09-987 and 09-991 (2011).
34. *Mitchell v. Helms*, 530 U.S. 793 (2000).
35. *Zobrest v. Catalina Foothills School District*, 509 U.S. 1 (1993). A similar decision in 1997 allowed a public school teacher to teach in a special program in a parochial school, *Agostini v. Felton*, 521 U.S. 203 (1997).
36. *Espinoza v. Montana Department of Revenue*, 591 U.S. (2020).
37. *Carson v. Makin*, 596 U.S. ____ (2022).
38. We will not cite all the cases here. See Abraham and Perry, *Freedom and the Court*, Chapter 6, for a summary of cases on this topic, especially Tables 6.1 and 6.2.
39. *Employment Division, Department of Human Resources of Oregon v. Smith*, 494 U.S. 872 (1990), 878–80. This case is often erroneously reported as having banned the religious use of peyote. In fact, the Court said: "Although it is constitutionally permissible to exempt sacramental peyote use from the operation of drug laws, it is not constitutionally required."
40. *City of Boerne v. Flores*, 521 U.S. 527 (1997); *Cutter v. Wilkinson*, No. 03-9877 (2005); *Gonzales v. O Centro Espirita Beneficente Uniao do Vegetal (UDV) et al.*, 546 U.S. 418 (2006). The Sherbert test requires that whenever the government limits religious expression, it must prove a compelling interest that is narrowly tailored to achieve that interest if a person is substantially burdened by the law (*Sherbert v. Verner*, 374 U.S. 398 [1963]).
41. *Burwell v. Hobby Lobby*, 573 U.S. 682 (2014).
42. In *Little Sisters of the Poor Saints Peter and Paul Home v. Pennsylvania*, 591 U.S. (2020), the Supreme Court upheld an administrative rule that overturned an Obama-era rule that had provided a workaround by having insurance pay directly for contraception for employees of private employers who objected to paying for it on religious grounds. The playground case, *Trinity Lutheran Church of Columbia, Inc. v. Comer*, 582 U.S. (2017), would appear to be an establishment clause case (can the state provide direct funds to a church?), but it was decided on free exercise grounds. This opens the door to a broader range of protections for religious activity. See Garrett Epps, "A Major Church-State Ruling That Shouldn't Have Happened," *The Atlantic*, June 27, 2017, www.theatlantic.com/politics/archive/2017/06/a-major-church-state-case-that-shouldnt-have-happened/531789 (accessed 10/18/17).
43. *Fulton v. City of Philadelphia*, 593 U.S. ____ (2021).
44. Jim Oleske, "Tandon Steals Fulton's Thunder: The Most Important Free Exercise Decision since 1990," SCOTUS Blog, April 15, 2021, www.scotusblog.com/2021/04/tandon-steals-fultons-thunder-the-most-important-free-exercise-decision-since-1990/ (accessed 1/12/22).
45. *Tandon v. Newsom*, 593 U.S. ____ (2021).
46. *National Federation of Independent Business v. Department of Labor, Occupational Safety and Health Administration*, 595 U.S. ____ (2022). However, the Court struck down the Biden administration's mandate for vaccinations or testing for large employers, but not on First Amendment grounds (see *Biden v. Missouri*, 595 U.S. ____ (2022).
47. *Masterpiece Cakeshop v. Colorado Civil Rights Commission*, 584 U.S. ____ (2018). In 2023 the Court ruled that a web designer did not have to create wedding websites for same-sex couples. However, the case was decided on the basis of free speech, rather than the free exercise clause. Refer to 303 *Creative LLC v. Elenis*, 600 U.S. 570 (2023).
48. *Police Department of Chicago v. Mosley*, 408 U.S. 92 (1972).
49. *United States v. O'Brien*, 391 U.S. 367 (1968); *Ladue v. Gilleo*, 512 U.S. 43 (1994).
50. *Schenck v. United States*, 249 U.S. 47 (1919), 52.
51. Alan Dershowitz, *Shouting Fire: Civil Liberties in a Turbulent Age* (New York: Little, Brown, 2002).
52. *Abrams v. United States*, 250 U.S. 616 (1919), 630–31.
53. *Dennis v. United States*, 341 U.S. 494 (1951).
54. *Brandenburg v. Ohio*, 395 U.S. 444 (1969).
55. *Snyder v. Phelps*, 131 S.Ct. 1207 (2011).
56. *Smith v. Goguen*, 415 U.S. 566 (1974).
57. *Tinker v. Des Moines School District*, 393 U.S. 503 (1969).
58. *Spence v. Washington*, 418 U.S. 405 (1974).
59. *Spence v. Washington*, 418 U.S. 409–10 (1974).
60. *Texas v. Johnson*, 491 U.S. 397 (1989).

61. *United States v. Eichman*, 496 U.S. 310 (1990).
62. David Wright, "Trump: Burn the Flag, Go to Jail," CNN, November 29, 2016, www.cnn.com/2016/11/29/politics/donald-trump-flag-burning-penalty-proposal/index.html (accessed 10/18/17).
63. *United States v. O'Brien*, 391 U.S. 367, 376 (1968).
64. *Walker v. Texas Division, Sons of Confederate Veterans*, 576 U.S. (2015).
65. Southern Poverty Law Center, "SPLC Reports Over 160 Confederate Symbols Removed in 2020," February 23, 2021 www.splcenter.org/presscenter/splc-reports-over-160-confederate-symbols-removed-2020 (accessed 1/12/22).
66. *Buckley v. Valeo*, 424 U.S. 1 (1976).
67. *Davis v. Federal Election Commission*, 554 U.S. 724 (2008).
68. *Citizens United v. Federal Election Commission*, 558 U.S. 310 (2010); *McCutcheon v. Federal Election Commission*, 572 U.S. (2014).
69. *McConnell v. Federal Election Commission*, 540 U.S. 93 (2003).
70. *Board of Regents of the University of Wisconsin System et al., Petitioners v. Scott Harold Southworth et al.*, 529 U.S. 217 (2000).
71. One example was a speech code adopted at the University of Michigan that prohibited "any behavior, verbal or physical, that stigmatizes or victimizes an individual on the basis of race, ethnicity, religion, sex, sexual orientation, creed, national origin, ancestry, age, marital status, handicap, or Vietnam veteran status" and "creates an intimidating, hostile, or demeaning environment for educational pursuits, employment or participation in University-sponsored extra-curricular activities." Kermit L. Hall, "Free Speech on Public College Campuses: Overview," www.firstamendmentcenter.org/speech/pubcollege/overview.aspx (accessed 2/10/08).
72. One of the authors of this book took Introduction to American Politics in that lecture hall, and the other has taught many classes in the room. For a description of the controversy, see Dwight Adams and Holly V. Hays, "IU: Room with Mural of KKK Rally Will No Longer Be a Classroom," *Indianapolis Star*, September 29, 2017, www.indystar.com/story/news/2017/09/29/indiana-university-no-longer-use-room-mural-showing-kkk-rally-classroom/717308001 (accessed 10/18/17).
73. Susan Svrluga and Danielle Douglas-Gabriel, "After Harvard and Penn resignations, who wants to be a college president?," *Washington Post*, January 12, 2024, www.washingtonpost.com/education/2024/01/12/college-presidents-pressures-harvard-penn/ (accessed 6/13/24).
74. Fabiola Cineas, "The failure of the college president: How the top campus job became so complex and public this year," Vox, June 7, 2024, www.vox.com/politics/354208/college-presidents-resigned-israel-palestine (accessed 6/13/24).
75. *City of St. Paul v. RAV*, 505 U.S. 377 (1992).
76. *Virginia v. Black*, 538 U.S. 343 (2003).
77. The Editorial Board, "Hate Speech on Facebook," *New York Times*, May 30, 2013, www.nytimes.com/2013/05/31/opinion/misogynist-speech-on-facebook.html (accessed 1/28/14).
78. Facebook "community standards" on hate speech, www.facebook.com/communitystandards (accessed 1/28/14).
79. Jeff Rosen, "Who Decides? Civility v. Hate Speech on the Internet," *Insights on Law and Society* 13:2 (Winter 2013): 32–36.
80. Mike Isaac, "Why Everyone Is Angry at Facebook over Its Political Ads Policy," *New York Times*, November 22, 2019, www.nytimes.com/2019/11/22/technology/campaigns-pressure-facebook-political-ads.html (accessed 1/29/20).
81. "Elected Officials Suspended or Banned from Social Media Platforms," Ballotpedia, January 4, 2022, https://ballotpedia.org/Elected_officials_suspended_or_banned_from_social_media_platforms (accessed 1/12/22).
82. *Packingham v. North Carolina*, 582 U.S. (2017).
83. *Mahanoy Area School District v. B. L.*, 594 U.S. ____ (2021).
84. *De Jonge v. State of Oregon*, 299 U.S. 353 (1937); *Edwards v. South Carolina*, 372 U.S. 229 (1963).
85. US Protest Law Tracker, International Center for Not-for-Profit Law, January 6, 2022, www.icnl.org/usprotestlawtracker/ (accessed 1/12/22).
86. *Dream Defenders v. DeSantis*, 4:21cv191-MW/MAF (N.D. Fla. Aug. 9, 2021), www.courthousenews.com/wp-content/uploads/2021/09/ruling-against-riot-law.pdf (accessed 1/13/22).
87. *Frisby et al. v. Schultz et al.*, 487 U.S. 474 (1988).
88. See UF Free Speech, Dialogue and Discourse, University of Florida, https://freespeech.ufl.edu/ for a discussion of all the related issues (accessed 3/7/18).
89. *McCullen v. Coakley*, 573 U.S. 464 (2014).
90. *New York Times Co. v. United States*, 403 U.S. 713 (1971).
91. *New York Times Co. v. United States*, 403 U.S. 713 (1971).
92. Quotation from James Risen, "Reporters Face New Threats from the Governments They Cover," *New York Times*, January 26, 2020, www.nytimes.com/2020/01/26/opinion/greenwald-brazil-reporter.html; also see Alex Emmons, "The Espionage Act Is Again Deployed against a Government Official Leaking to the Media," *The Intercept*, October 9 2019, https://theintercept.com/2019/10/09/the-espionage-act-is-again-deployed-against-a-government-official-leaking-to-the-media/ (both accessed 1/29/20).
93. *Chaplinsky v. State of New Hampshire*, 315 U.S. 568 (1942).
94. *Chaplinsky v. State of New Hampshire*, 315 U.S. 568 (1942).
95. *New York Times v. Sullivan*, 376 U.S. 254 (1964), cited in Abraham and Perry, *Freedom and the Court*, p. 193.
96. *Hustler v. Falwell*, 485 U.S. 46 (1988).
97. Jeffrey Toobin, "Gawker's Demise and the Trump-Era Threat to the First Amendment," *New Yorker*, December 19 and 26, 2016, www.newyorker.com/magazine/2016/12/19/gawkers-demise-and-the-trump-era-threat-to-the-first-amendment (accessed 10/16/2017).
98. "Melania Trump and *Daily Mail* Settle Her Libel Suits," *New York Times*, April 12, 2017, www.nytimes.com/2017/04/12/business/media/melania-trump-daily-mail-libel.html (accessed 10/16/17).
99. Adam Liptak, "Can Trump Change Libel Laws?," *New York Times*, March 30, 2017, www.nytimes.com/2017/03/30/us/politics/can-trump-change-libel-laws.html (accessed 10/16/17).
100. See Dareh Gregorian, "Trump Faces a Pile of Lawsuits as Depositions Begin," NBCNews.com, October 18, 2021, www.nbcnews.com/politics/donald-trump/trump-faces-pile-civil-lawsuits-depositions-begin-n1281612 for a list of the 10 civil suits that President Trump faced after he left office (accessed 1/13/22); Dan Mangan, "Trial for Trump Rape Defamation Lawsuit by Writer E. Jean Carroll Set for February," CNBC, July 19, 2022, www.cnbc.com/2022/07/19/trial-for-trump-rape-defamation-lawsuit-by-e-jean-carroll-scheduled.html (accessed 7/26/22). Kara Scannell, "Judge affirms $83.3 million verdict against Donald Trump in E. Jean Carroll defamation case," CNN, February 8, 2024, https://www.cnn.com/2024/02/08/politics/e-jean-carroll-judge-affirms-verdict/index.html (accessed 6/16/24).

101. *Valentine v. Chrestensen*, 316 U.S. 52 (1942).
102. *Virginia State Board of Pharmacy v. Virginia Citizens Consumer Council, Inc.*, 425 U.S. 748 (1976); *City of Cincinnati v. Discovery Network, Inc. et al.*, 507 U.S. 410 (1993).
103. *Central Hudson Gas & Electric Corp. v. Public Service Commission*, 447 U.S. 557 (1980).
104. *Matal v. Tam*, 582 U.S. (2017).
105. *Iancu v. Brunetti*, 588 U.S. (2019).
106. In 1996, Congress passed the Child Pornography Prevention Act. This law makes the possession, production, or distribution of child pornography a criminal offense punishable with up to 15 years in jail and a fine. However, two parts of the law were struck down by the Court for being "overbroad and unconstitutional." *Ashcroft v. Free Speech Coalition*, 353 U.S. 234 (2002).
107. *Jacobellis v. Ohio*, 378 U.S. 184, 197 (1964).
108. *Roth v. United States*, 354 U.S. 476 (1957).
109. *Miller v. California*, 413 U.S. 15 (1973).
110. *Federal Communications Commission v. Pacifica Foundation*, 438 U.S. 726 (1978).
111. *Federal Communications Commission et al. v. Fox Television Stations*, 556 U.S. 502 (2009).
112. *Federal Communications Commission and United States v. CBS Corporation*, 556 U.S. 1218 (2009).
113. *Federal Communications Commission v. Fox Television Stations*, 567 U.S. (2012); *Federal Communications Commission v. CBS Corporation*, no. 11–1240 (2012), writ of *certiorari* denied.
114. *United States v. Stevens*, 559 U.S. 460 (2010).
115. *Brown v. Entertainment Merchants Association*, 564 U.S. (2011).
116. David French, "Of Course the Second Amendment Protects an Individual Right to Keep and Bear Arms," *National Review*, April 13, 2016, www.nationalreview.com/2016/04/second-amendment-protects-individual-right-keep-bear-arms (accessed 3/29/18).
117. Dorothy Samuels, "The Second Amendment Was Never Meant to Protect an Individual's Right to a Gun," *The Nation*, September 23, 2015, www.thenation.com/article/how-the-roberts-court-undermined-sensible-gun-control/; John Paul Stevens, "Repeal the Second Amendment," *New York Times*, March 27, 2018, www.nytimes.com/2018/03/27/opinion/john-paul-stevens-repeal-second-amendment.html (accessed 3/29/18).
118. Gun Violence Archive, www.gunviolencearchive.org (accessed 1/13/22).
119. The FBI defines an active shooter as "an individual actively engaged in killing or attempting to kill people in a confined and populated area." For data on active shooters, see Federal Bureau of Investigation, Office of Partner Engagement, "Active Shooter Incidents 20-Year Review from 2000 to 2019," www.fbi.gov/file-repository/active-shooter-incidents-20-year-review-2000-2019-060121.pdf/view and "Active Shooter Incidents in the United States in 2020," www.fbi.gov/file-repository/active-shooter-incidents-in-the-us-2020-070121.pdf/view (both accessed 1/13/20).
120. Giffords Law Center, "Giffords Gun Law Center Gun Law Trendwatch: 2021 Year-End Review," https://giffords.org/lawcenter/trendwatch/giffords-law-center-gun-law-trendwatch-2021-year-end-review/ (accessed 1/13/22).
121. *District of Columbia v. Heller*, 554 U.S. 290 (2008).
122. *McDonald v. Chicago*, 561 U.S. 742 (2010).
123. Robert J. Spitzer, *The Politics of Gun Control* (Chatham, NJ: Chatham House, 1995). Also see www.bradycampaign.org/reforming-gun-industry-practices for a complete list of the cases (accessed 6/27/18). The two cases recognizing the individual right to bear arms were *United States v. Timothy Joe Emerson*, 46 F. Supp. 2d 598 (1999), and the D.C. Circuit Court case that was appealed in the landmark ruling *Parker v. District of Columbia*, 478 F.3d 370 (D.C. Cir. 2007).
124. *New York State Rifle & Pistol Association, Inc. v. Bruen*, 597 U.S. ___ (2022).
125. The second-place country to the United States is actually the Falkland Islands (at 62.1), but there are only 3,000 people in that nation. All data are from the Switzerland-based Small Arms Survey; see especially Aaron Karp, "Estimating Global Civilian-Held Firearms Numbers," June 2018, www.smallarmssurvey.org/fileadmin/docs/T-Briefing-Papers/SAS-BP-Civilian-Firearms-Numbers.pdf; for a complete list of nations, see www.smallarmssurvey.org/fileadmin/docs/Weapons_and_Markets/Tools/Firearms_holdings/SAS-BP-Civilian-held-firearms-annexe.pdf (both accessed 1/31/20).
126. *Gun Owners of America, Inc. v. Garland*, No. 19-1298 (6th Cir. 2021). *Garland v. Cargill*, Docket No. 22-976, June 14, 2024, https://www.supremecourt.gov/opinions/23pdf/22-976_e29g.pdf (accessed 6/16/24).
127. "Fact Sheet: Highlights from the Biden Administration's Historic Efforts to Reduce Gun Violence," White House Briefing Room, December 14, 2021, www.whitehouse.gov/briefing-room/statements-releases/2021/12/14/fact-sheet-highlights-from-the-biden-administrations-historic-efforts-to-reduce-gun-violence/ (accessed 1/14/22).
128. Jessica Bursztynsky, "President Biden Signs Bipartisan Gun Reform Bill into Law," CNBC, June 25, 2022, www.cnbc.com/2022/06/25/president-biden-signs-bipartisan-gun-reform-bill-into-law.html (accessed 7/26/22).
129. Giffords Law Center, "Post-*Heller* Litigation Summary," January 2022, https://giffords.org/lawcenter/gun-laws/litigation/post-heller-litigation-summary/ (accessed 1/13/22).
130. *New Jersey v. T. L. O.*, 469 U.S. 325 (1985); *Safford United School District No. 1 et al. v. Redding*, 557 U.S. 364 (2009).
131. See Abraham and Perry, *Freedom and the Court*, Chapter 4, for a discussion of these cases. The most recent case is *Kentucky v. King*, 563 U.S. 452 (2011).
132. *Florence v. Board of Chosen Freeholders*, 566 U.S. 318 (2012).
133. *Maryland v. King*, 133 S.Ct. 1958 (2013).
134. *Mitchell v. Wisconsin*, 588 U.S. (2019).
135. *Riley v. California*, 573 U.S. 373 (2014).
136. *United States v. Jones*, 565 U.S. 400 (2012).
137. *Carpenter v. United States*, 585 U.S. (2018).
138. *Merchant v. Mayorkas*, U.S. Court of Appeals for the First Circuit, No. 20-1505, 2020. The U.S. Supreme Court declined to hear the case on June 28, 2021 (see www.scotusblog.com/case-files/cases/merchant-v-mayorkas/; accessed 1/14/22).
139. *Mapp v. Ohio*, 367 U.S. 643 (1961).
140. *Herring v. United States*, 555 U.S. 135 (2009).
141. *Utah v. Strieff*, 579 U.S. (2016).
142. *Vernonia School District v. Acton*, 515 U.S. 646 (1995); *Board of Education of Pottawatomie County v. Earls*, 536 U.S. 832 (2002).
143. *Chandler v. Miller*, 520 U.S. 305 (1997).
144. National Public Radio, "Political Comebacks: The Art of the Putdown," *Morning Edition*, May 12, 2008, www.npr.org/templates/story/story.php?storyId=90337494 (accessed 5/7/20).
145. Leslie Cauley, "NSA Has Massive Database of Americans' Phone Calls," *USA Today*, May 11, 2006, p. 1.

146. Andrew Crocker and David Ruiz, "How Congress's Extension of Section 702 May Expand the NSA's Warrantless Surveillance Authority," Electronic Frontier Foundation, February 1, 2018, www.eff.org/deeplinks/2018/02/how-congresss-extension-section-702-may-expand-nsas-warrantless-surveillance (accessed 6/14/18). "Biden signs bill reauthorizing contentious FISA surveillance program," CBS News, April 20, 2024, https://www.cbsnews.com/news/biden-signs-bill-reauthorizing-fisa-surveillance-program-section-702/ (accessed 6/16/24).
147. Lorraine Woellert and Dawn Kopecki, "The Snooping Goes beyond Phone Calls," *Business Week*, May 29, 2006, p. 38; "Data Mining: Federal Efforts Cover a Wide Range of Uses," GAO Report 04-548, May 2004, www.gao.gov/assets/250/242241.pdf (accessed 5/13/14).
148. Anthony Cuthbertson, "AT&T Spying Program Is 'Worse Than Snowden Revelations,'" *Newsweek*, October 26, 2016, www.newsweek.com/att-spying-program-worse-snowden-revelations-513812 (accessed 10/23/17).
149. Jennifer Stisa Granick and Ashley Gorski, "How to Address Newly Revealed Abuses of Section 702 Surveillance," Just Security, Reiss Center on Law and Security at New York University School of Law, October 18, 2019; www.justsecurity.org/66622/how-to-address-newly-revealed-abuses-of-section-702-surveillance/ (accessed 1/31/20); Eric Lichtblau and James Risen, "Officials Say U.S. Wiretaps Exceeded Law," *New York Times*, April 16, 2009; for a good balanced discussion of the Section 702 certifications, see George Croner, "To Oversee or to Overrule: What Is the Role of the Foreign Intelligence Surveillance Court Under FISA Section 702?," Lawfare, May 18, 2021, www.lawfareblog.com/oversee-or-overrule-what-role-foreign-intelligence-surveillance-court-under-fisa-section-702 (accessed 1/14/22).
150. *Miranda v. Arizona*, 384 U.S. 436 (1966).
151. *New York v. Quarles*, 467 U.S. 649 (1984).
152. *Dickerson v. United States*, 530 U.S. 428 (2000).
153. *Benton v. Maryland*, 395 U.S. 784 (1969).
154. This "separate sovereigns" exception was established in *Abbate v. United States*, 359 U.S. 187 (1959), and recently confirmed in *Gamble v. United States*, 587 U.S. (2019).
155. *Kelo v. City of New London*, 545 U.S. 469 (2005).
156. National Conference of State Legislatures, "Eminent Domain Overview," January 1, 2012, www.ncsl.org/research/environment-and-natural-resources/eminent-domain-overview.aspx (accessed 1/31/14).
157. The 2017 case *Murr v. Wisconsin*, 582 U.S. (2017), involved a property owner who tried to sell a lot that was contiguous to another lot that he owned; he did not have to be compensated for the value of that lot when it was rendered worthless by a state regulation. The recent cases that ruled in favor of property owners were *Arkansas Game and Fish Commission v. United States*, 568 U.S. 23 (2012); *Koontz v. St. Johns River Water Management District*, 568 U.S. 936 (2013); and *Horne v. United States Department of Agriculture*, 569 U.S. 513 (2013).
158. *Cedar Point Nursery v. Hassid*, 594 U.S. ___ (2021). For an excellent analysis of the decision from a law professor who generally supports stronger property rights, see Josh Blackman, "*Cedar Point Nursery v. Hassid* Quietly Rewrote Four Decades of Takings Clause Doctrine," June 25, 2021, Reason.com, https://reason.com/volokh/2021/06/25/cedar-point-nursery-v-hassid-quietly-rewrote-four-decades-of-takings-clause-doctrine/; for a more critical view, see Ross Slaughter, "Property Owners Win Big in *Cedar Point Nursery v. Hassid*, June 23, 2021, https://onlabor.org/property-owners-win-big-in-cedar-point-nursery-v-hassid/ (accessed 1/14/22). Also, in 2019 the Court ruled that property owners who believe their property has been unfairly taken by local governments can sue for compensation directly in federal court without having to first bring the case in state court, which was a major victory for property owners (*Knick v. Township of Scott, Pennsylvania*, 588 U.S. ___ (2019)).
159. *Powell v. Alabama*, 287 U.S. 45 (1932).
160. *Gideon v. Wainwright*, 372 U.S. 335 (1963).
161. *Evitts v. Lucy*, 469 U.S. 387 (1985); *Wiggins v. Smith*, 539 U.S. 510 (2003). See Elizabeth Gable and Tyler Green, "*Wiggins v. Smith*: The Ineffective Assistance of Counsel Standard Applied Twenty Years after *Strickland*," *Georgetown Journal of Legal Ethics* (Summer 2004): 755–71, for a discussion of many of these issues.
162. Adam Liptak, "Justices' Ruling Expands Rights of Accused in Plea Bargains," *New York Times*, March 21, 2012, www.nytimes.com/2012/03/22/us/supreme-court-says-defendants-have-right-to-good-lawyers.html; the cases were *Missouri v. Galin E. Frye*, 566 U.S. 134 (2012) and *Lafler v. Cooper*, 566 U.S. 156 (2012) (accessed 1/14/22).
163. *Klopfer v. North Carolina*, 386 U.S. 213 (1967).
164. The law is 18 U.S.C. § 3161(c)(1) and the ruling is *Zedner v. United States*, 47 U.S. 489 (2006).
165. The case concerning Black Americans is *Batson v. Kentucky*, 106 S.Ct. 1712 (1986); the case about Latinos is *Hernandez v. New York*, 500 U.S. 352 (1991); and the gender case is *J.E.B. v. Alabama ex rel. T.B.*, 511 U.S. 127 (1994). Three more-recent cases affirming that peremptory challenges cannot be used in a racially discriminatory fashion are *Miller-El v. Dretke*, 545 U.S. 231 (2005); *Snyder v. Louisiana*, 552 U.S. 472 (2008); and *Flowers v. Mississippi*, 588 U.S. (2019).
166. *Peña-Rodriguez v. Colorado*, 580 U.S. (2017).
167. Data for 2021 are from "Executions Overview," Death Penalty Information Center, https://deathpenaltyinfo.org/executions/executions-overview; historical data are from "Executions by State and Year," www.deathpenaltyinfo.org/executions-year (accessed 1/14/22); *Hall v. Florida*, 572 U.S. 701 (2014).
168. Erik Eckholm, "One Execution Botched, Oklahoma Delays the Next," *New York Times*, April 29, 2014, www.nytimes.com/2014/04/30/us/oklahoma-executions.html (accessed 5/13/14).
169. *Furman v. Georgia*, 408 U.S. 238 (1972); *Gregg v. Georgia*, 428 U.S. 513 (1976).
170. *Moore v. Texas*, 581 U.S. (2017).
171. See Abraham and Perry, *Freedom and the Court*, pp. 72–73, for a discussion of the earlier cases, and Charles Lane, "5–4 Supreme Court Abolishes Juvenile Executions," *Washington Post*, March 2, 2005, p. A1, for a discussion of the 2002 and 2005 cases. The cases were *Atkins v. Virginia*, 536 U.S. 304 (2002); *Roper v. Simmons*, 543 U.S. 551 (2005); and *Kennedy v. Louisiana*, 554 U.S. 407 (2008).
172. *Jones v. Mississippi*, 593 U.S. ___ (2021).
173. *Griswold v. Connecticut*, 381 U.S. 479 (1965), 482–86.
174. *Griswold v. Connecticut*, 381 U.S. 479 (1965), 511–12.
175. *Roe v. Wade*, 410 U.S. 113 (1973), 129.
176. *Planned Parenthood of Southeastern Pennsylvania v. Casey*, 505 U.S. 833 (1992).
177. Erik Eckholm, "Access to Abortion Falling as States Pass Restrictions," *New York Times*, January 3, 2014, www.nytimes.com/2014/01/04/us/women-losing-access-to-abortion-as-opponents-gain-ground-in-state-legislatures.html (accessed 1/31/14).

178. *Whole Woman's Health v. Hellerstedt*, 579 U.S. (2016).

179. *Dobbs v. Jackson Women's Health Organization*, 597 U.S. ____ (2022); Annette Choi and Devan Cole, "See where abortions are banned and legal—and where it's still in limbo," CNN, May 2, 2024, https://www.cnn.com/us/abortion-access-restrictions-bans-us-dg/index.html (accessed 6/17/24).

180. *Bowers v. Hardwick*, 478 U.S. 186 (1986).

181. *Lawrence v. Texas*, 539 U.S. 558 (2003).

Take a Stand

a. Oral arguments in *U.S. v. Jones* (2012), November 8, 2011, www.supremecourt.gov/oral_arguments/argument_transcripts/2011/10-1259.pdf, p. 44 (accessed 4/9/18).

b. Gilad Edelman, "Can the Government Buy Its Way around the Fourth Amendment?," *Wired*, February 11, 2020, www.wired.com/story/can-government-buy-way-around-fourth-amendment/(accessed January 8, 2022).

c. "Wyden, Paul and Bipartisan Members of Congress Introduce The Fourth Amendment Is Not For Sale Act," April 21, 2021, www.wyden.senate.gov/news/press-releases/wyden-paul-and-bipartisan-members-of-congress-introduce-the-fourth-amendment-is-not-for-sale-act- (accessed January 8, 2022).

d. "You Have No Privacy—Get over It," Fox Business, March 4, 2016, www.foxbusiness.com/features/you-have-no-privacy-get-over-it (accessed January 8, 2022).

Chapter 5

1. Marianna Sotomayor, "Biden Condemns Death of George Floyd, Says Black Lives Are 'Under Threat,'" NBC News, May 27, 2020, www.nbcnews.com/politics/meet-the-press/blog/meet-press-blog-latest-news-analysis-data-driving-political-discussion-n988541/ncrd1215756#blogHeader (accessed 3/22/22).

2. Joe Biden, "President Biden's State of the Union Address," White House, March 1, 2022, www.whitehouse.gov/state-of-the-union-2022/ (accessed 3/22/22).

3. Nathaniel Rakich, "How Americans Feel about 'Defunding the Police,'" FiveThirtyEight, June 19, 2020, https://fivethirtyeight.com/features/americans-like-the-ideas-behind-defunding-the-police-more-than-the-slogan-itself/ (accessed 1/29/22).

4. There are eight commissioners on the U.S. Commission on Civil Rights, four appointed by the president and four by Congress. The commissioners serve six-year terms and do not require Senate confirmation, and no more than four members may be of the same political party.

5. Howard Dodson, "How Slavery Helped Build a World Economy," in Schomburg Center for Research in Black Culture of the New York Public Library, *Jubilee: The Emergence of African-American Culture* (Washington, DC: National Geographic Press, 2003).

6. Marc Howard Ross, *Slavery in the North: Forgetting History and Recovering Memory* (Philadelphia: University of Pennsylvania Press, 2018).

7. U.S. Census, *A Century of Population Growth: From the First Census of the United States to the Twelfth, 1790–1900*, Chapter 14, "Statistics of Slaves," www2.census.gov/prod2/decennial/documents/00165897ch14.pdf, p. 133 (accessed 1/30/22). Several non-southern states had almost no enslaved people: Massachusetts had one and Maine had two in the 1830 census, and Michigan, Ohio, and Wisconsin had a total of 76 enslaved people in various censuses after they became states.

8. Other provisions of the Compromise of 1850, which was a package of five bills, included creating the current boundaries for Texas as it dropped its claim to land in parts of five current states in exchange for the federal government's assumption of $10 million in debt from the old Texas Republic. Also, the trading of enslaved people, but not slavery itself, was abolished in the District of Columbia. See "The Compromise of 1850," Primary Documents in American History, Library of Congress, www.loc.gov/rr/program/bib/ourdocs/Compromise1850.html (accessed 2/23/22).

9. John W. Wright, ed., *New York Times 2000 Almanac* (New York: Penguin Reference, 1999), p. 165. Estimates from various online sources are quite a bit higher, averaging about 620,000 deaths.

10. Pema Levy, "How a Three-Word Phrase Sabotaged Black Voting Rights, and How They Can Be Reconstructed," *Mother Jones*, March/April 2021, www.motherjones.com/politics/2021/02/14th-amendment-section-2-mass-incarceration/ (accessed 2/1/22).

11. V. O. Key Jr., *Southern Politics in State and Nation* (New York: Knopf, 1949), p. 538. For example, the Louisiana grandfather clause read: "No male person who was on January 1, 1867, or at any date prior thereto, entitled to vote under the Constitution of the United States, wherein he then resided, and no son or grandson of any such person not less than twenty-one years of age at the date of the adoption of this Constitution . . . shall be denied the right to register and vote in this State by reason of his failure to possess the educational or property qualifications." Grandfather clauses as they applied to voting were ruled unconstitutional in 1915.

12. Chandler Davidson, "The Voting Rights Act: A Brief History," in *Controversies in Minority Voting: The Voting Rights Act in Perspective*, ed. Bernard Grofman and Chandler Davidson (Washington, DC: Brookings Institution, 1992), p. 21.

13. Equal Justice Initiative, *Lynching in America: Confronting the Legacy of Racial Terror*, 3rd ed. (2017), https://lynchinginamerica.eji.org/report/ (accessed 2/23/22).

14. "Indian Removal: 1814–1848," Public Broadcasting System, www.pbs.org/wgbh/aia/part4/4p2959.html (accessed 2/23/22).

15. Kevin Waite, "What Slavery Looked Like in the West," *Atlantic*, November 25, 2021, www.theatlantic.com/ideas/ archive/2021/11/native-americans-indigenous-slavery-west/620785/ (accessed 2/2/22).

16. Donald L. Fixico, "When Native Americans Were Slaughtered in the Name of 'Civilization,'" History.com, August 16, 2019, www.history.com/news/native-americans-genocide-united-states (accessed 2/23/22).

17. Bruce E. Johansen, *The Native Peoples of North America* (New Brunswick, NJ: Rutgers University Press, 2006); Russell Thornton, *American Indian Holocaust and Survival: A Population History since 1492* (Norman: University of Oklahoma Press, 1990), pp. 26–32; Henry F. Dobyns, *Their Number Become Thinned: Native American Population Dynamics in Eastern North America* (Knoxville: University of Tennessee Press, 1983).

18. One of the most horrifying examples of the brutal treatment of Native Americans was giving blankets that had been contaminated with smallpox to natives. There is at least one documented instance of this happening in 1763 (see Elizabeth A. Fenn, "Biological Warfare in Eighteenth-Century North America: Beyond Jeffery Amherst," *Journal of American History* 86:4 (March 2000): 1552–80; for a more general discussion of the evidence, see Patrick H. Kiger, "Did Colonists Give Infected Blankets to Native Americans as Biological Warfare?," History.com, November 25, 2019, www.history.com/news/colonists-native-americans-smallpox-blankets (accessed 2/1/22).

19. *Cherokee Nation v. Georgia*, 30 U.S. 1 (1831). This was the case in which the Supreme Court paved the way for the "Trail of Tears," saying that while it was sympathetic to the Cherokee Nation's case, it did not have jurisdiction in the case because of their status as a domestic dependent nation.

20. The Smithsonian Institution has recently digitized 374 ratified Native American treaties. While it is impossible to determine the precise number of treaties that were ignored or actively broken, scholarly consensus is that most of the treaties served the interests of the U.S. government and not the Native American tribes (Nora McGreevy, "Hundreds of Native American Treaties Digitized for the First Time," *Smithsonian Magazine*, October 15, 2020, www.smithsonianmag.com/smart-news/hundreds-native-american-treaties-digitized-and-online-first-time-180976056/ (accessed 2/1/22); Suzan Shown Harjo, *Nation to Nation: Treaties between the United States and American Indian Nations* (Washington, DC: Smithsonian Books, 2014).

21. "Land Tenure History," Indian Land Tenure Foundation, https://iltf.org/land-issues/history/ (accessed 2/2/22).

22. Ronald Mann, "Justices Toe Hard Line in Affirming *Reservation Status for Eastern Oklahoma*," SCOTUSblog, July 9, 2020, www.scotusblog.com/2020/07/opinionanalysis-justices-toe-hard-line-in-affirming-reservationstatus-for-eastern-oklahoma/ (accessed 2/2/22).

23. *McGirt v. Oklahoma*, 2020, 591 U.S., slip. op., p. 28. This was a rare case in which Justice Gorsuch voted with the four liberals and Justice Roberts was not in the majority in a 5–4 decision.

24. Andrea Smith, "Soul Wound: The Legacy of Native American Schools," *Amnesty International Magazine*, posted on News around Indian Country, Lara Trace Hentz, October 9, 2015, https://laratracehentz.wordpress.com/2015/10/09/soul-wound-the-legacy-of-native-american-schools/ (accessed 2/23/22).

25. Daniel M. Cobb, *Beyond Red Power: American Indian Politics and Activism since 1900* (School for Advanced Research Press, 2007); Roxanne Dunbar-Ortiz, *"All the Real Indians Died Off": And 20 Other Myths about Native Americans* (Boston: Beacon, 2016).

26. *United States v. Wong Kim Ark*, 169 U.S. 649 (1898).

27. Bilal Qureshi, "From Wrong to Right: A U.S. Apology for Japanese Internment," National Public Radio, August 9, 2013, www.npr.org/sections/codeswitch/2013/08/09/210138278/japanese-internment-redress (accessed 2/23/22).

28. *Trump v. Hawaii*, 585 U.S. (2018).

29. Kimmy Yam, "Anti-Asian Hate Crimes Increased 339 Percent Nationwide Last Year, Report Says," NBC News, January 31, 2022, www.nbcnews.com/news/asian-america/anti-asian-hate-crimes-increased-339-percent-nationwide-last-year-repo-rcna14282 (accessed 2/2/22).

30. Bruce Y. Lee, "Trump Once Again Calls Covid-19 Coronavirus the 'Kung Flu,'" *Forbes*, June 24, 2020, www.forbes.com/sites/brucelee/2020/06/24/trump-once-again-calls-covid-19-coronavirus-the-kung-flu/?sh=4af0c4201f59 (accessed 2/2/22).

31. This Day in History, "Abigail Adams Urges Husband to 'Remember the Ladies,'" Abigail Adams to John Adams, March 31, 1776, History.com, www.history.com/this-day-in-history/abigail-adams-urges-husband-to-remember-the-ladies (accessed 2/23/22).

32. *Bradwell v. Illinois*, 83 U.S. 130 (1873).

33. *Hoyt v. Florida*, 368 U.S. 57 (1961).

34. Lucian K. Truscott IV, "The Real Mob at Stonewall," *New York Times*, June 25, 2009, p. A19.

35. "LGBT" (various surveys), PollingReport.com, www.pollingreport.com/lgbt.htm; Justin McCarthy, "Gallup First Polled on Gay Issues in '77. What Has Changed?," Gallup, June 6, 2019, https://news.gallup.com/poll/258065/gallup-first-polled-gay-issues-changed.aspx; Justin McCarthy, "U.S. Support for Gay Marriage Stable, at 63%," Gallup, May 22, 2019, https://news.gallup.com/poll/257705/support-gay-marriage-stable.aspx (all accessed 2/23/22).

36. *Obergefell v. Hodges*, 576 U.S. (2015).

37. Sean Cahill, "Trump Administration Amasses Striking Anti-LGBT Record in First Year," *The Hill*, January 19, 2018, http://thehill.com/opinion/campaign/369790-trump-administration-amasses-striking-anti-lgbt-record-in-first-year (accessed 2/23/22). For a complete list, see "Trump's Record of Action against Transgender People," Center for Transgender Equality, https://transequality.org/the-discrimination-administration (accessed 2/3/22).

38. Mary Beth Musumeci et al., "Recent and Anticipated Actions to Reverse Trump Administration Section 1557 Non-Discrimination Rules," Kaiser Family Foundation, June 9, 2021, www.kff.org/racial-equity-and-health-policy/issue-brief/recent-and-anticipated-actions-to-reverse-trump-administration-section-1557-non-discrimination-rules/ (accessed 2/23/22).

39. For the executive order on transgender people in the military, see White House, "Executive Order on Enabling All Americans to Serve Their Country in Uniform," January 25, 2021, www.whitehouse.gov/briefing-room/presidential-actions/2021/01/25/executive-order-on-enabling-all-qualified-americans-to-serve-their-country-in-uniform/; for the executive order on preventing and combating discrimination on the basis of gender identity or sexual orientation, see White House, "Executive Order on Preventing and Combating Discrimination on the Basis of Gender Identity or Sexual Orientation," January 20, 2021, www.whitehouse.gov/briefing-room/presidential-actions/2021/01/20/executive-order-preventing-and-combating-discrimination-on-basis-of-gender-identity-or-sexual-orientation/; and on overturning Trump's HHS rule on health care, see Amy Goldstein, "Biden Administration Revives Anti-bias Protections in Health Care for Transgender People," *Washington Post*, May 10, 2021, www.washingtonpost.com/health/transgender-protection-hhs/2021/05/10/0852ce88-b17d-11eb-a980-a60af976ed44_story.html (all accessed 2/3/22).

40. "Charge Statistics, FY 1997 through FY 2023," U.S. Equal Employment Opportunity Commission, https://www.eeoc.gov/data/enforcement-and-litigation-statistics-0 (accessed 7/2/24). The number of charges was lower during the Trump years, averaging 69,468 cases during his presidency, and 84,743 for the four years before and two years after that.

41. "2023 Fair Housing Trends Report," National Fair Housing Alliance, https://nationalfairhousing.org/resource/2023-fair-housing-trends-report/ (accessed 7/2/24). 2022 had the highest number of cases ever reported at 33,007.

42. "Recent Accomplishments of the Housing and Civil Enforcement Section," U.S. Department of Justice, November 9, 2021, www.justice.gov/crt/recent-accomplishments-housing-and-civil-enforcement-section (accessed 2/3/22).

43. Davidson, "The Voting Rights Act," p. 22; also see U.S. Department of Justice, Civil Rights Division, "About Section 5 of the Voting Rights Act," www.justice.gov/crt/about-section-5-voting-rights-act (accessed 2/23/22), for a complete list of cases in which the Justice Department has denied "preclearance" of a change in an electoral practice under Section 5 of the Voting Rights Act. Note that in racially

homogenous single-member districts, candidates from historically marginalized groups usually win. But in at-large elections, in which representatives are elected citywide or countywide (and which thus may contain a racially diverse mix of voters from the districts making up the city or county), the majority-White voters can outvote the voters from historically marginalized groups and elect an all-White city council or school board.

44. "The Long Shadow of Jim Crow: Voter Suppression in America," Special Report, People for the American Way Foundation and NAACP, http://archive.fairvote.org/righttovote/PFAW-NAACP.pdf (accessed 2/23/22); "Election 2016: Restrictive Voting Laws by the Numbers," Brennan Center for Justice, September 28, 2016, www.brennancenter.org/analysis/election-2016-restrictive-voting-laws-numbers (accessed 2/23/22).

45. "Voting Laws Roundup: December 2021," Brennan Center for Justice, January 12, 2022, www.brennancenter.org/our-work/research-reports/voting-laws-roundup-december-2021. See the Brennan Center's review of recent academic research on the impact of these laws on turnout of voters from historically marginalized groups, "The Impact of Voter Suppression on Communities of Color," January 10, 2022, www.brennancenter.org/our-work/research-reports/impact-voter-suppression-communities-color (both accessed 2/3/22).

46. *Husted v. A. Philip Randolph Institute*, 584 U.S. (2018).

47. "Voting Laws Roundup: December 2021."

48. Carl Hulse, "After a Day of Debate, the Voting Rights Bill Is Blocked in the Senate," *New York Times,* January 19, 2022, www.nytimes.com/2022/01/19/us/politics/senate-voting-rights-filibuster.html (accessed 2/3/22).

49. Life expectancy data are from Elizabeth Arias, Betzaida Tejada-Vera, Farida Ahmad, and Kenneth D. Kochanek, "Provisional Life Expectancy Estimates for 2020," Centers for Disease Control and Prevention, July 2021, p. 2, www.cdc.gov/nchs/data/vsrr/vsrr015-508.pdf. Infant mortality numbers are from Donna L. Hoyert, "Maternal Mortality Rates in the United States, 2019," Division of Vital Statistics, National Center for Health Statistics, www.cdc.gov/nchs/data/hestat/maternal-mortality-2021/E-Stat-Maternal-Mortality-Rates-H.pdf (all accessed 2/3/22).

50. "Risk for COVID-19 Infection, Hospitalization, and Death By Race/Ethnicity," Centers for Disease Control and Prevention, February 1, 2022, www.cdc.gov/coronavirus/2019-ncov/covid-data/investigations-discovery/hospitalization-death-by-race-ethnicity.html (accessed 2/4/22).

51. For an application of these ideas to academic health centers, see Paris B. Adkins-Jackson, Rupinder K. Legha, and Kyle A. Jones, "How to Measure Racism in Academic Health Centers," *AMA Journal of Ethics* 23:2 (February 2021): E140–45, https://journalofethics.ama-assn.org/article/how-measure-racism-academic-health-centers/2021-02; also see Monique Tello, "Racism and Discrimination in Health Care: Providers and Patients," Harvard Health Blog, January 16, 2017, www.health.harvard.edu/blog/racism-discrimination-health-care-providers-patients-2017011611015 (both accessed 2/4/22).

52. See the National Resource Defense Council's program on environmental justice, www.nrdc.org/about/environmental-justice, and the Environmental Justice and Health Alliance for Chemical Policy reform's report "Who's in Danger? Race, Poverty, and Chemical Disasters," May 2014, http://comingcleaninc.org/assets/media/images/Reports/Who%27s%20in%20Danger%20Report%20FINAL.pdf (both accessed 2/23/22).

53. Steve Carmody, "5 Years after Flint's Crisis Began, Is the Water Safe?," National Public Radio, April 25, 2019, www.npr.org/2019/04/25/717104335/5-years-after-flints-crisis-began-is-the-water-safe (accessed 2/23/22).

54. Paul Egan, "Federal Judge Gives Final Approval to $626.25M Settlement in Flint Water Crisis," *Detroit Free Press,* November 10, 2021, www.freep.com/story/news/local/michigan/flint-water-crisis/2021/11/10/federal-judge-approves-settlement-flint-lead-poisoning-case/5556131001/ (accessed 2/4/22).

55. Frida Garza, "America's Dirty Divide: How Environmental Racism Leaves the Vulnerable Behind," *Guardian*, February 11, 2021, www.theguardian.com/us-news/2021/feb/11/environmental-racism-americas-dirty-divide; see the *Guardian*'s series on "America's Dirty Divide," www.theguardian.com/us-news/series/americas-dirty-divide; also see Hiroko Tabuchi and Nadja Popovich, "People of Color Breathe More Hazardous Air. The Sources Are Everywhere," *New York Times*, April 28, 2021, www.nytimes.com/2021/04/28/climate/air-pollution-minorities.html (accessed 2/4/22).

56. Anthony Nardone, Kara E. Rudolph, Rachel Morello-Frosch, and Joan A. Casey, "Redlines and Greenspace: The Relationship between Historical Redlining and 2010 Greenspace across the United States," *Environmental Health Perspectives* 129:1 (January 2021): 017006-1, https://ehp.niehs.nih.gov/doi/pdf/10.1289/EHP7495 (accessed 2/4/22).

57. Linda Villarosa, "Pollution Is Killing Black Americans. This Community Fought Back," *New York Times*, August 2, 2020, www.nytimes.com/2020/07/28/magazine/pollution-philadelphia-black-americans.html (accessed 2/4/22). Also note the examples of Native American resistance to the Keystone XL and Standing Rock pipelines noted above.

58. For a good overview and history, see David A. Harris, "Racial Profiling: Past, Present, and Future?," American Bar Association, *Criminal Justice Magazine* January 21, 2020, www.americanbar.org/groups/criminal_justice/publications/criminal-justice-magazine/2020/winter/racial-profiling-past-present-and-future/ (accessed 2/4/22).

59. Cristina Corbin, "Senate's Lone Black GOP Member Says Police Stopped Him 7 Times in a Year," Fox News, July 14, 2016, www.foxnews.com/politics/2016/07/14/senates-lone-black-gop-member-says-police-stopped-him-7-times-in-year.html (accessed 2/23/22).

60. Benjamin Weiser and Joseph Goldstein, "Mayor Says New York City Will Settle Suits on Stop-and-Frisk Tactics," *New York Times*, January 30, 2014, www.nytimes.com/2014/01/31/nyregion/de-blasio-stop-and-frisk.html (accessed 2/23/22).

61. For a summary of this research, see Radley Balko, "There's Overwhelming Evidence that the Criminal-Justice System Is Racist. Here's the Proof," *Washington Post*, September 18, 2018, www.washingtonpost.com/graphics/2020/opinions/systemic-racism-police-evidence-criminal-justice-system/ (accessed 2/4/22).

62. "Fatal Force," *Washington Post*, February 2, 2022, www.washingtonpost.com/graphics/investigations/police-shootings-database/ (accessed 2/4/22).

63. "Herstory," Black Lives Matter, https://blacklivesmatter.com/about/herstory (accessed 2/23/22).

64. Bill Chappell, "Derek Chauvin Is Sentenced to 22 1/2 Years for George Floyd's Murder," National Public Radio, June 25, 2021, www.npr.org/sections/trial-over-killing-of-george-floyd/2021/06/25/1009524284/derek-chauvin-sentencing-george-floyd-murder (accessed 2/4/22).

65. Janell Ross, "Police Officers Convicted for Fatal Shootings Are the Exception, Not the Rule," NBC News, March 13, 2019, www.nbcnews.com/news/nbcblk/police-officers-convicted-fatal-shootings-are-exception-not-rule-n982741 (accessed 2/23/22).

66. Lynne Peeples, "What the Data Say about Police Shootings: How Do Racial Biases Play into Deadly Encounters with the Police?," *Scientific American*, September 5, 2019, www.scientificamerican.com/article/what-the-data-say-about-police-shootings/ (accessed 2/23/22).

67. Federal Bureau of Investigation, "Hate Crime in the United States Incident Analysis," Crime Data Explorer, https://crime-data-explorer.app.cloud.gov/pages/explorer/crime/hate-crime (accessed 7/25/22).

68. Jesse McKinley and Glenn Thrush, "Buffalo Shooting Suspect Is Charged with Federal Hate Crimes," *New York Times*, June 15, 2022, www.nytimes.com/2022/06/15/nyregion/buffalo-shooting-hate-crime-charges.html (accessed 7/25/22).

69. Rosa Parks with James Haskins, *Rosa Parks: My Story* (New York: Dial Books, 1992), p. 116.

70. Clayborne Carson et al., eds., *The Eyes on the Prize Civil Rights Reader* (New York: Penguin Books, 1997).

71. *Boynton v. Virginia*, 363 U.S. 454 (1960).

72. David Halberstam, *The Children* (New York: Ballantine Books, 1999).

73. Matt Broomfield, "Women's March against Donald Trump Is the Largest Day of Protests in US History, Say Political Scientists," *Independent*, January 23, 2017, www.independent.co.uk/news/world/americas/womens-march-anti-donald-trump-womens-rights-largest-protest-demonstration-us-history-political-a7541081.html (accessed 2/23/22). Jeremy Pressman of the University of Connecticut and Erica Chenoweth of the University of Denver collected data on the Women's March, https://docs.google.com/spreadsheets/d/1xa0iLqYKz8x9Yc_rfhtmSOJQ2EGgeUVjvV4A8LsIaxY/edit#gid=0 (accessed 3/23/22). The low end of their estimate is 3,267,134, the high end is 5,246,670, and their "best guess" is 4,157,894.

74. "Dakota Access Pipeline in Operation after Months of Resistance," *PBS News Hour*, June 3, 2017, www.pbs.org/newshour/nation/dakota-access-pipeline-operation-months-resistance (accessed 2/23/22).

75. See Black Lives Matter, https://blacklivesmatter.com/ for more information about the movement, including the "Black Lives Matter 4-Year Anniversary Report" and news about recent events (accessed 2/23/22).

76. Beth Daley, "What If Tom Brady Took a Knee Instead of Colin Kaepernick?," The Conversation, October 21, 2021, https://theconversation.com/what-if-tom-brady-took-a-knee-instead-of-colin-kaepernick-169519 (accessed 2/4/22).

77. Larry Buchanan, Quoctrung Bui and Jugal K. Patel, "Black Lives Matter May Be the Largest Movement in U.S. History," *New York Times*, July 3, 2020, www.nytimes.com/interactive/2020/07/03/us/george-floyd-protests-crowd-size.html (accessed 2/23/22).

78. *Pearson v. Murray*, 169 Md. 478 (1936).

79. *Shelley v. Kraemer*, 334 U.S. 1 (1948).

80. *Brown v. Board of Education*, 347 U.S. 483 (1954).

81. *Brown v. Board of Education II*, 349 U.S. 294 (1955).

82. Paul Brest and Sanford Levinson, *Process of Constitutional Decision Making: Cases and Material* (Boston: Little, Brown, 1982), pp. 471–80.

83. *Swann v. Charlotte-Mecklenburg Board of Education*, 402 U.S. 1 (1971).

84. *Milliken v. Bradley*, 418 U.S. 717 (1974).

85. *Parents Involved in Community Schools Inc. v. Seattle School District*, 05-98 (2007); *Meredith v. Jefferson County (Ky.) Board of Education*, 551 U.S. 701 (2007).

86. *Heart of Atlanta Motel, Inc. v. United States*, 379 U.S. 241 (1964).

87. *Katzenbach v. McClung*, 379 U.S. 294 (1964).

88. *Griggs v. Duke Power*, 401 U.S. 424 (1971).

89. *Easley v. Cromartie*, 532 U.S. 234 (2001), rehearing denied, 532 U.S. 1076 (2001).

90. *Easley v. Cromartie*, 532 U.S. 1076 (2001).

91. Richard L. Hasen, "The Gerrymandering Decision Drags the Supreme Court Further into the Mud: Ignoring the Racial Redistricting Problem Won't Make It Go Away," *New York Times*, June 27, 2019, www.nytimes.com/2019/06/27/opinion/gerrymandering-rucho-supreme-court.html (accessed 2/23/22). The case is *Rucho v. Common Cause*, 588 U.S. (2019).

92. Amy Howe, "Court rules for South Carolina Republicans in dispute over congressional map," SCOTUSblog, May 23, 2024, https://www.scotusblog.com/2024/05/court-rules-for-south-carolina-republicans-in-dispute-over-congressional-map/ (accessed 7/5/24); the case was *Snyder v. United States*, 603 U.S. ___ (2024).

93. *Shelby County v. Holder*, 570 U.S. 529 (2013).

94. Carl Hulse, "After a Day of Debate, the Voting Rights Bill Is Blocked in the Senate," *New York Times*, January 19, 2022, www.nytimes.com/2022/01/19/us/politics/senate-voting-rights-filibuster.html (accessed 2/8/22).

95. *Brnovich v. Democratic National Committee*, 594 U.S. ___ (2021).

96. *Reed v. Reed*, 404 U.S. 71 (1971). As a young women's rights attorney, Ruth Bader Ginsburg wrote the plaintiff's brief in this case. She argued more than three hundred gender discrimination cases, including six before the Supreme Court, before becoming a federal judge.

97. *Frontiero v. Richardson*, 411 U.S. 677 (1973).

98. *Korematsu v. United States*, 323 U.S. 214 (1944).

99. *Trump v. Hawaii*, 585 U.S. (2018).

100. *Craig v. Boren*, 429 U.S. 190 (1976).

101. *Orr v. Orr*, 440 U.S. 268 (1979).

102. *United States v. Virginia*, 518 U.S. 515 (1996).

103. Joanna L. Grossman, "Policing Sexism at the Border: The Supreme Court's Decision in *Sessions v. Morales-Santana*," Verdict: Legal Analysis and Commentary from Justia, June 20, 2017, https://verdict.justia.com/2017/06/20/policing-sexism-border-supreme-courts-decision-sessions-v-morales-santana (accessed 2/23/22). The case is *Sessions v. Morales-Santana*, 582 U.S. (2017).

104. *Johnson v. Transportation Agency of Santa Clara*, 480 U.S. 616 (1987).

105. *Harris v. Forklift Systems*, 510 U.S. 17 (1993).

106. Danielle Bernstein, "#MeToo Has Changed the World—Except in Court Judges Continue to Enforce a Standard that Makes Proving Claims of Sexual Harassment Incredibly Difficult," *Atlantic*, August 13, 2021, www.theatlantic.com/ideas/archive/2021/08/metoo-courts/619732/ (accessed 2/8/22).

107. Jan Ransom, "Harvey Weinstein's Stunning Downfall: 23 Years in Prison," *New York Times*, March 11, 2020, www.nytimes.com/2020/03/11/nyregion/harvey-weinstein-sentencing.html (accessed 2/23/22).

108. Stephanie Zacharek, Eliana Dockterman, and Haley Sweetland Edwards, "Person of the Year 2017: The Silence Breakers," *Time*, http://time.com/time-person-of-the-year-2017-silence-breakers (accessed 2/23/22).

109. *Ledbetter v. Goodyear Tire & Rubber Co.*, 550 U.S. 618 (2007).

110. Julie Hirschfeld Davis, "Obama Moves to Expand Rules Aimed at Closing Gender Pay Gap," *New York Times*, January 29, 2016, www.nytimes.com/2016/01/29/us/politics/obama-moves-to-expand-rules-aimed-at-closing-gender-pay-gap.html (accessed 2/23/22).

111. White House, "Presidential Executive Order on the Revocation of Federal Contracting Executive Orders," March 27, 2017, https://trumpwhitehouse.archives.gov/presidential-actions/presidential-executive-order-revocation-federal-contracting-executive-orders/ (accessed 2/23/22).

112. White House, "Executive Order on Establishment of the White House Gender Policy Council," March 8, 2021, www.whitehouse.gov/briefing-room/presidential-actions/2021/03/08/executive-order-on-establishment-of-the-white-house-gender-policy-council/ (accessed 2/8/22).

113. "Women Present Widespread Discrimination at Wal-Mart," press release, April 28, 2003, www.walmartclass.com/staticdata/press_releases/wmcc.html (accessed 10/4/12).

114. David Savage, "Supreme Court Blocks Huge Class-Action Suit against Wal-Mart," *Los Angeles Times*, June 21, 2011. The case is *Wal-Mart v. Dukes*, 564 U.S. 338 (2011).

115. Michael Sainato, "Walmart Facing Gender Discrimination Lawsuits from Female Employees," *Guardian*, February 18, 2019, www.theguardian.com/us-news/2019/feb/18/walmart-gender-discrimination-supreme-court (accessed 2/23/22).

116. "Walmart, Inc. to Pay $20 Million to Settle EEOC Nationwide Hiring Discrimination Case," U.S. Equal Employment Opportunity Commission (EEOC), September 10, 2020, www.eeoc.gov/newsroom/walmart-inc-pay-20-million-settle-eeoc-nationwide-hiring-discrimination-case (accessed 2/8/22).

117. *Bowers v. Hardwick*, 478 U.S. 186 (1986), rehearing denied, 478 U.S. 1039 (1986).

118. *Romer v. Evans*, 517 U.S. 620 (1996).

119. *Lawrence v. Texas*, 539 U.S. 558 (2003). Because the basis for the decision was the due process clause of the Fourteenth Amendment and not the equal protection clause, this ruling upheld a civil liberty rather than a civil right. As such, it applied to all laws regarding sodomy, not just those that applied to gays. However, the decision has been widely regarded as a landmark civil rights case because it provided equal rights for gays.

120. The three cases are *Hollingsworth v. Perry*, 570 U.S. 693 (2013), *United States v. Windsor*, 570 U.S. 744 (2013), and *Obergefell v. Hodges*, 576 U.S. (2015).

121. Kenji Yoshino, "Is the Right to Same Sex Marriage Next?," *New York Times*, June 30, 2022, www.nytimes.com/2022/06/30/opinion/same-sex-marriage-supreme-court.html (accessed 7/25/22).

122. *Bostock v. Clayton* County, 590 U.S. (2020).

123. *Altitude Express Inc. v. Zarda*, 590 U.S. (2020); *R.G. & G.R. Harris Funeral Homes Inc. v. Equal Employment Opportunity Commission*, 590 U.S. (2020).

124. Quoted in Voting Rights Act Extension: Report of the Subcommittee of the Constitution of the Committee on the Judiciary, U.S. Senate, 97th Congress, 2nd session, May 25, 1982, S. Rept. 97-417, 4.

125. Drew S. Days III, "Section 5 Enforcement and the Justice Department," in *Controversies in Minority Voting: The Voting Rights Act in Perspective*, ed. Bernard Grofman and Chandler Davidson (Washington, DC: Brookings Institution Press, 1992), p. 52; Frank R. Parker, *Black Votes Count* (Chapel Hill: University of North Carolina Press, 1990), p. 1.

126. Davidson, "Voting Rights Act," p. 21.

127. "Fair Housing: It's Your Right," U.S. Department of Housing and Urban Development, www.hud.gov/program_offices/fair_housing_equal_opp/online-complaint (accessed 2/23/22).

128. Alexandra DeSanctis, "Would the Equal Rights Amendment Enshrine Abortion Rights in the Constitution?," *National Review*, February 17, 2020, www.nationalreview.com/2020/02/would-the-equal-rights-amendment-enshrine-abortion-rights-in-the-constitution/ (accessed 2/23/22).

129. *United States v. Morrison*, 529 U.S. 598 (2000).

130. *Board of Trustees of the University of Alabama v. Garrett*, 531 U.S. 356 (2001). Also, in *State of Tennessee v. George Lane and Beverly Jones*, 541 U.S. 509 (2004), the Court ruled that disabled people must have access to courthouses.

131. White House, "Remarks by the Reception Commemorating the Enactment of the Matthew Shepard and James Byrd Jr. Hate Crimes Prevention Act," October 28, 2009, https://obamawhitehouse.archives.gov/the-press-office/remarks-president-reception-commemorating-enactment-matthew-shepard-and-james-byrd- (accessed 4/18/18).

132. Barbara Sprunt, "Here's What the New Hate Crimes Law Aims to Do as Attacks on Asian Americans Rise," National Public Radio, May 20, 2021, www.npr.org/2021/05/20/998599775/biden-to-sign-the-covid-19-hate-crimes-bill-as-anti-asian-american-attacks-rise (accessed 7/25/22); H.R.8404 - Respect for Marriage Act, https://www.congress.gov/bill/117th-congress/house-bill/8404 (accessed 7/5/24).

133. Tim Mak, "Post-'Don't Ask,' Gay Navy Lt. Marries," Politico, September 20, 2011, www.politico.com/news/stories/0911/63909.html (accessed 2/23/22).

134. An early version of the ban was struck down by a federal court, but a revised version of the ban was upheld by the Supreme Court. Rebecca Kheel, "Navy Officer Sues Pentagon over Transgender Military Ban," *The Hill*, March 18, 2020, https://thehill.com/policy/defense/488240-navy-officer-sues-pentagon-over-transgender-military-ban (accessed 2/23/22).

135. White House, "Executive Order on Enabling All Qualified Americans to Serve Their Country in Uniform," January 25, 2021, www.whitehouse.gov/briefing-room/presidential-actions/2021/01/25/executive-order-on-enabling-all-qualified-americans-to-serve-their-country-in-uniform/ (accessed 2/8/22).

136. For a comprehensive assessment of Biden's first year in office on these issues, see "One Year Later: How the Biden Administration Is Doing on Civil Rights and Civil Liberties," American Civil Liberties Union, January 24, 2022, www.aclu.org/news/capital-punishment/one-year-later-how-the-biden-administration-is-doing-on-civil-rights-and-civil-liberties/ (accessed 2/8/22).

137. *Public Papers of the Presidents of the United States: Lyndon B. Johnson, 1965*, vol. 2, entry 301 (Washington, DC: Government Printing Office, 1966), pp. 635–40.

138. The first poll is from Lydia Sadd, "Americans' Confidence in Racial Fairness Waning," Gallup, July 30, 2021, https://news.gallup.com/poll/352832/americans-confidence-racial-fairness-waning.aspx?utm_source=alert&utm_medium=email&utm_content=morelink&utm_campaign=syndication; and the second is Nikki Graf, "Most Americans Say Colleges

Should Not Consider Race or Ethnicity in Admissions," Pew Research, February 25, 2019, www.pewresearch.org/fact-tank/2019/02/25/most-americans-say-colleges-should-not-consider-race-or-ethnicity-in-admissions/ (both accessed 2/8/22).

139. State of California, article 1, section 31.

140. The training program case was *United Steel Workers of America v. Weber*, 443 U.S. 193 (1979); the labor union case was *Sheet Metal Workers v. EEOC*, 478 U.S. 421 (1986); and the Alabama state police case was *U.S. v. Paradise*, 480 U.S. 149 (1987).

141. *Ricci v. DeStefano*, 557 U.S. 557 (2009).

142. *Regents of the University of California v. Bakke*, 438 U.S. 265 (1978).

143. *Hopwood v. Texas*, 78 F3d 932 (5th Cir. 1996).

144. *Smith v. University of Washington*, 233 F3d 1188 (9th Cir. 2000).

145. *Grutter v. Bollinger*, 539 U.S. 306 (2003), was the law school case, and *Gratz v. Bollinger*, 539 U.S. 244 (2003), was the undergraduate admissions case.

146. In *Bakke*, Justice Lewis Powell was the only member of the Court who held this position, even though it became the basis for all affirmative action programs over the next 25 years. Four justices in the *Bakke* decision wanted to get rid of race as a factor in admissions, and another four thought that the "strict scrutiny" standard should not even be applied in this instance.

147. *Shuette v. Coalition to Defend Affirmative Action*, 572 U.S. 291 (2014).

148. *Fisher v. University of Texas, Austin*, 579 U.S. 365 (2016).

149. *Students for Fair Admissions v. Harvard*, 600 U.S. 181 (2023); *Students for Fair Admissions v. University of North Carolina*, Docket 21-707 (2023).

150. "The Rights of Immigrants," American Civil Liberties Union, www.aclu.org/other/rights-immigrants-aclu-position-paper (accessed 2/8/22).

151. *Trump v. Hawaii*, 585 U.S. ____ (2018).

152. White House, "Proclamation on Ending Discriminatory Bans on Entry to the United States," January 20, 2021, www.whitehouse.gov/briefing-room/presidential-actions/2021/01/20/proclamation-ending-discriminatory-bans-on-entry-to-the-united-states/ (accessed 2/8/22).

153. James Vicini, "Supreme Court to Decide Arizona Immigration Law," Reuters, December 12, 2011, www.reuters.com/article/us-usa-immigration-arizona/supreme-court-to-decide-arizona-immigration-law-idUSTRE7BB0XJ20111212 (accessed 2/23/22).

154. *Arizona v. United States*, 567 U.S. 387 (2012).

155. Fernanda Santos, "Arizona Immigration Law Survives Ruling," *New York Times*, September 6, 2012, www.nytimes.com/2012/09/07/us/key-element-of-arizona-immigration-law-survives-ruling.html?r=0 (accessed 2/23/22).

156. Nicole Narea, "Poll: Most Americans Support a Path to Citizenship for Undocumented Immigrants," Vox, February 4, 2021 (accessed 2/8/22).

157. Emily Kassie, "Detained: How the US Built the World's Largest Immigrant Detention System," *Guardian*, September 24, 2019, www.theguardian.com/us-news/2019/sep/24/detained-us-largest-immigrant-detention-trump (accessed 2/23/22).

158. White House, "Preserving and Fortifying Deferred Action for Childhood Arrivals (DACA)," January 20, 2021, www.whitehouse.gov/briefing-room/presidential-actions/2021/01/20/preserving-and-fortifying-deferred-action-for-childhood-arrivals-daca/ (accessed 2/8/22).

159. "An Act Providing for the Collection of Data Relative to Traffic Stops," Massachusetts state law, Chapter 228 of the Acts of 2000, https://malegislature.gov/Laws/SessionLaws/Acts/2000/Chapter228 (accessed 2/23/22). See "NCSL Law Enforcement Statutory Database Narratives," National Conference of State Legislatures, www.ncsl.org/Portals/1/Documents/2021_Summit_Resources/NCSL-Law-Enforcement-Statute-Summaries.pdf (accessed 2/8/22).

160. "GLAAD Media Reference Guide - In Focus: Nondiscrimination Laws & the LGBTQ Community," GLAAD, www.glaad.org/reference/nondiscrimination (accessed 2/8/22).

Take a Stand

a. *Fisher v. University of Texas, Austin*, 579 U.S. 365 (2016).

b. *Students for Fair Admissions v. Harvard*, 600 U.S. 181 (2023); *Students for Fair Admissions v. University of North Carolina*, Docket 21-707 (2023).

c. *Shuette v. Coalition to Defend Affirmative Action*, 572 U.S. 291 (2014).

Chapter 6

1. Quoted in Mark Dawidziak, "Jon Stewart Blurs the Lines between Jester and Journalist," *Cleveland Plain Dealer*, March 28, 2019.

2. V. O. Key, *The Responsible Electorate: Rationality in Presidential Voting, 1936–1960* (Cambridge, MA: Harvard University Press, 1966).

3. Kathy Frankovic, "Why Won't Americans Get Vaccinated?," YouGov America, July 24, 2021, https://today.yougov.com/topics/politics/articles-reports/2021/07/15/why-wont-americans-get-vaccinated-poll-data (accessed 2/3/22).

4. For a review, see Arthur Lupia and Mathew D. McCubbins, *The Democratic Dilemma* (New York: Cambridge University Press, 1998).

5. Larry Bartels, "Partisanship and Voting Behavior, 1952–1996," *American Journal of Political Science* 44 (2000): 35–50.

6. Robert S. Erikson, Michael B. MacKuen, and James A. Stimson, *The Macro Polity* (New York: Cambridge University Press, 2002).

7. John Zaller, "Coming to Grips with V. O. Key's Concept of Latent Opinion" (unpublished paper, University of California, Los Angeles, 1998).

8. Morris Fiorina, *Retrospective Voting in American National Elections* (Cambridge, MA: Harvard University Press, 1981).

9. Virginia Sapiro, "Not Your Parents' Political Socialization: Introduction for a New Generation," *Annual Review of Political Science* 7 (2004): 1–23.

10. M. Kent Jennings and Richard G. Niemi, *Generations and Politics: A Panel Study of Young Adults and Their Parents* (Princeton, NJ: Princeton University Press, 1981).

11. Robert Putnam, *Bowling Alone: The Collapse and Revival of American Community* (New York: Simon and Schuster, 2000).

12. Richard G. Niemi and Mary Hepburn, "The Rebirth of Political Socialization," *Perspectives on Politics* 24 (1995): 7–16.

13. David Campbell, *Why We Vote: How Schools and Communities Shape Our Civic Life* (Princeton, NJ: Princeton University Press, 2006).

14. Sidney Verba, Kay Schlozman, and Henry Brady, *Voice and Equality: Civic Volunteerism in American Politics* (Cambridge, MA: Harvard University Press, 1995).

15. Paul Allen Beck and M. Kent Jennings, "Pathways to Participation," *American Political Science Review* 76 (1982): 94–108.

16. William Minozzi, Hyunjin Song, David M. J. Lazer, Michael A. Neblo, and Katherine Ognyanova, "The Incidental Pundit: Who Talks Politics with Whom, and Why?," *American Journal of Political Science* 64:1 (2020): 135–51.

17. Pew Research Center, "In Gay Marriage Debate, Both Supporters and Opponents See Legal Recognition as 'Inevitable,'" June 6, 2013, www.people-press.org/2013/06/06/in-gay-marriage-debate-both-supporters-and-opponents-see-legal-recognition-as-inevitable (accessed 2/3/22).

18. John Zaller, *The Nature and Origins of Mass Opinion* (New York: Cambridge University Press, 1992).

19. Richard Nadwau et al., "Class, Party, and South–Nonsouth Differences," *American Politics Research* 32 (2004): 52–67.

20. James H. Kuklinski et al., "Racial Prejudice and Attitudes toward Affirmative Action," *American Journal of Political Science* 41 (1997): 402–19.

21. Donald P. Green, Bradley Palmquist, and Eric Schickler, *Partisan Hearts and Minds* (New Haven, CT: Yale University Press, 2002).

22. For elaboration on this point, see William T. Bianco, Richard G. Niemi, and Harold W. Stanley, "Partisanship and Group Support over Time: A Multivariate Analysis," *American Political Science Review* 80 (September 1986): 969–76.

23. Lupia and McCubbins, *Democratic Dilemma*.

24. Jane Mansbridge, "Rethinking Representation," *American Political Science Review* 97:4 (2003): 515–28.

25. Zaller, *Nature and Origins of Mass Opinion*.

26. R. Michael Alvarez and John Brehm, *Hard Choices, Easy Answers: Values, Information, and American Public Opinion* (Princeton, NJ: Princeton University Press, 2002).

27. John Zaller and Stanley Feldman, "A Theory of the Survey Response: Revealing Preferences versus Answering Questions," *American Journal of Political Science* 36 (1992): 579–616.

28. Janet M. Box-Steffensmeier and Susan DeBoef, "Macropartisanship and Macroideology in the Sophisticated Electorate," *Journal of Politics* 63:1 (2001): 232–48.

29. Shanto Iyengar, Gaurav Sood, and Yphtach Lelkes, "Affect, not Ideology: A Social Identity Perspective on Polarization," *Public Opinion Quarterly* 76:3 (2012): 405–31.

30. R. Michael Alvarez and John Brehm, "American Ambivalence towards Abortion Policy: Development of a Heteroskedastic Probit Model of Competing Values," *American Journal of Political Science* 39:4 (1995): 1055–82.

31. Jens Hainmueller and Daniel J. Hopkins, "Public Attitudes toward Immigration," *Annual Review of Political Science* 17 (2014): 225–49.

32. Sophia Wallace and Chris Zepeda-Millán, *Walls, Cages, and Family Separation: Race and Immigration Policy in the Trump Era* (Cambridge: Cambridge University Press, 2020); David Redlawsk, Andrew Civettini, and Karen Emmerson, "The Affective Tipping Point: Do Motivated Reasoners Ever 'Get It'?," *Political Psychology* 31:4 (2010): 563–93.

33. Soumyajit Mazumder, "The Persistent Effect of US Civil Rights Protests on Political Attitudes," *American Journal of Political Science* 62:4 (2018): 922–35.

34. Mark R. Joslyn and Steven M. Sylvester, "The Determinants and Consequences of Accurate Beliefs about Childhood Vaccinations," *American Politics Research* 47:3 (2019): 628–49; James N. Druckman, Samara Klar, Yanna Krupnikov, Matthew Levendusky, and John Barry Ryan, "Affective Polarization, Local Contexts and Public Opinion in America," *Nature Human Behaviour* 5:1 (2019): 28–38.

35. Patrick Healy, Adrian J. Rivera, and Margie Omero, "These 14 Undecided Young Voters Are Starting to Change Their Minds," The New York Times, September 14, 2024 (accessed 9/15/24).

36. Graeme Blair, Alexander Coppock, and Margaret Moor, "When to Worry about Sensitivity Bias: A Social Reference Theory and Evidence from 30 Years of List Experiments," *American Political Science Review* 114:4 (2020): 1297–1315.

37. Nate Silver, "The Death of Polling Is Greatly Exaggerated," FiveThirtyEight, March 25, 2021, https://fivethirtyeight.com/features/the-death-of-polling-is-greatly-exaggerated/ (accessed 1/6/22).

38. George Ingram, "What Every American Should Know about US Foreign Aid," Brookings, October 19, 2019, www.brookings.edu/policy2020/votervital/what-every-american-should-know-about-us-foreign-aid/ (accessed 1/6/22).

39. Michael X. Delli Carpini and Scott Keeter, *What Americans Know about Politics and Why It Matters* (New Haven, CT: Yale University Press, 1997).

40. Delli Carpini and Keeter, *What Americans Know about Politics and Why It Matters*.

41. Nate Silver, "How FiveThirtyEight Calculates Pollster Ratings," September 25, 2014, http://fivethirtyeight.com/features/how-fivethirtyeight-calculates-pollster-ratings (accessed 2/3/22).

42. Lilliana Mason, *Uncivil Agreement: How Politics Became Our Identity* (Chicago: University of Chicago Press, 2015).

43. Steven W. Webster, *American Rage: How Anger Shapes Our Politics* (Cambridge: Cambridge University Press, 2020).

44. Alan I. Abramowitz and Steven W. Webster, "The Rise of Negative Partisanship and the Nationalization of US Elections in the 21st Century," *Electoral Studies* 41 (2016): 12–22.

45. Lilliana Mason, "'I Disrespectfully Agree': The Differential Effects of Partisan Sorting on Social and Issue Polarization," *American Journal of Political Science* 59:1 (2015): 128–45.

46. Shanto Iyengar and Sean J. Westwood, "Fear and Loathing across Party Lines: New Evidence on Group Polarization," *American Journal of Political Science* 59:3 (2015): 690–707.

47. For a review of the literature on trust in government, see Karen Cook, Russell Hardin, and Margaret Levi, *Cooperation without Trust?*, (New York: Russell Sage Foundation, 2005), as well as Marc J. Hetherington, *Why Trust Matters: Declining Political Trust and the Demise of American Liberalism* (Princeton, NJ: Princeton University Press, 2004).

48. William T. Bianco, *Trust: Representatives and Constituents* (Ann Arbor: University of Michigan Press, 1994).

49. Sean M. Theriault, *The Power of the People: Congressional Competition, Public Attention, and Voter Retribution* (Columbus: Ohio State University Press, 2005).

50. Thomas Rudolph and Jillian Evans, "Political Trust, Ideology, and Public Support for Government Spending," *American Journal of Political Science* 49 (2005): 660–71.

51. Patricia Moy and Michael Pfau, *With Malice toward All? The Media and Public Confidence in Democratic Institutions* (Boulder, CO: Praeger, 2000).

52. Erikson, MacKuen, and Stimson, *Macro Polity*.

53. James A. Stimson, *Public Opinion in America: Moods, Swings, and Cycles* (Boulder, CO: Westview, 1999).

54. Robert S. Erikson, Michael B. MacKuen, and James A. Stimson, "American Politics: The Model" (unpublished paper, Columbia University, 2000).

55. Christopher Wlezien, "The Public as Thermostat: Dynamics of Preferences for Spending," *American Journal of Political Science* 73 (1995): 981–1000.

56. Pew Research Center, "Public's Policy Priorities for 2019," January 24, 2019, www.people-press.org/2019/01/24/publics-2019-priorities-economy-health-care-education-and-security-all-near-top-of-list/pp_2019-01-24_political-priorities_0-02/ (accessed 2/3/22).

57. Leah Cardamore Stokes, *Short Circuiting Policy: Interest Groups and the Battle over Clean Energy and Climate Policy in the American States* (New York: Oxford University Press, 2020).

58. Larry Bartels, "Constituency Opinion and Congressional Policy Making: The Reagan Defense Buildup," *American Political Science Review* 85 (June 1991): 457–74; Jonathan Kastellec, Jeffrey R. Lax, and Justin H. Phillips, "Public Opinion and Senate Confirmation of Supreme Court Nominees," *Journal of Politics* 72 (2010): 767–84.

59. Lawrence R. Jacobs and Robert Y. Shapiro, *Politicians Don't Pander: Political Manipulation and the Loss of Democratic Responsiveness* (Chicago: University of Chicago Press, 2000).

Chapter 7

1. "Quotes," Goodreads, www.goodreads.com/quotes/9676544-fake-news-is-like-ice-once-it-comes-in-contact (accessed 2/15/22).

2. Madeleine Albright, *Fascism: A Warning* (New York: HarperCollins, 2018).

3. Kaleigh Rogers, "Why It's So Hard to Gauge Support for QAnon," FiveThirtyEight, June 11, 2021, https://fivethirtyeight.com/features/why-its-so-hard-to-gauge-support-for-qanon/ (accessed 1/13/22).

4. William H. Riker, *The Strategy of Rhetoric: Campaigning for the American Constitution* (New Haven, CT: Yale University Press, 1996).

5. Garry Wills, *Explaining America: The Federalist* (New York: Penguin, 2001).

6. Geoffrey R. Stone, *Perilous Times: Free Speech in Wartime from the Sedition Act of 1798 to the War on Terrorism* (New York: W. W. Norton, 2004).

7. John D. Stevens, *Sensationalism and the New York Press* (New York: Columbia University Press, 1991).

8. Robert C. Williams, *Horace Greeley: Champion of American Freedom* (New York: New York University Press, 2006).

9. Evan Thomas, *The War Lovers: Roosevelt, Lodge, Hearst, and the Rush to Empire, 1898* (New York: Little, Brown, 2010).

10. Gay Talese, *The Kingdom and the Power* (New York: Calder and Boyars, 1983).

11. The Project for Excellence in Journalism, "State of the News Media," www.pewresearch.org/topics/state-of-the-news-media (accessed 2/15/22).

12. The *Columbia Journalism Review* maintains a list of holdings for major media companies at Who Owns What, www.cjr.org/resources (accessed 2/15/22).

13. See Monkey Cage, washingtonpost.com/monkey-cage/ (accessed 1/21/22) and Mischiefs of Faction, mischiefsoffaction.com (accessed 1/21/22).

14. For details, see Your Local Epidemiologist, https://yourlocalepidemiologist.substack.com; Facebook, www.facebook.com/friendlyneighborepidemiologist/; and In the Pipeline, www.science.org/blogs/pipeline.

15. To see the difference between facts and opinions, take this Pew Research quiz: Pew Research Center, "Quiz: How Well Can You Tell Factual from Opinion Statements?," June 18, 2018, www.pewresearch.org/quiz/news-statements-quiz/ (accessed 2/15/22).

16. Timothy Bella, "Doctors Call out Spotify for Letting Joe Rogan Spread 'False and Societally Harmful' COVID-19 Claims," *Washington Post*, January 14, 2022, www.washingtonpost.com/arts-entertainment/2022/01/14/joe-rogan-spotify-doctors-covid-misinformation/ (accessed 1/24/22).

17. David Corn, "We Already Know That Trump Betrayed America," *Mother Jones*, May 2017, pp. 10–12.

18. Isabella Glogger and Lukas Otto, "Journalistic Views on Hard and Soft News: Cross-Validating a Popular Concept in a Factorial Survey," *Journalism & Mass Communication Quarterly* 96:3 (2019): 811–29.

19. Rebecca Hielweil, "Right-Wing Media Thrives on Facebook. Whether It Rules Is More Complicated," Vox, September 9, 2020, www.vox.com/recode/21419328/facebook-conservative-bias-right-wing-crowdtangle-election (accessed 2/9/22).

20. Patti M. Valkenburg, Jochen Peter, and Joseph B. Walther, "Media Effects: Theory and Research," *Annual Review of Psychology* 67 (2016): 315–38.

21. Natalie Stroud, *Niche News: The Politics of News Choice* (New York: Oxford University Press, 2011).

22. Lance Bennett, *News: The Politics of Illusion* (New York: Pearson, 2012).

23. Danny Hayes and Matthew Guardino, *Influence from Abroad: Foreign Voices, the Media, and U.S. Public Opinion* (New York: Cambridge University Press, 2013).

24. Matthew Baum, "Talking the Vote: Why Presidential Candidates Hit the Talk Show Circuit," *American Journal of Political Science* 49 (2005): 213–34.

25. Daniel Dale, "Fact Check: No, Biden Is Not Trying to Force Americans to Eat Less Beef," *CNN*, April 26, 2020, www.cnn.com/2021/04/26/politics/fact-check-biden-climate-plan-red-meat-hamburger/index.html (accessed 1/24/22).

26. Daniel Drezner, "Why Is the U.S. Intelligence Community So Chatty about Russia?," *Washington Post*, February 8, 2022, www.washingtonpost.com/outlook/2022/02/08/why-is-us-intelligence-community-so-chatty-about-russia/ (accessed 2/8/22).

27. Barton Gellman, "Code Name 'Verax': Snowden, in Exchanges with *Post* Reporter, Made Clear He Knew Risks," *Washington Post*, June 13, 2012, p. A1.

28. For a discussion of these concepts, see Mary Beth Oliver, Arthur A. Raney, and Jennings Bryant (Eds.), *Media Effects* (New York: Routledge, 2019). See also Andrew Guess, Kevin Munger, Jonathan Nagler, and Joshua Tucker, "How Accurate Are Survey Responses on Social Media and Politics?," *Political Communication* 36:2 (2019): 241–58; and Amos Tversky and Daniel Kahnemann, "The Framing of Decisions and the Psychology of Choice," *Science* 211 (1981): 453–58.

29. Markus Prior, "Media and Political Polarization," *Annual Review of Political Science* 16 (2013): 101–27.

30. Kevin Arceneaux et al., "The Influence of News Media on Political Elites: Investigating Strategic Responsiveness in Congress," *American Journal of Political Science* 60:1 (2016): 5–29.

31. Matthew S. Levendusky, "Why Do Partisan Media Polarize Viewers?," *American Journal of Political Science* 57:3 (2013): 611–23.

32. Kevin Arceneaux, Martin Johnson, and Chad Murphy, "Polarized Political Communication, Oppositional Media Hostility, and Selective Exposure," *Journal of Politics* 74:1 (2012): 174–86.

33. Hans J. G. Hassell, John B. Holbein, and Matthew R. Miles, "There Is No Liberal Media Bias in Which News Stories Political Journalists Choose to Cover," *Science Advances* 6:14 (2020): 234–42; Doron Shultziner and Yelena Stukalin, "Distorting the News? The Mechanisms of Partisan Media Bias and Its Effects on News Production," *Political Behavior* 43:1 (2021): 201–22.

34. Donald Trump, Twitter, February 17, 2017, 4:48 P.M., https://twitter.com/realDonaldTrump/status/832708293516632065 (accessed 6/2/20).

35. "The Top 25 Censored Stories of 2020 and 2021," Project Censored, www.projectcensored.org/category/the-top-25-most-censored-stories-of-2021/ (accessed 2/4/22).

36. Carl Bialik, "Scare Headlines Exaggerated the US Crime Wave," September 11, 2015, http://fivethirtyeight.com/features/scare-headlines-exaggerated-the-u-s-crime-wave (accessed 11/20/15).

37. Griffe Witte, "Homicide Rates Have Soared Nationwide, but Mayors See a Chance for a Turnaround in 2022," *Washington Post*, January 22, 2022, www.washingtonpost.com/nation/2022/01/21/homicide-rates-have-soared-nationwide-mayors-see-chance-turnaround-2022/ (accessed 2/4/22).

38. "Civil Rights Attorney Exposes Reason behind Nationwide Crime Spike," Fox News, January 16, 2022, www.foxnews.com/media/civil-rights-attorney-nationwide-crime-spike-gangs (accessed 2/4/2022).

39. Pew Research Center, "Press Widely Criticized, but Trusted More Than Other Information Sources," September 22, 2011, www.people-press.org/2011/09/22/press-widely-criticized-but-trusted-more-than-other-institutions (accessed 9/17/12).

40. Annie Linskey, Cleve R. Wootson Jr., Jeff Stein, and Brady Dennis, "After One Year in Office, What Has Biden Done about the Four Crises He Pledged to Address?," *Washington Post*, January 22, 2022, www.washingtonpost.com/politics/interactive/2022/biden-covid-race-economy-climate/ (accessed 2/8/22).

41. Markus Prior, "News vs. Entertainment: How Increasing Media Choice Widens Gaps in Political Knowledge and Turnout," *American Journal of Political Science* 49:3 (2005): 577–92.

42. Amy Mitchell et al., "Distinguishing between Factual and Opinion Statements in the News," Pew Research Center, June 18, 2018, www.journalism.org/2018/06/18/distinguishing-between-factual-and-opinion-statements-in-the-news/ (accessed 1/28/20).

43. Markus Prior, *Post-Broadcast Democracy: How Media Choice Increases Inequality in Political Involvement and Polarizes Elections* (New York: Cambridge University Press, 2007).

44. Pablo Boczkowski, *Imitation in an Age of Information Abundance* (Chicago: University of Chicago Press, 2010).

45. Amber E. Boydstun, *Making the News: Politics, the Media, and Agenda Setting* (Chicago: University of Chicago Press, 2013).

46. Jonathan Ladd, "Four Approaches to Providing Political News Given That So Many People Don't Want It," August 20, 2015, http://mischiefsoffaction.blogspot.com/2015/08/four-approaches-to-providing-political.html (accessed 2/8/22).

47. Thomas Patterson, "Bad News, Period," *Political Science and Politics* 29 (1996): 17–20.

48. Shanto Iyengar, Helmut Norpoth, and Kyu Hahn, "Consumer Demand for Election News: The Horserace Sells," *Journal of Politics* 66 (2004): 157–75.

49. Steve M. Barkin, *American Television News: The Media Marketplace and the Public Interest* (New York: Routledge, 2016).

50. Dhrumil Mehta, "The Media Has Really Neglected Puerto Rico," FiveThirtyEight, September 28, 2017, https://fivethirtyeight.com/features/the-media-really-has-neglected-puerto-rico/ (accessed 2/5/22).

51. Thomas E. Patterson, *The Vanishing Voter: Public Involvement in an Age of Uncertainty* (New York: Knopf, 2002); Joseph N. Cappella, and Kathleen Hall Jamieson, *Spiral of Cynicism: The Press and the Public Good* (New York: Oxford University Press, 1997).

52. Robert McChesney, *The Problem of the Media: U.S. Communication Politics in the 21st Century* (New York: Monthly Review Press, 2004).

What Do the Facts Say?

a. Stephanie Pagones,"America's Murder Rate Increase in 2020 Has 'No Modern Precedent,' Crime Analyst Group Finds," Fox News, January 21, 2021, www.foxnews.com/us/murder-rate-increase-2020-no-modern-precedent-crime-analyst-group-finds (accessed 2/4/22).

Chapter 8

1. Nancy Pelosi, "Transcript of Pelosi Weekly Press Conference Today," May 23, 2019, www.speaker.gov/newsroom/52319 (accessed 3/21/22).

2. Bernie Sanders, Twitter post, February 21, 2020, 8:02 p.m., https://twitter.com/berniesanders/status/1231021453270769664?lang=en.

3. Julia Azari, "Weak Parties and Strong Partisanship Are a Bad Combination," Vox, November 3, 2016, www.vox.com/mischiefs-of-faction/2016/11/3/13512362/weak-parties-strong-partisanship-bad-combination (accessed 3/21/22).

4. Nolan McCarty and Eric Schickler, "On the Theory of Parties," *Annual Review of Political Science* 21 (2018): 175–93.

5. David Karol, "Political Parties in American Political Development," *The Oxford Handbook of American Political Development* (2016): 473.

6. Joseph A. Schlesinger, *Political Parties and the Winning of Office* (Ann Arbor: University of Michigan Press, 1994).

7. Kenneth Benoit, "Duverger's Law and the Study of Electoral Systems," *French Politics* 4:1 (2006): 69–83.

8. William Nesbit Chambers and Walter Dean Burnham, *The American Party Systems: Stages of Political Development* (Oxford: Oxford University Press, 1966).

9. Ronald P. Formisano, *The Birth of Mass Political Parties* (Princeton, NJ: Princeton University Press, 2015); William T. Bianco, David B. Spence, and John D. Wilkerson, "The Electoral Connection in the Early Congress: The Case of the Compensation Act of 1816," *American Journal of Political Science* 40 (February 1996): 145–71.

10. John Aldrich, *Why Parties?: A Second Look* (Chicago: University of Chicago Press, Second Edition, 2012).

11. James MacPherson, *Battle Cry of Freedom: The Civil War Era* (New York: Oxford University Press, 1988).

12. Michael F. Holt, *The Rise and Fall of the Whig Party: Jacksonian Politics and the Onset of the Civil War* (New York: Oxford University Press, 1999).

13. David A. Bateman, *Disenfranchising Democracy: Constructing the Electorate in the United States, the United Kingdom, and France* (New York: Cambridge University Press, 2018).

14. Harold W. Stanley, William T. Bianco, and Richard G. Niemi, "Partisanship and Group Support over Time: A Multivariate Analysis," *American Political Science Review* 80 (1986): 969–76.
15. Eric Schickler, *Racial Realignment: The Transformation of American Liberalism, 1932–1965* (Princeton, NJ: Princeton University Press, 2016).
16. Hans Noel, *Political Ideologies and Political Parties in America* (New York: Cambridge University Press, 2014).
17. Ben Protess, Danielle Ivory, and Steve Eder, "Where Trump's Hands-Off Approach to Governing Does Not Apply," *New York Times*, September 10, 2017, www.nytimes.com/2017/09/10/business/trump-regulations-religious-conservatives.html (accessed 3/21/22).
18. Aldrich, *Why Parties?*
19. James L. Sundquist, *Dynamics of the Party System: Alignment and Realignment of Political Parties in the United States*, rev. ed. (Washington, DC: Brookings Institution, 1983).
20. David R. Mayhew, *Electoral Realignments: A Critique of an American Genre* (New Haven, CT: Yale University Press, 2002).
21. John H. Aldrich and Richard G. Niemi, "The Sixth American Party System: Electoral Change, 1952–1992," in *Broken Contract: Changing Relationships between Americans and Their Governments*, ed. Steven Craig (Boulder, CO: Westview, 1993).
22. Eric Schickler, *Racial Realignment: The Transformation of American Liberalism, 1932–1965* (Princeton, NJ: Princeton University Press, 2016).
23. Seth C. McKee, *Republican Ascendancy in Southern US House Elections* (New York: Routledge, 2018).
24. Daniel Schlozman, *When Movements Anchor Parties: Electoral Alignments in American History* (Princeton, NJ: Princeton University Press, 2015).
25. Jon F. Hale, "The Making of the New Democrats," *Political Science Quarterly* 110:2 (1995): 207–32.
26. James Monroe, *The Political Party Matrix: The Persistence of Organization* (Albany: State University of New York Press, 2001).
27. Gary Cox and Mathew McCubbins, *Legislative Leviathan: Party Government in the House* (Berkeley: University of California Press, 1993).
28. Marc Debus and Martin Gross, "Coalition Formation at the Local Level: Institutional Constraints, Party Policy Conflict, and Office-Seeking Political Parties," *Party Politics* 22:6 (2016): 835–46.
29. Matthew J. Lebo, Adam J. McGlynn, and Gregory Koger, "Strategic Party Government: Party Influence in Congress, 1789–2000," *American Journal of Political Science* 51:3 (2007): 464–81.
30. Nolan McCarty, *Polarization: What Everyone Needs to Know* (New York: Oxford University Press, 2019).
31. Donald Green, Bradley Palmquist, and Eric Schickler, *Partisan Hearts and Minds: Political Parties and the Social Identities of Votes* (New Haven, CT: Yale University Press, 2004).
32. Morris Fiorina, *Retrospective Voting in American National Elections* (New Haven, CT: Yale University Press, 1981).
33. Yphtach Lelkes and Sean J. Westwood, "The Limits of Partisan Prejudice," *Journal of Politics* 79:2 (2017): 485–501.
34. Alan I. Abramowitz and Steven W. Webster, "Negative Partisanship: Why Americans Dislike Parties but Behave Like Rabid Partisans," *Political Psychology* 39 (2018): 119–35.
35. Walter Dean Burnham, "The Reagan Heritage," in *The Election of 1988: Reports and Interpretations*, ed. Gerald M. Pomper et al. (Chatham, NJ: Chatham House, 1989).
36. Martin P. Wattenberg, *The Decline of American Political Parties: 1952–1994* (Cambridge, MA: Harvard University Press, 1996).
37. David S. Broder, *The Party's Over: The Failure of Partisan Politics in America* (New York: Harper and Row, 1971).
38. Donald P. Green and Bradley Palmquist, "Of Artifacts and Partisan Instability," *American Journal of Political Science* 34:3 (August 1990): 872–902.
39. Samara Kiar and Yanna Krupnikov, *Independent Politics: How American Disdain for Parties Leads to Political Inaction* (New York: Cambridge University Press, 2016).
40. Larry M. Bartels, "Partisanship and Voting Behavior, 1952–1996," *American Journal of Political Science* 44:1 (2000): 35–50.
41. Tiffany D. Barnes and Erin C. Cassese, "American Party Women: A Look at the Gender Gap within Parties," *Political Research Quarterly* 70:1 (2017): 127–41; Ryan Claassen, *Godless Democrats and Pious Republicans?: Party Activists, Party Capture, and the "God Gap"* (New York: Cambridge University Press, 2015).
42. Daniel Schlotzman, *When Movements Anchor Parties: Electoral Alignments in American History* (Princeton, NJ: Princeton University Press, 2015).
43. Matt Grossmann and David A. Hopkins, "Ideological Republicans and Group Interest Democrats: The Asymmetry of American Party Politics," *Perspectives on Politics* 13:1 (2015): 119–39.
44. Michael Barber and Jeremy C. Pope, "Does Party Trump Ideology? Disentangling Party and Ideology in America," *American Political Science Review* 113:1 (2019): 38–54; Eli J. Finkel, Christopher A. Bail, Mina Cikara, Peter H. Ditto, Shanto Iyengar, Samara Klar, Lilliana Mason, et al., "Political Sectarianism in America," *Science* 37:6516 (2020): 533–36.
45. Douglas Ahler and Guarav Sood, "The Parties in Our Heads: Misperceptions about Party Composition and Their Consequences," *Journal of Politics* 80:3 (2018): 964–81.
46. Marty Cohen et al., *The Party Decides: Presidential Nominations before and after Reform* (Chicago: University of Chicago Press, 2008).
47. Samuel Issacharoff, "Outsourcing Politics: The Hostile Takeover of Our Hollowed-Out Political Parties," *Houston Law Review* 54 (2016): 845–80.
48. Compiled from information available at Ballot Access News, www.ballot-access.org (accessed 2/18/18).
49. The Center for Responsive Politics, opensecrets.org (accessed 11/8/22).
50. John Gerring, *Party Ideologies in America, 1828–1996* (New York: Cambridge University Press, 2001).
51. Sam Rosenfeld, *The Polarizers: Postwar Architects of Our Partisan Era* (Chicago: University of Chicago Press, 2017).
52. Libertarian National Committee, "Elected Officials," www.lp.org/elected-officials (accessed 3/21/22).
53. Lee Drutman, *Breaking the Two-Party Doom Loop: The Case for Multiparty Democracy in America* (New York: Oxford University Press, 2020).
54. Gary Cox, *Making Votes Count: Strategic Coordination in the World's Electoral Systems* (Cambridge: Cambridge University Press, 1997).
55. Peter Hanson, *Too Weak to Govern: Majority Party Power and Appropriations in the U.S. Senate* (New York: Cambridge University Press, 2015).
56. Thomas B. Edsall, "GOP Gains Advantage on Key Issues, Polls Say," *Washington Post*, January 27, 2002, p. A4.

Take a Stand

a. Nelson Polsby, *Consequences of Party Reform* (New York: Oxford University Press, 1983).

b. Daniel A. Smith and Caroline J. Tolbert, *Educated by Initiative: The Effects of Direct Democracy on Citizens and Political Organizations in the American States* (Ann Arbor: University of Michigan Press, 2004).

Chapter 9

1. Donald Trump, Twitter, November 7, 2020, 4:53 P.M., https://twitter.com/realdonaldtrump/status/1325194709443080192 (accessed 11/17/20).
2. Quoted in Tim Alberta, "The Election That Broke the Republican Party," Politico, November 6, 2020, www.politico.com/news/magazine/2020/11/06/the-election-that-broke-the-republican-party-434797 (accessed 4/19/22).
3. Andrew Healy and Neil Malhotra, "Retrospective Voting Reconsidered," *Annual Review of Political Science* 16 (2013): 285–306.
4. David Mayhew, *Congress: The Electoral Connection* (New Haven, CT: Yale University Press, 1973).
5. For details on early voting, refer to the Early Voting Information Center at http://earlyvoting.net/ (accessed 4/5/22).
6. John DiStaso, "Exhaustive Investigation Reveals Little Evidence of Possible Voter Fraud in NH," WMUR Manchester, May 29, 2018, www.wmur.com/article/exhaustive-investigation-reveals-little-evidence-of-possible-voter-fraud-in-nh/20955267# (accessed 4/19/22).
7. United States Government Accountability Office, "Issues Related to State Voter Identification Laws," 2014, www.gao.gov/assets/670/665966.pdf (accessed 4/19/22).
8. Minor-party candidates are typically selected during party conventions.
9. Barbara Norrander, *The Imperfect Primary: Oddities, Biases, and Strengths of U.S. Presidential Nomination Politics* (New York: Routledge, 2019).
10. Marty Cohen, David Karol, Hans Noel, and John Zaller, *The Party Decides: Presidential Nominations Before and After Reform* (Chicago: University of Chicago Press, 2009).
11. Andrew J. Dowdle, Randall E. Adkins, Karen Sebold, and Jared Cuellar, "Forecasting Presidential Nominations in 2016: #WePredictedClintonANDTrump," *PS: Political Science & Politics* 49:4 (2016): 691–95.
12. Caitlin E. Jewitt, "Restoring Trust and Reducing Perceived Influence: Superdelegates and the 2020 Democratic Nomination," *Society* 57:6 (2020): 680–85.
13. FairVote, "Maine and Nebraska," www.fairvote.org/maine_nebraska (accessed 4/5/22).
14. Keith E. Whittington, "Originalism, Constitutional Construction, and the Problem of Faithless Electors," *Arizona Law Review* 59:4 (2017): 903.
15. William Josephson, "Senate Election of the Vice President and House of Representatives Election of the President," *University of Pennsylvania Journal of Constitutional Law* 11 (2008): 597.
16. Robert Erikson and Christopher Wlezien, *The Timeline of Presidential Elections: How Campaigns Do (and Do Not) Matter* (Chicago: University of Chicago Press, 2013).
17. Larry M. Bartels and Christopher H. Achen, *Democracy for Realists: Why Elections Do Not Produce Responsive Government* (Princeton, NJ: Princeton University Press, 2016).
18. Richard L. Fox and Jennifer L. Lawless, "To Run or Not to Run for Office: Explaining Nascent Political Ambition," *American Journal of Political Science* 49:3 (2005): 642–59.
19. Marian Currinder, *Money in the House: Campaign Funds and Congressional Party Politics* (New York: Routledge, 2018).
20. Jamie L. Carson, Eric J. Engstrom, and Jason M. Roberts, "Candidate Quality, the Personal Vote, and the Incumbency Advantage in Congress," *American Political Science Review* 101:2 (2007): 289–301.
21. For a discussion of Johnson's decision, refer to Robert A. Caro, *The Path to Power* (New York: Knopf, 1983).
22. David Karol, "Forcing Their Hands? Campaign Finance Law, Retirement Announcements and the Rise of the Permanent Campaign in US Senate Elections," *Congress & the Presidency* 42:1 (2015): 79–94.
23. Mayhew, *Congress.*
24. Sarah Binder and Mark Spindel, *The Myth of Independence: How Congress Governs the Federal Reserve* (Princeton, NJ: Princeton University Press, 2017).
25. Jonathan Krasno and Donald P. Green, "The Dynamics of Campaign Fundraising in House Elections," *Journal of Politics* 56 (1991): 459–74.
26. Norrander, *Imperfect Primary.*
27. Michael Babaro, "Candidates Stick to Script, If Not the Truth, in the 2016 Race," *New York Times*, November 7, 2015, www.nytimes.com/2015/11/08/us/politics/candidates-stick-to-script-if-not-the-truth-in-2016-race.html (accessed 4/19/22).
28. For details, refer to the House Ethics Committee guidelines at https://ethics.house.gov/campaign/campaign-work-house-employees (accessed 4/19/22).
29. Kevin Arceneaux, Johanna Dunaway, Martin Johnson, and Ryan J. Vander Wielen, "Strategic Candidate Entry and Congressional Elections in the Era of Fox News," *American Journal of Political Science* 64:2 (2020): 398–415.
30. Matt Bai, "Turnout Wins Elections," *New York Times Magazine*, December 14, 2003, p. 100.
31. Christopher Drew, "New Telemarketing Ploy Steers Voters on Republican Path," *New York Times*, November 6, 2006, www.nytimes.com/2006/11/06/us/politics/06push.html (accessed 4/19/22).
32. For a history of presidential debates, refer to the Commission on Presidential Debates site at www.debates.org (accessed 4/19/22).
33. For a video library of presidential campaign ads, refer to Museum of the Moving Image, "The Living Room Candidate: Presidential Campaign Commercials 1952–2012," http://livingroomcandidate.org (accessed 4/4/22).
34. Museum of the Moving Image, "The Living Room Candidate: 1964: Johnson vs. Goldwater," http://livingroomcandidate.org/commercials/1964/dowager (accessed 4/4/22).
35. Museum of the Moving Image, "Living Room Candidate: 1964: Johnson vs. Goldwater."
36. John Sides, Lynn Vavreck, and Christopher Warshaw, "The Effect of Television Advertising in United States Elections," *American Political Science Review* (2021): 1–17; Yanna Krupnikov, "When Does Negativity Demobilize? Tracing the Conditional Effect of Negative Campaigning on Voter Turnout," *American Journal of Political Science* 55:4 (2011): 797–813.
37. Richard Adams, "US Midterm Elections 2010: The 10 Worst Political Ads," *Guardian*, November 2, 2010, www.theguardian.com/world/richard-adams-blog/2010/nov/02/us-midterm-elections-2010-top-10-worst-political-ads (accessed 4/20/22).

38. Josh L. Kalla and David E. Broockman, "'Outside Lobbying' over the Airwaves: A Randomized Field Experiment on Televised Issue Ads," *American Political Science Review* (2021): 1–7.
39. David Doherty and E. Scott Adler, "The Persuasive Effects of Partisan Campaign Mailers," *Political Research Quarterly* 67:3 (2014): 562–73.
40. Josh L. Kalla and David Broockman, "The Minimal Persuasive Effects of Campaign Contact in General Elections: Evidence from 49 Field Experiments," *American Political Science Review* 112:1 (2018): 148–66.
41. Contribution and spending data are available from the Center for Responsive Politics at www.opensecrets.org.
42. Brian Stelter, "The Price of 30 Seconds," *New York Times*, October 1, 2007, http://mediadecoder.blogs.nytimes.com/2007/10/01/the-price-of-30-seconds (accessed 4/19/22).
43. Yasmin Dawood, "Campaign Finance and American Democracy," *Annual Review of Political Science* 18 (2015): 329–48.
44. Lynda Powell, *The Influence of Campaign Contributions in State Legislatures* (Ann Arbor: University of Michigan Press, 2012).
45. David Karol, "If You Think Super PACs Have Changed Everything about Presidential Primaries, Think Again," *Washington Post*, September 21, 2015, www.washingtonpost.com/blogs/monkey-cage/wp/2015/09/21/if-you-think-super-pacs-have-changed-everything-about-the-presidential-primary-think-again (accessed 3/20/22).
46. For a discussion, refer to Thomas Patterson, *The Vanishing Voter: Public Involvement in an Age of Understanding* (New York: Knopf, 2002), especially Chapter 1, "The Incredible Shrinking Electorate," pp. 3–22.
47. William H. Riker and Peter Ordeshook, "A Theory of the Calculus of Voting," *American Political Science Review* 62 (1968): 25–39.
48. Michael McDonald, The United States Elections Project, www.electproject.org (accessed 4/4/22).
49. Pew Research Center, "Regular Voters, Intermittent Voters, and Those Who Don't," October 18, 2006, www.pewresearch.org/wp-content/uploads/sites/4/legacy-pdf/292.pdf (accessed 4/19/22).
50. For a review of the literature on issue voters, refer to Jon K. Dalager, "Voters, Issues, and Elections: Are Candidates' Messages Getting Through?," *Journal of Politics* 58 (1996): 486–515.
51. Richard P. Lau and David P. Redlawsk, *How Voters Decide: Information Processing during Electoral Campaigns* (New York: Cambridge University Press, 2006).
52. Samuel Popkin, *The Reasoning Voter: Communication and Persuasion in Presidential Campaigns* (Chicago: University of Chicago Press, 1991).
53. Richard R. Lau and David P. Redlawsk, "Advantages and Disadvantages of Cognitive Heuristics in Political Decision Making," *American Journal of Political Science* 45 (2001): 951–71.

What Do the Facts Say?

a. See "Trump's Challenge: The President Dares Congress to 'Impeach This,'" Sean Hannity, October 1, 2019, https://hannity.com/media-room/trumps-challenge-the-president-dares-congress-to-impeach-this/ (accessed 5/14/22).

b. Philip Bump, "The Four Simple Reasons Trump's 'Impeach This' Map Doesn't Make Any Sense," *Washington Post*, October 1, 2019, www.washingtonpost.com/politics/2019/10/01/four-simple-reasons-that-trumps-impeach-this-map-doesnt-make-any-sense/ (accessed 5/14/22).

Chapter 10

1. Quoted in Naomi Jagoda, "Democrats Offer Bill to Undo Business Tax Provisions in Coronavirus Law," *The Hill*, https://thehill.com/policy/finance/494647-democrats-offer-bill-to-undo-business-tax-provisions-in-coronavirus-law (accessed 5/5/22).
2. Chuck Grassley, "Coronavirus-Damaged Businesses Deserve Financial Relief," www.grassley.senate.gov/news/news-releases/grassley-op-ed-coronavirus-damaged-businesses-deserve-financial-relief (accessed 5/5/22).
3. Jim Zarroli, "Even the Los Angeles Lakers Got a PPP Small Business Loan," National Public Radio, April 27, 2020, www.npr.org/sections/coronavirus-live-updates/2020/04/27/846024717/even-the-la-lakers-got-a-ppp-small-business-loan (accessed 5/5/22).
4. For an excellent summary of the details, see Steven M. Rosenthal and Aravind Boddupalli, "Heads I Win, Tails I Win Too: Winners from the Tax Relief for Losses in the CARES Act," Tax Policy Center, April 20, 2020, www.taxpolicycenter.org/taxvox/heads-i-win-tails-i-win-too-winners-tax-relief-losses-cares-act (accessed 5/5/22).
5. Joint Committee on Taxation, "Estimated Revenue Effects of the Revenue Provisions Contained in an Amendment in the Nature of a Substitute to H.R. 748, the 'Coronavirus Aid, Relief, and Economic Security ("CARES")' Act," JCX-11R-20, April 23, 2020, www.jct.gov/publications.html?func=startdown&id=5255 (accessed 5/5/22).
6. Alexis de Tocqueville, *Democracy in America* (originally published in 1835 and 1840; edition quoted here, Harvey C. Mansfield and Delba Winthrop, editors [Chicago: University of Chicago Press, 2000]), 182.
7. Robert A. Dahl, *A Preface to Democratic Theory* (Chicago: University of Chicago Press, 1951) and *Who Governs? Democracy and Power in an American City* (New Haven, CT: Yale University Press, 1961); David Truman, *The Governmental Process* (New York: Harper and Row, 1951).
8. Theodore Lowi, *The End of Liberalism: The Second Republic of the United States* (New York: W. W. Norton, 1979); E. E. Schattschneider, *The Semisovereign People: A Realist's View of Democracy in America* (Hinsdale, IL: Dryden, 1975).
9. Frank R. Baumgartner et al., *Lobbying and Policy Change: Who Wins, Who Loses, and Why* (Chicago: University of Chicago Press, 2009).
10. Lobbying regulations are often changed; the discussion here is just a general guide. For a summary of federal law, see "Lobbying Disclosure Act Guidance," Office of the Clerk, U.S. House of Representatives, January 31, 2017, https://lobbyingdisclosure.house.gov/amended_lda_guide.html; for state law, see Lobbying Regulation, National Conference of State Legislatures, www.ncsl.org/research/ethics/lobbyist-regulation.aspx (both accessed 5/5/22).
11. Nadja Popovich, Livia Albeck-Ripka, and Kendra Pierre-Louis, "The Trump Administration Is Reversing 100 Environmental Rules. Here's the Full List," *New York Times*, July 15, 2020, www.nytimes.com/interactive/2020/climate/trump-environment-rollbacks.html (accessed 5/5/22).
12. Monica Samayoa and Bradley W. Parks, "Biden Pumps the Brakes on More than 100 Trump Environmental Policy Decisions," Oregon Public Broadcasting, January 22, 2021,

www.opb.org/article/2021/01/22/biden-environment-climate-change-executive-order/ (accessed 4/6/22).

13. Frank Baumgartner and Beth Leech, *Basic Interests: The Importance of Interest Groups in Politics and in Political Science* (Princeton, NJ: Princeton University Press, 1999), p. 109.

14. Beth L. Leech et al., "Drawing Lobbyists to Washington: Government Activity and the Demand for Advocacy," *Political Research Quarterly* 58:1 (March 2005): 19–30.

15. OpenSecrets, "Bills," www.opensecrets.org/federal-lobbying/bills (accessed 5/5/22).

16. Project on Government Oversight, "Brass Parachutes: Defense Contractors' Capture of Pentagon Officials through the Revolving Door," November 5, 2018, https://s3.amazonaws.com/docs.pogo.org/report/2018/POGO_Brass_Parachutes_DoD_Revolving_Door_Report_2018-11-05.pdf (accessed 5/5/22).

17. Roxana Tiron, "Lockheed Martin Leads Expanded Lobbying by US Defense Industry," *Washington Post*, January 26, 2012, www.washingtonpost.com/business/economy/lockheedmartin-leads-expanded-lobbying-by-us-defenseindustry/2012/01/26/gIQAlgQtaQ_story.html (accessed 5/5/22).

18. However, the sector of "finance, insurance, and real estate" spent $502,107,659 on lobbying in 2019, which is a lot!

19. Tim LaPira, Lee Drutman, and Matthew Grossmann, "The Interest Group Top Tier: More Groups, Concentrated Clout," paper presented at the 2014 American Political Science Association Annual Meeting.

20. 2023 Ranked Sectors, OpenSecrets, https://www.opensecrets.org/federal-lobbying/ranked-sectors?cycle=2023; total spending on lobbying is from OpenSecrets, "Trends in Spending," www.opensecrets.org/federal-lobbying/trends-in-spending (both accessed 8/1/24).

21. For more on this argument, see Tim Harford, "There's Not Enough Money in Politics," *Slate*, April 1, 2006, www.slate.com/id/2138874 (accessed 5/5/22); and Stephen Ansolabehere, John M. de Figueiredo, and James M. Snyder, "Why Is There So Little Money in American Politics?," *Journal of Economic Perspectives* 17 (2003): 105–30.

22. See Black Lives Matter, https://blacklivesmatter.com/about/ (accessed 4/7/22).

23. Chime Asonye, "The Art of Black Lives Matter: Lessons for Organizations and Policymakers from the Streets," Brookings Institution, September 15, 2021, www.brookings.edu/blog/how-we-rise/2021/09/15/the-art-of-black-lives-matter-lessons-for-organizations-and-policymakers-from-the-streets/ (accessed 4/7/22).

24. Scott Ainsworth, *Analyzing Interest Groups: Group Influence on People and Policies* (New York: W. W. Norton, 2002).

25. Timothy LaPira and Hershel F. Thomas III, "Revolving Door Lobbyists and Interest Representation," *Interest Groups and Advocacy* 3 (2013): 4–29.

26. One hundred and six members retired in January 2019; 58 of those were employed by mid-2020, and 31 of those were employed in lobbying jobs. Data available at OpenSecrets, "Revolving Door: Former Members of the 115th Congress," www.opensecrets.org/revolving/departing.php (accessed 5/5/22).

27. Theodoric Meyer, "Has Trump Drained the Swamp in Washington?," Politico, October 19, 2017, www.politico.com/story/2017/10/19/trump-drain-swamp-promises-243924 (accessed 5/5/22).

28. Paul Waldman, "In Trump's Swamp, the Corporate Lobbyists Are in Charge," *Washington Post*, July 17, 2019, www.washingtonpost.com/opinions/2019/07/17/trumps-swamp-corporate-lobbyists-are-charge/; David Mora, "We Found a 'Staggering' 281 Lobbyists Who've Worked in the Trump Administration," Columbia Journalism Investigations, *ProPublica*, October 15, 2019, www.propublica.org/article/we-found-a-staggering-281-lobbyists-whove-worked-in-the-trump-administration (both accessed 5/5/22).

29. John M. Donnelly, "Pentagon Looks to Undo Parts of McCain Anti-lobbying Law," April 14, 2020, *Roll Call*, www.rollcall.com/2020/04/14/pentagon-looks-to-undo-parts-of-revolving-door-law/ (accessed 5/5/22).

30. "Executive Order on Ethics Commitments by Executive Branch Personnel," White House, January 20, 2021, www.whitehouse.gov/briefing-room/presidential-actions/2021/01/20/executive-order-ethics-commitments-by-executive-branch-personnel/ (accessed 4/7/22).

31. Robert H. Salisbury et al., "Who Works with Whom? Interest Group Alliances and Opposition," *American Political Science Review* 81 (1987): 1217–34.

32. Business-Industry Political Action Committee, "About BIPAC," www.bipac.org/about-us (accessed 5/5/22).

33. Chaoyuan She, "Social Media Dissemination of Counter Accounts and Stakeholder Support—Evidence from Greenpeace's 'Save the Arctic' Campaign on Facebook," *Accounting Forum* (2022), DOI: 10.1080/01559982.2021.2019524 (accessed 4/7/22).

34. Thomas Holyoke, "Choosing Battlegrounds: Interest Group Lobbying across Multiple Venues," *Political Science Quarterly* 56 (2003): 325–36.

35. Beth Kindig, "Microsoft Fairly and Squarely Beat Amazon in $10 Billion Pentagon Cloud Contract," MarketWatch, December 7, 2019, www.marketwatch.com/story/microsoft-fairly-and-squarely-beat-amazon-in-10-billion-pentagon-cloud-contract-2019-12-03. Amazon has sued in federal court, claiming that President Trump intervened to stop Amazon from getting the contract; see Aaron Gregg, "Microsoft Blasts Amazon's 'Sensationalist and Politicized Rhetoric' in Pentagon Cloud Lawsuit," *Washington Post*, February 11, 2020, www.washingtonpost.com/business/2020/02/11/microsoft-blasts-amazons-sensationalist-politicized-rhetoric-pentagon-cloud-lawsuit/ (both accessed 5/5/22).

36. AARP, "AARP Research," www.aarp.org/research/ (accessed 5/5/22).

37. James Q. Wilson, *Political Organizations* (New York: Basic Books, 1974).

38. AAA, Foundation for Traffic Safety, www.aaafoundation.org/home (accessed 7/29/16).

39. Kenneth Kollman, *Outside Lobbying: Public Opinion and Interest Group Strategies* (Princeton, NJ: Princeton University Press, 1998).

40. Jack Walker, *Mobilizing Interest Groups in America* (Ann Arbor: University of Michigan Press, 1991); Frank R. Baumgartner et al., *Lobbying and Policy Change.*

41. John P. Heinz, Edward O. Laumann, and Robert Salisbury, *The Hollow Core: Private Interests in National Policymaking* (Cambridge, MA: Harvard University Press, 1993).

42. Richard L. Hall and Alan V. Deardorff, "Lobbying as Legislative Subsidy," *American Political Science Review* 100 (2006): 69–84.

43. Hall and Deardorff, "Lobbying as Legislative Subsidy."

44. David Austen-Smith and John R. Wright, "Counteractive Lobbying," *American Journal of Political Science* 38:1 (1994): 25–44.

45. Yosef Getachew, Jonathan Walter, Beth Rotman, and Paul S. Ryan, "Broadband Gatekeepers: How ISP Lobbying and Political Influence Shapes the Digital Divide," Common

Cause, July 2021, p. 17, www.commoncause.org/wp-content/uploads/2021/07/CCBroadbandGatekeepers_WEB1.pdf (accessed 4/7/22).

46. Baumgartner and Leech, *Basic Interests*, p. 152.

47. Anthony Madonna and Ian Ostrander, "If Congress Keeps Cutting Its Staff, Who Is Writing Your Laws? You Won't Like the Answer," *Washington Post*, August 20, 2015, www.washingtonpost.com/news/monkey-cage/wp/2015/08/20/if-congress-keeps-cutting-its-staff-who-is-writing-your-laws-you-wont-like-the-answer/?utm_term=.d4773b24c7cf (accessed 5/5/22).

48. Rob O'Dell and Nick Penzenstadler, "You Elected Them to Write New Laws. They're Letting Corporations Do It Instead," *USA Today*, April 3, 2019, www.usatoday.com/in-depth/news/investigations/2019/04/03/abortion-gun-laws-stand-your-ground-model-bills-conservatives-liberal-corporate-influence-lobbyists/3162173002/ (accessed 4/7/22). The study was a joint investigation by *USA Today*, the *Arizona Republic*, and the Center for Public Integrity.

49. O'Dell and Penzenstadler, "You Elected Them."

50. Christine A. DeGregorio, *Networks of Champions: Leadership, Access, and Advocacy in the U.S. House of Representatives* (Ann Arbor: University of Michigan Press, 1992).

51. Daniel Carpenter, *The Forging of Bureaucratic Autonomy: Reputations, Networks, and Policy Innovation in Executive Agencies, 1862–1928* (Princeton, NJ: Princeton University Press, 2002).

52. Public Citizen, www.citizen.org (accessed 5/5/22).

53. Rick C. Wade, "Connecting Americans to Prosperity: How Infrastructure Can Bolster Inclusive Economic Growth," U.S. Chamber of Commerce, February 9, 2022, www.uschamber.com/diversity/rick-wade-congressional-testimony-connecting-americans-to-prosperity-how-infrastructure-can-bolster-inclusive-economic-growth (accessed 4/8/22).

54. Thomas T. Holyoke, "Interest Groups Going to Court," in *Interest Groups and Lobbying: Pursuing Political Interests in America*, 2nd ed. (New York: Routledge, 2020), pp. 230–257.

55. Paul Sabin, *Public Citizens: The Attack on Big Government and the Remaking of American Liberalism* (New York: W. W. Norton, 2021); Catherine Albiston, "Democracy, Civil Society, and Public Interest Law," *Wisconsin Law Review*, 2018: 187–214, https://heinonline.org/HOL/Page?collection=journals&handle=hein.journals/wlr2018&id=195&men_tab=srchresults (accessed 4/8/22).

56. Lauren Cohen Bell, *Warring Factions: Interest Groups, Money, and the New Politics of Senate Confirmation* (Columbus: Ohio State University Press, 2002).

57. Jesse Drucker, "The Tax-Break Bonanza inside the Economic Rescue Package," *New York Times*, April 24, 2020, www.nytimes.com/2020/04/24/business/tax-breaks-wealthy-virus.html (accessed 5/5/22).

58. Kevin W. Hula, *Lobbying Together: Interest Group Coalitions in Legislative Politics* (Washington, DC: Georgetown University Press, 1999).

59. Jeanne Cummings, "Word Games Could Threaten Climate Bill," Politico, June 9, 2009, www.politico.com/news/stories/0609/24059.html (accessed 5/5/22).

60. AARP, "NRTA Tips and Tool for Engaging Elected Officials Virtually," https://videos.aarp.org/detail/video/6196527077001/nrta-tips-and-tool-for-engaging-elected-officials-virtually (accessed 9/9/22).

61. Erica Chenoweth and Jeremy Pressman, "This Is What We Learned by Counting the Women's Marches," *Washington Post*, February 7, 2017, www.washingtonpost.com/news/monkey-cage/wp/2017/02/07/this-is-what-we-learned-by-counting-the-womens-marches/?utm_term=.4dd6925ad4a6 (accessed 5/5/22).

62. In addition to Planned Parenthood and the Natural Resources Defense Council, other supporting organizations included the AFL-CIO, Amnesty International USA, the Mothers of the Movement, the National Center for Lesbian Rights, the National Organization for Women, MoveOn.org, Human Rights Watch, Code Pink, Black Girls Rock!, the NAACP, the American Indian Movement, EMILY's List, Oxfam, Greenpeace USA, and the League of Women Voters.

63. Richard Fenno, *Home Style: U.S. House Members in Their Districts* (Boston: Little, Brown, 1978). See also Brandice Caines-Wrone, David W. Brady, and John F. Cogan, "Out of Step, Out of Office: Electoral Accountability and House Members' Voting," *American Political Science Review* 96 (2002): 127–40.

64. Emily Yoffe, "Am I the Next Jack Abramoff?," *Slate*, April 1, 2006, www.slate.com/id/2137886 (accessed 5/5/22).

65. Kollman, *Outside Lobbying*.

66. Eamon Javers and Meghna Maharishi, "How Google and Amazon Bankrolled a 'Grassroots' Activist Group of Small Business Owners to Lobby against Big Tech Oversight," CNBC Investigation, March 30, 2022, www.cnbc.com/2022/03/30/how-google-and-amazon-bankrolled-a-grassroots-activist-group-of-small-business-owners-to-lobby-against-big-tech-oversight.html (accessed 4/8/22).

67. Beth Daley, "How Airbnb and Uber Use Activist Tactics that Disguise Their Corporate Lobbying as Grassroots Campaigns," The Conversation, April 15, 2021, https://theconversation.com/how-airbnb-and-uber-use-activist-tactics-that-disguise-their-corporate-lobbying-as-grassroots-campaigns-158899 (accessed 4/8/22).

68. Climate Emergency Mobilization Team, Sierra Club, https://content.sierraclub.org/grassrootsnetwork/teams/climate-emergency-mobilization-team (accessed 4/8/22).

69. Gregory Calderia, Marie Hojnacki, and John R. Wright, "The Lobbying Activities of Organized Interests in Federal Judicial Nominations," *Journal of Politics* 62 (2000): 51–69.

70. C. Ryan Barber and Dave Levinthal, "'Dark Money' Groups Are Mobilizing around Biden's Nomination of Ketanji Brown Jackson to the Supreme Court," *Business Insider*, February 25, 2022, www.businessinsider.com/dark-money-biden-supreme-court-nominee-ketanji-brown-jackson-2022-2; Jamila Bey, "Anti-Abortion Groups Mobilizing against Judge Ketanji Brown Jackson," *Washington Informer*, March 11, 2022, www.washingtoninformer.com/anti-abortion-groups-mobilizing-against-judge-ketanji-brown-jackson/ (accessed 4/8/22).

71. *Citizens United v. Federal Election Commission*, 558 U.S. 310 (2010).

72. Data from OpenSecrets, www.opensecrets.org and the Federal Election Commission, www.fec.gov (accessed 11/8/20).

73. While this strategy means that the realtors have only a small impact on any given election, it is consistent with gaining favor with members of Congress, no matter who is in power.

74. All data are from OpenSecrets, "Political Action Committees (PACs)," www.opensecrets.org/political-action-committees-pacs/2020 (accessed 4/8/22).

75. John G. Matsusaka, "Direct Democracy and Fiscal Gridlock: Have Voter Initiatives Paralyzed the California Budget?," *State Politics and Policy* 5 (2005): 346–62; John Dinan, "State Constitutional Initiative Processes and Governance in the Twenty-First Century," *Chapman Law Review* 19:1 (2016): 61–108.

76. National Conference of State Legislatures, "The Term-Limited States," www.ncsl.org/research/about-state-legislatures/chart-of-term-limits-states.aspx (accessed 4/8/22).

77. "History of Marijuana on the Ballot," Ballotpedia, https://ballotpedia.org/History_of_marijuana_on_the _ballot (accessed 5/5/22).
78. "2020 Marijuana Legalization and Marijuana-Related Ballot Measures," Ballotpedia, https://ballotpedia.org/2020 _marijuana_legalization_and_marijuana-related_ballot _measures (accessed 5/5/22); Alex Leeds Matthews and Christopher Hickey, "More US states are regulating marijuana. See where it's legal across the country," CNN, April 19, 2024, https://www.cnn.com/us/us-states-where-marijuana-is -legal-dg/index.html (accessed 7/30/24).
79. Frederick J. Boehmke, "The Initiative Process and the Dynamics of State Interest Group Populations," *State Politics and Policy Quarterly* 8:4 (Winter 2008): 362–83.
80. John G. Matsusaka, *For the Many or the Few: The Initiative, Public Policy, and American Democracy* (Chicago: University of Chicago Press, 2004).
81. Elizabeth R. Gerber, *The Populist Paradox: Interest Group Influence and the Promise of Direct Legislation* (Princeton, NJ: Princeton University Press, 1999).
82. "California Proposition 56, Tobacco Tax Increase (2016)," Ballotpedia, https://ballotpedia.org/California _Proposition_56,_Tobacco_Tax_Increase_(2016) (accessed 5/5/22).
83. Baumgartner and Leech, *Basic Interests*, pp. 147–67.
84. Annual Budget from the Humane Society of the United States, Annual Report, 2021, p. 31, www.humanesociety.org /sites/default/files/docs/HSUS-HSI_AR21.pdf; lobbying expenses from OpenSecrets, "Client Profile: Humane Society of the US," www.opensecrets.org/federal-lobbying/clients /summary?cycle=2021&id=D000026546 (both accessed 9/9/22).
85. Lee Drutman, "The Solution to Lobbying Is More Lobbying," *Washington Post*, April 29, 2015, www.washingtonpost .com/blogs/monkey-cage/wp/2015/04/29/the-solution-to -lobbying-is-more-lobbying (accessed 5/5/22).
86. Keith E. Schnakenberg, "Informational Lobbying and Legislative Voting," *American Journal of Political Science* 61:1 (January 2017): 129–45.
87. Nicholas Fandos, "House Votes to Sharply Expand Concealed-Carry Gun Rights," December 6, 2017, *New York Times*, www.nytimes.com/2017/12/06/us/politics/house-concealed -carry-guns-nra-reciprocity.html (accessed 5/5/22).
88. Emma Leathley, "Net Neutrality," OpenSecrets, December 2017, www.opensecrets.org/news/issues/net_neutrality/ (accessed 5/5/22).
89. Eric Bradner, "Alabama Election: Doug Jones Scores Stunning Win, but Moore Won't Concede," CNN, December 13, 2017, www.cnn.com/2017/12/12/politics/alabama-senate-election -mainbar/index.html (accessed 5/5/22).
90. David Lowery, "Why Do Organized Interests Lobby? A Multi-Goal, Multi-Context Theory of Lobbying," *Polity* 39 (2007): 29–54.
91. Amy McKay, "Negative Lobbying and Policy Outcomes," *American Politics Review* 40 (2011): 116–46.
92. Jeffrey M. Berry, *The Interest Group Society* (New York: HarperCollins, 1997); Raymond A. Bauer, Ithiel de Sola Pool, and Lewis Dexter, *American Business and Public Policy* (New York: Atherton, 1963).
93. Kollman, *Outside Lobbying.*
94. Frank Baumgartner and Beth Leech, "Interest Niches and Policy Bandwagons: Patterns of Interest Group Involvement in National Politics," *Journal of Politics* 63 (2001): 1191–1213.
95. Martina Barash, "Bump-Stock Ban Remains as Appeals Court Splits on Gun Law," Bloomberg Law, December 3, 2021, https://news.bloomberglaw.com/product-liability-and-toxics -law/bump-stock-ban-remains-as-appeals-court-splits-on -gun-law (accessed 4/8/22); *Garland v. Cargill*, 602 U.S. 406 (2024).
96. Data from Yvonne Wingett Sanchez and Rob O'Dell "What Is ALEC? 'The Most Effective Organization' for Conservatives, Says Newt Gingrich," *USA Today*, April 3, 2019, www.usatoday .com/story/news/investigations/2019/04/03/alec-american -legislative-exchange-council-model-bills-republican -conservative-devos-gingrich/3162357002/ (accessed 8/23/22).

Take a Stand

a. Jacob Weisberg, "Three Cities, Three Scandals: What Jack Abramoff, Anthony Pellicano, and Jared Paul Stern Have in Common," *Slate*, April 9, 2006, www.slate.com/id/2140238 (accessed 5/5/22).
b. Herschel F. Thomas and Timothy M. LaPira, "How Many Lobbyists Are in Washington? Shadow Lobbying and the Gray Market for Policy Advocacy," *Interest Groups and Advocacy* 6:3 (2017): 199–214.

Chapter 11

1. Quoted in Morgan Gstalter, "Cruz: No Path to Citizenship for Dreamers," *The Hill*, January 25, 2018, https://thehill.com /latino/370771-cruz-no-path-to-citizenship-for-dreamers (accessed 3/15/22).
2. Quoted in Felicia Sonmez, "House Passes Immigration Bill to Protect 'Dreamers,' Offer a Path to Citizenship," *Washington Post*, June 4, 2019, www.washingtonpost.com /powerpost/house-poised-to-pass-immigration-bill-that -would-protect-dreamers/2019/06/04/bac5cf98-86d7-11e9 -a491-25df61c78dc4_story.html (accessed 3/15/22).
3. White House, "Statement by President Joe Biden on DACA and Legislation for Dreamers," July 17, 2021, www.whitehouse.gov /briefing-room/statements-releases/2021/07/17/statement-by -president-joe-biden-on-daca-and-legislation-for-dreamers/ (accessed 3/2/22).
4. Katie Reilly, "Here's What President Trump Has Said about DACA in the Past," *Time*, September 5, 2017, http://time. com/4927100/donald-trump-daca-past-statements/ (accessed 3/15/22).
5. Most of the poll questions specified the conditions of the DACA program for becoming a citizen: "To qualify, immigrants had to be under the age of 30 as of 2012, have no criminal record, and be a student, in the military, or have earned a high school diploma." A few only mentioned not having a criminal record. Refer to PollingReport.com, "Immigration/Border Security," www.pollingreport.com/immigration.htm for a record of the polls taken early in 2018 (accessed 3/15/22).
6. Daniel Hemel, "Candidate Kamala Harris Had a Plan to Help Dreamers. Why Not Use It?," *Washington Post*, January 20, 2022, www.washingtonpost.com/outlook/2022/01/20/dreamers -harris-citizenship-executive-action/ (accessed 3/2/22).
7. Sahil Kapur, "White House seizes on Mitch McConnell's remarks that Trump stalled action on border security," NBC News, April 26, 2024, https://www.nbcnews.com/politics /joe-biden/white-house-mitch-mcconnell-trump-stalled -action-border-rcna149331; Richard Cowan "'Dreamers' Left Out in the Cold by US Senate Border Bill," US News, Feb. 5, 2024 (both accessed 4/28/24).
8. The case is currently before the Fifth Circuit Court of Appeals. The earliest the Supreme Court would hear an appeal is 2025.

Refer to "DACA Court Case Updates: Summary of Litigation and Potential Supreme Court Case," February 2, 2024, FWD.us, https://www.fwd.us/news/daca-court-case/ (accessed 4/28/24).

9. Refer to Wendy J. Schiller and Charles Stewart III, *Electing the Senate: Indirect Democracy before the Seventeenth Amendment* (Princeton, NJ: Princeton University Press, 2015), for an analysis of Senate elections before the popular vote. Refer to Paul Gronke, *The Electorate, the Campaign, and the Office: A Unified Approach to Senate and House Elections* (Ann Arbor: University of Michigan Press, 2000), for research showing that the House and Senate elections share many similar characteristics. Refer to Richard F. Fenno, *Senators on the Campaign Trail: The Politics of Representation* (Norman: University of Oklahoma Press, 1996), for a good general discussion of Senate elections.

10. The poll data on Congress's general approval are from PollingReport.com; refer to www.pollingreport.com/CongJob.htm (accessed 3/2/22). The occupations poll was conducted by Gallup in December 2017; refer to http://news.gallup.com/poll/1654/honesty-ethics-professions.aspx (accessed 3/15/22).

11. "Congress Less Popular Than Cockroaches, Traffic Jams," Public Policy Polling, January 8, 2013, www.publicpolicypolling.com/pdf/2011/PPP_Release_Natl_010813_.pdf (accessed 3/15/22).

12. Claudine Gay, "Spirals of Trust? The Effect of Descriptive Representation on the Relationship between Citizens and Their Government," *American Journal of Political Science 46:4* (October 2002): 717–32.

13. Jennifer E. Manning, "Membership of the 118th Congress: A Profile," Congressional Research Service, April 29, 2024, pp. 7–8, https://crsreports.congress.gov/product/pdf/R/R47470 (accessed 4/30/24). In addition to those mentioned in the text, P.B.S. Pinchback was elected by the Louisiana state legislature in 1873, but he was not seated.

14. David T. Canon, *Race, Redistricting, and Representation: The Unintended Consequences of Black Majority Districts* (Chicago: University of Chicago Press, 1999); Katherine Tate, *Concordance: Black Lawmaking in the U.S. Congress from Carter to Obama* (Ann Arbor, MI: University of Michigan Press, 2014); Stella M. Rouse, *Latinos in the Legislative Process: Interests and Influence* (New York: Cambridge University Press, 2013); Michele L. Swers, *Women in the Club: Gender and Policy Making in the Senate* (Chicago: University of Chicago Press, 2013); Michele L. Swers, *The Difference Women Make: The Policy Impact of Women in Congress* (Chicago: University of Chicago Press, 2002).

15. R. Douglas Arnold, *The Logic of Congressional Action* (New Haven, CT: Yale University Press, 1990), pp. 60–71.

16. Richard F. Fenno, *Home Style: House Members in Their Districts* (Boston: Little, Brown, 1978).

17. David R. Mayhew, *Congress: The Electoral Connection* (New Haven, CT: Yale University Press, 1974).

18. Mayhew, *Congress*, p. 17.

19. Mayhew, *Congress*, p. 37.

20. Patrick J. Sellers, "Fiscal Consistency and Federal District Spending in Congressional Elections," *American Journal of Political Science* 41:3 (July 1997): 1024–41; Justin Grimmer, Sean J. Westwood, and Solomon Messing, *The Impression of Influence* (Princeton, NJ: Princeton University Press, 2014).

21. David T. Canon, "History in the Making: The 2nd District in Wisconsin," in *The Battle for Congress: Candidates, Consultants, and Voters*, ed. James A. Thurber (Washington, DC: Brookings Institution Press, 2001), pp. 199–238.

22. Gary C. Jacobson, *The Politics of Congressional Elections*, 5th ed. (New York: Longman, 2001), pp. 24–30.

23. Fenno, *Home Style*.

24. The trend has been an increasing gap between incumbent and challenger spending in the House, peaking at nearly 5–1 in 2016. However, in 2018 Democratic challengers raised almost as much as Republican incumbents ($1.86 million versus $2.26 million), reducing the overall gap to less than 2–1 (Democratic incumbents outspent Republican challengers by more than 7–1 in 2018). The gap was back to more than 4–1 in 2022. Refer to Center for Responsive Politics, "Incumbent Advantage," OpenSecrets.org, https://www.opensecrets.org/elections-overview/incumbent-advantage (accessed 4/30/24).

25. Morris Fiorina, *Congress: Keystone of the Washington Establishment*, rev. ed. (New Haven, CT: Yale University Press, 1989).

26. Michael C. Bender and Maggie Haberman, "Rally with Trump? Some G.O.P. Candidates Aren't Thrilled about It," *New York Times*, September 17, 2022, www.nytimes.com/2022/09/17/us/politics/trump-rally-republican-candidates.html (accessed 9/23/22).

27. "2020 Census: Apportionment of the U.S. House of Representatives," U.S. Census Bureau, April 26, 2021, www.census.gov/library/visualizations/2021/dec/2020-apportionment-map.html (accessed 3/4/22).

28. The language used by the Court in 1960 was "one-man, one-vote." The Court ruled in *Baker v. Carr*, 369 U.S. 186 (1962), that state legislative districts that were unequal in population violated the equal protection clause of the Fourteenth Amendment. *Wesberry v. Sanders*, 376 U.S. 1 (1964), applied the same principle to U.S. House districts.

29. *Davis v. Bandemer*, 478 U.S. 109 (1986); *Vieth v. Jubelirer*, 541 U.S. 267 (2004); *League of United Latin American Citizens v. Perry*, 548 U.S. 399 (2006).

30. The North Carolina case is *Rucho v. Common Cause*, 558 U.S. ____ (2019); this case was consolidated with the Maryland case, *Lamone v. Benisek* (No. 18-726), and was issued as a single opinion for both cases. 2022 district information is from Allan James Vestal, "States Are Redrawing Every Congressional District in the U.S. Here Is Where We Stand," Politico, September 1, 2022, www.politico.com/interactives/2022/congressional-redistricting-maps-by-state-and-district/ (accessed 9/23/22).

31. *Shelby County v. Holder*, 570 U.S. 529 (2013). The full citation for the North Carolina case is *Shaw v. Reno*, 509 U.S. 630 (1993).

32. *Allen v. Milligan*, 599 U.S. 1 (2023).

33. Hansi Lo Wang, "Judges block Louisiana's congressional map. A Supreme Court appeal is likely," National Public Radio, April 30, 2024, https://www.npr.org/2024/04/30/1247555372/louisiana-congressional-redistricting (accessed 4/30/24).

34. "Redistricting Commissions," BallotPedia, https://ballotpedia.org/Redistricting_commissions (accessed 4/30/24).

35. Refer to Kenneth R. Mayer and David T. Canon, *The Dysfunctional Congress: The Individual Roots of an Institutional Dilemma* (New York: Routledge, 1999), for an extended discussion of this argument.

36. Richard F. Fenno, "If as Ralph Nader Says, Congress Is the 'Broken Branch,' How Come We Love Our Congressman So Much?," in *Congress in Change: Evolution and Reform*, ed. Norman J. Ornstein (New York: Praeger, 1975), pp. 277–87.

37. Nicole Ogrysko, "Trump Signs Shutdown-Averting Spending Bills, Makes Federal Pay Raise Law," Federal News Service, December 20, 2019, https://federalnewsnetwork.com

/budget/2019/12/trump-signs-shutdown-averting-spending-bills-makes-federal-pay-raise-law/ (accessed 6/2/20).

38. Caitlin Emma, "House Swiftly Advances Behemoth $1.4T Spending Deal," Politico, December 17, 2019, www.politico.com/news/2019/12/17/house-passes-massive-deal-to-fund-government-and-avoid-shutdown-086514 (accessed 3/15/22).

39. Paul Kane, "The E-word Is Poised for a Capitol Hill Comeback," *Washington Post,* January 12, 2022, www.washingtonpost.com/politics/2022/01/12/earmarks-congress/. Refer to House Committee on Appropriations, "Transparency," https://appropriations.house.gov/transparency for the House requests and United States Senate Committee on Appropriations, "Congressionally Directed Spending Requests," www.appropriations.senate.gov/congressionally-directed-spending-requests for the Senate requests (accessed 3/8/22).

40. An important qualification to the norm was imposed by Republicans in 1995 when they set a six-year term limit for committee and subcommittee chairs.

41. Lisa Mascaro and Farnoush Amiri, "Kevin McCarthy ousted as House speaker in dramatic vote," PBS, October 3, 2023, https://www.pbs.org/newshour/politics/kevin-mccarthy-ousted-as-house-speaker-in-dramatic-vote (accessed 5/2/24).

42. Scott Wong, Ali Vitali, Rebecca Kaplan, and Kyle Stewart, "Rep. Mike Johnson elected 56th speaker of the House, ending weeks of GOP chaos," NBC News, October 25, 2023, https://www.nbcnews.com/politics/congress/mike-johnson-elected-new-speaker-house-vote-rcna122151 (accessed 5/2/24).

43. Carl Hulse, "McCarthy's Extraordinary Downfall Reflects an Ungovernable G.O.P.," *New York Times*, October 3, 2023, www.nytimes.com/2023/10/03/us/kevin-mccarthy-house-speaker.html (accessed 12/2/24).

44. Scott R. Meinke, *Leadership Organizations in the House of Representatives* (Ann Arbor: University of Michigan Press, 2019).

45. John Calhoun held the previous record of 31 from 1825–1832. Only 301 tie votes have been broken by the vice president in U.S. history. Refer to "Votes to Break Ties in the Senate," U.S. Senate, https://www.senate.gov/legislative/TieVotes.htm (accessed 5/2/24).

46. Michael Macagnone, "2021 Vote Studies: Party Unity Rates Underscore Polarized State of the Union," *CQ Magazine*, March 7, 2022, http://library.cqpress.com.ezproxy.library.wisc.edu/cqmagazine/weeklyreport117-000006471826 (accessed 9/23/22).

47. David W. Rohde, *Parties and Leaders in the Post-reform House* (Chicago: University of Chicago Press, 1991); Danielle M. Thomsen, *Opting Out of Congress: Partisan Polarization and the Decline of Moderate Candidates* (New York: Cambridge University Press, 2017).

48. David Rohde and John Aldrich, "The Transition to Republican Rule in the House: Implications for Theories of Congressional Politics," *Political Science Quarterly* 112:4 (Winter 1997–1998): 541–67.

49. Nelson W. Polsby, *Congress and the Presidency,* 4th ed. (Englewood Cliffs, NJ: Prentice Hall, 1986), p. 111.

50. James M. Curry and Frances E. Lee, *The Limits of Party: Congress and Lawmaking in a Polarized Era* (Chicago: University of Chicago Press, 2020).

51. Paul Steinhauser, "Obama 2014 Campaign Role: Fundraiser-in-Chief," CNN Politics, March 20, 2014, http://politicalticker.blogs.cnn.com/2014/03/20/obama-2014-campaign-role-fundraiser-in-chief (accessed 4/16/14).

52. Kathryn Watson, "Trump Addresses Record-Setting GOP Fundraiser," CBS News, March 20, 2018, www.cbsnews.com/news/trump-addresses-one-of-the-biggest-gop-fundraisers-of-the-year (accessed 6/7/18); Will Weissert and Zeke Miller, "Biden Posts $7.8M In-person Haul, Planning Bigger Money Push," Associated Press, May 13, 2022, https://apnews.com/article/2022-midterm-elections-biden-congress-c2c16dc44b0a8e8fe9e7889d417fcf25 (accessed 9/23/22).

53. Here is a list of the reasons Greene was removed from her committees: she "expressed support on social media for the assassination of Speaker Nancy Pelosi; agreed with those who said the mass shooting at Marjory Stoneman Douglas High School in Parkland, Fla., in 2018 was a 'false flag' operation; questioned whether a plane hit the Pentagon on 9/11; said President Barack Obama was Muslim; posted a photo of herself on Facebook holding a gun to images of Democratic Representatives Alexandria Ocasio-Cortez, Ilhan Omar, and Rashida Tlaib; mused that a space laser aligned with Jewish financial interests caused devastating wildfires in California; and aligned herself with QAnon, a baseless belief about an anti-Trump 'deep state' that engages in child sex trafficking and satanism." Chris Marquette, "House Votes to Strip Marjorie Taylor Greene of Committee Assignments," *Roll Call*, February 4, 2021, https://rollcall.com/2021/02/04/marjorie-taylor-greene-does-not-renounce-past-comments-as-house-moves-to-punish-her/ (accessed 3/8/22).

54. Robert Draper and Michael S. Schmidt, "Chief Witness Against Gaetz Is Cooperating with House Ethics Investigation," *New York Times*, February 9, 2024, https://www.nytimes.com/2024/02/09/us/politics/gaetz-sex-trafficking.html (accessed 5/6/24).

55. Dan Mangan, "Capitol Police Probing Claims GOP Lawmakers Gave Tours to Trump Supporters before Riot," CNBC, January 15 2021, www.cnbc.com/2021/01/15/gop-trump-supporters-tours-before-capitol-riot.html (accessed 3/8/22).

56. Clare Foran and Haley Talbot, "House votes to expel Santos from Congress in historic vote," CNN, December 1, 2023, https://www.cnn.com/2023/12/01/politics/george-santos-expel-resolution-vote/index.html (accessed 5/6/24).

57. This includes the Intelligence Committee, which is a permanent select committee but operates like a standing committee. Refer to United States Senate, "Committees," www.senate.gov/committees/ and United States House of Representatives, "Committees," www.house.gov/committees (accessed 3/8/22).

58. However, research shows that members of Congress do not confine their credit claiming to legislative activity that is rooted in committee work. Refer to Justin Grimmer, Sean J. Westwood, and Solomon Messing, *The Impression of Influence: Legislator Communication, Representation, and Democratic Accountability* (Princeton, NJ: Princeton University Press, 2014).

59. Keith Krehbiel, *Information and Legislative Organization* (Ann Arbor: University of Michigan Press, 1992).

60. Richard F. Fenno, *Congressmen in Committees* (Boston: Little, Brown, 1973).

61. Richard L. Hall, *Participation in Congress* (New Haven, CT: Yale University Press, 1996).

62. Grace Segers, Stefan Becket, and Melissa Quinn, "House Committee Approves Rules for Impeachment Vote," CBS News, December 18, 2019, www.cbsnews.com/live-updates/trump-impeachment-house-rules-committee-debate-live-updates-live-stream-2019-12-17/ (accessed 3/15/22).

63. Barbara Sinclair, *Unorthodox Lawmaking* (Washington, DC: CQ Press, 2000), p. xiv.

64. Hong Min Park, Steven S. Smith, and Ryan J. Vander Wielen, *Politics over Process: Partisan Conflict and Post-passage Politics in the U.S. Congress* (Ann Arbor: University of Michigan Press, 2017).

65. "Continuing Resolutions: Overview of Components and Practices," Congressional Research Service, Table 1, p. 11, https://crsreports.congress.gov/product/pdf/R/R46595 (accessed 5/6/24).

66. USA PATRIOT Act, Hearing before the Subcommittee on the Constitution, Civil Rights and Civil Liberties, Committee on the Judiciary, House of Representatives, September 22, 2009, www.gpo.gov/fdsys/pkg/CHRG-111hhrg52409/html/CHRG-111hhrg52409.htm (accessed 3/15/22).

67. Emily Cochrane and Jonathan Weisman, "Pelosi Delays Vote on $1 Trillion Infrastructure Bill," *New York Times*, November 15, 2021, www.nytimes.com/live/2021/09/30/us/government-shutdown-infrastructure (accessed 3/8/22).

68. Aidan Quigley, "House passes sweeping fiscal 2024 spending package," National Public Radio, March 22, 2024 (accessed 5/6/24).

69. Congressional Record, 46th Congress, 2nd session, April 22, 1880, p. 2661.

70. Howard H. Baker Jr., "Leaders Lecture Series Address to the Senate," July 14, 1998, www.senate.gov/artandhistory/history/common/generic/Leaders_Lecture_Series_Baker.htm (accessed 3/15/22).

71. Paul Kane, "Reid, Democrats Trigger 'Nuclear' Option; Eliminate Most Filibusters on Nominees," *Washington Post*, November 21, 2013, www.washingtonpost.com/politics/senate-poised-to-limit-filibusters-in-party-line-vote-that-would-alter-centuries-of-precedent/2013/11/21/d065cfe8-52b6-11e3-9fe0-fd2ca728e67c_story.html (accessed 3/15/22).

72. Matt Flegenheimer, "Senate Republicans Deploy 'Nuclear Option' to Clear Path for Gorsuch," *New York Times*, April 6, 2017, www.nytimes.com/2017/04/06/us/politics/neil-gorsuch-supreme-court-senate.html (accessed 2/20/18).

73. Lauren Peller, "House GOP opens up amendment process for first time in 7 years, allowing debate and delay," ABC News, January 26, 2023, https://abcnews.go.com/Politics/house-gop-opens-amendment-process-time-7-years/story?id=96636193; for data through the 117th Congress, refer to Donald R. Wolfensberger, "House Rules Data," Bipartisan Policy Center, June 30, 2022, https://bipartisanpolicy.org/report/house-rules-data/ (both accessed 5/6/24).

74. Philip Rucker and Robert Costa, "McCarthy's Comments on Benghazi Probe May Be a Political Gift to Clinton," *Washington Post*, October 1, 2015, www.washingtonpost.com/politics/mccarthys-comments-on-benghazi-probe-may-be-a-political-gift-to-clinton/2015/10/01/6ceb6e88-6857-11e5-9223-70cb36460919_story.html. For an account of the Ukraine investigation, refer to Jerrold Nadler, "Impeachment of Donald J. Trump, President of the United States," Report of the Committee on the Judiciary, House of Representatives, December 2019, https://docs.house.gov/billsthisweek/20191216/CRPT-116hrpt346.pdf (both accessed 3/15/22).

75. House Committee on Oversight and Reform, "Oversight of Trump Administration," https://oversight.house.gov/oversight-of-trump-administration (accessed 3/15/22).

76. "Read the full transcript from Hunter Biden's testimony," *Washington Post*, February 29, 2024, https://www.washingtonpost.com/politics/2024/02/29/hunter-biden-transcript/ (accessed 5/6/24).

77. Mathew McCubbins and Thomas Schwartz, "Congressional Oversight Overlooked: Police Patrol versus Fire Alarm," *American Journal of Political Science* 28:1 (February 1984): 165–77.

78. House Committee on the Judiciary, Hearing on "Oversight of the Department of Justice: Political Interference and Threats to Prosecutorial Independence," June 24, 2020, https://judiciary.house.gov/calendar/eventsingle.aspx?EventID=3034; House Committee on the Judiciary, Hearing on "Oversight of the Department of Justice," July 28, 2020, https://judiciary.house.gov/calendar/eventsingle.aspx?EventID=3140 (both accessed 3/15/22).

79. Select Committee to Investigate the January 6th Attack on the U.S. Capitol, https://january6th.house.gov/ (accessed 3/8/22).

80. Elizabeth Williamson, "Hundreds of Biden Nominees Stuck in Senate Limbo amid G.O.P. Blockade," *New York Times*, January 8, 2022, www.nytimes.com/2022/01/08/us/politics/biden-nominees-senate-confirmation.html; "Joe Biden has picked 631 nominees to fill key roles in his administration so far," *Washington Post*, May 6, 2024 (both accessed 5/6/24).

81. Maureen Chowdhury, Aditi Sangal, and Elise Hammond, "Senate kills articles of impeachment against Mayorkas," CNN, April 17, 2024, https://www.cnn.com/politics/live-news/alejandro-mayorkas-impeachment-trial-senate-04-17-24/index.html (accessed 5/6/24).

82. Farnoush Amiri, "House approves impeachment inquiry into President Biden as Republicans rally behind investigation," Associated Press, December 14, 2023, https://apnews.com/article/joe-biden-impeachment-inquiry-mike-johnson-94884b322da40ca9315ac5f4e73a3e86 (accessed 5/6/24).

83. The quote is from *Trump v. Vance*, 591 U.S. ____ (2020); the other case was *Trump v. Mazars USA, LLP*, 591 U.S. ____ (2020) (both accessed 3/9/22).

84. Because the case carried over into the Biden administration, the politics were strained: House Democrats continued to push for a broad-ranging subpoena, but Biden was worried about giving up too much ground given that Republicans could regain control of Congress in 2022. The compromise required limited testimony from McGahn but did not resolve the broader questions of executive privilege in this context. For an excellent discussion, refer to Jonathan Shaub, "Why the McGahn Agreement Is a Devastating Loss for Congress," Lawfare, May 19, 2021, www.lawfareblog.com/why-mcgahn-agreement-devastating-loss-congress (accessed 3/9/22).

85. Elizabeth McElvein and Benjamin Wittes, "Trump Loses Big on Executive Privilege," Lawfare, January 20, 2022, www.lawfareblog.com/trump-loses-big-executive-privilege; the Supreme Court's ruling is *Donald J. Trump, Former President of the United States v. Bennie G. Thompson, in His Official Capacity as Chairman of the United States House Select Committee to Investigate the January 6th Attack on the United States Capitol, et al.*, www.supremecourt.gov/opinions/21pdf/21a272_9p6b.pdf (both accessed 3/9/22).

86. Statistics and Historical Comparison, Govtrack.US, https://www.govtrack.us/congress/bills/statistics (accessed 5/7/24).

What Do the Facts Say?

a. "Senate by Population," https://docs.google.com/spreadsheets/d/1N4xCSR5NgoQykK_nQhkbdGd2WzLISD_t-DmUbfTFPfs/edit#gid=1813007479. For more historical data, refer to Lee Drutman, "The Senate Has Always Favored Smaller States. It Just Didn't Help Republicans Until Now," FiveThirtyEight, July 29, 2020, https://fivethirtyeight.com/features/the-senate-has-always-favored-smaller-states-it-just-didnt-help-republicans-until-now/ (both accessed 3/4/22).

Take a Stand

a. The warning against entering the "political thicket" comes from *Colegrove v. Green*, 328 U.S. 549 (1946).

Chapter 12

1. Quoted in Meagan Flynn and Allyson Chiu, "Trump Says His 'Authority Is Total.' Constitutional Experts Have 'No Idea' Where He Got That," *Washington Post*, April 14, 2020, www.washingtonpost.com/nation/2020/04/14/trump-power-constitution-coronavirus/ (accessed 5/11/22).
2. Quoted in Morgan Chalfant and Brett Samuels, "Trump Eases Back on Asserting Power over Governors on Reopening," *The Hill*, April 14, 2020, https://thehill.com/homenews/administration/492837-trump-eases-back-on-asserting-power-over-governors-on-reopening (accessed 5/11/22).
3. Philip Bump, "What Trump Has Undone," *Washington Post*, August 24, 2017, www.washingtonpost.com/news/politics/wp/2017/08/24/what-trump-has-undone/ (accessed 5/11/22).
4. Lori Cox Han and Caroline Heldman, eds., *Madam President? Gender and Politics on the Road to the White House* (Boulder, CO: Lynne Rienner, 2020).
5. John Aldrich, *Why Parties? A Second Look* (Chicago: University of Chicago Press, 2011).
6. Ernest R. May, "The Making of the Monroe Doctrine," in *The Making of the Monroe Doctrine* (Cambridge, MA: Harvard University Press, 2013).
7. Arthur M. Schlesinger Jr., *The Age of Jackson* (Boston: Little, Brown, 1945).
8. David Greenberg, "Lincoln's Crackdown," *Slate*, November 30, 2001, www.slate.com/id/2059132 (accessed 5/11/22).
9. Stephen Skowronek, *Building a New American State: The Expansion of National Administrative Capacities* (New York: Cambridge University Press, 1982).
10. Theda Skocpol, *Protecting Soldiers and Mothers: The Political Origins of Social Policy in the United States* (Cambridge, MA: Harvard University Press, 1995).
11. Alexander L. George and Juliette L. George, *Woodrow Wilson and Colonel House: A Personality Study* (Lexington, MA: Plunkett Lake, 2019).
12. Thomas J. Knock, *To End All Wars: Woodrow Wilson and the Quest for a New World Order* (New York: Oxford University Press, 1992).
13. Jeffrey W. Coker, *Franklin D. Roosevelt: A Biography* (Westport, CT: Greenwood, 2005).
14. Chester Pach and Elmo Richardson, *The Presidency of Dwight D. Eisenhower* (Lawrence: University Press of Kansas, 1991).
15. Richard E. Neustadt, *Presidential Power and the Modern Presidents: The Politics of Leadership from Roosevelt to Reagan* (1960; repr., New York: Free Press, 1991).
16. David E. Lewis, "Presidential Appointments and Personnel," *Annual Review of Political Science* 14 (2011): 47–66.
17. Christina M. Kinane, "Control without Confirmation: The Politics of Vacancies in Presidential Appointments," *American Political Science Review* 115:2 (2021): 599–614.
18. Kenneth Mayer, *With the Stroke of a Pen: Executive Orders and Presidential Power* (Princeton, NJ: Princeton University Press, 2001); Adam L. Warber, *Executive Orders and the Modern Presidency: Legislating from the Oval Office* (Boulder, CO: Lynne Rienner, 2006).
19. Brian Hallett, *Declaring War: Congress, the President, and What the Constitution Does Not Say* (New York: Cambridge University Press, 2012).
20. Frederick S. Tipson, "The War Powers Resolution: A Continuing Constitutional Struggle," in *Making Government Work: From White House to Congress*, ed. Robert E. Hunter (New York: Routledge, 2019), pp. 115–51.
21. Lewis Fisher and David G. Adler, "The War Powers Resolution: Time to Say Goodbye," *Political Science Quarterly* 113:1 (1998): 1–20.
22. William G. Howell and Jon C. Pevehouse, *While Dangers Gather: Congressional Checks on Presidential War Powers* (Princeton, NJ: Princeton University Press, 2007).
23. William G. Howell, *Power without Persuasion: The Politics of Direct Presidential Action* (Princeton, NJ: Princeton University Press, 2015).
24. Andrew Rudalevige, *Managing the President's Program: Presidential Leadership and Legislative Policy Formation* (Princeton, NJ: Princeton University Press, 2002).
25. Scott M. Guenther and Samuel Kernell, "Veto Threat Bargaining with a Bicameral Congress," *Political Research Quarterly* 74:3 (2021): 628–44.
26. Mitchell A. Sollenberger and Mark J. Rozell, *Executive Privilege: Presidential Power, Secrecy, and Accountability* (Lawrence: University Press of Kansas, 2020).
27. For a summary of the case, see Oyez, *United States v. Nixon*, 418 U.S. 683 (1974), www.oyez.org/cases/1973/73-1766 (accessed 5/11/22).
28. Mark J. Rozell, *Executive Privilege: The Dilemma of Secrecy and Democratic Accountability* (Baltimore, MD: Johns Hopkins University Press, 1994).
29. Richard W. Waterman and Yu Ouyang, "Rethinking Loyalty and Competence in Presidential Appointments," *Public Administration Review* 80:5 (2020): 717–32.
30. David E. Lewis, *The Politics of Presidential Appointments: Political Control and Bureaucratic Performance* (Princeton, NJ: Princeton University Press, 2010).
31. David E. Lewis, "Staffing Alone: Unilateral Action and the Politicization of the Executive Office of the President, 1988–2004," *Presidential Studies Quarterly* 35 (2005): 496–514.
32. Peter Baker, *Days of Fire: Bush and Cheney in the White House* (New York: Anchor, 2013).
33. Neustadt, *Presidential Power*.
34. Terry M. Moe and William G. Howell, "The Presidential Power of Unilateral Action," *Journal of Law, Economics, and Organization* 15 (1999): 132–46.
35. Mariana Alfaro and Eugene Scott, "More Than Two Dozen Senate Republicans Demand Biden Do More for Ukraine after Voting against $13.6 Billion for Ukraine," *Washington Post*, March 17, 2022, www.washingtonpost.com/politics/2022/03/17/republicans-ukraine-aid-vote/ (accessed 5/12/22).
36. These examples appear throughout Moe and Howell, "Presidential Power of Unilateral Action"; see also William G. Howell, "Unilateral Powers: A Brief Overview," *Presidential Studies Quarterly* 35:3 (2005): 417–39.
37. Andrew Rudalevige, *The New Imperial Presidency: Renewing Presidential Power after Watergate* (Ann Arbor: University of Michigan Press, 2005).
38. Michael Barber, Alexander Bolton, and Sharece Thrower, "Legislative Constraints on Executive Unilateralism in Separation of Powers Systems," *Legislative Studies Quarterly* 44:3 (2019): 515–48.
39. Christopher Deering and Forrest Maltzman, "The Politics of Executive Orders: Legislative Constraints on Presidential Power," *Political Research Quarterly* 52:4 (1999): 767–83.
40. David E. Lewis, *Presidents and the Politics of Agency Design: Political Insulation in the United States Government Bureaucracy, 1946–1997* (Palo Alto, CA: Stanford University Press, 2003).

41. David Epstein and Sharyn O'Halloran, *Delegating Powers: A Transaction Cost Politics Approach to Policy Making under Separate Powers* (Cambridge: Cambridge University Press, 1999).
42. William G. Howell, *Thinking about the Presidency: The Primacy of Power* (Princeton, NJ: Princeton University Press, 2015).
43. George C. Edwards III, *On Deaf Ears: The Limits of the Bully Pulpit* (New Haven, CT: Yale University Press, 2003).
44. George C. Edwards III, *Predicting the Presidency: The Potential of Persuasive Leadership* (Princeton, NJ: Princeton University Press, 2015).
45. Eric Berger, "Email Release Reveals Chaos Sowed by President Trump's Hurricane Tweets," Ars Technica, February 1, 2020, https://arstechnica.com/science/2020/02/email-release-reveals-chaos-sowed-by-president-trumps-hurricane-tweets/ (accessed 5/11/22).
46. Stephen Skowronek, *Presidential Leadership in Political Time: Reprise and Reappraisal*, 2nd ed., revised and expanded (Lawrence: University of Kansas Press, 2011).
47. Vicki Divoll, "Transcript: Eight Things I Hate about the Unitary Executive Theory," *Vermont Law Review* 38:1 (Fall 2013), 147–154, https://lawreview.vermontlaw.edu/wp-content/uploads/2014/01/06-Divoll1.pdf; Ilya Somin, "The Risks of the Unitary Executive," CATO Institute, August 31, 2018, www.cato.org/commentary/risks-unitary-executive; Noah Rosenblum, "The Antifascist Roots of Presidential Administration," *Columbia Law Review* 122:1 (January 2022), 1-86, https://search.library.wisc.edu/article/cdi_proquest_journals_2628334866.

Chapter 13

1. Robert A. Heinlein, *Stranger in a Strange Land* (1961; repr., New York: Berkley, 1983), p. 95.
2. Joseph A. Schumpeter, *Capitalism, Socialism and Democracy* (1943; repr., London: Routledge, 2013), p. 206.
3. David E. Lewis, "Deconstructing the Administrative State," *The Journal of Politics* 81:3 (2019): 767–89.
4. Peter B. Evans, Dietrich Rueschemeyer, and Theda Skocpol, *Bringing the State Back In* (New York: Cambridge University Press, 1985).
5. For a history of the FDA, see John P. Swann, FDA History Office, "History of the FDA," www.fda.gov/AboutFDA/History/FOrgsHistory/EvolvingPowers/ucm124403.htm (accessed 5/20/22).
6. Rachel Augustine Potter and Charles R. Shipan, "Agency Rulemaking in a Separation of Powers System," *Journal of Public Policy* 39:1 (2019): 89–113.
7. The *Federal Register* is available at www.federalregister.gov/ (accessed 9/24/24).
8. Audrey L. Gassman, Christine P. Nguyen, and Hylton V. Joffe, "FDA Regulation of Prescription Drugs," *New England Journal of Medicine* 376:7 (2017): 674–82.
9. Stephen Skowronek, *Building a New American State: The Expansion of National Administrative Capacities, 1877–1920* (New York: Cambridge University Press, 1982).
10. Gary J. Miller and Andrew B. Whitford, *Above Politics: Bureaucratic Discretion and Credible Commitment* (New York: Cambridge University Press, 2016).
11. Jason Webb Yackee and Susan Webb Yackee, "A Bias Towards Business? Assessing Interest Group Influence on the U.S. Bureaucracy," *Journal of Politics* 68:1 (2006): 128–39.
12. Juliet Eilperin and Steven Mufson, "Top Interior Official Who Pushed to Expand Drilling in Alaska to Join Oil Company There," *Washington Post*, September 4, 2019, www.washingtonpost.com/climate-environment/2019/09/04/top-interior-official-who-pushed-expand-drilling-alaska-join-oil-company-there/ (accessed 6/7/22).
13. William F. West, "Neutral Competence and Political Responsiveness: An Uneasy Relationship," *Policy Studies Journal* 33:2 (2005): 147–60; Max Weber, *Essays on Sociology* (New York: Oxford University Press, 1958).
14. Samuel Workman, *The Dynamics of Bureaucracy in the U.S. Government: How Congress and Federal Agencies Process Information and Solve Problems* (New York: Cambridge University Press, 2015).
15. Peter H. Schuck, *Why Government Fails So Often: And How It Can Do Better* (Princeton, NJ: Princeton University Press, 2015).
16. Karen Orren and Steven Skowronek, "Regimes and Regime Building in American Government: A Review of the Literature on the 1940s," *Political Science Quarterly* 113 (1998): 689–702.
17. Michael Nelson, "A Short, Ironic History of American National Bureaucracy," *Journal of Politics* 44 (1982): 747–78.
18. Nelson, "Short, Ironic History."
19. John H. Aldrich, *Why Parties?: A Second Look* (Chicago: University of Chicago Press, 2011).
20. Nelson, "Short, Ironic History."
21. W. Bartley Hildreth, *Handbook of Public Administration*, ed. W. Bartley Hildreth, Gerald J. Miller, and Jack Rabin, 4th ed. (New York: Routledge, 2021).
22. James Q. Wilson, "The Rise of the Bureaucratic State," in *The American Commonwealth*, ed. Nathan Glazer and Irving Kristol (New York: Basic Books, 1976).
23. Skowronek, *Building a New American State*.
24. Robert Harrison, *Congress, Progressive Reform, and the New American State* (New York: Cambridge University Press, 2004).
25. The National Archives and Records Administration has an excellent summary of the Pendleton Act at www.ourdocuments.gov/doc.php?flash=false&doc=48 (accessed 6/7/22).
26. B. Guy Peters and Jon Pierre, "Populism and Public Administration: Confronting the Administrative State," *Administration & Society* 51:10 (2019): 1521–45.
27. Ira Katznelson, *Fear Itself: The New Deal and the Origins of Our Time* (New York: W. W. Norton, 2013).
28. Theda Skocpol and Kenneth Finegold, "State Capacity and Economic Intervention in the Early New Deal," *Political Science Quarterly* 97 (1999): 255–70.
29. Erin Schickler and Devin Caughey, "Public Opinion, Organized Labor, and the Limits of New Deal Liberalism, 1936–1945," *Studies in American Political Development* 25:2 (2011): 162–89.
30. Ira Katznelson, Kim Geiger, and Daniel Kryder, "Limiting Liberalism: The Southern Veto in Congress, 1933–1950," *Political Science Quarterly* 108 (1993): 283–306.
31. Julian E. Zelizer, *The Fierce Urgency of Now: Lyndon Johnson, Congress, and the Battle for the Great Society* (New York: Penguin, 2015).
32. David T. Canon, *Race, Redistricting, and Representation: The Unintended Consequences of Black Majority Districts* (Chicago: University of Chicago Press, 1999).
33. Robert F. Durant, *Building the Compensatory State: An Intellectual History and Theory of American Administrative Reform* (New York: Routledge, 2019).
34. Theda Skocpol, *Social Policy in the United States* (Princeton, NJ: Princeton University Press, 2020).
35. Andrew Rudalevige, *Managing the President's Program: Presidential Leadership and Legislative Policy Formulation* (Princeton, NJ: Princeton University Press, 2018).

36. Andrew Rudalevige, "The Structure of Leadership: Presidents, Hierarchies, and Information Flow," *Presidential Studies Quarterly* 35 (2005): 333–60.
37. David E. Lewis, *Presidents and the Policy of Agency Design: Political Insulation in the United States Government Bureaucracy, 1946–1997* (Stanford, CA: Stanford University Press, 2003).
38. Yasmeen Abutaleb and Laurie McGinley, "Ousted Vaccine Official Alleges He Was Demoted for Prioritizing 'Science and Safety,'" *Washington Post*, May 5, 2020, www.washingtonpost.com/health/2020/05/05/rick-bright-hydroxychloroquine-whistleblower-complaint/ (accessed 6/7/22).
39. Terry M. Moe, "An Assessment of the Positive Theory of Congressional Dominance," *Legislative Studies Quarterly* 4 (1987): 475–98.
40. William A. Niskanen, *Bureaucracy and Public Economics* (Washington, DC: Edward Elgar, 1976); Robert Whaples and Jac C. Heckelman, "Public Choice Economics: Where Is There Consensus?," *American Economist* 49 (2005): 66–78.
41. Bill Heniff, Jr., Megan Lynch, and Jessica Tollestrup, "Introduction to the Federal Budget Process," *Congressional Research Service*, 2012.
42. Joel D. Aberbach, "The Political Significance of the George W. Bush Administration," *Social Policy and Administration* 39:2 (2005): 130–49.
43. David E. Lewis, "The Politics of Agency Termination: Confronting the Myth of Agency Immortality," *Journal of Politics* 64 (2002): 89–107.
44. Ronald A. Wirtz, "Put It on My . . . Er, His Tab: Opinion Polls Show a Big Gap between the Public's Desire for Services and Its Willingness to Pay for These Services," *Fedgazette*, January 2004, www.minneapolisfed.org/publications/fedgazette/put-it-on-my-er-his-tab (accessed 6/25/22).
45. James L. Perry and Annie Hondeghem, *Motivation in Public Management: The Call of Public Service* (Oxford: Oxford University Press, 2008).
46. Paul Light, *A Government Well-Executed: Public Service and Public Performance* (Washington, DC: Brookings Institution Press, 2003).
47. Dennis Cauchon, "Some Federal Workers More Likely to Die than Lose Jobs," *USA Today*, July 19, 2011, p. A1.
48. Ronald N. Johnson and Gary D. Libecap, *The Federal Civil Service System and the Problem of Bureaucracy* (Chicago: University of Chicago Press, 2007).
49. For the details of the Hatch Act, see Daniel Engber, "Can Karl Rove Plot Campaign Strategy on the Government's Dime?," *Slate*, April 21, 2006, www.slate.com/id/2140418 (accessed 6/7/22).
50. Nicole Ogrysko, "Energy Employee Banned for 3 Years after 'Flagrant' Hatch Act Violation," Federal News Network, January 16, 2020, https://federalnewsnetwork.com/workforce/2020/01/energy-employee-banned-for-3-years-after-flagrant-hatch-act-violation/ (accessed 6/7/22).
51. Timothy Noah, "Low Morale at Homeland Security," *Slate*, September 14, 2005, www.slate.com/id/2126313 (accessed 6/7/22).
52. For details on the SES, see U.S. Office of Personnel Management, www.opm.gov/policy-data-oversight/senior-executive-service/ (accessed 6/7/22).
53. "The Nominees Trump Tapped for Key Roles during His Term," *Washington Post*, www.washingtonpost.com/graphics/politics/trump-administration-appointee-tracker/database/?utm_term=.1b5914b69716 (accessed 6/4/22).
54. Lisa Rein and Juliet Eilperin, "White House Installs Political Aides at Cabinet Agencies to Be Trump's Eyes and Ears," *Washington Post*, March 19, 2017, www.washingtonpost.com/powerpost/white-house-installs-political-aides-at-cabinet-agencies-to-be-trumps-eyes-and-ears/2017/03/19/68419f0e-08da-11e7-93dc-00f9bdd74ed1_story.html (accessed 6/7/22).
55. Alexander Bolton, John M. De Figueiredo, and David E. Lewis, "Elections, Ideology, and Turnover in the U.S. Federal Government," *Journal of Public Administration Research and Theory* 31:2 (2021): 451–66.
56. Todd Frankel, "Why the CDC Still Isn't Researching Gun Violence, despite the Ban Being Lifted Two Years Ago," *Washington Post*, January 14, 2015, www.washingtonpost.com/news/storyline/wp/2015/01/14/why-the-cdc-still-isnt-researching-gun-violence-despite-the-ban-being-lifted-two-years-ago/ (accessed 6/7/22).
57. Umair Irfan, "'Climate Change' and 'Global Warming' Are Disappearing from Government Websites," Vox, January 11, 2018, www.vox.com/energy-and-environment/2017/11/9/16619120/trump-administration-removing-climate-change-epa-online-website (accessed 6/7/22).
58. John D. Huber and Charles R. Shipan, *Deliberate Discretion? The Institutional Foundations of Bureaucratic Autonomy* (New York: Cambridge University Press, 2002).
59. Anthony M. Bertelli and Kathleen M. Doherty, "Setting the Regulatory Agenda: Statutory Deadlines, Delay, and Responsiveness," *Public Administration Review* 79:5 (2019): 710–20.
60. Mathew D. McCubbins, Roger G. Noll, and Barry R. Weingast, "Structure and Process as Solutions to the Politician's Principal–Agency Problem," *Virginia Law Review* 74 (1989): 431–82.
61. Barry R. Weingast, "Caught in the Middle: The President, Congress, and the Political–Bureaucratic System," in *Institutions of American Democracy: The Executive Branch*, ed. Joel D. Aberbach and Mark A. Peterson (New York: Oxford University Press, 2006), pp. 312–43.
62. Keith Whittington and Daniel P. Carpenter, "Executive Power in American Institutional Development," *Perspectives on Politics* 1 (2003): 495–513.
63. Roger Noll, Mathew McCubbins, and Barry Weingast, "Administrative Procedures as Instruments of Political Control," *Journal of Law, Economics, and Organization* 3 (1987): 243–77.
64. Hannah Knowles, "Top Democrats Launch Investigation into Late-Night Firing of State Department Inspector General," *Washington Post*, March 16, 2020, www.washingtonpost.com/politics/2020/05/16/state-department-inspector-general-fired-democrats-decry-dangerous-pattern-retaliation/ (accessed 6/7/22).
65. Mathew McCubbins and Thomas Schwartz, "Congressional Oversight Overlooked: Fire Alarms vs. Police Patrols," *American Journal of Political Science* 28 (1984): 165–79.
66. McCubbins and Schwartz, "Congressional Oversight Overlooked."
67. Banks Miller, Brett Curry, and Joshua B. Kennedy, "The Role of Advisory Committees in Bureaucratic Oversight: The Case of AGAC," *Congress & the Presidency* 48:2 (2021): 195–218.
68. Terry M. Moe, "Political Control and the Power of the Agent," *Journal of Law, Economics, and Organization* 22 (2006): 1–29.
69. See David Weil, "OSHA: Beyond the Politics," *Frontline*, January 9, 2003, www.pbs.org/wgbh/pages/frontline/shows/workplace/osha/weil.html (accessed 6/7/22).

Chapter 14

1. Timothy Bella, "Critics Slam Cruz for Saying Biden's Vow to Nominate First Black Woman to Supreme Court Is 'Offensive,'" *Washington Post*, February 1, 2022, www.washingtonpost.com/politics/2022/02/01/cruz-black-woman-biden-supreme-court/ (accessed 3/29/22).
2. Cory Booker, "Booker Statement on the Nomination of Judge Ketanji Brown Jackson to the United States Supreme Court," February 25, 2022, www.booker.senate.gov/news/press/booker-statement-on-the-nomination-of-judge-ketanji-brown-jackson-to-the-united-states-supreme-court (accessed 3/29/22).
3. Nolan D. McCaskill, "In Coming Battle over Biden's Supreme Court Nominee, Republicans Seek Other Targets," *Los Angeles Times*, March 14, 2022, www.latimes.com/politics/story/2022-03-14/republicans-avoid-direct-criticism-supreme-court-nominee-judge-ketanji-brown-jackson (accessed 3/30/22).
4. Justice Gorsuch was confirmed by a 54–45 vote, Justice Kavanaugh by 50–48 (the lowest percentage of votes for a positive result in U.S. history), and Justice Barrett by 42–48.
5. Olafimihan Oshin and Jordain Carney, "Collins to Back Jackson for Supreme Court," *The Hill*, March 30, 2022, https://thehill.com/homenews/senate/600317-collins-to-back-jackson-for-supreme-court/ (accessed 3/31/22).
6. Debra Cassens Weiss, "Chief Justice Roberts Defends Judicial Independence after Trump's 'Obama Judge' Criticism," *ABA Journal*, November 21, 2018, www.abajournal.com/news/article/chief_justice_roberts_criticizes_trumps_reference_to_obama_judge_in_asylum (accessed 4/11/22).
7. Chandelis Duster, "Justice Amy Coney Barrett Says Supreme Court Is 'Not a Bunch of Partisan Hacks,'" CNN, September 13, 2021, www.cnn.com/2021/09/13/politics/amy-coney-barrett-supreme-court-not-partisan/index.html (accessed 3/30/22).
8. Adam Feldman and Jake S. Truscott, "Supreme Court Stat Review, October Term, 2023–2024," July 1, 2024, EmpiricalSCOTUS, p. 5, https://empiricalscotus.com/2024/07/01/2023-stat-review (accessed 10/3/24).
9. Ralph Ketcham, *The Anti-Federalist Papers and the Constitutional Convention Debates* (New York: Penguin Putnam, 2003), p. 304.
10. Lester S. Jayson, ed., *The Constitution of the United States of America: Analysis and Interpretation* (Washington, DC: U.S. Government Printing Office, 1973), p. 585.
11. David G. Savage, *Guide to the U.S. Supreme Court*, 4th ed. (Washington, DC: CQ Press, 2004), p. 7.
12. Savage, *Guide to the U.S. Supreme Court*, pp. 5–7.
13. Winfield H. Rose, "*Marbury v. Madison*: How John Marshall Changed History by Misquoting the Constitution," *Political Science and Politics* 36:2 (April 2003): 209–14. Rose argues that in a key quotation in the case Marshall intentionally left out a clause of the Constitution that suggests that Congress *did* have the power to expand the original jurisdiction of the Court. Other constitutional scholars reject this argument.
14. *Marbury v. Madison*, 5 U.S. 1 Cranch 137 (1803).
15. Revisionist historians, legal scholars, and political scientists have challenged the landmark status of *Marbury v. Madison*. For example, Michael Stokes Paulsen's *Michigan Law Review* article points out that *Marbury* was not cited in subsequent Supreme Court cases as a precedent for judicial review until the late nineteenth century. Legal scholars in the early twentieth century were the first to promote the idea that *Marbury* was a landmark decision. Paulsen also notes that when the opinion was delivered in 1803 it was not controversial. Even the Jeffersonian Democrats, who were at odds with Marshall's Federalists, thought that it was a reasonable decision and not the institutional power grab that is described in modern accounts. Finally, Marshall made a very narrow case for judicial review, arguing that the Supreme Court could declare legislation that was contrary to the Court's interpretation of the Constitution null and void only if it concerned judicial powers. Revisionists argue that what appear to be broad claims of judicial power in *Marbury* (e.g., the Court has the power "to say what the law is") are taken out of the context of a much narrower claim of power. Michael Stokes Paulsen, "Judging Judicial Review: *Marbury* in the Modern Era: The Irrepressible Myth of *Marbury*," *Michigan Law Review* 101 (August 2003): 2706–43.
16. Keith E. Whittington, "Judicial Review of Congress Database," https://scholar.princeton.edu/kewhitt/judicial-review-congress-database (accessed 3/30/22).
17. Bureau of Justice Statistics, "Federal Criminal Case Processing Statistics Data Tool," https://fccps.bjs.ojp.gov/home.html?dashboard=FJSP-Prosecution&tab=ProsecutionCourtsDefendantsChargedinCriminalCasesAdvanced (accessed 5/22/24). The numbers from 1998 to 2022 were 1,816,383 cases that had a plea out of 1,875,130 convictions, or 96.9 percent.
18. Brandon J. Murrill, "The Supreme Court's Overruling of Constitutional Precedent," Congressional Research Service, CRS Report R45319, September 24, 2018, https://fas.org/sgp/crs/misc/R45319.pdf (accessed 4/11/22). Another compilation of cases shows a similar pattern, but only about a 2:1 difference between cases decided after and before 1950; refer to Constitution Annotated: Analysis and Interpretation of the U.S. Constitution, Table of Supreme Court Decisions Overruled by Subsequent Decisions, Library of Congress, https://constitution.congress.gov/resources/decisions-overruled/ (accessed 5/22/24).
19. *Franchise Tax Board of California v. Hyatt*, 587 U.S. ___ (2019). For a discussion of the implications of this case, refer to Henry Gass, "Overruled: Is Precedent in Danger at the Supreme Court?," *Christian Science Monitor*, June 25, 2019, www.csmonitor.com/USA/Justice/2019/0625/Overruled-Is-precedent-in-danger-at-the-Supreme-Court (accessed 4/11/22).
20. *Lujan v. Defenders of Wildlife*, 504 U.S. 555 (1992).
21. *Food and Drug Administration v. Alliance for Hippocratic Medicine*, 602 U.S. 367 (2024).
22. The case concerning the bombing in Libya was *Kucinich v. Obama*, 821 F.Supp. 2d 110 (Dist. of Columbia 2011). The cases limiting taxpayers' standing to challenge laws they disagree with are *Flast v. Cohen*, 392 U.S. 83 (1968), and *Arizona Christian School Tuition Org. v. Winn*, 131 S.Ct. 1436 (2011).
23. "2022 Snapshot," Court Statistics Project, www.courtstatistics.org/csp-stat-nav-cards-first-row/csp-stat-overview (accessed 9/2/24). There was actually a 28 percent drop in cases in 2020 because of the COVID pandemic. By 2022, the most recent year for which data are available, the number of cases bounced back a bit, to 64.6 million, but were still well short of the pre-pandemic levels.
24. United States Courts, "Authorized Judgeships," www.uscourts.gov/judges-judgeships/authorized-judgeships (accessed 3/30/22).
25. The official name for each appeals court is the "United States Court of Appeals for the Circuit."
26. United States Courts, "Authorized Judgeships."
27. United States Courts, "The Federal Bench—Annual Report 2023," www.uscourts.gov/statistics-reports/federal-bench-annual-report-2023 (accessed 5/22/24).
28. *Ledbetter v. Goodyear Tire & Rubber Co.*, 550 U.S. 618 (2007).

29. The Eleventh Amendment does not mention lawsuits against a state brought in federal court by citizens of that same state. However, in *Alden v. Maine*, 527 U.S. 706 (1999), the Court extended the logic of sovereign immunity to apply to these cases as well. Then in *Franchise Tax Board of California v. Hyatt*, 587 U.S. (2019), the Court ruled that states cannot be sued by citizens in the courts of another state.
30. Brennan Center for Justice, "Judicial Selection: Significant Figures," April 14, 2023, www.brennancenter.org/our-work/research-reports/judicial-selection-significant-figures (accessed 5/22/24).
31. Brennan Center for Justice, "Judicial Selection."
32. Savage, *Guide to the U.S. Supreme Court*, p. 1003.
33. Allyson Escobar, "Why Do Catholics Make Up a Majority of the Supreme Court?," *America Magazine*, October 27, 2020, www.americamagazine.org/politics-society/2018/07/18/why-do-catholics-make-majority-supreme-court (accessed 4/11/22).
34. White House, "President Bush Discusses Judicial Accomplishments and Philosophy," October 6, 2008, https://georgewbush-whitehouse.archives.gov/news/releases/2008/10/20081006-5.html (accessed 4/11/22).
35. Paul Kane, "Reid, Democrats Trigger 'Nuclear' Option; Eliminate Most Filibusters on Nominees," *Washington Post*, November 21, 2013, www.washingtonpost.com/politics/senate-poised-to-limit-filibusters-in-party-line-vote-that-would-alter-centuries-of-precedent/2013/11/21/d065cfe8-52b6-11e3-9fe0-fd2ca728e67c_story.html (accessed 4/11/22).
36. John Roberts, "2023 Year-End Reports on the Federal Judiciary," U.S. Supreme Court, December 31, 2023, www.supremecourt.gov/publicinfo/year-end/2023year-endreport.pdf (accessed 5/30/24).
37. Supreme Court of the United States, *In Re Frederick W. Bauer*, On Motion for Leave to Proceed in forma pauperis, No. 99-5440, Decided October 18, 1999, per curiam, www.justice.gov/sites/default/files/osg/briefs/1990/01/01/sg900418.txt (accessed 4/11/22).
38. Roberts, "2023 Year-End Report on the Federal Judiciary."
39. *New Jersey v. New York*, No. 120 Orig., 118 S.Ct. 1726 (1998), and *Texas v. New Mexico*, 592 U.S. ___ (2020).
40. Henry J. Abraham, *The Judiciary: The Supreme Court in the Governmental Process*, 7th ed. (Boston: Allyn and Bacon, 1987), p. 25, says that original jurisdiction has been invoked "about 150 times." A Lexis search revealed an additional 27 original-jurisdiction cases between 1987 and December 2004. A search of the U.S. Supreme Court's website, www.supremecourt.gov, found 19 more original jurisdiction cases from 2005 to 2023.
41. Amanda L. Tyler, "Setting the Supreme Court's Agenda: Is There a Place for Certification?," *George Washington Law Review Arguendo* 78 (May 2010): 101–18.
42. Savage, *Guide to the U.S. Supreme Court*, p. 848.
43. Refer to Thomas G. Walker and Lee Epstein, *The Supreme Court of the United States: An Introduction* (New York: St. Martin's, 1993), pp. 80–85, for a more detailed discussion of these concepts and citations to the relevant court cases.
44. *Shaw v. Reno*, 509 U.S. 630 (1993).
45. *Elk Grove Unified School District v. Newdow*, 542 U.S. 1 (2004).
46. *Texas v. Pennsylvania*, 592 U.S. ___ (2020). For a discussion of the case, refer to Marcia Coyle, "Why Texas's Election Suit Failed to Reach First Base in the Supreme Court," Constitution Daily, National Constitution Center, December 14, 2020, https://constitutioncenter.org/blog/why-texass-election-suit-failed-to-reach-first-base-in-the-supreme-court (accessed 3/31/22).
47. *West Virginia v. Environmental Protection Agency*, 597 U.S. ___ (2022), Justice Elena Kagan dissent, p. 4.
48. Gregory A. Caldeira and John R. Wright, "The Discuss List: Agenda Building in the Supreme Court," *Law and Society Review* 24 (1990): 813; Benjamin Johnson, "The Supreme Court's Political Docket: How Ideology and the Chief Justice Control the Court's Agenda and Shape Law," *Connecticut Law Review* 50:3 (August 2018): 581–639.
49. Walker and Epstein, *Supreme Court*, p. 89; Ryan C. Black and Ryan J. Owens, *The Solicitor General and the United States Supreme Court: Executive Branch Influence and Judicial Decisions* (New York: Cambridge University Press, 2012).
50. U.S. Supreme Court, "The Court and Its Procedures," www.supremecourt.gov/about/procedures.aspx (accessed 4/11/22).
51. Lee Epstein et al., *The Supreme Court Compendium: Data, Decisions, and Developments*, 6th ed. (Washington, DC: CQ Press, 2015), Table 7-22.
52. Gregory A. Caldeira and John R. Wright, "*Amicus Curiae* before the Supreme Court: Who Participates, When, and How Much?," *Journal of Politics* 52 (August 1990): 803.
53. Richard L. Pacelle Jr., et al., "The Influence of the Solicitor General as Amicus Curiae on the Roberts Court, 2005–2014: A Research Note," *Justice System Journal* 38:2 (2017): 202–8.
54. Andrew Christy, "'Obamacare' Will Rank among the Longest Supreme Court Arguments Ever," National Public Radio, November 15, 2011, www.npr.org/blogs/itsallpolitics/2011/11/15/142363047/obamacare-will-rank-among-the-longest-supreme-court-arguments-ever (accessed 4/11/22).
55. U.S. Supreme Court, *Rules of the Supreme Court of the United States*, adopted April 8, 2019, effective July 1, 2019, www.supremecourt.gov/ctrules/2019RulesoftheCourt.pdf (accessed 3/21/20).
56. Savage, *Guide to the U.S. Supreme Court*, p. 852.
57. U.S. Supreme Court, "Argument Transcripts," www.supremecourt.gov/oral_arguments/argument_transcript/2019 (accessed 4/11/22).
58. Justice Jackson spoke 78,215 words in the 2023–24 term, Justice Gorsuch 51,073, and Justice Kagan 49,636. Jake S. Truscott and Adam Feldman, Empirical SCOTUS, https://empiricalscotus.com/2023-stats/ (accessed 5/30/24).
59. Garrett Epps, "Clarence Thomas Breaks His Silence," *Atlantic*, February 29, 2016, www.theatlantic.com/politics/archive/2016/02/clarence-thomas-supreme-court/471582/ (accessed 4/11/22).
60. For an interesting analysis of oral arguments during the pandemic, refer to Adam Feldman, "Results from the Court's Experiment with a New Oral Argument Format," SCOTUSblog, May 22, 2020, www.scotusblog.com/2020/05/empirical-scotus-results-from-the-courts-experiment-with-a-new-oral-argument-format/. On a lighter note, in addition to the normal problems of remote meetings, like forgetting to turn on your audio, there was one embarrassing moment when there was a distinct sound of a toilet flushing. Refer to Ariane de Vogue, "Supreme Embarrassment: The Flush Heard around the Country," CNN, May 6, 2020, www.cnn.com/2020/05/06/politics/toilet-flush-supreme-court-oral-arguments/index.html (both accessed 4/11/22).
61. "Why it's taking longer for the Supreme Court to hear oral arguments," PBS, January 22, 2023, https://www.pbs.org/newshour/politics/why-its-taking-longer-for-the-supreme-court-to-hear-oral-arguments (accessed 5/30/24).
62. Quoted in Savage, *Guide to the U.S. Supreme Court*, p. 854.

63. Richard J. Lazarus, "Back to 'Business' at the Supreme Court: The 'Administrative Side' of Chief Justice Roberts," *Harvard Law Review Forum* 129:33 (2015): 33–93.
64. Michael A. McCall and Madhavi M. McCall, "Quantifying the Contours of Power: Chief Justice Roberts & Justice Kennedy in Criminal Justice Cases," *Pace Law Review* 37:1 (2016): 115–74.
65. *Smith v. Allwright*, 321 U.S. 649 (1944).
66. Walker and Epstein, *Supreme Court*, p. 110.
67. Linda Greenhouse, "Chief Justice Roberts in His Own Voice: The Chief Justice's Self-Assignment of Majority Opinions," Yale Law School, Public Law Research Paper no. 496, August 15, 2013.
68. Savage, *Guide to the U.S. Supreme Court*, p. 854.
69. Lee Epstein, William M. Landes, and Richard A. Posner, "Are Even Unanimous Decisions in the United States Supreme Court Ideological?," *Northwestern University Law Review* 106:2 (2012): 702.
70. Adam Feldman and Jake S. Truscott, "Supreme Court Stat Review, October Term, 2023–2024."
71. Stephen Vladeck, *The Shadow Docket: How the Supreme Court Uses Stealth Rulings to Amass Power and Undermine the Republic* (New York: Basic Books, 2023).
72. John Ketcham, "Midnight Orders: Increased Use of the Shadow Docket Endangers the Supreme Court's Institutional Legitimacy," City Journal, Manhattan Institute for Policy Research, October 21, 2021, www.city-journal.org/supreme-court-shadow-docket-could-undermine-trust; Steve Vladeck, "The Supreme Court Doesn't Just Abuse Its Shadow Docket. It Does So Inconsistently," *Washington Post*, September 3, 2021, www.washingtonpost.com/outlook/2021/09/03/shadow-docket-elena-kagan-abortion/ (accessed 3/31/22).
73. Suzanne Monyak and Kimberly Strawbridge Robinson, "Biden Top Supreme Court Lawyer Laments Shadow Docket Effect," Bloomberg Law, May 2, 2024, https://news.bloomberglaw.com/us-law-week/biden-top-supreme-court-attorney-laments-shadow-docket-effect. For a complete listing of the emergency docket since 2021, refer to https://www.scotusblog.com/case-files/emergency/emergency-docket-2023/; https://www.scotusblog.com/case-files/emergency/emergency-docket-2022/; https://www.scotusblog.com/category/emergency-appeals-and-applications/ (accessed 6/3/24).
74. *Whole Woman's Health et al. v. Austin Reeve Jackson, Judge, et al.*, 594 U.S. ___ (2021), www.supremecourt.gov/opinions/20pdf/21a24_8759.pdf; the Wisconsin case was *Wisconsin Legislature et al. v. Wisconsin Elections Commission, et al.*, 595 U. S. ___ (2022), https://electionlawblog.org/wp-content/uploads/21A471-PC.pdf (both accessed 3/31/22).
75. U.S. Senate, Senate Judiciary Committee, "Texas's Unconstitutional Abortion Ban and the Role of the Shadow Docket," www.judiciary.senate.gov/meetings/texass-unconstitutional-abortion-ban-and-the-role-of-the-shadow-docket (accessed 3/31/22).
76. Lydia Wheeler, "Justices Forced to Explain Shadow Docket Rulings Under New Bill," Bloomberg Law, May 22, 2024, https://news.bloomberglaw.com/us-law-week/bill-forcing-justices-to-explain-shadow-docket-rulings-unveiled (accessed 6/3/24).
77. Thomas G. Hansford and James F. Spriggs, *The Politics of Precedent on the U.S. Supreme Court* (Princeton, NJ: Princeton University Press, 2006); Mark J. Richards and Herbert M. Kritzer, "Jurisprudential Regimes in Supreme Court Decision Making," *American Political Science Review* 96:2 (June 2002): 305–20.
78. In cases involving statutory interpretation, the language of the law passed by Congress would be the starting point. The logic of these various perspectives on constitutional interpretation generally applies to statutory interpretation as well.
79. Quoted in Lee Epstein and Thomas G. Walker, *Constitutional Law for a Changing America: Institutional Powers and Constraints*, 5th ed. (Washington, DC: CQ Press, 2004), p. 29.
80. The consolidated cases were *Bostock v. Clayton County, Georgia*, 590 U.S. (2020); *Altitude Express v. Zarda*, 590 U.S. (2020); and *R.G. & G.R. Harris Funeral Homes v. EEOC*, 590 U.S. (2020).
81. Emily Bazelon, "How 'History and Tradition' Rulings Are Changing American Law," *New York Times*, April 29, 2024, https://www.nytimes.com/2024/04/29/magazine/history-tradition-law-conservative-judges.html (accessed 6/3/24).
82. *United States v. Rahimi,* 602 U.S. ___ (2024).
83. Epstein and Walker, *Constitutional Law for a Changing America*, p. 31.
84. Seth Stern and Stephen Wermiel, *Justice Brennan: Liberal Champion* (Boston: Houghton Mifflin Harcourt, 2010).
85. Epstein et al., *Supreme Court Compendium*, Table 6-2.
86. Forrest Maltzman and Paul J. Wahlbeck, "Strategic Policy Considerations and Vote Fluidity on the Burger Court," *American Journal of Political Science* 90 (1996): 581–92; Forrest Maltzman, James F. Spriggs, and Paul J. Wahlbeck, *Crafting Law on the Supreme Court: The Collegial Game* (New York: Cambridge University Press, 2000), p. 33.
87. Lawrence Baum, *Judges and Their Audiences: A Perspective on Judicial Behavior* (Princeton, NJ: Princeton University Press, 2006).
88. Finley Peter Dunne, Paul Green, and Jacques Barzun, *Mr. Dooley in Peace and in War* (1898; repr., Champaign-Urbana: University of Illinois Press, 2001).
89. Robert Dahl, "Decision-Making in a Democracy: The Supreme Court as a National Policy-Maker," *Journal of Public Law* 6 (1957): 279–95, is the classic work on this topic. More recent work has challenged Dahl's methods but largely supports the idea that the Court follows the will of the majority.
90. Jeffrey A. Segal, Richard J. Timpone, and Robert M. Howard, "Buyer Beware? Presidential Success through Supreme Court Appointments," *Political Research Quarterly* 53:3 (September 2000): 557–73; Gregory A. Caldeira and Charles E. Smith Jr., "Campaigning for the Supreme Court: The Dynamics of Public Opinion on the Thomas Nomination," *Political Research Quarterly* 58:3 (August 1996): 655–81.
91. William Mishler and Reginald S. Sheehan, "The Supreme Court as a Countermajoritarian Institution? The Impact of Public Opinion on Supreme Court Decisions," *American Political Science Review* 87:1 (March 1993): 87–101.
92. Thomas R. Marshall, *Public Opinion and the Supreme Court* (Boston: Unwin Hyman, 1989), p. 12; as cited in Epstein and Walker, *Constitutional Law for a Changing America*, p. 92.
93. Matthew E. K. Hall, "The Semiconstrained Court: Public Opinion, the Separation of Powers, and the U.S. Supreme Court's Fear of Nonimplementation," *American Journal of Political Science* 58:2 (April 2014): 352–66; Matthew E. K. Hall, *The Nature of Supreme Court Power* (New York: Cambridge University Press, 2011).
94. *Stanford v. Kentucky,* 492 U.S. 361 (1989); *Roper v. Simmons,* 543 U.S. 551 (2005).
95. David O'Brien, *Storm Center: The Supreme Court in American Politics*, 4th ed. (New York: W. W. Norton, 1996), p. 276.
96. Helmut Norpoth and Jeffrey A. Segal, "Popular Influence in Supreme Court Decisions," *American Political Science Review* 88 (1994): 711–16.

97. While it is clear that the Supreme Court is at least somewhat sensitive to public opinion, the reverse does not appear to be true. A survey experiment had half the respondents read Chief Justice Roberts's admonition to President Trump about how there were not "Obama judges and Trump judges" and the other half did not see that statement. Both were shown a story about a federal court's decision on a political asylum case that President Trump was unhappy about to see if the respondents who read Roberts's statement would respond any differently than those who did not. There were absolutely no differences. However, another study by the same authors found that those who saw a speech by Justice Sotomayor were more likely than those who did not see the speech to think that law rather than ideology determined court decisions. Refer to David Fontana and Christopher Krewson, "Can the Supreme Court Learn to Speak Up for Itself?," *Washington Post*, February 26, 2020, washingtonpost.com/magazine/2020/02/26/can-supreme-court-learn-speak-up-itself/?arc404=true (accessed 4/11/22).
98. Thomas M. Keck, *The Most Activist Supreme Court in History: The Road to Modern Judicial Conservatism* (Chicago: University of Chicago Press, 2004).
99. Calculated by the author from data provided by Harold J. Spaeth et al., 2019 Supreme Court Database, Version 2019 Release 01, http://supremecourtdatabase.org (accessed 4/11/22).
100. Jeffrey Rosen, "Has the Supreme Court Gone Too Far?," *Commentary* 116:3 (October 2003): 41–42.
101. *National Federation of Independent Business v. Sebelius*, 567 U.S. 519 (2012).
102. Abby Phillip, Robert Barnes, and Ed O'Keefe, "Supreme Court Nominee Gorsuch Says Trump's Attacks on Judiciary Are 'Demoralizing,'" *Washington Post*, February 9, 2017, www.washingtonpost.com/politics/supreme-court-nominee-gorsuch-says-trumps-attacks-on-judiciary-are-demoralizing/2017/02/08/64e03fe2-ee3f-11e6-9662-6eedf1627882_story.html?utm_term=.ade3f9791d87 (accessed 4/11/22).
103. John Kruzel, "Democratic-backed US Supreme Court ethics bill passed by Senate panel," Reuters, July 20, 2023, https://www.reuters.com/world/us/senate-panel-set-vote-us-supreme-court-ethics-reform-2023-07-20/ (accessed 6/3/24).
104. Josh Gerstein, "Kagan enters fray over Congress' power to police Supreme Court," Politico, August 3, 2023, https://www.politico.com/news/2023/08/03/kagan-enters-fray-over-congress-power-to-police-supreme-court-00109770 (accessed 6/3/24).
105. Josh Gerstein, "6 things to know about the Supreme Court's new ethics code," Politico, November 13, 2023, https://www.politico.com/news/2023/11/13/supreme-court-ethics-code-what-to-know-00126962 (accessed 6/3/24).
106. Nina Totenberg, "Justice Alito declines to recuse himself in Jan. 6-related cases," National Public Radio, May 29, 2024, https://www.npr.org/2024/05/29/g-s1-1617/justice-alito-flags-jan-6 (accessed 6/3/24).
107. *Foster v. Neilson*, 27 U.S. 253 (1829).
108. *Charles B. Rangel v. John A. Boehner*, United States District Court for the District of Columbia, Civil Action No. 13-540, December 11, 2013, p. 48, https://ecf.dcd.uscourts.gov/cgi-bin/show_public_doc?2013cv0540-24 (accessed 4/11/22).
109. *Donald J. Trump v. United States*, 603 U.S. ____ (2024).
110. We thank Dan Smith for raising this point.

Take a Stand

a. Martin Kady II, "Justice Alito Mouths 'Not True,'" Politico, January 27, 2010, www.politico.com/blogs/politico-now/2010/01/justice-alito-mouths-not-true-024608 (accessed 4/11/22).
b. Donald J. Trump, Twitter, June 28, 2020, 10:08 A.M., https://twitter.com/realDonaldTrump/status/1273633632742191106 (accessed 6/17/20).

Chapter 15

1. Mitch McConnell, Twitter, May 15, 2020, 3:04 P.M., https://twitter.com/senatemajldr/status/1261371804133646337 (accessed 7/5/22).
2. Quoted in Erica Werner, Jeff Stein, and Rachael Blade, "McConnell Calls for Five-Year Lawsuit Shield for Businesses as Part of Next Coronavirus Bill," *Washington Post*, July 6, 2020, www.washingtonpost.com/us-policy/2020/07/06/congress-departed-two-week-recess-without-addressing-coronavirus-spikes-economic-strains/ (accessed 7/5/22).
3. Department of Labor, "Unemployment Insurance Weekly Claims," July 9, 2020, www.dol.gov/ui/data.pdf (accessed 7/5/22).
4. Kelsey Snell, "What's Inside the Senate's $2 Trillion Coronavirus Aid Package," National Public Radio, March 26, 2020, www.npr.org/2020/03/26/821457551/whats-inside-the-senate-s-2-trillion-coronavirus-aid-package (accessed 7/5/22).
5. Jeffrey Cheng, Dave Skidmore, and David Wessel, "What's the Fed Doing in Response to the COVID-19 Crisis? What More Could It Do?," Brookings Institution, June 12, 2020, www.brookings.edu/research/fed-response-to-covid19/ (accessed 7/10/20).
6. H.R.1319 - American Rescue Plan Act of 2021, 117th Congress (2021–2022), www.congress.gov/bill/117th-congress/house-bill/1319/all-actions?overview=closed&q=%7B%22roll-call-vote%22%3A%22all%22%7D (accessed 4/21/22).
7. "The Employment Situation, May 2022," Bureau of Labor Statistics, U.S. Department of Labor, April 1, 2022, www.bls.gov/news.release/pdf/empsit.pdf (accessed 4/21/22).
8. "Consumer Price Index, May 2022," Bureau of Labor Statistics, U.S. Department of Labor, April 12, 2022, www.bls.gov/news.release/pdf/cpi.pdf (accessed 4/21/22).
9. The classic article on deflation is Irving Fisher, "The Debt-Deflation Theory of Great Depressions," *Econometrica*, 1933, https://fraser.stlouisfed.org/docs/meltzer/fisdeb33.pdf. For articles on recent policies concerning deflation, see www.nytimes.com/topic/subject/deflation-economics (both accessed 7/5/22).
10. Daniel Yergin and Joseph Stanislaw, *The Commanding Heights: The Battle for the World Economy* (New York: Free Press, 2002), pp. 60–64.
11. Central Intelligence Agency, "Country Comparison: Distribution of Family Income, Gini Index," *World Factbook*, www.cia.gov/library/publications/resources/the-world-factbook/rankorder/2172rank.html (accessed 7/1/20).
12. The phrase comes from environmental economist E. F. Schumacher's influential book *Small Is Beautiful: Economics as If People Mattered* (New York: Harper and Row, 1973).
13. Jon Gertner, "The Rise and Fall of the GDP," *New York Times*, May 13, 2010, www.nytimes.com/2010/05/16/magazine/16GDP-t.html. For alternative measures of GDP, see Nikita Andester, "GDP Alternatives: 7 Ways to Measure a Country's

Wealth," June 10, 2019, https://ethical.net/politics/gdp-alternatives-7-ways-to-measure-countries-wealth/ (both accessed 7/5/22).

14. Congressional Budget Office, *The Budget and Economic Outlook: 2022 to 2032*, May 2022, Table 1-1, p. 7, www.cbo.gov/system/files/2022-05/57950-Outlook.pdf (accessed 9/28/22).

15. Dylan Matthews, "Modern Monetary Theory, Explained: A Very Detailed Walkthrough of the Big New Left Economic Idea," Vox, April 16, 2019, www.vox.com/future-perfect/2019/4/16/18251646/modern-monetary-theory-new-moment-explained (accessed 7/5/22).

16. Shaghil Ahmed, Carol Bertaut, Jessica Liu, and Robert Vigfusson, "Should We Be Concerned Again about U.S. Current Account Sustainability?," IFDP Notes, Board of Governors of the Federal Reserve System, March 9, 2018, https://doi.org/10.17016/2573-2129.42 (accessed 7/5/22).

17. "Biden Requires Infrastructure Projects to Use Steel and Iron Made in the U.S.," CBS News, April 18, 2022, www.cbsnews.com/news/infrastructure-biden-us-made-steel-iron/ (accessed 4/22/22). Critics say this is not a realistic goal because we cannot produce enough steel and other materials in the short term to cover the new construction. There is a waiver process that contractors can use if the U.S.-made materials are unavailable.

18. The classic work on the appropriations process in the pre-reform era is Richard F. Fenno's *The Power of the Purse: Appropriations Politics in Congress* (Boston: Little, Brown, 1966). D. Roderick Kiewiet and Mathew D. McCubbins reexamined the appropriations process in the post-reform era and found that the Appropriations Committees have maintained much of their power; see *The Logic of Delegation: Congressional Parties and the Appropriations Process* (Chicago: University of Chicago Press, 1991).

19. Bill Heniff Jr., "Congressional Budget Resolutions: Historical Information," Congressional Research Service, November 15, 2015, Table 12, p. 29, https://crsreports.congress.gov/product/pdf/RL/RL30297/27 (accessed 7/5/22). This study shows the failure to pass a budget resolution nine times from 1999 to 2016; Congress also failed to pass the resolution for the 2019–2023 fiscal years.

20. Stan Collender, "GOP-Led Budget Committees Have Just One Job . . . and Are Refusing to Do It," *Forbes*, April 22, 2018, www.forbes.com/sites/stancollender/2018/04/22/gop-led-budget-committees-have-just-one-job-and-are-refusing-to-do-it/#549a29aa5fb1; Stan Collender, "The Federal Budget Process Is Dead and Desperately Needs to Be Buried," *Forbes*, April 24, 2018, www.forbes.com/sites/stancollender/2018/04/24/the-federal-budget-process-is-dead-and-desperately-needs-to-be-buried/#82292162255d (both accessed 7/5/22).

21. The specific provision is paragraph (1)(E) of section 313(b)(1) of the Budget Control Act. James Thurber, "Centralization, Devolution, and Turf Protection in the Congressional Budget Process," in *Congress Reconsidered*, ed. Lawrence C. Dodd and Bruce I. Oppenheimer, 6th ed. (Washington, DC: CQ Press, 1997), pp. 325–46.

22. These figures exclude the Social Security surplus. Including Social Security, the government had a small surplus in 1969. See the CBO's historical budget data, www.cbo.gov/about/products/budget-economic-data#2 (accessed 7/5/22). For data before 1962, see the 1981 *Economic Report of the President* (Washington, DC: Government Printing Office, 1981), p. 316.

23. Robert Keith, "The Statutory Pay-As-You-Go Act of 2010: Summary and Legislative History," Congressional Research Service, April 2, 2010, https://budget.house.gov/sites/democrats.budget.house.gov/files/documents/CRS-stat-paygo.pdf (accessed 7/5/22). The programs and activities exempt from sequestration include Social Security and Tier I Railroad Retirement benefits; federal employee retirement and disability programs; veterans' programs; net interest; refundable income tax credits; Medicaid, the Children's Health Insurance Program (CHIP), the Supplemental Nutrition Assistance Program (SNAP), Supplemental Security Income (SSI), Temporary Assistance for Needy Families (TANF), and certain other low-income programs; and unemployment compensation, among others.

24. Congressional Budget Office, "H.R. 2, Medicare Access and CHIP Reauthorization Act of 2015," March 24, 2015, www.cbo.gov/sites/default/files/114th-congress-2015-2016/costestimate/hr22.pdf (accessed 7/5/22).

25. Congressional Budget Office, "The Effects of the Partial Shutdown Ending in January 2019," January 28, 2019, www.cbo.gov/publication/54937 (accessed 7/5/22).

26. Russell Berman, "The Trump Move That Democrats Want Biden to Copy: If Congress Won't Approve More COVID Funding, Should the President Go It Alone?," *The Atlantic*, April 18, 2022, www.theatlantic.com/politics/archive/2022/04/biden-trump-covid-democrats-wall/629581/ (accessed 7/5/22).

27. *Donald Trump v. Sierra Club*, 588 U.S. (2019) and *Donald Trump v. Sierra Club*, 591 U.S. (2020).

28. Pete Williams, "Supreme Court Cancels Arguments on Trump's Border Wall, 'Remain in Mexico' Policy," NBC News, February 3, 2021, www.nbcnews.com/politics/supreme-court/supreme-court-cancels-arguments-trump-s-border-wall-remain-mexico-n1256593 (accessed 4/22/22).

29. Rebecca Beitsch, "Supreme Court Dismisses House Democrats' Challenge to Trump Border Wall Moves," *The Hill*, October 12, 2021, https://thehill.com/regulation/court-battles/576325-scotus-dismisses-house-democrats-challenge-to-trump-border-wall/ (accessed 4/22/22).

30. Berman, "Trump Move."

31. The size of the tax cut was initially estimated at $1.5 trillion over 10 years by the nonpartisan Joint Committee on Taxation. A few months later, the Office of Management and Budget estimated the tax cut at $2.3 trillion, and then in April, the Congressional Budget Office estimated the 10-year cost at $1.9 trillion (www.cbo.gov/publication/53787). For a discussion of the tax cuts' short-term economic impact, see Indradip Ghosh and Shrutee Sarkar, "Tax Cuts to Boost U.S. Economy, but Benefits to Be Short-Lived: Reuters Poll," Reuters Business News, January 22, 2018, www.reuters.com/article/us-economy-usa-poll/tax-cuts-to-boost-u-s-economy-but-benefits-to-be-short-lived-reuters-poll-idUSKBN1FC0FX (both accessed 7/5/22).

32. Peter G. Peterson Foundation, "Two Years Later, What Are Economists Saying about the Tax Cuts and Jobs Act?," November 4, 2019, www.pgpf.org/blog/2019/11/two-years-later-what-are-economists-saying-about-the-tax-cuts-and-jobs-act (accessed 7/5/22); Filippo Occhino, "The Effect of the 2017 Tax Reform on Investment," Federal Reserve Bank of Cleveland, July 7, 2020, www.clevelandfed.org/newsroom-and-events/publications/economic-commentary/2020-economic-commentaries/ec-202017-effect-of-the-2017-tax-reform-on-investment.aspx (accessed 7/5/22); Howard Gleckman, "Despite Trump's Claims, It Is Hard To See Much Economic Impact Two Years after Passage of the Tax Cuts and Jobs Act," *Forbes*, February 5, 2020, www.forbes.com/sites/howardgleckman/2020/02/05/despite-trumps-claims-it-is-hard-to-see-much-economic-impact-two-years-after-passage-of-the-tax-cuts-and-jobs-act/#f8669747237b (accessed 7/5/22).

33. Ivalina Kalcheva, James M. Plečnik, Hai Tran, and Jason Turkiela, "(Un)intended Consequences? The Impact of the 2017 Tax Cuts and Jobs Act on Shareholder Wealth," *Journal of Banking and Finance* 118 (May 2020), https://escholarship.org/uc/item/8df0g46h (accessed 7/5/22).

34. Office of the United States Trade Representative, "About Us," https://ustr.gov/about-us (accessed 7/5/22).

35. National Economic Council, https://obamawhitehouse.archives.gov/administration/eop/nec (accessed 7/5/22).

36. See Charles M. Cameron, *Veto Bargaining: Presidents and the Politics of Negative Power* (New York: Cambridge University Press, 2000), for a general discussion of the strategic elements of issuing veto threats.

37. Federal Reserve, "The Structure and Functions of the Federal Reserve System," Federal Reserve Education.org, www.federalreserveeducation.org/about-the-fed/structure-and-functions (accessed 4/22/22).

38. William McChesney Martin, who was appointed by Harry Truman, served through the presidencies of Eisenhower, Kennedy, and Johnson and part of Nixon's first term. Paul Volcker served under Carter and Reagan, while Alan Greenspan's tenure spanned the presidencies of Reagan, Bush, Clinton, and the second Bush. Federal Reserve Board, "Board of Governors Members, 1914–Present," www.federalreserve.gov/aboutthefed/bios/board/boardmembership.htm (accessed 7/5/22).

39. "President Biden Nominates Jerome Powell to Serve as Chair of the Federal Reserve, Dr. Lael Brainard to Serve as Vice Chair," White House, Statements and Releases, November 22, 2021, www.whitehouse.gov/briefing-room/statements-releases/2021/11/22/president-biden-nominates-jerome-powell-to-serve-as-chair-of-the-federal-reserve-dr-lael-brainard-to-serve-as-vice-chair/ (accessed 4/22/22).

40. Federal Reserve Board, *Annual Report, 2023*, September 2024, Table G.10, p. 210, and Table G.12, p. 213, www.federalreserve.gov/publications/files/2023-annual-report.pdf (accessed 10/9/24).

41. Senator Sherrod Brown, Hearing on the Nomination of Jay Powell, Senate Banking Committee, November 28, 2017, www.banking.senate.gov/imo/media/doc/Brown%20Statement%2011-28-17.pdf (accessed 7/5/22).

42. Edward R. Tufte, *Political Control of the Economy* (Princeton, NJ: Princeton University Press, 1978); Douglas Hibbs, "The Partisan Model of Macroeconomic Cycles: More Theory and Evidence for the United States," *Economics and Politics* 6 (1994): 1–23.

43. Jim Granato, "The Effect of Policy-Maker Reputation and Credibility on Public Expectations," *Journal of Theoretical Politics* 8 (1996): 449–70; Peter Conti-Brown, *The Power and Independence of the Federal Reserve* (Princeton, NJ: Princeton University Press, 2016).

44. Jeanna Smialek, "Trump Says He Could Demote Fed Chair Powell, Risking More Market Turmoil," *New York Times*, March 14, 2020, www.nytimes.com/2020/03/14/business/economy/trump-powell-fed-chair.html (accessed 7/5/22).

45. U.S. Department of the Treasury, "Role of the Treasury," https://home.treasury.gov/about/general-information/role-of-the-treasury (accessed 4/22/22).

46. Bureau of Engraving and Printing, U.S Department of the Treasury, "Annual Production Reports," www.moneyfactory.gov/resources/productionannual.html; United States Mint, *2021 Annual Report*, January 2022, p. 9, www.usmint.gov/wordpress/wp-content/uploads/2021/12/2021-US-Mint-Annual-Report.pdf (both accessed 7/5/22).

47. Matthew Gualt and Kevin Truong, "COVID-19 Is Causing a National Coin Shortage," Vice, July 7, 2020, www.vice.com/en_us/article/8895e4/covid-19-is-causing-a-national-coin-shortage; Ben Luthi, "Are We Still in a Coin Shortage?," Dollars & Sense blog, SouthEast Bank, August 4, 2021, www.southeastbank.com/blog/dollars-sense-are-we-still-coin-shortage (accessed 4/22/22).

48. John Maynard Keynes, *The General Theory of Employment, Interest and Money* (1936; repr., New York: Macmillan, 2007).

49. Brian Domitrovic, "Trashing JFK's Tax Cuts, One of the Greatest Policy Successes of All Time," *Forbes*, March 12, 2013, www.forbes.com/sites/briandomitrovic/2013/03/12/trashing-jfks-tax-cuts-one-of-the-greatest-policy-successes-of-all-time/#347c0b863e2f (accessed 7/5/22).

50. In Laffer's original argument, there was only one tax rate. However, to apply the Laffer curve to the real world of tax policy, the theoretical argument must be presented in terms of the top marginal rate, which is the tax rate paid on the last dollars earned (and thus the rate that influences the marginal decision to work more or fewer hours). The end point of zero tax revenue associated with a 100 percent tax rate would be for Laffer's single tax rate, rather than the top marginal rate (because people would still work as long as they could keep some income in the marginal brackets below the top rate).

51. Arthur B. Laffer, "The Laffer Curve: Past, Present, and Future," Heritage Foundation Backgrounder #1765, June 1, 2004, www.heritage.org/research/reports/2004/06/the-laffer-curve-past-present-and-future (accessed 7/5/22).

52. These figures come from the Congressional Budget Office, "Historical Budget Data," www.cbo.gov/data/budget-economic-data (accessed 7/6/22). Tax revenue fell from 19.6 percent of GDP in 1981, the last year before the tax cuts went into effect, to 18.1 percent of GDP in 1988, the last year of the Reagan presidency. Individual income tax revenue fell from 9.3 percent to 8 percent of GDP over the same period, so most of the decrease in revenue was due to lower individual income taxes. While overall government spending did increase during the 1982–1983 recession, spending from the beginning of Reagan's term to the end dropped slightly, from 22.2 percent to 21.2 percent of GDP.

53. William G. Gale, "Did the 2017 Tax Cut—the Tax Cuts and Jobs Act—Pay for Itself?," Policy 2020 Brookings, February 14, 2020, www.brookings.edu/policy2020/votervital/did-the-2017-tax-cut-the-tax-cuts-and-jobs-act-pay-for-itself/ (accessed 7/5/22).

54. Congressional Budget Office, "An Update to the Budget and Economic Outlook: 2024 to 2034," June 2024, www.cbo.gov/publication/60419 (accessed 8/2/24).

55. Congressional Budget Office, "Update to the Budget and Economic Outlook," June 2024.

56. The "starve the beast" line is usually attributed to David Stockman and his book *The Triumph of Politics: The Inside Story of the Reagan Revolution* (New York: Avon Books, 1986), where "starving the budget beast" appears on p. 250. More recently, smaller-government proponents such as conservative political advocate Grover Norquist have embraced the concept.

57. U.S. Department of the Treasury Office of Tax Analysis, "Distribution of Tax Burden under Current Law, 2023," October 20, 2023, https://home.treasury.gov/system/files/131/Distribution-of-Tax-Burden-Current-Law-2024.pdf (accessed 8/5/24).

58. Robert McClelland and Nikhita Airi, "Effective Income Tax Rates Have Fallen for the Top One Percent Since World War II," Tax Policy Center, January 6, 2020, www.taxpolicycenter.org/taxvox/effective-income-tax-rates-have-fallen-top-one-percent-world-war-ii; the 2019 number comes from "Distribution of Tax Burden under Current Law, 2019," https://home.treasury.gov/system/files/131/Distribution-of-Tax-Burden-Current-Law-2019.pdf (accessed 4/22/22).

59. The details get a bit more complicated, but this is essentially how money is created. Banks generally must hold a reserve of 10 percent of all "demand deposits" (which is what economists

call checking accounts), so only $90,000 would actually be put into the money stream because the $10,000 reserve would have to come from money that someone deposited in the bank (as we will discuss below, the reserve requirement was reduced to zero on March 26, 2020). Also, the money supply would contract as you pay back your loan. The overall effect on the money supply has to take into account the "multiplier effect"—that is, the money you spend from your loan will get spent many times over. The computer store will take your $10,000 and deposit it in its bank, which allows that bank to make more loans, and so on.

60. Milton Friedman, "The Quantity Theory of Money: A Restatement," in *The Optimum Quantity of Money and Other Essays* (Chicago: Aldine, 1969), p. 52.

61. These figures are hypothetical. In reality, until the recent move to set the reserve requirement at zero, the Fed always had at least two different reserve requirements depending on the size of the bank, ranging from 3 percent to 26 percent at various points in our history. See Board of Governors of the Federal Reserve System, "Reserve Requirements," www.federalreserve.gov/monetarypolicy/reservereq.htm; and Joshua N. Feinman, "Reserve Requirements: History, Current Practice, and Potential Reform," *Federal Reserve Bulletin* (June 1993): 569–89, www.federalreserve.gov/monetarypolicy/0693lead.pdf (both accessed 7/5/22).

62. Bob Haber, "The Fed Fires 'The Big One,'" *Forbes*, March 16, 2020, www.forbes.com/sites/bobhaber/2020/03/16/the-fed-fires-the-big-one/#328525836aa8 (accessed 7/5/22).

63. In December 2002, the discount rate was effectively discontinued as an active policy tool and was pegged to 1 percent above the targeted FFR (which means that the "discount rate" is oddly named—it really should be called the premium rate). In the economic crisis of 2008–2009, the Fed temporarily dropped the difference between the FFR and the discount rate to 0.25 percent and then to zero in March 2020, in response to the COVID shutdown, where it remains today; see *Federal Reserve Bulletin*, December 2002, pp. 482–83. See also Federal Reserve, "The Discount Window and Discount Rate," www.federalreserve.gov/monetarypolicy/discountrate.htm (accessed 9/29/22).

64. "30-Year Fixed Rate Mortgage Average in the United States," and "Federal Funds Effective Rate," St. Louis Federal Reserve, https://fred.stlouisfed.org/series/MORTGAGE30US; https://fred.stlouisfed.org/series/FEDFUNDS (accessed 8/5/24).

65. Brian W. Cashell, "The Federal Government Debt: Its Size and Economic Significance," Report RL31590 (Washington, DC: Congressional Research Service, March 1, 2005), p. 9.

66. William Greider, *Secrets of the Temple: How the Federal Reserve Runs the Country* (New York: Simon and Schuster, 1987), pp. 295–98.

67. Board of Governors of the Federal Reserve System, "Credit and Liquidity Programs and Balance Sheets," "Recent Balance Sheet Trends," www.federalreserve.gov/monetarypolicy/bst_recenttrends.htm (accessed 5/5/22).

68. John B. Taylor, *Economics*, 4th ed. (New York: Houghton Mifflin, 2003), Chapter 10. Some economics textbooks also define regulation of externalities, such as pollution, as economic regulation.

69. *United States v. Microsoft*, 87 F. Supp. 2d 30 (D.D.C. 2000). For a detailed discussion of the case, see Alan Reynolds, *Microsoft Antitrust Appeal: Judge Jackson's "Findings of Fact" Revisited* (Washington, DC: Hudson Institute, 2002).

70. Bill Chappell, "EU Fines Google $1.7 Billion over 'Abusive' Online Ad Strategies," National Public Radio, March 20, 2019, www.npr.org/2019/03/20/705106450/eu-fines-google-1-7-billion-over-abusive-online-ad-strategies#:~:text=The%20European%20Commission%20is%20hitting,working%20with%20companies%20that%20had (accessed 7/5/22).

71. U.S. Patent and Trademark Office, "U.S. Patent Statistics Chart, Calendar Years 1963–2019," www.uspto.gov/web/offices/ac/ido/oeip/taf/us_stat.htm (accessed 5/5/22).

72. Daniel Carpenter and David A. Moss, eds., *Preventing Regulatory Capture: Special Interest Influence and How to Limit It* (New York: Cambridge University Press, 2014).

73. For a running list of changes to environmental regulations, see Nadja Popovich, Livia Albeck-Ripka, and Kendra Pierre-Louis, "The Trump Administration Is Reversing 100 Environmental Rules. Here's the Full List," *New York Times*, May 20, 2020, www.nytimes.com/interactive/2020/climate/trump-environment-rollbacks.html. The $1 billion in savings was cited in Juana Summers and Boris Sanchez, "EPA's Pruitt Fulfilling Trump's Anti-regulatory Agenda," CNN, April 3, 2018, www.cnn.com/2018/04/03/politics/scott-pruitt-donald-trump-environment-policy/index.html (both accessed 7/5/22).

74. "Tracking Regulatory Changes in the Biden Era," Center on Regulation and Markets, Brookings Institution, April 19, 2022, www.brookings.edu/interactives/tracking-regulatory-changes-in-the-biden-era/ (accessed 5/5/22).

75. Michael Hiltzik, "No Longer Termed a 'Failure,' California's Cap-and-Trade Program Faces a New Critique: Is It Too Successful?," *Los Angeles Times*, January 12, 2018, www.latimes.com/business/hiltzik/la-fi-hiltzik-captrade-20180111-story.html (accessed 7/5/22).

76. Bureau of Labor Statistics, "Measuring Green Jobs," www.bls.gov/green/ (accessed 7/5/22).

77. Lucien Georgeson and Mark Maslin, "Estimating the Scale of the US Green Economy within the Global Context," *Palgrave Communications* 5:121 (2019), www.nature.com/articles/s41599-019-0329-3#auth-1. Zineb Sqalli, Shalini Unnikrishnan, Nour Mejri, Patrick Dupoux, Robin George, and Younès Zrikem, "Why Climate Action Needs a Gender Focus," Boston Consulting Group, October 29, 2021, www.bcg.com/publications/2021/climate-action-impact-on-gender-equality (both accessed 5/5/22).

78. Bureau of Economic Analysis, "U.S. International Investment Position, 1st Quarter 2024 and Annual Update," June 26, 2024, www.bea.gov/data/intl-trade-investment/international-investment-position (accessed 8/5/24).

79. U.S. Department of Treasury, "Major Foreign Holders of Treasury Securities," https://ticdata.treasury.gov/Publish/mfh.txt; Treasury Direct, "Debt to the Penny," https://treasurydirect.gov/govt/reports/pd/pd_debttothepenny.htm (both accessed 8/5/24).

80. David E. Rosenbaum, "Free Trade Is Like Dry Water, Y'All," *New York Times*, December 19, 2004, www.nytimes.com/2004/12/19/weekinreview/free-trade-is-like-dry-water-yall.html (accessed 7/5/22).

81. Mark J. Perry, "Trump Is Completely Wrong about the U.S. Trade Deficit," *Los Angeles Times*, March 18, 2016, www.latimes.com/opinion/op-ed/la-oe-0316-perry-trade-benefits-20160316-story.html (accessed 7/5/22).

82. Laura He, "A US-China Trade War Is the Last Thing the World Economy Needs Now," CNN Business, May 19, 2020, www.cnn.com/2020/05/19/economy/us-china-trade-war-resume-coronavirus-intl-hnk/index.html (accessed 7/5/22).

83. Katie Lobosco, "Why Biden Is Keeping Trump's China Tariffs in place," CNN, January 26, 2022, www.cnn.com/2022/01/26/politics/china-tariffs-biden-policy/index.html (accessed 5/6/22).

84. David Ricardo, *The Principles of Political Economy and Taxation* (1817). Robert Torrens actually developed the point first in an 1815 essay on the corn trade, but Ricardo usually gets the credit because he explained it more fully.
85. This argument ignores transportation costs and the costs of shifting labor from one industry to another, but its logic is quite powerful. More intuitive, perhaps, is what happens when one nation has a large *absolute* advantage in the cost of production over another. In these situations, if there is free trade, most production of that good will shift to the country that can produce it more cheaply.
86. James McBride and Mohammed Aly Sergie, "NAFTA's Economic Impact," Council on Foreign Relations, July 26, 2016, https://css.ethz.ch/content/dam/ethz/special-interest/gess/cis/center-for-securities-studies/resources/docs/CFR-NAFTA%27s%20Economic%20Impact.pdf (accessed 7/5/22).
87. Suketu Mehta, "A Passage from India," *New York Times*, July 12, 2005, p. A21.
88. Yukon Huang and Jeremy Smith, "In U.S.-China Trade War, New Supply Chains Rattle Markets," Carnegie Endowment for International Peace, June 24, 2020, https://carnegieendowment.org/2020/06/24/in-u.s.-china-trade-war-new-supply-chains-rattle-markets-pub-82145 (accessed 7/5/22).
89. See Ronald Rogowski, *Commerce and Coalitions: How Trade Affects Domestic Political Alignments* (Princeton, NJ: Princeton University Press, 1986), for the constituency view. James Shoch, *Trading Blows: Party Competition and U.S. Trade Policy in a Globalizing Era* (Chapel Hill: University of North Carolina Press, 2001), pp. 13–19, reviews both explanations.
90. Judith Goldstein, *Ideas, Interests, and American Trade Policy* (Ithaca, NY: Cornell University Press, 1993).
91. American Recovery and Reinvestment Act of 2009 (Public Law 111–5), February 17, 2009, www.govinfo.gov/content/pkg/PLAW-111publ5/pdf/PLAW-111publ5.pdf (accessed 7/5/22).
92. Government Accountability Office, "Troubled Asset Relief Program Lifetime Cost," GAO-24-107033, December 2023, https://home.treasury.gov/system/files/256/GAO-Audit-TARP-Costs.pdf (accessed 8/5/24).
93. The one area of loans that has not turned a profit yet is loans to the auto industry. See U.S. Department of the Treasury, "TARP Tracker from November 2008 to March 2020."
94. Board of Governors of the Federal Reserve System, "Recent Balance Sheet Trends," July 25, 2018, www.federalreserve.gov/monetarypolicy/bst_recenttrends.htm (accessed 7/5/22).
95. U.S. Department of the Treasury, "The CARES Act Works for All Americans," https://home.treasury.gov/policy-issues/cares (accessed 11/12/20).
96. Jane Ihrig, Gretchen Weinbach, and Scott Wolla, "How the Fed Has Responded to the COVID-19 Pandemic," Federal Reserve Bank of St. Louis, August 12, 2020, www.stlouisfed.org/open-vault/2020/august/fed-response-covid19-pandemic (accessed 7/5/22).

Take a Stand

a. COP26 Goals, UN Climate Change Conference UK 2021, https://ukcop26.org/cop26-goals/ (accessed 5/6/22).
b. Emma Newburger, "A Carbon Tax Is 'Single Most Powerful' Way to Combat Climate Change, IMF Says," CNBC, October 10, 2019, www.cnbc.com/2019/10/10/carbon-tax-most-powerful-way-to-combat-climate-change-imf.html; for more general information on carbon pricing see the Carbon Tax Center, =www.carbontax.org/ (both accessed 5/6/22).
c. Kate C. Shouse et al., "U.S. Climate Change Policy," Congressional Research Service, October 28, 2021, https://crsreports.congress.gov/product/pdf/R/R46947 (accessed 5/6/22).
d. The two cases are *Massachusetts v. Environmental Protection Agency*, 549 U.S. 497 (2007), and *West Virginia v. Environmental Protection Agency*, ____ U.S. ____ (2022).

What Do the Facts Say?

a. Terry Jones, "National Debt: Will It Destroy America's Economy?," *Investor's Business Daily*, December 28, 2018, www.investors.com/politics/national-debt-economy-taxes/ (accessed 7/5/22).
b. Z. Byron Wolf, "Debt? What Debt? At $22 Trillion, Here's the Argument the National Debt Doesn't Matter," CNN, January 13, 2019, www.cnn.com/2019/01/13/politics/debt-spending-mmt/index.html (accessed 7/5/22).
c. Committee for a Responsible Federal Budget, "Why Should We Worry about the National Debt?," April 16, 2019, www.crfb.org/papers/why-should-we-worry-about-national-debt (accessed 7/5/22).

Chapter 16

1. Jon Greenberg, "Trump Wrongly Says End of Mandate Is 'Essentially' Obamacare Repeal," PolitiFact, December 21, 2017, www.politifact.com/factchecks/2017/dec/21/donald-trump/trump-wrongly-says-end-mandate-essentially-obamaca/ (accessed 7/5/22).
2. Greenberg, "Trump Wrongly Says End of Mandate."
3. Ed O'Keefe, "The House Has Voted 54 Times in Four Years on Obamacare," *Washington Post*, March 21, 2014, www.washingtonpost.com/blogs/the-fix/wp/2014/03/21/the-house-has-voted-54-times-in-four-years-on-obamacare-heres-the-full-list/ (accessed 7/5/22); Steve Benen, "On Groundhog Day, Republicans Vote to Repeal Obamacare," February 2, 2016, MSNBC, www.msnbc.com/rachel-maddow-show/groundhog-day-republicans-vote-repeal-obamacare (accessed 7/5/22).
4. Sylvia Mathews Burwell, "Impacts and Costs of the Government Shutdown," White House, November 7, 2013, https://obamawhitehouse.archives.gov/blog/2013/11/07/impacts-and-costs-government-shutdown (accessed 7/5/22).
5. Sarah Dutton, Jennifer De Pinto, Anthony Salvanto, and Fred Backus, "Poll: Congress, Tea Party Take Hits from Government Shutdown," CBS News, October 22, 2013, www.cbsnews.com/news/poll-congress-tea-party-take-hits-from-government-shutdown/ (accessed 7/5/22).
6. Joseph P. Williams, "Report: Obamacare Coverage Gains Are Eroding," *US News and World Report*, May 1, 2018, www.usnews.com/news/healthiest-communities/articles/2018-05-01/obamacare-gains-in-insurance-coverage-starting-to-erode-report-says (accessed 7/5/22).
7. The increase in overall enrolment were from more people being covered by Medicaid and by Basic Health Plans under the ACA. Aiden Lee, Rose C. Chu, Christie Peters, and Benjamin D. Sommers, "Health Coverage Changes Under the Affordable Care Act: End of 2021 Update," Office of the Assistant Secretary for Planning and Evaluation, Department of Health and Human Services, April 29, 2022, p. 10, https://aspe.hhs.gov/reports/health-coverage-changes-2021-update (accessed 6/10/22).
8. Katherine Keisler-Starkey and Lisa N. Bunch, "Health Insurance Coverage in the United States: 2023," United States Census Bureau, September 2024, Report Number P60-284, www2.census.gov/library/publications/2024/demo/p60-284.pdf (accessed 10/4/24).

9. Department of Health and Human Services, "In Celebration of 10 Years of ACA Marketplaces, the Biden-Harris Administration Releases Historic Enrollment Data," March 22, 2024, www.hhs.gov/about/news/2024/03/22/celebration-10-years-aca-marketplaces-biden-harris-administration-releases-historic-enrollment-data.html (accessed 8/6/24).

10. "President Biden to Sign Executive Orders Strengthening Americans' Access to Quality, Affordable Health Care," White House, January 28, 2021, www.whitehouse.gov/briefing-room/statements-releases/2021/01/28/fact-sheet-president-biden-to-sign-executive-orders-strengthening-americans-access-to-quality-affordable-health-care/ (accessed 6/13/22).

11. Louise Norris, "Obamacare's 'Subsidy Cliff' Eliminated for 2021 and 2022," HealthInsurance.org, December 7, 2021, www.healthinsurance.org/obamacare/beware-obamacares-subsidy-cliff/ (accessed 6/13/22).

12. Ashley Kirzinger, Isabelle Valdes, Alex Montero, Liz Hamel, and Mollyann Brodie, "5 Charts About Public Opinion on the Affordable Care Act," Kaiser Family Foundation Health Tracking Poll, February 22, 2024, www.kff.org/affordable-care-act/poll-finding/5-charts-about-public-opinion-on-the-affordable-care-act/ (accessed 8/6/24)

13. Theda Skocpol, *Social Policy in the United States: Future Possibilities in Historical Perspective* (Princeton, NJ: Princeton University Press, 1995), p. 37.

14. Franklin Delano Roosevelt's second fireside chat, "Government and Modern Capitalism," Washington, DC, September 30, 1934. For the full text, see John T. Woolley and Gerhard Peters, "The American Presidency Project," University of California, Santa Barbara, www.presidency.ucsb.edu/documents/second-fireside-chat (accessed 7/5/22).

15. Skocpol, *Social Policy in the United States*, pp. 145–60.

16. David M. Kennedy, *Freedom from Fear: The American People in Depression and War, 1929–1945* (New York: Oxford University Press, 2001); Byron W. Daynes, William Pederson, and Michael P. Riccards, eds., *The New Deal and Public Policy* (New York: St. Martin's, 1998).

17. Robert Dallek, *Flawed Giant: Lyndon Johnson and His Times, 1961–1973* (New York: Oxford University Press, 1998); Irving Bernstein, *Guns or Butter: The Presidency of Lyndon Johnson* (New York: Oxford University Press, 1996).

18. For a critical perspective on the Great Society, see Amity Shlaes, *Great Society: A New History* (New York: Harper, 2019).

19. Chesterfield Polkey, "New Rule on SNAP Work Requirements," National Conference on State Legislatures, March 20, 2020, www.ncsl.org/ncsl-in-dc/standing-committees/health-and-human-services/proposed-rule-by-usda-fns-and-snap.aspx; Lauren Bauer, Jana Parsons, and Jay Shambaugh, "Who Stands to Lose If the Final SNAP Work Requirement Rule Takes Effect?," Brookings Institution, April 6, 2020, www.brookings.edu/research/who-stands-to-lose-if-the-final-snap-work-requirement-rule-takes-effect/ (both accessed 7/5/22).

20. "D.C. Circuit Dismisses Appeal, Leaving in Place District Court Decision that Preserved Food Assistance for Approximately 700K Americans," Office of the Attorney General of the District of Columbia, March 24, 2021, https://oag.dc.gov/release/ag-racine-announces-successful-conclusion-lawsuit (accessed 6/13/22).

21. Office of the Assistant Secretary for Planning and Evaluation, "HHS Poverty Guidelines for 2024," U.S. Department of Health and Human Services, January 17, 2024, https://aspe.hhs.gov/topics/poverty-economic-mobility/poverty-guidelines (accessed 11/1/24).

22. Emily A. Shrider, U.S. Census Bureau, Current Population Reports, P60-283, *Poverty in the United States: 2023*, U.S. Government Publishing Office, Washington, DC, September 2024, p. 5, www2.census.gov/library/publications/2024/demo/p60-283.pdf (accessed 10/3/24).

23. These figures include income from capital gains. Thomas Blanchet, Emmanuel Saez, and Gabriel Zucman, "Who Benefits from Income and Wealth Growth in the United States?," University of California, Berkeley, https://realtimeinequality.org/ (accessed 8/10/24).

24. Blanchet, Saez, and Zucman, "Who Benefits."

25. Data from 2023 are from Blanchet, Saez, and Zucman, "Who Benefits"; data from 2022 are from Federal Reserve Board, "Survey of Consumer Finances (SCF), 2022," October 2023, www.federalreserve.gov/econres/scfindex.htm (both accessed 8/10/24).

26. Chase Peterson-Withorn, "The 2023 Forbes 400 List Of Richest Americans: Facts And Figures," *Forbes*, October 3, 2023, www.forbes.com/sites/chasewithorn/2023/10/03/the-2023-forbes-400-list-of-richest-americans-facts-and-figures (accessed 8/10/24).

27. Blanchet, Saez, and Zucman, "Who Benefits" (accessed 8/10/24).

28. The housing expenditure figures are from U.S. Department of Housing and Urban Development, "Fiscal Year 2022, Budget in Brief," March 2022, p. 8, www.hud.gov/sites/dfiles/CFO/documents/2022_Budget_in_Brief_FINAL.pdf. The top 20 percent figure is from Ilya Somin, "Mortgage Interest Deduction Mostly Benefits the Rich—End It," *The Hill*, November 6, 2017, http://thehill.com/opinion/finance/358922-mortgage-interest-deduction-mostly-benefits-the-rich-end-it. Data on tax expenditures are from Tax Expenditures, Department of Treasury, Table 2b, p. 29, December 2021, https://home.treasury.gov/policy-issues/tax-policy/tax-expenditures (all accessed 7/5/22). Note that tax expenditures for housing are lower as a result of recent changes in the tax law, because fewer people are itemizing due to the increase in the standard deduction and the cap on deducting state income taxes and local property taxes. However, given that wealthier people are more likely to itemize, tax expenditures on housing will be even more skewed toward the wealthy when new data are available.

29. Dean Baker, *The Conservative Nanny State: How the Wealthy Use the Government to Stay Rich and Get Richer,* Center for Economic and Policy Research, May 2006, https://deanbaker.net/images/stories/documents/cnswebbook.pdf (accessed 7/5/22).

30. Doug Bandow, "Corporate Welfare Lives On and On," Cato Institute, August 29, 2018, www.cato.org/publications/commentary/corporate-welfare-lives (accessed 7/5/22).

31. James Hohman, "State corporate welfare is undemocratic," *Fortune*, April 21, 2022, https://fortune.com/2022/04/21/state-corporate-welfare-undemocratic-usa-politics-business-james-hohman/ (accessed 6/16/22).

32. "The State of Tax Justice 2021," Tax Justice Network, November 2021, https://taxjustice.net/wp-content/uploads/2021/11/State_of_Tax_Justice_Report_2021_ENGLISH.pdf (accessed 6/16/22).

33. Congressional Budget Office, "The Distribution of Household Income, 2020," November 2023, Table C1, p. 27, www.cbo.gov/system/files/2023-11/59509-household-income_2019-2020.pdf (accessed 8/1/24).

34. Huaqun Li and Karl Smith, "Analysis of Sen. Warren and Sen. Sanders' Wealth Tax Plans," Tax Foundation, January 27, 2020, https://taxfoundation.org/wealth-tax/ (accessed 7/5/22).

35. Board of Governors of the Federal Reserve System, "Economic Well-Being of U.S. Households in 2020-May 2021," May 24, 2022, www.federalreserve.gov/publications/2021-economic

-well-being-of-us-households-in-2020-dealing-with-unexpected-expenses.htm (accessed 6/16/22).

36. Larry M. Bartels, *Unequal Democracy: The Political Economy of the New Gilded Age* (Princeton, NJ: Princeton University Press, 2008).

37. Joe Soss, *Unwanted Claims: The Politics of Participation in the U.S. Welfare System* (Ann Arbor: University of Michigan Press, 2000).

37. Greg Jaffe and Ed O'Keefe, "Obama Accepts Resignation of VA Secretary Shinseki," *Washington Post*, May 30, 2014, www.washingtonpost.com/politics/shinseki-apologizes-for-va-health-care-scandal/2014/05/30/e605885a-e7f0-11e3-8f90-73e071f3d637_story.html (accessed 7/5/22).

39. John Kelly, Jim Sergent, and Donovan Slack, "Death Rates, Bedsores, ER Wait Times: Where Every VA Hospital Lags or Leads Other Medical Care," *USA Today*, February 7, 2019, www.usatoday.com/in-depth/news/investigations/2019/02/07/where-every-va-hospital-lags-leads-other-care/2511739002/ (accessed 7/5/22).

40. "Examining Federal Efforts to Prevent, Detect, and Prosecute Pandemic Relief Fraud to Safeguard Funds for All Eligible Americans," Select Subcommittee on the Coronavirus Crisis, U.S. House of Representatives, June 14, 2022, https://coronavirus.house.gov/subcommittee-activity/hearings/covid-pandemic-relief-fraud-ppp-eidl (accessed 6/16/22).

41. Daniel P. Carpenter, *The Forging of Bureaucratic Autonomy: Reputations, Networks, and Policy Innovation in Executive Agencies, 1862–1928* (Princeton, NJ: Princeton University Press, 2001).

42. Michael Stratford, "Budget Fleshes Out Trump Higher Ed Agenda," Politico, February 13, 2018, www.politico.com/newsletters/morning-education/2018/02/13/budget-fleshes-out-trump-higher-ed-agenda-103874 (accessed 7/5/22).

43. Jennifer Selin, "Trump versus the States: What Federalism Means for the Coronavirus Response," The Conversation, April 17, 2020, https://theconversation.com/trump-versus-the-states-what-federalism-means-for-the-coronavirus-response-136361 (accessed 7/5/22).

44. For differences in state responses, see National Conference on State Legislatures, "State Action on Coronavirus (COVID-19)," July 13, 2020, www.ncsl.org/research/health/state-action-on-coronavirus-covid-19.aspx. For data on infection rates and death rates across the states, see Joe Fox et al., "At Least 132,000 People Have Died from Coronavirus in the U.S.," *Washington Post*, July 13, 2020, www.washingtonpost.com/graphics/2020/national/coronavirus-us-cases-deaths/?itid=hp_hp-top-table-main_gfx-virus-tracker%3Ahomepage%2Fstory-ans (both accessed 7/13/20).

45. Grace Ratley, "States Ranked by Age-Adjusted COVID Deaths," The Bioinformatics CRO, June 2, 2022, www.bioinformaticscro.com/blog/states-ranked-by-age-adjusted-covid-deaths/ (accessed 6/16/22).

46. For the current issues on which AARP is lobbying, see AARP, "Politics and Society: Advocacy," www.aarp.org/politics-society/advocacy/ (accessed 7/5/22).

47. See William T. Bianco, *Trust: Representatives and Constituents* (Ann Arbor: University of Michigan Press, 1994), Chapter 6, for a discussion of the repeal of the Catastrophic Coverage Act.

48. Steve Kelman, "'Reinventing Government,' 25 Years Later," FCW: The Business of Federal Technology, December 6, 2017, https://fcw.com/Articles/2017/12/06/Kelman-25-years-of-acquisition-reform.aspx?Page=1 (accessed 7/5/22).

49. Erich Wagner, "Biden's Management Agenda Puts Feds Front and Center," Government Executive, November 18, 2021, www.govexec.com/management/2021/11/bidens-management-agenda-puts-feds-front-and-center/186958/ (accessed 6/16/22).

50. James Q. Wilson, *Bureaucracy: What Government Agencies Do and Why They Do It* (New York: Basic Books, 1989).

51. For information on the pre-1994 policy, see U.S. Department of Agriculture, "USDA01: End the Wool and Mohair Subsidy," http://govinfo.library.unt.edu/npr/library/reports/ag01.html; for more on the current law, see U.S. Department of Agriculture, "2002 Farm Bill, Title 1: Commodities Programs," www.ers.usda.gov/webdocs/publications/42660/13771_ap022_6_.pdf. For a discussion of mohair and other subsidies, see George Will, "How American Government Became Encrusted with Subsidies," *National Review*, August 16, 2015, www.nationalreview.com/2015/08/government-growth-subsidies-sclerosis/ (all accessed 7/5/22).

52. The stages model was first presented in James E. Anderson, *Public Policy Making* (New York: Praeger, 1974). Also see Thomas R. Dye, *Understanding Public Policy*, 15th ed. (New York: Pearson, 2017).

53. HHS Press Office, "Trump Administration Announces $1.8 Billion in Funding to States to Continue Combating Opioid Crisis," September 4, 2019, www.hhs.gov/about/news/2019/09/04/trump-administration-announces-1-8-billion-funding-states-combating-opioid.html (accessed 7/5/22).

54. "Biden Administration Announces $1.5 Billion Funding Opportunity for State Opioid Response Grant Program," Department of Health and Human Services, May 19, 2022, www.hhs.gov/about/news/2022/05/19/biden-administration-announces-15-billion-funding-opportunity-state-opioid-response-grant-program.html (accessed 6/16/22).

55. "Overdose Death Rates," Figure 3, National Institute on Drug Abuse, National Institutes of Health, January 20, 2022, https://nida.nih.gov/research-topics/trends-statistics/overdose-death-rates (accessed 7/5/22).

56. John Kingdon, *Agendas, Alternatives, and Public Policy* (Boston: Little, Brown, 1984).

57. Frank R. Baumgartner and Bryan D. Jones, *Agendas and Instability in American Politics*, 2nd ed. (Chicago: University of Chicago Press, 2009); Nikolaos Zahariadis, "The Shield of Heracles: Multiple Streams and the Emotional Endowment Effect," *European Journal of Political Research* 54:3 (August 2015): 466–81.

58. Graeme T. Boushey, *Policy Diffusion Dynamics in America* (New York: Cambridge University Press, 2010). See U.S. Department of Justice, "AMBER Alert: America's Missing: Broadcast Emergency Response," https://amberalert.ojp.gov/#:~:text=Today%2C%20the%20AMBER%20Alert%20system,through%20the%20AMBER%20Alert%20system (accessed 7/5/22).

59. Charles R. Shipan and Craig Volden, "The Mechanisms of Policy Diffusion," *American Journal of Political Science* 52:4 (October 2008): 840–57.

60. Social Security expenses are published every year at "Social Security Administrative Expenses," Social Security Administration, www.ssa.gov/oact/STATS/admin.html (accessed 7/5/22). Expenses vary greatly for private retirement accounts, from hedge funds at the high end that have a 1.4 percent management fee and 16.2 percent performance fee (on average) to extremely low-cost index funds that may have fees as low as 0.1 percent.

61. Kathleen Romig, "Social Security Lifts More Americans above Poverty Than Any Other Program," Center on Budget and Policy Priorities, April 19, 2022, www.cbpp.org/research/social-security/social-security-lifts-more-americans-above-poverty-than-any-other-program (accessed 7/5/22).

62. Sue Hertz, "Millions of Baby Boomers Have Left the Workplace since 2020. Are They Coming Back?," *Washington Post*, February 25, 2022, www.washingtonpost.com/business/2022/02/25/great-resignation-older-workers/ (accessed 6/16/22).

63. Social Security Administration, *2024 OASDI Trustees Report*, May 7, 2024, Table V.A3, p. 98, www.ssa.gov/OACT/TR/2024/tr2024.pdf (accessed 8/10/24).

64. Social Security Administration, *2024 OASDI Trustees Report*, Table IV.B3, p. 64.

65. Emily A. Shrider, *Poverty in the United States: 2023*, p. 5.

66. In general, poorer people get back as much as they paid in plus interest much more quickly than wealthier people because of the progressive nature of the benefits. For a study on projected benefits that retirees will receive, see C. Eugene Steuerle, Damir Cosic, and Caleb Quakenbush, "How Do Lifetime Social Security Benefits and Taxes Differ by Earnings?," Urban Institute, February 2019, www.urban.org/sites/default/files/publication/99795/how_lifetime_ss_benefits_and_taxes_differ_by_earnings.pdf (accessed 7/5/22).

67. Social Security Administration, *2022 OASDI Trustees Report*, Table II.B1, p. 7, and Summary, pp. 5–6.

68. Social Security Administration, *2024 OASDI Trustees Report*, p. 4.

69. For a detailed account of the fiscal impact of the various proposals, see Charles Pineles-Mark, "Options for Social Security," Congressional Budget Office, March 8, 2017, www.cbo.gov/publication/52471 (accessed 7/5/22). Also see "Ten Options to Secure the Social Security Trust Fund," Committee for a Responsible Federal Budget, February 9, 2022, www.crfb.org/blogs/ten-options-secure-social-security-trust-fund (accessed 7/5/22).

70. Social Security Administration, *2024 OASDI Trustees Report*, Table V.A4, p. 101.

71. The National Commission on Fiscal Responsibility and Reform, "The Moment of Truth," White House, December 2010, www.washingtonpost.com/wp-srv/politics/documents/TheMomentofTruth.pdf (accessed 7/5/22).

72. Data for the United States are from "National Health Expenditure Projections 2023–2032," Centers for Medicare and Medicaid Services, June 14, 2024, www.cms.gov/data-research/statistics-trends-and-reports/national-health-expenditure-data/projected. Data for other countries are from Organization for Economic Cooperation and Development, Data Explorer, "Health expenditure and financing," https://data-explorer.oecd.org/vis?df[ds]=DisseminateFinalDMZ&df[id]=DSD_SHA%40DF_SHA&df[ag]=OECD.ELS.HD&df[vs]=1.0 (accessed 8/10/24).

73. "U.S. Uninsured Rate Drops by 26% Since 2019," Center for Disease Control, National Center for Health Statistics, June 18, 2024, www.cdc.gov/nchs/pressroom/nchs_press_releases/2024/20240618.htm (accessed 8/10/24).

74. Enrollment numbers are from "Medicaid and CHIP Enrollment, Trend Snapshot," www.medicaid.gov/medicaid/program-information/medicaid-and-chip-enrollment-data/report-highlights/index.html; Costs and reimbursements are from Department of Health and Human Services, Centers for Medicare and Medicaid Services, "Brief Summaries of Medicare and Medicaid," November 1, 2023, p. 25, www.cms.gov/files/document/brief-summaries-medicare-medicaid-november-1-2023.pdf (accessed 8/10/24).

75. Department of Health and Human Services, Centers for Medicare and Medicaid Services, "Brief Summaries of Medicare and Medicaid," pp. 31, 33–34.

76. Alison Mitchell, "Medicaid's Federal Medical Assistance Percentage (FMAP)," Congressional Research Service, July 29, 2020, https://fas.org/sgp/crs/misc/R43847.pdf (accessed 7/5/22).

77. Alison Mitchell, "Medicaid's Federal Medical Assistance Percentage (FMAP)," Congressional Research Service, July 29, 2020, https://fas.org/sgp/crs/misc/R43847.pdf; "Brief Summaries of Medicare and Medicaid," p. 31, www.cms.gov/files/document/brief-summaries-medicare-medicaid-november-15-2021.pdf (accessed 6/17/22).

78. Centers for Medicare & Medicaid Services, "March 2022 Medicaid and CHIP Enrollment Trends Snapshot," www.medicaid.gov/medicaid/national-medicaid-chip-program-information/downloads/march-2022-medicaid-chip-enrollment-trend-snapshot.pdf (accessed 7/18/22).

79. Michael Hiltzik, "Republicans Fund Children's Health Insurance Program, but Leave Their Local Health Centers in the Lurch," *Los Angeles Times*, January 23, 2018, www.latimes.com/business/hiltzik/la-fi-hiltzik-community-health-20180123-story.html (accessed 7/5/22).

80. *2024 Medicare Trustees Report*, June 2, 2024, pp. 208–210, www.cms.gov/oact/tr/2024 (accessed 8/11/24).

81. *2022 Medicare Trustees Report*, pp. 5–6, especially Figure I.1.

82. Peter Grier, "Health Care Reform Bill 101: Who Must Buy Insurance," *Christian Science Monitor*, March 19, 2010, www.csmonitor.com/USA/Politics/2010/0319/Health-Care-Reform-Bill-101-Who-must-buy-insurance (accessed 7/5/22). This article provides an excellent overview of the essential parts of the bill.

83. Congressional Budget Office, "Cost Estimates for H.R. 4872, Reconciliation Act of 2010 (Final Health Care Legislation)," March 20, 2010, www.cbo.gov/doc.cfm?index=11355 (accessed 7/5/22).

84. Ezekiel J. Emanuel, "Name the Much-Criticized Federal Program That Has Saved the U.S. $2.3 Trillion. Hint: It Starts with Affordable," Stat, March 22, 2019, www.statnews.com/2019/03/22/affordable-care-act-controls-costs/ (accessed 7/5/22).

85. David Nather and Susan Levine, "A Brief History of Obamacare Delays," Politico, March 25, 2014, www.politico.com/story/2014/03/obamacare-affordable-care-act-105036.html#ixzz33QRP8biR (accessed 7/5/22).

86. Centers for Medicare and Medicaid Services, "2020 Federal Health Insurance Exchange Enrollment Period Final Weekly Enrollment Snapshot," January 8, 2020, www.cms.gov/newsroom/fact-sheets/2020-federal-health-insurance-exchange-enrollment-period-final-weekly-enrollment-snapshot (accessed 7/5/22).

87. Medicaid.gov, "Medicaid Enrollment Data Collected through MBES, April–June 2019 Medicaid MBES Enrollment Report," June 2020, https://data.medicaid.gov/Enrollment/2019-3Q-Medicaid-MBES-Enrollment/avy5-4pxa/data (accessed 7/31/20).

88. Joseph R. Antos and James C. Capretta, "The ACA: Trillions? Yes. A Revolution? No," Health Affairs Blog, April 10, 2020, www.healthaffairs.org/do/10.1377/hblog20200406.93812/full/ (accessed 7/5/22).

89. Eligibility information for SNAP may be found at U.S. Department of Agriculture Food and Nutrition Service, "SNAP Eligibility," October 1, 2023, www.fns.usda.gov/snap/recipient/eligibility (accessed 8/12/24). Participation and benefits data are from U.S. Department of Agriculture Food and Nutrition Service, "SNAP Data Tables," May 2024, www.fns.usda.gov/pd/supplemental-nutrition-assistance-program-snap (accessed 8/11/24).
90. U.S. Department of Labor, "Unemployment Insurance Weekly Claims," August 8, 2024, www.dol.gov/ui/data.pdf (accessed 8/11/24).
91. Internal Revenue Service, "EITC Fast Facts," February 7, 2024, www.eitc.irs.gov/partner-toolkit/basic-marketing-communication-materials/eitc-fast-facts/eitc-fast-facts (accessed 8/11/24).
92. Internal Revenue Service, "EITC Fast Facts."
93. Maximum benefits are from Social Security Administration, "SSI Federal Payment Amounts for 2024," www.ssa.gov/oact/cola/SSI.html; average benefits and number of recipients are from Social Security Administration, "Monthly Statistical Snapshot, June 2024," www.ssa.gov/policy/docs/quickfacts/stat_snapshot (both accessed 8/11/24).
94. R. Kent Weaver, *Ending Welfare as We Know It* (Washington, DC: Brookings Institution Press, 2000).
95. Aditi Shrivastava and Gina Azito Thompson, "Cash Assistance Should Reach Millions More Families to Lessen Hardship," Center on Budget and Policy Priorities, February 18, 2022, www.cbpp.org/research/family-income-support/tanf-cash-assistance-should-reach-millions-more-families-to-lessen (accessed 6/17/22).
96. U.S. Department of Education, "About ED: Overview and Mission Statement," www.ed.gov/about/landing.jhtml?src=gu (accessed 7/5/22).
97. Trymaine Lee, "Has the World Gone Crazy over Common Core?," MSNBC, June 2, 2014, www.msnbc.com/msnbc/common-core-crazy-reactions-education-teachers (accessed 7/5/22).
98. National Conference of State Legislatures, "College and Career Readiness Standards Legislation," www.ccrslegislation.info/CCR-State-Policy-Resources/common-core-status-map (accessed 8/3/20).
99. For alternative perspectives on the Common Core, see Tom Loveless, "Common Core Has Not Worked," *Education Next* 20:2 (Spring 2020), www.educationnext.org/common-core-has-not-worked-forum-decade-on-has-common-core-failed/; and Michael J. Petrilli, "Stay the Course on National Standards," *Education Next* 20:2 (Spring 2020), www.educationnext.org/stay-course-on-national-standards-forum-decade-on-has-common-core-failed/ (both accessed 7/5/22).
100. U.S. Department of Education, "Race to the Top Fund," www2.ed.gov/programs/racetothetop/index.html (accessed 8/3/20).
101. Bill and Melinda Gates Foundation, "Grantmaking: Awarded Grants," www.gatesfoundation.org/How-We-Work/Quick-Links/Grants-Database (accessed 7/31/20).
102. Terry Gross, "From Slavery to Socialism, New Legislation Restricts What Teachers Can Discuss," Fresh Air, National Public Radio, February 3, 2022, www.npr.org/2022/02/03/1077878538/legislation-restricts-what-teachers-can-discuss; Jeffrey Sachs, "Steep Rise in Gag Orders, Many Sloppily Drafted," Pen America: The Freedom to Write, January 24, 2022, https://pen.org/steep-rise-gag-orders-many-sloppily-drafted/ (both accessed 6/17/22).
103. Hannah Natanson and Moriah Balingit "Caught in the Culture Wars, Teachers Are Being Forced from Their Jobs," *Washington Post*, June 16, 2022, www.washingtonpost.com/education/2022/06/16/teacher-resignations-firings-culture-wars/ (accessed 6/17/22).
104. Khristopher J. Brooks, "Rents are rising faster than wages across the country, especially in these cities," Moneywatch, CBS News, May 8, 2024, www.cbsnews.com/news/rent-cost-us-2024-housing-national (accessed 8/11/24).
105. "The Problem," National Low Income Housing Coalition, https://nlihc.org/explore-issues/why-we-care/problem (accessed 6/19/22).
106. This is the official government estimate. Other estimates are as high as 600,000. "HUD Releases 2021 Annual Homeless Assessment Report Part 1," Housing and Urban Development, February 4, 2022, www.hud.gov/press/press_releases_media_advisories/hud_no_22_022 (accessed 6/19/22).
107. "Housing Affordability Index," National Association of Realtors, April 2022, https://cdn.nar.realtor/sites/default/files/documents/hai-04-2022-housing-affordability-index-2022-06-10.pdf (accessed 6/19/22).
108. Katherine Schaeffer, "A Growing Share of Americans Say Affordable Housing Is a Major Problem Where They Live," Pew Research Center, January 28, 2022, www.pewresearch.org/fact-tank/2022/01/18/a-growing-share-of-americans-say-affordable-housing-is-a-major-problem-where-they-live/ (accessed 6/19/22).
109. Rachel M. Cohen, "The Simplest Fix to America's Rent Problem," *The Atlantic*, October 20, 2021, www.theatlantic.com/politics/archive/2021/10/universal-basic-rent-section-8-voucher/620429/ (accessed 6/19/22).
110. Jake Blumgart, "How Important Was the Single-Family Zoning Ban in Minneapolis?," Governing, May 26, 2022, www.governing.com/community/how-important-was-the-single-family-housing-ban-in-minneapolis; Christian Britschgi," Eliminating Single-Family Zoning Isn't the Reason Minneapolis Is a YIMBY Success Story," Reason, May 11, 2022, https://reason.com/2022/05/11/eliminating-single-family-zoning-isnt-the-reason-minneapolis-is-a-yimby-success-story/ (both accessed 6/19/22).

Take a Stand

a. National Conference of State Legislatures, "School Vouchers," www.ncsl.org/research/education/school-choice-vouchers.aspx#What%20States%20Have%20Done (accessed 7/5/22).
b. John F. Witte, *The Market Approach to Education: An Analysis of America's First Voucher Program* (Princeton, NJ: Princeton University Press, 2001).
c. *Zelman v. Simmons-Harris*, 536 U.S. 639 (2002).

Chapter 17

1. Madeleine Albright, *Fascism: A Warning* (New York: HarperCollins, 2018).
2. "Read Trump's Full Speech Outlining His National Security Strategy," PBS, December 18, 2017, www.pbs.org/newshour/politics/read-trumps-full-speech-outlining-his-national-security-strategy/ (accessed 6/27/22).
3. For an example of the isolationist approach, see Patrick J. Buchanan, *A Republic, Not an Empire: Reclaiming America's Destiny*, updated ed. (Washington, DC: Regnery, 2002).
4. The distinction was first made in E. H. Carr, *The Twenty Years' Crisis, 1919–1939: An Introduction to the Study of International*

Relations (London: Macmillan, 1939). Realism was elaborated as a general theory in Hans Morgenthau, *Politics among Nations: The Struggle for Power and Peace* (New York: Knopf, 1948). For a general overview, see Jonathan Haslam, *No Virtue like Necessity: Realist Thought in International Relations since Machiavelli* (New Haven, CT: Yale University Press, 2002).

5. John Mearsheimer, "America Unhinged," *National Interest*, January–February 2014, http://nationalinterest.org/article/america-unhinged-9639 (accessed 6/27/22).
6. Gilbert Felix, *To the Farewell Address: Ideas in Early American Foreign Policy* (Princeton, NJ: Princeton University Press, 1961).
7. A synoptic account of the United States as a world power, which takes the story up to the 2003 invasion of Iraq, is Niall Ferguson, *Colossus: The Price of America's Empire* (New York: Penguin, 2004).
8. Samuel Flagg Bemis, *John Quincy Adams and the Foundations of American Foreign Policy* (New York: Knopf, 1949); Ernest R. May, *The Making of the Monroe Doctrine* (Cambridge, MA: Harvard University Press, 1975). The latter stresses domestic political considerations and argues that the Monroe Doctrine was "actually the by-product of an election campaign."
9. Daniel M. Smith, *The Great Departure: The United States and World War I, 1914–1920* (New York: Wiley, 1965).
10. Thomas J. Knock, *To End All Wars: Woodrow Wilson and the Quest for a New World Order* (New York: Oxford University Press, 1992).
11. Margaret MacMillan, *Paris 1919: Six Months That Changed the World* (New York: Random House, 2001).
12. John M. Cooper, *Breaking the Heart of the World: Woodrow Wilson and the Fight for the League of Nations* (New York: Cambridge University Press, 2001).
13. John Lewis Gaddis, *Strategies of Containment: A Critical Appraisal of American National Security Policy during the Cold War* (New York: Oxford University Press, 2005).
14. Tony Smith, "Making the World Safe for Democracy in the American Century," *Diplomatic History* 23:2 (1999): 173–88.
15. Winston Churchill, "Sinews of Peace (Iron Curtain)," Westminster College, Fulton, Missouri, March 5, 1946, International Churchill Society, https://winstonchurchill.org/resources/speeches/1946-1963-elder-statesman/the-sinews-of-peace/ (accessed 6/27/22). See also Klaus Larres, *Churchill's Cold War: The Politics of Personal Diplomacy* (New Haven, CT: Yale University Press, 2002).
16. George F. Kennan, "The Sources of Soviet Conduct," *Foreign Affairs* 25:4 (July 1947): 566–82.
17. Robert L. Beisner, *Dean Acheson: A Life in the Cold War* (New York: Oxford University Press, 2006); Dean Acheson, *Present at the Creation: My Years in the State Department* (New York: W. W. Norton, 1969).
18. Michael J. Hogan, *The Marshall Plan: America, Britain, and the Reconstruction of Western Europe* (New York: Cambridge University Press, 1987). See also Martin Schain, ed., *The Marshall Plan: Fifty Years Later* (New York: Palgrave, 2001).
19. Marc Trachtenberg, *A Constructed Peace: The Making of the European Settlement, 1945–1963* (Princeton, NJ: Princeton University Press, 1999).
20. The balance of military power between NATO and the Warsaw Pact throughout the Cold War is traced in David Miller, *The Cold War: A Military History* (New York: St. Martin's Press, 1998).
21. Robert A. Packenham, *Liberal America and the Third World: Political Development Ideas in Foreign Aid and Social Science* (Princeton, NJ: Princeton University Press, 1973). For an overview, see David P. Forsythe, "Human Rights in U.S. Foreign Policy: Retrospect and Prospect," *Political Science Quarterly* 105:3 (Autumn 1990): 435–54.
22. Sergei N. Goncharov, John W. Lewis, and Xue Litai, *Uncertain Partners: Stalin, Mao, and the Korean War* (Palo Alto, CA: Stanford University Press, 1999).
23. James A. Bill, *The Eagle and the Lion: The Tragedy of American-Iranian Relations* (New Haven, CT: Yale University Press, 1988).
24. Lawrence Freedman, *Kennedy's Wars: Berlin, Cuba, Laos, and Vietnam* (Oxford, UK: Oxford University Press, 2002).
25. William J. Duiker, *Sacred War: Nationalism and Revolution in a Divided Vietnam* (New York: McGraw-Hill, 1995).
26. Henry Kissinger, *Years of Upheaval* (Boston: Little, Brown, 1982); Jussi Hanhimäki, *The Flawed Architect: Henry Kissinger and American Foreign Policy* (New York: Oxford University Press, 2004).
27. Raymond Garthoff, *Détente and Confrontation: American-Soviet Relations from Nixon to Reagan* (Washington, DC: Brookings Institution Press, 1994).
28. Bill, *The Eagle and the Lion.*
29. Odd Arne Westad, ed., *The Fall of Détente: Soviet-American Relations during the Carter Years* (Oslo, Norway: Scandinavian University Press, 1997).
30. Garthoff, *Détente and Confrontation.*
31. Philip Hanson, *The Rise and Fall of the Soviet Economy: An Economic History of the USSR from 1945* (London: Longman, 2003).
32. Francis Fukuyama, *The End of History and the Last Man*, updated ed. (New York: Free Press, 2006).
33. For a summary of American human rights policy, see John W. Dietrich, "U.S. Human Rights Policy in the Post–Cold War Era," *Political Science Quarterly* 121:2 (Summer 2006): 269–94.
34. Joseph Nye, *Soft Power: The Means to Success in World Politics* (New York: Hachette Book Group, 2009).
35. Chico Harlan, Loveday Morris, and Michael Birnbaum, "Protesters in Europe Push for a New Reckoning of Their Own Countries' Racism," *Washington Post*, June 7, 2020, www.washingtonpost.com/world/europe/george-floyd-protests-london-berlin-brussels-rome-madrid-police-racism-europe/2020/06/07/06c340c4-a829-11ea-b619-3f9133bbb482_story.html (accessed 6/27/22).
36. Samuel P. Huntington, *The Clash of Civilizations and the Remaking of World Order* (New York: Free Press, 2002).
37. Louis Fisher, *Presidential War Power* (Lawrence: University Press of Kansas, 2004).
38. John Mueller and Mark G. Stewart, *Chasing Ghosts: The Policing of Terrorism* (New York: Oxford University Press, 2015).
39. Arthur M. Schlesinger, *The Imperial Presidency* (Boston: Houghton Mifflin, 1973).
40. Terry Moe and William Howell, "Unilateral Action and Presidential Power: A Theory," *Presidential Studies Quarterly* 29:4 (1999): 850–72.
41. David Hoffman and David B. Ottaway, "Panel Drops Covert-Acts Notification; in Compromise, Bush Pledges to Inform Hill in All but Rare Cases," *Washington Post*, October 27, 1989, p. A1.
42. Dahlia Lithwick, "The Enemy Within," *Slate*, June 12, 2008, www.slate.com/id/2193468 (accessed 6/27/22).
43. Somini Sengupta, "As Musharraf's Woes Grow, Enter an Old Rival, Again," *New York Times*, April 6, 2007, p. A3; Leslie Wayne, "Airbus Seeks a Welcome in Alabama," *New York Times*, June 19, 2007, p. C1.
44. Pew Research Center, "U.S. Public Seldom Has Welcomed Refugees into Country," November 19, 2015, www

.pewresearch.org/fact-tank/2015/11/19/u-s-public-seldom-has-welcomed-refugees-into-country/ (accessed 6/27/22).

45. Joanna Piacenza, "Can You Locate Iran? Few Voters Can," Morning Consult, January 8, 2020, https://morningconsult.com/2020/01/08/can-you-locate-iran-few-voters-can/ (accessed 6/27/22).

46. For details, see Becky Little, "Most Young Americans Can't Pass a Test on Global Affairs—Can You?," *National Geographic*, September 13, 2016, https://news.nationalgeographic.com/2016/09/survey-geography-foreign-relations-americans-students/ (accessed 6/27/22).

47. Pew Research Center, "Public Opinion Six Months Later," March 7, 2002, www.people-press.org/2002/03/07/public-opinion-six-months-later/ (accessed 6/27/22).

48. A directory of NGOs can be found at the United Nations website, https://research.un.org/en/ngo (accessed 6/12/20).

49. See Amnesty International, "The Secretive and Illegal U.S. Programme of Rendition," April 5, 2006, www.amnesty.org/en/documents/amr51/056/2006/en/ (accessed 6/27/22).

50. United Nations, "Current Peacekeeping Operations," https://peacekeeping.un.org/en (accessed 9/13/22).

51. United States International Trade Commission, Official Harmonized Tariff Schedule 2022, www.usitc.gov/tata/hts/index.htm (accessed 6/6/22).

52. William B. Quandt, *Camp David: Peacemaking and Politics* (Washington, DC: Brookings Institution Press, 1986).

53. U.S. Department of State, *Treaties in Force*, January 1, 2019, www.state.gov/treaties-in-force/ (accessed 6/27/22).

54. Lisa L. Martin, "The President and International Commitments: Treaties as Signaling Devices," *Presidential Studies Quarterly* 35:3 (2005): 440–65.

55. Johanna Neuman and Megan K. Stack, "Americans' Beirut Exodus Underway; Hundreds Are Evacuated by Ship and Helicopter," *Los Angeles Times*, July 20, 2006, p. A10. The Clinton administration resorted to cruise missile attacks five times: three against Iraq (1993, 1996, 1998), one in 1995 against Bosnian Serb forces in the former Yugoslavia, and one against targets in Afghanistan and Sudan in 1998. James Mann, "Foreign Policy of the Cruise Missile," *Los Angeles Times*, December 23, 1998, p. 5.

56. A comprehensive account of the Afghanistan invasion and its aftermath is in Barnett R. Rubin, "Saving Afghanistan," *Foreign Affairs* 86:1 (January/February 2007): 57–78.

57. For an optimistic review, see Joseph E. Stiglitz, *Making Globalization Work* (New York: W. W. Norton, 2007).

58. Angelica LaVito, "Starbucks Is Opening a Store in China Every 15 Hours," CNBC, December 5, 2017, www.cnbc.com/2017/12/05/starbucks-is-opening-a-store-in-china-every-15-hours.html (accessed 7/6/20).

59. U. S. Special Trade Representative, "The People's Republic of China," https://ustr.gov/countries-regions/china-mongolia-taiwan/peoples-republic-china, accessed 6/5/22.

60. Benjamin Applebaum, "Perils of Globalization When Factories Close and Towns Struggle," *New York Times*, May 17, 2015, p. A1.

61. John Mueller, "Assessing Measures Designed to Protect the Homeland," *Policy Studies Journal* 38:1 (2010): 1–21; John Mueller, *Overblown: How Politicians, the Terrorism Industry and Others Stoke National Security Fears* (New York: Free Press, 2006).

62. Fred Kaplan, "North Korea's Nuclear Test Isn't as Dangerous as Kim Jong-un Wants Us to Believe," *Slate*, January 6, 2016, www.slate.com/articles/news_and_politics/politics/2016/01/north_korea_s_nuclear_test_isn_t_as_dangerous_as_kim_jong_un_wants_us_to.html (accessed 6/27/22).

Check Your Understanding Answer Key

Chapter 1

1. B
2. B
3. A
4. C
5. D
6. A
7. C
8. B
9. C
10. D
11. A
12. A

Chapter 2

1. A
2. C
3. B
4. C
5. A
6. B
7. D
8. C
9. D
10. B
11. A

Chapter 3

1. B
2. A
3. A
4. D
5. C
6. B
7. A
8. C
9. A
10. C

Chapter 4

1. B
2. A
3. D
4. C
5. B
6. A
7. C
8. B
9. C
10. D
11. A
12. B
13. B
14. B
15. A

Chapter 5

1. C
2. A
3. A
4. D
5. A
6. C
7. B
8. C

Chapter 6

1. A
2. B
3. B
4. C
5. D
6. D
7. A
8. C

Chapter 7

1. A
2. B
3. D
4. B
5. C
6. A
7. C
8. A

Chapter 8

1. B
2. B
3. C
4. A
5. C
6. D
7. D
8. D

Chapter 9

1. C
2. A
3. B
4. C
5. A
6. C
7. D
8. B

Chapter 10

1. B
2. D
3. A
4. B
5. C
6. C
7. A
8. B

Chapter 11

1. D
2. A
3. B
4. C
5. B
6. B
7. D
8. C

Chapter 12

1. C
2. D
3. C
4. A
5. A
6. B
7. D
8. B

Chapter 13

1. D
2. C
3. D
4. B
5. A
6. C
7. A
8. A
9. B
10. C

Chapter 14

1. A
2. B
3. D
4. D
5. B
6. A
7. D
8. C
9. C
10. B
11. A
12. B

Chapter 15

1. A
2. B
3. C
4. A
5. B
6. D

Chapter 16

1. A
2. B
3. D
4. C
5. A
6. B
7. B
8. D
9. B
10. C

Chapter 17

1. D
2. A
3. C
4. A
5. B
6. C
7. D
8. A

Credits

Text

Chapter 1, What Do the Facts Say? (p. 17, bottom): Map: "2020 Presidential Election, Purple America," by Robert J. Vanderbei, Princeton University. www.princeton.edu/~rvdb/JAVA/election2020/. Reprinted by permission of the author.

Figure 5.4 (p. 196): Map: Lifetime Wage Gap for Women Compared with Men, from "The Lifetime Wage Gap, State by State," National Women's Law Center, April 4, 2018. Reprinted by permission.

Figure 6.1 (p. 221): Graph adapted from "Majority of Public Favors Same-Sex Marriage, but Divisions Persist," Pew Research Center, Washington, DC (May 2019) www.pewresearch.org/politics/2019/05/14/majority-of-public-favors-same-sex-marriage-but-divisions-persist/. Reprinted with permission.

Figure 6.3 (p. 226): Graph adapted from "The Iraq War Continues to Divide the U.S. Public, 15 Years after It Began," Pew Research Center Fact Tank, Washington, DC (March 2018) www.pewresearch.org/fact-tank/2018/03/19/iraq-war-continues-to-divide-u-s-public-15-years-after-it-began/.

Figure 6.8 (p. 245): Graph adapted from "Economic Issues Decline among Public's Policy Priorities," Pew Research Center, Washington, DC (January 2018) www.people-press.org/2018/01/25/economic-issues-decline-among-publics-policy-priorities/. Reprinted with permission.

Table 7.1 (p. 261): Table adapted from "U.S. Media Polarization and the 2020 Election: A Nation Divided," Pew Research Center, Washington, DC (January 2020) www.journalism.org/2020/01/24/u-s-media-polarization-and-the-2020-election-a-nation-divided/.

Figure 7.1 (p. 273): Graph: "Tracking the Gun Control Conversation," www.thetrace.org/2018/05/parkland-media-coverage-analysis-mass-shooting/. Reprinted by permission of The Trace.

Table 9.5 (p. 356): Table adapted from "Faith and the 2016 Campaign," Pew Research Center, Washington, DC (January 2016) www.pewresearch.org/religion/2016/01/27/faith-and-the-2016-campaign/.

Figure 11.6 (p. 435): Graph: Liberal-Conservative Partisan Polarization by Chamber, from "Polarization in Congress," March 11, 2018, Jeffrey Lewis, Keith T. Poole, and Howard Rosenthal, voteview.com. Reprinted by permission.

Figure 15.9 (p. 613): Chart 1 in "The Crisis Is Over: It Is Time to End Experimental Monetary Policy," Norbert J. Michel, PhD, Backgrounder No. 3265, November 9, 2017, www.heritage.org/sites/default/files/2017-11/BG3265.pdf. Reprinted by permission of The Heritage Foundation.

Figure 17.1 (p. 684): Map: "U.S. Voters Were Asked to Identify Ukraine on the Map," Morning Consult, February 9, 2022. https://morningconsult.com/2022/02/09/can-americans-find-ukraine-on-a-map/. Reprinted by permission.

Photographs

Front Matter

Title spread: pp. ii-iii: Mark Kanning/Alamy Stock Photo. About the Authors: p. vi: William T. Bianco, photo by Paul B.; David T. Canon, photo by Kolin Goldschmidt, University of Wisconsin-Madison. Table of Contents: p. ix top: Ron Adar/Alamy Stock Photo; p. ix bottom: Jay Janner/Austin American-Statesman via AP; p. x: David Paul Morris/Bloomberg via Getty Images; p. xi top: Win McNamee/Getty Images; p. xi bottom: ZUMA Press Inc/Alamy Stock Photo; p. xii: Ringo Chiu via AP; p. xiii top: Susan Sheldon/Alamy Stock Photo; p. xiii bottom: SOPA Images Limited/Alamy Stock Photo; p. xiv top: Michael Le Brecht II/ABC News via ZUMA Press Wire/Alamy Stock Photo; p. xiv bottom: Storms Media Group/Alamy Stock Photo; p. xv top: UPI/Alamy Stock Photo; p. xv bottom: REUTERS/Alamy Stock Photo; p. xvi: Jabin Botsford/The Washington Post via Getty Images; p. xvii top: Planetpix/Alamy Stock Photo; p. xvii bottom: SAUL LOEB/AFP via Getty Images; p. xviii: Angel Valentin/The New York Times/Redux; p. xix: American Photo Archive/Alamy Stock Photo.

Chapter 1

Page 3: Ron Adar/Alamy Stock Photo; p. 5: MediaNews Group/Orange County Register via Getty Images; p. 8 (left): US Army Photo/Alamy Stock Photo; (right): ZUMA Press, Inc./Alamy Stock Photo; p. 10: Chip Somodevilla/Getty Images; p. 12: AP Photo/Evan Vucci, File; p. 13 (right): Eva Marie Uzcategui T./Anadolu Agency/Getty Images; p. 15 (left): Jeff Chiu/Associated Press; (middle): Cal Sport Media/Alamy Stock Photo; (right): Fox/Photofest; p. 18 (top): AP Photo/Odessa American, Courtney Sacco; (bottom): © Flip Schulke/CORBIS/Corbis via Getty Images; p. 20: Sipa USA/Alamy Stock Photo; p. 23: Xinhua/Alamy Stock Photo; p. 27: Shiiko Alexander/Alamy Stock Photo; p. 28: Ron Adar/Alamy Stock Photo.

Chapter 2

Page 33: Jay Janner/Austin American-Statesman via AP; p. 35: Album/Alamy Stock Photo; p. 38: Ian Dagnall/Alamy Stock Photo; p. 39: Library of Congress; p. 40: North Wind Picture Archives/Alamy Stock Photo; p. 44: Ailsa Mellon Bruce Fund/National Gallery of Art, Washington, D.C.; p. 49: Library of Virginia; p. 51: Library of Congress; p. 53: Library of Congress; p. 54 (top): Andrew W. Mellon Collection/National Gallery of Art, Washington, D.C.; (bottom): Library of Congress; p. 57 (Senate members): Dpa Picture Alliance/Alamy Stock Photo; (Bush): Draper, Eric, 1964-, Photographer/National Archives; (Obama): ZUMA Press, Inc./Alamy Stock Photo; (pen): imagenavi/Getty Images; (butterfly): Lightspring/Shutterstock (gavel): Spx Chrome/Getty Images; (Trump): Stone/Shutterstock; (border wall): Chess Ocampo/Shutterstock; (Supreme Court building): Glow Images/Getty Images; (Biden): White House Photo/Alamy Stock Photo; p. 58: Official White House Photo by Adam Schultz; p. 59: Rod Lamkey/CNP/MediaPunch/Alamy Stock Photo; p. 61: World History Archive/Alamy Stock Photo; p. 62: Jim Watson/AFP via Getty Images; p. 65: Porter Gifford/Corbis via Getty Images; p. 69 (both): Everett Collection, Inc./Alamy Stock Photo; p. 70: Norma Jean Gargasz/Alamy Stock Photo; p. 71: Jay Janner/Austin American-Statesman via AP.

Chapter 3

Page 77: David Paul Morris/Bloomberg via Getty Images; p. 79: AP Photo/Jae C. Hong; p. 83: AP Photo/Eric Gay; p. 84: Yaroslav Sabitov/YES Market Media/Alamy Stock Photo; p. 87: The Metropolitan Museum of Art, New York. The Edward W. C. Arnold Collection of New York Prints, Maps, and Pictures. Bequest of Edward W. C. Arnold, 1954 (54.90.491); p. 89: Library of Congress; p. 90: Everett/Shutterstock; p. 93 (Capitol): J Main/Shutterstock; (sticks): Ivana Star/Getty Images; (smokestack): Space Images/Getty Images; (carrot): Food Collection/Getty Images; (construction workers with solar panels): Cultura Creative RF/Alamy Stock Photo; (Trump): Stone/Shutterstock; (Biden): White House Photo/Alamy Stock Photo; (Supreme Court building): Glow Images/Getty Images; p. 94: GRANGER; p. 96: Mandel Ngan/Pool via AP; p. 99: Brandi Lyon Photography/Alamy Stock Photo; p. 102: Joe Raedle/Getty Images; p. 104: Justin Sullivan/Getty Images; p. 105: Andrew Caballero-Reynolds/AFP via Getty Images; p. 107: Allison Bailey/Alamy Stock Photo; p. 108: David Paul Morris/Bloomberg via Getty Images.

Chapter 4

Page 113: Win McNamee/Getty Images; p. 116 (top): Rick Barbero/The Register-Herald via AP; (bottom): William Thomas Cain/Getty Images; p. 123: (cake figurines): Thinkstock Images/Getty Images; (gavel): Spx Chrome/Getty Images; (scales): John Parra/Getty Images; (football): Danny E Hooks/Shutterstock; (pen): imagenavi/Getty Images; (boy): Stockbyte/Getty Images; p. 127: Matthew Staver/The New York Times/Redux; p. 130: Michael S. Williamson/The Washington Post via Getty Images; p. 131: Pablo Monsalve/VIEWpress via Getty Images; p. 133: Sipa USA/Alamy Stock Photo; p. 134: © ACLU 2022; photo by Danna Singer; p. 135: Xinhua/Alamy Stock Photo; p. 136: Shawn Thew/EPA-EFE/Shutterstock; p. 138: REUTERS/Alamy Stock Photo; p. 139: Anthony Pidgeon/Redferns/Getty Images; p. 142 (left): REUTERS/Alamy Stock Photo; (right): Erin Schaff/The New York Times/Redux; p. 144: Chip Somodevilla/Getty Images; p. 147: AP Photo; p. 148: Jason Reed/Reuters/Newscom; p. 149: Quang Ngo/Alamy Stock Photo; p. 150: Bettmann/Getty Images; p. 152: BearFotos/Shutterstock; p. 155: AP Photo/Michael Stravato; p. 157: Win McNamee/Getty Images.

Chapter 5

Page 163: ZUMA Press, Inc./Alamy Stock Photo; p. 165: Joshua Windsor/Alamy Stock Photo; p. 166 (left): agefotostock/Alamy Stock Photo; (right): Library of Congress; p. 167: Library of Congress; p. 168: Alpha Stock/Alamy Stock Photo; p. 169: AP Photo; p. 170: Brandon Bell/Stringer/Getty Images; p. 171: Everett Collection Historical/Alamy Stock Photo; p. 172: David Grossman/Alamy Stock Photo; p. 174: AP Photo/Julia Weeks; p. 177: AP Photo/Hillery Smith Shay; p. 180 (left): Eden Breitz/Alamy Stock Photo; (right): tetiana.photographer/Shutterstock; p. 182 (left): AP Photo/Bill Hudson; (right): Dom Slike/Alamy Stock Photo; p. 184: Don Cravens/Getty Images; p. 186: Robyn Beck/AFP via Getty Images; p. 187 (left): Bryan Woolston/REUTERS/Newscom; (right): AAraujo/Shutterstock; p. 189: AP Photo; p. 193: Kyodo via AP Images; p. 195: David Schaffer/Getty Images; p. 201: Chelsea Guglielmino/Staff/Getty Images; p. 202: ZUMA Press, Inc./Alamy Stock Photo; p. 206: Liu Jie Xinhua News Agency/Newscom; p. 207: Jose Luis Magana/Reuters/Newscom; p. 208: ZUMA Press, Inc./Alamy Stock Photo; p. 209: Nick Ut/Contributor/Getty Images; p. 210: ZUMA Press, Inc./Alamy Stock Photo.

Chapter 6

Page 215: Ringo Chiu via AP; p. 216: CALVIN AND HOBBES © 1994 Watterson. Reprinted with permission of ANDREWS MCMEEL SYNDICATION. All rights reserved; p. 217: AP Photo/Rogelio V. Solis; p. 218: Andrea Domeniconi/Alamy Stock Photo; p. 220 (left): Stephanie Keith/Getty Images; (right): AP Photo/Andrew Harnik; p. 223: Richard Levine/Alamy Stock Photo; p. 231 (phone): Tetra Images/Getty Images; (computer): Evirgen/Getty Images; (pencil eraser): Daniel Grill/Getty Images; (cell phone): John Lamb/Getty Images; (person with digital device): Josep Suria/Shutterstock; (pen): imagenavi/Getty Images; p. 237 (top): B Christopher/Alamy Stock Photo; (bottom): David McNew/Stringer/Getty Images; p. 240: Maidun Collection/Alamy Stock Photo; p. 246 (left): AP Photo/Mary Altaffer; (right): Tannen Maury/EPA/Shutterstock; p. 247: Ringo Chiu via AP.

Chapter 7

Page 253: Susan Sheldon/Alamy Stock Photo; p. 255: GRANGER; p. 256 (left): John Paul Filo/CBS via Getty Images; (right): Evan Agostini/Invision/AP; p. 259 (left): Richard Levine/Alamy Stock Photo; (right): Carl Court/Getty Images; (bottom): National Portrait Gallery, Smithsonian Institution; Frederick Hill Meserve Collection; p. 260: David Paul Morris/Bloomberg via Getty Images; p. 265: AP Photo/Julia Weeks; p. 269 (Biden): White House Photo/Alamy Stock Photo; (House members): Xinhua/Alamy Stock Photo; (finger): Klaus Vedfelt/Getty Images; (Capitol): J Main/Shutterstock; p. 270: Official White House Photo by Katie Ricks; p. 273: Hayk Shalunts/Alamy Stock Photo; p. 277: M4OS Photos/Alamy Stock Photo; p. 279: Stephen Lam/REUTERS/Newscom; p. 280: Susan Sheldon/Alamy Stock Photo.

Chapter 8

Page 285: SOPA Images Limited/Alamy Stock Photo; p. 287 (left): ZUMA Press, Inc./ Alamy Stock Photo; (middle): dpa picture alliance/Alamy Stock Photo; (right): Sipa USA/Alamy Stock Photo; p. 289: © CORBIS/Corbis via Getty Images; p. 290: Sarin Images/GRANGER; p. 292: AP Photo/Paul Sancya; p. 293: Andrew Spear for The Washington Post via Getty Images; p. 295: AP Photo/J. Scott Applewhite, File; p. 297: dpa picture alliance/Alamy Stock Photo; p. 299: Chris Hondros/Getty Images; p. 304: AP Photo/John Locher, File; p. 309 (Biden): White House Photo/Alamy Stock Photo; (Sanders): Matt Baron/Shutterstock; (Warren): Matt Baron/Shutterstock; (Buttigieg): ZUMA Press, Inc./Alamy Stock Photo; (Klobuchar): Michael Brochstein/Alamy Stock Photo; p. 310: Joyce Boghosian/ZUMA Press, Inc./Newscom; p. 311: Shutterstock; p. 313: SOPA Images Limited/Alamy Stock Photo; p. 318 (top): MediaPunch, Inc./Alamy Stock Photo; (bottom): SOPA Images Limited/Alamy Stock Photo.

Chapter 9

Page 323: Michael Le Brecht II/ABC News via ZUMA Press Wire/Alamy Stock Photo; p. 325: Associated Press; p. 326: UPI/Alamy Stock Photo; p. 328 (left): Ellen F. O'Connell/Hazelton Standard-Speaker via AP; (right): Marc Serota/Reuters/Newscom; p. 329 (left): AP Photo/LM Otero, File; (right): AP Photo/Eric Gay, File; p. 331: ZUMA Press, Inc./Alamy Stock Photo; p. 335: ZUMA Press, Inc./Alamy Stock Photo; p. 339: Andrew Cline/Alamy Stock Photo; p. 342: Tribune Content Agency LLC/Alamy Stock Photo; p. 344: Associated Press; p. 345: SOPA Images Limited/Alamy Stock Photo; p. 346 (both): Democratic National Committee/LBJ Library; p. 352: Drew Angerer/Getty Images; p. 354: John Spink/Atlanta Journal-Constitution via AP; p. 355: ZUMA Press, Inc./Alamy Stock Photo; p. 362: Photo by JIM WATSON/AFP via Getty Images; p. 364: Michael Le Brecht II/ABC News via ZUMA Press Wire/Alamy Stock Photo.

Chapter 10

Page 369: Storms Media Group/Alamy Stock Photo; p. 377: Tom Williams/Roll Call/Newscom; p. 378: Nicole S. Glass/Shutterstock; p. 380: Jim West/Alamy Stock Photo; p. 381: SOPA Images Limited/Alamy Stock Photo; p. 384: REUTERS/Alamy Stock Photo; p. 387 (highways): Ron Niebrugge/Alamy Stock Photo; (lobbyists): Pressmaster/Shutterstock; (congressional testimony): REUTERS/Alamy Stock Photo; (social media apps): True Images/Alamy Stock Photo; (Capitol): J Main/Shutterstock; (TV): KsanderDN/Shutterstock; (person watching TV): Cultura Creative RF/Alamy Stock Photo; (pen): imagenavi/Getty Images; (money): loskutnikov/Shutterstock; (person holding cell phone): John Lamb/Getty Images; (Manchin): Sipa USA/Alamy Stock Photo; (Sinema): Chip

Somodevilla/Getty Images; p. 389: AP Photo/Elaine Thompson; p. 390: Janine Wiedel Photolibrary/Alamy Stock Photo; p. 391: Ron Adar/Alamy Stock Photo; p. 394: Pacific Press Agency/Alamy Stock Photo; p. 398 (both): Jim West/Alamy Stock Photo; p. 400: JEMAL COUNTESS/UPI/Newscom; p. 401: Storms Media Group/Alamy Stock Photo.

Chapter 11

Page 407: UPI/Alamy Stock Photo; p. 409: Sarin Images/GRANGER; p. 413: Andrea Melendez—USA TODAY NETWORK; p. 416: Courtesy of Ari Berman; p. 418: Brian Hill/Daily Herald via AP; p. 423: Sipa USA/Alamy Stock Photo; p. 429 (both): United States Department of the Interior; p. 430: Tom Williams/CQ Roll Call via AP Images; p. 433: Anna Moneymaker/Getty Images; p. 436: ZUMA Press, Inc./Alamy Stock Photo; p. 437 (left): Abaca Press/Alamy Stock Photo; (right): JIM LO SCALZO/EPA-EFE/Shutterstock; p. 443 (House members): Xinhua/Alamy Stock Photo; (money): loskutnikov/Shutterstock; (Pelosi): UPI/Alamy Stock Photo; (Senate members): Dpa Picture Alliance/Alamy Stock Photo; (snacks): Oksana Mizina/Shutterstock; (Johnson): Sipa USA/Alamy Stock Photo; (Manchin): Sipa USA/Alamy Stock Photo; (Sanders): Matt Baron/Shutterstock; (Biden): White House Photo/Alamy Stock Photo; p. 447: Michael Nigro/Pacific Press/Shutterstock; p. 450: dpa picture alliance/Alamy Stock Photo; p. 451: UTC: UPI/Alamy Stock Photo.

Chapter 12

Page 457: REUTERS/Alamy Stock Photo; p. 459: Painting/Alamy Stock Photo; p. 460 (left): Everett Collection Historical/Alamy Stock Photo; (right): AP Photo/Bob Daugherty; p. 463: UPI/Alamy Stock Photo; p. 467 (Obama): ZUMA Press, Inc./Alamy Stock Photo; (Kerry): A Katz/Shutterstock; (smokestack): Space Images/Getty Images; (Senate members): Dpa Picture Alliance/Alamy Stock Photo; (Presidential seal): Nazlisart/Shutterstock; (Trump): Stone/Shutterstock; (Biden): White House Photo/Alamy Stock Photo; p. 470: American Photo Archive/Alamy Stock Photo; p. 474: Sipa USA/Alamy Stock Photo; p. 475: Al-Mayadeen via AP video; p. 477: Chip Somodevilla/Staff/Getty Images; p. 478 (left): Sipa USA/Alamy Stock Photo; (right): Planetpix/Alamy Stock Photo; (bottom): dpa picture alliance/Alamy Stock Photo; p. 481: American Photo Archive/Alamy Stock Photo; p. 483: NIH/Chiachi Chang; p. 486: UPI/Alamy Stock Photo; p. 487: REUTERS/Alamy Stock Photo; p. 488: REUTERS/Alamy Stock Photo.

Chapter 13

Page 493: Jabin Botsford/The Washington Post via Getty Images; p. 495: American Photo Archive/Alamy Stock Photo; p. 496: C. Morgan Engel/NCAA Photos via Getty Images; p. 499 (Capitol): J Main/Shutterstock; (EPA logo): United States Environmental Protection Agency; (gavel): Spx Chrome/Getty Images; (Obama): ZUMA Press, Inc./Alamy Stock Photo; (Trump): Stone/Shutterstock; (Biden): White House Photo/Alamy Stock Photo; p. 502: Dpa Picture Alliance/Alamy Stock Photo; p. 503: Charles Trainor Jr./Miami Herald/Tribune News Service via Getty Images; p. 504: North Wind Picture Archives/Alamy Stock Photo; p. 507: Justin Lane/EPA/REX/Shutterstock; p. 516: AP Photo/Andrew Harnik; p. 519: Andrew Holbrooke/Corbis via Getty Images; p. 520 (left): CFPB/Alamy Stock Photo; (right): Photo by Stefani Reynolds/AFP via Getty Images; p. 522: Storms Media Group/Alamy Stock Photo; p. 523: Jabin Botsford/The Washington Post via Getty Images.

Chapter 14

Page 529: Planetpix/Alamy Stock Photo; p. 530: B Christopher/Alamy Stock Photo; p. 533: North Wind Picture Archives/Alamy Stock Photo; p. 536: UPI/Alamy Stock Photo; p. 541 (Supreme Court building): Glow Images/Getty Images; (Constitution): Janece Flippo/Shutterstock; (gavel): Spx Chrome/Getty Images; (Pennsylvania district): United States Department of the Interior; p. 542: Sipa via AP Images; p. 544 (left): Patsy Lynch/Alamy Stock Photo; (right): Sipa USA/Alamy Stock Photo; p. 548: Janice and Nolan Braud/Alamy Stock Photo; p. 550: MICHAEL REYNOLDS/EPA-EFE/Shutterstock; p. 551: David Hume Kennerly/Getty Images; p. 553: Dana Verkouteren via AP; p. 555: Sipa USA/Alamy Stock Photo; p. 559: Bettmann/Getty Images; p. 564: John Badman/The Telegraph via AP; p. 566: Alex Wong/Getty Images; p. 567: Collection of the Supreme Court of the United States; p. 569: Bettmann/Getty Images; p. 570: Planetpix/Alamy Stock Photo.

Chapter 15

Page 575: SAUL LOEB/AFP via Getty Images; p. 576: Paulette Sinclair/Alamy Stock Photo; p. 578: PERO studio/Shutterstock; p. 584: Official White House Photo by Adam Schultz; p. 587 (pen): imagenavi/Getty Images; (thumb): PzAxe/Shutterstock; (House members): Xinhua/Alamy Stock Photo; (Capitol): J Main/Shutterstock; p. 590: White House Photo/Alamy Stock Photo; p. 592: Dpa Picture Alliance/Alamy Stock Photo; p. 593: Xinhua/Alamy Stock Photo; p. 601: Everett Collection, Inc./Alamy Stock Photo; p. 603: Bettmann/Getty Images; p. 604 (left): David R. Frazier/DanitaDelimont.com/Danita Delimont Photography/Newscom; (right): Dpa Picture Alliance/Alamy Stock Photo; p. 607: REUTERS/Alamy Stock Photo; p. 612: AP Photo/Lauren Victoria Burke; p. 614 (top): Andrew Harrer/Bloomberg via Getty Images; (bottom): SAUL LOEB/AFP via Getty Images.

Chapter 16

Page 619: Angel Valentin/The New York Times/Redux; p. 621: UPI/Alamy Stock Photo; p. 623: Everett Collection Inc./Alamy Stock Photo; p. 624: Jonathan Weiss/Alamy Stock Photo; p. 631: AP Photo/J. Scott Applewhite; p. 632: AP Photo/Rich Pedroncelli; p. 637 (elderly people): Everett Collection Historical/Alamy Stock Photo; (FDR): Science History Images/Alamy Stock Photo; (FDR signs legislation): Everett Collection Historical/Alamy Stock Photo; (Social Security card): Everett Collection/Shutterstock; (Obama): ZUMA Press, Inc./Alamy Stock Photo; (Social Security logo): USA Social Security Administration; (money): loskutnikov/Shutterstock; p. 638: Courtesy of Representative David Trone p. 645: Social Security Fix, by Brian Farrington © 2005 Cagle Cartoons; p. 649: Bill Clark/CQ Roll Call/Newscom; p. 656: REUTERS/Alamy Stock Photo; p. 657: Stephen Crowley/The New York Times/Redux; p. 658: Marilyn Humphries/Alamy Stock Photo; p. 659: Angel Valentin/The New York Times/Redux.

Chapter 17

Page 663: American Photo Archive/Alamy Stock Photo; p. 665: DOUG MILLS/The New York Times/Redux; p. 667: Rami Al-Sayed/AFP via Getty Images; p. 669: AP Photo; p. 671: F1 online digitale Bildagentur GmbH/Alamy Stock Photo; p. 672: Shutterstock; p. 673: Mohammed Mohammed Xinhua News Agency/Newscom; p. 674: Matteo Guedia/Alamy Stock Photo; p. 676: American Photo Archive/Alamy Stock Photo; p. 678: ZUMA Press, Inc./Alamy Stock Photo; p. 681 (Crimean peninsula): Peter Hermes Furian/Shutterstock; (UN logo): kckate16/Shutterstock; (pen): imagenavi/Getty Images; (troops): Alexander Ermochenko/EPA/Shutterstock; (Trump): Stone/Shutterstock; (Senate members): Dpa Picture Alliance/Alamy Stock Photo; (tank): REUTERS/Alamy Stock Photo; (NATO logo): Maxim Studio/Shutterstock; (Putin): EyePress/Newscom; (Biden): White House Photo/Alamy Stock Photo; (jet): Almaz Mustafin/Shutterstock; p. 682: AP Photo/Jose Luis Magana; p. 683: Sarah Silbiger-Pool/Getty Images; p. 686: Kevin Lim/The Straits Times/Sph/EPA-EFE/Shutterstock; p. 688: Stuart Walden/Alamy Stock Photo; p. 693: Keitma/Alamy Stock Photo; p. 694: Gilles Sabrie/The New York Times/Redux; p. 697: KCNA/UPI/Newscom; p. 698: American Photo Archive/Alamy Stock Photo.

Glossary/Index

Note: Page numbers in italics indicate figures, tables, and photographs.

A

Aid to Families with Dependent Children (AFDC), 623, 632, 653 The federal welfare program in place from 1935 until 1996, when it was replaced by TANF under President Clinton.

Bill of Rights, 48, 54–55, 64, 89, 114, 117, 118, 159, 165, 534 The first 10 amendments to the Constitution; they protect individual rights and liberties. *See also specific amendments*

block grants, 97 Federal aid provided to a state government to be spent within a certain policy area but that the state can decide how to spend within that area.

commerce clause, 64, 66, 90, 101–2 The part of Article I, Section 8, of the Constitution that gives Congress "the power to regulate Commerce . . . among the several States." The Supreme Court's interpretation of this clause has varied, but today it serves as the basis for much of Congress's legislation.

commercial speech, 138–39 Public expression with the aim of making a profit. It has received greater protection under the First Amendment in recent years but remains less protected than political speech.

common law, 536 Law based on the precedent of previous court rulings rather than on legislation. It is used in all federal courts and 49 of the 50 state courts.

competitive federalism, 99, 105–6 A form of federalism in which states compete to attract businesses and jobs through the policies they adopt.

concurrent powers, 80 Responsibilities for particular policy areas, such as transportation, that are shared by federal, state, and local governments.

confederal government, 81 A form of government in which states hold power over a limited national government.

confederations, 376 Interest groups made up of several independent, local organizations that provide much of their funding and hold most of the power.

conference, 295 The organization of Republicans within the House and Senate that meets to discuss and debate the party's positions on various issues in order to reach a consensus and to assign leadership positions.

conference committees, 438, 445–46 Temporary committees created to negotiate differences between the House and Senate versions of a piece of legislation that has passed through both chambers.

conservative, 20 The side of the ideological spectrum defined by support for lower taxes, a free market, and a more limited government; generally associated with Republicans.

constitutional authority (presidential), 462 Powers derived from the provisions of the Constitution that outline the president's role in government.

constitutional interpretation, 534 The process of determining whether a piece of legislation or governmental action is supported by the Constitution.

containment, 669, 670 An important feature of American Cold War policy in which the United States used diplomatic, economic, and military strategies in an effort to prevent the Soviet Union from expanding its influence.

cooperative federalism, 91, 94, 97, 108 A form of federalism in which national and state governments work together to provide services efficiently. This form emerged in the late 1930s, representing a profound shift toward less concrete boundaries of responsibility in national-state relations.

Council of Economic Advisers (CEA), 577, 590, 591 A group of economic advisers, created by the Employment Act of 1946, that provides objective data on the state of the economy and makes economic policy recommendations to the president.

hard money, 350 Donations that are used to help elect or defeat a specific candidate.

hard news, 278 Media coverage focused on facts and important issues surrounding a campaign.

hate speech, 132–33 Expression that is offensive or abusive, particularly in terms of race, gender, or sexual orientation. It is currently protected under the First Amendment.

head of government, 463 One role of the president, through which the president has authority over the executive branch.

head of state, 463 One role of the president, through which the president represents the country symbolically and politically.

hold, 448 An objection to considering a measure on the Senate floor.

horse race, 278 A description of the type of election coverage that focuses more on poll results and speculation about a likely winner than on substantive differences between the candidates.

hostile media effect, 270 The tendency of people to see neutral media coverage of an event as biased against their point of view.

I

idealism, 666, 667, 668 The idea that foreign policy decisions reflect normative goals such as justice, equality, and human rights.

ideological polarization, 238–40, 435, *435* Sharp differences in Americans' overall ideas of the size and scope of government.

ideology, 20, 371 A cohesive set of ideas and beliefs used to organize and evaluate the political world.

judicial restraint, 562, 565 The idea that the Supreme Court should defer to the democratically elected executive and legislative branches of government rather than contradicting existing laws.

judicial review, 63, 533, 679 The Supreme Court's power to strike down a law or an executive branch action that it finds unconstitutional.

Judiciary Act of 1789, 531, 533, 534 The law in which Congress laid out the organization of the federal judiciary. The law refined and clarified federal court jurisdiction and set the original number of justices at six. It also created the office of the attorney general and established the lower federal courts.

jurisdiction, 537–38 The sphere of a court's legal authority to hear and decide cases.

K

Keynesian economics, 595, 596, 597, 615 The theory that governments should use economic policy, like taxing and spending, to maintain stability in the economy.

L

latent opinion, 217 An opinion formed on the spot, when it is needed (as distinct from a deeply held opinion that is stable over time).

leaking, 265 The practice in which someone in government provides nonpublic information to a reporter, with the aim of generating press coverage favorable to the leaker's aims.

Lemon test, 124 The Supreme Court uses this test, established in *Lemon v. Kurtzman*, to determine whether a practice violates the First Amendment's establishment clause.

mass associations, 379–80, *380* Interest groups that have a large number of dues-paying individuals as members.

mass media, 254 Sources that provide information to the average citizen, such as newspapers, television networks, radio stations, podcasts, and websites. *See also* media

mass surveys, 228, 229, *229* A way to measure public opinion by interviewing a relatively small sample of a large population.

material benefits, 384 Benefits that are provided to individuals for joining a group, such as a coffee mug or a T-shirt, that are distinct from the collective benefits provided by the group.

***McDonald v. Chicago*, 142** The Supreme Court ruled in 2010 that the Second Amendment's right to keep and bear arms for self-defense in one's home is applicable to the states through the Fourteenth Amendment.

media conglomerates, 257 Companies that control a large number of media sources across several types of media outlets.

media effects, 267 The influence of media coverage on average citizens' opinions and actions.

Medicaid, 96, 97, 103, 461, 624, 633, 646–47 An entitlement program funded by the federal and state governments that provides health care coverage for low-income Americans who would otherwise be unable to afford health care.

Medicare, 13, 460, 588, 597, 599, 600, 620, 624, 628, 633, 640, 646–47 The federal health care plan created in 1965 that provides coverage for retired Americans for hospital care (Part A), medical care (Part B), and prescription drugs (Part D).

Miller Test, 139 Established in *Miller v. California*, this three-part test is used by the Supreme Court to determine whether speech meets the criteria for obscenity. If so, it can be restricted by the government.

Minority Leader, 432, 433, *433* The elected head of the party holding the minority of seats in the House or Senate.

National Security Council (NSC), 477, 483, 676, 677 An agency within the EOP that advises the president on matters of foreign policy.

national supremacy clause, 48, 82 The part of Article VI, Section 2, of the Constitution stating that the Constitution and the laws and treaties of the United States are the "supreme Law of the Land," meaning national laws take precedence over state laws if the two conflict.

natural rights, 39 Also known as "unalienable rights," these rights are defined in the Declaration of Independence as "Life, Liberty, and the pursuit of Happiness." The Founders believed that upholding these rights should be the government's central purpose.

necessary and proper clause, 58, 64, 82 The part of Article I, Section 8, of the Constitution that grants Congress the power to pass all laws related to its expressed powers; also known as the elastic clause.

negative partisanship, 298 Identification with a political party that is based on dislike of the other party rather than positive feelings about the party identified with.

New Deal, 70, 94, 97, 101, 289, *290*, 410, 460, 505–6, *506*, 542–43, 563, 622–23, 631, 637 The set of policies proposed by President Franklin Roosevelt and enacted by Congress between 1933 and 1935 to promote economic recovery and social welfare during the Great Depression.

New Jersey Plan, 45, 67 A plan that was suggested in response to the Virginia Plan; smaller states at the Constitutional Convention proposed that each state should receive equal representation in the national legislature, regardless of size.

***New York Times Co. v. United States*, 135–36** The Supreme Court ruled in 1971 that the government could not prevent the publication of the Pentagon Papers, which revealed lies about the progress of the war in Vietnam.

nominating convention, 306 A meeting held by each party every four years at which states' delegates select the party's presidential and vice-presidential nominees and approve the party platform.

norms, 21 Unwritten rules and informal agreements among citizens and elected officials about how government and society should operate.

notice-and-comment procedure, 496, 503, 519 A step in the rule-making process in which proposed rules are published in the *Federal Register* and made available for debate by the general public.

O

Office of Management and Budget (OMB), 477, 508, 590, 676 An office within the EOP that is responsible for creating the president's annual budget proposal to Congress, reviewing proposed rules, and performing other budget-related tasks.

omnibus legislation, 446 Large bills that often cover several topics and may contain extraneous, or pork-barrel, projects.

on background or off the record, 263 Describes comments a politician makes to the press on the condition that they can be reported only if they are not attributed to that politician.

open market operations, 603 The process by which the Federal Reserve System buys and sells securities to influence the money supply.

open primary, 305, 325 A primary election in which any registered voter can participate in the contest, regardless of party affiliation.

open rules, 448 Conditions placed on a legislative debate by the House Rules Committee allowing relevant amendments to a bill.

open seat, 339 An elected position for which there is no incumbent.

oral arguments, 552–55 Spoken presentations made in person by the lawyers of each party to a judge or an appellate court

permanent campaigns, 339–40, 410 The continual quest for reelection that is rooted in high-cost professional campaigns that are increasingly reliant on consultants and expensive media campaigns.

picket fence federalism, 91, 92 A more refined and realistic form of cooperative federalism in which policy makers within a particular policy area work together across the levels of government.

plaintiff, 535 The person or party who brings a case to court.

plea bargaining, 535 Negotiating an agreement between a plaintiff and a defendant to settle a case before it goes to trial or the verdict is decided. In a civil case, this usually involves an admission of guilt and an agreement on monetary damages; in a criminal case, this often involves an admission of guilt in return for a reduced charge or sentence.

pluralism, 44 The idea that having a variety of parties and interests within a government will strengthen the system, ensuring that no group possesses total control.

plurality voting, 314, 327 A voting system in which the candidate who receives the most votes within a geographic area wins the election, regardless of whether that candidate wins a majority (more than half) of the votes.

pocket veto, 445, 471, 472 The automatic death of a bill passed by the House and Senate when the president fails to sign the bill in the last 10 days of a legislative session.

police patrol oversight, 520–21 A method of oversight in which members of Congress constantly monitor the bureaucracy to make sure that laws are implemented correctly.

police powers, 80 Responsibilities that include the power to enforce laws and provide for public safety.

policy agenda, 634–35 The set of desired policies that political leaders view as their top priorities.

policy mood, 243, 244, 244, 245 The level of public support for expanding the government's role in society; whether the public wants government action on a specific issue.

political action committees (PACs), 292, 350, 350, 392–94, 403 An interest group or a division of an interest group that can raise money to contribute to campaigns or to spend on ads in support of candidates. The amount a PAC can receive from each of its donors and the amount it can spend on federal electioneering are strictly limited.

political appointees, 494, 516–17 People selected by an elected leader, such as the president, to hold a government position.

political socialization, 219 The process by which an individual's political opinions are shaped by other people and the surrounding culture.

politico, 413 A member of Congress who acts as a delegate on issues that constituents care about (such as immigration reform) and as a trustee on more complex or less salient issues (such as some foreign policy or regulatory matters).

politics, 9 The process that determines what government does.

popular sovereignty, 39 The idea that government gains its legitimacy through regular elections in which the people living under that government participate to elect their leaders.

popular vote, 331, *335* The votes cast by citizens in an election.

population, 228 The group of people whom a researcher or pollster wants to study, such as evangelicals, senior citizens, or Americans.

power of the purse, 58, 61, 588–89, 678, 680 The constitutional power of Congress to raise and spend money. Congress can use this as a negative or checking power over the other branches by freezing or cutting their funding.

precedent, 537, 558 A legal norm established in court cases that is then applied to future cases dealing with the same legal questions.

presidential approval rating, 483–84, *487* The percentage of Americans who think that the president is doing a good job in office. *See also* approval ratings

Q

R

random sample, 230, 232 A subsection of a population chosen to participate in a survey through a selection process in which every member of the population has an equal chance of being chosen. This kind of sampling improves the accuracy of public-opinion data.

rational basis test, 192, 197, 198 The use of evidence to suggest that differences in the behavior of two groups can rationalize unequal treatment of these groups.

realignment, 290–91 A change in the size or composition of the party coalitions or in the nature of the issues that divide the parties. Realignments typically occur within an election cycle or two, but they can also occur gradually over the course of a decade or longer.

realism, 666, 667 The idea that a country's foreign policy decisions are motivated by self-interest and the goal of gaining more power.

recess appointment, 464 Selection by the president of a person to be an ambassador or the head of a department while the Senate is not in session, thereby bypassing Senate approval. Unless approved by a subsequent Senate vote, recess appointees serve only to the end of the congressional term.

reconciliation, 448 Reconciliation allows for expedited consideration of certain tax, spending, and debt limit legislation. The main advantage of the procedure is that reconciliation legislation is not subject to filibusters in the Senate and therefore may be passed with simple majorities in the House and Senate.

redistributive tax policies, 16, 598–99 Policies, generally favored by Democratic politicians, that use taxation to attempt to create social equality (for example, higher taxation of the rich to provide programs for the poor).

redistricting, 423 Re-drawing the geographic boundaries of legislative districts. This happens every 10 years to ensure that districts remain roughly equal in population. *See also* gerrymandering

red tape, 502–3 Excessive or unnecessarily complex regulations imposed by the bureaucracy.

referendum, 395 A direct vote by citizens on a policy change proposed by a legislature or another government body. Referenda are common in state and local elections, but there is no mechanism for a national-level referendum.

regressive, 600 Describes taxes that take a larger share of poor people's income than wealthy people's income, such as sales taxes and payroll taxes.

regulation, 495, 604 A rule that allows the government to exercise control over individuals and corporations by restricting certain behaviors.

regulatory capture, 501 A situation in which bureaucrats favor the interests of the groups or corporations they are supposed to regulate at the expense of the general public.

remedial legislation, 101 National laws that address discriminatory state laws. Authority for such legislation comes from Section 5 of the Fourteenth Amendment.

republicanism, 38–39 As understood by James Madison and the framers, the belief that a form of government in which the interests of the people are represented through elected leaders is the best form of government. Our form of government is known as a republican democracy.

reserved powers, 48 As defined in the Tenth Amendment, powers that are not given to the national government by the Constitution, or not prohibited to the states, are reserved to the states or the people.

reserve requirement, 574, 602 The minimum amount of money that a bank is required to have on hand to back up its assets.

revolving door, 378–79 The movement of individuals from government positions to jobs with interest groups or lobbying firms, and vice versa.

***Roe v. Wade*, 12, 154–55, 156, 198, 555, 565** This 1973 Supreme Court case extended the right of privacy to a woman's decision to have an abortion while recognizing legitimate state interests in potential life and maternal health. The Court noted that the "relative weight of each of these interests varies over the course of pregnancy, and the law must account for this variability."

roll call vote, 433 A recorded vote on legislation; members may vote "yes," "no," or "present," or they may abstain.

runoff election, 327 Under a majority voting system, a second election is held only if no candidate wins a majority of the votes in the first general election. Only the top two vote-getters in the first election compete in the runoff.

S

salience, 399–400 The level of familiarity with an interest group's goals in the general population.

sample, 228, 230 Within a population, the group of people surveyed in order to gauge the whole population's opinion. Researchers use samples because it would be impossible to interview the entire population.

sampling error, 229, *229*, 229–30 The predicted difference between the average opinion expressed by survey respondents and the average opinion in the population, sometimes called the *margin of error*. Increasing the number of respondents lowers the sampling error.

select committees, 438, *450* Committees in the House or Senate created to address a specific issue for one or two terms.

selective incentives, 383 Benefits that can motivate participation in a group effort because they are available only to those who participate, such as member services offered by interest groups.

selective incorporation, 117–20, *120* The process through which most of the civil liberties granted in the Bill of Rights were applied to the states on a case-by-case basis through the Fourteenth Amendment.

semi-closed primary, 305, 325 A primary in which anyone who is a registered member of the party or registered as an Independent can vote.

senatorial courtesy, 545 A norm in the nomination of district court judges in which the president consults with their own party's senators from the relevant state in choosing the nominee.

seniority, 430 The informal congressional norm of choosing the member who has served the longest on a particular committee to be the committee chair. 4

"separate but equal" doctrine, 168, 507 The idea that racial segregation was acceptable as long as the separate facilities were of equal quality; supported by *Plessy v. Ferguson* and struck down by *Brown v. Board of Education*.

separation of powers, 7, 44, 55, 71 The division of government power across the judicial, executive, and legislative branches.

shadow docket, 557 The alternative path to the Supreme Court that involves emergency appeals of lower-court decisions. The cases do not involve a full briefing and oral arguments and often are unsigned opinions.

substantive due process doctrine, 197, 198 One interpretation of the due process clause of the Fourteenth Amendment; in this view the Supreme Court has the power to overturn laws that infringe on individual liberties.

substantive representation, 411, 413 Representation in which a member of Congress serves constituents' interests and shares their policy concerns.

supply-side economics, 595 The theory that lower tax rates will stimulate the economy by encouraging people to save, invest, and produce more goods and services.

symbolic speech, 130–31, 133 Nonverbal expression, such as the use of signs or symbols. It benefits from many of the same constitutional protections as verbal speech because of its expressive value.

T

tariff, 610, 611, 664, 672, 687, 688, 692, 693, 694 A tax levied on imported or exported goods.

Temporary Assistance for Needy Families (TANF), 97, 632, 653–54 The welfare program that replaced AFDC in 1996, eliminating the entitlement status of welfare, shifting implementation of the policy to the states, and introducing several new restrictions on receiving aid. These changes led to a significant decrease in the number of welfare recipients.

Three-Fifths Compromise, 43, 47, 49, *50*
The states' decision during the Constitutional Convention to count each enslaved person as three-fifths of a person in a state's population for the purposes of determining the number of House members and the distribution of taxes.

Tinker v. Des Moines School District*, 130, *559 In 1969, the Supreme Court ruled that students may wear armbands to protest the Vietnam War. The Court noted that the students "were not disruptive and did not impinge upon the rights of others" and therefore their conduct was protected by the First and Fourteenth Amendments.

trade deficit, 583–84, 608, *609*, 609–11
A measure of how much more a nation imports than it exports.

Treasury Department, 504, 591, 592, 593–94 A cabinet-level agency that is responsible for managing the federal government's revenue. It prints currency, collects taxes, and sells government bonds.

trustee, 411, 413 A member of Congress who represents constituents' interests while also taking into account national, collective, and moral concerns that sometimes cause the member to vote against the preference of a majority of constituents.

turkey farms, 516 Agencies to which campaign workers and donors can be appointed in reward for their service because it is unlikely that their lack of qualifications will lead to bad policy.

U

unfunded mandates, 96, 98, 108 Federal laws that require the states to do certain things but do not provide state governments with funding to implement these policies.

unified government, 295 A situation in which one party holds a majority of seats in the House and Senate and the president is a member of that same party.

unilateral action (national), 665 Independent acts of foreign policy undertaken by a nation without the assistance or coordination of other nations.

unilateral action (presidential), 480–81 Any policy decision made and acted upon by the president and presidential staff without the explicit approval or consent of Congress.

unitary executive theory, 481 The idea that the vesting clause of the Constitution gives the president the authority to issue orders and policy directives that cannot be undone by Congress.

unitary government, 80–81 A system in which the national, centralized government holds ultimate authority. It is the most common form of government in the world.

United Nations (UN), 460, 665, 665, 668, 669–70, 685, 686 An international organization made up of representatives from nearly every nation, with a mission to promote peace and cooperation, uphold international law, and provide humanitarian aid.

United States Trade Representative (USTR), 590, 611 An agency founded in 1962 to negotiate with foreign governments to create trade agreements, resolve disputes, and participate in global trade-policy organizations. Treaties negotiated by the USTR must be ratified by the Senate.

V

vesting clause, 463 Article II, Section 1, of the Constitution, which states: "The executive Power shall be vested in a President of the United States of America," making the president both the head of government and the head of state.

veto, 445, 462, 473, 591, 678 The president's rejection of a bill that has been passed by Congress. A veto can be overridden by a two-thirds vote in both the House and Senate.

Virginia Plan, 45, 46, 47, 67 A plan proposed by the larger states during the Constitutional Convention that based representation in the national legislature on population. The plan also included a variety of other proposals to strengthen the national government.

voting cues, 355–56 A plan proposed by the larger states during the Constitutional Convention that based representation in the national legislature on population. The plan also included a variety of other proposals to strengthen the national government.

W

X

Y

Z